THE OXFORD HANDBOOK

SHAKESPE

CW00816058

THE OXFORD HANDBOOK OF

SHAKESPEARE

Edited by

ARTHUR F. KINNEY

OXFORD
UNIVERSITY PRESS

OXFORD
UNIVERSITY PRESS

Great Clarendon Street, Oxford OX2 6DP

Oxford University Press is a department of the University of Oxford.
It furthers the University's objective of excellence in research, scholarship,
and education by publishing worldwide. Oxford is a registered trade mark of
Oxford University Press in the UK and in certain other countries

First published 2012
First published in paperback 2014

Published in the United States of America by Oxford University Press
198 Madison Avenue, New York, NY 10016, United States of America

British Library Cataloguing in Publication Data
Data available

Library of Congress Cataloging in Publication Data
Data available

ISBN 978-0-19-956610-5 (Hbk)
ISBN 978-0-19-870349-5 (Pbk)

PREFACE

The study of Shakespeare is rapidly changing. Scholars are redefining what he did and did not write, what it meant in his own time, and what it means to ours. Lines are being redrawn, even now; old stories are being told with new twists; our collective images of Shakespeare as a person and a poet are disintegrating and reforming. A new portrait of him has been proposed; scientific language study has assigned new writing to him and dismissed some earlier attributions; we know more about his professional associations, his playing companies, their repertoire, and the country routes they travelled; and we have learned far more about the social, political, religious, and economic times in which he lived and for which he wrote than at any time in the past. Within the Oxford Handbooks of Literature series, those devoted to the study of Shakespeare are designed to record past and present investigations and renewed and revised judgements by both familiar and younger Shakespearean specialists. Each of these volumes is edited by one or more internationally distinguished Shakespeareans; together, they comprehensively survey the entire field.

Arthur F. Kinney

In Memory of
ADAM MAX COHEN 1971–2010

ACKNOWLEDGEMENTS

I am grateful to the many co-authors of this volume and their many suggestions; for the editorial assistance of Jeffrey Goodhind, Thomas Warren Hopper, David Katz, Philip S. Palmer, and Timothy Zajac; and to the editors at Oxford University Press, especially Andrew McNeillie, Jacqueline Baker, Kathleen Kerr, Brendan Mac Evilly, Ruth Freestone–King, and Hayley Buckley.

—A. F. K.

Contents

PART III WORKS

PART IV PERFORMANCES

PART V SPECULATIONS

LIST OF ILLUSTRATIONS

Notes on Contributors

Arthur F. Kinney, Editor, is Thomas W. Copeland Professor of Literary History at the University of Massachusetts-Amherst and Director of the Massachusetts Center for Interdisciplinary Renaissance Studies. His most recent books include *'Lies Like Truth': Shakespeare, Macbeth, and the Cultural Moment* (2001), *Shakespeare by Stages* (2003), *Shakespeare's Webs* (2004); and *Shakespeare and Cognition* (2006). He is presently at work on *Shakespeare and the Mind's Eye*. He is a past trustee of the Shakespeare Association of America.

Melissa Aaron is a Professor of English in the Department of English and Foreign Languages at California Polytechnic State University at Pomona. Her book *Global Economics: a History of the Theater Business, the Chamberlain's/King's Men, and Their Plays, 1599–1642* (2005), is a history of 'Shakespeare's' theatrical company as a business. More recent essays include '"Beware at what hands thou receiv'st thy commodity": *The Alchemist* and the King's Men fleece the customers, 1610', *Inside Shakespeare: Essays on the Blackfriars Stage* (2006), and '"A Queen in a Beard": a Study of All-female Shakespeare Companies', *Shakespeare Re-dressed: Cross-Gender Casting in Contemporary Performance* (2008). Her most recent research is on the history of all-women Shakespeare companies and productions.

Ian Archer is Fellow, Tutor, and University Lecturer at Keble College, Oxford, and is the author of various books and essays on the social and political history of early modern London. He is Literary Director of the Royal Historical Society and Academic Editor of the Bibliography of British and Irish History.

Catherine Bates is Professor of Renaissance Literature and Head of Department at the University of Warwick's Department of English and Comparative Literary Studies. Her books include *The Rhetoric of Courtship in Elizabethan Language and Literature* (1992); *Play in a Godless World: The Theory and Practice of Play in Shakespeare, Nietzsche, and Freud* (1999); *Masculinity, Gender and Identity in the English Renaissance Lyric* (2007), and *The Cambridge Companion to the Epic* (2010). She is currently working on a book on representations of masculinity and the hunt in literature from *Sir Gawain and the Green Knight* to *The Faerie Queene*.

David Bevington is the Phyllis Fay Horton Distinguished Service Professor Emeritus in the Humanities at the University of Chicago. His books include *From 'Mankind' to Marlowe* (1962), *Tudor Drama and Politics* (1968), *Action Is Eloquence* (1985), *Shakespeare: The Seven Ages of Human Experience* (2005), *This Wide and Universal Theater:*

Shakespeare in Performance, Then and Now (2007), and *Shakespeare's Ideas* (2008). He is the editor of *Medieval Drama* (1975), *The Bantam Shakespeare*, and *The Complete Works of Shakespeare*, 6th edn. (2008). He is a senior editor of the Revels Student Editions, the Revels Plays, *The Norton Anthology of Renaissance Drama*, and the forthcoming Cambridge edition of the works of Ben Jonson.

Janet Clare is Professor of Renaissance Literature at the University of Hull. She formerly taught at University College Dublin. Among her publications are '*Art Made Tongue-Tied by Authority*': *Elizabethan and Jacobean Dramatic Censorship* (1999), *Drama of the English Republic, 1649–1660* (2002), and *Revenge Tragedies of the Renaissance* (2006). She has published numerous essays on Shakespeare and Renaissance drama, early modern women's writing, and drama and performance during the English Republic, 1649–1660.

Adam Max Cohen, Associate Professor of English, taught Shakespeare, Renaissance Literature, and Early Modern Cultural Studies at the University of Massachusetts, Dartmouth, until his death from brain cancer in January 2010 at age 38. As well as scholarly articles in *Sixteenth Century Journal, Journal of Early Modern Cultural Studies, Shakespeare Yearbook, Blackwell Companion to Tudor Literature*, and *Italian Culture in the Drama of Shakespeare & His Contemporaries*, Professor Cohen published three monographs with Palgrave Macmillan: *Shakespeare and Technology: Dramatizing Early Modern Technological Revolutions* (2006), *Technology and the Early Modern Self* (2009) and *Wonder in Shakespeare* (forthcoming).

Hugh Craig is Director of the Humanities Research Institute and Director of the Centre for Literary and Linguistic Computing at the University of Newcastle, Australia. He has published books on Sir John Harington and Ben Jonson and co-edited a collection of essays on Shakespearean authorship with Arthur F. Kinney. His current work is on linguistic individuality in the work of early modern English playwrights.

Brian Cummings is Professor of English at the University of Sussex and was founding Director of the Centre for Early Modern Studies, 2004–2008. He is the author of *The Literary Culture of the Reformation: Grammar and Grace* (2007), the editor, with James Simpson, of *Cultural Reformations: Medieval and Renaissance in Literary History* (2010), and has just completed an edition of *The Book of Common Prayer* for Oxford World's Classics. He is currently the holder of a Leverhulme Trust Major Research Fellowship for 2009–2012, researching his next book, *The Confessions of Shakespeare*.

Jane Hwang Degenhardt is Associate Professor of English at the University of Massachusetts-Amherst. Her work focuses on cross-cultural encounters in early modern drama and on the role of the popular theatre in shaping ideas about religious and racial differences. She is the author of *Islamic Conversion and Christian Resistance on the Early Modern Stage* (2010), and co-editor (along with Elizabeth Williamson) of *Religion and Drama in Early Modern England* (2011).

Christy Desmet is Professor of English at the University of Georgia, where she specializes in Rhetoric and Renaissance Studies. Her books include *Reading Shakespeare's*

Characters (1992), *Shakespeare and Appropriation* (with Robert Sawyer, 1999), *Harold Bloom's Shakespeare* (with Robert Sawyer, 2001), and *Shakespearean Gothic* (with Anne Williams, 2009). With Sujata Iyengar she is also founder and General Editor of *Borrowers and Lenders: The Journal of Shakespeare and Appropriation* (www.borrowers.uga.edu).

Lars Engle, author of *Shakespearean Pragmatism: Market of His Time* (1993), and an editor of *English Renaissance Drama: A Norton Anthology*, is department chair and James G. Watson Professor in English at the University of Tulsa. He has published essays on Shakespeare and his contemporaries in *PMLA*, *Shakespeare Quarterly*, *Shakespeare Survey*, *Studies in English Literature*, *Modern Philology*, *Exemplaria*, *Shakespearean International Yearbook*, and other journals and collections. A past trustee of the Shakespeare Association of America, in 2010 he served as the Lloyd Davis Professor of Shakespeare Studies at the University of Queensland.

Laura Estill is currently a Visiting Assistant Professor at the Université de Moncton, Campus d'Edmundston. She completed her doctorate at Wayne State University. Her dissertation, 'The Circulation and Recontextualization of Dramatic Extracts in Seventeenth-Century Manuscripts', focuses on issues of print and manuscript circulation, cultural and social history, and performed and literary texts. She is interested in what early modern audiences took, literally and figuratively, from the plays they watched and read. Her first essay, '*Richard II* and the Book of Life', is forthcoming in *Studies in English Literature*.

Brian Gibbons has been a General Editor of the New Cambridge Shakespeare since its inception, and also a General Editor of the New Mermaids since 1972. He was at the University of York, where he taught Shakespeare through theatre workshop classes, until he was appointed Professor of English at the University of Leeds, then at the University of Zurich, then the University of Münster. He has held visiting professorships at Lausanne, Geneva, Montpellier, and UCLA, and Fellowships at the Huntington Library and Folger Library. He is author of *Jacobean City Comedy* (1968, 1980), of *Shakespeare and Multiplicity* (1993, 2006), and of numerous articles; he edited the New Arden Shakespeare *Romeo & Juliet*, the New Cambridge Shakespeare *Measure for Measure*, and in the New Mermaids *The Revenger's Tragedy*, *The Duchess of Malfi*, and *The Way of the World*. He lives in Yorkshire.

Andrew Gurr is Professor Emeritus at the University of Reading, and former Director of Research at the Shakespeare Globe Centre, London. While at the Globe he spent twenty years chairing the committee that identified the Globe's shape and structure. His academic books include *The Shakespearean Stage 1574–1642*, now in its 4th edition; *Playgoing in Shakespeare's London*, now in its 3rd; *The Shakespearian Playing Companies: a History of The Shakespeare Company 1594–1642*, and most recently a history of *Shakespeare's Opposites: The Admiral's Men 1594–1625*, the company that performed at the Rose and the Fortune. He has edited several Renaissance plays, including Shakespeare's *Richard II*, *Henry V*, and the Quarto *Henry V* for the Cambridge Shakespeare editions, and is currently editing *The Tempest* for the New Variorum. He is a trustee of the Rose Theatre Trust.

Andrew Hadfield is Professor of English at the University of Sussex. He is the author of a number of works on early modern literature, including *Shakespeare and Republicanism* (2005, 2008), *Literature, Travel and Colonialism in the English Renaissance, 1540–1625* (1998, 2007), *Spenser's Irish Experience: Wilde Fruyt and Salvage Soyl* (1997), and *Literature, Politics and National Identity: Reformation to Renaissance* (1994). He is also editor of *Renaissance Studies* and a regular reviewer for *The Times Literary Supplement*. He is currently working on a biography of Edmund Spenser.

Andrew Hiscock is Professor of English at Bangor University, Wales. He has published widely on early modern literature, and his most recent monograph is *The Uses of This World: Thinking Space in Shakespeare, Marlowe, Cary and Jonson* (2004). He edited the MHRA's double issue of the 2008 *Yearbook of English Studies* devoted to Tudor literature, and is series co-editor for the *Continuum Renaissance Drama*, and co-editor of the academic journal *English*. His forthcoming monograph is entitled *Reading Memory in Early Modern Literature*.

Ton Hoenselaars is Professor of English Renaissance Literature and Culture at Utrecht University, the Netherlands. He is the president of the Shakespeare Society of the Low Countries and the European Shakespeare Research Association (ESRA). He has written extensively on Anglo-foreign relations and the reception history of Shakespeare worldwide. Books include *Images of Englishmen and Foreigners in the Drama of Shakespeare and his Contemporaries* (1992), *Shakespeare and the Language of Translation* (2004), *Shakespeare's History Plays: Performance, Translation, and Adaptation in Britain and Abroad* (2004), and *The Cambridge Companion to Shakespeare and Contemporary Dramatists* (2012). He is currently writing the cultural history of Ruhleben, the civilian internment camp for Britons in Berlin (1914–1918).

Adam G. Hooks is Assistant Professor of English at the University of Iowa, and an Associate Instructor at the UI Center for the Book. He has recently published essays on the early modern book trade in *Papers of the Bibliographical Society of America* and *Shakespeare Survey*, and was awarded the J. Leeds Barroll dissertation prize for 2010 by the Shakespeare Association of America. His current book project, *Vendible Shakespeare*, traces Shakespeare's career in print from the late sixteenth to the late seventeenth century, focusing on the various commerical and textual networks in which Shakespeare's works existed.

Grace Ioppolo is Professor of Shakespearean and Early Modern Drama in the Department of English Language and Literature at the University of Reading. Her publications include *Dramatists and Their Manuscripts in the Age of Shakespeare, Jonson, Middleton and Heywood: Authorship, Authority and the Playhouse* (2006), *Revising Shakespeare* (1991), and *Shakespeare Performed: Essays in Honor of R. A. Foakes* (2000). She has produced critical editions of Shakespeare's *King Lear* and *Measure for Measure*, and Middleton's *Hengist, King of Kent*. She is also the founder and director of the electronic archive www.henslowe-alleyn.org.uk. She is the General Editor of *The Complete Works of Thomas Heywood*, 10 vols. (forthcoming from Oxford University Press).

MacDonald P. Jackson is Professor Emeritus of English at the University of Auckland and a Fellow of the Royal Society of New Zealand. He is the author of *Defining Shakespeare: 'Pericles' as Test Case* (2003). He was an Associate General Editor of, and Contributor to, the Oxford *Thomas Middleton: The Collected Works* (2007), and the companion volume *Thomas Middleton and Early Modern Textual Culture*, and has been co-editor of two volumes of the Cambridge *Works of John Webster* (2003 and 2007). He has published widely not only on Shakespeare and his contemporaries but also on New Zealand literature.

James Kearney is Associate Professor of English at the University of California, Santa Barbara. He is the author of *The Incarnate Text: Imagining the Book in Reformation England* (2009), which won the CCL Book of the Year Award for 2009. His essays have appeared in the *Journal of Medieval and Early Modern Studies*, *English Literary Renaissance*, *Shakespeare Studies*, and the collection *Cultural Reformations: Medieval and Renaissance in Literary History*. He is currently working on a project concerning ethics and economics in the plays of Shakespeare.

Frederick Kiefer, Professor of English at the University of Arizona in Tucson, teaches Elizabethan and Jacobean drama. He is the author of *Fortune and Elizabethan Tragedy* (1983), *Writing on the Renaissance Stage: Written Words, Printed Pages, Metaphoric Books* (1996), and *Shakespeare's Visual Theatre: Staging the Personified Characters* (2003). He has also edited a collection of essays entitled *Masculinities and Femininities in the Middle Ages and Renaissance* (2009).

Roslyn L. Knutson, Emerita Professor of English at the University of Arkansas at Little Rock, is the author of *Playing Companies and Commerce in Shakespeare's Time* (2001), and *The Repertory of Shakespeare's Company, 1594–1613* (1991). She has published on theatre history in numerous journals, annuals, and essay collections including ones on the Queen's Men and Blackfriars Theatre. Her current projects include a repertorial analysis of the commercial theatrical marketplace in 1587–1593, when Christopher Marlowe's plays were new; and the wiki-style *Lost Plays Database* (www.lostplays.org), which she co-edits with David McInnis (University of Melbourne).

Douglas M. Lanier is Professor of English and Director of the London Programme at the University of New Hampshire. He has written widely on Shakespeare, contemporary popular adaptation and modern media, including *Shakespeare and Modern Popular Culture* (2002). He is currently working on two book-length studies, one on film adaptations of *Othello*, the other on disaffected intellectuals in early modern England.

Rebecca Lemon is the author of *Treason by Words: Literature, Law, and Rebellion in Shakespeare's England* (2006), as well as co-editor of *The Blackwell Companion to the Bible in English Literature* (2009), associate editor of *The Blackwell Encyclopedia of English Renaissance Literature* (forthcoming), and co-editor of the Shakespeare section of the journal *Blackwell Literature Compass*. Her essays on early modern literature, law, and political philosophy have appeared in numerous collections and journals. She is an Associate Professor of English at the University of Southern California.

Brian C. Lockey is Associate Professor of English Literature at St John's University in New York City. He is author of *Law and Empire in English Renaissance Literature* (2006), and his articles have appeared in *English Literary Renaissance*, the *Journal of the History of Ideas*, and the *Journal of Medieval and Early Modern Studies*. He has recently co-edited (along with Barbara Fuchs) a special issue of the *Journal for Early Modern Cultural Studies* on literary and historical perspectives on early modern Anglo-Spanish relations. He is currently writing a book tentatively entitled *Catholics, Royalists, and Cosmopolitans: Writing from the Margins of Renaissance England*.

Laury Magnus is Professor of Humanities at the United States Merchant Marine Academy at Kings Point, New York. Her work on Shakespeare includes the New Kittredge editions of *The Taming of the Shrew, Romeo and Juliet*, and forthcoming editions of *The Comedy of Errors* and *Measure for Measure*, as well as articles, reviews, and interviews in *Literature/Film Quarterly, Connotations, College Literature*, and *The Shakespeare Newsletter*. Her books also include a study of poetic repetition in early twentieth-century poetry and a co-translation of Ivan Goncharov's nineteenth-century Russian novel *The Precipice*. She is an Associate Member of the Columbia Shakespeare Seminar.

Lynne Magnusson is a Professor of English at the University of Toronto and Director of the Centre for Reformation and Renaissance Studies. She has published extensively on Shakespeare's language, early modern women's writing, the genre of the letter, and discourse analysis. The author of *Shakespeare and Social Dialogue* (1999), a co-author of *Reading Shakespeare's Dramatic Language* (2001), and co-editor of *The Elizabethan Theatre XI to XV*, she is completing a book provisionally entitled *The Transformation of the English Letter, 1520–1620* and editing the Norton Critical Edition of *Shakespeare's Sonnets*.

James J. Marino is Associate Professor of English at Cleveland State University, and the author of *Owning William Shakespeare: The King's Men and their Intellectual Property* from the University of Pennsylvania Press. His essays have appeared in *Shakespeare Quarterly, Renaissance Drama, The Oxford Handbook of Early Modern Theatre*, and elsewhere.

Arthur F. Marotti is Distinguished Professor of English at Wayne State University. He is the author of *John Donne, Coterie Poet* (1986), *Manuscript, Print and the English Renaissance Lyric* (1995), and *Religious Ideology and Cultural Fantasy: Catholic and Anti-Catholic Discourses in Early Modern England* (2005). He has also edited or co-edited nine collections of essays and numerous articles and book chapters on early modern English literature and culture. He is currently writing a book on the personal anthologizing of poetry in manuscript in early modern England.

Sonia Massai is Reader in Shakespeare Studies, King's College, London. Her research interests focus on Shakespeare in print and the reception of Shakespeare on stage, on screen, and across different languages and cultures. She is the author of *Shakespeare and the Rise of the Editor* (2007), and the editor of *World-Wide Shakespeares* (2005). Her editions of early modern plays include *Titus Andronicus* (2001), Thomas Heywood's *The Wise Woman of Hoxton* (2002), and John Ford's *'Tis Pity She's a Whore* (forthcoming). She is currently completing an edition of *The Paratext in English Printed Drama to the Restoration* for Cambridge University Press.

Matteo A. Pangallo is a doctoral candidate at the University of Massachusetts-Amherst, where he specializes in Renaissance dramatic literature and theatre history, text studies, and editorial theory. He holds an MA from King's College, London. He has published in the journals *Notes and Queries, Translation and Interpreting Studies, The Shakespeare Newsletter,* and in the essay collection *Divining Thoughts: Future Directions in Shakespeare Studies* (2007). His edition of Thomas May's *Tragedy of Antigone, the Theban Princesse* is forthcoming for the Malone Society. Currently he is working on a study of non-professional playwriting in early modern London.

Tanya Pollard is Associate Professor of English at the Graduate Center and Brooklyn College, City University of New York. Her publications include *Drugs and Theater in Early Modern England* (2005), *Shakespeare's Theater: A Sourcebook* (2003), and a number of essays on early modern theatre and medicine. She is currently writing a book on the the development of popular dramatic genres in early modern England and their debts to classical Greek plays and genre theory.

Catherine Richardson is Director of the Canterbury Centre for Medieval and Early Modern Studies and Senior Lecturer in Renaissance Literature at the University of Kent. Her research focuses on the material experience of daily life in early modern England on and offstage: on houses and furniture, and on the social, moral, and personal significance of clothing. She is author of *Domestic Life and Domestic Tragedy: The Material Life of the Household* (2006), and editor of *Clothing Culture, 1350–1650* (2004) and (with Tara Hamling) *Everyday Objects: Medieval and Early Modern Material Culture and Its Meanings* (2010).

Cathy Shrank is Professor of Early Modern Literature at the University of Sheffield. Her publications include *Writing the Nation in Reformation England, 1530–1580* (2004, 2006) and essays and articles on various early modern topics, including language reform, civility, travel writing, cheap print, mid-sixteenth-century sonnets, and Benson's 1640 edition of Shakespeare's *Poems*. With Mike Pincombe, she is co-editor of *The Oxford Handbook of Tudor Literature, 1485–1603* (2009). She is currently working on an edition of Shakespeare's poems for Longman Annotated English Poets and a monograph on non-dramatic dialogue in the sixteenth and early seventeenth centuries.

Alan Somerset is Professor Emeritus of English at the University of Western Ontario. He is the editor of *Shropshire* for Records of Early English Drama (1994, 2 vols.), as well as numerous articles, papers, and reviews on early theatres, theatre history, and Shakespeare. He is currently completing his edition of Staffordshire and Warwickshire for

REED. He continues to be engaged in creating, with Dr Sally-Beth MacLean, the 'Patrons, Performances and Playing Places Web Site' (http://link.library.utoronto.ca/reed); this site has been available to the public for over five years.

Fran Teague is the Josiah Meigs Professor of English at the University of Georgia. Her research interests include performance history and theory, as well as early modern women writers, and she has published and edited essays and books in both fields. Most recently, she published *Shakespeare and the American Popular Stage* (2006) and a chapter on early modern playhouses in *The Oxford Handbook of Early Modern Theatre*, edited by Richard Dutton (2009). She also works as a dramaturg and director.

Ann Thompson is Professor of English at King's College, London. She is a General Editor of the Arden Shakespeare and has (with Neil Taylor) edited all three texts of *Hamlet* for Arden (2006). Other publications include an edition of *The Taming of the Shrew* (1984, updated 2003), *Shakespeare's Chaucer* (1978), *Shakespeare, Meaning and Metaphor* (with John O. Thompson, 1987), *Teaching Women: Feminism and English Studies* (edited with Helen Wilcox, 1989), *Women Reading Shakespeare, 1660–1900* (edited with Sasha Roberts, 1996), and *In Arden: Editing Shakespeare* (with Gordon McMullan, 2003).

Jessica Wolfe is Associate Professor of English and Comparative Literature at the University of North Carolina Chapel Hill. She is the author of *Humanism, Machinery, and Renaissance Literature* (2004) and is completing a second book on the reception of Homer in the sixteenth and seventeenth centuries. She will be co-editing Thomas Browne's *Pseudodoxia Epidemica* for the new Oxford University Press edition of Browne's complete works; also in progress is a revised edition of *The Faerie Queene* for Penguin.

Tzachi Zamir is a philosopher and a literary critic affiliated to the Department of English and the Department of General and Comparative Literature at the Hebrew University of Jerusalem. His main publications include *Double Vision: Moral Philosophy and Shake-spearean Drama* (2006) and *Ethics and the Beast* (2007).

Adam Zucker is Associate Professor of English at the University of Massachusetts-Amherst, where he teaches courses on Tudor and Stuart drama and poetry. He is the co-editor, with Alan B. Farmer, of *Localizing Caroline Drama: Politics and Economics of the Early Modern English Stage* (2006), and the author of *The Places of Wit in Early Modern Comedy* (2011). Recent publications include essays on urban space in Julie Sanders (ed.), *Ben Jonson in Context* (2010) and on gambling in Amanda Bailey and Roze Hentschell (eds.), *Masculinity and the Metropolis of Vice, 1550–1650* (2010).

....

INTRODUCTION

....

ARTHUR F. KINNEY

IN the past 400 years over 100 documents relating to William Shakespeare have been recovered: he is the best known playwright of his time. There are church registries, deeds of property, tax certificates, marriage bonds, writs of attachment, and court records. Of the 230 plays still extant from that period, more than 15 per cent are wholly or partly his work, what Bill Bryson calls 'a gloriously staggering proportion'.[1] Only two of his plays—*Love's Labour's Won* and *Cardenio*—appear to be lost. What we have has been calculated as 884,647 words, composing 51,939 speeches spread over 118,406 lines excluding the sonnets and poems; and of those words the *Oxford English Dictionary* credits Shakespeare with the first recorded use of 2,035 of them—words such as *abstentious, critical, frugal, dwindle, extract, horrid, vast, hereditary, excellent, eventful, barefooted, assassination, lonely, well-read,* and *indistinguishable.* Even some of his earliest work—*Titus Andronicus* and *Love's Labour's Lost*—introduces 140 of them. What the accumulated records show, however, is not only someone astonishingly creative but also someone very complex.

According to the baptismal registers for the parish of Holy Trinity Church in Stratford-upon-Avon, Warwickshire, 'Gulielmas filius Johannes Shakespere' was received into the church on April 26, 1564, the same year Michelangelo and John Calvin died and Galileo was born: he shared the name William with 25 per cent of the other boys at the time. If this event followed custom, he was born three days earlier, on April 23, St George's Day, the same day he would die in 1616 at the age of 52. He was the

---

[1] Bill Bryson, *Shakespeare: The World as Stage* (New York: Atlas Books, HarperCollins, 2007), 19. The following statistics are also from Bryson. Other works consulted in writing this essay are: William Baker, *William Shakespeare* (London: Continuum, 2009); Jonathan Bate, *Soul of the Age: The Life, Mind, and World of William Shakespeare* (New York: Viking, 2008); E. K. Chambers, *William Shakespeare: A Study of Facts and Problems* (Oxford: Clarendon Press, 1930); S. Schoenbaum, *Shakespeare: His Life, His English, His Theater* (New York: Signet Classics, 1980); S. Schoenbaum: *William Shakespeare: A Documentary Life* (New York: Oxford University Press, 1975); S. Schoenbaum, *Shakespeare's Lives,* new edn. (Oxford: Clarendon Press, 1991); and Simon Trussler, *Will's Will: The Last Wishes of William Shakespeare* (Kew Gardens: National Archives, 2007).

third child and first son of John and Anne (or Agnes) Hathaway Shakespeare and the first child to survive childhood. Less than three months after his birth, the burial section of the parish register notes *Hic incepit pestis* (here begins plague) and the epidemic, which began that spring, spread rapidly in the autumn, taking the lives of at least 200 people, ten times the normal rate and one out of seven in the town; one of the Shakespeares' neighbours lost four children. We might speculate that, given such fierce danger, the Shakespeares harboured their new baby at the home of his maternal grandparents in nearby Wilmecote.

Shakespeare's father was then 34. He had grown up on a farm in the nearby village of Snitterfield before moving by 1552 to Stratford, a bustling market town of 1,200 people living in 240 households along a dozen streets. He must have arrived by 1552 when he paid a fine of twelve pence for allowing dirt to pile up in front of his house. He was first a craftsman, then a merchant, a glover, a wholesaler—and a usurer. He must have been successful from the start, for in 1556 he began a series of town appointments—first as the borough ale taster, supervising the measures and prices throughout Stratford, and then, successively, constable (doubtless superior to Dogberry); affeeror, one who issues fines not covered by statute; burgess; chamberlain, handling town finances and property; alderman; and finally, in 1568, when Shakespeare was 4, high bailiff (or mayor), a job in which he approved town funds for performances of visiting actors. They acted in Shakespeare's grammar school on Church Street: the Queen's players came in 1558-9; Worcester's Men in 1569 (for a year), 1574-5, 1576-7, 1580-1, and 1581-2; Leicester's Players in 1573-4, 1576-7; Lord Strange's Men in 1578-9, Essex's Men in 1578-9; Derby's Men in 1579-80; and Lord Bartlett's Men in 1579-80. Likely Shakespeare saw some of these plays as a boy and early teenager; he is also likely to have accompanied his father to the famous cycles of mystery plays in nearby Coventry, since their structure informs that of *The Comedy of Errors* and *Richard III*.

The records show that John Shakespeare never missed a town meeting. He was also saving and investing his money. In 1562 he purchased a home and garden in upscale Henley Street, a block from the town cross; in time he would buy the adjacent building also for his glover's shop. In 1575 he paid £40 for two more houses. But not all of his financial dealings were so respectable. Around 1569 he was prosecuted for usury and illegal practices in wool-dealing. He was accused again, and in one case fined, in 1570 and 1572. Late in 1578 he was borrowing money by selling land, mortgaging some of his wife's inheritance, and, in 1579, selling a share of his property in Snitterfield. In 1576 he withdrew from active church participation; in 1586 he was replaced as town alderman. In 1592 he was fined for recusancy, his name placed among those who were thought to forbear coming to church 'for feare of processe of debtte'. But his fortunes improved during the last decade of his life, perhaps with the help of his son. In 1596, following requests by him and by William, he was granted a coat of arms, becoming a gentleman of substance with 'lands and tenements of good wealth and substance' worth an impressive £500. (In time, William would have a coat of arms too, like his fellow players Richard Burbage, John Hemings, Augustine Phillips, and Thomas Pope.)

Shakespeare's mother was Mary Arden of Wilmecote, whose father Robert was Shakespeare's landlord. She was a descendant of an old provincial family living on a large farm at the edge of a rapidly diminishing Forest of Arden, a setting for *As You Like It*: John Shakespeare married up the social register as his son William would do. She bore eight children. Two were short-lived: Joan, baptized in 1558, died in childhood, and Margaret died in 1563, the year she was born. Following William there were Gilbert, a haberdasher, born in 1566 and buried in 1612; a second sister Joan, christened in 1569 who alone outlived William, finally residing in the house in Henley Street; Anne, born in 1571 and buried in 1579; Richard, born in 1574 and died in 1613; and the youngest, Edmund, who followed his brother William to London and became an actor too, and died in 1607 (perhaps a victim of the plague) and was buried there in Southwark Cathedral, some two days' horseride from Stratford and the graves of all his family. Of the eight children, only William and Joan married; and Joan, marrying a hatter, William Hart, remained childless at his death in 1616.

Although no records remain, William must have walked the four blocks to the King's New School, a public school for merchants' children, for his plays and poems lean heavily on the lessons of grammar, rhetoric, and logic that made up grammar-school curricula as well as readings of classical texts that are frequently alluded to in his works. School days went from six in the morning (seven in winter) until five at night with a break for lunch. They were generally conducted in Latin and Latin was spoken during recess. After learning Latin grammar, the students were taught rhetoric by way of declamations (formal speeches such as the funeral orations of Brutus and Antony in *Julius Caesar*); debate through Latin dialogue (as in the trial scenes of *Merchant of Venice* and *Othello* and *The Winter's Tale*), often through the speeches in the essays of Cicero often playing the part of historical figures. Besides such imitations—called *prosopopeia*—they also read (and acted) plays by Plautus (such as the *Menaechimi* used in *Comedy of Errors*) or Seneca (a basis for revenge tragedies like *Hamlet*). Here Shakespeare would have read his favourite writer, Ovid (whose *Amores* serve as a model for Shakespeare's sonnets and whose *Fasti* serves as a model for *The Rape of Lucrece*), whose *Heroides* is a model for letters in *King Lear* (and form a basis for female soliloquies of Helena, Cressida, and Cleopatra), and the whole idea of transformation, the subject of *Metamorphoses* (which appears in *Merry Wives of Windsor*, *The Tempest*, and, most especially, *A Midsummer Night's Dream*).

Customarily in sixteenth-century Stratford, men of 25 or 26 married women much younger than themselves (life expectancy for men was around 35). But Shakespeare was an exception: he was 18 when he married Anne Hathaway of neighbouring Shottery, aged 26, the daughter of a landed farmer to whom his father loaned money, in early December 1582. No marriage licence has survived, but there is a marriage bond that cost £40 (today, £10,000) that allowed the marriage to proceed with a single reading of the banns instead of the required three each Sunday and indemnified the church authorities against suits arising from this action. The ceremony was held five miles from Stratford in the chapel of Luddington, Temple Grafton, officiated by John Firth, whom one observer called a man of 'unsound religion'. (The marriage may well have followed a more private or public ceremony of handfasting or pledge of commitment.) Their first child, Susanna, was baptized six months later, on May 26, 1583. She was followed by the twins Judith and Hamnet, named for family friends Judith and Hamnet Sandler, a baker and his wife who lived on Bridge Street and probably served as godparents. They were baptized on February 2, 1585: Shakespeare was the father of three children before he was 21. There were no more children; Stratford registers show that mothers producing twins rarely had further offspring.

All known records of Shakespeare disappear from 1585 until 1592 when he appears in London as an actor and a collaborator writing *Henry VI*. In 1681 the biographer and gossip John Aubrey noted that Shakespeare was a schoolmaster in the country and recent elaborations have sought to have him follow the Jesuit Edmund Campion, briefly visiting Stratford, to Lancaster where he taught in a Catholic household. But there is no documentation for this. In these 'lost years' he is also said to have studied law, preparing him for the staging of *Comedy of Errors* at Gray's Inn, one of the Inns of Court (or law schools) in London; to have become a professional writer or scrivener like the playwright Thomas Kyd; or to travel in northern Italy, since he sets plays in Verona, Padua, and Venice; or to serve in the military in Flanders since he shows some knowledge of military life in the *Henriad* and elsewhere; or even sailing with Sir Francis Drake on the *Golden Hinde* since a number of plays concern sea voyages. All these are speculations only. Since playing companies often worked on the model of guilds and actors were expected to apprentice for seven years, perhaps that is where he was, playing and travelling with the Queen's Men or with Lord Strange's Men.

London was a city of about 200,000 some 85 miles southeast of Stratford; it took four days to walk there or two days on horseback (Shakespeare is said to have broken his trip by staying at the Golden Cross Inn at Oxford). It was the third largest city in Europe, after Paris and Naples: 448 crammed acres around the Tower of London and the old St Paul's Cathedral, roughly 100 parishes closed in by a town wall with various gates— Bishopsgate, Cripplegate, Newgate, Aldgate—that were locked at dusk and reopened at dawn. To one side lay Westminster, with its palace and Parliament House; to the north lay the suburb of Shoreditch; to the east and south lay the Thames, a wide river of heavy commerce that separated the city from Southwark, the home of the brothels, bearbaiting pits, prisons, lunatic asylums, unconsecrated graveyards, and, in time, public theatres. Inside the city walls, plays were staged in the large innyards of the Bel Savage, the Cross Keys, the Bell, and the Bull.

London's first true playhouse was the Red Lion, built in Whitechapel in 1567 by the entrepreneur John Brayne, when Shakespeare was three years old. It may not have lasted long, for within nine years Brayne, in partnership with his brother-in-law James Burbage, a carpenter and actor, was building the Theatre, an outdoor amphitheatre a few hundred yards north of the city near Finsbury Fields in Shoreditch that, for years, would be the main playhouse for Shakespeare and his company. Two years later, just up the road in Holywell, Philip Henslowe built a rival playhouse, the Curtain. Shoreditch, like Southwark, was a part of the 'liberties', jurisdictions free of the London city government, which refused to allow playhouses since they might cause the kind of unruly crowds that spread uprisings and the plague. (The only public activity the City Fathers permitted was churchgoing.) Not until 1595 with the building of the Swan did Southwark begin to displace Shoreditch as the main theatre district; it was preceded by Henslowe's Rose (1587), followed by the Globe, the Hope, and the Fortune.

Shakespeare joined Burbage's playing company at the Theatre in Shoreditch in 1592. The company was organized hierarchically: there were sharers (shareholders), actors, hired men, and apprentices. Master players signed the patent. Sharers split the profits after costs (Shakespeare took out one-twelfth of the shares). Other company members took constant inventory, purchased playbooks, selected routes for provincial travels to great halls of landed nobility and gentry and town halls of towns and villages, and scheduled performances. Hired men worked behind the stage, took tickets, and played walk-on parts or silent roles. Boy apprentices, playing the women's parts, received training, room, board, and clothing. The playing company helped the local economy by hiring a workforce, by paying taxes, and (in the case of the Fortune theatre), paying taxes for poor relief. Shakespeare probably made between £150 and £300 a year from his shares (equivalent to £30,000–£40,000 today).

He was also an actor; he is listed in documents from 1592, 1603, and 1608—the latter two as a member of the cast of Ben Jonson's *Every Man in His Humour* and *Sejanus His Fall*. Companies might keep as many as thirty plays in their active repertoire, so that actors could be asked to memorize as many as 15,000 lines at one time. Players rehearsed in the morning and played in the London public playhouses in the afternoon, or in provincial town halls and the great halls of noble estates in the evening. According to Philip Henslowe's *Diary*, the Admiral's Men performed 15 different plays in 27 playing days. A new play might be performed up to three times in a given year. The average play ran to about 2,700 lines, running about two hours or two and a half hours on stage, but recently unearthed evidence suggests some longer plays—like *Hamlet* and *Antony and Cleopatra*—might run four hours in both public and private playhouses. There is no primary documentation of Shakespeare as an actor, although John Davies of Hereford wrote in 1611:

> Some say (good Will) which I, in sport, do sing,
> Hadst thou not played some King parts in sport,
> Thou hadst been the companion for a King
> And, been a King, among the meaner sort:

He could represent a king, but also kingliness. Shakespeare may also have acted in the first play on which he collaborated: *1 Henry VI*, which opened in the first week of March 1592. It earned £3.16s.8d. at the opening and played fourteen times over the next four months. Henslowe's *Diary* also tells us that 'titus & ondrinicus' was played at the Rose on January 14, 1594. The play shows Shakespeare learning his craft in conjunction with his collaborator George Peele: where Peele has Tamora turn upon the Goths in Act 1, Shakespeare rounds out the play with Lucius and Marcus leaving Rome for the Goths; he counters Peele's Titus, willing to sacrifice his son Mutius at the start with Aaron's protection of his son near the end. Shakespeare's early work on the first tetralogy, in which each play was left unfinished for the next one to begin, may have also taught Shakespeare both the dramatic effect of inconclusiveness and the consequent desirability to involve the audience in formulating their own conclusions. That becomes an open invitation in *Henry V*: 'Can this cockpit hold the vasty fields of France?'; 'eech out our performance with your mind'. The same inconclusiveness aborts the marriages presumed at the end of *Love's Labour's Lost*, the unending competition between the Montagues and Capulets, the tales still untold by Horatio and Lodovico about the lives and significance of Hamlet and Othello.

And then, disastrously it must have seemed, Shakespeare's theatre career came to an abrupt halt in 1593, when for two years the plague in London prevented the staging of plays. More than half the theatres were closed and Shakespeare, now 29, turned to writing poetry under the patronage of Henry Wrothesley, third Earl of Southampton and Baron of Titchfield. He drew on Ovid for *Venus and Adonis* and on Livy and Ovid for *The Rape of Lucrece*, two longer narrative poems. The first of these established him as an important poet and outsold every other work of his published in his lifetime.

By 1595 he was back with his old playing company as the resident dramatist—what was termed an 'ordinary poet' who wrote two plays a year to his company's deadlines and with the company's particular actors in mind. The Burbage family owned half the shares and Richard Burbage was their leading actor: he was doubtless the King of Navarre, probably Benedick and Shylock, and almost certainly Prince Hal, Henry V, Hamlet, Othello, and Lear. It is more difficult to propose roles for others in the company—for Augustine Phillips; for John Heminge, a former grocer; for Henry Condell, initially a hired man; and for Thomas Pope. But the clown parts went to William Kempe, who played Launce, Lancelot Gobbo, and Dogberry and then, after he retired in 1599, Shakespeare wrote more serious cerebral clown parts for Robert Armin—Touchstone, Feste, Lear's Fool, Thersites.

The first decade, the 1590s, was a time when Holinshed's *Chronicles*, along with the histories of John Hall, William Camden, and Richard Grafton, were hugely popular as a consequence of the unexpected and miraculous defeat of the awesome Armada from Spain in August of 1588. England found herself a naval power and, as a country that wanted to know more about itself, was consumed in nation building. It is the time of Shakespeare's many history plays—the two tetralogies of *1, 2*, and *3 Henry VI* and *Richard III*; of *Richard II*, *1* and *2 Henry IV*, and *Henry V*—that explored troublesome times of the past while tracing the ancestral background of the Tudors; the plays concentrate on tumult and war while tracing the demise of a code of honour in favour of a pragmatic, even Machiavellian rule of power. At the end of the 1590s with the rising demands of the House of Commons and the lack of clear succession to an ageing and sickly Queen, plays dealt with change in leadership and even assassination: *Julius Caesar* and *Hamlet*. The Danish play, in fact, seems particularly pointed as it examined surveillance during the increasingly recognized systems of spying and counterspying by Sir Francis Walsingham and his successors and the treatment of prisoners by the Queen's torturer, Topcliffe. In 1596, *Romeo and Juliet* combined tragedy with a reference to a recent English earthquake and the sudden invasion of plague.

Yet, remarkably, the 1590s was also the time of Shakespeare's sunniest comedies—of *Comedy of Errors* and *The Taming of the Shrew*, of *Love's Labour's Lost* and *Midsummer Night's Dream* and *Merchant of Venice*; of *Much Ado about Nothing*, *The Merry Wives of Windsor*, and *As You Like It*. Shakespeare not only understood popular trends but (as later with tragedies and romances) had a hand on the nation's temperamental pulse and an eye for the market. He understood that the theatre was not only a place where history was taught but a place where social customs were learned and social behaviour was modelled. Nor was he one who declined to learn from his own successes. The successful use of twins in *Comedy of Errors* laid the groundwork for *Twelfth Night*; the failure of Hotspur to get reinforcement from Northumberland and Glendower was repeated in the failure of the Lord Governour of Harfleur to get expected and necessary support; the punishment of Malvolio anticipates the same scene with Parolles; the bed trick that permits the plot to work in *All's Well That Ends Well* also works in *Measure for Measure*. He learned to begin drama by an early interruption: Petruchio arriving in Padua, Hamlet arriving at Elsinore, a ship sailing past Prospero's island. He learned the dynamics of plot construction, cresting near the centre of Act 3. He learned how penetrating characterization can be realized within the talented strengths of his resident company, letting Kate and Petruchio reappear as Beatrice and Benedick and Lance reappear as Lancelot Gobbo. In the sudden miraculous reappearance of Rosalind at the end of *As You Like It*, he lay the groundwork for the reappearance of Helena, of Marina, and of Hermione. But he also learned how to dig deeply into the minds and passions of his characters, calibrating in Hamlet the fear and anxiety of the Ghost with the idea he represents, the unknown and undiscovered country of the mind. Shakespeare's discoveries meet up with our own: in Pistol he portrays post-traumatic stress disorder.

He juggled all his roles in the Lord Chamberlain's Men with those of characters and events in his life. In August 1596, his only son Hamnet died of unknown causes at the age of 11: he would have no male heirs to carry on the Shakespeare name. We do not know how he grieved, although lines in which Constance laments the death of young Arthur in *King John* may be a possibility:

> Grief fills the room of my absent child,
> Lies in his bed, walks up and down with me,
> Puts on his pretty looks, repeats his words,
> Remembers me of all his gracious parts,
> Stuffs out his vacant garments with his form;
> Then had I reason to be fond of grief,
> Fare you well.

Nevertheless, in nine months he was investing heavily in the future: in May 1597, he bought New Place, the second largest house in Stratford. It was brick and timber, with five gables, ten fireplaces, two barns, and an orchard on the corner of Chapel Street and Chapel Lane and across a side street from the grammar school. It had belonged to William Underhill, who had been poisoned the previous year by his eldest son Fulke, who would shortly be executed in Warwick for his crime. A short time later Shakespeare purchased the cottage across the road, presumably for a servant's quarters: like his father he saved his money and made investments in Warwickshire real estate; continuing only to rent various quarters in London while his family stayed in Stratford. The purchases of land in Shottery and Old Stratford came at a time of deep recession: three years of dearth had decimated crops and starvation was rampant; real wages declined to less than a third of what they were in buying power a century earlier; basic foodstuffs—peas, beans, cereals—had doubled in price and bread had risen by 400 per cent. The high bailiff called in all the grain supplies in and around Stratford to distribute them equitably and found that two citizens had been hoarding grain to drive up the price: one of them was William Shakespeare. In these two years, moreover—in 1597 and 1598—Shakespeare was defaulting on his London taxes and fined 5 shillings. In many respects, then, he was his father's son. He confirmed this by buying for his father the coat of arms that would descend to him.

During the night of December 28, 1598, Shakespeare's playing company, bolstered by a dozen or more workmen, secretly dismantled the Theatre in Shoreditch and trans-ported it across the Thames to Southwark, where they rebuilt it (overnight, it was said) and christened it the Globe: the lease had run out in Shoreditch and was not renewable, and the company leased the new land in Southwark for thirty-one years assigned to Cuthbert Burbage, his brother Richard, and five other members of the company. This is the 'wooden O' the Chorus pronounces in the Prologue to *Henry V* and for the opening months Shakespeare wrote that play as well as *Julius Caesar*, *As You Like It*, and began *Hamlet*: he must have been elated at this transfer and with New Place, because he was now writing at the top of his form. The first (bad) quarto of *Hamlet* was completed in 1601, a better quarto version by 1604; and in 1607 the first extant records of a performance documented that it was played on September 5 aboard a ship, the *Red Dragon*, off the shore of what is now known as Sierra Leone, forced there by a storm. 'We gave the tragedie of Hamlet', someone noted in the ship's log. And again, on September 31, the head of the ship invited a fellow captain 'to a fish dinner and had Hamlet acted abord . . . w[hi]ch [per]mit to keepe my people from idelness and unlaw-ful games or sleep'. By then, Shakespeare had become masterful in connecting symbolic words and thoughts, building his plays on metaphor—they are heavily metaphorical even for his day—and metonymy, what is seen and heard and what is realized like *bond* in *Merchant of Venice* or *blood* in the forthcoming *Macbeth*. It was his dramatic and enacted process, but decidedly more, it was a receiving and factoring process that, now throughout the plays, depended like their endings on the participation of his audience.

In the final years of Queen Elizabeth and the first years of James I, from 1601 to 1608, Shakespeare's plays reached their tragic apex with *Othello*, *Lear*, *Antony and Cleopatra*, and *Coriolanus*, speaking like James of power and empire. A darker tone invades the comedies of *Twelfth Night*, *Troilus and Cressida*, and *Measure for Measure* extending into the bitterness of *Timon of Athens* and the cynicism of *Troilus and Cressida* (where plague is displaced by syphilis). But even as he wrote these darker plays, he continued to push his money into home town investments. On May 1, 1602, he signed a deed of conveyance for 107 acres of land in Stratford, acquiring open fields north of Old Stratford for £320. In 1605, he bought from Ralph Huband a substantial share in Stratford tithes which paid him £60 per annum. In a sense, he was an opportunist: in 1594 and 1595 two 'disastrous fires' destroyed 200 buildings in the centre of town and displaced 400 people; by 1601, about 700 citizens of Stratford, roughly one-third of the town, were registered as paupers. But London was no better off; although records show that Shakespeare roomed as a lodger on Silver Street, London, with the Mountjoy family in 1603–4, he may have spent much of his time in Stratford. Once again plague broke out in London in 1603, taking 30,500 lives, and continuing for years. As a result, the theatres were closed within seven miles of London from May 1603 to April 1604; from May to September 1604; from October to December 1605: in the first six and a half years of James's reign theatres were only open a total of two years. Aside from the notations on Silver Lane, Cripplegate, there is no evidence that Shakespeare remained in the city. He may have made additions to Thomas Kyd's *The Spanish Tragedy* in 1604, becoming a play doctor. Now he wrote only one play a year, and his collaborations increased: *Timon of Athens* written with Thomas Middleton, *Pericles* written with the brothel-keeper George Wilkins, *Henry VIII* and *Two Noble Kinsmen* written with John Fletcher, his successor as the resident dramatist for the Lord Chamberlain's Company, made the King's Men by royal patent in 1603. Shakespeare's writing grew more complex and allusive, his single-authored works longer. They lacked the tight control of his earlier work. His company stayed active, performing before the court 187 times—a number greater than that of all the other companies' performances combined. Such performances might be with the court outside plague-ridden London as well as at Whitehall when the epidemic subsided, but there is no documentation that Shakespeare was present, and at least one scholar has speculated that Shakespeare retired to Stratford not in 1611 but in 1604.

On June 5, 1607, Susanna Shakespeare married Dr John Hall, ten years her senior. He was the most prominent and respected doctor in Stratford, treating his patients largely with herbal remedies, many of which he concocted. His case book, *Select Observations on English Bodies of Eminent Persons in Desperate Diseases*, was published decades later but reprints of one of his works are still available at his home, Hall's Croft, which is open to visitors, and still in much the way he left it in Stratford, two blocks from the site of New Place. But later that year, on September 5, Edmund died in London and was buried there, the only member of his family not laid to rest at Holy Trinity Church in Stratford.

The following year was similarly notable. Elizabeth Hall, Shakespeare's granddaughter, was christened on February 21. (She was also his last surviving descendant, dying unmarried in 1670). Little over a half-year later, on September 9, 1608, Mary Arden Shakespeare was buried. Somewhat earlier, Shakespeare sued a Stratford man for debt, the case winding on from December 17 to June 7, 1609. Things were brighter financially that year in London. The Blackfriars Theatre, located in the old Blackfriars monastery within the city walls, fell under royal control and the King's Men leased it from Richard Burbage and performed continuously there from the autumn of 1609 until the closing of all the theatres in 1642 at the outbreak of the Civil War. It was an indoor theatre and allowed the King's Men to play through the winter and in inclement weather. Rather than seating 3,000, as the Globe and other amphitheatres did, it seated only 600, including some who sat on the stage, sharing it with the actors. The darkened room was lit by candelabra, which had to be lowered periodically so that candles could be trimmed and relit, causing plays for the first time to be divided into acts. But the candelabra partially blocked the view from the higher seats, those that cost the most in the open-air theatres, and the pit, where groundlings stood at the Globe and elsewhere, became the most expensive location. This, and the size of the theatre, made the presentations far more intimate. On March 10, 1613, Shakespeare purchased the nearby Blackfriars Gatehouse from Henry Walker, an eminent London musician, for £140. He paid £80 down but neglected to pay on the mortgage, which remained unpaid at his death, thus preventing any future claims on the property by his heirs. He must have rarely used it, if at all; it was, at the time of probating his will, described as 'All that Messauge or ten[emen]t with thappurtenances wherein one John Robinson dwelleth, scituat, lyeing and being in the blackfriers in London nere the Wardrobe.'

Shakespeare drafted his will in January 1616 with his lawyer, Francis Collins, at a cost of £13.6s.8d. A month later, his second daughter Judith, already 31 and still unmarried, wedded a local vintner, Thomas Quiney. He was the son of Richard Quiney, one of Shakespeare's prosperous friends, but the marriage, to be performed during Lent, required a special licence that the couple failed to obtain and, as a consequence, were briefly excommunicated. They were probably anxious to complete the ceremony because on March 26 Quiney was arraigned for 'carnal intercourse' with Margaret Wheeler, who, as a result, had become pregnant. A month later she died in childbirth and Quiney confessed the charge of fornication in ecclesiastical court. Instead of public penance, he was given a fine of 5 shillings. Shakespeare changed his will so that Judith's inheritance was as executed by John and Susanna Hall; Quiney was offered £150 only if he equalled the amount as a part of the marriage.

Shakespeare's will is extant as a part of the National Archives. He left to his sister Joan Hart the house on Henley Street at a small rent as well as his clothes. He left his daughter Judith £100 as a marriage portion, interest on £150 for her children, the cottage on Chapel Lane, and a silver and gilt bowl; he left his only grandchild, Elizabeth Hall, 8 years old at his death, most of his silver and New Place on the death of her parents; he left the poor of Stratford a total of £10 (an unusually small sum); he left his friend Thomas Combe of Stratford his sword; he left Hamnet Sandler (who witnessed the will) and three of his fellow players (Richard Burbage, Henry Condell, and John Hemings) 28s.6d. each for memorial rings; William Walter of Stratford 20s.; and Susanna and John Hall, his executors, New Place, all his household goods, and any papers or books. Susanna received everything not mentioned. A later interlineation remembered his wife Anne, and he assigned to her, rather stingingly, the second best bed, and its furnishings. This last bequest has particularly puzzled scholars who suggest that it might be the marital bed which he and Anne shared and in which she conceived their children, the best bed reserved for guests as was the custom. It may also reflect Mary Shakespeare's own failing, since she was put into the care of Judith as the main executrix. This may (or may not) be in keeping with the fact that Anne seems to have been initially omitted from the will. She died in August 1623, just weeks before the splendid publication of the First Folio of her husband's *Works*.

The Workes of William Shakespeare, containing all his Comedies, Histories and Tragedies: Truly set forth, according to their first ORIGINALL begins with 'The Names of the Principall Actors in all these Playes' and divides the plays by genre, except for *Troilus and Cressida*, which appears to be a late addition. The printing was overseen by William Jaggard and his son Isaac, but the handsetting of the oversized 907 pages, begun in 1622 and finished two years later, using up to nine printers working in three printshops, was modelled on an earlier folio publication, *The Works of Benamin Ionson*. Condell and Hemings served as the editors, collecting from the company library what they thought to be the best versions, all of them therefore theatrically based. It was a magnificent and vital venture; without the editors saving the texts, we would be, without the Folio, without *Macbeth*; *The Tempest*; *Julius Caesar*; *The Two Gentleman of Verona*; *Measure for Measure*; *The Comedy of Errors*; *As You Like It*; *The Taming of the Shrew*; *King John*; *All's Well That Ends Well*; *Twelfth Night*; *The Winter's Tale*; *Henry VI, Part I*; *Henry VIII*; *Coriolanus*; *Cymbeline*; *Timon of Athens*; and *Anthony and Cleopatra*. *Pericles* was omitted. Ben Jonson wrote two memorial verses, and James Mabbe wrote one:

> To the memory of Master W. Shakespeare
> We wondered, Shakespeare, that thou went'st so soon
> From the world's stage to the grave's tiring-room.
> We thought thee dead, but this thy printed worth
> Tells thy spectators that thou went'st but forth
> To enter with applause. An actor's art
> Can die, and live to act a second part.
> That's but an exit of mortality;
> This, a re-entrance to a plaudity.

Shakespeare's scope and achievement were singular and recognized as such by his contemporaries. In 1598, Francis Meres had been the first, in *Palladis Tamia*, to point out Shakespeare's versatility. Edmund Bolton noted that 'this man, the sun of the stage, handles tragedy and comedy with equal skill'. And in 1638, the well-known poet Edmund Waller wrote,

> For thou couldst all *characters* impart,
> So none can render thing, who still escapes,
> Like Proteus in a variety of shapes,
> Who was nor this nor that, but all we find,
> And all we can imagine in mankind,[2]

deliberately echoing the opening Chorus in *Henry V*. All we can imagine.

But we imagine because his plays invite us to do that, whether we read them or see them or hear them. And there is much we still do not know. We do not know what he

---

[2] The references to Bolton and Waller are taken from Jeffrey Knapp, *Shakespeare Only* (Chicago, IL: University of Chicago Press, 2009), 28. The list of speculations at the end of the essay is an expansion of that given in Knapp, 19.

looked like. Candos never knew him. And Condell and Hemings, choosing a fronti-spiece for his *Works*, published a portrait by the Flemish engraver Martin Droeshut, who never saw Shakespeare either; and while his editors would be thought unlikely to publish a portrait that was misleading, it is starkly different from the pudgy burgher-like sculpture of Shakespeare in Holy Trinity Church in Stratford, erected by his neighbours and friends who did know him: they can't both be right. We do not know how to spell his name, since he spelled it at least six different ways (in an age when spelling seemed less significant). We do not know how he pronounced his name, as 'Shake' or 'Shack'. We have no autobiography, or notes, or diaries, or personal manuscripts. We do not know anything about his marriage, his relations with his wife, or his family life. We do not know how he spent his time or with whom he spent it. We do not know if he ever left England. We do not know if he ever apprenticed to his father or learned a trade or craft. We do not know how he spent his 'lost years'. We do not know what actors trained him. We do not know exactly what he wrote and in what order he wrote it. We do not know his religion or his politics. We do not know his sexual orientation. We do not know his social life in London or how long or where he lived there. Finally, we do not know the cause of his death. There is much room, therefore, to speculate.

What we know—beyond his glorious works—is that he was never imprisoned or censored. He was the only playwright of his time to have a lasting and stable relation-ship with a single company. And he was the only playwright who retired by choice, not by circumstance. In itself this is an enviable record.

What follows now in this volume are the considered observations of many of the most distinguished Shakespeareans looking in detail at all dimensions of his career and his work. While subjects were assigned to each of them, the coverage and perspective is wholly theirs.

PART I

TEXTS

CHAPTER 1

....

AUTHORSHIP

....

HUGH CRAIG

I. KINDS OF AUTHORSHIP

....

'AUTHORSHIP' in relation to Shakespeare can mean a number of things. There is, first of all, the question of whether the William Shakespeare who was christened in Stratford in April 1564, and whose death was recorded there in April 1616, in fact wrote the plays and poems we group together as 'Shakespeare'. While most of the people who go to 'Shakespeare' plays and read 'Shakespeare' works accept that William Shakespeare wrote them, as do almost all the scholars who are professionally concerned with these texts, there are some who doubt the connection and argue that some other person or persons is responsible. For these people this is the Shakespeare authorship question.

Then there is a second set of questions, focused more on 'authorship' than on Shakespeare: what does authorship mean in general, and what does it mean at any particular time and in any particular literary system? This has been the focus of a good deal of scholarly work and discussion. A range of views is current, from a traditional view that authorship is essentially the domain of an individual working independently to more recent conceptions that authorship is in its nature collaborative, driven more by social, technological, and institutional networks, and closely constrained by the *mentalité* of the era and by language itself. Then we need to consider local and historical factors. Plays, like film scripts, need a host of material resources and creative inputs before they can be realized in performance: in the theatre, the written text is just one input among many. In Shakespeare's time the playbook once bought by the theatre company was theirs to use, change, or dispose of, as they saw fit. Given these conditions, should Shakespeare be regarded as an 'author' at all? Plays were, of course, printed and sold as books as well as performed in Shakespeare's lifetime. How important was this alternative form of publication to Shakespeare? Should we think of him as writing plays for readers as well as playgoers?

A third area of authorship enquiry relates to the Shakespeare canon. Which of the works sometimes attributed to Shakespeare are apocryphal? Which plays are in fact collaborations? Which sections of plays outside the canon were in fact written by Shakespeare? How many works can be attributed to Shakespeare as sole author? Work in this area began in the eighteenth century and continues apace.

II. WHO WROTE SHAKESPEARE?

The idea that 'Shakespeare' was written by someone other than William Shakespeare of Stratford was first advanced, in print at least, in the nineteenth century. The favoured candidate was Francis Bacon, Viscount St Albans (1561–1626). The idea was pursued by an American, Delia Bacon, whose book on the subject was published in 1857. She scorned the notion that a lowly-born provincial man who had not been to university could have the knowledge of the law and of politics which is demonstrated in the plays. She found parallels in 'Shakespeare' to Bacon's other writings, and a match between the amplitude of the work and the achievements of Bacon's life.[1] In 1920 J. Thomas Looney presented a case for Edward de Vere, 17th Earl of Oxford (1550–1604), as the writer of the plays. Looney's evidence included parallels between Oxford's life experience and events depicted in the plays, and Oxford's activities as a poet. Looney was convinced that the true author of 'Shakespeare' must be, like Oxford, an aristocrat with a classical education. He suggested that the 'Shakespeare' plays usually dated after Oxford's death were in fact written before.[2]

The founder of psychoanalysis, Sigmund Freud, was converted to a belief in Oxford's authorship of 'Shakespeare' by reading Looney's book, and saw parallels between Oxford as a father of three daughters and King Lear, and between Oxford's marital experiences and Othello's. Freud found it 'inconceivable' that the writer had merely invented the powerful emotions in Shakespeare characters and felt that the parallels between Oxford's life experience and the preoccupations of Shakespeare's plays were overwhelming.[3]

Christopher Marlowe (1564–1593) was proposed as the author of 'Shakespeare' by Calvin Hoffman in 1955.[4] Hoffman put up a large prize, still unclaimed, to be awarded to the researcher who can prove conclusively that Marlowe is 'Shakespeare'.[5] Alden Brooks in *Will Shakspere and the Dyer's Hand* (1943) suggested that Sir Edward Dyer (1543–1607) wrote 'Shakespeare'. The cultured and well-travelled Roger Manners, 5th Earl of Rutland (1576–1612), has also had proponents.[6] A further recent candidate is Sir Henry Neville (1564–1615). Brenda James and William Rubinstein, writing in 2005,

---

[1] S. Schoenbaum, *Shakespeare's Lives* (Oxford: Clarendon Press, 1991), 389–90.
[2] Schoenbaum, *Shakespeare's Lives*, 431–4.
[3] Schoenbaum, *Shakespeare's Lives*, 442–4 and 442n.
[4] Schoenbaum, *Shakespeare's Lives*, 445–7.
[5] The Marlowe Society, 'The Hoffman Prize', www.marlowe-society.org/reading/info/hoffmanprize.html.
[6] Ilya Gililov, *The Shakespeare Game: The Mystery of the Great Phoenix* (New York: Algora, 2003).

contended that Neville's experiences, such as travel on the Continent and imprisonment in the Tower, correspond with uncanny exactness to the materials of the plays
and their order. Not all candidates are men. John Hudson has recently proposed
that Aemilia Lanyer (1569–1645) was in fact the author. He sees an extraordinary
number of connections linking Lanyer's life and interests with the contents of the
plays.[7] Two books, by Robin P. Williams and Fred Faulkes (2006), put forward Mary
Herbert, Countess of Pembroke, née Mary Sidney (1561–1621), as the true author of
'Shakespeare'.

The main bulwark against scepticism about the Stratford Shakespeare's responsibility for the plays and poems we know as 'Shakespeare' is the 1623 Folio. A folio volume is
an imposing physical object, and was associated with works of reference and authority.
The title of the 1623 example is *Mr. William Shakespeares Comedies, Histories, &
Tragedies*. The dedication, the preface, and five commendatory poems mention
Shakespeare as author by name. It was a notable public assertion of Shakespeare's
authorship, which would seem to leave little reason to doubt that the thirty-six plays
included were the work of the same William Shakespeare who had been the editors'
fellow-shareholder in the King's Men theatre company, and who had been the friend
and rival of the poet and playwright Ben Jonson, who signed two of the commendatory
poems. In addition, the name William Shakespeare is attached to many early printed
versions of Shakespeare works. *Venus and Adonis* (1593) and *The Rape of Lucrece* (1594)
were each published with a dedication signed 'William Shakespeare'. Quarto editions of
the plays from 1598 frequently have Shakespeare's name on the title-page.

In many respects attribution studies proceed independently of the debate about who
wrote 'Shakespeare'. The main tool for the attribution of a disputed passage to Shakespeare is comparison with well-accepted Shakespeare works, and the same procedures
would operate whoever is assumed to be actually holding the pen. But in one case there is
a convergence. A manuscript 'playbook' of the play *Sir Thomas More* survives. A series of
essays in a landmark volume from the 1920s edited by Alfred W. Pollard distinguished
various hands at work in the manuscript. One of them, known as 'Hand D', resembles
Shakespeare's signature, which is the only known handwriting of his that survives. On a
stylistic side, strong evidence from spelling and shared words and phrases links the
linguistic content of this part of the play to Shakespeare. If these two bodies of evidence
can be sustained, then the Hand D passages provide for once a link between 'Shakespeare' texts and William Shakespeare of Stratford.[8]

There is, then, a consistent and solidly substantiated network of evidence that
connects 'Shakespeare' to the actor, theatre shareholder and property-owner William

---

[7] Discussed in Michael Posner, 'Rethinking Shakespeare', *Queen's Quarterly* 115 (2008), 247–59.

[8] Alfred W. Pollard (ed.), *Shakespeare's Hand in the Play of 'Sir Thomas More': Papers* (Cambridge:
Cambridge University Press, 1923); MacDonald P. Jackson, 'The Date and Authorship of Hand D's
Contribution to *Sir Thomas More*: Evidence from "Literature Online" ', *Shakespeare Survey* 59 (2006),
69–78; Timothy Irish Watt, 'The Authorship of the Hand-D Addition to *The Book of Sir Thomas More*',
in Hugh Craig and Arthur F. Kinney (eds.), *Shakespeare, Computers, and the Mystery of Authorship*
(Cambridge: Cambridge University Press, 2009), 134–61.

Shakespeare. It would appear that it is the exceptional nature of the achievement that the plays and poems represent, rather than anything in the authorship facts themselves, which fuels the idea that someone other than the obvious and well-attested candidate wrote 'Shakespeare'. To some, it would seem, the towering edifice of the works requires a matching authorship romance. By necessity this narrative involves an extraordinary conspiracy, and requires its proponents to dismiss powerful external evidence and to contradict predecessors who were equally positive about some other candidate. It generally depends on a series of dubious coincidences and clues allegedly hidden within the poems and plays. The evidence produced is frequently of less interest than the motives of the advocates, such as a wish to deny the achievement represented by the Shakespeare canon to a commoner without a university education, and the assumptions underlying many of the arguments, like the conviction that literary work must always reflect the life of the writer.

III. What Kind of an Author was Shakespeare?

The idea of an author is necessarily many-layered. Thinking about the origins of literary works is fundamental to any theory of literature. The classicizing Renaissance promoted the notion of the author as an exceptional individual, creating works as much for posterity as for an audience of their own time, a law-giver and a landmark in a universal and transcendent shared literary enterprise. The Enlightenment sought to link a stable, well-defined author with a well-established and precisely defined *oeuvre* in print. The Romantic era added notions of aberrant, isolated, tortured, and gifted individuality. The mass print culture of the nineteenth century bound the idea of an author to the ultimate sole copyright and responsibility for a commercial object, the printed book. In the post-structuralist era beginning in the 1960s this composite and perhaps internally fractured notion that literary production was entirely dominated by the individual creator was challenged. A literary system based on a separate, unique, perceiving, and creating subject was duly replaced with a doctrine according to which social, historical, and institutional forces were paramount.

This changed idea of the author had special force for scholars working in the early modern period, Shakespeare's period, and in the drama, Shakespeare's main medium. Proponents argued that authorship in the modern sense did not come into being until literary work was established as personal property and incurred personal liability, in the late seventeenth and eighteenth centuries. Thus for Shakespeare in the late sixteenth and early seventeenth centuries a far less defined and much more collaborative idea of literary creation prevailed. In drama individual authorship was especially discounted. Putting on a play is inevitably a collective enterprise. In the London theatre of Shakespeare's day, it was argued, the performance came first, and any printed publication a distant second. In the overall economy of the Shakespearean theatre the author was only one among many contributors.

This would make Shakespeare not an author in the usual modern sense but one of a collective, providing a written 'playbook', which was one input among many others and which might then itself be trimmed or altered into a prompt book, or abandoned altogether for comic improvisation, for instance. This picture of a collaborative, rather than individualistic, mode of production has an attractively iconoclastic force, and is a stimulating alternative to the perhaps sometimes suffocating focus on a single point of origin for Shakespeare plays.

The ideas of collaborative production and the primacy of performance have consequences for the way Shakespeare's text is regarded. Margreta de Grazia has argued persuasively that it was Edmond Malone's Shakespeare edition of 1790 that was decisive in founding nineteenth- and twentieth-century Shakespeare studies, with its quest for authentic works and texts and for a biography based on reliable documents. Malone's edition also constructed for the first time a stable textual Shakespeare, which could be understood by way of a thinking, feeling author revealing himself to readers in the *Sonnets*.[9] While earlier commentators celebrated Malone's endeavour to produce a definitive text on consistent principles, de Grazia argues that Malone's enterprise was inevitably compromised by the fact that Shakespeare's texts were in their origins 'unfixed and unstable' in everything from spelling to the text of documents introduced in the course of the action.[10] To resolve the illogicality Malone had to construct an imagined exactly finished Shakespearean original manuscript, and an 'autonomous and entitled' creator.[11] This he did through his apparatus, with a chronology allowing the works to be seen in terms of development, through interconnecting the feelings and observations expressed by the speaker of the *Sonnets* with the dramatic works, and through the 'authentic' biographical materials offered. De Grazia says that the edition's apparatus hid from subsequent generations the reality of the 'erratic fecundity' and 'intractable deviations' in the Shakespeare text.[12]

It is worth returning from this picture of a labile and essentially unfixed text, and a collaborative author, to what contemporaries said about Shakespeare, and the views about authorship we can glean from his own work. There are some important surviving documents. In 1598, the clergyman Francis Meres published a collection of quotations and personal observations called *Palladis Tamia*. Shakespeare is mentioned many times in the section titled 'A comparative discourse of our English poets, with the Greek, Latin, and Italian poets'.[13] In these pages Shakespeare is certainly an author in the full sense, one of eight moderns mentioned as refining the English language as

---

[9] Margreta de Grazia, *Shakespeare Verbatim: The Reproduction of Authenticity and the 1790 Apparatus* (Oxford: Clarendon Press, 1991), 132–76.

[10] De Grazia, 222–3.

[11] De Grazia, 226.

[12] De Grazia, 223–5.

[13] Francis Meres, *Palladis Tamia, Wits Treasury* (London, 1598), sigs. Nn7r–Oo7r. The quotations in the rest of the paragraph all come from this section.

Homer and his successors enriched Greek, and Vergil and others Latin. '[S]weet witty Ovid' lives on in Shakespeare the poet, judging by the English poet's *Venus and Adonis*, *Rape of Lucrece*, and his as yet unpublished *Sonnets*. Plautus and Seneca excel in Latin for comedy and tragedy; in the same way Shakespeare is 'the most excellent' in the two genres in English, and Meres lists six Shakespeare comedies and six tragedies as evidence. There is no doubt that Meres aims to establish English writers as authors in the mode of Vergil and Ovid, places Shakespeare as an individual writer as high as any of his contemporaries, and attributes Shakespeare's prestige as much to his plays as to his poems.

In the *Sonnets* Shakespeare himself invokes the classical idea of an author whose works will live on beyond his own lifetime. For us the obvious vehicle for this persistence would be the printed book, but Shakespeare does not make this connection between immortality and publication in print. Sonnet 17, which anticipates a readership 'in time to come', talks of the physical form in which the lines will survive as 'papers, yellowed with their age'. This sounds like a manuscript rather than a printed book. Sonnets 77 and 122 refer to 'table-books', that is, blank manuscript books. In the plays Shakespeare characters rarely refer to print, and when they do the references are generally disparaging, connecting print with cheap popular ballads (*The Winter's Tale* 4.4.258–9) or with mechanically reproduced love letters (*The Merry Wives of Windsor* 2.1.71–6). In Shakespeare's dialogue the book is mostly something to write in with a pen, or a metaphorical Book of Life.

This indifference to print fits with the idea that Shakespeare took no interest in the printing of his plays, an idea that was well entrenched in Shakespeare studies until recently. Lukas Erne has argued against this view. He shows that ten of what seem to be the first twelve plays Shakespeare wrote for the Lord Chamberlain's Men were in print by 1602, following what looks like a calculated publication strategy.[14] This revision to the traditional account is now widely accepted.[15] One must also reckon with the dearth of later Shakespeare plays that were published in his lifetime, however. Of the sixteen Folio plays usually dated to 1600 or after, only three, *Hamlet*, *Troilus and Cressida*, and *King Lear*, had been printed when Shakespeare died in 1616. Many of the plays that we think of as central to Shakespeare's achievement, like *Twelfth Night*, *Macbeth*, *Othello*, *Antony and Cleopatra*, *Coriolanus*, and *The Tempest*, were available to Shakespeare's contemporaries only in performance. There is no direct evidence to suggest that Shakespeare concerned himself, as Jonson and Middleton did, with the way his plays appeared in print, or indeed with whether they appeared in print at all. While, as Erne points out, most of the plays Shakespeare wrote in the 1590s were printed, this was sometimes in forms so haphazard and garbled that he cannot possibly have been involved in supervising their passage through the press. Eighteen plays appear first in the 1623 Folio, and so would very likely have been entirely

---

[14] Lukas Erne, *Shakespeare as Literary Dramatist* (Cambridge: Cambridge University Press, 2003), 79–100.
[15] See, e.g., Patrick Cheney, *Shakespeare's Literary Authorship* (Cambridge: Cambridge University Press, 2008), 8–10.

unknown today but for Heminges and Condell's editorial labours. The *Sonnets* themselves were printed in 1609, but the consensus view is that this publication was not authorized by Shakespeare. Theatrical performance, which seems so ephemeral to us today, may well have been such an intense and all-consuming mode of presentation, and so gratifying in terms of audience response and commercial reward, that it satisfied Shakespeare's appetite for recognition, where others like Ben Jonson looked to readers of his printed works, in the present, and into a long and clearly imagined posterity.

Shakespeare is thus clearly not an author in the modern sense of someone who vests their artistic identity in a set of printed works, and maintains strict artistic and commercial control over them in everything from proofreading to contract negotiations. On the other hand, the collaborative Shakespeare in vogue in the 1980s and 1990s does not fit the facts very well either. This model made 'Shakespeare' merely a cipher under which to collect a certain body of work, and regarded the man himself as insignificant as a creator of meaning.

What is meant by Shakespeare as an author has of course been revised and reformulated since the era when he was a contemporary writer of plays and poems with an evolving career. Whatever the state of affairs during his active participation with the London theatrical world, from the time Shakespeare retired to Stratford, around 1612–13, the survival of his dramatic work necessarily depended more and more on the written form. Actors' memories and theatrical traditions no doubt provided some continuity beyond what was written down in playbooks and printed plays, but these informal connections suffered a major disruption with the closure of the theatres in 1642 and the dispersal of theatre companies that followed.

The outlines of 'Shakespeare' were reasonably clearly visible in the First Folio of 1623. Its editors were close friends and colleagues and are still our best witnesses to Shakespeare's authorship, in the sense of what he was and was not responsible for in the drama of the time, and the literary system he himself knew and his role in it as seen by contemporaries. Successive editions in many ways blurred these outlines, and editors and readers showed less interest in establishing the boundaries. Charles I read Shakespeare, as we know, but in the less careful Second Folio of 1632. London theatres reopened in 1660, and Shakespeare plays were a mainstay of productions, but the current Shakespeare was the Third Folio, whose second impression (1664) added six plays, none of them as we now think by Shakespeare, and these remained in the Fourth Folio of 1685. The *Sonnets* were read in the John Benson edition of 1640, which changed many of the pronouns of the 1609 edition to make the love object resolutely female. Adaptations of the plays, adding characters and songs, and even a happy ending to *King Lear*, were common. Accounts of Shakespeare's life revolved around a series of colourful incidents whose connections with actual events are now impossible to verify. Alexander Pope's edition, published from 1725, marks the outer limits of fluidity and plasticity in Shakespeare texts. Understanding the texts he inherited to be thoroughly corrupt, and trusting in his intuitions about which sections were Shakespeare's and which were not, he freely deleted and modified, and put sections he felt must be interpolations by others into footnotes.[16]

Pope's edition was controversial and a countervailing movement in favour of the 'restoration' of Shakespeare guided subsequent eighteenth-century editions, culminating in Malone's of 1790. De Grazia's view that Malone ushered in a new era of Shakespeare authorship, revolving around a fixed text and a single clearly defined originating consciousness, has already been mentioned. De Grazia highlights some of the paradoxes of Malone's endeavour to create a definitive Shakespeare out of shifting, inherently unstable texts and records. It is also possible that Malone's approach restored some of the overall shape and textual stability which seemed desirable to the Folio editors.

IV. THE SHAKESPEARE CANON

Shakespeare as author can also be defined purely by reference to his language. At the simplest level this is a network of preferences in vocabulary and grammatical constructions. Then there are characteristic expressions, figures of speech, and images. Shakespeare shared a common language with his contemporaries—necessarily so, if he was to communicate at all—but within this, like any writer, indeed like any user of the language, he made choices, as much unconsciously as consciously. We know from contemporary references that audiences recognized and discussed aspects of these individual styles. Examples are Marlowe's 'mighty line', cited in Jonson's poem to Shakespeare in the Folio, Jonson's own fidelity to real-life speech, alluded to scornfully in a satirical play of the period,[17] and Shakespeare's seductive eloquence, lauded in Meres's *Palladis Tamia* (quoted earlier).

All readers and listeners have the experience of hearing an authorial voice in a phrase, or in a favourite unusual word, or in a characteristic transition from one idea to another. It turns out that this kind of linguistic innovation is so marked and persistent that its traces in frequencies and distributions of individual words can be modelled statistically.[18] This allows us to compare our intuitions as readers about the authorship of speeches and scenes with an objective set of measures. It also shows that authorial style, in the sense of highly individualized and consistent language use, is a reality, and not a romantic or sentimental fiction. To illustrate: a Shakespeare passage is twice as likely to include the words *gentle* and *beseech* as a passage by one of his contemporaries.

---

[16] Details of the Restoration and eighteenth-century reception of Shakespeare in this paragraph are from Gary Taylor, *Reinventing Shakespeare: A Cultural History, from the Restoration to the Present* (New York: Weidenfeld & Nicolson, 1989), 9–99.

[17] Anonymous, *The Returne from Pernassus: Or the Scourge of Simony* (London, 1606), sig. B2v.

[18] Craig and Kinney (eds.), *Shakespeare, Computers, and the Mystery of Authorship*, 1–39.

Wealth, pride, and *lust*, on the other hand, are half as likely to turn up in a Shakespeare passage as in the rest.[19]

'Shakespeare' is a very large collection of plays by the standards of his contemporaries, as well as a respectably large collection of non-dramatic verse. There is good reason to think that Shakespeare was involved in the writing of forty-four plays. He may have been occasionally exceeded in sheer output by his peers—Thomas Heywood claimed in the preface to *The English Traveller* to have had 'either an entire hand, or at least the main finger' in 220 plays, though at the most generous estimate we have records of only forty-two of these, and surviving copies of only twenty-five[20]—but Shakespeare's is the largest surviving canon. The next largest is Middleton, whom the recent Oxford edition associates with thirty-one plays, as sole or joint author. The next after that is Jonson, with seventeen sole-author plays. Probably two factors are at work in this metric: Shakespeare was indeed exceptionally productive; and an unusual proportion of his dramatic work survives, because his plays were frequently printed in quarto editions before 1600, and it happened that his later plays were collected and printed after his death in the First Folio.

We need to make distinctions among the forty-four plays. A core group of twenty-eight surviving plays are widely accepted as entirely by his hand, if not entirely without challenge.[21] Beyond this, *Love's Labour's Won* seems to have been a single-author play but is lost. Another set of six plays seem to be collaborations in the straightforward sense that in them Shakespeare worked with another dramatist on a joint effort. Thus it is very likely that George Peele wrote part of *Titus Andronicus*, George Wilkins part of *Pericles*, Thomas Middleton part of *Timon of Athens*, and John Fletcher parts of *Henry VIII* and *Two Noble Kinsmen*. A third likely collaboration with Fletcher, *Cardenio*, is lost. With five plays we believe Shakespeare to have written a portion, but are uncertain of the number or identity of his collaborators.[22] *Measure for Measure* and *Macbeth* seem to be Shakespeare single-author texts with additions or revisions by Middleton. Finally, there is reason to believe there are two surviving plays to which Shakespeare added passages some time after their original performance: *The Spanish Tragedy*, more speculatively, and *Sir Thomas More*, now beyond reasonable doubt.

[19] These calculations are based on word counts in twenty-eight Shakespeare plays and ninety-one well-attributed single-author plays by others from the years 1580–1619.

[20] This is the tally of plays associated with Heywood in Alfred Harbage and S. Schoenbaum, *Annals of English Drama 975–1700* (Philadelphia: University of Pennsylvania Press, 1964), leaving aside pageants, 'classical legends', and the like.

[21] These are, in the order of composition given in Stanley Wells and Gary Taylor, *William Shakespeare: A Textual Companion* (Oxford: Clarendon Press, 1987): *Two Gentlemen of Verona, Taming of the Shrew, Richard III, Comedy of Errors, Love's Labour's Lost, Midsummer Night's Dream, Romeo and Juliet, Richard II, King John, Merchant of Venice, Henry IV Part 1, Merry Wives of Windsor, Henry IV Part 2, Much Ado about Nothing, Henry V, Julius Caesar, As You Like It, Hamlet, Twelfth Night, Troilus and Cressida, Othello, All's Well That Ends Well, King Lear, Antony and Cleopatra, Coriolanus, Winter's Tale, Cymbeline*, and *Tempest*.

[22] These are the three parts of *Henry VI, Arden of Faversham*, and *Edward III*.

This estimate of the Shakespeare canon rests on centuries of work by an extraordinary band of interested individuals. In Shakespeare's lifetime, as has already been mentioned, his works existed primarily as a large collection of play-scripts belonging to his theatre company, the Lord Chamberlain's Men, later the King's Men, some of which had been printed in various degrees of care and accuracy, and as a smaller assortment of printed and manuscript poems. The first attempt at collecting the plays was in 1619, when Thomas Pavier and William Jagger, printers and stationers put ten plays into a common format so that they could be bound together as a single volume, or sold separately.[23] This set included two plays now thought to be by others and several to which Pavier and Jagger did not in fact own publishing rights. Four years later two of Shakespeare's fellow-actors and shareholders, John Heminges and Henry Condell, published the First Folio, presenting thirty-six plays, eighteen never before published, and many of the others in new versions. In their dedication, and again in the preface, they say that since Shakespeare did not live to publish his writings himself, the task of collecting the plays and putting them in print has fallen to them as his friends. Heminges and Condell thus present themselves as Shakespeare's literary executors, and this strong connection is supported by Shakespeare's bequest to them, along with Richard Burbage, of money for funeral rings. None of the plays in their collection has been excluded from the modern canon, though scholars now agree that several of them contain work by other writers.

Over the last two and a quarter centuries, since, say, the founding of the New Shakspere Society in 1874, two broad tendencies have been evident in work on Shakespeare's canon. One of them is to confirm the integrity of the thirty-six plays in the Folio, to see a single authorial controlling influence through this stable set of dramatic works, and a largely uniform progress through time with each play as a milestone, surviving more or less intact from the moment of its first creation. Schoenbaum calls the proponents of this view the 'fundamentalists'.[24]

The other tendency is to see the Folio canon as a more arbitrary and questionable collection. Adherents of this second view argue that the volume may include sections, or at least layers, of work by others, beyond the well-attested collaborations, like *Henry VIII*, which do appear within its covers. These scholars were famously labelled 'disintegrators' by E. K. Chambers in his British Academy Shakespeare Lecture of 1924. Chambers identified some key beliefs, which lay behind their willingness to attribute parts of the canon to other authors. One was the notion that any departure from a fancied standard of Shakespearean greatness, and any local variation from regular patterns of metrical practice, necessarily indicated another hand at work.[25] The other was a 'doctrine of continuous copy' under which the Shakespeare texts that survive are

---

[23] The ten plays are *Henry V*, *Henry VI Part 2*, *Henry VI Part 3*, *King Lear*, *Merchant of Venice*, *Merry Wives of Windsor*, *Midsummer Night's Dream*, *Pericles*, *Sir John Oldcastle*, and *Yorkshire Tragedy*.

[24] S. Schoenbaum, *Internal Evidence and Elizabethan Dramatic Authorship: An Essay in Literary History and Method* (London: Edward Arnold, 1966), 137.

[25] E. K. Chambers, *The Disintegration of Shakespeare* (London: Oxford University Press, 1924), 10–13.

regarded as the product of revision by various hands and thus only imperfectly and indirectly related to a pure Shakespearean source.[26] Chambers declared that he was not arguing for 'the literal inspiration of the Folio', and he conceded that some of the plays in it may well not be entirely Shakespeare's, but he was determined to defend 'the structural outlines' of '[t]he rock of Shakespeare's reputation'.[27] Chambers's weighty defence of a largely unitary and unadulterated canon was widely influential[28] and pushed arguments extending the ambit of Shakespearean collaboration and revision to the fringes of Shakespeare discourse for several decades.

A related controversy in studies of the canon is between those who give credence to internal, stylistic evidence and those who do not. Schoenbaum gives the first two and a half decades of the twentieth century the somewhat ironical title of the 'Golden Age' of attribution based on style rather than documentary evidence.[29] Too often, as he shows, the tables of statistics of metrical patterns and the lists of rare words, parallel passages, and image clusters were merely 'impressionism rationalised'.[30] '[T]he deadly parallel', as Oliphant called it in 1923, was in disrepute as early as 1887, when A. H. Bullen compared it to handwriting evidence in a jury trial: 'it is always expected, it is always produced, and it is seldom regarded'.[31] Often enthusiasts failed to carry out what M. St C. Byrne called the 'negative check' to see if a phrase or wording was really characteristic and not a commonplace. She points out, too, that they often overlooked the fact that if a parallel might be a sign of common authorship, it might also be a plagiarism or a coincidence.[32]

On the other hand, as Schoenbaum acknowledges, the book edited by Alfred Pollard had succeeded in bringing the 'Hand D' passages from *Sir Thomas More* into the canon purely on the basis of internal evidence.[33] Brian Vickers has demonstrated how often scholarly work going back to the middle of the nineteenth century arrived at what now seem to be accurate divisions of collaborative plays between Shakespeare and other authors.[34] With searchable text provided by collections like Literature Online and Early English Books Online, present-day scholars have something like comprehensive coverage of surviving plays, so that negative controls can be watertight. Countable electronic text, allowing a statistical approach to word frequencies, offers a further step forward. With these resources it should be possible at last to pursue authorship questions 'upon a general and disinterested method, rather than along the casual lines

---

[26] Chambers, 17–22.

[27] Chambers, 15–16, 3.

[28] Schoenbaum, *Internal Evidence*, 108.

[29] Schoenbaum, *Internal Evidence*, 62.

[30] Schoenbaum, *Internal Evidence*, 75.

[31] E. H. C. Oliphant, 'How Not to Play the Game of Parallels', *JEGP* 28 (1929), 13; Bullen is quoted in Schoenbaum, *Internal Evidence*, 89.

[32] M. St C. Byrne, 'Bibliographical Clues in Collaborate Plays', *The Library*, 4th series, 13 (1932), 24.

[33] Schoenbaum, *Internal Evidence*, 107.

[34] Brian Vickers, *Shakespeare, Co-Author: A Historical Study of Five Collaborative Plays* (Oxford: Oxford University Press, 2002).

of advance opened up by the pursuit of an author for this or that suspected or anonymous play'.[35]

Looking in more detail at some of the outstanding problems in the canon, we can start with doubts about works usually printed in a collected edition. *A Lover's Complaint* is a case in point. There is strong external evidence connecting this poem with Shakespeare. It was published with the *Sonnets*, and is attributed to 'William Shakespeare' on its own separate title-page. On the other hand, if it is by Shakespeare, it is a departure from his regular style. Colin Burrow, editing the poems in 2002 for the Oxford edition, declared that studies by Kenneth Muir and MacDonald P. Jackson in the 1960s had concluded the attribution debate in favour of Shakespeare.[36] However, another eminent figure in Shakespeare authorship studies, Brian Vickers, has recently argued for John Davies of Hereford as the more likely author. In one section of his book on the topic Vickers sets out to show that the poem is distinct from Shakespeare in its vocabulary, its syntax, its verse, and in its use of some rhetorical figures and metaphor. He argues that the *Lover's Complaint* poet is much less skilful than Shakespeare in most of these areas.[37] A statistical study by Ward Elliott and Robert J.Valenza, applying a series of empirical tests to the poem, also declares the poem to be outside the range of Shakespeare's practice.[38] The debate is thus unresolved. Shakespeare studies in general seems able to tolerate this uncertainty. Complete Shakespeare editions almost invariably include the poem, and critical studies continue to declare confidently that 'Shakespeare' includes five printed poems, the two narrative poems, the *Sonnets*, *The Phoenix and the Turtle*, and *A Lover's Complaint*,[39] but only the occasional critical enterprise could be said to depend on the attribution for its validity.[40]

If *Lover's Complaint* illustrates that areas of doubt in Shakespeare attribution remain, even after the application of the most sophisticated and modern methods, then another area, dramatic collaboration, shows how some long-standing debates can reach closure. In his book *Shakespeare, Co-Author* Vickers deals with the five collaborations already mentioned—one each with Peele, Wilkins, and Middleton, and two with Fletcher—and, in the spirit of a medical metastudy, reviews previous studies, and adds new ones to show a convergence of differing approaches to a consensus not only on the partnerships involved, but on the divisions of the plays between the collaborators.

[35] Chambers, *The Disintegration of Shakespeare*, 13.

[36] Colin Burrow (ed.), *Shakespeare: The Complete Sonnets and Poems* (Oxford: Oxford University Press, 2002), 139.

[37] Brian Vickers, *Shakespeare, 'A Lover's Complaint', and John Davies of Hereford* (Cambridge: Cambridge University Press, 2007), 121–203.

[38] Ward Elliott and Robert J. Valenza, 'Did Shakespeare Write *A Lover's Complaint*? The Jackson Ascription Revisited', in Brian Boyd (ed.), *Words That Count: Essays on Early Modern Authorship in Honor of MacDonald P. Jackson* (Newark: University of Delaware Press, 2004), 117–39.

[39] E.g., Cheney, *Shakespeare's Literary Authorship*, 19, 34.

[40] Examples are John Kerrigan (ed.), *Motives of Woe: Shakespeare and the 'Female Complaint': A Critical Anthology* (Oxford: Clarendon, 1991), and Shirley Sharon-Zisser (ed.), *Critical Essays on Shakespeare's 'A Lover's Complaint': Suffering Ecstasy* (London: Ashgate, 2006).

The most straightforward cases of collaboration involve Shakespeare's younger contemporary John Fletcher (1579–1625). The title-page of the 1634 Quarto of *Two Noble Kinsmen* says the play was 'Written by the memorable Worthies of their time Mr John Fletcher and Mr William Shakespeare Gent[lemen]'. The play does not appear in the First Folio. A series of tests such as metre, the use of contractions, and vocabulary converge on a division of the play agreed on by modern scholars.[41] There is also general agreement that *Henry VIII* is a collaboration between the two playwrights; the division of the play proposed by Spedding in 1850 stands up well to modern testing.[42] The relative ease with which the divisions are established suggests that the two men generally worked on separate sections of the play, rather than jointly writing scenes or acts. It seems likely that there was a third Shakespeare–Fletcher collaboration, *Cardenio*, based on an episode from *Don Quixote*, which was published in an English translation in 1612. A play of this name was performed twice at court in 1613, although there is no evidence of publication.[43]

It now seems clear that Shakespeare worked as an anonymous collaborator on plays early in his career. He may well have contributed a section, but only a section, to *The Raigne of Edward III*, which was printed in 1595 but seems to have been performed earlier. Timothy Irish Watt has recently summed up and augmented the case for Shakespeare's part-authorship.[44] The three parts of *Henry VI* are dated to this period also. Confusion surrounds their authorship, however, and even the order in which they were written. Versions of part 2 and part 3 were published, without any indication of authorship, in 1594 and 1595. All three were included in the First Folio, so there is a prima facie case that Shakespeare was involved, but there is no agreement on how much, or about who his collaborators were, though Kyd, Marlowe, Peele, and Greene are most often mentioned by scholars.

Since the middle of the seventeenth century there has been a persistent strand of commentary linking Shakespeare with the anonymous play *Arden of Faversham*, first printed in 1592. Claims that the play is entirely by Shakespeare have been refined to suggestions that only some sections are his. There is by no means consensus—other candidates like Kyd continue to be put forward—but there are some strong connections with known Shakespeare in terms of style and imagery, confirmed by quantitative work in stylistics.[45]

[41] Brian Vickers, *Shakespeare, Co-Author*, 402–32.

[42] Vickers, *Shakespeare, Co-Author*, 332–402.

[43] G. Harold Metz (ed.), *Sources of Four Plays Ascribed to Shakespeare* (Columbia: University of Missouri Press, 1989), 257–83.

[44] Timothy Irish Watt, 'The Authorship of *The Raigne of Edward the Third*', in Craig and Kinney (eds.), *Shakespeare, Computers, and the Mystery of Authorship*, 116–32.

[45] Brian Vickers, 'Thomas Kyd, Secret Sharer', *Times Literary Supplement*, 18 April 2008, 13–15; MacDonald P. Jackson, 'Shakespeare and the Quarrel Scene in *Arden of Faversham*', *Shakespeare Quarterly* 57.3 (2006), 249–93; and Arthur F. Kinney, 'Authoring *Arden of Faversham*', in Craig and Kinney (eds.), 78–99.

Shakespeare may well have written the series of additions to Thomas Kyd's pioneering revenge play *The Spanish Tragedy* which were published in the 1602 edition of the play. In this case the external evidence points to Ben Jonson as the writer. Payments to Jonson for revisions to the play are listed in the diary of the theatre manager Philip Henslowe in 1601, but the additions include speeches of whimsical, ironical mental instability quite unlike anything in Jonson. Coleridge thought they were Shakespeare's work, and they share a number of unusual words and phrases with Shakespeare plays and poems.[46] A statistical analysis of patterns of word use, both function words and lexical words, supports the attribution to Shakespeare.[47]

In the late 1990s the claim that 'Shakespeare' should be extended to include a 1612 funeral elegy for William Peter, a little-known Devonshire gentleman, renewed the debate about the role of internal evidence in attribution. Donald W. Foster, the main proponent of the attribution, presented extensive data in a 1989 book showing that the poem fitted well within the 'Shakespeare' range on a number of linguistic markers such as the frequency of some common words and the frequency of some figures of speech. Foster says in fact that he was unable to find a Shakespeare test that the *Elegy* could not pass.[48] He summed up the case thus: the poem 'belongs hereafter with Shakespeare's poems and plays . . . because it is formed from textual and linguistic fabric indistinguishable from that of canonical Shakespeare'.[49] The only external evidence of any substance was the appearance of the initials 'W. S.' on the dedication to the poem. Most readers, meanwhile, agreed that the poem was laboured and dull, and saw no obvious connections with 'Shakespeare' in style, theme, or artistic stance. Richard Abrams, a second proponent of the attribution, responded that given the strength of the evidence for the inclusion of the poem in the canon, the rest of Shakespeare's works would just have to be read differently from now on.[50]

Doubters had had to rely on their impressions that the *Elegy*'s style was 'unShakespearean', and these were increasingly discounted. The poem began to appear in authoritative American Shakespeare editions like the Norton and the Riverside. The momentum was abruptly reversed in 2002, however, when G. D. Monsarrat published strong evidence in favour of another candidate, John Ford—mainly words and phrases in common with Ford poems written about the same time.[51] Foster and Abrams conceded shortly afterwards. The case illustrates some important methodological

---

[46] Warren Stevenson, *Shakespeare's Additions to Thomas Kyd's 'The Spanish Tragedy': A Fresh Look at the Evidence Regarding the 1602 Additions* (Lewiston, NY: Edwin Mellen, 2008).

[47] Hugh Craig, 'The 1602 Additions to *The Spanish Tragedy*', in Craig and Kinney (eds.), 162–80.

[48] Donald W. Foster, *Elegy by W. S.: A Study in Attribution* (Newark: University of Delaware Press, 1989), 147.

[49] Donald W. Foster, 'A Funeral Elegy: W[illiam] S[hakespeare]'s "Best-Speaking Witnesses"', *PMLA* 111 (1996), 1082.

[50] Richard Abrams, 'Breaching the Canon: *Elegy by W. S.*: The State of the Argument', *The Shakespeare Newsletter* (1995), 54.

[51] G. D. Monsarrat, 'A Funeral Elegy: Ford, W.S., and Shakespeare', *Review of English Studies* 53 (2002), 186–203.

considerations. Where an attribution relies on internal evidence, and connections are relative and comparative, one author may be the most likely candidate from those tested, but there is always the possibility of a new author from outside the set being stronger still. Once that author is included, or just taken seriously—Ford was in Foster's original control set, but not given anything like the same attention as Shakespeare—the claims of the first author look much less conclusive. Further, the lure of a Shakespeare discovery can lead to a gold rush mentality, which can tempt researchers into arranging tests to ensure the right result.[52]

There was a precursor to the *Elegy* episode in a controversy over a much shorter untitled poem beginning 'Shall I die? shall I fly?'. Gary Taylor, one of the editors of The Oxford Shakespeare, found the poem in the Bodleian Library in Oxford. The catalogue attributed the poem to Shakespeare. The poem was included in the 1987 Oxford edition, but its evident clumsiness and derivativeness and the paucity of persuasive parallels to 'Shakespeare' kept it out of the canon in any more general sense. Thomas A. Pendleton's collection of words that are used in the poem and in 'Shakespeare', but in different senses, is damaging for the attribution.[53]

A considerable number of anonymous and even well-attributed plays have been proposed for inclusion in the Shakespeare canon as wholly or partly by him. Like the apocryphal books of the Bible, they form a penumbra to the canonical works. One instance is *Edmond Ironside*, a late sixteenth-century history play which has survived in manuscript. E. B. Everitt put a case for Shakespeare's authorship in a 1954 book, mainly on the basis of verbal parallels with early canonical Shakespeare, and subsequently Eric Sams made his own arguments for the idea in a book and series of articles in the 1980s, again on the basis of internal evidence from vocabulary. Most other scholars reject the attribution.[54]

V. Conclusion

It is hard to exaggerate the cultural prestige that is invested in Shakespeare as an author. His works are invoked to guarantee the richness of the resources of the English language, to anchor English national pride, and as touchstones for the power of literature itself. They are read, performed, and studied to a degree that makes him outstanding even among the select band of national poets. A poem that is accepted as Shakespeare's is analysed with unparalleled intensity; the same poem, no longer

[52] Hugh Craig, 'Common-Words Frequencies, Shakespeare's Style, and the *Elegy* by W. S.', *Early Modern Literary Studies* 8 (2002), http://extra.shu.ac.uk/emls/081/craistyl.htm.

[53] Thomas A. Pendleton, 'The Non-Shakespearian Language of "Shall I Die?"', *Review of English Studies* 40 (1989), 323–51.

[54] For a discussion of Everitt and Sams, and a review of this authorship problem, see Philip S. Palmer, '*Edmond Ironside* and the Question of Shakespearean Authorship', in Craig and Kinney (eds.), 100–15.

attributed to Shakespeare, instantly loses its lustre. As a creator Shakespeare is both exceptional and representative. Defining him either as an independent author, or as essentially a member of a theatrical collective, affects the picture of literary creation in general. For many beyond the academy, questions about his identity, his moral character, and his politics must be resolved in a satisfactory direction to sustain general beliefs about humanity and culture.

Because so much is at stake, Shakespeare authorship throws the methods for arriving at the truth in a range of questions into extraordinary relief. These questions range from the attribution of a brief passage of dialogue to the nature of authorship itself. The cut and thrust of debate is intriguing, and there is no doubt that some fine intellects have given their best efforts in the quest to resolve some of the perplexing problems that arise. It is also remarkable how hard it is to rule out even wildly improbable hypotheses, and how far interpreters will go in building elaborate structures on uncertain foundations in attribution; and it is dismaying that doubts about what might seem to be obvious facts persist.

It is also worth noting that after several centuries of endeavour there has really been not so very much added, nor much taken away, from the first monument of Shakespeare authorship—the Folio volume of 1623, with its thirty-six plays presented as the work of a fondly remembered friend and colleague dead seven years before. No one has succeeded in ruling any of the Folio plays out of a collected Shakespeare: our best understanding is that he was involved in the majority of them as sole playwright, and in a minority as collaborator, or as the author of an earlier version later revised or supplemented by another. No whole play has been added to the canon, though there are a series of parts of other plays that can now be attributed to him, from the near-certain to the confidently ascribed. There is no equivalent to the Folio for the poems, but we can say that two long poems, a sonnet sequence, and a shorter poem stand clearly within the canon, and A Lover's Complaint, with some short poems published in a brief anthology, stand on the threshold; despite some urgent pleas for admission, no other poem has qualified.

The Folio also remains the best guide to Shakespeare authorship in terms of the identity of the author, and the idea of authorship itself. William Shakespeare is in the title, is presented throughout as the author, and is identified through the dedication, preface and commendatory poems with William Shakespeare the actor and King's Men shareholder, born in Stratford-upon-Avon. No challenge to these straightforward links between this individual and these works has been sustained. In the Folio volume Shakespeare appears neither as a solitary genius creating in isolation, nor as a mere functionary in a larger productive enterprise. He is presented simply as an exceptional theatre professional, admired by his peers both for his collegial ties and for his extraordinary talent.

CHAPTER 2

···

COLLABORATION

···

MacDONALD P. JACKSON

THE royal Chamber Accounts for 1613 record payments to the King's Men for performances of a play called by the scribe 'Cardenno' and 'Cardenna'. Thomas Shelton's English translation of the first part of Cervantes' *Don Quixote*, which contains 'The History of Cardenio', had been published the previous year. The natural presumption that this episode served as the lost play's source is confirmed by Humphrey Moseley's entry in the Stationers' Register on 9 September 1653 of a playscript designated 'The History of Cardennio, by M.ʳ Fletcher. & Shakespeare'. It appears never to have reached print and does not survive. But in 1727 Lewis Theobald presented at the Theatre Royal in Drury Lane his *Double Falshood; or, The Distrest Lovers*, which he claimed to have 'Revised and Adapted' from manuscripts descended from a Shakespearean original. Two successive issues of *Double Falsehood* (to modernize the spelling) were printed in 1728. Theobald conceded that some contemporaries thought *Double Falsehood* 'nearer to the Style and Manner of FLETCHER than of Shakespeare'. The majority opinion among modern scholars who have studied the question is that *Double Falsehood* was based on a version of the lost *Cardenio*, and that Moseley's ascription of that play to Shakespeare and Fletcher was correct.[1]

Believing this to be the case, Gary Taylor attempted a creative reconstruction of the original *Cardenio*. He was aided by careful study of the source episode in *Don Quixote*, of the ways in which eighteenth-century playwrights, such as Theobald, adapted plays of Shakespeare's time, and of the contrasting styles of Shakespeare, Fletcher, and Theobald. In May 2009, David Carnegie directed a short season of performances of Taylor's reconstructed *Cardenio* at Victoria University of Wellington, New Zealand.

---

[1] For the details in this paragraph, see E. K. Chambers. *William Shakespeare: A Study of Facts and Problems*, 2 vols. (Oxford: Clarendon Press, 1930), 1: 537–42; 2: 343; Stanley Wells and Gary Taylor (eds.), *William Shakespeare: The Complete Works* (Oxford: Clarendon Press, 1986 2nd edn. 2006), 132–3. A history of opinion on *Double Falsehood* is provided by G. Harold Metz (ed.), *Sources of Four Plays Ascribed to Shakespeare* (Columbia: University of Missouri Press, 1989), 255–93.

The script underwent many modifications as Taylor and Carnegie worked closely together in rehearsals.[2]

Cardenio and *Double Falsehood* illustrate various ways in which a playtext may be the work of more than one agent. Shakespeare and Fletcher collaborated on the writing of the original play. Theobald reworked a version of it that may well have already undergone alteration. Much later Taylor made his own substantial contributions, some of them in association with actors preparing the script for the stage. Of course, Theobald's intervention came over a century after initial composition, and Taylor's almost four centuries after, but the same processes occurred within the early modern period before the closing of the London theatres in 1642. Plays might be co-authored, adjusted by theatre-folk for performance, and afterwards augmented or revamped for revivals in new circumstances.

Investigating the input of persons other than playwrights to the scripts of plays is the province of textual criticism. 'Collaboration' is involved only in the broad sense in which drama is a collaborative art, so that actors, costumers, carpenters, book-holders, musicians, stagehands, and others join in the cooperative venture of bringing words on the page to life in the theatre. Nor is it helpful to regard the authors of source material as collaborators. Fletcher, Shakespeare, Theobald, and Taylor all drew on Shelton's English version of *Don Quixote*, so that at each stage of the play's evolution Cervantes served as what Harold Love, in *Attributing Authorship: An Introduction*, called a 'precursory author'.[3] But Cervantes' unwitting contribution to *Cardenio* and *Double Falsehood* was not, in any but the loosest of senses, collaboration.

Further, adaptation, rewriting, and augmentation of which the author or authors who first created a complete script were unaware must be firmly distinguished from the contemporaneous composition of a script by two or more playwrights working as a team, which is this chapter's main concern. The distinction has not always been appreciated. Jeffrey Masten, for example, asserts that 'collaboration was the Renaissance English theater's dominant mode of textual production'.[4] The claim rests on a misinterpretation of some educated guesswork by G. E. Bentley, who suspected that 'as many as half of the plays by professional dramatists' in the period 1590–1642 'incorporated the writing at some date of more than one man'.[5] But this formulation includes the reshaping of single-authored plays by subsequent revisers and providers of 'new additions'. Of surviving plays that were first performed during the years of Shakespeare's career as dramatist (1590–1614) and that are neither by him, nor mere closet dramas, nor anonymous, modern scholarship ascribes

[2] Papers from an international colloquium held in conjunction with the production will appear in a book edited by David Carnegie and Gary Taylor.

[3] Harold Love, *Attributing Authorship: An Introduction* (Cambridge: Cambridge University Press, 2002), 40–3.

[4] Jeffrey Masten, *Textual Intercourse: Collaboration, Authorship, and Sexualities in Renaissance Drama* (Cambridge: Cambridge University Press, 1997), 14.

[5] Gerald Eades Bentley, *The Profession of Dramatist in Shakespeare's Time, 1590–1642* (Princeton, NJ: Princeton University Press, 1971), 119.

some 20 per cent to more than one playwright.[6] The proportion is a little higher in the second half of the period than in the first, and in the following eight years—with the Fletcher–Massinger and Middleton–Rowley partnerships—it rises to 38 per cent.

In these terms, Shakespeare, seven of whose thirty-nine extant plays (18 per cent) are now widely thought to have been co-authored, is typical of his time. *1 Henry VI*, *Titus Andronicus*, and *Edward III* belong to his apprentice years, *Timon of Athens*, *Pericles*, *All Is True* (*Henry VIII*), and *The Two Noble Kinsmen* to his late maturity, from 1605–6 onward.[7] Of course, the lost plays of dual or multiple authorship for which Philip Henslowe's *Diary* recorded payments would swell the numbers of non-Shakespearean collaborations, and the co-written potboilers of the London entertainment industry may have been less apt than one-author plays to reach print and more apt to be published anonymously when they did. Moreover, the title-pages of play quartos sometimes bore one playwright's name when in fact two or more had shared the composition. But Jeffrey Knapp, in a cogent critique of Masten's influential book, has argued strongly that 'the primary theoretical model for playwriting throughout the English Renaissance was single authorship'.[8] It probably, as Knapp claims, predominated in practice too. Bentley's estimate, rightly understood, would support such a view.[9]

Clearly, however, collaborative playwriting was very common indeed and, like most other dramatists, Shakespeare engaged in it. One of the reasons for supposing that Moseley was right to credit Fletcher and Shakespeare with *Cardenio* is that the two men are known to have collaborated at about the right date. *The Two Noble Kinsmen*,

---

[6] The figures derive from the chronological table of plays in A. R. Braunmuller and Michael Hattaway (eds.), *The Cambridge Companion to English Renaissance Drama* (Cambridge: Cambridge University Press, 1990), 419–46. Using the same source, Philip C. McGuire shows that 'Collaborative dramatic writing was most intense in James' reign', when 'the King's Men's use of collaboratively written plays' increased both absolutely and relative to their rivals' ('Collaboration', in Arthur F. Kinney [ed.], *A Companion to Renaissance Drama* [Oxford: Blackwell, 2002], 540–52, at 543–4).

[7] Adding either *Cardenio* (lost except in Theobald's *Double Falshood*) or *Arden of Faversham* (not yet widely accepted as partly by Shakespeare) would raise the percentage to 20. Moreover, Shakespeare contributed one scene to a collaborative revision of *Sir Thomas More* (see below). Both *Macbeth* and *Measure for Measure* underwent some adaptation by Thomas Middleton before being included in the Shakespeare First Folio of 1623 (Gary Taylor and John Lavagnino [eds.], *Thomas Middleton: The Collected Works* [Oxford: Clarendon Press, 2007], 1165–201, 1542–85; and Taylor and Lavagnino, *Thomas Middleton and Early Modern Textual Culture: A Companion to the Collected Works* [Oxford: Clarendon Press, 2007], 383–98, 417–21). Brian Vickers, in his *Shakespeare, Co-Author: A Historical Study of Five Collaborative Plays* (Oxford: Oxford University Press, 2002), expertly summarizes the evidence for collaboration in *Titus Andronicus*, *Timon of Athens*, *Pericles*, *All Is True* (*Henry VIII*), and *The Two Noble Kinsmen*, and includes both an excellent chapter entitled 'Plot and Character in Co-Authored Plays: Problems of Co-ordination' (pp. 433–500) and a rebuttal of Masten, *Textual Intercourse* (pp. 5.27–41). His book obviates the need for a detailed account within this essay of the various stylistic and sub-stylistic discriminators.

[8] Jeffrey Knapp, 'What is a Co-Author?', *Representations* 89 (2005), 1–21, at 1.

[9] Practices may well have differed among different companies. The Admiral's Men, under Henslowe at the Rose Theatre, seem to have been especially dependent on collaboratively written scripts (Brian Vickers, *Shakespeare, Co-Author: A Historical Study of Five Collaboration Plays* [Oxford: Oxford University Press, 2002], 20).

printed in a quarto of 1634 with their names on the title-page, was first performed 1613–14.[10] *All Is True*, which unlike that play was included in the Shakespeare First Folio (1623), can confidently be dated 1613. It was not until the mid-nineteenth century that it was recognized as a collaboration with Fletcher. But both plays clearly exhibit the contrasting verse styles of the two men.

STYLE AND SIGNIFICANCE IN *THE TWO NOBLE KINSMEN*

Some modern theorists, deferring to Michel Foucault, would regard the previous section's last statement with extreme scepticism. Masten brands as futile any attempt to determine the shares of collaborating playwrights, because 'the collaborative project in the theatre was predicated on *erasing* the perception of any differences'.[11] But the differences between Shakespeare and Fletcher were not erased. The nineteenth-century essayist Thomas De Quincey judged Shakespeare's dramatic poetry in *The Two Noble Kinsmen* to be 'perhaps the most superb work in the language' and had no difficulty distinguishing it from Fletcher's.[12] And in its density, richness, and weight, Shakespeare's verse, which is far beyond Fletcher's range, conveys different attitudes to his material from those of Fletcher to his. Shakespeare, beginning and ending the play, dramatizes, in a sombre manner, events in Chaucer's *The Knight's Tale*. Fletcher develops several of these and is mainly responsible for a sub-plot suited to his gift for a mix of comedy and pathos. The distribution of scenes between the two men and their complementary perspectives on the whole story give the play its special quality. Contrast is built into its organization.

At the beginning of *The Two Noble Kinsmen* Theseus' wedding to Hippolyta is interrupted when three queens plead that he should resume war on Creon, who has refused burial to their husbands slain on the battlefields of Thebes. Theseus accedes to their request, is victorious, and captures the Theban warriors Palamon and Arcite. The main action turns on the rivalry of these cousins over Hippolyta's sister Emilia, with whom both fall in love at first sight, and culminates in a knightly contest set up by Theseus, with Emilia as the prize. Arcite no sooner wins than he dies when thrown off his horse, and so Palamon is awarded Emilia: the winner loses and the loser wins. In the

[10] Dates of first performance of Shakespeare's plays are taken from Wells and Taylor, *William Shakespeare: A Textual Companion*; dates for non-Shakespearean plays are from Alfred Harbage, rev. edn. S. Schoenbaum, *Annals of English Drama 975–1700* (London: Methuen, 1964).

[11] Masten, *Textual Intercourse*, 17.

[12] Quoted by Eugene Waith in Waith (ed.), *The Two Noble Kinsmen* (Oxford: Clarendon Press, 1989), 9–10. Waith's allocation of shares (p. 22) seems to me right, except that 5.1.1–17 (but no more of 5.1) is (in my view) Fletcher's. The Oxford *Collected Works*, numbering scenes in Act 5 differently, agrees with Waith, except that it denies Shakespeare 4.3. In the *Collected Works* Shakespeare's share ought to be: 1; 2.1; 3.1–2; 4.3; 5.1.18–67, 5.2–3; 5.5–6.

sub-plot the Jailor's Daughter falls mad with passion for Palamon, May Day is celebrated by morris-dancing rustics, and the Daughter's cure is effected when a Wooer of her own class gratifies her in the nobleman's guise.

Before the final combat, Arcite offers a long prayer to Mars, Palamon to Venus, and Emilia to Diana. Shakespeare is in each case the author, and his concerns in the play gather round the three aspects of human experience represented by these deities: war, valour, death, honour; romantic love, sexual obsession, marriage, new life; virginity, innocence, purity, and friendship. For him, Chaucer's tale is a fit vehicle for a poetic exploration of the paradoxes of desire in a world where good and ill become inextricably mingled. Shakespeare's comedies end in weddings, his tragedies in the formal removal of corpses. In *The Two Noble Kinsmen* gain and loss, wedding and funeral, combine at the end, as at the beginning. The pattern is unlike that of Shakespeare's late romances, in which a potentially tragic outcome is diverted toward a blissful comic resolution—a pattern adhered to in the sub-plot, though the Jailor's assurance that his Daughter is 'well restored, | And to be married shortly' (5.6.27–8) lacks the emotional amplitude of the endings of, for example, *Pericles* and *The Winter's Tale*.

The mood and atmosphere of Shakespeare's contribution to *The Two Noble Kinsmen* recall Prospero's famous 'We are such stuff | As dreams are made on' (*The Tempest*, 4.1.156–7). The last words that Shakespeare wrote for the stage are those with which Theseus sums up the action, as he addresses the immortal gods:

> O you heavenly charmers,
> What things you make of us! For what we lack
> We laugh, for what we have are sorry; still
> Are children in some kind. Let us be thankful
> For that which is, and with you leave dispute
> That are above our question.   (5.6.131–6)

La comédie humaine, with its passions, absurdities, and mysteries, is here viewed, as though from a distance, with a solemn resignation, acceptance, and, ultimately, gratitude—simply 'for that which is'. The lines are spoken by the Duke of Athens, but serve also as a moving valediction from their author.

Shakespeare's poetry, with its wealth of imagery and its wide range of reference, invests the story with a sense of real *gravitas*. Meaning is also conveyed in visual terms through ritual, pageantry, and tableaux, as when the three queens, dressed in funereal black, intrude upon the opening bridal procession, where the contents of the accompanying song reinforce the symbolism, as life and death are juxtaposed even in the catalogue of flowers: 'Oxlips, in their cradles growing, | Marigolds, on deathbeds blowing' (1.1.10–11). Significance is generated through the interweaving of action, spectacle, and language that carries a strong metaphorical charge. The queens' 'lords | Lie blist'ring fore the visiting sun, | And were good kings, when living' (1.1.145–7). The lines encapsulate volumes about the Fall of Princes. The Second Queen, kneeling before Hippolyta, entreats her to do likewise and plead their case before Theseus:

> Lend us a knee;
> But touch the ground for us no longer time
> Than a dove's motion when the head's plucked off;
> Tell him if he i'th' blood-sized field lay swoll'n,
> Showing the sun his teeth, grinning at the moon,
> What you would do.   (1.1.96–101)

The astonishing image of the beheaded dove, obviously drawn from a country-bred lad's first-hand experience, is grotesque but not gratuitous in envisaging brutal violence against the emblem of peace and love. And could there be a more vivid *memento mori* than the ghastly image of the dead king?

The salient features of Shakespeare's and Fletcher's contrasting verse styles have been well summarized by Brian Vickers in *Shakespeare, Co-Author*. Many are measurable. Although as his career progressed Shakespeare increased the proportion of double endings (where an extra unstressed syllable follows the pentameter), he never used them with the frequency of Fletcher, for whom the variation became the norm, with monosyllables (even quite weighty ones) often used for the purpose. Shakespeare runs the sense on from one line into the next more often than does Fletcher, whose rhythms, syntax, and vocabulary are far less varied. Fletcher's epithets and similes tend to be predictable. And of course trivial preferences over colloquial contractions, affirmative particles, verbal forms, and the like distinguish one man's writing from the other's. Concentrations of 'ye', and "em', for example, point to Fletcher, of 'hath' and 'doth' to Shakespeare. Fletcher prefers 'yes', Shakespeare 'ay'. Shakespeare, unlike Fletcher, is fond of unregulated auxiliary 'do', as in 'I do bleed' or 'I did begin', rather than 'I bleed' or 'I began'.

But a comparison of two speeches will illustrate the disparity between the two writers in poetic power.[13] In 1.1 Theseus at first insists that the solemnization of his marriage to Hippolyta must have precedence over the three queens' urgent requests. The First Queen objects:

> The more proclaiming
> Our suit shall be neglected. When her arms,
> Able to lock Jove from a synod, shall
> By warranting moonlight corslet thee; O when
> Her twinning cherries shall their sweetness fall
> Upon her tasteful lips, what wilt thou think
> Or rotten kings or blubbered queens? What care
> For what thou feel'st not, what thou feel'st being able
> To make Mars spurn his drum? O, if thou couch
> But one night with her, every hour in't will
> Take hostage of thee for a hundred, and
> Thou shalt remember nothing more than what
> That banquet bids thee to.   (1.1.173–85)

---

[13] Some of my points derive from discussions with the late Sydney Musgrove, as we prepared class notes for a course on Shakespeare's late plays.

The first three words complete a line that begins 'Or futurely can cope' at the end of Theseus' preceding speech, and so belong to one of only two lines that have double endings ('able' forming the other at 180). Only one line is end-stopped, that is, written so that the natural pauses in speech and thought coincide with the end of a line. Grammar often connects the last word of a line so intimately to the first word of the next line ('when | Her'; 'fall | Upon'; 'care | For'; 'able | To'; 'will | Take'; 'and | Thou') that the sense is welded into one, increasing momentum and enhancing coherence. To write such a sustained run-on passage without the verse collapsing into chaos demands great technical skill, especially since the speech conveys a tide of bitter emotion. In no two adjacent lines is the natural speech rhythm the same: the subtle variations of the almost completely regular lines 176–80 ('By . . . care') segue into the metrically turbulent, heavily stressed, 181–2 ('For . . . couch'). The effects are organically related to patterns of sense and emotion.

Characteristic are the semantically packed monosyllables, particularly active verbs, several with consonantal clusters—'lock', 'spurn', 'couch', 'feel'st'—alongside rarities such as 'warranting', 'synod', 'blubbered', and 'corslet'. The metaphorical structure is complex. Again images of love and war (Venus and Mars) are thrust into violent contrast. So the lover's 'arms' have the power to 'lock' the supreme god from the divine assembly ('synod', an official, remote word), and they 'corslet' what they embrace. The metaphor, in which a noun is turned into a verb, is from armour, the corslet being the plates that cover breast and back. Thus 'arms' and 'corslet' have double associations, of love and war. The bride herself is warrior-queen of the Amazons. The romantic 'moonlight' becomes a kind of formal licence ('warranting') to love. The next lines are richly sensual. 'Tasteful' has its etymological meaning of 'full of taste', here 'having intense capacity to taste', and the quarto's 'twyning' includes both 'twining' and 'twinning'. There are two pairs of lips in live contact, and the participle vividly evokes the real cherries dangling in pairs from their stalks, so that the effect is much more complicated than in Fletcher's clichéd 'cherry lips' at 4.1.74: in Shakespeare's formulation, cherries and lips intertwine in a delicious fusion of fruit and flesh! Then pictured in stark contrast are the rotting bodies of kings and the tear-stained, swollen faces of their widowed queens.

The syntax of lines 194–202 ('The . . . drum') is likewise varied and complex. In the quarto it is punctuated as a single intricate sentence: (1) main clause; (2) subordinate 'when' clause; (3) another subordinate 'when' clause; (4) a question; (5) another question; (6) a hanging absolute participial clause that includes (7) a double infinitive noun clause. The linked sequence, like the chain of images, ends with a vivid figure of war-god Mars, so inflamed by passion that he 'spurns' his martial drum. It is a tour de force, difficult to read and understand, and very demanding for an audience.

In the speech's final sentence ('O . . . to') love and war are yet again brought together in the image of taking hostage. If Theseus spends one night with his new bride, every hour will be so pleasurable as to make him spend a hundred more with her; but the suggestion is of a kind of warfare in which hostages are taken from Theseus, depleting his forces (as it were), his powers of action beyond the bridal bed. And in the last line 'banquet' links back to the 'cherries' of Hippolyta's lips. The opposition is between feasting on sensual delights, and so obliterating thoughts of anything else, and the call to a warrior-king's duty.

One of Fletcher's more eloquent passages of similar length points up the disparity between the two playwrights as poets. The imprisoned Arcite and Palamon join in despairing of their future:

> No Palamon,
> Those hopes are prisoners with us. Here we are,
> And here the graces of our youths must wither,
> Like a too-timely spring. Here age must find us
> And, which is heaviest, Palamon, unmarried—
> The sweet embraces of a loving wife
> Loaden with kisses, armed with thousand Cupids,
> Shall never clasp our necks; no issue know us;
> No figures of ourselves shall we e'er see
> To glad our age, and, like young eagles, teach 'em
> Boldly to gaze against bright arms and say,
> 'Remember what your fathers were, and conquer.'   (2.2.25–36)

Seven of the twelve lines have double endings, three of them monosyllables: 'find us', 'know us', and 'teach 'em' all typically consist of verb plus pronoun. The falling cadences help create the wistful tone. Nearly all the lines are end-stopped: most editors also place a comma after 'wife'. There are only mild variations from the metrical paradigm, such as the trochaic inversions of the first foot in 'Like a' and 'Loaden'. There are no physically 'packed' words, no double meanings. The syntax is simple, consisting mainly of a series of main clauses. Metre, vocabulary, and sentence structure together form a straightforward string of statements elaborating on the idea that the cousins, confined in jail, will never marry and have sons. Figurative language is restricted to similes—'Like . . . spring' in 28, 'like . . . eagles' in 34—and the epithets are as expected: 'embraces' are 'sweet', a 'wife' is 'loving', 'arms' are 'bright'. The god-figure Cupid is a decorative property, an attribute of a thousand wifely kisses, not an integrated symbol like Shakespeare's Mars. The passage elicits sympathy for the cousins and ends with a climax that is true to their nature and situation. On stage, it would be clearly comprehensible and doubtless more immediately effective than the Shakespearean passage. But there is little to stimulate the imagination.

In Arcite's prayer to Mars in 5.1, the god is 'Thou . . . that both mak'st and break'st | The stony girth of cities' (54–5), and the imperious Venus addressed by Palamon in 5.2 likewise creates and destroys. Nostalgia for the prelapsarian state symbolized by Diana is beautifully expressed in Emilia's treasured memories of her girlhood friendship with the dead Flavina (1.4.47–82), a more elaborate and delicate counterpart to Polixenes' description of the boyhood he shared with Leontes, when, like 'twinned lambs that did frisk i'th' sun', they 'knew not | The doctrine of ill-doing' (The Winter's Tale 1.2.69–72). Shakespeare could no more erase his poetic self from The Two Noble Kinsmen than Fletcher could emulate it. A Shakespearean set piece is like an operatic aria: though integral to the drama, it can, in its own right, stir the emotions, intellect, and imagination, and focus aspects of the playwright's vision. For instance, a more benign Venus emerges in the rapturous praise with which Arcite idealizes and deifies Emilia in 3.1.1–30. Queen of the May, she is transformed by the poetry into a veritable Flora in Botticelli's 'Primavera', and 'jewel | O'th' wood, o'th' world' besides. The way that 'wood' expands into 'world' beautifully mimics Arcite's surge of religious devotion.

Fletcher is at his most typical in such speeches as the soliloquy (the whole of 2.4) in which the Jailor's Daughter tells the audience how she came to fall in love with Palamon and how she delights in the daily routines that bring her into contact with him. Romantic adoration in Arcite is infatuation in the Daughter. She speaks with a childish simplicity. The breathless, staccato outpouring, while recognizably Fletcherian, is expertly organized to reveal character and advance the sub-plot, and the discrepancy between her feelings toward Palamon and his toward her makes for the kind of pathos in which Fletcher specializes. The incremental expansion of 'Then I loved him, | Extremely loved him, infinitely loved him' (14–15) is among his favourite tricks of style. The effect is very different from Arcite's 'O'th' wood, o'th' world'.

Nevertheless, reviewers have often regarded the Jailor's Daughter's sex-driven jour-ney from reckless adolescent exuberance through desperation into madness as the highlight of a stage production. Although her story is mainly Fletcher's province, her third soliloquy (another whole scene, 3.2), when she is alone at night in a wood, having failed to find Palamon, was written by Shakespeare, whose verse vividly evokes her dire predicament. But he has accommodated his style to Fletcher's to the extent of breaking the Daughter's thirty-eight lines into short, urgent, troubled units of speech. Her subsequent mania assumes a darker, more authentic air when Shakespeare takes over its dramatization in 4.3. Although the Daughter, as she first appears in Shakespeare's prose in 2.1, is far more sophisticated and literate than she becomes when next seen in Fletcher's 2.4, the playwrights clearly worked to a jointly considered plan. It is Fletcher who in 2.2 introduces the cousins' conflict between love and friendship and who develops it in 3.6, and it is he who contributes Emilia's long but inconclusive debate with herself over which of the two men she prefers. In both 2.2 and 3.6 there are Fletcher's trademark sudden reversals from one position, expressed in extravagant terms, to its opposite, creating a note of flippancy absent from Emilia's comparison of Palamon and Arcite in 5.5.41–55. The contrasts in situation, attitude, and behaviour of the two young women, so unequal in social class, are important in the overall scheme.

Yet collaboration between playwrights of such different temperaments and talents did make for inconsistencies in characterization. Fletcher's Palamon and Arcite, who luxuriate in self-pity (2.2) and josh each other about their former sexual conquests (3.3.28–42) are scarcely recognizable as the sturdy moralists of Shakespeare's 1.2 or 5.2.30–9. The knowing innuendo that Fletcher gives Emilia in 2.2.151–2 is foreign to Shakespeare's conception of her nature. Collaborating playwrights evidently first devised a 'plot' furnishing a detailed description of each scene or episode (Vickers 2002: 20–3), but to the actual composition of these they brought their individual values and skills. Fletcher was inclined to exploit his material for immediate theatrical effect, rather than in the interests of the whole.

ALL IS TRUE AND CARDENIO

The Two Noble Kinsmen is the sole extant play for which there is clear external evidence of Shakespeare's collaboration with another dramatist. But Fletcher's hand in *All Is True* is no less manifest. Shakespeare begins this play too, writing the first two scenes, but the final three scenes of Act 1 are Fletcher's. Disregarding prologues and epilogues (Fletcher's in both plays), Shakespeare's share of *All Is True* (1.1–2, 2.3–4, 3.2.1–204, 5.1), namely 42 per cent of the lines, was proportionally smaller than his share of *The Two Noble Kinsmen*, namely 46 per cent. Despite the enthusiasm of recent editors of *All Is True*, older views that in it 'Shakespeare's dramatic imagination was' not operating 'at anything like full pressure' seem warranted.[14] The play dramatizes events from a stretch of Henry VIII's reign, beginning with the meeting of Henry with Francis I of France on the Field of Cloth of Gold (1520) and ending with the birth and baptism of Elizabeth (1533).

The structure is unusual. Raphael Holinshed's *Chronicles* (second edition, 1587) is the source for the successive falls of the Duke of Buckingham, Queen Katharine, and Cardinal Wolsey—the three linked by Katharine's defence of Buckingham and by Wolsey's hubristic machinations—and for the coronation of Anne Boleyn and the christening of the daughter that she bears Henry. Interpolated into the final act from John Foxe's *Acts and Monuments* (first published 1563) is the abortive trial of Cranmer, who delivers the closing prophecy of the glories of Elizabeth and James. Spectacle, elaborately described in stage directions, is prominent: a masque of shepherds at Wolsey's banquet (1.4); processions from Buckingham's arraignment (2.1) and to Katherine's trial (2.4), Anne's coronation (4.1), and the christening (5.4); and the dying Katherine's vision (4.2).

The prologue promises tear-inducing *exempla* of 'how mightiness meets misery' (Prologue, 30), but this vague theme does not persist into Act 5. Rather, a stretch of history, treated in the spirit of Shakespeare's late romances, is manipulated into a pattern in which good providentially emerges from a medley of ills and the birth of the infant Elizabeth redeems old woes. Her christening, prompting Cranmer's vision of the future, performs a function similar to the unions of a younger generation, Florizel and Perdita or Ferdinand and Miranda. Henry's evolution as a monarch, freeing himself from Wolsey's domination, and the series of spiritual gains from worldly losses, are subsumed within this broad design.

All is true, so the title claims, but the play repeatedly gives us contradictory versions of the same event, character, or behaviour: the 'truth' seems to be a matter of 'on the one hand . . . on the other hand'. This is most blatantly the case in 4.2. Fletcher has Katherine sum up the dead Wolsey's character: he was ambitious, corrupt, ruthless. But her Gentleman Usher, Griffith, immediately voices a more charitable account of

---

[14] J. C. Maxwell (ed.), *Henry the Eighth* (Cambridge: Cambridge University Press, 1962), xxxii.

Wolsey's career, stressing his accomplishments and virtues. Fletcher has deliberately juxtaposed the two speeches, which are closely based on separate passages in Holinshed. In *The John Fletcher Plays*, Clifford Leech associates such a technique with 'Fletcher's way'.[15] But even in Shakespeare's *All is True* 1.1 Norfolk's enthusiastic description of the Field of Cloth of Gold as an occasion on which the English matched the French in opulent display is countered by Buckingham's splenetic repudiation of 'vanities' organized by Wolsey to further his own ambitions.

However, characterization, in particular, is affected by the co-authors' dissimilar verse styles. As Brian Vickers has pointed out, Shakespeare introduced and individualized all the main characters, 'leaving Fletcher to take care of their endings'.[16] As Buckingham, Wolsey, and Katherine fall from greatness, their personal identities are dissolved by the alchemy of Fletcher's verse. Renunciation, forgiveness, and acceptance become the keynotes. Fletcher's languid cadences, with their dying fall, are not unsuited to convey the changes in spiritual state, but they sentimentalize their speakers. At her trial in 2.4 Katherine is a forceful, intelligent, woman, engaging in passionate self-defence, with the regal dignity and strength of Hermione in *The Winter's Tale*, 3.2. Her sentences vary in form and length, often running across the line divisions, with mid-line pauses. The verse is subtle and vigorous. As the old Arden editor, Knox Pooler, remarked, in such Shakespearean passages 'the rhythm is the meaning and the emotion of the speaker expressed by sound; it changes with every change of feeling, with every hesitation and impulse'.[17] Fletcher's verse reduces the Katherine of 3.1 to a passive victim, even when she is indignant. Here she addresses the cardinals Wolsey and Campeius:

> The more shame for ye! Holy men I thought ye,
> Upon my soul, two reverend cardinal virtues—
> But cardinal sins and hollow hearts I fear ye.
> Mend 'em, for shame, my lords! Is this your comfort?
> The cordial that ye bring a wretched lady,
> A woman lost among ye, laughed at, scorned?
> I will not wish ye half my miseries—
> I have more charity. But say I warned ye.
> Take heed, for heaven's sake take heed, lest at once
> The burden of my sorrows fall upon ye.   (3.1.101–10)

Typical are the succession of double endings ('thought ye', 'virtues', 'fear ye', 'comfort', 'lady', 'warned ye', 'upon ye'), four with the pronoun 'ye' and three of those preceded by a verb, and the strings of small elaborations on a phrase: 'your comfort', for example, is varied as 'cordial that ye bring a wretched lady', 'wretched lady' as 'woman lost among

---

[15] Clifford Leech, *The John Fletcher Plays* (London: Chatto & Windus, 1962), 154.

[16] Vickers, *Shakespeare, Co-Author*, 486.

[17] C. Knox Pooler (ed.), *The Famous History of the Life of King Henry VIII* (London: Methuen, 1915), xxiii.

ye', 'lost among ye' as 'laughed at', and 'laughed at' as 'scorned'. Fletcher tends to pour all utterances into the same rhythmical mould.

Ralph Waldo Emerson found in Fletcher's style 'a trace of pulpit eloquence',[18] and this is appropriate enough to Archbishop Cranmer's oration over the new-born Elizabeth. Audiences have regularly been moved by its plangent strains, as also by the elegiac cadences of Katherine's valedictory speeches in 4.2. The play was evidently jointly plotted, and in 5.1 Shakespeare points forward to Fletcher's close. Fletcher's material is stageworthy, and Shakespeare seems to have been content to give his collaborator free rein, but the discrepancy between Shakespeare's and Fletcher's poetic styles has certainly not been 'erased'.

If *Double Falsehood* is an adaptation of a third (though first-written) Shakespeare–Fletcher collaboration, any account of the original *Cardenio* must be largely conjectural. Theobald's play contains many of the ingredients of Fletcherian tragicomedy and Shakespearean romance: wronged lovers, male rivalry, women endangered, madness, disguise (of a woman as a boy), pastoral scenes, and a complicated *Cymbeline*-like denouement in which lost young folk are restored to their fathers and couples reunited. The overall effect is more Fletcherian than Shakespearean, and Fletcher's verse style remains evident in much of the play's second half, as when Leonora, forsaken by Henriquez, laments:

> You maidens that shall live
> To hear my mournful tale when I am ashes,
> Be wise, and to an oath no more give credit,
> To tears, to vows—false both—or anything
> A man shall promise, than to clouds that now
> Bear such a pleasing shape and now are nothing.[19]

This wringing of pathos from lines in which a character imagines herself a posthumous exemplum is typical, and is closely matched in the Jailor's Daughter's fears of the consequences of her freeing Palamon in *The Two Noble Kinsmen*:

> If the law
> Find me and then condemn me for't, some wenches,
> Some honest-hearted maids, will sing my dirge,
> And tell to memory my death was noble,
> Dying almost a martyr.   (2.6.13–17)

Theobald, revising for the eighteenth-century stage, would have been less tolerant of Shakespeare's complex late poetry, and wholly Shakespearean lines are harder to identify. William Davenant's adaptation of *The Two Noble Kinsmen* as *The Rivals* (1664) retained some of Fletcher's share but left no line by Shakespeare intact. Nevertheless, the signs are that Shakespeare began *Cardenio* too, the bulk of the younger

---

[18] Quoted by Marco Mincoff, '*Henry VIII* and Fletcher', *Shakespeare Quarterly* 12 (1961), 239–60, at 248.

[19] Modernized from the second issue of the 1728 edition, 49, sig. E1.

dramatist's contribution belonging to 3.3 onwards. In all three collaborations with Fletcher, Shakespeare was more apt to reshape his sources, Fletcher to echo their wording.

Shakespeare's Collaborative Plays 1605–1607: with George Wilkins and with Thomas Middleton

While *The Two Noble Kinsmen*, *All Is True*, and (probably) *Cardenio* form a coda to Shakespeare's unaided late plays, *Pericles* (1607) is their precursor. In this case, Shakespeare wrote the last three acts, while the first two were written by George Wilkins, author of *The Miseries of Enforced Marriage* (1606), performed by the King's Men, and main co-author, with John Day and William Rowley, of *The Travels of the Three English Brothers* (1607).[20] *Pericles* retells the story, popular throughout Europe for a thousand years, of Apollonius of Tyre, as recycled by the medieval poet John Gower in his *Confessio Amantis*, and, in a prose version, by Laurence Twine. The old folk-tale is deeply rooted in the 'collective unconscious' of the ancient world, and much modern critical interpretation of the play, which adheres closely to the original, might equally well be addressing the Latin *Historia Apollonii Regis Tyri*.

Shakespeare's late plays cover two generations, in which infants grow to marriageable age. In *Cymbeline* and *The Tempest* Shakespeare solves the structural problem thus posed by loading the first act with narrative informing us of events long past. In *The Winter's Tale* a personified Time enters to fill the sixteen-year gap between Acts 3 and 4. In *All Is True* the child is born not at the beginning but at the end, and narrative is transformed into closing prophecy of her future reign. In *Pericles* the figure of Gower is resurrected to serve as choric presenter, whose quaint tetrameters guide the audience through time and space as the seafaring princely hero, after a false start, acquires a wife, begets a daughter, is separated from both, and is finally reunited with them.

Although Wilkins was a lesser dramatist than Fletcher, and *Pericles* is preserved only in a textually corrupt quarto (1609), it is, as T. S. Eliot declared, a 'very great play', building to two intensely moving recognition scenes that restore to Pericles his daughter Marina and his wife Thaisa, both supposed long dead.[21] The first holds audiences spellbound, as father and daughter inch their way toward realization of the other's identity and Pericles' spirit is drawn from despair to bliss. The second is treated economically, but Shakespeare can touch the heart with the simplest of speeches, as

---

[20] The evidence for the authorship of *Pericles* is most fully set forth in MacDonald P. Jackson, *Defining Shakespeare: 'Pericles' as Test Case* (Oxford: Oxford University Press, 2003), where the sources are also discussed, and the contrasting styles of Shakespeare and Wilkins analysed (pp. 149–65).

[21] For details concerning Eliot's statement see Jackson, *Defining Shakespeare*, 24 n. 40.

when Pericles draws Thaisa's attention to Marina, unseen by her mother since her birth at sea, and Thaisa responds 'Blessed, and mine own!' (Sc. 22.70).

Pericles derives its essential coherence from the Apollonius legend, which, despite its episodic nature, has its own inner dynamic. Wilkins dramatizes the young prince's discovery of incest between Antiochus and his daughter, his flight and his relief of famine at Tharsus, and the reversal of his fortunes when, shipwrecked on the coast of Pentapolis, he wins princess Thaisa as his bride. Wilkins's verse is halting, hobbled by sporadic rhyme, his manner sententious and prolix, his dramaturgy crude. But there are compensatory elements of the pictorial and emblematic; Wilkins can write lively colloquial prose (in Pericles' encounter with fishermen in Scene 5); and the scenes at the jovial King Simonides' court at Pentapolis have surprising theatrical vitality, with their parade of knights, banquet, and dance. Wilkins gets the events of Pericles' unmarried life onto the stage. Shakespeare takes over from Scene 11 (or Act 3) onwards, his imagination fully involved in the latter portion of the story, from Marina's birth and Thaisa's apparent death aboard a tempest-tossed ship, through Thaisa's miraculous recovery and her husband's and daughter's 'painful adventures', to the conclusion in which all three are 'crowned with joy at last' (Sc. 22.13). Once the fortunes of Marina (in particular) and Thaisa enter the tale, Shakespeare's superior architectonic skill is required for a less doggedly linear, more complex dramatic structure, as the focus shifts among father, mother, and daughter. Characters are more 'inwardly' observed. Shakespeare's superb poetry creates a sea-storm on the bare Globe platform, turns a boy actor lying in a wooden box into the lovely coffined queen whose eyelids 'Begin to part their fringes of bright gold' (Sc. 12.98) as she is revived by the physician-mage Cerimon, and conjures transcendental emotion from the blissful finale. The play benefits from the simple division of labour.

But there is nevertheless evidence that Wilkins, familiar with bawdy-house trade, contributed to the brothel scenes, in which Marina defends her chastity. This helps account for some anomalies surrounding Lysimachus' visit as a client in Scene 19.[22]

In *Timon of Athens* (1605–6) the collaborators' shares are more intertangled.[23] There are indications that the compilers of the Shakespeare First Folio (1623) had not originally intended to include this tragedy.[24] In 1968 Philip Edwards remarked that had it been omitted, 'We should not have known . . . of Shakespeare's power to write satirical merchant comedy in a style which only Middleton can equal.'[25] It is now clear that the 'brilliant' scenes admired by Edwards (3.1–3.3) are among those composed by Middleton himself.

---

[22] Jackson, *Defining Shakespeare*, 211–13.

[23] There is detailed information in Wells and Taylor, *William Shakespeare: A Textual Companion*, 501–2: Taylor and Lavagnino (eds.), *Thomas Middleton and Early Modern Textual Culture: A Companion to the Collected Works* (Oxford: Clarendon Press, 2007), 356–8; and Antony B. Dawson and Gretchen E. Minton (eds.), *Timon of Athens* (London: Arden Shakespeare, 2008), 401–7.

[24] Wells and Taylor, *William Shakespeare: A Textual Companion*, 127–8.

[25] Philip Edwards, *Shakespeare and the Confines of Art* (London: Methuen, 1968).

The plot is simple. Lord Timon, extravagantly bountiful, finds himself insolvent, is denied by the false friends from whom he seeks to borrow, withdraws to the wilderness and rails against humankind, until, all passion spent, he dies on 'the beachèd verge of the salt flood' (5.2.101). In the twentieth century, theories of the play's multiple authorship gave way to accounts that viewed it as 'unfinished' or related it to morality plays, *de casibus* tragedies, or 'shews' based on seasonal or diurnal myth. It is stylistically uneven in the extreme; scenes and characters—Alcibiades in 3.5, the Fool and Page in 2.2—are inadequately integrated into the action; there are puzzling structural anomalies, such as the failure of the Poet and Painter, whose entry is announced at 4.3.353, to appear until two unrelated episodes, covering two hundred lines, have intervened; there is muddle over the value of a talent; Timon is given two epitaphs.

Recent editors who accept the overwhelming case for Middleton having written about one-third of the play recognize that inconsistencies and loose ends in the Folio text have arisen through a process of co-authorship that had not reached the stage of a final combined effort to fully integrate individual scenes, episodes, and speeches and to ensure continuity. It seems probable that Middleton 'wrote his contributions after Shakespeare had stopped working on his'.[26] Middleton was responsible for 1.2, in which Timon as host is 'the very soul of bounty' (209) but we learn from his steward Flavius that the coffers are empty; for almost the whole of Act 3, in which Timon is refused financial aid, is pursued by creditors, and spurns all his guests at a mock-banquet, and in which the soldier Alcibiades is banished after offending the senate as he pleads for the life of a condemned friend; for portions of Act 4 in which Flavius appears (460–537); and for a few other short patches here and there.

Middleton thus created the scenes on which the play pivots, so that Timon the city-dwelling Philanthrope of Acts 1–2 turns into Timon the cave-dwelling Misanthrope of Acts 4–5, and Athenian captain Alcibiades is provoked into becoming his city's foe. Middleton was unrivalled at portraying unctuous hypocrisy and the scenes in which three of the destitute Timon's friends concoct pretexts for fobbing him off are in his satiric vein at its sharpest. The later, Shakespearean diatribes in which Timon redefines Renaissance cosmology in terms of 'thievery' are unmatched in fury outside *King Lear*. Between them the playwrights created a generic mix with its own peculiar flavour.

EARLY COLLABORATIONS

The plays discussed so far were composed for the King's Men late in Shakespeare's career, when his dramatic poetry—of which a sample from *The Two Noble Kinsmen*

---

[26] Taylor and Lavagnino, *Thomas Middleton and Early Modern Textual Culture*, 357.

has been analysed at some length—was highly distinctive. In his plays of the early 1590s it is often much less so. He had doubtless absorbed a range of styles as an actor. There is a stylistic sameness about much of the drama written at this time and playwrights freely borrowed one another's phrases and lines. The circumstances in which Shakespeare began to write for the theatre remain obscure, and the chronology of his earliest plays is uncertain. Yet some progress has recently been made. The revised Oxford *Complete Works* (2005) is the only edition to acknowledge *Titus Andronicus*, tentatively dated 1592, as 'by William Shakespeare, with George Peele', but the ascription has been fully substantiated. Peele, eight years Shakespeare's senior, began the play, composing the long first act and (probably) 2.1, 2.2, and 4.1, which initiates the counter-movement leading to Titus' shocking revenge for the atrocities committed against him and his family.

With the advent of a 'Theatre of Cruelty' in the mid-twentieth century, *Titus Andronicus*, frequently reviled as too replete with Senecan horrors to be substantially Shakespeare's, began to gain admirers. Returning Roman war hero Titus' insistence on carrying out his customary sacrifice of 'the proudest prisoner of the Goths' (1.1.96), Queen Tamora's eldest son, provokes extravagant reprisals on the Andronici by Tamora's Moorish lover Aaron. Titus' daughter Lavinia enters 2.4, '*her hands cut off and her tongue cut out, and ravished*', bodies are stabbed, throats cut, hands and heads lopped. In retaliation Titus slaughters Tamora's sons, bakes them in a pie, and serves it to their mother. In the opening scene, as the late emperor's two sons vie for succession, Titus is asked to 'help to set a head on headless Rome' (1.1.186), and in the final scene his brother Marcus considers 'how to knit' the 'broken limbs' of the state 'again into one body' (5.3.69–71). So the physical mutilations bear a metaphorical relationship to the body politic. Although Peele set the play's nightmare events in motion, as a dramatic action organized in terms of cause and effect it is structurally more sophisticated than any of his unaided works. Therefore Shakespeare must have taken a significant role in the plotting.

Peele's verse in *Titus Andronicus* is marked not only by striking verbal parallels with his known works but also by an un-Shakespearean avoidance of double endings, the repetition *ad nauseam* of a few common words and turns of phrase, a heavy use of vocatives, a 'lumbering way with rhetorical figures',[27] and various quantifiable features of vocabulary, grammar, function-word use, alliteration, metrics, and so on. The effect is of rhythmical and dramatic flatness and sameness. When Tamora meets Aaron in 2.3 the dialogue suddenly becomes lively and varied. The language is concrete and vivid. On a summer's day, when 'birds chant melody on every bush' and the 'snake lies rollèd in the cheerful sun', 'The green leaves quiver with the cooling wind, | And make a chequered shadow on the ground' (12–15). Tamora invites Aaron to sit with her and listen to 'the babbling echo' that 'mocks the hounds' in the nearby hunt, as their yelping answers 'the well-tuned horns', 'As if a double hunt were heard at once' (17–19), and

---

[27] Vickers, *Shakespeare, Co-Author*, 235.

recalls Aeneas and Dido's amorous encounter, 'curtained with a counsel-keeping cave' (24). The imagery and the inventive compound adjective are redolent of the younger Shakespeare at his most individual.[28] And Tamora's twenty-line speech is organized as a verse paragraph that ends by stitching together into a fancied post-coital lullaby the sounds of hounds, horns, and birds. The image of the snake is picked up in Aaron's reply. Tamora's thoughts are of love, his of vengeance, and so the snake lying 'rolled in the cheerful sun' becomes 'an adder when she doth unroll | to do some fatal execution' (36–7). Likewise, although the *mature* Shakespeare would not have written the speech in which Marcus bandages his mutilated niece in a swathe of Ovidian conceits, it is well beyond Peele's poetic powers (2.4.11–57).

In the opening act, Peele manages stage action which requires dialogue between characters on two levels and movement up and down (as he does at the beginning of *David and Bethsabe*), but it is only when Shakespeare takes over that scenes (notably 3.1) are shaped to an emotional climax, horrors are duly foreshadowed, characters become more than mere roles, and an audience's sympathies are engaged. Titus is no Lear, but his sufferings elicit compassion. In Shakespeare's hands Aaron the Moor, silent throughout Peele's 1.1, becomes a prime mover of the plot—and an exuberant fiend, brilliantly humanized by his solicitude for his illegitimate baby son. The achievement is uneven, but many elements of Shakespeare's later tragedies are here present in embryo.

While Peele and his more talented junior partner seem to have planned *Titus Andronicus* together, Shakespeare's contribution to *1 Henry VI* may not have belonged to the original play. Even E. K. Chambers,[29] who protested against excessive 'disinte-gration' of the Shakespeare canon, believed *1 Henry VI* to be of multiple authorship. But Andrew S. Cairncross's Arden editions of the three parts of *Henry VI* (1962–4) con-solidated a new orthodoxy—that they had been written in numerical order by Shake-speare alone as part of a coherent tetralogy ending with *Richard III*. It was not until 1995 that Gary Taylor effectively challenged this consensus, dating *1 Henry VI* after the other two parts, assigning Shakespeare 2.4 and 4.2–4.7.32, Thomas Nashe Act 1, and two unknown dramatists the remainder of the play.[30] Three scholars have since provided grounds for reaching substantial agreement with these conclusions. In a book-length analysis, full of new data, Paul Vincent modifies Taylor's findings by merging his two unknown dramatists into one and denying Shakespeare 4.6.[31] Brian Vickers and Marina Tarlinskaja deny him 4.7.1–32 as well.[32]

---

[28] For a few parallels with early Shakespeare works, see MacDonald P. Jackson, 'Determining Authorship: A New Technique', *Research Opportunities in Renaissance Drama* 41 (2002), 1–14, at 10–12.

[29] Chambers, *William Shakespeare: A Study of Facts and Problems*, 2: 277–95.

[30] Taylor, 'Shakespeare and Others: The Authorship of *Henry the Sixth, Part One*', *Medieval and Renaissance Drama in England* 7 (1995), 145–205.

[31] See Paul Vincent, *When 'harey' Met Shakespeare: The Genesis of the First Part of Henry the Sixth* (Saarbrücken: DVM Verlag Dr Müller, 2008).

[32] The results of Tarlinskaja's metrical analysis (part of a work 'in progress') were outlined by Vickers in 'Incomplete Shakespeare: Or, Denying Coauthorship in *1 Henry IV*', *Shakespeare Quarterly* 58 (2007), 311–52, at 343–5.

Evidence that Nashe was responsible for Act 1 is compelling: for example, the idiosyncratic phraseology is his; the jerky, disconnected verse with its superabundant grammatical inversions ('Sad tidings bring I to you out of France', 1.1.58) matches that of his *Summer's Last Will and Testament*; the numerous biblical and classical allusions (much less frequent in the rest of the play) are in his manner; and the stage directions beginning with 'Here' reflect his practice. Act 1 also borrows from recondite sources used elsewhere by Nashe but not by Shakespeare. Vincent argues, but without dogmatism, that *1 Henry VI* contains some revision by Shakespeare of the 'harey the vj' listed by Philip Henslowe and produced by Strange's Men at the Rose theatre on 3 March 1592, and that this had been co-written by Nashe and an anonymous dramatist.

Beginning with Henry V's funeral, the play dramatizes the struggles of an England weakened by civil quarrels to retain his conquests in France. Joan la Pucelle (Joan of Arc) rallies the French, while Lord Talbot is presented as the English hero. History is treated with considerable freedom. In Shakespeare's 2.4—the entirely fictional 'Temple Garden' scene—the symbolic plucking of red or white roses by nobles on opposing sides of the York–Lancaster divide adumbrates the Wars of the Roses. Shakespeare's 4.5 is clearly a replacement for 4.6, and his scenes in Act 4 expose the national shortcomings that result in the heroic deaths of Talbot and his son. Again, the Shakespearean material displays more vibrant images, more colourful vocabulary, more pointed couplets, and a stronger sense of the dramatic than is to be found in the rest of *1 Henry VI*. Talbot's extended analogy of his surrounded soldiers to a herd of deer 'bounded in a pale', with its apposite hunting terminology and typical pun on 'dear deer', is outside the scope of other playwrights at this time (4.2.45–54).[33]

The kind of scrupulous attribution study recently undertaken on *1 Henry VI* may yet demonstrate beyond reasonable doubt that Shakespeare was not the sole author of *The First Part of the Contention* and *Richard Duke of York* (2 and 3 *Henry VI*). But results may remain indeterminate if specific collaborators cannot confidently be identified, since it is always possible to suppose that writing less recognizably Shakespeare's than that of the scenes attributed to him in *1 Henry VI* simply belongs to a more primitive phase of his development.

A big step forward has been taken in *Shakespeare, Computers, and the Mystery of Authorship*, edited by Hugh Craig and Arthur F. Kinney.[34] Their team's methods, first tested on texts of known authorship, are based on counts of (a) lexical words and (b) high-frequency function words that are used significantly more often by one playwright than another. Besides giving broad support to the allocations made in the Oxford *Textual Companion* and *Complete Works*,[35] the results suggest that Marlowe

---

[33] The hunting terms are glossed in Edward Burns (ed.) *King Henry VI: Part 1* (London: Arden Shakespeare, 2000), 235. He might have added that 'a pinch' is a slight bite from a hound (*OED sb* 1).

[34] Craig and Kinney (eds.), *Shakespeare, Computers, and the Mystery of Authorship* (Cambridge: Cambridge University Press, 2009).

[35] Wells and Taylor (eds.), *William Shakespeare: A Textual Companion* (1987), and *eidem*, *William Shakespeare: The Complete Works* (Oxford: Clarendon Press, 1986; 2nd edn. 2005).

may have written some of the Joan of Arc material in *1 Henry VI* and some of the Jack Cade material in *2 Henry VI*.[36]

EARLY PLAYS NOT COLLECTED IN
THE FIRST FOLIO (1623)

Craig and Kinney also throw light on two early plays that, though absent from the First Folio, have long haunted the fringes of the Shakespeare canon: *Arden of Faversham*, published in a quarto of 1592, and *Edward III*, published in a quarto of 1596. In the nineteenth century, each was the subject of vigorous debate. The poet Swinburne championed the former's claims, but scorned the latter's.[37] The only external support for either comes from booksellers' unreliable catalogues of 1656.[38] There is now a measure of agreement, consolidated by Craig and Kinney, that Shakespeare wrote some of *Edward III*.[39] The revised Oxford *Complete Works* (2005) assigns him Scenes 2 (from the King's entrance before line 90), 3, 12, and 'possibly' 13 (1.2, 2.1–2, 4.4, 4.5 in other editions). In the first two, King Edward attempts in vain to seduce the Countess of Salisbury, after he has delivered her castle from Scots enemies allied with France. Once he has been taught, by the Countess's resourceful defence of her chastity, to master his adulterous passion, he pursues his claims to the French crown in a series of battles at which his son, the Black Prince, proves his valour. The main source, Berners' translation of Froissart's *Chronicles* (1523–5), is supplemented by Holinshed and, for the Countess scenes, by William Painter's *The Palace of Pleasure* (1575). As a chronicle history *Edward III* reads like a rudimentary forerunner of *Henry V*, but lacks the single big climax of an Agincourt. The scenes in which Edward woos the Countess have exceptional dramatic

---

[36] Craig and Kinney, *Shakespeare, Computers, and the Mystery of Authorship*, 40–77.

[37] Algernon Charles Swinburne, *A Study of Shakespeare* (London: Heinemann, 1918; first published Chatto & Windus, 1879), 128–41, 231–74.

[38] MacDonald P. Jackson, 'Shakespeare and the Quarrel Scene in *Arden of Faversham*', *Shakespeare Quarterly* 57 (2006), 249–93, at 253.

[39] For a history of opinion on the play's authorship and a discussion of sources see G. Harold Metz (ed.), *Sources of Four Plays Ascribed to Shakespeare* (Columbia: University of Missouri Press, 1989), 3–42; also Giorgio Melchiori (ed.), *King Edward III* (Cambridge: Cambridge University Press, 1998). Metrical data compiled by Philip Timberlake (*The Feminine Ending in English Blank Verse: A Study of its Use by Early Writers in the Measure and its Development in the Drama up to the Year 1595* [Menasha, WI: George Banta 1931], 77–80) and Marina Tarlinskaja ('Looking for Shakespeare in Edward III', forthcoming in *Shakespeare Yearbook* [private communication Sept. 2009]) support the Oxford ascription and suggest Shakespeare's possible involvement in Scenes 14–17, as do computerized investigations reported by Thomas Merriam (see '*Edward III*', *Literary and Linguistic Computing* 15 (2000), 157–86) and Ward E. Y. Elliot and Robert J. Valenza (see 'Two tough nuts to crack: did Shakespeare write the "Shakespeare" portions of *Sir Thomas More and Edward III*? Part 1 and Part II: Conclusion', *Literary and Linguistic Computing* 25 (2010), 67–83, 167–77. The Craig and Kinney team do not investigate the whole play, but support the ascription of the Countess scenes (2–3) to Shakespeare (Craig and Kinney, *Shakespeare, Computers, and the Mystery of Authorship*, 116–33).

and linguistic vitality, besides affording the play's sole touches of humour, while in Scene 12 Audley preaches the inevitability of death to Prince Edward in weighty lines that anticipate the Duke's homily to Claudio in *Measure for Measure*, 3.1. In both the Countess scenes and the war scenes at Poitiers (11 and 13) characters find themselves caught between the claims of conflicting oaths—a predicament explored in several of Shakespeare's earliest plays.

Edward III might have been composed almost any time between about 1588 and its entry on the Stationers' Register in December 1595. The domestic tragedy *Arden of Faversham* is indebted to an account in the 1587 edition of Holinshed's *Chronicle* of an actual crime—Thomas Arden's murder at the instigation of his wife Alice and her lover Mosby.[40] It has yet to gain admission to the canon, but is now knocking at the door. Jackson made out a case for Shakespeare's authorship of at least part of the play, notably the superb 'quarrel scene' between the two adulterers (Sc. 8), which ends with their reconciliation and the renewal of their murderous intent.[41] The independent lexical and function-word tests employed in the 'computational stylistics' of Craig and Kinney converge to confirm that Shakespeare was probably responsible for much of the middle of the play, from Scene 4 to Scene 9, a stretch of text corresponding to Act 3 in older editions.[42]

More firmly established is Shakespeare's collaboration with Henry Chettle, Thomas Heywood, and Thomas Dekker on the refurbishing of *Sir Thomas More*, extant only in a British Library manuscript. Shakespeare is almost certainly the famous 'Hand D' who contributed a scene in which More employs his oratory to quell a riot, and is the probable author of one soliloquy copied by a scribe.[43] The occasion of this revamping and of the composition of the original script (which is in the handwriting of the minor playwright Anthony Munday) are in dispute, but the most likely date of Shakespeare's contribution is around 1603–4. The concatenation of ideas and images in More's address to the mob is strikingly Shakespearean, as R. W. Chambers showed in a classic

---

[40] The fullest edition is M. L. Wine (ed.), *The Tragedy of Arden of Faversham* (London: Methuen 1973).

[41] MacDonald P. Jackson, 'Shakespeare and the Quarrel Scene in *Arden of Faversham*', *Shakespeare Quarterly* 57 (2006), 249–93; see also Jayne M. Carroll and MacDonald. P. Jackson, 'Shakespeare, *Arden of Faversham*, and "Literature Online"', *Shakespeare Newsletter* 54 (2004), 3–4, 6; Jackson, 'Compound Adjectives in Arden of Faversham', 51–4; and *idem*, 'Shakespearean Features of the Poetic Style of *Arden of Faversham*', *Archiv für das Studium der neueren Sprachen und Literaturen* 230 (1993), 279–304.

[42] See Craig and Kinney, *Shakespeare, Computers, and the Mystery of Authorship*, 78–99. There has been no secure identification of Shakespeare's collaborator or collaborators on *Edward III* or *Arden of Faversham*, though the Craig–Kinney team tested for Marlowe and Kyd in *Arden of Faversham*, and for Marlowe, Kyd, and Peele in *Edward III* (Craig and Kinney, at 99, 133).

[43] See MacDonald P. Jackson, 'The Date and Authorship of Hand D's Contribution to *Sir Thomas More*: Evidence from "Literature Online"', *Shakespeare Survey* 59 (2006), 69–78; *idem*, 'Is "Hand D" of *Sir Thomas More* Shakespeare's? Thomas Bayes and the Elliott–Valenza Authorship Tests', *Early Modern Literary Studies* 12.3 (2007), 11–36, http://purl.oclc.org/emls/12-3/jackbaye.htm; Craig and Kinney, *Shakespeare, Computers, and the Mystery of Authorship*, 134–61.

essay.[44] If Hand D is indeed Shakespeare's, this scene in *More* offers us the sole example, outside his signatures, of his penmanship and a glimpse into his playwriting workshop.[45]

CONCLUSIONS

What generalizations can be made about Shakespeare as collaborator? One concerns modes of operation. The normal division of labour was by scenes or substantial stretches of text. There is little evidence that Shakespeare and a co-author ever engaged in joint composition of individual speeches, though in *Timon of Athens* Middleton may have inserted a few short passages into scenes predominantly Shakespeare's, and in *Pericles* Shakespeare probably interpolated the famous 'blind mole' image into one speech by Wilkins (Sc. 1.143–5).

A more important finding is evaluative. Shakespeare wrote mainly poetic drama and his greatness as a dramatist is inseparable from his greatness as a poet. His dramatic verse is more flexible, vibrant, and expressive, and carries a heavier freight of meaning than that of his playwright contemporaries. Middleton's satirical cameos in Act 3 of *Timon of Athens*, mingling verse and prose, are the only scenes by a collaborator that Shakespeare could not have written better himself. The allocation of shares in Shakespeare co-authored plays does not *depend* on anybody's assessments of merit, but on a wealth of diverse quantifiable data. But value judgements need not be resisted. Shakespeare's dialogue is almost always superior, poetically and dramatically, to that of his co-authors. This superiority is not lost on experienced theatre goers. Reviewing a Royal Shakespeare Company production of *Pericles*, Robert Cushman remarked that after the first two acts 'the relief to the ear when we finally arrive at verse that moves in paragraphs instead of single lame sentences is hardly to be described'.[46] Some of Shakespeare's most densely concentrated passages in *The Two Noble Kinsmen* doubtless strain the capacities of an audience to the limit, but Emilia's account of her innocent love of Flavina, for example, is a gift to any actress with a feeling for poetry.

Emilia's speech is a wonderful piece of self-characterization. *Dramatis personae* acquire 'character' through the words and deeds given them by the playwright. The shallow natures of Lucullus, Lucius, and Sepronius in *Timon of Athens*, 3.1–3, are exposed by the glib and oily tones that Middleton's language generates for them. Fletcher's Jailor's Daughter in *The Two Noble Kinsmen* has a beguiling naiveté. But it

---

[44] Chambers, 'Shakespeare and the Play of *More*', in *Man's Unconquerable Mind* (London: Cape, 1939; rpt. 1952), 204–49.

[45] Shakespeare may have refurbished at least one other old play. Craig describes stylometric evidence that he wrote the famous 1602 'Additions' to Thomas Kyd's *The Spanish Tragedy* (Craig and Kinney, *Shakespeare, Computers, and the Mystery of Authorship*, 162–80).

[46] Review in the *Observer*, 8 April 1979, cited by Jackson, *Defining Shakespeare*, 150 n. 3.

is a feature of the collaborative plays that, in most modes, it is Shakespeare's, rather than his co-author's, dialogue that most effectively animates characters, confers complexity, and arouses empathy. Nineteenth- and early twentieth-century commentators who praised Shakespeare as the supreme master in the creation of 'life-like' characters were not wholly misguided.

Why, then, did Shakespeare collaborate? In the early 1590s, he may, as a mere tyro, have been obliged to in order to prove himself 'as well able to bombast out a blank verse as the best' of the University Wits. Shakespeare's beginnings in the theatre are still the subject of speculation, but for an actor turning playwright some joint generation of scripts would have been natural enough, as it was for Ben Jonson a few years later.[47] By the mid-1600s, Shakespeare's motives must have been different. Middleton wrote *A Yorkshire Tragedy* (1605) and *The Revenger's Tragedy* (1606) for the King's Men during the same period in which he contributed to *Timon of Athens* (1605–6).[48] The company may have been eager to strengthen the connection. It is possible also that Shakespeare found the Timon material intractable and recognized in Middleton a playwright capable of supplying the comic matter on which the plot could hinge. *Pericles* may well have begun as Wilkins' venture, in which Shakespeare joined him upon appreciating the potential of the Apollonius story. Collaboration with Fletcher during the years 1612–14 is readily explained. *The Tempest* (1611) was Shakespeare's last unaided play and Fletcher succeeded him as the King's Men's leading dramatist. The three co-authored works provided a natural transition from the old guard to the new. Although none of Shakespeare's collaborative plays rivals *Hamlet, Twelfth Night, 1* and *2 Henry IV, Antony and Cleopatra*, or *The Winter's Tale* in general esteem, the Shakespeare canon would be very much poorer without them.

---

[47] E. K. Chambers, *The Elizabethan Stage*, 4 vols. (Oxford: Clarendon Press, 1923), 3: 373–4.
[48] Taylor and Lavagnino, *Thomas Middleton and Early Modern Textual Culture*, 355–63.

CHAPTER 3

··

MANUSCRIPT CIRCULATION

··

ARTHUR F. MAROTTI AND LAURA ESTILL

In literary history and historical bibliography, Shakespeare's writing is associated with print culture—through the ('good' and 'bad') quartos of the plays, the various Folios or collected editions of his dramas beginning in 1623, the much reprinted narrative poems (*Venus and Adonis* and [*The Rape of*] *Lucrece*), Thomas Thorpe's 1609 Quarto of *Shakespeare's Sonnets*, John Benson's 1640 editorially-distorted *Poems: Written by Wil. Shake-speare*, and other printed texts such as William Jaggard's *The Passionate Pilgrim by William Shakespeare* (1599 and 1612) and Robert Chester's *Love's Martyr* (1601). Shakespeare's name, which became a marketable commodity in the late 1590s, also appears on the title-pages of editions of plays not written by, but attributed to, him— for example, *The First Part of the True and Honorable Historie of the Life of Sir John Oldcastle* (1600), *The London Prodigal* (1605), and *A Yorkshire Tragedy* (1608).

In his own lifetime, Shakespeare may have circulated some or all of his *Sonnets* in manuscript, as is suggested by Frances Meres's famous reference to the 'sugred *Sonnets* among his priuate friends' and William Jaggard's inclusion in his 1599 volume of versions of Sonnets 138 and 144 textually different from those found in the 1609 Quarto.[1] As Richard Dutton and Lukas Erne have recently argued, Shakespeare may have released into manuscript circulation reading versions of some of his plays.[2] But, unlike such authors as Sir Philip Sidney or John Donne, Shakespeare himself did not make extensive use of this medium of literary transmission—except, of course, in writing scripts for the theatre company in which he was a shareholder.

---

[1] *Palladis Tamia* (1598), in G. Gregory Smith (ed.), *Elizabethan Critical Essays*, vol. 2 (Oxford: Oxford University Press, 1904), 317.

[2] See Richard Dutton, 'The Birth of the Author', in Cedric C. Brown and Arthur F. Marotti (eds.), *Texts and Cultural Change in Early Modern England* (Basingstoke: Palgrave Macmillan, 1997), 13–78; and Lukas Erne, *Shakespeare as Literary Dramatist* (Cambridge: Cambridge University Press, 2003).

After the publication of his plays and poems, however, Shakespearean texts were available for excerpting and appropriation by those who kept commonplace books or who compiled collections of verse. Nevertheless, if we look for Shakespearean poems or for excerpts from the poetry and plays, we find relatively few examples in the manuscript remains of the period—at least by comparison with authors who loomed large in the system of manuscript transmission—for example, John Donne, Sir Walter Ralegh, Ben Jonson, Henry King, Richard Corbett, Thomas Carew, and Robert Herrick. Those who copied Shakespearean poems, plays, or excerpts, for the most part, used printed editions as their sources rather than manuscript documents. There are a few exceptions, but copying from print was the norm.

SHAKESPEARE'S POETRY IN MANUSCRIPT

In early modern English manuscript commonplace-book miscellanies and poetical anthologies, compilers and groups of compilers transcribed or had professional scribes record a variety of poems either passed on to them by others or composed by themselves. In this world of manuscript transmission (in which poems were often copied from printed texts), much lyric poetry from the period was preserved—pieces by well-known, canonical writers, but also by lesser-known poets or anonymous authors. Even poets whose work reached print form in their own lifetimes or shortly after their deaths—John Donne, Ben Jonson, Thomas Carew, and Henry King, for example—remained attractive to verse collectors in this system of literary transmission.

Given the cultural visibility of William Shakespeare both as a dramatist and poet, it might seem strange that such a small percentage of his work survives in manuscript documents from the period. With the possible exception of some of the songs from the plays, not many of Shakespeare's poems, plays, or dramatic excerpts have been preserved in this medium. This may be partly due to the availability in printed editions of the dramas and of *Venus and Adonis* and *Lucrece*, but, given Shakespeare's growing literary and cultural importance, it is still surprising how few times Shakespearean texts seem to have been recorded in sixteenth- and seventeenth-century manuscripts.

The shorter or longer non-dramatic poetry should be considered apart from the excerpts from the plays found in seventeenth-century manuscript collections, even though, especially in the cases of the two long narrative poems, commonplace-book compilers may have had the same motives for excerpting aphoristic or sententious passages from both kinds of writing. For purposes of this discussion, we omit two works that most specialists in the field would deny to Shakespeare, the lyric beginning 'Shall I die, shall I fly' and the funeral elegy for William Peter. We do, however, include the lyric 'When that thine eye hath chose the dame' (printed in *The Passionate Pilgrim by William Shakespeare* [1599 and 1612]).

This lyric, published in a textually garbled form in William Jaggard's *Passionate Pilgrim*, may or may not have been written by Shakespeare. It is found in complete form (with textual variants) in three different manuscripts: British Library MS Harley 7392 (fol. 43r–v), Folger MSS V.a.89 (pp. 25–6), and V.a.339 (fol. 191v), the first manuscript version appearing to be the least corrupt text.[3] This fifty-four-line piece was also used to fashion an eighteen-line poem that is found in British Library MSS Sloane 1792, fol. 11r–v and (minus two of the lines) Additional 30982, fol. 52v. In the former it reads:

Upon one that went a wooing

> The wiles and giles which women worke,
> Dissembled with an outward show:
> The trickes and toyes that in them lurke,
> The cocke that treads them cannot know.
> Have you not heard it saide full oft,
> A womans nay doth stand for nought.
>
> What though shee strive to try her strength,
> And bann and braule, and say thee nay;
> Her feeble force will yeld at length,[4]
> When craft hath taught her thus to say,
> Had women beene as strong as men,
> Good sooth you had not had it then.
>
> What though her cloudie lookes bee bent,
> Her stormie browes will calme eare night;
> And then to late shee will repent,
> that thus dissembled her delight;
> And twice desire eare it be day,
> That which with scorne shee put away.

This shorter poem not only has a title, but also reproduces three of the nine stanzas of the original in an altered order: lines 43–8, 31–6, 25–30.[5]

What we have here is a typical case of the kind of textual bricolage often practised in the manuscript system of literary transmission. Compilers of verse collections were free to copy from manuscript or printed sources; to alter the words of the texts they received; to add or subtract material; to excerpt, rearrange or conflate pieces; to provide titles for untitled poems. The collections of verse in which this excerpted, rearranged version of 'When that thine eye hath chose the dame' appears are among the many poetry anthologies associated with Christ Church, Oxford, in the second quarter of the seventeenth century. The first was compiled, as Peter Beal indicates, by one 'I. A.', a collector who also recorded a version of the Shakespeare sonnet that appeared in more

---

[3] See Arthur F. Marotti, 'The Cultural and Textual Importance of Folger MS V.a.89,' *English Manuscript Studies 1100–1700* 11 (2002), 70–92, at 74–9.

[4] This and the previous line are missing in the version of this poem found in BL MS Add. 30982.

[5] Though this excerpted piece is textually closest to the versions found in Jaggard's collection (the majority of whose pieces are not by Shakespeare), two of its phrases—'Good sooth' (l. 12) and 'cloudie lookes' (l. 13)—are unique readings.

manuscript copies than any other sonnet from the 154-poem collection, *Sonnet 2*.[6] The second was compiled by Daniel Leare, a distant cousin of that prominent Christ Church poet William Strode. In this poetical anthology, like so many others, older poetry reappears as examples of conventional wisdom or as aesthetic material to be experienced in a new way through a Caroline sensibility. Thus the basically Ovidian amorous counsel incorporated in these three stanzas of 'When that thine eye hath chose the dame' resembles other practical advice and cynical attitudinizing appreciated by young university men trying to acquire a veneer of sophistication and worldly wisdom. It is not just a case, however, of old wine in new bottles. Rather it is one of cultural and literary appropriation in a participatory system of manuscript literary transmission in which collectors could 'own' texts to a degree not possible in print culture. 'I. A.' or someone earlier along the line of manuscript transmission from which this text was obtained used a printed text of the poem to produce for manuscript retransmission a piece that was, in effect, a new artefact, a sampled old text put to new uses.

Shakespeare's two narrative poems from the 1590s, *Venus and Adonis* (1593) and *Lucrece* (1594) were a popular success in print. The former had some sixteen editions before 1636, while the latter had nine before 1655.[7] This meant that both texts were readily available in print over a broad time period running from the later Elizabethan through the early Stuart eras. As Sasha Roberts points out, both poems were excerpted in printed collections such as the late Elizabethan *England's Parnassus* (1600) and *Belvedere* (1600), the former containing some twenty-five passages from *Venus and Adonis* and thirty-eight from *Lucrece*, the latter with thirty-four and ninety-one respectively.[8] Both printed volumes treat the Shakespearean narrative poems as sources of sententious wisdom and as, in Roberts' words, 'illustrations upon a range of topics, largely reflecting the poem's themes'—enacting in print a process common in manuscript, the recording of memorable passages under commonplace categories or headings.[9] In a practice parallel to the marking of *sententiae* in some printed plays, the first edition of *Lucrece* highlights by the use of quotation marks some of the sententious statements in that poem, stimulating, perhaps, readers' desire to find wise and memorable sayings for their commonplace books: for example, 'The sweets we wish for, turne to lothed sowrs, | Euen in the moment that we call them ours.'[10]

---

[6] This compiler has been identified by Mary Hobbs, *Early Seventeenth-Century Verse Miscellany Manuscripts* (Aldershot: Ashgate, 1992), 118, as John Aubrey, a relative of his better-known namesake.

[7] John Jowett, William Montgomery, Gary Taylor, and Stanley Wells, (eds.), The Oxford Shakespeare: *The Complete* Works, 2nd edn. (Oxford: Clarendon Press, 2005), 223, 237. All passages from Shakespeare's printed works are taken from this edition.

[8] Sasha Roberts, *Reading Shakespeare's Poems in Early Modern England* (Basingstoke: Palgrave Macmillan, 2003), 93–4.

[9] Roberts, *Reading Shakespeare's Poems*, 96.

[10] *Lucrece* (1594), sig. G1v [ll. 867–8]. See G. K. Hunter, 'The Marking of *Sententiae* in Elizabethan Printed Plays, Poems, and Romances', *The Library* 6.3–4 (1951), 171–88. Henry Woudhuysen, 'The Foundations of Shakespeare's Text', *Proceedings of the British Academy* 125 (2004), 78, has noted the use in *Lucrece* of 'double opening inverted commas to signal . . . "sentences", that is, moral maxims to be especially noted by the reader for their serious wisdom'.

If we look at surviving seventeenth-century manuscript collections, we find an interesting group of passages recorded from the two narrative poems. As Roberts has noted, two kinds of excerpting of *Venus and Adonis* and *Lucrece* took place in manuscript and print documents: first, the memorable or shocking erotic passages, and second, the passages that might be valued for their aphoristic character.[11] And so, in Rosenbach MS 1083/16, p. 279, we find lines 17–18 and 233–4 of the poem modified to form an independent short amorous lyric:

Kissing: a song

Come sweet sit heere where neuer serpent hisses,
And being sate Ile smother thee with kisses,
Let me graze on thy lips, if those hills are too dry
Then Ile stray lower where the fountaines lye.

The section of the poem in which Venus offers an erotic tour of her body was obviously appealing to Henry Colling of St John's College, Cambridge, for he transcribed lines 229–40 in his papers, Cambridge University Library MS Mm.3.29, fol. 63v.[12] The same lines appear in a manuscript virginal book, Bibliothèque Nationale, Paris, Département de la Musique, MS Conservatoire Rés. 1186, fol. 56v.[13] A songbook marked 'Giles Earle his booke 1615' includes lines 517–22 set to music.[14] Three different manuscripts, probably compiled at Oxford, include lines 529–34 of the poem as a freestanding nocturne: Huntington MS HM 116, p. 32; Rosenbach MSS 239/27, p. 166 and 1083/16, p. 75.

The passages from *Lucrece* found in surviving manuscript documents include a combination in Peter Le Neve's verse manuscript, British Library MS Additional 27406, fol. 74r, of erotically titillating descriptions of Lucrece asleep naked in her bedchamber subject to Tarquin's 'greedy eyeballs' (l. 368), lines 365–71, 386–99, and 419–20.[15] At the other extreme, passages of moral passion and accusation uttered by Lucrece herself in her invective against 'Opportunity', lines 869–82 and 897–924, are recorded in Richard Waferer's compilation of verse and prose miscellany, British Library MS Additional 52585, fol. 54r–v. In lines 916–17, however, the original's 'My Collatine would else have come to me | When Tarquin did, but he was stayed by thee' is changed to 'my right noe wrong would ells haue falen to mee | but I perceive all this is doone by thee': it would

[11] Roberts, *Reading Shakespeare's Poems*, 83–4.

[12] See Hilton Kelliher, 'Unrecorded Extracts from Shakespeare, Sidney and Dyer', *English Manuscript Studies 1100–1700* 2 (1990), 163–88.

[13] Peter Beal, to whom we are indebted for access to his online *Catalogue of English Literary Manuscripts*, records this item and the other excerpts from Shakespeare's works, adding information that supplements that found in his earlier *Index of English Literary Manuscripts*, vol. 1, part 2 (London: Mansell, 1980).

[14] In his *Catalogue*, Beal records this, citing for this songbook the complete facsimile found in *English Song 1600–1675*, Elise Bickford Jorgens (ed.), vol. 1 (New York: Garland, 1986).

[15] Rosenbach MS 239/16, p. 146 has lines 386–95.

appear that whoever made this alteration wished to convert the narrative-specific passage into a more generally applicable set of moral observations. By appending 'Finis qd Mr Shakespeare' at the end of these selections, the compiler created the impression that what was recorded was that respected author's personal beliefs.

Very few of Shakespeare's sonnets were recorded in the manuscript anthologies, either before or after Thorpe's 1609 Quarto, which was not reissued, or after John Benson's unusual presentation of them in 1640 in conflated, titled, and lightly edited form in his *Poems: Written by Wil. Shakespeare. Gent.* Although there is internal evidence pointing to Shakespeare's sending handwritten sonnets to the male addressee of Sonnets 1–126 (in Sonnet 71, ll. 5–6, he says, for example, 'if you read this line, remember not | The hand that writ it'), we do not have manuscript copies of poems supposedly circulating before the publication of the 1609 Quarto or before Meres's 1598 reference to the sonnets' circulation. The alternate versions of Sonnets 138 and 144 in Jaggard's *Passionate Pilgrim* may be texts that were later revised, as Gary Taylor argues,[16] but, as scholars such as Katherine Duncan-Jones and Colin Burrow have suggested, their differences may be the result of textual corruption, as are those of the manuscript copies of Sonnet 2.[17]

Twenty-one different manuscripts postdate Thorpe's 1609 edition and preserve copies of, in total, eleven whole sonnets—Sonnets 2, 8, 32, 33, 68, 71, 106, 107, 116, 128, and 138:[18]

Bodleian MS Rawlinson Poetical 152, fol. 34: Sonnet 128
British Library MS Additional 10309, fol. 143: Sonnet 2
British Library MS Additional 15226, fol. 4v: Sonnet 8
British Library MS Additional 21433, fol. 114v: Sonnet 2
British Library MS Additional 25303, fol. 119v: Sonnet 2
British Library MS Additional 30982, fol. 18: Sonnet 2
British Library MS Sloane 1792, fol. 45: Sonnet 2
Folger MS V.a.148, fols. 22–3v: Sonnets 33, 68, and 107, plus excerpts from others
Folger MS V.a.162, fols. 12v and 26: Sonnets 32 and 71
Folger MS V.a.170, pp. 1673–4: Sonnet 2
Folger MS V.a.339, fol. 197v: Sonnet 138
Folger MS V.a.345, p. 145: Sonnet 2
London Metropolitan Archives MS ACC/1360/568, fol. [28v]: Sonnet 2
New York Public Library Music Division, MS Drexel 4257, No. 33: Sonnet 116
Univ. of Nottingham, Portland MS Pw V 37, p. 69: Sonnet 2

[16] Gary Taylor, 'Some Manuscripts of Shakespeare's Sonnets', *Bulletin of the John Rylands Library* 68 (1985–6), 210–46.
[17] Katherine Duncan-Jones (ed.), *Shakespeare's Sonnets*, The Arden Shakespeare (London: Thomson Learning, 1997), 453–62, and Colin Burrow (ed.), *The Complete Sonnets and Poems*, The Oxford Shakespeare (Oxford: Oxford University Press, 2002), 106–7, 690.
[18] We do not count the Drexel MS copy of Sonnet 116 because it is not, strictly speaking, the poem found in Thorpe's Quarto, but, instead, a new, longer musical version of the poem done by Henry Lawes. See Willa McClung Evans, 'Lawes' Version of Shakespeare's Sonnet CXVI', *PMLA* 51.1 (1936), 120–2.

Pierpont Morgan Library MS MA 1057, p. 96: Sonnet 106
Rosenbach MS 1083/16, pp. 256–7: Sonnet 106
Rosenbach MS 1083/17, fols. 132v–3: Sonnet 2
St John's College, Cambridge MS S.23 (James 416), fol. 38r–v: Sonnet 2
Westminster Abbey MS 41, fol. 49: Sonnet 2
Yale, Osborn MS b 205, fol. 54v: Sonnet 2[19]

By far the most transcribed poem is Sonnet 2, found in thirteen manuscripts. Presented as an anonymous piece and made to embody conventional belief that it is good to marry and have children, this sonnet from the initial group of poems addressed to a young man who resists marrying and perpetuating his lineage is changed into a poem addressed to a female reader needing to be persuaded to grant love.[20] In five of the manuscripts in which the poem appears, it has the title 'to one that would dye a Mayd' and in a sixth 'A Lover to his Mistres'.[21] The title of the poem in Rosenbach MS 1083/17, 'The Benefitt of Mariage', does not specify a female addressee, but, in the context of the love poems surrounding it, it would look like a poem addressed to a woman whose 'beauty' (l. 5) needs to be perpetuated. The title attached to this sonnet in several of the manuscript collections, 'Spes Altera', as Katherine Duncan-Jones points out, is a reference to Aeneas' son in Vergil's epic, the Latin phrase 'typical of the university and Inns of Court environment to which so many of the Jacobean and Caroline miscellanies belong'.[22] The most likely source text for the alternate version of Sonnet 2 appearing in manuscript is George Morley's manuscript, Westminster Abbey MS 41, which may have introduced the textual variants.[23] In most of the manuscripts in which we find copies of Sonnet 2 (especially those connected with that centre of manuscript circulation, Christ Church, Oxford), Shakespeare's poem is immersed in a body of witty University and cosmopolitan Caroline verse.[24]

In Folger MS V.a.345, the title of Sonnet 2 is 'Spes Altera A Song' and the poem is broken into three numbered quatrains and a numbered couplet. This demonstrates an association of some of Shakespeare's *Sonnets* with music in the seventeenth century.[25] In British Library MS Additional 15226, Sonnet 8 has the title 'In laudem Musice et opprobrium Contemptorii [*sic*] eiusdem' ('In praise of music and in reproach of the

---

[19] With the exception of the reference to the London Metropolitan Archive item, this list is derived from Beal's *Index*, 1.2.452–3. The additional item is part of his online *Catalogue*.

[20] Duncan-Jones, 453, says that, in this new context, the poem 'comes across as in effect an honorary "Cavalier" seduction lyric'.

[21] The first is the title in Westminster Abbey MS 41 and in several other manuscripts with Christ Church connections: BL MSS Add. 30982 and Sloane 1792, Folger MS V.a.170, and Yale Osborn MS b 205. The second is found in the University of Nottingham Portland MS Pw V 37.

[22] Duncan-Jones, 455.

[23] Duncan-Jones, 456, citing the unpublished work of Jeremy Maule.

[24] See Arthur F. Marotti, 'Shakespeare's Sonnets and the Manuscript Circulation of Texts in Early Modern England', in Michael Schoenfeldt (ed.), *A Companion to Shakespeare's Sonnets* (Oxford: Blackwell, 2007), 190–3, for more detailed discussion of the manuscript contexts of Sonnet 2.

[25] See Mary Hobbs, 'Shakespeare's Sonnet II: A "sugred sonnet"? ' *Notes and Queries* 224 (1979), 112–13.

despiser of the same'), and the poem is divided into three stanzas. Henry Lawes modified and expanded the text of Sonnet 116, arranging it as three six-line stanzas and producing a musical setting (NYPL MS Drexel 4237). Colin Burrow suggests that Sonnet 128 might have been copied into Bodleian MS Rawlinson Poetical 152 because of its musical allusions.[26] Many manuscript collections from the period identify their items as songs, and many specifically musical manuscripts survive from the period.[27]

The other sonnets that are recorded in manuscript are thematically varied and, like Sonnets 2, 8, and 116, take on new meanings in the context of the poems that surround them in various collections. For example, in Folger MS V.a.162, Sonnet 71 ('No longer mourne for me when I am dead') is preceded by a transcription of George Herbert's 'The Altar' (fol. 12v) and followed immediately by an anonymous poem 'Of Man' (fol. 13r–v), a context that highlights the poem's religious aspects. In the same manuscript, Sonnet 32 is preceded by a short religious poem apparently surviving in no other manuscript, 'Gods love' ('Noe mortall hath seen god, few heard him speake') (fol. 25v), which, like it, focuses on mortality. The version of Sonnet 138 transcribed in Folger MS V.a.339 seems to have been copied from *The Passionate Pilgrim*, since, in this manuscript, it comes after four other poems from that publication. It is followed by an interesting double sonnet in the Shakespearean form ('Before that antient time that man & wife') (fol. 198v) that maintains the cynical tone of Sonnet 138 and that fits the context of the other Caroline poems found in this manuscript anthology. Finally, Rosenbach Library MS 1083/16 fuses a textually variant version of Shakespeare's Sonnet 106 with a poem apparently written by William Herbert, Earl of Pembroke, who is perhaps the most likely addressee of the young-man sonnets ('When in the Annales of all-wasting time').[28]

One of the manuscripts containing verse from Shakespeare's sonnet collection (Folger MS V.a.148) is a student notebook with a variety of contents including notes on sermons and scriptural passages, on Hebrew grammar and astronomy, as well as a large number of epigrams and lyric poems by major and minor Caroline authors. Transcribing items from John Benson's edition, which includes poetry by authors other than Shakespeare, mostly from the Caroline period, the collector/scribe recorded, in addition to three complete sonnets (33, 68, 107), forty-eight poetic excerpts from the collection, including twenty-eight by Shakespeare ranging in length from a single phrase to two quatrains and a couplet. But he also occasionally modified them to craft independent clauses or memorable sayings out of grammatical fragments or compressed them to a shorter form. For example, he expanded the expression in the second line of Sonnet 97, 'the pleasure of the fleeting yeare' to 'Thou art the Pleasure of the fleeting yeare' (fol. 23). He

---

[26] Burrow, 106 n. 3.

[27] See Hobbs, *Verse Miscellany*, 93–6, 105–15.

[28] For an edition and discussion of this manuscript, see David Coleman Redding, 'Robert Bishop's Commonplace Book: An Edition of a Seventeenth-Century Miscellany' (PhD dissertation, University of Pennsylvania, 1960). Both the sonnet and the Pembroke poem appear separately in Pierpont Morgan Library MS MA 1057 (pp. 96, 140).

shortened lines 9–12 of Sonnet 28 to two lines: 'Clouds blot the heaven & make me flatter | The swart Complectiond night when sparkling stars twire' (fol. 23), and he reduced lines 10–12 of Sonnet 29 to 'To sing from sullen earth hymnes at heavens gate' (fol. 23). He obviously valued some sections of sonnets as aphorisms: for instance, 'The Canker bloomes have full as deepe a dy | As the Perfumed tincture of the roses' (Sonnet 54, ll. 5–6; fol. 22) and 'Love alters not with his briefe hours & weeks | But bears It out even to the Edge of Doome' (Sonnet 116, ll. 11–12; fol. 23). He was attracted to particular felicitous expressions such as 'Gilding the object whereupon It gazeth' (Sonnet 20, l. 6; fol. 22v) and 'Beaten & Chopt with Tan'd Antiquity' (Sonnet 62, l. 10; fol. 23). In the context of this student notebook, sonnets and sonnet-excerpts functioned the way other commonplace-book items functioned—as collected knowledge and wisdom, as rhetorically artful formulations, as cultural material ready for reuse by the educated collector. The scribe did record the name 'Shakespeare' on the first page of his sonnet-transcriptions, indicating perhaps not just authorship, but the printed source from which he obtained the items. A commonplace-book compiler often listed the sources of collected material—both the authorities being cited and the printed texts mined for valuable quotations. What was going on in the case of the student-compiler was not literary anthologizing in the modern sense, but acts of furnishing the mind with useful knowledge and language.

Although some scholars, such as John Kerrigan, have supported Gary Taylor's argument that the manuscript versions of the *Sonnets* show signs of the process of authorial revision, others, such as Katherine Duncan-Jones, cast doubt on this.[29] Given the changes to other texts resulting from memorial transcription, mistakes in copying, and deliberate scribal alteration of received material, one must be cautious about attributing textual variants to Shakespeare himself. The strongest evidence of authorial revision might be the alternate versions of Sonnets 138 and 144 appearing in the printed text, Jaggard's *Passionate Pilgrim*, which appeared *before* rather than, like the manuscripts, *after* Thorpe's 1609 Quarto.

There are some other poems associated with Shakespeare that appear in surviving manuscript documents from the period—for example, the epitaph on John Combe ('Ten in the hundred here lieth engraved'), which appears in Nicholas Burghe's large manuscript anthology, Bodleian MS Ashmole 38, p. 180, and Shakespeare's 'Epitaph on Himself' ('Good friend, for Jesus' sake forbear'), which was carved on his gravestone, but which also is attributed to him in Folger MSS V.a.180, fol. 79v and V.a.232, p. 63.[30] Other pieces have been claimed either in the seventeenth century or later as Shakespeare's, but, on the whole, the manuscript record of his verse is quite limited—a fact hard for modern admirers of Shakespeare to accept, since they think his culturally central status as an English author would have made his verse, especially his sonnets, more sought after by manuscript

[29] See John Kerrigan, (ed.), *The Sonnets and A Lover's Complaint* (New York: Viking, 1986), 428; Duncan-Jones, *Shakespeare's Sonnets*, 453. Kerrigan, 442, suggests that the Bod. MS Rawl. Poet. 152 version of Sonnet 128 is 'likely' an early version of that poem.

[30] See Burrow, 726–8.

compilers. The inescapable conclusion, as far as the first half-century following his death is concerned, is that his poetry, particularly his lyrics, did not have a strong presence in the manuscript literary culture of the time.

SHAKESPEARE'S PLAYS IN SEVENTEENTH-CENTURY MANUSCRIPTS

We do not have any of Shakespeare's plays or poems written in his own hand. Some scholars long for a Shakespearean holograph manuscript; as Leah Marcus puts it, the assumption is 'that if only we possessed some or all of the manuscript evidence, whether fair copy or foul papers, we would be brought considerably closer to the plays as the author intended them.'[31] Marcus points out, however, that having a holograph manuscript would not solve all editorial or interpretive problems with Shakespeare's works: rather, it could serve to complicate our understanding of Shakespeare. Furthermore, we do not have any of the Shakespearean manuscript part books that Elizabethan and Jacobean actors used to rehearse and perform, though we do have some manuscripts and printed texts that were marked up for possible use in the theatre.[32] Here we focus on the extant manuscripts that contain Shakespeare's poetic and dramatic work.[33]

Studies of the six surviving signatures of Shakespeare[34] have led to the identification of Shakespeare as a collaborator in the play *Sir Thomas More*. Beal asserts that the attribution of Hand D to Shakespeare in *Sir Thomas More* (British Library MS Harley 7386), found on folios 8 and 9, is 'virtually certain', although Peter Stallybrass and Margreta de Grazia argue that it 'rests upon shaky ground'.[35] *Sir Thomas More* was a collaborative effort, with Anthony Munday as the primary author, and revisions possibly made by Thomas Dekker, Thomas Heywood, Henry Chettle, and Shakespeare.[36] It is a text that reminds scholars that early modern theatre was inherently collaborative and challenges modern conceptions of authorship and authority.[37]

---

[31] Leah Marcus, 'The Veil of Manuscript', *Renaissance Drama*, NS, 30 (1999–2000), 116.

[32] See Simon Palfrey and Tiffany Stern, *Shakespeare in Parts* (Oxford: Oxford University Press, 2007),

[33] For a listing of known extracts and songs from Shakespeare's plays in manuscript not discussed in this chapter, see Beal's *Index*, 1.2.449–63. For a discussion of how Shakespeare's manuscripts might have circulated and an analysis of the documentary evidence surrounding Shakespeare, see Grace Ioppolo, *Dramatists and Their Manuscripts in the Age of Shakespeare, Jonson, Middleton and Heywood* (London: Routledge, 2006).

[34] See Beal, *Index* 1.2.449, for the list of these.

[35] Beal, *Index*, 1.2.449; Margreta de Grazia and Peter Stallybrass, 'The Materiality of the Shakespearean Text', *Shakespeare Quarterly* 14.3 (Fall 1993), 277.

[36] Vittorio Gabrieli and Giorgio Melchiori (eds.), *Sir Thomas More* (Manchester: Manchester University Press, 1990).

[37] See Jeffrey Masten's *Textual Intercourse: Collaboration, Authorship, and Sexualities in Renaissance Drama* (Cambridge: Cambridge University Press, 1997).

Early modern manuscript collections were also often the product of the scribal activities of more than one person.

There are nine seventeenth-century copies of entire Shakespeare plays in manuscript, all of which have received scholarly attention. Folger MS V.a.73 is a version of *The Merry Wives of Windsor* based on the Second Folio. Folger MS V.b.34, also called the Dering manuscript, contains an adaptation that combines both parts of *Henry IV*. The Douai manuscript (Bibliothèque Municipale, Douai, France, MS 787) contains six entire plays: *The Comedy of Errors, Twelfth Night, Julius Caesar, Macbeth, Romeo and Juliet,* and *As You Like It.* Folger MS V.a.85 has a copy of *Julius Caesar*, most likely related to the Douai manuscript. Each manuscript offers information that adds to our understanding of early modern theatrical practices and enhances our knowledge of oral and literate culture, while also deepening our understanding of Shakespeare's plays.

Based on the Second Folio of 1632, Folger MS V.a.73 (compiled c.1648–60) contains 500 variants from that text. Folger MS V.a.73 attempts to imitate a print version of *The Merry Wives of Windsor* with its format, which includes such elements as regular running titles, commendatory verse by Hugh Holland, and a hand that mimics print fonts. G. Blakemore Evans effectively argues that it is a literary manuscript because the writing is too cramped for a potential prompt book, yet he still believes that this manuscript might have been used indirectly in performance.[38] This manuscript also contains the first known list of 'drammatis persona' [*sic*] (fol. 1v) for this play, which suggests that it was designed for reading and not for performance. The list gives a brief description of each character, which shows how the characters were perceived in the seventeenth century. Bardolfe, Nym, and Pistoll are described as 'Hangers on'; the Host is 'A merry, conceited, ranting Inn-holder' (fol. 1v). These character descriptions offer clarification that would not be available to an early modern theatregoer (or someone reading the play in early print versions).

Folger MS V.a.73 shows how scribes changed the plays, making textual emendations and adding paratextual materials: the Dering MS (Folger MS V.b.34) offers a more drastic example of a play's malleability in manuscript culture. It contains a version of both parts of *Henry IV* abridged and adapted into one five-act play, using roughly 90 per cent of part one and 30 per cent of part two.[39] There are two hands in this manuscript: the first is generally accepted to be that of Edward Dering (1598–1644) and the second is probably that of a professional scribe. The manuscript was written in 1622 or in the first few months of 1623, before Shakespeare's works were published in the 1623 First Folio.[40] There were six quarto versions of *1 Henry IV* but only one quarto of

[38] G. Blakemore Evans, 'The Merry Wives of Windsor: The Folger Manuscript', in Bernhard Fabian and Kurt Tetzeli von Rosador (eds.), *Shakespeare: Text, Language, Criticism: Essays in Honour of Martin Spevack* (Zurich: Olms-Weidman, 1987), 57–79.

[39] John Baker, 'Found: Shakespeare's Manuscript of Henry IV', *Elizabethan Review* 4 (1996), 14–46.

[40] George Walton Williams and Gwynne Blakemore Evans (eds.), *The History of King Henry the Fourth, as revised by Sir Edward Dering, Bart.* (Charlottesville: University Press of Virginia, 1974), viii; Laetitia Yeandle, 'The Dating of Sir Edward Dering's Copy of "The History of King Henry the Fourth"', *Shakespeare Quarterly* 37.2 (Summer 1986), 224–6.

2 Henry IV published between 1598 and 1622. Dering's revision of the play shows that he, like the play-buying public, preferred the first part.

Unlike Folger MS V.a.73 and the Dering MS, the Douai MS was probably used for performances. Douai Public Library MS 787 contains complete copies of six Shakespearean plays (see above), as well as transcriptions of three Restoration plays: *Mithridates* by Nathaniel Lee, *The Indian Emperor* by John Dryden, and *The Siege of Rhodes* by William Davenant.[41] These plays were copied separately around 1694–5 and then bound into a single volume around 1697–9.[42] The Shakespeare plays were copied from the 1632 Second Folio, or from manuscripts copied from it. Evans suggests that the plays were copied from a marked-up version of the Second Folio, as there are few revisions on the page, but numerous alternate readings.

Like Cambridge and Oxford, the English college at Douai used 'dramatic exercises' as a way to test students.[43] The plays may also be related to the Catholic seminary and convent in Douai, perhaps demonstrating Catholic revision through the removal of jokes about 'holy bread' and nuns.[44] Many of the changes made to the plays in these manuscripts would have been helpful for performance and add to our knowledge of theatre history. For the Shakespeare plays, stage directions were often added to clarify the play; for the Restoration plays, the scribe simplified and corrected the stage directions.[45] The plays were also generally shortened: the longest play in the collection, *Romeo and Juliet*, was reduced the most (by 971 lines), and the shortest play, *The Comedy of Errors*, lost only eighteen lines. Ann-Mari Hedbäck suggests that certain emendations (such as altering the word 'ravish' in *Mithridates*) reflect Restoration tastes by making the plays more decorous. The changes made to the Douai manuscript suggest an English scribe concerned with Roman Catholic values, audience reception, and the realities of staging a play. These plays in manuscript shed light on theatricals in schools, Shakespeare on the Continent, and amateur performances of Shakespeare's plays.

Folger MS V.a.85 is the final extant manuscript containing an entire Shakespearean play (*Julius Caesar*), and is closely related to the Douai manuscript. This copy, like the copy at Douai, seems to have a theatrical provenance. In Folger MS V.a.85, *Julius Caesar* was originally attributed to 'Dyden' [*sic*], which meant that it was taken as the Dryden-Davenant *Caesar*.[46] Dryden's name was later erased and Shakespeare written in above it. Folger MS V.a.85, like the Douai manuscript, often modernizes Shakespeare's language. Along with the eighteenth-century manuscripts that follow it, Folger MS V.a.85 cuts 4.3.139–55, the scene where Brutus first tells the audience that Portia is

[41] G. Blakemore Evans, 'The Douai Manuscript—Six Shakespearean Transcripts (1694–95)', *Philological Quarterly* 41 (1962), 158–72.

[42] Ann-Mari Hedbäck, 'The Douai Manuscript Reexamined', *Papers of the Bibliographical Society of America* 73.1 (1979), 1–18.

[43] Evans, 'The Douai Manuscript', 165.

[44] Evans, 'The Douai Manuscript', 164.

[45] Evans, 'The Douai Manuscript', 164, and Hedbäck, 'The Douai Manuscript Reexamined', 17.

[46] G. Blakemore Evans, 'Shakespeare's *Julius Caesar*—A Seventeenth-Century Manuscript', *Journal of English and Germanic Philology* 41 (1942), 401–17.

dead. Evans suggests that this reflects seventeenth-staging practices.[47] This resolves the practical issue of Portia's 'repeated' death: later in the scene when Messala tells Brutus that Portia has died, it is news to the audience.

While there are only nine manuscripts with complete (or almost complete) versions of Shakespeare's plays, there are more than thirty extant manuscripts that contain parts of Shakespeare's plays. These vary in length from a single couplet (Bodleian MS English Poetry e. 97) or a single song (Folger MS V.a.38) to pages of extracts from multiple Shakespeare plays (British Library MS Lansdowne 1185). In the *Hesperides* manuscripts (Folger MSS V.b.93, V.a.75, and V.a.79–80), John Evans transcribed items from over 300 works, including thirty-six Shakespeare plays.[48] He arranged his excerpts under headings: for instance, below 'Condemne/d to death' (p. 143), he includes Hermione's proud, 'If I shall bee condemn'd upon surmizes (all proofes sleeping else; but what your jealousies awake), I tell you tis rigor & not law' (*WT* 3.2.110–14) and Buckingham's hopeless, 'My life is span'd allready, I am the shadow of poor Buckingham' (*HVIII* 1.1.224–5).

Other manuscript commonplace books arrange the extracts by play or author, rather than by subject matter. In Bodleian MS Sancroft 97, Archbishop Sancroft (1617–1693) chose to excerpt from a seemingly incongruous combination of plays, *A Midsummer Night's Dream*, 2 and 3 *Henry VI*, and *King Lear*. It is not unusual that he copies from a comedy, two histories, and a tragedy, since he does not copy for plot but for witty and sententious phrases. At times, like the student compiler of Folger MS V.a.148, Sancroft copies only a brief phrase, such as Puck's evocative image of 'black browd night' (*MND* 3.2.388; p. 79), and other times he copies longer passages, such as the fool's clever advice to King Lear, 'Have more than thou shewest, speake less than thou knowest, lend less than owest, ride more than thou goest, learn more than thou trowest, sett less than thou throwest, & thou shall have more than 2 tens to a score' (1.4.116–23; p. 81). Both Puck's phrase and the fool's speech are commonplace formulations.

Like many early modern manuscript compilers, Sancroft adapted Shakespeare's text when it suited him. He excerpted Isabella's soliloquy from *Measure for Measure* on her brother's support of her chastity:

> That had he twenty heads to tender down
> On twenty bloody blocks, he'ld yield them up,
> Before his sister should her body stoop
> To such abhorr'd pollution.   (2.4.180–3)

Sancroft changed the speech to a first person utterance: 'Nay had I 20 heads to tender down on 20 bloody blocks, | I'ld yeeld them up, before I'ld do't', and linked it with Isabella's later wish, 'Were it but my Life, | I'ld throw it down as frankly as a pin' (3.1.102–4; p. 85). Like most students in sixteenth- and seventeenth-century grammar

---

[47] Evans, 'Shakespeare's *Julius Caesar*', 411.

[48] For a detailed discussion of the relation of these manuscripts, see Tianhu Hao's dissertation, '*Hesperides, or the Muses' Garden*: Commonplace Reading and Writing in Early Modern England' (Columbia University, 2006).

schools, Sancroft was probably taught to keep a commonplace book to provide material for later use in conversation or writing.[49] John Marston satirizes this practice with his character Luscus in *The Scourge of Villainy*, who 'hath made a common-place booke out of plaies', which he uses to embellish his daily speech; he 'speakes in print'.[50] Sancroft probably altered Shakespeare's text to make it more useful to him. For instance, he took Launcelot's emphatic denial of Shylock, 'if I serve not him, I will run as far as God has any ground' (*MV* 2.2.104–5) and rearranged it into a general expression of dislike: 'I'll run as far as G. hath any ground rather than—', a phrase that could be completed in different ways to suit a variety of situations (p. 85).

Sancroft kept multiple manuscripts with dramatic excerpts. Bodleian MS Sancroft 97 is a primarily prose miscellany that contains excerpts from religious tracts and romances as well as Shakespearean excerpts. In MS Sancroft 97, he copied as prose short commonplaces from plays. In MS Sancroft 53, a verse miscellany, he collected longer extracts from plays rather than commonplaces; he copied the song 'Hark, hark, the lark' from *Cymbeline* (2.3.19–25) and Iago's speech, 'She that was ever fair and never proud' from *Othello* (2.1.151–63). He treated these excerpts like poems, titling them and writing them as verse. Unlike Sancroft MSS 97 and 53, Sancroft MS 29 mainly consists of drama, including more than thirty pages of Shakespearean extracts that have been overlooked by scholars to date. In it, Sancroft primarily collected commonplaces, arranging the first sixty pages under commonplace headings: for instance, 'Go kindle Fire with Snow' (2.7.19), a phrase from *The Two Gentlemen of Verona*, is listed under the heading 'Impossible' (p. 29). Most of the Shakespearean extracts, however, are gathered by play instead of under headings. Sancroft's manuscripts demonstrate multiple ways compilers copied selections from Shakespeare: verbatim or altered, in prose or in verse, by heading or by play, in brief phrases or entire speeches.

Like Sancroft, Abraham Wright (1611–1690), in British Library MS Additional 22608 made editorial changes when copying texts. Roberts points out that Wright changed Iago's 'Even now, now, very now, an old black ram | Is tupping your white ewe' to 'A ramme is said to tupp ye ewe. And a horse to couer a mare' (fol. 83v), which removes the racial slur.[51] Wright not only excerpts from many plays (including Shakespeare's) but also comments on them. These include eleven plays by James Shirley and six plays by Francis Beaumont and John Fletcher, but only two by Shakespeare, *Othello* and *Hamlet*.[52] *Hamlet* is afforded only about two pages of manuscript, whereas Wright

---

[49] For more on the role of commonplacing in education, see Mary Thomas Crane, *Framing Authority: Sayings, Self, and Society in Sixteenth-Century England* (Princeton, NJ: Princeton University Press, 1997), and Ann Moss, *Printed Commonplace-Bookes and the Structuring of Renaissance Thought* (Oxford: Clarendon Press, 1996).

[50] See Tiffany Stern's *Making Shakespeare: From Stage to Page* (New York: Routledge, 2004) for more examples of seventeenth-century references to theatre and commonplace books.

[51] Roberts, *Reading Shakespeare's Poems*, 122.

[52] For a complete transcription of Wright's extracts from *Hamlet* and *Othello*, see James G. McManaway, 'Excerpta Quaedam per A. W. Adolescentem', in Thomas P. Harrison et. al. (eds.), *Studies in Honor of DeWitt T. Starnes* (Austin: University of Texas Press, 1967), 117–29.

focuses on *Othello* for about three pages, which is about the average length he devoted to each play (Shirley's *Hyde Park* and Webster's *White Devil* receive only one page, but Jonson's *Bartholomew Fair* six pages). Wright famously criticizes *Hamlet* as 'But an indifferent play, [the] lines but meane' (fol. 85v), but is more generous in his description of *Othello*, which he sees as 'A very good play both for lines and plot, but especially [the] plot' (fol. 84v).[53]

While it is clear that Wright and Sancroft used print sources for their Shakespearean extracts (at times giving page numbers for their sources), some compilers took notes while attending performances. For example, Edward Pudsey's Bodleian MS English Poetry d. 3 (compiled *c.*1600–13) includes excerpts from *Othello* (written *circa* 1603, published 1622).[54] He might have taken a table-book to the performance, then recopied his notes into his commonplace book.[55] Pudsey's book, unlike Sancroft MS 29, is not composed primarily of dramatic extracts: he demonstrates his passion for reading by excerpting from a wide spectrum of genres and topics: poetry (Sidney, Ralegh), history (Livy, Guicciardini), morals (Bacon), geography (Torquemada), religion (Lodge), and drama (Shakespeare, Jonson, Middleton, and others).

While finding extracts from Shakespeare alongside other selections from literature, science, and religion is not unusual, it is unusual to find illustrated Shakespearean extracts. The Longleat manuscript is one folio leaf with a drawing at the top that includes extracts from *Titus Andronicus* below it. It contains Tamora's speech pleading for her son's life (1.1.104–20) and Aaron revelling in his wickedness (5.1.124–44). It begins with a stage direction that does not appear in any of the early print versions of the play: 'Enter Tamora pleadinge for her sonnes going to execution', and ends with a speech-prefix for Alarbus, who does not have any lines in the play. The drawing at the top of the manuscript, as many scholars point out, does not dramatize an actual moment that would have occurred on stage during a performance of *Titus*. It depicts two guards in Roman garb on the left: these are sometimes identified as two of Titus' sons. In the middle stands a man, often identified as Titus, wearing laurels and holding a large staff, facing a woman on her knees with her hands clasped, Tamora, 'pleadinge' for Alarbus. On the right are two men, bound and on their knees, probably Chiron and Demetrius. On the far right stands a black man holding a sword, pointing, probably Aaron the Moor. This manuscript has been interpreted many ways: as representing

---

[53] For a complete transcription of Wright's comments on *Othello*, *Hamlet*, and other plays, see Arthur C. Kirsch, 'A Caroline Commentary on the Drama', *Modern Philology* 66.3 (1969), 256–61.

[54] See Juliet Rees, 'Shakespeare and Edward Pudsey's Booke, 1600', *Notes and Queries* 39.3 (1992), 330–1. See also Rees's (née Gowan) 'An Edition of Edward Pudsey's Commonplace Book (c. 1600–1615) from the Manuscript in the Bodleian Library' (MPhil thesis, University of London, 1967).

[55] For more information on table-books, see Peter Stallybrass, Roger Chartier, J. Franklin Mowery, and Heather Wolfe, 'Hamlet's Tables and the Technologies of Writing in Renaissance England', *Shakespeare Quarterly* 55.4 (2004), 379–419.

more than one scene from the play, as symbolically reflecting the action in the play, or as portraying the staging and theatricality of the play.[56]

Songs from Shakespeare's plays circulated in both literary and musical manuscripts, sometimes with music. Tracing the manuscript transmission of songs from plays, however, differs from tracing manuscript transmission of speeches or dialogue because Renaissance playwrights, including Shakespeare, often used pre-existing songs. This means that a compiler might be deliberately including the song from the play, or that he might not even have known the song was associated with Shakespeare. For instance, Desdemona's 'The poor soul sat sighing by a sycamore tree' (*Othello* 4.3.40–8), is a fragment of a song that Shakespeare probably did not write. A more complete version of this song is found in British Library MS Additional 15117.[57] This manuscript, however, does not offer a clear source for Shakespeare, simply an analogue. John H. Long explains how Shakespeare manipulated the source song and shows other 'Willow songs' contemporary to this ballad.[58]

While 'The Willow Song' from *Othello* offers a clear example of Shakespeare's use of a popular ballad in his plays, the attribution of other songs is more problematic. For example, 'It was a lover and his lass' from *As You Like It* (5.3.15–38) might have been written by Shakespeare or by Thomas Morley, or it might have been a collaboration.[59] Morley published the song with music in *The First Book of Ayres* in 1600, close to the date of the play's composition and original performance. This song is found in the Leyden MS, a verse miscellany with Scottish provenance (National Library of Scotland Advocate's Library MS 5.2.14, fol. 18r–v).[60] This manuscript contains only a vocal line (that matches Morley's print source), but, since some critics believe that Morley's tune was used for the original performance of the play, or that Morley borrowed the lyrics from Shakespeare, they can only speculate whether the compiler considered this song one of Shakespeare's when copying it. It is entirely possible that the compiler of the Leyden manuscript did not include this as a specifically Shakespearean piece, as there is no attribution, the music is Morley's, and there are no other songs from Shakespeare plays in this songbook.[61]

Unlike the compiler of the Leyden MS, the compiler of British Library MS Egerton 2421 (perhaps Francis Norreys and/or Henry Balle) deliberately collected Shakespeare's songs in his verse miscellany, grouping five songs from *The Tempest* and titling them

---

[56] Richard Levin, 'The Longleat Manuscript and *Titus Andronicus*', *Shakespeare Quarterly* 53.3 (2002), 323–40.

[57] This version is transcribed in Peter J. Seng, *The Vocal Songs in the Plays of Shakespeare: A Critical History* (Cambridge, MA: Harvard University Press, 1967), 195–6.

[58] John H. Long, *Shakespeare's Use of Music: The Histories and Tragedies* (Gainesville: University of Florida Press, 1971), 98–9.

[59] See Seng, *Vocal Songs*, 87–90 and 97–100 for a summary of the authorship problems of this song.

[60] The Leyden manuscript is reproduced in Jorgens, *English Song*, vol. 11.

[61] In Morley's print edition, 'It was a lover and his lass' is attributed to Morley without mention of Shakespeare or *As You Like It*.

'Songs [out of] Shakespeare,' with the subtitle, 'The Tempest'.[62] The compiler numbers each song and lists the character who sings it. Similarly, Anne Twice's manuscript, New York Public Library Drexel MS 4175, shows an interest in collecting songs from plays, by collecting six songs from plays and masques including *The Winter's Tale*. Bodleian MS Mus. D. 238 contains sixteen songs from dramatic sources, including *The Winter's Tale* and *The Tempest*. Twice's music book and Bodleian MS Mus. D. 238 include musical notations for the songs, which implies that they were copied from print music books, whereas British Library MS Egerton 2421 both records the lyrics and the names of the singers, implying that a print version of the play was used as a source. Songs from *The Tempest* circulated more widely than other songs and extracts from Shakespeare's plays: they are also found in Edinburgh University Library MS Dc.1.69, pp. 87–8;[63] Bodleian MSS Donation c. 57 fol. 75 and Music d. 238, 87–8; British Library MSS Additional 29396, fol. 110, and Harley 3991, fol. 83v; Folger MSS V.a.411, fols. 9v–13v, and W.b.515, 5; New York Public Library MS Drexel 4041, fols. 67v–8, Yale Music Library Misc. MS 170 Filmer MS 4, 4/a fol. 20v, 4/b fol. 14v, 4/c fol. 20; and University of Texas at Austin MS (Killigrew, T)/Misc./B, fol. 65v.

The print music for Shakespeare's songs often copied into music manuscripts was written by noted seventeenth-century composers. John Wilson (1595–1674) wrote settings for 'Take, oh take these lips away' (4.1.1–7) from *Measure for Measure*, a song that also appears in Fletcher's *The Bloody Brother or Rollo, Duke of Normandy*. Robert Johnson (*c*.1583–1633) composed music for performances of Shakespeare's plays; he perhaps wrote the original music to *The Winter's Tale*. At times, even Shakespeare's non-musical works were used as libretti for composers: for instance, Cesare Morelli set Hamlet's speech 'To be or not to be' to music in the late seventeenth century (Magdalene College, Cambridge, Pepys Library MS 2591).[64] In both music manuscripts and miscellanies, complete songs are more common than extracts from songs. In general, songs from plays were more popular than other dramatic extracts, possibly because they could be more easily memorized.

If we look at the range of manuscript documents in which Shakespeare's poetic and dramatic writing is preserved, we see different purposes at work, different marks of authorship, different cultural and literary contexts in which the texts were defined and recoded. Some collectors and scribes copied poems and extracts for their aphoristic value; others for their aesthetic merit; others for both purposes, treasuring the felicitous expression of conventional (or unconventional) wisdom. Some submerged the items as anonymous pieces in a larger collection of both ascribed and unascribed work, while others invoked Shakespeare's name either to identify a source or to acknowledge his

---

[62] The songs collected are 'Full fathom five thy father lies' (1.2.399–409); 'The master, the swabber, the boatswain, and I' (2.2.45–54); 'No more dams I'll make for fish' (3.1.179–86); 'Honour, riches, marriage-blessing' (4.1.106–17); and 'Where the bee sucks, there suck I' (5.1.88–96), fols. 6v–7.

[63] Following 'Where the Bee Sucks' (p. 88) are additional stanzas on a second page also numbered 88. See the facsimile in Jorgens, *English Song*, vol. 8.

[64] MacDonald Emslie discusses this and other blank verse speeches used as recitatives in 'Pepys' Shakespeare Song', *Shakespeare Quarterly* 6.2 (1955), 159–70.

cultural prestige. Some jotted down only a brief phrase or couplet from Shakespeare; others diligently copied out entire plays. Some recorded texts that either they or their sources verbally changed or adapted for new purposes, treating the Shakespearean text not as a pure original not to be corrupted, but as something to be appropriated, altered, and used as one saw fit. The texts in their printed forms, which were the sources for almost all of the manuscript copying, thus became more malleable in the system of manuscript transcription and transmission, an environment in which textuality, authorship, and reader-roles were defined differently than they were in print culture.

CHAPTER 4

....

QUARTO AND FOLIO

....

ANN THOMPSON

WHICH SHAKESPEARE?

....

As audience members, we are used to a play such as *Hamlet* being different every time we see it. Of course every production is different, but even different performances of what is ostensibly the same production will be slightly different on different nights, sometimes in trivial ways (an actor skips a line), sometimes in more important ones (an understudy takes on a major role). Film might seem to offer a greater degree of stability, but even then we find variations such as the longer and shorter versions of Kenneth Branagh's 1996 film, and there has been a bewildering variety of recent adaptations. In a piece published in *Around the Globe*, the magazine of Shakespeare's Globe Theatre, a few years ago, Tony Howard wrote

> Recently, details emerged of five forthcoming films to be based on *Hamlet* alone: a version set in Spain at the time of the Armada, a rewrite told from the King's point of view (with William Shatner as Claudius), a Japanese cartoon, an experimental update set in a gay bar, and a comedy *Hamlet* featuring Halle Berry as Ophelia in a fast-food joint.

He went on to reassure his readers

> I'm not sure if I was more disappointed or relieved to find that these rumours all originated in a website 'dedicated to the dissemination of misleading information'. But Christopher Walken really *has* just appeared in a *Macbeth* set in a hamburger franchise, and the point of the hoax was that it could easily be true.[1]

But beyond the fact that there have always been different readings, interpretations, and adaptations of *Hamlet*, what I intend to focus on in this essay is that, from early on in the seventeenth century, there have always been different versions of the text itself. And this is true, not just of *Hamlet*, but of about half of the plays in the Shakespeare canon.

---

[1] Tony Howard, 'Tragedy Transplanted', *Around the Globe* 23 (Spring 2003), 28–9.

Film and theatre directors today are likely to be explicit about the textual choices they have made. Kenneth Branagh indicates in the published screenplay of his 1996 film that it is based on the First Folio of 1623: 'Nothing has been cut from this text, and some passages absent from it (including the soliloquy "How all occasions do inform against me" . . .) have been supplied from the Second Quarto (an edition of the play which exists in copies dated 1604 and 1605).'[2] In 2004, two stage versions demonstrated a similar awareness of conscious decisions having been made. In the programme for Trevor Nunn's production at the London Old Vic starring Ben Whishaw, an essay significantly entitled 'Director's Cut' (an allusion of course to cinema where we have become used to different versions, alternative endings, and so forth), explains that Nunn

> has used the First Folio as his main text, with occasional divergences. However, in the case of Hamlet's famous lines to Horatio about there being 'more things in heaven and earth' which goes on in the Folio: 'Than are dreamt of in your philosophy' he prefers another edition [in fact the Second Quarto] which uses instead 'our philosophy', because this tells us more about their relationship; they are two close friends and students studying the same subject.[3]

Many, if not most, audience members would not have been aware of this choice, but they might have noticed one of larger significance. The programme essay continues

> [Nunn] is also very conscious of the fact that, in this production, he is contributing to the ongoing debate as to where the most famous speech in the English language should come in the play. Hamlet's soliloquy, 'To be or not to be', traditionally appears in a place which is difficult to justify in terms of either the character or the narrative itself. . . . [It] comes only a few lines after the previous soliloquy, 'O what a rogue and peasant slave am I', at the end of which Hamlet has a positive plan of campaign: 'The play's the thing | Wherein I'll catch the conscience of the King'. He is patently intent on action here. Then, only 50 lines later, he is discussing whether or not he should take his own life. This is an uncomfortable development. . . . So Nunn has taken the controversial decision to move the soliloquy.

Although the essay is not explicit on this point, Nunn moved 'To be or not to be' to one scene (but about 500 lines) earlier, to precisely where it appears in the First, so-called 'Bad', Quarto of 1603. Michael Boyd, directing Toby Stephens for the Royal Shakespeare Company in the same year, made the same decision about 'To be or not to be', a 'controversial decision', which has in fact become almost conventional: British examples in the second half of the twentieth century include Michael Benthall directing John Neville at the Old Vic in 1957, Tony Richardson directing Nicol Williamson at the Roundhouse in 1969, Ron Daniels directing Mark Rylance at the Royal Shakespeare Company in 1989, and Matthew Warchus directing Alex Jennings at the Royal Shakespeare Company in

---

[2] Kenneth Branagh, *Hamlet: Screenplay and Introduction* (London: Chatto & Windus, 1996), 175. for more on quartos and folios, see below, pp.76–8.

[3] Unpaginated theatre programme for this production. The actor Samuel West has said to me that when he played Hamlet in the Royal Shakespeare Company production in Stratford-upon-Avon and London in 2001–2, his director, Steven Pimlott, made the same change for the same reason.

1997. It happened again when Gregory Doran directed David Tennant in 2008; indeed, when I reviewed the production directed by Michael Grandage and starring Jude Law at Wyndham's Theatre, London, in the Donmar West End season in 2009, I felt obliged to remark that 'To be or not to be' appeared, for once, in its 'traditional' place.[4]

Something that was (or should have been) much more controversial about Michael Boyd's production in 2004 was that he included a version of a scene between the Queen and Horatio which is unique to the First Quarto. It comes after Hamlet has taken ship for England and immediately after Ophelia's mad scene. It contains an abridged version of narrative material found in three different places in the longer texts: 4.6 and 4.7 where Horatio and the King respectively receive and read letters from Hamlet concerning what has happened to him since he was dispatched to England, and the beginning of 5.2 where Hamlet gives Horatio a fuller account of his voyage. This scene also contains three crucial narrative elements that are not found in the other texts: Horatio tells the Queen about Hamlet's discovery of the 'packet' sent by the King containing orders for his execution, she reaffirms her support for her son (which in this text she has previously expressed in the closet scene), and she expresses her intention to hide her knowledge and her feelings from her husband: 'I will soothe and please him for a while.' In the First Quarto, this scene, in which Horatio and the Queen meet, apparently in secret, to conspire in support of Hamlet, is followed by the parallel scene in which Laertes and the King conspire against him.[5]

What is going on here and how do we, as readers, performers, or indeed editors, cope with such radical differences between the texts? How do we choose which text to read, perform or edit? As is already apparent, you do not have to dig very deeply into the question of Shakespeare's texts to discover that they are multiple and complicated. Publishers make apparently conflicting claims in support of the superior authority of the versions they print, and the last twenty or thirty years have seen a bewildering variety of choices offered to potential purchasers of plays.

PUBLISHING SHAKESPEARE SINCE 1986

In the 1980s, the editors of The Oxford Shakespeare *The Complete Works* (Stanley Wells and Gary Taylor, with John Jowett and William Montgomery) championed the versions of the plays printed in the 1623 First Folio, mainly on the grounds that they are 'the more

---

[4] British Shakespeare Association journal *Shakespeare* 5 (2009), 448–50.

[5] This is Scene 14 in the Q1 text in the Arden edition of *Hamlet: The Texts of 1603 and 1623* edited by Ann Thompson and Neil Taylor (London: Thomson Learning, 2006). References to the First Quarto and First Folio texts of *Hamlet* are to this volume; references to the Second Quarto are to its companion volume, the Arden *Hamlet*, also edited by Ann Thompson and Neil Taylor (London: Thomson Learning, 2006).

theatrical versions' in every case, and arguing that, in the case of the plays that exist in very different forms in earlier quartos, especially *2 Henry IV, Hamlet, Troilus and Cressida, Othello,* and *King Lear,* the Folio text represents an authorial revision and hence takes precedence.[6] They were, nevertheless, prepared to draw extensively on readings from the 'good' quartos when preparing texts of individual plays, and even took the radical decision to print two texts of *King Lear,* the 1608 Quarto as well as the 1623 Folio version, on the grounds that the revisions in this case were more substantial than in the cases of the other multiple-text plays.[7] Reflecting on their edition in 1990, they noted that 'It now seems obvious that we should have included two texts of *Hamlet,* as we did of *King Lear,* a Folio-based version and one based on Q2', but they did not follow this up.[8] Nevertheless, it should be emphasized that this was the most radical edition of the *Complete Works* ever attempted and that it and its accompanying volume, *William Shakespeare: A Textual Companion,*[9] revolutionized the field. Disappointingly, however, the publishers of the Norton Shakespeare, who based their edition on the Oxford text, were apparently so nervous about presenting their reader with two texts of *King Lear* that they included a third text, a 'traditional' conflated one.[10]

An apparently even more radical line was taken by the editors of the 2007 Macmillan | RSC (Royal Shakespeare Company) *Complete Works* (Jonathan Bate and Eric Rasmussen) who, we are told, 'have edited the First Folio as a complete book, resulting in a definitive *Complete Works* for the twenty-first century'. This was actually a much easier task than the Oxford editors had set themselves, since the Macmillan | RSC editors made far less use of the quartos. They presented this as a purification of the text, stripping away centuries of editorial interference: 'starting with Nicholas Rowe in 1709 and continuing to the present day, Shakespeare editors have mixed Folio and quarto texts, gradually corrupting the original *Complete Works* with errors and conflated textual versions'.[11]

The claim being made here is that editors, for three centuries, have behaved just like Kenneth Branagh and Trevor Nunn and, while choosing one version as their basic text (often referred to by editors as their 'copy-text'), have felt free to adopt different readings and additional passages from other versions. Editors have been more cautious than the directors and performers, usually restricting their choices to the First Folio

---

[6] For further discussion of authorial revision, see the essay by Grace Ioppolo in this volume.

[7] This issue is discussed extensively by all the contributors to Gary Taylor and Michael Warren (eds.), *The Division of the Kingdoms: Shakespeare's Two Versions of 'King Lear'* (Oxford: Clarendon Press, 1983).

[8] See the Introductions to 'The History of King Lear: The quarto Text' and 'The Tragedy of King Lear: The Folio Text' in *William Shakespeare: The Complete Works,* Stanley Wells and Gary Taylor with John Jowett and William Montgomery (eds.) (Oxford: Clarendon Press, 1986), 909, 943. Also Wells's and Taylor's reflections in 'The Oxford Shakespeare Re-viewed' by the *Analytical and Enumerative Bibliography* 4 (1990), 6–20.

[9] Gary Taylor and Michael Warren (eds.) (Oxford: Clarendon Press, 1987).

[10] Stephen Greenblatt, Walter Cohen, Jean E. Howard, and Katharine Eisaman Maus (eds.), *The Norton Shakespeare based on the Oxford Edition* (New York: Norton, 1997).

[11] These claims are made on the cover of the hardback edition.

and the 'good' quartos: I do not, for example, know of any edition of the longer texts of *Hamlet* that moves 'To be or not to be' or prints the unique scene from the First Quarto. Such texts, which combine readings from more than one early source, are indeed known as 'conflated texts' and were overwhelmingly the most common kind of editions of Shakespeare before the 1980s.[12]

But while Oxford and Macmillan, in their different ways, championed the Folio, other publishers have aimed to give readers access to the early quartos. In the 1990s, Harvester Wheatsheaf published a series under the general heading 'Shakespearean Originals: First Editions' and explained on the back covers

> This controversial new series raises a fundamental question about the authenticity of Shakespeare's texts as we know them today. In a radical departure from existing series, it presents the earliest known editions of Shakespeare's plays—which differ substantially from the present versions—and argues that these are the most 'authentic' documents we have.

This series includes not only some quartos previously dismissed as 'bad', such as the 1603 *Hamlet*, and the 1594 *The Taming of A Shrew*, both edited by Graham Holderness and Bryan Loughrey (1992), but also some quartos generally accepted as 'good', such as the 1608 Quarto of *King Lear*, edited by Graham Holderness (1995), and the 1622 *Othello*, the last quarto to appear before the 1623 Folio, edited by Andrew Murphy (1995). They even included some texts that appear for the first time in the Folio, such as *Antony and Cleopatra*, edited by John Turner, and *Twelfth Night*, edited by Laurie E. Osborne (both 1995).

Cambridge University Press also inaugurated an 'Early Quartos' series in the 1990s, with a somewhat more modest claim on their back covers:

> The surviving early quartos of Shakespeare's plays are gaining the attention of scholars as authoritative texts with independent integrity. Indispensable to advanced students and textual scholars, they are not readily available. Alongside standard volumes in the new Cambridge Shakespeare, editions of selected quartos are now published in critical, modern-spelling form, complete with collations, textual notes and substantial introductions.

Rather than aiming to oust traditional versions of Shakespeare's texts 'as we know them today', the Cambridge Quartos merely bid to exist 'alongside standard volumes'. The series again includes *A Shrew* (edited by Stephen Roy Miller, 1998), *Hamlet* (edited by Kathleen O. Irace, 1998), *Othello* (edited by Scott McMillin, 2005), and *King Lear* (edited by Jay L. Halio, 1994).

Arden has turned out to be, at the time of writing, the only edition to publish not two but all three texts of *Hamlet* (in 2006) with full commentaries and editorial apparatus in its main series, and that required my co-editor Neil Taylor and I to argue our case

---

[12] For a history of the construction of the conflated text of *Hamlet* since Nicholas Rowe in 1709, see Barbara Mowat, 'The form of *Hamlet*'s Fortunes', *Renaissance Drama* 19 (1988), 97–126.

extensively with the publisher and the other General Editors. The Arden third series had previously published conflated texts of *Othello* (edited by Ernst Honigmann, 1997) and *King Lear* (edited by R. A. Foakes, 1997), though the latter used an ingenious system of superscript Qs and Fs to indicate the beginning and end of words or passages found only in the Quarto or Folio text. This resulted in Lear's last speech appearing thus:

> And my poor fool is hanged. No, no,[F] no[F] life!
> Why should a dog, a horse, a rat have life
> And thou no breath at all? [Q]O[Q] thou'lt come no more,
> Never, never, never, [F]never, never.[F]
> Pray you undo this button. Thank you, sir.
> [Q]O o o o.[Q]
> [F]Do you see this? Look on her: look, her lips.
> Look there, look there![F]

While this is admirable as a way of making it very obvious to readers how the editor has constructed his text by conflating two early versions, I am not sure if I would want to read *King Lear* for the first time in this edition: the Qs and Fs can seem intrusive.

It was made clear to other editors of multiple-text plays still in production that *Hamlet* was to be seen as a one-off exception. The reasons were fundamentally commercial ones: the publishers could envisage members of their core market (students, for example) buying two books called *Hamlet* (we could not persuade them to let us have three, so we compromised by printing Q2 as a 'core' volume, with 'the texts of 1603 and 1623' as a companion volume) but not two books called *Troilus and Cressida*.

WHAT ARE FOLIOS AND QUARTOS ANYWAY?

Folios are books made out of large sheets of paper folded in half to create two leaves or four pages. In the early modern period this format would typically be chosen by printers for expensive and prestigious projects such as historical or theological works or collected editions of canonical authors. The book we refer to as 'the First Folio' (routinely abbreviated to F1 or just F) is the earliest collected edition of Shakespeare's plays, put together by his friends and fellow-actors, John Heminges and Henry Condell, in 1623, seven years after his death. It was an ambitious publishing project for the time but was presumably a success because a second edition (F2) appeared only nine years later in 1632.

The First Folio contains thirty-six plays divided into three generic categories (Comedies, Histories, and Tragedies). It includes all the plays that are generally ascribed to Shakespeare today, apart from *Pericles* and *The Two Noble Kinsmen*, both late works thought to have been written in collaboration, the first with George Wilkins and the second with John Fletcher. The First Folio does however include *Henry VIII*, another play written in collaboration with Fletcher, and *Timon of Athens*, in which Thomas Middleton is thought to have had a major hand. Middleton is also thought by modern scholars to have contributed to *Macbeth* and *Measure for Measure*, two more First Folio plays, and the debate continues about whether other collaborators contributed to some of Shakespeare's earliest efforts, the *Henry VI* plays and *Titus Andronicus*. The First Folio almost did not include *Troilus and Cressida*, which does not appear in the prefatory 'Catalogue' or list of contents and which seems to have been added at a very late stage, perhaps after some copies of the volume had gone on sale.[13]

Quartos are books made out of the same large sheets of paper as folios, but now folded in half twice to make four leaves or eight pages. In the early modern period individual plays were printed in quarto format and about half of Shakespeare's plays (eighteen of them, many in more than one edition) had appeared in this form before his death in 1616. Texts of his two long poems, *Venus and Adonis* and *The Rape of Lucrece*, had also appeared in quarto format, but their presentation to readers was very different, giving rise to the long-held notion that Shakespeare was interested in publishing his poems as literary texts but not his plays. The poems were carefully printed by Shakespeare's friend and fellow-citizen from Stratford-upon-Avon, Richard Field, and furnished with signed dedications to an aristocratic patron, the Earl of Southampton. The plays seem much more carelessly printed, by twenty different publishers, and have no dedications, prefaces, epistles from the author, or other forms of material now known as 'paratexts', meaning additional or secondary matter existing alongside a primary text.

In some cases it seems clear that the first version of a play to appear in print was an unauthorized text, perhaps a bootlegged one, which was quite quickly followed by a superior, more accurate and usually longer version. Examples of this would include the drastically abbreviated texts of *Romeo and Juliet* and *Hamlet*, published in 1597 and 1603 respectively, and soon followed by longer versions in 1599 and 1604/5.[14] The title-page of the 1599 text of *Romeo and Juliet* claims that it is 'newly corrected, augmented and amended', while that of the 1604/5 *Hamlet* claims that it is 'newly imprinted and enlarged to almost as much againe as it was, according to the true and perfect Coppie'. Some of the statements made on title-pages in this period turn out not to be true: title-pages seem to have been used for advertising purposes and claims about novelty, correctness, and length could be exaggerated, but this one is accurate: Q2 Hamlet is indeed twice the length of Q1. These later texts, referred to as 'good' quartos must have been published with the consent of Shakespeare's company and indeed Shakespeare

---

[13] Other texts absent from the First Folio, which are beginning to appear in Shakespeare series, are *Edward III*, edited by Giorgio Melchiori for Cambridge in 1998 and forthcoming from Arden, edited by Richard Proudfoot and Nicola Bennett, and *Cardenio* or *Double Falsehood* (the play survives only as an eighteenth-century adaptation by Lewis Theobald), now published by Arden, edited by Brean Hammond, 2010.

[14] As Kenneth Branagh (quoted above on 72) notes, some of the extant copies of Q2 (in fact three) are dated 1604 while the others (in fact four) are dated 1605. It seems that printing began in 1604 and continued into 1605 with someone altering the date during the process.

himself, in an effort to supplant the 'bad' quartos and compete with them in the marketplace.[15]

These quartos don't even necessarily specify the author: seven of Shakespeare's plays, including not only his early and very successful tragedy, *Titus Andronicus*, and the popular *Henry VI* plays, but also the more mature works, *Romeo and Juliet*, *Richard II*, and *King Henry IV, Part One*, appeared anonymously, and it was not until 1598 that the title-page of a quarto of *Love's Labour's Lost* mentioned, in small type, that it had been 'Newly corrected and augmented *By W. Shakespere*'. Quarto title-pages, which were used as a form of advertising, do however often mention the acting company that had performed the play. *Titus Andronicus*, for example, was offered in print in 1594 'As it was Plaide by the Right Honourable the Earle of *Darbie*, Earle of *Pembrooke*, and Earle of *Sussex*, their seruants', and *Richard II* was offered in 1597 '*As it hath been publikely acted by the right Honourable the Lorde Chamberlaine his Seruants*'. It would seem then that these texts were designed to appeal to playgoers who had seen a performance and wanted to purchase 'the book of the play' as a souvenir, and to those who had not been able to go to the theatre but had heard of these famous companies. Again some of these claims were false or dubious ones: the 'bad' 1603 Quarto of *Hamlet* gave the author and the company ('his Highnesse seruants') correctly but added that the play had been performed 'in the two universities of Cambridge and Oxford', for which there is no evidence.[16]

WHAT DO EDITORS DO?

It will already be apparent that for roughly half of Shakespeare's plays we have only a single text, that of the First Folio, so an editor has no choice and must just try to present the best version of the Folio text. Even then, s/he must often correct errors of transcription where the text seems to make no sense, and errors of lineation where the printers have set verse as prose to save space or prose as verse to fill up space. In most of the complete works and series I have been discussing, editors must modernize punctuation, spelling, and capitalization, all of which can involve some difficult decisions. They must also insert stage directions to clarify the action on stage for readers, perhaps most frequently by adding entrances and exits and by indicating to whom a line or speech is addressed and whether it is an 'aside', that is, a line or speech that is not meant to be heard by other characters on stage.[17]

[15] Lukas Erne has argued, using this and other evidence, that Shakespeare was in fact more interested in publishing 'literary' versions of his plays than has usually been supposed. See his book *Shakespeare as Literary Dramatist* (Cambridge: Cambridge University Press, 2003).

[16] Curiously, the first performance of *Hamlet* of which we have a specific record took place not in London but on board a ship anchored off the coast of Africa in 1607: see the Arden edition (as cited in n. 5 above), 53–5.

[17] In my recent experience as a General Editor I have found some volume editors reluctant to add 'aside' stage directions on the grounds that they are modern intrusions, despite the fact that Alan C.

When faced with plays that exist in more than one early text, an editor who does not have the luxury of printing multiple texts has to make a decision as to which text to print, usually on the grounds that it is the one closest to Shakespeare's manuscript; but in recent years, as I have said in the case of The Oxford Shakespeare, the argument that one text is closer to the theatre than another has become important. And having chosen a text, this editor has to decide whether to stick to it as if it were the only existing text of the play or to adopt readings from other texts, thereby creating a conflated text to a greater or lesser degree. It is very tempting, when confronted by two 'good' texts of a play, as one is with Hamlet, to turn to the other text when the first one seems to make no sense. We tried not to do this, but only to emend when we felt we had no choice. For example, in Hamlet's first soliloquy, when he laments in Q2 that 'the Everlasting had not fixed | His canon "gainst seale slaughter"' (1.2.131–2), we felt that we would have emended to 'self-slaughter' even without that reading existing in F, since the context makes it clear that Hamlet is talking about suicide and 'seale' for 'self' is an understandable misreading. More controversially, we did not emend Hamlet's comment in Q2 on his decision not to kill the King when he is praying; 'Why this is base and silly, not revenge' (3.3.79) to the Folio's 'Why this is hire and salary, not revenge'. One might prefer the F reading, but the Q2 reading can be defended (assuming that 'silly' means something like 'feeble-minded' as it does at 5.5.25 of Richard II) and we were trying not to produce a conflated text.

In a one-play-per-volume series such as Arden, Oxford, or Cambridge, an editor is also required to provide a full commentary on the text, sometimes justifying textual choices or emendations, but also fulfilling a host of other functions such as providing glosses for archaic or difficult words, explaining complicated syntax, noting sources and other intertextual allusions, explicating historical references, suggesting possibilities for stage action, and so forth. All the time, an editor must be aware of the immense heritage of contributions by his or her predecessors, and that he or she constitutes what Stanley Wells called 'one thin layer in the coral reef of editorial effort'.[18] In the case of a play like Hamlet, which has such an enormous and rich 'afterlife', the editor can try to give a flavour of this, indicating, for example, the importance of the pictorial tradition for the drowning of Ophelia, or the influence on stage designers, especially in the former Soviet Union and Eastern Europe, of the line (found only in the Folio text), 'Denmark's a prison' (2.2.242). This very close engagement with the text, and the commitment to commenting on it at all levels, can be one of the most challenging and rewarding aspects of the editorial role, though it receives far less attention than the higher profile issue of the establishment of the text itself.

In the case of preparing commentaries on the Arden Hamlet texts, we were of course much concerned with textual questions and were surprised to find how often editors who affirmed their commitment to the Folio text as Shakespeare's own revision and

Dessen and Leslie Thomson note 550 examples of 'aside' in their A Dictionary of Stage Directions in English Drama, 1580–1642 (Cambridge: Cambridge University Press, 1999), 15–16.

[18] Stanley Wells, Re-editing Shakespeare for the Modern Reader (Oxford: Oxford University Press, 1984), 3.

'last intention' (not just Wells and Taylor in the Oxford *Complete Works*, but also Philip Edwards in his 1985 edition for Cambridge and G. R. Hibbard in his 1987 edition for Oxford) nevertheless adopted numerous Q2 readings on what seemed often to be partly subjective grounds. For example, when Horatio describes to Hamlet the effect on Marcellus and Barnardo of seeing the Ghost in 1.2, he says in F that 'they bestilled | Almost to jelly with the act of fear, | Stand dumb and speak not to him' (1.2.201–3), where 'bestilled' seems a perfectly acceptable reading, meaning 'made motionless'. But Wells and Taylor, Edwards, and Hibbard all prefer Q2's 'distilled', meaning 'dissolved' or 'reduced'. And when Hamlet is describing the performance of the Player in 2.2, he says in F that 'from her working, all his visage warmed' (2.2.548), which seems acceptable, meaning 'his face flushed', but again all three Folio-favouring editions prefer the Q2 reading, 'his visage wanned', meaning 'his face turned pale'. Similarly, editors who ostensibly privilege Q2 nevertheless take many readings from F. Harold Jenkins, for example, in his 1982 Arden edition, emends Marcellus's reference to 'cost of brazen cannon' at 1.1.72 to F's 'cast of brazen cannon'; he also emends Hamlet's line to the Ghost about the sepulchre 'Wherein we saw thee quietly interred' at 1.4.49 to F's 'Wherein we saw thee quietly inurned'.[19] All of these variant readings can be (and are) explained as errors of transcription, but my point is that if the other text did not exist as an alternative, these editors would probably have let the readings of their respective copy-texts stand. One would suppose that both F and Q2 were unusually corrupt texts from the sheer number of readings of this kind imported from one to the other by editors who, while claiming to be presenting what they see as the best single text are actually conflating on many occasions.

Sometimes, but quite rarely, an editor has the privilege of intervening in the ongoing tradition of a play with a new reading or suggestion. In an interview with Ron Rosenbaum, Harold Jenkins expressed his delight when watching Kenneth Branagh's 1996 film of *Hamlet* and hearing Laertes say to the King when they are planning to kill Hamlet:

> It warms the very sickness in my heart
> That I shall live and tell him to his teeth,
> 'Thus diest thou'.   (4.7.53–5)

The word 'diest' is an editorial emendation or invention, first adopted in the 1964 reprint of John Dover Wilson's 1934 Cambridge edition: the Q2 text has 'didst' and the F text has 'diddest'. Jenkins was convinced that Shakespeare must have written 'diest' and that editors had recovered a lost authorial intention.[20] Curiously, he did not support this reading from Q1 where Leartes [sic] says he is glad 'That I shall live to tell him, thus he dies' (15.5), but few editors have used Q1 for anything other than stage directions.

[19] Harold Jenkins (ed.), *Hamlet*, Arden Shakespeare, 2nd series (London: Methuen, 1982).
[20] Ron Rosenbaum, 'Shakespeare in Rewrite', *The New Yorker* (13 May 2002), 68.

I have felt equally pleased when I have seen in productions of *The Taming of the Shrew* that the character who is prevailed upon to pretend to be Lucentio's father, Vincentio, in 4.2 is played as a Merchant and not a Pedant. He is called a Pedant in F and all subsequent editions, but I argued in my 1984 edition of the play for Cambridge that someone who copied the text and tidied it up for printing chose the wrong profession of the two offered by Biondello ('a marcantant or a pedant', 4.2.63), probably influenced by the unfamiliarity of the word 'marcantant', Biondello's version of the Italian 'mercatante'. The character's itinerary, which includes Rome and Tripoli, seems more like that of a merchant than that of a pedant, and this is supported by his reference to the 'bills for money by exchange | From Florence' which he has brought to Padua. Finally, we already have one pedant in the play (Lucentio in disguise), so it seems unlikely that the motif would be repeated.[21]

Editing itself, obviously enough, has its own history, and the field has been a particularly contentious one over the last thirty years. It had seemed dull territory when I was choosing a topic for my PhD back in 1969, and I rejected the suggestion of my supervisor, Richard Proudfoot, that I should edit a play in the so-called Shakespeare Apocrypha. By the time I accepted the commission to edit *The Taming of the Shrew* for Cambridge in the late 1970s it seemed a much more exciting field to get into, and by the early 1990s I was delighted to find myself not only joining Richard as a General Editor of the Arden series but also taking on the *Hamlet* edition. I shall try to sketch some aspects of what had changed.

EDITING AND UNEDITING

A curious phenomenon of the 1980s and 1990s was the number of books published about editing Shakespeare and other early modern authors by people who did not themselves actually engage in editing.[22] Other scholars examined the history of editing, particularly in the eighteenth century,[23] yet others questioned the assumptions of the twentieth-century 'New Bibliographers' (notably Fredson Bowers, W. W. Greg, A. W. Pollard, and John Dover Wilson) and in particular challenged their theories about 'bad' quartos.[24] Perhaps

---

[21] See further discussion of this point in my edition (2003 updated version), 'List of Characters' (45), 4.2.71 SD (123) and 'Textual Analysis' (157–8).

[22] See, e.g., these works on the textual situation of *King Lear*: Peter W. M. Blayney's *The Texts of* King Lear *and Their Origins* (Cambridge: Cambridge University Press, 1982); P. W. K. Stone, *The Textual History of* King Lear (London: Scolar Press, 1980); and Steven Urkowitz, *Shakespeare Revision of* King Lear (Princeton, NJ: Princeton University Press, 1980).

[23] E.g., Peter Seary, *Lewis Theobald and the Editing of Shakespeare* (Oxford: Oxford University Press, 1990); Margreta de Grazia, *Shakespeare Verbatim: The Reproduction of Authenticity and the 1790 Apparatus* (Oxford: Oxford University Press, 1991).

[24] E.g., Kathleen O. Irace, *Reforming the 'Bad' Quartos: Performance and Provenance of Six Shakespearean First Editions* (Newark: University of Delaware Press, 1994); Irace would go on to edit

the most puzzling aspect of this was the avowed belief in 'unediting', a kind of anti-editing movement that viewed all editorial intervention with suspicion as attempts to impose stability on what was intrinsically unstable and, moreover, as ways of aggrandizing the power of the editors themselves as members of an intellectual elite.[25]

The net result of the combination of all these different contributions to textual studies was however to overturn a major tenet of 'New Bibliography', namely that by studying different versions of a text an editor can reconstruct a single (lost) original and arrive at a confident assertion of having discovered the author's final intentions. On the negative side, the outcome would logically be a return to original or facsimile texts, devoid of editorial intervention, or an anarchic situation whereby all texts are equal and terms like 'good' and 'bad' become inappropriate. (I remember inventing the designation 'textually challenged' myself to avoid the term 'bad'.) On the positive side, we are now in a situation where the fluid and unstable nature of early modern texts (especially dramatic texts) is fully recognized and all texts, even 'bad' ones, can be examined as valuable documents in their own right rather than be dismissed out of hand.

WHAT MIGHT HAPPEN NEXT IN EDITING?

There has been, as I hope I have shown, a high level of intellectual engagement with editing since the 1980s and a prodigious output of books and essays about editing as well as editions themselves. This has not been limited to Shakespeare but has included, most notably, the appearance of the magnificent and monumental first *Collected Works of Thomas Middleton* and its companion volume, *Thomas Middleton and Early Modern Textual Culture*, edited by Gary Taylor and John Lavagnino with P. Jackson, John Jowett, Valerie Wayne, and Adrian Weiss.[26] Other major editions of non-Shakespearean texts are ongoing, but it is clearly the case that, for commercial reasons, publishers would prefer to invest in yet another Shakespeare series than to take a risk on any of his lesser-known contemporaries. (It should be said, however, that the publishers of the Arden Shakespeare have been prepared to invest in a new 'Arden Early Modern Drama' series, the first three volumes of which appeared in 2009.)

Within the Shakespeare canon some plays are of course more commercially viable than others: it takes more work to edit a textually difficult but relatively unpopular play such as *Troilus and Cressida* or *Pericles* than it does to edit a textually straightforward

---

Q1 *Hamlet* for Cambridge in 1998. See also Laurie E. Maguire, *Shakespearean Suspect Texts: The 'Bad' Quartos and Their Contexts* (Cambridge: Cambridge University Press, 1996).

[25] Influential studies here would include Randall McLeod [also Random Cloud], 'The Marriage of Good and Bad Quartos', *Shakespeare Quarterly* 33 (1982), 421–31; Leah Marcus, *Unediting the Renaissance: Shakespeare, Marlowe, and Milton* (New York and London: Routledge, 1996).

[26] Gary Taylor, et al. (eds.), *Collected Works of Thomas Middleton*, 2 vols. (Oxford: Oxford University Press, 2007).

but popular play such as *Twelfth Night* or *Macbeth*, but the publishers can allow the big-selling titles to subsidize the others, and a series such as Arden depends heavily on its backlist for sales: Kenneth Muir's 1951 Arden edition of *Macbeth*, for example, is still a big seller, despite competition from Nicholas Brooke's 1990 edition from Oxford and A. R. Braunmuller's 1997 edition from Cambridge.

At the time of writing, the future of electronic presentation of editions is still unclear. Shakespeare's texts have been available in digital form for a long time now and it is obviously possible to display textual variants onscreen by allowing a reader to click on 'Q' or 'F' to bring up a reading. When preparing our three-text *Hamlet*, we toyed with the idea of publishing the 1603 and 1623 texts in the form of a disk to accompany a one-volume version of Q2 rather than as a separate volume, but technology changes so quickly that obsolescence is a real problem: we assume at least a twenty-year shelf life for an edition published in book form, but would a disk published in 2006 even be readable in 2026? From the publishers' point of view online editions suffer from the usual drawback that, with so much free material on the internet, it is difficult to persuade people to pay for anything, however good the quality.

Editions published in book form are themselves changing. The second series of the Arden Shakespeare assumed a relatively elite, well-educated, and primarily British readership who had a good knowledge of English literature and the Bible and could cope with French, Latin, and even Greek quotations in commentary notes without the need of a translation. We assume a wider, more international, and more diversely educated readership for the third series including, for example, readers who are more familiar with Shakespeare's plays on film and television than they are with them in the theatre.

As a General Editor of the Arden series I have tried, with my colleagues, to encourage volume editors to pay more attention to the plays in performance (not just theatre but film and television) than was required of editors of previous series. Even a stage history was optional in the Arden second series (there is none in Jenkins' *Hamlet*), but it is now an important aspect of any Introduction, and ideally it should go beyond the Anglo-American tradition, though this can be challenging because of the accessibility (or even existence) of appropriate archives. We have also encouraged editors to engage with their play as a text for the stage throughout their commentary notes. A further aspect of the new theatre-consciousness of the series is the obligation to provide a casting chart and to calculate the minimum number of actors required to perform any play, given early modern practices in relation to casting and doubling. Such charts are necessarily speculative (one has to assume, for example, that every line of a text is spoken, which seems unlikely in the case of very long texts such as Q2 or F *Hamlet* or Q or F *King Lear*), but they require attention to the pragmatics of the theatre and can sometimes throw up interesting insights, such as the fact that the actor in *Hamlet* least able to double in another part is the actor of Horatio.[27]

---

[27] See Appendix 5, 'Casting', in the 2006 Arden *Hamlet* (as cited in n. 5 above), 553–65. Strictly speaking, the actor of Horatio could play Reynaldo in 2.1 and the Captain in 4.4. The actor who plays Hamlet could play both of these parts and in addition Francisco in 1.1 and the Sailor in 4.6. The actor

We have also tried to encourage editors to make their editorial procedures more transparent. We felt that the routine practice of the Arden second series of opening the Introduction with a detailed textual discussion, sometimes running to over fifty pages, did not invite readers, especially student readers, to engage with this material. So we suggest in the Editorial Guidelines that, in addition to providing a detailed textual discussion somewhere in the edition (possibly as an appendix and certainly not as the opening section of the Introduction):

> Discussion of the text should include a facsimile page, or section of a page, of the earliest edition(s) with a 'demonstration' of what is involved in producing a modern edited text. If possible, it should illustrate some specific point(s) of difficulty or interest. Matters that could be mentioned with reference to the facsimile page include spelling (especially where modernization involves loss of ambiguity), punctuation, layout and stage directions.[28]

My own students have told me that they have found the results of this exercise enlightening, for example in the case of the Arden *Tempest*[29] and the Arden *Twelfth Night*,[30] and that they have been able, for the first time, to understand exactly what it is that editors undertake to do. At MA level, increasing numbers of them choose to edit a scene from an early modern play as an alternative to writing a conventional essay, so the whirligig of time seems to be coming around.

To conclude: the ongoing fascination with editing (to which even unediting, paradoxically, bears witness) must have something to do with how non-dogmatic it has become. There is something about its necessarily empirical nature that saves it from some of the dangers of 'true believer' writing that has threatened literary theory in our time. And it is a pleasure to achieve a result which will be, ideally, enjoyable, and useful to the reader.

---

who plays the Queen could also play all four of these minor parts. Of course the actors playing Hamlet and the Queen rarely if ever double, but it remains striking that the actor of Horatio should be such a special case.

[28] Arden Third Series Editorial Guidelines, April 2004, section 13e.

[29] Virginia Mason Vaughan and Alden T. Vaughan (eds.), *The Tempest*, (London: Thomas Nelson, 1999): see 'Editorial Practice' and ''Cruxes', 130–8.

[30] Keir Elam (ed.), *Twelfth Night* (London: Cengage Learning, 2008): see 'The Text and Editorial Procedures', 355–79.

CHAPTER 5

....

REVISION

....

GRACE IOPPOLO

'You could for a need study a speech of some dozen or sixteen lines which I would set down and insert in't, could ye not?'

'Let those that play your clowns speak no more than is set down for them.'[1]

JUDGING from his two comments above, Hamlet seems to have had a rather strict idea about how to revise, as well as to 'set down' and permanently establish, the text of a play. His first comment comes in 2.2 when he asks the travelling players if they can perform the old play of *The Murder of Gonzago*, which he knows well enough to revise by inserting into it some dozen or sixteen lines of his own composition. The second comment comes in 3.2 when he lectures the same players on the 'purpose of playing', by which time he envisions himself not only as an occasional reviser but as chief actor, director, and dramatist of the plays in their repertory. It is worth considering whether Shakespeare draws here from his own career, beginning as a reviser of old, stock plays like *The Murder of Gonzago*, who then moved on to writing and revising his own plays. The two comments emphasize that Shakespeare, like Hamlet, expected an accomplished poet, and not actors, some of whom he even fondly admired, to make cuts, additions, alterations, amendments, augmentations, or any other form of revision to a play, and thus 'set down' its text, when the original author or authors were not available.

By the time Shakespeare came to write *Hamlet* he had spent about ten years in professional theatre as an actor and dramatist. He may have begun his career not only by rewriting and adapting old and seemingly authorless plays but by cutting, adding to, and otherwise revising those of senior colleagues with whom he was directly collaborating. By 1601 or 1602, he was a dramatist who worked without collaborators in the composition and revisions of plays. He evidently was so assured of the financial rewards of his profession that he, uniquely among dramatists, had begun to invest in

---

[1] Shakespeare, *The Tragedy of Hamlet, Prince of Denmark*, in *William Shakespeare: The Complete Works*, Stanley Wells and Gary Taylor (eds.) (Oxford: Clarendon Press, 1986), 2.2.541–3, 3.2.38–9.

two different consortia: first in 1594 as a shareholder in the Lord Chamberlain's, later the King's, Men, and second in 1599 as a shareholder in the Globe Theatre. By the end of the next decade he added another consortium to his list, for in 1608 he became a shareholder in the Blackfriars theatre. He therefore came to sell his plays and their performances to companies and theatres in which he was a shareholder.[2] He also received further income when he and the other shareholders in his acting company sold his plays to printers, and even if his share were only one-eighth of 40 shillings, a contemporary rate for a printer's purchase of a playtext,[3] those 5 shillings were his.

Thus, even by the composition of *Hamlet*, Shakespeare was firmly in the position to lecture the audience as well as actors and other theatre personnel on who, exactly, should add even as little as a dozen or sixteen lines to a play. It clearly was not the clowns, even when the company was travelling and far away from the company's resident dramatist. By this time, Shakespeare would not have been obliged generally or in specific cases to surrender control of his playtexts once they reached the theatre and were later printed, watching helplessly as his texts were altered, cut, added to, or mangled by interfering actors, company scribes, 'bookkeepers', who kept track of the company 'book' (or prompt book), or printers and compositors, as critics once believed.[4] In fact, Shakespeare would have had tremendous financial incentive, not to mention artistic desire, to help prepare and maintain his texts to the best advantage for production and later publication, and this preparation would have included their revision.

In sum, Shakespeare was a very shrewd businessman, and his revision of his own plays was a sound business investment, a fact that needs more emphasis because centuries of critics and admirers have burdened Shakespeare with the title of the world's greatest playwright and natural genius who was much too brilliant in the act of writing to need to revise then or later. This burden was built on a superb piece of publicity and advertising in the 1623 First Folio by John Heminges and Henry Condell, Shakespeare's fellow-shareholders and actors, who boasted, 'What he thought he

---

[2] I am very grateful to Herbert Berry and to Andrew Gurr who clarified for me five years ago the very complicated issues relating to the three consortia. See Berry's discussion of these financial arrangements in Glynne Wickham and Herbert Berry, *English Professional Theatre 1530-1660* (Cambridge: Cambridge University Press, 2000), 493-5, 502-3. Berry accepted that the financial shares for the first Globe were similar to those documented for the second Globe, hence the Burbages had larger shares than other investors, including Shakespeare. Gurr is more cautious in *The Shakespeare Company, 1594-1642* (Cambridge: Cambridge University Press, 2004), 85-119. Also see Grace Ioppolo, *Dramatists and their Manuscripts in the Age of Shakespeare, Jonson, Middleton and Heywood: Authorship, Authority and the Playhouse* (London: Routledge, 2006), 140-2.

[3] See Peter W. M. Blayney, 'The Printing of Playbooks', in John D. Cox and David Scott Kastan (eds.), *A New History of Early English Drama* (New York: Columbia University Press, 1997), 383-422.

[4] Such beliefs were common among 18th- and 19th-century editors of Shakespeare's plays; see for example the editions of Shakespeare's *Works* by Nicholas Rowe (1709), Alexander Pope (1725), Samuel Johnson (1765), Edmond Malone (1790), and John Payne Collier (1842). These critical beliefs were re-examined with the rise of the 'new bibliography' in the early twentieth century through the use of scientific and systematic examination and finally overturned with the publication of E. A. J. Honigmann's groundbreaking book on theatrical and literary revision, *The Stability of Shakespeare's Text* (London: E. Arnold, 1965), and the debate beginning in the 1980s about revision in *King Lear* (see below).

uttered with that easiness that we have scarce received from him a blot in his papers.' But this claim was probably as exaggerated, and false, as their other implication that many of the plays in the First Folio had been previously published from 'divers stolen and surreptitious copies, maimed and deformed by the frauds and stealths of injurious impostors'.[5] As some of these previously printed plays had been typeset from theatrical manuscripts that the two men and their fellow-actors had used at the Globe, Blackfriars, and elsewhere, and other plays had been typeset directly from Shakespeare's foul papers, these First Folio statements need to be viewed as great advertising copy and nothing more. As company managers, Heminges and Condell would have routinely commissioned company dramatists, including Shakespeare, to make 'addicians' to or 'mend' or 'alter', to use Philip Henslowe's terms, existing playtexts, as well as to supply new plays, and such revised playtexts were not ordinarily surreptitious, maimed, or deformed.

Overwhelming evidence in the early printed quarto and First Folio texts of Shakespeare, and in the dramatic manuscripts and printed texts of contemporary colleagues or collaborators such as Anthony Munday, Thomas Heywood, Ben Jonson, John Fletcher, Thomas Middleton, and Philip Massinger, demonstrates that years after their original composition and performance authors considered their playtexts to be fluid documents that they could reclaim as their own.[6] Further evidence of such an authorial belief, and sometimes a demand, appears in account books, letters, contracts, receipts, bills, and other archival records of a variety of early modern English theatre personnel and entrepreneurs. At any stage during and after the completion of a play, including after its submission to the Master of the Revels, and during or after rehearsal, public or private performance, a later revival, or after being printed, Shakespeare and any other dramatist could once again pick up a playtext and rework it if they needed to or if they wanted to.

Whether minute or large-scale, authorial revision proves that the exact state of a text, word for word, was of enormous concern to a dramatist and an acting company, even many years after that play's composition and original staging. Such concern is explicit in the King's Men's complaint to the Lord Chamberlain in 1637 that 'corruption', including unauthorized revision, in the texts of plays printed without the company's permission led to 'the iniury and disgrace of the Authors'.[7] Numerous dramatists returned to their plays, sometimes years later in the case of John Bale, who rewrote his play *King Johan* for performance before Queen Elizabeth, or Philip Massinger, who

---

[5] 'To the Great Variety of Readers', *Mr William Shakespeares Comedies, Histories & Tragedies* (London: Isaac Jaggard and Ed. Blount, 1623), sig. A3.

[6] In this essay, my discussion of the manuscripts of Shakespeare's contemporary dramatists draws on my personal examination of over 140 early modern English dramatic manuscripts located in the UK and USA. I discuss at length the evidence of revision in many of these manuscripts in *Dramatists and their Manuscripts*, as well as in *Revising Shakespeare* (Cambridge, MA: Harvard University Press, 1991), and my Malone Society Reprints edition of *Hengist, King of Kent by Thomas Middleton* (Oxford: Oxford University Press, 2004).

[7] National Archives, Kew (formerly PRO), LC 5/134/178. W. W. Greg provides a transcript of the letter in *Collections Vol. II. Part III* (N. 71 in the Malone Society Reprints Series) (Oxford: Oxford University Press, 1931; rpt. New York: AMS Press, 1985), 384-5.

hand-corrected editions of his plays after they had been printed.[8] Even though dramatists surrendered their financial claim to a play when they sold it to an acting company, they did not surrender their artistic claim to it, especially if they still worked occasionally or full-time with that company. In fact, while any given play was in rehearsal or performance, dramatists were often writing new plays, alone or in collaboration, for that company and could often be found dining, drinking, gossiping, fighting, or even co-signing payment slips or bail receipts with company actors. So it was not difficult for actors or company personnel or even the censor to locate dramatists with whom they worked. At least one Master of the Revels, Sir Henry Herbert, wrote notes to authors about censorious material in the plays that he was in the act of reading and licensing, so he obviously assumed that authors, and not company bookkeepers (who kept charge of the master 'book' or prompt-copy) would revise the text to incorporate the cuts that he demanded. Other authorial revisions appear to have been custom-made to suit not the censor's but the actors' demands, for example to praise a new monarch, perform in a new theatre, or ease a new actor into a role.

Although dramatists worked collaboratively with theatre personnel and censors to prepare a text for performance, this collaboration left the responsibility for the composition and revision of the play's content, including dialogue, plot, characters, and structure, entirely up to dramatists. These dramatists were evidently expected, as part of their contractual duties or for their own artistic interests, to 'perfit', i.e. perfect, the text, to use a term of the dramatist and experienced acting-company manager Robert Daborne,[9] even after the text entered the playhouse. But dramatists not only revised when compelled to, as a result of censorship or of the desire of the actors to pass an old play off as a new one, but when they wanted to. They also did not always consider changes made between foul papers and fair copies to be 'improvements', and fair-copied texts were not necessarily 'better' than foul-paper texts. Evidence in extant autograph foul-paper and fair-copied manuscripts, as well as the censors' records and other archival documents, remind us that playtexts took a circular, and not a linear path: they did not move from author to censor to acting company to audience, acquiring nothing but non-authorial revisions, but could circulate back at any or every stage to the author for his revisions, large or small.

The Business of Revision

The substantial archive of papers of the theatrical entrepreneur Philip Henslowe and the actor and entrepreneur Edward Alleyn demonstrates that actors, dramatists, company

---

[8] See Barry B. Adams (ed.), *John Bale's King Johan* (San Marino, CA: Huntington Library Press, 1969), and W. W. Greg, 'Massinger's Autograph Corrections in *The Duke of Milan*' and 'More Massinger Corrections', in J. C. Maxwell (ed.), *Collected Papers*, (Oxford: Clarendon Press, 1966), 110–48.

[9] See Dulwich College Library MS 1: Articles 70, 71, available online at www.henslowe-alleyn.org.uk.

managers, theatre owners, and other personnel lived in a highly interdependent and financially competitive theatrical business world. These men often moved casually or deliberately among companies, theatres, and professions over short or long periods of time. Many of those who began their careers in the Elizabethan period often continued in the same or different capacities in the Jacobean period. In effect, everyone, including Shakespeare, knew everyone else, and more importantly they knew what everyone else was doing and how much they were being paid to do it. They also had daily access to plays in manuscript, either as actors, dramatists, company sharers, managers, or theatre owners, and these manuscripts contained minor and major revisions.

Even as a young apprentice, Shakespeare would have been familiar with the three categories of revision to existing plays for which Philip Henslowe and others who commissioned plays paid dramatists: 'addicians', 'mending', and 'altering'. An 'addician' could consist of one or more new speeches, passages or scenes, or simply a new prologue or epilogue. Often these were for particular performances at court or a stately home in front of a monarch or peer, who would have expected some personal reference at the beginning or end of the play. 'Mending' would probably require the dramatist to rework or repair some small portion of a play, while altering could involve small or large changes. Mending or altering an existing play took considerably less time and earned less remuneration, at the rate of 10 to 20 shillings, than writing a new play, at the rate of £7 and upwards.[10]

Whenever possible, Henslowe appears to have commissioned the original authors to deal with plays that needed mending, altering, or additions. His *Diary* repeatedly makes clear that other company personnel, including scribes, bookkeepers, company managers, and senior or junior actors, were not employed to perform revisions to playtexts, even though many of these personnel were already under contract or indebted to him in some way. Henslowe, who was exceptionally careful about spending money, obviously considered revision to be the responsibility of professional writers and was willing to pay them to do this work. Actors could, of course, embellish or change the script during performance, as Hamlet complains of the clowns, but such wholesale alteration or revision of the original text could have placed the acting company in jeopardy of defying the censor's licence of the text as originally written. But as Hamlet knows, actors on provincial tour far from the censor's London base could take far more liberties with their texts. In the case of Edward Alleyn's own 'part', or script, of the play *Orlando Furioso*, the actor made only minor and occasional corrections and notations, partly in the form of stage directions that increase his character's emotional outbursts. He probably made these revisions in consultation with the scribe who made corrections and insertions into a few gaps of dialogue.[11] But by the time Alleyn came to perform this role, the play's author, Robert Greene, was

---

[10] See throughout *Henslowe's Diary*, R. A. Foakes (ed.), 2nd edn. (Cambridge: Cambridge University Press, 2002). Digital images of each page of the original manuscript of the *Diary* can be viewed at www.henslowe-alleyn.org.uk.

[11] Dulwich College Library MS 1: Article 138, available online at www.henslowe-alleyn.org.uk. Also see Greene, *The Historie of Orlando Furioso* (London: 1594), and W. W. Greg, *Two Elizabethan Stage Abridgements: The Battle of Alcazar & Orlando Furioso* (Oxford: Clarendon Press, 1923), 133–4. Greg offers a parallel text of the part and the printed play on 142–201.

not involved with Alleyn's acting company, which may, in fact, have bought the play second-hand. Thus, even as a lead actor and company sharer, and commissioner of plays by dramatists, Alleyn did not overhaul, alter, adapt, or 'contaminate' the text of this script, of one of his most famous roles, even when the original author was not available.

The professional revision of plays was time-consuming and required skill, concentration, and experience. In a 1614 letter to Henslowe, Robert Daborne writes of the 'extraordynary payns' he has taken in revising his new tragedy *Machiavell and the Devil* during its composition.[12] His comments, frequently echoed by other Elizabethan and Jacobean dramatists in play prefaces, prologues, epilogues, and even in dialogue, show authors more determined to craft and perfect a play reflecting their artistic designs than quickly producing an updated or corrected acting text. Dramatists insisted that integrity and authority were vital parts of the 'general *Scope* and purpose of an *Author*', as Ben Jonson argued in his 1601 satire *Poetaster*, the title of which refers to an incompetent dramatist.[13] Jonson also explicitly acknowledged that he made a gift of his authority through the process of playwriting, including through revision, and he was always ready to complain in play prefaces, inductions, epilogues, and even in dialogue when his own words had been replaced by those of an interloper.[14] Professional dramatists knew that company scribes would, for example, regularize, correct, or add speech-prefixes and stage directions for actor entrances, stage properties, and music but would allow the author to make minor or major revisions to dialogue or structure, as evidenced by such manuscript plays as *The Wasp*, *The Lady Mother*, and *John of Bordeaux*. In fact, an examination of the different hands in such manuscripts clearly shows that the roles of author-reviser and scribe were clearly demarcated, with authors revising and scribes correcting.[15]

Of course, company dramatists could rework other dramatists' plays that were already in the repertory, as is made clear in 1640 in a series of legal documents about Richard Brome's previous contracts with the Salisbury Court theatre owners and actors. In addition to writing new plays, for which he agreed to use 'his best Arte and Industrye' and 'applie all his studdye and Endeauors', Brome agreed to make 'divers scenes in ould revived playes for them and many prologues and Epilogues to such playes of theires, songs, and one Introduccion'. Brome clearly did not enjoy reworking others' plays, for he complained that such revision took up 'as much

[12] Dulwich College Library MS 1: Article 81, available online at www.henslowe-alleyn.org.uk.

[13] See Jonson, *Poetaster* (London: 1602), sigs. L2–2v.

[14] See especially the 1602 Quarto of *Poetaster* and the text of the play in *The Works of Beniamin Ionson* (London: 1616), and the text of *Bartholomew Fair* in *The Works of Benjamin Jonson: The Second Volume* (London: 1640).

[15] Alnwick Castle MS 507; British Library MS Egerton 1994; and Alnwick Castle MS 507. Also see J. W. Lever and Gary Proudfoot (eds.), *The Wasp or Subject's Precedent* (Oxford: Oxford University Press, 1976); Arthur Brown (ed.), *The Lady Mother by Henry Glapthorne* (Oxford: Oxford University Press, 1959); William Lindsay Renwick and W. W. Greg (eds.), *John of Bordeaux* (Oxford: Oxford University Press, 1936).

tyme and studdy as twoe ordynarie playes might take vpp in writing'.[16] Thomas
Middleton probably agreed with Brome, at least in *Hengist, King of Kent*, because he
has thieves stage an old play of *The Cheater and the Clown* which has been badly
revised by actors, with the result that a mayor in the audience shouts out, 'A pox of
your new additions! They spoil all the plays that ever they come in!'[17] New additions
had to be carefully done, preferably by the original author, and if he was not available,
an experienced and skilled dramatist who was.

The Business of Shakespearean Revision

Only manuscripts in an author's hand or in a scribal hand with annotations by an
author can truly tell us how, when, and why authors made revisions to playtexts
(authorial and scribal manuscripts do not, as a rule, show minor or major revisions
in non-authorial hands). In the case of Shakespeare, we are limited to studying his fair
copy of his addition on three leaves to the collaborative manuscript of *Sir Thomas
More*. For a glimpse of his foul papers, we need to examine the early quarto and First
Folio texts of his plays, which were printed from foul papers. These texts show the same
types and patterns of authorial revision as seen in the manuscripts of his contemporary
dramatists, many of whom served as Shakespeare's colleagues throughout his career
and as collaborators at the beginning or end of it. Signs of authorial reworking during
the composition of foul papers include false starts, duplications, 'ghost' characters who
are listed in stage directions but never speak, confusions in character names and
interactions, vague stage directions, missing entrance or exit directions, and inconsistent notation of the beginnings and ends of acts or scenes.

That Shakespeare sometimes, and perhaps routinely, produced such inconsistencies
is suggested by the difficulty the compositors had in reading his handwriting in the foul
papers of *Romeo and Juliet*, from which they set the second Quarto. This Quarto was
evidently printed to supersede the first Quarto, printed from an unauthorized and
heavily-cut text used for provincial touring. These foul papers, at least, were messy,
somewhat disordered, and often illegible, and are thus in fact similar to Thomas

---

[16] National Archives, Kew (formerly PRO) Req. 2/662. For transcriptions of these documents, see
Ann Haaker's excellent article, 'The Plague, the Theater and the Poet', *Renaissance Drama* NS 1 (1968),
283–306; she discusses their history, noting that Charles W. Wallace discovered them among National
Archives, Kew (formerly PRO) records and that his transcriptions are among his papers in the Wallace
Collection at the Henry E. Huntington Library. However, the Wallace Collection has been recatalogued
since Haaker saw it, and Wallace's transcript of the Heaton–Brome case can now be found in Wallace
Collection Box 9, Shelfmark BV13b. Also see Ioppolo, *Dramatists and their Manuscripts*, 45–53;
G. E. Bentley, *The Profession of Dramatist 1590–1642* (Princeton, NJ: Princeton University Press, 1971)
112–11; and Wickham and Berry, *English Professional Theatre 1530–1660*, 657–64.

[17] Middleton, *Hengist, King of Kent*, Grace Ioppolo (ed.), in Gary Taylor and John Lavagnino (eds.),
Thomas Middleton: The Collected Works (Oxford: Oxford University Press, 2007), 5.1.325–6.

Heywood's extant foul-paper manuscript of *The Captives*.[18] Like his contemporaries, Shakespeare was a working man of the theatre, and he worked as his colleagues and collaborators worked. He composed a text, rewriting or rethinking it before and after it was read by the censor and after performance, copying it again, and in the process sometimes polishing and refining it and sometimes allowing it to stand with other errors or inconsistencies. Many of these errors or inconsistencies are not apparent in performance. If he did not go back after composition and clean up or correct all of them in his foul papers, it was most likely because he knew that he would write out his own fair copy of his foul papers or assist a scribe in doing so. Shakespeare could have made his corrections and further revisions in that fair copy, leaving his foul papers uncorrected. Like King's Men's colleagues such as Jonson and Middleton,[19] Shakespeare may have seen his playtexts as flexible and variable, and never quite finished, whether in manuscript or print.

The early printed texts of some of his plays printed from foul papers particularly show uncorrected and inconsistent *currente calamo* revisions, that is, changes while composing, as in this passage, printed with cramped type, in the 1600 first Quarto of *A Midsummer Night's Dream*:

> Lovers, and mad men haue such seething braines,
> Such shaping phantasies, that apprehend more,
> Then coole reason euer comprehends.The lunatick,
> The louer, and the Poet are of imagination all compact.
> One sees more diuels, then vast hell can holde;   5
> That is the mad man.The louer, all as frantic,
> Sees *Helens* beauty in a brow of *Ægypt*.
> The Poets eye, in a fine frenzy, rolling, doth glance
> From heauen to earth, from earth to heauen. And as
> Imagination bodies forth the formes of things   10
> Vnknowne: the Poets penne turns them to shapes,
> And giues to ayery nothing, a locall habitation,
> And a name. Such trickes hath strong imagination.[20]

---

[18] As Arthur Brown, in his preface to his Malone Society Reprints edition of *The Captives by Thomas Heywood* (Oxford: Oxford University Press, 1953), xii, notes, it is 'unlikely' that there was ever a rougher authorial draft behind this foul-paper manuscript. Also see Greg's discussion of the play as foul papers in *The Shakespeare First Folio* (Oxford: Clarendon Press, 1955), 109, and Grace Ioppolo, *Dramatists and their Manuscripts*, 94–9. On the printing of the second Quarto of *Romeo and Juliet*, see John Jowett's Textual Introduction to *Romeo and Juliet* in Stanley Wells, Gary Taylor, John Jowett, and William Montgomery (eds.), *William Shakespeare: A Textual Companion* (Oxford: Clarendon Press, 1987), 288–90.

[19] Jonson insisted that the scribe copying out his masque *The Gypsies Metamorphosed* record in the margin the revisions for subsequent performances; Middleton helped to circulate six variant manuscripts of his notorious play *A Game at Chess*. See Jonson, *The Gypsies Metamorphosed*, ed. George Watson Cole (New York: Modern Language Association, 1931), and Grace Ioppolo, *Revising Shakespeare*, 65–77.

[20] Shakespeare, *A Midsommer nights dreame* (London: 1600), sigs. G2–G3r.

In this passage, the third and fourth lines are noticeably hypermetric, that is, they have too many syllables for a pentameter line. The eighth and following lines are similarly hypermetric, leading the scholars Arthur Quiller-Couch and John Dover Wilson to argue persuasively that Shakespeare originally wrote this passage to compare the lover and the lunatic, and that he made *currente calamo* revisions in the margin to include the poet in the comparison. Shakespeare evidently left the lines hypermetric in his foul papers, and when the compositor came to set the type for them, he followed the text exactly as written without correcting it either. Further mis-lining in the entire scene also suggests marginal additions and revisions throughout.[21] When the play was reprinted many years later in the 1623 First Folio from a theatrical manuscript, the first set of hypermetric lines had been carefully corrected, no doubt by Shakespeare, to:

> Then coole reason euer comprehends.
> The Lunaticke, the Louer, and the Poet,
> Are of imagination all compact.

The second set of hypermetric lines has been corrected to:

> The Poets eye in a fine frenzy rolling, doth glance
> From heauen to earth, from earth to heauen.
> And as imagination bodies forth the forms of things   10
> Vnknowne: the Poets penne turns them to shapes.[22]

Shakespeare's later integration of these revisions into proper blank verse lines implies that he paid very careful attention to the formality of his written text and how it appeared, not only to the actors, who needed to recite pentameter lines, but to his later theatrical and literary audiences, who did not, but who expected Shakespeare to be able to do so.

At least sixteen other plays were almost certainly printed from Shakespeare's foul papers: the first Quartos of *Titus Andronicus, Hamlet, Love's Labour's Lost, 1 Henry VI, 2 Henry VI, Romeo and Juliet, Richard II, 3 Henry VI, 2 Henry IV, The Comedy of Errors, Much Ado About Nothing, Henry V, Troilus and Cressida*, and *King Lear*; and the First Folio texts of *All's Well That Ends Well* and *Antony and Cleopatra*.[23] As with the first Quarto of *A Midsummer Night's Dream*, these texts show, to varying degrees, authorial errors, false starts, loose ends, duplications, inconsistencies, and other confusions in plot, setting, character, dialogue, speech-prefixes, and stage directions that come from a composing author rethinking and reworking his text. Clearly Shakespeare did not write out and keep the first thing that came into his head but kept going back to

---

[21] See Quiller-Couch and Wilson (eds.), 'Notes' to *A Midsummer Night's Dream* (Cambridge: Cambridge University Press, 1924), 138–41.

[22] *Mr William Shakespeares Comedies, Histories, & Tragedies* (London: 1623), sig. O2.

[23] For thorough discussions of the printing and signs of authorial and non-authorial revision of Shakespeare's plays, see W. W. Greg, *The Shakespeare First Folio* and the individual textual introductions to plays in Wells and Taylor, *William Shakespeare: A Textual Companion*.

insert, in a sense, speeches of some dozen or sixteen, or another number, of lines as he composed.

Plays with surviving texts printed both from foul papers and partially or wholly from a theatrical book to which Shakespeare contributed at some point, such as *Titus Andronicus, A Midsummer Night's Dream, Love's Labour's Lost, The Merry Wives of Windsor, Much Ado About Nothing, The Merchant of Venice, Troilus and Cressida, 2* and *3 Henry VI, Richard III, Richard II, 1* and *2 Henry IV, Henry V,* and *Romeo and Juliet, Hamlet, Othello,* and *King Lear,* can reveal even more about Shakespeare's revision after composition or performance. As noted above, some revisions may have been made in response to demands from the censor or for some other externally-imposed reasons. For example, complaints by the Cobham family about the comic portrayal of their esteemed ancestor, Sir John Oldcastle, in the *Henry IV* plays were most likely the cause of Shakespeare's alteration of the character's name from Oldcastle to Falstaff. To emphasize the change, Shakespeare apparently added the rather awkward line, 'Olde-castle died Martyre, and this is not the man', when referring to Falstaff in the last few lines of the Epilogue to *2 Henry IV*.[24] But Shakespeare neglected to remove a few other references to Oldcastle in speech-prefixes and dialogue in the manuscripts used to print quartos of the two plays. Shakespeare, or his acting company, also appears to have been forced to cut the politically dangerous deposition scene of 3.3 from the early printed quartos of *Richard II*, and possibly from performances, until after the death of Elizabeth I, who was rumoured to have taken great offence to it. But other revisions were not made to suit censorship, but as in *A Midsummer Night's Dream*, to suit Shakespeare's changing and evolving artistic concerns. Plays including *The Tempest, Coriolanus, Julius Caesar, Antony and Cleopatra, Twelfth Night,* and *All's Well That Ends Well*, which were not printed in early quartos but in the Folio for the first time, may also show internal signs of later revisions and not just revision during composition.

If we are to judge by his revisions in the form of an addition to the manuscript 'book' of the *Sir Thomas More*,[25] Shakespeare was evidently very careful, at least early in his career, in making fair copies of his foul papers, but these fair copies were not without 'blots' or revisions, as Heminges and Condell claimed in the First Folio. Although this manuscript eventually came to be termed a complete 'book' on its wrapper, intended to be used to transcribe other copies of the play, including the playhouse 'plot' and actors' 'parts' and to prompt actors during performance, it contains numerous inconsistencies, incomplete corrections, and confusions acquired as the play was repeatedly revised to suit the censor. The play's primary author, Munday, and the

[24] *The Second part of Henrie the fourth* (London: 1600), sig. L1v.
[25] British Libary MS Harley 7368. For a discussion of this manuscript, see especially W. W. Greg (ed.), *The Book of Sir Thomas More* (Oxford: Oxford University Press, 1911); Peter W. M. Blayney, The *Booke of Sir Thomas Moore* Re-Examined', *Studies in Philology* 69 (1972), 167–91; and Scott McMillin, *The Elizabethan Theatre and The Book of Sir Thomas More* (Ithaca, NY: Cornell University Press, 1987).

other revisers, Chettle, Heywood, and Dekker, were regularly contracted by Henslowe to write plays for the Admiral's Men and other companies, either alone or in collaboration, and thus would have been experienced both in writing new plays and revising old ones that would suit the censor. Both Dekker and Shakespeare, at least, were experienced dramatists with the Chamberlain's/King's Men. Three non-authorial hands, including that of a bookkeeper and the censor Sir Edmund Tilney, also appear in the manuscript.

Only the additions by Heywood are foul papers, while the original play by Munday and the additions by Shakespeare, Dekker, and Chettle are authorial fair copies of foul papers. Shakespeare's portion especially shows the type of deliberately written and elaborately flourished letter forms of an author writing carefully and slowly and not cursively.[26] Thus Shakespeare is copying here, not composing. Most major alterations in these three sheets are in the hand of a bookkeeper or playhouse scribe who has changed some speech-prefixes and cut some lines. All the occurrences of revision are typical of extant manuscripts such as Massinger's *Believe as You List* and Heywood's *The Escapes of Jupiter* in which a bookkeeper has lightly annotated the authors' mostly fair copy.[27] However, in *Sir Thomas More*, Shakespeare also made an interlinear revision, which was deleted by the bookkeeper, most likely after the bookkeeper's first attempt to revise the lines by deleting them. In these 147 lines in Shakespeare's hand there are approximately 19 single words (or parts of single words) which he corrected or subtly revised.

Thus, the idea that authorial fair copies, however neatly written, not to mention foul papers, would be perfect or even without 'a blot' cannot be substantiated in any of the authorial fair copies of Munday, Dekker, and Chettle, or Shakespeare in the manuscript of *Sir Thomas More* or of Massinger, Jonson, and Middleton, for example, in their manuscripts. What fair copy manuscripts repeatedly and consistently show are the types of small and seemingly inconsequential revisions that appear in these three Shakespearean leaves of *Sir Thomas More*. More importantly, Shakespeare does his revision here after the bookkeeper has read through the text. Thus, these three leaves and many others in this manuscript emphasize that the bookkeeper worked with, and not against, revising dramatists, especially those collaborating with other dramatists. In fact, Shakespeare's methods of working here suggest that he made or accepted changes in theatrical business such as speech-prefixes and stage directions that the bookkeeper and other colleagues suggested. In effect, Shakespeare did not simply compose this addition as a revision but helped prepare it for seamless integration into production and performance; that is, he 'perfected' his portion of the text, to use Daborne's term, as much as possible. Such collaboration with playhouse personnel would be especially profitable when the revising dramatist was himself an entrepreneur, as Shakespeare increasingly was.

[26] See Ioppolo, *Dramatists and their Manuscripts*, 102–9.

[27] British Library MSS Egerton 2828 and 1994. Also see C. J. Sisson (ed.), *Believe as You List by Philip Massinger* (Oxford: Oxford University Press, 1927), and Henry D. Janzen (ed.), *The Escapes of Jupiter* (Oxford: Oxford University Press, 1978).

The argument that Shakespeare revised his plays not only in his foul papers and during his fair copying of them but some years after their original composition was successfully re-examined in the 1980s, using the first Quarto and Folio texts of *King Lear* as an exemplum. Even though scholars had been willing to accept that Shakespeare had revised *Othello* after composition, they resisted the idea of large-scale revision in *King Lear*, perhaps because this play is now seen as Shakespeare's greatest artistic achievement.[28] The subsequent acceptance that Shakespeare revised that play and others, including *Hamlet*, after composition has encouraged scholars to re-evaluate major and minor variants between quarto texts or between quarto and folio texts of the same play as revisions, especially when they maintain the artistic and stylistic coherence of the play. The changes made between the two texts of *King Lear*, for example, show an author returning to his text to make careful, consistent, and intelligent changes to his major characters, notably Lear.

For example, the confrontation between Cordelia and Lear in 1.1 becomes more intense but also more painful in revision. In the Quarto, when Lear asks her, 'What can you say to win a third, more opulent | Then your sisters', she replies, 'Nothing my Lord'. His response is 'How, nothing will come of nothing, speake againe'.[29] However, in the Folio the scene runs as follows:

> LEAR: What can you say, to draw
> A third, more opulent, then your Sisters? speake.
> COR.:   Nothing my Lord.
> LEAR: Nothing?
> COR.:   Nothing.
> LEAR: Nothing will come of nothing, speake again.[30]

Lear's offer in the Folio, but not in the first Quarto, to give Cordelia another chance to amend her first proffer of 'Nothing' is a small but telling moment. Not only does the stand-off establish that Cordelia sees herself as equal to Lear, in responding simply 'Nothing' to his 'Nothing', with no acknowledgement of his rank or her affection, but that Cordelia is truly her father's daughter, and is as stubborn and inflexible as he is.

Such small additions in the Folio, however, seem to be carefully balanced with small cuts elsewhere. For example, in 2.2 in the first Quarto when Lear finds his servant Kent, disguised as Caius, stocked, Lear refuses to believe that his daughter Regan and son-in-law Cornwall are responsible. Lear says to Kent, 'No.' Kent's response of 'Yes', provokes Lear's reply, 'No I say'. Kent answers, 'I say yea'. Lear then states, 'No no, they would not'. Kent responds, 'Yes they haue', causing Lear to explode with the statement, 'By Jupiter I sweare no' as the beginning of a six-line speech of anger and frustration

---

[28] On the cultural shift in attitudes to *King Lear*, see R. A. Foakes, *Hamlet versus Lear: Cultural Politics and Shakespeare's Art* (Cambridge: Cambridge University Press, 1993).

[29] *Mr William Shak-speare: His True Chronicle Historie of the life and death of King Lear and his three Daughters* (London: 1608), sig. B2. Further references will be made parenthetically in the text.

[30] *Mr William Shakespeares Comedies, Histories, & Tragedies*, sig. 2q2v.

(sig. E3r). The Folio passage differs here substantively from the first Quarto only in the cutting of Lear's, 'No no, they would not' and Kent's response, 'Yes they haue' (sig. 2r recto). Perhaps Shakespeare felt a need in the Folio to show a firm and slightly extended confrontation between a father and daughter early in the play but a more rushed one later between a ruler and a servant. In fact, the Folio shows the majority of its major cuts later in Acts 3 and 4, by which time the mock-trial of Goneril and Regan in 3.6 by Lear, Poor Tom, and the Fool seems to be superfluous, or too physically demanding for the actor playing Lear, who has to use tremendous concentration and energy through-out the scenes on the heath and in the hovel in Act 3.

Yet, by the time he came to revise the play, Shakespeare appears to have been more interested in focusing on parent–child cruelty in the scene immediately following the mock-trial, that is, the blinding of Gloucester in 3.7. In the first Quarto, this scene, which has left critics and audiences in shock since the play's composition, allows two servants to remain behind after Gloucester's blinding to follow him and 'fetch some flaxe and whites of egges to apply to his bleeding face' (sig. H2). In the Folio, these lines have been cut, further intensifying the horrific actions. Pity may be in short supply in *King Lear*, but it appears more often in the first Quarto than in the Folio, including when in 4.3, a scene cut entirely from the Folio, Kent and a Gentleman prepare the audience for Cordelia's return after an absence of four acts by narrating her pity and compassion toward her father's condition.[31]

It is not clear whether Shakespeare considered his text of *King Lear* as it came to be printed either in the first Quarto or the First Folio to be 'better' than the other. Certainly he considered them to be different states or versions of his text, as did Ben Jonson in the composite manuscript of *The Gypsies Metamorphosed* and Middleton in the six variant manuscripts of *A Game at Chess*. These states could evolve and change as needed, acquiring some dozen or sixteen lines of insertion or deletion as playing conditions and authorial design required. Shakespeare revised at least *Hamlet* and *Othello*, as well as *King Lear*, through small- and large-scale revision some years after their original composition in order to reshape the plays artistically and possibly to respond to changes within and outside his acting company and playhouses. He cut major speeches or entire scenes in other plays, including Hamlet's speech of 'How all occasions do inform against me' in 4.4 in *Hamlet*, and altered single words elsewhere that reshape characters, plot, and structure. These changes show a revising and experienced dramatist who is exceptionally concerned with maintaining the unity and consistency of the formal elements of his plays, even to the smallest degree. This concern may be financial but it is certainly also artistic.

Of course, some of the changes to the manuscripts used to print folio texts may have been made after the end of Shakespeare's financial involvement with the King's Men or after his death. But other revisions may have been made much earlier with his consent,

---

[31] For a discussion of the varieties of revision in King Lear, see Gary Taylor and Michael Warren (eds.), *The Division of the Kingdoms* (Oxford: Clarendon Press, 1983); Steven Urkowtiz, *Shakespeare's Revision of King Lear* (Princeton, NJ: Princeton University Press, 1980); and Ioppolo, *Revising Shakespeare*.

especially as he was frequently staging these texts with his Chamberlain's/King's Men colleagues. The fact that a printed text is 'clean' actually cannot prove that it was printed from a scribal rather than authorial manuscript or that it lacks revision. Sir Henry Herbert was asked by the King's Men to relicence a manuscript of *The Winter's Tale* in 1623 because the 'allowed' book licenced by his predecessor had been lost.[32] But how long it had been lost is not clear, and it could have been recopied some years earlier than 1623. During this recopying it could have been updated, altered, cut, added to, or changed in a variety of ways, particularly in regards to suiting current theatre personnel, performance venue, topical issues, or audience taste. If a company acquired or commissioned plays that could be performed in sequence with existing plays, such as chronicle histories, the old or new plays could be adapted or revised to fit the plays together into a coherent sequence, and such revision would have been done by as accomplished and experienced a dramatist as possible. When quarto and First Folio plays show signs of non-authorial revision by printers and theatre company personnel, such as scribes, to suit different performance or printing conditions, including the expurgation of oaths after 1606, these revisions tend to be slight and seamless. On the other hand, adaptors tended to overhaul an existing play into their own creation. Scribes were much more conservative when copying an author's foul papers or fair copies, or another scribe's fair copy, usually confining themselves to regularizing performance features of the text, as King's Men scribe Ralph Crane did, for example.[33] This is surely something that Hamlet understood.

Although Hamlet appears to have had a strong opinion about non-authorial revision, his author had a stronger one that, not ironically, superseded Hamlet's. Shakespeare revised Hamlet's offer to revise *The Murder of Gonzago* by inserting a revision into Hamlet's offer of revision. To be specific, in the second Quarto of the play, printed from Shakespeare's foul papers, Hamlet asks the players, 'You could for neede study a speech of some dosen lines, or sixteen lines, which I would set downe and insert in't, could you not?' In the First Folio text, printed from a theatrical manuscript showing Shakespeare's later revisions throughout, Hamlet asks, 'You could for a need study a speech of some dosen or sixteen lines, which I would set downe, and insert in't? Could ye not?' The first Quarto, printed from a reconstructed text that had been heavily cut for provincial playing, mostly follows the Folio text here: 'And could'st not thou for a neede study me | Some dozen or sixteene lines, | Which I would set downe and insert'.[34] The substantive and accidental variants in the second Quarto and

---

[32] See Joseph Quincy Adams (ed.), *The Dramatic Records of Sir Henry Herbert, Master of the Revels, 1623-1673* (New Haven, CT: Yale University Press, 1917), 25; N. W. Bawcutt (ed.), *The Control and Censorship of Caroline Drama, The Records of Sir Henry Herbert, Master of the Revels: 1623-73* (Oxford: Clarendon Press, 1996), 142.

[33] On Ralph Crane's career, see T. H. Howard-Hill, 'Ralph Crane, Shakespeare's Earliest Editor', *Shakespeare Survey* 44 (1992), 113–29, and 'Crane's 1619 "Promptbook" of *Barnavelt* and Theatrical Processes', *Modern Philology* 86 (1988), 146–70.

[34] *The Tragicall Historie of Hamlet* (London: 1604), sig. F4v; *Mr William Shakespeares Comedies, Histories, & Tragedies*, sig. Oo4v; *The Tragicall Historie of Hamlet* (London: 1603), sig. E4v.

First Folio versions of these lines about inserting lines suggests that Shakespeare, the author, felt free to revise Hamlet the character's revision. But Shakespeare lets stand in the three texts, without any substantive variants, Hamlet's complaints about the clowns speaking more than is set down for them. Even in the act of revising *Hamlet*, Shakespeare obviously had not changed his mind about objecting to non-authorial revisions but ultimately proved that authors and not the roles they create, or the actors who play them, have the final, or perhaps not so final, say on what is 'set down' and firmly established in a playtext.

CHAPTER 6

···

DRAMATIC METRE

···

MATTEO A. PANGALLO

[Q]ue quien con arte agora las escribe muere sin fama...
[He that writes according to the rules dies without fame...]
—Lope de Vega, *El Nuevo Arte de hacer Comedias* (1609)[1]

HAMLET'S advice to the players famously admonishes them to temper their performances to the demands of decorum and verisimilitude; component to that truthfulness is the quality of 'trippingly' pronouncing their speeches. The overall aim, he reminds them, must be 'smoothness' (3.2.1–8). These kinesthetic terms—'trippingly' and 'smoothness'—are conventional characterizations of metred language throughout the period. More particular, however, is Hamlet's earlier, explicit reference to metre. Upon learning that the players are approaching, Hamlet enumerates how he will satisfy each of the stock characters. He concludes that 'the Lady shall say her mind freely, or the blank verse shall halt for't' (2.2.325–6). Hamlet draws a direct connection between free speech—that is, emotionally truthful speech—and the 'smoothness' of blank verse. In other words, the smoothest blank verse is the least theatrical, the most natural (acoustically and emotionally), and therefore the most invisible; writing effective stage poetry, as one early critic puts it, is the 'art of veiling art'.[2]

While critics often point out that Hamlet's theatrical tastes run closer to Jonson than Shakespeare, the observation he makes here accords well with Shakespeare's own tendencies as a dramatic poet. Throughout his career, Shakespeare constantly worked toward developing metred language that would best capture the aural effects of natural, spoken English. As he experimented, borrowed, and revised, Shakespeare continuously revisited the sound of his characters' speeches, flexing their metred language as far as possible in pursuit of the most honest rhythms achievable. Taking

---

[1] Trans. J. W. H. Atkins, *English Literary Criticism: The Renascence* (London: Methuen and Company, 1955), 239.

[2] M. A. Bayfield, *A Study of Shakespeare's Versification* (Cambridge: Cambridge University Press, 1920), 48–9.

the iambic pentameter line as his starting point, Shakespeare found that adding or omitting syllables, inverting or reordering stresses, splitting lines between characters, and alternating between verse and prose could achieve specific dramaturgical effects, including the establishment of mood, thematic conceit, characterization, and, most crucially, a sense of naturalness to the sound of actors' speeches. As his abilities as an actor and dramatist developed—along with his awareness of the abilities of his fellow company members and the desires of his audiences—Shakespeare's use of these variants increased and his verse gradually ceded its metrical regularity to syntactical fluency. Through 'trippingly' metred language, the phrase came to dominate the flow of Shakespeare's dramatic poetry, replacing the iambic pulse and the pentameter length as the driving engine of verse speeches.

Recent criticism of Shakespeare's dramatic verse has highlighted the extent to which he experimented with the pliability of metre over the course of his career. The substantial body of work produced by poet, critic, and scholar George T. Wright, culminating with his essential book *Shakespeare's Metrical Art*, establishes quite clearly the degree to which Shakespeare aimed

> always at variety, grace, energy, elevation, verisimilitude (the speechlikeness of the line generally), and dramatic expressiveness [by] deploy[ing] strategically his different kinds of lines, his metrical variations, and his two orders of meter and phrase. The verse that results never loses its connections with the rhythms of spoken English. It is formed, determined, by its constant obligation to maintain a creative equilibrium between two poles of linguistic force: the continually recurring metrical pattern and the rhythmic phrase.[3]

Wright analyses the sounds of Shakespeare's verse and how it shifts from an early model of (mostly) metrical conformity to a more experimental model of metrical freedom. In the process, he identifies the slight changes Shakespeare makes to his verse—his short and long lines, his use of trochees, his purposeful syllabic ambiguity, and his shifting of the caesura. Analysis of these variants shows how, both within plays and between them, the 'text changes metrical modes (or shifts to prose) as a landscape changes, not whimsically but *in response to pressures*'.[4] The successful verse dramatist commands metre; instead of simply picking phrases to fit the metre, the metre is bent to fit the phrases. Rather than simply following the prescribed traditions, the successful verse dramatist liberates the text from them when a particular effect is needed; patterns are used for the purpose of *breaking* them when needed. It is this quality of plasticity and dynamism that makes Shakespeare's line so lifelike: 'the verse reflects this playwright's alert observation of how people speak—and change their speech as circumstances, occasions, and settings keep changing'.[5] In a similar vein, Russ McDonald has studied Shakespeare's prosodic artistry on a verbal level, demonstrating, for example,

---

[3] George T. Wright, *Shakespeare's Metrical Art* (Berkeley: University of California Press, 1988), 281.

[4] George T. Wright, 'Troubles of a Professional Meter Reader', *Shakespeare Reread: The Texts in New Contexts*, (Ithaca, NY: Cornell University Press, 1994), 56–76, at 75, emphasis added.

[5] Wright, *Shakespeare Reread*, 59.

that his increasingly sophisticated and varied line reflects specific thematic, as well as dramaturgical, needs in the plays.[6]

Underpinning the aesthetic criticism of literary scholars such as McDonald and Wright lies a body of careful statistical analysis from linguists such as Marina Tarlinskaja. In her important study *Shakespeare's Verse: Iambic Pentameter and the Poet's Idiosyncrasies*, Tarlinskaja subjects the plays in Shakespeare's canon—in tandem with works by other poets, for purposes of comparison—to a series of metrical tests designed to identify patterns in key aspects of the verse.[7] Her quantification of stress patterns in Shakespeare's line over time accords with the long-recognized growth of his metrical freedom; perhaps more groundbreaking is her demonstration of the ways in which rhythms in particular plays are often tied to structural forms, grammatical features, and even characters, their types, and their emotional transitions.

For obvious reasons, a vast body of material relating Shakespeare's metre to performance has poured forth from modern theatrical practitioners and scholars. Some have historicized the issue of metrical efficacy, using qualities in the poetry to attempt a better comprehension of how early modern plays *sounded* on their original stages, what techniques their performers may have employed, and what their audiences may have craved.[8] Others have argued for importing this historical evidence into modern performances; many theatre scholars and practitioners have cultivated from Shakespeare's purposeful metre methodologies by which performers might deliver the words of the play with fluency, understanding, and life.[9] Despite the marked morphologic and phonemic change English has undergone, many of Shakespeare's metrical devices still function as they were designed to function 400 years ago—a testament to the versatility, vitality, and dramaturgically *affective* nature of Shakespeare's dramatic verse.

[6] Russ McDonald, *Shakespeare and the Arts of Language* (Oxford: Oxford University Press, 2001), 89; see also 95–6. See also Wright (1988), 257–63.

[7] Marina Tarlinskaja, *Shakespeare's Verse: Iambic Pentameter and the Poet's Idiosyncrasies* (New York: Peter Lang, 1987).

[8] See, for example: J. L. Styan's *Shakespeare's Stagecraft* (Cambridge: Cambridge University Press, 1967), esp. 141–92; Richard Flatter's *Shakespeare's Producing Hand* (New York: Norton, 1948); and Bertram Joseph's *Acting Shakespeare* (New York: Theatre Arts Books, 1960), 20–81.

[9] See, Thomas Turgeon, *Improvising Shakespeare: Reading for the Stage* (New York: McGraw-Hill, 1997), 132–54; Patsy Rodenburg, *Speaking Shakespeare* (New York: Palgrave Macmillan, 2002), 84–107; Edward S. Brubaker, *Shakespeare Aloud* (Lancaster: E. S. Brubaker, 1976); Delbert Spain, *Shakespeare Sounded Soundly* (Santa Barbara, CA: Garland-Clarke, 1988); Robert Cohen, *Acting in Shakespeare*, 2nd edn. (Hanover, NH: Smith and Kraus, 1991), esp. 168–201; Peter Hall, *Shakespeare's Advice to the Players* (New York: Theatre Communications Group, 2003), 15–46; and John Barton's highly influential *Playing Shakespeare* (New York: Random House, 1984), 3–55.

BLANK VERSE ON THE EARLY
MODERN STAGE

Unrhymed iambic pentameter made its premiere on the English stage in parts of Sackville and Norton's 1562 *Gorboduc*.[10] Over the following two decades the form came to dominate English stage poetry because of its suitability to English speaking patterns and expressive effects, culminating in 1587 with the Inns of Court tragedy *The Misfortunes of Arthur*, the first English play entirely in iambic pentameter. The powerful iambic pulse coupled with the malleable decasyllable made blank verse irresistible to stage poets seeking a medium capable of delivering to a crowded inn-yard, hall, or amphitheatre, a wide range of emotions—from the subtle to the roaring. Nonetheless, most early verse dramatists conformed their phrases to their lines; little effort was made to break free from the steady, weak–strong beat that arose as a result of matching end-stopped phrases and sentences to the regular decasyllabic line. English poets—particularly stage poets—had to confront the hard fact that many phrases in English do not fit the ideal form of ten syllables; thus the caesural pause was used to break the line in an increasing range of places, allowing for phrases of almost any length *within* the pentameter frame.[11] Furthermore, because iambic pentameter cannot be divided into two exactly symmetrical rhythmic units, the caesural pause in blank verse is always displaced from the middle of the line—producing a sound similar to the naturally asymmetric rhythm of spoken English.[12]

In the hands of many early dramatists—Marlowe and Kyd especially—this blank verse line was put to evocative, though often radically histrionic, use.[13] Marlowe in particular heightened the emotional pitch of his characters through the hammering force of ornate and polysyllabic words melded forcefully onto the iambic pulse of his blank verse.[14] Some of his contemporaries, especially those writers who prided themselves on their university education, decried this style of poetry as abuse, not use, of blank verse. Though he does not mention him by name, Nashe presumably refers to Marlowe when he decries late-sixteenth-century dramatists as

---

[10] The form first appeared in English, however, in the Earl of Surrey's translation of parts of Books II and IV of Virgil's *Aeneid*, published in 1556 as part of the highly popular *Tottel's Miscellany*.

[11] Ants Oras, *Pause Patterns in Elizabethan and Jacobean Drama* (Gainesville: University of Florida Press, 1960).

[12] Wright, *Shakespeare's Metrical Art*, 4–5.

[13] On the deliberate poetic self-display of the early Elizabethan dramatists, see John Baxter's *Shakespeare Poetic Styles: Verse into Drama* (London: Routledge & Kegan Paul, 1980), 168–95.

[14] The resulting speeches lend themselves to the bombastic style of performance for which Marlowe's plays became famous; as Tarlinskaja observes, the Marlovian line 'probably required a particular style of declamation and a specific intonation' (p. 181). See Wright, *Shakespeare's Metrical Art*, 95–9.

idiote art-masters, that intrude the[m]selves to our eares as the alcumists of eloquence; who . . . think to outbrave better pens with the swelling bumbast of a bragging blanke verse [and] spacious volubilitie of a drumming decasillabon.[15]

Though disdainful, Nashe's comments highlight the intense aural force of Marlowe's 'mighty line' (as Jonson termed it). Joseph Hall echoed this critique when he correlated Marlowe's verse style with the capacity of metred language to, in effect, hypnotize an audience (another frequent trope in contemporary references to metred language in performance):

> There if he can with termes Italianate,
> Big-sounding sentences, and words of state,
> Faire patch me up his pure *Iambick* verse,
> He ravishes the gazing Scaffolders . . .[16]

Hall's scorn is not reserved for Marlowe alone; his impressions of dramatic poetry are generally not favourable. He critiques it for being a paid—and hence mercenary—art, but also for the 'easy' nature of writing blank verse, the old-fashioned nature of writing in rhyme, and the often awkward, foreign-sounding phrases selected to fit the constraints of the strict iambic metre:

> Too popular is *Tragicke Poesie*,
> Strayning his tip-toes for a farthing fee,
> And doth besides on *Rimelesse* numbers tread,
> Unbid *Iambicks* flow from careless head.
> Some braver braine in high *Heroick* rimes
> Compileth worm eate[n] stories of olde tymes . . .
> . . .
> Then straines he to bumbast his feeble lines
> With farre-fetcht phrase . . .[17]

Robert Greene defended his own preference for prose by mocking Marlowe's verse for its simplicity ('English blanck verse . . . is the humor of a novice') and literal bad taste:

> [His] verses jet upon the stage in tragicall buskins, everie worde filling the mouth like the faburden [faux-bourbon] of Bo-Bell . . .[18]

Notwithstanding the rebukes of classicists and moralists, the 'unbid iambicks' of the 1570–80s enjoyed great popularity with audiences. Even some of Shakespeare's early plays—particularly *Titus Andronicus* and the first history tetralogy—reproduce the sounds of Marlovian and Kydian verse; clearly the apprentice dramatist carefully

---

[15] Thomas Nashe, 'To the Gentlemen Students of both Universities.' *Menaphon* by Robert Greene (London: 1589), sig. **r. This is likely the earliest reference to unrhymed iambic pentameter as 'blank verse'.

[16] Joseph Hall, *Virgidemiarum* (London: Robert Dexter, 1597), sig. B5.

[17] Joseph Hall, *Virgidemiarum*, sig. B6v.

[18] Robert Greene, *Perimedes the blacke-smith* (London: 1588), sig. A3r.

listened to and mimicked the successes of his contemporaries. Greene, writing to the university-trained dramatists, claimed of the young Shakespeare, '[he] supposes he is as well able to bombast out a blanke verse as the best of you'.[19] This success, and Shakespeare's initial imitations of it, came about, not despite early blank verse's fustian rattle and thump, but because of it, because it was exciting and impassioned, because it was strange and unnatural, and, importantly, because its presentational nature suited the kinds of characters speaking it. In the mouths of stock types, with great emotional pitch but little depth, verse that flatly declares its status as verse sounds fitting and decorous. When the dramatists of the 1590s set to work with their metrical inheritance it was this sense of the importance of *decorum* that still prevailed—though, in the hands of Shakespeare especially, what kind of verse they considered decorous changed radically. For Shakespeare's increasingly complex, multifaceted, and internally contradictory characters, a different kind of metrical tune was required: one that took advantage of the regular iambic beat and the standard five-foot length by deploying purposeful variations to those patterns. These variations accumulate and collaborate to create rhythms comparable to English speech, resulting in a representational style; this was the sound required by the truthful, deep, and increasingly realistic characters with which Shakespeare began to people the stage.[20]

In Shakespeare's prosody, theatrical effect stems from deviations from the norm because it is those deviations that give the characterization its depth, the action its direction, and, almost always, the poetry its meaning.[21] Metrical variations invest energy into the dramatic moment by defying audiences' aural expectations and taking speeches' rhythms in unanticipated, but naturally plausible, directions. Shakespeare was increasingly aware of this dramatic potential in variant metre: the range and rate of its use expanded exponentially as his career progressed. As F. E. Halliday puts it, 'Shakespeare gradually at first, then more and more rapidly, . . . modified the restrictive metrical conventions [and] transformed the plainsong, the monophonic verse of Marlowe into a new polyphonic or contrapuntal poetry of interwoven rhythms.'[22]

In order to make his dramatic verse resemble spoken English, Shakespeare exploited the flexibility of iambic pentameter through numerous metrical, or, as McDonald calls them, 'acoustic' variations.[23] Though it is often difficult to determine whether a variation was intended by the dramatist or merely a flaw in an early text, many

---

[19] Robert Greene, *Greenes' groats-worth of witte* (London: 1592), sig. F1v.

[20] Russ McDonald, Stanley Wells and Lena Cowen Orlin (eds.), 'Shakespeare's verse', in *Shakespeare: An Oxford Guide* (Oxford: Oxford University Press, 2003), 79–92. See also Wright, *Shakespeare's Metrical Art*, 90.

[21] Mark Womack, 'Shakespearean Prosody Unbound', *Texas Studies in Language and Literature* 45.1 (2003), 1–19, refers to Shakespeare's verse as offering 'all the comforts of regularity with all the energy of irregularity' (p. 12), an interpretation that links the 'smooth and tame' rhythm of iambic pentameter with audience appeasement and the disruption of that rhythm with the kinetic, often conflicting, power that makes drama dramatic.

[22] Womack, 'Shakespearean Prosody', 27.

[23] 'Shakespeare's Verse', 83.

frequently used metrical techniques stand out for the meaningful ways in which they enrich, enhance, and even create character, emotion, action, or tone. While we must be careful not to ascribe a one-to-one correlation between a specific type of variation and a specific quality of meaning, these variations produce sufficient complications to the standard blank verse line to stand out as clear markers of the threads Shakespeare wove together to fashion the fabric of his plays.[24]

Dramatists were aware of the ways performed metre could create certain effects on stage. Nabbes, for example, writes of his 1639 *The Unfortunate Mother*, 'Here is no sence that must by thee be scann'd, | Before thou canst the meaning understand.'[25] The play is written in irregular blank verse and uses many of the same variants Shakespeare and others used; the crucial difference, however, is that it was never acted (though Nabbes may have intended it for performance). In other words, 'scan[ning]' metred language for 'sence' is an attribute of a play *in* performance. Metrical variants, for Nabbes, convey their meanings aurally.

Though Shakespeare uses many different types of variants to create specific aural meanings, those explored here represent some of the most common and efficacious aspects of what Patrick Cheney terms Shakespeare's 'poetical dramaturgy'.[26]

SHORT LINES

Lines short of the ten syllables typical of iambic pentameter leave an audible gap in the flow of a speech, offering a potential opening for a physical gesture, a loaded pause, or some other non-verbal performative action. The particular functions of such a brief metrical gap vary depending on the context in which it appears, though it frequently

---

[24] Metrical variations in dramatic verse undeniably affect the performance of the text, but they only carry meaning in their relationship to the context within which they occur. Divorced from their place in a speech, a scene, a role, a play, or even a dramatist's career, variants cannot be said to carry transcendent meanings. One specific variant, for example, the substitution of a trochaic foot for an iamb, can result in two very different effects and two different semantic loads in two different contexts. On this subject, see Wright 'Troubles', 72; Tarlinskaja, 'Shakespeare's Verse', 232–3, and especially 287–329; also Womack *passim*, Ellen Spolsky, 'The Limits of Literal Meaning', *New Literary History* 19 (1988), 419–40. Womack attempts to refute 'the persistent belief that metre's primary function is, or ought to be, a mimetic one' (p. 2) and argues that 'metre need not reinforce meaning to have value' (p. 3). But this does not adequately address the ability of metre—particularly metre in performance—to become meaning, not in a semantic sense, but in a dramatic sense. Womack refers to Shakespeare's mimetic metre as a 'literary achievement' and claims that '[p]rosody unbound to meaning increases the complexity of a literary experience' (p. 7). The suggestion that associating meanings with metrical devices merely makes metre 'a redundant expression of content' (p. 9) neglects the fact that much of the dramaturgical content in Shakespeare's plays can *only* be inferred through performative interpretations of the language and prosody. The nature of dramatized poetry compels rhythmic figures to carry content meaning beyond mere euphony.

[25] Thomas Nabbes, *The Unfortunate Mother* (London: 1639), sig. A3r.

[26] Patrick Cheney, 'Poetry in Shakespeare's Plays', in Cheney (ed.), *The Cambridge Companion to Shakespeare's Poetry* (Cambridge: Cambridge University Press, 2007), 221–40, at 228–9.

emphasizes by contrast the words immediately surrounding it.[27] It might add an ominous weight to a tense moment, as when Gloucester—misled by Edmund—sentences any person helping Edgar evade justice:

> That he which finds him shall deserve our thanks,   [10 syllables]
> Bringing the murderous coward to the stake;   [10 syllables]
> He that conceals him, death.   [6 syllables]
>
> *(King Lear* 2.1.60–2)

Truncation can also produce a comedic effect. For example, after thirty-three exhaustingly tangential lines, the Nurse in *Romeo and Juliet* takes an unexpected pause:

> 'Shake', quoth the dove-house! 'Twas no need, I trow,   [10 syllables]
> To bid me trudge;   [4 syllables]
>
> *(Romeo and Juliet* 1.3.35–6)

The silence following 'trudge' prompts the audience, and Lady Capulet, to assume the garrulous old woman has finished her reminiscence: she has not. The narrative resumes in the next line and continues for fourteen more, the short line offering a brief (and humorous) metrical respite.

Shakespeare also increasingly used monosyllabic feet for deliberate effect; this line-shortening device omits half a foot by packing one powerful, monosyllabic word into a whole measure. It often lends itself to emphatic lists, sudden interjections, or, as in this example from *Coriolanus*, aggressive repetitions (feet divisions are marked by /):

> Kill, / kill, / kill, / kill, / kill him!
> *(Coriolanus* 5.6.130)[28]

As the examples from *Lear* and *Romeo and Juliet* show, a speech's generic context can change the ramifications for a short line. The position of the gap within the line also influences meanings for the pause. For example, a missing beat at the start—a 'headless line'—can suggest a loss for words followed by a burst of speech; this might be caused by any number of factors, such as anger, fear, or, as in this example from Mercutio, impatience (the gap is indicated by ˆ):

---

[27] George Wright, 'An Almost Oral Act: Shakespeare's Language on Stage and Page', *Shakespeare Quarterly* 43.2 (1992), 159–69, suggests, also, that short lines are used simply for 'practical business' because they sound 'perfunctory and barren of...authenticity' (p. 163). Often catalectic lines adjoin stage actions, such as entrances and exits, suggesting that the physical business is a sort of kinesthetic verse line shared with the short verbal verse line.

[28] Wright, *Shakespeare's Metrical Art*, 179, scans the ultimate foot of this line as the final 'kill' (a monosyllabic foot), followed by 'him' as a double-ending (on which, see below); here the line is scanned with the final foot 'kill him' as a resolving spondee, which would seem to better sustain the angry energy of the speech. The speech prefix for this line ('*All Consp*[*irators*]'), however, complicates any effort to scan the line for performance.

> ˆWhere the dev'l should this Romeo be?
> (*Romeo and Juliet* 2.3.1)[29]

Similarly, a mid-line gap generates a flicker of hesitation, allowing the speaker to ramp up into the second half of the line. Wright terms these 'broken-backed lines' and observes that they often relate to 'shifts from one kind of syntax to another.'[30] He gives, as an example, the loaded gap that separates York's suspicious rhetorical question from his demand for proof:

> Yea, look'st thou pale? ˆLet me see the writing.
> (*Richard II* 5.2.57)

The imperative phrase pointed up by the pause becomes an aggressive thrust for York, who repeats his demand to 'see the writing' three more times in the next eleven lines.

Frequently one character's short line will be metrically completed by the following speaker. This conversational sharing of one verse line between two or more speakers generates speed and intensity, but also offers an added layer of meaning and (potentially) conflict. In these exchanges, Shakespeare often uses the dynamic nature of the metre to imply an intrinsic relationship between the speakers. For example, the combination of a plea tied metrically to an interrupting rebuke, which is then tied to another plea, in the following passage deftly characterizes the speakers: the Steward speaks with selfless, passionate honesty; Timon blinds himself to his precarious position and the lifestyle that has brought it about.

> TIMON: You make me marvel wherefore ere this time
> Had you not fully laid my state before me,
> That I might so have rated my expense
> As I had leave of means.
> STEWARD: You would not hear me.
>   At many leisures I proposed—
> TIMON: Go to.
> Perchance some single vantages you took,
> When my indisposition put you back,
> And that unaptness made your minister
> Thus to excuse yourself.
> STEWARD: O my good lord,
> (*Timon of Athens* 2.2.121–9)

Shakespeare's use of shared lines to link adjacent speeches with a powerful kinetic energy increased over his career (see below). It also set him apart from his predecessors: 'the long individual speeches that defined and dominated Marlowe's theatre have given

---

[29] This line, and the one following, are given as verse in the First Quarto and by many modern editors; they are given as prose in the later quartos and Folio, as well as in the Oxford *Complete Works*, which sets 'dev'l' as 'devil'.

[30] *Shakespeare's Mertical Art*, 176.

way to duets, trios, or even larger ensembles'.[31] The shared line became, through Shakespeare's dramaturgy, a means of increasing the dialogic quality of what was heard on the early modern stage:

> [D]rama presents human beings bound to each other by speech, not merely declaiming but defining themselves through words they speak to and receive from one another. Speech breeds speech, requires it, goads it, desires it—in life as in drama—and the shared line only realizes more intently that condition of being bound together in a common action that the play as a whole affirms.[32]

By combining shared lines with the meaningful pause of the broken-backed line, Shakespeare could create a condensed but evocative rhythmic connection between characters. This dual variant is particularly well suited to dramatic irony, that is, when one character spontaneously decides to withhold important information from another:

> VIOLA: My father had a daughter loved a man
>   As it might be, perhaps, were I a woman
>   I should your lordship.
> ORSINO: ˆAnd what's her history?
>   (*Twelfth Night* 2.4.107–9)

The dramatic flow of this exchange will shift depending on which character 'takes' the mid-line pause: if the hesitation is Viola's it might derive from the sudden realization that she has possibly revealed too much; if it is Orsino's, it might be symptomatic of a sudden suspicion at what she has just said (or, alternatively, he may remain completely oblivious and the pause arises simply from his waiting to see if she will continue speaking). In *Othello*—a play that Wright notes is 'rich' with short shared lines[33]—the tension of the hesitation before Iago responds to Othello's question about Cassio marks almost the very start of the protagonist's tragic downfall:

> OTHELLO: Is he not honest? ˆ
> IAGO: Honest, my lord?
>   (*Othello* 3.3.105–6)[34]

As in the example from *Twelfth Night*, the missing beat falls upon an important accent (the central ictus of the line), effectively punctuating Iago's momentary pause as he perhaps searches for precisely the right word without tipping his hand.

This metrical flexibility echoes spoken English, but it has the added benefit of contributing a rich ambiguity to the reading, allowing actors to make various choices that, while upheld by the verse, can greatly change the nuanced meanings of the

---

[31] George T. Wright, 'Shakespeare's Metre Scanned', in *Reading Shakespeare's Dramatic Language: A Guide*, Sylvia Adamson et al. (eds.), (London: Thomson Learning, 2001), 51–70, at 59.

[32] Wright (1988), 138–9.

[33] *Shakespeare's Metrical Art*, 181.

[34] The Oxford *Complete Works* sets these lines as prose, though other parts of Iago and Othello's exchange at this point in the scene are given as shared verse lines.

exchange. This metrically-orchestrated freedom lends a feeling of truthfulness to the spoken exchange. Another technique that produces this effect is the use of what Wright calls 'squinting lines'[35]—three or more short lines apportioned between two or more speakers which can be combined in two or more ways. This results in a quick exchange tied together with an 'earned' pause, a meaningful beat that draws attention to a sudden or important point of dramatic tension, transition, or emotion. For example, in *The Tempest*, Sebastian thrusts Alonso with a litany blaming the King for the shipwreck and Ferdinand's death. At the conclusion of the speech, his final short line is followed by two short lines, one from Alonso and one from Gonzalo, creating a set of squinting lines:

> SEBASTIAN: The fault's your own.
> ALONSO: So is the dear'st o'th' loss.
> GONZALO: My lord Sebastian,
>   The truth you speak doth lack some gentleness
>   (*The Tempest* 2.1.140–2)[36]

Alonso's line seems to bite into Sebastian's with its spondaic first foot, as if the King is lashing out at his tormentor; Gonzalo's ensuing short line thus suggests a pause either after Alonso's line (perhaps the old adviser waits to ensure that the King has stopped speaking) or between his own lines (perhaps escorting Sebastian out of the King's earshot). But the squinting lines also offer the opposite reading: if Sebastian's line is short and there is a pause between his speech and Alonso's, the momentum of the litany is broken by suspenseful silence as the audience (and the other characters) wait to see how the King will respond. When that response comes off aggressively, Gonzalo rapidly intervenes, cutting off a potential fight among the castaways.

These performative choices are speculative; however, the metrical variation of adjoining short lines recurs so frequently that it is undeniably a deliberate instrument in Shakespeare's orchestration. Occasionally the number of squinting lines exceeds three, affording performers even more options for imbuing their verse with realistic rhythms:

> PORTIA: But in the cutting it, if thou dost shed
>   One drop of Christian blood, thy lands and goods
>   Are by the laws of Venice confiscate
>   Unto the state of Venice.
> GRAZIANO: O upright judge!
>   Mark, Jew! O learned judge.
> SHYLOCK: Is that the law?
> PORTIA: Thyself shalt see the act;
>   (*The Merchant of Venice* 4.1.306–12)

---

[35] *Shakespeare's Metrical Art*, 103.

[36] The Oxford *Complete Works* eliminates the possibilities of the 'squinting lines' here: Sebastian's line is adjoined to the end of his preceding short line ('Than we bring men to comfort them.') making an hexameter; Alonso's is joined to Gonzalo's as a long shared line.

Editors typically join Portia and Graziano's speeches and Shylock and Portia's, leaving Graziano's final line two feet short; a heavily loaded pause results, prompting all eyes to turn expectantly to Shylock.[37] This lineation is plausible, but it is only one possibility of several. Shakespeare's short and shared lines are sufficiently malleable to meet multiple interpretive needs and still sound truthful to the patterns of spoken English.

LONG LINES

Just as lines often fall short of the ideal pentameter length, some break the boundaries and run long; just like short lines, these long lines can be associated with various performable qualities, such as tempo, emotion, action, and characterization. Such hypermetrical lines are often found when characters feel an unbearable compulsion to express themselves vigorously:

> QUEEN: O, I am pressed to death through want of speaking!
> Thou, old Adam's likeness, set to dress this garden,
> How dares thy harsh rude tongue sound this unpleasing news?
> (*Richard II* 3.4.73–5)

The second and third lines pack in an assertive twelve syllables each: the second adds an extra stressed syllable at the start and ends with an extra unstressed syllable; the third is an alexandrine—a variant often used for lines carrying too much matter for pentameter to bear.

The double-ending effect caused by the extra unstressed syllable in the Queen's first and second lines was a prevalent variant in Shakespeare's mid-career and late plays. The results of this double-ending vary depending upon context: they may lend the speech a sense of uncertainty, incompleteness, gentleness, or even distraction. The early modern prosodist George Puttenham felt that the extra weak syllable tagged on after a strong penultimate syllable causes a kind of falling into emptiness: 'the sharpe accent . . . doth so drowne the last, as he seemeth to passe away in maner unpronounced.'[38] Wright points out that, when they appear in clusters, such endings make the verse sound 'more speechlike, *less* patterned, exactly because, as in phrases of ordinary speech, rhyme is absent and the final unstressed syllables fail to match.'[39] In *The Winter's Tale*, Leontes slips in and out of double-ending lines (among other variants) as he bounces between tormented fantasies of his wife's imagined infidelity and struggling rationalizations of his son's paternity (extra unstressed syllables are underlined):

---

[37] The Oxford *Complete Works* sets Portia's and Graziano's as a shared line but leaves Graziano's second line, Shylock's, and Portia's following line all short and unshared.

[38] Quoted in Wright *Shakespeare's Metrical Art*, 161.

[39] *Shakespeare's Metrical Art*, 162.

> Thou want'st a rough pash and the shoots that I have,
> To be full like me. Yet they say we are
> Almost as like as eggs. Women say so,
> That will say any thing. But were they false
> As o'er-dy'd blacks, as wind, as waters, false
> As dice are to be wished, by one that fixes
> No bourne 'twixt his and mine, yet were it true
> To say this boy were like me. Come, sir page,
> Look on me with your welkin eye. Sweet villain,
> Most dear'st, my collop! Can thy dam—may't be?—
> Affection, thy intention stabs the centre.
>   (*The Winter's Tale* 1.2.130–40)

Metrically scattered speech is only one manifestation of the King's mental unrest, but such variants serve as outward representations of his condition just as gestures or facial expressions might. Symptoms of his jealousy appear, not just in what he says, but in how he says it.

A lingering quality can be heard, also, in the occasional triple-ending line. In English, many words and phrases resolve with two weak accents on the penultimate and ultimate syllables; Shakespeare sometimes places these at the end of a line, sustaining sound past the pentameter border. The purposes for this are as varied as those of the double-ending, though the overflowing line inexorably, subtly draws attention to the word in question. For example, Ursula's teasing of the hidden Beatrice concludes by dallying on an important triple-ending word:

> She cannot be so much without true judgement,
> Having so swift and excellent a wit
> As she is prized to have, as to refuse
> So rare a gentleman as Signor Benedick.
>   (*Much Ado About Nothing* 3.1.88–91)

Referring to Benedick only by his name—as she does earlier (line 3.1.37)—would supply Ursula with a line of perfect iambic pentameter; instead, she uses the added 'Signor' to displace Benedick's triple-ending name to the conclusion of the line, tauntingly pointing it up as bait for Beatrice.

Shakespeare also frequently lengthens lines by using an epic caesura—an added unstressed syllable immediately before the caesura. As with the double-ending, the frequency with which Shakespeare used the epic caesura increased into the middle of his career, no doubt because he found the device hospitable to the copious enjambment that dominated the middle plays. The extra weak syllable followed by the mid-line break almost always compels a pause that 'ruffles the current' of the line, adding emotional weight or tension[40] (the caesura is marked by |):

---

40 Wright, *Shakespeare's Metrical Art*, 166.

What's the boy Malcolm?
Was he not born of wom<u>an</u>? | The spirits that know
(*Macbeth* 5.3.3–4)

The epic caesura adds a note of irony by inflecting an uncomfortable (that is, metrically unresolved) beat after Macbeth asks the question that will finally prove fatal.

Varying line length can impose an affective quality beyond merely regulating tempo and pauses. For example, juxtaposing a long line against a short line can convey the different emotional states of speakers, and suggest the conflict generated by those states:

GERTRUDE: This bodiless creation ecstasy is very cunning in.
HAMLET: Ecstasy?
My pulse as yours doth temperately keep time,
(*Hamlet* 3.4.129–31)[41]

Hamlet's abrupt, hyperbolically short repetition of his mother, following her hypermetrical outburst, underscores the friction of the scene and subtly (unknowingly?) belies his assertion that either are 'temperately keep[ing] time'.

END-STOPPING AND ENJAMBMENT

As noted, the epic caesura lends itself to enjambed lineation; thus, as the frequency of epic caesurae increases in Shakespeare's plays, so too do the number of mid-line to mid-line, mid-line to full-line, or full-line to mid-line phrases that are the hallmark of the flowing, enjambed style. The number of enjambed lines as a percentage of total verse grows dramatically, with an early play such as *Love's Labour's Lost* at 5.5 per cent and a late play such as *Winter's Tale* at 47.2 per cent; likewise, the percentage of lines with mid-line stops climbs from early lows of 1.2 per cent in *Comedy of Errors* to highs of 62 per cent in *Tempest*.[42] Comparing two speeches, one from an early comedy and one from his last, evinces the two extremes of heavily end-stopped verse and heavily enjambed verse that marked the spectrum of his career. They also reveal how—contrary to expectations—end-stopped lines can demand speed in delivery, while enjambment might move more slowly. Both speeches make use of rhetorical repetition, but the structures of phrasing and pointing in each are radically different. The first, from *The Comedy of Errors*, builds upon a sequence of nearly precise iambic pentameter lines; nearly every strong punctuation mark (colons, semicolons, and periods) falls at the end of a line and all lines but one

---

[41] This lineation occurs only in the 1623 Folio; both the Second Quarto and Folio set Gertrude's line as one line of verse, but only the Folio provides Hamlet's 'Ecstasy?'. Most editions flatten the exchange into more regular metre, either omitting Hamlet's 'Ecstasy?' or, as in the Oxford *Complete Works*, splitting Gertrude's between 'ecstasy' and 'is' and joining the second half to Hamlet's 'Ecstasy?', for a pentameter followed by a shared short line.

[42] George H. Browne, *Notes on Shakspere's Versification*, 4th edn. (Boston: Ginn and Company, 1901), 25.

are so marked, while every light punctuation mark (here, commas) but for one falls within a line. As is typical in speeches from the early plays, the symmetry of metre and phrase reinforces, rather than contradicts, the polished feel of the narrative, paralleling the play's own balanced structure of plots, characters, and even stage actions. In performance, the speech has an enforced, pulsing, and highly artificial rhythm in which, as Wright observes, each line is clearly audible as a line:[43]

> Returned so soon? Rather approached too late.
> The capon burns, the pig falls from the spit.
> The clock hath strucken twelve upon the bell;
> My mistress made it one upon my cheek.
> She is so hot because the meat is cold.
> The meat is cold because you come not home.
> You come not home because you have no stomach.
> You have no stomach, having broke your fast;
> (*Comedy of Errors* 1.2.43–50)

This end-stopped style does not result in a plodding tempo; rather, the rapid nature of Dromio's speech, particularly the layered anadiplosis of ll. 47–50, provokes Antipholus finally to stop him with the order, 'Stop in your wind, sir.'

Contrasting with this speech, Antonio's carefully paced prelude to treason uses line breaks to slowly dangle the second half of potentially dangerous phrases just out of reach of the dullard Sebastian, drawing his (and the audience's) ears closer:

> She that is Queen of Tunis; she that dwells
> Ten leagues beyond man's life; she that from Naples
> Can have no note—unless the sun were post—
> The man i'th' moon's too slow—till new-born chins
> Be rough and razorable; she that from whom
> We all were sea-swallowed, though some cast again—
> And by that destiny, to perform an act
> Whereof what's past is prologue, what to come
> In yours and my discharge.
> (*The Tempest* 2.1.251–9)

Enjambment helps the syntax flow from line to line, but the pace—controlled by so many monosyllabic words—slows to a conspiratorial crawl as Antonio tests to be sure he has not misjudged his puppet. As with Dromio's speech, Antonio's is marked by mid-line caesurae; his, however, introduce phrases that overrun the line-ends. The dramatist has not abandoned his instruments—he has, in the seventeen years and twenty-nine intervening plays, learned to rearrange their parts for a radically different orchestration.

---

[43] 'Shakespeare's Metre', 61.

Syllabic Density

A further indicator of Shakespeare's evolving metrical style is evident in the increasing precision with which he employs patterns of syllabic density for dramaturgical effect. Syllabic density relates to the placement of words with certain syllabic values and structures at specific places in the pentameter line; this purposeful placement can reinforce the iambic pulse or it can complicate or even contradict it. If the syllabic value of a word challenges the metrical value of its location in the line, the aural effect that results seems contrapuntal. Whether that counterpoint is harmonious or discordant depends, of course, upon the context. Again, examining two similar speeches from different points in Shakespeare's career demonstrates the importance of this metrical technique and how much it changed as Shakespeare gained in experience.

One subject of fascination for Shakespeare throughout his career is how a classical orator could seize control of a restless, unguided mob and manipulate them to his ends through only the power of his words. An example of this may be found in the initial line of Antony's funeral oration:

> Friends, Romans, countrymen, lend me your ears.
> (*Julius Caesar* 3.2.74)

The verbal construction of Antony's line begins with a *tricolon crescens*, steadily building from one syllable ('Friends'), to two ('Romans'), to three ('countrymen'), up to the caesura; it then bursts out with an imperative phrase of four monosyllables. Metrically, these words contradict the iambic pulse, but they do so with an organized and emphatic pattern, lending an aggressive syntactical counterpoint to the metre. This contrasts sharply with the disorganized syllabic counterpoint in a similar line that was a predecessor to (if not outright rough draft for) Antony's:

> Romans, friends, followers, favourers of my right,
> (*Titus Andronicus* 1.1.9)

Phrasally (though neither metrically nor grammatically) Bassianus' line follows a similar structure (three plural nouns in a list followed by a four-word phrase), but it lacks the oratorical force of Antony's crescendo. The disruption of the iambic pulse is not coupled with a deliberate pattern of syllabic density. It is not difficult to speculate, from these aural shows of power alone, which of the two Roman princes will prevail in his respective play. This tendency to organize and complicate the pattern of syllabic units against accentual units, sometimes quite elaborately and sometimes quite subtly, quickly increased over Shakespeare's career.

VARYING THE IAMBIC PULSE

By occasionally substituting non-iambic feet into his verse, Shakespeare added complexity and layers of acoustic meaning to speeches. Inverting the iambic pulse by inserting a trochaic foot is particularly common, especially in the first foot of lines, and serves a number of purposes, from seizing attention, to putting emphasis upon a minor word, to generating tension, conflict, or contrast. The emphatic trochee that opens *Richard III*, for example, seizes the stage in much the same way that the protagonist will eventually seize the throne:

> Now is the winter of our discontent
> Made glorious summer by this son of York;
> (*Richard III* 1.1.1–2)

Completely eliminating the weak beat by using a spondee punctuates the sentiment immediately preceding or following the foot. The spondaic 'Ay, there's' in Hamlet's meditation on suicide is not, in itself, a particularly emphatic phrase, but as an abrupt spondee it serves to show that his inner thoughts have spontaneously stuck upon the phrase immediately before it in the line:

> To sleep, perchance to dream. Ay, there's the rub,
> (*Hamlet* 3.1.67)

The conversion of an iamb to a dactyl speeds the word out of the actor's mouth with great emotional intensity. McDonald notes, for example, that the double dactyls of Lear's challenge to the storm—followed by two spondees of parallel imperatives—results in a 'bombastic inversion [resulting in] a tripping measure that communicates Lear's state of madness':[44]

> Rumble thy bellyful; spit, fire; spout, rain.
> (*King Lear* 3.2.14)

Piling up variant feet, especially trochees and spondees, produces a powerful turbulence, but it also results in speeches that strike the ear as highly spontaneous and thus more realistic. In Macbeth's hastily devised excuse for having killed the grooms guarding Duncan, variant feet are layered so thickly and with such prominence (four lines start with hurried trochees and one with a timid pyrrhus) that the speech seems almost to broadcast the thane's agitated, internalized guilt:

> Who can be wise, amazed, temp'rate, and furious,
> Loyal and neutral, in a moment? No man.
> Th'expedition of my violent love
> Outran the pauser, reason. Here lay Duncan,

---

[44] 'Shakespeare's Verse', 88–9.

His silver skin laced with his golden blood,
And his gashed stabs looked like a breach in nature
For ruin's wasteful entrance; there the murderers,
Steeped in the colours of their trade, their daggers
Unmannerly breeched with gore. Who could refrain,
That had a heart to love, and in that heart
Courage to make 's love known?

> (*Macbeth* 2.3.108–18)[45]

Varied metre, frequent overrunning of the pentameter ejambments, mid-line phrase starts, late caesurae—all of these reinforce Macbeth's sense that, as he claims, his actions, his words, and his thoughts, 'outran the pauser, reason.'

VERSE AND PROSE

All of these variants rely on slight deviations to serve as either symptom or cause of a performable quality. On a more fundamental level, of course, there is an even larger metrical choice that the dramatist must make: whether a speech will be verse or prose. Prose cannot be dismissed as a lesser medium; often early critics attempted to relegate prose to a lower category of writing by assuming it was straightforward, unorchestrated speech. Scholars such as Brian Vickers, Kenneth Hudson, and Jonas Barish have shown that Shakespeare took just as much care with the acoustic aesthetics of his prose as he did with his verse. What matters, dramaturgically, is less whether a passage is verse or prose and more the shift between the two modes, with the corresponding 'change in theatrical mood' that follows.[46] It is the energy of this shift—like the energy produced by other variants—that creates dramaturgical meaning.

Throughout the first two acts, and part of 3.1, of *Measure for Measure*, the Duke uses blank verse, no matter the context or characters with whom he speaks. Even when disguised as a friar, the Duke's methodical, carefully-laid plan is expressed in methodical, carefully-laid metre. This measured speech is abandoned, however, when he overhears Isabella tell Claudio of Angelo's demands. Still disguised, the Duke steps forward and finally uses prose, hastily improvising as he is forced to change his hitherto assiduously scripted plot. After this point, the Duke often slips into prose. The new dialect seems to signal his liberation from the belief that everything must operate (like ideal verse) according to a predesigned plan; as successive disruptions interfere with his plan, the prose-speaking Duke is able to extemporize around them.

Even the speech of minor characters is carefully arranged to take advantage of the meanings communicated by the prose–verse shift. The boatswain in *The Tempest*,

---

[45] For additional metrical analysis of this speech, see Wright, *Shakespeare's Metrical Art*, 232–4.

[46] Styan, *Shakespeare's Stagecraft*, 158; see 158–63 and G. L. Brook's *The Language of Shakespeare* (London: Deutsch, 1976), 160–1, for more on meaningful verse–prose shifts.

for example, follows the rules of decorum at the start of the play, bellowing orders to his sailors in prose and, at first, matching the blank verse addressed to him by the nobles with his own. When his commands are not obeyed, however, he switches back to prose—his language of command—to address his passengers, and it is this style in which he is still speaking when the ship (supposedly) sinks. In the final scene the boatswain reappears, but once more addressing the nobles in verse. The change he has undergone is not one of recalcitrance and disrespect to obedience and deference but one of anger and fear to compassion and wonder, a reversal that manifests itself in the very style in which he speaks. In these examples, and so many others, metrical variants are tactics that contribute dramaturgical meaning to the performance.

TRENDS

Scholars have long observed certain trends in Shakespeare's verse over his career; most associate those trends with his increasing capacities and his command over the tools of the stage poet.[47] Halliday, for example, uses guild imagery to explain the transformation: '[T]he difference between the verse of Shakespeare's *apprenticeship* and of his complete *mastery* is so immense that it is essential.'[48] The dramatist's increasing capacity to bend his metre for dramatic purposes is usually taken as a mark of professionalism and his status as a 'practical man of the theatre'. Undoubtedly, as Shakespeare sought a style more closely resembling the natural rhythms of spoken English, his conformity to metrical norms decreased and his variants increased to as much as once in every five lines.[49] The ideal iambic pentameter line, 'a kind of *figure* for natural speech',[50] dissolved within the sentence—the form of natural speech.[51]

It is true that elements of Shakespeare's metre gradually changed as he sought greater acoustic verisimilitude. But not all trends were a result of this pursuit: certain metrical features changed without respect to the context of the dramatist's career. For example, eighteenth-century critics often assumed that Shakespeare employed fewer and fewer rhymes as he matured; while true in the aggregate, this does not accurately describe a trend (see Figure 6.1).[52] A more compelling cause for the use of rhyme in a

---

[47] For a challenge to the idea that Shakespeare greatly altered his verse, see Dorothy Sipe's *Shakespeare's Metrics* (New Haven, CT: Yale University Press, 1968) and Spain, *Shakespeare Sounded*, 6.

[48] F. E. Halliday, *The Poetry of Shakespeare's Plays* (New York: Barnes and Noble, 1964), 23, emphasis added.

[49] Wright, *Shakespeare's Metrical Art*, 105.

[50] Wright, *Shakespeare's Verse*, 255, emphasis added.

[51] For a comparison of Shakespeare's styles to the stress patterns of spoken English, see Tarlinskaja, 54–5.

[52] See, for example, Russ McDonald, *The Bedford Companion to Shakespeare* (Boston: Bedford Books, 1996), 219–20. On Shakespeare's rhymes see Frederic Ness's *The Use of Rhyme in Shakespeare's Plays* (New Haven, CT: Yale University Press, 1969) and Lorna Flint's *Shakespeare's Third Keyboard: The Significance of Rime in Shakespeare's Plays* (Newark: University of Delaware Press, 2000).

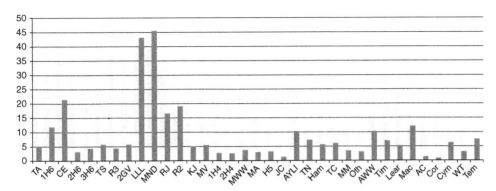

FIGURE 6.1. Percentage of rhymed lines within total line count

play may relate to genre, rather than date: on average, rhymed lines comprise nearly 14 per cent of a Shakespeare comedy, compared to only between 5 and 6 per cent in a history, tragedy, or tragicomedy. But neither genre nor date is entirely reliable as a variable correlating to the use of rhyme; for example, the early history play *Richard II* uses nearly twice as many rhymed lines as a percentage of its total as the late comedy *All's Well That End's Well*. Likewise, the atypical amount of prose in the mid-career comedies *Much Ado About Nothing* and *Merry Wives of Windsor* results in a paucity of rhyme at that point in his career.

Certain features of Shakespeare's verse, however, do change in a way that suggests a relationship with his evolving dramaturgical sensitivity. These trends reveal what Halliday referred to as Shakespeare's shift 'from artifice and diffuseness ... to a dramatic naturalism and concentration'.[53] The chart of double-endings demonstrates that after the middle of his career, Shakespeare often ended lines with a naturalistic added syllable (see Figure 6.2). Further, in the middle of his career, Shakespeare frequently employed prose more often than verse in a given play (see Figure 6.3).[54] Into the late plays, the ratio of prose to verse wanes to the same levels seen in the early plays. One explanation for this may be that Shakespeare's experiments with blank verse and prose eventually merged in his loose, late verse style, a style in which—like prose—the phrase operates relatively free from the constraints of strict iambic pentameter.[55] As Wright puts it, 'in the language he prepared for the stage, probably to make it more like ordinary English speech, the evidence seems overwhelming that Shakespeare increasingly cultivated both metrical and syllabic conventions aimed at making the verbal texture *less obviously iambic*.'[56] His late verse sounded enough like prose that the use of prose was unnecessary; Shakespeare could achieve, or even surpass, the liberated sense of prose through the plasticity of his verse.

[53] Halliday, 27.
[54] Data from McDonald (1996), 219–20, refigured here into percentages.
[55] Kenneth Muir, 'Shakespeare the Professional', *Shakespeare Survey* 24 (1971), 40.
[56] (1988), 150, emphasis added. See also 213.

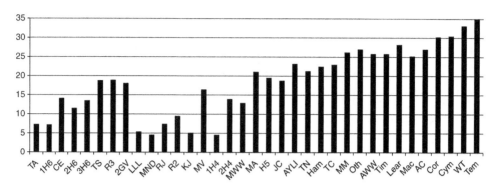

FIGURE 6.2. Percentage of double-ending lines within total line count

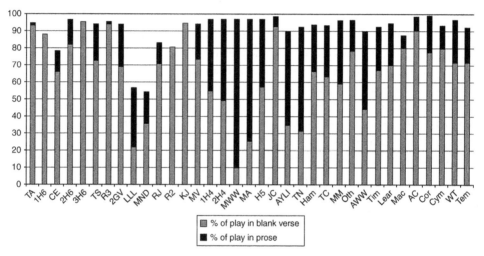

FIGURE 6.3. Prose v. blank verse

A rising and falling trend can be seen, also, in the relative number of blank verse lines that incorporate an epic caesura (see Figure 6.4).[57] The number of epic caesurae per verse line peaks with *Othello*, but then, like the rate of prose in the plays, decreases. As noted, the epic caesura is useful in constructing an enjambed line as it allows for a natural flow of phrase from mid-line to mid-line. Certainly the rate of enjambment steadily increased over the late plays. Why, then, did the number of epic caesurae decline? It is possible that as Shakespeare used enjambment more frequently he became more adept at building the unstopped line without the need for the added weak beat before the mid-line pause. The epic caesura was, in effect, an early aid as the dramatist experimented with enjambment; once he could achieve the effect with sufficient dexterity, it no longer became necessary.

---

[57] Data for this and the following variant charts from Wright, *Shakespeare's Metrical Art*, 292–5, refigured here into percentages.

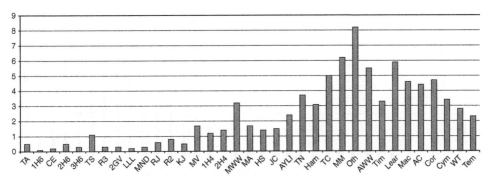

FIGURE 6.4. Percentage of epic caesurae within blank verse

Nearly concurrent with the rise and fall of the line-lengthening epic caesura is the rise and fall of the short line. Interestingly, while the relative number of short lines decreased in the late plays, the rate of shared lines steadily rose to the end of Shakespeare's career (see Figure 6.5).

Many of the peaks in the use of shared lines are, perhaps not surprisingly, plays that centre on one or more romantic couples (for example, *Taming of the Shrew, Midsummer Night's Dream, Much Ado About Nothing, Antony and Cleopatra*). Shakespeare clearly found the device an increasingly reliable tool, not just for pacing, but also—as noted above—for instilling verbal exchanges with dramatic tension and emotional realism.

Counting up the distribution of variants provides a broad view of how Shakespeare's prosodic style evolved (or, in some cases, did not evolve). Analysing specific speeches offers a closer look at some of these broad trends. The following passages are from three plays that represent distinct stages of Shakespeare's career. Though all three are 'classical', they are radically different types of plays within that genre: the first is a bloody revenge tragedy, the second, a geopolitical love tragedy, and the third, a romantic tragicomedy.

The speeches are all delivered in response to a common cue: the horrifying sight of extreme violence exercised upon the body of someone whom the speaker holds dear (or, in the third example, *supposedly* the body of someone whom the speaker holds dear). Rather than speeches of action—in which we might have difficulty disentangling the *character's* premeditated style from the *dramatist's* imposed style—these are speeches of reaction, of immediate and (theatrically) spontaneous emotion. We are justified, then, in expecting the language and variants in these passages to be 'honest', that is, true portrayals of the dramatist's understanding of verisimilitude in speech. The characters are, as Hamlet would put it, speaking 'freely', without rationalization or predetermined rhetorical objectives, and their verse may be expected, therefore, to reflect the dramatist's understanding of the sound of lifelike, viscerally flowing speech.

The first example comes from Titus' reaction to seeing his daughter after Chiron and Demetrius have brutally mutilated her:

> Speak, Lavinia, what accursed hand
> Hath made thee handless in thy father's sight?

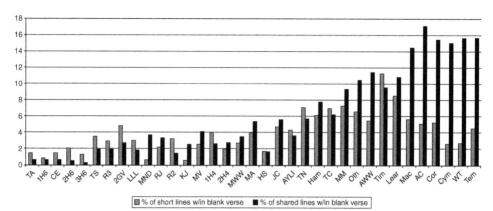

FIGURE 6.5. Short lines and shared lines

> What fool hath added water to the sea,
> Or brought a faggot to bright burning Troy?
> My grief was at the height before thou cam'st,
> And now like Nilus it disdaineth bounds.
> Give me a sword, I'll chop off my hands too,
> For they have fought for Rome, and all in vain;
> And they have nursed this woe in feeding life;
> In bootless prayer have they been held up,
> And they have served me to effectless use.
> Now all the service I require of them
> Is that the one will help to cut the other.
> 'Tis well, Lavinia, that thou hast no hands,
> For hands to do Rome service is but vain.
> (*Titus Andronicus* 3.1.66–80)

But for a few inversions, the iambic pulse is steady; but for one short and one long line, the pentameter length is maintained. As in the example from *Comedy of Errors*, repetition—especially the questions that start the speech—underlines the rhetorical point but without conveying a realistic emotional response. The caesurae fall in their conventional mid-line place, all but two lines are end-stopped, and all of the heavy punctuation falls at the end of a line; cumulatively, these qualities produce a prosodically steady and measured speech in which the rhythm dominates over the phrase. Rather than showing the character's emotional state, the poetry simply explains it. In every metrical sense, this is a typical early Shakespearean speech.

By mid-career, Shakespeare's ability to convey emotional shock through metrical variants became more pronounced. When the battle-scarred Antony expires before her eyes, Cleopatra's language and heart break simultaneously:

> Noblest of men, woot die?
> Hast thou no care of me? Shall I abide
> In this dull world, which in thy absence is

No better than a sty? O see, my women,
The crown o'th' earth doth melt. My lord?
O, withered is the garland of the war,
The soldier's pole is fall'n. Young boys and girls
Are level now with men. The odds is gone,
And there is nothing left remarkable
Beneath the visiting moon.
                    (*Antony and Cleopatra* 4.16.61–70)[58]

Her first line is shared with Antony's last line ('I can no more.'), her words effectively completing her lover's final breath. As with Titus, the repetitive questions addressed to the unresponsive body lend pathos to the unfulfilled exchange—a dialogue that will never be completed. Here, however, the questions slip along the line, from the end to the middle to the end again, just as Cleopatra's attention slips from the body to her attendants and back. Again, the iambic pulse is mostly intact and only one line extends beyond the pentameter length; two fall short of the decasyllabic ideal, most notably the final line, which collapses as she swoons. Despite this largely regular metre, the syntax moves jaggedly against the lines: four of the lines enjamb and more than half of the heavy punctuation falls within a line. Even the caesural pause is displaced slightly late in the first two lines and in the fifth, another feature of Shakespeare's developing style.[59] In contrast to Titus' speech, Cleopatra's has begun to find emotional force, expressive effect, and heightened realism in the competition of line against phrase.

The final example comes from *Cymbeline*, when Innogen awakens beside the headless body of a man she assumes to be Posthumus (actually Cloten, wearing Posthumus' garments):

A headless man? The garments of Posthumus?
I know the shape of 's leg; this is his hand,
His foot Mercurial, his Martial thigh,
The brawns of Hercules; but his Jovial face—
Murder in heaven? How? 'Tis gone. Pisanio,
All curses madded Hecuba gave the Greeks,
And mine to boot, be darted on thee! Thou,
Conspired with that irregulous devil Cloten,
Hath here cut off my lord. To write and read
Be henceforth treacherous! Damned Pisanio
Hath with his forged letters—damned Pisanio—
From this most bravest vessel of the world
Struck the main top! O Posthumus, alas,
Where is thy head? Where's that? Ay me, where's that?

---

[58] The question mark following 'lord' (1.65) and the comma following 'war' (1.66) are from the 1623 Folio text; the Oxford *Complete Works* point these, respectively, with an exclamation mark and a period—both of which considerably, and needlessly, change the nuance of the line's delivery and meaning.

[59] George Wright, 'The Play of Phrase and Line in Shakespeare's Iambic Pentameters', *Shakespeare Quarterly* 34.2 (1983), 147–58, 150 and 152.

> Pisanio might have killed thee at the heart
> And left thy head on. How should this be? Pisanio?
> 'Tis he and Cloten. Malice and lucre in them
> Have laid this woe here. O, 'tis pregnant, pregnant!
> (*Cymbeline* 4.2.310–27)[60]

Once more the speaker's horror manifests itself in a sequence of questions, though here they are far more abrupt. These questions are accompanied by many of the syntactical features common to the late plays, such as a peppering of incomplete or phrase-length sentences within a single line and crowded bursts of monosyllables. Metrically also the speech typifies Shakespeare's later style. The modulation of line length through double- and triple-endings lends the speech a sense of agitation. Repeated words combine with enjambment and phrases, even sentences entirely internal to one line to create the effect that Innogen is unable to control her speech. Like Cleopatra, she shifts focus so rapidly over an enjambed line that the listener might have difficulty following her thoughts. The constant shifting of metrical and phrasal currents, with compressed grammatical constructions and powerful inversions of iambs, reinforces this sense of distraction. Metrically variant phrases—such as the trochee–spondee 'Struck the main top!'—complicate the rhythm of the line, providing acoustic and dramatic energy, but also occur almost at random, making the character's disorientation *felt* by the audience as well. So many phrases resolving at midline and refusing to obey the pentameter generates what Halliday describes as a 'double movement' of metre against syntax—the hallmark of the late style. These passages show how the shift from early plays to late was one of 'the line . . . ced[ing] a good deal of its authority to the sentence [and a] movement from uniformity to irregularity'.[61]

Another way to characterize this change is one of increasing representation and decreasing presentation. Titus' speech tells us what he is thinking and feeling; the metre is simply a means of explaining that information. Much of Cleopatra's and essentially all of Innogen's speeches, however, *show* what the characters are thinking and feeling; the metre in these instances serves not merely as a means for communicating feeling or even as expressing the emotion: it *is* the emotion.

In some respects, Shakespeare took far more risks with his metre than many of his contemporaries; M. A. Bayfield, for example, found that in his early career Shakespeare used hypermetrical feet more often than any other writer but Greene, and that by the end of his career Shakespeare surpassed even him.[62] But looking more broadly, Tarlinskaja has shown that Shakespeare's metrical development was largely in accord with industry-wide trends in dramatic prosody over the Elizabethan–Jacobean period; his increasingly liberated style matched the larger shift from the rigidity of the Norton

---

[60] Again, the question mark after 'heaven' (1.314) has been retained from the Folio text; the Oxford *Complete Works* points this with an exclamation mark, needlessly changing the sense of the line.

[61] McDonald, *Shakespeare and the Arts*, 96.

[62] Tarlinskaja, 8; cf. 15. See also Tarlinskaja, *Shakespeare's Verse*, 188; she notes that Massinger also came close to matching Shakespeare.

and Sackville line to the remarkably loose and natural line of Webster.[63] In fact, in some respects, Shakespeare's later metrical style was more conservative than what the new generation of professionals, such as Fletcher, was writing.[64] Whether Shakespeare was leading the larger trend toward 'efficacy' and verisimilitude in stage poetry or whether he was following it is not clear, but he was metrically a 'son of his time, very much in the mainstream of Elizabethan–Jacobean rhythmical practice'.[65]

By the end of his career, Shakespeare wrote in a style that, embracing the 'autonomy of the phrase' against the line, married both meaning and metre.[66] For the audience listening to one of Shakespeare's late plays, the fabric of the verse became more than just a means for receiving words and more than just a means for 'intensifying, reinforcing, or qualifying semantic or dramatic meanings'.[67] The fabric of the verse became the expressive fabric of the play's meaning itself, even if, by the late plays, it was difficult even for a contemporary audience to distinguish individual lines of verse *as* lines. Shakespeare's skill in varying his metre produced a poetry capable of revealing matter and, ultimately, creating dramatic effects and meanings. The 'secret' of Shakespeare's greatest poetry is not just, as Emerson contended, 'that the thought constructs the tune', but that the thought and the tune are one and the same.[68]

---

[63] Tarlinskaja, 44–5 and 92. See also Wright, *Shakespeare's Metrical Art*, 93.

[64] Tarlinskaja, *Shakespeare's Verse*, 207; cf. 333, 336, and 338.

[65] Tarlinskaja, 54.

[66] Wright 'Play of Phrase', *Shakespeare's Metrical Art*, 156 and 261. See also Tarlinskaja, *Shakespeare's Verse*, 120, 156, 173, 339–43, and 345–6.

[67] Wright, 'Troubles', 73.

[68] Ralph Waldo Emerson, 'Shakspeare; or, the Poet', in Joel Porte, *Emerson* (New York: Literary Classics of America, 1989), 713.

CHAPTER 7

....

BOOK TRADE

....

ADAM G. HOOKS

In 1601, Thomas Wright lamented and enumerated the ways the world led one to sin, coupling 'obscenous and naughty Bookes' with 'stageplayes, and such impure exercises', both of which 'corrupt extreamly all good manners'. To purchase these 'dregges of mens wits' was actually to commit an act of theft, for those who did so were 'robbing their owne soules of grace and goodnesse' (sigs. X6–X7). Three decades later, William Prynne reiterated this polemical commonplace in his infamously verbose attack on plays in performance and, notably, in print, where they became naughty books themselves. For Prynne, printed plays were *vanities* or *idle recreations* with no redeeming worth or value, and to sell them was thus 'fraudulent and sinfull' (1633 edn., sig. 5Z2). While Wright and Prynne roundly condemned this sinful swindling of souls, the language of commerce employed by both discloses the disquieting economic reality they were forced to confront. As Prynne vainly complained, 'Play-books' were 'now more vendible than the choycest Sermons' (sigs. *3–*3v).

The problem for Prynne was not purely, or even primarily, the popularity and profitability of printed playbooks. The dynamics of the capitalist market had radically redefined the very conditions and constituents of value by granting priority to commercial rather than spiritual concerns. By promoting and selling these vendible vanities, the London book trade was willingly and wilfully capitalizing on the calculated exchange of spiritual health for financial wealth. A book's profit, in an ethical sense—its potential to edify and educate—was superseded and yet determined by its commercial profitability. Intrinsic worth or aesthetic merit did not essentially or primarily establish a book's quality; rather, this worth or merit depended on and was defined by its fiscal viability. To be vendible was to be valuable. Adhering to this system of value may have risked one's eternal reward, but it could ensure a rich earthly compensation in return. Wright's denunciation of these impious pamphlets attempted to rectify this imbalance, as he opposes them to the 'thousandes of spirituall Volumes', such as sermons, Bibles, and prayer books, which 'surpasse the other in number, in efficacie, in learning'. These 'spirituall Volumes' were in no danger of being outnumbered, for Prynne's contention notwithstanding, religious works were ubiquitous in the bookshops of early modern

London. Even though there were fewer 'naughty Bookes' in print, both Wright and Prynne worried about their potentially outsized impact on a perilously corruptible reading public. Though Wright argued that the disparity in efficacy and learning between the two kinds of books prohibited any meaningful comparison, the very presence of his denunciation acknowledges the undeniable power of profane pamphlets. The lamentably palpable appeal of these 'other' pamphlets led to an enviable notoriety, and the accusations aimed at the supposedly sinful, self-interested stationers and the eager consumers they supplied were often tinged with jealousy.

Although Wright did not name any of the 'light and wanton Poets' (sig. X6v) he deplored, his indictment would have served as an apt appraisal of the contemporary reputation of William Shakespeare, chief writer of 'stageplayes' for the Lord Chamberlain's Men and notorious author of 'obscenous' erotic poetry. Now central to the literary canon, not to mention school curricula, at present Shakespeare's texts are viewed neither as impediments to virtue nor as idle recreations. However, this was not the case in his own time. In the late sixteenth and seventeenth centuries, Shakespeare was variously known as a honey-tongued love poet, as the writer of several history plays that featured compelling central characters, as a decidedly downmarket purveyor of fantastical romances, and as the dramatist responsible for plays that we now know he did not even write. These multiple authorial personae, none of which correspond to the literary genius we are familiar with today, were all created and capitalized on by the book trade in the course of conducting the everyday transactions typical of its business. For stationers, Shakespeare's works were not great books; they were good business.

Shakespeare depended on the book trade in two senses. As a writer, he existed in and engaged with a fertile textual environment, and his avid reading habits and active imagination are revealed in his poems and play-scripts, which derive from yet wholly transform the source material on which they are based. As a published author, though, Shakespeare—or, more accurately, the various versions of Shakespeare—were produced by commercial and textual networks that both fostered and took advantage of his success. Shakespeare was a distinctly vendible commodity, and his value—the authorial status and artistic merit ascribed to him—was inextricably tied to his commercial viability. His identity and reputation in the world of print were generated and inflected by the intersecting and interdependent systems of economic and aesthetic value. To think about Shakespeare and the book trade thus requires that we attend to how the stationers of early modern London employed his texts to further their own economic ends. To understand the relationship between these two corporate entities, we must focus on how the interests of the individuals and institutions of the book trade shaped Shakespeare, rather than on how Shakespeare may have used the technology of the trade to fulfil the literary ambition sometimes attributed to him. Indeed, because Shakespeare himself kept silent on the matter, we can only access whatever ambitions he may have had through the efforts of the stationers who risked their livelihood (and perhaps their spiritual well-being) by investing in the publication of his poems and plays. Shakespeare provided a steady source of income for many members of the book trade, and in return they invented and reinvented his reputation as an author, inaugurating the long and far from inevitable process that ensured his everlasting fame.

Shakespeare inhabited the world of print as immediately and enduringly as he did the theatre. There is by now a well-established body of scholarship that locates Shakespeare and his works within the collaborative conditions of the book trade, among the scribes and compositors, printers and publishers, binders and booksellers, customers and collectors who made the buying and selling of Shakespeare their business. Once marginalized as the arcane domain of editors and bibliographers, charged with the task of providing an accurate text so that critics could get on with the real intellectual work of interpreting and illuminating those texts, this brand of scholarship is now securely situated in the mainstream of early modern studies. The New Bibliography of the early twentieth century provided the foundations on which much of this work continues to rely, establishing the evidentiary bases and methodological practices that institutionalized Shakespearean textual scholarship.[1] However, motivated by a desire to determine the authentic text of Shakespeare's plays—the text as Shakespeare initially intended it, before his manuscript copy (which does not survive) was obscured by the necessary collaborations of the playhouse and the printing house—the New Bibliographers also instituted a number of misleading yet persistent critical narratives. Even as they focused their attention on the material practices of the book trade, their efforts were aimed at and altered by a valorization of Shakespeare as a single authorial agent. In the late twentieth century, work loosely characterized under the rubric of the New Textualism greatly expanded our knowledge of the ways in which Shakespeare's plays were collaboratively produced, in the process overturning many of the pre-existing narratives of textual scholarship.[2] Early contributions to this research focused on the variant versions of some of Shakespeare's plays, which were explained through the idea of authorial revision, thereby allowing us access to the plays as performed and adapted, perhaps by Shakespeare himself.[3] The focus on Shakespeare largely upheld the New Bibliography's model of single authorship, though, in contrast to other work that decentred the author, focusing instead on the ways Shakespearean authorship and authority were constructed—that is, on how Shakespeare became 'Shakespeare'—and the concomitant elevation of the ephemeral

---

[1] The New Bibliographers included W.W. Greg, A.W. Pollard, J. D. Wilson, and R. B. McKerrow, among others. On the history and influence of the New Bibliography, see Paul Werstine, 'Narratives about Printed Shakespeare Texts: "Foul Papers" and "Bad Quartos"', *Shakespeare Quarterly* 41.1 (1990), 65–86, and Laurie Maguire *Shakespearean Suspect Texts: The 'Bad' Quartos and Their Contexts* (Cambridge: Cambridge University Press, 1996).

[2] Margreta de Grazia and Peter Stallybrass ('The Materiality of the Shakespearean Text', *Shakespeare Quarterly* 44.3 (1993), 255–83) coined the term. The New Textualism was indebted to post-structuralist theoretical movements within early modern studies, particularly New Historicism, and to the sociology of texts within bibliography, identified with the work of D. F. McKenzie and Jerome J. McGann. The various strands of the history of the book, or print culture studies, associated with Roger Chartier, Robert Darnton, and Elizabeth L. Eisenstein, mark the point of origin or inspiration for much of this work.

[3] This work led to the inclusion of two texts of *King Lear* in The Oxford Shakespeare; see Gary Taylor and Stanley Wells, *William Shakespeare: A Textual Companion* (Oxford: Oxford University Press, 1987).

genre of drama to a fittingly literary status—that is, how the plays were transformed in the transition from stage to page.[4]

Recent work has continued to revise and refine what has become the new orthodoxy by investigating the various practices of textual production and reception, exploring and exploiting the critical and interpretive potential of focusing not on authors but rather on other agents such as readers or publishers.[5] This important research has begun to change the way we classify, and thus interpret, literary texts, and in considering Shakespeare's *plays* as *books*, it has been most productive in adjusting how we think about printed drama in particular. Critical work remains to be done on the relationship between drama's appearance in print and its perceived literary status, since the category of the literary was much less defined, and much more complicated, in the early modern period than many scholars have assumed. Print did not immediately or inevitably confer upon drama the high literary status it has since achieved. Rather, printed drama emerged as a category unto itself—distinct from other poetic genres, and distinctively profitable.

This is not to say that Shakespeare himself has entirely disappeared from early modern textual studies—far from it. Another strand of scholarship has reclaimed Shakespeare as a deliberately active participant in the processes that have been separated from him.[6] Accompanied by a revitalization of attribution studies (the attempt to determine exactly which parts of collaborative plays were written by Shakespeare) as well as a renewed interest in Shakespearean biography, this strand reincorporates Shakespeare into the narrative of the New Bibliography, and seems particularly indebted to post-Romantic notions of authorship. Although attending to both the poems and the plays, this recent work still isolates the poems as the product of a wholly autonomous artist, whose authority can then be transferred to the plays, which are in this view similarly characterized as autonomous literary creations. The recent attention to Shakespeare's career as a poet, and his poetic oeuvre, has certainly been welcome, since Shakespeare was known throughout his lifetime (and beyond) as a poet, with a distinct style and a beloved brand. However, his roles as a poet and as a playwright were

[4] David Scott Kastan rebranded this kind of scholarship the 'New Boredom', as a way of foregrounding the detailed historical particularity of this work (*Shakespeare After Theory* [New York: Routledge, 1999], 18). Representative studies include Kastan, *Shakespeare and the Book* (Cambridge: Cambridge University Press, 2001); Douglas Brooks, *From Playhouse to Printing House* (Cambridge: Cambridge University Press, 2000); and Jeffrey Masten, *Textual Intercourse: Collaboration, Authorship, and Sexualities in Renaissance Drama* (Cambridge: Cambridge University Press, 1997).

[5] For an overview of recent developments, see Marta Straznicky (ed.), *The Book of the Play: Playwrights, Stationers, and Readers in Early Modern England* (Amherst: University of Massachusetts Press, 2006); see also Zachary Lesser, *Renaissance Drama and the Politics of Publication* (Cambridge: Cambridge University Press, 2004); Tiffany Stern, *Making Shakespeare: From Stage to Page* (New York: Routledge, 2004); Heidi Brayman Hackel, *Reading Material in Early Modern England: Print, Gender, and Literacy* (Cambridge: Cambridge University Press, 2005); Sonia Massai, *Shakespeare and the Rise of the Editor* (Cambridge: Cambridge University Press, 2007).

[6] The most significant recent studies are Lukas Erne *Shakespeare as Literary Dramatist* (Cambridge: Cambridge University Press, 2003); Patrick Cheney, *Shakespeare, National Poet-Playwright* (Cambridge: Cambridge University Press, 2004); and *idem*, *Shakespeare's Literary Authorship* (Cambridge: Cambridge University Press, 2008).

not determined by Shakespeare alone. He was not a solitary literary genius producing, propagating, and authorizing both poems and plays. Rather, in print, both the poems and the plays—and Shakespeare's career as a poet and a playwright—were produced collaboratively by the agents working in, and the economic conditions of, the early modern book trade.

Sweet Shakespeare

The poem that earned Shakespeare the title of a poet (and a 'light and wanton' one at that) was his debut in print, *Venus and Adonis*, a narrative poem that expands on an episode from Ovid's *Metamorphoses*. When it initially appeared in 1593, it was an immediate success, and its impact on Shakespeare's reputation simply cannot be overstated. *Venus and Adonis* was by far the most popular (and profitable) of Shakespeare's works: no fewer than ten editions were published during his lifetime, with a further six extant editions through the seventeenth century, in total almost twice the number of his most successful play.[7] Shakespeare was recognized first and foremost as a poet—a distinctly Ovidian poet primarily associated with the scandalous subjects of *Venus and Adonis*. Venus' erotic blazon of herself—suggestively urging Adonis to 'Graze on my lips, and if those hills be dry, | Stray lower, where the pleasant fountains lie'—was perhaps the most oft-cited, and certainly the most infamous, passage from Shakespeare in the early modern period.[8] The fashionable, delectable poem made Shakespeare's fame, and it remained the quintessential Shakespearean work for years to come.

Venus and Adonis has also retained a special place in critical accounts of Shakespeare's career and development as a writer. Imitating and amplifying its Ovidian model, the poem directly demonstrates the formative poetic and thematic influence Ovid exerted over Shakespeare from the very beginning of his professional life. The Ovidian motto on the title-page of *Venus and Adonis*—the only such motto ever to appear on any of Shakespeare's printed works—seems to confirm this artistic affinity: '*Vilia miretur vulgus: mihi flavus Apollo | Pocula Castalia plena ministret aqua*'. Taken from the first book of the *Amores*, the motto is usually glossed with Christopher Marlowe's translation of the lines: 'Let base-conceited wits, admire vilde things | Fair Phoebus lead me to the Muses' springs'. The Castalian fountain was sacred to the Muses and to the god of poetry, Apollo ('Fair Phoebus'), and so the motto boldly proclaims Ovid as a source both of inspiration and of poetic ambition. How it may have been construed by contemporaries is another matter, though. The motto and the elegy it was taken from were well-known statements of poetic power, and it circulated widely, including

---

[7] Andrew Murphy, *Shakespeare in Print* (Cambridge: Cambridge University Press, 2003).

[8] Sasha Roberts, *Reading Shakespeare's Poems in Early Modern England* (Basingstoke: Palgrave Macmillan, 2003), 85.

as the preface to an anthology of classical texts known to every boy who had attended grammar school. The association with Ovid could have deleterious effects, too. Ovid was a culturally contested figure whose love poetry, in particular, evoked the same moral consternation directed at wanton pamphlets like *Venus and Adonis* itself, and attempts were made at prohibiting, or at least mitigating, Ovid's lascivious provocations, either by banning the publication of the love poetry, or more commonly, by attaching moralizing glosses to English translations. (It was not by chance that the volume in which Marlowe's rendition of the *Amores* was first published, c.1599, was censored.) These attempts were unsurprisingly unsuccessful, as the popularity of *Venus and Adonis,* and the plethora of other Ovidian poems that appeared in the 1590s, so clearly attests.

That *Venus and Adonis* appeared during an outbreak of plague, when the London theatres were closed, has led many to interpret the '*vulgus*' mentioned in the motto as a reference to the vulgar business of the commercial theatre in which Shakespeare was quickly advancing, and from which, according to this version of events, he was attempting to distance himself. There is little reason to think so, however, since the vocations of poet and playwright were not mutually exclusive. The title-page motto was indeed accompanied by a dedication to the Earl of Southampton, signed by Shakespeare, bolstering the idea that the poem was planned as a dignified bid for aristocratic patronage, thereby gaining (or at least claiming) a greater degree of authorial status than was available to a workaday dramatist. This is surely the most plausible explanation, but the poet's attempt to secure a patron did not require a rejection of his professional obligations in the theatre, for which, after all, he had just written the equally Ovidian *Titus Andronicus*. Furthermore, the attempt did not lead straightforwardly to the achievement of either increased status or a steady income from a patron. Although Southampton was becoming known as a sympathetic supporter of prospective protégés, very little had previously been dedicated to him, at least in part because the young earl was in dire financial straits. Shakespeare continued a public affiliation with the earl the next year, in 1594, dedicating to him *The Rape of Lucrece,* his second published poem and presumably the '*graver labour*' he had promised in the epistle to *Venus and Adonis*. That he did so may indicate that Shakespeare had received something from Southampton in return, but even so, there is no further record of transactions between the two after the initial dedication of *Lucrece*. If a desire for patronage and prestige did motivate Shakespeare's dedications, it was a desire he seems to have abandoned relatively quickly. He soon shifted his attention to his professional role in the theatre, leaving the business of propagating his fame as a poet to the stationers who continued to publish and profit from the two poems. The conventional critical narrative that locates in the poetry a Shakespeare in complete artistic control of his creations, desiring and designing a career as a published author, neglects the fact that the book trade was just as collaborative an environment as the theatre, even if those collaborations took different forms. The reception of his poems and the interpretation and construction of his status depended on much more than an implied interpersonal interaction between poet and patron.

There is one further biographical coincidence that has inhibited a full recognition of the commercial context that produced Shakespeare's poetry, partially obscuring how Shakespeare the poet was made. The printer of both *Venus and Adonis* and *Lucrece*, the successful and well-connected Richard Field, happened to hail from Stratford-upon-Avon, Shakespeare's hometown. Since Field was not otherwise an obvious choice—he was not often involved with this kind of vernacular poetry—the most likely scenario is that Shakespeare did indeed bring his debut poem to Field. But Field was not simply a convenient conduit through which Shakespeare made it into print; once Field entered *Venus and Adonis* in the Stationers' Register, it became his property, subject to his own interests and concerns. Field was not simply the *printer*—the stationer who actually produced the physical artiefact—but also the *publisher*, responsible for laying out the initial capital, hiring a printer (in this case himself), and securing a *bookseller* to serve as the wholesaler.[9] In this respect, Field's importance extends beyond his Stratford origins to include his partnership with John Harrison, the bookseller of *Venus and Adonis*. It was Harrison who entered *Lucrece* in the Stationers' Register in 1594, and who soon after acquired *Venus and Adonis* from Field. Harrison hence became the publisher of Shakespeare's poems, while continuing to hire Field as the printer. It was also for Harrison that Field printed a three-volume set of Ovid's complete works, in Latin. In Harrison's bookshop, Shakespeare's two poems stood side by side with their classical models, thereby providing a strikingly material manifestation of the Ovidian milieu in which Shakespeare's poems circulated—a milieu that becomes not only more visible but also tangible by looking beyond any personal relationship that may have existed between Shakespeare and Field.

Shakespeare's printer and publisher also shaped the two poems in another significantly material way, designing nearly identical title-pages that made them a conspicuously matched set. *Lucrece* was never as popular as its more renowned precursor, although the nine editions that appeared through the seventeenth century do equal the most popular of Shakespeare's plays. While the myth of Lucretia could be found in a number of sources, including Ovid, the more ponderous and political *Lucrece* was prefaced by a prose argument, derived from Livy, which outlined the narrative's potentially republican implications. Nevertheless, it was visibly presented and often perceived as a companion piece to *Venus and Adonis*, as another characteristically Shakespearean work. By the end of the decade, Shakespeare was thoroughly identified as an Ovidian poet, to the extent that Francis Meres could remark that the 'sweet wittie soule of Ouid liues in mellifluous & hony-tongued *Shakespeare*,' mentioning both *Venus and Adonis* and *Lucrece* by name.[10] Shakespeare's identification with Ovid had thus become both material and metaphysical.

---

[9] On the distinctions among these three roles, see Peter W. M. Blayney 'The Publication of Playbooks', in *A New History of Early English Drama*, John D. Cox and David Scott Kastan, (eds.) (New York: Columbia University Press, 1997), 383–422. On the importance of publishers, see Zachary Lesser, *Renaissance Drama and the Politics of Publication* (Cambridge: Cambridge University Press, 2004).

[10] Meres, *Palladis Tamia* (London, 1598), sig. Oo1v.

Just as important as the invocation of Ovid was the term 'sweet'. The customary adjective used to describe a certain pleasing smoothness of poetic style, 'sweet' was the term most commonly applied to Shakespeare in his time, usually in conjunction with his poetry. The desirable quality of sweetness was by no means limited to Shakespeare—it was often ascribed to a range of other popular and stylistically sophisticated writers, from poets to preachers—but it did denote the particular appeal of his verse. When printed commonplace books began using the published work of contemporary vernacular writers at the turn of the century, they overwhelmingly relied on those who had already been branded 'sweet'. The verse produced by 'hony-tongued' poets was distinctly quotable, and could thus be repurposed and repackaged to serve a variety of uses. Shakespeare's two poems proved to be attractive sources, and extracts from them far outnumber those taken from the few plays that had reached print by this time.[11] By using the work of Shakespeare, these printed books further contributed to his burgeoning authorial reputation.

The lack of control over his own reputation, and the comparative power of the book trade, is demonstrated by the ensuing success of Shakespeare's sought-after brand, which was soon extended by other stationers. In addition to identifying Shakespeare with Ovid, Francis Meres offered a tantalizing glimpse at Shakespeare's hitherto unpublished work, mentioning 'his sugred Sonnets among his priuate friends' alongside the two celebrated best-sellers (sig. 201v). Customers unable to get their hands on one of the copies circulating in manuscript did not have to wait long, though. In 1599, *The Passionate Pilgrime* appeared in print, a collection of poems that included two of these 'sugred Sonnets', variant versions of what we now know as Sonnets 138 and 144, along with three sonnets from the recently published play *Love's Labour's Lost* (1598). While attributed to Shakespeare on the title-page, most of the volume consists of non-Shakespearean poems, notably several pastiches on the theme of *Venus and Adonis*. Published by William Jaggard, a stationer who would remain in the Shakespeare business for over two decades, *The Passionate Pilgrime* was undoubtedly an attempt to capitalize on Shakespeare's established fame as a poet. The volume was sold, by no coincidence, at the shop of William Leake, who had by that time acquired the publishing rights to *Venus and Adonis*. Jaggard smartly started the volume by grouping together most of the actual Shakespearean compositions, with the two unpublished sonnets given pride of place. Jaggard has been maligned for this seeming act of deception, profiting from Shakespeare while diluting the quality of his poetry by mixing it with the work of poets who have failed to achieve an eminence similar to Shakespeare's. This early embarrassment has often been explained away, in order to preserve Jaggard's later, more laudable involvement with Shakespeare, which will be addressed below. But Jaggard was simply engaging in normal business practices, producing the kind of collection that was popular in the 1590s. Indeed, Jaggard should

---

[11] Roger Chartier and Peter Stallybrass, 'Reading and Authorship: The Circulation of Shakespeare 1590–1619', in *A Concise Companion to Shakespeare and the Text*, Andrew Murphy, (ed.) (Oxford: Blackwell, 2007), 35–56.

be vindicated, since *The Passionate Pilgrime* was a key constituent of Shakespeare's poetic identity at the turn of the century. And it would continue to be so: Jaggard republished the volume in 1612, sweetening the deal by explicitly advertising '*Certaine Amorous Sonnets, | betweene* Venus *and* Adonis, | *newly corrected and aug- | mented. | By W. Shakespere.*' Shakespeare of course had nothing to do with either correcting or augmenting the volume; Jaggard here used the most common, if misleading, of marketing tactics. But not everyone was pleased by this tactic, and Jaggard seems to have taken Shakespeare's name off the title-page after objections were raised by Thomas Heywood, whose poetry had been appended to the augmented edition. Heywood refused to be annexed to, or usurped by, Shakespeare's authorial prominence, but he also reported Shakespeare's own displeasure with Jaggard's little volume. Despite— or indeed because of—Shakespeare's apparent objection, *The Passionate Pilgrime* shows the agency, the importance, and the success of stationers in fashioning Shakespeare's authorial identity.

The extent to which the 'sweet' Shakespearean persona shaped this identity is shown by the reception of his plays, particularly those with thematic, stylistic, or formal connections to the poetry, like *Romeo and Juliet* and *Love's Labour's Lost*. The first extant edition of the latter, published in 1598, was the first printed play to bear Shakespeare's name on the title-page (once again, as the corrector and augmenter, leading scholars to believe that a previously published edition of the play has been lost, along with the labours of love). A year later, three of the sonnets interspersed in the play reappeared in *The Passionate Pilgrime*. In context, the extracted sonnets—composed by Berowne, Longaville, and Dumaine—simultaneously mock and exemplify the conventions of the love sonnet. After hearing Berowne's sonnet, for example, the pedant Holofernes judges that it lacks 'elegancie, facilitie, and golden cadence of poesie', proclaiming instead that '*Oviddius Naso* was the man' (sigs. E1v–E2r). On stage, the episode is a pointedly ironic appraisal of Shakespeare's own 'poesie' as well as his poetic model. In print, though, the sonnet became an accepted part of Shakespeare's poetic work, furthering Shakespeare's identification with this particular form.

Although the complete collection of what we now know as Shakespeare's 154 sonnets did not reach print for another decade, in 1609, even the earlier scattered sonnets helped to constitute his renown, and his value as a commodity in the book trade. Once again, as with the earlier narrative poems, critical attention has been focused on whether or not Shakespeare authorized the publication of the sonnets, and what this might tell us about the sonnets themselves, and about his ambition as a poet. The desire to find Shakespeare within the sonnets derives from the post-Romantic tradition of reading the sonnet as a more personally revealing form than the playscript, which requires the writer to produce a number of different characters. However, even if Shakespeare personally assembled and authorized the collected sonnets, the printed collection was still shaped by the conventions of the sonnet sequences of the period— and the investment of a stationer. Whatever Shakespeare's role in their publication may have been (and there is no definitive evidence that he was involved in any way), his collection of sonnets was an important, and long-awaited, part of his reputation in print. The title-page prominently presents the volume as *Shake-speares Sonnets*, the name here as much a marker of authorial possession as a shrewd marketing device intended to whet the appetite of customers for what they could finally find inside: as the title-page further promises, these sonnets were 'Neuer before imprinted.'

The publisher of the *Sonnets*, Thomas Thorpe, took the liberty of attaching a dedication that over the years has garnered as much attention and speculation as the poems that follow it. The epistle, taking the form of an inscription, is infamously addressed to 'THE. ONLIE.BEGETTER.OF. | THESE.INSVING.SONNETS', cryptically referred to only as 'MR W.H.' The owner of these initials is unknown; it could be a patron, whom the 'EVER.LIVING.POET' apparently promised 'ALL.HAPPINESSE' and even 'ETERNI-TIE' itself. However, it is not Shakespeare who does the promising in this preface; rather, it is Thorpe, who signs off as 'THE.WELL.WISHING | ADVENTVRER.IN. | SETTING. | FORTH. | T.T.' 'Setting forth' was a standard phrase for the process of printing a text, and so Thorpe here claims responsibility for making the *Sonnets* public. By calling himself an 'adventurer', Thorpe also draws attention to the commercial enterprise of publication—of the risk and potential reward of selling Shakespeare's sonnets (*OED*, 'adventurer,' 4). The transactions are Thorpe's, rather than Shakespeare's; economic and material, rather than personal and authorial. Despite the critical effort expended to locate Shakespeare behind this epistle—an effort that exposes our desire for a Shakespeare who fully determined the conditions of authorship and all that entails—we should not overlook the role of Thorpe and his fellow 'adventurers', who actually ensured that the ever living poet would indeed continue to live in print.

SWAGGERING SHAKESPEARE

Meres may have begun his praise of Shakespeare by admiring his 'sweet' Ovidian poetry, but he quickly followed by naming Shakespeare the 'most excellent' for both comedy and tragedy on stage, citing the models of Plautus and Seneca, along with a substantial list of examples from the promising playwright's repertoire. Shakespeare first appeared in print as a poet, but this identity existed alongside his growing renown as a working—and as a published—dramatist. In print, plays like *Love's Labour's Lost* and *Romeo and Juliet* supplied readers with another source of Shakespearean sweetness. Others, however, promoted a somewhat different version of Shakespeare, one increasingly known for plays based on the chronicles of English history, and featuring compelling, captivating central characters.

Shakespeare's career as a playwright in print began almost simultaneously, if less conspicuously, with his career as a published poet. In 1594, the year *Lucrece* appeared, two Shakespeare plays reached the London bookstalls, albeit with no visible link to the dramatist. The title-page of 'THE | MOST LA- | mentable Romaine | Tragedie of Titus Andronicus' advertised the play's extensive theatrical history, naming three different acting companies—but no playwright. That same year, Thomas Millington, one of the stationers selling *Titus*, published 'THE | First part of the Con- | tention betwixt the two famous Houses of Yorke | and Lancaster' (what we now call *2 Henry VI*), providing a thorough plot summary on the title-page, but again with no mention of a dramatist. The next year Millington published the continuation, 'The true Tragedie of Richard | Duke of Yorke' (*3 Henry VI*), explicitly linking the play to its precursor by referring to '*the whole contention*' between the houses of Lancaster and York. Although Millington was an early investor in the Shakespeare business, he seems to have been either unaware of, or uninterested in, the possibility of promoting Shakespeare himself. Indeed, while Millington's investment helped reveal the appeal of a published Shakespeare play, his greater contribution was to help establish the viability of printed plays as a category of books. When Millington began selling plays in 1594, he was taking a risk on an uncertain commodity. He could not have known that 1594 would in fact be a watershed year for printed playbooks, witnessing an unprecedented surge in publication that suddenly and strikingly demonstrated their commercial potential.[12] The potential prominence of Shakespeare, or for that matter of any writer, as a published playwright depended on the established profitability of printed plays themselves. Once again, in the book trade, viability equals vendibility.

Millington first brought Shakespeare's plays to the bookshops, but the most sustained, significant, and successful investment in Shakespeare's plays was made by the bookseller and sometime publisher Andrew Wise. In 1597 Wise published 'THE | Tragedie of King Ri- | chard the se- | cond' (*Richard II*), and 'THE TRAGEDY OF | King Richard the third' (*Richard III*), and added 'THE | HISTORY OF | HENRIE THE | FOURTH' (*1 Henry IV*) the next year. These three titles would prove to be the three most popular of Shakespeare's plays in print, and indeed they were among the most popular of all printed playbooks in the period.[13] How Wise came to acquire these plays is uncertain, but he certainly knew how to make the most out of these properties once they came into his possession. Like Millington, Wise first published his three plays without attributing them to Shakespeare. When his initial stock quickly sold out, Wise reissued the plays almost immediately, with one noteworthy alteration: he added Shakespeare's name to the title-pages, indicating that he, and more importantly that his customers, recognized an emerging brand. Once Shakespeare's plays had been shown to be profitable, his name could be recognized and exploited as a marketing tactic. Indeed, Wise found Shakespeare's plays to be such reliable and attractive commodities that he added to his stock in 1600, publishing 'THE | Second part of Henrie | the fourth', and 'Much adoe about | Nothing', both of which he connected to his three best-sellers by including the playwright's name. These two plays were not as popular as their predecessors, but Wise continued to maximize his investment in

---

[12] Alan B. Farmer and Zachary Lesser, 'The Popularity of Playbooks Revisited', *Shakespeare Quarterly* 56.1 (2005), 1–32.

[13] *Richard II* would be published a total of six times through the seventeenth century; *Richard III* eight times; and *1 Henry IV* nine times. According to Farmer and Lesser, only 7.2 per cent of playbooks reached a sixth edition; 3.4 per cent reached an eighth edition; and only 1.9 per cent a ninth edition. (Farmer and Lesser, 'The Popularity of Playbooks Revisited').

Shakespeare by making minor corrections in the reprinted editions, even advertising them with the inflated claim that they had been 'Newly corrected' by Shakespeare.[14]

Wise's wildly successful series of Shakespeare plays augmented his reputation in print. No longer simply sweet, Shakespeare was now associated with a succession of sensational characters. Shakespeare's plays participated in the 1590s vogue for stories about the reigns of English monarchs from the recent past, in the process helping to consolidate that popular genre. They proved most memorable, however, for the exploits of distinctive characters such as the eponymous villain of *Richard III* and the roguish thieves who stole the *Henry IV* plays, Falstaff and Pistol. Wise cannily capitalized on such star turns by describing their onstage exploits on the title-pages of his editions, displaying their names more prominently than that of their creator, and Shakespeare's success in print was closely tied to their notoriety. The profitable profligacy of Falstaff became something of a franchise: *1 Henry IV* advertises the '*humorous conceits of Sir* Iohn Falstaffe', and on the title-page of *2 Henry IV* he is joined by his tavern companion, '*Swaggering* Pistoll'. Falstaff was subsequently given top billing in his very own play, which we know now as the *Merry Wives of Windsor*, but which was published in 1602 as 'A | Most pleasant and | excellent conceited Co- | medie, of Syr *Iohn Falstaffe*', where he is once again joined by the 'swaggering vaine of Auncient | *Pistoll* '. The marketing strategies used to promote the printed editions of these plays reveal a Shakespeare identified not with the qualities of his honeyed verse, but rather with the identifiable traits of his idiosyncratic characters.

Proclaiming Shakespeare's authorship of his plays seems an obvious tactic to us, but dramatic authorship was at the time a promising, though unproven, venture. The sudden surge in Shakespeare's visibility as a published playwright has typically been taken as the mark of his rising stature as an author, and even as a rise in status of the concept of dramatic authorship itself.[15] This attractive narrative, whereby Shakespeare single-handedly converts drama into a literary genre, conflates the canonical value drama has subsequently achieved with the more immediate marketing tactics used by stationers to sell a newly viable class of printed playbooks. For Andrew Wise, Shakespeare's name may have had as much to do with capitalizing on his concurrent fame as a poet, as with distinguishing and promoting Shakespeare as a playwright. Printed playbooks, and the playwrights they named, were emerging as a distinct category of books, however. As has been demonstrated, William Prynne was right, correctly detecting that playbooks were indeed more vendible than sermons.[16] While sermons still came out ahead in the sheer number of first editions, playbooks were actually more popular, since they were reprinted at a much higher rate. Reprint editions were more profitable than the first edition, since stationers did not have to worry about one-time expenses such as acquiring manuscript copy or entering the title with the Stationers' Company.[17] Reprint editions

---

[14] Massai, *Shakespeare and the Rise of the Editor* (Cambridge: Cambridge University Press, 2007).

[15] Lukas Erne, *Shakespeare as Literary Dramatist* (Cambridge: Cambridge University Press, 2003).

[16] Farmer and Lesser, 'The Popularity of Playbooks Revisited'.

[17] Peter W. M. Blayney, 'The Publication of Playbooks', in *A New History of Early English Drama*, John D. Cox and David Scott Kastan, (eds.) (New York: Columbia University Press, 1997), 383–422.

were also easier to produce, since compositors could use copy that was already printed. And, of course, the very presence of a reprint edition indicates not only that the print run of the first edition had sold well, but that the publisher deemed it profitable to produce a new edition, thereby supplying the continuing demand for the title. While the outlook of any single playbook was uncertain, on the whole, playbooks outperformed the market average, and thus came to be considered a sound investment, particularly when a stationer could rely on the renown of an established writer. Shakespeare's plays were among the most popular, helping to reinforce the profitability of the commercial category of playbooks, as well as his own authorial brand—a brand desirable enough that it expanded beyond the bounds of what Shakespeare actually wrote.

BAD SHAKESPEARE

The book trade may have established the commercial, and hence the conceptual, viability of plays in print, but the way this was accomplished has often earned stationers the reproach of modern scholars for mangling and mishandling Shakespeare's master-pieces. Editors in particular have berated the printers of the early quartos, assailing their moral culpability for violating Shakespeare's textual corpus in language not unlike that used by Prynne and his fellow polemicists. At times, critics have equated the authenticity of Shakespearean texts with undisputed, and hence uncontaminated, Shakespearean authorship. The New Bibliographers created the category of so-called 'bad' quartos, abridged editions of plays such as *Hamlet* and *Romeo and Juliet* with jumbled syntax or garbled diction. These 'bad' quartos were usually attributed to greedy minor actors, who were accused of poorly recreating a playscript from memory—a process known as 'memorial reconstruction'—and selling it to a similarly suspect stationer for a quick profit. The irregularities of these texts were deemed inadequate and inferior to the 'good' versions found in later quartos or in the First Folio. The compilers of the Folio—the landmark collection of Shakespeare's plays published in 1623—denigrated some of the earlier quartos as 'stolne, and surreptitious copies,' conveniently offering instead the 'True Originall Copies' of the plays as Shakespeare had first written them, a distinction that the New Bibliographers were all too eager to affirm.[18] The moralistic terminology surrounding these supposedly corrupt texts and the equally corrupt agents blamed for their creation largely governed the critical and editorial discourse until recently. Scholars have now realized that these 'bad' quartos cannot be discounted, since they may

---

[18] The New Bibliographers created yet another category, authorial 'foul papers', to describe Shakespeare's own working drafts, prizing these manuscripts (which were necessarily imaginary, since manuscripts in Shakespeare's hand do not survive except for a few lines of *Sir Thomas More*) above scribal 'fair copies', playhouse 'promptbooks', and of course the 'memorial reconstructions' of actors. For an analysis of the evidence—or lack thereof—to support these categories, see Werstine, '"Foul Papers"', and Laurie Maguire, *Shakespearean Suspect Texts: The 'Bad' Quartos and Their Contexts* (Cambridge: Cambridge University Press, 1996).

represent texts closer to what was actually performed in the theatre, while in print they constituted a tangible part of Shakespeare's authorial reputation. 'Bad' Shakespeare was still Shakespeare, and an accurate account of his work demands attention to the currency of these quartos in his time.

The worst of the 'bad' quartos is *Pericles*, a play that was excluded from the First Folio altogether, and the only 'bad' Shakespearean text that never appeared in a longer, 'good' version. First published in 1609 as 'THE LATE, | And much admired Play, | Called | Pericles, Prince | of Tyre', it has long been anything but 'admired', suffering more critical derision than any other Shakespeare play, and occupying a particularly precarious position in the canon. The text of *Pericles* is admittedly confusing and often impenetrable, vexing the efforts of editors and inhibiting a close, or even adequate, consideration of the play. The genre of the play has also caused consternation. An especially scattered example of the geographically and chronologically far-flung stage romance—not usually considered a typical Shakespearean genre—*Pericles* sits a bit uneasily alongside other, more beloved late plays like *The Winter's Tale* and *The Tempest*. The most significant problem *Pericles* presents, though, is that Shakespeare wrote only a little more than half of the play, working with a collaborator whose reputation is unsavoury, to say the least. Shakespeare's partner in composing *Pericles* was George Wilkins, a minor writer better known for owning a brothel. Wilkins also attempted to cash in on his dramatic collaboration with Shakespeare by producing a prose pamphlet version of the play, *The Painfull Aduentures of Pericles Prince of Tyre*, published a year before the play in 1608. The alleged immorality of Wilkins has tainted not only *Pericles*, but the very idea of Shakespearean collaboration. Indeed, critics have often suggested that the play was excluded from the Folio because it was a collaborative work, or more precisely, because it was a *more* collaborative work than other plays. Far from being an anomalous and nearly non-Shakespearean product, however, *Pericles* was entirely consistent with—even characteristic of—the conditions and practices of both the theatre and the book trade. Shakespeare often collaborated with other dramatists, and we know that he knew Wilkins personally. Further, while it was not very common for a play to be adapted into a prose pamphlet, other kinds of stories or events frequently appeared in multiple print genres. If there is a problem with *Pericles*, it should not be blamed on Wilkins.

Pericles may now be classified as bad on nearly every level—a corrupt, collaborative, and uncharacteristic play—but it was undeniably popular in Shakespeare's time. In fact *Pericles* was one of the most identifiably Shakespearean works; it may show us an unfamiliar Shakespeare, but one nevertheless rooted in the customary conditions of textual production, particularly within the early modern book trade. It was published a total of six times in the seventeenth century, including twice in its first year—a feat matched only by *Richard II* and *1 Henry IV*. Despite the fact that Shakespeare wrote only part of *Pericles*, in print it belonged solely to him: the title-page advertises the play as 'By William Shakespeare'. The publisher of *Pericles*, Henry Gosson, specialized in timely, ephemeral pamphlets that capitalized on popular or notorious events, and the immediate notoriety of *Pericles* certainly fit his business model. Gosson had previously published a play written by Wilkins alone, which may explain how he acquired the copy. His decision to advertise *Pericles* as a Shakespeare play may have been based on his recognition—and acquisition—of Shakespeare's more established brand.

The subsequent history of *Pericles* in print is also notable, as the play participated in further incarnations of 'bad' Shakespeare. In 1619, William Jaggard, publisher of *The Passionate Pilgrime*, printed a series of ten previously published plays for Thomas Pavier. The series, now known as the Pavier Quartos, was intended to be a small Shakespearean collection, starting with a combined text of *2* and *3 Henry VI*, retitled 'The | Whole Contention | betweene the two Famous | Houses, LANCASTER and | YORKE', with continuous signatures.[19] The third play was *Pericles*, published separately, but designed to be sold either by itself, or bound together with *The Whole Contention*. Thereafter, though, the remaining seven plays were published independently, several with misleading imprints, a seeming act of deception that has cast a shadow of corruption over the entire enterprise. A number of the Pavier Quartos are 'bad' texts, later superseded by other versions. Even worse, two of the ten plays were not written by Shakespeare at all: 'A | YORKSHIRE | TRAGEDIE' and 'The first part | Of the true & hono- | rable history, of the Life of | *Sir Iohn Old-castle*', an alternative version of the life of the historical figure who had inspired the creation of Falstaff. However, when *A Yorkshire Tragedy* was first published in 1608, it was advertised as '*VVritten by* VV. Shakspeare', and while *Old-castle* had appeared anonymously, the attribution to Shakespeare shows how thoroughly the character of Falstaff had become identified with the playwright.

Now the attribution of spurious plays to Shakespeare looks devious, but at the time the texts were accepted as his, and they comprised a part of Shakespeare's reputation in print. The attributions look 'bad' when judged by modern principles of textual authenticity, but not when assessed by early modern standards. Writers did not own their texts; stationers did, and they could market their properties however they pleased. *Pericles* may have been excluded from the First Folio, but it was eventually included in the second issue of the Third Folio (1664) along with six other plays previously attributed to Shakespeare. In the world of print, all of these contributed to the Shakespearean personae. *Pericles* is the only one of these plays now accepted as part of the canon; the other plays of the so-called 'apocrypha' have more or less fallen from view, although the Shakespearean canon, and thus our idea of the Shakespearean, continues to be negotiated to this day.

BIG SHAKESPEARE

The criticism aimed at Pavier's scheme to produce a Shakespearean collection has as much to do with their size—quarto rather than folio—as with the false dates in their

---

[19] Andrew Murphy, *Shakespeare in Print* (Cambridge: Cambridge University Press, 2003); John Jowett, *Shakespeare and Text* (Oxford: Oxford University Press, 2007).

imprints. But in 1619 Pavier could not have known that only four years later his partner Jaggard would be involved in producing the First Folio, and he certainly could not have known that the Folio would eventually become the most fetishized book in literary history. The Folio was compiled by fellows from Shakespeare's theatre company, and produced by a syndicate of stationers including William Jaggard and his son Isaac, and Edward Blount, one of the leading literary publishers of the time. Whereas Shakespeare's plays had previously been published in the smaller, more ephemeral quarto format, they were now published in a format usually reserved for larger, more serious works. Critics have long considered the monumental and consciously com-memorative Folio as the epitome and the embodiment of the literary status of Shake-speare and of early modern drama. The book's publication has been seen as marking the moment of Shakespeare's elevation as a literary author, and the concomitant conversion of plays into a respectable literary genre. The Folio has been meticulously and repeatedly examined, and the story of its production and its cultural afterlife has been well chronicled.[20]

The Folio's ultimate triumph, however, has obscured the fact that its success—both commercial and conceptual—was neither assured nor immediate. The compilers' pref-atory epistle testifies to their anxiety, pleading with potential customers, 'whatever you do, Buy'. Their plea underlines the risky nature of their venture in publishing the first collection consisting only and entirely of printed plays from the professional theatre. The volume's contents were dictated as much by commercial as commemorative considerations: the syndicate scrambled to secure the rights to plays they did not own, and the exclusion of the poems may in part be explained by their ongoing profitability in their own right. In some ways, the First Folio was actually a failure. It seems not to have been an unqualified success in the bookstalls; the estimated print run of about 750 copies sold out and warranted a second edition nine years later, a span of time that has been variously characterized by critics as indicating both quick and sluggish sales. Neither did it definitively determine Shakespeare's oeuvre—either the works attributed to him, or the generic designations of those works. The book was aimed at an upscale market, but the more affordable individual copies of a handful of plays continued to circulate, along with his poetry. Even John Smethwick, a member of the Folio syndicate, thought it worth his while to mitigate his financial risk in the volume by reprinting quarto editions of his two proven Shakespearean properties, *Hamlet* and *Romeo and Juliet*. It was this trade in single, more widely accessible playbooks that would ultimately consolidate a distinct category of printed drama, laying the groundwork for a rudimentary form of specifically dramatic criticism, which defined Shakespeare's primary authorial identity as that of a playwright, rather than as a poet.[21] The trade in single playbooks flourished throughout the seventeenth century, alongside but separate from the succession of Folios that has

[20] For an overview, see Blayney, 'The Publication of Playbooks', and Anthony James West, *The Shakespeare First Folio: The History of the Book*, 2 vols. (Oxford: Oxford University Press, 2001–3).

[21] Adam G. Hooks, 'Booksellers' Catalogues and the Classification of Printed Drama in Seventeenth-Century England', Papers of the Bibliographical Society of America 102.4 (2008), 445–64.

dominated critical narratives. The publishers and booksellers who continued to invest in these single editions fostered the first critical attempts at enumerating and classifying the entire body of English printed drama in the late seventeenth century, attempts that perforce relied on the profusion of quarto playbooks rather than the few single-author folio collections. The Shakespeare Folio did not single-handedly raise the literary status of drama; rather, Shakespeare's status as a playwright depended upon the emergence of a coherent and distinctive category of printed drama, and the nascent criticism focused on that category. The Folio only gained the critical and cultural esteem it now holds once Shakespeare's place as the pre-eminent English author was firmly established later in the eighteenth century, when by no coincidence, the volume's monetary value among collectors began to increase exponentially.

William Prynne completed his polemic just a year after the appearance of the Second Folio (1632), and he was keenly aware, and considerably anxious about, the differences between the big Shakespeare book and the abundance of little playbooks. Prynne observed with alarm that 'Some Play-books' had 'growne from Quarto into Folio', noting with a perceptive eye that 'Shackspeers Plaies are printed in the best Crowne paper, far better than most Bibles', an accurate bibliographical description of the Second Folio (1633: sig. 2*6v). Prynne here identified what the folios are usually thought to have accomplished: that the transition from stage to page quite literally transformed and elevated Shakespeare's plays, above even the Bible—fitting for what has become a secular scripture. However, Prynne was concerned not with literary status but with ethical and spiritual worth, and the stationers of London had once again subverted his system of value with the very materials of their trade. Worse yet, these big books 'beare so good a price and sale' that even smaller bibles 'hardly finde such vent as they'. The tactile quality and commercial viability of the Second Folio disturbed Prynne, although considering its limited print run, this disturbance was perhaps more in principle, the very existence of the Folio outweighing its potential to inflict harm on its buyers. More pressing for Prynne was the prevalence of 'Quarto-Play-bookes', which 'have come forth in such abundance, and found so many customers, that they almost exceede all number'. Prynne nevertheless cited a number, claiming that 'Above forty thousand Play-bookes have beene printed and vented within these two years', a remarkably accurate figure in what was the most active period of playbook publication the market had yet seen.[22] What Prynne found to threaten the greater good of readers is exactly what those readers found appealing—and what the book trade found to be profitable. Prynne would be horrified, but the book trade's investment in Shakespeare's plays, and the profit they gained in return, made possible the profit we now derive from Shakespeare, in every sense of the word.

---

[22] Brayman Hackel, *Reading Material in Early Modern England*, 76–7; Farmer and Lesser, 'The Popularity of Playbooks Revisited'.

CHAPTER 8

....

EARLY READERS

....

SONIA MASSAI

While there are some basic continuities in the ways in which people process texts, almost every aspect of reading has undergone profound historical transformations as we have moved from a culture in which [early modern] readers take hold of texts for specific purposes to one in which texts generally take hold of readers who may not be looking for anything beyond 'a good read'.[1]

READING in the early modern period involved engaging in a range of activities which are no longer commonly associated with the private and mostly silent consumption of books among modern readers. Commenting on the significance of the pointing hands, or manicules, drawn in the margins of humanist manuscripts and, subsequently, in early modern English texts, William Sherman describes reading in the period as a self-conscious 'manipulation of information', which involved 'selecting, ordering, and applying resources gleaned from a wide variety of texts'. Deriving from '*manus*, the Latin word for "hand"', manipulating information literally meant both 'taking the text *in hand* and fitting it to the purpose *at hand*'.[2]

This active engagement with texts explains why early modern manuscripts and printed books are often heavily marked and annotated. The marks and annotations inscribed by early modern readers in their books show the extent to which reading was aimed at identifying useful and edifying precepts or memorable and elegant conceits. What readers gleaned from their encounters with texts (or what they copied in their table-books while watching plays or listening to sermons) was often transcribed in common–place books, helpfully defined by Ann Moss as 'collection[s] of notes from reading and other sources that the compiler might want to recall, and reuse, at a later date'.[3] This

---

[1] William H. Sherman, *Used Books: Marking Readers in Renaissance England* (Philadelphia: University of Pennsylvania Press, 2008), xvi.

[2] Sherman, *Used Books*, 47.

[3] Ann Moss, *Printed Commonplace Books and the Structuring of Renaissance Thought* (Oxford: Clarendon Press, 1996), v.

proactive approach to reading was one of the most tangible legacies of humanist pedagogy. Although humanist scholars recommended the application of this type of reading to the study of classical texts in schools and at universities, readers of vernacular and recreational literature deployed similar strategies. Telling in this respect is a copy of John Donne's 1633 *Poems* where an early reader has added several commonplace headings, thus showing how 'an "aesthetic" text becomes useful'.[4] Similarly, as Hilton Kelliher explains, sixty-three lines copied from *1 Henry IV*, possibly as early as the late 1590s, in British Library Additional MS 64078, 'tacitly confir[m] that the authoritative voice of human experience was to be heard not solely in the classical authors, who were studied in schools and universities . . . , but also in the vernacular poetry and drama of the day.'[5]

It is therefore worth bearing in mind that Shakespeare's works started to circulate as manuscript and printed artiefacts, as individual editions and short extracts in literary anthologies or private miscellanies at a time when vernacular literature and English drama were in the process of being elevated to the status of classical texts. Although classical scholars and university-educated writers often mocked the efforts of those involved in the transformation of commercial drama from an oral and popular form of entertainment into reading texts,[6] the strategies deployed by Shakespeare's stationers and by his early readers show that his work was increasingly presented to and appropriated by readers as literature.

Shakespeare's elevation to the status of 'national poet' dates back to the eighteenth rather than the seventeenth century.[7] However, by 1609 he was compared to Terence and Plautus[8] and by 1623 he was canonized through the first collected edition of his dramatic works, the First Folio, aptly described by Gary Taylor as a monumental publishing venture, which did not reflect but rather constructed Shakespeare's reputation as a modern classic.[9] By focusing on 'the intellectual and material activities on both

---

[4] Bradin Cormack and Carla Mazzio, *Book Use, Book Theory: 1500–1700* (Chicago, IL: University of Chicago Press, 2005), 25.

[5] Hilton Kelliher, 'Contemporary Manuscript Extracts from Shakespeare's *1 Henry IV*', *English Manuscript Studies* 1 (1988), 177. For other early manuscript quotations from Shakespeare, see Juliet Gowan, '"One Man in His Time": The Notebook of Edward Pudsey', forthcoming in the *Bodleian Library Record*.

[6] For more details about the presentation of early modern plays written for the commercial stage as reading texts and contemporary attacks against the literary ambitions of early modern dramatists and their stationers, see Zachary Lesser and Peter Stallybrass, 'The First Literary *Hamlet* and the Commonplacing of Professional Plays', *Shakespeare Quarterly* 59 (2008), 371–420. Lesser and Stallybrass's work qualifies the more commonly held view that 'play texts . . . had not yet fully made the transition from the ephemera of an emerging entertainment industry to the artifacts of high culture' (David Scott Kastan, 'Plays into Print: Shakespeare to His Earliest Readers', in Jennifer Andersen and Elizabeth Sauer [eds.], *Books and Readers in Early Modern England* (Philadelphia: University of Pennsylvania Press, 2002), 23–41, at 38).

[7] See, for example, Michael Dobson, *The Making of the National Poet: Shakespeare, Adaptation and Authorship, 1660–1769* (Oxford: Clarendon Press, 1992).

[8] See the address 'A neuer writer, to an euer reader. Newes', included in the second issue of *Troilus and Cressida* (1609, STC 22331), which is discussed in more detail later in this essay.

[9] Gary Taylor, 'Why Publish Shakespeare's Works?', in 'The McKenzie Lectures', delivered at the University of Oxford in February 2006.

sides of the early modern printing press',[10] on those who transformed Shakespeare's works into reading texts and those who read them, this essay considers how these texts were presented to their first readers and how some of these early readers responded to them.

IMPLIED READERS

Several features in the material and the bibliographical make-up of early modern printed books, including their format, layout, and paratextual materials, such as dedicatory epistles, addresses to the reader, lists of errata, and glosses, suggest the target readership envisaged by those who produced them.[11] Shakespeare's plays were first published as small pamphlets, thin booklets in quarto or octavo format, which were roughly the size of modern pocket-size paperbacks—although quartos tended to be slightly larger and square in shape. Single-edition playbooks were mostly sold unbound and were relatively cheap to buy.[12] Recent scholars have contested our understanding of this type of play-books as ephemeral,[13] but they were undoubtedly less likely to survive than larger or more substantial books, unless they were bound by their readers and owners with other pamphlets. The process of elevation of English commercial plays to the status of literary drama is not only documented by the increasing presence of dramatic extracts in early literary anthologies,[14] but also by the fact that single-edition playbooks started to be

[10] Heidi Brayman Hackel, *Reading Material in Early Modern England: Print, Gender and Literacy* (Cambridge: Cambridge University Press, 2005), 8.

[11] William H. Sherman, *John Dee: The Politics of Reading and Writing in the English Renaissance* (Amherst: University of Massachusetts Press, 1995), rightly complained that 'the pages of Reader-Response works are peopled with every kind of reader except the real and historical: Freund lists the mock reader (Gibson), the implied reader (Booth and Iser), the model reader (Eco), the super-reader (Riffaterre), the inscribed or encoded reader (Brooke-Rose), and the ideal reader (Culler)' (55). Since then, several studies cited elsewhere in this essay have helpfully focused on actual early modern readers. However, it is still important to focus on the moment of production of early modern books and on how these books were presented to their readers, in order to establish how they were at least meant to be read and by whom, while bearing in mind that reading practices and book ownership often departed from how authors and publishers meant their books to be received and used by their readers.

[12] For more details about the economics of dramatic publication see Peter Blayney, 'The Publication of Playbooks', in John D. Cox and David Scott Kastan (eds.), *A New History of Early English Drama* (New York: Columbia University Press, 1997), 383–422; Alan B. Farmer and Zachary Lesser, 'The Popularity of Playbooks Revisited', *Shakespeare Quarterly* 56 (2005), 1–32; Peter Blayney, 'The Alleged Popularity of Playbooks', *Shakespeare Quarterly* 56 (2005), 33–50; and Alan B. Farmer and Zachary Lesser, 'Structures of Popularity in the Early Modern Book Trade', *Shakespeare Quarterly* 56 (2005), 206–13.

[13] See, for example, Henry Woudhuysen, 'Early Play Texts: Forms and Formes', in *In Arden: Editing Shakespeare, Essays in Honour of Richard Proudfoot* (London: Thomson Learning, 2003), 48–61, and Alan B. Farmer, 'Shakespeare, Revision, and the Ephemerality of Playbooks', delivered at the International Shakespeare Conference, Shakespeare Institute, Stratford-upon-Avon, August 2008.

[14] For a full discussion of early literary anthologies, which included extracts from Shakespeare's plays, see Peter Stallybrass and Roger Chartier, 'Reading and Authorship: The Circulation of Shakespeare, (1590–1619)', in Andrew Murphy (ed.), *A Concise Companion to Shakespeare and the Text* (Oxford: Blackwell, 2007), 35–56.

collected and bound together in larger volumes by owners of substantial private libraries. Sir Edward Dering (1598–1644), for example, paid regular visits to the London theatres and purchased as many as 220, or 240, playbooks between 1619 and 1624, including two copies of Shakespeare's First Folio. Dering's detailed 'Booke of expences' shows that by spring 1624 he had bound his playbooks into fourteen volumes.[15] Similarly, 'A Catalogue of my Ladies Bookes at London' lists the titles of the 241 books purchased by Frances Egerton, Countess of Bridgewater (1583–1636), throughout most of her adult life, including 'Diuers Playes by Shakespeare'.[16] As Heidi Brayman Hackel explains, the date '1602' placed next to this entry suggests that this item was 'perhaps a volume in which diverse separate Quartos were bound together, the first of which was printed in 1602'.[17]

Specimens of cheaply produced playbooks have undoubtedly survived mostly because they started to be collected by gentlemen and gentlewomen readers who could afford to buy them in bulk and have them bound into substantial volumes for their private libraries. However, early modern single-edition playbooks were primarily meant to offer their readers an affordable record of a theatrical event.[18] The prominence accorded on their title-pages to the name of the acting company and sometimes to the playhouse where the play had originally been staged suggests that the target readers were eager playgoers who had probably seen the plays performed in the London playhouses in the first place. Accordingly, the earliest editions of Shakespeare's plays, like the vast majority of editions of plays written for the commercial stage and printed in the 1590s, provide clues about their theatrical provenance but do not mention the name of their author(s). The title-page of *Titus Andronicus* (1594, STC 22328), for example, does not mention Shakespeare (or his collaborator, George Peele),[19] but lists as many as three acting companies—'the Right Ho- | nourable the Earle of *Darbie*, Earle of *Pembroke*, and Earle of *Sussex* their Seruants'—with whom Shakespeare was most probably associated before he joined the Chamberlain's Men in 1594. And it was the patronage of the Lord Chamberlain which was to remain a constant feature on the title-pages of Shakespeare's plays even after 1598, when Shakespeare's name started to be included more regularly.[20]

---

[15] T. N. S. Lennam, 'Sir Edward Dering's Collection of Playbooks, 1619–1624', *Shakespeare Quarterly* 16 (1965): 145–53.

[16] Manuscript lists of plays, probably meant to be bound together, can also be found on the verso of the title-page and on the verso of the last page of the Garrick copy of the First Quarto of *The Merchant of Venice* held at the British Library (1600, C34k22).

[17] Brayman Hackel, *Reading Materials*, 166.

[18] See, for example, Richard Hawkins's address to the reader in his edition of *Philaster* (1628), where he identifies his target readership with the 'Seeing Auditors, or Hearing Spectators' who watched the play in the theatre (sig. A2v).

[19] George Peele is believed to have written Act 1 and shorter passages at the beginning of Acts 2 and 4. Alternatively Shakespeare may have revised a play originally written by Peele. For more details, see Brian Vickers, *Shakespeare, Co-Author: A Historical Study of Five Collaborative Plays* (Oxford: Oxford University Press, 2002), 148–243.

[20] See, for example, Lukas Erne, 'The "Making" of Shakespeare', in his *Shakespeare as Literary Dramatist* (Cambridge: Cambridge University Press, 2003), 56–77. However, even at the height of Shakespeare's popularity in print in the late 1590s and early 1600s, the Lord Chamberlain's name features on fifteen title-pages of editions of Shakespeare's plays and Shakespeare's name only on eleven of them.

The absence of the name of the author(s) and the foregrounding of the commercial stage on the title-pages of early single-edition playbooks do not necessarily suggest that they were presented to their readers as devoid of literary value as reading texts. Editorial pledges included on the title-pages of five out of the twenty editions of Shakespeare's plays published before 1623 draw their readers' attention to the 'augmented' or 'enlarged' copy from which they were set. The title-page of the 1598 quarto edition of *Love's Labour's Lost*, for example, specifies that the text of this 'PLEASANT | Conceited Comedie' had been 'Newly corrected and augmented'. Unfortunately, no earlier edition of this play is extant and the meaning and accuracy of this editorial pledge cannot be verified. However, the differences between Burby's 1599 edition of *Romeo and Juliet*, which is described on the title-page as being *'Newly corrected, augmented, and | amended'*, and the First Quarto edition, which was partly printed and published by John Danter in 1597, are significant enough to suggest the use of different manuscript copies. Burby's edition provides a fuller printed version of the play, thus justifying the editorial pledge included in its title-page. Similarly, the Second Quarto edition of *Hamlet*, printed by James Roberts for Nicholas Ling in 1604-5, boasts on its title-page to be 'Newly imprinted and enlarged to almost as much | againe as it was, according to the true and perfect | Coppie'. Once again, this claim is supported by the range of variants between this edition and the first edition also published by Nicholas Ling in 1603. The origins of these variant texts have been subject to much debate.[21] What is undisputable is that Burby's and Ling's decision to invest their capital to secure a fuller manuscript version of these plays must have reflected their expectation that their readers would appreciate and buy a 'newly corrected' and 'enlarged' edition.

Editorial pledges on the title-pages of Shakespeare's early editions extend to the quality and accuracy of the texts preserved in them. Even before the official rise of the editorial tradition at the beginning of the eighteenth century, when named editors of Shakespeare started to claim intellectual and commercial ownership of their editorial labours, the texts of commercial plays were routinely, if lightly, corrected prior to being submitted or resubmitted to the press.[22] The earliest instance of an editorial pledge signalling correction of copy on the title-page of an English commercial play can be found in the Second Quarto edition of Shakespeare's *1 Henry IV* (1599). The emendations are fairly local but nonetheless significant and involve changes in stage directions and speech prefixes, which improve the dramatic consistency of the fictive world of the play.[23] Similarly, the Third Quarto editions of *2* and *3 Henry VI*, which were published for Thomas Pavier in 1619 as *The vvhole contention betvveene the tvvo famous houses,*

---

[21] For recent contributions to the debate, see Laurie Maguire, *Shakespearean Suspect Texts: The 'Bad' Quartos and their Contexts* (Cambridge: Cambridge University Press, 1996), and Paul Werstine, 'A Century of "Bad" Quartos', *Shakespeare Quarterly* 50 (1999), 310–33.

[22] For a systematic study of the annotation of dramatic copy for the press in the sixteenth and seventeenth centuries, see Sonia Massai, *Shakespeare and the Rise of the Editor* (Cambridge: Cambridge University Press, 2007).

[23] For a more detailed discussion of these emendations, see Massai, *The Rise of the Editor*, 102–5.

Lancaster and Yorke, are advertised as being 'newly corrected and | enlarged' on their title-pages. Once again, the emendations are sporadic and affect mostly speech prefixes and stage directions.[24] Besides, at least on one occasion, the text of the dialogue in *2 Henry VI* is changed to emend York's genealogy. In short, the stationers who published the Second Quarto edition of *1 Henry IV* and *The Whole Contention* must have decided to invest time and effort in preparing Shakespeare's texts for the press, because of their readers' interest in 'newly corrected' texts.[25]

Another indication of the increasingly literary status accorded to the early editions of Shakespeare's plays, and to early modern playbooks more generally, is the use of commonplace markers, starting with Ben Jonson's *Every Man Out of his Humour* in 1600.[26] As Zachary Lesser and Peter Stallybrass have recently reminded us, '[i]n the years immediately following [1600], there was a sea change in the kinds of vernacular poesy printed with commas, inverted commas, or a change in font to demarcate *sententiae*' and 'a large number, probably the great majority, of those books originated as plays from the professional theatres'.[27] Lesser and Stallybrass reach two important conclusions. Firstly, they argue that 'playbooks [were] marked as literary, but not by being distanced from their origins in the professional theatre'.[28] Secondly, they

[24] For a more detailed discussion of these emendations, see Massai, *The Rise of the Editor*, 121–32.

[25] For more details about editorial pledges in non-Shakespearean playbooks, see Sonia Massai, 'Editorial Pledges in Early Modern Dramatic Paratexts', in Helen Smith and Louise Wilson (eds.), *Renaissance Paratexts* (Cambridge: Cambridge University Press, 2011), 141–61.

[26] The first study of commonplace markers in early modern English playbooks was George K. Hunter, 'The Marking of Sententiae in Elizabethan Printed Plays, Poems, and Romances', *The Library* 5th series, 6 (1951–2), 171–88. See also Margreta de Grazia, 'Shakespeare in Quotation Marks', in Jean I. Marsden (ed.), *The Appropriation of Shakespeare: Post-Renaissance Reconstructions of the Works and the Myth* (New York: St. Martin's Press, 1991), 57–91.

[27] Lesser and Stallybrass, 395.

[28] Lesser and Stallybrass, 409. Lesser and Stallybrass do point out that the two Shakespeare plays that were printed with commonplace markers prior to 1623—*Hamlet* and *Troilus and Cressida*—are also the two plays whose early editions signal an attempt to distance them from the commercial stage. The title-page in the First Quarto of *Hamlet* (1603) reveals its literary ambitions by alluding to the fact that the play had been performed not only in London but 'also in the two V- | niuersities of Cambridge and Oxford'. The Second Quarto (1604–5) goes even further by replacing the play's theatrical credentials with the exceptionally detailed editorial pledge quoted above: 'Newly imprinted and enlarged to almost as much | againe as it was, according to the true and perfect | Coppie'. Similarly, when *Troilus and Cressida* was first printed in 1609, a variant title-page was used to replace the standard reference to theatrical provenance—'*As it was acted by the Kings Maiesties* | seruants at the Globe'—with an allusion to its literary qualities—'THE | Famous Historie of | Troylus *and* Cresseid. | *Excellently expressing the beginning* | of their loues, with the conceited wooing of | *Pandarus* Prince of Licia'. Copies with the variant title-page also include a new 'Epistle' headed 'A neuer writer, to an euer reader. Newes', where the play is described as 'not . . . sullied, with the smoaky breath of the multitude . . . neuer stal'd with the Stage, | neuer clapper-clawd with the palmes | of the vulgar, and yet passing full of | the palme comicall'. Having denied a link with the commercial stage, this preface compares the play to 'the best Commedy in *Terence* or *Plautus*', thus inviting its readers to view it as a modern classic. However, as Lesser and Stallybrass rightly explain, the anti-theatrical bias in the early editions of these two plays is exceptional, both in relation to the rise of Shakespeare in print and in light of the widespread commonplacing of playbooks in the same period.

convincingly attribute the commonplacing of early playbooks to their publishers or to annotating readers associated with their publishers rather than to their authors (Ben Jonson and John Marston being two notable exceptions). Lesser and Stallybrass' attribution of commonplace markers is corroborated by the fact that Shakespeare, unlike Ben Jonson, wrote no prefaces to distance his printed dramatic works from the stage. Even more crucially, the number of first editions of Shakespeare's plays dropped dramatically after 1600, at a time when his name was accorded unprecedented prominence on the title-pages of Jacobean editions of plays like *King Lear* (1608), where the name 'M. William Shak-speare' is set in large type at the top of the title-page. Even the publication of *The Sonnets* in 1609 did not prompt Shakespeare to write dedicatory epistles, as he had done for *Venus and Adonis* and *The Rape of Lucrece* in 1593 and 1594. Although the lack of a dedication signed by Shakespeare may suggest that the 1609 edition was published without his authorization, it is perfectly in keeping with Shakespeare's consistent lack of a direct engagement with the publication of his works after 1593–4. It would therefore seem reasonable to conclude that the concerted effort to present Shakespeare's plays to his early readers as literary texts, often reissued in 'newly corrected' or 'newly augmented' editions, should be attributed to the foresight and entrepreneurship of his stationers rather than to Shakespeare himself.

ANNOTATING READERS

The literary aspirations of those who prepared Shakespeare's plays for the press were not wasted on those early readers who marked and annotated them. Annotation was more frequent in non-literary books, which were explicitly meant to inform professional practice—law and medical books—or to teach practical skills—conduct books or manuals. Besides, as Sherman puts it, 'fewer marked early modern books survive than unmarked ones because use destroys books'. Sherman also reminds us that the systematic 'destruction of manuscript annotations . . . in the nineteenth century, when printed leaves were washed and bleached in a concerted effort to "clean" the margins of books' has had an impact on the amount of annotations that has survived in all early modern books, including playbooks.[29] Nonetheless, the marks and annotations left behind by early readers of Shakespeare are extensive and significant enough to confirm the growing reputation of Shakespeare's plays as reading texts throughout the seventeenth century.

The amount and range of annotations in the early editions of Shakespeare's plays can now be more easily studied and discussed thanks to a pioneering digitization project led by the British Library, which has made 107 copies freely accessible online.[30]

---

[29] Sherman, *Used Books*, 4.

[30] 'Shakespeare in Quarto' is only one of several databases called 'Treasures in Full', which are also freely accessible online at http://www.bl.uk/treasures/treasuresinfull.html. For a detailed discussion of early annotating readers of Shakespeare's poems, see Sasha Roberts, *Reading Shakespeare's Poems in*

In these copies, manuscript commonplace markers and corrections far outnumber theatrical annotations, thus suggesting that early readers did care about the accuracy of the text and that they read it as a source of profitable and memorable quotations, as well as a record of a theatrical event. Only one copy records details of a Restoration production of *The Merchant of Venice* (1637, BL C34k24)—an early hand added the name of the actors next to the name of the characters, including Mrs Barry as Portia— while two copies of *1 Henry IV* display attempts to provide lists of dramatis personae. On the verso of the title-page of the George III copy of the Sixth Quarto (1633, BL C12g21), an unidentified hand started to write under 'Dramtis Personae' the names of 'Henry ÿ 4th King of England', 'Prince Henry his son', and 'John of Gaunt Duke of Lancaster', possibly conflating John of Gaunt, uncle to Richard II and father to Henry Bolingbroke, with Prince John, son to Henry Bolingbroke, who went on to become King Henry IV, and brother to Prince Henry, who would succeed his father as Henry V. This reader had little or no familiarity at all with the printed text of the play. Another hand supplied a fuller list of dramatis personae on the verso of the title-page of the Garrick copy of the Seventh Quarto (1632, BL C34k10). What is striking about this list is the omission of Lady Percy and Lady Mortimer, which along with the confinement of 'Sr John Fastaff' and his associates, described as 'highwaymen', to the bottom of the list,[31] suggests a strikingly hierarchical and gender-biased approach to the play.[32]

Except for a handful of annotations showing some alertness to the printed texts as theatrical scripts,[33] most markings left by early readers focus more consistently on their literary qualities. The main aim of these manuscript corrections is generally not to *amend* the text by referring to other editions of the same play in order to recover a

Early Modern England (Basingstoke: Palgrave Macmillan, 2003). The most recent analysis of early annotating readers of the Folio editions of Shakespeare's dramatic works is Jean-Christophe Mayer's paper 'Shakespeare's Commonplacing Readers', presented at the 'Shakespeare Reconfigured' Conference, held at the University of York on 9–10 October 2009.

[31] The relative marginality of Falstaff's character, which suggests the extent to which modern readers' approaches to this play have changed, is also noted by Hilton Kelliher in his essay on 'Contemporary Manuscript Extracts from Shakespeare's *Henry IV*', where he explains that the interests underlying these extracts 'include the commonwealth and its great ones, war, dishonour, fear and cowardice', while 'Falstaff, the presiding comic genius of Shakespeare's play, surprisingly provided not one sentiment worthy of record' (162). These extracts are also discussed in David Scott Kastan (ed.), *Henry IV, Part 1*, The Arden Shakespeare, 3rd series (London: Thomson Learning, 2002), Appendix 3, 350–2.

[32] The 'Hostess' is the only female character included in a line of unnamed and minor characters at the bottom of the page.

[33] In the Halliwell-Phillipps copy of the First Quarto of *King Lear* (1608, BL C34k17, sig. I2), an early hand underlines '*Edmund*' and correctly writes '*Edgar*' above it in the stage direction '*Enter Gloster and Edmund*' at line 31; in the same copy, the same hand adds a missing speech prefix—'Bast.'—on sig. C1. Another speech-prefix 'Hspur.' is added by an early hand in the Garrick copy of the Second Quarto of *1 Henry IV* (1599, BL C34k6, sig. B4v). In the Halliwell-Phillipps copy of the First Quarto of *Hamlet* (1603, BL C34k1, sig. F3), an early hand highlights an inconsistency in the stage direction announcing the entrance of the characters in the dumbshow in Act 3: 'Duke & / Dutchese sh^d be as below'. In the Garrick copy of the Third Quarto of *Hamlet* (1611, BL C34k4, N4v), an early hand adds a stage direction: '[?] lose his rapier and take | vp the contrary'.

more authoritative reading,[34] but to *perfect* it. Contemporary usage of the verb 'to perfect' signals the intervention of an annotating reader, whose main concern is to replace obvious mistakes or unsatisfactory words or phrases with alternative readings, even when the new reading radically departs from the text preserved in earlier editions or what may reasonably be assumed to have been in the printer's copy.[35] While some of the manuscript corrections preserved in the copies digitized by the British Library are fairly straightforward,[36] others reveal sophisticated and well-educated readers engaged in *perfecting* Shakespeare's language. In the Folger copy[37] of the First Quarto of *Titus Andronicus*, an early hand has crossed out 'obsequies' in Lavinia's lines 'Lo at this Tombe my tributarie teares, | I render for my brethrens obsequies' and replaced it with 'exequies'. As Jonathan Bate explains in his edition of this play, '"exequies" [is] the correct classical Latin word for "funeral rite" [while] "obsequies" is a corrupt medieval Latin form, which in Elizabethan usage often meant "commemorative rites performed at the grave"'.[38] This annotating reader knew Latin and was fastidious enough to feel obliged to replace an authoritative reading with an etymologically accurate alternative. Also noteworthy is the fact that this astute reader felt no compunction in correcting the text by radically altering it. One such correction occurs on sig. D4v, line 23, when Martius describes Bassanius as lying 'bereaud in blood'. Modern editors tend to emend 'bereaud in blood' to read 'berayed in blood' ('berayed' meaning defiled), following an emendation first adopted by John Dover Wilson.[39] '[B]erayed' could have easily been misread by the compositor who set this line in the First Quarto as 'bereaud'. However, the early reader who emended this line suggested an elegant, but radically different, solution, crossing out 'bereaud in blood' and writing 'heere reav'd of lyfe' in the margin.

Other types of markings suggest the extent to which Shakespeare's early playbooks were increasingly read as literary works by readers who were looking for morally edifying or witty quotations to remember or to copy in their commonplace books.

[34] The only exception might be a correction in the Garrick copy of the Fourth Quarto edition of *Hamlet* (1622, BL C34k3, sig. F3v), where an early hand crosses out 'office and' and writes 'despis'd | loue' in the margin, next to Hamlet's line 'The pangs of office and the Lawes delay'.

[35] For more details on the practice of perfecting the printer's copy for the press, see Massai, *The Rise of the Editor*, 1–38.

[36] In the Garrick copy of the Third Quarto of *The Merry Wives of Windsor* (1630, BL C34k28, sig. H3), the nonsensical 'gold' is emended to read 'cold'. Also predictable, although signalling an alert reader, are two corrections in the Halliwell-Phillipps copy of the Sixth Quarto of *Richard III* (1622, BL C34k50, sig. G3 and sig. G4v). The first correction replaces 'brother' with 'mother', as Richard insinuates that his brother Edward may have been conceived outside wedlock, while feigning some reluctance to question his mother's chastity publicly, since, as he puts it, 'my mother [not my brother] liues'. The second correction adds 'tell' to Catesby's line 'Ile him what you say my Lord.'

[37] Copies of editions not held at the British Library were supplied by partner libraries, including the Folger Shakespeare Library, Washington, DC, the Bodleian Library, Oxford, the National Library of Scotland, Edinburgh, and Edinburgh University Library.

[38] Jonathan Bate (ed.), *Titus Andronicus*, The Arden Shakespeare, 3rd series (London and New York: Routledge, 1995), 138.

[39] John Dover Wilson (ed.), *Titus Andronicus*, The New Shakespeare (Cambridge: Cambridge University Press, 1948).

Manicules are, for example, drawn in the margins of the Halliwell-Phillipps copy of the First Quarto of *Hamlet* (1603, BL C34k1, sigs. E3, E3v, F2, and F2v). Their position reveals an early reader interested in passing references to classical drama, to the acting profession in late republican Rome, and to Hamlet's lesson to the actors. This copy of the First Quarto of *Hamlet* also includes marginal crosses and copious underlining of other passages which attracted this reader's attention. However, the use of manicules is particularly telling because it establishes a connection between classical and late Elizabethan drama. This connection in turn reinforces Lesser and Stallybrass's views discussed above, according to which both the paratextual features of this edition of *Hamlet* and the literary ambitions of the agents involved in its publication were aimed at presenting it as a literary text.[40]

Other commonplace markers include marginal commas,[41] and, more frequently, crosses and straight lines drawn next to the dialogue. Straight lines are effectively used to highlight two passages in the Folger copy of the Third Quarto of *Richard II* (1598 White STC 22309). The first passage is itself a commonplace: 'The loue of wicked men conuerts to feare, | That feare to hate, and hate turns one or both | To worthy danger and deserued death' (sig. H2v). The second passage neatly sums up the tragic implications of Richard's enforced abdication: '*King* Doubly diuorc't, (badde men) you violate | A twofold marriage, betwixt my Crowne and me, | And then betwixt me and my married wife. | Let me vnkisse the oath betwixt thee and me: | And yet not so, for with a kisse t'was made' (sig. H2v). The use of straight lines in the Halliwell-Phillipps copy of the Sixth Quarto of *Richard III* (1634, BL C34k50) is strikingly similar. Two lines in the final speech delivered by Hastings convey a proverbial sentiment about the futility of titles and power: 'O momentary state of worldly men, |Which we more hunt for, then the grace of heauen' (sig. G2). Three earlier lines, also spoken by Hastings, reflect his inability to read Richard's intentions, hypocrisy being Richard's defining trait as a villain: 'I thinke there is neuer a man in Christendome, | That can lesser hide his loue or hate than he: | For by his face straight shall you know his heart'(sig. G1v). The use of straight lines in these copies of *Richard II* and *Richard III* shows the effective economy of reading strategies aimed at extrapolating short passages applicable to general sentiments or tropes ('The loue of the wicked' or the 'momentary state of wordly men') or to a character's defining qualities or circumstances.[42]

---

[40] Another manicule is drawn next to Longaville's warning, 'Looke how you but[t] your selfe in these sharp mockes', in the Garrick copy of the Second Quarto of *Love's Labour's Lost* (1631, BL C34k21, sig. H1).

[41] Several marginal commas are added to a heavily annotated copy of the First Quarto of *King Lear* (1608, BL C34k17). A single pair of marginal commas are inscribed in the George III copy of the Second Quarto of *Merchant of Venice* (1600[1619], BL C12g31, sig. C1).

[42] Crosses and vertical lines are by far the most popular commonplace markers used by Shakespeare's early readers in the copies of the playbooks digitized by the British Library. See also the Malone copy of the First Octavo edition of *3 Henry VI* (1595, Bodleian Arch.G f.1 sig. E2), where this type of marking is used at a pivotal moment in the play when Clarence turns his back on Warwick to rejoin his brothers and the Yorkist faction (the first straight line is drawn next to Edward's lines 'Et tu Brute, wilt thou stab *Caesar* too? | A parlie sirra to *George* of Clarence'), and next to the stage direction that follows—'Sound a

The vast majority of markings and annotating readers in copies of Shakespeare's early playbooks digitized by the British Library cannot be dated or identified. However, there are interesting exceptions. Sometimes a marked-up copy includes a date, as with the George III copy of the Second Quarto of *Romeo and Juliet* (1599, BL C12g18), where the same ink used for crosses, asterisks, brackets, and other symbols next to the dialogue seems to have been used to add a date—'Agst 30. 1623'—underneath the word 'FINIS' on sig. M2. Several early readers signed their names on their playbooks,[43] and some of them are female readers. The dated inscription 'Sarah Downes her Booke | 1709' on the verso of the title-page in the Garrick copy of the Fourth Quarto edition of *Romeo and Juliet* (1622, BL C34k56, sig. A1v) can be compared with another signature by the same reader, dated eleven years earlier, which most probably shows a younger Sarah Downes first claiming ownership of her book (sig. L4v).[44] The signature 'Elizabeth | Smith' is barely visible on the verso of the last page of the second quarto of *Othello* (1630, BL C34k34) and is unlikely to have been inscribed by the neater (and later) hand that transcribed one leaf missing from this copy (sigs. C4 and C4v). Also difficult to attribute are several commonplace markers (mostly crosses) in the Garrick copy of the Eighth Quarto edition of *1 Henry IV*, because this copy has two signatures, 'Eliz. Mary Croussmaker | her Booke 174[6]' on its title-page and 'Richard Hawkins' on the last page (sig. K4v).[45]

Parlie, and *Richard* and *Clarence* whisper to- | gither, and then Clarence takes his red Rose out of his | hat, and throwes it at *Warwike.*' Crosses are also copiously used in the Garrick copy of the First Quarto of *The Merchant of Venice* (1600, BL C34k22).

[43] Signatures are often found on title-pages: see, for example, the signatures 'J[?] Fleming' in the George III copy of the First Quarto edition of *3 Henry VI* (1600, BL C12h9); 'Edward Nedham' in the George III copy of the Second Quarto edition of *A Midsummer Night's Dream* (BL C12g30); or 'John Bancroft' in the Garrick copy of the Fifth Quarto of *Richard II* (1615, BL C34k44). Occasionally signatures are found at the back of playbooks, as with 'Tho Webbe' and 'Wi[ll]iam Edwards' on the verso of the last page of the George III copy of the Second Quarto of *The Merchant of Venice* (1600[1619] BL C12g31, sig. K4v).

[44] The name 'John' is also visible on the same page.

[45] Copies of Shakespeare's early single-text editions not included in the 'Treasures in Full: Shakespeare in Quarto' digitization project at the British Library may well preserve better evidence to establish how specific categories of readers read them. So far, only a handful of female readers of Shakespeare's First Folio have been identified and studied in depth. See, for example, Roberts, *Reading Shakespeare's Poems*, 57–8:

> Mary Lewis, First Folio (Folger First Folio 51) contains annotations to *Hamlet* and *Titus Andronicus* in a late seventeenth century italic hand. . . . The annotations reveal a careful and active reader of the plays, fully prepared to emend the text and with a command of basic Latin (which need not, of course, preclude the work of a woman). In *Hamlet* corrections and emendments are inserted—such as 'solid Flesh' to 'sallowed Flesh' in 1.2.219—and lines are highlighted with a fist, while in *Titus Andronicus* lines are emended, minor corrections made, speech prefixes added and meanings altered.

For other evidence of ownership and provenance and readers' markings in the four seventeenth-century Folio editions of Shakespeare's dramatic works, see Anthony James West, *The Shakespeare First Folio: The History of the Book*, vol. 2: *A New Worldwide Census of First Folios* (Oxford: Oxford University Press, 2003).

By far the most rewarding exemplar for a close analysis of ownership and early reading practices is the Halliwell-Phillipps copy of the First Quarto edition of *King Lear* (1608, BL C34k17), because it preserves copious annotations as well as including multiple signatures—'Thomas Middleton'; 'John Cooper'; 'Richard [from?] Mary'; 'Mary'; and 'John Cooper' again—followed by dates—'1688' and 1667'—on the verso of the last page (sig. L4v). The bulk of the annotations falls into three broad categories: commonplace markers, corrections, and glosses. By far the most interesting annotations are brief marginal glosses in Latin added by another learned reader, who, like the reader of the Folger copy of the First Quarto of *Titus Andronicus* discussed above, used his classical erudition to read and annotate the printed text of a vernacular play. These Latin glosses are primarily used to signal changes of speakers: 'ad Regē Gal.' (to the French King) and 'loq. ad Emundū' (spoken to Edmund) are, for example, added next to Lear's half-line 'For you great King' (sig. B3v) and Cornwall's half-line 'farewell my Lord of *Gloster*' (sig. H1). The same hand glosses Albany's reference to 'this paper' in the final scene by adding 'sc. her lett' | to Gloster' ('sc.', or *scilicet*, is Latin for 'namely') and Edgar's recollection of his encounter with Kent in the same scene by adding 'Kent sc.' after 'came there in a man' (sigs. L2, L2v).[46]

Also significant in this copy of *King Lear* is the copious use of marginal commas or underlining for quotable passages spoken both by Lear and his supporters and by morally flawed, if not openly amoral, characters. Among the marked passages spoken by Lear and his supporters, a few are worth mentioning because they are still readily associated with the play, including Kent's 'anger has a priuiledge' (sig. E1v), Edgar's 'Who alone suffers suffers, most in't mind' (sig. G4v), Lear's 'through tattered raggs smal vices do appeare' (sig. I4), Cordelia's 'Time shal vnfould what pleated cūning hides' (sig. B4v), or even the Captain's 'I cannot draw a cart, nor eate dride oats, | If it bee mans worke ile do't' (sig. K4v). However, several passages spoken by Lear's opponents were also marked-up, including Edmund's 'This policie of age makes the world bitter to the best of our times' (sig. C1v) and Regan's 'how in a house | Should many people vnder two commands | Hold amytie, 'tis hard, almost impossible' (sig. F2).

Marked passages were often copied in commonplace books and extrapolated from their original context, so there is nothing exceptional about this reader singling out lines spoken by characters who do not share the same values and views. However, contrary to a still commonly held assumption about the selective and therefore arguably patchy engagement of commonplacing readers with their texts, this reader was not insensitive to the dramatic coherence of the play as a whole. As Peter Mack helpfully points out,

> Some historians have characterised the Renaissance approach to reading...as reading in fragments....By this method, the text is decomposed into a personal dictionary of quotations....While it is certainly true that the emphasis on

---

[46] Other Latin tags can be found on E2v, F2, and F3v.

commonplace books and *moral* [sic] *sententiae* could encourage reading in fragments, this picture needs to be balanced against evidence of approaches to reading
focused on the text as a whole.[47]

The reader of this copy of *King Lear* was clearly reading the play to find memorable
passages in it, but also as a dramatic and a reading text in its own right. This reader was
sensitive to who spoke what lines to whom, as suggested by the fact that he added a
missing speech prefix (sig. C1v), altered a stage direction by replacing Edmund with
Edgar (sig. I2), and used Latin tags, as mentioned earlier, to signal changes of address in
two speeches (sigs. B3v and H1).

Also remarkable is the level of attention bestowed on the text of the play, as shown by
dozens of local (and often unnecessary) corrections. In keeping with other annotators
discussed earlier, the corrector of this copy of *King Lear* intervened either to emend
straightforward typographical errors and to normalize spelling and syntax,[48] or to perfect
viable readings. Like other early annotators, this reader displayed an appropriative,
rather than a reverential, attitude toward Shakespeare's text and felt at liberty to perfect
it, often at the expense of metre or the slightly more archaic flavour of Shakespeare's
language. On sig. B2v, for example, 'tyme' is unnecessarily added to 'And as a stranger to
my heart and me, | Hould thee from this tyme for ever'.[49] Particularly telling are
occasions when this reader takes the trouble to change the text to replace the original
with a synonym, as on sig. D1v, where 'I should bee false perswaded' is emended to read
'I should bee halfe persuaded'. Other changes are prompted by words which must
have already started to come across as archaic, as when 'derogate' is replaced by

[47] Peter Mack, 'Rhetoric, Ethics and Reading in the Renaissance', *Renaissance Studies* 19 (2005), 3.

[48] On sig. B2v, 'Be *Kent* vnmannerly, when *Lear* is man' is emended to read 'Be *Kent* vnmannerly,
when *Lear* is madd'; on sig. D1v, 'bit off be' reads 'bit off by'; on sig. D2 'thourt' is modernized and reads
'thwart'; on sig. D2v 'you cast' is correctly rearranged as 'cast you' and the tense of the verb 'praise' is
normalized to read 'praised'; on sig. E2 'That stands' is correctly emended to 'Then [Than] stands'; on
sig. E3 'Dost' is normalized to 'Doth'; the missing preposition 'to' is added to 'To knee to his throne' on
sig. F2; 'wanderer' becomes plural on sig. F4v; 'beniflicted' on H4 becomes 'benifitted', 'benefacted' being
the alternative reading preferred by modern editors; on the same page the nonsensical 'Human' is
correctly emended to read 'Humanity' and on sig. H4v 'streme' is also correctely emended to 'strooue';
'at each' on sig. I3 becomes 'at least', while modern editors prefer 'at length' or 'alenth', unless they decide
to retain 'at each'; 'fell' is normalized to read 'fallne' and 'borne' to 'bourne' on the same page; on sig. I3v
'I ever inch a King' becomes 'I every inch a king'; 'do shake the head heare of pleasures' is also correctly
amended to read 'does shake the head hearing of pleasures' on sig. I3v; 'I am only sorrow' is normalised
to read 'I am only sorry' on sig. K1 and '*Venter*' to '*Ventering*' (modern editors tend to prefer 'Venture')
on sig. K1v; on sig. K2, 'Had you not bene' becomes more straightforward as 'Had he not bene' and 'you'
and a final question mark are added to Cordelia's line 'Sir know me'; the nonsensical 'sleach and fell' is
amended to read 'flesh and fell' on sig. K4; and 'As bent to proue' becomes 'Are bent to proue' on sig. L2.

[49] A similar correction occurs on sig. D2, where 'it' is added to 'men so disordered... that this our
court... showes | like a riotous Inne; epicurisme, and lust make it more like a tauerne...'. Other
unnecessary emendations include, for example: 'cold neglect' for 'couldst neglect' on sig. B4; 'as you are
old and reuerend, you should be wise' for 'as you are old and reuerend, should be wise' on sig. D1v;
'misinstruction' for 'misconstruction' on sig. E2; 'tye all my haire with knots' for 'elfe all my haire in
knots' on sig. E3; and 'that thy being some say of breeding breathes' becomes 'that thy being somewhat of
breeding breathes', while 'By right of knighthood' is changed to 'My right of knighthood' on sig. L2.

'degenerate' (sig. D2), while other corrections spoil a trope or image, as on sig. D2v, where 'vntented' in 'the vntented woundings of a fathers cursse' becomes 'vntainted'.

More crucially, like other correctors discussed earlier, this reader replaces obvious mistakes with alternatives, which cannot be justified as a compositorial misreading of the printer's copy, because they are typographically too different. On sig. G1, for example, 'crulentious storme' becomes 'truculent storme'. Modern editors prefer 'contentious' because 'contentious' has exactly the same number of letters in it as 'crulentious' and 'u' | 'n' and 'l' | 't' would have looked quite similar in Elizabethan secretary hand, thus justifying the assumption that the compositor who set this page may have failed to decipher 'contentious' and set it as 'crulentious'.[50] If the dates added at the end of this volume are at all indicative of when this copy of *King Lear* may have been so thoroughly annotated, the reader would have had access to the text of the play as printed in the four subsequent folio editions published in the seventeenth century. However, like other early correctors, this reader consulted no other editions to recover more authoritative readings.[51] This reader's aim was to perfect, rather than to correct, his copy of *King Lear*. This fundamental difference in early readers' approaches to Shakespeare's text should not detract from our appreciation of the effort invested in the marking, annotating, and perfecting of the early editions. Although not comparable to the level of annotation in more established literary genres, the annotations discussed in this section show that Shakespeare started to be read by literary-minded readers well before the establishment of the Shakespeare myth and the editorial tradition in the eighteenth century.

Commonplacing Readers

Private notebooks or early literary anthologies in print were the products of a process of textual consumption that combined reading and writing practices. These collections have traditionally attracted little sustained critical and editorial attention, because editors regard them as devoid of any textual authority and literary critics as mere exercises in imitation rather than creative appropriation. Even while emphasizing the proactive approach of early readers to their books, Bradin Cormack and Carla Mazzio

---

[50] On sig. L1, 'conspicuate' is emended to read 'conspirator', but modern editors tend to prefer 'conspirant' on the same principle, 'conspirant' being typographically closer to what this word would have looked like when written in Elizabethan secretary hand (the letter 'c' looked like a modern handwritten 'r' and the whole word was probably spelt 'conspirante').

[51] On sig. E2 'dialogue' becomes 'dialect', and on sig. H3v 'desire' becomes 'dislike', as in the Folio. However, the context makes these corrections possible without reference to the Folio, while the correction of 'Hard is thequesse [sic] of their great strength' to 'Hard is the conquest of their great strength' on sig. K3v suggests that this reader was trying to make sense of the text preserved in this copy, without having access to the Folio, where 'Heere' rather than 'Hard' logically relates to both 'guesse' and 'By diligent discovery' in the next line.

describe commonplace reading as 'highly prescribed, "common" in the sense that it filtered one's reading through social norms that determined which textual elements were significant and which were not'.[52] Similarly, Steven Zwicker has argued that commonplace reading before the mid-seventeenth century consisted essentially in 'identifying, acquiring, and replicating the wisdom of the text'.[53] Other scholars have conversely remarked on how idiosyncratic commonplace practices during the early modern period actually were. Kevin Sharpe has, for example, demonstrated that while 'what the compiler copied was extracted from a common storehouse of wisdom, the manner in which extracts were copied, arranged, juxtaposed, cross-referenced or indexed was personal and individual'.[54]

Closer attention to the context within which Shakespearean extracts were copied by early commonplacing readers shows how their practices were not only idiosyncratic but also transformative. If commonplacing practices reduced the source text to fragments lifted out of their original context, the fragments often cohered into new composite texts and acquired different meanings and resonances. The final section of this essay focuses on representative examples of passages copied from *The Rape of Lucrece*, by far the most frequently commonplaced work by Shakespeare during his lifetime and throughout the seventeenth century.[55] Passages copied in two notebooks, a 1630s miscellany belonging to Peter and Oliver Le Neve (British Library Additional MS 27406) and the 'Waferer Commonplace Book' (*c*.1591–1627, BL Additional MS 52585), would seem to reflect the two most common strategies through which early readers appropriated this poem. As Roberts explains,

> the rights and wrongs of Lucrece's suicide took second place to aphorisms on such topics as thought, time, opportunity and the responsibility of princes. In so doing the particular circumstances of Lucrece's fate were transformed into general remarks applicable to all. Some readers, however, were drawn to more worldly concerns: the poem's description of the naked female body laid open to the male gaze. Reworking Shakespeare's description of Lucrece lying 'like a virtuous monument' (391), they appropriated Shakespeare's 'graver labour' for recreational and erotic ends.[56]

The passages copied in these two notebooks would also seem to have been read either as amorous, voyeuristic, and recreational or as grave, sombre, and elegiac.[57] However,

---

[52] Cormack and Mazzio, *Book Use*, 70.

[53] Steven N. Zwicker, 'The Constitution of Opinion and the Pacification of Reading', in Kevin Sharpe and Steven Zwicker (eds.), *Reading, Society and Politics in Early Modern England* (Cambridge: Cambridge University Press, 2003), 295–316, at 300.

[54] Kevin Sharpe, *Reading Revolutions: The Politics of Reading in Early Modern England* (New Haven, CT: Yale University Press, 2000), 278.

[55] As Roberts explains, '[b]y comparison with other writers—such as Donne, Jonson, Ralegh, Carew, Herrick, William Strode and Henry King—Shakespeare wielded only a minor presence in early modern manuscript culture: his growing importance in the canon of 16- and 17-century English literature was a phenomenon specific to print' (*Reading Shakespeare's Poems*, 9–10).

[56] Roberts, *Reading Shakespeare's Poems*, 15.

[57] Roberts, *Reading Shakespeare's Poems*, 140.

when read within the sequence of the other quotations within which they are included, they no longer look so starkly different.

In the 'Waferer' notebook, five stanzas on 'Opportunity' ('O opportunitye thy guilt is greate', fols. 54v, 55; ll. 876–82, 897–924)[58] are introduced by the earlier stanza from *The Rape of Lucrece*—'Vnruly blasts waite on the tender springe' (ll. 869–75)—and are sandwiched between Nicholas Breton's 'Come solemn Muse and help me sing' (printed in *Brittons bowre of delights*, 1591) and Robert Southwell's 'Upon the Image of Death' (printed in *Moeoniae* in 1595). As Roberts points out, the reader who transcribed Shakespeare passages omitted two stanzas where sexual violations and Lucrece's rape are mentioned as prime examples of how opportunity conspires with those who oppress the weak. As a result, the passages copied in this notebook read as a generic invective against opportunity, which destroys 'What Vertue breedes' and life itself, 'or else his quality'. In Breton's poem, death is the target of the poet's complaint: the death of the beloved 'kills his life, or else his quality' and death in turn becomes the only end 'devoutly to be wished'. Southwell's poem is a prayer invoking God's intercession to help the speaker accept the inevitability of death and prepare for it ('graunt grace therefore o God y^t I | my life maye mende seth I must dye', fol. 55v).

Breton's and Southwell's poems are in turn preceded and followed by other poems. Sir Edward Dyer's 'The lowest trees have tops' and another unattributed poem, starting with the line 'This prouerbe olde full longe agoe', open the sequence (fols.53v, 54). Dyer's poem is a celebration of love as the empowering force that ennobles even the lowliest of creatures and, simultaneously, an elegy about 'true harts', who 'haue eares & eyes' but 'noe tongs to speake' and so 'theye heare & see & sigh' and then inevitably 'they breake' (fol. 53v). The anonymous poem is another invective, this time against 'shadowes', which, like opportunity in Shakespeare's poem, are accused of betraying and destroying the virtuous and the weak ('By helpe of shadowe thus it goese | the poore mans cause is overthrone | . . . true men are hanged strong theves let goe', fol. 54). The sequence ends with three further poems: a prayer in verse attributed to 'Tho: Churchman', starting with the line 'Repent oh Englande nowe repent' and ending with God's summoning of all souls to be judged before Him (fols. 55, 55v); another unattributed poem, starting with the line 'Layde in my restles bedd' (fol. 56v); and the wooing and crowning of Phillida as 'the Ladie of the maye' (fol. 57) taken from Nicholas Breton's *Entertainment at Elvetham* (1591). The unattributed poem is another meditation upon the futility of human desires. Conventionally, it mentions 'the little boye' who 'doth wishe of god to escape the rod | a tall yonge man to be', the 'younge man' who 'would be a ritch ould man | to lyue & lye at rest', and the 'olde man' who 'would be a litle boye againe | to lyue so longe the more'. Coming after all the other poems, Breton's second extract in this sequence acquires a sombre register, love being, like virtue, particularly vulnerable to the blows inflicted by death and opportunity.

---

[58] Line numbers for passages in *The Rape of Lucrece* refer to Colin Burrow (ed.), *Complete Sonnets and Poems*, The Oxford Shakespeare (Oxford: Oxford University Press, 2002).

Overall, this sequence represents a strikingly coherent collection of extracts, sharing a mournful concern for the transient quality of human endevours and the vulnerability of virtue. Besides, all extracts are described at the bottom of folio 53 as 'divers ditties to be sung & plaid upon Instrumts', thus suggesting that the context of their consumption was more likely to be social and communal recitation than silent and private reading. Within this context, the passages from *The Rape of Lucrece* function as a grave reminder of the plight of the human condition, which remains central even in devotional poems where the emphasis shifts to the ultimate need to accept and prepare for death.

The passages from *The Rape of Lucrece* copied in the Le Neve notebook (fols. 74, 74v) would seem to set a radically different tone. They are drawn from the section of the poem that describes Lucrece asleep on her bed and Tarquin transfixed by 'her azure veines, her alabaster skin, | Her corrall lips, her snow-whight dimpled chin' (ll. 365–71; 386–99; 419–20). As Roberts observes, the compiler 'altered the pronouns as if to create the impression of a shared erotic scene between a "faire" man and a woman lying in bed' and concludes that '[i]n contrast to the grave tone struck by [the Waferer] extract', these passages 'appear to have more to do with reading for pleasure than profit'.[59] However, when read within the context of the larger group of verse and prose extracts taking up folios 74 to 87, these passages can be seen to perform a similarly edifying function.

An earlier stanza from *The Rape of Lucrece*—'W^t win I, if I gaine ye things I seeke?' (ll. 211–17)—is copied at the top of folio 74v. By inverting the order in which this stanza and the previous passages appear in Shakespeare's poem, the compiler shows that moral reflection—'Who buyes a minutes mirth to wayle a weeke | Or sels eternitie to get a toy?'—follows the consummation of an illicit passion. This stanza strikes a note that resounds through most of the short poems and extracts that follow. Appeals to shun vice and to die a good, Christian death and eminent examples of how great spirits conquer death are the main topics of roughly half of the poetic extracts in this section of the notebook. This stanza from *The Rape of Lucrece* is followed by 'An Epitaph vpon Niobe', a paradoxical meditation on the mystery of a 'carkasse' (Niobe's body) turned into its own 'tombe', the 'tombe' containing no 'carkasse' and the 'carkasse' having no 'tombe' besides itself. Four further lines of verse headed 'Death' end by reassuring the reader that 'good men but see death, ye wicked tast it'. Next comes a very popular poem, written 'Vpon Queene Elizabeths death', variously attributed to John Taylor, 'the Water-Poet',[60] to Thomas Heywood,[61] or to Thomas Dekker,[62] and ending with a couplet celebrating Elizabeth as supreme sovereign on earth and now 'second maid' in heaven. Immortality is also the chief reward for the 'younge man of great hope' commemorated in the next four lines of verse—'Shorte was thy life, | Yet livest thou

---

[59] Roberts, *Reading Shakespeare's Poems*, 140.

[60] Mackenzie Edward Charles Walcott, *The Memorials of Westminster* (London: 1851), 36.

[61] This poem is attributed to Thomas Heywood the *Scriptorium: Medieval and Early Modern Manuscripts Online* database based on the Faculty of English, University of Cambridge at http://scriptorium.english.cam.ac.uk/manuscripts/images/index.php?ms=Add.8640&page=10.

[62] Joshua Eckhardt, *Manuscript Verse Collectors and the Politics of Anti-Courtly Love Poetry* (Oxford: Oxford University Press, 2009), 61.

ever, | Death hath his due, | Yet diest thou never'. On folio 75, a poem 'On Princ ˆHenry'
is spoken by his tomb—'Here is shrind celestiall dust'—and revisits the mystery of an
ultimately empty grave—'And I keepe it but in trust'— thus recalling both Niobe's
tragic metamorphosis into stone and the other (nameless) young man's release from
the bounds of mortality.

The recurrent concern with death, which emerges in many of the extracts and short
poems included in the Le Neve miscellany, makes the passages from *The Rape of
Lucrece* seem more sombre and in keeping with the extracts copied in the Waferer
commonplace book. Even the first cluster of quotations on folio 74 is not entirely
amorous and recreational in tone, due to the prominence given in the first stanza to the
'high treason' that misleads the male lover's heart and the dangerous quality of his
trespass, as 'wickedly he stalkes' into his beloved's chamber. Besides, this first cluster of
quotations from *The Rape of Lucrece* is linked to the final stanza on folio 74v by the
twelve lines of unattributed verse copied on the bottom half of folio 74. These lines
seem to function as a warning that the dangers attending on the consummation of illicit
desires are not dispelled by the break of day. This unattributed extract represents
'wakfull morninge' as she leaves her 'odoriferous bed' in the East and evokes memories
of other trespasses by mentioning Phaeton and Phoebus' chariot in the opening line.

A pervasive preoccupation with physical and spiritual death as the result of a failure or
betrayal of virtue links the passages copied from *The Rape of Lucrece* in both notebooks.
What changes is their overall register. While the poems and extracts in the 'Waferer'
commonplace book are predominantly mournful and elegiac, the passages copied in the
Le Neve notebook are plaintive but keenly aware of the beauty, as well as the dangers,
implicit in human experience, and confident in a second life to come. Passages about
death and the moral failures leading to spiritual death are interspersed with moving
extracts celebrating natural beauty and the passing of time, evocatively headed 'The
Sunset' (fol. 75v), 'Almost night', 'A cleare night', and 'Day breake', to name but a few.
Finitude in the Le Neve notebook is also fundamentally comic, not only because of the
prospect of a second life to come (as in Dante's *Divine Comedy*), but also because of
grotesque and parodic elements, which lighten its overall tone. In a short poem headed
'On a Scould' (fol. 75), for example, the hope of a good death and the mystery of the
resurrection are not 'devoutly to be wished': 'Here lies a woman noe man can deny it |
Shee rests in peace although shee lived unquiet | Her husband prayes if by her grave you
walke | You'l gently tread for if shee wake sheele talk.'

Closer attention to the context within which Shakespearean extracts were copied
shows broadly similar approaches to individual texts. The commonplacing of passages
from *The Rape of Lucrece* in these two notebooks confirms the currency of Gabriel
Harvey's reference to this poem as appealing to 'the wiser sort'.[63] However, even
broadly similar commonplacing approaches to individual texts produced idiosyncratic

---

[63] Clement Mansfield Ingleby, *The Shakespeare Allusion Book*, 2 vols. (London: 1909), 1: 56.

collections of extracts, within which passages from the same source text acquired different layers of meaning or registers. As Joshua Eckhardt has recently argued,

> Poetic meaning need not be limited to what a poet puts into a poem, what a reader gets out of it, or what a critic finds in it alone. A poem's full significance, rather, may extend beyond its text to the affiliations and resonances that it develops among other texts and its various contexts, no matter how local or even physical.[64]

It would therefore seem appropriate to conclude that a close analysis of how early readers read Shakespeare highlights significant and consistent approaches and practices that are no longer familiar to us. The stationers who published single-text editions of his dramatic works often felt no need to include his name on the title-page; as a result early modern readers of quarto editions of *Romeo and Juliet* prior to 1623 may not have read this play as a play by Shakespeare, bizarre as this notion may sound to readers of Shakespeare in the twenty-first century. Annotating readers felt at liberty to perfect Shakespeare's language and commonplacing readers often ignored essential aspects of Shakespeare's works—Lucrece in *The Rape of Lucrece* or Falstaff in *1 Henry IV*. However, the approaches and practices considered in this chapter should not suggest that early readers read Shakespeare in predictable ways. The 'Waferer' and the Le Neve notebooks, where extracts from *The Rape of Lucrece* show a similar approach to the poem, but a very different appreciation and redeployment of similar topics, are a testimony to what William Sherman charmingly describes as the 'ineluctable specificity of readers and readings'.[65]

---

[64] Eckhardt, *Manuscript Verse Collectors*, 13–14.
[65] Sherman, *Used Books*, xvi.

PART II

CONDITIONS

CHAPTER 9

···

ECONOMY

···

IAN W. ARCHER

In common with most early modern people of his class Shakespeare would have understood 'economy' primarily in terms of 'oeconomy' (an English rendering of the Greek term 'oikonomia'), or household management rather than what we think of as 'the' economy.[1] The household was not only a unit for reproduction; it was also conceived as the basic unit of production in society. According to Xenophon, whose *Treatise of the household* was first translated into English in 1532 and went through at least six editions in the sixteenth century, 'commonly goods and substance do come into the house by the labour and pain of the man, but the woman for the most part is she that keepeth and bestoweth it where need is' (STC 26075: fol. 11v). That basic gendered division of labour, transmitted from the classical sources into the godly conduct manuals, which proliferated during Shakespeare's lifetime, belied a messier reality, where women were much more engaged in paid (but often less visible) work, but it sets out an ideal of the male breadwinner directing the household, and a man's standing in the community, his 'credit' would depend to a large degree on his success in fulfilling this role. Households were fragile units, vulnerable to disruption by the death of a spouse and the strains of providing for too many non-productive children, and subject to wider economic forces, which might threaten their viability. Nor were all men necessarily well-suited to the discharge of their patriarchal obligations; improvidence might cause the resources of the household to be wasted; character defects might make it difficult for the husband to exercise the necessary authority over his wife.[2]

We do not know what combination of factors brought about the arrest of Shakespeare's father's social ascent. John Shakespeare was the son of a Snitterfield

---

[1] Alexandra Shepard, 'Manhood, Credit and Patriarchy in Early Modern England c.1580–1640', *Past and Present* 167 (2000), 75–106, and Shepard, *Meanings of Manhood in Early Modern England* (Oxford: Oxford University Press, 2003).

[2] Keith Wrightson, *Earthly Necessities: Economic Lives in Early Modern Britain* (New Haven, CT: Yale University Press, 2000), 30; Natasha Korda, *Shakespeare's Domestic Economies: Gender and Property in Early Modern England* (Philadelphia: University of Pennsylvania Press, 2002), 25–31.

husbandman and migrated to Stratford-on-Avon, setting up as a glover by 1552. His marriage represented a very modest move up the ladder; Mary Arden was the daughter of his landlord, a relatively prosperous husbandman (with inventoried wealth at death of £77.10s.10d. Robert Arden was perhaps a notch above the Shakespeares in the social pecking order) and she brought a modest amount of land in Wilmcote into the marriage. He prospered in the 1560s and 1570s, diversifying his economic activities into wool dealing, property management, and possibly moneylending, and moving through a succession of offices in Stratford: chamberlain (1561–5), alderman from 1565, and bailiff in 1568–9, a sign that he was in good standing with his neighbours. Frg. But things had turned sour by his son William's late teens. John got into debt, and in 1578 mortgaged the property at Wilmcote to his wife's brother-in-law, and forfeited it when he defaulted on the debt; that he was singled out among the aldermen for exemption from the poor rate signalled a real loss of standing, for rate-paying was an element in social status; in 1586 he was eased off the town council.[3] What had gone wrong? It was probably not because of recusancy (John's claim in 1591 that he did not go to church for fear of arrest for debt may have been genuine and not a cover for Catholicism); perhaps, as Stephen Greenblatt speculates (on the basis of his son's preoccupation with alcohol abuse), he had a drinking problem;[4] but more likely he simply over-extended his operations. The webs of credit in which sixteenth-century businessmen were enmeshed meant that default by debtors could endanger the viability of one's own operations. In London between 1586 and 1614 no fewer than 13 per cent of tradesmen's estates showed inventoried goods worth £1,000, but negative wealth once their debts had been factored in; this made them extraordinarily vulnerable to credit crunches.[5] How many might face the grim message that Timon received, 'the greatest of your having lacks a half | To pay your present debts'? (*Timon of Athens*, 2.2.141–2).

His father's loss of social standing seems to have made a lasting impression on Shakespeare. The family pursued litigation between 1588 and 1598 to recover the lost land at Wilmcote, but it was fruitless. Nevertheless a recovery of status was signalled in 1596 when John was granted a coat of arms, achieving gentry status. The grant which rehearses his father's and grandfather's service to Henry VII, the association with the Ardens whose lineage dated back to the Conquest, and reputed him to be worth £500, was a piece of fiction, but no worse than many the heralds colluded in. There is no evidence of service to the Tudor crown; John's own office-holding days were long past; Mary Arden came from an extremely lowly branch of the Ardens, and the estimate of John's income was wildly exaggerated. We cannot doubt that William had played the major part in securing the grant. But the key to gentility in England lay in the mastery

---

[3] M. Eccles, *Shakespeare in Warwickshire* (Madison: University of Wisconsin Press, 1961); Robert Bearman, 'John Shakespeare: a Papist or Just Penniless?', *Shakespeare Quarterly* 56 (2005), 411–33.

[4] Greenblatt, *Will in the World. How Shakespeare became Shakespeare* (New York: W. W. Norton, 2004), 68–71.

[5] Richard Grassby, 'The Personal Wealth of the Business Community in Seventeenth Century London', *Economic History Review*, 2nd series, 23 (1970), 220–34.

of the social codes that went with the status. As Sir Thomas Smith put it, 'to be short, who can live idly and without manual labour, and will bear the port, charge and countenance of a gentleman: he shall be called master . . . and shall be taken for a gentleman'.[6] Shakespeare's social pretensions were to be mocked by his fellow dramatists. In *Every Man Out of his Humour*, Ben Jonson has one of the buffoon Sogliardo's friends suggest the mocking motto 'not without mustard' for his coat of arms, probably a snide remark on Shakespeare's newly adopted motto, 'Non sanz droict' (not without right). But playing the part of 'William Shakespeare of Stratford on Avon gentleman', as he could now describe himself, required money. The grant of arms testifies to his social ascent and successful management of his household economy.

How had he done it? Obviously not through inheritance, for that had been wasted. Nor through the other conventional means of a favourable marriage. Philip Henslowe's business career benefited from his marriage to his master's widow (in marrying a widow he was following a practice common among London tradesmen, 25 per cent of whose first marriages took this form); the actor Edward Alleyn was to gain a boost by marrying Henslowe's step-daughter, cementing their alliance. By contrast, Shakespeare's marriage in 1582 to Anne Hathaway hardly brought large resources into the household: her father had promised her 10 marks (£6.13s.4d.) on her marriage. Probably the downwardly mobile Shakespeares did not have much leverage on the marriage market in the 1580s, and in any case William married younger than was normal. He was just 18 at the time of the marriage (the average age of male marriage in Elizabeth's reign seems to have been ten years later). Anne was eight years older; the household therefore violated one of the principles of household order, that there should not be a marked disparity in ages, and that preferably the husband should be a couple of years older. Unfortunately we know all too little about the functioning of the Shakespeare household. It was unusual in that William spent so long away in London while Anne was based in Stratford, perhaps enlarging her role, for she would have managed the servants, which one would expect in a household from a couple of this social standing, certainly by the later 1590s. And if the Shakespeares participated in Stratford's malting business (as it seems they might have given the eighty bushels revealed to be in their possession in the 1598 survey), who ran it on a daily basis, if not Anne? But we know nothing of the domestic economy of Shakespeare's household, nor of Anne's possible participation in the Stratford marketplace.

Thanks to the ingenious work of a number of historians who have modelled theatrical finances by means of extrapolation from Philip Henslowe's accounts of takings from the Rose theatre we can make some informed guesses as to the sources of Shakespeare's income. The bulk of his wealth did not derive from writing plays, the payments for which (if Henslowe was typical) averaged £5. Thomas Dekker never made more than £20 a year from writing for the Rose. Rather the key to Shakespeare's wealth lay in his position as a player shareholder. He was one of the eight shareholders in the

---

[6] Mary Dewar, *Sir Thomas Smith 'De Republica Anglorum'* (Cambridge: Cambridge University Press, 1982).

Lord Chamberlain's company formed as part of the reorganization of theatrical companies in 1594. We do not know how he raised the capital required for the initial investment (probably £50), but he may have borrowed it, and he may have had help from aristocratic patrons like Southampton. The return on that investment depended on the amount of playing. The shareholders were entitled to half the takings from the galleries, plus the pennies paid by the standing spectators in the pit, and it has been estimated that each shareholder would have received £60 per annum. When Richard and Cuthbert Burbage confronted the problem of raising the cash to pay for the removal of the timbers from the Theatre and the construction of the Globe in February 1599, they hit upon the solution of bringing in five of the player shareholders, each of whom stumped up £100. Shakespeare joined Augustine Phillips, Thomas Pope, William Kempe, John Heminges, and the Burbages as housekeepers, entitling him to a share in the playhouse rents (the other half of the income from the galleries), which amounted to about £80 per annum for each shareholder, from which the costs of housekeeping had to be deducted. From 1608 the profits would have been boosted when Shakespeare also became an investor in the Blackfriars theatre. Andrew Gurr concludes that by 1613, when he probably sold up, Shakespeare was making up to £200 per annum from his theatrical activities.[7] This was an income appropriate to a middling gentleman.

One of the hallmarks of his rising status was his investment in property in and around Stratford. In May 1597 he acquired New Place, a three-storey ten-roomed brick and timber house, with its sixty-foot frontage on Chapel Street; in September 1602 he acquired cottages in Chapel Lane, possibly to extend the New Place property. His Stratford friends were speculating in 1598 that 'our countryman Mr Shakespeare is willing to disburse some money upon some odd yardland or other at Shottery or near about us'; in the event Shakespeare did not make his purchases until a few years later. In May 1602 he spent £320 on four yardlands (107 acres of arable and 20 acres of pasture) in Old Stratford purchased from John and William Combe. Another substantial investment was the half share of the tithes of Old Stratford, Welcombe, and Bishopton that he purchased for £440 in 1605, yielding an income of £60 per annum.[8]

One wonders how our view of Shakespeare might be altered if an account book were uncovered. It would add flesh to the picture which is emerging of a man embedded in the economic structures of both metropolitan and provincial life, drawing income from a variety of sources.[9] For many years Henslowe's reputation suffered because his business ledger revealed a man for whom the theatre was just one element in a multiple business enterprise: he was a rentier, pawnbroker, an investor in his brother's iron

---

[7] Andrew Gurr, *The Shakespeare Company, 1594–1642* (Cambridge: Cambridge University Press, 2004), 85–119; Susan Cerasano, 'Theatre Entrepreneurs and Theatrical Economics', in Richard Dutton (ed.), *The Oxford Handbook of Early Modern Theatre* (Oxford: Oxford University Press, 2009).

[8] Eccles., *Shakespeare in Warwickshire*, 86–7, 92, 100–2.

[9] E. A. J. Honigmann, 'There is a World Elsewhere: William Shakespeare, Businessman', in Werner Habicht, D. J. Palmer, and Roger Pringle (eds.), *Images of Shakespeare: Proceedings of the Third Congress of the International Shakespeare Association* (Newark: University of Delaware Press, 1988).

foundries, and possibly as interested in bear baiting as drama. We have perhaps got beyond the sweeping Victorian denunciations of Henslowe as an 'old, pawnbroking, stage-managing, bear-baiting usurer',[10] as we have come to realize that his behaviour was not untypical, though elements of the picture find their way into the popular consciousness, as his representation in John Madden's film *Shakespeare in Love* (1998) shows. The more successful of Shakespeare's contemporaries like Edward Alleyn also kept their options open. The theatre was in fact a risky business, and diversifying investments was a means of spreading risk. Shakespeare was no exception.

It is also clear that Shakespeare's circle of friends included several Stratford business-men, lawyers, and gentlemen. If his will is anything to go by his theatrical ties had weakened as the Stratford ones strengthened. He left two marks each to buy memorial rings 'to my fellows John Heminges, Richard Burbage and Henry Condell',[11] but also remembered were Anthony Nash, a gentleman who farmed the tithes for Shakespeare, William Reynolds, another local gentleman, and Hamnet Sadler, a Stratford baker. The overseers were Thomas Russell, a prosperous gentleman reputedly worth £12,000, and the attorney Francis Collins, who became town clerk of Stratford in 1617. We know that Shakespeare was close to other leading Stratford families. Thomas Green, the town clerk from 1603, lived at New Place from 1609 and was on good terms with 'my cousin Shakespeare'.[12] The mercer Richard Quyny, in London in October 1598 on a trip to petition for a reduction in Stratford's tax quotas, had sought to borrow money from him ('Loving countryman, I am bold of you as of a friend, craving your help with £30'; p. 93), and his son Thomas was to marry Judith Shakespeare, though this was not a match of which her father approved. Shakespeare was apparently in with the Combes. John Combe, a moneylender and local landowner, had sold him the land in Old Stratford in 1602 and bequeathed him £5 in 1614; his brother Thomas held the other share of the tithes owned by Shakespeare; another Thomas was bequeathed Shakespeare's sword (p. 119–21).

Just occasionally we get glimpses of Shakespeare's involvement with these men, and he seems very much to be of their class. In the same letter to Quyny in which he refers to Shakespeare's possible interest in land purchases in 1598, Abraham Sturley writes,

> he thinketh it a very fit pattern to move him in the matter of our tithes. By the instructions you can give him therefore, we think it a fair mark to shoot at, and not impossible to hit. It obtained would advance him indeed and would do us much good. (p. 92)

[10] F. Fleay, *Chronicle History of the London Stage 1559–1642* (London: Reeves and Turner, 1890), 94; R. A. Foakes and R. T. Rickert (eds.), *Henslowe's Diary* (Cambridge: Cambridge University Press, 1961); Natasha Korda, 'Household Property, Stage Property: Henslowe as Pawnbroker', *Theatre Journal* 48 (1996), 185–95.

[11] E. K. Chambers (ed.), *William Shakespeare. A Study of Facts and Problems*, 2 vols. (Oxford: Clarendon Press, 1930), 2: 170–4.

[12] Eccles, *Shakespeare in Warwickshire*, 116–29. Further citations given parenthetically in the text.

Here is the mix of calculation and friendship, mutuality and self-interest which characterized the dealings of early modern businessmen. Are we right to detect Shakespeare's reputation for hard-headedness in financial matters in Sturley's sceptical reply to Quyny's news that Shakespeare was willing to help with the £30 loan: 'that our countryman Mr William Shakespeare would procure us money, I will like of as I shall hear when, and where, and how'?[13]

It is striking that Shakespeare did nothing to oppose the enclosure of Welcombe proposed in 1614 (among others) by William Combe, the nephew of his old friend John, and bitterly opposed by the Stratford corporation. This was a matter on which local feelings ran extraordinarily high. Other landowners opposed the scheme. Lord Compton was reminded of his promise to the country at the last digging, a reference to the disturbances in Warwickshire as part of what is known as the Midlands Rising of 1607, a popular protest movement against enclosures. When the Stratford men came to fill in the ditches he had prepared, Combe set his men upon them 'while he sat on horseback and said they were good football players', calling them 'puritan knaves', and telling one of his tenants that 'if he sowed his said wheat land he would eat it up with his sheep'. The bailiff of Stratford complained that Combe's conscience was blinded 'as it seemeth with a desire to make yourself rich by other men's loss'. Here was a classic depopulating enclosure opposed by commons and elite, occurring within a few years of a major popular uprising, which had prompted the sympathetic portrayal of grain rioters in the opening scene of *Coriolanus*. The Stratford corporation pleaded with Shakespeare not to cooperate, and his friend Thomas Greene seems to have made a personal appeal, but the enclosers had taken care to offer him financial guarantees that his interests in the Welcombe tithes would not be affected, and he did not lift a finger to oppose the scheme.[14] Here Shakespeare apparently sided with the forces of capitalist progress against the commons.

So, in contemporary terms, Shakespeare was a successful practitioner of 'oeconomy'. From a rather unpromising start he had prospered, lifting up his family's social status, achieving an income of probably £300 per annum, and dying as a prosperous gentleman, with bequests with a cash value of £350 in his will, and an estate conservatively valued at £1,200. He had done so by a mix of canny investments, participating both in the commercializing entertainment industry in London, and investing in landed property the value of which (as we shall see) was steadily increasing. Upwardly mobile, he was one of the beneficiaries of the new economic opportunities of Elizabethan and early Stuart England, and as such a target for moralists and satirists: 'With mouthing words that better wits have framed | They purchase lands, and now Esquire are made' (2 *Return*, ll. 1927–8). But the question arises as to the degree to which Shakespeare's drama was inflected by the economic issues of the day, and if so, in what ways.

In recent years a number of literary critics have been impressed by the conjunction between the appearance of the commercial theatres and the economic changes (often

[13] Alan Stewart, 'Shakespeare and the Carriers', *Shakespeare Quarterly* 58 (2007), 431–64.
[14] Eccles, *Shakespeare in Warwickshire*, 136–8.

referred to in a kind of shorthand as the transition from feudalism to capitalism) occurring in England at this time. Bruster notes the coincidences of chronology between the construction of the Royal Exchange (a combination of shopping mall and business centre) in 1566–7 and the opening of the Red Lion Theatre in 1567, and the launching of the East India Company and the building of the Globe (both joint stock ventures) in 1599. The theatres were part of 'a larger historical trajectory: the dawn in London of institutionalized capitalism'.[15] Jean-Christophe Agnew suggested that the theatre was

> a laboratory of representational possibilities for a society perplexed by the cultural consequences of nascent capitalism'.[16] David Hawkes claims that the theatre was 'portrayed as a metonym for the market economy and therefore as complicit in the destruction of the feudal order and the 'natural' social relations it supported. . . . It has become a critical commonplace that the concern with shifting identities and 'self-fashioning' that characterises the drama of the period somehow reflects the breakdown of stable feudal relations and the sense of a natural God-given order in the world which such relations foster.[17]

This critical tendency has become subsumed within what is called the 'new economic criticism', although the eclecticism of the approaches adopted has led some to doubt its coherence as a critical movement.[18]

The homologies between theatre and market are certainly compelling. They were standard elements in the anti-theatrical discourse where it was often not so much the plays that were the problem, but the fact that one was paying for them. For Stephen Gosson, the playhouses were 'the very markets of bawdry, where choice without shame hath been as free as it is for your money in the Royal Exchange, to take a short stock, or a long, a falling band or a French ruff'.[19] Thomas Dekker wrote that

> the theatre is your poets' Royal Exchange upon which their muses (that are now turned to merchants) meeting, barter away that light commodity of words for a lighter ware than words, plaudits and the breath of the great beast, which (like the threatening of the two cowards) vanish all into air)[20]

In condemning the plasticity of theatrical identities the moralists also turned to commercial images, Gosson comparing the player to 'a merchant's finger that stands sometimes for a thousand, sometimes for a cipher'.[21]

---

[15] Douglas Bruster, *Drama and the Market in the Age of Shakespeare* (Cambridge: Cambridge University Press, 1992), 4.

[16] Jean-Christophe Agnew, *Worlds Apart: The Market and the Theater in Anglo-American Thought, 1550–1750* (Cambridge: Cambridge University Press, 1986), 54.

[17] David Hawkes, *Idols of the Marketplace: Idolatry and Commodity Fetishism in English Literature, 1580–1700* (Basingstoke: Palgrave Macmillan 2001), 88.

[18] Bruster, *Drama and the Market in the Age of Shakespeare.*

[19] W. C. Hazlitt (ed.), *The English Drama and Stage under the Tudor and Stuart Princes, 1543–1664* (London 1869), 214–15.

[20] Dekker, Thomas, *The Gull's Horn Book* (1609), 27.

[21] Hazlitt, *The English Drama and Stage under the Tudor and Stuart Princes*, 166.

Recent work by theatre historians has complicated the relationship between the theatres and capitalism. It is possible that the development of commercial playing was driven by pressures from the court as much as by the marketplace. The proliferation of playhouses in the 1570s was probably encouraged by the Queen's ministers anxious to cut the costs of the Revels Office by outsourcing productions; many of the overheads of court entertainments could be passed on to the theatrical companies.[22] The teleological accounts of commercial playing have a strong metropolitan bias, which has been called into question by the work of the Records of Early English Drama project. With at least twenty-five companies regularly touring the provinces in the 1590s, one might question whether playing in London really was more remunerative than playing in the provinces. London playing companies were fragile affairs as the various crashes of 1593–4 all too clearly demonstrated. It is true that the theatres were run as business enterprises, and there were important spin-off effects such as the employment generated for the watermen of London, but with annual turnovers at each of the amphitheatres of between £1,400 and £1,700 in the 1590s (maybe rising to £2,000 at the beginning of the 1600s), they were hardly major components of the wider London economy.[23] The volume of cloth exports in the 1560s has been conservatively estimated at £1m; a recent estimate puts the domestic market for clothing at a minimum of £3m at the turn of the century; the stock subscribed for the first East India Company voyage in 1601 was £68,373; in 1617 the Company raised £1.629m from 954 subscribers.[24] These are all perhaps rather unfair comparators, but playgoing was only a tiny element of the consumption habits of members of the elite: at 1s. to 2s. per theatrical visit for the best seats (minimum admission prices at the Cockpit and Blackfriars were 6d.) one would have to attend an awful lot of plays to match the kind of spending the elite undertook on building, clothing, jewels, and plate. The development of the theatre undoubtedly represented a step-change in the commercialization of leisure but its wider significance should not be exaggerated.

Another problem with some of the work exploring the relationship between the economy and the theatre is that it too frequently draws upon models of economic change with which historians are uncomfortable, and it is perhaps for this reason that historians have so rarely engaged with it. The transition from feudalism to capitalism is regularly invoked though the terms are rarely explained, and a rather compressed chronology is implied. Agnew describes the period 1550–1650 as one where 'the disruptive and transformative power of market exchange were first brought home to Britons'; these were 'years of expansion and differentiation of trade, of unprecedented prosperity and depression in the textile industry, of unrelenting inflation, and of the

---

[22] W. R. Streitbger, 'Adult Playing Companies to 1583', in Richard Dutton (ed.), *The Oxford Handbook of Early Modern Theatre* (Oxford: Oxford University Press, 2009), 19–35.

[23] Gurr, *The Shakespeare Company, 1594–1642*, 105–11.

[24] Ian W. Archer, 'Commerce and Consumption', in Norman Jones and Susan Doran (eds.), *The Elizabethan World* (Oxford: Blackwell, forthcoming); W. R. Scott, *The Constitution and Finance of English, Scottish, and Irish Joint Stock Companies to 1720*, 3 vols. (Cambridge: Cambridge University Press, 1910–12), 1: 148; 3: 465.

seemingly inexorable commodification of land and labor'.[25] For Natasha Korda the same period may be 'broadly defined by the dissolution of the monasteries, the breakdown of the medieval manorial system of agriculture, the enclosure of land, the decline of subsistence farming as arable land was converted to pasture, the expropriation of the agricultural population from the land, and the bloody legislation criminalizing the population'; it was a period of 'transition to a market economy'; 'household production was gradually being replaced by nascent capitalist industry'.[26] For Lena Orlin the 'exploding availability of material goods in the early modern period' represented a pervasive 'cultural preoccupation'.[27]

While historians might agree with the broad trajectory of change outlined in these views (and they all come from critics that social, economic, and cultural historians of the period would be well advised to read), their language would be more cautious, and they would insert many (doubtless irritating) qualifications. They would want to clarify the chronology of change. Sometimes reading the literary critics one gets the impression that the transition from feudalism to capitalism, or the rise of the market economy, or the consumer revolution occurred in Shakespeare's lifetime. This is not the case. One of the leading economic historians of the Middle Ages argues that medieval England was a highly market-oriented society.[28] That London in 1300 was a larger city than when Shakespeare arrived in it in the 1580s suggests that the market mechanisms to feed and clothe a large population were well developed at an early stage.[29] It is true that inflationary pressures in the late sixteenth century were serious, but the depression in real wages may not have been as great as was once thought, and in any case the size of the wage-dependent population is questionable because many craftsmen remained self-employed. Estimates of the proportion of poor in the population have been down-scaled; perhaps 5–7 per cent of households were dependent on regular relief from neighbours, another 20 per cent or so hovered on the margins of subsistence. Vagrants loomed large in elite phobias but their numbers were not overwhelming. The shift away from household production is likewise much exaggerated: there were big employers like the East India Company docks, and miners were being reorganized into larger units as the industry became more heavily capitalized, but the bulk of industrial production continued to take place within a domestic setting, albeit with the supply of raw materials increasingly controlled by merchant entrepreneurs. As for agrarian change, the force of landlord entrepreneurialism was frequently blunted by paternalistic considerations as well as institutional constraints (the legal obstacles in the way of

[25] Agnew, *Worlds Apart*, 7–8.

[26] Natasha Korda, *Shakespeare's Domestic Economies: Gender and Property in Early Modern England* (Philadelphia: University of Pennsylvania Press, 2002), 19, 36, 160–1.

[27] Lena Orlin, *Private Matters and Public Culture in Early Modern England* (Ithaca, NY: Cornell University Press, 1994), 255.

[28] Richard Britnell, *The Commercialisation of English Society 1000–1500*, 2nd edn. (Manchester: Manchester University Press, 1997).

[29] Derek Keene, 'Material London in Time and Space', in Lena Orlin (ed.), *Material London, c.1600* (Philadelphia: University of Pennsylvania Press, 2000).

wholesale revisions of tenures). The disappearance of the peasantry was a protracted process. In some areas the consolidation of holdings was well advanced by 1550; in others smallholdings proliferated in the later sixteenth century, the real process of consolidation was delayed until the years after 1650 when lower agricultural prices made smaller units less viable. Much of rural England had already been enclosed by 1500; enclosure often took place by agreement between peasants (as seems to have been the case in the Arden family) rather than being imposed by a depopulating landlord; enclosure in the sixteenth century was a more regionally specific problem (particularly in the Midlands where the lack of water communications incentivized sheep farming given the relatively higher costs of transporting wheat than wool). While trade was beginning to diversify, France, Germany, and the Low Countries still accounted for over three-quarters of cloth exports in 1600.[30] There is considerable conceptual muddle over the consumer revolution, several historians confusing luxury spending by the elite with the broader culture of consumption, which would constitute the true revolution. William Harrison's account of growing standards of domestic comfort is much cited, and while it is true that probate inventories show clearly the multiplication of consumer goods, the scale of the phenomenon should not be exaggerated. Kent probate inventories listed 92 per cent of linen in 1600, but only 44 per cent feather beds and 37 per cent cushions; in Cornwall the impact of consumerism was less marked with 59 per cent listing linen, 33 per cent feather beds and 12 per cent cushions.[31] It is also worth stressing that there were some significant weaknesses in market mechanisms in early seventeenth-century England. Remedies for debtors and creditors were very limited: as the experience of Shakespeare's father shows raising money on mortgages was highly risky, rendering one liable to forfeiture of the property on a short-term loan. Bills of exchange and promissory notes were negotiable only to a limited extent. Commercial and contract law were still in a pretty primitive state. As Leinwand remarks, Agnew was guilty of premature dating of across the board 'liquidity of the commodity form'.[32]

It is not that historians deny the processes of change, though literary critics might be forgiven for complaining that they are guilty of privileging the local, contingent, and variable, at the expense of the big picture. But they tend to start not with commerce, credit, and markets, but with the way in which the economy responded to the demographic changes, which are curiously overlooked as motors of change in the models influencing much of the literary scholarship. In the course of Shakespeare's lifetime the population of England rose from 3.06m to 4.51m, putting immense pressure

[30] Joan Thirsk (ed.), *The Agrarian History of England and Wales*, vol. 4: *1500–1640* (Cambridge: Cambridge University Press, 1967); Keith Wrightson, *Earthly Necessities: Economic Lives in Early Modern Britain* (New Haven, CT: Yale University Press, 2000).

[31] Georges Edelen (ed.), *William Harrison. The Description of England* (Ithaca, NY: Cornell University Press, 1968); Mark Overton et al., *Production and Consumption in English Households, 1600–1750* (London: Routledge, 2004).

[32] Theodore Leinwand, *Theatre, Finance and Society in Early Modern England* (Cambridge: Cambridge University Press, 1999).

upon landed resources, and causing inflation. The key to success or failure for the peasantry was whether one had access to sufficient land to produce a surplus for sale on the market, and the crucial dividing line may have been that between yeomen and husbandmen. Subsistence farmers were vulnerable to extra calls on family incomes (for example, additional children) and to the vagaries of the harvest. There was a strong possibility that they would have to consume their seed corn to survive a difficult year; they might be able to carry the resulting burden of debt for a while, but repeated harvest failures such as occurred in the 1590s might force them into the ranks of the labouring poor. Yeomen farmers, on the other hand, were much better placed to benefit from rising agricultural prices, and some of them were able to move over the course of several generations into the ranks of the gentry. Historians, following Keith Wrightson,[33] have dubbed this process 'social polarization'. It will do as a shorthand for the changes of the period, but it needs to be appreciated that there were very considerable regional variations; smallholdings were much more resilient in areas with extensive common rights such as fenland and forest communities, or where significant by-employments were available through rural industries, and here polarization was less marked, though there might still be large numbers of poor cottagers.

In 1520, the proportion of people living in towns of over 5,000 people was 5 per cent; by 1600 it had risen to 8 per cent, but the vast majority of this growth was accounted for by London, which had a population of around 50,000 in 1550 and 200,000 in 1600. To some extent London's growth was parasitic on the provincial economy, its merchants exploiting their locational advantages with respect to the entrepots in the Low Countries and northern Germany, sucking away trade from the provincial ports like Southampton. As the period progressed the beneficial effects of London's growth may have been more apparent as import-led growth fuelled spin-off industries like sugar refining and shipbuilding, and as the stimulating effects of London demand began to percolate through the provinces. The switch from wood to coal as the capital's primary source of fuel entailed considerable increases in the output of the northeastern coalfields (shipments to London tripled in the twenty years after 1580), and stimulated a large carrying trade down the east coast.[34] The intensification of market relations between the capital and the provinces is evident in the transactions conducted by Richard Quyny, Stratford's man of business in London in the later 1590s. He buys groceries, clothes, and books for family members, assists a fellow townsman in seeking an apprenticeship for his son, and arranges to pay debts to London drapers for a kinsman.[35]

For medium-sized market towns like Stratford, the Elizabethan and early Stuart experience was mixed. On the best estimates, Stratford's population grew from 1,450 to

[33] Keith Wrightson, *English Society 1580–1680* (London: Hutchinson, 1982).

[34] Peter Clark (ed.), *The Cambridge Urban History of Britain*, vol. 2: *1540–1840* (Cambridge: Cambridge University Press, 2000); Wrightson, *Earthly Necessities*; A. L. Beier and Roger A. P. Finlay, *London 1500–1700: The Making of the Metropolis* (London: Longman, 1986).

[35] Eccles, *Shakespeare in Warwickshire*, 96–7.

2,500 between 1563 and 1598, but much of this may have been the result of an influx of subsistence migrants from the countryside rather than reflecting a buoyant economy. Its position on the boundary between the wood pasture district of the Arden and the Fielden arable areas of southern Warwickshire should have strengthened its marketing role, but there were complaints of the collapse of traditional industries.[36] 'The said town', its governors alleged in 1591, 'is now fallen much into decay for want of such trade as heretofore they have had by clothing and making of yarn employing and maintaining a number of poor people by the same which now live in great penury and misery by reason they are not set on work as they have been'.[37] The town, already in very serious difficulties because of two fires in 1594 and 1595 (reportedly responsible for £12,000 worth of damage), suffered from famine in 1596–7, and social relations were fraught with tension. As the ranks of the poor swelled to 400 by 1598, the town authorities took stern measures against immigration and unlicenced alehouses. The poor saw members of the town elite, including Shakespeare's associates Richard Quyny and Abraham Sturley, profiting from their dealing in grain (malting was a mainstay of the Stratford economy) and grew 'malcontent', one of them, a shoemaker, saying that 'he hoped within a week to lead some of them in a halter', meaning the maltsters, another, a weaver, saying that 'if God send my lord of Essex down shortly [he hoped] to see them hanged on gibbets at their own doors'. Some among the elite showed little sense of social responsibility. Thomas Rogers, the bailiff in 1595, we are told, was guilty of forestalling the market, 'and he doth say that he will justify it, and he careth not a turd for them all'.[38] The Midland Revolt of 1607 gave the representation of the conflict over the food supply between patricians and plebeians in *Coriolanus* considerable topicality, but Shakespeare's experience of the confrontational politics of subsistence in the Stratford of the 1590s was probably another element in his shaping of the episode.

It was therefore a period of considerable economic change (although not quite of the kind and at the speed some of the criticism suggests) with serious implications for the pattern of social relations. But did these changes really engage Shakespeare's imagination? There are occasional vivid scenes from the world of work, for instance as Hamlet describes Denmark's war economy, 'such daily cost of brazen cannon | And foreign mart for implements of war, | . . . such impress of shipwrights' (*Hamlet* 1.1.72–4), in which audiences might have recalled the large-scale operations of the Royal Ordnance in the Minories close by the Tower and the naval dockyards at Deptford. We glimpse the growing availability of consumer goods when the merchant Gremio boasts of his 'house within the city':

---

[36] Alan Dyer, 'Crisis and Recovery. Government and Society in Stratford, 1540–1640', in Robert Bearman (ed.), *The History of an English Borough. Stratford on Avon, 1196–1996* (Stroud: Alan Sutton for the Shakespeare Birthplace Trust, 1997).

[37] Levi Fox (ed.), *Minutes and accounts of the Corporation of Stratford-upon-Avon*, vol. 5: *1593–1598* (Stratford-upon-Avon, 1990), 115–16.

[38] E. I. Fripp, *Master Richard Quyny. Bailiff of Stratford-upon-Avon and friend of William Shakespeare* (Oxford: Oxford University Press, 1924), 103, 125–6.

> My hangings all of Tyrian tapestry.
> In ivory coffers I have stuff'd my crowns,
> In cypress chests my arras counterpoints,
> Costly apparel, tents, and canopies,
> Fine linen, Turkey cushions boss'd with pearl,
> Valance of Venice gold in needlework,
> Pewter and brass, and all things that belongs
> To house or housekeeping.
> (*The Taming of the Shrew*, 2.1.345–52)

Gremio's inventory perhaps surpasses the levels of luxury to be found in even the wealthiest of London merchant houses in the late 1590s (their furnishings were rather less exotic), but it does carry echoes of William Harrison's account of the 'great provision of tapestry, turkey work, pewter, brass, fine linen, and thereto costly cupboards of plate.[39] In Autolycus's pack with its sheets, haberdashery, fashion accessories, and ballads we get a vivid glimpse of the means by which consumer goods circulated from London through the network of chapmen.

Images drawn from the world of material goods, traffic, and exchange are found throughout the works. Greenblatt has noted how his experience of his father's gloving business provided a rich range of images from the leather trades.[40] Wooing is often referred to as a commercial venture. Troilus describes his pursuit of Cressida:

> Her bed is India; there she lies, a pearl.
> Between our Ilium and where she resides
> Let it be called the wild and wand'ring flood,
> Ourself the merchant, and this sailing Pandar
> Our doubtful hope, our convoy and our barque.   (1.1.100–14)

Romeo tells Juliet 'were thou as far | As that vast shore washed with the farthest sea, | I should adventure for such merchandise' (2.24–6). Bassanio hopes that by 'adventuring' to Belmont, he will be able to repay his debt to Antonio, gaining a lady 'richly left' whose 'sunny locks | Hang on her temples like a golden fleece' (1.1.143, 161, 169–70). Falstaff pursues Mrs Page as 'a region in Guiana all gold and bounty' (1.3.361–2). *The Taming of the Shrew* and *The Merry Wives of Windsor* explore, as Natasha Korda has shown, the dynamics of the household economy with which this chapter opened.[41] It is also true that the world of commerce and money-lending is central to *The Merchant of Venice*, *The Comedy of Errors*, and *Timon of Athens*. The commercial imagery in *Troilus and Cressida* is so pervasive that the war between Troy and Greece might be conceived of as 'an amplified struggle between merchant powers' (Bruster, *Drama and the Market*: 102); Troy could be a figure for mercantile London, 'this great Grandmother of Corporations, Madame Troynovant'[42] as Dekker put it.

---

[39] Edelen, *William Harrison. The Description of England.*
[40] Greenblatt, *Will in the World*, 55–6.
[41] Korda, *Shakespeare's Domestic Economies.*
[42] Bowers 1953–1961, 1: 181.

But the fact of the matter is that Shakespeare never wrote a city comedy, the genre in which other writers found the most appropriate vehicle for the exploration and negotiation of the tensions wrought by economic change—the closest he got was *The Merry Wives*.[43] Shakespeare shows little interest in how his characters make their money. As Lena Orlin writes, 'we don't know what skills of huswifery and industry Mistresses Ford and Page practise, what trades Masters Ford and Page pursue, or how the Pages have accumulated wealth of sufficient magnitude to make their daughter a prize on the marriage market'.[44] Petrucchio, we learn, has 'better'd' his estate (*The Taming of the Shrew* 2.1.118), but we don't know how. The two feuding households of the Montagues and Capulets are not clearly situated in Verona's economic system. How does the Old Shepherd in *The Winter's Tale* rise from 'very nothing' to an 'unspeakable estate' (4.2.39-40) such that he can host the lavish sheep-shearing festival? The fortunes of Shakespeare's characters are more usually presented as a result of ethical choices rather than the result of economic processes. So Poor Tom's descent from servingman to Bedlam beggar is the result of pride, lust, and drunkenness (*King Lear* 3.4.79-86), the classic moralists' explanation of vagrancy in terms of moral failings rather than economic victimization. Timon's bounty is brought to an end by his creditors, for he is in debt to usurers, with his lands as collateral for his debts, but the message is that Timon falls because of his prodigality (his 'raging waste': 2.1.4) and his failure to see the greed and avarice that were masked by the hollow courtesies of civil society: 'it grieves me to see so many dip their meat in one man's blood' (1.2.39-40) remarks the philosopher Apemantus of the false friends and flatterers who abuse Timon's hospitality.

Where Shakespeare did adopt a commercial backdrop, it is not always as clearly delineated as it might have been. Lisa Jardine has noted the difference between the specificity in the depiction of mercantile activities in Marlowe's *Jew of Malta* as compared to Shakespeare's rather sketchier vision of the realities of trade in *The Merchant of Venice*. We learn that Barabas has ships coming in from Cairo and Alexandria and a factor in Hormuz on the Persian Gulf; his ships are laden 'with riches, and exceeding store | Of Persian silks, of gold, and orient pearl'; lying 'in the Malta road', their 'bills of writing' (required for customs administration) are ready; the custom comes 'to more | Than many merchants of the town are worth'; the transportation of his goods requires sixty camels, thirty mules, and twenty wagons (*The Jew of Malta*, 1.1.45, 50, 57, 65-6). Barabas is plausibly presented as the arch merchant intelligencer, with good knowledge of fortifications and international diplomacy. In what Jardine calls the 'diabolical merchant-usurer-intelligencer'[45] one is reminded of the towering figure of Elizabethan commerce, Sir Thomas Gresham, who combined all those roles. The trading practises and commercial relations of Shakespeare's Venetians are much less visible. Antonio's argosies to Tripolis, Mexico, the Indies, and England do not map

---

[43] Lena Orlin, 'Shakespearean Comedy and Material Life', in R. Dutton and J. E. Howard (eds.), *A Companion to Shakespeare's Works*, vol.3: *The Comedies* (Oxford: Blackwell, 2003), 159–81.

[44] Orlin, 'Shakespearean Comedy and Material Life', 160.

[45] Jardine (1996), 99–100, 103.

easily onto the trading patterns of either late-sixteenth-century Venice or England. We learn that Bassanio has 'disabled' his estate by conspicuous consumption beyond his 'faint means' (1.1.123, 125) but little more about his economic circumstances. Perhaps this is why critics differ over whether he should be seen as a gentleman prodigal, a proto-bourgeois adventurer, or the classic gentry amateur investor in privateering enterprise.

Shakespeare did occasionally stick his neck out with hard-hitting observations on contemporary social and economic processes. This is most obvious in *As You Like It* with scenes set in the Forest of Arden. The wood to which the banished duke has retreated with his companions serves as a refuge from the 'painted pomp' (2.1.3) of the 'envious court' (2.1.4), where they live as a fellowship of 'co-mates and brothers in exile' (2.1.1) enacting what Peter Holbrook has called 'an egalitarian social fantasy'.[46] But the social realities of the forest stand in counterpoint to this idealized vision of social harmony and mutuality. The shepherd Corin tells us that he is 'shepherd to another man | And do not sheer the fleeces that I graze' (2.4.77–8). He has been reduced to the status of a wage labourer, a classic victim of the depopulating landlord, a man of 'churlish disposition' who neglects the conventional paternalistic obligations of 'deeds of hospi-tality' (2.4.79, 81), and proposes to sell the estate. The result will be a deserted village: 'By reason of his absence there is nothing | That you will feed on' (2.4.84–5). The spectre of vagrancy haunts the play. The new man Oliver du Bois, succeeding to his father, old Sir Rowland, alienates the faithful family retainer Adam, 'a man not for the fashion of these times | Where none will sweat but for promotion' (2.3.60–1), and victimizes his younger brother denying him the gentlemanly education that was his due, and keeping him 'like a peasant' (1.1.64). The options facing these displaced persons are grim. Orlando remon-strates with Adam when he suggests they turn to the road:

> What wouldst thou have me go and beg my food,
> Or with a base and boisterous sword enforce
> A thievish living on the common road?   (2.3.325)

But he accepts the force of necessity and joins Adam. The 'uncouth forest' resembles a 'desert' (2.6.6, 16) and Adam is reduced to near starvation, telling his new master, 'I can go no further. Oh, I die for food! Here I lie down and measure out my grave' (2.6.1–2). In this play Shakespeare gets close to the misery of the 1590s, displacement, vagrancy, and starvation, but he offers little in the way of solution. Corin's farm is saved by an act of *noblesse oblige* by Celia but nothing is done at the end of the play to right Arden's economy, just as Shakespeare stood aside over the Welcombe enclosures.

Some critics have seen Shakespeare developing a critique of capitalism in *Troilus and Cressida* and *Timon of Athens*.[47] The pervasive commercial imagery drives home

---

[46] Peter Holbrook, 'Class X: Shakespeare, Class, and the Comedies', in Richard Dutton and Jean E. Howard (eds.), *A Companion to Shakespeare's Works*, vol. 3, *The Comedies* (Oxford: Blackwell, 2003), 67–89, at 80.

[47] Douglas Bruster, *Drama and the Market in the Age of Shakespeare* (Cambridge: Cambridge University Press, 1992); Karl Klein (ed.), *Timon of Athens* (Cambridge: Cambridge University Press, 2001); Hugh Grady, '*Timon of Athens*: The Dialectic of Usury, Nihilism and Art', in R. Dutton and

the message that human relationships have become commodified. We have already seen how Troilus conceives of his relationship with Cressida as a quest for an Indian pearl; the image is reused of Helen of Troy: 'why, she is a pearl | Whose price hath launched above a thousand ships, | And turned crowned kings to merchants' (2.2.82–4). As Bruster points out he is recalling Marlowe's line, 'Is this the face that launched a thousand ships' but in changing price to face, Shakespeare points up how 'ascribed worth replaces essential value'.[48] Hector debates with Troilus on the nature of value, seeking to question Troilus' relativism ('what's ought but as 'tis valued?', 2.2.51) with the argument that value is an inherent quality. 'But value dwells not in particular will. It holds his estimate and dignity | As well wherein 'tis precious of itself | As in the prizer' (2.2.52–5). Timon continues the debate in his diatribe against the alienating effects of gold, in two speeches that made a powerful impression on Karl Marx: 'much of this will make | Black white, foul fair, wrong right, | Base noble, old young, coward valiant' (4.3.28–30). Gold has the transformative power to turn negative qualities into their opposites; ethical values are exposed as contingent and dependent on material self-interest: 'This yellow slave | Will knit and break religions, bless th'accursed, | Make the hoar leprosy adored, place thieves, | And give them title, knee, and approbation | With senators on the bench' (4.3.34–8). Gold's power is so disruptive of human relationships that 'beasts | May have the world in empire' (4.3.394–5). The play has already demonstrated the way in which money distorts social interactions: the beneficiaries of Timon's bounty who mouth the platitudes of hospitable reciprocities are in reality bloodsuckers who will turn on him as soon as it is advantageous.

But the question remains as to whether Shakespeare intends a systematic critique of capitalism. We can agree with Bruster that *Troilus and Cressida* 'echoes traditional reservations over mercantile exchange and merchant adventurism locating some of the city's ills in the uncontrolled dynamism of the market', but that is not the same as a full-blown critique of the system.[49] Indeed the language of commerce in the play perhaps functions as a vehicle for the critique of devalued human relationships, which on the surface after all is the matter of the play, rather than the pervasive language of commodification being intended as an indicator of the corrosive nature of capitalism. Likewise, the message of Timon may be one of individual failing and personal responsibility. Timon has failed to use his wealth in moderation; he has flouted the basic classical and biblical ethical codes.[50] According to Aristotle, generosity was a mark of honour, but its potential varied according to one's means; while the Bible warned of Tyre, 'the crowning city, whose merchants are princes, whose traffickers are

J. E Howard (eds.), *A Companion to Shakespeare's Works*, vol. 1: *The Tragedies* (Oxford: Blackwell, 2003), 430–51.

   [48] Bruster (1992), 104.

   [49] Bruster, *Drama and the Market in the Age of Shakespeare*, 99, 117.

   [50] Philip Brockbank, *On Shakespeare: Jesus, Shakespeare, and Karl Marx, and other Essays* (Oxford: Blackwell, 1989).

the honorable of the earth', but which the Lord purposed to lay waste 'to stain the pride of all glory', so that 'after the end of seventy years shall Tyre sing as a harlot' (Isaiah 23).

In any case as some critics have come to recognize early modern capitalism was not anonymized but communal.[51] As the work of Craig Muldrew has demonstrated, the whole system depended on personal relationships. In an underdeveloped credit system, loans had to be guaranteed by sureties, individuals who would stand to pay up if the debtor defaulted. This meant that one's credit was bound up intimately with one's personal standing in the community; hence men's anxieties on reputation focused on their economic self-sufficiency, while women's concentrated more on their sexual honesty.[52] Credit relationships were often deeply personal, operating through ties of kinship and friendship and sustained by sociability, hence Quyny's appeal to his 'countryman' and invocation of the ties of friendship when asking Shakespeare for money. Antonio captures something of this when he promises Bassanio his 'purse' and his 'person' (1.1.138), but the play which came closest to delineating the realities of commercial relationships is *The Comedy of Errors* where, as Curtis Perry has shown, interpersonal trust is 'an essential part of the way Ephesian business is conducted',[53] and the farce in the play is built around the disruption of these fragile networks of exchange built upon trust. Antipholous Ephesus's 'reverend reputation' and 'credit infinite' (5.1.5–6) is enough to ensure that he gets the gold chain form Angelo before paying for it; when Angelo learns that he will not be paid for the chain he is most concerned with the damaging effect on his reputation should his circumstances become public knowledge: 'Consider how it stands upon my credit' (4.1.68).

Douglas Bruster has recently noted the different intellectual currents in the new economic criticism, a division between what he calls the 'reckoned' and the 'rash', the former positivistic, quantitative, historicist, specific, and seeing the economic as an object, the latter more theoretically engaged, thematic, epistemic in its historical orientation, generalizing, and seeing economic as a metaphor. It is a helpful distinction and evident in the works this chapter has discussed.[54] Bruster implies no value judgement, but historians will have more affinity with the reckoned approach, which perhaps explains why so much of the criticism has passed them by. Perhaps they will pay more attention if the two approaches fertilized each other; a little more clarity over terms (feudalism, capitalism, consumerism), and an acknowledgement of the messiness of the historical process could yield critical dividends.

---

[51] Leinwand, *Theatre, Finance and Society in Early Modern England*; Richards (2002); Curtis Perry, 'Commerce, Community, and Nostalgia in *The Comedy of Errors*', in Linda Woodbridge (ed.), *Money and the Age of Shakespeare* (Houndmills: Palgrave Macmillan, 2003), 39–51.

[52] Craig Muldrew, *The Economy of Obligation: the Culture of Credit and Social Relations in Early Modern England* (Basingstoke: Macmillan, 1998); Alexandra Shepard, 'Manhood, Credit and Patriarchy in Early Modern England c.1580–1640', *Past and Present* 167 (2000), 75–106.

[53] Perry, 'Commerce, Community, and Nostalgia in *The Comedy of Errors*', 42.

[54] Bruster 'On a Certain Tendency in Economic Criticism of Shakespeare', in Linda Woodbridge (ed.), *Money and the Age of Shakespeare* (Houndmills: Palgrave Macmillan, 2003).

CHAPTER 10

....

STATUS

....

JAMES KEARNEY

NOT WITHOUT MUSTARD

....

IN Ben Jonson's *Every Man Out of his Humour* (1599), Sogliardo—a rube with money—
buys a coat of arms and gentle status. For £30, he has purchased the ability, as he says,
to 'write myself gentleman now'.[1] The ensuing discussion of the absurd design of the
coat of arms prompts one of Sogliardo's interlocutors to suggest that the heraldic 'word'
or motto accompanying the arms should be 'Not without mustard' (3.1.244). To get the
joke, we need to know that Jonson's mustard is allusive and has multiple referents. In
literary London of the 1590s, 'Not without mustard' was already a punch line, first used
in Thomas Nashe's *Pierce Penniless* (1592). In *Pierce*, Nashe tells the tale of a 'young heir
or cockney' who goes to sea to make his fortune. When a storm threatens shipwreck
and he sees his fellow sailors praying for deliverance, he vows—'in a desperate jest'—
never again to eat dried cod. Since salted fish—such as dried cod (or haberdine)—was
the common fare of sailors and something that a man at sea would probably
prefer never to encounter again, his offering is a mockery of the earnest vows of
his compatriots.[2] Once the skies clear and he has safely made it to the shore,
however, he equivocates on even this mild vow of abstinence, adding an addendum
to his oath by crying out 'Not without mustard, good Lord, not without mustard'.[3]
Playing on the comic resonance the rallying cry 'Not without mustard' might have for

[1] Ben Jonson, *Every Man Out of his Humour*, ed. Helen Ostovich (Manchester: Manchester
University Press, 2001), 3.1.213–14. Subsequent citations from *Every Man Out of his Humour* refer to
this edition and will be cited in the text.
[2] On the significance of dried codfish both in this episode and in the period generally, see Edward
Test, 'The Tempest and the Newfoundland Cod Fishery', in Barbara Sebek and Stephen Deng (eds.),
Global Traffic: Discourses and Practices of Trade in English Literature and Culture from 1550 to 1700 (New
York: Palgrave Macmillan, 2008), 201–20.
[3] Thomas Nashe, *The Unfortunate Traveler and other Works*, J. B. Steane (ed.) (New York: Penguin
Books, 1985; first published 1972), 66–7.

parts of his audience, Jonson deploys the allusion to Nashe's irreverent sailor to place the 'essential clown' Sogliardo in a tradition of ne'er-do-wells and would-be social climbers.[4] As Jonson uses it, however, the joke is not simply a bit of clever recycling but a newly current punch line that takes a well-aimed shot at his fellow playwright, William Shakespeare.

The editorial and critical tradition explains Jonson's barbed reference by directing us to certain details of Shakespeare's biographical record. In 1575 or 1576 Shakespeare's father, John Shakespeare, applied for what is technically 'armigerous status', what we might call the right to bear a coat of arms, or—in Sogliardo's terms—the right to 'write [oneself] gentleman'. This request was either denied or ignored by the College of Arms and its leading officer, the Garter Principal King of Arms; perhaps the application fell on deaf ears because the claim was not strong enough or the offered 'fee' was not large enough.[5] In any case, the appeal lay fallow for twenty years until it was cultivated once again by John's son, William. In 1596 William Shakespeare seems to have succeeded in obtaining for his father the right to sign himself 'gentleman'; and, of course, the status so obtained for the father would, in theory, be inherited by the dutiful son. The application was vetted and the arms—with the device of a falcon shaking a spear— granted by William Dethick, the Garter Principal King of Arms at the time. Dethick was evidently notorious for granting armigerous status to dubious claimants; for the right price, you too could be a gentleman. In 1602 Ralph Brooke, the York Herald, 'prepared charges against Dethick . . . for having improperly granted arms to some twenty-three "mean" individuals'. Among these twenty-three individuals, Brooke named John Shakespeare, by then deceased.[6] Brooke evidently felt that Dethick abused his position by elevating the 'meaner sort'—such as players—to armigerous status. As G. Blakemore Evans and J. J. M. Tobin note, 'in a manuscript volume now in the Folger Shakespeare Library . . . Brooke made a sketch of the Shakespeare arms and below it sneeringly wrote "Shakespeare ye Player | by Garter [i.e. Dethick]" '.[7] We do not know what became of Brooke's charges; all we know is that the status of the Shakespeares as 'gentle' was contested. In light of this fraught history, the 'word' or motto chosen to accompany the coat of arms strikes a suitably defensive posture: 'non sanz droict' ('not without right').[8] This contested status and defensive posture are, of course, ripe for mockery. And in Jonson's comedy, the adamant claim 'not without right' becomes the absurd cry 'not without mustard'. The reference to mustard also seems to play on the fact that the predominant colour in the design for Shakespeare's coat of arms was gold. By

[4] Jonson, *Every Man*, List of Characters, l. 74.

[5] For details of the biographical record discussed here, see Samuel Schoenbaum, *William Shakespeare: A Documentary Life* (New York: Oxford University Press, 1975), esp. 27–40; 161–81.

[6] G. Blakemore Evans and J. J. M. Tobin, 'Grant of Arms to John Shakespeare' in Appendix C of G. Blakemore Evans et al. (eds.), *The Riverside Shakespeare*, 2nd edn. (Boston: Houghton Mifflin, 1997), 1954.

[7] Evans and Tobin, 'Grant of Arms to John Shakespeare', 1954.

[8] On the coat-of-arms episode, see Schoenbaum, *Documentary Life*, 166–73; Evans and Tobin, 'Grant of Arms to John Shakespeare', 1953–54; Katherine Duncan-Jones, *Ungentle Shakespeare: Scenes from His Life* (London: Arden Shakespeare, 2001), 82–103.

having his 'essential clown' Sogliardo purchase a coat of arms and by then associating those arms with the motto 'not without mustard', Jonson seems to mock Shakespeare's pretentions to 'right' as the equivalent of mustard gilding dried and salted fish.[9]

In his catalogue of 'the character of the persons' appended to *Every Man Out of His Humour*, Jonson describes Sogliardo, as 'so enamoured of the name of a gentleman that he will have it though he buys it' (ll. 74–6). The critique here is twofold and pushes in different directions: Sogliardo is someone 'enamoured of the name of a gentleman', a figure who reveres status; he is also someone without respect for tradition and authority, a figure base or cynical enough to flout the entire system of social differences. He worships status; however (or therefore), he is willing to corrode its value by purchasing it. It is far from clear how to read Jonson's intention in his mocking allusion to Shakespeare, but from Jonson forward, the episode of the coat of arms has frequently been used as a means of defining Shakespeare vis-à-vis status. Two recent biographers offer duelling portraits of Shakespeare, and in diagnosing the reasons lying behind the purchase of the coat of arms, they seem to find the Shakespeare for whom they are looking. In *Ungentle Shakespeare: Scenes from His Life*, Katherine Duncan-Jones depicts Shakespeare as, among other things, a brash and tough-minded social climber; she reads the coat of arms episode as telling with respect to his desire for status, speculating that Shakespeare found it 'mortifying to be able to articulate the innermost thoughts of kings and noblemen, both in writing and acting, and yet have no "name" or status in private life'.[10] In *Will in the World*, Stephen Greenblatt finds a much kinder and gentler Shakespeare; he reads the effort to claim armigerous status as part of a strongly nostalgic and sentimental desire to restore a world lost due to John Shakespeare's fall into financial difficulty.[11] The problem with these attempts to divine Shakespeare's perspective on status from the coat of arms episode is that there is so little real information with which to work. All the episode really tells us is that Shakespeare valued armigerous status for his father or himself or his progeny at a certain price, and was not above treating that status as a good to be purchased. And if he anticipated the mockery of someone like Jonson, this also was a price he was willing to pay for the particular commodity he was purchasing. My point is not to bury or praise Shakespearean biography; the genre necessitates a certain amount of speculation concerning the motives of the biographical subject, and scholars like Duncan-Jones and Greenblatt certainly offer plausible narratives that work with the limited evidence we have. In an enquiry into Shakespeare and status such as this, however, it is important to point to the limits of the biographical record. One of the troubling consequences of pursuing a biographical line with limited

---

[9] On the ongoing contretemps between Shakespeare and Jonson, see James Bednarz, *Shakespeare and the Poets' War* (New York: Columbia University Press, 2001).

[10] Duncan-Jones, *Ungentle Shakespeare*, 83.

[11] The chapter in which Greenblatt addresses these issues is entitled 'The Dream of Restoration' in his *Will in the World: How Shakespeare became Shakespeare* (New York: Norton, 2004), 54–86.

evidence is that the 'facts' produced are then available to be pressed into service when reading the plays. This is not to say, however, that biography is a dead end in considerations of Shakespeare and status. On the contrary, if the biographical information is not robust enough for us to speculate about the thoughts and feelings of Shakespeare in the way that the genre of biography seems to mandate, this same information does open out onto history in striking ways.

Shakespeare's England is often depicted as occupying a transitional moment between a modern society that sees itself as organized according to economic wherewithal and a medieval society that understood itself to be organized according to social function.[12] That modern taxonomies of social difference are anachronistic in early modern England is, of course, well known. The discourse of 'class' with which we are so familiar, a discourse that differentiates between social groups on fundamentally economic grounds and presumes a certain consciousness of class identity, only emerges in the eighteenth century. And if the discourse of class is anachronistic, the medieval conception of a society organized according to 'estates' also fails to describe how society was organized or perceived in the early modern period. Indeed, the traditional notion of the three estates—the fighting, praying, and labouring classes—was already breaking down well before the sixteenth century; with the ongoing erosion of the military function of the aristocratic class and the reconceptualization of the clergy necessitated by the Reformation and Counter-Reformation, the three estates model seems to have been more or less abandoned in late sixteenth-century England. To oversimplify a complex historical question, early modern England is then no longer a society that can be described in terms of estates, and not or not yet a society that can be described in terms of class. Early modern writers attempting to offer a taxonomy of English society still used the term 'estate' or 'state', but deployed it not to depict a society organized according to function but a hierarchical society organized according to notions of rank and order.[13] In his *Description of England* (1577), William Harrison attempts to explain English society in a chapter tellingly entitled 'Of Degrees of People in the Commonwealth of England'.[14] Harrison's chapter is devoted to cataloguing and describing what

---

[12] In my understanding of status in early modern England I am particularly indebted to the following: David Cressy, 'Describing the Social Order of Elizabethan and Stuart England', *Literature and History* 3 (1976), 29–44; J. A. Sharpe, *Early Modern England: A Social History 1550–1760* (London: Edward Arnold, 1987), esp. 127–224; Alexandra Shephard, 'Poverty, Labour and the Language of Social Description in Early Modern England', *Past and Present* 201 (2008), 51–95; Keith Wrightson, 'Estates, Degrees, and Sorts: Changing Perceptions of Society in Tudor and Stuart England', in Penelope Corfield (ed.), *Language, History, and Class* (Oxford: Blackwell, 1991), 30–52; Wrightson, *Earthly Necessities: Economic Lives in Early Modern Britain* (New Haven, CT: Yale University Press, 2000), esp. 132–226. Also see the collection *The Middling Sort of People: Culture, Society, and Politics in England, 1550–1800*, Jonathan Barry and Christopher Brooks (eds.) (New York: St Martin's Press, 1994).

[13] See Wrightson, 'Estates, Degrees, and Sorts'.

[14] William Harrison, *The Description of England*, Georges Edelen (ed.) (Ithaca, NY: Cornell University Press, 1968), 94–123. Harrison's *Description* first appeared in Holinshed's *Chronicles* in 1577. Famously, Harrison's chapter on 'Degrees of People in the Commonwealth of England' is virtually

amounts to a descending hierarchy from monarch to wage labourer, and his use of the word 'degree' is symptomatic of a move away from a language of function to a reifying language that treats status itself as the organizational principle of society. If there is no longer any pretence that social function determines status, this hierarchical model is nonetheless traditional and, in theory, static. At the same time, there is open acknowledgement both of the pre-eminence of economic considerations and of the fact that new money is dissolving traditional social arrangements. In a wry aside, Harrison notes that although merchants are to be catalogued alongside citizens and are, therefore, considered lower on the social scale than gentlemen, 'they often change estate with gentlemen, as gentlemen do with them, by a mutual conversion of the one into the other'.[15] If his manner of calculating 'degrees of people' in England follows the traditional view that land rather than money remains the measure of status, Harrison's description also illustrates the extent to which money manages to create its own rules.

According to Harrison, 'we in England divide our people commonly into four sorts, as gentlemen, citizens or burgesses, yeomen, and artificers or laborers'.[16] It is important to note that Harrison's taxonomy does not include the large population of unemployed poor, usually pejoratively labelled as vagrants or 'sturdy beggars'. The societal animus against the unemployed and indigent meant that Harrison's description—like the social world in which they lived—simply had no place for them.[17] As I have argued elsewhere, the spectre of the growing demographic group of the idle and indigent meant that so-called 'honest labour' gained social currency in early modern England.[18] One can see this in Harrison's approving if patronizing description of the fourth sort, which includes 'day laborers, poor husbandmen, and some retailers (which have no free land), copyholders, and all artificers, as tailors, shoemakers, carpenters, brickmakers, masons, etc.' This group comprises those who work the land of others and those who sell their labour or the fruits of their labour either for a wage or some other form of compensation. Yeomen are country farmers who—as 'freemen born English'—'have a certain pre-eminence and more estimation than laborers and the common sort of artificers, and these commonly live wealthily, keep good houses, and travail to get riches'. Like yeomen, citizens and burgesses are characterized as 'free' although their place tends to be 'within the cities' rather than the country. This freedom tended to mean that they were employers rather than employees, and this grouping included merchants as well as the relevant members of guilds. The final, and in Harrison's account most important, group is the 'gentlemen'. This designation includes

---

identical to material published in Sir Thomas Smith's *De Republica Anglorum*. Mary Dewar makes a convincing case that Harrison's text was written first. See 'A Question of Plagiarism: The "Harrison Chapters" in Sir Thomas Smith's *De Republica Anglorum*', *The Historical Journal* 22.4 (1979), 921–9.

[15] Harrison, *Description of England*, 115.

[16] Harrison, *Description of England*, 94.

[17] Harrison does, however, have a chapter ostensibly devoted to provisions made for the poor, which offers a description of the underclass. Harrison, *Description of England*, 180–6.

[18] James Kearney, 'Idleness', in Brian Cummings and James Simpson (eds.), *Cultural Reformations: Medieval and Renaissance in Literary History* (Oxford: Oxford University Press, 2010), 570–88.

'gentlemen of the greater sort' ('dukes, marquises, earls, viscounts, and barons'), the lesser gentry ('knights, squires'), and 'last of all, they that are simply called gentlemen'.[19] Harrison's description of those 'that are simply called gentlemen' is of particular interest here:

> Whosoever studieth the laws of the realm, whoso abideth in the university giving his mind to his book, or professeth physic and the liberal sciences, or . . . can live without manual labor, and thereto is able and will bear the port, charge, and countenance of a gentleman, he shall for money have a coat and arms bestowed upon him by heralds (who in the charter of the same do of custom pretend antiquity and service and many gay things), and thereunto being made so good cheap, be called master, which is the title that men give to esquires and gentlemen, and reputed for a gentleman ever after. Which is so much the less to be disallowed of for that the prince doth lose nothing by it . . . No man hath hurt by it but himself who peradventure will go in wider buskins than his legs will bear or, as our proverb saith, now and then bear a bigger sail than his boat is able to sustain.[20]

Although there is a certain amount of irony in this report on the state of gentlemanly status (simply 'pretend antiquity and service and many gay things' and one can be 'made . . . good cheap'), Harrison seems remarkably sanguine about the porous borders of the gentlemanly class.

The strange thing about the case of William Shakespeare is that in the course of his life he seems to have occupied roles up and down the hierarchical ladder of states or degrees. A player—which is how a professional social taxonomist like Ralph Brooke defined Shakespeare—was technically an 'artificer' and so was lumped in with the wage labourers, poor husbandmen, and servants. Shakespeare, of course, was not simply a player; he was also an entrepreneur and astute businessman as well as a celebrated poet and playwright. Famously, he became a shareholder in his theatrical company and ultimately the Globe and Blackfriars theatres as well. By the end of his life, he was not only a landholder but a savvy player in the real estate markets of both London and Warwickshire.[21] And when Shakespeare wrote his will, he began—with the blessing of William Dethick, at least—by styling himself a gentleman: 'I, William Shakespeare, of Stratford upon Avon in the county of Warwick, gentleman'.[22] But perhaps Shakespeare's career is not so strange. If Shakespeare's biographical record seems to suggest a certain amount of social mobility, or at least a man who was able to wear many proverbial hats, his case is not anomalous. If most people in early modern England probably lived more stable and stationary lives than Shakespeare, it is also true that

---

[19] Harrison, *Description of England*, 118, 117, 115, 94.

[20] Harrison, *Description of England*, 113–14.

[21] See Schoenbaum, *Documentary Life*, 161–92; and Theodore Leinwand, 'Shakespeare and the Middling Sort', *Shakespeare Quarterly* 44.3 (Autumn, 1993), 288–9.

[22] See Schoenbaum, *Documentary Life*, 242–6; see also E. A. J. Honigmann, '"There is a World Elsewhere": William Shakespeare, Businessman', *Images of Shakespeare: Proceedings of the Third Congress of the International Shakespeare Association*, Werner Habicht, D. J. Palmer, and Roger Pringle (eds.) (London: Associated University Presses, 1988), 40–6.

most could be categorized in a variety of different ways depending on the perspective from which they were viewed and the criteria used to 'see' them. Moreover, it would be relatively easy to find numerous careers like that of Shakespeare, especially in and around London. Was early modern England then a society more conducive to social mobility than descriptions like Harrison's suggest? Yes and no. If the situation is more fluid and complex than a relatively rigid description like Harrison's suggests, it remains true that, by and large, people died within the same social grouping into which they were born.

Social historians have recently asked us to question the seemingly fixed hierarchy implicit in the language of degree. While this language is regularly deployed in formal descriptions of English society like Harrison's, there is not much evidence that this language was used in everyday practice or that people in early modern England commonly thought of themselves in these terms. To complement and modify the language of degrees deployed by heralds and scholars, Keith Wrightson points us to the prevalent language of 'sorts' as a 'simpler, cruder, and more effective vocabulary' that people of early modern England deployed in everyday settings 'to describe the essential distinctions of their social world'. For Wrightson 'relative status' in early modern England 'emerged from the interplay of a range of variables (of which wealth was the single most important), in a process of social assessment which was, and remained, largely informal'.[23] Harrison himself uses the language of sorts in his *Description of England*, both in his initial taxonomy—'We in England divide our people commonly into four sorts'— and in other less gradated formulations: 'the greater sort', 'the vulgar and common sorts'.[24] As Harrison uses the language of sorts in his initial formulation concerning the division of England, it does not suggest a grouping related to political interest or economic power but a grouping according to *kinds*. The language of 'sorts' as used here is wonderfully malleable as it seems to imply something naturalized and arbitrary all at once. In the latter formulations, Harrison uses what seems to be a commonplace language of sorts, which suggests a more flexible and informal means of describing place in society. The fundamental distinction here is between the 'better' or 'richer sort' and the 'poorer' or 'meaner sort'. It has become customary among scholars to observe that Harrison's fourfold division is subtended by a more fundamental division between the noble and the ignoble, the gentle and the commons. It is important to note that this is not quite how this more commonplace language of sorts seems to work in Harrison, or, indeed, how it works in Wrightson's account. For Wrightson,

> the distinction between the 'better sort' and the 'meaner sort' was not simply a distinction between gentlemen and the common people . . . Its political sociology was more complex. For the 'better' and 'richer' sorts included also the local notables of England's towns and villages, those whose property gave them prominence in local life, and a growing part also in the government and administration of their townships and parishes . . . In short, the 'better sort' were a composite group of local notables distinct from both the greater gentry and the mass of the common people.

[23] Wrightson, 'Estates, Degrees, and Sorts', 44.
[24] Harrison, *Description of England*, 94, 121; also see Wrightson, 'Estates, Degrees, and Sorts', 45–6.

They were those alternatively described as the 'substantial men of the parish' or the 'principal' or 'chief inhabitants'.[25]

The language of sorts is useful in thinking about the Shakespeares as a family who would consider themselves among the 'better sort' and who want to maintain and solidify that position. Before his fall into financial difficulty in the 1570s, John Shakespeare would certainly have been considered one of the 'substantial men of the parish'; a property owner and shopkeeper, a dealer in commodities, a constable and an alderman, he seems to have been one of the 'chief inhabitants' of Stratford.[26] And after his rise, William Shakespeare would also have been considered and considered himself one of the so-called 'better sort'. The language of sorts seems to open up a space for something between the 'meaner sort' and the 'gentry', and later in the seventeenth century a new category would emerge in descriptions of English society: the 'middling sort'.[27] Although he does not use the term, Harrison's *Description* already seems to be carving out a space for the 'middling sort'. His fourfold taxonomy becomes twofold insofar as he seems to align both 'citizens' and 'yeomen' with the gentry and over and against the 'meaner sort'. He is quick to define these middle categories as adjacent to the gentry; the 'fourth and last sort of people', however, seems to be of a different kind, insofar as they 'have neither voice nor authority in the commonwealth, but are to be ruled and not to rule'.[28]

The careers of both John and William Shakespeare then situate the Shakespeare family within a particular social milieu. For large portions of their lives, Shakespeare and his father could describe themselves as being of the 'better sort' but not of the gentry. Moreover, although one could argue that a certain *kind* of social mobility is part of their experience and understanding of rank and status, one could also argue that the fundamental 'status' of John and William Shakespeare never really changed, that they simply remained men of the 'middling sort' despite the changes in their financial fortunes over time and the different hats that they wore in their lifetimes. And in this they seem to be typical; even the attempt to acquire a coat of arms seems *de rigueur* for men of this station who found themselves with a dimly plausible genealogical claim and some disposable income. Theodore Leinwand captures Shakespeare's multitude of social roles and stable social identity beautifully:

> Situated below the Warwickshire Grevilles but above the county poor, below Henry Wriothesley, third earl of Southampton (to whom he dedicated his long narrative poems), but above those who paid a penny or two at the Globe, Shakespeare's precise socioeconomic position seems both securely among the middling sort and anything

[25] Wrightson, 'Estates, Degrees, and Sorts', 47–8.

[26] Schoenbaum, *Documentary Life*, 27–40. See also Leinwand, 'Shakespeare and the Middling Sort', 288.

[27] On the 'middling sort', see the collection of essays *The Middling Sort of People*, Jonathan Barry and Brooks Leinwand (eds.), 'Shakespeare and the Middling Sort'; Wrightson, 'Estates, Degrees, and Sorts', 49–52; and *Earthly Necessities*, 182–201.

[28] Harrison, *Description of England*, 118.

but precise. He was a capitalist and a client, a popular playwright and one of the King's Men, a rentier, an owner, and an investor; he succeeded on the manor and in the market, was armigerous and yet subdued to his craft. Like the theater business and like his times, he embodied but could not resolve economic and social differences.[29]

Shakespeare's career is idiosyncratic in its particulars but not atypical in the range of possibilities for someone of the 'middling sort'. And in this he mirrors his audience.

The majority of those frequenting plays performed at public venues like the Globe were, broadly speaking, of the 'middling sort'. Pointing to the rise of 'a large urban artisan class, chiefly in London, a citizen class of merchants and manufacturers in the major cities and ports', and 'an increasingly literate class of schoolmasters, scriveners and clergy', Andrew Gurr observes that 'almost all of these distinct classes in the middle stratum can be found amongst Shakespearean playgoers'. Indeed, 'though the complete social range' of playgoers extends 'from earls and even a queen to penniless rogues', the composition of this middle stratum 'broadly defines the composition of a majority in the London playhouse audiences'.[30] To suggest that both Shakespeare and the majority of his audience were part of some hard-to-define 'middling sort' is, however, not an argument for the emergence of a proto-middle class. As Gurr notes, in early modern England, 'there was nothing like the amorphous "middle class" which provides the bulk of modern theatre audiences'.[31] One of the reasons the language of 'sorts' may have been seized upon is precisely because it is imprecise, because it is usefully malleable. The 'better sort' and the 'meaner sort' (and later in the seventeenth century, the 'middling sort') were moving targets, shifting reference and significance depending on who was speaking. Nor is this an argument for an incipient class consciousness among the 'middling sort'. The language of sorts was useful because it allowed commoners of substance to align themselves with the nobility over and against the 'meaner sort'. And this aligning of interests with the ruling class is arguably one of the draws of the theatre. As mentioned above, players were technically classified as artisans (Harrison's fourth and lowest sort), but they were often ridiculed and disparaged as 'rogues and vagabonds'. The dubious status of players was one of the reasons they needed the protection of a noble patron. Shakespeare's theatrical company enjoyed the patronage of first the Lord Chamberlain and then the King; required on occasion to sing for their supper at court, they were then liveried servants in the ostensible employ of powerful benefactors. Paul Yachnin has made a compelling argument that the theatre's 'commodification of social prestige was a key element in the development of the drama'.[32] One way to cast oneself in the role of the 'better sort' was to align oneself with the great through the consumption of luxury goods like the theatre.

[29] Leinwand, 'Shakespeare and the Middling Sort', 288–9.

[30] Andrew Gurr, *Playgoing in Shakespeare's London*, 2nd edn. (Cambridge: Cambridge University Press, 1996), 50.

[31] Gurr, *Playgoing in Shakespeare's London*, 50.

[32] Paul Yachnin and Anthony Dawson, *The Culture of Playgoing in Shakespeare's England: A Collaborative Debate* (Cambridge: Cambridge University Press, 2001), 41.

If a given Shakespearean play might reach—in its various performances—most 'degrees' of London society, it seems only fitting that all degrees of society be represented in these plays. This, however, was one of the reasons the theatre was attacked in the period. In an historical moment in which the stratifications of society were fundamental to social life, when sumptuary laws determined how one could dress and conduct oneself, it seemed bizarre to some that players, mere artisans, could portray those of superior social station. David Scott Kastan has equated this kind of social role-playing with the cross-dressing of the early modern stage, suggesting that we see the portrayal of everything from clowns to kings by Elizabethan and Jacobean players as a kind of social cross-dressing:

> social crossdressing, legally prohibited on the streets of London, was of course the very essence of the London stage. Actors crossdressed with every performance . . . On stage, men of "inferior degree" unnervingly counterfeited their social betters, imitating not merely their language and gestures but their distinctive apparel . . . Understandably, then, the theater, with its constitutive transgressions, was a politically charged arena in an age when social identities and relations seemed distressingly unstable.[33]

And this politically-charged arena was not simply a place where status could be portrayed, where different sorts of person could be represented. We should refrain from reading the early modern stage as a place where playwrights simply brought to life the taxonomy of society we find in something like Harrison's *Description*. The early modern stage was necessarily a place where status was shaped and interrogated, defined, and redefined. It does not follow, however, that the theatre was somehow authentic in its representation of social life. Status on the Shakespearean stage was mediated by a host of factors: commercial prospects, audience expectations, generic forms, the history of theatre, the changing personnel and practices of the acting companies. If the early modern theatre was an alternative arena for the description 'Of Degrees of People in the Commonwealth of England', it was one with a particular set of limitations and possibilities.

In the second half of this essay, I turn to some of the more charged depictions of status on the Shakespearean stage.[34] Articulations of status are, of course, everywhere in

[33] David Scott Kastan, 'Is There a Class in This (Shakespearean) Text?' *Renaissance Drama* 24 (1993), 105.

[34] In my understanding of Shakespeare and status, I am particularly indebted to the following: Ralph Berry, *Shakespeare and Social Class* (Atlantic Highlands, NJ: Humanities Press International, 1988); William Carroll, *Fat King, Lean Beggar: Representations of Poverty in the Age of Shakespeare* (Ithaca, NY: Cornell University Press, 1996); Richard Helgerson, *Forms of Nationhood: The Elizabethan Writing of England* (Chicago, IL: University of Chicago Press, 1992); Jean Howard, *The Stage and Social Struggle in Early Modern England* (New York: Routledge, 1994); Kastan, 'Is There a Class'; Leinwand, 'Shakespeare and the Middling Sort'; Louis Montrose, *The Purpose of Playing: Shakespeare and the Cultural Politics of the Elizabethan Theatre* (Chicago, IL: University of Chicago Press, 1996); Annabel Patterson, *Shakespeare and the Popular Voice* (Cambridge, MA: Blackwell, 1989); Phyllis Rackin, *Stages of History: Shakespeare's English Chronicles* (Ithaca, NY: Cornell University Press, 1990); and Paul Yachnin and Anthony Dawson, *The Culture of Playgoing*.

Shakespeare's works, but there are certain plays in which the playwright seems to apply pressure to conventional notions of state and degree, plays in which he seems particularly interested in prodding and interrogating notions of status from a variety of angles. I briefly address four such plays: *2 Henry VI*, *The Merchant of Venice*, *King Lear*, and *The Tempest*. These are works that span the length of Shakespeare's career as a dramatist and touch on his major generic commitments: history, comedy, tragedy, and romance. Although I proceed from early plays to late, I do not attempt to create a narrative or make a case for a particular development of ideas over time. The approach is illustrative and exploratory rather than diagnostic or comprehensive. By probing the career of Shakespeare at different points, I hope to examine the various and conflicting ways in which he attends to status.

STATUS STAGED

Shakespeare seems to have made his name as a dramatist, in part, with his not inconsiderable contributions to the new genre of the English history play in the 1590s. And the history depicted in these plays is primarily the political history of the chronicles, a history defined by the actions of the ruling class. In the First Folio the titles of the plays are assigned to the monarch who reigns during the action depicted, and as Richard Helgerson observes, in 'Shakespeare's English history plays . . . England seems often to be identified exclusively with its kings and nobles. The story of their conflicts and conquests is its story'.[35] And yet Shakespeare arranges for other voices to be heard: a French peasant girl with visions of God, a rebellious mob with visions of Cockayne, a tavern full of the 'meaner sort', and a fat, fallen knight with delusions of grandeur. Status is called into question most directly by that rebellious mob in *The First Part of the Contention of the Two Famous Houses of York and Lancaster* (or *2 Henry VI*), even if that rebellion is consigned both to the dust heap of history and to the play's comic sub-plot.[36] In Act 4 of the play, Jack Cade and his 'ragged multitude' burst onto the stage to offer a utopian social vision in which the dissolution of property rights ('henceforward all things shall be in common', 4.7.17) and the attendant legal documentation ('Burn all the records of the realm', 4.7.12–13) will lead to a society without status ('All the realm shall be in common', 4.2.70) and its markers ('I will apparel them all in one livery', 4.2.75–6).[37] If the expressed desire is to dissolve traditional relations between person and property, Cade nevertheless frames the rebellion through his

---

[35] Helgerson, *Forms of Nationhood*, 195.

[36] On the ways in which the subversive energies of the rebels are contained by genre, see Rackin, *Stages of History*, 204–22.

[37] William Shakespeare, *The Complete Works*, Stanley Wells and Gary Taylor (eds.), 2nd edn. (Oxford: Oxford University Press, 2005). All citations from Shakespeare's plays refer to this edition and will be cited in the text.

(wonderfully absurd) genealogical claims to the throne, and, therefore, within the traditional terms that defined status: 'My father was a Mortimer...My mother a Plantagenet...My wife descended of the Lacys...Therefore am I of an honourable house' (4.2.40–50) ('Non sanz droict', indeed!). Cade's genealogical claims are undermined by his own men and refuted unequivocally by Sir Humphrey Stafford: 'Villain, thy father was a plasterer; | And thou thyself a shearman' (4.2.131–2). In his response to Stafford, the mercurial Cade changes tack entirely: 'And Adam was a gardener' (4.2.132). Cade here echoes the rallying cry of the rebellion of 1381, the preacher John Ball's well-known adage, 'When Adam delved and Eve span | who then was a gentleman?' Cade's rhetorical turn to Genesis is a radical return to origins, in which degree and distinction are erased by a common—in both senses of the term—human genealogy. Confronting some of the paradoxes of a rigidly hierarchical and Christian society, Cade first claims status by genealogy and then erases the distinctions of status by an even more ancient genealogy. Cade's turn to humanity's common origins in a Christian Eden is an inversion of the hilarious chop logic of the gravedigger in *Hamlet*, who claims that 'There is no ancient gentlemen but gardeners, ditchers and gravemakers' (5.1.29–30). Of the same profession as Adam—the man of 'earth'—these labourers too must be counted gentle. Moreover, since Adam was, as 'the Scriptures says', a digger, he must have been a 'gentleman', indeed, 'the first that ever bore arms' since he obviously could not 'dig without arms' (5.1.33–7). In both tragedy and history, Shakespeare has the commoner make a radical and droll claim to equality; for Cade, however, the road back to 'ancient freedom' is paved not only with clownish sophistry, but also with the burnt remains of books and the heads of clerks and lawyers.

In the depiction of Cade and his rabble, scholars have found evidence both of Shakespeare's commitment to a populist agenda and of his contempt for the 'meaner sort' as illiterate clowns with a chilling penchant for violence.[38] The play itself, however, seems to gain dramatic power in these scenes precisely by balancing farce and social critique. In fact, at times it seems that the more absurd the logic of Cade and the rebels, the greater weight the critique underlying their actions carries. Cade's outrageous condemnation of Lord Saye, for instance, can be staged with a menacing edge because both the violence threatened and the underlying social concerns are all too real:

> It will be proved to thy face that thou hast men about thee that usually talk of a noun and a verb and such abominable words as no Christian ear can endure to hear. Thou hast appointed justices of peace to call poor men before them about matters they were not able to answer. Moreover, thou hast put them in prison, and, because they could not read, thou hast hanged them when indeed only for that cause they have been most worthy to live.   (4.7.35–43)

---

[38] For a range of responses to the problem of Shakespeare's Cade, see Carroll, *Fat King, Lean Beggar*, 127–57; Helgerson, *Forms of Nationhood*, 195–245; Patterson, *Shakespeare and the Popular Voice*, 32–51; Rackin, *Stages of History*, 204–22; and Wilson, *Will Power: Essays on Shakespearean Authority* (Detroit, MI: Wayne State University Press, 1993), 26–44.

Beneath the comic absurdity and the anti-humanist cant, one can hear the playwright ventriloquizing outrage at a system in which the illiterate are not merely powerless before a legal and documentary culture in which they cannot participate, but in which the lack of letters could cost the 'meaner sort' their lives. When Cade claims that Lord Saye has hanged poor men because they could not read, he refers to the legal recourse of the literate to the 'benefit of clergy'. Initially instituted to ensure that the clergy would retain the privilege of being tried by an ecclesiastical court, the 'benefit of clergy' was eventually extended to all who could demonstrate the ability to read Latin. By the sixteenth century, secular courts had begun employing 'benefit of clergy' to deliver the guilty but literate from the frequently exercised death penalty. Being able to read the Latin of the 'neck-man's verse' became the means to a very literal salvation. When Cade condemns Saye for his affiliations with a culture of literacy, the gallows humour is enhanced by the fact that the absurdity and injustice of Cade's verdict simply mirrors the absurdity and injustice of the contemporary legal system. In the Jack Cade scenes of *2 Henry VI*, Shakespeare is neither simply lampooning the 'meaner sort' nor tying his wagon to their cause. He is ventriloquizing a very real outrage so that he can entertain his audience both with the clownish antics of Cade's 'ragged multitude | Of hinds and peasants' and with the contradictions, paradoxes, and injustices endemic to the social system in which both ragged multitude and audience lived (4.4.31–2).

If the history plays put the English social system on stage in particularly direct ways, Shakespeare also seems to have been interested in exploring status by imagining the social dynamics of other people, other places. In *The Merchant of Venice*, for instance, he turns to the urban and commercial space of Venice to depict a place in which social distinction is fluid and social identity fragile. An unlikely romantic comedy hung on a revenge plot fuelled by bigotry and animosity, *The Merchant of Venice* has become a text that is most often and quite fruitfully analysed in relation to questions of religion and ethnicity. Shakespeare's *Merchant*, however, is not merely concerned with religious identity and *ressentiment*; it is also a meditation on the complex social dynamics at play between usurer and merchant, prosperous merchant and insolvent gentleman, gentle-man adventurer and noble heiress to land and great wealth, and so on. Indeed, there is something almost schematic about the various 'sorts' of person inhabiting the play, not to mention the transparent way in which setting is pressed into the service of the play's concern with socioeconomic status and its discontents. Pairing the economically diverse and dynamic urban centre of Venice with the static and nostalgic vision of landed aristocracy in Belmont, Shakespeare juxtaposes seemingly incompatible visions of socioeconomic structure. In Venice one is defined by the manner in which one engenders wealth; however much the merchant would like to differentiate himself from the usurer, for instance, Antonio and Shylock are men defined by their occupational pursuit of wealth. Portia, by contrast, is defined *as* wealth, and wealth of a particular kind:

> In Belmont is a lady richly left,
>
> . . .
>
> Nor is the wide world ignorant of her worth,
> For the four winds blow in from every coast
> Renownéd suitors, and her sunny locks
> Hang on her temples like a golden fleece,
> Which makes her seat of Belmont Colchis' strand,
> And many Jasons come in quest of her.   (1.1.161–72)

Invoking the romance tradition through the figure of Jason, Bassanio casts himself as the bold adventurer and Portia as the precious object of his heroic enterprise. The easy misogyny of casting the woman as a prize to be won dovetails with traditional conceptions of status in which personal identity is locked into inherited 'place' (in both senses of the term) as the source of social function and status. Belmont is a hazy evocation of the world of the landed aristocracy, a world where property confers and conflates political authority and social identity. Belmont is both a possession and a political entity and Portia is—for the time being at least—Belmont.

If Belmont is an idealized vision of a feudal world in which person seems coterminous with landed property, Venice is a society in which economic status and social relations are fluid. Borrowing against Antonio's good name, Bassanio takes to the seas in hopes of winning his fortune. Antonio scatters his wealth to the four corners of the globe, with the expectation that returns on various ventures will more than counterbalance some not unexpected losses. Shylock weighs status by the measure of credit— 'Antonio is a good man' (1.3.12)—and thus by attending to precise fluctuations within the ebbs and flows of fortune. Jessica flees her father's house, appropriates her own dowry, and—while cross-dressed—seems to give herself away to her husband. The status of each of these Venetian figures is defined both by the manner in which they do and do not obtain wealth and by the vagaries of economic fortune in a modern urban setting like Venice. And each is threatened by the prospect of financial disaster and loss of status. The seeming inevitability of the romance plot sometimes obscures the fact that Bassanio faces a future in which he not only is in ever greater debt but also no longer has the hope of 'lady richly left' to save him; given that his social status at the beginning of the play is defined in part by the hope of future prospects through marriage, he risks much in accepting the terms of the casket test. Shylock and Antonio obviously must contend with the prospect of economic ruin—not to mention death— depending on the outcome of the trial scene. Jessica and Lorenzo do, in fact, seem to lose all due to their excessive prodigality in the aftermath of their nuptials. They are first redeemed by Portia's generosity—she takes Lorenzo on as her steward essentially—and then by the gifts extorted from Shylock: half of his estate to Antonio to have 'in use, to render it | Upon his death unto the gentleman | That lately stole his daughter' (4.1.380– 2); and 'all he dies possessed' of 'Unto his son, Lorenzo, and his daughter' (4.1.386–7). Indeed, the fact that all of these characters are redeemed in one way or another by Portia, the landed aristocrat, speaks to the kind of fantasy enacted in the endgame of *The Merchant of Venice*. That endgame seems to suggest that traditionally-conceived aristocratic status—and the fabulous wealth that would ideally attend such status—trumps all. And yet before we arrive in Belmont for the final act, Shakespeare gives the audience a play in which status is defined and redefined in complex and dynamic ways; it is accepted complacently, desired fervently, seized at great risk, lost and redeemed. Above all the play dramatizes the way wealth defines status and governs relationships. In the various plots, status is dynamically related to notions of friendship and love, and in the world of this play friendship and love can never be dissevered from conceptions of property and money.

Naturalized conceptions of status are subjected to devastating critique in *King Lear*. The play begins with the Earl of Gloucester awkwardly acknowledging his relationship to his 'natural' son, the bastard Edmund. When Kent asks Gloucester, 'Is not this your son, my lord?' (1.1.7), the discomfited response, filled with defensive joking and posturing, is painful to the audience both onstage and off.[39] In the first few lines of the play, Shakespeare manages to introduce the figure of the bastard as a problem for the proper ordering of society. For noblemen like Gloucester and Kent, social relations are founded on unambiguous claims to land and clear lines of inheritance. Indeed, these men are so associated with their land and place that they need no other name. As Margreta de Grazia observes, 'the given names of all the highborn male characters in the play are dropped so that person and property are synonymous'.[40] Given names are not for the Kents and Gloucesters, Cornwalls, and Albanys; they are reserved for women and stewards and sons who have not yet inherited. The situation is more complex for the son who should never inherit; Edmund obviously has a name and no title, but, as de Grazia notes, the 'speech prefixes of the Quarto and Folio distinguish Edmund with no proper name but rather with his legal status—Bastard, short for "unpossessing bastard" (2.1.67), identifying him with his incapacity to inherit land'.[41] Since a figure like Edmund troubles the idealized, if not the legal, language of property and inheritance, he must be disavowed as well as disinherited, which is why Edmund has been kept away from court 'nine years' and, as Gloucester assures Kent, 'away he shall again' (1.1.31–2). Neither fully acknowledged nor easily dismissed, the bastard threatens the logic of the social order even before Edmund decides to challenge it directly. And in the manifesto-like soliloquy in which he commits his services to a Nature and natural law that he perceives as having priority and authority over 'the plague of custom' and the 'curiosity of nations' (1.2.3–4), Edmund simply denies that there is anything natural in the normative mode of succession.

The main plot of *King Lear*, of course, begins with the problem that Edmund embodies so economically in that opening scene: the problem of succession. Like Edmund, Lear is a man who will take the social order into his own hands and reshape

---

[39] All citations of *King Lear* are to the Folio version unless otherwise noted.

[40] Margreta de Grazia, 'The Ideology of Superfluous Things: *King Lear* as Period Piece', in Margreta de Grazia, Maureen Quilligan, and Peter Stallybrass (eds.), *Subject and Object in Renaissance Culture* (Cambridge: Cambridge University Press, 1996), 17–42, at 27.

[41] De Grazia, 'The Ideology of Superfluous Things', 27.

it for his own ends. Anticipating his own death, Lear will divide his inheritance, divide his patrimony and his kingdom, among his three daughters. The love test is a way to ritualize this gift even as he contravenes the customs of inheritance with which Shakespeare's audience would have been familiar. Unlike Edmund, however, Lear has faith in the social order he flouts, believes that status is a function of his person rather than of his relative place. And so he believes that he can be a king without a kingdom:

> Only we shall retain
> The name, and all th' addition to a king. The sway,
> Revenue, execution of the rest,
> Belovèd sons, be yours; which to confirm,
> This coronet part between you.   (1.1.135–9)

Trusting that he can relinquish those things that underpin power—land and men—and retain the 'name, and all th' addition to a king', Lear becomes an object lesson in believing too well in status and the social identity it confers. The fool will relentlessly insist that Lear's actions and beliefs prove him a fool ('All thy other titles thou hast given away', 1.4.144[42]), and the rest of the play will confirm this judgement. Yet Kent does, or claims to, find 'authority'—that which he 'would fain call master'—in Lear's 'countenance' (1.4.27–30). And Cordelia does return in an attempt to redeem her father and restore her King. Modern readers and audiences have a tendency to see these choices and these relations as primarily personal and affective, but they also reflect an obligation to the order of things. Kent and Cordelia do not simply champion Lear, do not simply act out of love of an old man more sinned against than sinning; they act out of fealty and filial obligation. Their actions uphold a particular and traditional way of life. Lear's belief in a naturalized status is then warranted to the extent that his subjects believe in the same. Of course, this is cold comfort to a man who thought he was king even without a crown. Late in the play the mad Lear articulates the bitter wisdom he has gained: 'Thou hast seen a farmer's dog bark at a beggar? . . . And the creature run from the cur, there thou mightst behold the great image of authority. A dog's obeyed in office' (4.6.150–5). As Edmund saw, authority is simply convention, a product of 'the plague of custom' and the 'curiosity of nations'. In *King Lear* Shakespeare systematically subjects status to the vagaries of fortune and a corrosive scepticism that reveal it to be nothing without the necessary props to sustain it: 'an O without a figure' (1.4.174–5).

The late plays that we have—since the nineteenth century—called romances, return to the idealized aristocratic realm of places like Belmont. *Pericles* and *Cymbeline* and, to a lesser extent, *The Winter's Tale* inhabit this realm so fully that they seem to dramatize a one-class society.[43] True to romance form, shepherdesses and peasants and young women in brothels turn out to be aristocratic offspring who simply need to find their

---

[42] In this instance, I am quoting the Quarto version of *King Lear*.

[43] For a suggestive argument that early modern England was, in fact, a one-class society, see Peter Laslett, *The World We have Lost* (New York: Scribner, 1965).

way home. To the extent that *The Tempest* offers an alternative to such a realm, it does so through the irreverence of the sailors in the opening scene and the insurrection of the clowns. From the first exchange of the play—the master's call for the 'Boatswain!' and the boatswain's response: 'Here, Master'—Shakespeare stages the kind of hierarchical relation that he will explore throughout *The Tempest* (1.1.1–2). As the play opens, this social structure seems to work exactly as it should, as master, boatswain, and the cohort of mariners coordinate their efforts to battle the elements. The simple hierarchical organization of the ship, however, is complicated when the King's party enters. Responding to the crisis at hand, the boatswain is deeply unimpressed by the powerful passengers and responds to their intrusive requests with disdain: 'Hence! What cares these roarers for the name of king? To cabin! Silence; trouble us not' (1.1.15–17). Personified, the angry waves become 'roaring' or rebellious subjects who care not for the privilege and presumption of royal authority.[44] If the Boatswain seems to anticipate Prospero's Ariel in his subservient and efficient relation to the shipmaster, he anticipates Prospero's Caliban in his vexed relation to the King's entourage. The poisonous repartee that the Boatswain and the King's men engage in resonates throughout the play as they clash over labour ('You mar our labour', 1.1.12), employ the language of cursing ('A plague upon this howling!' 1.1.35; 'bawling, blasphemous, incharitable dog!' 1.1.39–40; 'hang, you whoreson insolent noisemaker!' 1.1.42–3), and discuss the relation between character and fate ('he hath no drowning mark upon him; his complexion is perfect gallows', 1.1.28–9; 'I'll warrant him for drowning', 1.1.44; 'He'll be hanged yet', 1.1.55). When Sebastian curses him, the Boatswain responds with the simple directive— 'Work you, then' (1.1.41). The Boatswain's injunction to work is wonderfully biting since it draws the audience's attention not merely to the uselessness of the King's entourage but to their dependence on the Boatswain's labour for their very survival. And the Boatswain can refuse to recognize the authority of the royal entourage because the King and his men are literally out of their element. The discourse of authority and power that they enjoy on land becomes, on the sea, an inflated rhetoric that provides them little profit, other than the ability to curse. Of course, in the very next scene the audience learns that the roaring waves not only cared for 'the name of king' but were concerned with this particular King. The noble passengers are not saved by the labour of the mariners but by the power of Prospero, the author of the storm. Nevertheless, this conception of labour as the repressed foundation of aristocratic idleness is evoked throughout the play. Foregrounding the fact that the idle aristocrats are dependent upon the work of the mariners, this opening scene launches the play's exploration of the ways in which aristocratic privilege and noble idleness are subtended and sustained by the labour of others.

Arising from injustice and culminating in farce, the insurrection of Caliban and the clowns seems to reprise Cade's rebellion in a variety of ways. Unlike Cade, however,

---

[44] See David Norbrook's excellent '"What Cares these Roarers for the Name of King?": Language and Utopia in *The Tempest*', in Gordon McMullan and Jonathan Hope (eds.), *The Politics of Tragicomedy: Shakespeare and After* (London: Routledge, 1992), 21–54.

Caliban is not often considered in relation to early modern notions of status, as he seems to stand outside traditional social rankings altogether. Scholars and critics tend to read both *The Tempest* and Caliban through the lens of developing notions of race and the ideological demands of empire, the strangeness of new worlds and the familiar viciousness of the old. But Caliban is also one of Shakespeare's experiments in status. His claim to sovereignty of the isle ('This island's mine, by Sycorax my mother', 1.2.333)—a claim based on European notions of inheritance—places him in a line of contenders and pretenders to various thrones scattered throughout Shakespeare's dramatic works. And if his political claims place him within a tradition of heroes and clowns who would be king, his nostalgia for the place in Prospero's household that he once held positions him as a servant fallen out of favour. The mocking designation of Caliban as a 'servant monster' by Stephano and Trinculo seems telling in this respect (3.2.3, 4, 8). Scholars have done terrific work positioning Caliban in relation to descriptions of the indigenous inhabitants of the New World, 'wild' or 'savage' figures from the romance tradition, the philosophical tradition's conception of the natural slave, but Caliban is also quite simply a servant, a member of a household. And the fact that early modern England was a society predicated on service and relationships between masters and servants has received significant scholarly attention in recent years.[45] In *Shakespeare, Love and Service*, David Schalkwyk contends that

> Service was such a prevalent condition in early modern England that for a long time its very obviousness rendered it invisible to literary scholars. It was the dominant condition that tied people to each other and the framework that structured the ways in which they lived such relationships . . . Most of the population [of early modern England] would therefore have been in service at some point, and for many that condition would have been permanent.[46]

Service relationships complicate our understanding of the language of 'class' or 'degree' or 'sorts' precisely because service cuts across such lines. Service transcends taxonomies of status, and yet service relationships, it would seem, are necessarily central to perceptions of status within early modern culture. Seeing Caliban as an Old World servant as well as a New World monster—however we interpret the term—would help us reconsider certain aspects of *The Tempest*. We often assume, for instance, that the attempt on Miranda's virtue threatens distinctions between self and other, European and non-European, Christian and non-Christian. From the perspective of a Prospero, however, it also seems possible that the attempt is a horrific abuse of the privileged proximity to the family that servants enjoy; it is then less a violation of the natural order

---

[45] On service and servants in Shakespeare and early modern England, see Mark Thornton Burnett, *Masters and Servants in English Renaissance Drama and Culture: Authority and Obedience* (New York: St Martin's Press, 1997); David Evett, *Discourses of Service in Shakespeare's England* (New York: Palgrave Macmillan, 2005); David Schalkwyk, *Shakespeare, Love and Service* (Cambridge: Cambridge University Press, 2008); and Judith Weil, *Service and Dependency in Shakespeare's Plays* (Cambridge: Cambridge University Press, 2005).

[46] Schalkwyk, *Shakespeare, Love and Service*, 19.

than a fundamental violation of the social order of the household. Caliban is kin to Shakespearean outsiders like Shylock and Othello, to be sure, but in his political claims and vexed relation to household he can also be productively related to those figures—like a Cade or a Malvolio—who challenge or violate notions of 'place'.

Status in Shakespeare is a protean topic and so, in conclusion, I turn briefly to one of Shakepeare's most protean characters: Autolycus. Thief, peddler, conman, vagabond—the Autolycus we meet in the fourth act of *The Winter's Tale* is an extravagant and entertaining avatar of the 'meaner sort'. He too, however, once served at court: 'I have served Prince Florizel, and in my time wore three-pile, but now I am out of service' (4.3.13–14). When scholars say that there is little social mobility in early modern England, they primarily mean upward social mobility. As the early modern theatre was constantly reminding its audience, however, the vagaries of fortune can bring anyone low. Neither William nor John Shakespeare ever rose as high as Autolycus or fell so far, but, as we have seen, the relative social mobility evoked by the figure of Autolycus was not unfamiliar to the Shakespeare family. At the end of the play, Autolycus seems to miss his chance to rise yet again, to engineer a return to court and his former status. In this he is outdone by the father and son team, the clown and the old shepherd, who have by the end of the play been miraculously (and amusingly) raised to the status of 'gentleman born' (5.2.133). Although the shepherds reach this 'preposterous estate' through 'fairy gold' and 'strange fortune' rather than an application to the College of Arms, it is difficult not to see a self-deprecating and deflated version of Shakespeare and his father in this pair of country bumpkins who stumble into wealth and status (5.2.45–6; 3.3.19; 2.3.179). And, indeed, as Patricia Parker observes, in a brilliant reading of the preposterous, or the rhetorical figure of *hysteron proteron* (putting the cart before the horse) in Shakespeare,

> the Shepherd son's 'preposterous' suggests not simply a rise from low to high . . . but also *hysteron proteron* in a specifically temporal form. Just lines before his apparent malapropping of 'preposterous' for 'prosperous', this son remarks 'I was a gentleman born before my father' . . . an 'unnatural' ordering in which son precedes father rather than the other way round.[47]

Not unlike Shakespeare in some sense, the clown achieves the status of being a 'gentleman born'—with all the irony that the phrase accrues in this context—before his father. If the hierarchical structure of Shakespeare's society means that such topsy-turvy events were by definition preposterous, they were also increasingly available to the prosperous and the 'better sort'.

If Autolycus is left out of the whitewashing of social difference in the final act of *The Winter's Tale*, this seems fitting. Like the theatre he seems, at times, to represent, Autolycus is of all states and degrees and none. Like Prince Hal who is 'so . . . proficient' he can 'drink with any tinker in his own language' (*1 Henry IV* 2.5.17–19), Autolycus

---

[47] Patricia Parker, 'Preposterous Events', *Shakespeare Quarterly* 43.2 (1992), 187–8.

seems able to talk to, and past, all degrees of society, to bridge the gaps between rich and poor, better and meaner, even as he picks pockets indiscriminately. And this slyly metatheatrical figure seems to embody the stage's ability to conjoin high and low, to insinuate itself into any setting, any place, through craft and guile, imagination and will. Throughout his dramatic career, Shakespeare attends to status in a seemingly endless number of ways; if this 'infinite variety' suggests a protean and bottomless topic, Shakespeare also seems to want to insist on the theatre's ability to encompass it. Like Autolycus, the theatre can speak to all sorts in their own language. And at the end of the day, the theatre, like Autolycus, has no true place; it is—in its various incarnations—beyond traditional notions of status, even if its practitioners must contend with the realities of a complex and contentious social realm.

CHAPTER 11

···

DOMESTIC LIFE

···

CATHERINE RICHARDSON

THIS is an essay about four of the houses which Shakespeare built—Othello's house, in which we finally see him together with Desdemona in a perversion of a wedding night, Capulet's house in *Romeo and Juliet*, where his 'old accustomed feast' takes place and where Romeo and Juliet spend the night together, Mr Ford's house in *The Merry Wives of Windsor* in which the fat knight Falstaff is thrown into a laundry basket and then beaten as a witch, and Petruccio's house in *The Taming of the Shrew*, where he takes his new bride Katherine to tame her before allowing her to return to Padua. My aim is to explore what we know about these houses: how they are built—the form of their stage representation—and then what *work* they do as spaces within the plays in which they appear—how they shape the action by providing it with a context.

Domestic life in drama is about family business within the household, for instance Hamlet's impassioned argument with his mother in her closet, or Lear's exploration of the fraught 'relationship among various conceptions of dwelling place and home'.[1] Domestic life provides a contrast to its opposites: to public acts, to outside spaces, and to extraordinary emotions—Shakespeare's lyrical descriptions of the journeys of hearts and minds. They take their meaning from and are shaped in relation to the comforting regularity and normality of domestic life, that baseline of human activity. Without it, settings like Lear's formless heath and actions like Macbeth's murder of Duncan would lose some of their sense of poignancy and rupture.

Domestic life takes shape on the stage as a series of actions, emotions, and allegiances particular to a specific and bounded place. And in early modern England, those meanings had a very precise political edge. Across the period, a series of critical commonplaces revolved around home life—that a man's house was his castle, and that the household was akin to a commonwealth in which the role of the head of the house (if not his particular person) resembled the rule of the king within his kingdom and Christ over his church. Under James I, these ideas crystallized into a political ideology of rule. They gave

---

[1] Heather Dubrow, *Shakespeare and Domestic Loss: Forms of Deprivation, Mourning and Recuperation* (Cambridge: Cambridge University Press, 2003), 5.

household action a considerable authority and a weight and moment in relation to concepts of communal order and disorder, which it retained for the next century.[2]

Houses were prominent in economic terms too. The early modern period witnessed a drawn-out shift in modes of production, in which the household moved from being the location within which the things that households needed were produced, to being a site for the display of goods manufactured and purchased outside. At the same time, houses were changing shape: open central halls, so important to the way social relations were conducted in medieval England, were being ceiled over, and the series of chambers which were created above made segregated sleeping possible. And the things with which houses were filled expanded enormously during the period in which Shakespeare was writing his plays.[3] A growing urban mercantile elite measured their rising social status through their possession of greater numbers of household furnishings—of linen table cloths, silver spoons, cushions, and window curtains, for instance. As a result, as Natasha Korda puts it, the 'relations between subjects within the home became increasingly centered around and mediated by objects.'[4]

OTHELLO

Almost every scene in Shakespeare's plays might be said to be about domestic life—about the frustrations, confusions, and joys of people's relations to family, love, and household. But exploring the implications of domesticity is different to depicting familial life within a material space: the realities of the household ground action in a particular way. In *Othello*, the lack of a concretely realized domestic space for the newlyweds throughout the majority of the play makes palpable the increasing distance between them. Lena Cowen Orlin points out that 'while Desdemona moves away from a space governed by her father, she does not move to one governed by her husband'. Between the window at which Brabanzio appears in 1.1 and the chamber in which Desdemona dies in 5.2 there are only hints of a tangible domestic life. And these hints are complex and confusing. Orlin traces the meaning of the name of the inn at which the couple are lodging in Venice—the Sagittary—a name which she connects to the centaur, shooting evil arrows of envy, and she points out that the location of their Cyprus lodgings is vague too: 'as the tragedy unfolds, our fix on Othello and Desdemona's residence slips.'[5]

---

[2] For more on these ideas see Lena Cowen Orlin, *Private Matters and Public Culture in Post-Reformation England* (Ithaca, NY: Cornell University Press, 1994), ch. 2.

[3] For more information, see Catherine Richardson, *Domestic Life and Domestic Tragedy in Early Modern England: The Material Life of the Household* (Manchester: Manchester University Press, 2006), ch. 2.

[4] Natasha Korda, *Shakespeare's Domestic Economies: Gender and Property in Early Modern England*, (Philadelphia: University of Pennsylvania Press, 2002), 8.

[5] Orlin, *Private Matters*, 193, 197, 223. She points out the connection to the 'Centaur' of *The Comedy of Errors*, 198.

Othello's exchange with Emilia, his wife's maid, at the start of 4.2 suggests the most significant kind of representation of domestic life in the play to date—the imagined interior. Emilia assures him that she has witnessed everything which has passed between Desdemona and Cassio: 'I heard | Each syllable that breath made up between 'em' (4.2.4–5), that her mistress did not send her out of the way '[t]o fetch her fan, her gloves, her mask, nor nothing' (4.2.10), and that there was 'no harm' (4.2.4) in any of it. But Othello cannot believe the innocent domestic life Emilia presents him with. As Iago works on Othello's jealousy, he does so by forcing him to imagine the adultery his wife is committing—to believe in it by making an image of it in his head which then becomes like a memory. In 3.3 Iago begins the process of imagined intimacy by giving a visceral portrait of his own night with Cassio, when he says he 'lay his leg o'er my thigh' (3.3.428) as they shared a bed. And then in 4.1 Othello himself imagines Cassio to be telling Iago 'how [Desdemona] plucked him to my chamber' (4.1.138–9). The fact that Othello plays out this scene in his own, as opposed to Cassio's, chamber draws attention to the room as the centre of the married domestic life which has become so problematic for the couple. As 'there can be no ocular proof of innocence',[6] nothing he can see or imagine which will prove Desdemona true, the imagined confirmation of her falseness takes on the corresponding strength of positive proof. Iago finally puts all these images together to produce a representation of the location of murder: 'Strangle her in her bed, even the bed she hath contaminated' (4.1.202–3).

These conjured intimacies in imagined chambers colour the material reality of the chamber, which the audience finally sees onstage in 4.2. The scene is domestic in the sense that we see a household in operation: its head gives orders to its servant; at several points in the scene Emilia exits on errands and then re-enters shortly afterwards, her movement emphasizing the exigencies of domestic service. At one point, Othello commands Emilia to 'Leave procreants alone, and shut the door, | Cough or cry "Hem" if anybody come.' (4.2.30–1). The attention paid to the doors of the house makes clear the fundamental nature of domestic space—that it is not communal, that its owners can control who enters from outside. And yet in spirit this scene is a perversion of domesticity. Othello's allusion to procreation is a double-edged reference to the couple's newly-married state and to casual sex, and he pays Emilia for her 'pains' in turning the key and keeping their counsel as though she were a bawd in a brothel. The domestic location becomes ironic in relation to the ideas that circulate there, as Othello uses the audience's first invitation into his house to call his wife 'whore'.

Lisa Jardine has argued that the movement of Othello's accusation of adultery, from the privacy of domestic space in 4.2 after he has sent Emilia away, to her repetition of it to Iago later in the scene, fundamentally changes the quality of the insult, turning it into a legally-actionable slander. It is, she says, 'the spilling-over of private exchange into a public space . . . which alters the nature of the incident, and turns it from verbal abuse into event in the communal sphere.' From this point on, she argues, Desdemona's

---

[6] Orlin, *Private Matters*, 226.

failure to rebut this accusation formally leads Othello to act in 'complete certainty of her guilt' and to murder her not out of jealousy, but for her adultery.[7] This argument draws our attention to a contemporary sensitivity to the division between outside and inside, to the quality of action which takes place in both, and to the ability of space fundamentally to alter the interpretation of action.

In this final crescendo of the play, then, inside and outside are carefully patterned. But there are also material connections between the scenes that make it clear that domestic life continues uninterrupted even when the audience is seeing the street outside. After Othello's exit, Desdemona asks Emilia to, 'Prithee tonight | Lay on my bed my wedding sheets, remember' (4.2.107–8), and when Emilia mentions the sheets again in 4.3, saying that she has laid them upon the bed, Desdemona asks her '[i]f I do die before thee, prithee shroud me | In one of these same sheets' (4.3.23–4). The continuation of domestic routine across the play's final movement gives power and momentum to the immanent tragedy and a coherence, a palpability, to domestic space itself.

The material stuff of the household at this point in the play both 'confirms the sense of an established household'[8] and comments ironically upon its hospitality, upon the marriage bond which it should nurture. But the sheets which form the symbolic focus of, and material context for, the final stages of Desdemona's life are also personal objects, peculiar to Desdemona as well as suggestive of her marriage. As such, they are connected, by their status as objects and their position within the narrative as 'much talked about' things, to the handkerchief which she loses in 3.3.

Natasha Korda argues that the play's interest in these objects is part of a larger linking of 'the modalities of overvaluation and undervaluation' of things. She connects these questions of valuation to race and gender: 'both women and Africans were in varying ways vilified as being attached in the wrong way or to too great an extent to material objects'. Jealousy, Korda argues, is 'an affliction arising from the institution of private property', and for her Desdemona's death is brought about by the fact that '[t]he discourse of jealousy as predicated on the institution of private property would ... seem to depend upon the equation of women with objects of property'.[9] So for Korda these intense meditations on domestic objects have an economic underpinning.

But the sheets are also a part of the poetry of grief and loss—more properly domestic discourses. Desdemona's talk of death, of shrouds, and of the maid's role in the laying out of bodies, generates her recollection of another maid:

> My mother had a maid called Barbary.
> She was in love, and he she loved proved mad
> And did forsake her. She had a song of willow.
> An old thing 'twas, but it expressed her fortune,
> And she died singing it. That song tonight
> Will not go from my mind. (4.3.25–30)

---

[7] Lisa Jardine, *Reading Shakespeare Historically* (London: Routledge, 1996), 32.

[8] Orlin, *Private Matters*, 225.

[9] Korda, *Domestic Economies*, 112–14, 138.

Desdemona's speech about Barbary is connected to the various biographies which the play offers for the handkerchief that Desdemona loses: it is a condensed narrative of origins. Barbary's experience explains Barbary's song, gives it a history, gives it an emotional context, and demonstrates its potential significance. It also gives Desdemona a history, a connection to this woman in the past and to her practices and her ways of coping with or externalizing grief. This appearance of the past in the present, providing ways out of emotional crisis, routes through by way of domestic practices, is a defining feature of family life. And Desdemona's singing of the song literally performs her past, staging for the audience one of the aspects of domestic life that is so hard to show on stage—the history of a family which cumulatively gives its members identity in the present every time it is brought to mind.

This recollection and the song that it generates are a part of the wandering thoughts that give the scene its pathos and gender it female. It is not shaped by the linear course of action and its discourses do not impart information that is essential to the plot—it contrasts strongly with the scenes of Iago's machinations, for instance. Rather, it moves as Desdemona's mind, distracted by grief, works out a pattern of association that connects ideas, emotions, and music going back across the years. In this sense it is a mimetic representation of the 'polytemporality' of memory, and its pace is slow and circular.[10]

Household things intervene: Desdemona asks Emilia to 'Give me my nightly wearing, and adieu' (4.3.15) and then later asks her, 'Prithee unpin me' (4.3.20). 'Shall I go fetch your nightgown', Emilia asks; 'No. Unpin me here' (4.3.33), her mistress replies. In between these everyday questions about the practicalities of dressing and undressing, the two women discuss Othello's behaviour and whether or not Desdemona would have been better off if she had never met him. '[U]npin me here' comes half way through Desdemona's assertion that 'even his stubbornness, his checks, his frowns . . . have grace and favour in them.' Their discussion weaves the weightiness of the current situation into the practice of domestic life; the analysis of a fledgling marriage is seamed together with the everyday tasks which should make up its foundation within the household.

When he returns in 5.2, having witnessed the violent confusions of murder in the dark from his window in the intervening scene, Othello enters a space calmed by songs of mourning. And this stillness is intensified by his entry 'with a light. [He draws back a curtain, revealing] Desdemona asleep in her bed.' Desdemona and Emilia's conversation was domestic in the sense that it did not rise above the quotidian in its scope. They were focused upon personal things, upon the things of the household, and did not appear to see the wide scope of macrocosmic meaning which tragedy opens up. But Othello's language is strikingly different from theirs: 'It is the cause, it is the cause, my soul. | Let me not name it to you, you chaste stars.' Emilia has set this scene—she has laid the wedding sheets in which the audience now sees Desdemona asleep on the bed, she has unpinned her mistress's outdoor clothing and dressed her in the smock that she

---

[10] For theories of polytemporality and the actions of fragments of the past in the present see Jonathan Gil Harris, *Untimely Matter in the Time of Shakespeare* (Philadelphia: University of Pennsylvania Press, 2009).

now wears. And within this chamber whose quotidian routines we have witnessed, Othello's soliloquy opens out to address his soul and the stars in the poetry of tragedy. His speech itself performs that movement from the domestic to the eternal as he uses the pragmatism, the repeatability of the action of extinguishing a light like the one in his hand as a way of exploring the action of murder: 'Put out the light, and then put out the light' (5.2.7). In a familiar early modern thought process, he moves from the domestic and material to the eternal and impalpable.

This pairing of the household as the 'here and now' and the implications of tragedy, caught in the constraints of an eternal judgement to come, continues throughout the scene. Emilia's presence outside the door keeps bringing the elemental language of murder back down to its domestic scope:

EMILIA: (*within*) I do beseech you
That I may speak with you. O, good my lord!
OTHELLO: I had forgot thee.—O, come in, Emilia.—
Soft, by and by. Let me the curtains draw.

(5.2.110–13)

Like the interstitial pragmatism of the unpinning of Desdemona's gown, the cries of her maid from outside the door fade in and out of Othello's consciousness. Represented textually by the dash, domestic life calls stridently, insistently, from the margins of Shakespeare's tragedies.

Othello offers only failed households, then: Brabantio's attempt to protect his daughter by keeping her inside, trusting the physical containment which the house offers rather than its affective domestic ties, fails to contain her;[11] Othello's endeavour to build for himself an identity as a householder rather than a soldier is a disaster. Orlin sees the play as being about 'Male collapse under the burdens of oeconomic responsibility', and Heather Dubrow points to the breakdown of 'the role of guardian, so central to early modern male subjectivity' in Shakespeare's plays.[12] The sense of a domestic life, which failed to establish itself as a series of routines and processes, is represented materially in 5.2. The marriage bed is finally visible to the audience as a deathbed, defiled, its meaning erased, but still materially present in the sheets on which husband and wife lie together in a final kiss. This material remnant stands testimony to a domestic future which has been cut off, its presence eloquently demonstrating an absence.

ROMEO AND JULIET

We see Capulet's house much earlier on in *Romeo and Juliet*, as his wife enters with the Nurse in 1.3, asking her 'where's my daughter? Call her forth to me.' This is a domestic

---

[11] Orlin, *Private Matters*, 218.
[12] Orlin, *Private Matters*, 195; Dubrow, *Domestic Loss*, 108.

scene in the sense that three women are on stage talking more or less pertinently about marriage. It reworks in comic vein some of the techniques of Desdemona and Emilia's winding conversation about marriage as it follows the routes of Capulet's wife's and the Nurse's recollections. But the specific location is not given in the name of a room or the use of domestic props—this express materializing only takes place at its very end when Peter enters:

> Madam, the guests are come, supper served up, you called, my young lady asked for, the Nurse cursed in the pantry, and everything in extremity. I must hence to wait. I beseech you follow straight.   (1.3.101–5)

In this brief speech, slipped into the discussion of Juliet's marriage like Emilia's unpinning, the rest of the house is brought rhetorically onto the stage as a series of interdependent locations and domestic processes.

A similar scene is played at 1.5, where servingmen *'come forth with napkins'* and Peter asks 'Where's Potpan, that he helps not to take away? He shift a trencher, he scrape a trencher!', and then later 'Away with the joint-stools, remove the court-cupboard, look to the plate' (1.5.6–7). Such speeches make it clear to the audience that the domestic context is *constructed*—produced through the actions of Peter and his fellows, who order goods in relation to their master's wishes and perform a range of processes such as the preparation of marzipan (1.5.8). These scenes are almost metatheatrical—as actors use props to build a domestic scene, so too do household servants in the theatre of elite hospitality. They give the energy of animation and preparation to the play's onward movement toward the feast, and they serve as a way of demonstrating the wealth of a household with such servants and the bounty of Capulet's hospitality.

But like *Othello*, *Romeo and Juliet* sets its quest for a future, for a domestic life for its eponymous protagonists, within the context of a very public violence. The play opens with 'civil strife' caused by the casual meeting of the Capulet and Montague servants as they walk the streets of Verona. By contrast, Capulet is seen in 1.2 handing invitations to his servant to be delivered around the town 'and to them say | My house and welcome on their pleasure stay' (1.2.34–5). The household should be the place where guests can be controlled and therefore violence avoided for the sake of celebration and mirth. But just as the feast is 'old-accustomed' so the feud is an 'ancient grudge', and Tybalt's violent interventions threaten the rules of hospitality. On hearing Romeo's voice in praise of Juliet he immediately calls for his rapier and quarrels with Capulet about the right course of action. 'I would not', says his uncle, 'for the wealth of all this town | Here in my house do him [Romeo] disparagement.' (1.5.6–70). Unlike Othello's slander of his wife, Capulet shows a sensitivity to the quality of household conduct—he is aware of the particular kind of behaviour which fittingly defines an elite house. Tybalt's trespass against the authority of his host and elder is interestingly patterned against the springing into life of Romeo's illegitimate love.

And there are further familial contexts for that moment of love at first sight. Like Desdemona's tale of Barbary, discussions of familial celebration and violence both bring a time-depth to the meeting of Romeo and Juliet. In addition to his wife's many references to his age and infirmity, Capulet's discussions with his cousin deepen this sense as the feast begins in 1.5: 'Nay, sit, nay, sit, good cousin Capulet, | For you and I are past our dancing days. | How long is't now since last yourself and I | Were in a masque?' (1.5.30–3). In a kind of reminiscing which harks back to the Nurse's ways of marking time in 1.3, they discuss what was presumably the last family marriage:

> CAPULET'S COUSIN: By'r Lady, thirty years.
> CAPULET: What, man, 'tis not so much, 'tis not so much.
> 'Tis since the nuptial of Lucentio,
> Come Pentecost as quickly as it will,
> Some five-and-twenty years; and then we masqued.
> CAPULET'S COUSIN: 'Tis more, 'tis more. His son is elder, sir.
> His son is thirty.
> CAPULET: Will you tell me that?
> His son was but a ward two years ago.
>
> (1.5.33–41)

Since their last dance, then, Lucentio has died and his son has come of age. This is the immediate context for Romeo's first glance at Juliet—he is an intruder into this space of family memory and hence family identity. Lucentio's story, like the tale of Susan, Juliet's nurse's daughter, is left a blank. These other family stories, fleetingly alluded to—cut in two dimensions like funeral effigies—show how much the wider Capulet family has been diminished. Their briefly introduced vignettes of lineage suggest the way families become narrowed down to a point by death and they give full meaning to Romeo's and Juliet's position as representatives of the houses of Montague and Capulet.

Within these various constructions of the familial and material house of Capulet, Romeo and Juliet share their sonnet of developing attraction. But it is a brief moment of poetic concord in between the anger of Tybalt and her father and her mother's summons—'Madam, your mother craves a word with you' (1.5.110), the Nurse interrupts. And it is at this point in the play that the position of domestic life shifts. Rather than the pragmatics of household life appearing within the more central business of the play as Peter's interruption did within discussion of Juliet's wedding, now Romeo and Juliet's relationship itself develops in fits and starts, moulded and shaped in its duration if not in its quality by the demands of the Capulet household.

When they meet again of course, Juliet is still inside the house and Romeo is below in the garden. And it is the Nurse once again who is calling her, practically-speaking presumably to go to bed, but symbolically to attend to the domestic business of the Capulets rather than her love for a Montague: 'Anon, good Nurse!' (2.2.179), and then 'I come, anon' (2.2.192), and 'By and by I come' (2.2.195). Our view of Capulet's house from this point onwards is a very different one to that which the feast was set up to give. It is characterized by the window at which Romeo sees Juliet, and from which he eventually leaves at dawn on the morning after their marriage night—two appearances which mark the brief duration of a relationship played out between them. These are night meetings, taking place under cover of a darkness that should ensure that the couple do not come up against the other members of the household, and the heat of Verona's sunshine is brought inside as imagery of light which radiates outwards: 'But soft, what light through yonder window breaks? | It is the east, and Juliet is the sun.' (44–5). It is the light of Capulet's house which gives the illusion that Juliet is backed by the rising sun at night. And that light of domestic life going on inside stands as a context for the couple's more intimate meetings.

From the great chamber in which the feast takes place to the window of Juliet's chamber, our view of Capulet's house changes dramatically in scale. The feast is explicitly intended to put many of Verona's women on show: 'At my poor house look to behold this night | Earth-treading stars that make dark heaven light (1.2.22–3), Capulet says, and suggests that Paris 'hear all, see, | And like her most whose merit most shall be' (1.2.28–9). Benvolio, in his turn, counsels Romeo to use the feast to compare Rosaline with 'all the admired beauties of Verona . . . And I will make thee think thy swan a crow.' (1.2.86–9). The list of families named to be invited and the men about whom Juliet quizzes the Nurse as cover for her urgent questioning about Romeo's identity as the guests leave show a world of possibility within which the story we watch is just one version of fate. To this large and open stage belong the preparations for feasting and the frenetic activities of household servants. But the domestic space which Romeo carves out with Juliet has a much tighter focus. Its intensity is that of tragedy and its domesticity is not the productive, quotidian kind, but rather the privacy of an unassailable space. Montague's description of Romeo in the first scene of the play comes closest to describing this kind of bounded location: 'Away from light steals home my heavy son, | And private in his chamber pens himself, | Shuts up his windows, locks fair daylight out, | And makes himself an artificial night' (1.1.134–7).

But these kinds of space are two sides of the same coin, or rather two rooms in the same house, and the domestic preparation which created the one pushes, at first gently and comically but then with increasingly tragic pressure, upon the other. Moving from the centre of the mansion to its periphery means moving from the comic to the tragic in theatrical mode, and from the materiality of napkins and joint-stools to the ethereality of the play's huge imagistic register of sky and stars. This kind of movement requires a change of focus worthy of Mercutio's descriptions of the minute Queen Mab. It shifts from large scene with small props to small scene with large conceptual universe. But it is the location within Capulet's house that joins all these aspects of domesticity together, which insists that the one be seen against the other. Domestic life anchors the macrocosmic language of tragedy, showing how its characters' bodies are circled by obligation and time, even as their souls struggle to rise beyond them, and the tension between language and location underwrites the bitterness of tragedy.

THE MERRY WIVES OF WINDSOR

If the household provided a central, bounded location within which tragedies could be played out and given meaning, then it is its *processes* which are vital to the development of comedy. In *The Merry Wives of Windsor* the household is the centre around which the marriage plot for Anne's hand and the shaming of the lecherous Falstaff revolve. The Fords' and the Pages' are households of middling status—ones which need servants such as John and Robert (who carry out the buck-basket) to run them, but whose organization is clearly under the control of their mistresses. Mistress Ford is quite firm in her sarcasm to her husband as he quizzes the servants carrying the buck-basket with Falstaff inside it—'How now? Whither bear you this?' (2.3.146), he asks— 'Why, what have you to do whither they bear it?', she replies, 'You were best meddle with buck-washing!' (2.3.148–9). While tragedies often explore patriarchal authority over the household, comedies more frequently consider female domestic skill.

Rather than the wars or feuds of tragedy which supply the context for the meaning and interpretation of domesticity, it is the contests of social status which provide the controlling dynamic for *Merry Wives*. The play opens, for instance, with a lengthy discussion of the exact social standing of Robert Shallow, esquire, 'Justice of Peace and Coram' (1.1.4–5), 'and a gentleman born' (1.1.7), whose ancestors have, for three hundred years, borne the 'dozen white luces' in their coat of arms (1.1.14). The point of this list of elements of status and the longevity of families is to give Shallow a sense of his own worth in relation to Falstaff, who is a knight. This posturing for status also extends to the plot for the hand and dowry of Anne Page—'seven hundred pounds of moneys, and gold and silver' (1.1.46–7). Faced with the prospect of a joining of households in marriage, Page's criticism of Fenton, the courtier suitor, is that 'he shall not knit a knot in his fortunes with the finger of my substance' (3.2.68–9)—shall not use Anne's dowry to underpin his own status. The question of 'substance', of the palpable materiality of things, is raised by the way social status is displayed within communities, and it becomes crucial to the play's comedy. Both humour and the comedic shape of the play—its movement toward marriage—are tied up with the social significance of domestic goods.

The really concentrated period of domestic work that is actually performed in front of the audience is the first scene in which Falstaff is ejected from Master Ford's house, and the comedy is of an intensely physical, almost slapstick kind. Coming right in the middle of the play, 3.3 is also its most energetic scene. It begins with the rapid fire of commands by which households are organized:

MISTRESS FORD:	What, John! What, Robert!
MISTRESS PAGE:	Quickly, quickly! Is the buck-basket —
MISTRESS FORD:	I warrant.—What, Robert, I say!
MISTRESS PAGE:	Come, come, come!

(3.3.1–4)

The unfinished sentences offer the same kind of mimesis of household speed and the dovetailing of different actions which characterized the comic episodes of domestic preparation in *Romeo and Juliet*. Falstaff himself adds to the energy of the scene in the repetition involved in his panic to ram himself into the buck-basket: 'Let me see't, let me see't, O let me see't! I'll in, I'll in' (3.3.127–8), and Mistress Ford issues orders with rapidity: 'What, John! Robert, John! Go take up these clothes here quickly. Where's the cowl-staff? Look how you drumble!' (3.3.138–41). The fermented vigour of domestic process generates a particular kind of physical, material comedy.

The scene shows us the wives' total command of domestic processes and their close familiarity with them—they have these routines at their fingertips and can adapt them to suit the pressing needs of the occasion. Many scholars have commented on the domestic forms which Mistress Page and Mistress Ford's shaming of Falstaff takes. Wendy Wall, for instance, argues that 'the play deflates his bodily pretensions by making him into manageable domestic goods', and that 'the depiction of moral ordering never strays too far from that of domestic labour . . . Undertaking Falstaff's reformation, the wives move between figurative and literal acts of purgation, with the result that the household swells to define the ethics and boundaries of the community.'[13] Women's domestic labour works literally to expel and then clean Falstaff, and in so doing it works metaphorically to cleanse the household of his lewd desires.

There is an inherent tension, however, in the comic uses of household process in the service of the taming of men. Natasha Korda explains the developing role of the early modern housewife: 'Housewifery, in *Merry Wives of Windsor*', she says, 'is depicted as a task requiring a particular kind of gaze, one that is both vigilant and discriminating.' Women were to ensure that the goods, which defined the status of their household and generated and guaranteed the routines through which it operated, were repeatedly 'looked to'—that they kept an eye on all their husbands had. And yet 'the assertive manner of looking necessitated by this role', was 'a mode of looking dangerously at odds with the shy, retiring gaze traditionally associated with feminine modesty' and it rendered 'the housewife vulnerable to allegations of impropriety'.[14] The anxieties which these kinds of 'looking after property' provoked were profound.

In 3.3 such apprehensions about women's relationship to domestic goods take on a concrete, material expression. As John and Robert take Falstaff out of the house in the basket, Ford, thinking he is still to be found inside, orders his friends and neighbours: 'Here, here, here be my keys. Ascend my chambers, search, seek, find out.' (3.3.155–6). Ford's domestic openness is, however, strikingly and consistently censured: 'You wrong yourself too much' (3.3.158–9) says Page; 'You do yourself mighty wrong' (3.3.197) his wife adds. When he comes back onto the stage after entering all the private rooms of the house, Evans says, 'If there be any pody in the house, and in the chambers, and in the coffers, and in the presses, heaven forgive my sins at the day of judgement!' (3.3.200–2). All the spaces of the house in which valuable domestic goods might be stored have been checked, but in so doing, Ford has opened his house up to his neighbours in what they clearly feel is an unseemly way. At the second scene of Falstaff's shaming, Ford, always one step behind his wife, has the basket searched and orders 'Pluck me out all the linen' (4.2.137). Literally airing his dirty washing in public,

---

[13] Wendy Wall, *Staging Domesticity: Household Work and English Identity in Early Modern Drama* (Cambridge: Cambridge University Press, 2002), 116–7.

[14] Korda, *Domestic Economies*, 76, 85.

emasculating himself by performing women's work, degrading himself by messing with dirty objects, he is told by Shallow: 'This wrongs you' (4.2.142).

But Evans, in one of his strange uses of English, makes a more troubling comment: ''Tis unreasonable: will you take up your wife's clothes?' (4.2.129–30). There is an innuendo here—Ford is literally lifting the clothes in the basket, perhaps the linens worn close to her body, but the suggestion is that this is like lifting the clothes she is wearing, exposing her body to his neighbours' view. As Ford approaches the house Falstaff suggests, in his panic, 'I'll creep up into the chimney' (4.2.48), while Mistress Page suggests he should 'Creep into the kiln-hole' (4.2.51). These warm, productive spaces of the household become associated with the body of the woman who controls them and organizes the processes of their use, and entertaining the idea of the fat knight's entry into them raises several images of defilement. In this play, then, illicit sexuality is investigated through the careful exploration of domestic goods.

Infidelity, as a result, is presented as an attack on just such goods. As Falstaff boasts big about his impending liaison with Mistress Ford to her disguised husband, he first points out the connection between sexual attraction and financial wealth: 'They say the jealous wittolly knave hath masses of money, for the which his wife seems to me well favoured' (2.2.262–3)—in other words, his wife's physical attractiveness is generated by her husband's money. And his next image connects women and goods in a striking way: 'I will use her as the key of the cuckoldly rogue's coffer' (2.2.261–4). It is the physicality of this idea, the sense that the word 'use' does not only metaphorically mean 'persuade' or 'deceive', but that it literally refers to something much more physical, which so unpleasantly connects Mistress Ford's body to the wealth of her husband's house.

Ford himself uses another striking image of defilement in his frantic, frenetic soliloquy after Falstaff's departure: 'See the hell of having a false woman! My bed shall be abused, my coffers ransacked, my reputation gnawn at' (2.2.282–4). He moves from the bed which stands metaphorically for his wife's chastity to the coffers which Falstaff had suggested her adultery would unlock, to the tarnishing of his reputation, which he envisages in terms of the kind of assault which domestic goods regularly suffered at the mouths of hungry vermin if they were not kept in chests and coffers. In the companion piece to this scene, in which he hears of Falstaff's latest assignation with his wife, he says of himself, 'There's a hole made in your best coat, Master Ford.' (3.5.130). Again, it is through the spoiling of those things which demonstrate social status that Ford articulates his fear of his wife's honesty. Othello's sentiment in a similar position is rather different: 'I had rather be a toad | And live upon the vapour of a dungeon | Than keep a corner in the thing I love | For others' uses.' (3.3.274–7), he says. The difference between imagining a 'corner' and expressing emotion through the image of the 'coffer' clarifies the distinction between seeing home as a metaphor for ownership of a woman in marriage, and seeing goods as a metaphor for the value of the household, which a wife must organize and protect. Characters think with things in *Merry Wives*; they express emotion and negotiate relations through them.

THE TAMING OF THE SHREW

Like *Othello*, *The Taming of the Shrew* defers its richest representation of the *practice* of married domestic life until the end of the play. But whereas in the tragedy this generates a sense of the impossibility of a quotidian existence for its central characters, in the comedy it makes a more pragmatic point about how long it takes to get domestic life right. In one way, *Taming* is all about the definition of the kind of behaviour which is appropriate for elite householders. The Induction posits this as a kind of dramaturgical question—'can you make a lord by dressing a man as one'—which the main action continues to interrogate as Tranio dresses as his master and the Pedant dresses as his master's father. It is when the characters offer a successful imitation of another person, by acting, for instance, like their master, that the comic plot advances. The effectiveness of these illusions is inherent in the way they link dress and action: clothing and the behaviour appropriate to it are essential to guarantee reputations—to certify the young and old men's assertions of identity. It is things and the activities and conduct that they generate that create a convincing representation of social status on the stage.

The play's most insistent interrogation of the qualities of elite identity takes place around the joining together in matrimony of Petruccio and Katherine. From the very start of the play, when we see Katherine offering to 'comb [Hortensio's] noddle with a three-legged stool, | And paint your face, and use you like a fool' (1.1.64–5), household objects are used as a way of defining behaviour. Unlike the sumptuous objects mentioned by the Lord of the Induction and picked up again in Gremio's discussion of his household in 2.1, the three-legged stool is a distinctly folksy, unrefined piece of furniture. The object and the behaviour in which it is employed, in other words, are similarly inappropriate to a woman of Katherine's status. Petruccio's mis-identification of her shows this clearly: 'I find you passing *gentle*. | 'Twas told me you were *rough*, and coy, and sullen, | And now I find report a very liar, | For thou art pleasant, gamesome, passing courteous . . . thou with mildness entertain'st thy wooers, | With *gentle* conference, soft, and affable' (2.1.237–46). Kate's roughness is at odds with her gentility. When, later on, she tries to argue for the appropriateness of a cap: 'This doth fit the time, | And gentlewomen wear such caps as these' (4.3.69–70), Petruccio makes the obvious retort: 'When you are gentle you shall have one, too, | And not till then' (4.3./1–2). Behaviour appropriate for the 'gentle' is a kind of domestic completeness in which objects, routines, and behaviours are all suitable to one another in their refinement.

So, like *Merry Wives*, *Taming* explores the ways in which status is constructed and guaranteed by its material manifestations through a representation 'cluttered with references to and displays of objects, and especially household furnishings'. As Lena Orlin argues, 'objects . . . expand in significance to create the illusion of a little world'.[15]

---

[15] Lena Cowen Orlin, 'The Performance of Things in *The Taming of the Shrew*', *Yearbook of English Studies*, Early Shakeseapre Special Number, 23 (1993), 167, 172.

Attention to things in the play, for some writers, has indicated the force of economic relationships beyond the couple's household. Korda argues that Shakespeare's tale of taming differs from its precursors in being an '*embourgeoisement* of the story', demonstrating 'a shift in *modes of production* and thus in the very terms through which domestic economy is conceived'. She explores the distinction between goods produced within the home and those purchased outside it, tying Petruchio's punning on Katherine's name ('For I am he am born to tame you, Kate, | And bring you from a wild Kate to a Kate | Conformable as other household Kates' [2.1.268-70]) to this wider economic movement: 'household cates ... are not proper to or born of the domestic sphere, but are produced outside the home by the market. They are by definition extra-domestic or to-be-domesticated'.[16] Now that domestic objects were largely bought outside the household, rather than being manufactured within it, the way women managed goods—the behaviours they developed around things—were more important than the way they *made* things. Cates privilege 'delicacy of form over domestic function'— they shape an aesthetic in which appearance rather than use defines value. Just as these goods' worth lies in the aesthetic value of their surface appearance, so Kate's behaviour is to be altered to something precious in its outer face, in the way it reflects her husband's status in the community.

For the majority of this play then, as for most comedies, the clear and pressing sense of the domestic interior, which helps to generate the intensity of tragedy, is dissipated into household objects. Possessions become the governing metaphor for explicating the role of women, and the nature of marriage as a liaison between the relative statuses of the men with whom they are associated as daughters and wives. But 4.1 and 4.3 of *Taming* are different. They are positioned between the reported scene of Petruccio and Katherine's marriage and the final consummatory marriage feast which, although it in fact celebrates other nuptials, symbolically brings their wedding to a close. In the long section of the play which draws out the space between the different elements of the ceremony, the taming of the shrew is played out in full within Petruccio's house.

Rudely, Petruccio has rejected his new family's nuptial hospitality ('my haste doth call me hence' [3.3.60]) and instead offers the audience a substitute, 'negative' celebration. Having set out on his adventures at the start of the play, he apparently takes Kate all the way back home to the house that used to be his father's but is now his. The arc of his travel, then, is from home as relatively 'untried' master of the house, to adventure and the acquisition of a wife, to home as a married man. And this movement sets his house up as a space for the achievement of maturity, a space of education, which mirrors Baptista's comic version of an 'academy for ladies' staffed by disguised lovers.

Within the house, attention to materiality, to the physical, sensual experience of things, is developed as a method of taming. As the mutton is served, Petruccio exclaims, ''Tis burnt, and so is all the meat' and, throwing the food down, 'take it to you, trenchers,

---

[16] Korda, *Domestic Economies*, 62, 52, 60.

cups, and all, | You heedless jolt-heads and unmannered slaves' (4.1.147–52). The focus on the names of things here—trenchers, cups—draws attention to its actuality, to the real presence of the food, which is now taken away from Kate. This process of display and then removal is continued rhetorically by Grumio in 4.3 as he offers her a neat's foot, a 'fat tripe finely broiled' (4.3.20), and a piece of beef and mustard, but finds reasons not to fetch any of them for her. 'Go, get thee gone, thou false, deluding slave' she replies to him, 'That feed'st me with the very name of meat' (4.3.31–2). Food is removed from Kate as part of the process of taming her which Petruccio transfers from his elite skills in training falcons: 'My falcon now is sharp and passing empty, | And till she stoop she must not be full-gorged, | For then she never looks upon her lure' (4.1.176–8), he says in soliloquy. His attitude toward the material things of the household, then, is not a puritanical renuncia-tion of domestic culture, but rather a process which keeps it in sight but out of hand—which increases rather than eliminates the appetite. The things which are consumed in wealthy households are central to his attempts to reform Katherine's behaviour into a series of appropriately controlled responses.

Grumio's excuse for failing to meet his master at the park when the newlyweds arrived at the house is instructive here: 'Nathaniel's coat, sir, was not fully made, | And Gabriel's pumps were all unpinked i'th' heel. | There was no link to colour Peter's hat, | And Walter's dagger was not come from sheathing' (4.1). In other words the household staff lacked crucial elements of their liveries: 'There were none fine but Adam, Ralph, and Gregory. | The rest were ragged, old, and beggarly' (4.1.118–23). Rather than reflecting the nature of their master's domestic status as 'fine' (in its dual meanings of both 'finished' and 'consummate in quality') they appeared 'beggarly'—lacking a household of any kind. Like Petruccio himself as he is described arriving at his wedding, and like Kate in her shrewishness, the household remains unfinished. It is in need of the kind of finishing, of perfecting, which attends to the detail of elite appearance and makes 'all ready and all things neat' (4.1.102). In *Taming* as in *Merry Wives*, then, domestic process alters behaviour, and household routine makes Kate's image more suitable to her own and her husband's status.

It is in this domestic space, in process between Petruccio's domestic life as a son and as a master, set temporally between their marriage and their life together as a couple, that Kate is finally tamed. The house is a space in which Petruccio's rules can apply, and the image of domestic control we have as he (impatiently) orders his servants, serves to guarantee that they will assist him in his project to tame his new wife. In terms of the play's consideration of behaviour appropriate for elite men and women, the house functions rather like an intellectual proposition—a 'what if' space—in which behaviour can be altered, one which is artificially isolated from society as a whole. In this way it echoes the Induction, and the pairing of the two houses as spaces for creating social change gives domestic life in the play a dynamic character, showing it to be dedicated to the production of elite identity.

Hortensio's entry noticeably changes the dynamic: as an outsider to the household, neither master nor servant, his arrival signals the beginning of the movement toward Baptista's wedding feast. There, Kate can manipulate outer show—marshalling behaviour as she does the trappings of elite finery; showing herself perfected, aesthetically whole in a way which links domestic objects to conduct in order to complete the image of the elite wife. Smoothly, perhaps glibly, she can run through the speeches belonging to her part, including the *pièce de résistance*, 'Thy husband is thy lord, thy life, thy keeper . . .' (5.2.151).

CONCLUSION

Politics and economics mix with intense emotion in the portrayal of domestic life, then. The time-depth of its fundamentally physical presence—the palpable touch of family past and future, of status and identity experienced—is present either as a comfortingly familiar hold or a vice-like grip upon the characters. But the stability of these houses is also in question—lodging and owning a property are contrasted in all but *Romeo and Juliet*, as the plays probe the stability and rootedness of domestic life in a period where 'house' meant both ancient family and physical building.

As households sever and re-form, or try to grow, like Romeo and Juliet's domestic space, inside the old family home, the roles of men and women in organizing domestic life also come into question. Women's connection with these spaces forms part of the working out of new domestic roles in a changing economy, and the moral dimension of their association with household space is striking. But, as Heather Dubrow has argued, we also 'need to extend the gendering of the domestic to look more closely at its connections to male subjectivity and male bodies'.[17] The role of household guardian, so central to patriarchal projects, is evident in men's often belligerent policing of domestic behaviour.

The dynamic of emotion which is out of control and the bounded domestic space in which it is played out is perhaps the strongest connection between the plays studied here: from Romeo and Juliet's explosive young love and Tybalt's fury to Othello's and Ford's irrational jealousy and Katherine's shrewishness, those who control the household try to manage excessive and damaging emotional intensity. Genre determines domestic efficacy: emotion is more or less susceptible to household routine, more or less able to be altered by the processes of domestic life in comedy and tragedy. If the buck-basket stands as an image of the efficiency of domesticity in combating negative emotion in comedy (instrument of the 'double excellency' in which Ford and Sir John are both shamed [3.3.167]), then perhaps Juliet's position at the window is an equally evocative image of the inadequacy of domesticity in tragedy, where deeds and their ramifications sidestep routine and its constant surveillance, growing unseen out of range of the call of the household.

Ford's domestic hysterics shows how the household can provide a focus, not only as a space for emotion but also as a way of shaping it, of thinking through deeply personal and emotive issues. Domestic life, as process, routine, interpersonal

---

[17] Dubrow, *Shakespeare and Domestic Loss*, 79.

relations or household things, becomes one element in a metaphor. As a quotidian thing it provides a springboard to think through, beyond the materiality of day-to-day existence, to less mundane matters. The distance between a candle and a life (*Othello* 5.2) might be huge, but Shakespeare repeatedly makes that leap. And in doing so, he ties the material culture of the stage—the domestic props which his audience can see in front of them—to the imaginative universe of his poetry, which takes its shape within their imaginations.

CHAPTER 12

....

GENDER

....

ANDREW HISCOCK

[. . .] in Stage Playes for a boy to put [on] the attyre, the gesture, the
passions of a woman; for a meane person to take vpon him the title of a
Prince with counterfeit porte, and traine, is by outwarde signes to shewe
them selues otherwise then they are, and so with in the compass of a lye,
which by Aristotles iudgement is naught of it selfe and to be fledde.

—Stephen Gosson[1]

AT the dawn of the modern age, Freud famously contended in one of his *New
Introductory Lectures* entitled 'Femininity' that 'When you meet a human being, the
first distinction you make is "male or female?" and you are accustomed to make the
distinction with unhesitating certainty.'[2] Such an appetite for crisp cultural distinctions, which can be made with 'unhesitating certainty', was clearly thwarted for an
Elizabethan like Stephen Gosson when he entered a built environment wholly devoted
to the business of pretence, concealment, and performance—the early modern playhouse. In his *Playes Confuted in Fiue Actions* (1582) Gosson described an extravagantly
lawless place in which male acting companies impersonated figures of all ranks, ages
and nations . . . and of both sexes. Surely, such environments could signal the disintegration of all social discipline—and Gosson was not alone in his thinking. There were
other Elizabethans working themselves up into similarly heady passions. John Rainolds
barked in *Th'ouerthrow of stage-playes* that 'the apparell of wemen [. . .] is a great
provocation of men to lust and leacherie: because a womans garment beeing put on a
man doeth vehemently touch and moue him with the remembrance & imagination of a
woman; and the imagination of a thing desirable doth stirr vp the desire'.[3] And, earlier

---

[1] See S. Gosson (1582), *Playes Confuted in fiue actions*, sig. C5r.

[2] See S. Freud (1964), *The Standard Edition of the Complete Psychological Works of Sigmund Freud*,
vol. 22: *New Introductory Lectures on Psycho-Analysis and other Works*, James Strachey et al. (trans.)
(London: Hogarth Press, 1964), 113.

[3] John Rainolds , *Th'overthrow of stage-playes* (London: 1599), 97.

in Elizabeth's reign, the venerable voice of 'Age' in a tract by John Northbrooke declared himself, 'persuaded that Satan hath not a more speedie way and fitter schoole to work and teach his desire, to bring men and women into his snare of concupiscence and filthie lustes of wicked whoredome, than those places and playes, and theatres are'.[4] These shrill voices (with their disarmingly intimate knowledge of the sins of temptation) indicate, if nothing else, that a concern with the imaginative possibilities of all kinds of cultural performance (of gender-swapping, cross-classing, racial impersonation, feigned travel and so on), which the playhouse offered, clearly dates from the period itself when the writings of Shakespeare and his contemporaries were being staged and read—and the scholarly debate surrounding the challenges which early modern theatre posed shows no signs of flagging.

Gender-based Shakespearean scholarship has remained one of the liveliest, most popular and most diverse areas of enquiry among academics, directors, audiences, and students in recent decades, and the limits of time and space mean that I can by no means exhaust the multifarious nature of the subject in this chapter. Nonetheless, the opportunity to contemplate the great variety of what has become one of the dominant fields in Shakespeare studies remains illuminating. An abiding interest in gender in terms of an examination of culturally constructed 'difference' (articulated as 'masculinity' and 'femininity') and the social pressures deployed to enforce normative gendered identities (through the promotion of these fictions of difference) has stimulated generations of critics, theatre companies, audiences, and students to engage in wide-ranging forms of textual analysis and cultural critique linked to Shakespearean writing. Such enquiries might consider the ways in which arbitrary operations of differentiation (often linked to contrasting anatomical interpretations of the male and female body) have resulted in societal structures underpinned by egregious examples of unwarranted privilege, omission, and neglect. Indeed, pursuing such questions in *A bride-bush, or A wedding sermon* (1617) William Whately contended that 'the wife being resolued that her place is the lower, must carry herselfe as an inferiour. It little bootes to confesse [the husband's] authority in word, if shee frame not to submission in deede'.[5]

Elsewhere, the concern has been to scrutinize the cultural constructions of meaning and power mediated *through* Shakespeare: the ways in which this seemingly unassailable, immutable, universal cultural icon has been appropriated globally, and the ways in which his writings have been exploited in the service of very different political ideologies down the centuries. These ideologies have shaped, and continue to shape, the cultural formulation of 'literature' per se and, more particularly with reference to this discussion, the subject of 'Shakespeare' in terms of school and

---

[4] See, respectively, J. Rainolds (1599), *Th'overthrow of stage-playes*, 97; J. Northbrooke (1577), *Spiritus est vicarius Christi in terra*, 59–60.

[5] W. Whately, *A bride-bush, or A wedding sermon compendiously describing the duties of married persons: by performing whereof, marriage shall be to them a great helpe, which now finde it a little hell* (1617), 37.

university curricula, funded research, editing practices, acting repertoires, and audience expectations.

GENDER-BASED CRITICISM: AN HERMETICALLY SEALED CATEGORY?

In *Julius Caesar*, Portia remonstrates with her secretive husband 'I grant I am a woman, but withal | A woman well reputed, Cato's daughter' (2.1.293–4), whereas Ophelia goes much further in diversifying the identities of Hamlet in the later tragedy to courtier, soldier, scholar: 'Th'expectancy and rose of the fair state. | The glass of fashion and the mould of form' (3.1.154–6). In such dramatic narratives Shakespeare raises thorny questions about the human appetite for a repertoire of selves and about the ideological pressures which may excite this need.

Critics have often remained perplexed by the multifariousness of the politics of identity in Shakespearean writing, and frequently the decision has been to adopt a multi-focal vision on questions of gender. The fraternization between gender-based criticism and research enquiries highlighting issues of sexuality, class, race, and history, for example, has fluctuated enormously over past decades—and there appears little enduring critical consensus on how to proceed. In the event, as we shall see, the many and variously proposed disciplinary boundaries have rarely been policed in the manner that some critics would have wished as gender-based analysis of Shakespeare has developed over time.

THE PLAYHOUSE AND GENDER PERFORMANCE

One favoured departure point for a consideration of the politics of gender in Shakespeare's writing has remained a focus upon the acting conventions in the public playhouse. Theatres, such as the Rose and the Globe, did not seek to blur the distinctions between fictive experience and the conditions of existence on offer to its audiences beyond the *wooden O*: all-male companies in broadly contemporary costume experimented in all manner of gendered, racialized, socially-mobile theatrical narratives. Yet these same actors frequently interacted with each other and the audience in verse, staged asides, or soliloquies for the audience's benefit. Indeed, at the close of *As You Like It*, Rosalind engages directly with the possibility that audience responses might be governed by gendered allegiances: 'I charge you, O women, for the love you bear to men, to like as much of this play as please you. And I charge you, O men, for the love you bear to women...that between you and the women the play may please' (Epilogue, 11–16). In the course of performance, these same audiences might be transported to a multitude of locations without elaborate props ('So this is Tyre, and this the court'—*Pericles* Sc. 3.1), or invited to consider by Ross in *Macbeth* 'by th'clock 'tis day, | And yet dark night strangles the travelling lamp' (2.4.6–7). Meanwhile, the thrust stage might allow spectators to view not only the dramatic action, but also other members of the audience in the same line of vision. Nevertheless, whatever the troublesome questions that remain concerning the diverse representations of gendered experience in Shakespeare's theatre, it remains inarguable that his texts clearly had currency for the society in which they were produced, irrespective of the distance or proximity between the dramatic worlds conjured up by actors and those inhabited by the broader community of playgoers.

It may be, of course, that the theatrical conventions of gendered impersonation were simply experienced as exactly that by at least some playgoers—perhaps distantly resembling the imaginative leaps in which audiences have engaged when encountering the performance of 'breeches' roles in contemporary traditions of British pantomime, castrato parts played by women in modern productions of early opera, or the stagings of Chinese opera before the 1930s. However, at least some early modern figures (such as Gosson, Rainolds, and Northbrooke) felt that the scrambling of normative codes of gender and moral expectation on the early modern stage warranted vigorous comment, and a good measure of more recent Shakespearean criticism has been similarly minded. Indeed, the texts themselves constantly urge us to attend to the adoption or imposition of gendered identities: in *The Taming of the Shrew*, for example, Petruchio wishes to fashion out of the male actor playing his wife 'a second Grissel' (2.1.290), whereas the male actor playing Princess Innogen in *Cymbeline* is instructed 'You must forget to be a woman' (3.4.155) in order to pass him-her-self off safely as Fidelio.

Successive generations of critics have inevitably been drawn to explore the dramatic challenges posed by these unending cycles of gendered performance: might not this convention of female impersonation constitute a means of examining and interrogating cultural appetites for schemes of gendered difference? an opportunity to consider the fragility and/or reversibility of any gender performance? an erotic stimulus for members of either or both sexes of the audience? a focus for the wider study of the ways in which theatrical and textual cultures may be coercive or subversive with reference to prevailing ideologies at work within a given society? The critical jury has still yet to arrive at a verdict, but Barbara Hodgdon, for example, has argued that 'In Shakespeare's theatre of gender, the most obvious signs were voice and costume'[6]—yet even these cultural markers may be decoded in a number of different ways. Is the 'gracious silence' of Coriolanus' wife, Virgilia, less gender-marked than the volubility of Rosalind in *As You Like It*?—'Do you not know I am a woman? When I think, I must speak' (3.1.244–5). In *Twelfth Night*, Viola (as Cesario) laments 'I see disguise thou art a wickedness' (2.2.27), yet Falstaff eagerly dons women's clothing when cornered in a Windsor household: 'My maid's aunt, the fat woman of Brentford, has a gown above' (*The Merry Wives of*

---

[6] B. Hodgdon, 'Sexual Disguise and the Theatre of Gender', in A. Leggatt (ed.), *The Cambridge Companion to Shakespearean Comedy* (Cambridge: Cambridge University Press, 2002), 179–97, at 181.

Windsor 4.2.67–8). Hamlet gives a consummate performance at court in his 'inky cloak', yet Caliban dismisses the aristocratic garments, which so dazzle the eyes of European servants, as 'trash' (*The Tempest* 4.1.223).

Furthermore, we should not think of a theatre experience in which all attentions were uniformly upon the stage. Despite the claims of those such as Gosson and Rainolds, one wonders to what extent gender impersonation remained uppermost in the early modern playgoer's mind. John Donne bemoaned, 'How many times go we to Comedies, to Masques, to places of great and noble resort, nay even to Church onely to see the company?'[7] Yet if William Prynne lamented that 'Stage-playes devirginate unmarried persons, especially beautifull, tender Virgins who resort to them (which I would our female Play-haunters; and *their Parents* would consider:) that they defile their soules with impure carnall lusts; and so let in eternall death upon them,'[8] such sentiments do not appear to have dissuaded members of either sex from flocking to the theatres to taste its forbidden fruits.

GENDER CRITICISM AND THE BODY: 'IS THIS THY BODY'S END?'

As a growing number of discussions have indicated, the best preserved theatres from the early modern period were often built for the express purpose of anatomical study. There is now a wealth of scholarship devoted to the ways in which Shakespeare's writing acknowledged medical theorizing of the body (inherited from antiquity), which focused upon discourses of balance, lack, and excess. Excess or physical largesse is, of course, something which is perennially associated with the *miles gloriosus* Sir John Falstaff, memorably described by Prince Hal as one who 'sweats to death, | And lards the lean earth as he walks along' (2.3.16–17). And Gail Kern Paster, for example, has stressed the wider currency of the medical theorizing of anatomy and the humours in Shakespeare's writing, pointing out that in *The Taming of a Shrew*, 'it is Katherine's excessive choler, uncontained and unsocialised, that Petruchio must regulate—a process complicated and underscored by the play's emphasis on his own humoral imbalance. If her taming entails his self-taming, the play nonetheless endorses his retention of choler as a prerequisite to, and the biological basis of, male mastery'.[9]

[7] J. Donne, *The Sermons of John Donne*, George R. Potter and Evelyn M. Simpson, (eds.), vol. 4 (Berkeley: University of California Press, 1959), 176.
[8] W. Prynne *Histrio-mastix The players scourge, or, actors tragaedie* (1633), 340–1.
[9] G. K. Paster, *Humoring the Body: Emotions and the Shakespearean Stage* (Chicago, IL: University of Chicago Press, 2004), 86.

More generally, the body can become a focus of consuming interest in Shakespearean narrative. The popularity of *Venus and Adonis* in the early modern period is not in doubt. It ran to some ten editions during his own lifetime, and a further five by 1637— and the goddess's erotic ambitions occupy a good deal of the poetic intrigue:

> 'Fondling,' she saith, 'since I have hemmed thee here
> Within the circuit of this ivory pale,
> I'll be a park, and thou shalt be my deer.
> Feed where thou wilt, on mountain or in dale;
> > Graze on my lips; and if those hills be dry,
> > Stray lower, where the pleasant fountains lie.   (229–34)

It may be that a sexual immaturity, a fear of physical intimacy, an absence of erotic interest, and/or extravagant narcissism are among the motivations that prevent Adonis from accepting this invitation and, at the poem's conclusion, this fugitive from love finds himself speared on the tusks of a slavering boar. The extent to which *Venus and Adonis* invites readers to sanction, condemn, or interrogate departures from prevailing expectations of gendered/sexualized performance remains an area of animated critical discussion. However, the narrative poem has also continued to excite interest in the ways in which early modern schemes of gender difference were often legitimized by aligning them closely with affirmations about the human form—a marker that has remained crucial to the cultural formulation of selfhood down the ages. In this context, Venus' performance might usefully be contrasted with the rather more coy offering from the warrior Coriolanus, who bids for the Roman consulship by participating in the city's rituals which seek to unveil his distressed body: 'Kindly! Sir [. . .] I have wounds to show you, which shall be yours in private. Your good voice, sir; what say you?' (2.3.75–7).

Indeed, at times of crisis the early modern body might more generally become an object of intense surveillance as evidence was sought to safeguard the purity and integrity of the wider community: refusing to be harried by her 1559 Parliament into wedlock, Elizabeth proclaimed, 'this shalbe for me sufficient, that a marble stone shall declare that a Queene, having raigned such a tyme, lived and dyed a virgin'.[10] Elsewhere, looking back to gender expectations inherited from Aristotelian writings, early modern manuals often presented the unruly female body as a departure from the authoritative and legible male template, and subject to all kinds of mysterious and unpredictable transformations. Clearly influenced by such received thinking that linked the changeful female anatomy with an innate appetite for sexual change, Leontes (believing himself a cuckold) rails in *The Winter's Tale* that there is 'No barricado for a belly' (1.2.205).

Culturally stylized accounts of the body also frequently recur as key components in early modern formulations of political theory and discipline. Not unrepresentatively, John Speed proclaimed at the opening of his richly presented map collection *The Theatre of the Empire of Great Britain* (1611) that 'The State of euery Kingdome well

---

[10] T. E. Hartley, *Proceedings in the Parliaments of Elizabeth I*, vol. 1, 1558–1581 (Leicester: Leicester University Press, 1981).

managed by prudent gouernment, seems to me to represent a Humane Body, guided by the soueraignty of the *Reasonable Soule*'.[11] If the human form thus expressed meta-phorically the body politic (as in the case of Menenius' fable in *Coriolanus*) and, as the Book of Genesis informed, was in miniature an *imago Dei*, this completed, scrutable, admirable form was that of the male body. Hamlet exults, 'What a piece of work is a man! . . . in action how like an angel, in apprehension how like a god—the beauty of the world, the paragon of animals!', but 'frailty' is reserved for the 'name' of woman (2.2.304–8, 1.2.146). Early modern expectations of heroic (often 'forceful', if not 'physi-cal') performances of masculinity are widely in evidence throughout Shakespeare's writings. This thematic concern has often dominated critical accounts of *The Taming of the Shrew*, as we have seen; and in Shakespeare's last Roman tragedy, it quickly becomes apparent as the bloodied hero emerges from the sack of the Volscean city, Corioli, that the violence in which he has just participated has certainly 'invigorated' him—indeed, enabled him to engage in a new birthing narrative as he is transformed from Caius Martius into Coriolanus. And this textual preoccupation with the male body's perceived propensity for physical and verbal violence (often connoting an appetite for cultural change and power assertion) feeds the development of many of the intrigues of the later romances. In *Cymbeline*, for example, the mental responses of the thwarted clown prince Cloten converge effortlessly upon a profoundly troubling fantasy of physical violation:

> With that suit [of Posthumus'] upon my back, will I
> ravish her—first kill him, and in her eyes; there shall she see
> my valour, which will then be a torment to her contempt. He
> on the ground, my speech of insultment ended on his dead
> body, and when my lust hath dined—which, as I say, to vex her
> I will execute in the clothes that she so praised—to the court
> I'll knock her back, foot her home again. She hath despised
> me rejoicingly, and I'll be merry in my revenge.   (3.5.137–45)

GENDER CRITICISM AND EARLY MODERN ESSENTIALISM

The cultural formulation of radically imbalanced power relations between the sexes has endured as a primary interest in gender-based criticism of Shakespeare. Essentialist discourses relating to the attributes of masculinity and femininity were already well established in antiquity. Much of the rationale for interpretations of female physical weakness as an index of moral and intellectual weakness came from popular readings of Aristotle on the biology of animals: 'whenever the sexes are separate the female

---

[11] John Speed (1611), *The theatre of the empire of Great Britaine*, 1.

cannot generate perfectly by herself alone, for then the male would exist in vain, and nature makes nothing in vain. Hence in such animals the male always perfects the work of generation, for he imparts the sensitive soul';[12] and from familiar *topoi* in Scripture: 'But I would have you know, that the head of every man is Christ; and the head of every woman *is* the man'.[13]

The lifting of proofs from ancient texts was inevitably highly selective, but many early modern voices were eager to demonstrate the 'naturalness' and 'legitimacy' of female subordination in the social order by citing such authorities. The state-commissioned Tudor homily on marriage stressed that 'the woman is a weake creature, not endued with like strength and constancy of mind; therefore they be sooner disquieted, and they be the more prone to all weake affectations & dispositions of the mynde, more than men be . . . [Saint Peter] sayth . . . that the woman ought to haue a certayne honour attributed to her, that is to say, she muste be spared and borne with, the rather for that she is the weaker vessel, of a frayle heart, inconstant, and with a worde soone stirred to wrath'.[14] Indeed, Antigonus is vigorously chastised by his wrathful sovereign in *The Winter's Tale* when he admits his inability to restrain his wife—'When she will take the rein I let her run' (2.3.51). Investing in the cultural projection of the feminine in terms of lack, absence, and inadequacy, the political theorist Sir Thomas Smith submitted that 'God hath giuen to the man great wit, bigger strength, and more courage to compell the woman to obey by reason or force, and to the woman bewtie, faire countenaunce, and sweete wordes to make the man to obey her againe for loue. Thus ech obeyeth and commaundeth other'.[15] More crisply, Thomas Overbury stated of a 'Good Woman' that the husband's 'good becomes the businese of her actions . . . her chiefest vertue is a good husband. For *Shee is Hee*'[16]—and these are certainly sentiments which Shakespeare's Petruchio endorses in the *The Taming of the Shrew*: 'For I am he am born to tame you, Kate, | And bring you from a wild Kate to a Kate' (2.1.268–9).

In *The Rape of Lucrece*, the violated heroine scrutinizes a 'skilful painting'. It depicts the Trojan war and offers to the viewer's eye the dynamic performances of 'sly' Ulysses, 'grave' Nestor, and 'bold' Hector in contrast to the tableaux of spectating women—of 'Trojan mothers' and 'despairing' Hecuba (1366 ff.). And, more generally, it is evident that the visual arts of the early modern period remained richly sensitive to the communication of gender in terms of Aristotelian antitheses, as may be witnessed in

---

[12] Aristotle, Generation of Animals, in A. L. Peck (trans.), Loeb Classical Library 366 (Cambridge, MA: Harvard University Press, 1942), 1.1150.

[13] 1: Corinthians 11.3.

[14] 'Homilee', see 'an Homilee of the state of Matrimonie', in *The second tome of homilees of such matters as were promised, and intituled in the former part of homilees. Set out by the auothoritie of the Queenes Maiestie; and to be read in every paraishe church agreeably* (1571; 1st pub. 1562), 480.

[15] T. Smith, *De republica Anglorum. The maner of gouernment or policie of the realme of England* [. . .] (1583), 13.

[16] T. Overbury, *A wife now the widow of Sir Thomas Ouerburie Being a most exquisite and singular poeme, of the choyse of a wife. Whereunto are added many witty characters* [. . .] (1614), sig. C2v.

the woodcut illustrations from Henry Peacham's emblem collection *Minerua Britanna* (1612) (see Figure 12.1). In such enormously popular collections, gendered codes of ethical idealism circulated for a diverse readership, both literate and illiterate; and perhaps one of the most striking aspects of early modern literature is how often such cultural assumptions were articulated in a host of different genres. In his pedagogic treatise *Positions* (1581), for example, Richard Mulcaster stressed for his readers' edification that the 'bodies [of] the *maidens* be more weake, most commonly euen by nature, as of a moonish influence'.[17] In this context, we might recall that at the opening of *The Winter's Tale* the eloquent Queen Hermione is demonized as sexually incontinent by her crazed husband: Leontes believes that her persuasive rhetoric deployed for another man has placed the performance of his own masculinity in question ('Women say so, | That will say anything' (1.2.132–3)), and has served to compromise her erotic allegiances. Yet in this instance, it is the unruly king whose mind and body are (mis)governed by the changeful moon, as Paulina acknowledges: 'These dangerous, unsafe lunes i'th'King, beshrew them!' (2.2.33). When marital relationships become central narrative preoccupations for Shakespeare, the textual drama is often monopolized by masculinist appetites for sexual ownership and power play, as the beleaguered Othello confirms: 'I had rather be a toad | ... than keep a corner in the thing I love | For others' uses' (3.3.274–7). This is not simply a question of asserting exclusive rights over the woman's access to sexual experience, but an anxiety-ridden bid to control her access to language, society, and memory, and to ensure that she fulfils her role to complete the patriarch's staging of his masculinity in society. Moreover, from the perspective of the early modern judiciary, as Richard Allestree stressed in *The whole dvty of man* (1658), 'The corrupting of a mans wife, enticing her to a strange bed, is by all acknowledged to be the worst sort of theft, infinitely beyond that of the goods'.[18]

The sexual violation of the female body is indeed not only explored in terms of profound physical and mental trauma for the victim in Shakespearean narrative, but frequently with an emphasis upon the feverish and competing bids for patriarchal appropriation of its meanings. In *The Rape of Lucrece* the heroine responds to the crime ultimately by taking her own life, yet the poem urges us to revisit the vexed narrative in which the rape and its consequences come to serve as a moment of textual and political parturition. Lucrece's violation is linked initially to her assumption of a more dynamic textual and political role. However, her access to a public voice is withdrawn not only through her subsequent act of self-destruction, but also through the male exploitation of her suffering for the purposes of founding the Roman Republic. The profoundly troubling nature of this patriarchal consumption of the woman's victimized body is also made explicit by Shakespeare in another Roman

---

[17] R. Mulcaster, *Positions wherein those primitiue circumstances be examined, which are necessarie for the training vp of children, either for skill in their booke, or health in their bodie* [...] (1581), 176.

[18] See Richard Allestree, *The whole dvty of man necessary for all families with privated devotions for severall occasions* (1658), 227.

FIGURE 12.1. Henry Peacham, *Minerua Britanna or A garden of heroical deuises furnished, and adorned with emblemes and impresas of sundry natures, newly devised, moralized and published* (1612), 147, 158.

narrative of the 1590s, *Titus Andronicus*. Here, the violent traumas endured by the protagonist's daughter are once again inextricably linked with the collapse of the body politic: in this harrowing tragedy poised between unexpected moments of pathos, horrifying violence, and bleak farce, the defiled Lavinia is murdered by her own father ('Die, die, Lavinia, and thy shame with thee; | And, with thy shame, thy father's sorrow die!), and her ravishers minced up and 'both bakèd in this pie, | Whereof their mother daintily hath fed, | Eating the flesh that she herself hath bred' (5.3.45–6, 59–61).

GENDER CRITICISM AND QUEER THEORY

The Elizabethan polemicist Phillip Stubbes chose to interpret the contemporary theatre industry specifically in terms of sexual deviance when he asked his readers to 'marke the flocking and running to Theaters & curtens, daylie and hourely, night and daye . . . Than these goodly pageants being done . . . euery one brings another homeward of their way verye freendly, and in their secret conclaues (couertly) they play the *Sodomits*, or worse'.[19] And there has indeed been growing interest in the ways in which the early modern

[19] Phillip Stubbes, *The Anatomie of Abuses* (London, 1583), sigs. L8r–v.

playhouse may have critiqued and even challenged heteronormative pressures of sexual identification. The intense emotional investment which Antonio yields to Bassanio in *The Merchant of Venice* ('My purse, my person, my extremest means | Lie all unlocked to your occasions' (1.138–9)) and another Antonio offers to Sebastian in *Twelfth Night* ('If you will not murder me for my love, let me be your servant' (2.1.31–2)) has regularly given pause for thought in modern theatre productions and in critical debate. In a discussion of *The Merchant of Venice*, for example, Alan Sinfield radically unsettles the narrative movement toward heterosexual coupledom in this comedy, submitting archly that 'for most audiences and readers, the air of "happy ending" suggests that Bassanio's movement toward heterosexual relations is in the necessary, the right direction (like Shylock's punishment, perhaps)'.[20]

In terms of the late Elizabethan society in which these plays were first produced, it remains clear that the subject of same-sex relations had sufficient currency to be treated in such works as Richard Barnfield's *The affectionate shepheard* (1594), and satirized in John Marston's *The scourge of vilaine* (1598) and Edward Guilpin's *Skialetheia* (1598). And the Shakespearean corpus of plays and poems continues to offer ample opportunity for this critical approach. In the midst of *Troilus and Cressida*'s lightly classicized world characterized by frantic sexual exchanges, Pandarus declares that he 'could live and die i'th'eyes of Troilus' (1.2.239–40). The young heroine often renders her uncle a fine target for ridicule for herself and her intimates, but he is nevertheless afforded a sustained power of intervention in the play's ongoing interrogation of dissident sexualities. Equally interestingly in this context of problematizing sexual prerogatives, in *Coriolanus* the Volscian leader Aufidius pleads with the hero, 'Let me twine | Mine arms about that body . . . more dances my rapt heart | Than when I first my wedded mistress saw | Bestride my threshold' (4.5.107–8, 117–19). And in the late collaborative work *The Two Noble Kinsmen*, Emilia is shown to remember with fondness her passionate friendship with Flavia: 'Loved for we did, and like the elements, | That know not what, nor why, yet do effect | Rare issues by their operance, our souls | Did so to one another' (1.3.61–4). At such moments, theatre audiences are clearly urged to match Emilia's poignant emotional engagement with the subsequent depiction of the intense commitment which the eponymous heroes, Palamon and Arcite, make to each other. The prospect of marriage at the close of this tragicomedy ('Is this winning?' (5.5.138)) fails to eclipse the heroic potential, which has been regularly linked in the preceding narratives with same-sex relations. Tellingly, at the denouement, Palamon is found to mourn 'That we should things desire which do cost us | The loss of our desire' (5.6.110–11).

Influenced by post-structuralist analytical strategies, queer theorists have sought to read the figuring of erotic desire in Shakespearean texts *against the grain* in creative and provocative ways: yet the difficulty of this commitment is often underlined by the critics themselves. Thus, in the endeavour to interrogate the orthodoxies of the heterosexist framework embedded in early modern textual cultures, Valerie Traub

---

[20] A. Sinfield, 'How to Read *The Merchant of Venice* without being Heterosexist', in K. Chedgzoy (ed.), *Shakespeare, Feminism and Gender* (Basingstoke: Palgrave Macmillan, 2001), 115–34, at 120.

acknowledges that her consideration of 'lesbian desire' inevitably confronts difficulties in seeking to apply modern sexual templates onto the past, 'extrapolat[ing] a cultural *presence* from a discursive *silence*'.[21]

Gendered Performances and Gendered Spaces

When questioned why he is not 'afield' with the other Trojan warriors, the harassed Troilus concedes that 'womanish it is to be from thence' (1.1.107), and this irrepressible concern with the regulation of gender in terms of cultural representation and locale is afforded a voice throughout the corpus of Shakespeare's writing and, indeed, the wider textual cultures of early modern Europe. The Continental Reformist Heinrich Bullinger affirmed that 'What so euer is to be done wythout ye house that belongeth to the man, & the woman to study for thynges wythein to be done',[22] and it is precisely this gendered division of the social environment that is placed under intense scrutiny in a play such as *Timon of Athens*. As his assumed identity of munificent patron splinters beneath the weight of misfortune, Timon turns to the equally forceful masculine persona of a railing Jeremiah in the later phases of the play. However, when he encounters the residue of his former life in the shape of the 'poor steward' Flavius, Timon (like Coriolanus in a similar situation) bears witness to the collapse of all codes of cultural distinction: 'What, dost thou weep? Come nearer then; I love thee, | Because thou art a woman, and disclaim'st | Flinty mankind' (4.3.483–5).

Many critical discussions of such exchanges bear witness to the influence of Judith Butler's theorizing of the constructedness and provisionality of gender performance and domains, and these discursive emphases can offer illuminating insights into Shakespearean narratives in general. In the bitter struggles enacted in *King John*, for example, to penetrate the confines of the city of Angers, the walled settlement becomes a coveted space and a proving ground for factions vying to perform their masculinity for wider cultural consumption and to legitimize their claims to royalty through combat at arms. At the beginning of Act 2 the feminized city still has 'those sleeping stones | That as a waist doth girdle [it] about', but if Angers fails to 'open [the] gates and give the victors way', then (the belligerent John warns) it will prove impossible 'To save unscratched your city's threatened cheeks' (2.1.216–17, 324, 225). In the later *Julius Caesar*, this negotiation with explicitly gendered space is played out under equally compelling

---

[21] Valerie Traub, 'The (in)significance of "Lesbian" Desire in Early Modern England; in Susan Zimmerman (ed.), Erotic Politics: Desire on the Renaissance Stage (Ithaca, NY: Cornell University Press, 1992), 150–69; 164.

[22] H. Bullinger, *The golden boke of christen matrimonye moost necessary [and] profitable for all the[m], that tentend to liue quietly and godlye in the Christen state of holy wedlock* [. . .] (1542), sigs. L3r–L3v.

terms within the intimacy of a marriage. The furtive Brutus is upbraided angrily by Portia, 'Dwell I but in the suburbs | Of your good pleasure?' From this perspective, if she is thus denied access to her husband's innermost thoughts, she must belong to the unsavoury subculture which inhabited the peripheries (or 'liberties') of most early modern cities: 'If it be no more, | Portia is Brutus' harlot, not his wife' (2.1.284–6).

With regards to the performative question of gendered identity, early modern authors themselves were clearly keenly sensitive to the fragility of any social performance, and the constant need for rehearsal and fine-tuning. In *Hero-Paideia: of the Institution of a Young Nobleman* (1607), for example, James Cleland was at pains to demonstrate the theatrical demands which life in society imposed: 'Many men seeing you passe by them, will conceive presently a good or bad opinion of you. Wherefore yee must take very good heed unto your feete, and consider with what grace and countenance yee walke'.[23] One of the most evident Shakespearean locations where these kinds of gender negotiations are foregrounded is in the *Sonnets*. Here, the 'tender churl' at the beginning of the collection is enjoined to fulfil his masculine self and to expend his 'unused beauty' through the performance of 'increase' (Sonnets 1, 4). However, by the close of the 1609 sonnet sequence, with its consuming interest in the 'master-mistress' of desire (Sonnet 20), the reader may be drawn to identify the collapse, rather than the occlusion, of early modern schemes of gender expectation: the erstwhile patterns of distinction between the sexes are now frequently eroded ('On both sides thus is simple truth suppressed. | . . . I lie with her, and she with me' (Sonnet 138)) or poignantly reversed: ' "I hate" from hate away she threw, | And saved my life, saying "not you" ' (Sonnet 145).

Gender, Empathy, and Character Criticism: Past and Present

The frequent psychological narrativization (nay, novelization) of the Sonnets by critics down the centuries in terms of an erotic and starkly gendered triangulation among the Young Man, Dark Lady, and the Poet-Speaker links with a broader (and seemingly insatiable) critical preoccupation with characterization itself within Shakespearean gender studies. The publication of Juliet Dusinberre's *Shakespeare and the Nature of Women* in 1975 is taken widely by scholars to mark a watershed moment in the development of theorized gender criticism, but the promotion of character as a major route of entry into dramatic narrative has a long ancestry within this critical approach.[24] One of the earliest critics to bequeath her responses to posterity was the writer Margaret Cavendish, and she marvelled in her collection *Sociable Letters* (1664),

---

[23] J. Cleland, *Hero-Paideia: of the Institution of a Young Nobleman* (1607), 170.

[24] Juliet Dusinberre, *Shakespeare and the Nature of Women* (London: Macmillan, 1975; rpt. New York: St. Martin's, 1996).

'Who would not think [Shakespeare] had been such a man as his Sir *Iohn Falstaff*...
one would think that he had been Metamorphosed from a Man to a Woman, for who
could Describe *Cleopatra* Better than he hath done.'[25] In the eighteenth century, this
kind of attention to gender identification and affect continued to form an important
strand of Shakespearean criticism. Elizabeth Montagu's *An essay on the writings and
genius of Shakespear* (1769) broached questions of poetics and dramatic structure, but
also invited her readers to engage with 'the mild, the virtuous, the gentle Brutus':
indeed, 'at Rome, we become Romans; we are affected by their manners; we are caught
by their enthusiasm'.[26]

The traumatized Hamlet himself clearly communicates the power of performance to
move the audience and to stimulate powerful modes of empathy ('all his visage
wanned, | Tears in his eyes, distraction in's aspect' (2.2.555–6)), and at the close of *As
You Like It* Rosalind explicitly highlights this resource which lies *in potentia* in
performance: 'My way is to conjure you; and I'll begin with the women' (Epilogue,
10–11). For many generations of critics, an attention to what we might now term gender
criticism was, and is, inextricably linked to the dramatic representation of character.
Dusinberre's sanguine presentation of an enlightened Bard ('The feminism of Shakespeare's time is still largely unrecognised. . . . The drama from 1590 to 1625 is feminist in
sympathy.') repeatedly invited readers to blur the distinctions between the realms of
dramatic intrigue and those of our everyday selves: 'Shakespeare knew that the tough
intellect behind the raillery of the court ladies in *Love's Labour's Lost*, or of Beatrice and
Rosalind, or behind the self-awareness of Helena in *All's Well That Ends Well* had
plenty of basis in real life.'[27]

However, the plays themselves problematize repeatedly such gender expectations. At
the close of *As You Like It*, Rosalind expressly teases the audience with the hypothesis
'If I were a woman' (Epilogue, 15–16), and Shakespeare's last tragic heroine imagines
herself performed at a later time by 'some squeaking Cleopatra boy' (5.2.216). Unsurprisingly, there has emerged a growing resistance to critical approaches, which navigate
questions of gender by concentrating on transhistorical schemes of 'innately' male or
female experience and by presenting female characters notably as foci for pathos and
empathy. In an account of *The Two Gentlemen of Verona*, Lisa Jardine cautioned that
'we should be extremely wary of such a reading, which imputes peculiarly female
insight to Julia, or to Silvia via Julia's masquerade';[28] and, more recently, Dympna
Callaghan has underlined that 'there is a level at which [Shakespeare's Cressida] refers
not to women but to the masculinities she negotiates. Certain characters, especially the

[25] M. Cavendish, *CCXI Sociable letters written by the thrice noble, illustrious, and excellent princess,
the lady Marchioness of Newcastle* (1664) 246.

[26] E. R. Montagu, *An essay on the writings and genius of Shakespear, compared with the Greek and
French dramatic poets* (1769), 246.

[27] J. Dusinberre, *Shakespeare and the Nature of Women* (Basingstoke: Macmillan, 1996) 1, 5, 2.

[28] L. Jardine, 'Boy Actors, Female Roles, and Elizabethan Eroticism', in D. S. Kastan and P. Stallybrass
(eds.), *Staging the Renaissance. Reinterpretations of Elizabethan and Jacobean Drama* (New York/
London: Routledge, 1991), 57–67, at 67.

cross-dressed heroines of the profoundly homoerotic comedies, of which Rosalind in *As You Like It* is the preeminent example, may not have been representations of women at all'.[29] The slippery nature of gendered identities has already been highlighted in the *Sonnets* where readers are asked to attend to 'the master-mistress' of desire, yet in a host of other works, such as *Twelfth Night* for example, audiences encounter precisely the same difficulties as gender expectations (rather than coherently gendered selves) are vigorously interrogated: 'One face, one voice, one habit, and two persons, | A natural perspective, that is and is not' (5.1.213–14).

GENDER AND GENRE

Polonius famously juggles with all manner of generic hybrids in his introduction of the visiting players to the court at Elsinore ('tragedy, comedy, history, pastoral, pastoral-comical, tragical historical, tragical-comical-historical-pastoral' (2.2.397–400)), and the manner in which genre expectation may encourage audiences to revisit questions of gender expectation endures as a source of critical debate. It is certainly clear, for example, that the Shakespearean history play compels audiences to concentrate frequently upon male-dominated power relations that seek at the very least to margin-alize—but often to demonize or infantilize—women to the margins of that society. In *Richard III* the grieving Lady Anne is wooed disarmingly swiftly by her antagonist as the funeral cortège of Henry VI passes through the streets of London. Her energetic participation in the seductive rhythms of their stychomythic exchanges ('I would I knew thy heart', ''Tis figured in my tongue' (1.2.180–1)) may enact the collapse of her selfhood or, equally persuasively, constitute the vehicle by which she comes to appre-hend the breadth of her own ambition. Anne may be tempted by the prospect of exchanging her victim status for a coronet and a renewed identity in the remorseless cycle of courtly power games, but the predatory Richard reminds the audience that she has no hope of escaping from the ranks of the exploited: 'I'll have her, but I will not keep her long' (1.2.217).

Interestingly, contemporary psychoanalytical criticism has often been at the fore-front of this scholarly desire to concentrate upon questions of gender in terms of textual taxonomies and of collective (rather than individual) experiences of cultural control, interpellation, and agency. Madelon Gohlke Sprengnether, for example, has offered sustained analyses of the relations between gender and genre,[30] and attended to

---

[29] D. Callaghan, *Shakespeare Without Women. Representing Gender and Race on the Renaissance Stage* (London: Routledge, 2000), 13. Indeed, equally persuasively, when she turns her attention to *Twelfth Night*, Callaghan discovers a Malvolio who is 'at the centre of a plot where femininity is little less than an impossible condition, and female authority a ridiculous one' (p. 42).

[30] M. G. Sprengnether, 'Annihilating intimacy in *Coriolanus*, in Mary Beth Rose (ed.), *Women in the Middle Ages and the Renaissance: Literary and Historical Perspectives* (Syracuse, NY: Syracuse University Press, 1986), 89–112.

the 'structures of consciousness' in Shakespearean tragedy whose dramatic intrigues repeatedly present their audiences with pervasive fantasies of 'feminine betrayal'.[31] More generally, Shakespeare's characters may draw our attention to the signs and meanings associated with genre/gender distinctions, and invite us to consider the degree to which the plays themselves negotiate such discourses. In the second Induction to *The Taming of the Shrew* we are duly informed that the players are come 'to play a pleasant comedy' (Ind.2.126), whereas in *Love's Labour's Lost* Biron suspects himself implicated in 'a Christmas comedy', yet subsequently discovers the collapse of gender and genre conventions at the play's finale: 'Our wooing doth not end like an old play. | Jack hath not Jill. These ladies' courtesy | Might well have made our sport a comedy' (5.2.463, 861–3). The fragility of all such expectations and, equally importantly, our abiding need to construct defining discourses of genre are repeatedly placed under the microscope in Shakespearean drama, and nowhere is this made more entertainingly apparent than in the confusions of *A Midsummer Night's Dream*. Here, the *rusticus* Bottom remains convinced that the mechanicals will stage 'a sweet comedy', whereas the sophisticate Theseus later retorts acidly that 'if he that writ it had played Pyramus and hanged himself in Thisbe's garter, it would have been a fine tragedy' (4.2.40, 5.1.351–3).

'A LITTLE MORE THAN KIN AND LESS THAN KIND': GENDER, LANGUAGE AND PSYCHOANALYSIS

Freud assured his readers that 'the whole progress of society rests upon the opposition between successive generations'[32] and we encounter the trauma of such cultural experience across all genres in Shakespeare's writing. In this context, we may be reminded, for example, of Cordelia's notable defiance of the paterfamilias Lear ('I love your majesty | According to my bond; nor more nor less' (1.1.92–3)) and the princely bridegroom Florizel's refusal to fulfil his filial duty:

POLIXENES:	Have you a father?	
FLORIZEL:		I have. But what of him?
POLIXENES:	Knows he of this?	
FLORIZEL:		He neither does nor shall.
		(4.4.390–3)

---

[31] M. G. Sprengnether, '"I wooed thee with my sword": Shakespeare's Tragic Paradigms', in R. McDonald (ed.), *Shakespeare. An Anthology of Criticism and Theory 1945-2000* (Oxford: Blackwell, 2004), 591–605, at 594–5.

[32] See 'Family Romances', in *Sigmund Freud: On Sexuality*, A. Richards (ed.), Penguin Freud Library, vol. 7 (Harmondsworth: Penguin, 1991), 221.

For many psychoanalytic critics such moments of rupture in the social fabric of Shakespeare's dramatic worlds offer penetrating insights not necessarily into an individual consciousness, but into, what Sprengnether named, 'structures of consciousness'. The contrary motions of human desire and need lie inevitably at the heart of any successful dramatic narrative, and in both comedy and tragedy Shakespeare gravitates obsessively to the moments of fissure (provisional or otherwise) occasioned in patriarchies by power transferrals—transferrals which are signalled by acts of betrothal, marriage, inheritance, and estrangement, for example. In *Romeo and Juliet*, when Paris is proposed as a possible suitor, the young (and initially dutiful) heroine responds to her mother, 'I'll look to like, if looking liking move: | But no more deep will I endart mine eye | Than your consent gives strength to make it fly' (1.3.99–101). Shakespeare's early tragic protagonists are surreptitious for a large measure of the play in resisting the erotic choices imposed upon them by the tribal politics of Veronese society. In the later *King Lear*, the patriarch encounters open sedition to his commands from the very outset, and his response to this defiance of his authority is to reshape his daughter's psychic and cultural identity through language: she finds herself 'Unfriended, new-adopted to our hate' and alienated to the community of 'The barbarous Scythian' (1.1.203, 116) whose savagery had been made infamous for millennia by the topographies of Herodotus.

Physically and mentally, Cordelia is swiftly sited on the desolate margins of this dramatic environment. However, quite apart from violent dismembering of the royal family, at the opening of the tragedy we are also compelled to attend to the fundamental investment which Lear makes in words (rather than deeds) to communicate his authority. Believing he can continue to control the allegiances and ambitions of his court and nation with the transformative alchemy of royal utterance, the ageing monarch disposes of his lands and obligations to the greedy hands of his elder daughters. In reality, the progressive collapse in the interdependency of the cultural values of service and respect (at all ranks of society) leads not only to a violent scrambling of the social hierarchy, but also to a radical diversification of gender- and class-marked identities available in this divided realm. Whilst the dramatic attention afforded to Gloucester's family frequently forces audiences to ponder the ethics surrounding the practices of fealty and social mobility, Shakespeare's narrative also focuses squarely upon the newly instituted female access to language and power. France initially wonders whether it is Lear or Cordelia who has acted in a manner 'so monstrous' as to undo irrevocably the family of the British nation (1.1.216). Nonetheless, it swiftly becomes apparent that the next generation of female rulers is determined to enforce the contractual donation of royal authority and to test its terms and conditions rigorously: 'I pray you, father, being weak, seem so' (2.2.374).

The ongoing critical interest in the psychological intelligibility of Shakespearean narrative is often intimately linked with the 'psychic' drama embodied in language itself. At the close of *Henry V*, the protagonist's prospective bride may be infantilized in a comic interlude at the close of the play ('Your majesty shall mock at me; I cannot speak your England'), yet the audience is never encouraged to underestimate the linguistic (and mental) strain of a young woman compelled to embody an accommodation with a foreign invader: 'Is it possible dat I sould love de *ennemi* of France?' (5.2.102–3, 169–70). In *A bride-bush* (1617), William Whately warned that 'The wiues tongue towards her husband must bee neither keene, nor loose' (p. 38), and it may be that early modern conduct-books argued so energetically for separately gendered spheres of cultural activity because there was precious little evidence of it beyond their pages. Sixteenth- and seventeenth-century society appeared to cherish such 'proverbial' knowledge as *many women, many words; many geese, many turds* and *free of her lips, free of her hips,* and these acute anxieties surrounding the speaking woman clearly relate closely to the depictions of Margaret in *Richard III*, Volumnia in *Coriolanus*, and Hermione in *The Winter's Tale*, for example.

By way of conclusion to this section, it is interesting to note that the cultural theorist Dick Hebdige has highlighted how 'Subcultures [may be seen to] represent "noise" (as opposed to sound)',[33] and such enquiries continue to offer rich insights into the ways in which the politics of gender and language may be dissected in Shakespeare. Carla Mazzio, for example, has intriguingly drawn attention to the 'inarticulate as a central subject of cultural history', and to the strategic amnesia of many forms of early modern writing when considering the linguistic status of those who may find themselves marginalized by identities signalled in terms of region, rank, profession, compromised ethical and affective states, and gender.[34] Indeed, more generally, it is clear that Shakespearean writing is keenly sensitive to the linguistic tactics a culture may adopt in order to subdue and/or alienate its unruly members, as may be witnessed in the capture and alienation of Parolles in *All's Well that Ends Well*:

> *They seize and blindfold him*
> PAROLLES: O, ransom, ransom, do not hide mine eyes.
> INTERPRETER: *Boskos thromuldo boskos.*
> PAROLLES: I know you are the Moscows regiment,
>   And I shall lose my life for want of language.
>   If there be here German or Dane, Low Dutch,
>   Italian, or French, let him speak to me,
>   I'll discover that which shall undo the Florentine.
>   (4.1.67–74).

Parolles' masculinist bravado is punctured remorselessly in this comic ambush and psychoanalytic criticism has been particularly persuasive in unveiling such gender-marked and class-marked operations of power in Shakespearean narrative. In her landmark study *Suffocating Mothers: Fantasies of Maternal Origin in Shakespeare's Plays, Hamlet to The Tempest*, for example, Janet Adelman remains illuminating in her attention to the ways in which *Timon of Athens* might be viewed as Shakespeare's 'most

---

[33] See D. Hebdige (2005), 'Subculture' (pp. 355–71), in R. Guins, and O. Z. Cruz (eds.), *Popular Culture. A Reader* (London/Thousand Oaks/New Delhi: Sage), 355.

[34] C. Mazzio, *The Inarticulate Renaissance. Language Trouble in an Age of Eloquence* (Philadelphia: University of Pennsylvania Press, 2009), 1.

ruthless exposure of the fantasy of male bounty', and indeed to the progressive 'excision' of female power from the body politic in *Macbeth*.[35] More widely, the question of the relative paucity of matriarchs in Shakespeare and the various formulations of maternal agency continue to lie at the heart of scholarly debate surrounding dramas as different in focus and emphasis as *The Comedy of Errors*, *Richard III*, the late romances, and *Hamlet*. Yet it is perhaps in *Coriolanus* that this dramatic debate is most spectacularly staged, as Volumnia unceasingly determines to focus all her psychological resources on defining and controlling her son's public *persona*. In her 'mind's eye' she confesses to her daughter-in-law, 'Methinks I hear your husband's drum, | See him pluck Aufidius down by th'hair' (1.3.31–2). The mental trauma and misgiving with which parents view their offspring enter the adult world of emotional autonomy and, indeed, of sexuality is made apparent throughout Shakespeare's tragedies and late romances. Lear had hoped to remain in the 'kind nursery' of Cordelia's care, yet Volumnia appears unable or unwilling to divorce Rome's insatiable blood lust and starkly polarized gender expectations from the crippling intimacy of an indissoluble union of parent and child:

> VIRGILIA: His bloody brow? O Jupiter, no blood!
> VOLUMNIA: Away, you fool! It more becomes a man
> Than gilt his trophy. The breasts of Hecuba
> When she did suckle Hector looked not lovelier
> Than Hector's forehead when it spit forth blood
> At Grecian sword, contemning.
> (1.3.40–5)

It is the hero's inability to reconcile his patrician hubris and familial allegiances with his stunted (and socially produced) appetites for physical and verbal violence that leads ultimately to the violation of his Roman identity and his destruction: 'There's no man in the world | More bound to's mother, yet here he lets me prate | Like one i'th'stocks' (5.3.159–61). The emphases of these kinds of Shakespearean gender-based enquiries can often point not only to the ways in which the performance of subjectivity in Shakespearean narrative may enhance our understanding of the possibilities of human agency, but also to the radical instability of selfhood itself in these textual worlds.

SHAKESPEARE AND GENDER CRITICS: PRESENT AND FUTURE

The multifariousness of signs and meanings linked to the figuration and interrogation of gender prerogatives in Shakespearean writing has meant that there is no risk at all

---

[35] Janet Adelman, *Suffocating Mothers: Fantasies of Maternal Origin in Shakespeare's Plays, Hamlet to* The Tempest (New York: Routledge, 1992), 165, 145.

that gender-based criticism need have any fear of foreclosure or displacement. Critics, students, actors, and audiences of Shakespeare continue to reflect upon the variant, deviant, and endlessly mobile ways in which historically-produced constructions of femininity and masculinity may be digested within societies past and present. In addition to the perspectives outlined above, the plurality of Shakespearean formulations of gendered identity also continues to be informed and enriched by growing emphases upon the practices of translation and reading, theoretical constructions of race and empire, the challenges of eco-criticism and presentism, and, of course, by the bewildering expansion in the modes of multimedia adaptations of his texts.

And so we return to the enquiry with which this discussion began—the performative. At the opening of this discussion it was the company of early modern critics railing against the impersonation of women on the stage which made its presence felt, and thus it may be timely to close pondering some English encounters with alternative theatrical traditions. When the traveller and writer Thomas Coryate (1577?–1617) lodged in Venice, he declared, '[I] saw women acte, a thing that I neuer saw before, though I haue heard that it hath beene sometimes vsed in London, and they performed it with as good a grace, action, gesture, and whatsoeuer conuenient for a Player, as euer I saw any masculine Actor'.[36] However, if Coryate remained full of wonder at such a spectacle, it should give us pause that this was clearly not the case back in his native land some two decades later in 1629 when his compatriots encountered both sexes acting on the stage:

> [...] certaine vagrant French players, who had beene expelled from their owne contrey, and those women, did attempt, thereby giving just offence to all vertuous and well-disposed persons in this town, to act a certain lacivious and unchaste comedye, in the French tonge at the Blackfryers. Glad am I to saye they were hissed, hooted, and pippin-pelted from the stage [...][37]

---

[36] T. Coryate, *Coryats crudities hastily gobled vp in five moneths trauells in France, Sauoy, Italy* [...] (1611), 247.

[37] Thomas Brande 8 Nov 1629, Quoted in A. Gurr, *Playgoing in Shakespeare's London* (Cambridge: Cambridge University Press, 2004), 283.

CHAPTER 13

....

LANGUAGE

....

LYNNE MAGNUSSON

HISTORY AND LANGUAGE-GAMES
....

ANY attempt to explain Shakespeare's language or explore his linguistic innovation needs to come to terms with a major historical problem. 'Look how you drumble!' remarks Mistress Ford in *The Merry Wives of Windsor* to her poor servants, John and Robert, when they are tasked to carry off to the laundress in Datchet Mead the heavy buck-basket that conceals Falstaff amidst the dirty laundry.[1] But 'What is "drumble"?', one wonders. No problem, says the Arden gloss. 'Drumble' is 'lag, move slowly (*OED* *v*.[1] 1)'.[2] This type of citation—and far more elaborate variations on it, yoking, for example, *OED* 32*a* with *OED* 14*b* to pin down exact discriminations of meaning for the wordplay—has become the gold standard for annotating the challenging vocabulary in recent Shakespeare editions. Something apparently quite similar happens in the Latin lesson that is brought out onto the open street in Act 4, Scene 1, when William's schoolmaster, the Welsh parson Sir Hugh Evans, enquires:

	What is '*lapis*', William?
WILLIAM:	A stone.
EVANS:	And what is 'a stone', William?
WILLIAM:	A pebble.
EVANS:	No, it is '*lapis*'. I pray you remember in your prain.
WILLIAM:	'*Lapis*'.
EVANS:	That is a good William.

(4.1.28–34)

[1] 3.3.141. Unless otherwise noted, quotations are from Stanley Wells, Gary Taylor, John Jowett, and William Montgomery (eds.), William Shakespeare, *The Complete Works*, 2nd edn. (Oxford: Clarendon Press, 2005). I am grateful to Alan Bewell, Carol Percy, David Schalkwyk, and Paul Stevens for their helpful conversation and comments and to the Killam Foundation and the SSHRC of Canada for research-grant support.

[2] Giorgio Melchiori (ed.), *The Merry Wives of Windsor*, The Arden Shakespeare, 3rd series (Surrey: Thomas Nelson, 2000), 220.

What is on show here is a historically specific language-game intended to help cultivate the boy's linguistic resources but which, the scene suggests, may not be functioning wholly adequately for William. This particular performance in language, the master's routinized exercise in the 'posing of parts', is set in motion in response to a reservation William's father has raised about his education. The immediate trigger is his mother's request to Sir Hugh: 'my husband says my son profits nothing in the world at his book. I pray you ask him some questions in his accidence' (4.1.13–15). That is, William is being drilled in, and expected to recall answers word-for-word from, William Lily and John Colet's *A Shorte Introdvction of Grammar*, the foundational Elizabethan grammar-school text setting out (in English) the Latin parts of speech. That we are meant to see the limitations of this exercise is strongly suggested by its circularity and how it demands that the child turn off his linguistic curiosity and the sensible act of comprehension that explains 'a stone' by its approximate equivalence to 'a pebble'. What we can easily recognize as our own historically-situated language-game does resemble Sir Hugh's procedure insofar as it calls upon the authority of a book, but, for us, there is no requirement to 'remember in your prain'. If our Arden gloss is not close at hand when we reread or rehear the scene of Falstaff's ignoble exit from Ford's house, we can readily access '*OED* drumble *v*.[1] 1' at need and online, on our iPhone or BlackBerry Web browser. Not only the word 'online' but also the attendant language-game of consulting *OED Online* for a precise meaning of this word, first recorded in this sense in *Merry Wives* and discriminated from 'drumble *v*.[1] 2' as used by Fulke in 1579 and Nashe in 1596 to mean 'drone, [or] mumble', would be as alien to Shakespeare and his characters as 'drumble' and the posing of Latin parts are to us. And, as for William, there may be something in the *OED* language-game that is short-changing our own action of comprehension and engagement with Shakespeare's language.

The difficulties people encounter these days in reading or hearing a Shakespeare play make us increasingly aware—at least in certain ways—of historical differences and language change. At the same time, we have seen major advances in recent years in tools, competencies, and technology to assist us in reaching back into the past and recovering Shakespeare's language. After depending on Abbott's *Grammar* for over 100 years, we now have two new comprehensive Shakespearean grammars and the authoritative *Cambridge History of the English Language*.[3] These can make it much easier for us to be aware of key differences between the grammar of Shakespeare's early modern English and our own present-day English, whether the well-known choice of 'thou' and 'you' for the second-person singular pronoun, the alternative inflexions '-st' for the second-person singular verb ('thou liest') and '-th' for the third-person singular verb ('it sufficeth'), or the persisting use of possessive 'his' where we would use 'its' for inanimate or non-human reference ('his edge' to refer to a knife's

---

[3] E. A. Abbott, *A Shakespearian Grammar*, 3rd edn. (London: Macmillan, 1870); N. F. Blake, *A Grammar of Shakespeare's Language* (Basingstoke and New York: Palgrave Macmillan, 2002); Jonathan Hope, *Shakespeare's Grammar* (London: Arden Shakespeare, 2003); Roger Lass (ed.), *The Cambridge History of the English Language*, vol. 3: *1476–1776* (Cambridge: Cambridge University Press, 1999).

edge).[4] To help us with vocabulary, not only has the *OED* gone online, but it is easily searchable in ways that allow anyone to generate, with astonishing speed, a listing of the English words first recorded in any particular Shakespeare play or major poem. The list for *The Merry Wives of Windsor* is especially interesting for its colloquial flavour, including 'dickens', 'farm-house', 'buck-washing', 'bold-beating', 'frampold', 'dry-nurse', 'bodikin', 'eye-wink', 'go-between', 'hodge-pudding', 'ouphe', 'sprag', 'bully-rook', 'Jack-a-Lent', 'whoa', 'nayword', and the contracted interjection "'Slid', in addition to the more predictable new words formed with familiar prefixes and suffixes like 'dishorn', 'uncape', 'unconfinable', 'unpitifully', 'unduteous', 'unfool', 'fixture', 'scholarly', 'shelvy', and 'wittolly', and then a small sprinkling of words adapted from Latin like 'labras', 'eryngo', and the play's ultimate show-word 'anthropophaginian'. The play is less reliant on Latin derivatives of the kind that heighten the language of *Macbeth* ('assassination', 'incarnadine', 'multitudinous'), add resonance to the classical setting of *Troilus and Cressida* ('assubjugate', 'corresponsive', 'indistinguishable', 'multipotent'), or obtrude the learned pretensions of characters in *Love's Labour's Lost* ('apostrophe', 'infamonize', 'peregrinate', 'preambulate').[5]

David Crystal has recently produced a number of popular studies aimed at making people more aware of Shakespeare's influence in introducing and disseminating new English words and even at reconstructing historical pronunciation. It is becoming easier and easier to have handy information (even cocktail party sound-bites) available about Shakespeare's words, information about his vocabulary that Shakespeare himself, living without English dictionaries let alone searchable databases, could never have acquired. 'Of the 2,200 words in the *OED* whose first recorded use is in Shakespeare,' Crystal tells us, 'about 1,700 are plausible Shakespearean inventions—words like *anthropophaginian, assassination, disproperty, incardinate, insultment, irregulous, outswear,* and *uncurse*—and about half of them stayed in the language'. By his calculation, he claims the remarkable 'fact that 1,700 is approaching 10 per cent of his known vocabulary', estimated at 'about 20,000' words.[6] Furthermore, with the more widespread availability of facsimile editions of early printed texts, often read online, more people are encountering directly linguistic differences in the form of the highly variable spelling or variant orthographic conventions of the Elizabethan age, and Crystal has

---

[4] For a helpful brief guide, see Sylvia Adamson, 'Understanding Shakespeare's Grammar: Studies in Small Words', in S. Adamson, L. Hunter, L. Magnusson, A. Thompson, and K. Wales (eds.), *Reading Shakespeare's Dramatic Language: A Guide* (London: Arden Shakespeare, 2001), 210–36.

[5] Among the most helpful compilations of Shakespeare's neologisms or first-recorded word uses is Appendix III in Jürgen Schäfer, *Shakespeares Stil* (Frankfurt am Main: Athenäum Verlag, 1973), 204–20; Bryan A. Garner, 'Shakespeare's Latinate Neologisms', and 'Latin-Saxon Hybrids in Shakespeare and the Bible', rpt. in Vivian Salmon and Edwina Burness (eds.), *A Reader in the Language of Shakespearean Drama* (Amsterdam and Philadelphia: John Benjamins, 1987), 207–28 and 229–34; on word-formation, see Vivian Salmon, 'Some Functions of Shakespearian Word-Formation', in Salmon and Burness (eds.), *Reader*, 193–206; and Terttu Nevalainen, 'Shakespeare's New Words', in Adamson et al. (eds.), *Reading Shakespeare's Dramatic Language*, 237–55.

[6] David Crystal, *'Think on my Words': Exploring Shakespeare's Language* (Cambridge: Cambridge University Press, 2008), 9, 4.

taken the helpful step of familiarizing the general reader with 'Shakespearean graph-ology'.[7] Although, as academic disciplines, literary studies and linguistics have not been close partners of late, new branches of historical language study have emerged, including historical sociolinguistics and historical pragmatics. Along with their meth-odological advances, both fields have built up historical corpora of early modern English texts in various genres that potentially make available a very rich comparison base for Shakespeare's language.[8]

Paradoxically, the new tools, competencies, and technologies aimed at decreasing distance from Shakespeare's language also function to increase distance by anesthetiz-ing us to, or making us short-sighted about, important kinds of difference. Many of the newer tools are constructed out of, or enabled by, the sedimented layers of language change intervening between Shakespeare's language and our own, changes that make our various linguistic cultures and language-games radically different from those of Shakespeare and his age. In general terms, what stands between us are the advancing stages of standardization (under way in Shakespeare's time), the codification of English in dictionaries and grammars, the prescriptivism associated with the eighteenth-century's construction of consistency as correctness, and media changes over time. Hence the validity of Jonathan Hope's recent observation that 'We are used to historicizing Shakespeare in every respect except his language'.[9] This is partly the case because the New Historicism developed as an alternative to the prevalent modes of language study and tended to construct language and history as opposites. But it is also due to the complicated situation that arises when the flux of language is both the medium and object of our study. My point is that in our encounters with Shakespeare's texts, in our attempts to explain his language, we need to be aware of the cultural scene of language as a critical part of the historical context. As hermeneutic theory has suggested, this cannot be accomplished without an effort being made to recognize and accommodate the separate horizons shaping our own linguistic understanding and that adumbrated in the text. In what follows, I want to suggest that Shakespeare's English comedy, The Merry Wives of Windsor, is a good place to begin such a process, especially if we work toward a comparison and accommodation of what I will call 'miscompre-hension sequences' within the play and between us and the play. My analysis consists of four parts: first, an overview of how the Windsor community in The Merry Wives of Windsor negotiates language change; second, the example of Mistress Quickly's

---

[7] Crystal, 'Think on my Words', 42–63.

[8] For introductions to these fields, see Terttu Nevalainen and Helena Raumolin-Brunberg, Historical Sociolinguistics: Language Change in Tudor and Stuart England (London: Longman, 2003), and Susan M. Fitzmaurice and Irma Taavitsainen (eds.), Methods in Historical Pragmatics: Approaches to Negotiated Meaning in Historical Contexts (Berlin: Mouton de Gruyter, 2007).

[9] Jonathan Hope, 'Shakespeare and Language: An Introduction', in Catherine M. S. Alexander (ed.), Shakespeare and Language (Cambridge: Cambridge University Press, 2004), 1. This essay emphasizes key differences between the language of Shakespeare's time and ours and has been influential on my thinking for this chapter.

resourceful meaning-making in the extended miscomprehension sequence of the Latin lesson; third, an account of how the interaction of orality and literacy in Shakespeare's day shapes language use and word coinage, with Quickly as our 'go-between'; and, fourth, Shakespeare's interest in language change associated with miscomprehension sequences across media, or 'speaking in print'. In this way, I hope to bring us to a better understanding of what we might mean by 'Shakespeare's language'.

LIVING WITH CHANGE: MISCOMPREHENSION SEQUENCES IN *THE MERRY WIVES OF WINDSOR*

There is no better place to look for a characterization of the lived experience of the English tongue on native soil in Shakespeare's time than to *The Merry Wives of Windsor*. It is the only comedy written by Shakespeare to be set in an English town, and at the heart of its comedy are some of the most salient conditions of the evolving language. In its portrayal of the heterogeneity of the linguistic community, the comedy foregrounds the huge amount of variation that was encompassed within the emerging unity of the English tongue. At the same time, it dramatizes a kind of consciousness or semi-consciousness about change in the language. In particular, it takes as its subject the very situation that has so often been advanced as a principal condition of possibility both for the flourishing of English Renaissance literature and for Shakespeare's art— that is, the huge influx of new words into the language as the use of English spread to encompass more fields of experience. More new words were introduced into the English language during the Renaissance, from about 1500 to 1660, than in any other period of its history. Shakespeare's writing career coincided with the peak of this influx. Using the evidence of the *Chronological English Dictionary*, Bryan A. Garner claims that 'from roughly 1588 to 1612, 7,968 neologisms were brought into English' and 'thirty percent of all of the Renaissance neologisms appeared'.[10] In exploring Shakespeare's engagement with the situation of rapid change in the English lexicon, it is important to think not only about his own word coinages but also about how he adopted and recirculated other recent or unusual words. *The Merry Wives of Windsor* quite explicitly explores how the variously positioned English speakers and users in the play respond to linguistic flux, to this remarkable pace of change. The comedy of language in *Love's Labour's Lost*, which has received more attention, also treats the growth of the English lexicon, but in a more rarified way. Focusing attention on Armado's inkhorn terms and Holofernes's Latinisms, it attends to the more directly engineered areas of the lexicon, to vocabulary of the kind that learned writers were self-consciously introducing and publishing in their writings, what sociolinguists term 'change from above'. *The Merry Wives* responds much more directly to experience on the ground, as

---

[10] Garner, 'Shakespeare's Latinate Neologisms', 209.

felt in a living speech community, and it takes seriously 'change from below'.[11] Complicated and often hilarious interactions are continually being triggered as one character's coinages, novel or unfamiliar words, and creative, fuzzy, mistaken, or unexpected uses of existing words prompt the disoriented reaction of another character, followed usually by some effort at coordination, and the realignment of a communication that has been going off-track. These double-takes over words—the mistakings, verbal 'translations', repair or realignment sequences or alternatively (where verbal cozening is highlighted) sequences of misrepair—are at the very centre of this play, making it what Giorgio Melchiori so aptly termed 'the Comedy of English'.[12] Here are a few basic examples of the miscomprehension sequences:

> BARDOLPH: And being fap, sir, was, as they say, cashiered. And so
>   conclusions passed the careers.
> SLENDER: Ay, you spake in Latin then, too. But 'tis no matter.
>
> (1.1.162–4)

> HOST: . . . A word, Monsieur Mockwater.
> CAIUS: Mockvater? Vat is dat?
> HOST: Mockwater, in our English tongue, is valour, bully.
> CAIUS: By Gar, then I have as much mockvater as de Englishman. Scurvy jack-dog
>   priest!
>
> (2.3.52–7)

> MISTRESS PAGE: . . . unless he know some strain in me that I know not myself, he
>   [Falstaff] would never have boarded me in this fury.
> MISTRESS FORD: 'Boarding' call you it? I'll be sure to keep him above deck.
>
> (2.1.84–7)

> ANNE: What is your will?
> SLENDER: My will? 'Od's heartlings, that's a pretty jest indeed! I ne'er made my will
>   yet, I thank God; I am not such a sickly creature, I give God praise.
> ANNE: I mean, Master Slender, what would you with me?
>
> (3.4.54–8)

Shakespeare brings to life the community and the vernacular of a small rural English town within striking distance of the capital, quite surprisingly, by representing a collision of micro-languages. We have, as title characters, two well-spoken citizen wives who are literate and skilful readers of letters (Mrs Page and Mrs Ford); their articulate husbands; a voluble and socially aspiring housekeeper whose experience of language, I will argue, is oriented by orality (Mrs Quickly); a parson speaking a Welsh–English dialect who doubles as the town school's Latin master (Hugh Evans); a schoolboy being inculcated in Latin language-learning (William Page); an inveterate neologizer and respected community member who is Host of the Garter Inn; a French immigrant doctor who is a new user of English (Dr Caius); a dim-witted country gentleman confounded by the polysemy of simple English words (Slender). Filling out the diversity and social range, we have an

---

[11] Nevalainen and Raumolin-Brunberg, *Historical Sociolinguistics*, 28.

[12] Melchiori, 'Introduction', *The Merry Wives of Windsor*, 5. As Melchiori remarks, this 'attention to the linguistic factor' is a quality of the Folio text of 1623 (9), and many of the passages I discuss in this chapter do not appear at all in the shorter Quarto of 1602.

impoverished aristocrat and suitor to a citizen daughter whose language injects a courtly note (Fenton); Justice Shallow, oddly imported (together with his deer park) from Gloucester; and a variety of male household servants, including 'Ay, forsooth'-saying Simple. Contributing still further both to the shifting composition of the community and its linguistic variety are visitors and transients, including the famous decadent knight who exploits his 'scholarly' linguistic mastery (1.3.2) in a master-scheme to cozen the towns-people (a Sir John Falstaff much altered from the history plays); Falstaff's dismissed attendants representing an underworld sub-culture allying aggression with novel in-group linguistic usages (Pistol, Bardolph, and Nym); and even a gang of German horse-thieves. In part, the continual collision of languages is the trigger in this play for hilarious comedy, as where Slender mistakes Bardolph's flashy words like 'fap' and 'cashiered' for Latin, or where Evans's accent, characteristically reversing voiced and unvoiced consonants, turns the dignified 'vocative' case of the Latin lesson into the obscene 'focative' (4.1.45). But, read as a study of English, the exuberant linguistic display has a lot more to tell us.

Synchronic variation and diachronic change are characteristics of all natural lan-guages, so that to characterize the experience of English that *The Merry Wives* is representing requires not only that we attend to the fact of heterogeneity but that we ask how heterogeneity is being patterned, what differences are being strongly marked. Changes that have occurred in English since Shakespeare's time affect the kinds of variation that are most noticeable to us, so we need to be conscious of our own situated viewpoint. I have suggested that the quality of our own encounter with Shakespeare's language and/or his community members' multiple languages is deeply affected by changes related to processes of standardization reducing types of variation and render-ing English more homogeneous, by codification rendering English an explicitly 'ruled' language, abundantly supplied with dictionaries and grammars, and by prescriptivism, associating consistency with correctness. For example, while by 1600 written English was in some ways well advanced in the process of standardization reducing variation, with London Chancery scribes having homogenized copying practices beginning around 1430 and with William Caxton adopting London speech as the printing norm later in the same century, spelling remained highly variable.[13] Jonathan Hope has suggested that the variant spellings of words and names occurring in abundance on the same page or even in the same line of text, so noticeable to modern-day readers, would likely have gone largely unnoticed by early modern readers.[14]

In terms of spoken language, one might expect a strong marking of regional accents and dialects when heterogeneity is represented on stage, given, for example, the printer William Caxton's observation a century earlier of how radically 'comyn englysshe that is spoken in one shyre varyeth from another',[15] making England what the

---

[13] David Crystal, *The Cambridge Encyclopedia of the English Language* (Cambridge: Cambridge University Press, 1995), 54.

[14] Hope, 'Shakespeare and Language', 4–6.

[15] Quoted from Manfred Görlach, *Introduction to Early Modern English* (Cambridge: Cambridge University Press, 1991), 217.

seventeenth-century lexicographer Thomas Blount called a 'self-stranger Nation'.[16] Hope, however, has remarked on how little attention regional dialect receives in Shakespeare's plays.[17] Even in *The Merry Wives of Windsor*, where phonetic variation is strongly salient in representing Dr Caius as a speaker of French-inflected and Hugh Evans as a speaker of Welsh-inflected English, it is actually functioning less to register the heterogeneity of accents and pronunciations within the English tongue than to mark off the boundaries of an emergent hypothesized and recognizable homogeneity—an inclusive national language.[18] This is the Shakespeare play that explicitly postulates such an entity as 'the King's English'. It is significant that it is Mistress Quickly who uses this phrase in relation to her master, the Frenchman, Doctor Caius: 'here will be an old abusing of God's patience and the King's English' (1.4.4–5). Mistress Quickly certainly does not use the phrase to signify what H. W. and F. G. Fowler meant at the outset of the twentieth century when they produced guides to *The King's English* to set off one 'superior' or 'correct' variety from other less prestigious versions of English spoken within the same political realm. Intervening between the play's linguistic attitudes and Fowler's are eighteenth-century formulations about 'correctness' like Lord Chesterfield's:

> The language of the lower classes is, of course, to be avoided because it is full of barbarisms, solecisms, mispronunciations, and vulgar words and phrases, all of which are the marks of 'a low turn of mind, low education, and low company.' . . . 'ordinary people in general speak in defiance of all grammar, use words that are not English, and murder those that are.'[19]

In *The Merry Wives*, the King's English incorporates the language of Chesterfield's 'ordinary people'. That is not to say there is no reference to a standard of correctness in the play, but the corrector is Hugh Evans, influenced by his Latin training, and, when he corrects English usage, he always gets it wrong. Mistress Quickly means 'the King's English' to be inclusive of a Windsor housekeeper's, cook's, or launderer's usage (that is, her own) as well as of all the other highly variegated non-foreign speakers' usages in the community. In this play, the 'King's English' registers a recognition among the Windsor community not of a correct or prestige language but of a shared language, a language the members of the community hold in common even as they muddle through their continual misunderstandings.

The differences that are strongly marked and explored in the Windsor community are social and educational. As I will argue in the next sections of this chapter, the variegated linguistic profiles of the community members are affected by the competition between English and Latin promoted by grammar-school education, the

---

[16] Thomas Blount, *Glossographia* (1656), Dedicatory poem, quoted from Paula Blank, *Broken English: Dialects and the Politics of Language in Renaissance Writings* (London: Routledge, 1996), 17.

[17] Hope, 'Shakespeare and Language', 6.

[18] On language and nation, see Richard Helgerson, 'Language Lessons: Linguistic Colonialism, Linguistic Postcolonialism, and the Early Modern English Nation', *The Yale Journal of Criticism* 11 (1998), 289–99.

[19] J. H. Neumann (quoting Chesterfield's letters), 'Chesterfield and the Standard of Usage in English', *Modern Language Quarterly* 7 (1946), 466.

competition between orality and literacy, and the varying levels of exposure to the developing culture of print. Elsewhere I have written about how the hierarchical social relations as exhibited in dialogic interaction in Shakespeare's plays and Elizabethan culture are constructed by means of anticipatory and coordinated politeness strategies that divide and differentiate speakers' styles.[20] Here the linguistic construction of relations in the social community turns more on moments of transculturation, verbal encounters whereby speakers negotiate communication in a kind of contact zone involving disorienting miscomprehensions and subsequent adjustments to the alien words of the others. In a community where everyone is talking different localized languages, the verbal negotiations among them entail shifts and realignments that potentially have consequences not only for comprehension and the constitution of a shared English tongue but also for the repair of the relationships and the construction of intersubjective identity.

Indeed, the play brings into focus the relationship between language and community in a number of innovative ways. Although Shakespeare is himself the literary writer more universally recognized than any other for his individual agency in shaping language, this play places a strong focus on the collective linguistic agency of the community. First, from the opening utterance of the play ('Sir Hugh, persuade me not'), there is an emphasis on language as communal action in the form of rhetorical persuasion. While Cicero claimed that the eloquence of the great orator was what brought people together and sustained civil communities, this play insistently explores how the goodwill negotiations among people in everyday conversation—even in acts of mediation that fail to bridge differences fully—are the social rhetoric that sustains civil community.[21] It is a play in which threatened violence always gives way to words, as where the Host insists that the duelling Evans and Caius be disarmed: 'Let them keep their limbs whole, and hack our English' (3.1.71–2). Second, and more radical, there is a focus on the agency of the community in language innovation and change. Rather than the English tongue being imagined as a given, as a fully realized system (or *langue*) out of which each user (except the most brilliantly innovative) finds the tools for his or her *parole* or individual utterance, tools which he or she uses more or less competently, the play seems to present the language as always in a process of negotiation in speech interactions of essentially productive misunderstanding.[22] Thus, these interactions function both as moments of language acquisition and adjustment for individuals and as contributions to the flux or the creative changes in the language. In these microcosms of linguistic change and innovation, the play assesses the collaborative participation of the entire community, including its least educated members, in the making and transforming of English.

[20] Lynne Magnusson, *Shakespeare and Social Dialogue: Dramatic Language and Elizabethan Letters* (Cambridge: Cambridge University Press, 1999).

[21] Cicero, *De Inventione*, H. M. Hubbell (trans.) (Cambridge, MA: Harvard University Press, 1949), 5–9.

[22] For a recent study that posits language as an evolving and flexible system of this kind, see Robin Cooper and Ruth Kempson (eds.), *Language in Flux: Dialogue Coordination, Language Variation, Change and Evolution* (London: King's College, College Publications, 2008).

THE LATIN LESSON AND MISTRESS QUICKLY'S
MEANING-MAKING: HEARING WITH EARS

Much attention has been paid to Mistress Quickly's role in the Latin lesson—the play's most extended miscomprehension sequence—as an ideologically gendered representative of the 'mother tongue', set in demeaning opposition to the authority of Latin, as it is reinforced by a humanist 'pedagogical economy of men and boys'. Bringing the Latin lesson out onto the Windsor street, Shakespeare clearly stages a central shaping force on the language of his day, the competition between classical Latin in the classroom and English in most walks of life. Patricia Parker characterizes Quickly's linguistic profile in terms of her 'extravagantly errant female speech', emphasizing her ungovernable tongue and its association both with her lack of education and with the vernacular's errant inclination to descend into obscenities. Furthermore, she is consistently read as a 'seemingly irrepressible producer of malapropisms'.[23] Here I want to shift the emphasis, first, to her mechanisms for interpreting other people's words and, later, to a rethinking of the category of 'malapropisms' so often associated with Quickly's coinages. I would argue that what Shakespeare dramatizes above all in his representation of Mistress Quickly's resourceful acts of comprehension is her positioning as a language user oriented to orality within an overall linguistic community profiled (like Shakespeare's own cultural world[24]) as in transition between orality and literacy. In his study of *Orality and Literacy*, Walter J. Ong has asked, 'without dictionaries, written grammar rules, punctuation, and all the rest of the apparatus that makes words into something you can "look" up, how can literates live?'[25] This is not an idle question: we need an answer in order to begin to understand the horizon of expectations and competencies in relation to early modern English that Shakespeare and his characters could have inhabited. Some of them were oral in orientation and some literate, but even the most educated could not have consulted an English grammar book before the appearance of William Bullokar's *Bref Grammar for English* in 1586 or an English dictionary before Robert Cawdrey's *A Table Alphabeticall* in 1604. Mistress Quickly is such an interesting character because she shows us precisely how one could operate in such a culture as a fairly advanced language user whose primary experience is oral.

The 'hearing-dominance'[26] in her world of thought and expression shows itself in her first intervention into the Latin lesson's 'posing of parts', an intervention framed as a variation upon the play's characteristic miscomprehension sequence:

---

[23] Patricia A. Parker, *Literary Fat Ladies: Rhetoric, Gender, Property* (London: Methuen, 1987), 27.
[24] Hope, 'Shakespeare and Language', 3.
[25] Walter J. Ong, *Orality and Literacy: The Technologizing of the Word* (London: Methuen, 1982), 14.
[26] Ong, *Orality and Literacy*, 121.

EVANS: William, how many numbers is in nouns?

WILLIAM: Two.

MISTRESS QUICKLY: Truly, I thought there had been one number more, because they say "Od's nouns'.

EVANS: Peace your tattlings!

(4.1.19–23)

Here, as elsewhere, Mistress Quickly's meaning-making process has recourse to oral sayings as repositories of knowledge. She is probably completely right in her memory that people say 'od's-Nownes' (as spelled in the Folio). As our own linguistic culture's knowledge repository, the online *OED*, tells us, the oath or asseveration, 'By God's wounds' was subjected to innumerable variations, contractions, and truncations in early modern English. Often contracted as 'swounds' or 'zounds', it could have been heard onstage in Marlowe's *Faustus* as 'swowns, boy', or, earlier in the century, in Udall's *Royster Doister*, as 'Kocks nownes what meanest thou man.' *The Merry Wives* itself demonstrates the extreme variability of simple oaths and exclamations, especially those invoking and often euphemizing God as a proper name for the Christian deity. Indeed, Mistress Quickly had been within hearing when Slender, wooing Anne Page, used the same truncated name to swear on "Od's heartlings' (3.4.55). Quickly seems not, however, to have heard or remembered 'od's-Nownes' so much as an oath as the kind of compound word that telescopes and, so, packages to store in memory, an assertion or proposition.[27] She unpacks it as if it were a memory-device for the knowledge-bite, 'nouns are odd in number'. An outsider to Evans's Latin language-game, which requires of Will citations from Lily's 'Accidence', the printed rules about Latin inflexions, her grasp of meaning is nonetheless no more flawed than Master Evans's. If she lacks knowledge of the categories for Latin noun inflexions, the Welsh parson's habitual attachment of plural 's' endings to English abstract nouns and his repeated use of the singular verb 'is' with plural subjects suggests that he has no capacity to transfer his bookish Latin knowledge of 'number' to the context of his own English usage.

More characteristic of what this scene highlights in Quickly's procedure for con-structing words and construing meaning than a 'malapropping tongue'[28] is her dependence on the ear. Consider how she frames her understanding on what she hears about the accusative forms of Latin articles:

EVANS: That is a good William. What is he, William, that does lend articles?

WILLIAM: Articles are borrowed of the pronoun, and be thus declined. *Singulariter nominativo*: 'hic, haec, hoc'.

EVANS: *Nominativo*: 'hig, hag, hog'. Pray you mark: *genitivo*: 'huius'. Well, what is your accusative case?

WILLIAM: *Accusativo*: 'hinc' —

[27] Terttu Nevalainen, 'Early Modern English Lexis and Semantics', in Lass (ed.), *The Cambridge History of the English Language*, 3: 408.

[28] Patricia Parker, '*The Merry Wives of Windsor* and Shakespearean Translation', *Modern Language Quarterly* 52 (1991), 226, 233, 237.

> EVANS: I pray you have your remembrance, child. *Accusativo*: '*hing, hang, hog*'.
> MISTRESS QUICKLY: 'Hang-hog' is Latin for bacon, I warrant you.
> EVANS: Leave your prabbles, 'oman!
>
> (4.1.34–45)

Quickly's exact replication of Evans' 'hang-hog' suggests that she hears with greater accuracy or aural distinction-making even than the boy William. When Will offers up '*Accusativo*: "*hinc*"' (and not '*hing*'), he demonstrates that he has heard his master's repeated recitation of declensions in the schoolroom, at least in part, with his eyes, visualizing the graphic form as it appears in his grammar-book of the word that Evans's accent re-forms. (I say in part, because the joke also involves Will's replication of a grammar error presumably deriving from Evans's classroom recitations, substituting the erroneous '*hinc/g*' for the masculine accusative form '*hunc*'.) Will is thus represented as developing a literate mechanism for 'hearing with eyes', a mechanism that visualizes words in a way that Shakespeare exposes in Sonnet 23 as a strange phenomenon. The sonnet contrasts the experience of hearing an actor's oral performance on stage with reading a poet's written expression in a 'book': 'O learn to read what silent love hath writ; | To hear with eyes belongs to love's fine wit.' (13–14). In Will's unsteady performance, Shakespeare brings out not just the strangeness of handwritten script, but the strange way that learned Latin presented in a printed book can begin to refashion and textualize the experience of language.[29]

That writing and reading affect a person's language and thought is not a new idea, but the way in which *The Merry Wives of Windsor* explores the intersubjective experience of a diversified English speech community in transition between orality and literacy is worth more careful attention. In accounting for how Mistress Quickly not merely constructs the compound word she hears as 'hang-hog' but construes its meaning, we need to look again to the kind of knowledge she brings with her to unpack the compound word, a word she half-hears and half-produces in this interaction. Oral cultures enshrine wisdom in formulaic sayings and proverbs, and, as some expert annotators of this scene have noted, the sense of the line depends on the saying, 'Hog is not Bacon till it be well hanged'.[30] Despite Quickly's creativity with word coinage here, and the fact that the compound, joining a verb and a noun, follows a plausible pattern for early modern English word formation analogous to 'chokeapple' or 'rattlesnake',[31] 'hang-hog' does not appear among Shakespeare's coinages or nonce words recorded in the *OED* or in Jürgen Schäfer's listing of compounds first recorded in the play, including the not dissimilar 'bold-beating', 'bully-rook', 'go-between', and 'hodge-pudding' (perhaps on Quickly's own authority since she identifies it as 'Latin' or, more ambiguously in the Folio, 'latten'). But far from illustrating Quickly's 'outrageous' or 'obscene' Englishings,[32] it illustrates a number of elements of an oral orientation to language that Ong and others have excavated. As Ong explains, 'oral

---

[29] Ong, *Orality and Literacy*, 130.
[30] Ong, *Orality and Literacy*, 35; Melchiori, *The Merry Wives of Windsor*, 241.
[31] Nevalainen, 'Early Modern Lexis and Semantics', 412–13.
[32] Parker, 'Shakespearean Translation', 226–7.

cultures must conceptualize and verbalize all their knowledge with more or less close reference to the human lifeworld, assimilating the alien, objective world to the more immediate, familiar interaction of human beings'.[33] Some annotators of *Merry Wives* have noted that the hoggish proverb circulated not merely as a saying but also as a clever story associated with Queen Elizabeth's first Lord Keeper of the Great Seal, Sir Nicholas Bacon, thus linking it to the Elizabethan human lifeworld of Shakespeare's original audiences. As the story goes, when a thief called Hog was brought before Bacon, he tried to escape sentencing by claiming kinship with the judge: the magistrate's clever comeback was framed, like Quickly's verbal compound, out of the proverb, 'Hog is not Bacon till it be well hanged'. Even the dismissive Evans seems to recognize the basis in 'parable' ('prables' in the Folio) of Quickly's coinage.

In other words, Quickly's portrayal in this scene can help us to understand how strange and different from our own linguistic horizon and experience of verbal interaction it might be to take in words primarily through one's sense of hearing. Just as Sonnet 23 makes literacy strange by minting the phrase to 'hear with eyes', this play makes orality strange when it obtrudes Pistol's seemingly redundant phrase, 'He hears with ears', an expression Evans greets with exasperation: 'The tevil and his tam! What phrase is this? "He hears with ears"! Why, it is affectations!' (1.1.136–8). But Parson Evans's response is itself obtuse, oblivious as the town's 'celestial' (3.1.98) should not be to the scriptural intertexts placing value on oral tradition (the Litany's 'O God, we have heard with oure eares, and our fathers have declarid unto us the noble workes that thou dyddest in their dayes, and in the olde tyme,' drawn from Psalm 44).

Mistress Quickly as 'Go-Between': Orality and Literacy in Transition

To understand Quickly's linguistic positioning, however, it is not enough to identify or isolate her as an oral subject. As we shall see, Shakespeare represents her own speech almost as a record of transculturation, as a meeting place of words from the different cultural worlds of oral and literate experience. She is also represented as a 'go-between' in the Windsor community, carrying messages between Falstaff and the wives, between Anne Page and her suitors. While in Falstaff's eyes, this situates her as a convenient pander, the dramatic focus is by no means on arranging sexual liaisons. Representing Quickly as the play's messenger continues the emphasis on a linguistic culture in transit between orality and literacy. In a play full of letters, with a strong accent on their circulation and reception, she plays an interesting role. For the citizen wives—like the female recipients of letters represented in seventeenth-century Dutch paintings—the receipt and response to letters is a defining event in this play, situating Mistress Page

---

[33] Ong, *Orality and Literacy*, 42.

and Mistress Ford not merely by class but also, significantly, as the kind of women whose lifeworld encompasses reading and writing. David Cressy estimates that, at the outset of Queen Elizabeth's reign, only about 20 per cent of Englishmen and 5 per cent of Englishwomen could both read and write, growing to about 30 per cent of men and 10 per cent of women by 1640, although with evidence of significantly higher rates in London.[34] Because most of our commerce with the Elizabethan world is mediated by written words, it is easy to take them for granted as the functional medium of the period. But this is very misleading. Shakespeare actually represents the wives' literacy as an exciting novelty, partly through the juxtaposition made to Quickly's word-world. In the embroidered account of Mistress Ford's enviable life that Quickly invents for Falstaff, not merely have there 'been knights, and lords, and gentlemen, with their coaches' pursuing her, but she has received 'letter after letter' (2.2.63–5). 'Here: read, read' (2.1.51) is indeed what the excited Mistress Ford had urged Mistress Page to do in the preceding scene, and the play makes one of its most interesting dramatic episodes out of the wives' experience of reading their near-identical seduction letters from Falstaff. The episode provides a variation on the play's characteristic miscomprehension sequence, although it turns not so much on disorientation by a singular word as on the disorienting effect of the letter's discourse as a whole. The emphasis here is on a kind of intersubjective adjustment triggered by the alien language of Falstaff's written message. His words make Mistress Page re-examine her own 'conversation' (encompassing her self-presentation both in language and behaviour): 'What an unweighed behaviour hath this Flemish drunkard picked, i'th' devil's name, out of my conversation, that he dares in this manner assay me? . . . What should I say to him? I was then frugal of my mirth, heaven forgive me' (2.1.21–6). Remarking on how Falstaff's written message 'makes me almost ready to wrangle with mine own honesty', Mistress Page concludes, 'I'll entertain myself like one that I am not acquainted withal' (2.1.81–3).

This formulation of the idea that writing and reading can make one self-conscious in a surprising new way echoes a meditation on written ideas occasioned in Shakespeare's Sonnet 77 by the poet's gift of a notebook to his friend. The poem reflects on the novelty of the experience of writing and reading just as we today might reflect on changes to cognition or subjectivity arising from how the new digital media are transforming our experience of language:

> Look what thy memory cannot contain
> Commit to these waste blanks, and thou shalt find
> Those children nursed, delivered from thy brain,
> To take a new acquaintance of thy mind.   (9–12)

Written script—here the reader's own writing, for Mistress Page the written words of another—can make one know one's mind (or the 'mind' of another) in an unaccustomed way. It is fruitful to compare the repeated proud claim of Mistress Quickly to

[34] David Cressy, *Literacy and the Social Order: Reading and Writing in Tudor and Stuart England* (Cambridge: Cambridge University Press, 1980), 176.

know another person's mind, presumably through intimate oral disclosures, that concludes the preceding scene. 'Truly an honest gentleman', she says of the courtier, Fenton, 'but Anne loves him not, for I know Anne's mind as well as another does.—Out upon't, what have I forgot?' (1.4.158–60). Through such juxtapositions, *The Merry Wives* invites us to reflect on how written language and oral language shape knowledge of minds and selves in different ways, partly by how each medium affects the role of memory. Shakespeare seems fascinated by how written script releases one from the mental exertions of memory, allows one to slow down, objectifying one's words and so nursing or developing the products of one's cognition like children separate from oneself, with the effect that a new phase of reflection opens up, when, through the medium of written words, one can meet up again 'and take a new acquaintance of [one's] mind'.

Where does Quickly stand in relation to these mental arrangements, this interbreeding of language and consciousness? One of the seemingly loose ends for which *The Merry Wives of Windsor* is notorious is that the first letter 'dispatched', to use one of the play's favourite words, is actually addressed to Mistress Quickly by Sir Hugh Evans, although we never see her read or even receive the letter. Evans tells Simple, the letter-bearer, the letter's contents ('to desire and require her to solicit your master's desires to Mistress Anne Page' (1.2.9–10)), and Simple, questioned later about his errand both by Quickly and Dr Caius, repeats the message by mouth ('To desire this honest gentlewoman, your maid, to speak a good word to Mistress Anne Page for my master in the way of marriage' (1.4.77–9)), and is sent back with Quickly's oral message for Evans ('Tell Master Parson Evans I will do what I can for your master' (1.4.31–2)). This may seem very curious and haphazard to us, but Shakespeare lived in a world where, among people who received and even sent letters, some read and some did not, and this is the world being portrayed in *The Merry Wives*. This, in fact, would seem to be the point of Quickly's remarks, including their vague reference to the contents of a letter, when she arrives to lay the groundwork to trick the twice-tricked Falstaff a third time: 'Sir, let me speak with you in your chamber. You shall hear how things go, and, I warrant, to your content. Here is a letter will say somewhat. Good hearts, what ado here is to bring you together!' (4.5.114–17). Recent work on early modern epistolary culture has emphasized how a messenger's speech may supplement a written letter, but here Mistress Quickly offers the written letter she carries from one or other of the wives as an unnecessary supplement to the primacy of her own oral communication.

If the miscomprehension sequences of the Latin lesson help us to see Quickly's adaptive behaviour as a kind of transculturation process, her finest speeches place on exhibit the linguistic products of her experience of moving between different linguistic cultures. Her report to Falstaff on Mistress Ford's disposition is a prime example:

> Marry, this is the short and the long of it. You have brought her into such a *canaries* as 'tis wonderful. The best courtier of them all, when the court lay at Windsor, could never have brought her to such a *canary*. Yet there has been knights, and lords, and gentlemen, with their coaches; I warrant you, coach after coach, letter after letter,

gift after gift, smelling so sweetly, all musk; and so rustling [*rushling* in F1], I warrant you, in silk and gold, and in such *aligant* terms, and in such wine and sugar of the best and the fairest, that would have won any woman's heart; and, I warrant you, they could never get an *eye-wink* of her. (2.2.59–70; emphasis added)

Quickly seems to have listened with admiration to the speech of the ladies whose lifestyles she so admires and to have appropriated their words 'quandary' (accented at the time, the *OED* tells us, on the second syllable) and one or both of 'elegant' and 'eloquent'. She has heard these posh words 'with ears', recognizing them as associated with what we take to be very different words, 'canary' and 'alicant', both words for exotic wines and probably familiar to her in relation to her fondness for comforts like sharing 'a posset [milk and wine] . . . soon at night, in faith, at the latter end of a seacoal fire' (1.4.7–8).[35] Having heard (or misheard) words approximating 'canaries' and 'alicant' used in alien contexts in the women's speech about mental disposition and sophisticated terminology, she extends the meanings of her own familiar words as if they are metaphors, transferred from their literal sphere of comforting alcoholic lubrication to elucidate less material conceptions in the fresh realms of the other women's worlds, worlds that give shape to her aspirations and desire. In her appetite for fine expression, I find no sign of the linguistic insecurity or anxious struggle to conform that sociolinguists identify as hypercorrection. Her word coinages or adaptations may supply comedy, but they are also a resourceful—even creatively risk-taking— use of language.

To label and dismiss these uses as 'malapropisms' may be to mishear what the play tells us about Quickly's linguistic resources and about Shakespeare's own language-world, a world in which people's conversations regularly negotiated the contact zone between orality and literacy. The very idea of 'correct' and 'incorrect' word choice from a well-regulated and well-documented English lexicon on which the concept of the 'malapropism' depends is alien to Shakespeare's time. The eighteenth-century sense of 'linguistic law and order'[36] did not obtain. Patterns of word formation were not so tightly regulated, and, without dictionaries to consult, Shakespeare's contemporaries could happily coin many different formally related words without clear differences in meaning, no one of which could be identified as the 'correct' choice.[37] As part of our own linguistic heritage from the eighteenth century, a prescriptive notion of correctness is so engrained in how we make sense of words that, like the precise discriminations of word meanings in *OED*, it both assists and obfuscates our struggle to historicize and understand the language of an Elizabethan play. Indeed, reading a modernized and annotated edition of *The Merry Wives of Windsor*—the text we need in order to overcome the difficulties created by historical change—we can never escape

---

[35] For these discriminations of word meaning, see Melchiori's very helpful notes, *The Merry Wives of Windsor*, 181–2.

[36] Manfred Görlach, 'Regional and Social Variation', in Lass (ed.), *The Cambridge History of the English Language*, 3: 465.

[37] Nevalainen, 'Early Modern English Lexis and Semantics', 334.

the ideology of the 'incorrect' or 'correct' English word. The words have all been regularized and sorted for us in advance into these categories, with novel uses like 'hang-hog' or 'aligant' attributed to Quickly, or mistakes like Evans's 'plessing' edited so as to best exhibit their deformity and novel uses allotted to Shakespeare like 'the firm *fixture* of thy foot' (3.3.57–8) presented so as to exhibit correctness and an *OED* pedigree. Most scholars who have studied his vocabulary have found at least some evidence of the 'licentious Use of Words' of which William Warburton accused him in his edition of 1747.[38] Even Garner, who quotes with approbation Joseph T. Shipley's celebration of Shakespeare as 'the greatest word-maker of them all', explains why Shakespearean coinages like 'disquantity', 'dishorn', 'immoment', 'exceptless', and 'unsphere' are what H. W. Fowler would have called 'abortions', outraging principles of Latin word formation.[39] My point is that it may be helpful to think more in terms of a continuum rather than a clear-cut division between Quickly's verbal behaviour and Shakespeare's own overreaching and risk-taking verbal invention.

SPEAKING IN PRINT: MISCOMPREHENSION ACROSS MEDIA

One other significant strand of *The Merry Wives*, which extends its rich exploration of how interactions between literacy and orality shape the linguistic culture of Windsor, treats oral performances arising out of written scripts and printed books.[40] For Shakespeare, whose working life consisted in producing scripts for oral performance, how this manner of transmission affected language must have been a subject of special fascination. In his early collaborative play *1 Henry VI*, a debate between two characters, the Bishop of Winchester and the Duke of Gloucester, considers this special situation of speech that reproduces writing:

> WINCHESTER: Com'st thou with deep premeditated lines?
> With written pamphlets studiously devised?
> Humphrey of Gloucester, if thou canst accuse . . .
> Do it without invention, suddenly,
> As I with sudden and extemporal speech
> Purpose to answer what thou canst object.
> GLOUCESTER: Presumptuous priest . . .
> Think not, although in writing I preferred
> The manner of thy vile outrageous crimes,

---

[38] Quoted from W. F. Bolton, *Shakespeare's English: Language in the History Plays* (Cambridge, MA: Blackwell, 1992), 78.

[39] Garner, 'Shakespeare's Latinate Neologisms', 211, 215.

[40] Adam Fox, *Oral and Literate Culture in England, 1500–1700* (Oxford: Clarendon Press, 2000), describes a society in which 'speech, script, and print infused and interacted with each other in a myriad ways' (p. 5).

> That therefore I have forged, or am not able
> Verbatim to rehearse the method of my pen.
>   (3.1.1–13)

In place of what Winchester requests, not studied text but 'sudden and extemporal speech', Gloucester offers as a rough equivalent the oral rehearsal, 'verbatim' or word for word, of what he has written in his book. 'Verbatim' is oddly used here, for it is more usually applied to the transmission or reproduction of written texts, either by accurate word-for-word copying or by literal translation from one language to another. Clearly, a verbatim or word-perfect recitation of his written script is not what Winchester is asking for, and the debate encourages reflection on the disparity. The idea that print culture promotes 'verbatim' transmission of words is explicitly registered in *The Merry Wives of Windsor* when the wives discover that Falstaff has sent them duplicate seduction letters: 'Letter for letter, but that the name of Page and Ford differs. . . . I warrant he hath a thousand of these letters, writ with blank space for different names—sure, more, and these are of the second edition. He will print them, out of doubt—for he cares not what he puts into the press' (2.1.67–75).[41] Here a link is made not between print and extemporal speech but between print and engineered or falsified emotion. The wives are perceptive in recognizing a new use of language promoted by the increasing ubiquity of print transmission—a kind of synthetic personalized address, the forerunner of the kind of messages we routinely encounter today in the mass-produced letters or emails sent out by businesses and charities. In a related vein, but without Falstaff's connivance, Slender aspires in his wooing of Anne Page to the manufacture of extemporal speech and emotion from a book, although he has misplaced both the 'book of songs and sonnets' and 'the book of riddles' that enter his mind as potential helps (1.1.181–4).

We have seen how verbatim recitation from a Latin book is demanded in Evans's pedagogy, following the method of the Elizabethan grammar school aimed at civilizing the English schoolboy and fashioning a transculturated subjectivity, a consciousness imbued with the language and culture of the classical period. In contrast to this oral performance that requires deliberate replication of the printed text, Shakespeare introduces a scene in which the haphazard meditation of Parson Evans's extemporal speech draws together mixed-up citations from books. This is the strange scene in which the bookish Evans (literally carrying a book according to a stage direction most modern editors provide) expresses his disorientation and muddled emotions as he prepares himself for the anticipated duel with Dr Caius. Nervously awaiting his adversary, he curiously mixes up (in addition to his voiced and unvoiced consonants) his words for the humours, remarking, 'Plesse my soule: how full of Chollors I am, and trempling of minde: I shall be glad if he haue deceiued me: how melancholies I am'. Then, almost as if to illustrate Bakhtin's contention that internal language and consciousness consist of social dialogue, that people's words are always 'half someone else's

---

[41] On print technology, reproduction, and *Merry Wives*, see Elizabeth Pittenger, 'Dispatch Quickly: The Mechanical Reproduction of Pages', *Shakespeare Quarterly* 42 (1991), 389–408.

words',[42] he recites, sings, or mis-recites Christopher Marlowe's famous verses from *England's Helicon*, mixing them up in a curious miscomprehension sequence with a line from Sternhold and Hopkins's metrical version of Psalm 137: "Plesse my soule: *To shallow R[iu]ers to whose falls: melodious Birds sings Madrigalls: There will we make our Peds of Roses: and a thousand fragrant posies. To shallow*: 'Mercie on mee, I haue a great dispositions to cry. *Melodious birds sing Madrigalls:—When as I sat in Pabilon: and a thousand vagram Posies. To shallow, &c.*'.[43] In Evans's rendition, not only does the joyful riverbank setting of 'Come live with me' mutate into the melancholy river scene of the metrical Psalm ('When as we sate in Babylon the riuers round about, | And in remembrance of Sion the tears of grief burst out'), but the word 'fragrant' transmutes into the coinage 'vagram'.[44] The logic of this hybrid creation is related not only to Evans's dialect confusion of f's and v's, which allows him to associate 'fragrant'/ 'vagrant' with the homeless status of the biblical exile—and his own emotional dis-orientation. We are accustomed to admiring Shakespeare's linguistic genius in com-posing speeches and soliloquies in *King Lear* and *Hamlet* that suggest the 'mind in motion'; here we have a humbler but nonetheless impressive language of interiority, a book-muddling stream-of-consciousness that is a convincing forerunner of modernist moments in T. S. Eliot's *The Waste Land*. What is still more remarkable is that we also have—here as with Mistress Quickly's inventions, despite their different linguistic profiles—a speculative meditation on the psychology of word coinage. Evans's coinage 'vagram' arises, like Quickly's coinages 'hang-hog' and 'canaries', out of a historically specific instance of social dialogue involving a situation of miscomprehension and reorientation. Shakespeare's play offers lessons in word derivation that are not to be found in the *OED*, demonstrations of how ordinary people in his day could coin words, add to the expressiveness of their own linguistic resources, and even make small changes to the English tongue in response to their everyday needs and desires. These lessons are by no means the whole story about the English tongue in Shakespeare's day or about Shakespeare's linguistic artistry within his historical context, but they should encourage us to listen in Shakespeare's other plays for the stories about language that may be both obscured and enlivened by our own positioning in the English of our day.

[42] M. M. Bakhtin, 'Discourse in the Novel', in Michael Holquist (ed.), *The Dialogic Imagination: Four Essays* (Austin: University of Texas Press, 1981), 293.

[43] For this episode I quote from Charlton Hinman, *The First Folio of Shakespeare*, intro. Peter W. M. Blayney, The Norton Facsimile, 2nd edn. (New York: Norton, 1996), 48 (3.1.11–13 and 15–25), since the regularization of the modern text obscures my points.

[44] For these identifications and quotations, I am indebted to Melchiori, *The Merry Wives of Windsor*, 202.

CHAPTER 14

....

DRAMATURGY

....

BRIAN GIBBONS

Shakespeare's plays are not in the rigorous and critical sense either tragedies or comedies, but compositions of a distinct kind; exhibiting the real state of sublunary nature, which partakes of good and evil, joy and sorrow, mingled with endless variety of proportion and innumerable modes of combination.

—Dr Samuel Johnson[1]

I. Mingling

....

SHAKESPEARE is nowhere more Elizabethan than in his readiness to 'mingle' different generic and stylistic elements in his plays: he deploys a wide range of contrasting codes, varying his choice and interweaving them in patterns that are for each play unique. But the dramaturgy of the Elizabethans, the general Elizabethan idea of theatre, did not survive beyond the third quarter of the seventeenth century. This is easier to overlook because Shakespeare's sheer prestige, his poetry, his characters, have ensured his plays an unbroken performance history from that day to this. But this is not true of non-Shakespearean Elizabethan plays; their thin and intermittent performance history shows us how deep was the disruption that separated Elizabethan dramaturgy from what has come afterwards.

By the third quarter of the seventeenth century, educated English writers had succumbed to French influence; they assumed the Elizabethan playwrights (with the exception of Ben Jonson) had been ignorant or unskilful in attempting classical form, as it is seen in French drama of Molière, Corneille, and Racine. Thus Dryden explained his adaptation of *Troilus and Cressida*:

---

[1] Preface to *The Plays of William Shakespear* (1765), in W. K. Wimsatt (eds.), *Dr Johnson on Shakespeare* (Harmondsworth: Penguin Books, 1969).

I undertook to remove that heap of rubbish under which many excellent thoughts lay wholly buried. Accordingly I new modelled the plot, threw out many unnecessary persons...I made with no small trouble an order and connexion of all the scenes, removing them from the places where they were inartificially set...so that there is a coherence of 'em with one another and a dependence on the main design: no leaping from Troy to the Grecian tents and thence back again in the same Act...the beginning scenes of the fourth Act are either added or changed wholly by me, the middle of it is Shakespeare altered, and the whole fifth Act, both the plot and the writing are my own additions.[2]

But what was the Shakespearean alternative to Dryden's orderly scheme? Elizabethan playwrights sought to project multiple aspects of a situation. Conventional Elizabethan dramatic narratives deliberately tend to extravagance, in time, space, and incident, and involve multiple locations. Sam Mendes, a modern director of Shakespeare's *Troilus and Cressida* at The Swan Theatre, Stratford-upon-Avon, felt that its Elizabethan-style playing space enabled him to present the essential features of this Elizabethan kind of theatre, to achieve everything Dryden did not—'the fluid and simple technique of shifting from one world to another, to be both epic and domestic...from the inside of a tent onto the battle plains of Troy, and then back into a man's mind...it is not an illusory space, its a very honest space, but it is a space which fires the imagination.'[3]

Shakespeare's early practice, as we see it in *King Henry VI*, demonstrates in simpler form the technique he handles so fluidly in *Troilus and Cressida*. In *King Henry VI* Shakespeare confers on the stage architecture a variety of temporary locational meanings, as at the beginning of Part 1, successively Westminster Abbey, the walls of Orleans, the Tower of London, the walls of Orleans, within the Countess of Auvergne's castle, the Temple garden, a room within the Tower. (These are locations which the text establishes with emphasis, however much they superficially resemble the imaginary locations of outmoded editorial tradition.) Shakespeare's dramaturgy here can be compared to the manner in which the pageants of the medieval mystery plays passed in order before their spectators, not to be viewed naturalistically but as marking salient points in a narrative. Shakespeare's montage technique in *King Henry VI* presents the spectators, in up-to-date sixteenth-century dialectical style, with a complex pattern of likenesses and differences between successive groups and locations, the juxtaposition of which constitutes a dialectic about power, nationality and honour, embedded in the narrative.

Although otherwise something completely different, the comedy *Love's Labour's Lost* can clearly be identified as dialectical in this sense, since Shakespeare devises an action derived from dialogic thinking: two alternative ways of life—learning and love—are tested, both found inadequate, and the third term—love through prolonged moral

[2] 'Preface to *Troilus and Cressida*' (London: 1679), in James Kinsley and George Parfitt (eds.), *John Dryden, Selected Criticism* (Oxford: Oxford University Press, 1970), 159–62.
[3] Sam Mendes, in an interview with Peter Holland, *Shakespeare Survey* 47 (1994), 121.

askesis—is the proposed solution. At the far end of Shakespeare's career in *Antony and Cleopatra* a multiplicity of viewpoints is presented directly from the outset, in the opening scene, which is framed by the Roman soldiers Demetrius and Philo who uncomfortably watch, and interpret for the audience (who can also see for themselves), the behaviour of Antony and Cleopatra. What is fundamental is that Shakespeare sees all his dramatic material in terms of *equity*, the principle of placing any given human philosophical question or principle in a specific lived context, where every principle has to be tested, and a situation should be seen from multiple points of view.

I begin with an obvious multiplicity in Shakespeare, that concerning plot. This will lead to the rhetorical tradition of dialectic informing the plays, aimed not to resolve debate and provide a single answer, but to lay bare the complex nature of the case. Further senses of multiplicity will be pursued, more closely woven in the language, both verbal and theatrical, expressive of ambivalence and multivalence.

II. MULTIPLE PLOTS

Until the mid-1930s when the pioneering work of M. C. Bradbrook and William Empson overturned it,[4] the prevailing scholarly and critical view of the Elizabethan multiple-plot was hostile. Richard Levin cites representative scholars from 1886 to 1936 (including the illustrious T. S. Eliot), all of whom affirmed that in these plays the sub-plot was alien matter illegitimately attached to the main action;[5] indeed one editor, E. H. C. Oliphant, in his 1929 anthology *Shakespeare and His Fellow Dramatists*—intended for the college classroom—actually printed a warning line in the margin alongside sub-plot episodes in the plays, recommending they be omitted, since this would 'add greatly' to appreciation of the play.

Behind such views lay, ultimately, Aristotle, in the *Poetics*. Sir Philip Sidney in 1581–3 had censured the earlier phase of Elizabethan drama for breaking tragedy's decorum, which he said 'should be still maintained in a well raised admiration' and never, as did early Elizabethan tragedies, mingle 'kings and clowns' or match 'hornpipes and funerals'. This was in *An Apology for Poetry*,[6] written c.1581–3, first printed in 1595, a year or so before *Romeo and Juliet*. I would not put it past Shakespeare (who glances at *An Apology* in the Act 4 Chorus in *King Henry V*) to be alluding to *An Apology* in Act 4, Scene 5 of *Romeo and Juliet*, where one of the musicians hired for Juliet's wedding celebrations complains, when Juliet's death is announced, that they must now pack up their pipes. The juxtaposition of opposites, hornpipes and funerals, is indeed a central

---

[4] Respectively, *Themes and Conventions of Elizabethan Tragedy* (Cambridge: Cambridge University Press, 1935), and *Some Versions of Pastoral* (London: Chatto & Windus, 1935).

[5] *The Multiple Plot in English Renaissance Drama* (Chicago, IL: University of Chicago Press, 1971), 2–3.

[6] Quotations from Geoffrey Shepherd (ed.), Sir Philip Sidney, *An Apology for Poetry* (Manchester: Manchester University Press, 1973), 135.

characteristic of the play, which is a powerful example of generic mingling. It begins as apparently a romantic comedy but in Act 3 a random encounter of young hotheads sparks a street brawl and suddenly two men lie dead. That Romeo is merely banished for a killing half-acknowledges that this is no right tragedy, and seems to promise tragicomic reconciliation. Yet Shakespeare, having hinted at tragicomedy, soon disrupts it with an extraordinary sequence of accidents at rapidly accelerating speed, ending in multiple deaths. The insistent colliding of different generic rules is a calculated element in Shakespeare's grander ambition, to produce on the one hand an excitingly unpredictable switchback of lifelike accident and coincidence, and on the other, the almost Kydian frame-plot bolstered by a Chorus, bluntly insisting that the fault lies in their stars and not in themselves. Arthur Brooke, the author of Shakespeare's main source, *The Tragicall Historye of Romeus and Juliet*, described the theme in his 'Address to the Reader' as 'a couple of unfortunate lovers, thralling themselves to unfortunate desire'. London citizens, like Elizabethans generally, had conservative attitudes.[7] Shakespeare's main change to Brooke was to introduce a counter-theme upholding the power of love against parental authority. This was deliberately controversial: his design was dialectical, hence the ubiquity of antithetical patterns in his tragedy.

A play with a multiple plot needs to be controlled to have a coherent shape. The simplest and least significant mode of linking different plots is that in which individuals from different plots are friends, neighbours, or blood relatives, making probable their coming together at crucial points in the drama. Jonson's *Bartholomew Fair* is a rare example that uses geography for simple linking: it is the public occasion, the annual August 24 fair at Smithfield in London, which attracts so many unconnected individuals and is the cause of the integration of the numerous plots (one could compare Lovewit's house in Jonson's *The Alchemist* and, perhaps, the forest in *As You Like It*).

At a higher level is the causal mode, where a character or event in one plot directly affects another plot. Such links must be built into the onstage action, and have the effect of combining plots in mutual interaction. In *Much Ado* the Beatrice–Benedick courtship makes contact with the Hero–Claudio action at three stages: in the conspiracy in 2.1., in 4.1. when Beatrice asks Benedick to kill Claudio, and in the final scene when Hero and Claudio intervene to resolve the action. Earlier critics, says Levin, seem to have regarded the causal mode as the only means of integrating a multiple-plot play;[8] they complained that the two plots were not properly connected or unified when all they meant was that one line of action did not significantly affect the other.

Yet if the sub-plot does make any substantive contribution to the work as a whole, it must be in terms of a broader conception of unity, 'encompassing more complex and more important modes of integration' (Levin, op. cit, 9).[9] This is the province of the

---

[7] See Andrew Gurr, *Playgoing in Shakespeare's London*, 3rd edn. (Cambridge: Cambridge University Press, 2004), esp. 180–4.

[8] Richard Levin, *The Multiple Plot in English Renaissance Drama* (Chicago, IL: University of Chicago Press, 1971).

[9] Levin, *The Multiple Plot in English Renaissance Drama*, 9.

formal mode of integration, which includes all the analogical relationships between plots, which are to be inferred from the sequence of alternating scenes, although they must be abstracted and compared as complete wholes to be fully comprehended. Analogies may be negative as well as positive; they may involve both parallels and contrasts: thus the two families of Lear and Gloucester are in obvious respects parallel, but also contrasted in that the main plot is more serious and more internalized than the sub-plot. This even determines the choice of scenes to be dramatized: in the main plot the deaths of Goneril and Regan are not shown, but the focus is on Lear's tragic end, whereas in the sub-plot Gloucester's death is not shown but reported, and the triumph of Edgar and defeat of Edmund are shown, but in a non-tragic resolution.

The formal mode raises much more interesting questions, since it can be inferred in plays where the plots deal with quite different areas of experience and starkly contrasting modes, superficially not linked at all. Shakespeare's favoured comic structure is a three-level hierarchy. In *A Midsummer Night's Dream* a range of styles is set in counterpoint while Shakespeare mingles three plots: his main plot, the course of true love for two pairs of well-born Athenian young lovers; a second plot presenting the quarrel of the fairy king and his queen; a third plot, low comedy concerning Athenian tradesmen who rehearse and perform a ludicrous love tragedy of 'Pyramus and Thisbe'. It is worth pointing out that when Shakespeare deploys two or three plots in a play they are presented as running simultaneously; he further reinforces the implicit analogies, positive and negative, by arranging the sequence of scenes so that each in turn is devoted to a different plot.

Some formal relationships involve significant ambivalences and ironic tensions, particularly in the case of a highly romantic or heroic main plot with a sub-plot presenting a debased, cynical, or parodic version of the same action. In plays where the distance between the two plots is increased, the low comedy's crude pantomime may serve only to confirm the superior values of the main plot—as for instance in the heroical romance *Sir Clyomon and Sir Clamydes*. When the wandering knight Clamydes makes his proud first entrance, he then calls back offstage to some 'fellow': the fellow (Subtle Shift) then enters '*backwards, as though he had pulled his leg out of a mire, one boot off*'. This is in structural terms a perfect parodic inversion of the hero's impressive entrance which the audience has just seen, yet it is merely a sight-gag, conventional to the clown's role. Its dramatic purpose is to get a laugh. However, it does not initiate a sustained critical view of the heroic from below. On the contrary, clownishness attracts to itself the audience's urge to laugh and ridicule, thereby ensuring admiration for the heroic: contrast the much more amplified, complex relationship of the lyrical young heroine and her prosaic old Nurse in *Romeo and Juliet*.

III. THE PLAY OF IDEAS

Marlowe, in *Dr Faustus* for instance, and Shakespeare much more widely in *King Henry IV*, interweave with the main plot substantial low-comedy episodes, to create sustained ironic patterns of analogy. The result is a cumulative ambivalence that plays over the drama as a whole. Shakespeare in *King Henry V* puts the doctrine of the monarchy's sacredness in a testing context, a debate between the disguised king and common soldiers the night before the battle. That night scene (4.1) is not in his main source, Holinshed. Shakespeare invents it, taking the desacralization process far into Machiavellian territory. In flat contradiction to this, however, the battle of Agincourt itself is endowed with mythic status: Shakespeare suppresses reference to Henry's use of hidden archers and protective stakes—a 'politike invention' as Holinshed calls them— which played a crucial part in the historical victory. Thus Shakespeare's Agincourt is made to appear to be a victory against impossible odds and is felt and claimed as miraculous. This ambivalence is typical of the play's general dialectical mode. When Henry V proposes a military expedition to France it is seen from disconcertingly multiple aspects: the new King is personally challenged at home as well as abroad, so that chivalric and patriotic attitudes are starkly juxtaposed to politic calculation and acquisitive opportunism. To the end, the play offers a double perspective, the Chorus reminding us that after Henry V's success, France would be lost and England itself would eventually unravel in a civil war—'Which oft our stage has shown'. Every kind of border would then crumble: as Andrew Marvell's bleak words in the 'Horatian Ode' insist:

> For those do hold or break,
> As men are strong or weak.[10]

A. P. Rossiter's 1951 essay 'Ambivalence: the Dialectic of the Histories' was a landmark in modern recognition of this great double-play's double nature;[11] recently Phyllis Rackin has offered a yet darker view, that the plays 'constituted an area for ideological contest'—locating in *King Richard II* the arrival of Machiavellian secularism and the irreversible development of statecraft and realpolitik.[12] William Empson in 1935 suggested that in *Troilus and Cressida* a primitive form of hidden causal connection linked very different plots: Cressida's infidelity will bring about Troy's fall. Indeed plots concerned with quite different areas of experience may be linked at the psychological or anthropological level, as in *Cymbeline*,[13] where Shakespeare mingles primitive dramatic kinds, including the folk-play[14] and the medieval saints play, with

---

[10] See Brian Gibbons, 'The Wrong End of the Telescope', in J-P. Maquerlot and Michèle Willems (eds.), *Travel and Drama in Shakespeare's Time* (Cambridge: Cambridge University Press, 1996), 141–59.

[11] A. P. Rossiter, *Angel with Horns* (London: Longmans, 1961).

[12] *Stages of History* (London: Routledge, 1991), 222.

[13] See the discussion in the 'Introduction' in both Roger Warren (ed.), *Cymbeline* (Oxford: Oxford University Press, 1998), and Martin Butler (ed.), *Cymbeline* (Cambridge: Cambridge University Press, 2005).

[14] Guiderius, one of the royal brothers exiled in Wales, when challenged by Cloten (4.2.70 ff.) beheads him with Cloten's own sword, then jokes that the head is a mere 'empty purse' and chucks it in a stream. There is extreme contrast between the primitive folk-tale callousness of this episode and the ensuing episode of Imogen's waking beside the headless bloody trunk she takes to be her beloved Posthumus. See Brian Gibbons, *Shakespeare and Multiplicity* (Cambridge: Cambridge University Press, 1993), 35–41.

sophisticated Jacobean courtly manners, to effect in Innogen his most advanced experimental representation of a heroine's subconscious. There is also a spectacular descent of a god, bearing a prophecy.

Creative reinvigoration of received conventions is a marked feature of another later tragicomedy, *The Winter's Tale*. Structurally this has a double action divided by Time the Chorus. Part 1, the movement in Sicily from court to country and from kings to shepherds, is reversed in Part 2, a movement in Bohemia from country to court and from shepherds to kings, as in a diptych or pair of hinged mirrors. And this double pattern is repeated in other terms: the repetition in the second Part of stories, characters, events, motifs, and even individual words from the first Part, thereby composing patterns of likeness-with-difference; of conceits which are far-fetched over a gap between Sicily and Bohemia, winter and spring, tragedy and comedy. Patterns may begin in language, to be realized later in stage images: as with the sombre words of the 'marble-breasted' Leontes gazing at the statue of his wife Hermione— 'does not the stone rebuke me | For being more stone than it?' (5.3.37–8). This subconsciously prepares an audience for the *coup de théâtre*, Shakespeare's surprise happy ending: the Gallatea-like metamorphosis of the statue into life.

Coleridge memorably claimed for Shakespeare 'the power of reducing multitude into unity of effect, and modifying a series of thoughts by some one predominant thought or feeling'.[15] In the plays this highest mode of integration may be understood by referring to Harry Levin's concept of 'overplot', signifying an abstract topic, quite above the level of story, that generates the activity of the drama and serves as a fixed point of reference for it. In the case of *Troilus and Cressida* the overplot would be 'those principles of social and cosmic order that Ulysses enunciates'.[16]

IV. DEBATE DRAMA AND DIALECTIC

At this point, it is appropriate to turn to rhetoric, which was, in the sixteenth century, a central part of the English education syllabus. It comprised a system of exploring, processing, and shaping information in dialectical terms. The aim was to teach how to make one side of a debatable question as plausible as possible, and then turn around and make the other side seem just as plausible. This was not something only lawyers had to be able to do when preparing their cases in defence and prosecution: all Elizabethan writers were taught techniques of dialectics, amplification, and copious-ness. Pre-eminent among the rhetorical textbooks was the *de Copia* by Erasmus. In Book 2 Erasmus gives many and varied suggestions and practical exercises through which a writer may learn how to amplify things: for instance, the student is to practise

---

[15] S. T. Coleridge, 'On Shakespeare as Poet', in Terence Hawkes (ed.), *Coleridge on Shakespeare* (Harmondsworth: Penguin Books, 1969), 69.

[16] Harry Levin, 'The Shakespearean Overplot', *Renaissance Drama* 8 (1965), 63–71.

enlarging a narrative in terms of the *persons* concerned by specifying, in turn, their race, country, sex, age, education, culture, physical appearance, fortune, position, quality of mind, desire, experiences, temperament, understanding, and name. One can see how relevant such an exercise could be for a would-be author of fiction: it requires the writer to give a general question a specific, concrete context, creating individualized characters and locating them in a specific situation, a narrative, a time, and a place. And something else—to embody an abstract moral question in fictional form is not only to render the issue more apprehensible. To dramatize it in specific human terms is to make it more debatable, more open to question.

In this period of early sixteenth-century humanism, English drama in Interlude-form is conceived of as a medium of liberal enquiry in both the sociological and cognitive senses: one where the playwright is free to pursue ethical and scientific questions. Plays were literally constructed as questions: they begin with a proposition and develop it through a process of enquiry, using topics to reach a more comprehensive proposition. The aim is to discover the most comprehensive truth, not merely that one side or the other is right; hence the answer usually embraces both. John Heywood's *Witty and Witless* is an entertaining illustration of the essential pattern. The first half of the play presents two inadequate young men in a superficial argument: James, too aware of his own cleverness, defends the proposition 'Better ys for a man that may be wyttles then wytty' and John, earnest but dull, tries to rebut it. They take, as successive topics, temporal wealth, pain, and pleasure.[17] The play allows the paradox that witless is better than witty to be proved by pure wit. On a more serious philosophical level it adjusts the antithetical vision originally proposed by supplying (through a third person, Jerome, who arrives in the middle of the play) the middle term that is missing in the first debate: as Joel Altman observes, 'Jerome's wisdom subsumes the innocence of Witless and the experience of Witty, yet is superior to both. This third term, which unites apparent opposites, is typical of the synthetic vision of these interludes.' Altman also notes (p. 112) that 'The pattern is apparently the archetype of a comedy derived from dialogic thinking which refuses to abandon either of its original terms, and seeks a

[17] Joel Altman, *The Tudor Play of Mind* (Berkeley: University of California Press, 1978), 108–12, summarizes *Witty and Witless* as follows: James begins by arguing that fools live carefree whereas witty men have to scrape together a living. John concedes this security to fools but declares the fool may suffer the whip. They turn to the next topic, pain. James claims that the labourer suffers as much as the fool, and the witty man suffers from disappointment just as the witless one does. John claims victory since James concedes that it is as good to be witless as witty. James replies that comparing a labourer to a student shows that mental pain is worse than physical; and since fools are incapable of mental labour, fools cannot suffer as witty men do. They move to the topic of pleasure. James proposes that the highest pleasure is salvation, and fools like children are saved by baptism alone whereas the witty are saved only if they do well. This seems to prove the thesis, but now enters a third person, Jerome. He invokes a conclusive counter-thesis, that it is not wit but wisdom that makes men wise; if a man's rational soul lies unused, as in a fool, that man is no better than a beast. As for the life to come, the wise man who performs good works will merit a higher place in heaven, and should he sin may earn salvation through sincere repentance.

tertium quid that will fuse and complete them.' It persists all the way to *Love's Labour's Lost.*[18]

In Shakespeare the voice of detached critical commentary is often embodied in a figure completely of his own invention or much developed by him from his sources: such figures share characteristics with the conventional Fool but are more fully drawn as characters and more important dramatically—they include Jack Cade (*King Henry VI*), the Bastard Falconbridge (*King John*), Berowne (*Love's Labour's Lost*), Benedick (*Much Ado*), Falstaff (*Henry IV*), Parolles (*All's Well*), Thersites (*Troilus and Cressida*), Lucio and even Barnardine (*Measure*), Edmund (*King Lear*), Iago (*Othello*), Caliban (*The Tempest*)—typically these figures are unconventional, outspoken, and theatrically attractive, ready with direct address to the audience to insist on being heard. In *King Henry V* the equivalent is the group of common soldiers who debate with a disguised King Henry in 4.1., a scene which does not advance the plot, but spaciously explores through debate the idea of a king and his subjects. Aristotle specifies that plot is the prime embodiment of the action and this is the actual practice of ancient Greek drama. Through plot the meaning radiates into character and language. Such a pyramid of emphasis ensures genuine unity of action. But in Elizabethan construction, with its independent parts and coordinated accents, unity of action is not really possible—as Bernard Beckerman points out in his classic analysis, *Shakespeare at the Globe.*[19] The structure of incidents does not implicitly contain the total meaning of the play. Character and thought have degrees of autonomy; they are not subordinate to, but coordinate with, plot (although the critic Schücking[20] found it a weakness that Shakespeare tends to develop individual scenes at the expense of the whole: 'a tendency to episodic intensification').

In *Romeo and Juliet* the independent voice is Mercutio (greatly developed from a hint in Shakespeare's source, Arthur Brooke), and associated with him is the play's extraordinary amount of parody—a brilliant feature of other plays in this period, *Love's Labour's Lost* and *A Midsummer Night's Dream*. Parody has a significant function in the subtler linking of different character-groups and sub-plots as well as in keeping an audience conscious of the overplot. Through Mercutio, Shakespeare subjects the love-rhetoric of Romeo himself, at its height, to unmerciful parody: Romeo, hidden in the Capulet orchard, exults at the sight of Juliet at the window:

---

[18] As to the issue of open endings in Shakspeare—endings which in some ways are not endings—Dr. Johnson remarked in his 'Preface to Shakespeare' that in many of the plays 'the latter part is evidently neglected . . . his catastrophe is improbably produced or imperfectly represented'; but Johnson did not pause to consider how an incomplete or inconclusive ending may by that very means constitute a completed representation of a complex situation that resists full resolution (as happens, for instance, in *Love's Labour's Lost* and, arguably, *Troilus and Cressida*). Johnson also perhaps underplayed the importance for Shakespeare, when dramatizing a familiar story, of making changes to invigorate, to make it new, uncovering new truths by running counter to the predictable.

[19] Beckerman, *Shakespeare at the Globe 1599–1603* (New York: Macmillan, 1962).

[20] *Character Problems in Shakspeare* (New York, 1922), 114, from Bernard Beckerman, *Shakespeare at the Globe 1599–1603*, 45.

> It is my lady, O it is my love,
> O that she knew she were   (2.2.10–11)

Yet only moments before (in a pre-echo), Mercutio was bawdily parodying Romeo's predilection for the exclamatory 'O'—

> O Romeo, that she were, O that she were
> An open arse and thou a poperin pear!   (2.1.37–8)

Mercutio makes a no less lewd pun (on 'pricksong') in his quick-fire parodic mime of the gallant swordsman Tybalt:

> O, he's the courageous captain of compliments: he fights as you sing pricksong, keeps time, distance and proportion. He rests his minim rests, one, two, and the third in your bosom: the very butcher of a silk button—a duellist, a duellist . . .'

Parody and mockery in Shakespeare serve to reflect critically on the character who utters them as well as on the victim they unkindly skewer, as when Romeo overhears Mercutio mocking his 'O's (2.1.37–8) and remarks of his friend 'He jests at scars that never felt a wound' (2.2.1). But in Shakespeare's intensely intricate scheme there is a further irony in this, since Romeo cannot guess that Mercutio is going to feel a wound, no mere scratch, from Tybalt's claw, a wound that will never leave a scar because Mercutio barely has time to jest at it before it takes his life:

> No 'tis not so deep as a well nor so wide as a church door but 'tis enough, 'twill serve. Ask for me tomorrow you shall find me a grave man.   (3.1.97–9)

It is this ambivalent sudden event that Shakespeare places at the centre of the action.

V. COUNTER-NARRATIVES

Shakespeare's Chorus declares *Romeo and Juliet* to be (as most audiences know very well already) a story of 'star-crossed lovers' who met a tragic end. Yet plays are written in the present tense and for live performance: as the present-day playwright Michael Frayn remarks: 'in the theatre one feels (or one should, surely) that these events are occurring *now*, that things might go one way or another'.[21] The poignancy of *Romeo and Juliet* is precisely that its action comes so close to ending happily. In *Julius Caesar* it is this idea of unpredictability that Shakespeare places in the audience's minds early on, when an anxious Brutus meditates prospectively:

> Between the action of a dreadful thing
> And the first motion, all the interim is
> Like a phantasma or a hideous dream   (2.1.63–5)

---

[21] *The Human Touch* (London: Faber and Faber, 2006), 254. Frayn had, in 1998, written *Copenhagen*, a play based on the history of the atom bomb.

This is the passage Hazlitt quotes when defining poetry's essence as the creation of the spirit of life and motion in depicting events, as they unfold: 'it is during the progress, in the interval of expectation and suspense, while our hopes and fears are strained to the highest pitch of breathless agony, that the pinch of the interest lies'.[22]

Out of the tension between what is foretold and what actually happens from moment to moment, much audience excitement is generated. Telescoping the time-frame and highlighting surprises are key strategies where the story is already world-famous, as with *Julius Caesar*, and *Troilus and Cressida*, and *Antony and Cleopatra*; in other cases, Shakespeare spices his sources with alterations calculated to enhance tension. Thus the old play of *King Leir* ends happily, not desperately; in *Pandosto*, the source of *The Winter's Tale*, the equivalent of the jealous king Leontes is not cured, but commits suicide; of Macbeth the chronicles record that after he became king he ruled well for ten years, whereas Shakespeare drastically shortens the time and deletes the good rule; in Cinthio's version of the Othello story, Desdemona's death is at first accepted as an accident and much time elapses before Othello is arrested; he is tortured but then released to live on in exile; and more time elapses before, eventually, Desdemona's family have him murdered. There again Shakspeare's changes are radical. In *Hamlet* Shakespeare begins with the Ghost and his scheme for revenge—thus recalling the frame-plot of Kyd's *The Spanish Tragedy*. In Kyd's tragedy the ghost of Andrea is memorably present observing events, and at the conclusion of the frame-plot expresses his satisfaction: 'blood and sorrow finish my desires' (4.5.2); but Shakespeare's Ghost, after intervening in the middle of the action and thus keeping up the expected parallel to Kyd, is neither heard nor seen again. By his absence, his silence, Shakespeare intensifies what is obscure, what is questionable, and new, in this tragedy.

Consider Shakespeare's *Julius Caesar*. As Wellington said of the Battle of Waterloo, it is 'a damn'd close-run thing' that the assassination of Julius Caesar actually happens. In the build-up to it (3.1.), the morning of the Ides of March, Shakespeare crowds into some fifty lines thunder and lightning, Caesar's wife Calpurnia crying out in a nightmare, Caesar's three-times repeated rejection of her pleas—and his rejection of the advice of the augurers—not to go to the Capitol; then Calpurnia again, this time on her knees, pleading that he send Mark Antony instead, and Caesar abruptly giving in without explanation! That decision is no sooner made than Decius enters—Decius, the conspirator who had assured the anxious Cassius that, whatever the auguries, he would bring Caesar to the Capitol. With near-contemptuous ease Decius takes Calpurnia's nightmare image of Caesar's statue spouting blood and reinterprets it as a happy augury. Caesar gives in to him (so much for Caesar's claim to be 'constant as the northern star'). Shakespeare allows a moment's pause and then tightens suspense again, with Artemidorus announcing to the audience his plan to stop Caesar on the way and expose the plot. The Soothsayer passes by: he too intends to warn Caesar as he comes along. The stage clears. A flourish, then Caesar enters in procession. He brushes

---

[22] 'On Poetry and Poets', in William Hazlitt, *Lectures on the English Poets* (London: 1818).

aside the Soothsayer and impatiently refuses to read the warning note Artemidorus presses on him: 'What? Is the fellow mad?' As the assembly gathers, Cassius is alarmed at a remark passed by Popillius: 'I wish your enterprise today may thrive'—will he betray the conspiracy? And when they see Popillius going up to Caesar, the conspirators panic—and this in the last moments before they must strike!

In a central scene of *Othello*, 4.1., Iago quick-wittedly improvises when the unexpected happens, but the real cause of his success is chance: sheer multiple coincidence. Iago goads Othello to a paroxysm of frenzied jealousy at Cassio. Othello falls unconscious—for no more than a minute or so—but *exactly* in that minute Cassio chances to arrive, and then leaves before Othello revives (4.1.46). Had Othello been able to confront him, he might have realized Cassio was innocent. Iago now tells Othello to conceal himself and to *watch* as Iago induces Cassio to *tell* of having Desdemona. Out of earshot, Othello will only be able to watch Cassio's gestures, having been primed by Iago how to interpret them. The audience do hear Iago talk to Cassio: not of Desdemona, but of Bianca. Then (of all people) who should happen to appear but Bianca herself, petulantly brandishing the handkerchief and thrusting it into Cassio's hand as she exits! Iago gets rid of Cassio, turns and tells Othello that what he saw was indeed Cassio 'laughing at his vice'—Iago reinforces the deception:

IAGO: And did you see the handkerchief?
OTHELLO: Was that mine?
IAGO: Yours, by this hand. And to see how he prizes the foolish woman your wife!
She gave it him, and he hath giv'n it his whore.

(4.1.169–73)

They agree that Othello shall strangle Desdemona 'this night' while Iago takes care of Cassio.

It is the sheer recklessness of Iago and the precariousness of his grip—improvisation after improvisation—that keeps an audience aware of the likelier outcome, that he will fail, that Desdemona will be vindicated, that the implicit counter-narrative is going to prevail. Iago's playlet with Cassio has a very simple design and he directs the theatre audience to read it simply: as Cassio shall smile, Othello shall go mad; but we should notice that from the theatre audience's point of view the episode is far from simple. It does grimly expose, in Iago's skilful performance, new levels of his malignity, but there is something comic exposed, too, when we see that he is surprised by Bianca's entry, and there is more comedy in his further surprise (and relief) as he sees how perfectly her intervention is fitting his plot. Othello's inability to *hear* Cassio makes him appear a fool whereas Cassio's inability to *see* Othello makes him appear foolish too: the symmetry is also reminiscent of comedy. Then Bianca's entry adds a comic effect in openly showing up an embarrassed Cassio: can this be Cassio's supposedly doting Bianca, the one whom Cassio has just been imitating for Iago's amusement, hanging and lolling and weeping upon him? Nevertheless, there is nothing comic about Bianca's effect on Othello; it is decisive. It confirms his fear that Desdemona has shamed him, and that this cannot be kept secret. The accidental coincides with the fatal. The episode is a cunningly wrought perspective that shows from one side grotesque comedy, from the opposite side hell: 'I will chop her into messes. Cuckold me!' And yet the scene is not done yet; a plan is no sooner sketched—Othello to strangle Desdemona in her bed, Iago to take care of Cassio—when another interruption occurs: ''Tis Lodovico— | This comes from the Duke. See, your wife's with him' (4.1.210–11).

Iago spells it out so pointedly we may infer that he fears Othello is overwrought—he needs warning to sleek o'er his rugged looks. Certainly Lodovico's is an emblematic entrance, emphasized by its interrupting effect, and bespeaking in Lodovico the authority of Venice, now reimposing itself on the anarchy in Cyprus. Othello takes the Duke's letter and goes a little apart to read it—apart enough for the others to begin a conversation without disturbing him, yet close enough for him to overhear some of it. This spatial separation of Othello (stressed by implicit stage directions in the dialogue) serves ironically to recall for the audience, possibly for Othello too, his isolation and eavesdropping on Cassio a few minutes previously. The implicit parallel in the situations subliminally works on his overheated imagination, so that even without Iago's prompting he now interprets what is said as another playlet, this time exposing Desdemona.

Cause in Shakespeare, Beckerman objects, often does not have sufficient weight to produce the effect it does, as with the handkerchief in *Othello*, while in *King Lear* the events leading to Cordelia's death are without cause unless you accept chance as cause: it is by chance that she is captured and by chance that Edmund confesses too late.[23]

It is a too-hasty decision *not* to act (Pompey can't concentrate) that marks a crucial turning point in *Antony and Cleopatra*. During the drunken feast of the world-sharers, hosted by Pompey on his galley (2.7), Menas makes repeated efforts to get his master Pompey to listen to his urgently whispered plan: he wants to cut the cable and then the throats of his guests, thereby making Pompey 'lord of all the world'; Menas shows how simply the whole course of history may be changed if you pick the right moment, but Pompey rejects the idea out of hand: he is the host; honour forbids. He impatiently rejoins the party; and so Antony, Lepidus, and Caesar never find out how close a shave they had, and the next we hear of Pompey (3.5) he's been murdered.

In such instances there is an ostensible disproportion between the weighty consequences and the light cause: but to modern sensibilities, and after two World Wars, this may be seen as ironically reflecting the real world. A small exemplary anecdote: during the British seaborne invasion of Egypt (November 6–7) in the 1956 Suez crisis, the British commander General Keightley, with his ADC, set off from his headquarters ship, at dusk in a small motorboat, to direct operations ashore. On the way the engine failed and the small boat began to drift. No radio signals could be sent. For a long and anxious time the General was completely isolated and helpless, adrift in the dark, with the entire future of the invasion in the balance. The Egyptian location, together with the mixture of implausible chance and possible grave consequences, gives the event a distinctly Shakespearean character.[24]

---

[23] One could add the appearance in *The Winter's Tale* of a bear, which chances also to be hungry yet seizes scrawny old Antigonus, leaving the plump royal baby Perdita to survive and become a heroine.

[24] Chance in the form of the weather in the English Channel played a decisive role in the failure of the Spanish Armada in 1588, and in the success of the Allied invasion of Normandy in 1944: see in Robert

VI. Delusion, Magic, Madness, as Parallel Narratives

Marlowe in *Dr Faustus* had presented in Mephistophilis a figure who is corporeal, sharing with Faustus the location of his study, and simultaneously a supernatural spirit who declares he is in hell. Marlowe does not abandon—on the contrary, he insists on—the medieval conventions of the psychomachia, in which the allegorical mode is dominant and which do not depend on specified time, place, or individuality; but at the same time Marlowe presents a sixteenth-century, specifically German cultural context and location and a Faustus in whom the drama is internalized, a Faustus who is an individual and a psychological hero. Shakespeare may have found this conception particularly significant, for in *King Richard III*, whatever the importance we may wish to ascribe, with Bernard Spivack, to the allegory of evil, the psychological interest of the characterization is acute, and it is significant that the stage appearance of the supernatural is restricted to within Richard's dream.

The experience of being possessed becomes an important motif in Shakespearean drama, beginning in *The Comedy of Errors* where it is associated with Christian belief in demons as well as ordinary obsessive mania. It is in familiar surroundings, the street outside her own house, that Adriana, the wife of Ephesian Antipholus, comes upon her husband (2.2.100)—at least, she believes it is he, though as the audience knows, it is actually a complete stranger, his long-lost identical twin newly arrived in the town. She upbraids him for his neglect: 'Ay, ay, Antipholus, look strange and frown'. Her terms have unintended ironic aptness: 'O, how comes it | That thou art then estranged from thyself?' This approach from such an attractive woman bewilders him, understandably, though some things she says do get his attention—'this body consecrate to thee . . . ruffian lust . . . harlots . . . the crime of lust . . . thy true bed'. His blunt reply, 'Plead you to me, fair dame? I know you not', stuns her with its apparent brutal denial of her identity as reflected in him. As for him, his confusion only deepens:

> What, was I married to her in my dream?
> Or sleep I now, and think I hear all this?'   (2.2.173–4)

Given the neutrality of the Elizabethan stage, conventions for establishing location are basic—'Well, this is the Forest of Arden'—and as a rule accepted, though Sidney objects to plays with multiple locations because 'the player, when he cometh in, must ever begin with telling where he is, or else the tale will not be conceived'.[25] But there is great interest in cases where the characters are disoriented, are in the grip of dream,

Crowley (ed.), *What If?* (London: Macmillan, 2001), the essays by Geoffrey Parker and Stephen E. Ambrose, 139–54, 341–8, respectively.

[25] Sidney, *Apology*, in Shepherd (ed.), 134.

deception, delusion, or madness. Shakespeare progressively exploits the possibilities of interplay between regular and distorted perceptions of location.

In *Romeo and Juliet* a contrast in locations is the means to introduce the hero: first the stage is filled with the noisy, brutal communal life of the city streets, then the absent hero is described in a remote, silent location—a grove of sycamore before dawn, which, we are told, he alternates with the 'artificial night' of his shuttered chamber. Verona's communal sense of ordinariness, of everyday plain reality, provokes the creation of rival dreamworlds, the world of Mercutio's mind, of the lovers' shared ecstasy, and the worlds of misery each lover endures alone.

Romeo reassures Juliet that he is safe from her kinsmen: 'I have night's cloak to hide me from their eyes', and she in turn defends her boldness: 'Thou knowst the mask of night is on my face' (2.1.117, 127). It is not simply that with the mask of night they reveal their inner selves, it is rather that they discover new selves in the different location of dream, which is kept private from the other characters. This new self, this awareness of being in a rival world beyond a local habitation and a name, involves sacrifice, but it is the locus for whatever affirmation the hero or heroine makes in the face of death.

Yet the play has no actual supernatural persons; by contrast in *A Midsummer Night's Dream* the location of the wood near Athens, which Bottom the amateur actor-director at first considers 'a marvellous fit place for our rehearsal', is then shown to be an abode of fairies who, by a further paradox, celebrate it for being natural, 'where the wild thyme blows | Where oxlips and the nodding violet grows' (2.1.249–50). Nevertheless the nature of the location, once called in question, stays unstable whoever is present, fairy or mortal or both simultaneously—natural and supernatural, familiar and magical. Bottom's humble, downright convenient shape may be restored to him at the end, but his inner disorientation persists. Shakespeare uses the comic mode teasingly, to keep the issue unfathomable; Act 3 Scene 1 begins when the solid figure of Bottom makes his entrance, leading his mates in search of somewhere to rehearse 'Pyramus and Thisbe'. Quince looks round: 'here's a marvellous convenient place for our rehearsal'. 'This green plot shall be our stage, this hawthorn brake our tiring house' (3.1.2–4). Here, in its simplest possible form, was how location was conventionally indicated on the Elizabethan stage; but a complicating ironic layer is added, over the heads of these fictional characters: for while the theatre spectators are duly imagining the rush-strewn stage to be a green plot, Bottom is imagining the green plot to be a rush-strewn stage; and while the theatre audience is imagining this actor to be an Athenian weaver, the Athenian weaver himself wants to be imagined as an actor, and one worthy to play Pyramus.

Jonson's comedy *The Alchemist* was performed by Shakespeare's company in 1610, near in time to *The Tempest*. In both plays a solitary location serves to bring a number of sub-plots together: Shakespeare presents an almost-desert island somewhere in the Mediterranean, where a white magician casts his spells to effect spiritual alchemy on his subjects, while Jonson presents a temporarily vacated house in London's Black-friars, where con artists fake alchemical magic to extract gold from leaden-witted gulls. *The Alchemist* begins with the bogus alchemist, Subtle, reminding his accomplice, Face, that he has already made him metaphorically a subject of alchemical transmutation, 'sublimed', 'exalted' and fixed', wrought to 'spirit, to quintessence', remote from the base condition in which he was found, among 'brooms and dust and wat'ring pots'; and that Subtle's 'art' can make them finer yet. The main plot involves their pretence, to the variety of credulous investors they attract, that the day of alchemical projection is at hand, to make everyone limitlessly rich. The accelerating sequence of interruptions of one sub-plot by another, and the imminent risk to Subtle and Face of exposure and collapse, which each of these interruptions presents, leads to the climax, a spectacular interruption as the 'great works' fly '*in fumo*' (that is, as a pot explodes in the kitchen) thereby dispersing all the creditors. The rogues' plot itself is then, at its very zenith, interrupted by the unexpected return of the house's owner, Lovewit, who takes their prize. (Lovewit's absence and return constitute a vestigial frame-plot.) Thus the gigantic fantasy enacted in his house vanishes as if it had all been illusion. Although an audience finds no difficulty in enjoying the idea that the laboratory 'within' is only the house kitchen, it is less easy to think of it as also the foul rag-and-bone shop of the backstage area at the playhouse—Jonson's added metatheatrical joke.

In these two plays, both Jonson and Shakespeare certainly do take remarkable risks as playwrights, and require highly-visible risks to be taken by the actors in performance. While *The Alchemist* may not present, in terms of spectacle, such obvious challenges as *The Tempest* does with its monsters and drolleries, nevertheless Jonson's play is in its own terms hazardous: its intricate construction and hectic pace make tremendous demands on the spectators' concentration and on the actors' versatility and exactness. If a single entrance cue is missed the whole play can collapse.

The opening scene of *The Tempest* directly represents a ship in a storm, something Shakespeare had studiously avoided in *The Comedy of Errors* and *The Winter's Tale* where the story features actual shipwrecks. The Globe may have been a non-scenic stage, but for *The Tempest* Shakespeare evidently required actors to be recognizable as mariners—heaving on ropes, climbing up and down ladders, opening hatches, shouting to make themselves heard, deafened by backstage thunder and alarmed by lightning-flashes and soused from above with water. The language—evidently Shakespeare requires it to be audible above the theatre's special effects—compares the waves to insurgents and the storm-tossed ship to a state imperilled by malignant fortune or bad captainship. Spectators can accept this familiar theatrical code, but, when the second scene begins, the code is changed: Prospero explains to Miranda that the spectacular storm was magical illusion. There was no real storm, no wreck, no drowning. Well, this isn't fair. Spectators may be fools for parting with their money to see a play with a tempest in a non-scenic theatre, but here in this second scene even that contract is broken: the storm that seemed in the first place real and only in the second place emblematic, now has to be reread, in the light of Prospero's explanation, as in the first place emblematic and in the second place only illusory. The Globe groundlings' naive taste—as represented by, say, the likes of Trinculo—is first solicited but then dismissed by Shakespeare's new interruptive style. Various kinds of imaginative and theatrical experience are got under way, interrupted, transformed and exalted, constituting a process of refining (in alchemical terms) for Prospero's base enemies and, at another level, for the play's spectators too. In this sense Shakespeare in *The Tempest* seems at times curiously, possibly mischievously, Jonsonian.

Hamlet begins with the most vague and archaic of outdoor locations, a castle platform, in the night, bitter cold, guarded by armed soldiers who have Italian or Latin names. Not until after the Ghost has come and gone is the ground even clearly identified as Denmark. The play's location, Elsinore Castle, while having emblematic significance,[26] is established with near-Jonsonian concern for detail when the characters refer to its particular parts as familiar features of a shared everyday life: as when Ophelia tells of sewing in her chamber and being suddenly affrighted by Hamlet, his doublet all unbrac'd, or when Hamlet tells Gertrude, as he gets hold of Polonius's corpse: 'I'll lug the guts into the neighbour room', and later describes its location, 'as you go up the stairs into the lobby' (3.4.186; 3.4.36). Hamlet, giving Osric his assent to the duel, gestures casually to the familiar location: 'Sir, I will walk here in the hall' (5.2.134). A central scene, 3.4, is located in Gertrude's bedchamber, and features the appearance of the Ghost to Hamlet. Gertrude claims she neither sees nor hears it:

> HAMLET: Do you see nothing there?
> GERTRUDE: Nothing at all; yet all that is I see.
> HAMLET: Nor did you nothing hear?
> GERTRUDE: No, nothing but ourselves.
>
> (3.4.122–4)

She diagnoses Hamlet as suffering from hallucination, 'the very coinage of your brain', a 'bodiless creation' (3.4.128–9). If Gertrude's diagnosis of mental illness may give Hamlet pause, Shakespeare is deliberately giving the spectators a jolt too, thrusting in the Ghost and his plot, this musty medieval remnant, into the fast-moving, sophisticated, new psychological theatre, where the stabbing of Polonius behind the arras forms a climactic, multiple metaphor for Claudius's success in stage-managing the transformation of Hamlet's home into a booby-trapped maze of killing jokes.

Apart from the issue of censorship, it is as if Shakespeare saw particular artistic challenges in supernatural material in itself, as well as in the received medieval conventions for representing it. Shakespeare's confining the ghosts to within Richard III's dream does not accord equal status to supernatural characters, so they do not disrupt the conventions by which the natural location of the scene is established. Shakespeare establishes for them an alternative decorum; there will be later plays where an alternative *imagined* location makes a claim on our attention equal to, or greater than, the scenic location already established in the spectators' minds—as with the dizzying unreal precipice of Dover cliffs, or that bare anonymous tract—the bleak winds do sorely ruffle, for many miles about there's scarce a bush—where for a time hallucination possesses and disorients Lear, transporting him to a region of demons, and hell fire, and tears that scald like molten lead.

---

[26] See Anne Lancashire, 'The emblematic castle in Shakespeare and Middleton', in J. C. Gray (ed.), *Mirror up to Shakespeare* (Toronto: University of Toronto Press, 1984), 223–42.

To conclude: Shakespeare's multiplicity is ultimately a mode of apprehending, it is a searching discourse accommodating afresh, for each play, differing ideas, voices, and ways of being. In *Hamlet* there can be no question that the Ghost is accepted by spectators: it is a triumph of Shakespeare's manipulative power over them, a power derived from his unique instrument, a mixed-genre, multiple dramatic mode. Exactly because—when all's done—this was a theatre, an 'unworthy scaffold', in which the word was king, Shakespeare was free to make Elizabethan spectators imagine they saw whatever he chose: but today, when set-designers provide a specific consistent cultural location—say, Edwardian England—then the essentially eclectic, mingled drama of Shakespeare is obscured; and with it is obscured the question which Shakespeare's dramaturgy is designed to compose: how is Hamlet, how is any of us, to reconcile the acute inconsistencies in man's perception of the world? And that *is* a question.

CHAPTER 15

....

CENSORSHIP

....

JANET CLARE

CONTROL AND REGULATION

....

ELIZABETHAN censorship in the decades preceding and coinciding with Shakespeare's early career evolved in response to the rapid growth of theatre production. The first public theatre, the Red Lion, was erected in 1567, quickly followed by the Theatre, the Curtain and the Rose, allowing the travelling companies to have permanent stages on which to perform the plays in their repertoire. It has been estimated that by the mid-1590s as many as 8,000 spectators could have been watching plays in the open-air London amphitheatres at any one time. Faced with such an unprecedented increase in theatrical activity, the state sought to regulate the operation of playhouses and acting companies and to check the contents of plays before granting a licence for their performance. The precaution accords with Francis Bacon's axiom in relation to dramatic poetry: 'The minds of men are more open to impressions and affections when many are gathered together than when they are alone'.[1]

The early playhouses were built outside the City of London boundaries and their regulation fell to the Justices of the Peace of Middlesex and Surrey. From time to time, however, the Privy Council intervened to limit or suppress performances following specific complaints or intelligence brought to them of performances, which had elicited an unruly audience response. The most often cited of such instances is in 1597 after a performance at the Swan by Pembroke's Men of a play called *The Isle of Dogs*. From scattered sources, including Privy Council records, the 'diary' of Philip Henslowe, and allusions to the play by its authors, Thomas Nashe and Ben Jonson, we know about the stir caused by the performance and about the state response to what was held to be a seditious play. Following investigations into the production, conducted in part by the notorious intelligencer Richard Topcliffe, playing was suspended and the Justices were

---

[1] *The Advancement of Learning*, s.2, ch. 13, in J. Spedding, R. L. Ellis, and D. D. Heath (eds.), *Works*, 7 vols. (London, Longmans, 1858–61), 4: 316.

ordered to demolish all the playhouses, an order which was not, however, implemen-ted.[2] In the context of the law of real property, such an injunction was probably unenforceable in the first place, and one can only speculate that it was issued as a display of power and a deterrent. Frustratingly for a study of early modern censorship, but hardly surprisingly, the play is lost. Since Nashe and Jonson were imprisoned, Pembroke's Men disbanded, and the Swan theatre had ceased to be the home of an established company, there could be no thought of publishing a play which had brought all this about. Perhaps there had never been much of a playbook, anyway, since according to Nashe the actors created the last four acts, which, complained Nashe, 'bred both their trouble and mine too'.[3] Topcliffe was ordered to discover how many copies of the play had been distributed and to whom, while Nashe's lodgings were searched.[4] It is highly probable that any play manuscript and contingent docu-ments of plot and parts were immediately destroyed.

The regulation of playhouses and companies is less significant, however, to the narrative of government surveillance of dramatic production than the perusal and licensing of plays prior to performance. From the very beginning of Elizabeth's reign, the subject and content of plays were restricted; so much is evident from a proclama-tion 'Prohibiting Unlicensed Interludes and Plays Especially on Religion' issued in 1559 during the first year of the Queen's reign.[5] The proclamation is inclusive in its restrictions: local officials were instructed not to permit 'any play wherein either matters of religion or of the governance of the estate of the commonweal shall be handled or treated'. Documents of control are of course intimately bound up with political culture; they need to be historicized and questions asked about the political contingencies which brought them about. This early Elizabethan proclamation is clearly significant in the context of Reformation politics. In succeeding her Catholic sister Mary I and Mary's Spanish consort Philip II of Spain, Elizabeth reversed the doctrinal direction of religious policy, and consequently religious drama had to be brought into line with the shift back to Protestantism. During her reign we see the steady erosion of the medieval mystery cycles, the great religious dramas performed by the craft guilds in the major English cities. The mystery plays at first suffered piecemeal censorship of doctrinal issues—the veneration of the saints, the cult of the Virgin Mary, transubstantiation—and then total suppression.[6] Generally speaking, the popular drama of Shakespeare's time steered well clear of religious and doctrinal matters,

[2] *Acts of the Privy Council 1597* (hereafter *APC 1597*), in J. R. Dasent (ed.), *Acts of the Privy Council of England* 32 vols. (London: 1890–1907).
[3] *Lenten Stuffe*, in R. B. McKerrow (ed.), *The Works of Thomas Nashe*, 5 vols. (Oxford: Blackwell, 1958), 3: 154.
[4] *APC 1597*, 27, 338.
[5] *Tudor Royal Proclamations*, Paul L. Hughes and James F. Larkin (eds.), 3 vols. (New Haven, CT: Yale University Press, 1964–9), 2: 115–16.
[6] See, for example, Lawrence M. Clopper (ed.), *Records of Early English Drama: Chester*, (Manchester: Manchester University Press, 1979), 110, 114, and *Records of Early English Drama: York*, Alexandra F. Johnson and Margaret Rogerson (eds.), 2 vols. (Manchester: Manchester University Press, 1979), 1: 331–2.

possibly a consequence of silent censorship, but, as we shall see, it was less successful in negotiating political and ideological boundaries, which were by their nature less stable and definite.

The most significant document circumscribing theatrical and dramatic practice is the commission of 1581 granted to Edmund Tilney, who had been appointed Master of the Revels two years previously. The Office of the Revels had been created originally to facilitate entertainment for the monarch and the court: a development which is briefly alluded to in *A Midsummer Night's Dream* when Duke Theseus commands Philostrate, his Master of the Revels: 'stir up the Athenian youth to merriments' (1.1.12) in order to while away the tedious days before the celebration of his marriage to Hippolyta. Moreover, as the patent granted in 1574 to Leicester's Men demonstrates, plays performed by travelling players strictly could be performed only with the licence of the Master of the Revels.[7] The actual commission of 1581 extends the office from manager of court entertainment to theatrical censor. Quite new to the Office are the powers vested in Tilney to 'warn, command and appoint':

> All and every player or players with their playmakers, either belonging to any nobleman or otherwise bearing the name or names of using the faculty of playmakers or players of Comedies, Tragedies, Interludes or what other shows soever from time to time and at all times to appear before him with all such plays, Tragedies, Comedies or shows as they shall have in readiness or mean to set forth and them to present and recite before our said servant.[8]

From Tilney's considerable markings on the manuscript of what is known as *The Book of Sir Thomas More*,[9] it is clear that the stipulation in his Commission that the players should in person recite their plays before the Master of the Revels had been modified. At some point censorship must have moved from an oral to a written practice, although we can speculate that oral directives accompanied the playbook as it changed hands. On the crucial matter of what the censor is actually to censor, the commission is vague. The Master is 'to order and reform, authorise and put down as shall be thought meet or unmeet unto himself or his said deputy in that behalf'. Whether or not it was designed as such, it was certainly to prove useful for the substance of censorship to be left open and indeterminate, thereby allowing the Master of the Revels to intervene and exercise his powers in response to current political exigencies. The dynamics of censorship, as evinced in dramatic manuscripts, in the differences between printed texts, and in recorded reactions to provocative plays—such as the lost *Isle of Dogs*, *Eastward Ho* (the work of a collaboration among Jonson, Marston, and Chapman), Chapman's *Byron*, Jonson's *Sejanus*, and Middleton's *A Game at Chess*—demonstrate how varied could be the concerns of early modern censorship.

---

[7] E. K. Chambers, *The Elizabethan Stage*, 4 vols. (Oxford: Oxford University Press, 1923), 2: 87–8.

[8] Quoted in Janet Clare, *Art Made Tongue-Tied by Authority: Elizabethan and Jacobean Dramatic Censorship*, 2nd edn. (Manchester: Manchester University Press, 1999), 32–3. Spelling has been modernized.

[9] The title was added by a scribe; 'book' means the script or the prompt-book.

IMPLEMENTATION

The Book of Sir Thomas More

No play of Shakespeare's survives in manuscript to tell us what the Master of the Revels may have objected to in his work or what Shakespeare's company, the Lord Chamberlain's Men, later the King's Men, may have decided to cut in anticipation of the censor's objections. On the contrary, Shakespeare's early encounter with censorship may have been as a writer brought in to make good textual depredations caused by censorship. One such text, which has survived in manuscript, was a late Elizabethan play[10] by a consortium of dramatists which follows the career of Henry VIII's Chancellor, Thomas More, who refused to accept the king's break with Rome and his adoption of the title Supreme Head of the Church of England. The play telescopes two disparate narratives: the May Day riots of 1517 against foreigners in London, which Thomas More attempted to quell, and the Reformation politics of Henry's break with Rome, leading to More's execution in 1534. Thus, two alleged acts of treason are represented. The insurgents themselves were seen as traitors because their uprising is directed against the nationals of countries friendly to the King (they are referred to as 'Frenchmen' and 'strangers', but Tilney changes the reference to 'Lombards'). The other incidence of treason focuses on Thomas More himself. More becomes a traitor for denying the King's supremacy in matters spiritual as well as temporal. Despite the cautious and dramatically abbreviated handling of More's principled stand against the King, the Master of the Revels objected to its representation on the stage. In a Privy Council scene, More is depicted with the Bishop of Rochester: both are refusing to subscribe to unspecified 'articles' (4.1.), identified as the Oath of Supremacy and the Act of Succession. More resigns his office of Lord Chancellor and is put under arrest at his home in Chelsea. Tilney has marked the scene for omission and has written the marginal note 'All Alter'. This is the last amendment to the text which is definitely in Tilney's hand.

Dramatically, there is less focus on Thomas More as a morally intransigent statesman and more on his role, earlier in the reign of Henry VIII, as sheriff in London attempting to pacify May Day riots against foreigners. In fashioning More rather more

---

[10] The date is open to dispute. Vittorio Gabrieli and Giorgio Melchiori believe the play was written no later than 1593, although the revisions must have been made some time later. See Gabrieli and Melchioli (eds.), *Sir Thomas More* (Manchester: Manchester University Press, 1992), 11–12. References are from this edition. Scott McMillin argues that the original play and the Hand D addition were written in the early 1590s; following censorship the book was laid aside and revised for performance by the Admiral's Men in the early 1600s ('*The Book of Sir Thomas More*: Dates and Acting Companies', in T. H. Howard-Hill (ed.), in *Shakespeare and Sir Thomas More: Essays on the Play and its Shakespearian Interest*, [Cambridge: Cambridge University Press, 1989], 131–51). John Jowett in the forthcoming Arden edition argues for a later date for the play's composition and censorship, seeing the play as part of the early seventeenth-century dramatic interest in the reign of Henry VIII. I am grateful to Professor Jowett for allowing me to see his work in advance of publication.

as a folk hero than a Catholic martyr, it would seem that the dramatists who collaborated on the play were consciously avoiding the controversial political aspects of their subject's career, tacitly acknowledging the ideological sensitivity of the material and the possible reactions of the censor. It is equally clear that, in planning to represent on the stage popular rebellion against an immigrant workforce, the dramatists badly misjudged the mood of authority. The depiction of the riots in London against 'aliens' provoked a draconian response from Tilney, and it is probable that his response was shaped by the topicality of the material. In May 1593, for example, a manifesto urging an attack on the 'strangers' was posted on the wall of the Dutch churchyard in Austin Friars, which warned—in rhetoric evocative of the insurgents in *Thomas More*—that unless the migrants were made to depart 'apprentices will rise to the number of 2,336. And [they] will down with the Flemings and strangers'. The Council ordered searches and countenanced torture to discover the perpetrators of the libels against the foreign communities from which the state derived so much advantage.[11] If the play came before the Master of the Revels at this time, it would undoubtedly have been regarded as fuelling antagonism against the migrants, and Tilney's rigorous censorship can be seen as part of wider measures to curb such hostilities. Throughout the manuscript, he demanded changes and made excisions to scenes alluding to the rebellion. He has marked for omission the entire first scene of the play, in which the London artisans are depicted as blatantly wronged: in that scene Francis de Bard abducts Doll Williamson and Caveler steals two doves, which have been purchased in Cheapside by Doll's husband. Tilney objected to this sympathetic representation of the origins of the uprising as well as to the actual rebellion, as is apparent from his marginal directive:

> Leave out the insurrection wholly and the cause thereof and begin with Thomas More at the mayor's sessions with a report afterwards of his good service done being Shrive of London upon a mutiny against the Lombards only by a short report and not otherwise at your own perils.   E. Tilney

Before the depiction of the insurrection, there is occasional censorship, notably where the earls of Shrewsbury and Surrey comment on the restiveness of the Commons, using expressions such as 'dangerous times', 'frowning vulgar brow', 'distracted countenance of grief', and 'displeased commons of the city' (1.3). Here Tilney has written in the margin, 'Mend this'. One or more leaves of the manuscript have been lost and thus the scene depicting the riot by the apprentices is incomplete, breaking off when the threats of the insurgents against the strangers are at their most violent and resuming with the laying down of weapons after More's appeal to the crowd. The tenor of the censored episode is characterized by Lincoln's rousing and ironic speech to the populace which even today has a familiar ring:

---

[11] See Andrew Petegree, *Foreign Protestant Communities in Sixteenth Century London* (Oxford: Oxford University Press, 1986), 292.

Come gallant bloods, you, whose free souls do scorn
To bear th'enforced wrongs of aliens.
Add rage to resolution, fire the houses
Of those audacious strangers [...]
Shall those enjoy more privilege than we
In our own country? Let's then become their slaves.
Since justice keeps not them in greater awe,
We'll be ourselves rough ministers at law.[12]

Lincoln's inflammatory words have limited impact on the crowd, who soon begin to fear for their lives, but they were forceful enough to disturb Tilney, who has marked for omission all that is extant of the scene.

Censors are not in the least interested in what constitutes a good play, and this is very much in evidence in Tilney's imperatives: entire scenes are to be omitted and replaced simply by reports of the events they represent. George Chapman was to complain a decade later that following the intervention of the Master of the Revels his *Byron* plays were 'poor dismembered poems'.[13] This is far more the case with *The Book of Sir Thomas More*. The censor left the play in a mutilated condition, and if all his strictures were obeyed, nearly a quarter of the play would have been lost. Additions and revised passages suggest that some attempt was made to salvage the play, although how immediate this was to Tilney's censorship is open to question.

The manuscript of *Sir Thomas More* with its excisions poses an enormous challenge to modern editors. Moreover, inserted into the original manuscript are six additional passages in five different hands, designated A, B, C, D, and E, which are recastings of original scenes marked for omission, extensions of certain other scenes, or allegedly reconstructions of scenes from the original manuscript which had been lost.[14] Hand D is attributed to Shakespeare.[15] Various hypotheses have been advanced about the additional passages and whether they pre- or postdate Tilney's censorship. Only one of the additional sheets, which contains an elaborate reworking of the incomplete apprentice riot, is directly relevant to Tilney's objections. As several scholars have commented, if this is consequent on Tilney's censorship, the revisers pay comparatively little heed to his injunctions. Lincoln's rousing speech quoted above appears in both the original manuscript and in the revised version in Hand B. Tilney objected to the use of the word 'strangers', changing it to 'Lombards', yet 'strangers' is used seven times in the addition made by Hand D in which More pacifies the insurgents. At the same time, it could be argued that Shakespeare's addition has been in part undertaken in recognition of censorship. Although the term 'stranger' is reiterated in the Hand D passage, seemingly disregarding Tilney's objection, it is employed as part of More's rhetorical

---

[12] See Gabrieli and Melchiori, 'Rejected or Alternative Passages', 209.

[13] Dedication to Sir Thomas Walsingham, *The Conspiracy and Tragedy of Charles Duke of Byron Marshall of France* (London: 1608).

[14] See *The Book of Sir Thomas More*, W.W. Greg (ed.), Malone Society Reprints (Oxford: Oxford University Press, 1911), Introduction, viii–ix.

[15] In the Revels edition the scene written by Hand D corresponds to 2.3.1–159.

strategy to elicit sympathy for the foreigners and the emphasis is on More's subduing of the riot by entreating the rioters to be calm and compassionate.[16] But, above all, the warning which finally persuades the rebels to be 'rul'd' by More lies in the speech on kingship and divine right with its assertion that by rising against the King, who has been lent 'his throne', 'his sword', and his 'own name' by God, they are in fact rising against God himself. Their insubordination is jeopardizing their souls. In this passage the stress has shifted from the grievances of the commons to respect for order and degree and the heinousness of rebellion. Even if the scene was written in ignorance of Tilney's precise stipulations,[17] Hand D gave the company what they needed: a politically orthodox scene to counter popular xenophobia.[18] Nevertheless, the passages may have offered insufficient ideological counterweight to the forceful representation of treason elsewhere in the play, since there is little evidence that the play was performed, at least not in the period immediate to Tilney's censorship.[19]

The directives and textual excisions evident in the manuscript of *Sir Thomas More* indicate some of the preoccupations of late Elizabethan censorship. Even sixty years after the event, More's opposition to the King against the backdrop of Reformation politics was judged too sensitive or provocative for performance. Shakespeare only dramatized the reign of Henry VIII—in his last history play—almost a decade after the end of the Tudor dynasty with the death of Elizabeth I in 1603. Throughout the 1590s it was feared that public order would break down. Besides the repeated protests at foreign and refugee communities, there were other disturbances caused by worsening economic circumstances in the capital.[20] That a popular, disaffected figure might emerge to offer leadership and articulate grievance was a fear conveyed in 1599 by Robert Cecil: 'When has England felt any harm by soldiers or gentlemen, or men of worth . . . Some Jack Cade or Jack Straw and such rascals are those that have endangered the kingdom.'[21] Fear of popular protest or riot seems to have extended to its representation on the stage. No play of the period endorses rebellion and when uprisings, such as those led by Jack Cade and Jack Straw, are depicted they have a comic element, almost parodying rebel causes.

[16] The definition 'stranger' was not necessarily pejorative. In 1593 in his defence in Parliament of Protestant immigrants Sir John Woolley argued 'in the days of Queen Mary when our cause was as theirs is now, those countries did allow us that liberty which now we seek to deny them. They are strangers now, we may be strangers hereafter. So let us do as we would be done to'. Quoted by Pettegree, 291. The designation is similarly nuanced by Shakespeare's More.

[17] Scott McMillin, 71.

[18] Some such scene must have been in the original play since the Mayor praises More for having preserved the City from 'a most dangerous fierce commotion' (2.3.190).

[19] McMillin argues that the play written in the early 1590s was revised a decade later and performed by the Admiral's Men at the Fortune. The only evidence for performance is the occurrence of the name of the actor Thomas Goodale.

[20] See Peter Clark, *The European Crisis of the 1590s: Essays in Comparative History* (London: Allen and Unwin, 1985), 50–4.

[21] *Calendar of State Papers, Domestic Series*, 1598–1601 (hereafter *CSPD*), CCLXXIII, 352.

TEXTUAL TRACES

From the evidence of the playbook of *Sir Thomas More* Shakespeare emerges fairly early in his career in the role of an adapter of dramatic writing in response to or mindful of its political exigencies. Had some of his own plays of the same period survived in manuscript, showing cuts made by, or in other cases, anticipation of censorship a different perspective might be offered.[22] In the absence of a manuscript disclosing censorial interference with a play, printed texts may also, by their anomalies and variations, suggest some censorship of the copy-text. A number of the English history plays composed during the 1590s were published in different editions, and although the textual discrepancies may seem slight or insignificant, from the nature of the subject matter they may with some confidence be ascribed to the interference of the censor. In general, censored material appears to have been included or reinstated when the copy-text consisted of authorial papers or when, as for example in the case of *Richard II*, publication occurred at a date considerably later than that of its first performance. With time and distance we may surmise that such material might lose its provocative edge and be restored later in the play's theatrical life. Conversely, a play, scene, or line may inadvertently become topical. Generally speaking, in this period the closer a copy-text is to performance the more likely it is to transmit incursions of censorship.

Here it is useful to distinguish between theatrical and literary censorship in the Elizabethan and Jacobean periods.[23] Initially, the licensing of plays for stage and for publication came under different auspices. Plays for the stage were perused and licensed by the Master of the Revels, and of the few extant dramatic manuscripts that have been censored some display the markings of successive Masters of the Revels: Tilney, George Buc, and Henry Herbert. Plays intended for publication had to be entered into the Stationers' Register for the registration of copyright and this could only be done once the work had been authorized by an ecclesiastic press licenser, the Archbishop of Canterbury or Bishop of London, or one of his subordinates. In theory, then, plays were subject to more rigorous censorship than any other genre because of the twofold process of censorship. On occasions, however, the authority of the Master of the Revels alone seems to have sufficed, as certain playbooks are entered in the Stationers' Register with the allowance merely of one of the wardens of the company. Presumably the stationers had tacitly accepted the stage licence, and any attendant manuscript deletions and alterations, in lieu of ecclesiastical sanction. By 1606 the Revels Office seems to have extended its official power to include licensing

---

[22] See Grace Ioppolo, *Dramatists and their Manuscripts in the Age of Shakespeare, Jonson, Middleton and Heyward: Authorship, Authority and the Playhouse* (London: Routledge, 2006).

[23] See Cyndia Clegg, *Press Censorship in Elizabethan England* (Cambridge: Cambridge University Press, 1997), 57–65.

for publication, for it is from this date that George Buc's name appears in the Register as the source of authorization.

As to the impression made by censorship on Shakespeare's writing, most of the evidence can be deduced only from a close analysis of different editions of plays whose variants suggest the intervention of the censor. Censorial interference would seem to have occurred early in Shakespeare's career. The two latter plays of his first trilogy, *2* and *3 Henry VI*, exist in earlier editions, *The First Part of the Contention of the Two Famous Houses of York and Lancaster* (1594) and *The True Tragedy of Richard Duke of York* (1595), and some small variations between the texts can be interpreted as traces of censorship.[24] In dramatizing the 'contention' between York and Lancaster which was to lead, some would argue providentially, to the defeat of Richard III and the establishment of a new dynasty with the Queen's grandfather Henry VII, Shakespeare was dealing with one of the most sustained and bloody conflicts of English history. Moreover, in representing the defeat of Henry VI, Shakespeare engaged with the highly controversial matter of the deposition of a king. In 1600, when the historian John Hayward was on trial for writing an allegedly seditious history, *The First Part of the Life and Reign of King Henry IV*, one of the charges put to him by the Lord Chief Justice was that he had maintained 'that it might be lawful for the subject to depose the king' and had added 'many persuadings in allowance thereof'.[25] It may be assumed that fears expressed about the ideological implications of written history were similarly aroused by the performance of history.

In the Henry VI plays, although there is no indication that the deposition of Henry VI prompted censorship, the ignominious treatment of the King by the Yorkist faction may have caused some muting of the text. At one point in *The First Part of the Contention*, after York has killed Clifford, he challenges the absent King. 'Come fearful Henry grovelling on thy face, | Yield up thy crown to the Prince of York' (sig. H3r). This humiliating challenge does not appear in the Folio *Henry VI*, the copy-text of which is thought to be theatrical.[26] Absent also in the latter is Warwick's exhortation that York should usurp the crown while Warwick will 'rouse the bear, | Environed with ten thousand ragged-staves' in York's defence. The 'bear' alludes to Warwick's decorative standard, while the image captures the fearful spectre of a popular uprising. That the Folio text represents a text that has encountered some censorial interference is substantiated by changes to the representation of the Cade rebellion and the absence of allusions to the Irish rebellion. Both plays offer a counter-revolutionary view, in that Cade's rebellion and pretensions to the crown are presented as a travesty of York's. There are, however, signs that Cade's rhetoric has been toned down in the Folio text, notably in the scene where Cade, in parlay with Stafford, retaliates that it is the King

---

[24] The Oxford editors adopt the titles by which the plays were first known, although the edited texts are those of the Folio.

[25] *CSPD 1598–1601*, CCLXXIV, 404.

[26] The names of the actors Bevis and Holland as among Cade's followers are included at the beginning of 4.2, which suggests that the text has been prepared for performance.

who should seek pardon from him, rather than the other way round; the threat 'bid the king come to me . . . or otherwise I'll have his Crown tell him, ere it be long' (sig. F4v) is missing in *The Contention*, as is his rallying call to his followers 'now we'll march to London, for tomorrow I mean to sit in the king's seat at Westminster' (sig. F4v). There are also changes to the Irish rebellion which provides York with an army. *The Contention* alludes to the rebel leader 'Wild O'Neill', who is described as leading a stubborn, uncontrolled, and proud army and representing a real threat. The Folio, on the other hand, contains only one specific reference to the Irish, as the Cardinal admonishes the squabbling Suffolk and York that the 'uncivil kerns of Ireland are in arms'. The differences between the texts in the representation of the Irish rebellion, specifically the absence of O'Neill, can be accounted for by assuming that censorship of the 1590s text was transmitted to the performance-based text published in 1623. In the mid-1590s, Hugh O'Neill, Earl of Tyrone, head of one of the most powerful of the Anglo-Irish clans, was mobilizing forces against the English with the ambition of making Ulster an independent kingdom.[27] He accorded himself the title of 'the O'Neill' and with it almost monarchical status. In England he was declared a traitor, although successive attempts to subdue his campaign failed, culminating in what was perceived as the dishonourable truce of the Earl of Essex with Tyrone in 1599. The attempt of the Elizabethan state to subdue Ireland was so sensitive to disadvantageous comment that by the end of the decade it was forbidden 'on pain of death, to write or speak of Irish affairs'.[28] As Andrew Hadfield has commented, it is perhaps no accident that not one serious treatise on or history of Ireland was published in that decade.[29] Shakespeare's short but crucial account of the Irish rebellion in the reign of Henry VI had resonances that invited censorship at a moment when Irish confrontation came to present ever more threats to crown ascendancy.

The most often cited case of Elizabethan censorship is that of *Richard II*, a play that depicts the deposition of Richard II by his cousin Henry Bolingbroke and culminates in the murder of Richard at Bolingbroke's instigation. Richard's reign had been dramatized before in the anonymous plays *Thomas of Woodstock* and *The Life and Death of Jack Straw* and his downfall had been recalled in non-dramatic literature, notably *The Mirror for Magistrates*, as exemplifying the consequences of tyrannical rule and the turn of Fortune's wheel. But no surviving play of the period represents the King on the stage surrendering—as he maintains—his God-given power to a political opponent who is only indirectly in line to the succession.

Censorship of the play can be inferred from the publication of different texts. In all three Elizabethan editions of *Richard II* the lengthy scene in which the King is deposed, familiar to modern spectators and readers, is absent from the play. The scene, which brings

[27] See Stephen O'Neill, *Staging Ireland: Representations in Shakespeare and Renaissance Drama* (Dublin: Four Courts, 2007), 69–90. O'Neill argues that while the Folio text may appear to be 'toned down', in the earlier text there is a definite sense that the crisis will be averted. Both texts show anxiety about the representation of the Irish war.

[28] *CSPD 1598–1601*, CCLXXI, 225.

[29] 'Censoring Ireland in Elizabethan England, 1580–1600', in Hadfield (ed.), *Literature and Censorship in Renaissance England* (London: Palgrave Macmillan, 2001), 151.

together King Richard and his cousin, Henry Bolingbroke, soon to be crowned Henry IV, was only restored to the play in the Jacobean edition of 1608. Dramaturgically, there is great contrast between the histrionic Richard, who luxuriates in the grief of his downfall, and the near silent Bolingbroke, who watches Richard playing out his doom. Moreover, the iconography of the scene is startling as Richard hands over his crown and sceptre to Bolingbroke, making his forced deposition seem more like a willing abdication:

> BOLINGBROKE: Are you contented to resign the crown?
> RICHARD: Ay, no; no, ay; for I must nothing be;
>   Therefore no, no, for I resign to thee.
>   Now mark me how I will undo myself.
>   I give this heavy weight from off my head,
>   [*Bolingbroke accepts the crown*]
>   And this unwieldy sceptre from my hand,
>   [*Bolingbroke accepts the sceptre*]
>   The pride of kingly sway from out my heart.
>   With mine own tears I wash away my balm,
>   With mine own hands I give away my crown,
>   With mine own tongue deny my sacred state,
>   With mine own breath release all duteous oaths.
>   All pomp and majesty I do forswear.
>
> (4.1.190–201)

The title-page of an extant Quarto draws attention to the new material and its recent staging: 'With new additions of the Parliament Scene, and the deposing of King Richard. As it hath been lately acted by the King's Majesty's Servants, at the Globe'. Critics and editors generally accept, however, that the addition to the 1608 text does not actually represent new writing, but the restoration of lines removed from the play in the previous decade.

The play had been licensed for publication on 29 August 1597.[30] In this instance, authority to publish was granted by one of the wardens of the Stationers' Company and not by an ecclesiastical licenser. Although it was not uncommon for plays to be entered under the hands of wardens, a warden did not officially have the power to censor the work he licensed for publication. In all likelihood the warden accepted that *Richard II* had already been scrutinized by the Master of the Revels and that provocative material had been removed prior to performance and thus the censored performance text of the play made its way into print.

Clearly, in representing, if not directly articulating, a doctrine of resistance to tyranny, Shakespeare was engaging with sensitive ideological issues. However unjust the monarch, rebellion against him contravened the Elizabethan code that subjects should not oppose wicked or tyrannical kings, but instead trust their fate to providence. The Master of the Revels, as theatrical censor, could hardly alter the facts of a history

---

[30] Edward Arber, *A Transcript of the Registers of the Company of Stationers of London, 1554–1640,* 5 vols. (London: privately published, 1874–84), 3: 23.

play—Richard II numbered among the few English kings deposed from the throne—but he could suppress the stage spectacle of a ritualized dethronement. The fact that the deposition scene was not restored to the play until 1608 and that, despite its early popularity, there were no further editions of the play between 1597 and 1608 implies that at a time of uncertain succession and political tension *Richard II* was perceived as potentially complicit with the ambitions of pretenders to the throne and that therefore it constituted part of an oppositional discourse.[31]

The play as a whole is ambiguous about the deposition of the King. Other passages in the play argue against any transgression of authority, and there are resonances of the Shakespearean passage in *Sir Thomas More* when More argues that the insurgents are in 'arms 'gainst God' (2.3.103). John of Gaunt refuses to respond to the Duchess of Gloucester's plea to avenge the death of her husband, Thomas of Woodstock:

> JOHN OF GAUNT: God's is the quarrel; for God's substitute,
> His deputy anointed in his sight,
> Hath caused his death; the which if wrongfully,
> Let heaven revenge, for I may never lift
> An angry arm against His minister.
>
> (1.2.37–41)

Yet, Gaunt's articulation of Tudor-style passive obedience serves only to reveal how harmful and disabling such a belief can be in actuality: Gaunt's loyalty reduces him and his fellow citizens to impotence in the face of mounting injustices. Similarly, the Bishop of Carlisle's denunciation of Bolingbroke and his passionate articulation of the doctrine of non-resistance before Richard's deposition (4.1.105–40) falls on deaf ears. Carlisle's prophecy that 'the blood of England shall manure the ground' does not impinge on Bolingbroke's advance to power which is, to all intents and purposes, achieved without impediment. Although the lines of Gaunt and of Carlisle have little bearing on the outcome of events, they do, nonetheless, point to dramatic circumspection in varying the perspectives offered on Richard's deposition and thus to a mitigation of the subversive subject matter of the play.

Another play written in the 1590s, Christopher Marlowe's *Edward II*, also shows a King losing his grip on power through misrule, leading to his deposition and murder. As far as we know, Marlowe's tragedy, published after his death, encountered no official opposition to performance or publication, and this has encouraged inferences of leniency or inconsistency of censorship.[32] There is, however, a crucial difference in the shape of the plays' narratives. In *Edward II* the usurper Mortimer is arrested and

---

[31] It is well known that the Lord Chamberlain's Men were specially commissioned 'to play the deposing and killing of King Richard II' on the eve of the Essex rebellion. Brought to trial, one of the actors, Augustine Phillips, maintained that they had wanted to play something else—*Richard II* being 'long out of use'—but agreed to perform it when they were offered forty shillings above the usual rate. *CSPD 1598–1601*, CCLXXVIII, 578.

[32] See Richard Dutton, *Mastering the Revels: the Regulation and Censorship of English Renaissance Drama* (Basingstoke: Macmillan, 1991), 125.

executed on the order of the murdered king's heir, and the play's final tableau presents the king's hearse, on which lies the head of the traitor. This is very different from *Richard II*, in which there is no public humiliation of the traitor and no restitution of legitimate God-given authority. Edward also recognizes that the presence of his son ensures the continuation of his line: 'So shall not Edward's vine be perished, | But Edward's name survive though Edward dies' (5.2.47–8). Richard's death, on the other hand, is the death of his line, and the link between Richard as the last Plantagenet and Elizabeth I as the last Tudor would not have been lost on contemporaries. All in all, it is not difficult to see why the censor should intervene in *Richard II* and not in Marlowe's play, and his different responses give an indication of the reigning sensibilities.

The late-Elizabethan close surveillance of theatre production is further illustrated in one of the sequels to *Richard II*, *2 Henry IV*. The two plays on Henry IV dramatize what the chroniclers described as a troubled reign: Richard II is rehabilitated in memory and the King faces challenges to his authority from the nobility. *2 Henry IV* re-presents the opposition to Henry IV witnessed in *1 Henry IV* with the exception that the rebel faction is now led by the Archbishop of York and is lent a better cause than the Percy rebellion in *1 Henry IV*. In the second part, the rebels are defeated, not by heroic action as in Part 1, but by Prince John's shameless betrayal of his word after the Archbishop's party have in good faith laid down their arms. Prior to this, the Archbishop eloquently defends his opposition:

> Hear me more plainly.
> I have in equal balance justly weighed
> What wrongs our arms may do, what wrongs we suffer,
> And find our griefs heavier than our offences.
> We see which way the stream of time doth run,
> And are enforced from our most quiet shore
> By the rough torrent of occasion,
> And have the summary of all our griefs,
> When time shall serve, to show in articles,
> Which long ere this we offered to the King,
> And might by no suit gain our audience.   (4.1.66–76)

The first published text of *2 Henry IV* appeared in 1598, and in this version of the play, which is considerably shorter than the Folio text, these lines do not appear. Although the omission could be a cut for performance, it is surely not accidental that, like other missing Quarto passages, it relates to grievance and rebellion against the king. Another such passage is the Archbishop's earlier allusion to disaffection with Henry IV and nostalgia for the reign of Richard II:

> Let us on,
> And publish the occasion of our arms.
> The commonwealth is sick of their own choice [. . .]
> What trust is in these times?
> They that, when Richard lived, would have him die

Are now become enamoured on his grave.
Thou that threw'st dust upon his goodly head,
When through proud London he came sighing on
After th'admired heels of Bolingbroke,
Cri'st now, 'O earth, yield us that King again,
And take thou this!' O thoughts of men accursed!
Past and to come seems best; things present, worst.

(1.3.85–108)

The Quarto omission would appear to be part of a serial change to mute the representation of the rebellion and to suppress the persuasive articulation of the rebels' cause. Other cuts include the Earl of Morton's reflection that the 'bishop turns insurrection to religion' (1.1.200) and Bardolph's allusion to the insurrection as 'this great work— | Which is almost to pluck a Kingdom down' (1.3.48–9). Certainly, 2 Henry IV is one of the few plays of the period to represent a convincing assault on the Crown, and in the context of the late 1590s it would not be surprising that the play should encounter censorship.

Shakespeare's last Elizabethan history play was Henry V, and in many respects this play, in its patriotic celebration of Henry's victories against the French, would seem one of the least likely of dramas to incur censorship. But the play was composed and performed at the new Globe playhouse in charged and volatile political times. The Earl of Essex, the Queen's favourite, had been dispatched to Ireland to defeat the Earl of Tyrone, and one of the few topical references in Shakespeare is made in the fifth Chorus, which compares Henry to Essex and projects the Earl's triumphant return from Munster:

But now behold,
In the quick forge and working-house of thought,
How London doth pour out her citizens.
The Mayor and all his breathren, in best sort,
Like to the senators of th'antique Rome
With the plebeians swarming at their heels,
Go forth and fetch their conqu'ring Caesar in—
As, by a lower but high-loving likelihood,
Were now the General of our gracious Empress—
As in good time he may—from Ireland coming,
Bringing rebellion broachèd on his sword,
How many would the peaceful city quit
To welcome him!   (5.0.22–34)

As has been observed, Henry V (as it appears in the Folio) derives something of its appeal from public sensitivity to Essex's campaign in Ireland.[33] Such optimism and

---

[33] See Christopher Highley, *Shakespeare, Spenser and the Crisis in Ireland* (Cambridge: Cambridge University Press, 1997), 135. The high expectations of Essex, which chime with the language of the Chorus, are conveyed in a speech delivered by the Lord Chamberlain, 28 November 1599: 'with such a spirit as my Lord of Essex, the army sent to Ireland might have passed through Spain and endangered the kingdom', *CSPD*, CCLXXIII, 351.

confidence were short-lived as news of what was seen as Essex's dishonourable truce with Tyrone reached London, and as the General fell from the favour of his 'gracious Empress' hasty alterations must have been made to *Henry V*. Essex's disgrace does not account for the omission of the entire Chorus from the early text of *Henry V*; but any lines which might cause an association between the heroic Henry and the now traitor Essex would have been suspect. The exuberant mood and tone of the Chorus with its celebration of nationhood was ill-timed in the context of current colonialist failures, and it was presumably excised—by the censor or in anticipation of censorship—because it was no longer in the right key.

One of the features of artistic censorship is that it is not governed by abiding or consistent principles and concerns. Changes in religious, domestic, and foreign policy helped to dictate censorship, as did the ascendancy of particular factions at court. A reference, allusion, or dramatic episode may pass without comment in one context, but may be judged libellous, offensive, even treasonous in another. A familiar example of this is Shakespeare's original naming of Falstaff in *1* and *2 Henry IV* as Oldcastle, a name which he took over from a pre-text *The Famous Victories of Henry the Fifth*, having loosely modelled Hal's drinking companion and surrogate father on the character in that play. Such an ignoble stage representation of a Lollard martyr celebrated by John Foxe was apparently judged slanderous by Oldcastle's descendants, and at some stage in the play's performance history, though apparently after stage licensing, the character was renamed Falstaff.[34] It is interesting that no such pressures were brought to bear on *The Famous Victories*, where the name of Oldcastle remains in the text. This may simply be because Oldcastle is usually referred to as 'Jockey' and so the revered family name does not resonate much on stage or in the text. Neither is Oldcastle so prominent a character as Falstaff. But as with most cases of early modern censorship, the censorship of *1 Henry IV* is very much tied to the moment of production: William Brooke, Lord Cobham, Oldcastle's descendant, was Lord Chamberlain for eight months from August 1596, at which time the play was enjoying great success. *The Famous Victories*, on the other hand, would have been licensed and performed a decade earlier and, once licensed for performance, it did not, in this period, need to be relicensed for publication.

JACOBEAN CENSORSHIP

The accession of James I in 1603 stimulated a considerable change in the configuration of theatre practice and the preoccupations of censorship. Shakespeare's company was

---

[34] See Clare, '*Art Made Tongue-Tied by Authority*', 76–9; Peter Corbin and Douglas Sedge, *The Oldcastle Controversy: Sir John Oldcastle, Part I and The Famous Victories of Henry V* (Manchester: Manchester University Press, 1991), 9–12; David McKeen, *A Memory of Honour: The Life of William Brooke, Lord Cobham*, 2 vols. (Salzburg: Institut für Anglistik und Amerikanistik, 1986), and Gary Taylor, 'The Fortunes of Oldcastle', *Shakespeare Survey* 38 (1985), 85–100.

promoted to the King's Men and their leading rival, the Admiral's Men, came under the patronage of Prince Henry. The Queen gave her patronage to the Earl of Worcester's Men and to the Children of the Chapel. For a brief period censorship seems to have been relaxed, perhaps because the job of the Master of the Revels was temporarily split. The patent awarded to the Children of the Queen's Revels in 1604 entrusted the 'approbation and allowance' of plays to the poet and dramatist Samuel Daniel, apparently as a result of the Queen's direct intervention.[35] Playwrights were clearly testing the new political waters: Marston, Jonson, Chapman, and the lesser known John Day all produced plays satirizing, with various degrees of obliquity, the court and the King and the King's Scottish favourites. With some relaxation of censorship and divided authority, provocative plays may have got through the licensing system—*Eastward Ho* was not, in fact, submitted for licence—but once reports had been made of their contents, reprisal followed. Jonson and Chapman were imprisoned for their part in the composition of *Eastward Ho*. Several of the actors who had performed in Day's *Isle of Gulls* were imprisoned[36] and the Queen's Company was deprived of its royal patronage. George Buc succeeded Edmond Tilney as Master of the Revels in 1606, and from manuscript evidence of his censorship—notably in an unnamed play, probably by Middleton,[37] and in *The Tragedy of Sir John van Olden Barnavelt* by Massinger and Fletcher—Buc acted to suppress material which undermined the authority and interests of the Crown.

Apart from the initial, but temporary, division in the power of the Master of the Revels, the system of Elizabethan censorship remained in place. Curiously, one of the few new directives related to swearing and blasphemy on the stage. The Act to Restrain the Abuses of Players, passed in 1606, might suggest legislative measures to curb satire, but its ambit is fairly local. Players were banned from the use of 'the holy Name of God or of Christ Jesus , or of the Holy Ghost or of the Trinity'. The Act can be seen as a gesture toward Parliamentary Puritans who had repeatedly objected to the profanity of the stage. Its impact seems to have been minimal, limited to the excision of oaths, either in the playhouse or by the Master of the Revels. One of the more interesting cases showing the effects of the Act concerns the text of Marlowe's *Doctor Faustus*, which was published in 1616 consequent to a Jacobean revival. The relationship to the earlier text published in 1604 is complex; only relevant here is the muting

[35] Chambers, *The Elizabethan Stage*, 2: 49.

[36] Sir Edward Hoby wrote to Thomas Edmondes that the play had been discussed in the Commons and consequently 'sundry were committed to Bridewell'. See Thomas Birch, *The Court and Times of James the First*, 2 vols. (London, 1848), 1: 60–1.

[37] The play has been known as *The Second Maiden's Tragedy*—the title given to it by Buc when he licensed it in 1611. See *The Second Maiden's Tragedy*, Anne Lancashire (ed.), (Manchester: Manchester University Press, 1978). Cuts and censored passages are in Appendix A. However, Julia Briggs, in her edition for the Oxford Middleton, calls the play *The Lady's Tragedy* and helpfully provides parallel texts to enable the reader 'to see how a Jacobean tragedy, written for the King's Men at the height of their success, underwent processes of censorship, addition, and revision before and during rehearsal'. See Gary Taylor and John Lavagnino (eds.), *Thomas Middleton: The Collected Works* (Oxford: Clarendon Press, 2007), 833–906.

of doctrinal allusions, which would seem to have been dictated by the terms of the Act. Faustus apprehends heaven and hell in the final soliloquy; yet these are differently nuanced in the two texts. He calls on Christ's blood in both versions: but there is no evocation of the blood streaming in the firmament in the later text, which also omits the line which contains Faustus's plea: 'Yet for Christ's sake, whose blood hath ransomed me'.[38] In the pre-1606 text Faustus imagines God thus: 'And see where God stretcheth out his arme, And bends his ireful browes' (ll. 1468–9). In comparison, the 1616 text is depersonalized and less immediate: 'And see a threatening arme, an angry Brow'. Earlier Reformation censorship had prohibited the appearance of the deity, while the censorship of *Doctor Faustus* suggests further inhibition in restricting graphic evocations of or iconographic references to the deity.

Comparatively few of Shakespeare's Jacobean plays were published prior to the Folio, which limits the opportunity to explore their possible censorship. But there is every indication that as the leading dramatist of the King's Men he was highly conscious of the bounds of censorship. Unlike Jonson, Marston, and Middleton, Shakespeare appears to have experienced no investigations into the purport of his plays. He did not write for the children's companies, who were known for their provocative and audacious productions, and again, unlike major competitors, he was not attracted to satire.

One play which does appear to have encountered some censorship, or was at least revised in deference to official suggestion, is *King Lear*. The play was published in a Quarto text of 1608 in a version which is substantively different from that of the Folio.[39] It is currently thought that the latter is a performance-oriented revision of the Quarto and as such would incorporate any censorial interventions. One of the most notable divergences between the texts is in the representation of the French invasion in support of Lear, led by Cordelia and her husband, the King of France. In the Folio, allusions to French military support have been removed to the extent that an entire scene (Sc. 17) between the disguised Kent and a Gentleman, reporting the return of the King of France to confront internal dissent, has gone. Also omitted is Albany's reference to the French invasion which, with some misgivings, he must oppose:

> Where I could not be honest
> I never yet was valiant. For this business
> It touches us as France invades our land:
> Yet bold's the King, with others whom I fear,
> More just and heavy causes make oppose
>
> (Sc. 22, 2.25–9)

---

[38] An earlier 'B' text omission is similar: the Old Man's reminder of Christ's atonement: 'But mercy Faustus of thy Saviour sweet | Whose blood alone must wash away thy guilt' (1312–14). See W. W. Greg, *Doctor Faustus 1604–1616: Parallel Texts* (Oxford: Clarendon Press, 1950). All quotations are from this edition.

[39] The two texts, *The History of King Lear* and *The Tragedy of King Lear* are printed and given independent status in the Oxford Shakespeare.

On a general comparison of the two texts, it is notable how in the Quarto Cordelia and the King of France invade with the express purpose of claiming Cordelia's portion of the kingdom, which is then modified to a quest to avenge Lear. The King retires to France to settle his own internal disputes and Cordelia is left with the foreign army, represented on the stage as the direction makes clear: 'Alarum. The powers of France over the stage, Queen Cordelia with her father in her hand' (Sc. 23). The corresponding Folio direction (5.2) has no reference to the constitution of Cordelia's army. Various hypotheses have been made about the promptings for such a serial change to Cordelia's role.[40] Censorship must number strongly among them. Jacobean foreign policy, in contradistinction from the warmongering rhetoric of the previous decade, was directed toward European peace and alliance. *King Lear*, in its depiction on stage of a French invasion, even one prompted to restore the rightful king, may well have caused some disquiet. There is now near-consensus that Shakespeare revised the play and, as the serial change to the French invasion suggests, one of the pressures behind the revision may well have been to expunge as far as possible any mention of war with France. Other omissions in the Folio point to and substantiate the case for censorship. In *The History of King Lear* in an early scene between Lear and his fool, the latter's ditty, in which he claims that Lear's actions have made the King as much a fool as the Fool, prompts Lear's 'Dost thou call me fool, boy?' (Sc. 4). The ditty, Lear's response, and the Fool's ironic retort that he does not have a monopoly on foolishness—lords and great men would not allow it—are missing from the later text. Such references are provocatively topical: James I had been described as the wisest Fool in Christendom and the granting of monopolies to royal favourites was much resented by those who were excluded from the privilege. In all likelihood, George Buc, who licensed the play, excised the passage.

This essay has sought to demonstrate how censorship involves contiguous processes of control, implementation or practice, and compliance. Documents of control have survived; manuscripts and other contemporary materials record implementation, while manuscript markings and textual discrepancies indicate the direction of censorship operative during Shakespeare's working life. Its primary concerns evidently relate to the maintenance of public order and the preservation of the monarchy and its interests, both domestic and foreign. The preoccupations of censorship were bound up with current pressure points, whether those were anti-alien riots, the Irish war, the question of the succession or the cementing of European alliances. Levels of censorship were not consistent and, again, can be seen to relate to the political pressures of the moment: the late Elizabethan period can be seen as fairly repressive, the early Jacobean much less so. What is less easy to assess is compliance. To what extent did dramatists work within the parameters of censorship? Here attention has to be directed at negotiation and the way playwrights developed strategies to circumvent censorship. As Jonson's prologue in *Poetaster* makes clear, situating the play in the ancient world or in an imaginary

---

[40] See Gary Taylor and Michael Warren (eds.), *The Division of the Kingdoms: Shakespeare's Two Versions of King Lear* (Oxford: Clarendon Press, 1983), 75–117.

European court licenced some freedom. Similarly, as we have seen in *Sir Thomas More* and *Richard II*, plays juxtapose the orthodox and the unorthodox so that meaning remains elusive, and, as some commentators have maintained, may have been tacitly understood by dramatist and censor as denoting the way to work within the system.[41] Commercial pressures must also, however, be taken into the equation; dramatists had to negotiate with their audiences. The Prologue to Day's *Isle of Gulls* (1606) neatly encapsulates one of the dilemmas of the early modern playwright. The play begins with two gentlemen—seated on the stage as auditors—questioning one of the players, acting as Prologue, what the play is about. Referring to the echo of the notorious play of the previous decade, *The Isle of Dogs*, the first gentleman asks 'But why doth he call his play *The Isle of Gulls*, it begets much expectation'. The Prologue denies that the play contains any current political associations, maintaining that it does not 'figure any certain state, or private government'. The first gentleman is unconvinced and persists in his suspicion of the playwright's intentions: 'Out a question, he hath promised thee some fee thou pleadest so hard for him'. Finally, the Prologue replies in mock exasperation: 'Alas, Gentlemen, how is't possible to content you? You will have railing, and invectives, which our author neither dares nor affects . . . yet all these we must have, and all in one play, or, 'tis already condemned to the hell of eternal disgrace.' (1.0.29–75). Audiences demanded plays which were referential and satirical in their dramatic intentions. This guaranteed commercial success, but only at the attendant risk of the play's censorship or post-performance suppression. The relationship between playwright and audience, on the one hand, and playwright and censor, on the other, is governed by a set of expectations which have elements of a contract, but one which is destabilized by the dynamics of circumstance and substance. The conflicting artistic, commercial, and political interests which governed playwriting, its production, and regulation, ensured that censorship could never be entirely contractual.

---

[41] See Annabel Patterson, *Censorship and Interpretation: The Conditions of Writing and Reading in Early Modern England* (Madison: University of Wisconsin Press, 1984).

PART III

WORKS

CHAPTER 16

....

THE EARLY SHAKESPEARE

....

DAVID BEVINGTON

SOME time around 1590, quite possibly earlier, Shakespeare arrived in London at the age of 26 or so and began his career as playwright and actor. Detailed information on the very early years in London continues to elude us, but we do know that by 1592 he had attracted the unfavourable attention of his fellow dramatist Robert Greene. Shortly before he died in poverty that year, Greene lashed out at 'an upstart crow beautified with our feathers, that with his "Tiger's heart wrapped in a player's hide" supposes he as well able to bombast out a blank verse as the best of you, and, being an absolute *Johannes Factotum*, is in his own conceit the only Shake-scene in a country'.[1] Christopher Marlowe, Thomas Nashe, and George Peele were thus warned to beware of an obstreperous newcomer in their midst.

Lukas Erne has cogently argued that Henry Chettle's apology for this outburst in his *Kind-Heart's Dream* (late 1592) is addressed not to Shakespeare, as is often supposed, but to Peele.[2] Still, Greene's tirade itself is unmistakably an attack on Shakespeare. The 'Tiger's heart wrapped in a player's hide' parodies 'O tiger's heart wrapped in a woman's hide!' from *3 Henry VI* or *Richard, Duke of York* (1.4.138), and 'Shake-scene' can hardly be intended for someone else. As Erne argues, the passage is of great importance in establishing Shakespeare's presence in the London theatrical world by the time of the attack. 'By 1592', writes Erne, 'Shakespeare had possibly completed or was at least well advanced in the writing of his first tetralogy, the most ambitious of his theatrical projects up to that point.'[3] The parodied line is from the last of the three *Henry VI* plays. Critics disagree as to whether Greene's animus is directed against plagiarism or merely pride,[4] but at all events it is prompted by envy of a new playwright

[1] See, D. Allen Carroll (ed.), *Greene's Groatsworth of Wit, Bought with Million of Repentance* (1592), (Binghamton, NY: Medieval and Renaissance Texts and Studies, 1994), 131–45.

[2] Lukas Erne, 'Biography and Mythography: Rereading Chettle's Alleged Apology to Shakespeare', *English Studies* 5 (1998), 430–40.

[3] Erne, 'Biography and Mythography', 430.

[4] See Carroll (ed.), *Greene's Groatsworth*.

with a reputation for opportunistic facility in writing. Shakespeare, in Greene's estimation, is not one of the well-educated University Wits like Marlowe, Nashe, Peele, and of course Greene himself, but is instead one of the 'rude grooms' and 'puppets' who are nothing better than 'antics garnished in our colours'.

Although Greene's mean-spirited estimate of Shakespeare is surely not one that we share today, it affords a useful point of departure for a study of the early Shakespeare as a budding dramatist who was astonishingly adept at various forms of collaboration. He may have co-written plays with some of the writers already mentioned, including Peele in *Titus Andronicus* (though Jonathan Bate emphatically disagrees)[5] and Nashe in *1 Henry VI.*[6] Peele and Nashe have been proposed as possible contributors to *2 Henry VI*, along with none other than Greene himself.[7] Edmond Malone, in the eighteenth century, conjectured that Greene's complaint of plagiarism was prompted by Shakespeare's having rewritten a version of *3 Henry VI* to which Peele, Marlowe, and Greene were the original contributors; more recently, John Cox and Eric Rasmussen consider it more likely that Shakespeare 'shared the composition of *3 Henry VI* with indeterminate others' than that he wrote it all by himself.[8] Brian Vickers argues for collaborative writing primarily in *Titus Andronicus* and then in the later *Timon of Athens* (with Thomas Middleton), *Pericles* (with George Wilkins), and *Henry VIII* and *The Two Noble Kinsmen* (with John Fletcher).[9] Collaboration must have taken other forms as well, in the close interaction in rehearsal and performance between writer and actors, with Shakespeare well situated in both camps.[10] Most important of all, perhaps, Shakespeare clearly absorbed a great deal of what he learned about playwriting from writers in the field, including Thomas Kyd and John Lyly, as well as from his reading.

Shakespeare's major dramatic genres, from the very beginnings of his career as writer, are comedy, English history, and tragedy. The 1623 Folio confirms this pattern by printing its collection of his plays in these three groupings. To be sure, anomalies and ambiguities appear with increasing frequency in his later work: is *Troilus and Cressida* a dark comedy, or classical history play, or bleak tragedy? Is *Henry VIII* a

---

[5] Brian Vickers, *Shakespeare, Co-Author: A Historical Study of Five Collaborative Plays* (Oxford and New York: Oxford University Press, 2002), 148–243, and Jonathan Bate (ed.), *Titus Andronicus*. The Arden Shakespeare, 3rd series (London: Routledge, 1995), 2–3.

[6] Edward Burns (ed.), *King Henry VI Part I*, The Arden Shakespeare, 3rd series (London: Thomson Learning, 2000), 73–83, and Gary Taylor, 'Shakespeare and others: the authorship of *Henry the Sixth, Part I*', *Medieval and Renaissance Drama in England* 7 (1995), 145–205.

[7] Ronald Knowles (ed.), *King Henry VI Part II*, The Arden Shakespeare, 3rd series (London: Thomas Nelson, 1999), 111–22. F. P. Wilson, *Marlowe and the Early Shakespeare* (Oxford: Clarendon Press, 1953), 104–5, is sceptical.

[8] John D. Cox and Eric Rasmussen (eds.), *King Henry VI Part III*, The Arden Shakespeare, 3rd series (London: Thomson Learning, 2001), 44–9.

[9] See Vickers, note 5 above.

[10] See Jeffrey Masten, 'Playwriting: Authorship and Collaboration', in *A New History of Early English Drama*, John D. Cox and David Scott Kastan (eds.), (New York: Columbia University Press, 1997), 357–82; and Gordon McMullan, ' "Our whole life is like a play": Collaboration and the Problem of Editing', *Textus* 9 (1996), 437–60.

history play or late romance? Are *Measure for Measure* and *The Winter's Tale* more tragicomedy than comedy? Why is *Cymbeline* printed last among the tragedies? At the start of Shakespeare's career, on the other hand, the distinctions in genre seem more clear, as though Shakespeare approached his task as dramatist with the purpose of contributing to and reshaping these genres to his own purposes. Comedy and English history plays occupied his attention especially: he would write approximately ten romantic comedies in the decade of the 1590s, give or take a year or two, and nine English history plays, both sorts of plays more or less evenly spaced over the decade. Tragedy, for the most part, would be a chief focus in later years, though tragic materials are plentifully explored in the early history plays.

Shakespeare's writing of romantic comedies does not involve significant elements of shared writing. It does, on the other hand, reveal an intense interplay between Shakespeare and the kinds of plays he saw on stage and in which he may well have acted. This brilliant self-education embraced models of widely disparate theatrical traditions, both classical (or neo-classical) and native, as though Shakespeare saw himself as a young dramatist who could coalesce and refashion different kinds of stage comedy into a genre that would be pre-eminently his own.

What then was the shape of comedy on the English stage round 1590 as Shakespeare prepared to take it up as a vehicle for his own writing? A prevailing genre of comedy in sixteenth-century England had been the morality play, in which a beleaguered young protagonist, well-intended but weak in his resolve, capitulated to the gleeful insinuations of the tempter Vice. After scenes of rioting and misconduct, the Mankind figure was eventually won again to virtue by moral abstractions like Mercy, Perseverance, and Truth. Such plays often took on political and religious colouration as England veered back and forth from Catholic to Protestant to Catholic to Protestant. The Vice figures could represent the abuses of either side, depending on the polemical stance of the dramatist, the acting company, and the patron.

In the years that preceded Shakespeare's entry on the scene, new dramatists adapted comedy to more socially recognizable scenarios. They did so with the morality play as one model, while at the same time finding other appealing kinds of comedy in fictional romance, in classical and neo-classical drama, and still more. They were able to exploit these new opportunities with vigour and hope of economic success because London was rapidly becoming a thriving locale for theatrical activity. The troupes of perhaps six or eight adult male actors and one or two boys who had toured the provinces with their moralities and other fare increasingly discovered that London audiences were far more numerous and enthusiastic than the actors had previously encountered. New theatrical buildings began to emerge, prominently including the place known as the Theatre, just outside London's walls to the north, which had been erected by James Burbage in 1576.

The playwrights who flocked to this bright but competitive opportunity included the writers named above. Robert Greene wrote a number of comedies, including *Friar Bacon and Friar Bungay* (c.1589), in which Margaret, the fair maid of Fressingfield, is the embodiment of a romantic dream: wholesome, self-assured, witty, patient, good-natured both chaste and emotionally responsive, and thoroughly English, she manages to capture the heart of an earl and marries him in defiance of social norms. George Peele's *The Old Wives Tale* (*c*.1588–94) offers a medley of romantic folk tales about two brothers in search of their sister, a sorcerer, an old man who has been turned into a bear, his beautiful but mad lady named Venelia, and much more. John Lyly wrote a series of plays for the court of Elizabeth I that were very popular with the courtly set, including *Endymion* (1588), about a shepherd who worshipfully loves the moon—i.e. Cynthia, a stand-in for Elizabeth herself. Thomas Nashe's *Summer's Last Will and Testament* (1592) was a masque-like entertainment describing the process in which Summer, sensing himself to be on the verge of death, reviews the performances of those who have served him and eventually bestows his crown on Autumn. Marlowe's *The Jew of Malta* (*c*.1589–90), though nominally a tragedy, revels in the savage humour of the Vice-like Barabas and his slave, Ithamore. A comedy called *Fedele and Fortunio*, performed at court in the early 1580s, was essentially a translation of Pasqualigo's *Il Fidele* in the vein of Italian neo-classical comedy. George Gascoigne's earlier *Supposes*, 1566, performed at Gray's Inn, was similarly a free translation of a neo-classical comedy, *I Suppositi*, by Ludovico Ariosto. (We will return to this play in relation to *The Taming of the Shrew* below.) Comedy was thus extraordinarily varied in its forms on the English stage of the 1580s. One might say that it was somewhat unformed in its differing manifestations, as though waiting for a genius like Shakespeare to put some of its pieces together.

EARLY COMEDIES

A good place to begin is with *The Comedy of Errors*. It is not necessarily his first romantic comedy; no mention of it appears until Innocents Day, 28 December 1594, when a 'Comedy of Errors (like to Plautus his *Menechmus*)' was performed by professional actors at Gray's Inn in London as part of that institution's seasonal festivities. The play may have been written earlier. What it afforded Shakespeare, at any rate, was an opportunity to adapt the genre of classical and neo-classical comedy to the English tastes and predilections of his London audience.

Actually, *The Comedy of Errors* is a combination of elements from not one but two plays by the Latin comic dramatist Plautus (*c*.254–184 BC): the *Menaechmi*, and *Amphitruo*.[11] The first of these is about twins who are separated by misadventure at sea (*Menaechmi* means 'twins'). When the travelling twin comes to the town where his

---

[11] Richard Dutton, '*The Comedy of Errors* and *The Calumny of Apelles*: An Exercise in Source Study', in Richard Dutton and Jean E. Howard (eds), *A Companion to Shakespeare's Works*, vol. 3: *The Comedies* (Oxford: Blackwell, 2003), 307–19, makes a persuasive argument that *The Comedy of Errors* is also indebted to *The Calumny of Apollo*. On Shakespeare's complicating the plot of his Plautine source by greatly enlarging 'the scope of the whole dramatic structure', see T. G. Bishop, *Shakespeare and the Theatre of Wonder* (Cambridge: Cambridge University Press, 1996), 74–91.

lookalike brother dwells, the traveller is repeatedly mistaken by the townspeople for the resident they know well, resulting in a succession of comic mix-ups. Eventually the confusion is cleared up and the two long-separated twins are happily reunited.

What Shakespeare does with this plot device is to elaborate its comic elements and to domesticate its humour. Whereas the travelling twin in Plautus is accompanied by a single servant, Shakespeare introduces another lookalike twin as servant to the resident brother. The opportunities for mistaken identity are thereby hilariously multiplied. Even their masters cannot tell them apart. Then, too, Shakespeare's version adds romantic and domestic elements that are largely absent in his Latin sources. Antipholus of Ephesus, where the action takes place, is married to a woman whose sister lives with them and who becomes the object of ardent devotion by the newly arrived Antipholus of Syracuse; once the mix-ups are resolved, the travelling Antipholus can now settle down to presumed marital bliss. Plautus' wryly sardonic depiction of a courtesan and her household is largely replaced by a more softening approach to sexual conduct: Shakespeare's Antipholus of Ephesus does consider shifting his attentions to the Courtesan when he is denied entrance to his own house, but the resolution of the plot emphasizes domestic harmony and loyalty to marriage vows. The dual identity of the two servants leads to a comic impasse borrowed by Shakespeare from Plautus' *Amphitruo*: the servant of Antipholus of Ephesus is locked out of his master's house and must plead for admittance with the servant of the travelling Antipholus, who, with his master, has been mistakenly invited to take up residence there.

No less importantly in the anglicizing of the Latin play, Shakespeare outfits his version with a frame-plot that is borrowed from the old story of Apollonius of Tyre (to which Shakespeare would later return in *Pericles*). The father of the twin Antipholi, having been separated for many years from his wife and children and servants, turns up in Ephesus, where he is arrested and sentenced to die in one day's time if he is not ransomed by a large payment, his only offence being that he is of Syracuse and thus an enemy of the city of Ephesus. This threat of death hovers over the play until it is effortlessly resolved at last by the discovery that his long-lost wife is really the Abbess of Ephesus. The ending of this frame-plot thus accentuates the reunion of a long-separated married couple in the context of religious faith. Moreover, the device of the one-day delay in the threatened execution gives to this play a perfectly regular neo-classical structure fashioned along the lines of neo-Aristotelian prescriptions that a play should extend its single action over no more than a single day and locate itself in one place; *The Comedy of Errors* centres its action in Ephesus from start to finish, while indications of the time of day move the plot precisely forward from morning to noon to two o'clock and eventually to sundown. This neo-classical structure further enables Shakespeare to employ a stage setting that is at least close to that of his Plautine original: the action takes place in an open locale with houses facing on the street. The house of Antipholus of Ephesus is visible throughout, with the establishments of the Courtesan and of the Abbess close at hand. Never again does Shakespeare model a play on such a closely contained classical model, while at the same time transporting the play's mores and humour into a more recognizably English environment.

The Two Gentlemen of Verona, also of early date, turns toward prose fiction and pastoral romance for its romantic saga of competitive love and friendship. Among the many translations of fictional narratives from Spain, France, and Italy that were being introduced into England with increasing frequency in the late sixteenth century, two were especially useful to Shakespeare for this play: Jorge de Montemayor's Spanish pastoral, *Diana Enamorata*, translated into French in 1578 and 1587 and into English by Bartholomew Yonge (not published until 1598, but begun some nineteen years earlier, according to Yonge), and the story of Titus and Gisippus, translated from Boccaccio's *Decameron* and published in Sir Thomas Elyot's *The Book Named the Governor* in 1531. The first of these tales provided Shakespeare with the model for his dramatization of male inconstancy in love. Like Proteus in Shakespeare's play, whose name betokens inconstancy, the Felix of *Diana Enamorata* is sent off to court to prevent his marrying the orphaned Felixmena, who thereupon disguises herself as a young man named Valerius in order that she may follow after her wooer. Overhearing a conversation in which Felix lays amorous siege to a courtly lady named Celia, the disguised Felixmena takes service with Felix and is sent on embassages of courtship to Celia. This story closely parallels that of Proteus and Julia in *The Two Gentlemen*, but lacks an equivalent for Valentine, Proteus's loyal friend, whose lady-love Silvia is then courted by the fickle Proteus. Here Shakespeare turned to the story of the noble friendship of Titus and Gisippus in Elyot's *The Governor*, in which Gisippus, about to marry the woman whom they both love, offers to let Titus take his place on the marriage night. Titus later reciprocates this extraordinary generosity by proposing that he be executed for a murder of which Gisippus has been wrongly accused. Richard Edwards's play about *Damon and Pythias* (c.1565) offered still another model of selfless friendship.

Shakespeare's tactic here is typical of the way he proceeds to fashion a structure of romance in his early comedies: he combines two or more plots in ways that dramatize conflicts between rival ethical value systems.[12] Both Julia and Silvia are constant, loyal, and long-suffering. They seem to know perfectly who they are and what they desire, namely, to be bound in an eternal marriage to the young men they love. They are all that the fantasizing male imagination might crave: they are beautiful, well born and well educated, patient, forgiving, and always a source of support and encouragement. Oddly, as suggested above, Shakespeare's admiring portraiture of young women may owe something to Robert Greene's romantic comedies, including *Friar Bacon and Friar Bungay*, with its wholesome idealization of Margaret as an unspoiled beauty of the English countryside not unlike Shakespeare's Julia and Silvia, and, later on, Portia in *The Merchant of Venice* and Rosalind in *As You Like it*. Perhaps Greene's churlish resentment of Shakespeare as newly-arrived playwright in the early 1590s was occasioned in part by Greene's perception that he had already encountered something like

---

[12] See Jeffrey Masten, 'The Two Gentlemen of Verona', in Dutton and Howard (eds.), 3: 266–88, and Arthur F. Kinney, 'Shakespeare's *Comedy of Errors* and the Nature of Kinds', *Studies in Philology* 85 (1988), 25–52.

the Shakespearean heroine in his, Greene's, own work. (Unless, that is, *Two Gentlemen* preceded *Friar Bacon*; the dating is uncertain.)

The men in *Two Gentlemen*, unlike the patient and loyal young women, are caught up in unceasing conflicts with each other and themselves. Proteus is not proud of betraying his dear friend Valentine by doing everything in his means to steal away Valentine's lady love. Only when Valentine demonstrates utter selflessness by offering to let Proteus have Silvia after all does Proteus come to his senses, inspired to respond in kind by such a demonstration of true friendship. 'All that is mine in Silvia I give thee', declares Valentine (5.4.83), much to the distress of Julia and presumably Silvia as well, neither of whom has been consulted! Valentine's noble conduct also prompts Silvia's father, the Duke of Milan, to relent in his opposition to the marriage of Silvia to her Valentine. Love finally triumphs, in ways that capitalize upon Shakespeare's ingenious weaving together of two plot sources with their variations on the theme of love and friendship.

No less characteristic of early Shakespearean romantic comedy is the plentiful admixture of clownish antics by servants. As in *The Comedy of Errors*, where the Dromios swap outlandish puns with their masters and are comically beaten for things they haven't done (since one servant is constantly being mistaken for the other), and where the ridiculous conjuring schoolmaster named Doctor Pinch offers an especially amusing role for an expert comedic actor, Lance and Speed capitalize in *The Two Gentlemen* on juicy opportunities for funny business. Lance's monologue with his dog Crab on the eve of their departure from Verona to Milan (since Lance is Proteus's servant and must accompany him on this journey) is comically brilliant. Lance reproaches his dog for being a hard-hearted cur unable to share in the unhappiness on this sad occasion. Lance dramatizes the scene of grieving by letting his shoes take the place of various members of Lance's family, tears flowing from their eyes, while the dog 'all this while sheds not a tear nor speaks a word' (2.3.30–1). Later, in Milan, Lance offers to take the punishment on himself that is about to be meted out to Crab for having urinated on a gentlewoman's farthingale (4.4.1–38). This is all so hilarious that one can understand why the film *Shakespeare in Love* brings on Lance and Crab, to the vast amusement of Queen Elizabeth (played by Judi Dench), who readily appreciates that dumb animals can steal a scene in the theatre.[13] Yet these scenes are far more than mere comic relief, whatever that phrase is supposed to mean. Lance's selfless offer to suffer punishment in Crab's place is a delicious parody of Valentine's offer to step aside in favour of the wishes of his friend, Proteus. Crab is Lance's best friend, and friends should be prepared to do anything for each other.

The term 'romantic comedy' is beginning to take on a sonorous richness of meaning. It connotes romance in the sense of travel and adventure, as in Valentine's thoroughly improbable sojourn with brigands or outlaws in a forest region on the frontiers of Mantua, or in Julia's perilous journey to Milan in disguise as a young man, so

---

[13] See Marjorie Garber, 'Shakespeare's Dogs', in Jonathan Bate, Jill Levenson, and Dieter Mohl (eds.), *Shakespeare and the Twentieth Century: The Selected Proceedings of the International Shakespeare Association World Congress, Los Angeles, 1996* (Newark: University of Delaware Press, 1998).

anticipatory of the tribulations of the four young lovers in the forest near Athens in *A Midsummer Night's Dream*, or Rosalind's and Celia's escape into the Forest of Arden in *As You Like It*. Romance also connotes erotic entanglement and sexual rivalry. The term 'comedy' points to the happy resolution of romantic conflict in these plays, with the rediscovery and reunion of those who have long been separated (as in *The Comedy of Errors*, pointing forward to *Twelfth Night*), and with forgiveness, and often with marriage and the overcoming of parental opposition (as in the case of Silvia in *Two Gentlemen* and of Hermia in *A Midsummer Night's Dream*). The term 'comedy' also points in the direction of slapstick humour, with comic drubbings of servants and punning wordplay. The genre of comedy lends itself well to satirical portraits of humorous types, such as the foolish love-rival Thurio in *The Two Gentlemen*, the goofy schoolmaster Pinch in *The Comedy of Errors*, and the greasy kitchen-wench named Luce or Nell in the same play who evidently has her eye on Dromio of Syracuse, or perhaps both servants. In Shakespeare, the satirical portraits tend to be genial. They are part of a congenial and warm-hearted world where ridiculous mix-ups are an everyday occurrence and where mean-spirited impulses are overwhelmed by a surprising generosity.

Love's Labour's Lost demonstrates all these qualities of romantic comedy, even if the marriages at the end must be postponed. Here, although Shakespeare is seemingly indebted to no single source or pair of sources, he appears to have learned a lot from John Lyly, whose courtly comedies, including *Campaspe, Sappho and Phao, Galatea, Midas,* and *Endymion*, were sensationally successful in the decade of the 1580s before Shakespeare began making his mark as a dramatist. The fantastical Spaniard, Don Armado, is especially close to Lyly's Sir Tophas (in *Endymion*) in his enervated lovesickness, his pompous self-importance, his cowardice papered over with comic bravado, and his torturing of the English language. Like Sir Tophas, Don Armado is accompanied by a pert page, Moth, who helps us to see what is so absurd in the Spanish Don and his helpless prostration as wooer of the dairymaid, Jaquenetta. The portrait reaches back through Lyly's Sir Tophas to Chaucer's Sir Thopas and to the *miles gloriosus* or braggart soldier of Plautus' Roman comedy.

The play abounds in other genially satirical portraits as well. The denizens of the never-never land of Navarre include a pedantic schoolmaster named Holofernes and a Latin-loving curate named Nathaniel, both of whom are so pleased with their verbal ingenuity that they produce some of the most egregious alliterative wordplay in all Shakespeare. Holofernes discourses archly on how 'The preyful Princess pierced and pricked a pretty pleasing pricket', and goes on to point out that appending an 'l' to the word 'sore' will produce 'sorel', i.e. a buck in its third year. The nearly pointless punning on 'sore' goes on for several lines (4.2.56–61). A witless constable, Dull, adds to the verbal confusion when, for example, he mistakes Nathaniel's Latin *haud credo*, i.e. 'I cannot believe what you just said', for something like 'auld grey doe' in their conversation about hunting (4.2.11–20). The cheeky clown or rustic named Costard is also much given to maladroit wordplay, as when he misinterprets Don Armado's 'I will enfranchise thee' as meaning, 'O, marry me to one Frances!' and misunderstands Berowne's offer of a 'remuneration' as signifying a coin of that name (3.1.118–68). All this adds up to what

William Carroll has aptly titled 'The Great Feast of Language in *Love's Labour's Lost*'.[14] No other play by Shakespeare is quite as word conscious.

These are satirical portraits, capitalizing on the 'humours' or pet obsessions and characteristic postures of the various characters, somewhat in the vein of Edmund Spenser's Braggadocchio in Book II of *The Faerie Queene*, of which Spenser observes that the best kind of comedy is sharply satirical comedy, provoking scornful laughter at the various sorts of ridiculous behaviour that sensible and well-educated persons must learn to eschew. Ben Jonson and George Chapman, among others, were to adopt this mode of satirical comedy as the mainstay of their comic writing in the later 1590s. Not coincidentally, *Love's Labour's Lost*, in its Lylyan style of Euphuistic mannerism, is closer than most of Shakespeare's plays to the satirical drama written for the Elizabethan court and for well-heeled sophisticated audiences who saw their plays indoors in the so-called 'private' theatres such as Blackfriars and similar playhouses. Shakespeare shows early on that he is adept at satirical writing when it suits his dramatic purposes.

At the same time, *Love's Labour's Lost* revels in the comedy of romantic misunderstanding. In the fairyland world of Navarre, the young king of that principality and his three companions resolve never to converse with women for three years while they dedicate themselves to serious study, only to be foiled in their determination by the arrival of the Princess of France and her three ladies-in-waiting on a diplomatic mission from the court of France. From the very first we perceive, of course, that the two sets of four young persons are destined to pair off two by two. We see, moreover, that the young women already have fixed their gazes on the unsuspecting males they have chosen to be their companions for life. The women are never flustered, or gushy, or overwhelmed by the emotion of love; to the contrary, they seem coolly bent on marriage as a suitable destiny. The women have nothing to learn about themselves; they are self-possessed, amused by the situation in which they find themselves, and bent on torturing the young men with pert repartee and with playful disguises until they have beaten the males into a kind of submission.

For their part, the men are chiefly unaware of who they are and what they want. They fool themselves into thinking that they can get along without women. Even Berowne, the most self-aware of the lot, falls prey to romantic longing for young Katharine, whose dark complexion and scornful wit constantly remind Berowne of how he has enslaved himself to anxiety and frustration. The young men try to conceal their shameful infatuations from one another, only to revel in those passions once they have found each other out. Absurdly confident now that they can win the ladies with their irresistible charms, the men have to be taken down a few pegs and forced to delay marital happiness until they have come to a better understanding of what marriage entails. They have been tricked into perjuring themselves in their solemn vows to abstain from love. The theme of perjury nicely links this main

---

[14] William C. Carroll, *The Great Feast of Language in 'Love's Labour's Lost'* (Princeton, NJ: Princeton University Press, 1976). See also Keir Elam, *Shakespeare's Universe of Discourse: Language-Games in the Comedies* (Cambridge: Cambridge University Press, 1984), esp. 251–75.

romantic plot to the verbal excesses of the below-stairs characters. All ends in a delicious play-within-the-play finale consisting of a spoof on the theme of 'The Nine Worthies', in which the more ridiculous characters of the play impersonate Hector of Troy, Alexander the Great, Pompey, Hercules in his infancy, and still others for the wry amusement of the gentlemen and ladies. All are gathered on stage for this finale, thus juxtaposing and harmonizing the elements of which this confection is composed: genial satire, love interest, adventure in a strange foreign land, and verbal and physical horseplay. Once again Shakespeare's approach to romantic comedy has proven to be varied and multiform.

The Taming of the Shrew offers a quintessential solution in Shakespeare's search for a pattern in his developing genre of romantic comedy. It combines a neo-classical plot of young lovers outmanoeuvring parental opposition with a thoroughly native English saga of wife-taming, and frames the whole enterprise with a little glimpse of English country life in the vicinity of Stratford-upon-Avon, Shakespeare's home town. The play thus embraces the model that Shakespeare has employed in the neo-classically inclined *The Comedy of Errors* along with the freer forms of *The Two Gentlemen* and *Love's Labour's Lost*. Many of the character types of those plays are once again in full view.

The love story of Lucentio and Bianca and of her other wooers is closely borrowed from Ludovico Ariosto's *I Suppositi* (1509), which had been colloquially translated by George Gascoigne as *The Supposes* in 1566. Through Ariosto, the story type reaches back to Plautus' *Captivi* and Terence's *Eunuchus*. As in those source plays, Shakespeare's Baptista Minola is a widower father burdened with the responsibility for finding a mate for his attractive daughter, Bianca. (Bianca's sister, Kate, belongs to the other plot and is not in Ariosto.) Bianca has to put up with the attentions of an aged, wealthy wooer, Gremio, who is thus not unlike Ariosto's Doctor Cleander, even if Gremio is not as disagreeable and malodorous as that miserly lawyer. Bianca has another wooer as well, the flea-brained Hortensio, who has no counterpart in Ariosto; Shakespeare characteristically multiplies the motifs he derived from his sources, as he did in *The Comedy of Errors* by providing two comic servants rather than one. Bianca secretly prefers to be wooed by the young Lucentio, who has traded places with his witty servant Tranio in order to gain access to the house of Baptista as a tutor for the young daughter. As in Ariosto, Lucentio is in fact well born, so that the father's vexation on discovering that his daughter has a secret admirer is easily dispelled at last by providing Lucentio with legitimate wealth and position. To be sure, the Ariosto plot offers more of a threat to comic happiness than in Shakespeare's more cheerful version: the young lady in Ariosto is actually having an affair with her secret lover, who is thereupon thrown into prison by the irate father. The young woman is aided in her amorous scheming by a nurse. Shakespeare redirects the moral atmosphere of this affair for the presumably decorous tastes of his London audience.

The wife-taming saga of Katharine or Kate and her self-assured wooer, Petruchio, has no single source in classical literature or in continental fiction. The story is essentially a folk legend, set down in English and Scottish ballads like 'The Wee Cooper of Fife' and 'The Wife Wrapped in Wether's Skin'. In a version of about 1550 identified by Richard Hosley,[15] a shrewish wife is beaten by her husband and wrapped in the raw salted hide of an old plow-horse named Morel, with the justification that the husband is exercising his right as a farmer to thrash his own animal's skin. The tale is pointedly devised as an object lesson for henpecked husbands. Petruchio's treatment of Kate in Shakespeare's play is less harsh, to be sure, but it still derives its energies from male phobias about domineering women. Interpretation of Kate's final submissive gesture at the end of the play is highly controversial today, but one can at least say that Shakespeare offers a presumably instructive contrast of Kate and her sister: Bianca appears to be the more tractable and modest to her wooers, but in the last analysis she reveals a wilful temperament in refusing to obey her new husband (as does the Widow in her marriage with Hortensio), whereas Kate seems to have settled for the role of obedient wife as a means of keeping peace in her marriage.

The frame-plot or Induction of the play features an itinerant tinker named Christopher Sly, who is tricked by a practical-joking lord into believing that he, Sly, has awakened from an amnesiac dream and is in fact a wealthy lord himself for whom the performance of *The Taming of the Shrew* is an idle evening's entertainment. The motif of dreaming encourages the audience to meditate on playacting as illusion and thus a reflection of the illusory nature of life itself, as in *A Midsummer Night's Dream*. *Taming* is perhaps Sly's dream, and ours as well. Whether Sly disappears halfway through the play, as in the version we have, or was intended to remain throughout as an observer, is hard to determine. Certainly, in any case, the Induction material transports us to a thoroughly English environment. Sly identifies himself as 'old Sly's son of Burton Heath' and an acquaintance of 'Marian Hacket, the fat alewife of Wincot' (Induction, 2, 17–20). These villages are in the vicinity of Stratford-upon-Avon. *The Taming of the Shrew* adroitly links a neo-classically derived plot with romantic plot material and with elements of the English countryside that Shakespeare knew so well.

EARLY HISTORIES

As Greene's rueful comment in 1592 makes clear, Shakespeare had clearly become identified with the English history play by that date, having written most or all of the three *Henry VI* plays by then. His models in the way of English history plays were few indeed, apart from the rollicking anonymous *The Famous Victories of Henry the Fifth*, written some time in the 1580s. That play was to become a source for Shakespeare's tetralogy of the late 1590s relating, in four sequential plays, the story of Henry IV's coming to the throne in 1399 and his son's rise to his glorious kingship as Henry V. This saga lies beyond the scope of this present chapter. *Famous Victories* was nevertheless

---

[15] Richard Hosley, 'Sources and Analogues of *The Taming of the Shrew*', *Huntington Library Quarterly* 27 (1963–4), 289–308. The ballad is titled *A Merry Jest for a Shrewd and Curst Wife Lapped in Morel's Skin, for Her Good Behavior*, printed c.1550.

also an important precedent for Shakespeare's first tetralogy of the early 1590s, with its three plays centred on the reign of Henry VI and then a fourth play about the short but eventful reign of Richard III from 1483 to 1485.[16] *Famous Victories* offered a model of a loose-knit chronicle history of late fourteenth- and early fifteenth-century England, making free with historical fact and interlacing its depiction of political and military history with legendary and humorous accounts of the major figures, especially Prince Hal in his reckless companionship with the Falstaff-like Sir John Oldcastle.

The English history play is an odd genre. Although the 1623 Folio conveniently divides Shakespeare's works into comedies, histories, and tragedies, Renaissance classical theories about drama distinguished between comedy and tragedy with no room for something like English history. Indeed, the the English history play had no formal structure of the sort that Aristotle or neo-Aristotelian critical analysis could formulate into a coherent pattern. When Frances Meres undertook, in 1598, to list Shakespeare's works up to that time, arranging them according to comedies and tragedies, he categorized *Henry IV* as a tragedy along with *Richard II, Richard III, King John*, and *Titus Andronicus*, despite the fact that the *Henry IV* plays celebrate the King's successful defeat of rebellion and the coming to power of Henry V. To be sure, some of these plays describe themselves as tragedies in their published Quarto titles as, for example, *The Tragedy of King Richard the Third* and *The Tragedy of King Richard the Second* (both in 1597), but in the 1623 Folio these same plays are more descriptively entitled *The Life and Death of Richard the Third* and *The Life and Death of Richard the Second*, while still others are matter-of-factly called *The First Part of King Henry the Fourth* and *The Second Part of King Henry the Fourth*. (Their quarto titles are similar: *The History of Henry the Fourth* and *The Second Part of the History of King Henry the Fourth*.) The first published version of *2 Henry VI* in 1594 was called *The First Part of the Contention betwixt the Two Houses of York and Lancaster*; the first version of *3 Henry VI* was called *The True Tragedy of Richard Duke of York*.

What then is the genre of the English history play? What the editors of the First Folio evidently saw was that Shakespeare had written ten plays on English history, eight of which formed a continuous historical narrative from the late reign of Richard II to the reign of Richard III (approximately 1397 to 1485), and that all ten could simply be listed in chronological order from the reign of King John (early thirteenth century) to the reign of Henry VIII and the birth of the Princess Elizabeth in 1533. The English history play was thus not really a dramatic genre so much as an arrangement by historical

---

[16] F. P. Wilson, *Marlowe and the Early Shakespeare* (see n. 7 above), noting that *Famous Victories* is 'the only play of this kind' based on English history to have preceded Shakespeare's English history plays, and that *Famous Victories* is 'a play of incredible meanness … written in bad prose, one imagines, because the compiler could not rise to bad verse' (106), does not hesitate to give Shakespeare the supreme role in the fashioning of this dramatic genre that was to become so quickly popular on the London stage. So much, in Wilson's view, for the 'old view' that the chronicle play, 'inspired by the patriotic feeling that swept the country before and after the Armada, was first lifted into the dignity of historical tragedy by Marlowe [in *Edward II*] and that Shakespeare profited from his example' (104). Instead, Wilson maintains, Marlowe is 'following the example which Shakespeare had already set' (90–1).

subject matter. As David Kastan has cogently observed, history itself is open-ended and apt to be indeterminate in its beginnings and ends; it is a process more than a literary form.[17] The very titling of the plays, naming the kings in succession, is determined more by chronological sequence than by the events of the plays themselves; Henry VI is hardly the central figure in the three plays named for him.

Where then did the concept of the English history play arise, and in what way was Shakespeare a major—perhaps *the* major—contributor? Other historical plays had been written by the early 1590s, of course, though not generally on English history: plays about Ajax and Ulysses, Caesar and Pompey, Dido of Carthage, Philotas (who was convicted of conspiring against the Emperor Alexander), Marius and Sulla (from Roman history of 88 to 83 BC), Catiline, Cyrus the Great, and still others. A Latin *Richardus Tertius* was acted at St John's College, Cambridge, in 1580, though not published until the late nineteenth century, so that it may have been unknown in London in the 1590s.

More promising as source material, perhaps, were the dramatizations of biblical history in the great cycle plays of late medieval England, with their all-encompassing narrative extending from the creation of the universe to the day of doom, laying heavy emphasis on the birth, ministry, crucifixion, and resurrection of Christ. Here lay a dramatic model of epic scope that included many wonderful stories of Noah, John the Baptist, Mary the mother of God, Pontius Pilate, vigorously enlivened by comic portrayals of Cain or Herod or Mary's husband Joseph. The narrative subject was, to be sure, distant from that of late medieval English history, but the overarching theme of *divina commedia* and eventual salvation for the human race achieved through heavenly intercession and atonement offered a native-born and ecclesiastically inspired structure that could be used to interpret English history as ultimately meaningful and divinely sanctioned.

The astonishingly successful *Tamburlaine* plays of Christopher Marlowe (1587–8) offered Shakespeare yet another model in quite a different vein. Tamburlaine was a heroic figure in an iconoclastic mode, trampling underfoot the kings and emperors of the Middle East and then of eastern Europe as he rose from lowly shepherd to invincible conqueror. Even though he eventually had to face the unavoidable reality of death in the loss of his beloved Zenocrate and then his own last fatal illness, his challenge of the gods themselves seemed otherwise unanswered. The first *Tamburlaine* play, performed and published free-standingly without its sequel, provided no assurance that such irresistible ambition would have to face any day of reckoning, human or otherworldly. Edward Alleyn was evidently great in the role. Shakespeare must have seen the performance.

Most of all, Shakespeare clearly made extensive use of the second edition of Raphael Holinshed's *Chronicles of England, Scotland, and Ireland*, published in 1587 as the impending crisis of the Spanish Armada (1588) drew near. The year 1587 also saw the

---

[17] David Scott Kastan, *Shakespeare and the Shapes of Time* (Hanover, NH: University Press of New England, 1982).

execution of Mary Queen of Scots, Elizabeth I's Catholic first cousin, and (despite her denials) the focus of an increasingly intense series of conspiracies against Elizabeth's life culminating in the so-called Babington conspiracy of 1586. The papacy had declared Elizabeth a proscribed heretic; anyone taking away her life was offered assurance of spiritual reward. English Catholics, many of them no doubt loyal to Elizabeth as queen despite their religious affiliation to the Roman Catholic Church, were under intense suspicion as the well-publicized preparation for the Armada invasion proceeded. Philip of Spain and his generals assumed that English Catholics would come over to their side once the invasion had begun. These were the crises of the time in which Shakespeare took up the subject of England's fifteenth-century civil wars.

Holinshed's compilation of *Chronicles* contained within its capacious boundaries much of Edward Hall's *The Union of the Two Noble and Illustre Families of Lancaster and York* (1542). This work had been written explicitly to glorify the Tudor monarchy by demonstrating how Henry Tudor, Queen Elizabeth's grandfather, had consolidated the two warring houses of Lancaster and York by uniting his Lancastrian descent with the Yorkist pedigree of the young woman he married, Elizabeth of York, daughter of Edward IV and sister of the two princes, Edward V and Richard, who had presumably been murdered in the Tower of London at the behest of their uncle Richard III. Hall's providential reading of English history took the story back to Henry Bolingbroke's seizing of the kingship from his first cousin, Richard II, in 1399, an event that was often interpreted as bringing down on the English people the wrath of the Almighty and a resulting half-century and more of civil strife that could be brought to an end only when Henry Tudor stepped forward to challenge and defeat Richard III at Bosworth Field in 1485. The providential reading was manifestly a work of propaganda for the Tudor monarchs, and did not go unchallenged as an interpretation of history, but it was enduringly popular in Elizabethan England because it justified the coming to power of a royal dynasty that had resulted in Elizabeth I's long continuance in office (since 1558) and in England's triumph over the Spanish Armada in 1588. That event was clearly providential, in the eyes of most English people, and so, by extension, was the process by which Henry VII had ascended the throne in 1485.

Shakespeare, in his early English history plays, makes some use of Hall's providentialism for his overall artistic purposes while also interrogating that thesis on the level of day-to-day conflict. (Providentialism will be even less in evidence in the English history plays about Prince Hal that Shakespeare will write in the later 1590s.) Henry Ansgar Kelly has effectively demolished E. M. W. Tillyard's once-traditional reading of the history plays as straightforward expressions of the Tudor myth.[18] The *Henry VI* plays were performed individually in Shakespeare's day, not, as is often the case today, in a closely packed sequence, and as individual plays they offer a ceaseless and dismaying representation of war and civil strife.

---

[18] Henry Ansgar Kelly, *Divine Providence in the England of Shakespeare's Histories* (Cambridge, MA: Harvard University Press, 1970); and E. M. W. Tillyard, *Shakespeare's History Plays* (London: Chatto & Windus, 1944 and 1961).

1 Henry VI, covering roughly the years from Henry V's death in 1422 down to the fall of Lord Talbot in 1453, shows the English army fighting well at first against a craven French enemy but ultimately overwhelmed at Bordeaux because political infighting at home has deprived the English soldiers of needed support in the field. Young Henry, pious and innocent, is unable to stem the bickering between the Lancastrian and Yorkist factions. The result is the death of Talbot and his brave son John, and the loss of English territories in France. Henry's final surrender in this play is his marriage to Margaret of Anjou, an impecunious Frenchwoman who offers no political advantage to the English through this union and who is indeed brought over to England by the Duke of Suffolk in order that he may enjoy her as his mistress. Transgressive women loom large in this play, not only in Margaret but also in Joan of Arc, who subdues the French dauphin with her nefarious charms, and in the Countess of Auvergne, who tries without success to subdue Lord Talbot. Inverted structures of gender are symptomatic of an enervation and decay eating at the heart of England's greatness.

2 Henry VI thus begins on a note of helpless disorder that is merely the sad prelude of worse to come. The honest and courageous Duke Humphrey of Gloucester, uncle and Lord Protector to the young king, falls victim to the machinations of his enemies at court, including the Dukes of Buckingham, Somerset, and York, who bury their own political differences for the time being while they conspire to rid the kingdom of a Protector whose main fault in their eyes is simply that he strives for justice and thus stands in the way of their ruthless scheming. Humphrey's marriage to Dame Eleanor Cobham, whose own ambitions have prompted her to traffic with sorcerers, leaves Humphrey open to his enemies. Once again the motif of the domineering woman manifests its baleful presence. The commoners, encouraged by factionalism at court, grow restive; their strident demands that Suffolk be banished are symptomatic of a profound social disorder that subsequently erupts in the extra-judicial assassination of Suffolk and then in the Cade Rebellion of 1450.[19] To magnify the horrors of this mob attack on London, Shakespeare conflates accounts of the Cade Rebellion itself with details drawn from the Peasants' Revolt of 1381. To be sure, the commoners are not primarily to blame; Richard Plantagenet, the Duke of York and standard-bearer of the threatening Yorkist claim to the throne, eggs on Jack Cade with the Machiavellian intent of unleashing chaos so that Richard can move in with his Yorkist supporters to challenge the weak Lancastrian Henry VI. Open civil war is about to begin. Any sense of providential purpose is nowhere to be found.

The civil war itself is the oppressive theme of *3 Henry VI*. It takes the form of reciprocal slaughter between the Lancastrians on one side and the Yorkists on the other: an Edward for an Edward, a Richard for a Richard. One especially emblematic scene is that in which poor King Henry, banished from the field of battle in Yorkshire by his managerial wife Margaret, sits on a molehill and meditates on the vanity of human wishes while he beholds the spectacle of a son who has unknowingly killed his own father and a father who has unknowingly killed his own son (2.5). Perjury

---

[19] See Thomas Cartelli, 'Suffolk and the Pirates: Disordered Relations in Shakespeare's *2 Henry VI*', in Dutton and Howard (eds.), vol. 2: *The Histories*, 325–43.

abounds, as major figures like the Duke of Clarence and the Earl of Warwick betray their oaths by shifting sides between the Yorkist and Lancastrian factions. Peace is achieved at last in *3 Henry VI*, but only because the Yorkists have finally triumphed in the reciprocating violence. Richard of Gloucester, who emerges in this play as a fierce warrior on behalf of his older brother Edward and will soon be King Richard III, caps the terror of this civil war by slaughtering the defenceless King Henry VI in the Tower, just as he and his brothers Edward and George, Duke of Clarence, have stabbed the captured Lancastrian Prince Edward at the battlefield of Tewkesbury in 1471 (5.5). Richard's gloating soliloquy, in which he vows to achieve the English crown by whatever means necessary, reveals him as a practised Machiavel who knows only too well how to 'wet my cheeks with artificial tears, | And frame my face to all occasions' (3.2.184–5). Richard's ominous presence unsettles any hope that the cessation of hostilities can bring with it any lasting or meaningful peace.

Indeed, *Richard III* begins on this disarming note. Richard sardonically opens the play by saluting the 'glorious summer' of York that has ended their long 'winter of discontent', but his purpose is only to use the occasion for his own malign and murderous plotting. In rapid succession he suborns the murder in prison of his older brother, the Duke of Clarence; persuades the widow of Prince Edward of Lancaster to leave off her holy duty to her dead father-in-law and marry Richard instead; and sows factionalism at court between the Queen's kindred and her many political enemies. Richard need not proceed directly against King Edward IV, for that dissolute monarch has brought upon himself an early death by his dissipations and by his extraordinarily imprudent marriage to the destitute widow of a Lancastrian officer instead of to the sister-in-law of the King of France. The new Queen's rapid promotion of her brother and sons is galling to important courtiers like Lord Hastings and the Duke of Buckingham because the Queen's kindred are commoners unworthy of such elevation in rank. Edward's rash marriage has cost him the loyalty of the Earl of Warwick and Edward's brother the Duke of Clarence; the marriage amounts in their view to one more sad confirmation of the enervating surrender of susceptible males to the wiles of controlling women, like that earlier marriage of the young Henry VI to Margaret of Anjou.

Margaret is still around in *Richard III*, a dowager widowed former queen, politically powerless but gifted with an angry power of prophecy. Other women in this play join her in a chorus of prophetic utterances, designed both to warn the political leaders of England to beware of offending heaven by entering into cynical agreements with dangerous men and to pronounce a series of curses on Richard as one on whom 'Sin, death, and hell have set their marks' (1.3.293).[20] For much of the play, to be sure, Richard seems unstoppable in his striving for supreme power. He deceives his brother George into thinking he can count on Richard for aid. He manages the seemingly impossible task of persuading the Lady Anne to marry him despite his having killed her

---

[20] See Kathryn Schwartz, 'Vexed Relations: Family, State, and the Uses of Women in *3 Henry VI*', in Dutton and Howard (eds.), vol. 2: *The Histories*, 344–60.

husband and father-in-law. He fools Hastings by conspiring with him to destroy the Queen's kinfolk, only to order the execution of Hastings when that gentleman appears unwilling to go along with any plan to seat Richard as king in place of the legitimate heir of the Yorkist line, his young nephew Edward. With Buckingham's able assistance, Richard bamboozles the Londoners to join in acclaiming him as monarch. This steady march toward supremacy might well seem, up to this point, to confirm an audience's bleak assessment that an evil spirit is in control of England's fraught destiny.

Belatedly, however, *Richard III* allows the audience to see that a happier destiny for England has only been awaiting its champion in the person of Henry Tudor, Earl of Richmond. Once he is king, Richard can prevail only through hatred and intimidation. He alienates even his loyal supporter, the Duke of Buckingham. Soon, and inevitably, the baleful power that has raised itself to such heights begins to topple. Unbeknownst to himself, Richard's villainies have achieved what can be viewed ironically as a blessing in disguise. One by one, Richard's victims—Clarence, Hastings, the Lady Anne, the Queen's kindred, Buckingham—come to realize that they are being justly punished for their own perjuries. They are truly penitent, and accept fully the blame for what they should have known how to avoid. For Richard, on the other hand, conscience can only prove to be a torment. Burdened with the curse that is pronounced by his own mother, he must face, in a nightmarish dream, the ghosts of the victims who have come back from the dead to tell him that he will fall in battle at the hands of the Earl of Richmond, whom destiny has sorted out to be the nemesis of the doomed villain.

Historically, Henry Tudor's claim to the English throne was laughable. His grandfather, a Welsh gentleman named Owen Tudor, had married Katherine of Valois after she had been left a widow by her husband Henry V's untimely death in 1422. On his mother's side, Henry Tudor was descended from John of Gaunt, father of Henry IV, but only on the side of the bar sinister: Gaunt had sired three sons with his mistress, Catherine Swynford, wife of a minor English knight and sister-in-law, as it happened, of the great poet Geoffrey Chaucer. These offspring of John of Gaunt and Catherine had been honoured with aristocratic titles and high church offices, but they and their descendants were explicitly barred from inheritance of Gaunt's title and any claim to royal succession. Thus Henry Tudor had no real claim to the throne at all. Yet not many valid claimants were still alive, owing to the reciprocal bloodbath of the civil wars; Richard had done well his job of clearing out the underbrush, even if he thought he was doing it for his own advancement. To be sure, Edward IV's daughter Elizabeth was still alive, but she was a woman, and at all events Henry Tudor co-opted this line of succession by marrying Elizabeth once he had become King Henry VII.

Historians generally agree that Richard III was no worse a person or a king than his successor. Richard III may in fact have been responsible for the killing of his two nephews whose claim to the Yorkist lineage stood in the way of his own, but even if he did so he was guilty of nothing more heinous than Henry VII's own grim determination to see to it that no rival claimants to the throne were allowed to threaten his royal tenure. Lambert Simnel, declaring himself to be the Earl of Warwick, was imprisoned and then given a job in the royal kitchen as spit-turner. Perkin Warbeck, alleging himself to be descended from Edward IV and thus heir to the throne, made two attempts at uprising and was imprisoned in the Tower along with a genuine claimant to the throne, Edward, Earl of Warwick, with whom he tried to escape confinement. Warbeck was recaptured and executed by hanging in 1499. Arguably, both Henry VII and Richard III before him were doing what any monarch had to do in the wake of so many decades of civil strife and contesting candidacies for the throne.

Why Shakespeare chooses in *Richard III* to blacken the character of Richard well beyond any reliable historical indications while simultaneously glorifying the Earl of Richmond as a pious, popular, and successful hero is a matter of concern to anyone wondering if Shakespeare is guilty of toadying to the Tudor monarchy. Several defences can be proposed. Elizabeth I was greatly admired by many of her subjects. England's victory under her rule against the Spanish Armada was widely understood to be a manifestation of God's special grace. Surely, then, the Tudor rulers who had delivered England from God's enemies by means of the Reformation and the defence of Protestantism against the Catholic powers of Europe were the agents of divine purpose. Henry VII's irregular accession to the throne in 1485 had to be legitimized as the consequence of a heaven-sent plan of deliverance from civil war, once the English people had bled for their folly and had learned repentance.

More largely for our purposes here, perhaps, such an overview of England's civil wars as culminating in divine rescue through Henry Tudor gave Shakespeare an overarching architectonic structure for his four-play series of history plays from *1 Henry VI* to *Richard III*. In retrospect, the horrible sufferings depicted in the three earlier plays of this series could be seen as preparation for a harmonizing resolution that would belatedly find meaning and explanation for that suffering. Such a story line was essentially that of a *divina commedia*, not unlike that of the English religious cycles. Artistically, it offered a pattern of cohesion and closure for what at first had looked chaotic.

At the same time, we must not overemphasize the role of providential design in Shakespeare's early history plays. They are also vibrantly historical, keenly fascinated with human behaviour in a time of great national crisis. The story of civil war is above all a story of struggles for power among proud, imperfect men and women. Richard himself is presented in *Richard III* as both a living demon and a psychologically complicated human being. He is denounced as a 'dreadful minister of hell' (1.2.46), an 'elvish-marked, abortive, rooting hog', the 'slave of nature and the son of hell' (1.3.225–7), a 'poisonous bunch-backed toad' (1.3.244), and much more. The play seriously poses a question: is Richard's behaviour a humanly plausible reaction to his being despised by others, or was he pre-existently evil, born with teeth in his head as a sign of his being an emissary of the devil? Correspondingly, the play is ambivalent as to whether his baleful rise to power and his subsequent fall are to be explained in human and historical terms or whether these things are the consequence of the prophetic curses that are pronounced by Queen Margaret and by Richard's own mother, the Duchess of York. Part of the play's extraordinary dramatic excitement, and the fascination of its central character, arises from the suspended uncertainty as to whether we are witnessing secular history or a confirmation of how divine purpose manifests itself in human events.

Scholars and critics are uncertain as to whether *1 Henry VI* is the first written play of the series or whether it may have come after the original versions of Parts II and III known as *The First Part of the Contention* and *The True Tragedy of Richard Duke of York*. The current consensus favours the latter hypothesis, though I remain sceptical. The text of Part I is certainly defective, with Shakespeare arguably as contributor to some of the most effective passages, such as the scene in the Temple Garden when the factions of Lancaster and York declare open hostilities (2.4), and the sequence of action at Bordeaux depicting the brave deaths of Lord Talbot and his son John (4.5–7). The imperfections of a probable collaboration might seem the plausible consequence of an early effort when Shakespeare and his colleagues were still struggling to work out what an English history play should be like. The lack of any reference to Lord Talbot in Part II does not seem inexplicable in a work of loose construction. Samuel Johnson, in the eighteenth century, was content with the notion that the three plays read sequentially enough in their episodic rendition of so much fifteenth-century history. The issue is perhaps not very important.

What does matter is that Shakespeare's four-play historical sequence was largely if not wholly in place by the time Greene attacked him in 1592, and had achieved a great success. Thomas Nashe testified in that same year: 'How would it have joyed brave Talbot (the terror of the French) to think that after he had lain two hundred years in his tomb, he should triumph again on the stage, and have his bones new embalmed with the tears of ten thousand spectators at least (at several times) who, in the tragedian that represents his person, imagine they behold him fresh bleeding'.[21] The English history play had developed a form suitable to this popular new genre that was to remain a staple of London drama throughout the 1590s. Perhaps too, as Gary Taylor plausibly speculates,[22] Greene's attack persuaded Shakespeare that he would do well to set aside his collaborative writing in favour of pursuing what was by now his own distinctive contribution to the writing of plays. He did not object to collaboration as such, and would return to it at the end of his writing career, but for the long interim at the height of his career he preferred being on his own.

REVENGE TRAGEDY

Titus Andronicus, Shakespeare's only tragedy of these early years, may well have been another collaboration, as we have seen. To be sure, his early history plays were sometimes labelled as tragedies in their titles, but the overall shape of the first tetralogy, ending happily with the coming to power of Henry VII, identifies the whole more as a kind of tragicomedy. *Titus Andronicus* is a tragedy in the more formal sense of the term. It is based on a kind of Roman history, though invented and even at times

---

[21] Thomas Nashe, *Pierce Penniless, His Supplication to the Devil* (London: 1592).
[22] See Gary Taylor, 'Shakespeare and Others', cited in note 6 above, esp. 148–9.

fantastical. Shakespeare and his collaborator or collaborators seem to have had access to some prose chapbook and/or ballad that had assembled a fable about ancient Rome made out of mythologies that embodied motifs of rape, dismemberment, and the eating of one's children's flesh as found in Ovid's *Metamorphoses*, Seneca's *Thyestes*, and still other sources.

As an experiment with the genre of tragedy, the play stands alone in Shakespeare's work of the early 1590s. It is a revenge tragedy, in the tradition of Seneca and also of Kyd's *The Spanish Tragedy*, and as such it raises interestingly problematic issues of sympathy with the protagonist.[23] Titus Andronicus is a worthy tragic hero in a number of ways: he is a military leader who has defended Rome against 'the barbarous Goths' (1.1.28) and who is selflessly patriotic to the extent of losing most of his twenty-five sons in battle. Being valiant and uncorrupt, he is a suitable candidate for the imperial diadem of Rome. Yet when he is offered the crown in the play's opening scene, he stands aside in favour of Saturninus, son of the late Emperor of Rome. His only wish is to bury his dead sons with honour. Things quickly go wrong. He acquiesces in the execution of Alarbus, eldest son of the captured Tamora, Queen of the Goths, when Titus' surviving sons demand a reprisal for the deaths of their brethren in battle. 'O cruel irreligious piety!' exclaims Tamora. Her son Chiron echoes the sentiment: 'Was never Scythia half so barbarous' (1.1.130–1). And indeed an audience is bound to feel the force of this condemnation of vengeful execution of a prisoner taken in battle.

No less unfortunate is Titus' agreeing to the new Emperor's proposal that Titus' daughter, Lavinia, become Empress, despite her being engaged to the Emperor's younger brother, Bassianus. When Bassianus undertakes to seize Lavinia as his own, with the active support of Titus' sons, Titus stabs and kills the son, Mutius, who thus stands in his way. He has thus demonstrated his loyalty to the new Emperor, but at the expense of this violence against his own offspring and in defiance of Lavinia's preference for Bassianus. To make matters worse, the Emperor Saturninus almost instantly becomes lustfully obsessed with the sexually seductive, villainous Tamora. She, for her part, is soon carrying on an affair with a Machiavellian Moor named Aaron, with whom she ultimately has a half-caste child. Titus has alienated his family and has delivered himself into the hands of ruthlessly vengeful enemies.

Despite these flaws in his role as protagonist, Titus quickly gains audience sympathy as his persecutors relentlessly pursue their cause of vengeance and wanton destruction. Tamora's sons, Chiron and Demetrius, encountering Bassianus and Lavinia in a forest during a hunt, stab Bassianus, and ravish Lavinia, severing her hands and cutting out her tongue to prevent her from naming her assailants. Aaron entices Titus' sons, Martius and Quintus, to a concealed pit, into which they fall, whereupon Aaron accuses them of the murder of Bassianus to the Emperor Saturninus. Cynically offered a chance by Aaron to send a hand of one of his family members to the Emperor as ransom for the imprisoned Martius and Quintus, Titus cuts off his own hand, only to learn that the

---

[23] See Fredson T. Bowers, *Elizabethan Revenge Tragedy, 1587–1642* (Princeton, NJ: Princeton University Press, 1940).

offer was a ruse. The violence in this early tragedy is unusually nightmarish and grotesque. Lavinia onstage with stumps for hands and bleeding from the mouth is a pitiable sight indeed, calculated to arouse audience outrage at her enemies. Chiron and Demetrius are gloating villains, sinister and obscene. Aaron is the fearful caricature of a murderous and lustful Moor.

In a revenge tragedy of this sort, as in *The Spanish Tragedy*, events are sure to turn at last against the wrongdoers. Titus and his beleaguered clan discover the necessity of fighting cunning deception with equal cunning. Once Lavinia has been taught to reveal the names of her ravishers by guiding a stick in the sand, holding one end in her mouth and moving the stick by her stumps, Titus becomes the full-fledged avenger. Feigning madness in the person of Revenge, he tricks Tamora's sons into allowing themselves to be bound and gagged, whereupon he cuts their throats while Lavinia obligingly holds a basin in her stumps to receive the blood. Dressing himself as a cook, Titus feasts the unsuspecting Emperor and Tamora with the flesh of her sons baked in a pie, whereupon he stabs Tamora, Saturninus stabs Titus, and Lucius kills Saturninus. A great tumult ushers in a sombre resolution of the conflict. Aaron is to be set breast-deep in earth and famished until he dies. Tamora's body is to be thrown forth 'to beasts and birds to prey' (5.3.197).

When Shakespeare came to write *Hamlet* some decade or so after *Titus*, he gave his audiences another tragedy in the revenge genre that had become so popular, but did so in a way that handled the matter of audience sympathy for the revenging protagonist in a profoundly different manner. Titus becomes so immersed in bloody violence himself by the end of his play that an audience is bound to be distanced from the presentation. The result is ironic, at times almost wryly amusing in its garish excesses. *Hamlet*, though a revenge play, finds a way for its protagonist to carry out his ghostly father's command to 'revenge his foul and most unnatural murder' (1.5.25) as an act prompted by Providence and almost without premeditation. It is as though Shakespeare had pondered the artistic difficulty of the revenge play through his own experience as a writer and that of others, and had found a new path.

The genre of tragedy, after another tentative though quite wonderful venture in *Romeo and Juliet* some time in 1594–6, was to become a major vehicle for Shakespeare's supreme achievements at the very end of the 1590s and in the first decade of the seventeenth century: *Julius Caesar* (1599), *Hamlet* (c.1600–1), *Othello* (c.1603–4), *King Lear* (c.1605–6), *Macbeth* (c.1606–7), *Antony and Cleopatra* (c.1606–7), *Timon of Athens* (c.1605–8), and *Coriolanus* (c.1608). The collaborative and early *Titus Andronicus* pointed the way and posed some fascinating questions, but it also seems to have represented an artistic undertaking that Shakespeare was prepared to postpone for later years.

CHAPTER 17

MIDDLE SHAKESPEARE

JAMES J. MARINO

THE PLAYWRIGHT AS CELEBRITY

WHICH was the first of Shakespeare's middle plays? Where did the beginning of his career end, and the middle of his career begin? Such riddles have no answers except those set by the asker. My charge to discuss the middle plays demands that I begin as arbiter of how far my charge extends. I have chosen to take the 'middle' period to mean the fertile expanse of years during which William Shakespeare was inarguably *a* dominant and arguably *the* dominant influence upon English stagecraft. At the beginning and end of his writing life Shakespeare was a talented but not predominant figure, creating highly original work but not setting theatrical fashions. But between Shakespeare's journeyman days and his years as an elder statesman came a decade and more of artistic and professional ascendancy, during which he was the most successful working playwright in England. During that period, Shakespeare was rebuked under no other man's genius, no longer Marlowe's junior competitor and not yet Fletcher's senior colleague. If Shakespeare's middle plays seem in some ways the most 'Shakespearean', then Shakespeare himself might be imagined as fundamentally a middle playwright. He occupies a transitional role in the history of early English drama, between the establishment of the playhouse's basic conventions and the final establishment of its generic norms. The fundamental grammar of theatrical poetry was created during Shakespeare's twenties and its final idiom set in his later forties. The interim was very much his.

Shakespeare's era of pre-eminence did not make him immune to influence. Rather, he gained pre-eminence by digesting and reshaping other playwrights' influences into work that was distinctively his own. The public sign and proof of Shakespeare's mastery was dramaturgical innovation; whatever he had borrowed he had bettered, and made into something unlike what had come before. Shakespeare and his acting partners in the Lord Chamberlain's Men undertook a series of ground-breaking experiments in dramatic storytelling as part of their theatrical rivalry with the Lord Admiral's Men.

In the later 1590s, Shakespeare and his fellows occupied the artistically progressive position, creating distinct artistic identities for both the company and its poet. Shakespeare made himself the leading playwright of his generation in those years by grounding his appeal in newness and implicitly opposing himself to his contemporaries. For a few years, at least, he bestrode his living rivals like a colossus. Of his competitors only George Chapman and the young Ben Jonson would produce anything dramaturgically original during the late 1590s, and Jonson brought his freshest work to Shakespeare and the Chamberlain's Men.[1] By the end of the decade Shakespeare was the most celebrated playwright in England and easily the most prosperous, rich when all the rest were poor. That the most affluent stage poet of that day was also the most original is no accident. Shakespeare had the luxury of commissioning his own work while his peers created the plays their customers demanded, reliable dramas that fitted easily with the Admiral's Men's established practices. Shakespeare supplied his partners with custom work precisely to upstage that well-worn aesthetic.

During James I's reign, Shakespeare gradually ceased to occupy the forward cultural position, as a generation of newer playwrights positioned themselves as the champions of innovation and increasingly cast Shakespeare as a representative of the old guard. His ambitious younger rivals viewed (or purported to view) Shakespeare as part of the very theatrical generation which he had represented himself as opposing, an establishment figure aesthetically aligned with Heywood and Dekker and Kyd. During the first decade of the 1600s Shakespeare responded with complex, original work that absorbed his junior rivals' critiques on one hand but on the other engaged in a searingly powerful debate with his own earlier dramatic style.

When William Shakespeare began writing plays is lost to history. When he became famous for writing plays is surprisingly easy to pinpoint. In 1598 Shakespeare's name begins appearing on playbooks' title-pages (three in 1598 alone) and contemporary witnesses begin mentioning him as a playwright.[2] Earlier witnesses had only identified Shakespeare with his erotic verse, and these new witnesses continue to do so. To assert Shakespeare's authorship of plays was originally to associate those plays with fashionable love poetry. But in 1598 that association became widespread. At the outset of his fame as a playwright, every witness to his dramatic career mentions three specific works: *Venus and Adonis*, *Richard III*, a play that looks backward to reinvent earlier traditions, and *Romeo and Juliet*, which looks forward to Shakespeare's innovative middle style: freely experimenting with genre, capitalizing on Shakespeare's personal fame as love poet, and slyly responding to the repertory of the Lord Admiral's Men.

---

[1] Jonson was so new to the scene in 1598 that Francis Meres praised him only for his tragedies, and not his comedies.

[2] Early witnesses to Shakespeare as a playwright include John Weever, Francis Meres, Gabriel Harvey, and an unknown scribe, all writing in 1598 or later. See E. K. Chambers, *William Shakespeare: A Study of Facts and Problems*, 2 vols. (Oxford: Clarendon Press, 1930), 2: 193–201, and Francis Meres, *Palladis Tamia; Wits Treasury*, Facs., intro., Arthur Freeman (New York: Garland, 1973), 280–4. The famous earlier reference to the 'upstart crow, beautified with our feathers', who is the only 'shake-scene in a country' does not use Shakespeare's actual name.

OUTLIVING MARLOWE

Romeo and Juliet is both wildly original and openly preoccupied with the influence of Christopher Marlowe. Shakespeare famously rewrites one mighty line from Marlowe's *Jew of Malta* into something mightier still. Barabas the Jew, standing beneath a window waiting for his daughter to appear, asks:

> But stay, what star shines yonder in the east?
> The lodestar of my life, if Abigail.   (2.1.41–2)[3]

Romeo, waiting beneath another window, asks a pointedly similar question:

> **But** soft, **what** light through **yonder** window breaks?
> It is the east, and Juliet is the sun.
> Arise fair sun, and kill the envious moon . . .   (2.1.44–6)[4]

Shakespeare has actually regularized Marlowe's scansion a bit; the first syllable of 'window' bears unambiguous stress while the stress upon 'in' is merely positional, and Shakespeare's 'through' is naturally unstressed in a way that 'shines' cannot quite be. The change does not merely overtop Marlowe's line but performs a kind of metrical *recusatio*, demonstrating Shakespeare's ability to match Marlowe at Marlowe's game before moving on to play his own. Since *The Jew of Malta* had been a staple at the Rose playhouse throughout the early 1590s, the reference would have been extremely clear to Shakespeare's original audiences, and their memory of Marlowe's line would be prompted by the visual echo of the earlier tableau. Shakespeare's version rereads Marlowe's scene and forces subsequent viewers to see it through the perspective of the later one; Romeo is not so much shadowed by Barabas as Barabas and Abigail are uncomfortably eroticized by Shakespeare's echo of them. Marlowe has been so effectively rewritten that Shakespeare seems to be influencing the play he imitates.

But this swift, sharp gesture toward Marlowe is only one part of Shakespeare's long public re-imagination of the Admiral's Men's repertory. It is widely noted that *The Merchant of Venice* responds to the main action of *The Jew of Malta*, just as *Richard II* openly reworks Marlowe's *Edward II*. And citations of Marlowe run through Shakespeare's work in the later 1590s. Pistol emphatically if inaccurately quotes *Tamburlaine, Part 2* in *2 Henry IV* (2.4.140–4). *As You Like It* alludes to Marlowe's death and quotes his *Hero and Leander*: 'Dead shepherd, now I prove thy saw of might | Whoever loved that loved not at first sight?' (3.5.82–3). *Hamlet* features a visiting troupe of actors capable of reciting 'Aeneas' tale to Dido' much as it is recited in Marlowe's *Dido, Queen of Carthage* (2.2.426–7, 430–98). Marlowe was apparently very much on Shakespeare's

---

[3] For ease of reference, all quotations from plays by Shakespeare's contemporaries are taken from David Bevington et al. (eds.), *English Renaissance Drama. A Norton Anthology* (New York: Norton, 2002).

[4] All quotations from Shakespeare are taken from Stephen Greenblatt, et al. (eds.), *The Norton Shakespeare: Based on the Oxford Edition*, 2nd edn. (New York: Norton, 2008).

mind, but more was at stake than individual rivalry. The Marlovian allusions usually come alongside allusions to other playwrights and other plays, and especially Admiral's Men's plays. Pistol garbles Tamburlaine's words while obsessively quoting other grandiloquent military dramas from the Admiral's Men's repertory, notably George Peele's *Battle of Alcazar* and his lost *The Turkish Mahomet* (2.4.130–74). Marlowe's love poetry and death come up in a play adapted from a romance by sometime-playwright Thomas Lodge, with a main love plot that parodies Robert Greene's *Orlando Furioso*. *Hamlet* is deeply engaged with Thomas Kyd's seminal revenge play *The Spanish Tragedy*. Shakespeare's business is not with one formidable peer but with his whole generation of playwrights. Marlowe, Kyd, Peele, Greene, and Lodge make a nearly complete roster of Shakespeare's original peer group, including nearly every professional dramatist whose name had appeared on a printed play before Shakespeare's had.

There are many elements of his contemporaries' basic style that Shakespeare did not contest. He maintains the established storytelling grammar of dialogues, soliloquies, and asides, while looking for different ways to use those narrative tools. He draws upon the same sources for plots that his peers do. Iambic pentameter mixed with prose had become the standard theatrical measure and Shakespeare continued to use it as his metrical baseline. As his verse became more relaxed, more flexible, and less heavily end-stopped, his prosody began to set him apart from the inescapable regularity of earlier pentameter drama. The plays that established blank verse as a playhouse staple bore the burden of establishing its firm, unrelenting beat in every playgoer's ear; Shakespeare, writing in his middle career for listeners who had grown accustomed to that underlying rhythm, was free to sweeten his thunder. He was no longer limited to drumming heroic speeches, and therefore no longer needed percussively heroic speakers.

The Admiral's Men built much of their repertory around heroic, bombastic pentameter lines, and especially around Tamburlaine and his theatrical kindred: virile warrior heroes, often from the Muslim East, who combine triumphant martial rhetoric with thrilling drum-beat verse. This type also recurs in Shakespeare's middle plays, but not to triumph. The Prince of Morocco in *The Merchant of Venice* is one such visitor from the competing repertory, swearing

> By this scimitar,
> That slew the Sophy and a Persian Prince
> That won three fields of Sultan Suleiman,
> I would o'erstare the sternest eyes that look,
> Outbrave the heart most daring on the earth,
> Pluck the young sucking cubs from the she-bear,
> Yea, mock the lion when 'a roars for prey,
> To win thee, lady.   (2.1.24–31)

The lady, of course, is not so to be won, and Morocco is hopelessly out of place; Shakespeare's comedy is holding his rivals' tragedies up to affectionate mockery. But Hotspur in *1 Henry IV* is surely in the right genre for a heroic soldier eager

> To pluck bright honour from the pale-faced moon,
> Or dive into the bottom of the deep,
> Where fathom-line could never touch the ground,
> And pluck up drownèd honour by the locks,
> So he that doth redeem her thence might wear,
> Without corrival, all her dignities.   (1.3.200–5)

The poetry here is admirable, and the Hotspur himself generally admired by the play's other characters. Hotspur is not a parodic version of the Admiral's Men's warlike heroes. He is an exemplary version. He embodies ideals of military and political leadership that are repudiated by his self-destruction and a set of literary and theatrical values that Shakespeare deliberately ironizes. The play admits the appeals of Hotspur and of his gloriously egocentric verse, but offers spectators a subtler model of rhetoric and leadership in the person of Prince Henry. Hotspur and Tamburlaine purport to be entirely and transparently themselves, while Henry is from his first appearance in *1 Henry IV* a performer self-consciously creating effects. Henry is calculating rather than impulsive, politic rather than sincere, complicated and subtly strategic even when he seems most simple and direct. While Shakespeare's Henry V has been read as a myth of idealized English kingship, he presents an alternative to the naive authoritarian fantasies offered at the Admiral's Men's Rose, which imagined action heroism as leadership. Shakespeare would continue to examine and deflate that popular warlord fantasy throughout his career, with his portrayals growing increasingly dark.

Nonetheless, the old martial heroes continued to hold sway with the Admiral's Men's audience for the rest of Shakespeare's career; even when it had become mildly unfashionable, the heroic repertory was never unprofitable. If the Admiral's Men's approach did not evolve, one explanation is that they had no desire to tamper with a successful formula. Another is that the truly innovative playwrights who had created that formula for them were gone. Marlowe, Kyd, Greene, Peele, and Thomas Watson were dead. Lodge seems to have given up writing plays. Shakespeare's most important close contemporaries were George Chapman and Michael Drayton, who like Shakespeare had reputations as non-dramatic poets and who, like nearly every other working playwright, laboured for the Admiral's Men. Francis Meres's *Palladis Tamia* (1598) features Shakespeare prominently in his lists of leading dramatists, but the rest of the playwrights Meres names fall into three basic categories: gentlemen amateurs, dead men who had written Admiral's Men's plays, and living playwrights still writing Admiral's Men plays.[5] All but two of the playhouse dramatists Meres names contributed to the Admiral's Men's inventory. The exceptions were the disgraced Thomas Nashe and Shakespeare himself. And until 1598 we cannot name any Chamberlain's Men playwright but Shakespeare; the second identifiable contributor, Jonson, gave the troupe one comedy in 1598 and a second in 1599. Shakespeare stood apart from the rest

---

[5] Meres, 282, 283.

of his generation in the 1590s because nearly all of them were working for his competition.

Shakespeare did have collaborators, of various kinds, and he was not responsible for creating his company's repertory single-handedly. A few anonymous Chamberlain's Men's plays made their way into print, including *A Warning for Fair Women* (1599), *A Larum for London* (1602), and *Thomas, Lord Cromwell*, by 'W. S.' (1602). Presumably the company had a number of other plays that are now lost. And Shakespeare need not even be imagined penning every single word of the plays in his canon; strong arguments have been made for other hands in a number of Shakespeare's plays, although scholars still tend to find such collaboration chiefly in Shakespeare's less well-loved plays and in cases where the surviving text appears problematic.[6] Moreover, the nature of the early modern playhouse assured that plays would continue to be tweaked and revised over time, whether by Shakespeare or by others. Shakespeare was never his company's sole playwright, but he was its signature playwright.

What Shakespeare enjoyed was the liberty to impose his own artistic identity upon his company's plays and repertory, although neither the authority nor the labour of composition was ever his alone. The precise internal arrangements of the Lord Chamberlain's Men are beyond recovery, but Shakespeare's position as player, shareholder, and playwright ensured some degree of integration between writing decisions and management decisions, an integration that allowed the company's dramaturgy to develop and evolve as their principal poet's did. The Chamberlain's Men could promote themselves by promoting Shakespeare; they appreciated the market value of artistic innovation. The dramaturgy of the Admiral's Men, whose playwrights did not participate in the company's profits or decisions, was comparatively static. Playwrights served the the Admiral's Men as vendors, trying to suit their product to the company's known preferences. Offering the actors variations on what had succeeded before made the sale easier, and working within comfortable formulas made it easier to split the work of writing a play among several writers and complete it quickly. Although the Admiral's Men's house style had initially coalesced around the work of a few major talents, it had become functionally anonymous. Even the contributions of a poet like Drayton are difficult to distinguish from those of his fellows. The company's artistic identity derived from its actors and their established repertory; the writing was aimed at maintaining that identity. The Chamberlain's Men identified themselves with a newer aesthetic, and Shakespeare brought their evolving style to both new plays and old ones.

---

[6] Brian Vickers, for example, argues for collaboration in 'probably eight surviving plays—*1 Henry VI*, *Edward III*, "The Booke of Sir Thomas More", *Titus Andronicus*, *Timon of Athens*, *Pericles*, *Henry VIII*, *The Two Noble Kinsmen*, and perhaps one now lost—*Cardenio*' (*Shakespeare, Co-Author: A Historical Study of Five Collaborative Plays* [Oxford: Oxford University Press, 2002], 137). Gary Taylor and John Lavagnino, editing the *Collected Works of Thomas Middleton* (Oxford: Clarendon Press, 2007), identify Thomas Middleton as a co-author of *Timon* and as the 'adapter' of Shakespeare's *Macbeth* and *Measure for Measure*.

MAKING IT NEW

Some of Shakespeare's writing time during the company's first decade was undoubtedly spent on revision. In almost every case where some form of a Shakespeare play pre-dates the creation of the Chamberlain's Men, that play's earliest documented form is notably different from the canonical text printed later. (The main exception is *Titus Andronicus*, whose text is largely stable.) Nineteenth-century critics, following Edmond Malone, tended to view these early printings as Shakespeare's sources or early drafts, and Malone himself argued specifically that Shakespeare had revised the *Henry VI* plays. Twentieth-century critics, beginning with the New Bibliographers, tended to view these early variants as derived (often illegitimately) from already-completed Shakespearean originals, a view that maximizes Shakespeare's personal literary author-ity but involves a number of chronological and evidentiary embarrassments. The plausibility of that later narrative varies greatly from play to play; it is hardly incontro-vertible in the best cases, and in others it is nearly impossible to make work.

It is hard to argue plausibly that the old anonymous plays *King Leir, The Troublesome Reign of King John*, and *The Famous Victories of Henry V* represent pirated versions of Shakespeare's *King Lear, King John*, and his plays about Henry IV and Henry V. These plays are now widely, albeit not unanimously, understood as sources that Shakespeare drastically reworked, as he is widely considered to have rewritten an earlier version of *Hamlet*. How many old plays he revised is an argument for another chapter, but in some cases Shakespeare was clearly collaborating diachronically with an earlier playwright, building upon elements of the older work to create a new whole. Most of the plays he began with were old-fashioned compared to Marlowe's or Kyd's, many dating from the heyday of the Queen's Men in the 1580s. Rewriting them allowed Shakespeare to expand his partners' repertory of new plays more quickly, even as they appealed to audiences' memories of old favourites. The resulting works leap-frogged the Admiral's Men's dramaturgy, turning pre-Marlovian chestnuts into post-Marlovian experiments.

The work of making these old plays new required an education in dramatic structure. The revisions are far more extensive and complicated than the routine patches, additions, and alterations perennially made to early modern plays. While the connections between *The Famous Victories* and Shakespeare's own history plays, or between *King Leir* and *King Lear*, are undeniable, the differences between them are profound. Shakespeare's histories expand the material covered in *The Famous Victories* to fifteen acts rich in secondary plots and supporting characters; both versions are structured around Henry V's character arc, beginning and ending it in the same place, but Shakespeare covers far more ground along the way. Shakespeare develops the central character arc at greater length and in greater detail, making it strong enough to bear the weight of the plays' new material without being overwhelmed. If Falstaff is the figure of copious, proliferating narrative, the Prince embodies the implacable, indispensable principle of formal structure, relentlessly turning each episode or digression into one more forward step toward the story's preordained end.

King Lear adds a new B plot, borrowed from another source and elaborately ramified, to the older *King Leir*; complicates the play's A plot slightly and profoundly enriches its language; and then meticulously intergrafts the two plots. *The Taming of the Shrew* seems to apply the same revision strategies to the Pembroke's Men's play called *The Taming of a Shrew*, although twentieth-century editing tradition views the Pembroke's Men's play as derived from Shakespeare's. Whoever did the rewriting proceeded much as Shakespeare would later proceed with *King Leir*: retaining the best moments and basic structure of the A plot but thoroughly complicating and improving its language while replacing the original B plot with a new one borrowed from an upscale literary source, subsequently developed, and methodically connected to the A plot so that the jointwork does not show. If this labour was undertaken to turn Shakespeare's *Taming of the Shrew* into *The Taming of a Shrew*, then the labour was poorly spent. If Shakespeare remodelled *The Taming of a Shrew* into *The Taming of the Shrew*, he knew what he was doing.

These deep, wide-ranging revisions differ strikingly from the documented revisions that the playhouse financier Philip Henslowe commissioned for the Admiral's Men's *Doctor Faustus* and *The Spanish Tragedy*. Those 'additions' are chiefly extensions and interpolations, adding new scenes to old plays without any deliberate reconsideration of the whole. *Doctor Faustus* gains several new scenes of clowning, while a number of existing speeches and scenes are retouched; the additions to *The Spanish Tragedy* are almost entirely new scenes for Hieronimo, the leading man. These mid-scale revisions only address dramatic structure by default, moderately burdening the plays' construction with the weight of new material. The overall narrative is not expanded or reorganized to integrate the added scenes and the play is left to sag very slightly in the middle. The revisions to *Doctor Faustus* and *The Spanish Tragedy* are like adding a new room to an existing building. Shakespeare's revisions are like incorporating a Tudor country house into a newer and grander edifice. The resulting house preserves features of the original but is renovated and integrated into a larger, more modern whole. Shakespeare's *Lear* could claim to be both an old landmark and a state-of-the-art creation.

Only a deep understanding of dramatic construction permits renovation on such a scale. One needs to know what features can be changed or discarded and what load-bearing elements must be preserved and reinforced. And the builder needs to understand how the new, larger whole will cohere. Shakespeare was not a contractor; he was an architect. He was allowed more scope to remodel and reimagine his company's plays than poets hired for discrete 'additions' could ever have had. As part-owner of his rehabilitated properties, Shakespeare had time to learn their construction intimately and the luxury of implementing his most ambitious remodelling in sucessive stages if he liked. Revisions could continue for years, as long as Shakespeare grasped the underlying structure.

The same profound grasp of dramatic architecture that marks Shakespeare's revision projects can be seen in the new plays of his middle period. Grasping how a house is designed and how to rebuild it also means grasping how a new house may be built. Shakespeare had thought deeply about how to integrate parts that lacked any original or natural relationship into a unified and seemingly coherent whole. He had also learned to use repeating words and images to bind disparate components of a play together. Shakespeare's motifs are structure as well as style. They actively bind plots and sub-plots, scenes and actions, into an apparently organic whole. The well-studied keywords and image clusters in *King Lear* (the images of animal violence, the eyesight and blindness motif, the play's ongoing rumination on the word 'Nature') run through every part of the work, whether taken from *King Leir* or introduced from another source, so that the resulting drama seems to be all of one piece. The same techniques that allowed Shakespeare to create a sense of dramatic unity from originally independent units allowed him to create a feeling of dramatic cohesion from stylistically diverse and apparently irreconcilable elements. English plays had always thrived on generic and stylistic multiplicity, but during his thirties Shakespeare artfully raised England's hybrid theatre to a nearly infinite variety, cross-breeding styles, genres, and moods to create subtle tonal effects. Shakespeare's early plays had fitted clearly into genres and relatively unified styles: *The Comedy of Errors*, the *Henry VI* plays, and *Titus Andronicus* are as straightforward examples of comedies, histories, and tragedies as Shakespeare provides. But in his middle career, confident in his ability to sustain dramatic cohesion, Shakespeare was free to experiment with the tragical-comical-historical-pastoral mode.

The plays of his middle period can hold together with sketchy and haphazard plotting; *As You Like It*, *Twelfth Night*, and *The Merry Wives of Windsor* make more sense on stage than in any plot diagram. They can contain almost painfully divergent emotional notes; *Twelfth Night*'s combination of seduction, horseplay, musical melancholy, and unrepentant cruelty can not be explained by any set straightforward critical prescriptions. A play like *1 Henry IV* may be a comedy, tragedy, and history at the same time, although the prescribed betrothal is forestalled until the end of *Henry V*. Hamlet may play the clown in the midst of his revenge tragedy before dispensing metatheatrical strictures about clowning. Yet these plays hold together better than plays constructed from more obvious blueprints.

Perversely, the complexity and multiplicity of such plays seem out of reach for many dramas that were actually composed by multiple writers, who needed to make sure their individual contributions would fit together properly. The audience's sense of cohesion had to be guaranteed by the visible mechanisms of strong plot, clear genre, and unified poetic style. Shakespeare could dispense with these obvious devices, or with the novice prescriptions of the Aristotelian unities, and rely on techniques that make an audience feel artistic cohesion without realizing why. Repetition of words, motifs, and structural elements works upon audiences subliminally, allowing auditors to experience a work's wholeness intuitively despite a lack of signposts. Indeed, such repetition becomes strangely more effective when the obvious signposts are removed, so that the audience apprehends the formal cohesion unconsciously rather than noticing it consciously; structure that is felt but not seen is experienced as 'natural'. Shakespeare's early modern reputation as an unlearned genius stems from misunderstandings of his approach to dramatic form. His tendency to hide the strong formal structures beneath the surface of his plays and to hold his works together with patterns that are not apparent to the casual listener creates the impression that he uses no art at all. Such apparent spontaneity requires far more craftsmanship than more obviously crafted works. Shakespeare's methods are no less mechanical or technical than his rivals', but the technical mechanisms are subtler.

And yet some of the subtlest mechanics are also some of the most durable. Because Shakespeare achieves many of his effects cumulatively, by weaving a network of repeated sounds and images throughout each work, those effects become fairly robust, capable of surviving further rounds of revisions without any catastrophic loss of power. Shakespeare worked with the expectation that his plays would continue to be rewritten and adjusted by various hands: by his fellow actors, by his own pen, and perhaps by subsequent writers. He was the plays' signature author, but not the sole one. If he felt that a literary effect was crucial to a play's success, Shakespeare had to weave that effect through the fabric of the play so thoroughly that only a nearly complete rewriting of the script would unravel the pattern.

King Lear takes some of its artistic cohesion and emotional colour from its recurring patterns, but the power of each motif does not reside in any particular instance of that motif. Nor do Shakespeare's motifs depend on any specific number of repetitions, because the listener is not meant to count them consciously. The pattern will persist if one image, or more than one, is incidentally cut from the play. Since the repetition needs only to reach a certain critical mass, the optimal count of repetitions is necessarily approximate, a range rather than a numeral: often enough to work upon the listener's mind as a pervasive element of the drama, but not so often as to become obvious and thus appear counterproductively artificial. Within that range, there is room to cut some instances of any one motif while reducing the motif's power only slightly if at all.

Although any alteration in a literary text inevitably changes meaning, Shakespeare's plays are designed to tolerate alterations with a minimal loss of effectiveness. They are robust: meant to wear well over many years in many weathers and to be patched easily as needed. Shakespeare's works are not the brittle masterpieces prized by critics who identify the well-crafted text as the one that would be damaged by the change of a single word. Shakespeare's plays are crafted so well that they are hard to damage. This is surely true of *King Lear*, whose revised Quarto and Folio texts retain their essential power and identity, despite the many illuminating differences between them. It is true of *Hamlet*, which is palpably *Hamlet* in either the Second Quarto or the Folio texts and which works on stage whether Hamlet speaks the 'How all occasions inform against me' soliloquy or not. The last four centuries of editing, conflating, and performing testify to the remarkable durability of these plays, which have kept their power over audiences although the precise text being acted changes with almost every production. Ever since Nahum Tate's version of *King Lear* with its happy ending gave ground to relatively more faithful texts in the nineteenth century, critics have been keenly aware of how hard Shakespeare is to improve. But it is also important to acknowledge the even more fundamental lesson of the past 400 years: a Shakespeare play is astonishingly hard to ruin.

THE ONLY LOVE GOD

The core of Shakespeare's initial literary celebrity was his renown as a love poet. *Venus and Adonis* continued to be his best-selling work throughout the 1590s and indeed through the rest of his life, and the publication of *The Passionate Pilgrim* in 1599 confirmed his ongoing public reputation for love poetry. *The Passionate Pilgrim* treats him as England's foremost love poet, aggregating the amorous verse of several other poets including Marlowe under the banner of Shakespeare's authorship. Any plausibly decent love poem, even Marlowe's 'Passionate Shepherd to His Love', counts as a 'Shakespeare' poem to the compilers, because 'Shakespeare' was a synecdoche for love poetry.

Shakespeare's company took both commercial and artistic advantage of his special fame. Almost every play that Shakespeare originated between 1594 and the end of Elizabeth's reign, which is to say every play that has no earlier dramatic precursor, is occupied with the question of love; witness not only *Romeo and Juliet* but *Love's Labour's Lost*, *A Midsummer Night's Dream*, *The Merchant of Venice*, *Much Ado About Nothing*, *As You Like It*, *Twelfth Night*, *All's Well That Ends Well*, and *The Merry Wives of Windsor*. (The glaring exceptions are *Julius Caesar* and *Richard II*, the latter a prequel to the Henry V material.) The Lord Chamberlain's Men were evidently confident that playgoers would pay to hear 'Sweet Master Shakespeare' demonstrate the art of eloquent wooing. Meanwhile Shakespeare's works were drawing on the style and vocabulary of the contemporary English love lyric in ways that were unprecedented on the stage.

Love plots had always been essential components of playhouse drama, but the actual poetry of the obligatory love scenes had been relatively stilted and compressed. The love material in *The Spanish Tragedy* and *Friar Bacon and Friar Bungay*, to choose a tragic and a comic example, can barely approach the routine quality of later Elizabethan love scenes. Lovers in Marlowe's plays speak in the tyrant's vein, with the same heroic megalomania that marks their other speeches. Tamburlaine may boast his love for Zenocrate, but those boasts are essentially announcements, not seductions. And there is an enormous distance between *Edward II*'s 'Come, Gaveston, | And share the kingdom with thy dearest friend,' (1.1.1–2) on the one hand and 'Come live with me and be my love' on the other. The question here is not the playwrights' facility with love verse, but the distinctions that they observed between dramatic and lyric decorum. Marlowe keeps the style of his masterful erotic verses separate from that of his epic and historical tragedies, just as Drayton abstains from his lyric style while writing plays for the Admiral's Men. Marlowe mocks the very idea of incorporating the lyric within his tragedy, with Ithamore spouting a parody of Marlowe's 'The Passionate Shepherd to

His Love' in *The Jew of Malta* (4.2.97–107). Part of Marlowe's multifaceted joke is that such language does not fit a tragic stage, even a stage capacious enough to encompass Barabas and Ithamore's macabre clowning, and so Ithamore's attempt to speak lyrically makes him ridiculous. When Marlowe's characters speak of love, they speak in the terms of empire, triumph, and destruction. Even Faustus's ardent question about 'the face that launched a thousand ships | And burned the topless towers of Ilium', obsesses on epic violence and serves to introduce a long monologue about Homeric mayhem (5.1.90–109). Marlovian lovers invoke Jove more than they mention Cupid. If they can hear a nightingale they take no notice.

The lush, erotic style of Shakespeare's famous 'lyric period' breaks down this generic decorum so thoroughly and radically that it has become hard to see the rules that he was breaking. Shakespeare does not limit himself to brief inset lyrics, as earlier playwrights had. Instead he saturates his plays of the later 1590s with the tropes and diction of the love lyric, and his sweetly amorous verse offers no boundary to contain those lyrical elements. It is tempting to argue that Shakespeare is 'lyricizing' English drama as Mikhail Bakhtin describes literary genres becoming 'novelized', but the better analogy is with Bakhtin's description of the novel absorbing and digesting other genres. Shakespeare demonstrates that the theatre can adopt the voice of any literary genre it pleases, and this may be his most radical breach of generic decorum. Intermingling comedy and tragedy, the prescribed kinds of drama, was a refinement upon old popular tradition, but writing drama in the mode of an entirely different poetic kind was undiscovered country. Moreover, by drawing so extensively upon lyric Shakespeare aligned himself with the moderns rather than the ancients. The Elizabethan love poem, what Sidney calls 'that lyrical kind of songs and sonnets', was distinct from the classical lyric (itself poorly theorized by texts such as Aristotle's *Poetics*) and descended from *Trecento* Florence rather than imperial Rome. Shakespeare's lyric phase proclaims him a deeply vernacular playwright: fashionable, contemporary, and owing as much to Wyatt and Surrey as to Ovid.

The stage naturally interrogated love lyric's premises. The perpetually-suffering Petrarchan lover does not fit easily into the structures of comedy or tragedy, both of which prescribe some end to his pleasing pains. And Shakespeare remorselessly probes and undermines exhausted tropes, serially demolishing outworn conventions in order to erect comparatively fresher and more authentic-seeming ones. Romeo abandons his shopworn Petrarchanism so that Shakespeare may set a new standard for love verse; Benedick rejects even that standard to woo in eccentric prose. Meanwhile, plays demanded that the Petrarchan beloved be dramatized in her own right, rather than contained in a sonneteer's monologues. Shakespeare's middle plays are filled with heroines like Olivia, Rosalind, and Beatrice who speak pointedly to their wooers about the conventions of wooing. When Rosalind gives tutorials on proper courtship, she discourses with her tongue rather than with her eyes.

But the lyric enlarged the drama as well. It seems obvious in retrospect to put fashionable love verse in the mouths of comic lovers, but those intricate, extended expressions of love create an improved illusion of emotional depth. Shakespeare's comic heroes and heroines speak of love more feelingly than either plot or Plautus really demands. And the lyric palette's power to express sophistication and reflection creates new possibilities for depicting introspective tragic characters who appear to have complex inner lives. Shakespeare's *Richard II*, for example, is a major break from chronicle history tradition: a historical tragedy perversely suffused with the style of love lyric, deliberately violating the expectations of genre. The lyricism allows Shakespeare to build a successful drama around a passive hero, whose main role in the plot is to suffer rather than to act. Because within the lyric mode reflection itself is action, Shakespeare's Richard always has plenty to do: to meditate upon his situation, elaborate his feelings, order and frame events in poetic figures. Richard is not an active king by the standards of historians or stage heroes, but Shakespeare makes him actively reflective. In creating such a king, Shakespeare began refining techniques that would make his later tragic heroes seem to cogitate and brood, as if they had interior lives and consciences to make them cowards. Shakespeare's Macbeth strikes most readers as more inward-looking and more psychologically complicated than his Richard III, written only a decade or so earlier. The central difference between the characters is a decade of increasingly evocative, because essentially lyrical, speech upon the stage.

Through with Love

William Shakespeare did not remain the glass of fashion in the playhouse, and the Elizabethan love lyric did not remain in vogue. Shakespeare's personal success reached a height which left him little further to climb. The building of the Globe playhouse in 1599 with Shakespeare as an investor gave him a secure financial and institutional position. He quite literally owned a piece of the landscape. The ascension of James I in 1603 and accompanying translation of the Lord Chamberlain's Servants into the King's Servants at once recognized and prescribed the company's pre-eminence. It would be hard to imagine a greater success from the vantage of Shakespeare's early career, and no easily visible steps remained for his career to further ascend. And when Shakespeare had no higher to climb, it was inevitable that newer playwrights would begin to come closer to his success.

The company's competition did not surrender the field. After the construction of the Globe, the Admiral's Men built a new playhouse, the Fortune, and their Rose was leased to another company, Worcester's Men, who purchased several old Admiral's Men's plays. Moreover, the Lord Chamberlain's Men's star clown, William Kemp, left the group and after a certain interim joined Worcester's Men. Critics have traditionally argued that Shakespeare begins to write a new kind of clown roles for Kemp's replacement, Robert Armin, a narrative recently complicated and re-theorized by the work of Richard Preiss.[7] Armin needed to play Kemp's old roles effectively while continuing to create a new aesthetic, an artistic problem faced by Shakespeare's company as a whole.

---

[7] Richard Preiss, 'Robert Armin Do the Police in Different Voices', in Peter Holland and Stephen Orgel (eds.), *From Performance to Print in Shakespeare's England* (Basingstoke: Palgrave Macucillan, 2006), 208–27.

The Chamberlain's Men now had two sets of rivals who acted the traditional early 1590s repertory in the traditional early-1590s style, and England's most famous clown had defected to one of them. On the other hand, there was a revival of children's playing companies, with two indoor theatres featuring new companies of boys. The boys' plays were commissioned from artistically ambitious playwrights including Jonson, Chapman, Marston, Middleton, Beaumont, and Fletcher, who dispensed with old-fashioned stage clowning entirely. These newer dramatists seem to have enjoyed higher profiles than the Admiral's Men's playwrights did, and the famous Poetomachia or 'Poet's War' that Jonson, Marston, and Dekker briefly waged among themselves (with glances at and the occasional topical glance from Shakespeare) suggests how dramatists could use the boy companies to publicize themselves.

Around 1600, Shakespeare and the Lord Chamberlain's Men occupied the aesthetic middle of the London stage, between the artistic conservatism of the other two adult companies and the freshly minted repertories of the two children's companies. The Shakespeare plays most confidently dated to this period are masterful reinventions of established genres, and 'Friendly Shakespeare's Tragedies' seemed to Anthony Scoloker a perfect synthesis of artistry and popularity, able 'to please all'.[8] *Henry V* represents the final triumph of Shakespeare's new military hero, the patriotically Machiavellian and rhetorically generous anti-Tamburlaine. *Hamlet*, which alludes to both the company's adult and adolescent rivals, is a brilliant deconstruction of the old-fashioned revenge tragedy, dramatizing the avenger's rumination as action; Hamlet wishes 'with wings as swift | As meditation or the thoughts of love' to 'sweep to his revenge' (1.5.29–31) before discovering the agonizing speed of meditation and thought. *As You Like It* sets the comic and pastoral modes against themselves; aristocrats in rustic disguises encounter genuine shepherds, the satiric truth-tellers come in more than one unreliable, mutually incompatible model, and the proliferating lovers and love games expose one another as variably ridiculous but invariably ruled by artifice. *As You Like It* holds a mirror up to genre.

But the newer generation of writers who especially thrived in the boys' playhouses viewed Shakespeare as simply the leader of the older generation they strove to displace. When Beaumont mockingly quotes Hotspur's speech about 'plucking bright honor from the pale-faced moon' in *The Knight of the Burning Pestle* (Induction, 79–83), it is clear that Beaumont does not view Hotspur as a response to the ranting Admiral's Men's tradition but as an extension of it. Jonson lumps Shakespeare's *Titus Andronicus* with Kyd's *Spanish Tragedy*, implying that Shakespeare himself had not moved on from the early style of his generation. And John Webster praises Shakespeare faintly for his 'happy and copious industry' along with Dekker and Heywood, playwrights for companies that had originally been the Admiral's and Worcester's Men.[9] Such ambitious dramatists faulted Shakespeare for his lack of classicism, beginning the long discourse of Shakespeare as a natural, untutored genius. Jonson writes about Shakespeare's 'small Latin and less Greek' in the opening pages of the 1623 Folio, and Beaumont hopes in an epigraph that he might 'from all learning keep these lines as

---

[8] *Daiphantus* (1604), sig. E4v, quoted in Chambers, *William Shakespeare*, 2: 214–15.
[9] *Bartholomew Fair*, Induction, 105–9; *The White Devil*, 'To the Reader'.

clear | as Shakespeare's best are, which our heirs shall hear'.[10] Shakespeare's innovative violations of classical prescriptions were construed by his younger rivals, who espoused clearer generic boundaries and stricter decorum, as simple ignorance of the rules.

The fashionable new poets also stressed their individual poetic styles, which required emphases on stylistic unity and on a fixed, authorial text. The new idea of the 'dramatic poem' as distinct from the performance text was a necessary prerequisite to the invention of dramatic poets as elite cultural figures. The newer poets' insistence on their authority over the play, like the Admiral's Men's assertions of their authority over playwrights, meant an emphasis on plotting and on relatively clear generic boundaries. While the Admiral's Men had stressed plot and genre to facilitate piece-work, 'dramatic poets' stressed them to highlight the author's handiwork. Structuring a play with a web of motifs that the audience would not consciously perceive would never do for the younger dramatists, who needed their artistry credited. Nor were they interested in robust effects that could survive repeated revisions; because they saw revision as diminishing their authority, they asserted the fragility of their dramatic poems, their vulnerability to tampering. They did not value Shakespeare's novel techniques because articulating aesthetic prescriptions was central to their own cultural authority, and artistic rules that had not yet been codified could not advance their programme. *Ars celare artem* is a motto for artists whose reputation is secure. Jacobean playwrights structured their plays with easily apprehensible rules because they needed their artistry apprehended.

Shakespeare responded to this younger generation by paying even less obedience to generic decorum. *Troilus and Cressida* is the least easily categorized of all of Shakespeare's plays, described as a comedy in quarto publication and included among the tragedies in 1623. It is explicitly classical and satirical but undermines both classicism and satire: its epic story is thoroughly subverted, generic classifications flouted, and at the end satire is allowed neither a secure vantage for critique nor the comfortable satisfaction of laughter. *Troilus and Cressida* critiques the playwrights who were critiquing Shakespeare, and the traditionalists as well. (Thomas Dekker and Henry Chettle had written a *Troilus and Cressida*, now lost.) It continues Shakespeare's dissection of the Admiral's Men's soldier-heroes on a new front; Hector is the most genuinely admirable warrior in Shakespeare, whose murder undermines the values to which the play's characters pretend allegiance but also the traditional repertory's cult of soldiership and Jonson's fetish for the ancients.

But more importantly, *Troilus and Cressida* is an early landmark in Shakespeare's extended critique of his own amorous drama, a critique he develops more effectively than Jonson or Beaumont could. Shakespeare's Jacobean period constitutes a staged reconsideration of his previous decade's work. Part of this grows naturally from his earlier sceptical interrogations of the love-poetry conventions he was using, but in *Troilus and Cressida* courtship is itself the problem, and no improvement in poetic technique can alter the fundamental corruption of its nature. Troilus and Cressida are

[10] Chambers, *William Shakespeare*, 2: 224.

allowed to woo almost as eloquently as any Shakespearean lovers, but instead of being ennobled by the poetry they speak, they reveal love poetry's moral failures.

Shakespeare's erotic palinode continues through *Measure for Measure*, *Othello*, and *Antony and Cleopatra*. *Measure for Measure* cannot imagine a couple whose wooing fully observes the commandments of sexual morality, except (perhaps) for Isabella and the Duke, whom it cannot imagine actually wooing. Only a marriage proposal divorced from any previous courtship is depicted as completely untainted by sexual impropriety, a formulation as undeniable as it is absurd. *Othello*, on the other hand, depicts characters deeply and self-destructively committed to idealized love. Othello's essentially Petrarchan language of superlatives and extremes, which allows no term between hell and heaven or between incarnate angels and whores, makes him susceptible to Iago's corrosive, cynically materialist perspective (itself a borrowing from fashionable Jacobean satire). Othello stands convicted both as a lover, believing the hoary tropes of erotic poetry too literally, and as a decayed soldier, a still-more-diminished echo of Tamburlaine and his tribe. *Antony and Cleopatra*, too, focuses on Antony's decline both as warrior and as lover. The play suggests that those two roles might be fundamentally incompatible (calling 'Eros, mine armor, Eros!' [4.4.1] raises pointed doubts), but insists that age diminishes the lover and the soldier alike. Enobarbus' claim of Cleopatra that 'Age cannot wither her nor custom stale, | Her infinite variety' (2.2.240–1) is a poignantly self-deceiving half-truth, true at best about love poetry instead of lovers. No art can preserve Cleopatra in despite of time, except literature. Whether the conventions of erotic encomia are so infinitely variable that they can never be exhausted is a question Shakespeare leaves unanswered.

Which shall I call the last of Shakespeare's middle plays? *Coriolanus*, Shakespeare's final tragedy, offers a convenient ending place. Its title character is the last of Shakespeare's dangerously unreliable military heroes, a lineage involving Othello and Antony but also Macbeth and Alcibiades. In the latter half of Shakespeare's career, these figures become progressively less engaging; Coriolanus has all of Hotspur's redoubtable energy but fewer of his charms. Shakespeare's self-destructive soldiers seem less and less designed to woo spectators from the conservative repertory derived from the old Admiral's Men and more tailored to the new audience for scepticism and classical decorum. The thundering Marlovian heroes had never left the London playhouses, but their share of the market had shrunk to an irreducible core that could not be lured away. The meaningful competition was with the younger playwrights and younger companies.

That competition came to an end or at least to a new phase in 1608, when the leading company of children was officially disbanded and the King's Men took over the Blackfriars playhouse. The remaining years of Shakespeare's career were occupied by the integration of the old boys' company resources—their actors, their audience, their playwrights, and their plays—into the King's Men's enterprise. John Fletcher, who would succeed Shakespeare as the King's Men's signature playwright, entered the company's orbit around this time. The middle of Shakespeare's working life, the years when he set his company's literary direction, came to a discreet and lucrative end.

CHAPTER 18

POETRY

CATHERINE BATES

IN the sweltering summer of 1592, an outbreak of plague struck the city of London and, while a menace to which the city was always prone, it spread on this occasion with such speed and virulence that the authorities were obliged to close the theatres for fear of contagion. Shakespeare—not yet thirty, relatively new to London, and with a promising career still largely ahead of him—was forced to look around for an alternative source of income, and, like his contemporary Christopher Marlowe, who found himself in a similar position, he turned to poetry. This was a time-honoured move. A choice and well-turned poem—if it caught the eye of a wealthy patron—might with luck and skill bring its author to the attention of someone in a material position to reward him. In the months that followed, both men wrote long, narrative poems on erotic themes: Marlowe, *Hero and Leander*, and Shakespeare, *Venus and Adonis*. Marlowe's poem— which was left unfinished at the poet's untimely death a few months later—remained unpublished until 1598; but Shakespeare's—which was dedicated to a fashionable young aristocrat, the Earl of Southampton—was published in 1593. It was never out of print thereafter, at least not during its author's lifetime nor for several decades after that, going through at least eleven editions before 1620, and another five before 1640. It was still in demand in 1675. It inspired a host of imitations and has the singular fame of having been more alluded to than any other text that Shakespeare wrote.[1] By any standards *Venus and Adonis* was a success, and it is worth reminding ourselves— especially given the tendency to award a greater precedence to the plays—that in his own time Shakespeare's poems were held in the highest esteem and that, to his contemporaries at least, the figure they praised as the 'mellifluous and hony-tongued Shakespeare' was a poet as much as anything else.[2]

---

[1] See *The Shakespeare Allusion-Book: A Collection of Allusions to Shakespeare from 1591 to 1700*, 2 vols., rev. edn., John Munro, reissued with a preface by Sir Edmund Chambers (London: Oxford University Press, 1932).

[2] Francis Meres, *Palladis Tamia* (London: 1598), in G. Gregory Smith (ed.), *Elizabethan Critical Essays*, 2 vols. (Oxford: Oxford University Press, 1904), 2: 317.

Venus and Adonis presents itself as being different from the drama in every possible way: it appeals to a different kind of audience, offers a different kind of content, and promotes a quite different kind of author.[3] Where the dramatist had to direct his words to a playhouse audience that was, in social terms, highly mixed—to appeal to the 'unskilful' spectators no less than to the 'judicious' (often, as Hamlet was to complain, with mixed success)—the poet, by contrast, could be fairly confident that he was addressing only the latter.[4] He was writing for a readership and thus, by definition, for a far more self-selecting group. With the theatre audience temporarily unavailable to him, Shakespeare shrewdly redirected his words to an audience of a quite different class, the gentlemen readers who browsed the printers' stalls and booksellers' shops in St Paul's churchyard—a clientele he could safely assume would be elite, educated, literate, and male. What he offered them in his poetry was material they would find immediately recognizable and familiar: stories drawn from the literary classics that made up the core curriculum of a Renaissance education and which they would all have learned in their country houses, or at grammar schools and at the universities, and which they would have continued reading in the literary circles at Westminster or the Inns of Court. Of course the stage plays drew on the same material—in some cases, on identical sources—but with poetry the pitch was quite different. Unlike the playwright, the poet need not fear that his words would be wasted on the unappreciative multitude—'caviary to the general', as Hamlet put it—for he was directing his words far more pointedly at a target audience: the discerning few (*Venus and Adonis* was caviar to the cognoscenti).[5] The poet could thus afford to engage his readers in a more self-conscious, knowing, and collusive relation, and to be more demanding of them, confident that his allusions would be spotted, jokes appreciated, and literary frame of reference valued and understood. That *Venus and Adonis* received more allusions than anything else Shakespeare wrote testifies to the success of his strategy, for these were the kind of readers who, in their copy-books and in their own imitations and tributes, left their literary appreciation on record.

Shakespeare also used *Venus and Adonis* to launch himself on the literary scene and to present himself in a way that, at the time, was not available to him as a writer of plays. In the early 1590s stage plays still ranked very low in the literary hierarchy and with *Venus and Adonis* Shakespeare seized the opportunity to conform to the prejudices of the age. The poem's Dedication opens with a quotation from Ovid's *Amores* that, as well as displaying the author's literary credentials, appears to dismiss in one breath the—actually rather successful—plays he had written to date (*The Two Gentlemen of Verona*, *The Taming of the Shrew*, the *Henry VI* trilogy, and *Richard III*): 'Vilia

---

[3] See Patrick Cheney, *Shakespeare, National Poet-Playwright* (Cambridge: Cambridge University Press, 2004), for the alternative view that Shakespeare's roles as poet and playwright were less distinct and more coterminous.

[4] *Hamlet* 3.2.26. All references to the plays are taken from G. Blakemore Evans, et al. (eds.), *The Riverside Shakespeare*, 2nd edn. (Boston: Houghton Mifflin, 1997).

[5] *Hamlet* 2.2.437.

miretur vulgus: mihi flavus Apollo | Pocula Castalia plena ministret aqua' [Let the common herd be amazed by worthless things; but for me let golden Apollo provide cups full of the water of the Muses].[6] Instead, the poem that follows is offered as contrastingly 'high' art, its author clearly differentiated from the debased figure of the dramatist and presented as a member of the educated elite whose aureate verse will be read and appreciated only by those in the know. In the dedicatory epistle that follows, Shakespeare describes *Venus and Adonis* as 'the first heir of my invention', not because the plays he had written were not equally the products of his brain, but because he could not be seen to say as much. The point of *Venus and Adonis* was to showcase its author's status and talent—a blatant piece of self-fashioning, an advertising campaign for one. Again, it is testimony to the success of this marketing strategy that, within a few years, the literary value of Shakespeare's stage plays would rise to the point that they too could be presented to the world as serious reading matter: 'Reade him, therefore; and againe, and againe', as the editors of the First Folio would urge their prospective customers in 1623.[7] This new artistic legitimacy of stage-plays was to a large extent founded on the reputation Shakespeare had built up for himself as a professional print poet.

VENUS AND ADONIS

Shakespeare took the story of Venus and Adonis from Ovid's *Metamorphoses*, where it forms the last of a series of cautionary tales that warn of the disasters and unhappiness that accompany heterosexual love. These tales, which come in Book X of Ovid's poem, are narrated by the figure of Orpheus, who, embittered by the loss of his wife Eurydice, resolves to give up that love forever and uses the stories to justify his decision to turn thereafter to the love of boys. Shakespeare's poem, too, ends on a cautionary note— with Venus prophesying that 'Sorrow on love hereafter shall attend' (l. 1,136)—but in adapting Ovid's tale for his own purposes Shakespeare makes a small but crucial change: one that his gentlemen readers would immediately have picked up. In Ovid's version, Adonis is Venus' partner in love: he and the goddess are joined in a willing, consensual, and mutually satisfying relation, and the story is an unhappy one because Adonis is tragically killed, gored to death by a boar while out on a hunting expedition. In Shakespeare's version, Adonis is not Venus' partner in love: he is a sexually immature, indeed, untried youth who has no interest in love or sexual desire and who successfully resists the goddess's declarations and fervent approaches to the end. He still dies, gored by a boar while hunting, but he dies without ever having given Venus what she wants. This puts a whole new gloss on Ovid's tale, turning a tragedy of

---

[6] All references to the poems are taken from Colin Burrow (ed.), *The Complete Sonnets and Poems* (Oxford: Oxford University Press, 2002), 173.

[7] Preface to the First Folio, reproduced in *The Riverside Shakespeare*, 63.

loss into a comedy of non-fruition. The original Ovidian story thus gets overlaid with a patina of Petrarchanism, the mode that, in imitation of Petrarch's foundational sonnet sequence, the *Rime sparse*, had since the fourteenth century come to dominate European lyric (and had, more locally, just burst upon the English literary scene with the publication in 1591 of Sidney's *Astrophil and Stella*, an event that sparked the 'sonnet craze' of the early 1590s). Persuasion and frustration were the essence of this mode, in which the lover typically assured an idealized beloved of his worth and devotion and besought her to look kindly upon him and return his affections, all, for the most part, to no avail.

Much of the humour of *Venus and Adonis* derives from the witty role reversal Shakespeare creates by making Venus the subject rather than the object of desire: 'She's love, she loves, and yet she is not loved' (l. 610). As the impassioned suitor, Venus now takes on a role that had been perfected by generations of Petrarchan poets. Despite her insistence and flattery (and her powers as a goddess notwithstanding), Venus proves quite incapable of winning Adonis' love, and as the poem proceeds she woos him with increasing desperation, her claims of attractiveness and irresistibility being undermined all the more comically by their demonstrable failure to impress. Gender stereotypes are reversed, too, to equally comical but also explicitly erotic effect, as a masculinized Venus—big, red, and hard—presses herself (quite literally) upon the yielding, maidenly boy whose dimpled and ultimately wounded body is full of orifices, concavities, and holes. If Venus takes up position as the importunate lover, Adonis falls into place as the typical sonnet mistress. Virtuous, virginal, and cold, he spends most of the poem resisting her demands and asking her to stop, only making minimal concessions (such as allowing her to kiss him) on condition that afterwards she leave him alone. Having said that, there is at the same time much in Shakespeare's play with power relations that also conforms to the Petrarchan game-plan, for his oversized Venus still has much in common with the conventional sonnet Lady, who similarly towers over her lover and issues him with commands (albeit not to love), while his feminine Adonis is not unlike the typical Petrarchan lover, who is equally weak, ineffectual, and 'unmanly', and no more successful in achieving his aims. Superimposing a Petrarchan scenario onto an Ovidian story allowed Shakespeare to take an altogether irreverent look at the lyric tradition of his time and to send up its sometimes precious solemnities to hilarious effect.

It also allowed him to present two quite serious preoccupations that, as we shall see, resurface in his poetry again and again. The first of these was a fascination with language—an often heady sense of the limitless possibilities and sheer productivity of this medium, the writer's infinite resource. The second was a more detached and reserved take on language—a distinct sense of the liabilities that inhere within a medium that could by turns entrap, distract, misrepresent, or amount to nothing. In *Venus and Adonis* Shakespeare made use of the formula—tried and tested in Renaissance sonnet sequences—that frustrated desire leads to eloquence. Met with rejection, the lover must redouble his/her efforts and, in the bid to win the other over (now more determined than ever in the face of a challenge), the words just flow. Adonis' reluctance gives Venus the cue for speechifying and she duly mounts a barrage of arguments that are designed to refute all opposition: her status as goddess, her beauty, her previous conquests, the advisability of seizing the day, the naturalness of sexual desire, the advantages to be had in enjoying her love, the perils of resisting it. Since it further limits his power to satisfy Venus' desire, Adonis' death provides an occasion for still more talk: expressions of inexpressible grief, curses, laments, and self-reproaches. All of this takes up a large part of the poem and, indeed, expands by some ten times or more the rather spare 100 or so lines in Ovid's original. It is typical of her volubility that, as if impatient with single measures, Venus talks multiples: she lures Adonis not with one but with 'A thousand honey secrets' (l. 16), offering him her heart in return for a 'thousand kisses' (l. 517) or 'twenty hundred' if he defaults (l. 522). She is also a great one for lists, coming up with seven things her former lover Mars did with her (ll. 105–6), fifteen different ways in which she is not unattractive (ll. 133–7), six inducements to seize the day (ll. 163–5), five ways of complaining that Adonis is cold (ll. 211–13), ten mortal ailments to contrast with Adonis' heavenly beauty (ll. 739–44), and seven things with which to appease Death (ll. 1,013–14). Not satisfied with one example when several will do, Venus' whole tendency is toward linguistic expansiveness. Hers is one of the 'copious stories' that lovers typically tell and that (as the narrator drily puts it) 'End without audience, and are never done' (ll. 845–6). It is, in other words, an exercise in *copia*, the rhetorical art of amplification that was enshrined in Erasmus' *De Copia* (first published in 1512 and much revised and enlarged thereafter), one of the key textbooks of the Renaissance schoolroom that taught boys how to embellish their writing style and show off their linguistic facility by finding 100 different ways of saying the same thing.

Since the poem was designed to show off its author's rhetorical skill, Venus' gushing speech—which graphically conjures the inexhaustible possibilities of language—could be seen as providing the perfect platform (and its popularity as proof of its success). Within the terms of the poem, however, all this rhetoric amounts to very little. Venus' words do not persuade Adonis to love her (quite the reverse), and his answers, in turn, have no effect whatsoever in shutting her up. Indeed, an inverse relation seems to exist between anything actually happening in the poem and the volume of words it generates. As Adonis sternly tells the goddess, he will not be moved even 'If love hath lent you twenty thousand tongues, | And every tongue more moving than your own' (ll. 775–6). As if to demonstrate the ineffectiveness of his remark, however, Venus seems to take him up on his challenge a bare fifty lines later: '"Ay me", she cries, and twenty times, "woe, woe", | And twenty echoes, twenty times cry so' (ll. 833–4). By my calculation, that makes 8,000 cries (or 16,000, if you count 'woe' only once). The exponential repetition of a single word might not seem the height of rhetorical resourcefulness, but it serves to pass on Venus a symbolic judgement. For it aligns her with Narcissus' unsatisfied lover, the wood nymph Echo, who, in another of Ovid's stories, fades away to a mere voice for the lack of an answering love. Venus' largely self-generated monologue suggests that what she is really in love with is the sound of her own voice, with all the implications that has for a poet who is using that voice as a way of showcasing his own rhetorical talent. The hint of narcissism is never very far away.

In comparison with this disproportion between action and words, the poem presents us with a series of animal participants whose actions, by contrast, are unaccompanied by any such verbal clutter. First and foremost, there is the boar who, in the midst of all this verbiage, makes refreshingly short work of Adonis; but there is also Adonis' stallion who, in a few brief and happy stanzas (ll. 259–324), spies, chases, and mounts a mare; and in one of Venus' lengthiest digressions, an unforgettable vignette of the hunted hare (ll. 673–708). In addition, there is a whole menagerie of beasts and birds to whom Venus and Adonis are variously compared (snail, falcon, eagle, vulture, dab-chick, deer, doe, fawn, and so on). The point of these creatures is not, I think, to invite moralizing inferences on the 'bestial' nature of sexual desire, but rather to draw out the definitive difference that exists between humans and animals. The animals in the poem are presented as stable behavioural archetypes that are guaranteed to act in certain ways according to their nature or 'kind': boars kill, vultures attack, hares run, and so on. Unlike their animal counterparts, however, human beings are born into language and, for better or worse, their subjectivity and desire are irremediably structured by it. With the actions of the human characters (and for the sake of argument I am including Venus here), language inevitably intervenes. Language comes first: it is what makes the concept of 'action' possible at all, and what—as several celebrated protagonists would soon articulate in a number of Shakespeare's plays—often stands in the way of an action actually being performed. *Venus and Adonis* makes great play of this, presenting us—in its huge wall of words that gets in the way as much as it impresses or delights—with a sense that, if we can be the masters of language (as the aureate poet was undoubtedly trying to be), we can also be its subjects, and that the resulting condition can be turned as much to negative as to positive effect.

THE RAPE OF LUCRECE

The Rape of Lucrece—another long, narrative poem that was published the following year (1594)—relates to *Venus and Adonis* in many ways as a sister poem or companion piece. It was published by the same printer and dedicated to the same patron: indeed, the address to the Earl of Southampton in the earlier poem cannily gave advance notice of the later by advertising readers of a 'graver labour' to come. It, too, was written when the theatres were closed (the plague continued into a second year). It draws on the same stock of classical material that would have been familiar to any beneficiary of a humanist education—Ovid again (this time the *Fasti*) and Livy's history of Rome—and, in publication terms, it was also a success, running through eight editions before 1640. It tells a similar story of aggressive sexual desire directed at an unwilling party and shares many of the earlier poem's metaphors of sexual predation. True, it does not share the gender reversals of *Venus and Adonis*. In this case, sexual power is entirely embodied in the figure of the male, and the terrible consequences of his exercise of that power—quite different from the titillating but ultimately inconsequential fumblings of Venus—are what give *Lucrece* its altogether 'graver' tone: a tragic poem to match the other's comic representations. But the preoccupations with language—its powers and dangers—are equally in evidence. Indeed, the ratio between actions and words is, if anything, even more strained in this poem where the action, albeit swift and brutal, generates a still greater amount of talk. The rape itself is barely described, but it is preceded by Tarquin's lengthy debate with himself and Lucrece's increasingly desperate pleas that he desist, and is followed by her even lengthier lament. At 1,855 lines, *Lucrece* is nearly half as long again as the earlier poem.

The story *Lucrece* tells recounts events that marked a turning point in early Roman history. In 509 BC, Tarquinius Sextus—son of the tyrannical king of Rome (also called Tarquinius)—raped Lucretia, the wife of one of his nobles, upon which the victim committed suicide but not before urging her husband and men folk to avenge the crime. The populace, seeing this abuse of power as symptomatic of the tyrannical regime under which they languished, used the occasion to rise up against the ruling family and, having successfully ousted them, to establish a quite different political order. From that point, Rome became a Republic. The relation between private and public—between what might at first appear, however terrible, to be an essentially domestic tragedy, and the large-scale public events of civil disorder and regime-change to which it led—had numerous literary and historical precedents, the most important of which, arguably, was the abduction of Helen that had given rise to the Trojan War some seven centuries earlier. In Shakespeare's poem, the ravished Lucrece spends a sizeable part of the narrative (ll. 1,366–582) gazing on a mural that depicts the fall of Troy and identifying with the routed city and its shattered human inhabitants. Behind this scene stands another key literary moment when, in Virgil's *Aeneid*, Aeneas similarly gazes—and weeps—upon a visual representation of the Trojan War in which he had been a participant and from which he had come out on the losing side. His own imperial mission to found the city of Rome is perceived by the inhabitants of Latium—to whose land he comes as claimant and whose princess, betrothed to a local prince, he takes for himself—as a sinister rerun of the original Trojan crime of stealing a woman who belongs to someone else, with all the political fallout that such an action was expected to entail. Of course, this time round Aeneas comes out on the winning side and much of Virgil's epic is devoted to justifying his actions and proving his defeated opponents wrong. The point, however, is that in *Lucrece* Shakespeare selected the kind of story that inevitably brought with it an extensive literary history. This tale of a sexual depredation that leads to radical civil conflict not only drew on Shakespeare's immediate sources in Ovid and Livy but also came with heavy-duty literary historical precedents attached. Indeed, to Homer and Virgil we should also add Chaucer and Gower, who wrote their own versions of the Lucrece story in *The Legend of Good Women* and the *Confessio Amantis* respectively. One of the noticeable things about Shakespeare's poem is the way its protagonists behave less like early Romans and more like characters in a medieval romance or complaint poem—the result of its blithe combination of Roman Stoicism with chivalric feudalism. This kind of anachronism results (much as it did in *Venus and Adonis*, with its mixture of Petrarch and Ovid) when it is literary precedence that matters, not historical verisimilitude. Ironically, the key relation in *The Rape of Lucrece* is not so much that between Tarquin and Lucrece— consequence-laden though that is—but that between Shakespeare's poem and the numerous inter-texts to which it obsessively answers and speaks.

The poem exhibits this preoccupation with words largely through its two protagonists. Tarquin and Lucrece seem incapable of seeing events clearly. Indeed, both insist on viewing the situation they are in through the lens of literary re-workings of their own and similar stories, some of which precede and some of which long postdate them historically. Numerous parallels are drawn between the two characters and various animal archetypes—Tarquin is a lion, a dog, a hawk, a wolf to Lucrece's lamb, and so on—but, as in *Venus and Adonis*, neither of them acts with the immediate behavioural instinct of such creatures. Instead, they are entirely hung up, as animals would never be, on verbal constructions—both of themselves and of the other—and these seem to constitute their whole fixation and drive. Thus in Shakespeare's poem Tarquin does not desire Lucrece because he has seen her in any straightforward way and, for example, been overwhelmed by her beauty. He desires her because he has first heard a glowing report of her delivered by her husband, as it were second-hand. It is not her chastity itself but explicitly 'that *name* of "chaste"' (l. 8, emphasis added) that piques his interest and stirs his lust. When Tarquin does meet Lucrece for the first time, it is not a woman that he sees but a literary cliché: 'This silent war of lilies and of roses, | Which Tarquin viewed in her fair face's field, | In their pure ranks his traitor eye encloses' (ll. 71–3). He cannot see past this and, as far as he is concerned, there is nothing behind this mask. Encrusted with metaphor, Lucrece's face hardens into a heraldic shield emblazoned with the colours red and white. Depersonalized, she becomes a purely poeticized object of desire, and yet this is what seems decisive in hardening her attacker's resolve. Indeed, this metaphor seems not only to construct his view of Lucrece but to provide Tarquin with a distinct role for himself, for the actions he takes are largely dictated by it. Seeing Lucrece's visage as 'heraldry' (l. 64), rather than as the face of a beautiful woman, means that he essentially sees her as a challenge to arms. She represents a foe the defeat of whom is necessary proof of his valour as a knight. Although Tarquin admits that, were it to be discovered, the rape would stain his own reputation and deface his own coat of arms with an indelible mark of shame—'"O shame to knighthood, and to shining arms!"' (l. 197, Shakespeare's feudalizing of Roman history being much in evidence here)—he is nonetheless obliged to rise to the challenge his own metaphor has laid down for him. This is why the various arguments he mounts against raping Lucrece come to nothing and why he goes ahead anyway. Indeed, once resolved to act, he presents the rape to himself as a kind of heroically martial deed. Breaking into Lucrece's bedroom, he sees her sleeping body as a vulnerable city that invites his conquest. Her breasts are 'round turrets' (l. 441) which his hand did 'scale' (l. 440). Upon her breast, his hand is a 'Rude ram to batter such an ivory wall!' (l. 464), and feeling the beating of her heart 'moves in him more rage and lesser pity | To make the breach and enter this sweet city' (ll. 468–9). He begins the assault like a soldier laying siege to a city—'First, like a trumpet doth his tongue begin | To sound a parley to his heartless foe' (ll. 470–1)—and declares that he comes 'to scale | Thy never-conquered fort' (ll. 481–2). The inappropriateness of the imagery shows the extent to which Tarquin is bound by the literary metaphor he is living inside, for he is acting out the role of the soldier-lover who assails his beloved and lays siege to the fort of her chastity. He could snap out of it if he wanted to—a metaphor, after all, is just a metaphor—but he chooses not to and is thus obliged to proceed to the bitter end. After the rape, Tarquin's lusts are said to have got the better of his soul and to have 'battered down her consecrated wall' (ll. 723), suggesting a strange kind of identification between himself and the victim on whom he has just mounted this kind of attack. Such, Shakespeare seems to be implying, is the force of metaphor, but its literalization as rape makes the deadly effect of that force abundantly clear.

For her part, Lucrece seems no less subject to the pressures of literary precedence than her attacker. She too insists on conforming to type and seeing herself as a ransacked city, even though it is by no means in her interests to do so. Indeed, she uses this literary motif as a justification for taking her own life. Describing her despoiled body in the third person, she ruminates:

> 'Her house is sacked, her quiet interrupted,
> Her mansion battered by the enemy;
> Her sacred temple spotted, spoiled, corrupted,
> Grossly engirt with daring infamy.
> Then let it not be called impiety
>   If in this blemished fort I make some hole
>   Through which I may convey this troubled soul'. (ll. 1,170–6)

Before she plunges the knife into her body, effectively finishing off what Tarquin had begun, Lucrece goes to gaze on an elaborate painting of Troy that depicted the city as it was surrounded by Greeks, come to avenge the Trojan outrage and 'For Helen's rape the city to destroy' (l. 1,369). Clearly, the comfort she finds in the images (if it can be called that) comes from self-identification: she sees herself in the tragic figure of Hecuba, in every individual she 'finds forlorn' (l. 1,500), but above all she sees herself as the ravaged city—'so my Troy did perish' (l. 1,547). Applied to her own situation, this metaphor is deeply illogical, but it is also profoundly telling. For it implies that Lucrece identifies herself with the guilty party—with the Trojans who had stolen Helen from her husband, much as Tarquin had ravished her—and that her destruction is therefore to some extent justified. The discomfort this reading is likely to create in the reader seems, once again, to suggest Shakespeare's preoccupation with the sheer power that metaphor is capable of exerting. Both his characters, arguably, are hidebound by literary precedents: beholden to ancient, long-inherited, and multiple repeated images that—however anachronistic, clichéd, or inappropriate to themselves—put ideas into their heads, fix them into set positions, and incite them to perform actions and reactions that are, in both cases, demonstrably self-destructive. Lucrece might be the victim of Tarquin, but both could be said to be the victims of metaphor.

SONNETS AND *A LOVER'S COMPLAINT*

....

The *Sonnets* and *A Lover's Complaint* were published together in a single quarto volume in 1609 and, in terms of publication history, they differ from the narrative poems that preceded them in several striking ways. The salient facts of *Venus and Adonis* and *The Rape of Lucrece* are indisputable, open to view, and clear as day. We know when Shakespeare wrote them, who published them (he took them to Richard Field—a fellow citizen of Stratford who had moved to London—and authorized if not oversaw their printing), and to whom they were dedicated. By comparison, the circumstances that surround the *Sonnets* and its accompanying complaint poem are shrouded in darkness. Although there is evidence that some of the sonnets were circulating 'among his priuate friends' in the late 1590s—and two of them appeared in *The Passionate Pilgrim*, a miscellany of poems by various hands, some anonymous, published in 1599—we do not know precisely when Shakespeare wrote either these or the rest of the sequence.[8] The 1609 volume was published by Thomas Thorpe—a London printer who had something of a reputation for publishing material he did not own—and it is yet to be established whether the *Sonnets* were published with their author's permission or whether the order in which they appear is his. The mysterious dedication, signed by the printer, 'To the onlie begetter of these insuing sonnets, Mr. W. H', subsequently launched one of the most celebrated wild goose chases in literary history and, while a number of candidates of varying plausibility have been suggested (including the Earl of Southampton), 'W. H.' has never satisfactorily been identified.

There are other differences, too. *Venus and Adonis* and *The Rape of Lucrece* had cannily tapped into the literary tastes of the moment, combining the new fashion for Ovidian narratives with other well-recognized literary forms, above all the craze for Petrarchan sonnets that had been galvanized by the publication of *Astrophil and Stella* in 1591.[9] By the time Shakespeare's own *Sonnets* came out, some fifteen or sixteen years later, this craze was well and truly over, making them look, from the perspective of the first decade of James I's reign, like a strangely archaic Elizabethan relic. Perhaps for this reason, they were a publishing failure. Where the narrative poems had made a splash and run through numerous editions to satisfy eager public demand, the *Sonnets* volume—never reprinted (or not until the eighteenth century)—caused barely a ripple and sank without trace: if *Venus and Adonis* received more allusions than anything else

---

[8] Meres, op. cit. The two sonnets published in 1599 were those that the 1609 volume numbered as 138 and 144. Sonnet 107 makes reference to the death of Queen Elizabeth and therefore postdates 1603. Other than that, there is little besides stylometric evidence with which to date the *Sonnets*.

[9] Between 1592 and 1597 around seventeen amorous sonnet sequences were published in London, including: Samuel Daniel, *Delia* (1592); Henry Constable, *Diana* (1592); Barnabe Barnes, *Parthenophil and Parthenophe* (1593); Thomas Lodge, *Phillis* (1593); Giles Fletcher, *Licia* (1593); Michael Drayton, *Idea's Mirror* (1594); anon., *Zepheria* (1594); E. C., *Emaricdulfe* (1595); Edmund Spenser, *Amoretti* (1595); Bartholomew Griffin, *Fidessa* (1596); R[ichard] L[inche], *Diella* (1596); William Smith, *Chloris* (1596); Richard Barnfield, *Cynthia* (1595); and R[obert] T[ofte], *Laura* (1597).

Shakespeare wrote, the *Sonnets* and *A Lover's Complaint* received the least. By a strange irony—although one that serves only to reinforce the contrast—the narrative poems remain (in spite of a recent revival of scholarly interest) of concern largely to the academy, whereas Shakespeare's *Sonnets* have become by far his most popular work and, in the hard terms of global sales, scoop an impressive market share. They regularly outsell anything else he wrote, including the best known of the plays. Nevertheless, these differences aside, the *Sonnets* and *A Lover's Complaint* share with the narrative poems the same preoccupations with language we have been tracing here, and bear witness, like them, to a self-consciousness about the writer's medium, and a response to its power that combines pride and reserve in equal measure.

The 154 poems that make up the *Sonnets* fall into three distinct, and distinctly unequal, groupings. The first 126 are directed to a figure who is variously addressed as a 'master mistress' (Sonnet 20), 'beauteous and lovely youth' (Sonnet 54), 'sweet boy' (Sonnet 108), and 'lovely boy' (Sonnet 126); Sonnets 127 to 152 are addressed to a female 'mistress'; and Sonnets 153 and 154, which involve racy mythological fables about Cupid, are based on the style of the Greek poet Anacreon, and follow the pattern set by previous poets, chiefly Samuel Daniel and Edmund Spenser, who had in the early to mid-1590s used similarly light lyrics to mark the transition from a sonnet sequence to an ensuing longer poem.[10] An abiding feature of the first and longest series of sonnets is the poet's repeated assertion that the quality of his own verse will immortalize the youth and beauty of the young man it addresses and thus capture for eternity qualities that are otherwise inevitably destined physically to decay. In the first seventeen sonnets, the young man is commanded to reproduce his physical beauty physically—by engendering children—and to this end the poet mounts many of the arguments that Venus had put to Adonis in the earlier narrative poem. As in the latter, however, the youth's refusal to be so persuaded gives birth to a different kind of progeny—more poetry—and, although the poet feigns regret at the youth's disinclination to get on with the serious business of peopling the world, there is a sense in which it serves his turn very well indeed. Producing children is presented as being a superior way ('mightier', 'more blessèd') of reproducing the qualities of youth and beauty than the poet's modestly self-deprecated 'barren rhyme'—the perpetuation of a blood line (or 'lines of life') as being better than any lines the poet may write with his 'pupil pen' (Sonnet 16)—yet the modesty topos is, as always, disingenuous. For, described as 'barren' and as a mere stripling or 'pupil', the poet's pen has, of course, a great deal in common with the young man it is describing, except that, unlike him, it is busily reproducing poem after poem. In a slightly earlier sonnet, natural reproduction is compared to a giant printing house in which self-propagation is metaphored as a successful print run—'Thou shouldst print more, not let that copy die' (Sonnet 11) —as if to suggest that in fact printed poetry is a much more secure way of ensuring a lasting legacy than the hazards of biological

---

[10] Daniel marks the transition between his sonnet sequence, *Delia*, and the complaint poem that follows with an anacreontic ode; Spenser, that between his sonnet sequence, the *Amoretti* and the *Epithalamium* or wedding poem that follows with four anacreontic poems.

reproduction. In Sonnet 17, the poet again deprecates his own verse on the grounds that future readers will doubt its fulsome praise could possibly be true (they will dismiss it as 'a poet's rage' or the 'stretchèd metre of an antique song'), but even if the young man did go ahead and father a child, as the poet is ostensibly insisting he should, there is no suggestion that the poetry would stop. On the contrary, the future child and the poems are presented as continuing side by side—'You should live twice, in it, and in my rhyme'—as equal and alternative co-heirs.

From its introduction in the opening set of sonnets, this theme continues throughout the remainder of the young man sub-sequence and finds itself expressed in some of the best-known poems. The youth's 'eternal summer shall not fade' because it is guaranteed to last forever in the poet's 'eternal lines', and so long as those lines are read, so long they will live and thus give 'life to thee' (Sonnet 18): a statement that has the advantage of being entirely self-fulfilling. All things are subject to decay but 'My love shall in my verse ever live young' (Sonnet 19). The beloved will always 'live in this', the poem we are reading, for 'Not marble, nor the gilded monuments | Of princes shall outlive this pow'rful rhyme, | But you shall shine more bright in these contents | Than unswept stone besmeared with sluttish time' (Sonnet 55). Time will of necessity destroy everything, 'And yet to times in hope my verse shall stand' (Sonnet 60) and 'in black ink my love may still shine bright' (Sonnet 65). 'Your monument shall be my gentle verse, | Which eyes not yet created shall o'er-read, | And tongues-to-be your being shall rehearse' (Sonnet 81). 'I'll live in this poor rhyme . . . And thou in this shalt find thy monument, | When tyrants' crests and tombs of brass are spent' (Sonnet 107). Behind these statements of poetic confidence stand literary precedents, the echoing of which serves only to reinforce the argument: Ovid, who famously concluded the *Metamorphoses* by claiming that the poem would go on to perpetuate his fame for all time, and Petrarch, whose own sonnet sequence routinely conflated the name of the beloved, Laura, with the *lauro* or laurel leaf that signified poetic fame, as if the two were inseparable if not one and the same.

Against these assertions of poetic pride, however—both in Shakespeare's sonnets and, indeed, in the literary precedents to which he alludes—there speaks a powerful counter voice. The great poetic 'monument' that promises to outlast the most magnificent of tombs, for example, turns out to be nothing more substantial than a trust that, in future times, the poems will come to be read out loud: 'You still shall live (such virtue hath my pen) | Where breath most breathes, even in the mouths of men' (Sonnet 81). Words suddenly seem a lot less solid as they threaten to melt away or evaporate into thin air—mere speech—much as Petrarch's solid achievement of winning the laurel of poetic fame (he was crowned poet laureate in Rome in 1341) had similarly seemed less stable when, as happens periodically in his sonnet sequence, the *lauro* dissolves into another pun on his beloved's name: *l'aura*, the breeze. Similarly, for all the power of its self-certification, the statement 'such virtue hath my pen' really only begs the question, rather as, in the penultimate line of his own great literary bow-out, Ovid disconcertingly injects a moment of doubt that potentially threatens to upset everything: 'perque omnia saecula fama | siquid habent veri vatum praesagia, vivam '[And time without all end | (If poets as by prophecy about the truth may aim) | My life shall everlastingly be lengthened still by fame]'.[11] Much virtue in If, as Touchstone would say.[12] Such prophecies of enduring fame might fulfil themselves every time the poem is read, but they can just as equally cancel themselves out entirely. If the poem remains unread, no one will be any the wiser.

Accompanying the numerous statements that claim that poetry can defeat or conquer time, then, are alternative statements to the effect that either it can't or, even if it can, that this isn't always a good thing. A theme to which the young man sonnets revert again and again is the impossibility of capturing in verse the living, breathing, and evanescent qualities of beauty and youth with which the poet is largely concerned. The very thing that gives poetry its durability—the fact that it can fix a moment or a description in words so that, mounted and framed, as it were, it can be reproduced and handed down in perpetuity—can also militate against its ability to deal with qualities that evade fixture or that move or change. A poem can arrest a moment of perfection, certainly—'When I consider every thing that grows | Holds in perfection but a little moment . . . Then the conceit of this inconstant stay | Sets you most rich in youth before my sight' (Sonnet 15)—but it can also freeze that moment, lock it in time, and so fail to do justice to the nature of experience that is necessarily subject to constant change (it's no accident, of course, that Ovid's claim to enduring fame comes at the end of a poem devoted entirely to the principle of metamorphosis). With typical economy, Shakespeare encapsulates the problem with a simple pun. In sonnet 78, he assures the young man that, where other poets might reach for elaborate metaphors in order to praise him, he has no need of doing so. He claims to renounce all such art, for 'thou art all my art'. Verb and noun for a moment coincide, so that the other's existence—his very being—merges briefly with the poet's art. For a moment, they are co-extensive: the beloved and the poem both by definition 'are', allowing the poet's art to metamorphose briefly into a living, breathing thing. The moment however is transitory, for although the poem will continue to exist long after the young man has ceased to exist—the great claim to monumentality—it will thereby, of necessity, cease to coincide with the living man. As a result, the statement will forever after be a form of a lie. Art cannot 'be' in the same way as the beloved, precisely because it is fixed and does not change. It can survive death but it does not live (memorial art always has a whiff of the mausoleum about it). Sonnet 115 addresses a similar problem. Not even the most ardent poem can capture an experience of love that is constantly changing and growing over time. 'Those lines that I before have writ do lie', the poet avers, because earlier declarations that 'I could not love you dearer'—however sincerely meant at the time—turn out to be falsified by later proofs that his devotion has indeed increased in depth and intensity. Later superlatives give the lie to earlier ones. The poet cannot in all honesty say '"Now I love you best"' because the fleeting present can never be captured in words that, once

---

[11] Metamorphoses, XV. 993–950, trans. Arthur Golding (London: 1567), Madeleine Forey (ed.), Metamorphoses (Harmondsworth: Penguin, 2002), my emphasis.

[12] As You Like It 5.4.103.

written down, stay the same. Instead, he is forced to acknowledge that 'then might I not say so, | To give full growth to that which still doth grow'. Love, after all, was classically depicted as a young boy as if to indicate that it is in a permanent state of growth.

In *The Rape of Lucrece*, Shakespeare had explored the dangers of metaphor and what can happen when individuals find themselves trapped inside metaphors that, because ossified and fixed, fail to adapt to or correlate truly with their unique, lived experience. A similar concern surfaces in the young man sonnets. About two-thirds of the way through the sub-sequence, a number of poems refer to a rival poet with whom the speaker seems to be in some kind of competition for love and literary reward. The identity of this figure has set off another wild goose chase, not dissimilar to that after Mr. W. H. Whoever he may have been, however, there is another rival poet in the sequence whose identity is all too clear—indeed, quite explicit—and that is the personified figure of Time. In the early sonnets, 'time's pencil or my pupil pen' (Sonnet 16) are both presented as being unable to reproduce the young man's qualities as well as his fathering of children would—but in the course of the sequence they come to represent two quite different modes of writing. Thus Time's 'hand'—the word could mean both hand and handwriting—is repeatedly described as drawing or engraving lines upon the face of youth and beauty: carving wrinkles in the beloved's brow and drawing 'lines there with thine antique pen' (Sonnet 19), delving 'the parallels in beauty's brow' (Sonnet 60), much as 'Time's injurious hand' has already done in the (older) speaker's case, having 'filled his brow | With lines and wrinkles' (Sonnet 63). By means of this cruel script—that marks the passage of years indelibly on a person's skin—'Time's fell hand' (Sonnet 64), like 'winter's ragged hand' (Sonnet 6), can thoroughly deface a face.

Throughout the sequence, Time is presented as a monstrous force—an unconquerable enemy that corrodes, devours, and destroys—with whom the poet is locked in combat, fiercely opposing the power and immortality of his art. Yet there is also a sense in which Time remains the superior artist: not simply because the poet himself must die, but because the wrinkles on a human face tell another and arguably more truthful kind of poem. Neither static nor fixed, these lines are the result of growth and continue to change as a person continues to grow. In other words, Time's mark-making can capture process in a way the poet's cannot: it can inscribe a body that is still living and changing without having to impose upon it some artificial arrest. Time-as-poet can thus truthfully say 'thou art all my art' because only with its alternative kind of body poem—the lined face—can art and being coincide once again. To this extent, the poet must concede to his rival, and, for all his protestations to the contrary, we can't help wondering whether Time's isn't perhaps a more eloquent kind of line.[13]

The sonnets that follow the young man poems differ from them in a number of ways—most notably in being addressed to a woman and in cultivating an edgier, more

[13] Compare Paulina's praise of the artist who fashions the wrinkled 'statue' of Hermione: 'So much the more our carver's excellence, | which lets go by some sixteen years, and makes her | As she lived new' (*The Winter's Tale* 5.3.30–32).

bristling, and at times harshly excoriating sexual tone—but these preoccupations about art, and what it can and cannot do, nonetheless remain a primary concern. In the sonnet that announces the new sub-sequence, the poet introduces the new object of desire as a mistress whose eyes are said to be 'raven black' (Sonnet 127): a description that has subsequently sent critics and biographers scouring sixteenth-century London for a Dark Lady with whom Shakespeare might have had intimate relations (wild goose chase number three). What the Sonnet is concerned with, however, is not whether the woman in question had black eyes but whether beauty is something that can be defined in poetic terms and, if so, whether poetry has the power to say what beauty is (it is concerned, that is, with entirely literary considerations). The poem situates itself within a literary tradition that had its own very well-established definitions of female beauty and that had for centuries prioritized the 'fair', in both senses of that word. As a result, 'In the old age black was not counted fair': indeed, it was branded beauty's opposite. The challenge the Sonnet sets itself, therefore, is to overturn this centuries-old poetic tradition and, effectively, to make black white. '*Therefore* my mistress' eyes are raven black', the poet declares (emphasis added), not because they necessarily were but because it was a poetic triumph to be able to say so and to bring off such an outrageous turnaround well. Whatever the colour of her eyes, then (or, indeed, whether there was ever even a mistress at all), Sonnet 127—and much of the sub-sequence that follows— remains a largely literary exercise. There is an element of self-conscious poetic imita-tion going on here, as well. In *Astrophil and Stella*, Sidney had similarly presented an unconventionally black-eyed mistress and set himself the task of praising as beautiful something traditionally understood as its contrary: 'When Nature made her chiefe worke, *Stella's* eyes, | In colour blacke, why wrapt she beames so bright?' (*AS* sonnet 7). The remainder of this sonnet sets out to answer this rhetorical question and concludes that Nature executed this cheeky reversal precisely in order to display her "miraculous power" over literary convention: 'That whereas blacke seemes Beautie's contrary, | She even in blacke doth make all beauties flow'. Nature trumps generations of lesser poets by spectacularly turning their precious terms of reference on their heads. Black is thereby given a new currency and in Sidney's sequence this gives rise to a series of increasingly ingenious conceits: Stella's eyes are black in mourning for the lovers they have killed (*AS* 7), they are 'blacke beames' that 'burning markes engrave' in her lover's side (*AS* 47), they are 'seeing jets, blacke, but in blacknesse bright' (*AS* 91).[14]

In a gesture that combines respectful imitation with a bid for poetic one-upmanship, Shakespeare offers his own literary conceits in order to account for the blackness of his own mistress's eyes. In sonnet 132, for example, he declares that they 'Have put on black, and loving mourners be, | Looking with pretty ruth upon my pain', and urges her otherwise unpitying heart to mourn for him as well. In Sonnet 127, to return to that poem, he presents a highly complex conceit that stands to some extent as a direct answer to Sidney's challenge. And yet in so doing it also, curiously, both asserts and

---

[14] Quotations from W. A. Ringler (ed.), *The Poems of Sir Philip Sidney* (Oxford: Clarendon Press, 1962).

undermines the poet's claims to the superiority of his own art at the same time. In this case the mistress's eyes are said to be black because they are in mourning: not on this occasion for the lover, but rather for a proper definition of beauty. What might seem 'fair' can no longer be called that, nor can it be taken to signify beauty, because modern women are using cosmetics to paint their faces, thereby falsifying their natural looks by artificial means: 'For since each hand hath put on Nature's power, | Fairing the foul with Art's false borrowed face, | Sweet beauty hath no name, no holy bower, | But is profaned' (Sonnet 127). These women have taken the role of artist upon themselves, but their handiwork—the result of the paint applied by their 'each hand' to their faces—is distinctly inferior to Nature's. As in the earlier sonnets that had described Time's hand drawing lines on the human face, so here Nature is given the edge over the merely human artists. It is not the women who define what beauty is (on the contrary, they distort or conceal it): it is Nature. Like Time, Nature alone is truthful, and it is therefore only she who can say what beauty is and give it its proper 'name'.

At first glance this might seem a pretty conceit to the effect that 'my mistress' does not use cosmetics and is all the more beautiful for that. In fact, however, something more serious (and more self-consciously literary) is going on: a deep reserve about what the human artist—whether a female 'painter' or a male poet—is ultimately able to achieve. Many of the sonnets that follow are concerned with truth and falsehood—'For I have sworn thee fair: more perjured eye, | To swear against the truth so foul a lie' (Sonnet 152)—as if the poet wanted in some way to go back and denounce the very conceits that had cleverly made white of black or fair of foul. In what is arguably Shakespeare's most famous sonnet—'My mistress' eyes are nothing like the sun' (Sonnet 130)—the move is to down tools and stop writing poetry altogether: to undo conceit, to deride metaphor, to cease imitating other poets, and to concede all power to Nature as the superior artist who wins the day because she needs no art at all. The mistress does not need a poem because she is one already and is as beautiful 'As any she belied with false compare'. This anti-poetic impulse might seem to undermine poetic cleverness or to jeopardize statements of poetic confidence and pride, but it injects a level of self-questioning and self-examination that serves, perhaps, rather to deepen and enrich the poetry than to cancel it out.

A Lover's Complaint—the 329-line poem that follows on immediately from the sonnet sequence—has suffered a long history of neglect (it was for many years disregarded or passed over as being of doubtful authenticity), even though it explores these literary preoccupations quite as incisively as any of Shakespeare's other poems. Spoken for the most part by an unnamed female complainant, who laments her seduction at the hands of an unscrupulous young man, the poem directly follows the mode established by Samuel Daniel, who had similarly appended a female complaint poem, 'The Complaint of Rosamund', to the end of his sonnet sequence *Delia* (1592). Like the latter (and, indeed, like others in the same mode), Shakespeare's poem points up an ironic relation between a sonnet tradition that was predicated on winning the beloved's 'favour' and what the consequences of such a conquest might look like if it were seen from the woman's point of view.[15] In this case—as the 'fickle maid' (l. 5) of his text bitterly tears up the various poems and tributes that her lover used to seduce her— sonnets of the kind we have been reading over the preceding pages end up at the bottom of a river, any claims to monumentality or perpetuity they may have made being unceremoniously sepulchred 'in mud' (l. 46). Seen from the perspective of someone who has been abused by it, perhaps being shredded and cast out onto the elements is indeed the proper fate of a sonnet tradition that had been inspired at the outset by Petrarch's *Rime sparse* ('scattered rhymes'). Like the characters in the preceding sonnet sequence, the woman herself is marked by experience and age: although some vestiges of her former beauty show through the 'lattice of seared age' (l. 14), her face is also lined by Time, as if to reiterate that Time has superiority over anything a human hand could write.

At one level, the woman's story might appear to demonstrate the power of words, since the 'papers' (l. 6), 'folded schedules' (l. 43), 'letters' (l. 47), and 'lines' (l. 55) that she tears have evidently achieved their aim: they have shown considerably more persuasive force in winning her 'favour', for example, than anything Venus might have tried on Adonis. However, a closer look at the poem reveals that the poems and other tributes the seducer gave the woman—and that she is busy tearing up and throwing away—were not in fact written by him to her at all (as one might have assumed), but, rather, were written to him by other infatuated women and then passed on by him to her, as it were, second-hand: '"Look here what tributes wounded fancies sent me"', she quotes her seducer as saying,

> "'Of pallid pearls and rubies red as blood . . .
> And lo, behold these talents of their hair,
> With twisted metal amorously impleached,
> I have received from many a several fair,
> Their kind acceptance weepingly beseeched
> With the annexions of fair gems enriched,
> And deep-brained sonnets that did amplify
> Each stone's dear nature, worth, and quality'"
>
> (ll. 197–8, 204–10)

These 'sonnets' clearly had the power to move and persuade—having received them from her seducer, the woman promptly yields and 'my white stole of chastity I daffed' (l. 297)—and yet that power is emphatically *indirect*. The sonnets were as useless as such poems generally are in persuading their direct addressee (it is not a question, therefore, of 'strong' female writers reclaiming the pen or giving voice to their own desires, for the poems had very little effect in making the young man give them his heart). But they are strangely effective when directed to someone else.

Much of the trouble this 'enigmatic' poem has caused critics and readers in the past, I think, is a consequence of this unexpected turn of events, for it opens up a distinctly

---

[15] Other examples include Thomas Lodge, whose sonnet sequence *Phillis* (1593) is followed by 'The Tragical Complaint of Elstred', and Richard Barnfield's *Cynthia* (1595), which is followed by the 'Legend of Cassandra'. For an anthology of other examples, and an introductory essay on the form, see John Kerrigan (ed.), *Motives of Woe: Shakespeare and 'Female Complaint'* (Oxford: Clarendon Press, 1991).

murky scenario in which the power of words is very much in evidence but is mediated, made indirect, and turned to largely negative effect.[16] This reversal constitutes, perhaps, Shakespeare's last dig at the Petrarchan tradition. In the *Sonnets* he had skewed that tradition by addressing his poems first to a man, and then to a woman who was not ideal. In *A Lover's Complaint* he has women addressing sonnets to a man who is not ideal, and whose failure to be ideal is demonstrated in the use he puts those same sonnets to seduce a woman who is not ideal. In place of the more normal scenario in which male poets wrote sonnets about desirable women and circulated them among themselves—to advertise their skills and make claims about the immortality of their art—we have one in which sonnets about a desirable yet detestable man are written by women and end up in a woman's hands, where they prove to be highly destructive, but are also very effectively destroyed.

[16] I have treated this poem at greater length in my *Masculinity, Gender and Identity in the English Renaissance Lyric* (Cambridge: Cambridge University Press, 2007), 174–215.

CHAPTER 19

....

LATE SHAKESPEARE

....

ADAM ZUCKER

WRITING about Shakespeare's later drama *in toto* is a complicated business. Four of the six surviving plays that he wrote and co-wrote between 1607 and 1613 are beautiful companions for one another. The works we've come to know, for better or for worse, as the romances—*Pericles*, *Cymbeline*, *The Winter's Tale*, and *The Tempest*—sit together like circles in a dense Venn diagram, the themes, language, forms, and historical engagements of each overlaying those of the others.[1] Understanding Shakespeare's 'late plays' as a simple, unified category would be an entirely reasonable thing to do, if we were left only with these four. But in a sign of Shakespeare's difficult truth, in a sign of his implication in the same kinds of cultural and economic networks that enmeshed his competitors and partners in the stage trade, in a sign, that is, of Shakespeare's utter ordinariness, students of his late plays must come to terms with two co-authored final efforts—*The Two Noble Kinsmen* and *Henry VIII*—that are decidedly different from each other and from the four other plays that fall under the rubric of this chapter. This is not to say that *The Two Noble Kinsmen* and *Henry VIII* are lesser plays than the others—far from it. But at the risk of further strengthening a somewhat arbitrary boundary that has organized Shakespeare scholarship for decades, I will consider those two in a coda here, after I've explored the others. Setting apart the two plays we know Shakespeare co-wrote with John Fletcher does, in the end, give us a chance to think carefully about the assumptions we make concerning his artistry and our

Thanks to Matteo Pangallo, who assisted me with the research for this essay, and to James Egan for challenging me as an undergraduate to write about the politics of *The Tempest*.

[1] 'Romance' is a debated term in Shakespeare scholarship. It has been applied to the late plays for nearly 200 years, but Shakespeare himself would not have used the word this way. For the sake of brevity, I am side-stepping the debate. See these excellent discussions of the term as it has been applied to Shakespearean drama and to European literature more generally: Gordon McMullan, *Shakespeare and the Idea of Late Writing: Authorship in the Proximity of Death* (Cambridge: Cambridge University Press, 2007), 68–78; Benedict Robinson, *Islam and Early Modern Literature: The Politics of Romance from Spenser to Milton* (New York and London: Palgrave Macmillan, 2007), esp. 1–26; and on a more general level, Northrop Frye, *The Anatomy of Criticism* (Princeton, NJ: Princeton University Press, 1957).

own relationship to it. It is a kind of thinking all of Shakespeare's later plays demand from us, regardless of whether or not we choose to see them as a coherent group.[2]

FANTASY AND THE TRAGICOMIC

The simplest thing to be said about *Pericles, Cymbeline, The Winter's Tale*, and *The Tempest*—Shakespeare's romances—is that they are fantastic. This is true not only because they are wonderful, striking works of art, but also because they are dominated by a feeling of fantasy, what Mark van Doren called the 'wide world of imaginable event' rather than strictly practical, plausible causes leading to reasonable effects.[3] A woman who seems to have died giving birth to her daughter on board a storm-tossed ship is thrown overboard in a coffin. Still unconscious, she washes ashore in Ephesus where she is resuscitated and becomes a priestess of Diana. Years later, she is reunited with her family. Two young princes are kidnapped by a bitter courtier and raised through adolescence in a cave in Wales, perfectly placed, as it turns out, to rescue their disguised sister from a barbarous suitor, then repel an entire army of invading Romans. A shepherdess May Queen is courted by the disguised prince of Bohemia, who flees with her to Sicily to escape the wrath of his father. It turns out that he has fallen in love with the long-lost heir to the Sicilian throne, uniting the ruling families of the two kingdoms and healing an old wound. Each of these events is, generously speaking, unlikely, yet they form the basic substance of Shakespeare's plot lines. They make these late plays most similar to our modern iterations of the genre we've stopped calling romance, and now know as fantasy. Twenty-first-century audiences quickly recognize the strategy at work in Shakespeare's late plays—it is shared by the novels of Tolkein and C. S. Lewis—and our responses to them are often linked to our tolerance for the emotional aesthetics of the impossible.

It is our challenge as students, critics, readers, and audience members to appreciate these fantasies for their internal style and logic on the one hand, and for their contextual influences and references on the other. These subjects cannot be entirely separated, but in keeping with the goals of this handbook, I will focus more carefully here on the former. I in no way wish to dismiss the fact that these plays were, and continue to be, embedded in material and political relations that are all too often masked, as Gordon McMullan has pointed out, by readings that focus on their emotional and/or aesthetic qualities.[4] In fact, as some of the best contemporary

---

[2] Recent work that has shaped my discussion here includes Simon Palfrey, *Late Shakespeare: A New World of Words* (Oxford: Oxford University Press, 1997); Peter Platt, *Reason Diminished: Shakespeare and the Marvelous* (Lincoln: University of Nebraska Press, 1997); the essays collected in Jennifer Richards and James Knowles (eds.), *Shakespeare's Late Plays: New Readings* (Edinburgh: Edinburgh University Press, 1999); Russ McDonald, *Shakespeare's Late Style* (Cambridge: Cambridge University Press, 2006), 1–27; McMullan, *Late Writing*.

[3] Mark van Doren, *Shakespeare* (New York: Henry Holt and Company, 1939), 293.

[4] McMullan, *Late Writing*, 7–8.

criticism has demonstrated (I refer the reader to my notes throughout), these more abstract qualities tend to be treated in the plays as precisely historical, and deeply political. With that in mind, I'll begin here with a bit of theatre history that any student of Shakespeare's later plays should know. A crucial contextual influence on these plays comes from the community of the King's Men—Shakespeare's playing company—and from the changing tastes of its audiences. The second decade of the seventeenth century saw the emergence of John Fletcher as the King's Men's leading playwright. While Shakespeare was writing *Cymbeline* and *The Winter's Tale*, Fletcher (along with one of his many collaborators, Francis Beaumont) was toying with a new style of drama characterized by intricate plotting, outlandish eroticism, and political intrigue. The unsettling sexual and governmental problems in these plays are often interdependent, and they are often resolved in climactic scenes featuring a series of unexpected revelations and unmaskings. In *A King and No King*, for example, a tyrannous King who has ordered his subjects to approve of his planned incestuous marriage to his sister is suddenly revealed to be a changeling, and thus not related to the woman he wants to marry. In the printed edition of one of his earliest experiments with this kind of plotting, *The Faithful Shepherdess*, a translation of *Il Pastore Fido* by Guarini, Fletcher provides a brief excursus on its genre, using the term 'tragie-comedie' to describe it:

> A tragie-comedie is not so called in respect of mirth and killing, but in respect it wants deaths, which is inough to make it no tragedie, yet brings some neere it, which is inough to make it no comedie: which must be a representation of familiar people, with such kinde of trouble as no life be questioned, so that a God is as lawful in this as in a tragedie, and mean people as in a comedie.   (sig. 2v)[5]

Shakespeare's plays from this period cannot strictly be called 'tragicomedies' if we use Fletcher's definition, insofar as he shows little compunction about killing off characters—the entirely sympathetic Mamillius and Antigonus die in *The Winter's Tale*; the rather less likable Cloten is decapitated in *Cymbeline*. But it is clear that Fletcher and Shakespeare were involved in a shared set of stylistic experiments and renovations during this overlapping part of their careers.[6] Eventually, like many of the

---

[5] John Fletcher, *The Faithfull Shepheardesse* (London: 1610).

[6] On Jacobean tragicomedy, see Robert Henke, *Pastoral Transformations* (London: Associated University Presses, 1997); Gordon McMullan, *The Politics of Unease in the Plays of John Fletcher* (Amherst: University of Massachusetts Press, 1994); Verna A. Foster, *The Name and Nature of Tragicomedy* (Burlington, VT: Ashgate, 2004); and two excellent collections of essays, Gordon McMullan and Jonathan Hope (eds.), *The Politics of Tragicomedy: Shakespeare and After* (London and New York: Routledge, 1992); and Subha Mukherji and Raphael Lyne (eds.), *Early Modern Tragicomedy* (Cambridge: D. S. Brewer, 2007). On the influence of Guarini on Shakespeare, Beaumont, and Fletcher see Lee Bliss, 'Tragicomic Romances for the King's Men: 1609–1611', in A. R. Braunmuller and J. C. Bulmer (eds.), *Comedy from Shakespeare to Sheridan: Essays in Honor of Eugene Waith* (Newark: University of Delaware Press, 1986), 148–64; and Raphael Lyne, 'English Guarini: Recognition and Reception', *The Yearbook of English Studies* 36 (2006), 90–102. The most recent works on the subject show a sensitivity to the ways mixed forms can resonate with paradoxical or complex historical relations: see, for example, Valerie Forman, *Tragicomic Redemptions: Global Economics and the Early Modern English Stage* (Philadelphia: University of Pennsylvania Press, 2008); and Zachary

other major playwrights working between 1610 and 1625, Shakespeare would closely collaborate with Fletcher on several plays. But even before this, we can see Shakespeare working out the aesthetic possibilities of formal mixture and the near-death narrative that interested Fletcher. Marina and Thaisa in *Pericles*; Innogen[7] and Posthumus in *Cymbeline*; Hermione and Perdita in *The Winter's Tale*; Ferdinand, a boatload of sailors, Miranda, and even Prospero in *The Tempest*: each of these characters is either brought close to death or is assumed to have died by others in their respective plays; each is revealed (or reveals themselves) to have lived miraculously, often by art or magic. Each becomes a healing force for communities and individuals that have assumed themselves to be permanently bereft. There is, in other words, a tragicomic tone to be found in Shakespeare's late plays, a tone that is equally the product of his interest in working with a younger playwright and in writing for his changing audiences at the Globe, the Blackfriars theatre, and at court. These plays are the work of a writer enmeshed in a cultural field, a profession, a living, shifting theatre scene. They help us see very clearly the ways in which Shakespeare's brilliance was part and parcel of his ordinary aims and practices, and in that way among others, they are inspiring.

'LIE THERE, MY ART.'

In the final scene of *The Tempest*, the deposed Duke of Milan, Prospero, draws a magical circle on the ground. He sends his fairy minion Ariel off to find the party of wandering aristocrats and courtiers he has marooned upon his island, then vows to give up magic forever:

> ... this rough magic
> I here abjure; and when I have required
> Some heavenly music—which even now I do—
> To work mine end upon their senses that
> This airy charm is for, I'll break my staff,
> Bury it certain fathoms in the earth,
> And deeper than did ever plummet sound
> I'll drown my book.   (5.1.50–7)[8]

Prospero's promise to surrender his powers has become one of the foremost clichés in the teaching and performance of Shakespeare's last plays. These lines are often seen as a set of overlapping and reflective goodbyes: one from Prospero the magician, about to

Lesser, 'Tragical-Comical-Pastoral-Colonial: Economic Sovereignty, Globalization, and the Form of Tragicomedy', *ELH* 74 (2007), 881–908.

    [7] I use the Oxford editors' spelling of the name.

    [8] All citations of Shakespeare's work are taken from the Oxford Shakespeare: Stanley Wells, Gary Taylor, John Jowett, and William Montgomery (eds.), *Complete Works* (Oxford: Oxford University Press, 1986).

board Alonso's ship and leave us stranded on an island with Caliban; one from Shakespeare, who—a certain argument goes—uses Prospero as a stand-in for himself in order to bid adieu to his career as a playwright for the public stage; and occasionally, in the context of a course-ending lecture, one from the teacher, imagining for a moment that his or her own lessons have left a roomful of students, like Alonso, Sebastian, Antonio, and the others who wander into Prospero's charmed circle, utterly transfixed.

This seductive mix of pedagogical and biographical possibilities has managed to obscure some very basic facts about Shakespeare's life and work. First and foremost, he wrote brilliantly for the King's Men after *The Tempest* was performed. Second, and this may be more to the point, we have absolutely no evidence whatsoever that Shakespeare imagined that his career as a playwright was winding down in 1611 or had ended by 1613. Barring a prophetic power that even the most reverential biographer would be reluctant to grant him, Shakespeare certainly did not know as he wrote *The Tempest* and the plays that followed it—*The Two Noble Kinsmen* and *Henry VIII*—that he would die in 1616. Following our desire to see the last plays Shakespeare wrote as a stylistically, generically, or thematically coherent group, we have created for ourselves what McMullan has called an 'idea' of lateness.[9] That is to say, readers of Shakespeare's last plays tend to interpret them as if he himself knew that they were late, as if Shakespeare saw that his career was nearing its end, and as if this knowledge would inspire in him the need to create a fitting style or image set for a properly reflective, considered coda on his brilliant corpus of plays and poetry. He did not do this, and without our studious efforts to read this narrative into his work, he could not have been imagined to. We are all partners, in other words, in the meanings of Prospero's goodbye.

This is not to say that *The Tempest*, like the rest of Shakespeare's later drama, fails to reflect upon the act of giving up a certain kind of creative power. In many ways, Prospero's revocation of his magic is the signature move of the play—a crucial moment of comic release—and if we approach it as such, we can begin to see it as a decent introduction to Shakespeare's late plays for reasons that are something other than biographical. In each of the romances, a ruler or a monarch surrenders some aspect of his power. Pericles, the Prince of Tyre, twice leaves his kingdom in the hands of his councillors and drifts around the Mediterranean. Cymbeline, the King of the Ancient Britons, first follows the poor advice of his Queen, then agrees to pay tribute to Caesar, despite having defeated his army in battle. And Leontes, the King of Sicilia in *The Winter's Tale*, gives himself over to the punishing guidance of Paulina after the presumed death of his wife, thrusting his realm into a 16-year-long period of stasis and mourning. These are certainly not identical situations, and as I explore each play below, it will become clear that the outcomes of these moments of abdication, surrender, and acquiescence create very different kinds of political and theatrical narrative. But we should see Prospero's revocation as an example of this pattern. The fantasies of

---

[9] McMullan, *Late Writing, passim*.

Shakespeare's late plays all reflect on the act and meanings of royal compromise and human surrender.[10]

I have suggested that this element of surrender in *The Tempest* has comic overtones, in a generic sense. Prospero's move to un-magic himself creates a conventional narrative moment of resolution and release similar to Viola's removal of her disguise in *Twelfth Night* or the Shepherd's revelation of Perdita's true identity in *The Winter's Tale*. It is a moment, in other words, that dissolves a crucial obstacle to the play's desired ends of dynastic continuity, familial harmony, and homecoming. To see why this is so, we need simply to acknowledge that the central problem in *The Tempest* might be the unmitigated authority of Prospero himself.[11] Though the image of him as a gentle, paternal Shakespeare substitute tends to obscure this possibility, the strength of his magic is absolutely terrifying. He is unnaturally powerful, more powerful, in fact, than any of Shakespeare's other human characters. Setting aside his ability to call up storms and control various spirits, he is, in his own telling of it, capable of necromancy: in the lines that immediately precede those I've given above, he boasts that at his bidding, graves 'Have waked their sleepers, oped, and let 'em forth' (5.1.49).[12] While we are spared this vision of literal human decay during the play, we do get a detailed sense for Prospero's firm control over every character on the island. He tells his daughter, Miranda, 'Thou art inclined to sleep', and she nods off at his command (1.2.185). He threatens Ariel repeatedly with tortuous imprisonment, and Ariel jumps to do his bidding. And while the pinches and cramps to which Caliban, Stephano, and Trinculo are subjected might be seen as a kind of humorous punishment for their drunken uprising, their pain seems quite real. 'Hark', says Ariel, listening as the three rebels are chased off stage by joint-grinding goblins, 'They roar' (4.1.26). Prospero is right to call his magic 'rough'—its force comes in part from its implicit violence and its irresistible efficacy.

That combination creates a controlling authority so entirely impervious to the will of other men and women that, despite the ways Prospero chooses to use it over the course of the play, it exists outside of ordinary political considerations. It is, in other words,

[10] My take on the politics of these plays has been deeply influenced by Constance Jordan, *Shakespeare's Monarchies: Ruler and Subject in the Romances* (Ithaca, NY: Cornell University Press, 1997). See also Amelia Zurcher, 'Untimely Monuments: Stoicism, History, and the Problem of Utility in *The Winter's Tale* and *Pericles*', *ELH* 70 (2003), 903–27.

[11] This observation drives the analysis of the play's relationship to the acts and language of colonialism. See, for example, Paul Brown, '"This thing of darkness I acknowledge mine": *The Tempest* and the Discourse of Colonialism', in Jonathan Dollimore and Alan Sinfield (eds.), *Political Shakespeare: New Essays in Cultural Materialism* (Manchester: Manchester University Press, 1985), 48–71; and, for a spectrum of related perspectives, Peter Hulme and William H. Sherman (eds.), *The Tempest and its Travels* (Philadelphia: University of Pennsylvania Press, 2000). Recent contributions include Julia Reinhard Lupton, 'Creature Caliban', *Shakespeare Quarterly* 51 (2000), 1–23; Barbara Fuchs, 'Conquering Islands: Contextualizing *The Tempest*', *Shakespeare Quarterly* 48 (1997), 45–62; and Jean Feerick, '"Divided in Soyle": Plantation and Degeneracy in *The Tempest* and *The Sea Voyage*', *Renaissance Drama* 35 (2006), 27–54.

[12] These lines are inspired by a speech of Medea's in the *Aeneid*, one of many allusions to that work in *The Tempest*. See David Scott Wilson-Okamura, 'Virgilian Models of Colonization in Shakespeare's *Tempest*', *ELH* 70 (2003), 709–37.

ideologically incompatible with mundane systems of government. As the story of Sycorax, Caliban's banished witch of a mother, suggests, there is no place for actual magic in the ordinary realms of Naples, Milan, or Algiers (where Sycorax once lived). Prospero's power belongs to the Island alone, and in order for him to return home— indeed, in order for him to be considered a sympathetic character in any sense—he must leave it behind. More so than the dynastic marriage of Miranda to Ferdinand, more so even than the half-hearted repentance of Alonso and Antonio for their collusion against Prospero (the latter is, after all, entirely silent on the matter, even after he has been confronted with his misdeeds), magical authority itself is the knot that must be untied for the narrative lines of the play to straighten themselves out. *The Tempest* earns its accidental place as the first play listed under the heading of 'Comedies' in the 1623 Folio the moment that Prospero—romance hero, *senex*, magical Machiavel—promises to break his staff and become, simply, a human being.

PERICLES

Of the three remaining romances, *Pericles* sits at the farthest remove both in time and in style from *The Tempest*, despite some shared material. Pericles, the wandering Prince of Tyre, is both tortured and redeemed by the precise elements of the world that Prospero controls with his magic: storms at sea; relationships between fathers and daughters; the ebbs and flows of power in the political firmament of the coastal Mediterranean. Marina, Pericles' daughter, reveals these points of contact in her earliest lines. She is in Tarsus, where her father left her fourteen years earlier, and she is mourning both the death of the nursemaid that has raised her and the more general misfortune that has marked her life:

> Ay me, poor maid,
> Born in a tempest when my mother died,
> This world to me is as a lasting storm,
> Whirring me from my friends   (Sc. 15, 69–72)

Moments later, Marina is attacked by a killer employed by her surrogate mother, then rescued by pirates, only to be sold into sexual slavery in Mytilene. The word 'whirring' is a fitting one here, especially in this unusual transitive usage. While *The Tempest* is shaped by Prospero's tight, effective dominance and Shakespeare's uncharacteristically strict temporal and spatial limits in his plotting, *Pericles* is wild, loose, and wide-ranging, whirring us along with its characters from setting to setting, from challenge to challenge, and, ultimately, from crushing disasters to a series of reunions that gesture in their choppy ways to the overwhelming power of fortune and Providence in the lives of all humans, potentates or no. In many ways, the vision of human agency traced out in *Pericles* reads like *The Tempest* in reverse: no human in the play can raise the dead, and no one can cast spells to control the storms that fuel the plot.

This sense of antithesis with *The Tempest* might also apply to some basic compositional facts that make *Pericles* a play defined by syncreticism and mixture. First and
foremost, it is one of the many Shakespeare plays we know to have been co-authored:
the current consensus has it that George Wilkins was the author of the play's first two
acts and many of the interstitial lines delivered by the choral figure, Gower.[13] Second,
Pericles might offer the best example of Shakespeare's life-long interest in writing plays
shaped by stylistic hybridity and compilation. Like *Hamlet* and *Twelfth Night* and
Measure for Measure, among others, *Pericles* offers a jumble of dramatic and poetic
textual traditions. The travel narratives popular in the day mix with a brothel scene
lifted from satirical city comedy; a chivalric jousting tournament sits side by side with
debates on the role of a ruler's counsellors taken from political tragedies of irrational,
lust-struck tyrants. And though there is something abrasive about the shifts in tone that
accompany these transitions from style to style and from place to place (not to mention
from author to author), they help *Pericles* stand out as the play of Shakespeare's most
clearly marked by the highly episodic structures of other kinds of verse and prose
romance. As in *The Faerie Queene* and Sidney's *Arcadia*, cause-and-effect relations
binding events together in the play are considerably less important than individual
events themselves.

The distribution of the play's action all over the eastern Mediterranean creates a
scatter-shot political investigation.[14] Each scene, each setting contains its own rulers
who buffet Pericles and his family members with punishments and rewards, threats
and alliances. We meet over the course of the play a paranoid King of Antioch—he
sends an assassin after Pericles following the prince's discovery of the truth about the
King's incestuous relationship with his daughter; a kinder King of Pentapolis, whose
daughter Thaisa becomes Pericles' wife after our hero washes ashore there with just
enough armour to triumph in a tournament of foreign knights; the governors of a
famine-stricken Tarsus who become foster parents for Marina, Pericles' daughter, then
attempt to have her murdered; and the urban administrator of Mytilene, who is
introduced as a brothel-going lecher but is converted by Marina's piety into a suitable
husband for her. This diffusion of sites and authorities is matched by Pericles' multiple
revocations of his own powers as Prince. While Prospero's decision to give up his
magic is singular and entirely his own, Pericles twice leaves his kingdom in the hands of
his counsellors in order to reckon with forces that are entirely out of his control: in the
first act to escape the machinations of Antiochus; in the fourth to retrieve, then, when
he is told she is dead, to mourn over Marina. After this final crushing blow, Gower, the
play's choral figure, describes a Periclean mode of storm-creation in grief:

[13] On the authorship of *Pericles*, see MacDonald P. Jackson, *Defining Shakespeare: Pericles as Test
Case* (Oxford: Oxford University Press, 2003).

[14] On the settings of *Pericles*, see Linda McJannet, 'Genre and Geography: the Eastern Mediterranean
in *Pericles* and *The Comedy of Errors*', in John Gillies and Virginia Mason Vaughan (eds.), *Playing the
Globe: Genre and Geography in English Renaissance Drama* (Newark, NJ: Associated University Presses,
1998), 86–106.

> He swears,
> Never to wash his face nor cut his hairs.
> He puts on sackcloth and to sea he bears
> A tempest which his mortal vessel tears,
> And yet he rides it out   (Sc. 18, 28–32)

This is the only kind of tempest Pericles can call up. By the beginning of Scene 21, he is 'driven by the winds' at sea, silent, unshaven, peripatetic, and devastated by the destruction of his family. He is a prince in name only, his governmental and practical power abandoned entirely.

Fittingly for a play that gives us multiples of nearly everything within it, the final portion of *Pericles* brings its family back together with two consecutive climactic reunion scenes. The first occurs in Mytilene, as a hirsute Pericles encounters Marina, listens to her story, and realizes that she has not died in Tarsus. As Marina speaks and is revealed to him, Pericles becomes increasingly entranced by the sound of what he calls 'the music of the spheres' (Sc. 21, 216), evoking a kind of aesthetic encounter that will become a crucial element in the conclusions of Shakespeare's later romances. The series of accidents and episodes that lead to this moment of reunion are configured here as a coalescing concert, a bit of art that can be understood as such only in its completion. Pericles' experience of the aesthetics of reunion lulls him to into a peaceful sleep, during which the goddess Diana appears to him in a dream and tells him to visit her temple at Ephesus. Messengers from the Greco-Roman pantheon appear in each of Shakespeare's later romances: in this case, Diana enables the play's second climax, as Pericles and Marina find Thaisa alive and well serving as a priestess in the temple.[15] The tempest in which Marina was born turns out to have been the force that washed Thaisa in her coffin onto the shores of Ephesus, where Cerimon was able to save her. By the end of *Pericles*, the powers of nature and politics alike have aligned to present to us a moral vision of, as Gower puts it in the play's epilogue, 'Virtue preserved from fell destruction's blast, | Led on by heaven and crowned with joy at last' (Sc. 22, 111–12). This vision of virtue preserved is, of course, also a vision of a family preserved: as we've already begun to see, Shakespeare's romances are as concerned with the intimate relationships between husbands and wives, parents and children, as they are with those between rulers and subjects, the divine and the earthly, masters and slaves.

CYMBELINE

Cymbeline is the only one of Shakespeare's late romances that is set on British soil, and it reads as a decidedly different kind of play than the others as a result.[16] It leaves

---

[15] See Elizabeth F. Hart, '"Great is Diana" of Shakespeare's Ephesus', *Studies in English Literature* 43 (2003), 347–74.

[16] I am classifying *Henry VIII* here as a history play, although, as I'll discuss at the end of this chapter, it does incorporate romance conventions.

behind the punishing storms of the Mediterranean for material drawn from chronicle history, and its convoluted plot centres, as in earlier history plays, on the preservation and transmission of British sovereignty. The threats imposed upon the Crown are, on the one hand, external—a Roman army approaches to extract an agreed-upon tribute from Cymbeline, King of the ancient Britons—and on the other, internal—Cymbeline's Queen plots to supplant Innogen, the rightful heir to the throne and Cymbeline's child from an earlier marriage, either by poisoning her or by marrying her off to her idiotic son, Cloten. The Queen has also counselled the King to deny Rome its tribute—she is, in that sense, directly responsible for the disruptive and unlooked-for war in the play's final act. In *Cymbeline*, the King's political weaknesses are caused not by grief or disaster, but by a lack of good counsel—a problem that will be staged in much more dramatic fashion in *The Winter's Tale*.[17]

The disturbances within the kingdom are adumbrated through the elaborate story of Innogen and her husband Posthumus Leonatus, who is not quite noble enough to be married to the heir to the throne, despite their love for one another. We can see in their travails Shakespeare's most intricate and, some might say, most overwrought plotting. Complexity is in many ways the basic point of the play: any plot summary of *Cymbeline* necessarily defies pith. To protect the King's bloodline (and to clear the way for Cloten), Posthumus is banished to Rome, where he meets a conniving courtier named Giacomo. Giacomo wagers with Posthumus that he might travel to England and seduce Innogen, and upon his return, he convinces Posthumus that he was successful (he was not). Distraught, Posthumus sends a letter to his servant Pisanio ordering him to kill Innogen. Pisanio instead warns her of the plan. Innogen ends up wandering the Welsh countryside dressed as a page, where she encounters her two long-lost brothers who have been raised for the past twenty years in a cave by Belarius, a banished courtier who kidnapped them to punish Cymbeline. They do not know that they are princes. Innogen does not know that they are her brothers. Her brothers do not know that she is a woman. Soon, they do not know that she is still alive: Innogen drinks a liquid she has received from Pisanio, who received it from the Queen, who told him it was a restorative medicine, though she in fact believed it to be mortal poison given to her by a doctor, who in turn had tricked her by giving her a harmless but very effective sleeping potion. The princes lay the seemingly dead Innogen down alongside the headless corpse of the Queen's stepson, who had gone in search of Innogen wearing Posthumus' clothes in order to rape her, but who insulted one of the wild princes and was killed for his pains. Innogen wakes up, believes herself to be next to the corpse of her lover, and in the midst of her despair agrees to become a Roman general's assistant. All this occurs in the play's first three and a half acts. To describe the rest of the plot would be a lengthy mistake. Suffice it to

---

[17] On the politics of *Cymbeline* and its visions of British nationhood, see Jodi Mikilachki, 'The Masculine Romance of Roman Britain: *Cymbeline* and Early Modern English Nationalism', *Shakespeare Quarterly* 46 (1995), 301–22; Andrew Escobedo, 'From Britannia to England: *Cymbeline* and the Beginning of Nations', *Shakespeare Quarterly* 59 (2008), 60–87.

say that Posthumus, the banished Belarius, and the two cave-raised princes turn back an entire Roman army on their own, then converge alongside nearly every other living character from the play in a climactic scene that may be the most difficult moment in the entire Shakespearean canon to stage successfully for a modern audience. To get a sense for why this is so, we need only look to Cymbeline's befuddled reaction to an abbreviated description of the play's narrative he hears as his family is reunited. He speaks like a stand-in for a confused audience member (or perhaps, a confused reader of the exposition I've just given):

> When shall I hear all through? This fierce abridgement
> Hath to it circumstantial branches which
> Distinction should be rich in. Where, how lived you?
> And when came you to serve our Roman captive?
> How parted with your brothers? How first met them?
> Why fled you from the court, and whither? These,
> And your three motives to the battle with
> I know not how much more should be demanded,
> And all the other by-dependences,
> From chance to chance. But nor the time nor place
> Will serve our long inter'gatories.   (5.3.384–94)

The King's interest in 'all the other by-dependences, | From chance to chance' that go unspoken in the final scene is a signpost of sorts, directing us toward the aesthetic strategy of a play that often seems to lack one. More than any of the other late romances, *Cymbeline* is an exercise in complexity for its own sake, a play made ornate with 'circumstantial branches' to please an audience that enjoyed elaborate and unlikely plotting onstage. This is not a quality that modern audiences have been trained to appreciate—quite the opposite. In a 2007 staging of *Cymbeline* by the Cheek by Jowl company at the Brooklyn Academy of Music, the audience laughed out loud during the climactic final scene when Posthumus struck Innogen in her disguise as the page Fidele. 'Shall's have a play of this?' asks an angry Posthumus when Innogen interrupts his lament for her, 'Thou scornful page, | There lie thy part' (5.4.228–9). This is in many ways the most shocking moment of the play, an encapsulation of the violence threatened by and often explicitly underpinning the political and erotic relationships staged in early modern tragicomedy and in Shakespeare's later drama more generally. But for audience members who no longer feel emotion in the aesthetics of accident and error, Posthumus' slap across the face of his disguised, presumed dead wife is entirely laughable.

Of course, changing audiences will always find new meanings or affect in old plays— this is as it should be. But to understand Shakespeare's late plays and *Cymbeline* most of all, it is necessary to see the ludicrous as potentially luminous. In making the King an inquisitive audience member for its own narrative, *Cymbeline* suggests as much, staging an appreciative response to the twists and turns of its plot. Immediately after the lines I've given above, the King's speech turns from question-asking to pleasurable experience, from wondering about cause and effect to feeling wonder or awe at unlikely, fortunate resolutions.[18] 'See,' Cymbeline commands his court:

> Posthumus anchors upon Innogen
> And she, like harmless lightning, throws her eye
> On him, her brothers, me, her master, hitting
> Each object with a joy; the counterchange
> Is severally in all. Let's quit this ground,
> And smoke the temple with our sacrifices.   (5.4.395–400)

Cymbeline looks at Innogen, while she looks at those around her. The other characters on stage do the same. A repentant and forgiven Giacomo; a vanquished but also satisfied Roman general, Lucius (after his Queen dies offstage admitting her perfidy, Cymbeline decides to pay tribute to Rome to avoid further battles, despite his victory); a relieved and restored Posthumus whose marriage to Innogen can stand now that her elder brothers have returned to become heirs to the throne in her place; the forgiven Belarius, preserver of Cymbeline's bloodline and the British polity more generally— each of these characters stare at one another silently. What Cymbeline calls 'the counterchange' between them all is a mutual vision shared by the audience: the sight of reunion, forgiveness, and harmony. It is joined by the promised scent of smoke rising in the temples at Lud's town, the taste of the 'feasts' proposed by Cymbeline to celebrate the peace with Rome, and, of course, the sound of the poetry that has marked these final moments.[19] We are presented here with a more complex and diverse expression of 'the music of the spheres' heard by Pericles. A soothsayer witnessing the scene suggests that 'The fingers of the powers above do tune | The harmony of this piece' (5.4.477–8). His pun on piece/peace yokes together political fantasy and aesthetic form, rendering the play's historical engagements and its art simultaneous and nearly identical. A rich, sensual consolidation resolves the 'long inter'gatories' that Cymbeline suggests cannot be properly staged. The asking and answering of questions is not quite the point of *Cymbeline*: we are to take it in, to sense it, and if we are lucky, to wonder that it could have been dreamed up at all.

THE WINTER'S TALE

The Winter's Tale does not lack for its share of the ludicrous. The selective appetite of a Bohemian bear—it prefers to eat the full-grown Antigonus instead of the infant

---

[18] My ideas about 'wonder' as a defining element of the romances are indebted to Platt, *Reason Diminished*. For Platt, wonder functions as 'an ongoing inquiry and an aesthetic astonishment, both caused by an acceptance of an openness to the previously unimaginable' (p. 125).

[19] On the aural quality of the later plays' concluding scenes, see McDonald, *Shakespeare's Late Style*, 214–18.

Perdita—ends up being the key to the survival of the royal house of Leontes in Sicily. But unlike *Cymbeline*, *The Winter's Tale* does not revel in complex absurdity for its own sake. Though it shows signs of the narrative strategies that shaped the earlier romances, and though it presents another version of the investigation of absolutism staged in *The Tempest*, the often exaggerated features of Shakespeare's later drama take on a subtler cast here.[20] The jolting shifts from setting to setting to setting that create the Mediterranean mélange in *Pericles* are modulated into a simpler journey from the court of Leontes in Sicily to Bohemia and back; the increasingly bizarre course of events that leads to the familial, political, and romantic reconciliations in *Cymbeline* is distilled down to one or two odd coincidences; and, perhaps most importantly, the vision of an omnipotent magician controlling everything around him with unquestioned purpose at the centre of *The Tempest* is written into this earlier play as both the cause and the subject of a striking critique of authoritarian rule. The ultimate solution to the political and emotional turmoil staged in the play also gives us Shakespeare's most precise depiction of the social potential for aesthetic experience to remake the world: the famous statue scene in Act 5 is the epitome of the later plays' interest in art's practical role in human relations.

The play opens with the familiar figure of a man possessed by an entirely irrational kind of jealousy. Leontes wrongly suspects that his very, very pregnant wife Hermione is about to bear the child of his close friend Polixenes, the King of Bohemia, who has been visiting for the past nine months. Leontes is Othello without an Iago: his suspicions are entirely self-generated and entirely self-confirmed. No one else in his court sees what he sees, but as Leontes is quick to point out as he sends Hermione to prison, it is within his rights to demand that they do:

> Why, what need we
> Commune with you of this, but rather follow
> Our forceful instigation? Our prerogative
> Calls not your counsels, but our natural goodness
> Imparts this; which, if you, or stupefied,
> Or seeming so in skill, cannot or will not
> Relish a truth like us, inform yourselves
> We need no more of your advice. The matter,
> The loss, the gain, the ord'ring on't
> Is all properly ours.   (2.1.162–70)

There are the seeds here of the lectures Prospero delivers to Ariel or Caliban about his magical hold over them. Without these explicitly supernatural overtones, however, Leontes's harangue reads as a fairly typical expression of early modern political theory. The English King could be (and often was) envisioned as an absolute monarch who was under no obligation to listen to the councillors that typically helped him or her with the

---

[20] On the relation of *The Winter's Tale* to the genre of romance more generally, see Steven R. Mentz, 'Wearing Greene: Autolycus, Robert Greene, and the Structure of Romance in *The Winter's Tale*', *Renaissance Drama* 30 (1999–2001), 73–92.

day-to-day organization of policy and governance. In practice, the ruler of a centraliz-
ing English state could never govern successfully without these councillors. But the
theories of kingship and rule in Shakespeare's day—especially those favoured by James
I himself—made room for that possibility.[21] In a fashion only hinted at in the figures of
Antiochus and Cymbeline in the earlier romances, The Winter's Tale engages with
these ideas by directly taking up one of the central motivations of political tragedy in
the Renaissance: the passions of monarchs make them susceptible to error and
misdeed; and under certain interpretations of the law, there is in the end no appropriate recourse for subjects victimized by such tyrants. The first half of The Winter's Tale
depicts the horrifying outcomes of this problem. Hermione gives birth to a daughter in
prison, and Leontes orders the infant abandoned to the fates in some far-off place. He
then presides over a treason trial called to session against his wife, still weak from
childbirth, during which she is allowed no defence beyond her own. Under these
conditions, there is no logical way for Hermione to argue on her own behalf: 'mine
integrity, | Being counted falsehood, shall, as I express it, | Be so retrieved' she
complains (3.2.25–7). The trial's inevitable outcome notwithstanding, Hermione's
performance features a beautiful mixture of forensic rhetoric and impassioned lyricism.
She and Paulina have both caught the attention of contemporary critics drawn to the
play's interest in women's speech at a moment in history that featured a strong
ideological commitment to feminine chastity defined, in part, by silence.[22] Both
women resist in language the violence of the state; and Paulina is eventually able to
redirect that violence toward its embodied source, Leontes.

Paulina's rise to power begins when a Delphic oracle resolves Hermione's trial. In a
calmer, quieter version of the showy set-pieces from the other romances during which
the gods descend to speak with mortals, Apollo in The Winter's Tale never actually
appears: his oracle simply reveals that Hermione is innocent, that Leontes is not, and
that there will be no heir to the Sicilian throne until 'that which is lost'—the infant girl
Leontes has banished and presumably killed—is found (3.2.133). Leontes stupidly
denounces the oracle, and immediately loses what's left of his family. The prince
Mamillius dies offstage, and Hermione collapses at the news, apparently dead as well.
This scene takes us closer to pure tragedy than any other of the romances. It also
marks the beginning of the shift in the play from its tragic narrative of tyranny and
infanticide toward the comic reconciliations and reunions to come. But unlike

---

[21] For a pithy overview of this topic, see Stephen Orgel's introduction to The Oxford Shakespeare: The
Winter's Tale (Oxford: Oxford University Press, 1996), 12–16; William Morse, 'Metacriticism and
Materiality: The Case of Shakespeare's The Winter's Tale', ELH 58 (1991), 283–304.

[22] See, for example, Lynn Enterline, '"You speak a language that I understand not": The Rhetoric of
Animation in The Winter's Tale', Shakespeare Quarterly 48 (1997), 17–44; Kathleen Kalpin, 'Framing
Wifely Advice in Thomas Heywood's A Curtaine Lecture and Shakespeare's The Winter's Tale', Studies
in English Literature 48 (2008), 131–46; M. Lindsay Kaplan and Katherine Eggert, '"Good queen, my lord,
good queen": Sexual Slander and the Trials of Female Authority in The Winter's Tale', Renaissance Drama
25 (1994), 89–118; and, in a slightly different but no less striking analysis, Amy L. Tigner, 'The Winter's Tale:
Gardens and the Marvels of Transformation', English Literary Renaissance 36 (2006), 114–34.

Fletcherian tragicomedy—and unlike *Pericles* and *Cymbeline*—which feature drastic and sudden moments of narrative redirection, *The Winter's Tale* dilates this moment of transition, slows it down, and makes the suffering of Leontes its point. The King devotes his life to grieving over the bodies of his family members—'Once a day I'll visit | The chapel where they lie, and tears shed there | Shall be my recreation' (3.2.236–8)—and Paulina, who has chastised Leontes throughout the play, becomes his sole guide. When we next see him at the beginning of the fifth act, Leontes has spent sixteen years in mourning. The councillors he ignored at the beginning of the play now beg him to remarry and provide political stability with a new heir; but Leontes obeys Paulina, who demands that he preserve the terms set out by the oracle: there will be no heir to the throne until the lost child is found.

With the apparent death of Hermione, Shakespeare thrusts the audience into a fairy tale world of lost children and divided families, a world where a kingdom is frozen in time as its ruler surrenders his basic governmental responsibilities and succumbs to personal grief. This is the world of a 'winter's tale'—a phrase that was used in Shakespeare's day to describe precisely the kind of children's story or fable the play brings into being. And while nothing is particularly magical or fantastical in the first three acts of the play, a change in setting and tone occurs at the end of the third act that introduces an entirely new set of images and themes. Antigonus arrives with the infant Perdita on the coasts of Bohemia (coasts that signify our entry into a strictly imaginary world: Bohemia, as Shakespeare likely knew, is landlocked). As he lays down the baby, a bear chases him offstage and devours him. For a moment, the audience is left staring at a swaddled infant, alone in a field, abandoned to the elements. Then the energies of fantasy take over. A shepherd finds Perdita and decides to raise her as his own. As his son describes the unpleasant end of Antigonus, the shepherd holds up the swaddled infant and speaks the pivot point of the play: 'Thou metst with things dying, I with things newborn' (3.3.109–10). With this, *The Winter's Tale* leaves death and tragedy behind for song, dance, flower garlands, and young love.

Near the beginning of *Cymbeline*, as Innogen reckons with her father's banishment of Posthumus, she invokes a pastoral world as a potential refuge from the political realities that vex their love: 'Would I were | A neatherd's daughter, and my Leonatus | Our neighbour shepherd's son' (1.1.149–51). There are similar gestures toward these sentiments in the piscatorial scene in *Pericles*, in the story of the kidnapped princes in *Cymbeline*, and in the basic premise of the isolated Island in *The Tempest*. The fourth act of *The Winter's Tale* takes up the fantasies of escape inherent to pastoral in a more conventional fashion.[23] A brief choral monologue from the allegorical figure of Time pushes the action forwards sixteen years, and the audience is treated to a vision of

[23] The best contemporary work on pastoral in Shakespeare's romances is Henke, *Pastoral Transformations*. See also the general studies in Paul Alpers, *What is Pastoral?* (Chicago, IL: University of Chicago Press, 1996); William Empson, *Some Versions of Pastoral* (London: Chatto & Windus, 1935); and Raymond Williams, *The Country and the City* (Oxford: Oxford University Press, 1973).

prince Florizel—the son of Polixenes—disguised as a peasant and courting Perdita, who has no idea she is a princess. She is dressed instead as a mock May Queen, and presides with touching irony over a sheep-shearing festival. Men and women dance, buy ballads, and scatter flowers; even the disguised Polixenes, spying on his son, playfully banters with the rustics he encounters. The green world festivities, however, come to a crashing halt with the re-emergence of the play's interest in the twinned logics of domestic and political patriarchy. Polixenes unmasks himself, forbids the planned marriage between Florizel and Perdita, and threatens the Shepherd, Perdita's foster father, with death. A strange reversal of perspective takes place: the young lovers are encouraged to flee to Sicily, in the hopes that Leontes might shelter them from the wrath of Polixenes. Sicily, in other words, becomes the wished-for green world or place of escape in relation to the spoiled Bohemian pastoral scene. There is no perfect isolation from the mundane and the oppressive in *The Winter's Tale*. Imperfection marks its imagined worlds—even in the midst of a summertime celebration—and the place of safety is always somewhere else.

The convergence of all the play's characters in Sicily creates a scene of mutual recognition and resolution that refines what some readers take to be the excesses of *Pericles* and *Cymbeline*. Rather than staging two recognition scenes as in *Pericles* or risk flooding a single scene with a superflux of revelation as in *Cymbeline*, Shakespeare has two characters describe the discovery of Perdita's identity in a conversational report. As a result, his characters' reactions to an unlikely story become as important as the story itself:

> ... the changes I perceived in the King and Camillo were very notes of admiration. They seemed almost with staring on one another, to tear the cases of their eyes. There was speech in their dumbness, language in their very gesture; they looked as they had heard of a world ransomed, or one destroyed. A notable passion of wonder appeared in them; but the wisest beholder that knew no more but seeing could not say if th'importance were joy, or sorrow—but in the extremity of the one it must needs be.   (5.2.11–21)

The unnamed gentlemen having this conversation are guides not only to the emotions of the play's final scene, but to the purposes of tragicomedy more generally in the period. The 'passion of wonder' is central to the genre and to the conclusions of Shakespeare's late plays; the confusion over the nature of that passion is central as well. Joy? Sorrow? We cannot know. Instead, what the gentlemen call 'extremity' is the hoped-for response to the ends of these plays. Exceptional artifice is meant to inspire emotion, or, as Paulina puts it in the last scene of the play, to 'Strike all that look upon with marvel' (5.3.100).

The last event of the play is an emblem for all that Shakespeare works toward in his later drama. Paulina brings the assembled characters to her gallery, where she unveils a statue of the presumed-dead Hermione. It is wrinkled, and life-like, and Leontes believes that it breathes. Paulina suddenly presents herself as a Prospero-like magician who can make the statue move, though she assures the onlookers that she is not 'assisted | By wicked powers' (5.3.90–1). She calls for music, and as it begins, the statue descends. It is the living Hermione, who has been hidden for sixteen years, waiting for Apollo's prophecy to come true. 'If this be magic', says an overwhelmed and grateful Leontes, 'Let it be an art lawful as eating' (5.3.110–1). Sustenance and pleasure are joined in Paulina's art, which turns out, in the end, to be a rough version of the arts of narrative and theatre. She has told Leontes the story of his crimes for years and years; here, in the end, she stages his redemption. Paulina's *tableau vivant* is a work of art that changes the world, that heals the broken family of Sicily, and that restores Leontes to his proper place. Antigonus and Mamillius are still dead: the flaws that occur over the passage of time cannot be entirely undone. But Paulina's arts—as lawful as eating—have helped transform a tyrant into a humble king and a grateful husband; her statue, both an image of death and an enactment of rebirth, epitomizes the trajectories of tragicomedy and its political, domestic fantasies.

JOHN FLETCHER'S COLLABORATOR

It is not surprising that critics have read Prospero as a stand-in for Shakespeare. His god-like mastery in *The Tempest* confirms a certain kind of fantasy that many lovers of Shakespeare entertain at one point or another: the fantasy that Shakespeare's art might in some small way bring order to the world, might teach us the lessons we need to learn to live properly within it, and might, in the end, show the tyrants and Machiavels who live among us the errors of their ways. It is, however, a mistake to think of Shakespeare and his later work in these terms. Romanticizing the moral or political power of the romances is very much in the spirit of the plays themselves, but doing so obscures some of the crucial lessons of Shakespeare's own art and of his career more generally. If we want Shakespeare's work to serve as something other than an idealized model of genius unobtainable, we need simply to expand our range of analysis beyond the four romances to include *The Two Noble Kinsmen* and *Henry VIII* (and, peripherally, the lost *Cardenio*). These last plays, simply in the basic facts of their composition, make good on the promise of the romances, showing that drama in and of itself can be a productive enactment of the aesthetic, historical relationships it stages.

In the final scene of *Henry VIII*, a crowd of Londoners clambers for a view of the infant princess Elizabeth, a swaddled baby held up, like Perdita in *The Winter's Tale*, as a promise of future plentitude and political calm. 'In her days', says Thomas Cranmer as he blesses her, 'every man shall eat in safety | Under his own vine what he plants, and sing | The merry songs of peace to all his neighbours' (5.4.33–5). *Henry VIII* has more in common with Shakespeare's earlier history plays than it does with *The Winter's Tale*, but the mixture of pastoral lyricism and political dream-weaving in Cranmer's vision of Elizabeth's future reign chimes with the prophecies issued by Jupiter, Apollo, Iris, Ceres, and Juno in Shakespeare's romances. The King's response suggests that the energies of romance live on in Shakespeare's final effort at staging history: 'Thou speakest wonders', Henry says (5.4.55), then leads the crowds offstage for a shared holiday. Surely, Shakespeare was interested in the promise of new life and familial continuity at the end of his career. Surely, in a play populated by the well-remembered ancestors of living audience members—figures from the not-very-distant past—he sought to use the formal conventions of romance to flatter England's noble families. But for all this, Cranmer's blessing and Henry's admission of wonder—such typically Shakespearean dramatic moments—were almost certainly not written by Shakespeare. They have been assigned to John Fletcher, a dramatist who stands as a crucial reminder that whatever else we might think about Shakespeare's brilliance, his insight, and his artistry at the end of his career, we should keep in mind that he never did anything entirely on his own.[24]

This observation has a certain commonsense ring to it, but readers of Shakespeare's late plays do not always keep it in mind: 'If we use the word Shakespeare in the interpretation of this [final] sequence of plays', writes one critic, 'it should be used as we use the word "God": to signify that principle of unity and coherence within apparent multiplicity and disorder'.[25] This is an exaggerated version of the kind of analysis Shakespeare's final plays inspire but, ultimately, deny to us. 'Shakespeare' will continue to be a convenient 'principle of unity' in all kinds of ways, but the later plays become richer artefacts when they are understood with diverse kinds of collaboration, rather than unity, in mind. As Jeffrey Masten and others have shown us, collaboration defines both the practical production and the semantic effect of early modern drama, especially (though not exclusively) in print.[26] Take, for example, *The Two Noble Kinsmen*, co-written by Fletcher and Shakespeare in late 1612 or 1613. First and foremost, the play is a retelling of *The Knight's Tale* from *The Canterbury Tales*: Chaucer is a third co-author. The title-page of the 1634 edition of the play leaves Chaucer out of the picture, but it is nonetheless an anomaly in the Shakespearean canon, insofar as Shakespeare's name appears along with Fletcher's—the same cannot be said of the first printing of *Henry VIII* in the 1623 Folio, and the many playwrights we know to have shaped Shakespeare's plays are similarly unnamed in other editions. This shared authorial attribution indicates only a fraction of the people involved in the creation of *The Two Noble Kinsmen*. Two other names appear on the title-page: John Waterson, who decided it was a worthwhile investment to publish the play, and Thomas Cotes, who was hired to

[24] For a review of attribution studies and *Henry VIII*, see Gordon McMullan (ed.), *Henry VIII*, The Arden Shakespeare, 3rd series (London: Thomson Learning, 2000), 180–99, 448–9.

[25] G. Wilson Knight, *The Crown of Life: Essays in Interpretation of Shakespeare's Final Plays* (London: Methuen, 1947), 29.

[26] Jeffrey Masten, *Textual Intercourse: Collaboration, Authorship, and Sexualities in Renaissance Drama* (Cambridge: Cambridge University Press, 1997). For different perspectives on collaborative production in early modern drama, see McMullan, *Late Writing*, 225–54; David Scott Kastan, *Shakespeare and the Book* (Cambridge: Cambridge University Press, 2001), 14–49; Lucy Munro, *The Children of the Queen's Revels: A Jacobean Theatre Repertory* (Cambridge: Cambridge University Press, 2005). For current work on the question of authorial collaboration in a Shakespearean context, see Hugh Craig and Arthur F. Kinney (eds.), *Shakespeare, Computers, and the Mystery of Authorship* (Cambridge: Cambridge University Press, 2009).

print it. The labourers who worked for the printer are nowhere listed, but the quirks of printshop practice usually shape language and punctuation as the manuscript copy of a play is set into type. And what of the manuscript used to create the 1634 edition? Scholars believe that it bore signs not only of Shakespeare's and Fletcher's script, but also of practical playhouse annotations made during past performances—perhaps one in 1613 and another in 1625–6.[27] When we consider how many people may have had a hand in editing the script in the twenty years that passed between its likely date of composition and its first printing, we are faced with another range of collaborators: actors, whose alterations to their parts may have made their way into the manuscript; the Master of the Revels, a representative of the Crown who licensed plays for production and who was not shy about making changes to scripts; other playwrights who may have been asked to change elements of the play when it was revived in the 1620s. And we cannot discount the possibility that one of the authors (more likely Fletcher, who was active with the King's Men until his death in 1625) revised the original manuscript over time, making an older and more experienced author a collaborator with his past self.

Again: it would be a mistake to romanticize the motivations of these contributors, writers, printers, and players. The agents of theatrical culture were most certainly in it for the money—a final crowd of collaborators might be located in the theatregoers and book-buyers whose tastes always shaped the output of the King's Men and the publication choices made by stationers. But for all this, the creation of a play, a playtext, or a theatrical performance is necessarily enmeshed in a cultural field that depends on multiplicity to bring into the world the aesthetic experiences that the late plays so often stage in their conclusions. Shakespeare is never solely responsible for these experiences. They come into being in crowds. And as we look over the wondrous conclusions of the late plays we see those crowds depicted. In the romances, nearly every living character gathers together to bear witness to marvels; huge crowds of celebratory spectators form in *Henry VIII* and *The Two Noble Kinsmen* to celebrate (and, in the case of the latter, to mourn as well). Masses and masses of people endorse these final scenes. We might feel ourselves to be a part of them. Shakespeare's late drama places us in a crowd gazing upon a wondrous event. At the same time, these plays direct our attention to the operation of wonder on all those who witness wonders alongside us. By yoking our experience to those of the staged characters, by suggesting that their transformations might be ours as well, these late plays push us to take the political, historical ramifications of fantasy quite seriously, to acknowledge the aesthetic power of tragicomedy, and, most of all, to marvel at the implicit force of theatre's sensuous, material narratives.

---

[27] Lois Potter (ed.), *The Two Noble Kinsmen*, The Arden Shakespeare, 3rd series (London: Thomson Learning, 1997; 2002), 128–9.

PART IV

PERFORMANCES

....

CHAPTER 20

LOCAL RECORDS

....

ALAN SOMERSET

MANY years ago, when I was beginning my career-long series of visits to local record offices in England, record-office staff members commonly distinguished between 'real researchers' (harmless drudges like myself, working on such large projects as local political histories or early public entertainments) and 'just genealogists'. The latter were considered an inferior breed, amateurish dabblers, whose research goal (family history) was adjudged trivial. This condescension toward genealogical research was unwise and has since been discarded, because genealogists have proven to be staunch contributors, supporters, and defenders of record-office budgets and facilities. Seen from the point of view of Shakespeare scholarship it was also unfair, because investigation into records connected to Shakespeare began with genealogy, and was for centuries driven by genealogy.

In the beginning there was no life of Shakespeare, and this state of affairs continued for over ninety years; the issue can be neatly traced by pursuing the question, when was Shakespeare born (and when and how did the knowledge of his birth date come to light)? Shakespeare himself, questioned late in life, was apparently unable to give exact details, because he, like most people, then lacked (and had no need of) the wallet-loads of records, all requiring precise birthdates, that we carry (birth certificates, pension certificates, drivers' licences, and the like). Called to testify in the 1612 Court of Requests case of Stephen Belott vs. Christopher Mountjoy, Shakespeare's age is recorded, in his deposition dated May 7, 1612, as 'of the age of xlviij yeres or thereaboutes'.[1] This formula, 'or thereaboutes', is common in court documents of the time because people knew approximately, but not exactly, how old they were. Thomas Fuller, first to attempt a biography in *The Worthies of England* (1662), apparently was ignorant of Shakespeare's dates, even his date of death (visible on his monument in Holy Trinity Church).[2] In

---

[1] Court of Requests Process Book, National Archives Public Record Office, Req. 1/183, f. 269; quoted in David Thomas, *Shakespeare in the Public Records* (London: HMSO, 1964), 29.

[2] See Samuel Schoenbaum, *Shakespeare's Lives*, 2nd. edn. (New York: Oxford University Press, 1991), 84. Cf. his *William Shakespeare: A Documentary Life* (New York: Oxford University Press, 1975), 23. I am greatly indebted to Schoenbaum's monumental and painstaking scholarship for many details of

Gerard Langbaine's *An Account of the English Dramatic Poets* (1691) the death date has been discovered, but about the birth Langbaine says only that Shakespeare 'was born at Stratford upon Avon in Warwickshire'. Nicholas Rowe, gathering materials for his 'Some Account of the Life . . .' prefacing his 1709 edition of the plays, was the first to have recourse to the local records, but not in person: he employed the aged actor Thomas Betterton to travel to Stratford and examine the parish register. This recourse to what we would now title a 'research assistant' sometimes (as in the present case) has unfortunate results. Betterton made numerous errors and misinterpretations in his transcriptions from the register, but he at least supplied Rowe with a more precise date: 'April 1564'. Full information lay some time in the future. In 1769 the vicar of Holy Trinity, Stephen Nason, transcribed the records of 'the Shakespeare family' (again, not wholly without error); he sent one copy of his notes to David Garrick and another to the local headmaster, Joseph Greene. Greene sent the notes to an antiquarian friend, James West, who in turn placed them in the hands of George Steevens. Through Steevens they finally saw the light of day, being printed in the edition of Shakespeare's plays that he published in 1773 with Samuel Johnson. At this point, 157 years after the playwright's death, the date of his birth (inferred from the baptismal date, April 26, 1564) was suggested as April 23, 1564, a date now fixed by tradition.[3] Only 157 years, and the labours of over a half-dozen antiquaries, were needed to bring this to light.

Nicholas Rowe's meagre 'Some Account of the Life . . .' remained standard for the eighteenth century, although it was based on only eleven biographical facts, two (the baptism and burial) from the parish register, and of the others, eight being mistaken and one doubtful. Remarkable genuine discoveries dot the eighteenth century: Shakespeare's will, discovered in 1747, first saw print in 1763, the Blackfriars Gatehouse mortgage deed bearing Shakespeare's signature was unearthed in 1768, and in 1795 the Blackfriars conveyance, also signed by Shakespeare, turned up. A fascinating progression of discovery received powerful support, in 1790, from Edmond Malone and this carries us through the nineteenth and twentieth centuries. Rather than recount this course of discovery, let us look at its results, recently summarized by Robert Bearman: there now exist seventy-nine documents bearing Shakespeare's name. The Shakespeare Birthplace Trust holds thirty, the National Archives (Public Record Office) holds thirty-five, and the remaining fourteen are scattered in various repositories.[4] Does it seem, then, that we can put away our magnifying glasses, and turn our weary eyes to some other pursuit? Not likely. In an engaging lecture delivered in 1981, 'All That Is Known Concerning Shakespeare', Samuel Schoenbaum teases the reader with hints of

---

Shakespeare's biography, its sources in local records, and the dates and identities of the original researchers.

[3] Robert Bearman, *Shakespeare in the Stratford Records* (Stroud: Sutton, 1994), 12–13. Nason's notes were auctioned at Phillips in London on 19 March 1992; Bearman presents new information about them to correct a few particulars in Schoenbaum.

[4] Bearman, *Stratford Records*, p. viii.

recent discoveries, or discoveries perhaps to come.[5] Before looking at a few aspects of that quest, and some of the notable participants, there remains an important issue about Shakespeare's birth date that continues to occupy modern scholarship.

It is important to keep the provenance of a documentary discovery in mind. The dates at which details about Shakespeare's birth date were made public (April 1564 [in 1708], and April 23 1564 [in 1773]) render suspect any claim that bases itself upon supposed earlier knowledge of either date. The 'Sanders Portrait', itself a documentary record of potentially great importance, has teased the curiosity of art historians and Shakespeare biographers for the last ten years. Its claim to be a portrait of Shakespeare has been much debated, and stoutly defended. Its pigments, and the wooden panel on which it is painted, both establish that the portrait dates from the earlier seventeenth century.[6] The claim that it is a portrait of Shakespeare, however, depends solely upon a small paper label affixed to the back, much perished, that reads:

> Shakspere
> Born April 23—1564
> Died April 23—1616
> Aged 52
> This Likeness taken 1603
> Age at that time 39 *years*

The claim that this is a contemporary or very early label has been hotly contested. The date of the linen rag paper, even if it could be established, means nothing, because of the ease with which one can avail oneself of early paper. But finally one has to question how, in any case, any early writer of the label could have come upon the evidence of that birth date, which was fixed in April 1564 only in 1709, and on April 23 1564 only in 1773.[7]

Forgery, which entered the world of Shakespeare's records almost from the beginning of investigating records, needs some discussion because of its attractiveness as a means of promoting one's view of Shakespeare and enhancing one's own reputation, and on the other hand because of its pernicious effect on the whole world of record searching, interpretation and reception. Forgeries come in several varieties; first are misattributions to Shakespeare of works written by other hands. From the quarto of *Locrine* (1595) and with increasing frequency in the early seventeenth century, we find plays that claim authorship, by 'W. S.' on their title-pages, and several that claim to be by 'William Shakespeare.' As C. F. Tucker Brooke, the editor of *The Shakespeare Apocrpypha* (1908) succinctly put it, 'Each generation has attributed to the poet, in good faith or in fraud, tentatively or with conviction, the authorship of plays with

---

[5] In Ronald Dotterer (ed.), *Shakespeare: Text, Subtext, and Context* (London: Associated University Presses, 1989), 15–30.

[6] Stephanie Nolen, *Shakespeare's Face* (Toronto: Knopf, 2002), 27–65, discusses the evidence.

[7] Alan Somerset, '"Label me a Sceptic", Tentatively—I Think', International Conference, 'Picturing Shakespeare', University of Toronto, November 2002. Subsequently published on Canadian Shakespeares website, University of Guelph: http://www.canadianshakespeares.ca/multimedia/imagegallery/m_i_13.cfm.

which his name had not previously been connected.'[8] (Might we not add poems, as well as plays?)

Forging of artefacts with supposed Shakespeare associations is where our trail of forgery really begins, with the manufacture of bugle purses, mulberry memorabilia, courting chairs, gloves, and other bric-a-brac to astonish gullible early visitors to Stratford-upon-Avon following the 1769 Jubilee, and to separate them from their money. The motive that underlies such relics is familiar from the traffic in supposed religious relics, such as the shroud of Turin or the bed where George Washington slept.

Falsified documents (forgeries proper) may be created out of whole cloth, the claim being that the document itself, the paper or parchment, is genuine along with its contents. On the other hand, there are genuine documents (like Henslowe's *Diary*) that have been adulterated by spurious additions. Finally, there are 'fabrications' based on claims that a document exists or existed containing certain information, but the document cannot now be found. It is the last two classes of forgeries that are most problematic and pernicious, continuing to trouble scholarship even today.

The first remarkable forger of Shakespeare documents, William-Henry Ireland, visited Stratford with his father, Samuel Ireland, in 1793. The course of his brief but spectacular career need not detain us long because he, being amazingly incompetent and foolhardy, quickly came to naught. Samuel was a Shakespeare bardolator and collector possessed with extraordinary enthusiasm, whose appetite was whetted by his Stratford sojourn. There he met one John Jordan, a local wheelwright and purveyor of spurious Shakespeare artefacts, including copies of the poet's (forged) signature: Samuel Ireland yearned to unearth some scrap of writing associated with Shakespeare (a desire that we will meet again). William-Henry, no doubt anxious to please, saw his chance (or perhaps we might better say, his 'sucker'?). His career is not without many moments of amusement, and it has been often recounted, most recently by Patricia Pierce.[9] I wish only to reflect briefly on ways that the story reflects upon Shakespeare and local records. First, his tools of forgery.[10] William-Henry obtained, from a book-binder, a formula to make authentic-looking old ink that darkened after being warmed before a flame—not the genuine article, but good enough in days before chemical analysis. His job gave him access to aged parchment documents that provided a ready supply of blank leaves, and for old paper he excised all the flyleaves and blank leaves from old folios and quartos in a bookshop. Second, he began with an unadventurous, easily deniable forgery, inserting a spurious leaf, a dedication, into an existing old quarto volume. His first imposition was readily accepted by Samuel Ireland; having primed the market, William-Henry went on to 'discover' a series of twenty-three Shakespearean documents for his father. The first, a deed signed by Shakespeare and

---

[8] C. F. Tucker Brooke (ed.), *The Shakespeare Apocrypha* (Oxford: Clarendon Press, 1908), p. vii.

[9] Patricia Pierce, *The Great Shakespeare Fraud: The Strange, True Story of William-Henry Ireland* (Stroud: Sutton, 2004).

[10] Details of his methods are found in William-Henry Ireland's *The Confessions of William-Henry Ireland. Containing the Particulars of His Fabrication of the Shakespeare Manuscripts* (London: 1805).

John Heminge, with seals affixed, was submitted by Samuel to the College of Heralds and pronounced by them to be genuine; 'expertise' could be hoodwinked, because William-Henry was no slouch as a forger.

Samuel Ireland began as a believer and quickly became to a degree complicit with his son's series of forgeries, lured by hopes of profit and fame. He had a reputation as a bookman and expert collector, so his *imprimatur* assisted the deception. Samuel began to allow public access, for a fee, to his rarities from February 1795, but he never allowed open or unrestricted access, nor did he allow access to the most notable Shakespearean scholars of the day, George Steevens and Edmond Malone. Why not? Father and son became co-conspirators, as shown by the twelfth forgery, a pair of notes between the Earl of Leicester and William Shakespeare. One of these was dated 1590, and Samuel Ireland instantly saw the error because he knew the earl had died in 1588 (the forgeries are littered with similar blunders). William-Henry offered to burn the paper, but his father demurred, and they agreed that the date should be ripped off. Profit provides a powerful motive.

Not everyone wanted to believe, and exposure followed open revelation; Samuel Ireland, over his son's objections, published the documents in December 1795, with facsimiles. There Edmond Malone had all the evidence he needed, and by the end of March 1796 he published his devastating *An Inquiry into the Authenticity of Certain Miscellaneous Papers*, whereupon the bubble was burst. One wonders that it continued for over a year.

A second early forger displayed similarly amazing audacity; about John Payne Collier it is difficult to be at all charitable, because his deceptions still affect modern scholarship. He achieved much eminence as an editor, biographer, and historian of the English drama before 1642. As Arthur Freeman states, 'he wrote, or edited, or contributed to some ninety-five separately printed works, many of which are still of great service'.[11] He must be credited with a number of genuine and important manuscript discoveries, such as the *Diary* of John Manningham, discovered in the British Museum. Collier's early reputation was impeccable; he used it to gain access to collections including (1) the great collection of theatrical records at Dulwich College, including Philip Henslowe's theatrical *Diary* and the papers of his son-in-law, the notable actor Edward Alleyn; (2) the registers of the Company of Stationers, wherein much crucial evidence about early printed books is found; (3) the library of Lord Francis Egerton, later Earl of Ellesmere, at Bridgwater House; (4) the State Paper Office (later the Public Record Office and now The National Archives); and (5) the library of the Duke of Devonshire. Given free run in these repositories, Collier perpetrated manifold deceptions to support his own theories about the life and writings of Shakespeare and the

[11] Arthur Freeman, 'A New Victim for the Old Corrector' [rev. of Dewey Ganzel, *Fortune and Men's Eyes: The Career of John Payne Collier*], *Times Literary Supplement* (April 22, 1983), 391. An exchange of letters ensued in the *TLS*: Ganzel's response to this review (May 20, 1983, 516), was answered by Freeman (June 3, 1983, 573). Ganzel responded further (June 24, 1983, 667), and was answered by Freeman (July 8, 1983, 729), who had the last word in the exchange.

history of the theatre before 1642. He interspersed forged insertions into documents in all these collections, and in some collections (chiefly among the Egerton manuscripts) he introduced documents created wholly by himself. Other forgeries have turned up in materials not associated with those repositories, such as eighty-three forged ballads in an early commonplace book.[12] As Charles M. Ingleby wrote of Collier's forgeries in the Alleyn *Memoirs* and Henslowe's *Diary*, 'we know that the great literary slug has crawled over both. What wonder if we shall still be able to trace his slime.'[13]

The list of Collier's forgeries, proven or suspected, continues to grow. A listing compiled in 1930 by E. K. Chambers numbers over forty documentary sources with which Collier is known to have interfered.[14] More have since turned up, or have been suspected, and the search continues. The latest investigation, Arthur and Janet Freeman's recent and magisterial *John Payne Collier: Scholarship and Forgery in the Nineteenth Century*, presents an account of Collier's whole scholarly career, with its undoubted contributions of value, against the context of his vigorous and active career as a forger. The Freemans list fifty-seven physical forgeries and seven unlocated possible forgeries, while at the same time exonerating Collier from eleven mistaken accusations of forgery. There may be more—as the Freemans point out, one cannot make a determination when one is faced with a claim based on a document that is now missing.[15] Once a document is known to have been in Collier's hands, or even in the same room as Collier, it must remain under suspicion. The carelessness with which documents used to be stored away uncatalogued, and made easily available without supervision, to persons like Collier, was an invitation to the unscrupulous. I have devoted much research labour over the last twenty-five years to provincial and national record collections (which are now usually under close and professional supervision). I must say that the ever-present possibility of forgery troubles me whenever I meet an insertion, an erasure, a change of ink, or the like. I ask myself, was John Payne Collier, or one of his ilk, ever here? Luckily for my project, Records of Early English Drama (REED), Collier was not interested in provincial theatre records, although such local records have not been immune to tampering.[16]

[12] Giles Dawson, 'John Payne Collier's Great Forgery', *Studies in Bibliography* 24 (1971), 1–26, shows that Collier copied eighty-three early ballads into the 'Hall Commonplace Book' (now Folger MS V.a.339), and that they are probable forgeries, in the same hand as the corrector of the Perkins Folio.

[13] C. M. Ingleby, ms supplement to A Complete View of the Shakespeare Controversy. Quoted in Schoenbaum, *Shakespeare's Lives*, 264.

[14] E. K. Chambers, *William Shakespeare: A Study of Facts and Problems*, vol. 2 (Oxford: Clarendon Press, 1930), 384–93.

[15] Arthur and Janet Ing Freeman, *John Payne Collier: Scholarship and Forgery in the Nineteenth Century*, 2 vols.(New Haven, CT: Yale University Press, 2004). For the listings of forgeries, suspects, and red herrings see 2: 1031–41.

[16] The 'Wakefield forger' inserted spurious evidence into Wakefield Burgess Court Rolls to suggest that Wakefield, Yorks, was the home of a cycle of religious plays. The imposture held sway for eighty-five years, but was eventually exposed by Barbara D. Palmer, '"Towneley Plays" or "Wakefield Cycle" Revisited', *Comparative Drama* 21.4 (1987–8), 318–49.

Collier's exposure was delayed because of his reputation, and because he could claim to be a victim of fraud, rather than its perpetrator. He finally initiated a deception too large, an attempt to interfere with the texts of Shakespeare's plays. He claimed to have bought a copy of the Second Folio (1632) which upon examination proved to contain more than 20,000 annotations in an early handwriting; this story strains credulity as even his allies and later defenders have admitted.[17] Collier controlled access, exhibited the volume to select groups of antiquaries, but only for brief periods under carefully controlled conditions, and he attempted to keep the volume, the 'Perkins Folio', away from public view by giving it (or selling it) to the Duke of Devonshire, whose library at Devonshire House was closed to access. Why attempt this brazen forgery? Collier published one full-length book, *Notes and Emendations to the Text of Shakespeare, from Early Manuscript Corrections in a Copy of the Folio, 1632, in the Possession of J. Payne Collier* (1853), and he based two lavish editions of Shakespeare partly on these 'discoveries.' Herein may lie one motive, as John Velz has argued; the market in Shakespeare editions was crowded (as it is today), so it was well to have the sort of 'edge' that these emendations gave to an edition, especially since Collier claimed exclusive ownership of them. He pre-empted the market.[18] *Cui bono?*

Truth eventually came to light after 1858 when the Duke died and his successor loaned the Folio to the British Museum; examination quickly resulted in the conviction that the annotations are forgeries, could not be in a hand of the seventeenth century, and could not survive microscopic and chemical scrutiny. The vehemence of the subsequent attack upon Collier by C. M. Ingleby and others was fuelled by anger, because Collier was a respected member of the community of Shakespeare scholars, and his crimes represented a case of *trahison des clercs*. Also consider the damage done by him; as I stated earlier, his forgeries, known or suspected, continue to afflict scholars working in the period, particularly those whose searches lead them to any library or collection in which Collier is known to have worked. And one must constantly wonder, how many less-ambitious forgers have roamed, undetected, through record offices large and small?

A final type of forgery, claims made about a document now lost, brings us to a life record supposedly connected to Shakespeare, the 'Spiritual Testament of John Shakespeare', that continues to perplex, because much is unclear about the story of its discovery and its transmission. It purports to have been discovered in 1757 between the rafters and the tiling of the birthplace by one Thomas Moulton, a bricklayer, who retained possession (which seems strange); he claimed to have shown it to his daughters on its discovery (again strange, since in 1757 the eldest daughter was under a year old and the other two were yet to be born). It was some years later given to one Mr Payton, a Stratford alderman. Payton allowed John Jordan to copy it in 1784 (minus the first leaf, lacking by then) and Jordan attempted unsuccessfully to publish his

---

[17] John Velz, 'The Collier Controversy Redivivus' [rev. of Dewey Ganzel, *Fortune and Men's Eyes: The Career of John Payne Collier*], *Shakespeare Quarterly* 36 (1985), 106.

[18] Velz, 'Collier Controversy', 112.

transcription. We encountered Jordan earlier as a fraudster, and forger of Shakespeare signatures, so his involvement here raises suspicions. Thomas Moulton died in 1788, and thereafter was (conveniently?) unavailable to answer questions, so the provenance of the record became untraceable. Malone heard about the document, and at his request it was sent to him by Payton. Malone printed the document in the introduction to his 1790 edition of the works of Shakespeare. He later came to doubt the validity of the document, because Jordan's transcription, which Malone subsequently examined, by then included the supposed missing first leaf, and Malone was unsatisfied by Jordan's evasive answers about how he came to have this. In 1796, in his volume that exposed the Irelands, Malone retracted his attestation of the document and announced that he had obtained documentary evidence proving the document was a fake. In the event he never published this. As well, the original handwritten copy of the testament has vanished, although Jordan's transcript survives.[19]

The spiritual testament raises many problems, not the least of which is that its disappearance prevents us from looking at handwriting, watermarks, paper, and other possible evidence of its provenance. It could not have been an autograph, because John Shakespeare apparently could not write but signed documents with his mark, a drawing of a glove. In 1923 the document was proven not to be an invention because a Spanish version attributed to Cardinal Carlo Borromeo of Milan, dated 1661, was discovered in the British Library. An English-language version was acquired by the Folger in 1966 bearing the date 1635, and a later one has turned up dated 1638. The only Italian version to have turned up is not attributed to Borromeo, so the formulary need not necessarily be by him or predate his death in 1585. Its attribution perhaps resulted from his canoniz-ation in 1611. The printed versions are formularies—the document leaves blanks for its owner to sign his or her name in two places, and the document, thus personalized, was intended to be carried by the signator and buried with him/her. John Jordan's transcript clearly shows him at his inventive best, because his version of the first leaf bears no relationship to the original as contained in the two versions of the printed formularies.

Theories abound, and in the absence of Malone's documentary evidence we will never be able to discern if this document is a forgery (as Malone came to believe, and many after him have agreed) or if it is genuine. Recently Robert Bearman published his study of the evidence, which led him to the conclusion that Jordan, or a scribe employed by him, had come upon a printed version of the formulary, missing its first leaf, and made it into a Shakespeare document by copying it out in manuscript, inserting John Shakespeare's name (including its insertion in several places where the formulary text does not call for it). Thus the immortal bard was given a Catholic connection, through his father. Jordan then created a false provenance for the docu-ment (with the help of others), and offered it to the world.[20] If Bearman is right, forgery

---

[19] Schoenbaum, *William Shakespeare: A Documentary Life*, 41–6, prints the text and discusses its early history.

[20] Robert Bearman, 'John Shakespeare's "Spiritual Testament": A Reappraisal', *Shakespeare Survey* 56 (2003), 184–202.

here has resulted, as elsewhere, from a desire to create a Shakespeare in tune with the forger's own desires. The whole affair is, it seems, a reminder that the Shakespeare world is not yet free of the possible influence of literary forgery.

Let us return now to the more prosaic and certainly more painstaking world of local records research, and Shakespeare within it, by remembering that we must keep in mind the linked issues of selectivity and inclusiveness. Within the confines of a single lifetime ('dinners, and suppers, and sleeping hours excepted') one's ability to survey and digest the mountains of material available in local record offices is limited, so where does one start and stop? Within the REED project (and its immediate predecessor, the Malone Society collections series), organizing the project by county or borough provides a means of assembling a team of researchers to carry the project through, but even then a project continues to be beset with the difficulties arising from unstable funding, mortality, and the like. *Ars longa, vita brevis.* Establishing parameters of selection is inevitably necessary; one can only wonder at the ambitions of some earlier researchers. But we have to examine their (and our) implicit or announced principles of selection critically, asking if they are sound and appropriate. And finally, given that any records project can never be final or complete, we have to face the objections of those who wonder if records research is ultimately capable of success, and if so in what terms.

To frame this discussion of Shakespeare and local records I wish to pose a large question: to what degree were the Lord Chamberlains' Men/King's Men affected, in their provincial travels, by what Jonas Barish termed the 'anti-Theatrical Prejudice'?[21] That is, how often, and when and where, did they have the experience while travelling of being dismissed or prevented from performing, and how often were they paid to go away without performing? Were there boroughs that they might have avoided visiting because those civic authorities prohibited civically-sponsored performances? A subsidiary but important question is proportionately how frequently did this happen? This subsidiary question, of course, requires us to ascertain how often the Lord Chamberlains' Men/King's Men are recorded as having performed, so we will have to try to gain a rounded picture of the activities of the company over its history. And to ensure that our picture is accurate, proportionate and fair we need to look at the activities of the other companies of travelling players, who number over six hundred (besides those performance or other incidents which are recorded, for various reasons, without a named patron—there are over 1,700 records so far discovered in this category). We need, in other words, to investigate and analyse analogies, to include the widest possible context; thus we result in a huge question which ultimately bears upon Shakespeare at numerous points because it concerns many conditions of his professional life. It is not yet near an answer.

Before 1887 there simply was no way whatsoever to begin to answer any part of this question because the records upon which answers must be based lay unpublished and unexamined in provincial borough offices and muniment rooms. The saga begins with

---

[21] Jonas Barish, *The Anti-Theatrical Prejudice* (Berkeley: University of California Press, 1985).

an encyclopedist, James Orchard Halliwell-Phillipps, who I suggested years ago was 'the first REED researcher'; he deserves to be thus regarded because of his work in the Stratford-upon-Avon archives, and his methodical wider forays into provincial record repositories.[22] Although research into borough records began earlier with Betterton in 1707–8, and Malone who spent time at Stratford searching in the 1790s, with Halliwell-Phillipps it became more ambitious and systematic. He was the first curator and cataloguer (unpaid) of the riches of the Stratford Corporation records. In Stratford, and in all boroughs within a forty-mile radius, Halliwell-Phillipps examined every document that dated from 1585 to '1614, or thereabouts', because he was driven by the hope of finding therein Shakespeare's signature, or at least his name or some other evidence of the bard's activities. The biographical urge that brought Thomas Betterton to Stratford in 1708 is still the motive driving Halliwell-Phillipps, and in his case it was to become a 'tunnel vision' that constricted him, as we shall see.

Halliwell-Phillipps began his wider surveys in the 1860s and continued, on and off, for over twenty years, devoting part of each summer to turning over old provincial borough records, examining the records of, he claims, 'upwards of seventy towns.' Selection came into play here, since Halliwell-Phillipps confined himself to Town minute books and Treasurers' or Chamberlains' accounts. He made notes, transcribing brief extracts from the records onto small slips of paper. At the end of all this searching, in his own words, his project was a failure; he failed to find a Shakespeare signature or even 'some notice of the great dramatist himself . . . a minute investigation failed to unearth a single allusion to him'. He was looking for the wrong reasons, asking the wrong question, in a Shakespeare-limited, biography-driven search. This conviction of failure led Halliwell-Phillipps to leave his findings largely unpublished, pasted over-lapping onto pages, like shingles on a roof, in the unsorted and chaotic manuscript scrapbooks now in the Folger Shakespeare Library. These contain over 1,200 notices of dramatic activity.[23] He did publish his findings related to the Lord Chamberlains' Men/King's Men, in *The Visits of Shakespeare's Company of Actors To the Provincial Cities and Towns of England* (1887), giving the company a quixotic new title and presenting to the world the first published theatre extracts from local records. This little book of 48 pages provides us with a start toward an answer to our question, because in it one finds numerous records for the company, from all over England. Halliwell-Phillipps organized his materials by location, arranged the extracts chronologically, and included some details from the records themselves. You would have to read the whole book carefully, pencil and notebook in hand, to ascertain the numbers of dismissals, but you would be able to do it. You would come up, alas, with nothing definitive, because Halliwell-Phillipps's researches were incomplete and not always accurate. For Stratford, including only references to 'Shakespeare's Company of Actors' meant that he

---

[22] He was originally Halliwell, and changed his name following the death of his father-in-law in 1872.

[23] Alan Somerset, *Halliwell-Phillipps Scrapbooks: An Index* (Toronto: REED, 1979), presents a computer-based index on microfiche. See also my 'James Orchard Halliwell-Phillipps and his Scrapbooks', *REED Newsletter* 2(1979), 8–17.

excluded two records in which the town council prohibited payments to any and all companies, in 1602 and 1611–12;[24] his decision to stop reading in 1614–15 meant that he missed the one explicit reference to the King's Men, in 1622–1623, when they were paid to depart the town without playing.[25] Valuably, Halliwell-Phillipps's little book gave a start by exciting the curiosity of later researchers about the riches that awaited discovery; his scope was very narrowly focused, but his range over 'upwards of seventy towns' continues to amaze.

The issue that looms here, of course, is how wide must a search be? What is 'enough' context? We next pursue our large question by glancing at successive forays into the contents of provincial archives (not always, however, into the archives themselves). We must keep the issue of context before us. John Tucker Murray's *English Dramatic Companies 1558–1642*, 2 vols. (1910), was a study undertaken as a PhD dissertation at Harvard, which its author ruefully admits could have taken several lifetimes to complete. He presents his material in two formats; first, he has arranged the data by company (royal companies, greater men's companies, lesser men's companies, and children's companies), dividing them into London companies and non-London companies, and constructing a brief chronology for each company. Here we encounter a hierarchy that recurs elsewhere—London adult companies are given pride of place, and the chronology of company activities is most important. Also, in his first section by company we detect a decline in interest, evidenced by presentation of the detailed findings in tabular format, without details. The information supplied is scanty, omitting to note the amounts of payments or their purpose, whether payments for performance or to depart without playing. So we cannot answer our question from his pages. In the second volume the data are all presented again, this time chronologically under borough (or, rarely, household), but here other problems appear: inaccuracy and incompleteness. One notes, repeatedly, that records that appear under borough have not been extracted to appear where they should, under company, in volume one. I did a careful check against his pages (2: 389–95) when I was editing the Shrewsbury records for my REED volume, and found that a dismaying 62 per cent of his entries contained inaccuracies. For the King's Men, Murray's first reference (2: 392) is inaccurate: the Shrewsbury reference cannot be from 1602–3 (although that is the accounting year of the record), because the King's Men did not become so until April 17, 1603, so the correct date range is April 17 to September 28, 1603. Again, Murray lists Shrewsbury in both 1609–10 and 1610–11 as being on the company's itinerary, but my Shropshire REED volume does not. The borough's annual 'finished' accounts present inclusive entries for these years that go something like this: 'Item to the kings, queens, princes and other noble mens players 20 s.' However, there also exist for the years in question the actual payment claim-chits, which Murray apparently did not examine; those for 1609–10, for example, specify that the entire sum of 20 shillings was spent on only one

---

[24] Stratford, Shakespeare Birthplace Trust; Council Book, BRU 2.2, 1593–1628, ff. 95, 220.

[25] Stratford, Shakespeare Birthplace Trust; Chamberlains' Accounts, BRU 4.2; 1622–49, f. 1. These records will appear in my forthcoming edition of the Warwickshire/Staffordshire records, for REED.

troupe, the players of the Lord President. So there are 'ghosts' that have to be winkled out of the records before we can have confidence in the data. Murray's transcribed records stop before 1616, although the announced limits of his book, and the Shrewsbury records, go to 1642. Did he run out of steam? Looking at Stratford-upon-Avon (the borough with greatest Shakespeare connections) his records stop at 1596–7, so he does not include the two borough prohibitions against paying players in the guildhall, from 1602 and 1611–12. As well, the one explicit reference to the King's Men from 1622 is again missing; these omissions suggest that he has copied his extracts from Halliwell-Phillipps, rather than consulting the records themselves. One meets Murray's presence when scanning the pages of borough records, where one finds large strokes in soft pencil in the margins opposite relevant records, marking them so that either he (or more likely, a research assistant) could return to transcribe the details.

Continuing this brief survey of previous local records researchers brings us to two monumental reference works of the last century. First, E. K. Chambers's *The Elizabethan Stage* presents us with narrative accounts of the histories of each company with a London connection (he had no interest in any company unless it had such a connection, a narrow scope).[26] His narrative proceeds chronologically, and Chambers concentrates attention solely on geography, looking at where a company toured in a given year, putting that information together with records of court performances and other documentation of the life-history of the company. He does not distinguish performance payments from payments to depart without playing, but simply presents evidence about where the company visited. The precise dates of visits within a given year are often simply impossible to ascertain because the original documents are annual accounts without internal dates; hence the constructed chronologies are sometimes suspect. Chambers reveals that he has not consulted local records at all, but often follows Murray; for Shrewsbury he gives the year of the King's Men's visit to Shrewsbury as 1602–3, and he adds two other references, one of whose dates differs from Murray's. Chambers, of course, limited himself to Shakespeare's lifetime, and the account is carried forward by G. E. Bentley in *The Jacobean and Caroline Stage*. Here the chronological narrative account of the company's activities deals only with London and court records, while the evidence for the company's tours is presented in tabular form only. The payment amounts are omitted. Bentley has cast his net beyond Murray, and suggests that Murray missed much. He also alludes, at the foot of a tabular list of 'Provincial Notices', to the possibility of a second King's company, operating only in the provinces, as opposed to 'the London company'.[27] I suggest that a main reason for presenting the data in such an unappetizing, even indigestible form is that these scholars, particularly Bentley, were not very interested in provincial activities. We will return to this a little later, but first a few words about two recent and authoritative

---

[26] E. K. Chambers, *The Elizabethan Stage*, 4 vols. (Oxford: Clarendon Press, 1923). His exclusion of non-London companies renders useless his findings to reconstruct activities for particular localities. For Norwich, to take one example, Chambers excluded 80 of 100 records.

[27] G. E. Bentley, *The Jacobean and Caroline Stage*, 7 vols. (Oxford: Clarendon Press, 1941–68), 1: 92–3.

investigators of provincial playing, one using a company-centred approach and the other based upon localities.

Professor Andrew Gurr's recent book *The Shakespeare Company 1594–1642* is reminiscent, in its title, of Halliwell-Phillipps's pioneering work. Gurr includes a section on 'Travelling'.[28] He bases his account on records so far published by REED, and presents a narrative in which he sometimes includes amounts of payments, but more often does not. He goes much further into the question of multiple troupes after 1615 bearing identities as the King's Men, a subject alluded to by Bentley as we saw, and he is very careful to note instances where the company was asked to depart without playing, usually with a payment. The locality-based investigations were those undertaken by the Malone Society in its 'Collections' series; these ceased publication when REED began issuing its volumes, and one reason was doubtless the greater inclusiveness of the latter.[29] The volume where we may make a comparison is instructive. Giles Dawson's *Records of Plays and Players in Kent* excluded, as Dawson notes, some classes of performers such as waits and trumpeters, and his 211 pages are dwarfed by James Gibson's REED edition that covers only that part of the county lying in the diocese of Canterbury but totals over 1,800 pages.[30]

I suggested above that many scholars have not been very attracted by provincial activities. Of course, in accounts of London-based royal companies such as the King's Men, provincial activities will take second place; however, beyond this the idea grew that the provinces were uninteresting because nothing ever happened there, and that provincial tours were avoided, by London companies, unless unavoidable. Here is Bentley on the subject:

> there is no evidence that touring was ever very profitable, and it was certainly uncomfortable in the mire and the rain. . . . [it was] an unpleasant and comparatively unprofitable expedient to compensate for London misfortunes . . . permission to play was sometimes granted . . . [but] often they were not allowed to play at all . . . there is little evidence that the local authorities received the travelers with enthusiasm . . .[31]

He depicts what happened, in his view, when a troupe arrived at a borough and sought permission to play; he quotes from two records wherein permission was granted or a payment was made, as opposed to thirteen examples in which players were refused, arrested, placed under control, or otherwise harassed (pp. 177–84). Obviously, a hard and perilous existence (a 13.2 per cent success rate is implied by his examples). Is the picture

---

[28] Andrew Gurr, *The Shakespeare Company 1594–1642* (Cambridge: Cambridge University Press, 2004), 54–69.

[29] D. Galloway and J. Wasson (eds.), *Records of Plays and Players in Norfolk and Suffolk, 1330–1642*, Malone Society Collections XI (Oxford: Oxford University Press, 1981), was the last of these volumes.

[30] Giles E. Dawson (ed.), *Records of Plays and Players in Kent, 1450–1642*, Malone Society Collections VII (Oxford: Oxford University Press, 1965).

[31] G. E. Bentley, *The Profession of Player in Shakespeare's Time, 1590–1642* (Princeton, NJ: Princeton University Press, 1984), 177.

accurate, or does it arise from anti-provincial bias? This issue about a supposed anti-theatrical prejudice, particularly biased against the provinces, led to asking the large question that took us to this survey of provincial records investigators. Looked at together then, and leaving aside the Malone Sociey volumes, what do the results gathered by these five (Halliwell-Phillipps to Gurr) show us? There are a total of 213 visits by the Lord Chamberlains' Men/King's Men that occur in one or another of their accounts, with of course a great degree of duplication which I had to eliminate to arrive at that figure. Of these, sixteen (7.5 per cent) are requests to depart without playing, all but two of which included a payment. Of these sixteen, there are two instances where cities (Worcester and Norwich) twice in one year paid the players to depart. You can't blame a troupe for trying! This is ultimately not the final answer because this collection of 213 records, in these varying sources, is full of inaccuracies and incompleteness, and this is where the REED project enters the picture. To reiterate, the payment to depart from Stratford in 1622 is missing from all listings—'payd to the kinges players for not playinge in the hall vj s.'! Why was this missed? Halliwell-Phillipps was not interested in reading beyond his announced interest in the period 1585–1614, so he never saw the entry; I think I am safe in supposing that none of the others consulted the original documents. Clearly the need for comprehensive data is apparent. Attempting to survey stable data as completely as possible, a number of years ago I went systematically through the entire REED collection then existing (I did not survey the Malone Society Collections volumes because of doubts, mentioned above, about their completeness). I don't recommend this exercise to others, since it took me several weeks to complete. I included all records, whether or not a patron was mentioned in connection with a troupe. The result was startling, and a tribute to comprehensive data—taking the whole period to 1642 into consideration, and looking at all types of travelling entertainers, I discovered that visiting performers successfully obtained a civic permission and/or reward in about 95 per cent of visits. So, there are some stunning misconceptions about the provinces to be overturned!

There is now a quicker and far easier means to survey the company-related data, to gain an answer to my question as it relates to the Lord Chamberlains' Men/King's Men, for any and all other companies with named patrons. The REED Patrons and Performances Web Site grew from the conviction that something had to be done to make the REED materials easily accessible, and beginning in 1985 we began to construct databases to allow analysis of the data. The internet has provided wonderful capacities to manage and divulge data quickly over great distances, and the REED Patrons and Performances Web Site Project takes advantage of all these developments. I'm the co-director, with Professor Sally-Beth MacLean, of this project, which we see as complementing the REED records. The URL is: http://link.library.utoronto.ca/reed. The website aims to deliver the information collected in the published REED volumes about performers who had patrons, their patrons, their performances, and performance spaces across England and Wales (outside London) before 1642, and to augment this information with much new research into performers' itineraries, patrons' biographical details, performance venues, and more. The objects are to make the REED research more widespread, to facilitate research, and to enable new kinds of research. This carries us well beyond Shakespeare and local records; quickly to give an answer from the website about performances versus dismissals so far recorded for all patronized companies, the figures are: there are 1,882 performances, 76 dismissals and 36 regulations about performances. But to return to Shakespeare, from our dataset thus far what can we say about the activities of 'Shakespeare's Company of Actors'? Again, my question: how often, and when and where, did Shakespeare's Company of Actors experience the 'anti-theatrical prejudice' while travelling? And proportionately how frequently did this happen? There are 125 records for the Lord Chamberlains' Men/King's Men in the REED database so far, of which nine are dismissals. In summary, no matter which dataset one selects, the results are far different from those implied by Bentley!

One thread we have been pursuing is the question of selectivity and completeness, governed by our understanding of the purpose and relevance of the materials we are collecting. We have seen how records investigators have imposed various parameters upon themselves—limiting to Shakespeare's Company of Actors (Halliwell-Phillipps), limiting to London-connected companies (Chambers, Bentley, and to an extent the Malone Society and Murray), or limiting to patronized companies (the REED Patrons and Performances Web Site). Each selection proceeds from an (implied) purpose, and imposes limits on the types of questions that the extracted records will enable one to ask. At this point in the development of local records research into professional acting companies, it seems to me that two purposes underlie the collecting and analysis of present and further evidence. First is a sort of 'rescue mission', undoing past biases against the provinces as backwaters. Second (and this underlies the question I framed earlier to guide our survey), is the desire to create as comprehensive a picture as possible of pre-Restoration professional drama as a performed art, in its economic, social, and religious settings in provincial localities. We are no longer led by Halliwell-Phillipps's dream of a Shakespeare signature, a Shakespeare reference, a large breakthrough discovery. We resign ourselves to unearthing tiny fragments of data—a payment record here, a court appearance there—because such pieces of information, aggregated together, help to piece together the large picture of the world in which Shakespeare pursued his professional life.

But can these fragments ever deliver the picture? Only the REED editions themselves hold out the promise of comprehensiveness, because they promise to present, locale by locale, volume by volume, all evidence of provincial dramatic, entertainment and ceremonial activity before 1642. But is 'completeness' itself a dream, impossible of attainment?[32] Briefly to survey the current situation, 200 years after the publication of the first Shakespeare record, there exist 79 documents bearing Shakespeare's name (and containing 6 examples of his signature), and there are 213 provincial

[32] Theresa Coletti, 'Reading REED: History and the Records of Early English Drama', in Lee Patterson (ed.), *Literary Practice and Social Change in Britain, 1380–1530* (Berkeley: University of California Press, 1990), 248–84.

records of the Lord Chamberlains' Men/King's Men. Beyond these direct records there are 1,860 records of other companies in the provinces, or upwards of 3,500 if one includes records wherein a patron is not named. Looking mainly at London-related evidence (but with some attention to the provinces) a recent collection, *English Professional Theatre, 1530–1660*, comprises 517 records, or groups of records, from the period.[33] Taken together, are these 'comprehensive'? No, because there remain many important questions to be asked.

Earlier I mentioned two records in which the Stratford council prohibited payments to any companies, in 1602 and 1611–12; and in 1622–3 the council paid the King's Men to depart without playing. The first two of these, bearing no patron's name, will not appear in the REED Patrons and Performances Web Site, but all three will appear in the volume. There remain questions. Why make the prohibition order twice? And the third record, the only payment to depart made at Stratford, demands explanation because of its singularity. Did other companies simply not visit Stratford? Or were they simply shown the door, rewardless? Or was the council, in 1622–3, under particularly Puritan leadership? Or did companies perform, on other occasions, at other unrecorded venues in the town?

Over the puzzling question of other possible performance spaces, beyond town halls or private houses, looms the larger question: how did companies make a living in the provinces? An active and prominent company, touring widely, might in a year accrue a total of six to a dozen records of performance payments; out of the total rewards therein recorded, there is no way that a company could have avoided starvation. So there must be a big piece of the picture missing, a lot of records that we know nothing about! Dawson pointed to one example, from March 1596, where a court document indicates that the Queen's Men were in Canterbury, but the borough accounts that survive for the year make no mention of a payment to the company. As Dawson notes, there are twenty-one years before 1601 for which Canterbury accounts survive, but without payments to any troupe.[34] I am attracted by Andrew Gurr's suggestion that, particularly when town civic spaces began to become less assured, the travelling companies resorted to using inns.[35] Was this the case at Canterbury? Did they always, or often, use inns? This scenario is rejected by other scholars, who point out the lack of evidence to back it up. There is, of course, well-documented London evidence of inn-yard theatres. Whether or not they provided the inspiration for the design of the earliest purpose-built outdoor theatres has again been hotly contested, but that debate lies outside this discussion. In a review of that controversy a number of years ago, Donald F. Rowan pointed hopefully to the possibility of provincial evidence and proclaimed: 'I am confident that the thorough search of the provincial records being

[33] Glynne Wickham, William Ingram, and Herbert Berry (eds.), *English Professional Theatre, 1530–1660* (Cambridge: Cambridge University Press, 2000).

[34] Dawson, *Plays and Players in Kent*, xxvi.

[35] Gurr, *The Shakespeare Company*, 64.

mounted by REED will turn up more records of performance in the inn-yards.'[36] Alas, experience of three decades of record searching, including my own, has proved otherwise. No records have turned up, because there are no record sources in which to look—the business accounts of inns, alehouses, and other places of public resort have simply vanished. No records, no history—we cannot complete the picture of provincial performance conditions, or assume that our picture is complete. We remain baffled by incomplete evidence.

This need to supply context, to interpret the records, is demonstrated by returning finally to the first local document to excite Shakespearean interest: the parish register. The baptism of Susanna Shakespeare, only six months after the wedding of her parents, has aroused much comment, but it was only in 1994 that some insight was furnished by local context—Robert Bearman pointed out that in the register for 1582 five other offspring were produced before nine months of marriage, nine children were born 'after a more respectable interval', and for another six there is no evidence either way (presumably because these parents' marriages occurred elsewhere).[37] Another unanswered question from the register: why were there no further children after the birth of the twins, Hamnet and Judith, in 1585? This was unusual, and invites speculation about marital estrangement. Perhaps a medical condition arising from carrying twins to term is to blame, but Bearman's research suggests that this is unlikely. Between 1560 and 1600 eighteen sets of twins in Stratford's parish register survived the first three months of infancy, and in ten of these cases further children followed.[38] Contextual evidence may assist with interpretation, but as in both of these register entries, it may be impossible to reach final conclusions. Estrangement may also be suggested by the intriguing, interlineated bequest on the last page of Shakespeare's will: 'Item I gyve vnto my wife my second best bed with the furniture'. Exactly how we follow that, by looking at contextual evidence, to a conclusion is a subject far too wide for this chapter; suffice it to say that many questions must remain without answers.[39]—for 'real researchers', and even for 'just genealogists'.

---

[36] Donald F. Rowan, '"Inns, Inn-Yards, and Other Playing Places"', *The Elizabethan Theatre IX*, G. R. Hibbard (ed.) (Port Credit: P. D. Meany, 1981), 19.

[37] Bearman, *Shakespeare in the Stratford Records*, 6.

[38] Bearman, *Shakespeare in the Stratford Records*, 8.

[39] E. A. J. Honigmann and S. Brock, *Playhouse Wills, 1558–1642: An Edition of Wills by Shakespeare and his Contemporaries in the London Theatre* (Manchester: Manchester University Press, 1993).

CHAPTER 21

....

PATRONAGE

....

ANDREW GURR

OFFICIAL REGULATION OF PLAYING COMPANIES

....

AT the beginning of the final Act of *A Mad World, my Masters*, a feast is prepared. The host, Sir Bounteous, is offered a play by a group claiming to be travelling players. He asks their leader 'Whose men are you, I pray?' (5.1.43). This was the standard question for any group of travelling players. Whose servants they were determined their status and their legitimacy. The notorious highwayman Gamaliel Ratsey, according to a fiction told soon after his execution in 1606,[1] when staying at a country inn asked a company of travelling players 'whose men they were, and they answered they served such an honorable Personage'. Subsequently he met them again at another tavern, in disguise as a different person, and found they were now acting 'not in the name of the former Noblemans servants. For like Camelions they had changed that colour; but in the name of another, (whose indeede they were) although afterwardes when he heard of their abuse, hee discharged them, and tooke away his warrant. For being farre off, (for their more countenance) they would pretend to be protected by such an honorable man, denying their Lord and Master; and comming within ten or twenty miles of him againe, they would shrowd themselves under their owne Lords favour.' Throughout the later Tudor and early Stuart period all playing companies were known by their patron's name. At least ostensibly they were his 'servants'. Having a noble patron or master gave them legitimacy in English law.

Up to the middle of the sixteenth century in England, local authorities, lords and mayors, controlled their localities through the country and ran their laws. From then on, however, as the Henrician Reformation strengthened its grip on government, central authority in London began to assume more and more power, gradually imposing direct control over the whole country. The history of how companies of

---

[1] *Ratsey's Ghost* (1603), sig. A3v.

players grew with the aid of their patrons is an exemplar of how English government changed between the 1530s and 1642.

In the 1530s, Henry VIII's Reformation acts took the supervision of plays and performances out of the hands of the Catholic Church and gave it to the state, represented by peers of the realm and local mayors or magistrates. Various laws, embodied in the series of 'Actes concernyng punysshement of Beggers & Vacaboundes' first instituted in 1531 and extended and elaborated throughout the Tudor period, started under Elizabeth in 1559 to pick out the travellers who toured with plays or music or other forms of public entertainment. Attempts to restrict the groups offering plays or music who were in the habit of taking their skills round the country were made in London before 1550, but in the wake of Elizabeth's new institution of the Book of Common Prayer, and its expectation of religious conformity, a royal Proclamation (509, 16 May 1559) introduced state censorship for plays. It declared that

> the tyme wherein common Interludes in the Englishe tongue are wont usually to be played, is now past untyll All Halloutyde, and that also some that have ben of late used, are not convenient in any good ordred Christian Common weale to be suffred. The Quenes Majestie doth straightly forbyd all maner Interludes to be playde eyther openly or privately, except the same be notified before hande, and licensed within any Citie or towne corporate, by the Maior or other chiefe officers of the same, and within any shyre, by suche as shalbe Lieuetenauntes for the Quenes Majestie in the same shyre, or by two of the Justices of peax inhabyting within that part of the shire where any shalbe played.[2]

A revised statute of 1572, elaborated in 1576, removed from the rights of any gentleman below the rank of baron the right to patronize a company of players, although the Privy Council retained the capacity to override the law if it chose. Its chief concern was to restrict the travelling companies, and to put control in the hands of central government. The appointment of a new Master of the Revels with overall command of playing in 1578 affirmed the need for such an official and functional role.

This wish for centralized control had already been asserted on May 10 1574, when the first royal patent was issued to a playing company, the Earl of Leicester's players. Besides overriding the Statute about vagabonds, it gave the company leave

> to use, exercise, and occupie the arte and facultye of playenge Commedies, Tragedies, Enterludes, stage playes and other such like as they have alredie used and studied, or hereafter shall use and studie, aswell for the recreacion of oure loving subjectes, as for oure solace and pleasure when we shall thincke good to see them, as also to use and occupie all such Instrumentes as they have alreadie practised, or hereafter shall practise, for and during our pleasure. And the said Commedies, Tragedies, Enterludes, and stage playes, to gether with their musicke, to shewe, publishe, exercise, and occupie to their best commoditie during all the terme aforesaide, aswell within oure Citie of London and liberties of the same, as also within the liberties and fredomes of anye oure Cities, townes, Bouroughes &c whatsoever as without the same, thoroughte oure Realme of England. Willynge

---

[2] E. K. Chambers, The Elizabethan Stage, 4 vols. (Oxford: Clarendon Press, 1923), 4: 263.

and commaundinge yow and everie of yowe, as ye tender our pleasure, to permytte and suffer them herein withoute anye yowre lettes, hynderaunce, or molestacion duringe the terme aforesaid, anye acte, statute, proclamacion, or commaundement heretofore made, or hereafter to be made, to the contrarie notwithstandinge. Provyded that the said Commedies, Tragedies, enterludes, and stage playes be by the master of oure Revells for the tyme beynge before sene & allowed, and that the same be not published or shewen in the tyme of common prayer, or in the tyme of great and common plague in oure said Citye of London.[3]

The Revels Office, first established under Henry VIII in 1545, now took on a new onus. The first Master of the Revels to be given the right to control all playing, Sir Edmund Tilney, held his post from 1578 until his death in 1610. As the Leicester's Men's patent indicated, his commission, issued in December 1581, required him to

warne commaund and appointe in all places within this our Realme of England, aswell within francheses liberties as without, all and every plaier or plaiers, with their playmakers, either belonginge to any noble man or otherwise, bearinge the name or names of using the facultie of playmakers or plaiers of Comedies, Trage- dies, Enterludes or what other showes soever, from tyme to tyme and at all tymes to appeare before him with all suche plaies, Tragedies, Comedies, or showes as they shall have in readinesse or meane to sett forth, and them to presente and recite before our said Servant or his sufficient deputie, whom wee ordayne appointe and aucthorise by these presentes of all such showes, plaies, plaiers, and playmakers, together with their playing places, to order and reforme, auctorise and put downe, as shalbe thought meete or unmeete unto himselfe or his said deputie in that behalfe. And also likewise we have by these presentes aucthorised and com- maunded the said Edmunde Tylney that in case if any of them, whatsoever they bee, will obstinatelie refuse, upon warninge unto them given by the said Edmunde or his sufficient deputie, to accomplishe and obey our commaundement in this behalfe, then it shalbe lawful to the said Edmunde or his sufficient deputie to attache the partie or parties so offendinge, and him or them to commytt to warde, to remaine without bayle or mayneprise untill such tyme as the same Edmunde Tylney or his sufficient deputie shall thinke the tyme of his or theire ymprisonment to be punishement sufficient for his or their said offences in that behalfe, and that done to inlarge him or them so being imprisoned at their plaine libertie, without any losse, penaltie, forfeiture or other daunger in this behalfe to be susteyned or borne by the said Edmunde Tylney or his deputie, Any Acte Statute Ordynance or provision heretofore had or made to the contrarie hereof in any wise notwithstandinge.[4]

Tilney's job was specific, and overrode the various provisions against playing groups in the statute against travelling beggars and vagabonds. Under Tilney's guidance the regime soon imposed its control. Local authorities such as those in Leicester in 1583

---

[3] Quoted in Gurr, *The Shakespearean Stage 1574–1642*, 4th edn. (Cambridge: Cambridge University Press, 2008), 42.

[4] Chambers, *The Elizabethan Stage*, 4: 286–7.

recorded his insistence that only plays with his signature on them and his word that he had 'allowed' them for playing could be staged in their town, although Bristol tried to stick with the older order, declaring in 1585 that it was the mayor who had the power to censor any plays before they could be performed in the town.[5] Tilney not only read and censored playbooks; he licensed all the companies that had noble patrons, tried to regulate where any company could play, especially in London, and exercised his duty to license every form of public performance. He took a fee for all such activities, as well as spending up to five months each year organizing the winter revels at court, choosing which plays and which companies should present their plays before the queen and her courtiers each year.

Tilney did far more than impose central authority on the local councils. Much of his real power was imposed on playing in London, where the city fathers were developing a strong animosity against playing at the inns inside the city. For all his title, which made him officially just the Master of the royal Revels, for the court's programme of entertainment through the Christmas holiday season, he did everything he could to keep the companies coming to and playing before the public of London.

For this he had a sound practical reason. Mounting anything in the older tradition of masques (usually known as masks in Elizabethan times) was extremely expensive, even when the students of an Inn of Court or some extravagant courtier paid the basic cost of the show. Using professional playing companies for the court's entertainment was much cheaper, and Tilney had a pressing need to keep his costs down. And there were issues of court politics, with the wealthier and more pushy figures exhibiting their riches by getting their own shows mounted, whether as masques or, increasingly, with plays by the companies that flaunted their names. These rivalries were part of the reason why, with support from some major Privy Councillors, in 1583 Tilney established a single dominant group of the best players from each of the pre-eminent companies, the Queen's Men.[6] This group culled the best two or three players from each of the four leading professional companies of the time.

Patrons from the Nobility and the Queen's Intervention

The Queen's Men were a crucial intervention for the professional playing groups. Their establishment was the first open sign of royal support for playing, and it secured the status and to some extent the quality of what the professionals could offer in the subsequent great years of growth in acting and plays. Tilney gave the new group,

[5] See Gurr, *The Shakespearian Playing Companies* (Oxford: Clarendon Press, 1996), 38–9.

[6] The history of this company and the political situation that brought it into being, is told in Scott McMillin and Sally-Beth MacLean, *The Queen's Men and Their Plays* (Cambridge: Cambridge University Press, 1998).

markedly bigger than its peers with twelve sharers, the exclusive right to perform at the best inns in the city of London, the Bull and the Bell. The Bull had an outdoor venue in its yard, the Bell a large hall upstairs. One was for use in the summer, the other in winter. This innovation was part of a lengthy governmental process, widespread in all business activities of the time, awarding monopolies to specific groups in return for the central control that such privileges allowed the government. Companies such as the Stationers' and the Queen's Company as a playing company emerged out of the same central government interest: gaining control through censorship of everything said and published in public. In varying forms, as the quality of individual companies fluctuated, this system lasted through Elizabeth's reign and beyond.

The idea of a professional company with royal support was used again eleven years later. In 1594, two Privy Councillors imitated the inauguration of the Queen's Company as an attempt to monopolize professional playing in a double form. Tilney's own master, the Lord Chamberlain, and his son-in-law tried to solve the constant problem visited on the Council by Guildhall's flow of complaints over players performing in London by setting up two new playing companies and giving their own names to them as patrons. That was how the Lord Chamberlain's Men and the Lord Admiral's Men came into being. Together their monopoly of playing made them the most successful and durable pair of acting companies London has ever enjoyed. Henry Carey, Tilney's direct master, had kept James Burbage as his servant ever since the Queen's Men were set up, and his son-in-law Charles Howard, the Lord Admiral, had kept England's most celebrated player, Edward Alleyn, wearing his livery for a similar period. The two Privy Councillors used their servants to lead one company at Burbage's eighteen-year-old Theatre in the suburbs of Middlesex, where the Lord Mayor had no authority, and the other at the Rose on Bankside in Surrey, which was similarly free from mayoral control. Thenceforth all other companies were banned from playing in London, and no playing was permitted at any of the inns inside the city, the chief cause of the Lord Mayor's recurrent complaints.

One major problem with the Elizabethan form of control by noble patrons was that when the patron died the company did too. Leicester's Men flourished until their lord died in 1586, when they had to dissolve and re-form themselves under another patron. Towards the end of the great plague epidemic of 1593–4 disruption resulting from the deaths of several major patrons struck a number of the companies trying to establish themselves in London. The Earl of Sussex died on December 14, 1593, and Lord Strange, by then the Earl of Derby, on April 14, 1594. His older brother, running his own company, had died on September 23 of the previous year. With so many patrons dying within a few months of each other, the losses caused chaos among the acting groups. Derby's widow tried to keep her dead husband's group going for a while, but in reality it was the two Privy Councillors, Lord Hunsdon and the Lord Admiral, who retrieved the situation for the players. They gathered up senior players from all the groups whose patrons had died recently and put them into two new companies, making themselves their patrons.

The chief effect of this 'duopoly' was, most conspicuously, the exclusive right they gained for the next six years to perform in the court's Christmas festivities. Between Christmas 1594 and 1600 the Lord Chamberlain's Men played at court twenty-four times and the Admiral's fourteen. No other company had even a single performance. The one exceptional season was 1596–7, when the Chamberlain's took all six performances, conceivably because they had just lost Henry Carey, their first patron, and even more onerously, had also lost the Blackfriars indoor playhouse, built for them in 1596.

This duopoly system broke up in 1600, when a new company belonging to a pushy new patron set itself up in the east of the city, and two boy companies that had been closed down in 1590 were revived with new membership. Three years later the controls exercised by the Elizabethan patronage system were replaced entirely. Within a month of his arrival in London King James made himself patron of the Lord Chamberlain's Men, and soon after gave the Admiral's Men to his elder son, and the third company, Worcester's Men, to his wife as patron. Thereafter the only companies licensed to perform in London had royal patrons. James's other two children, Elizabeth and Charles, acquired their own companies in 1608 and 1610. From then on the Revels Office, after some fiddling with the surviving boy companies, tried to sustain no more than four companies in all playing in London. That royal takeover of patronage, sustained in different forms when the at first childless Charles inherited the throne in 1625, made the royal protection of professional companies set up under Elizabeth a fatal alliance for all the playing companies. The identification of the court with the love of plays was what led to the closure of all playing for eighteen years when Parliament took control of London from the king in 1642.

It was of course not just the great who were seen as patrons of the theatre, and it was not the celebrities who gave their names to the great companies whose patronage secured their livings. When playing his mountebank act on stage Volpone addresses his audience as 'my worthy patrons', and many prefaces to books, including playbooks, wrote of their readers as their patrons. Audiences at plays, paying the actors to entertain them, were more immediate if less affluent as patrons than any of the great who gave their names to their acting companies. What little evidence there is about the relations of the lords who gave their names to their 'servants' as acting companies indicates that normally they paid them nothing, and only rarely summoned them to provide entertainment for their own households.[7] In a letter to the Earl of Leicester on behalf of the company that he gave his name to, in 1572, James Burbage asked for the renewal of his patronage in the wake of the revised statute limiting retainers. The letter affirmed

> not that we meane to crave any further stipend or benefite at your Lordshippes hands but our lyveries as we have had, and also your honors License to certifye that

---

[7] Sally-Beth MacLean in her analysis of records about the Earl of Leicester's company, which included James Burbage, suggests that he never once made direct use of them.

we are your household Servaunts when we shall have occasion to travayle amongst our frendes.[8]

It was Leicester who secured the first 'patent' for his acting company two years later.

Travelling Country Groups
and Musicians

Most of the small groups that toured with their plays or other forms of entertainment in the centuries leading up to the Tudor period gradually disappear from the records as central government restricted the rights of patronage to higher and higher levels of the nobility. Nonetheless, it was a widespread custom for major figures throughout the country to run groups of different kinds of entertainer. Tudor patrons recorded in the archives of Bristol, a major seaport, included in their names, besides the royal musicians and trumpeters and various bearwards and jugglers, playing companies wearing the liveries of the earls of Bath, Derby, Essex, Hertford, Huntingdon, Leicester, Nottingham (the Lord Admiral), Oxford, Pembroke, Shrewsbury, Sussex, Warwick, and Worcester, along with the Lords Abergavenny, Berkeley, Chandos, Clinton, Cobham, Compton, Cromwell, Darcy, Hunsdon (the Lord Chamberlain), Morley, Mountjoy, Rich, Sheffield, Stafford, and Strange, plus a few lesser nobles, and players from two cities, Coventry in 1570–1, and the singing waits of Hereford in 1579–80.

Patrons with playing groups noted throughout the county of Devon, again along with the travellers who wore royal livery, included the earls of Essex, Leicester, Norfolk, Nottingham, Oxford, Sussex, Warwick, and Worcester, and the lords Bath, Berkeley, Chandos, Clifford, Dudley, Hunsdon, Latimer, Montagu, Mountjoy, Sandys, Sheffield, Stafford, Stourton, and Strange. Sir Francis Drake, when he was mayor of Plymouth in 1594, had a company of musicians, and Richard Hawkins was patron to groups of trumpeters and waits who visited Plymouth in the 1590s. In the northern port of Newcastle, playing companies with earls as their patrons included Bedford's, Derby's, Hertford's, Huntingdon's, Leicester's, Lincoln's, Nottingham's, Pembroke's, Sussex's, and Worcester's. Companies of the Lords Bartholomew, Darcy, Dudley, Hunsdon, Monteagle, Morley, Ogle, Stafford, and Willoughby were also recorded, plus groups from Hull and from Durham. Across the county of Shropshire, besides the royal companies, playing groups who visited were patronized by the earls of Essex, Leicester, Nottingham, Oxford, and Worcester, and the lords Abergavenny, Beauchamp, Berkeley, Burghley, Chandos, Darcy, Hunsdon, Morley, Stafford, Strange, and Willoughby. Other individuals, of less high standing, tended to patronize small companies of musicians rather than performers of plays.

---

[8] Chambers, *The Elizabethan Stage*, 2: 586.

One major difference between the small groups of musicians and the companies of players seems to be that while their patrons regularly used music to entertain themselves and their friends, and paid for it, the players were expected to find their own sources of income. Some groups remained fairly local to their lord, and gave him whatever entertainment he required of them, but other groups ranged more widely in search of employment. We know that, for instance, Lord Berkeley was a generous benefactor of his musicians, giving them an annual gift of money plus other gratuities, but between 1600 and 1605 he only paid his players twice.[9] We cannot be sure whether this practice was a cause, or an effect, of the likelihood that players could find employment around the country with more ease than musicians. Some touring groups do seem to have combined playing with the offer of music by individuals or small groups accompanying them.

The forms of patronage given to these groups of different size and capacities must have been much more varied than the extant records show. Suzanne Westfall has an incisive chapter on the broad and deep spread of the complex functions of patronage in a collection of essays about theatre patronage in early modern English society. She pointedly quotes Guy Fitch Lytle, who wrote that 'patronage in the sixteenth century was an inherited muster of laws, properties, obligations, social ligatures, ambitions, religious activities, and personal decisions that kept a complex society working'.[10] The intricate forms of social relations in English society through this time make the patronage of playing companies an intricate and diverse subject for study, and one that stands out on its own in strange and distinctive ways. What gradually brought this complex social system down was firstly the centralization of control, and secondly, the takeover by King James of patronage for all the London-based companies by himself and his immediate family.

THE MASTER OF THE REVELS AS CONTROLLER AND CENSOR

The playing companies suffered far more than any of the other types of entertainer from intervention by central government over what could be performed. The Master of the Revels took no interest in the activities of the many musical groups that toured the country, even the royal trumpeters. Musicians might use their patron's name to advertise their own status as much as the name of the man they worked for, but the tunes they entertained their audiences with were not considered dangerous in the way

---

[9] Peter Greenfield, 'Touring', in Richard Dutton (ed.), *The Oxford Handbook of Early Modern Theatre* (New York: Oxford University Press, 2009), 293.

[10] Ch. 1, p. 20, in Paul Whitfield White and Suzanne R. Westfall (eds.), *Shakespeare and Theatrical Patronage in Early Modern England* (Cambridge: Cambridge University Press, 2002), esp. 20–42.

that words so easily could be. Moreover the playing companies grew substantially in size up to 1593, and the writers changed what they provided accordingly. Furthermore, as new playhouses grew up around London, the demand for new plays grew mightily. Since the same audiences were flocking to the same places to see what was on offer, the playing companies had to find a constant flow of new plays for them. One effect of this was that gradually the significance of patrons shrank as the power of money in Londoners' pockets began to affect the priorities of the players. Patrons remained vital as protective devices, but not as major financiers for the players.

In *A Midsummer Night's Dream* Theseus asks Philostrate, who as his chamberlain is his usual provider of court entertainment, to tell him what plays or masques are on offer to fill the time up to his wedding with Hippolyta. His own previously cited scorn for 'the lunatic, the lover and the poet' as authors of love-stories he sets aside so that some local 'mechanics' might present one from a variety of stories based on Ovid, the classical underwriter of the whole play. Such activities were in the tradition of major wedding celebrations and other festive occasions, such as Sir Bounteous's feast in *A Mad World my Masters*. Sir Bounteous takes in a group who he assumes have passed by his house casually, on the off-chance of earning money for an evening's entertainment. Others would come by invitation, as the London companies often did. The Shakespeare company played for the lawyers at Gray's Inn at Christmas 1594 and at the Middle Temple for Candlemas in February 1602, and between December 28, 1595 and January 6, 1596, when they played at court, they seem to have taken *Titus Andronicus* north to perform it at Exton Hall in Rutland. The Admiral's Men also played for the Middle Temple in 1613. Such invitations resulted from their repute as players with good plays, although it is possible that the first such invitation to the Chamberlain's Men, at Christmas 1594, was because the new company had as its patron a lord who was himself a member of Gray's Inn, and attended the Prince of Purpoole's celebrations. Such an invitation would have been a tacit compliment to the lord who graced their feast.

Many attempts have been made to identify Shakespeare's plays as being originally composed as entertainment for special occasions such as weddings. Through much of the nineteenth century attempts were made to fiddle the date of *The Tempest* in order to prove that its Act 4 masque was written to adorn the marriage of James's daughter Elizabeth to the Elector Palatine in February 1613. For *A Midsummer Night's Dream* alone as many as fourteen different weddings have been claimed as the most likely stimuli for its composition. The date of *The Merry Wives of Windsor* is still subject to contention in a flurry of attempts to make it fit the award of the Garter to the company's patron, George Carey, at Windsor in 1597. The idea that any play might have been written entirely for any such one-off event shows a misunderstanding of the radical change that had taken place over the previous two decades, when the power of noble patrons was supplanted by the power of audience purses in London. That power was still manifest at court, which sponsored masques and shows like those designed for the Queen in 1578 at Kenilworth or at Elvetham in 1591. But the London players now made the daily performances in their purpose-built playhouses their top priority. Their chief patrons were now the city's audiences.

LONDON AND THE DEVELOPMENT OF THE
PROFESSIONAL PLAYING COMPANIES

The conflicts over playing in London that we are all familiar with were repeated in varying forms and degrees of intensity throughout the country. The recurrent antipathy toward playing shown by successive Lord Mayors of London was well reproduced in varying degrees of intensity by mayors of the major cities such as Bristol, Norwich, Coventry, and equally in smaller and more localized authorities, as the REED records show. But from the inauguration of the Queen's Men in 1583 the old civic tradition of controlling plays and playing even in London increasingly came into opposition with central authority. As playing companies took on royal protection their size grew, and the Privy Council's determination to restrict the number of companies licensed by the Revels Office only to those players who were nominally the servants of a great lord meant that all creative novelty was in the hands of the major companies protected by the Revels. All new plays had to be licensed for public performance by the Master. And the 1580s was the decade when great new plays began to appear. Kyd's *Spanish Tragedy*, Marlowe's *Tamburlaine* and *Dr Faustus*, and a host of imitations toured the country as they came to fame in London.

Another factor that contributed to the reduction in the number of patronized companies must have been the growth through that spectacular decade of the number of players used by the best companies. This was obviously stimulated in the first place by the formation of the Queen's Men in 1583 as a group of twelve sharers, instead of the eight that normally toured with plays in the earlier years under Elizabeth. While in their early years they ran as a single major company they took on their tours plays with a bigger cast list than ever before. In the years up to 1594 a distinctive number of plays were written for what have been called the 'large' companies, where between twenty and thirty players could appear on stage at the same time.

By 1590, at least four companies staged plays that called for an exceptionally grand number of players: Lord Strange's, the early Admiral's, and Pembroke's Men, besides the Queen's. The fourteen or so plays which demand such numbers include *Friar Bacon and Friar Bungay*, *1 Henry VI*, *2 Henry VI*, *3 Henry VI*, *Edward I*, *Edward II*, *The Massacre at Paris*, *Edward III*, *Titus Andronicus*, *2 Seven Deadly Sins*, and *Sir Thomas More*. This radical growth in resources and ambitions for staging came to an end before 1594, after which the two licensed companies each ran a repertory making fewer demands for players. From then on the norm ran at about fifteen players for each play, plus perhaps under special needs a few mute walk-ons (the Admiral's 'plots' in places specify gatherers to bulk up the numbers for processions).

With this increase in size of plays through the 1580s went, what we must assume was, a drastic increase in quality. Only from the mid-1580s and after did plays acquire the fame that got them into public notice and print. Kyd, Marlowe, and Shakespeare supplied their companies with plays that enabled them to build themselves a fame and audiences that secured their status for the next seven decades. At the same time they created an appetite that they fed on, and that fed on their products. Where through the previous decades they had toured the country with no more than two or three plays to satisfy the once-a-year tastes of the towns they passed through, in London they had huge audiences demanding novelty every week or so. Philip Henslowe's records for the Admiral's Men from 1594 onward show that Londoners satisfied their taste for novelty with a different play every day throughout the year, in a repertory that ran over thirty plays each year, half of them new. The first twenty or so years of that great period of playwriting produced the classics that kept the London stage going until Parliament's division from the court stopped all playing. Long before that happened, London's audiences had become the real patrons of the players.

THE BOY COMPANIES UNDER KING JAMES

The short history of the boy company that performed at the Blackfriars theatre from 1600 to 1608 is a paradigm for the complex story of Jacobean patronage. The boys' first official name, under Elizabeth, was Children of the Queen's Chapel Royal. When King James came to the English throne they were given the new name Children of the Queen's Revels, with Queen Anne making herself their personal patron, and Samuel Daniel as their controller. When he and they lost that title, they became the Children of the Revels, an odd reversion, since the Revels Office seems for some years to have had no authority over their doings.[11] It also made them the first company not to have a patron's name in their title. They were subsequently known by their playhouses as the Children of the Blackfriars, and later the Children of the Whitefriars.[12] This sequence, over less than a decade, took them from having a royal name on their escutcheon to being known only by the name of their playhouse. That reflects precisely the shift of title for almost every playing company from patron to playhouse between 1600 and 1642. Only the King's Men, unique in owning and performing in two playhouses season by season, retained their royal title throughout that time.

The story of the Blackfriars boy company has a special value in showing why such a change of names and values took place through the Jacobean period. Both the Paul's and Blackfriars companies started by flaunting their status as users of indoor playhouses by declaring that they were playing 'privately', not in the common and 'public' amphitheatres. Ben Jonson issued his first Chamberlain's Men's play, *Every Man in his Humour*, early in 1601 as 'publicly' acted, and issued his *Cynthia's Revels* later in the same year as '*privately acted in the* Black-Friers *by the* Children *of her* Majesties *Chappell*'. He used the same adjective for *Poetaster* in the following year. Paul's followed suit by issuing *Blurt Master Constable* in 1602 '*As it hath bin sundry times*

---

[11] See Richard Dutton, 'The Revels Office and the Boy Companies, 1600–1613: New Perspectives', *English Literary Renaissance* 32 (2002), 324–51.

[12] These are the names listed by Mary Bly, 'The Boy Companies, 1599–1613', in *The Oxford Handbook of Early Modern Theatre*, 138.

privately acted by the Children of Paules'. Dekker published *Satiromastix*, his answer to *Poetaster*, in 1602, '*As it hath bin presented publikely*, by the Right Honorable the Lord Chamberlaine his Servants; and privately, by the Children of Paules'.[13] This distinction began a publishing tradition of asserting outdoor playhouses as 'public' while indoor venues were 'private' that lasted till late in the 1630s. To a large extent it became a point of snobbery to claim that the indoor playhouses hosted shows that were not for the general public. It always ignored the requirement that you must pay for admission to either kind of playing site. But it seems to have begun from the assumption, not necessarily the Master's own view, that the plays and playhouses used by the boy companies did not need licensing by the Revels as the adult companies and their plays did.

Boy companies were always seen as coming under the authority of the Master of the Revels, judging from a Privy Council order to the Lord Mayor of 24 December 1578, when he is told that all the companies designated by the Master to perform at court should be allowed to play 'within the Cittie'.[14] Over the years he does seem to have licensed several of their plays for performance, though not *Eastward Ho!* and several others. Jonson, who was probably the instigator of the 'private' label, did later claim that the Master had 'allowed' both *Cynthia's Revels* and *Poetaster*. The chief anomaly over Tilney's exercise of control over the boy companies is Queen Anne's appointment of Daniel in 1603 with the distinctive, and for the time unique, duty of licensing her boy company's plays for public performance. Daniel got the boys and himself into trouble late in 1604 with his own *Philotas*, which was generally thought to be about the Essex conspiracy, and although the fracas that caused was strong enough to make Anne withdraw her patronage from the company he may have continued long enough in his licensing role to allow such other troublesome plays as *The Isle of Gulls* and *Eastward Ho!* to hit the Blackfriars stage in 1605 and 1606.

It is not clear when Tilney really imposed his censorship on the boy company's plays. The ostensible value of differentiating between 'public' and 'private' shows disappeared once the King's Men took over the Blackfriars playhouse in 1608, although for the next thirty years the difference was frequently reasserted on play title-pages. By the second decade of the seventeenth century the difference between the two kinds of playhouse was a far more potent factor in identifying the quality of a particular playing company or repertory than the title of the patron that the company ran under.

ROYAL PATRONAGE UNDER THE EARLY STUARTS

The King's Company did get help from their patrons in various ways and at various times, particularly during the longest of the many painful blockages placed on public

---

[13] The first (1603) Quarto of *Hamlet* used both terms, when Gilderstone tells Hamlet that 'the principall publike audience that came to them, are turned to private playes, and to the humour of children'.

[14] Chambers, *The Elizabethan Stage*, 4: 278.

performance by reason of the epidemics of plague. In 1630, King Charles gave them £100 to see them through that year's closure. King James had backed them in January 1619, when a complaint by the residents of Blackfriars led to an order by the Common Council of London banning playing there. After the closure for the death of Queen Anne in March they were issued with a new patent affirming their right to play at both their playhouses. By this time the companies were known rather by the name of the playhouse they performed at than by the name of their royal patron. Not for the first time under the Stuarts, as had been done for the Blackfriars boy company, it was the Revels Office that awarded the company its own name in place of any specifically named patron. For years after Anne's death in March 1619 the new Master of the Revels, Henry Herbert, baldly called the former Queen's Men 'the players of the Revels'.

Sometimes, though not as frequently as is usually assumed, when their companies staged performances at court the royal patrons went to watch them performing. That was certainly the expectation laid on the younger Stuarts. In the first Christmas season the nine-year-old Prince Henry was present for seven plays, including all five staged by his own new company, the former Admiral's Men playing at the Fortune. Otherwise, attendance by royal patrons at performances by particular companies was surprisingly random.

For most of James's reign all the companies licensed to play in London operated under royal patronage. Playing was seen from on high as a royal self-indulgence. James's son Prince Charles, however, when he assumed the crown in 1625, had only his new wife as a potential patron, so from then on two companies were awarded the King and Queen as their patrons, while until their first son was old enough the other companies ran without any formal patronage, though they were still tightly controlled by the Master of the Revels. Initially the new King and Queen gave their names to the companies occupying the two superior indoor playhouses, the Blackfriars and the Cockpit. The other companies did at times acquire names from other patrons, including the young Prince Charles, but by then they were mostly known by the playhouse they used for their performances.

The Role of Patrons and
their Companies

In recent years the role of patrons in the early modern theatre has been caught up in debates about the economics of theatre, with all the differences in political and sociological bias that that subject invites. As can be seen from this account, patronage always worked to support playing through political muscle rather than financial backing. Work on the economics of patronage and professional playing drifts very quickly into the sociology and economics of public (and private) theatre audiences.

Douglas Bruster[15] and others have done much good work on the finances of the playing companies and their social function in London. An impressive amount of information about payments by city authorities and by the owners of great houses such as Chatsworth or Lord Berkeley's Caludon and Berkeley Castle is accumulating from the REED studies of provincial playing.[16] Yet in the nature of political power it is no easier to identify the precise economic effect of a patron on an individual company and its financial health than it is to know exactly how any lines of a play would have been spoken on a stage of the time. Imprecision is the name of all such games.

We can see that the role of patrons and their companies varied widely over time, of course, particularly between the period when great Elizabethan nobles used them to display their own stature and the Jacobean period when the royal family became patrons of all the London-based companies. Under Elizabeth, it has been reckoned that 'the patron's role was partly to provide economic opportunities for his favored servants; it was also to act as a powerful courtier, manipulating the players for his own ends'.[17] From 1583 that dual role slowly faded under pressure from the Privy Council, concerned for less than obvious reasons to defend professional playing against Guildhall's hostility, and their more obviously well-motivated policy to institute central control and censorship through the Master of the Revels. Thereafter, playing in London and elsewhere became increasingly firmly a process fostered and protected by royalty, whether as formal patrons or simply through the fact of their patronage, and the regular use of the court through the winter months and on the occasion of special visitations for royal performances. In 1642 this royal protection turned against the playing companies, when Parliament took over control of London.

---

[15] *Drama and the Market in the Age of Shakespeare* (Cambridge: Cambridge University Press, 1992).

[16] An outstanding account of the role of Tudor and Jacobean patrons is by Alan Somerset, 'Not just Sir Oliver Owlet: From Patrons to "Patronage" of Early Modern Theatre', in *The Oxford Handbook of Early Modern Theatre*, 343–61. He notes (349) that the 30 companies running theatre activities in London had only 48 individual patrons, 13 of them royal.

[17] Kathleen McLuskie and Felicity Dunsworth, 'Patronage and the Economics of Theater', in John D. Cox and David Scott Kastan (eds.), *A New History of Early English Drama* (New York: Columbia University Press, 1997), 429. This essay is more concerned with the economics of theatre than with the economics of patronage, which it largely dismisses as a non-existent feature of the time.

CHAPTER 22

....

REPERTORY SYSTEM

....

ROSLYN L. KNUTSON

> The ideal of my work would be reached if I could give for every play, from the opening of the theatres in 1576 to their closure before the civil wars in 1642, the authorship in each instance, the date of original production, the theatre at which it was acted, the company by whom it was played, the relation it bore to other plays and to dramatic history generally.
>
> —Frederick Gard Fleay, *A Biographical Chronicle*
> *of the English Drama, 1559–1642*, 2 vols.
> (London: Reaves and Turner, 1891), 1: 2

In that 'relation it bore to other plays', F. G. Fleay provided the *desideratum* for repertory studies with one adjective missing: scholars in the field would like to know also the *commercial* relation a given play bore to its contemporaries. Historically, in Shakespeare studies, authorship has mattered more than the commercial context in which an author's plays were performed. However, since the 1960s theatre historians have promoted company ownership, venue, and repertorial context as partners with authorship in the assessment of the value of a given play. For Shakespeare's plays, there is still work to do revising the traditional author-centric model in order to view the plays in a repertory of offerings being given by a particular company at a particular venue in a theatrical marketplace shared by some number of competitive player organizations. The purpose of this chapter is to participate in this work by considering Shakespeare's plays as commodities in a thriving commercial environment. Taking a roughly chronological frame, the following discussion will present issues being investigated in repertory studies as they pertain to the early years of Shakespeare as dramatist, the decade of his membership in the Chamberlain's Men, and his continuation with that company as it became the King's Men. Necessarily, much of what follows is guesswork, as there is little data and too few instances in which the evidence fits together to provide some level of certainty. So this is the challenge: to adduce what theatre historians know in broad terms about the perspective of repertorial practice on the commercial life of Shakespeare's plays.

1583 AND THE QUEEN'S MEN

For every aspect of early modern theatre history including repertory studies, the most important event in Shakespeare's early career is the formation of the Queen's Men. Scott McMillin and Sally-Beth MacLean provide the narrative relevant here: Sir Francis Walsingham authorized Edmund Tilney, Master of the Revels, to form the company; Tilney drafted top players from existing troupes; the company dominated the theatrical scene at court; on tour, their receipts were consistently higher than those of other companies; in London, they played at City inns as well as playhouses in the suburbs; they developed a distinctive 'medley' style; and their texts incorporated the political and religious agendas of their patron.[1] No one knows when Shakespeare first took notice of the Queen's Men. A popular belief is that by 1587 he had joined the company as player and play-patcher. But it is not necessary to make Shakespeare a Queen's man to assess his grasp of their repertory and its competition within and across company lines.

The first question to ask in a repertory study is 'what did the company play?' For the Queen's Men, as for all companies not represented in Philip Henslowe's *Diary* (see below), an answer is complicated by issues of date and venue. McMillin and MacLean assemble an A-list of nine plays unarguably owned by the Queen's Men: *Clyomon and Clamydes* (Q1599); *The Famous Victories of Henry V* (S. R., May 14, 1594, Q1598); *Friar Bacon and Friar Bungay* (S. R. May 14, 1594, Q1594); *King Leir* (S. R. May 14, 1594; Q1605); *The Old Wives Tale* (S. R. April 16, 1595; Q1595); *Selimus* (Q1594); *The Troublesome Reign of King John* (Q1591); *Three Lords and Three Ladies of London* (S. R. July 31, 1590, Q1590); and *The True Tragedy of Richard III* (S. R. June 19, 1594, Q1594).[2] But they are thwarted by an absence of evidence on when the plays were new and where they were performed. A welcome exception is *The Famous Victories of Henry V*, which can be dated in performance in mid-1587 by way of *Tarlton's Jests* (1613). The 'excellent Iest of *Tarlton* suddenly spoken' relates that Tarlton, having on this occasion to double the part of the Lord Chief Justice with his own in a performance at the Bull Inn in Bishopsgate, was cuffed by John Bentley, who played Prince Hal. The anecdote gives the play a *terminus ad quem* because Bentley was killed by fellow player John Towne in June of 1587, but it does not necessarily identify the debut season. The remaining plays on McMillin and MacLean's A-list are customarily dated between 1570 and 1594, the vagueness of which is not helpful to a discussion of the company's repertory in any given year. By a quirk of fate, we know more about the plays post-1587 than those on which the Queen's Men first commanded the theatrical marketplace, but fortunately

---

[1] *The Queen's Men and their Plays* (Cambridge: Cambridge University Press, 1998).

[2] For further discussion of the Queen's repertory, see McMillin and MacLean, *The Queen's Men and their Plays*, esp. 91–3 and 121–54; and Roslyn Knutson, 'The Start of Something Big', in Helen Ostovich et al. (eds.), *Locating the Queen's Men: Material Practices and Conditions of Playing, 1583–1603* (Aldershot: Ashgate, 2009), 99–108.

(given the repertorial perspective here) those plays seem also to be the ones Shakespeare knew best.

For a complex of reasons, the hegemony of the Queen's Men was challenged in 1587–8. This fact raises a question about theatrical competition that repeatedly bedevils repertory studies: in what commercial context was a given company at work? In terms specific to the Queen's Men, what other plays did they have, and what were the contemporaneous offerings of companies in competition with them? From the names of the Queen's players given in the license of the Court of Aldermen[3] we know that Edmund Tilney drained significant talent from existing companies in 1583, specifically from Warwick's Men (John Dutton), Sussex's Men (John Adams, Richard Tarlton), and Leicester's Men (William Johnson, John Laneham, Robert Wilson). On the one hand, this information opens the possibility that the players brought some of the repertory from their old companies with them to the Queen's Men. On the other, we have to wonder what competition remained for the Queen's Men to face outside their own offerings. McMillin and MacLean, reinforcing the traditional line of scholarship, argue that the politicians behind the creation of the Queen's Men meant to constrain the burgeoning theatrical marketplace by creating a crown-protected monopoly. Yet other companies did not wither away. The REED 'Patrons and Performances Web Site', linked to data from the Toronto-based project Records of Early English Drama (REED), lists nearly ninety performances outside of London, 1583–6, by roughly twenty companies, at least eight of which had or were likely to have had appearances at London venues.[4] One London document suggesting an active theatrical scene is a letter dated June 18, 1584 from William Fleetwood, the City Recorder, who complains that James Burbage had arrogantly refused a summons, justifying his insubordination by saying 'he was my Lo[rd] of Hunsdons man', whereas the players of Lord Arundel and the Queen's Men had been cooperative.[5] In a document corroborating a busy London marketplace, the London Common Council objected to a petition c. November 1584 from the Queen's Men 'to excercise [i.e. play] within the Cittye' with the complaint 'that the last yere when such toleration was of the Quenes players only, all the places of playeing were filled with men calling themselues the Quenes players'.[6] Apparently, therefore, even though the political fiat to create an *uber-*company in the Queen's Men was powerful and instantaneous, other companies remained and with them opportunities for repertorial competition.

The Queen's Men are given credit for inventing the English chronicle play, allegedly to boost not only patriotic fervour but also the Queen's brand of Protestantism. For students of the repertory the question now becomes what dramatic formulas in this genre and others were replicated in the offerings of those troupes on tour and at the

---

[3] Glynne Wickham, Herbert Berry, and William Ingram (eds.), *English Professional Theatre 1530–1660* (Cambridge: Cambridge University Press, 2000), 210.

[4] http://link.library.utoronto.ca/reed/.

[5] E. K. Chambers, *The Elizabethan Stage*, 4 vols. (Oxford: Clarendon Press, 1923), 4: 298.

[6] Chambers, *The Elizabethan Stage*, 4: 299, 302.

numerous London playhouses and inns. The existence of plays such as *Locrine* and *Edmond Ironside* shows that other history plays shared the marketplace with those of the Queen's, and there is every reason to assume that folk material such as that in *Old Wives Tale* and hybrid elements of the moral play and estate satire as in *The Three Lords and Three Ladies of London* had counterparts on offer at London and provincial venues. Furthermore, these plays undoubtedly had outstanding, often starring, parts for clowns, even though the Queen's Men had the *sui generis* Richard Tarlton and his closest compeer, John Adams. Thus, as is so often the case, because too few plays survive, and too few of those that do can be dated with any confidence or ascribed to a given company, it is impossible to prove but nonetheless reasonable to assert that, when Shakespeare began to notice the Queen's Men in performance, he would have seen their influence reach beyond the chronicle history.[7]

And then came Christopher Marlowe. A fascinating but unanswerable question with repercussions for Shakespeare studies and repertorial competition is how Marlowe and the Admiral's Men came together for the debut of *Tamburlaine the Great*, perhaps in 1587. One popular theory is that Edward Alleyn was the draw. A lad of 16 in January 1583 when his initial company of Worcester's Men was licensed, Alleyn became an Admiral's man *c*.1586, and he would retain that lord's patronage throughout his career. Understandably, scholars have been unable to resist a narrative in which Marlowe wanted this young, tall, talented player for the part of Tamburlaine. McMillin and MacLean turn the question around and ask why Marlowe did not choose to sell to the Queen's Men; their answer is that the dramaturgy of that company—with its medley style and versification—would have seemed too vaudevillian. They see the Queen's Men as consequently spending the years following 1587 playing defence against the Marlovian blitzkrieg: *Tamburlaine*, part two; *The Jew of Malta*; *Doctor Faustus*. It is not certain that the Admiral's Men had the latter two plays, but it is certain that the Queen's Men did not. And, though the Queen's Men had had Thomas Kyd write for them in their early years, they are not assigned *The Spanish Tragedy*, its lost prequel ('The Comedy of Don Horatio'),[8] the discrete text of its embedded play, *Soliman and Perseda*, or the putatively Kydian 'Hamlet'.[9] Besides the prolific Anonymous, who trafficked indiscriminately with all companies, the major contributors to repertorial competition during the Queen's Men's prime that can be linked to specific plays were George Peele and Robert Greene. Yet only *Friar Bacon and Friar Bungay* by the latter and *Old Wives Tale* by the former were certainly the Queen's property. By 1592, the Queen's Men are perceived as in decline in terms of the London marketplace. They may have experienced a burst of commerce in 1595–6, perhaps at the opening of the Swan playhouse (see below), but otherwise their participation in repertorial

---

[7] See Meredith Anne Skura, *Shakespeare the Actor and the Purposes of Playing* (Chicago, IL: University of Chicago Press, 1993), for further influence from plays by the Queen's Men.

[8] I mark lost plays with quotation marks, and plays surviving in text or manuscript with italics.

[9] Lukas Erne states flatly that 'none of his [Kyd's] extant plays can in any way be convincingly linked to' the Queen's Men (*Beyond The Spanish Tragedy: A Study of the Works of Thomas Kyd* [Manchester: Manchester University Press, 2001], 163).

competition is measurable solely in the provinces, where for another decade they remained 'the best known and most widely travelled professional company in the kingdom'.[10]

Where was Shakespeare when the Admiral's Men first performed *Tamburlaine the Great*? Or in 1590, when it was published with its second part? It is impossible here to calibrate the influence of the theatrical environment of 1587 or 1590 on the young playwright in any detail. Countless scholars have addressed that influence on the Shakespearean canon and on individual plays, the latest being Robert A. Logan in *Shakespeare's Marlowe*;[11] but even a short list of recent work becomes very long, very fast. For the Queen's Men, the obvious influence was on the history play. McMillin and MacLean note that 'Shakespeare did not lift the comedies of the Queen's Men'.[12] But that statement would probably be revised significantly if an accurate list of their repertory survived.

1592 AND HENSLOWE'S *DIARY*

Whatever the proximity of Shakespeare to or distance from the activities at a playing venue previously, scholars generally agree that he was in London, fully invested in a theatrical life, in 1592. His presence is deduced from an entry on March 3, 1592 of the play, 'harey the vj', in the book of accounts kept by Philip Henslowe, who had built the Rose playhouse in 1587 with financial help from John Cholmley, a grocer. Henslowe had the playhouse remodelled in 1592, and he began on February 19 to make daily entries in a ledger (familiarly known as Henslowe's *Diary*) including the name of the company leasing the playhouse, the date of performance, the title of the play, and his receipts per day. The set of performances that includes 'harey the vj', which is generally believed to be the initial piece of Shakespeare's serial on the reign of Henry VI and the Wars of the Roses, was given by Lord Strange's Men, who continued at the Rose through June 22. Strange's Men had been on the theatrical landscape for some several years by 1592, often playing with—perhaps even merging with—the Admiral's Men. They would continue an affiliation, particularly with Edward Alleyn, until 1593 (they became the Earl of Derby's Men in September 1593 at the elevation of their patron to the earldom). Almost nothing is known of their repertory until they appear in Henslowe's records at the Rose. Presumably they shared plays as well as players with the Admiral's Men, in which case they would have performed works by Marlowe, Peele, Greene, and others now unidentifiable. Did they then also acquire pre-1592 plays by Shakespeare, perhaps *Two Gentlemen of Verona*? Their main competition for those earlier works should have been the

---

[10] McMillin and MacLean, *The Queen's Men and their Play*, 67.

[11] *Shakespeare's Marlowe: The Influence of Christopher Marlowe on Shakespeare's Artistry* (Aldershot: Ashgate, 2007).

[12] *The Queen's Men and their Plays*, 166.

Queen's Men, but the evidence of company ownership for too many plays is too tenuous to provide more than a few circumstantial clues.

Henslowe provided four months' worth of performances by Strange's Men in the spring of 1592, plus another month at Christmastide (December 29, 1592–February 1, 1593). These records are the first evidence of the early modern repertory system in action, and the first of a Shakespearean play in repertory. Now generally accepted as the industry norm,[13] the system has the following features: (1) almost daily playing, even occasionally on Sunday, (2) a scheduling of offerings in rotation but in no consistent pattern except to produce variety, and (3) frequent initial showings of new plays, with increasing distance between shows as the run winds down. These principles are observable in the debut of *Henry VI* ('harey the vj'). It was introduced on Friday, March 3, and played again on Tuesday and Saturday of the following week. It was offered once in the third week, once in the fifth and subsequent weeks, with a few weeks blank, for a total of fifteen performances. The play was continued in the winter run with two performances on January 16 and 31, 1593. When introduced on March 3, *Henry VI* was marked 'ne'. With residual scepticism, scholars have accepted the obvious reading of the annotation as the sign of a new play,[14] a distinction *Henry VI* shares with four titles in 1592. Nineteen additional plays, apparently old by 1592, fill out the repertory of twenty-four plays in the spring season.

In comparison with the number of English chronicle plays owned by the Queen's Men, the repertory of Strange's Men in Henslowe's *Diary* has just two: *Henry VI* and the lost 'Harry of Cornwall'. But it is rich in plays of diverse genres with exotic foreign sites, including *Orlando Furioso*, *The Jew of Malta*, *A Looking Glass for London and England*, and *The Massacre at Paris*. Lawrence Manley explores a predilection for pyrotechnics that characterizes a number of the offerings including Shakespeare's play: 'Fire, fireworks, the threat of fire, and above all the threat and the actual simulation of burning people alive are astonishingly prominent in the company's repertory'.[15] His observation illustrates a trend in repertory studies revived by McMillin and MacLean in their characterization of the Queen's Men: to identify the personality of a given company by way of 'those special characteristics which gave the company its identity—its acting style, its staging methods, its kind of versification, its sense of what constituted a worthwhile repertory of plays'.[16]

---

[13] It was not always so. See R. A. Foakes (ed.), *Henslowe's Diary*, 2nd edn. (Cambridge: Cambridge University Press, 2002), pp. xxix–xxx, and Roslyn Knutson, *The Repertory of Shakespeare's Company, 1594–1613* (Fayetteville: University of Arkansas Press, 1991), 16–19, on the rehabilitation of Henslowe's reputation.

[14] For the range of opinions on 'ne', see Foakes, *Henslowe's Diary*, pp. xxxiv–xxxv.

[15] Lawrence Manley, 'Playing with Fire: Immolation and the Repertory of Strange's Men', *Early Theatre* 4 (2001), 115–29, at 116.

[16] *The Queen's Men and their Plays*, p. xii. The desire to identify the personality of a company is not new. Nineteenth-century theatre historians defined the personality of the Chamberlain's/King's Men by Shakespeare's plays and their supposedly sophisticated appeal. For evidence of this opinion, see Robert B. Sharpe, *The Real War of the Theaters* (Boston: D. C. Heath, 1935).

This search for a company personality has significant implications. It implies a coherence in a company's acquisitions and scheduling that transcends a merely commercial desire to entertain through diversity. Also, it risks scholars reading the repertory to fit preconceived opinions. Henslowe's playlists for Strange's Men illustrate some of the hazards. One is the number of lost plays. Greg identified probable narrative sources for a number of these lost plays, but for many he could find nothing. Frequently he fell back on F. G. Fleay's habit of identifying plays with similar subject matter as the same play. Obviously, plays about which nothing is known, and plays possibly misidentified, cannot count heavily in the construction of the company's personality, yet such dubiously identified items are in the majority for all companies. A second hazard is the presence of other companies' plays in the repertory. At least five of Strange's nineteen old plays had belonged to another company first. To some degree, then, the personality of Strange's Men—and any company in its early years—is contingent on the personality of the troupes from which it acquired scripts second-hand.

Even given the problems of lost and recycled plays, a few patterns of commercial import do emerge. One is the tendency to market multi-part plays as a serial. Strange's Men performed the two-part 'Comedy of Don Horatio' and *Spanish Tragedy* in tandem four times, but also as discrete plays. The Admiral's Men did likewise with serial plays, for example the two parts of *Tamburlaine* and 'Caesar and Pompey'. However, in a case such as 'The Seven Days of the Week', the second part seems to be a substitute for the ageing first part.[17] Another commercial relationship in Henslowe's playlists, 1592–7, is a tendency to cluster plays with similar motifs in a quasi-serial relationship. Strange's Men, for example, scheduled *The Jew of Malta* three times on the afternoon following 'Muly Mollocco' (with which it shares the geography of the Mediterranean) and once following 'Machiavel' (with which it shares the Machiavellian character). On May 29, 30, and 31, 1592, the plays appear as a trio. The Admiral's Men sometimes played *Doctor Faustus* with other 'doctor' or 'wise man' plays, and they occasionally paired 'Mahomet' with part one of 'Godfrey of Bulloigne'. In one fine moment in 1595, the Admiral's Men combined the marketing strategies of genuine serials and similar motifs: on the afternoons of May 20, 21, 22, and 23 they performed part one of 'Hercules', part one of *Tamburlaine*, part two of *Tamburlaine*, then the 'ne' part two of 'Hercules'. This sequence looks very like the company was advertising its new action-figure hero (Hercules) by way of the long-poplar Marlovian one.

By continuing Shakespeare's *Henry VI* into the Christmas season of 1592–3, Strange's Men engaged at least one company—Pembroke's Men—in repertorial competition in London by means of Shakespeare's plays. Pembroke's Men are likely to have been formed in early autumn 1592, though their origin is murky.[18] They are notorious among

---

[17] Inexplicably, the second part of 'Seven Days of the Week' did not last long in performance. It received only two performances (January 22 and 26, 1596), although its receipts averaged a respectable 42s. to Henslowe.

[18] For variant birth narratives, see Chambers, *The Elizabethan Stage*, 2: 129–31, and Andrew Gurr, *The Shakespearian Playing Companies* (Oxford: Clarendon Press, 1996), 266–71.

companies in 1593 because, according to Henslowe in a letter to Edward Alleyn dated September 28, they ran into financial trouble late in the summer and had to pawn their 'parell for ther carge'.[19] Several of their plays were printed subsequently, including the Quarto versions of *2 Henry VI* and *3 Henry VI*: titled in these printings *The First Part of the Contention Betwixt the Two Famous Houses of York and Lancaster* (*The Contention*) and *The True Tragedy of Richard Duke of York* (*True Tragedy*). For this moment in theatre history, then, Shakespeare's plays were in competition with each other across company lines by way of the discrete plays in the 'Henry VI' serial. But, as is so often true, we know nothing about the heat such competition might have generated. Pembroke's Men also owned *The Taming of a Shrew* (*A Shrew*, Q1594). Was Shakespeare's *Taming of the Shrew* in the repertory of another company when Pembroke's were playing *A Shrew*? Had Shakespeare's even been written yet? Similar questions apply to the competitive engagement of other apparent duplicates, for example *Friar Bacon and Friar Bungay*, a Queen's play, with the 'Friar Bacon' in the repertory of Strange's Men (which might be a play featuring Friar Bacon but called in manuscript *John of Bordeaux*).

1594 AND THE CHAMBERLAIN'S MEN

The company of Chamberlain's Men that Shakespeare joined was formed by early June 1594. Theatre historians have always believed that the company acquired Shakespeare's old plays when they acquired *him*. They are probably right, although there is no documentary proof (it is just too odd to think of the Queen's Men or Pembroke's in the provinces or at the Swan in 1595 playing *Two Gentlemen of Verona* and *Richard III*, while Shakespeare's company played the newly acquired *Romeo and Juliet* at the Theatre).[20] Scholars have also believed that the Chamberlain's Men needed few additional plays to compete—indeed, to triumph—in the theatrical marketplace because they had Shakespeare's plays as the backbone of their repertory. But that belief has changed, due largely to the rehabilitation of Henslowe's *Diary* as evidence of an industry-wide repertory system. Nevertheless, there is little documentary guidance to confirm the wholesale application of repertory principles in Henslowe's *Diary* to the Chamberlain's/King's Men. Some of the knottier problems of applying the repertorial system illustrated in the *Diary* to Shakespeare's company include a discussion of the marketing of Shakespeare's plays within their own repertory and in the larger commercial landscape of London, the court, and the provinces.

Let us begin with how the Chamberlain's Men acquired Shakespeare's plays in 1594. Andrew Gurr claims that the company was given them.[21] According to his theory of a duopoly, the Lord Admiral and Lord Chamberlain gave Marlowe's plays to the

---

[19] Foakes, *Henslowe's Diary*, 280.

[20] However, Holger Schott Syme argues precisely that in 'Three's Company'; Alternative Histories of London's Theatres in the 1950s', *Shakespeare Survey* 65 (2012), 269–89.

[21] *The Shakespeare Company 1594–1642* (Cambridge: Cambridge University Press, 2004), p. xiii.

Admiral's Men and Shakespeare's to the Chamberlain's. Someone must then have rounded up the plays from their current owners and delivered them to the newly formed companies. A narrative friendlier to entrepreneurial enterprise is that players joining the new companies brought scripts including Shakespeare's with them. One of those players could have been Shakespeare himself. Unfortunately, we know very little about property and ownership issues in regard to playtexts. Henslowe's record of purchases, 1597–1603, suggests that companies owned plays, but a few professionals, including Edward Alleyn, Martin Slater, and Christopher Beeston, owned plays also.[22] It is not entirely clear which plays *were* Shakespeare's in 1594. Was *Titus Andronicus* 'his'? Scholars, reopening the issue of Shakespeare as collaborator, complicate matters for students of the repertory for this reason: he probably wrote a scene or two in other plays such as *Edward III*. Should we then assume that they journeyed to the Chamberlain's Men also because of the parts by his hand, as *Henry VI* and *Titus Andronicus* apparently did?

Henslowe gives an initial list of the Chamberlain's repertory by recording the titles of eight plays performed at the playhouse in Newington by 'my Lord Admeralle men & my Lorde chamberlen men' from June 3 to 13, 1594. Because four of these plays show up immediately in Henslowe's lists for the Admiral's Men on their return to the Rose on June 15, scholars have reasonably assigned the remaining four to the repertory of the Chamberlain's Men: 'Hester and Ahasuerus', *Titus Andronicus*, 'Hamlet', and 'the tamynge of A shrowe'.[23] In addition, they must have acquired more old scripts, but to guess at these we have to guess also at the chronology and provenance of the plays in question. Two examples will have to suffice. *Mucedorus* was printed in 1610 with a title-page advertisement of the King's Men, but it was an old play then, having been printed also in 1598 and 1606. Alfred Harbage assigns it to 1590 in his *Annals of English Drama, 975–1700*. If that date is close, it is reasonable to assume that the Chamberlain's Men acquired it in their first year or two of business. Another possibility, *A Knack to Know a Knave*, is a candidate on different circumstantial evidence. Henslowe entered it as 'ne' in the 1592 run of Strange's Men at the Rose (June 10). It was printed in 1594 with a title-page advertisement both of Edward Alleyn and William Kemp. The play did not go with Alleyn to the Admiral's Men, but that company did acquire *A Knack to Know an Honest Man*, a play that capitalized on its predecessor in title, though not otherwise ('ne,' October 22, 1594). It is reasonable to assume that the Admiral's Men were responding to a revival of *A Knack to Know a Knave* in the repertory of the Chamberlain's Men, with a reprise by Kemp of the merriments advertised on the 1594 title-page.

The company also acquired new plays. For most of these, we can be relatively confident of their newness and ownership by the Chamberlain's Men, but an

---

[22] In a deed of sale dated January 3, 1588/9, Richard Jones sells his share in playbooks, apparel, and other property to Edward Alleyn (W. W. Greg [ed.], *Henslowe Papers*. [London: A. H. Bullen, 1907], 31), but was Alleyn buying these wares for himself or for his company?

[23] Even though Henslowe records 'the tamynge of A shrowe', Shakespearean scholarship usually reads this entry as an error for *The Taming of the Shrew*.

assignment to a given repertorial year remains largely guesswork. For the years up to 1603, the list is short enough to provide in full: *A Warning for Fair Women* (1597–8); *Every Man In his Humour* (1598–9); *Every Man Out of his Humour*, 'Cloth Breeches and Velvet Hose', and *A Larum for London* (1599–1600); *The Freeman's Honor* and *Thomas Lord Cromwell* (1600–1); *Satiromastix* (1601–2), *The Merry Devil of Edmonton* and 'Stuhlweissenburg' (1602–3); and *The Fair Maid of Bristow*, *The London Prodigal*, and *Sejanus* (1603–4). To this list should be added Shakespeare's new plays, starting with *Romeo and Juliet*. Also, to provide any semblance of a repertory schedule, we need to consider the issue of revivals and mislabelled plays. One lesson of Henslowe's *Diary* is that companies returned their successful plays to the stage. We can track a few revivals of plays by Shakespeare and others from court documents such as the Revels Accounts of 1604–5; but for those routine second and third runs of previously popular plays, we have little other than their reprinting to suggest a continued stage life. Another lesson from Henslowe is variant titles. No doubt some of the Chamberlain's lost plays are concealed by casual reports that use alternative titles. For example, did a play called 'Love's Labour's Won' exist? Francis Meres thought so, but scholars have disagreed.[24] When the Chamberlain's Men gave a performance of 'Oldcastle' at their patron's London house in March 1600 to entertain a foreign dignitary, Louis Verrey-ken, were they performing the now-old *1 Henry IV* or a new spin-off that corrected the *faux pas* of Falstaff's original name?[25] When the players complained in the new Induction to *The Malcontent* in 1604 that the children's company had taken their 'Jeronimo', were they referring to an actual play? And, when Dudley Carleton called the play performed by the company on New Year's night 1604 at court 'Robin Goodfellow', did he really mean *A Midsummer Night's Dream*?[26]

This repertory list, partial and flawed as it is, makes possible an enquiry into the repertorial commerce of Shakespeare's company. However, such an enquiry presupposes that the principles extrapolated from Henslowe's *Diary* are both reliable and applicable to the Chamberlain's Men and other adult professional troupes with a significant London presence. Even if that supposition is valid, we have to recognize certain extenuating circumstances. For one, if other companies had repertories as large as that of the Admiral's Men, the number of plays now lost is huge. Second, if these plays once existed, someone must have written them. Who would that have been? In the records for 1597–1603, Henslowe names men we would not identify as dramatists without his entries—for example, William Bird, who would otherwise be known only as a player; and William Haughton, whom we would not know at all. Undoubtedly dramatists named in Henslowe's *Diary* wrote for other companies, but assigning every one of them to double or triple duty cannot fill the blanks of lost dramatists, unless

---

[24] Roslyn L. Knutson, 'Love's Labor's Won in Repertory', *Publications of the Arhansas Philological Association* 11, (1985), 45–57, 45–6.

[25] Knutson, *The Repertory of Shakespeare's Company*, 95–7.

[26] E. K. Chambers, *William Shakespeare: A Study of Facts and Problems*, 2 vols. (Oxford: Clarendon Press, 1930), 1: 362.

they—like Thomas Heywood—wrote some several hundred plays. Third, how much interpretive weight can playing schedules at the Rose sustain? The temptation to over-read a coincidence of scheduling as a calculated marketing strategy is great. It is dicey enough to read intentionality into Henslowe's records (as above, with the 1595 cluster of the pairs of *Tamburlaine* and 'Hercules' plays); if we do so for Shakespeare's company and its competitors, we must be careful not to attribute more managerial planning and execution than Henslowe's records may support.

Proceeding cautiously, therefore, we may explore the options the Chamberlain's Men might have considered as they assembled a season of offerings in 1594, based on the repertory list conjectured above (the Newington plays, Shakespeare's, and a few imports from defunct companies). Most obvious is the challenge presented by the tetralogy on the Wars of the Roses. If the Chamberlain's Men presented these in tandem for four afternoons of any given week, would that have been too much of a good thing? This number of history plays raises another question: would having the *Henry VI–Richard III* plays in-house have made the acquisition of other history plays such as *Edward III*, *George a Greene*, or *Edward II* more attractive, or less so? A lot of history plays have very little history in them. *George a Greene*, for example, focuses on the commoner-hero, who is more of a patriotic bully than warrior; his adventures, as in his defence of his girlfriend against the jealousies of Robin Hood's Maid Marian, turn the chronicle matter into folktale. Similarly, *A Knack to Know a Knave* is a history play only in the names of a few characters (King Edgar, Bishop Dunston); its hybrid of estate satire and moral allegory—with the merriments of the trio of tradesmen billed on the title-page with William Kemp as 'the men of Goteham'—perhaps negated its perception as history. In tragedies, the Chamberlain's Men appear to have had considerable diversity. Two old plays, both in the popular revenge formula, have the very different settings of ancient Rome and medieval Denmark. A third, 'Hester and Ahasuerus', doubled as a history play through its biblical source; if it followed 'The Book of Esther', it would have juggled romantic, political, and religious narrative threads. With the arrival of Shakespeare's bittersweet romance, *Romeo and Juliet*, the tragedic holdings were further diversified. What the Chamberlain's Men seem *not* to have had was competition for the Mediterranean generic hybrids in the Admiral's repertory (i.e. *Tamburlaine*, 'Mahomet', *The Jew of Malta*, the two-part 'Godfrey of Bulloigne'). Such a vacuum offers two choices: we can decide, as scholars used to do, that the company disdained such matter as too down-market, or we consider likely titles among lost and unattributed plays. A possible contender is 'The Tartarian Cripple', registered at Stationers' Hall at the same time and by the same stationers as *Every Man In his Humour* (August 14, 1600).[27] For comedies, the Chamberlain's Men had *Two Gentlemen of Verona* as well as a 'Shrew' play on hand. The fact that Shakespeare wrote more comedies right away—e.g. *The Comedy of Errors*, *Love's Labour's Lost*, and its sequel—

---

[27] Roslyn L. Knutson, 'Evidence for the Assignment of Plays to the Repertory of Shakespeare's Company', *Medieval and Renaissance Drama in England* 4 (1989), 63–89, at 78.

suggests an awareness on his or the company's part that half of the Admiral's offerings were some version of a comedic formula.

Signs of commercial competition across company lines are, understandably, based on even more guesswork than theories of the Chamberlain's marketing of their own repertory. Suffice it here to note some possibilities constructed out of surviving data. One is the aforementioned apparent referentiality, though by title alone, of *A Knack to Know a Knave* (Chamberlain's) and *A Knack to Know an Honest Man* (Admiral's). Another centres on the printing of *The Famous Victories of Henry V* in 1598. If this printing is a sign of recent stage life, and *if* that life was its old owners in a reconstituted troupe at the newly-built Swan,[28] then the introduction of 'harey the v' on November 28, 1595 looks like the Admiral's Men's commercial response. Shakespeare's own sequence mining the narrative of the Queen's play, which comes along at about the same time, extends the interplay of competition to the Chamberlain's Men. Furthermore, there are spin-offs: not only *The Merry Wives of Windsor*, but also the two-part play on Sir John Oldcastle acquired by the Admiral's Men in early autumn 1599, which explicitly refers to Falstaff. The Admiral's *Oldcastle* pair, later altered for Worcester's Men,[29] heightens the appeal of identifying the play performed at the Lord Chamberlain's house for the Dutch politician in 1600 as yet another 'Oldcastle' play.

Similarly tantalizing commercial relationships across the offerings of the companies are plausible throughout the years of Shakespeare's career and beyond. One cluster is the new fashion of domestic relations such as *A Warning for Fair Women* and *All's Well that Ends Well* with the Chamberlain's Men; *Patient Grissil* and 'Page of Plymouth' with the Admiral's Men; and *A Woman Killed with Kindness* and *How a Man May Choose a Good Wife from a Bad* with Worcester's Men. A well-documented referentiality connects Jonson's *Poetaster* at Blackfriars with Dekker's *Satiromastix*, both with Paul's Boys and the Chamberlain's Men. Still another harkens back to the matter of the Wars of the Roses. Shakespeare's plays were old, but their reprinting in 1600 (in their quarto versions, *The Contention* and *True Tragedy*) implies fresh stage life; Q3 of *Richard III* appeared in 1602. The Admiral's Men had two plays now lost in the spring of 1600, 'Owen Tudor' and 'Henry Richmond' (the latter tagged as a second part). The former play told some part of the narrative of Henry VI's mother's second husband, grandfather to Henry Richmond, later Henry VII. At the Battle of Mortimer's Cross, Tudor, a Lancastrian, was beheaded on the order of Edward of York. Derby's Men had a two-part play named *Edward IV* (Q1600), but in many ways it looked rather to Jane Shore, the subject of a play by Worcester's Men in May 1603. By this time (June 22, 1602), the Admiral's Men had paid Ben Jonson for a new play, 'Richard Crookback'.

---

[28] William Ingram, *A London Life in the Brazen Age: Francis Langley 1548–1602* (Cambridge, MA: Harvard University Press, 1978), 115–20.

[29] Foakes, *Henslowe's Diary*, 216.

1603 AND THE KING'S MEN

If the change in patrons from the Lord Chamberlain to James I had an effect on the repertory practices of Shakespeare's company, no traces of those effects remain. Plague returned in the spring of 1603, but the companies had long ago developed ways to cope. As servants of the Crown, the King's Men now received an additional aid: a stipend in lieu of suspended court performances. In 1604, the court returned to London, and by chance the Revels Accounts for that holiday season survive. These appear to offer evidence of repertorial practice; however, we may not want to look too closely because the Revels listing gives mixed support to claims formulated here about repertorial playing habits. On the one hand, that list makes it look as though the company counted as heavily on plays by Shakespeare as scholars of the nineteenth century thought it did. Of the eleven performances scheduled during the period from All Hallows through Shrove Tuesday, Shakespeare's plays were scheduled on eight of those dates.[30] On the other hand, the list is contrary to the old-fashioned view that the King's Men depended on new plays, by Shakespeare or others. Only two—*Othello* and *Measure for Measure*—are thought to be in their maiden run (the age of 'The Spanish Maze' is unknown). Indeed, some of the old plays were quite old. *The Comedy of Errors* and *Love's Labour's Lost* were about ten years old; *The Merchant of Venice* was eight; the newest of the old plays, *Henry V* and *Every Man Out of his Humour*, were five. More disconcerting than the preponderance of Shakespeare's plays and old plays, however, is the treatment of serials. Though the King's Men revived *Henry V*, they did not accompany it with either of its serial parts (parts one and two of *Henry IV*); rather, they chose its spin-off, *The Merry Wives of Windsor* (November 4, 1604), which they played both before and two months separated from its cousin (January 7, 1605). By this choice, they lost not only the popular transformation of the prodigal Prince Hal into the national hero of Henry V but also all context for the reprobate Falstaff. The company did choose both of Jonson's 'humours' plays, but they did not play them in serial order, scheduling *Every Man In his Humour* more than three weeks later than its titular mate. And they did not pair 'Love's Labour's Lost' with its sequel. There is some comfort for the guesswork here about lost plays by dramatists unidentified in the appearance of 'The Spanish Maze', otherwise unknown. Also, the Revels offerings have the kind of generic diversity consistent with repertories generally in Henslowe's *Diary*: one tragedy (*Othello*), one history (*Henry V*), and the rest comedies (with the genre of 'The Spanish Maze' unknown). But that distribution may have had more to do with court tastes than repertorial practice, as the other companies performing that holiday season also presented comedies ('How to Learn of a Woman to Woo', Thomas Heywood, Queen Anne's Men; *All Fools*, George Chapman, Children of the Queen's Chapel).

---

[30] There were eight playing dates, but only seven plays were scheduled because *The Merchant of Venice* was played a second time.

The major question about repertorial practice by the King's Men—indeed perhaps the only question of real significance—concerns their acquisition of the Blackfriars Playhouse. By 1609, Henry Evans, who had acquired the Blackfriars for a company of boys in 1600, had turned the lease back to the Burbages. When the surcease of plague allowed the companies to resume business,[31] the King's Men took up the lease and now had two playhouses: the outdoor venue of Globe, and the indoor venue of Blackfriars. Since the time of Edmond Malone (1790) scholars have accepted that the King's Men divided the playing year between their two houses, playing at Blackfriars in the winter and at the Globe in summer.[32] In an influential essay in 1948, G. E. Bentley argued that the company began in 1609 to develop new repertorial practices to take advantage of this opportunity. One of those was to create a two-tier repertory, with the most sophisticated plays designated 'for the elegant new theatre' and the old-fashioned plays for the noisy groundlings at the Globe.[33] Another was to seek out dramatists who already wrote for a higher class of audience such as Ben Jonson and the collaborative team of Francis Beaumont and John Fletcher; Shakespeare himself, in Bentley's view, would 'write henceforth with the Blackfriars in mind and not the Globe'.[34] Although Andrew Gurr has dismissed Bentley's argument as 'long…discredited',[35] he is nonetheless the most vocal supporter of the Blackfriars as the holy grail of venues to which Shakespeare's company had aspired since James Burbage bought the property in February 1596.[36] He identifies a range of theatrical effects that would have been unwelcome in the small enclosed space of Blackfriars, including noisy alarums and the Jacobean equivalent of the smell of napalm in the morning.[37]

Yet several aspects of existing evidence make problematic the case of a divided repertory. One, of course, is an absence of repertory lists for any given year. When something similar to such a list does appear, as in the notebooks of Simon Forman, the evidence is not definitive. In terms of venues and seasons, Forman's entries show that he went to the Globe in the spring months (April, May) of 1610 and 1611; in terms of a tiered repertory, Forman saw one play written before the company owned Blackfriars

---

[31] See J. Leeds Barroll, *Politics, Plague, and Shakespeare's Theater: The Stuart Years* (Ithaca, NY: Cornell University Press, 1991), on likely interruptions of playing because of plague, post-1609.

[32] The authority for seasons split between summer and winter is James Wright's *Historia Histrionica* (London: 1699), in which characters reminisce in a fictional conversation about the theatrical world before the English Civil War (Roslyn L. Knutson, 'What if there wasn't a "Blackfriars Repertory"?' in Paul Menzer [ed.], *Inside Shakespeare: Essays on the Blackfriars Stage* [Selinsgrove: Susquehanna University Press, 2006], 54–60, at 54–5). See Knutson, 'Two Playhouses, Both Alike in Dignity', *Shakespeare Studies* 30 (2002), 111117, for a contrarian view on the company's seasonal use of the two playhouses.

[33] Bentley, 'Shakespeare and the Blackfriars Theatre', *Shakespeare Survey* 1 (1948): 38–50, at 43.

[34] Bentley, 'Shakespeare and the Blackfriars Theatre', 46.

[35] Gurr, *The Shakespearian Playing Companies*, 367.

[36] See, for example, Andrew Gurr, 'London's Blackfriars Playhouse and the Chamberlain's Men', in Paul Menzer (ed.), *Inside Shakespeare: Essays on the Blackfriars Stage* (Selinsgrove: Susquehanna University Press, 2006), 17–30. For a contrarian view, see Roslyn L. Knutson, 'What was James Burbage *Thinking*???', in Peter Kanelos and Matt Kozusko (eds.), *Thunder at a Playhouse: Essays on Shakespeare and the Early Modern Stage* (Selinsgrove, PA: Susquehanna University Press, 2010).

[37] Gurr, *The Shakespearian Playing Companies*, 367–8.

(*Macbeth*), two that might otherwise be considered Blackfriars quality (*Cymbeline* and *The Winter's Tale*), and a filler putatively suited to the commoner outdoor-playhouse market, 'Richard the 2'. Another problem is the evidence of staging in texts. The fact that most plays were published long after their composition and were thus vulnerable to interpolated changes from untraceable sources makes connections between repertory choices and venues a complicated issue, lending itself to contrary interpretations. A third is title-pages. In a perfect world, plays written for and performed at one venue or another would so advertise themselves on publication, but the plays of the King's Men published after 1609 show no such consistency. For four plays by Beaumont and Fletcher, for example, all of which by Bentley's view should have been written for Blackfriars, *The Maid's Tragedy* and *Thierry and Theodoret* conform by advertising that playhouse on their title-pages in 1619 and 1621 respectively. However, *A King and No King* and *Philaster* advertise the Globe; subsequently reprinted, both advertise both playhouses.

In the minds of many scholars, performances at court come close to approximating the high-class repertory that the King's Men allegedly designated for Blackfriars. Gurr, in fact, has claimed that the Master of the Revels '[f]rom 1615 onwards . . . only ever chose plays for performance at court that came from the indoor playhouses'.[38] Support for this claim does not come from the two records of court performance, Accounts of the Office of the Chamber and Accounts of the Office of the Revels. The Chamber Accounts do specify that the King's Men gave fourteen performances in 1615–16, thirteen in 1616–17, eighteen in 1617–18, eight in 1618–19, and eleven in 1619–20, but only in 1618 are the plays named: *Twelfth Night* and *The Winter's Tale* at Eastertide and *The Merry Devil of Edmonton* on May 15.[39] Given this paucity, we may be excused for falling back on earlier evidence when the King's Men had the lease on Blackfriars and when the Chamber Accounts are detailed. In 1611–12, the company performed five plays, plus two with Queen Anne's Men (e. g., Heywood's *Silver Age*). These five—*The Tempest, The Winter's Tale, A King and No King, The Twins Tragedy*, and *The Nobleman*—may very well have been part of a 'Blackfriars repertory', though none was published with a title-page advertisement of the Blackfriars until 1625 (*A King and No King*, Q2). But in 1612–13, the King's offerings at court were eclectic. In addition to repeats of the five plays from the previous court season, five plausibly 'Blackfriars' plays were performed (*Philaster, The Maid's Tragedy, The Captain, The Alchemist*, 'Cardenio'), but another five written long before the acquisition of the indoor venue were also given: *Much Ado About Nothing* (listed a second time as 'Benidicte and Betteris'), *The Merry Devil of Edmonton*, 'The Moore of Venice' (*Othello*), 'Sʳ John Falstafe' (taken to be one of the 'Henry IV' plays or *The Merry Wives of Windsor*), 'Caesars Tragedye' (taken to be *Julius Caesar*), and 'Hotspurr' (taken to be *1 Henry IV*). And finally, the King's Men gave two plays about which we know nothing but which by their titles do

[38] Andrew Gurr, 'Shakespeare's Playhouses', in David Scott Kastan (ed.), *A Companion to Shakespeare* (Oxford: Blackwell, 1999), 362–76, at 372.

[39] David Cook and F. P. Wilson (eds.), *Dramatic Records in the Declared Accounts of the Treasurer of the Chamber 1558–1642*, Malone Society Collections VI, 1 (1961), 60–74.

not sound specifically groomed for sophisticated tastes: 'The Knot of Fools' and 'A Bad Beginning Makes a Good Ending'. More than a decade after the King's Men acquired Blackfriars, Henry Herbert, the new Master of the Revels, provided lists of plays censored, plays licensed, and plays presented at court. In a representative year, 1623–4, he identified six court dates for which the King's Men performed four plays.[40] The new comedy, *Maid of the Mill* (three performances), had been licensed the previous August, and Herbert did not then specify the playhouse for which it was meant.[41] The lost play, 'The Buck is a Thief', does not appear in Herbert's list of newly licensed plays. Herbert labelled *More Dissemblers besides Women* an old play newly licensed.[42] The fourth play that holiday season was the perennial favourite *The Winter's Tale*. From these lists collectively, it appears that the King's Men after the acquisition of Blackfriars kept a repertory remarkably similar to the mix of new and old plays, of genres and popular subjects, that they had kept since their opening for business in 1594 at Burbage's Theatre in Shoreditch.

Fleay's *desideratum*, to learn as much about every single play as possible, remains the research goal for repertory studies. The data assembled by the massive archival project, Records of Early English Drama, have opened up provincial civic halls and aristocratic great houses to consideration as frequent and desirable venues, extending a once London-centric field of study to the whole of Britain, and even Europe. The 'Patrons and Performances Web Site' makes that REED material available with the click of a mouse; another Web resource, the 'Lost Plays Database,' performs a similar service for the data on lost plays. Scholars with fresh tools for determining authorship have rattled our assumptions about the ubiquity of collaboration and challenged an all-too-comfortable assumption that company ownership of a given play may be deduced from its authorship. Research into the lives of players and theatrical entrepreneurs has provided new contexts in which to evaluate questions of class and financial status among the men who made their livings, even fortunes, in the playhouse world. A reorientation of theatre history from individual dramatists to company organizations has raised the profile of the battery of plays such companies performed, making it possible to argue that plays once dismissed as insignificant to company business or lost might in fact have been crucial to a company's professional identity and financial success. In such an environment, Shakespeare's plays, far from being marginalized by studies with a repertory focus, are provided a commercial theatrical context with many of their key relationships yet to be identified.

---

[40] Joseph Quincy Adams (ed.), *The Dramatic Records of Sir Henry Herbert* (New Haven, CT: Yale University Press, 1917), 50–1.

[41] Adams, *The Dramatic Records of Sir Henry Herbert*, 25.

[42] Adams, *The Dramatic Records of Sir Henry Herbert*, 26.

CHAPTER 23

....

THEATRE AS BUSINESS

....

MELISSA AARON

THE study of Shakespeare's company as a business is relatively recent: it is not so long ago that the 'commercial' focus of the Admiral's Men was unfavourably contrasted with the more 'artistic' focus of the Chamberlain's or King's Men, Shakespeare's company. But the business of Shakespeare's company cannot be viewed in a vacuum. The very conditions of its existence arose from a specific moment in economic and cultural history. The increasing economic centralization of England in London created a market large enough for luxury goods and services such as the theatre. Older guild structures provided a foundation for theatrical businesses to build upon: many actors and sharers in theatrical companies remained members of various guilds, such as the Drapers or the Grocers. Newer economic organizations such as the joint stock corporation also provided models for theatrical businesses: investors in the East India Company and in the King's Men alike were called 'full sharers and adventurers'. A shift to a cash, and later to a credit economy gave audiences literally the currency to pay for admission to public theatres. In addition to this new public market, playing companies were able to expand their traditional markets of touring and private performance. The courts of King James, and later King Charles, provided another market for the company's work: one that represented a larger portion of the company's business as time went on, possibly to its detriment.

Adverse economic conditions did not automatically translate to poor financial performance for the King's Men. John Maynard Keynes suggested that 'we were just in a financial position to afford Shakespeare when he presented himself', but Douglas Bruster has pointed out that this is not so. England produced Shakespeare when she could least afford him: Shakespeare became a sharer and the Chamberlain's Men achieved dominance after a prolonged plague closure in 1593 and during a time of poor harvests and economic dearth.[1] As the 1590s went on, the Chamberlain's Men

---

[1] John Maynard Keynes, *A Treatise on Money, Vol. 2, The Applied Theory of Money*, 154, cited in Douglas Bruster, *Drama and the Market in the Age of Shakespeare* (Cambridge: Cambridge University Press, 1992) 18.

maintained a virtual duopoly with the Admiral's Men and moved to the Globe Theatre in 1599, a building owned by a consortium of the company sharers.[2] In 1603, the company was given a royal patent as the King's Men and performed more frequently at court. Plague and civil unrest usually spelled economic difficulties, true—as Leeds Barroll has demonstrated, plague could have a devastating effect on the theatre business—but despite several financial setbacks during the early 1600s, a lengthy lawsuit during the acquisition of the Blackfriars Theatre as an additional playhouse, and the burning of the Globe in 1613, the company increased its financial stability, rebuilding the Globe, adding more sharers, and dividing its time between two playhouses.[3]

The business and legal documentation available is limited, and analysis requires a certain amount of speculation. No ledger or inventory has survived from Shakespeare's company. Most analyses of the Chamberlain's/King's Men's finances depend on documents connected to other theatrical companies and speculation about how closely their business transactions resembled these of Shakespeare's company. Some of the business documents of Philip Henslowe and of Edward Alleyn have survived: a large book containing Henslowe's financial transactions, theatrical and otherwise, commonly known as *Henslowe's Diary*, and Alleyn's inventories of props and company-owned costumes. The resulting financial picture of the Rose and Fortune theatres and of the Admiral's/Prince's Men is often extrapolated to Shakespeare's company. There are no contracts for a poet-in-ordinary to a theatrical company, and the closest remaining document is a lawsuit by Queen Henrietta Maria's Men against Richard Brome for non-performance of duties from 1638, considerably after Shakespeare's death, but assumptions about Shakespeare's duties as a poet in the playing company to which he belonged are usually hypothesized backwards from this lawsuit.[4]

Lawsuits are also very important in assigning the value of shares in both the playing company, the Chamberlain's, later the King's, Men, and in the theatres, the Globe and the Blackfriars, and in providing details of income and expenses.

VALUATION, INVESTMENT, AND OWNERSHIP

It is commonly said that Shakespeare's company owned the Globe, but that is inaccurate. There were two separate groups: the sharers and the housekeepers. Sharers were

---

[2] Andrew Gurr, *The Shakespearian Playing Companies* (Oxford: Oxford University Press,1996), 65; Roslyn Landers Knutson, *Playing Companies and Commerce in Shakespeare's Time* (Cambridge University Press, Cambridge, 2001), 36–7. Gurr suggests the duopoly began in 1594; Knutson suggests the relationship between the Admiral's Men and the King's Men was as cooperative as it was competitive.

[3] J. Leeds Barroll, *Politics and Plague in Shakespeare's Theatre: The Stuart Years* (Ithaca, NY: Cornell University Press, 1991).

[4] Ann Haaker, 'The Plague, the Theatre, and the Poet,' *Renaissance Drama* n.s. 1 (1968), 283–306, cited in Gurr, *Shakespearian Playing Companies*, 431.

stakeholders in the theatrical company. Most of them were actors and were jointly responsible for production expenses: the purchase of playtexts, costumes, lights, and hiring personnel. Housekeepers were part-owners of a theatre building or buildings—in Shakespeare's case, the Globe Theatre and later the Blackfriars. Housekeepers were responsible for land-rent, maintenance, and other expenses directly related to the upkeep of the building itself. Shakespeare's company was unusual in the number of sharers who were also housekeepers. Some playing companies had a member or two connected with someone who owned a theatre: Edward Alleyn, the lead actor of the Admiral's Men, was the son-in-law of Philip Henslowe, who owned the Rose and later the Fortune. After Alleyn retired from acting in 1603 and shifted his energies to being a theatrical entrepreneur, there was almost no overlap between playing company and theatre ownership until Alleyn sold the Fortune to some of the sharers in the Prince's Men in 1618, an arrangement that ended when the Fortune burned in 1621. In some cases, there was no overlap between the sharers in the company and the owners of the buildings at all. The income and expenses from both groups must therefore be calculated separately in order to gain a picture of Shakespeare's company as a business.

The sharers in the Chamberlain's and the King's Men were drawn from the principal actors. At some point, perhaps at the death or departure of a sharer, a member of the company would be given the opportunity to acquire a share in the company, and hence, he would be a 'sharer and adventurer'.

The number of sharers among the company varied: in the early years of Shakespeare's time with the company, the 1590s, it averaged between eight and ten. By 1610, there were thirteen; after Shakespeare's retirement and death, the number increased. By 1619, there were sixteen; and in 1624, at the time that *A Game At Chesse* was played, the number had risen as high as twenty-one.[5] The value of a share in the company also fluctuated. Most estimates of the value of shares in the company and in the theatres are taken from a series of lawsuits: *Ostler v. Heminges* (1615), *Witter v. Heminges and Condell* (1620), and the *Sharers' Papers* (1635).

The value of housekeeping shares in the theatre buildings is easier to estimate. The cost of building the first Globe in 1599 was £700. There were originally seven house-keepers in 1599: the Burbage brothers, Cuthbert and Richard, retained ownerships of half the Globe, worth £175 apiece. The remaining half was divided into five equal parts worth £70 each, bought by William Shakespeare, John Heminges, Augustine Phillips, Thomas Pope, and William Kempe. Kempe asked his fellow housekeepers to buy him out within a few days of signing the initial contract. An individual share in the Globe Theatre at initial offering was therefore worth £87.10s.[6]

The Blackfriars Theatre was initially an outright purchase by James Burbage for £600 1597 and meant to serve as a replacement for the Theatre when he lost the

---

[5] Gurr, *Shakespearian Playing Companies*, 388.

[6] Melissa D. Aaron, *Global Economics: A History of the Theater Business, the Chamberlain's/King's Men, and their plays* (Newark: Delaware University Press, 2005) 38, 51–2.

ground-lease. The residents of Blackfriars blocked any efforts by the Chamberlain's Men to use the theatre directly, so James's sons Richard and Cuthbert were forced to lease the theatre to Henry Evans, who ran the theatre as a venue for the Children of the Queen's Revels. The boys' company did not do well financially, and Evans made numerous attempts to terminate the lease. When the boys' company finally failed, partly driven out of business by King James, the Burbages agreed to terminate the lease and return the theatre to use for the adult company. In order to pay for necessary renovations, the Burbages drew up a new lease agreement. Several sharers of the King's Men—Heminges, Shakespeare, Condell, and William Sly—and Thomas Evans, possibly connected to Henry Evans, formed a syndicate who would be responsible for the £40 annual rent, maintenance, and renovation costs, and who would share in the profits.

THEATRE BUILDINGS, ADMISSIONS PRICES, AND PLAYING SEASONS

Income from the public audiences was clearly dependent upon theatre capacity, the price of admissions, and the number of days the company could perform. The two major types of theatre buildings during Shakespeare's time were the large outdoor playhouses, known as amphitheatres, and the indoor hall playhouses. As Andrew Gurr has pointed out, the King's Men were unusual in having access both to an indoor and an outdoor playhouse.

The best information about the cost, structure, and layout of the Globe Theatre is not from the Globe Theatre at all, but from the Fortune Theatre, built the year after the Globe by Henslowe for the use of the Admiral's Men, the chief rival to Shakespeare's company. Henslowe and Alleyn signed a building contract with Peter Street, who had also built the Globe. The records kept by Henslowe and Alleyn help calculate the precise cost of building the theatre: £440 to Street and £80 additional costs, including 'pd for the Removinge of the Donge wth the carte . . . xs[10s.]', which Alleyn estimated was a total of £520. The Fortune contract mentions the Globe no fewer than four times, and in every instance, it emphasizes that the Fortune is to be built in the same proportion and style as the Globe, except that the stage and the stage pillars are to be square.

The amphitheatres could hold substantial audiences. The second Globe, built in 1614, once held up to 3,000 people; 2,000 is a more reasonable estimate for the first Globe. The cost for admission and standing in the yard was one penny, so gross takings at the first Globe might be up to 2,000 people paying a minimum of a penny apiece. Thomas Platter, in his *Travels in England*, seems to suggest a series of incremental payments: 'Thus anyone who remains on the level standing pays only one English penny, but if he wants to sit, he is let in at a further door and there he gives another penny. If he desires to sit on a cushion in the most comfortable place of all, where he not only sees everything well but can also be seen, then he gives yet another English penny at another door.'[7] An audience member intending at first only to pay one penny could then be persuaded to spend more for a better spot, a stool, a cushion, and also refreshments.

The audience capacity at the Blackfriars was approximately 500, or an eighth that of the Globe. The minimum admission at the Blackfriars was sixpence, or six times the minimum price at the Globe Theatre, to sit in the highest part of the theatre; a seat at a bench in the pit was a shilling, so gross takings at the Blackfriars might be up to 500 audience members paying a minimum of sixpence up to a shilling, eighteen pence, or more. Unlike the Globe, audience members could also sit on stools on the stage, where their feathered hats, clouds of tobacco smoke, and audible commentary became part of the performance whether the players and the rest of the audience liked it or not. It is possible to make too much of the social distinctions between the Globe and Blackfriars audiences; wealthy and well-connected people did attend the Globe, at least during Shakespeare's time. However, it is impossible to deny that the higher admission costs constituted a barrier for the less affluent of the Globe audience, and while there are records of both Queen Anne and Queen Henrietta-Maria attending the Blackfriars, it is unlikely that any member of the royal family attended the Globe.

For some time, the King's Men ran the Globe and the Blackfriars seasonally. The Globe, with its outside exposure, larger capacity, and greater dependence on natural light, was well suited to summer audiences, whereas the Blackfriars was better suited to the winter, where the players and audience would be shielded from inclement weather and where the audience could afford to pay the difference in cost necessitated by fewer seats and more artificial lighting. Most theatre historians suggest that performances at both theatres began in the early- or mid-afternoon, when there was still some natural light.

Theatre historians have also estimated a varying number of performing days per year. Players were prohibited by an order of the Privy Council from playing on Sundays, during Lent, or on holy days on penalty of a fine, although players also flouted these rules on occasion. Eliminating Lent and Sundays leaves a maximum of 276 days on which the company might play; most scholars assume fewer than that, from 200 to 240 days per year.[8] The London theatres were sometimes closed by the authorities for plague or for other reasons. During some years, including the mid-1590s, there were no plague closures; in other unlucky years, the theatres were almost entirely closed. Leeds Barroll has documented the devastating effect of plague on the King's

---

[7] Cited in Aaron, 45 n. 61.

[8] 276 is a very, indeed an unrealistically, large number of playing days. I assume a 240-day playing season in *Global Economics*, 51, as does James W. Forse in *Art Imitates Business: Commercial and Political Influence in Elizabethan Theatre* (Bowling Green, OH: Bowling Green State University Press, 1993); Thomas W. Baldwin posits a 233-day playing season in *The Organization and Personnel of the Shakespearean Company* (Princeton, NJ: Princeton University Press, 1927). Forse, Baldwin, and I base those calculations from the records of the Admiral's Men and extrapolating them to the Chamberlain's Men. Gurr postulates a smaller 200-day playing season (*The Shakespeare Company*, 97).

Men during the early Stuart era, which increased the company's dependence on the King's gifts to them. The theatres were also closed for occasions of public mourning, or because of civil unrest, and occasionally these reasons might be compounded into extremely long closures. When Queen Elizabeth died in 1603, the public theatres were initially closed for public mourning, but a particularly virulent outbreak of plague extended the closure for many months. Between 1608 and 1610, the public theatres were closed for eighteen months, opened, and re-closed after the death of Henry, Prince of Wales in November of 1610. In 1625, in an echo of the events of 1603, the public theatres once again closed in order to memorialize the death of the monarch and remained closed because of a lengthy and virulent outbreak of plague, which among other things robbed the King's Men of John Fletcher, their poet-in-ordinary. The closing of the theatres in 1642 was ostensibly for reasons of civil unrest, though probably it was intended to be permanent. The estimated number of playing days per year must be taken as an average and not as a stable number.

INCOME

Sources of income included the gross intake from attendees at public performances, which was split between the sharers and the housekeepers according to an established formula; income from performances at court and royal gifts; performances at other venues, such as the Inns of Court; touring, and more speculative forms of income such as the profits realized by the sale of fruits, nuts, and tobacco in the public theatres.

The number of performances, was therefore a major variable in the sharers' and in the housekeepers' incomes. At the Globe, the playing company was entitled to all the receipts from the yard, and to half of the take from the galleries. The housekeepers were entitled to the remaining half from the galleries. Estimating company income for both the sharers and the housekeepers is extremely speculative during the 1590s and early 1600s; it depends largely upon reading Henslowe's diary entries and assuming they are analogous to finances at the Globe. Henslowe reports gallery receipts from the Rose at about £20 a week. James H. Forse and Thomas W. Baldwin have suggested that the gallery receipts amounted to two-thirds of the total take. If the gallery take was £20, and the yard take was £10, for a total of £30 a week, and one assumes a playing year of roughly forty weeks per year, the annual gross would have been £1,200: £800 for the playing company and £400 for the housekeepers. After 1603, plague closures and the 1607 addition of the Blackfriars makes estimating company income more complicated.

The sharers in the playing company had sources of income not connected with the theatres. The Chamberlain's and King's Men were sometimes to perform in front of private, non-royal audiences, such as the performance of *Twelfth Night* at Middle Temple Hall on February 2, 1602. The company were asked to perform plays at court during the Christmas and Shrovetide seasons at £10 per performance. During James's and Charles's reign, royal performances formed a larger amount of their work, as the number of court appearances increased: 12 in 1608-09, 13 in 1609-10, 15 in 1610-11, and 20 in 1612-13. The King's Men were also hired to appear in court masques, such as *The Masque of Oberon*, 1610-11.[9]

The King's Men also received direct gifts from their patron, the King, especially during difficult years in which the company could not perform owing to outbreaks of the plague. The first of these payments was made in 1603, during the long closure beginning with Queen Elizabeth's death. This payment of £100 amounted to the equivalent of an eighth of the gross the company would have earned at the Globe: such subsidies continued through the early Stuart era.

There are a variety of opinions on how large a place touring held in the Chamberlain's Men's overall income. During the 1590s, there are only 11 recorded instances of their having performed on the road, and one of those includes Kempe's famous Nine Day's Wonder, when he danced from London to Norwich. The Admiral's Men had much more extensive tours during this time. The number of performances on the road for Shakespeare's company goes up in the 1600s, when the closure of the London theatres made performing outside London more desirable and necessary. The REED volumes have added to the picture of touring as a source of income: much work has been done by Alan Somerset on this element of the company's business.[10] The picture is slightly complicated because there might be three or four companies calling themselves the King's Men in the countryside at any time. There are documented visits to the country: there are also, in the 1630s, numerous instances of the company being paid not to play, for fear of spreading the plague or for political reasons.[11]

The company owned the playbooks they had purchased, but there is no indication that they frequently profited from their publication. They had the right to insist that the plays not be printed without their permission, and they were able to block publication of Pavier's collection of their plays in 1619. Peter Blayney claims that the King's Men were paid a lump sum of £50 or less for the copies and printing rights of the First Folio of 1623, and that the publisher, Jaggard, had the rights to the profits.[12] If he is right, then the sale of playbooks cannot have been a frequent source of income.

Money from concessions is a much more speculative source of income. Once again, this is partially surmised from Henslowe's extant business records and the presence of an alehouse on the Rose's grounds. According to Paul Hentzner and Thomas Platter, contemporary playgoers, we know that apples, pears, nuts, bottle ale, and tobacco were

---

[9] Malone Society Collections (*MSC*) VI: *Declared Accounts of the Treasurer of the Chamber* (Malone Society, Oxford, 1962), 56–9.

[10] J.A.B. Somerset, '"How Chances It They Travel?": Provincial Touring, Playing Places, and the King's Men,' *Shakespeare Survey* 47 (1994), 45–60.

[11] Gurr, *Shakespearian Playing Companies*, 390–1.

[12] Peter W. M. Blayney, *The First Folio of Shakespeare* (Washington, DC: Folger Shakespeare Library, 1991), 2.

sold.[13] More recent excavations at the sites of the Rose and the Globe theatres have revealed the remains of shellfish in addition to a larger variety of nuts and dried fruits. What we do not know is how much each of these items cost or how much profit they represented. Gurr assumes for the sake of overall speculation a sum of £35 per annum during the 1590s and £40 per annum during the 1610s and 1620s, stating clearly that these numbers are 'purely hypothetical'.[14] Gurr also suggests that the profits from these sales went to the playing company, noting that Henslowe does not make entries based on food sales. However, the housekeepers were responsible for upkeep and maintenance on the theatres, which would include the damage and dirt caused by permitting eating and drinking, and the *Sharers' Papers* of 1635 estimated the housekeepers' income from the taphouses on the Globe property at 20 to £30 per annum, so it seems likely that this source of income belonged to the housekeepers and not to the sharers. Other than that, it is almost impossible to document other than to note that these were an additional source of income.

EXPENSES

The personnel of the Chamberlain's Men were made up of the sharers, hired men and women, and apprentices. The sharers generally took the most important roles and split the expenses and profits. Shakespeare's company was unusual in having among its sharers a resident playwright, or poet-in-ordinary, who was responsible for writing new plays and revising old ones.[15] After Shakespeare's retirement and death, the company continued this practice: the poets-in-ordinary following Shakespeare were John Fletcher, Phillip Massinger, and James Shirley. The hired men and women included players, a bookkeeper, men to do backstage chores such as placing large items of furniture onstage and firing cannon, tirewomen who costumed the cast, and people stationed at the various doors to collect admissions to the playhouse and to rent stools, cushions, and other amenities. Finally, there were the boy players. They were not apprenticed to the company, but to individual sharers, who trained them for future careers as players. Food, housing, clothing and education were the responsibility of the sharer to whom the boy was apprenticed, and the sharer was reimbursed for the boy's work for the company.

The sharers did not have to be compensated for acting. Playing companies always worked in repertory, so personnel were compensated by the week and not by the

---

[13] Paul Hentzner, 'A Journey into England. By Paul Hentzner, in the year 1598', trans. Horace Walpole, *Fugitive Pieces on Various Subjects by Several Authors*, vol. 2 (London: 1761), 267–70, cited in Aaron, *Global Economics*, 49 n. 64.

[14] Gurr, *The Shakespeare Company*, 106, 117.

[15] Gurr, *The Shakespeare Company*, 149–53.

performance. Hired men might receive between five and ten shillings a week; fines would be levied for missing rehearsals or performances or for losing parts or costumes.[16] Masters of boy apprentices might be paid three shillings per week, as Henslowe was in 1597: there are other contracts in Henslowe's *Diary* that suggest slightly larger payments.[17] Assuming ten hired men and four boys, the costs for wages might be between 72 and 112 shillings per week.

Musicians were probably hired separately. Many sharers or hired men had the ability to play musical instruments, as well as dance and fence. There would be no need to hire musicians for court performances or to take musicians on tour, as royal and noble households had musicians of their own. Musicians would only be hired for performances at the Globe or at the Blackfriars, and since songs were usually sung to already-popular melodies, there would be no need for musicians to rehearse with the company. They might have been hired on a per-performance basis, and therefore it would be extremely difficult to establish how much the company spent on musicians per year or what percentage of their expenses it represented.

Costumes were also a large expense for the company. There was no such thing as a production with a suite of purpose-built costumes in the professional theatre during Shakespeare's lifetime; such things were common in the court masque, but not on the public stage. The first purpose-built suite of costumes was probably for the 1624 play *A Game At Chesse*, under an unusual set of circumstances: a play that was expected to make a great deal of money in a short period of time, necessitating a larger than usual cast, special purchases, and probably special costumes.

Costumes could be acquired second-hand. Platter stated that servants sold garments given them by their masters and mistresses to the playing companies, as sumptuary laws forbade them to wear such clothing themselves.[18] Henslowe was, among other things, a pawnbroker, and acquired unredeemed clothing, which he then sold to the Admiral's Men. Some costumes may also have been direct gifts; for example, it has long been speculated that the bear costumes from the 1610 *Masque of Oberon* were given to the King's Men and reappeared in a new production of *Mucedorus* and in *The Winter's Tale*. In the Caroline era, well after Shakespeare's death, the King's Men received extravagant gifts of complete sets of costumes. Queen Henrietta Maria gave the costumes from her own 1632 production of *The Shepherd's Paradise* to the King's Men, who used them for Fletcher's *The Faithful Shepherdess.* John Suckling donated the costumes from his court production of *Aglaura* in 1638, including clothing with real gold lace. Stage costumes

---

[16] Chambers, *The Elizabethan Stage* vol. 2. (Oxford: Clarendon Press, 1923), 255–7. Missing a performance incurred a fine of 20s. Removing a costume or wearing it out of the playhouse incurred a fine of £40.

[17] Chambers, vol. 1, 370–1. There are several records of these apprenticeship documents recorded in Henslowe's *Diary*.

[18] Thomas Platter, *Thomas Platter's Travels in England 1599*, trans. Clare Williams (London: Jonathan Capre, 1937), 167.

usually used copper lace, which was considerably cheaper, and it was rightly noted that this gift, worth £300 or £400, was 'an unheard-of extravagance'.[19]

Because there is only one inventory of a company's clothing, Edward Alleyn's, theatre historians can only estimate which costumes the company would have owned in common. Adult professional actors owned their own kit, which might include musical instruments, weapons, and costumes. Alleyn's inventory includes unique specialist items no actor would be expected to own, such as 'i hary the viii gowne', 'a cardinals gowne', 'angels silk', and costumes for specific characters: 'Faustus Jerkin his clok', and 'a cloth of silver for pan'. Also prominent in the inventory are items for the apprentices to wear, for example 'wemens gowns', 'a colored bugell for a boye', 'red velvet for a boye', and 'red payns for a boye w^t yelo scalins'. It would have made more sense for the company to acquire women's and boys' clothing and continue to use them as apprentices grew too old for those roles. Even with re-use and acquisition at second-hand, costuming was a major expense, as the heavy £40 fine levied on a hired man who removed a costume from the theatre indicates.

Play-scripts were also a very large expenditure for a theatre company. Here we have very few records of purchasing plays for Shakespeare's company, but we do have records for the Admiral's/Prince's Men. Because Shakespeare's company had a poet-in-ordinary among their sharers, they would have saved the expense of paying for at least one or two plays a year. Henslowe's *Diary* shows payments for plays at £6 apiece; later, the cost went up to £10. It used to be estimated that the company bought only six new plays a year; Roslyn Knutson has estimated twenty per year, a much higher number, and more likely to be correct.[20] Even subtracting Shakespeare's two plays a year and assuming a lower £6 per play payment, over £100 per year would have been spent on acquiring new plays.

Gurr has argued that the King's Men changed its purchase of new plays as time went on. Continuing to retain a poet-in-ordinary and the acquisition of a large repertory of plays, many of which were revived in later years, may have reduced the total expenditure on play-scripts. It is also important to emphasize that once the purchase had been made, the play was not the property of the poet, but of the company, and the company could then do with it as they pleased.

The company also had to purchase properties, such as beds, tombs, a bar for court scenes, and hand props. Here again, Henslowe's inventory is helpful, as it lists crowns, a bear's head, a lion's skin, 'j gowlden flece', and some more unusual items. Some of the props are clearly from recognizable plays, including 'Tamberlyne brydell', 'i dragon in fostes', 'i cauderm for the Jewe'. Since there is no equivalent list for the King's Men, evidence must come from indications in the text. It is obvious, for example, that they possessed a skull, and possibly an entire skeleton for the 'bony lady' in *The Revenger's Tragedy*, but

[19] The Rev. Mr. Garrard, *The Earl of Strafford's Letters and Dispatches*, William Knowles (ed.), 2 vols. (London: 1739), 2: 150; cited in Aaron, 193.

[20] Knutson, *The Repertory of Shakespeare's Company, 1594–1613* (Fayetteville: University of Arkansas Press, 1991), 32.

whether it was real or not and where they acquired it is a mystery. Internal evidence also suggests that there were many props they re-used. Some of the props would have been standard: the large props, such as the bar, the bed, and the state; and the hand props, such as cups, crowns, and mirrors.[21]

The company was also required to pay for lighting. R. B. Graves has listed various lighting methods, including natural light, simple lamps made of fat with a rag in it, candles of tallow or wax, torches, and tapers. The picture is complicated, because Elizabethan and Jacobean theatre workers used the terms for different lights indiscriminately: torches were called tapers, candles were torches, and any and all of them were simply 'light'. Graves indicates that tallow candles were four pence per pound in 1600, with six or eight candles in a pound. Wax candles were four or five times more expensive than tallow candles. They were commonly reserved for liturgical use, and it is unlikely that they were used for professional performances during Shakespeare's lifetime. The Globe could make use of natural light, but so could the Blackfriars, as it had large casement windows. Lighting expenses went up considerably during the period, and represented a larger percentage of company expenses in the 1630s. The expense was borne entirely by the playing company at the Blackfriars, which was one of the complaints in the 1635 *Sharers' Papers*. At Salisbury Court in 1639, the housekeepers bore half the cost: two to four dozen candles per performance for an estimated 10s. per day.[22]

By contrast the housekeepers' expenses were relatively simple. They were responsible for repair and maintenance to the buildings, for ground rent, and for licensing the theatre. Repairs and maintenance fluctuated over time. Building the Globe itself was a one-time expense of £700, including payments to Peter Street, the builder, and materials. When the Globe burned down in 1614, the housekeepers paid to rebuild it with a new fireproof tile roof, at a cost of £1,400. Renovating the Blackfriars Theatre in 1608 for the purposes of company use was also quite expensive. What repairs and maintenance would have cost in a less expensive year is more speculative. Ground rent for the Globe paid to Nicholas Brend was £14.10s. in 1599–1600. Licensing fees paid to the Revels Office were £3 a month in 1599–1600, dramatically up from three shillings a month in 1591–2.

Expenses for the housekeepers remained fairly stable, except for renovation, restoration, or even, in one case, rebuilding. The basic expenses such as maintenance and rent were more or less the same. The annual lease for the Blackfriars, for example, only went up £10 over the course of twenty years. The expenses for the sharers increased dramatically over time. The shift to the Blackfriars necessitated a higher expenditure on candles, and the more elitist audience there grew to expect production values closer to those they saw at court. Sometimes they were literally what they had seen at court, as when courtly costumes migrated to the public stage, but keeping the production values consistent was costly. Expense for costumes, lighting and other

---

[21] Henslowe, *Diary*, 319–21.

[22] R. B. Graves, *Lighting the Shakespearean Stage, 1567–1642* (Carbondale: Southern Illinois University Press, 1999) 23, 17–18, 129–30.

visual elements became larger budget items: the *Sharers' Papers* set the total annual expenses at £900 per year. .

LAWSUITS

Lawsuits are possibly the most useful index the theatre historian has to the change of the company's business practices over time. The most important in relation to the Chamberlain's/King's Men are *Allen v. Burbage* (1597), *Keysar v. Burbage* (1610), *Ostler v. Heminges* (1615), *Witter v. Heminges and Condell* (1620), and the *Sharers' Papers* of 1635. Although several of them were filed after Shakespeare's departure from the company, many provide information from previous years that are helpful in understanding company structure during the late 1590s and early 1600s.

Allen v. Burbage reflects the challenges presented to the Chamberlain's Men when the theatre they had been playing in lost its ground lease. Giles Allen owned the land on which the theatre stood and sued the Burbages for removing the timbers from the theatre and using them to build the Globe on the South Bank; he also demanded 40 shillings for trampling the grass.

Keysar v. Burbage concerns the renovation of the Blackfriars Theatre and the formation of the Blackfriars Syndicate: Heminges, Condell, Sly, Shakespeare, and Thomas Evans, who bought shares in the theatre. Robert Keysar had taken over the management of the Children of the Queen's Revels, the children's company who had played in the theatre, from Henry Evans. Claiming that he had bought a share from John Marston for £100, and that he had been responsible for the expenses of training the children's company in the interim, he sued the syndicate for a one-sixth share in the theatre or its monetary equivalent. The syndicate pointed out the difference between owning shares in the Children of the Revels and the theatre itself; noted that Keysar's estimation of £1,500 profit was grossly inflated; and demanded that the suit be thrown out. Keysar suggested in his response that the Blackfriars syndicate had paid all the private playhouses in London to remain closed for one full year with the sole intent of ruining him financially, an excessive claim which would have required the company to have been responsible for the plague as well. Whether it was because of Keysar's blatant overreaching or for some other reason, the suit was apparently settled out of court.

Both *Ostler v. Heminges* and *Witter v. Heminges and Condell* provide lists of the housekeepers over time and provide estimates of the value of shares. Thomasina Ostler sued her father John Heminges for a share in the Globe, and John Witter sued John Heminges and Henry Condell for the share in the theatre he claimed to have acquired through marrying Augustine Phillips's widow, Anne. *Ostler v. Heminges* sets the value of a fourteenth share of the Globe at £20 and a seventh share of the Blackfriars at £20, which would have made the annual value of the Globe £280 and of the Blackfriars £140. *Witter v. Heminges and Condell* sets the value of a share of the Globe at £30 or more, placing the annual value between £420 and £560. *Witter v. Heminges and Condell* explains the system of sharing, but it also demonstrates the difficulties of using lawsuits as a guideline for share values. Witter was an unreliable witness, omitting the fact that he had mortgaged the share, abandoned Anne, and left her for John Heminges to bury, which calls his estimate of £30 or more per share into question. These lawsuits also document the difficulty posed by the alienation of shares in the theatre through marriage and inheritance: almost all the shares in the theatres had originally been owned by sharers in the playing company, but as time went on, this ceased to be the case.

The *Sharers' Papers,* not properly a lawsuit but an appeal to the Court, further demonstrates this difficulty, as the shares in the Globe and in the Blackfriars were increasingly not owned by sharers in the King's Men, but by the heirs of the house-keepers. In 1635, three members of the King's Men—Robert Benefield, Heliard Swanston, and Thomas Pollard—complained to the Lord Chamberlain's office that they had ex-pected, as senior members of the playing company, to have been given the opportunity to purchase shares in the Globe and the Blackfriars. They maintained that the expenses of the sharers had increased dramatically over time, while the expenses for the housekeepers had not; the sharers had expenses between £900 and £1,000 a year or £3 a day, not counting costumes and scripts, while the Housekeepers' rent was a mere £65 per year. The acting company was earning only a quarter of the profits, while in their view doing all the work. They also pointed out that with the exception of two members of the company, John Lowin and Joseph Taylor, and the older player John Shanks, all of the shares were now owned by people who were not actors or the king's servants, and demanded that some of these shares be sold to them.

The Burbages countered that they had inherited the theatres, or shares in the theatres, from their family; John Shanks added that if the Lord Chamberlain's office admitted Swanston, Pollard, and Benefield's suit, there would never be an end to the financial wrangling and chaos. In the event, Shanks was proved right: between increased production costs, a narrowing audience, and difficulties with internal orga-nization, the King's Men lacked the financial strength to withstand the external pressures brought to bear in the 1640s.

Ultimately, studying the business practices of the Chamberlain's and the King's Men and the syndicates that owned the Globe and the Blackfriars provides a valuable light on the conditions which helped produce Shakespeare's plays and the milieu in which they were first performed.

CHAPTER 24

....

FOREIGN WORLDS

....

JANE HWANG DEGENHARDT

As Shakespeare was writing plays for the English stage, England was advancing its position on the world stage through overseas exploration and commerce. In 1580, Sir Francis Drake became the first Englishman to circumnavigate the globe successfully. His triumphant return helped galvanize support for later exploratory and commercial ventures, and made him a national legendary figure—but also a controversial one—for years to come. Earlier examples of successful commercial and colonial ventures led by the Spanish and the Portuguese incentivized the English to follow suit. Although the English still played only a small role in the arena of international maritime trade, they began in the late sixteenth century to penetrate the rich markets of the eastern Mediterranean and to undertake exploratory ventures in the Far East and the Americas. Newly obtained knowledge of these foreign worlds informed and transformed a wide range of English cultural media, including travel narratives, cartographical materials such as globes and maps, and popular stage plays performed in the public theatres.

This chapter will consider some of the ways that Shakespeare's plays registered England's growing awareness of the foreign worlds beyond its borders by incorporating topical references and by projecting in less direct ways English fantasies and apprehensions about cross-cultural commerce, travel, and exploration. In particular, it will consider the significance of the Mediterranean world, which was a place of central importance to Shakespeare both because of its rich classical legacies and its contemporary hubs of East–West commerce, newly accessed by the English. After offering an overview of English trade in the Mediterranean and forays into other geographical regions, I examine some of the ways that Shakespeare's settings evoke foreign worlds—both old and new—through richly layered temporal resonances. A brief case study of *Twelfth Night* demonstrates how contemporary geopolitical resonances might offer deeper insight into Shakespeare's foreign settings and their animation of temporal, geographical, and imperial border zones. In addition, this chapter considers the process by which the distances and displacements associated with travel to faraway places were translated onto the stage—from the globe to the Globe, as it were. It demonstrates how the task of representing foreign worlds stretched the limitations of the stage and reshaped theatrical conventions, ultimately introducing audiences to new pleasures in observing the imperfect contrivances of dramatic enactment and the heightened stakes of reconciliation and homecoming as sources of generic resolution.

English Commerce and Exploration

During the time Shakespeare's plays were first being written and performed, England's overseas ventures were most profitably directed at the southeastern Mediterranean, including the Levant and the northern coast of Africa. Primarily controlled by the Ottoman Empire, direct trade in these areas was largely inaccessible to the English until the early 1570s, due to the impossibility of competing with the Venetians, who had negotiated exclusive trading rights with the Ottomans. Venice's defeat by the Turks in Cyprus in 1571, combined with Antwerp's collapse as the major northern entrepot, created a rare opportunity for England to break into the Mediterranean trade. The Anglo-Spanish War as well as the weakening holds of Spain and Portugal within the eastern territories also helped bolster England's presence in the Mediterranean. Queen Elizabeth actively pursued diplomatic relations with the Ottoman Empire and Morocco, and she appointed English consuls in Cairo, Alexandria, Aleppo, Damascus, Algiers, Tunis, and Tripoli. By establishing direct trading relations in these regions, the English did away with their former reliance on intermediaries for obtaining a wide range of luxury goods, including silks, carpets, cloths, oils, wines, currants, pepper, cloves, nutmegs, cinnamon, ginger, sugar, indigo, and other spices. The growth of luxury consumption across Europe drove the profitability of these particular commodities and created lucrative markets for their re-export within Europe.

England's commerce in the Mediterranean contributed to a major shift in its commercial orientation away from a reliance on cloth exports and toward a reliance on the importation of raw goods for domestic manufacturing, broad home consumption, and re-export to Europe and eventually the New World.[1] The second half of the sixteenth century and the opening decades of the seventeenth century saw the founding of the great joint-stock companies, the Muscovy Company in 1555, the Levant Company in 1592, the East India Company in 1599, and the Virginia Company in 1609. By far, England's trade in the Levant represented the most profitable branch of its overseas commerce during the period between 1580 and 1620. In particular, the merging of the

[1] For a history of this commercial shift and the rise of the joint stock companies, see Robert Brenner, *Merchants and Revolution: Commercial Change, Political Conflict, and London's Overseas Traders, 1550–1653* (Princeton, NJ: Princeton University Press, 1993). For a discussion of the East India Company's reorientation of trade around imports and re-exports, in place of English exports, see K. N. Chaudhuri, *The English East India Company: The Study of an Early Joint-Stock Company, 1600–1640* (New York: August Kelley, 1965).

Venice and Turkey companies into the Levant Company strengthened the English Levant trade by forging a monopoly that dissolved competition between the two companies. With its commercial advances in the eastern Mediterranean, England exchanged its passive role within Europe's trading system for an active role in the global system.

England's new role in Mediterranean trade brought with it a new set of cross-cultural encounters that helped reorient its view of itself in relation to the rest of the world. In particular, the English became aware of the far larger, wealthier, and more powerful Ottoman Empire, which controlled the majority of trade taking place in the Levant and along the Barbary Coast of Africa through tributary relationships. News reports and prayers offered at church repeatedly reminded the English of the Ottoman Empire's imperial ambitions and its increasing incursions on European territories. Contemporary territorial threats added to a long history of Christian–Muslim warfare, including the Crusades as well as more recent sixteenth-century struggles over the Mediterranean islands of Rhodes, Malta, Crete, Sicily, and Cyprus. By the early seventeenth century, a text such as *The estates, empires, & principallities of the world* ominously reported that the Ottoman Empire's imperial dominion extended 3,000 miles 'from Buda to Constantinople', as well as across the northern coast of Africa from Alexandria to the border of Morocco.[2] In taking up the rhetoric of the Crusades, many early modern writers interpreted Ottoman imperialism as a religious threat to all of Europe, lamenting the loss of a united Christendom because of the fracturing effects of the Reformation. Nevertheless, the perceived benefits of trade prompted the English to seek diplomatic relations with the Ottoman Empire and to devote substantial resources toward commerce in the Mediterranean. The desires and anxieties attendant upon Mediterranean trade helped set the scene for a proliferation of Muslim characters on the English stage as well as the production of numerous plays featuring intercultural conflicts between Christians and Turks in Mediterranean settings.

During this period English overseas aspirations were not solely directed at the Mediterranean world. The English pursued a number of ventures in the Americas, hoping to follow in Spain's footsteps. Richard Eden's 1555 translation of Peter Martyr d'Anghera's *Decades of the Newe Worlde* encouraged the English to support and emulate the Spanish in their colonial conquests of America. While Eden's text appeared under the reign of Queen Mary and was influenced by an Anglo-Spanish alliance created by the Queen's marriage to Philip II, in subsequent years the English viewed their colonial obligations in the New World as a means of containing Spain's dominance there and defending the Protestant Reformation abroad. Queen Elizabeth took up this charge during her reign and authorized royal patents for half-brothers Humphrey Gilbert and Walter Ralegh's voyages to the New World in the late 1570s and 1580s. Ralegh's attempt to set up an English colony in Virginia was later publicized by Thomas Harriot, who reported on his experience as part of Ralegh's expedition. First

---

[2] Pierre d'Avity, *The estates, empires, & principalities of the world*, trans. E. Grimstone (London: 1615), 936.

published as a small pamphlet in 1588 and expanded in 1590 with detailed engravings that compared the native Americans to the ancient Scottish Picts, Harriot's report encouraged future colonial ventures by emphasizing America's abundance of natural resources and assuaging anxieties about hostility among the natives.[3]

Other early modern reports of English ventures in the New World played up the advantages of colonialism, but they also reflected its difficulties and in some cases drew suspicions. As Mary Fuller has argued, Raleigh's voyage to Guiana in 1596 produced a text (*Discoverie of Guiana*) with an agenda similar to Harriot's, promising gold mines more lucrative than Peru's. Later called upon to authenticate this account, Ralegh received permission to undertake a second voyage to Guiana in 1618, but he succeeded only in attacking the Spanish-occupied town of San Thome and did not find the lucrative gold mine of El Dorado. After a long history of treason charges and conflicts with the Crown, he was ultimately executed by King James after his return to England. While Raleigh's efforts in the New World were largely unsuccessful, they helped pave the way for later English explorers such as John Smith, who established the first permanent English settlement at Jamestown in 1607. Smith's writings sought to incentivize other English settlements in the New World with optimistic accounts such as the story of his rescue by Pocahontas, but they also detail his first-hand experiences with captivity, mutiny, conflicts with native Americans, and numerous hardships. In general, colonial prospects in the New World generated some impassioned publicity in England but went largely unrealized until the later seventeenth century—a fact that has been distorted by tendencies to magnify claims of English empire and transatlantic expansionism in the early modern period. English explorers had tremendous difficulty attaining sufficient public or private support to effectively pursue settlements in the New World. While America looms large in modern accounts of English empire, during Shakespeare's time it was viewed as a risky investment for overseas ventures and an inconvenient obstacle to the more desirable wealth of Cathay and the Far East. Indeed, many of the voyages to America were funded with the intention of discovering a passage to the East.[4]

Attempts to discover a northwest passage to the Far East also inadvertently facilitated the opening of English trade with Muscovy and Persia in the 1550s. Seeking a route to the spices and gold of the Far East that was free from Portuguese interference, the Muscovy Company helped establish direct trade with Russia, which centred on the import of naval supplies and furs. Soon after, the Company founded a direct overland trade with Persia via Russia, and sent six voyages to Persia between 1557 and 1570. When the Turks cut off the overland route from Russia to Persia in 1570, the English pursued an alternate route via the Mediterranean Sea, eventually leading to the founding of the Turkey Company in 1580–1, a development characterized by historian Robert Brenner

---

[3] *A Brief and True Report of the Newfoundland of Virginia* (London: 1588, 1590).

[4] Consider for example the title of Humphrey Gilbert's report of his voyage to America: *Discourse of a discoverie for a new passage to Cataia* (London: 1576).

as 'the decisive step in the Elizabethan expansion'.[5] Travels and exploration in Russia and Persia were publicized to English readers through accounts such as Giles Fletcher's *Of the Russe Common Wealth* (1591) and pamphlets detailing the travels of Robert Shirley.

Despite the high desirability of its trade, the Far East and, in particular, the Moluccas Spice Islands of the Indonesian archipelago, remained largely out of reach to the English during the late sixteenth and early seventeenth centuries.[6] Under licence from the Muscovy Company, Martin Frobisher led three ventures to establish a northeast trade route to the Indies between 1576 and 1578, but these expeditions repeatedly landed in Canada. Drake reached the Moluccas during his circumnavigation of the globe in 1579, and sent members of his crew ashore on the island of Ternate, where they spoke with the sultan about taking over the clove trade from Portuguese control. Held back by mutual suspicions and a lack of formal authorization from the Queen, Drake's men did not finalize an agreement, though Drake's success in finding the Spice Islands inspired others in England to continue to pursue trade there. Subsequent attempts to break into the Indonesian spice trade were thwarted, however, by difficulties in securing funding for expeditions and aggressive competition from the Dutch, who had discovered the best route to the Far East by sailing around the Cape of Good Hope. In India, which was often conflated with the Moluccas by early modern writers, English advances were quite limited during the time Shakespeare was writing. In 1607, directors of the East India Company made contact with the Gujarati port of Surat, and in 1615 they dispatched a ship directly from Surat to England, but it took many years for the English to establish firm commercial footholds in Surat and Agra. This slow progress may help to put into context the seemingly casual reference to an Indian boy in *A Midsummer Night's Dream*. While Oberon and Titania's conflict over the boy seems to imply their sense of entitlement to this prized commodity, in actuality, direct access to Indian commodities proved as elusive to the English in 1596 as the boy himself, whose body never appears on the stage.[7] Similarly, English participation in the emerging sub-Saharan African and West Indian slave trades remained quite limited during the early modern period. John Hawkins led several English slaving voyages in 1560s to the Guinea coast and the Spanish West Indies, but these efforts were effectively abandoned by the 1570s and did not resume until after 1650.

---

[5] Brenner, *Merchants and Revolution*, 16.

[6] On the Moluccas, see Robert Markley, *The Far East in the English Imagination* (Cambridge: Cambridge University Press, 2009), ch. 1; Jerry Brotton, *Trading Territories: Mapping the Early Modern World* (London: Reaktion Books, 1997), ch. 4; and Kenneth Andrews, *Trade, Plunder and Settlement: Maritime Enterprise and the Genesis of the British Empire 1480–1630* (Cambridge: Cambridge University Press, 1984), 265–70.

[7] For influential discussions of the play's reference to the Indian boy, see Ania Loomba, 'The Great Indian Vanishing Trick—Colonialism, Property, and the Family in *A Midsummer Night's Dream*', in Dympna Callaghan (ed.), *A Feminist Companion to Shakespeare* (Malden, MA: Blackwell, 2000), 163–87; and Shankar Raman's psychoanalytic reading of the Indian boy in *Framing India* (Stanford, CA: Stanford University Press, 2001), ch. 6.

FANTASIES, REALITIES, AND RISKS

As this cursory sketch of England's overseas activities during Shakespeare's time suggests, English ventures into foreign worlds were generally characterized by struggle and disappointment rather than confidence and mastery. Although John Dee, a mathematician and adviser to Queen Elizabeth, coined the term 'British Empire' in 1576, the state of British imperialism at the time was extremely tentative and undeveloped. Occupying a peripheral position on the rim of northern Europe, England entered late upon the imperial scene and had been largely eclipsed by the Spanish, Portuguese, and Dutch. This is not to say that the English did not imagine themselves as future colonizers or produce a substantial volume of writings expressing the fantasy of imperial conquest. Colonial struggles closer to home to contain the Welsh, Scots, and Irish within an emerging British nation initiated a process that the English hoped to extend farther afield. A play such as *Henry V* illustrates the difficulties of subsuming England's internal colonies under one body politic through its depiction of highly distinct Welsh, Irish, and Scottish subjects. The desire for empire was richly articulated across a wide range of cultural media, including popular drama, but the reality was that England could not compete with other European countries, much less with the immense and powerful Ottoman, Persian, and Mogul empires outside of Europe. As critics such as Jerry Brotton have now amply demonstrated, the East was perceived to be dominant over the West during Shakespeare's time, and even the notion that the European Renaissance originated exclusively in Italy is largely misleading.[8] Rather, the Renaissance period was characterized by East–West exchange and collaboration, producing a wealth of artwork, technological inventions, and writings that integrated influences from Africa, the Levant, and the Far East. Within this cross-cultural Renaissance, England assumed a belated and struggling role.

If England entered the world stage during Shakespeare's time, it did so by virtue of its growing participation in the Mediterranean trade, rather than its colonial efforts or its imperial prowess. In the words of historian Kenneth Andrews, the English 'put colonization well below trade and plunder in their priorities. Their primary objective from about 1580 down to 1630 was oriental trade.'[9] But England's shifting reliance on eastern commerce was associated with both substantial risk and controversy. For one, the dangers of travel in the Mediterranean were significant. The limitations of maritime technology rendered journeys long and arduous, and the chances of getting thrown off course or shipwrecked were high. Seamen often experienced disease, hunger, conflict over victuals, and mutiny. In addition, piracy and plunder—particularly along the Barbary Coast of Africa—proved to be constant threats. English seamen were vulnerable not only to Muslim corsairs, who threatened enslavement and forced conversion to Islam, but to

[8] Jerry Brotton, *The Renaissance Bazaar: From the Silk Road to Michelangelo* (Oxford: Oxford University Press, 2002).

[9] Andrews, *Trade, Plunder and Settlement*, 356.

attacks by Spanish, Italian, and other Christian ships. In many cases piracy afforded a more profitable profession than legitimate trade, and numerous Englishmen took up its practice and reaped its benefits. The adventures of life on the seas and the moral vicissitudes of Christian renegades informed a popular genre of stage plays that fictionalized the exploits of real-life adventurers such as Thomas Stukeley, John Ward, Francis Drake, and the Shirley brothers. While none of Shakespeare's plays fits squarely into the genre, several plays such as *Othello* and *The Tempest* contain recognizable elements of the adventure drama, or else feature the odd sea captain (consider the pirate's head in *Measure for Measure*, the sea captain in *Twelfth Night*, and the merchant who is delayed from his voyage to Persia in *The Comedy of Errors*) or threatening Mediterranean port (consider Mytilene in *Pericles*).

In addition to the physical dangers of conducting maritime trade in the Levant and along the Barbary Coast, risks associated with economic investment in foreign imports created controversy about global trade. Some worried that the investment of English bullion in global trade would compromise England's pressing need to defend its own borders. Others worried about the potential moral hazards of cross-cultural trade for both the individual seafarer and the English nation as a whole. William Harrison's *Description of England*, which was incorporated into Raphael Holinshed's *Chronicles* (1577, 1587), expresses suspicions about the effects of foreign trade on the English character. Many others worried that English expenditures overseas would not be sufficiently recouped in the form of viable profits. *The Merchant of Venice* dramatizes this anxious possibility through its repeated references to Antonio's foreign ventures, which tie his 'means' up 'in supposition': 'he hath an argosy bound for Tripolis, another to the Indies, . . . a third at Mexico, a fourth for England, and other ventures he hath squandered abroad' (1.3.16, 17–20).[10] Although Antonio claims that his exposure is minimized because his 'ventures are not in one bottom trusted | Nor to one place', the dispersal of his capital so diffusely around the world requires him to relinquish his control over it (1.1.42–3). Over the course of the play, news of Antonio's losses at sea continues to pour into the Rialto, and the stakes of such losses are weighed in the threat to Antonio's very flesh, which he has waged against these overseas investments. We do not get to see Antonio's ships at sea or their far-flung destinations, but we do see the potential effects of their loss played out in Venice and in the human drama that unfolds between friends and enemies at home. As Valerie Forman has recently shown, the English stage responded to England's new economic practices by producing a genre of plays that transformed losses into gains by following a tragicomic arc.[11] Although for Forman, *The Merchant of Venice* does not adhere entirely to this generic model, it does assuage anxieties about overseas investments by showing that Antonio's economic

---

[10] All line references to Shakespeare's plays correspond to John Jowett, William Montgomery, Gary Taylor, and Stanley Wells (eds.), *The Oxford Shakespeare Complete Works* (Oxford: Oxford University Press, 2005).

[11] Valerie Forman, *Tragicomic Redemptions: Global Economics and the Early Modern English Stage* (Philadelphia: University of Pennsylvania Press, 2008).

fortunes ultimately fall under the protection of Christian providence. He not only profits from his bond with Shylock, he learns in the final act of the play that 'three of [his] argosies | Are richly come into harbour suddenly' (5.1.276–7). This 'sudden' reversal of fortune, which allows Antonio to 'read for certain that [his] ships | Are safely come to road', amounts to a kind of miracle, reflecting the grave uncertainties and suspicions associated with overseas trade (5.1.287–8).

Another concern related to foreign trade had to do with its effects on London as a rising world city and temporary home to a growing number of immigrants. London's transformation during this period was fostered by its spectacular demographic and economic growth. Its population tripled between the years 1520 and 1600, with thousands of people migrating yearly to London from other parts of the country. By 1600, London was the third largest city in Europe, surpassed only by Naples and Paris. The expansion of English mercantile activity, primarily in the Mediterranean, contributed significantly to London's rise as a world city and to its emerging cosmopolitanism.[12] In 1568, Thomas Gresham built the Royal Exchange, modelled on the great trading bourses on the Continent, to serve as a gathering place for international merchants. The Royal Exchange figured prominently in city comedies such as William Haughton's *Englishman for My Money* (1598) and Thomas Heywood's *If you Know Not Me You Know Nobody, Part II* (1606). Jean Howard argues that it came to symbolize 'London's pride in its growing role as an international entrepot' as well as its 'anxiety about the traffic with strangers that such a role mandates'.[13] Due to its shifting commercial status, London attracted increasing numbers of foreign visitors, including traders and diplomats who populated the Royal Exchange, official places of business, and the London theatres as well.

Scapegoats for the problems relating to overcrowding, grain shortages, and poverty included not only the labourers who had migrated to London from other parts of Britain and Europe, but also London's growing community of alien merchants. As Ania Loomba has observed, 'England displayed an increasing hostility to, and anxiety about, the presence of outsiders within its borders, even as it sought to expand its own frontiers'.[14] In turn, movements emerged that sought to circumscribe the legal and economic rights of outsiders. In 1596 and again in 1601, Queen Elizabeth issued open letters to the Lord Mayor of London commanding the expulsion of 'blackmoores' from the land. Given the 'divers blackmoores brought into this realme, of which kind of people there are already here to manie' and the recent increase to the English population, Elizabeth expressed concern for the 'people of our own nation' who for lack of work 'fall to idlenesse and to great extremytie'.[15] Reaction against the influx of foreigners in London thus resulted in a form of colour-based discrimination. According to

---

[12] Crystal Bartolovich, '"Baseless Fabric": London as a "World City"', in Peter Hulme and William H. Sherman (ed.), *The Tempest and Its Travels* (London: Reaktion Books, 2000), 13–26.

[13] Jean Howard, *Theater of a City: The Places of London Comedy, 1598–1642* (Philadelphia: University of Pennsylvania Press, 2007).

[14] Loomba, 'The Great Indian Vanishing Trick', 155.

[15] *Acts of the Privy Council of England*, ns 26 (1596–7), John Roche Dasent (ed.) (London: Mackie & Co., 1902), 16–17, 20–1.

Emily Bartels, Queen Elizabeth's move to deport London's Moors to Spain and Portugal also served a specific practical purpose in offering the Moors in exchange for the redemption of English captives from Spain.[16] Apparently, during his final voyage of 1595–6, Drake attacked the Spanish-occupied West Indian town of Rio de la Hacha and captured a number of Moors—an occurrence referred to in Elizabeth's 1596 letter. While ostensibly aimed at redressing the displacement of English subjects from jobs taken by Moorish immigrants, Elizabeth's deportation orders were informed by Anglo-Spanish hostilities being played out in foreign commercial and colonial spaces. Thus, Elizabeth's move to rid London of these outsiders responded to the effects of global commerce in more ways than one.

TRAVEL WRITING AND THE ENGLISH TRAVELLER

England's new role in global trade had a direct impact on cultural life, the evidence of which survives in a diverse range of texts from the period. Global trade affected not only the materials and experiences of everyday life, but also the cultural fantasies of the English and their shifting view of the world around them. As I have been implicitly suggesting, popular media such as the plays performed on the public stage assumed a vital role in making sense of this new world and reconciling England's place within it. Another popular medium that flourished due to England's growing interest in cross-cultural commerce and exploration was travel writing. Within a relatively short period of time, English publishers produced a diverse array of travel books written by a wide range of travellers—some leading state-authorized ventures, others travelling for leisure, others working in the crews of merchants ships, and still others forced to travel because of religious exile or captivity. Travel books also served a broad range of purposes, reporting on past voyages, appealing for funding for future expeditions, providing navigational and other practical information, and telling stories of exotic places and dangerous exploits purely for entertainment.

Richard Hakluyt's massive compilation of the full range of narratives in *The Principall Navigations, Voyages, and Discoveries of the English Nation* (1589, 1598–1600) provided an archive of past and present English voyages that was oriented around promoting patriotic support for future voyages. Like *The Merchant of Venice*, it linked commerce with Christian providence, and more specifically aligned English commercial and proto-colonial expansion with the Protestant cause. The first edition of Hakluyt's compilation covered ninety-three voyages and spanned 1,500 years; by the time of his second edition, eleven years later, the number of voyages included had

---

[16] Emily Bartels, *Speaking of the Moor: From Alacazar to Othello* (Philadelphia: University of Pennsylvania Press, 2008), ch. 4.

doubled. While Hakluyt claimed that his collected narratives all possessed a certain truth value grounded in the actual experiences of their authors, these kinds of claims were becoming as commonplace as the perception that travel writing was nothing but fabrication and lies. Featuring authors ranging from John Mandeville to Walter Ralegh. Hakluyt's collection reflected the capacious range of travel writing that circulated in the period and its blurring of the line between truth and fiction.

If travel narratives attracted suspicions about their veracity that in some ways enhanced their popular appeal, the travelling persona also emerged as a kind of performative trope in the period. English travellers such as Fynes Moryson, Thomas Coryate, William Lithgow, George Sandys, Henry Blount, and many others wrote books that followed similar conventions but also exhibited highly distinct narrative voices. In turn, English travellers were perceived by popular audiences in a variety of ways. Some like Francis Drake and the Shirley brothers were celebrated as national heroes. Strategically marketed to cultivate their legendary potential, these figures attained near-celebrity status, while at the same time offering examples of how landless men or second sons could rise in social status, or even become landed through colonial plantations. On the negative side, the social climbing associated with travel also fuelled anxieties about the English traveller's susceptibility to degeneration, his loss of English-ness, his indiscriminate assimilation of foreign influences, and at worst, his risk of becoming a lawless renegade. Travellers such as Thomas Coryate and John Taylor made light of these anxieties, self-consciously playing up their eccentricities to provide amusement to readers. A woodcut illustration of Coryate balancing precariously atop an elephant in India depicted in ways both provocative and unthreatening the dis-placement of Englishness in a foreign world.[17] Similarly, English travellers who re-invented themselves through foreign fashions became a source of parody. Portia's dismissal of her English suitor in *The Merchant of Venice* seems to evoke comically anxieties about the hybridization of the English subject due to the effects of travel and trade: 'How oddly he is suited! I think he bought his doublet in Italy, his round hose in France, his bonnet in Germany, and his behaviour every where' (1.2.70–3). Such parodies seem equally invested in exposing English susceptibility to foreign influences and mocking illegitimate class pretensions made possible through foreign travel and trade. A text such as *Coryat's Crudities* (1611) played up the pretensions of an aristo-cratic world traveller to comic effect through Coryates self-mocking performance and the inclusion of panegyric verses appended to the text. Assuming a more serious response to anxieties about the effects of foreign influences on English gentlemen, Roger Ascham's *The Scholemaster* (1570) attacked 'Italianate Englishmen,' whose bodies and souls were corrupted through travel, and asserted the virtues of staying at home to receive one's education in England.

Many other writers attempted to dissuade English travel by emphasizing its physical and moral risks. Thomas Nashe's *The Unfortunate Traveler* (1594) offers a purely

---

[17] See *Thomas Coriate traveller for the English wits: greeting from the Court of the Great Mogul* (London: 1616), title-page.

fictional account of one Jack Wilton's adventures in France, Germany, and Italy that depicts travel as dangerous and corrupting. The book seems to suggest that the best way to experience the world is not to travel but simply to stay home and read about it. Of course, the dangerous exploits and death-defying escapes described in travel narratives were exactly what made people want to read Nashe's book and why travel was such big business for publishers of books and pamphlets. A wealth of travel and captivity narratives describing torture, enslavement, and forced conversion in the dominion of the Ottoman Empire elevated the potential dangers of travel to an extreme level.[18] These stories not only detailed the physical hardships inflicted by merciless Turks, but also described the terrifying possibility of being converted to Islam, or 'turned Turk'—a fate that was understood to be worse than death. As Desdemona's entrancement by Othello's traveller's history demonstrates, stories of travel and travail were powerfully seductive. And for most audiences, travel narratives offered the excitement and suspense of travel without the risks of death or conversion.

THE ROLE OF THE STAGE

At a time when travel was dangerous, impractical, and relatively rare, the stage played a significant role in bringing the world home to English audiences. In addition to addressing audiences' curiosities about foreign worlds, it afforded travel without travail. Although small numbers of English travellers were venturing to increasingly distant reaches of the world, most English theatregoers would never leave England. The same was true of playwrights like Shakespeare, whose knowledge of foreign places was based on travel narratives, chronicles, newsbooks, hearsay, maps and atlases, and other plays and literary texts. By contrast, London theatres themselves were increasingly visited by foreign travellers, merchants, and diplomats. In 1599, the Swiss physician Thomas Platter attended two plays, a cockfight, and a bearbaiting in London, and subsequently observed in his journal, 'With these and many more amusements the English pass their time, learning at the play what is happening abroad . . . since the English for the most part do not travel much, but prefer to learn foreign matters and take their pleasures at home.'[19] Platter characterized as 'English' the tendencies both to stay home and to learn about the world by going to the theatre. An outpouring of plays between 1580 and 1610 featured travel to distant places and were known by titles such as *Fortune By Land and Sea*, *The Travails of the Three English Brothers*, *John Mandeville*, *Captain Thomas Stukely*, *The New World's Tragedy*, *The Fair Maid of the West*, *Eastward Ho!*, *The Four Prentices of London*, and, of course, *The Tempest* and *Pericles*

---

[18] See Nabil Matar, *Islam in Britain 1558–1685* (Cambridge: Cambridge University Press, 1998), and Daniel Vitkus, *Turning Turk: English Theater and the Multicultural Mediterranean* (New York: Palgrave Macmillan, 2002).

[19] *Thomas Platter's Travels in England, 1599*, trans. Clare Williams (London: Jonathan Cape, 1937).

(as well as many others). Collectively, these plays express a wide range of views about travel, including fantasies of mastery, pronounced anxieties about cross-cultural contact, excitement about the unknown, caution about the dangers of travel, and reassurance in the form of exemplary models and Christian providence.

Even plays not overtly concerned with travel engaged English interests in foreign worlds in numerous ways. The majority of Shakespeare's plays are set in foreign or otherworldly settings and often in past temporalities, thus exhibiting a layering of ancient and topical resonances. In addition, the materials of global trade frequently found their way into the fictions, as well as the property and costume inventories, of Shakespeare's plays and are casually referred to by characters both high and low. In *The Comedy of Errors*, Antipholus of Ephesus offers instructions for locating his purse of ducats in a desk 'that's covered o'er with Turkish tapestry' (4.1.104). His possession of a Turkish tapestry seems both unremarkable and temporally disorienting, given the play's ostensible setting in ancient Ephesus. Perhaps similarly, King Lear's objection to 'the fashion of [Edgar's] garments', which he presumes Edgar will say are 'Persian', displaces a reference familiar to the English through contemporary eastern trade onto Lear's eighth-century BC reign (3.6.37–9). Other plays invoked English desires for foreign commodities by drawing attention to their absence on the stage. In *Measure for Measure*, Pompey the clown describes serving stewed prunes in dishes that 'are not China-dishes', but 'good dishes' nonetheless (2.1.92). His reference to Chinese porcelain as a standard for judging his own household items reflects chinaware's inflated value and relative inaccessibility at the time. By contrast, a prop such as Othello's handkerchief suggests its vulnerability to all sorts of contextual reinscriptions through its very commonality and lack of distinction.[20] The handkerchief's contradictory histories as a gift given by an Egyptian to Othello's mother and as an object sewn by a sibyl from the silk of 'hallowed' worms and 'dy'd in mummy' seem to establish its elusive and mysterious origins while also refering to materials and processes that assumed new significance for the English because of eastern trade (3.4.73–4). At once a common trifle and a rare gift with 'magic in the web of it', the handkerchief demonstrates the potential for an object's value to become destabilized as the result of promiscuous travel from place to place, and it may also stand in for the human subject's susceptibility to being reconstituted as the result of travel across cultural boundaries (3.4.69).

Shakespeare's plays also reflect the ways that innovations in the development of globes, maps, and atlases registered and helped shape new conceptions of the world and England's place within it. As Brotton has shown, terrestrial globes started to become popular in the first decades of the sixteenth century.[21] As exemplified in images such as Hans Holbein's portrait of *The Ambassadors* (1533), the globe came to function as a shorthand for European claims of conquest and awareness of an expanding world.

---

[20] For a reading of the fluctuating value (both economic and religious) of Othello's handkerchief as it circulates between multiple social spheres, see Elizabeth Williamson, *The Materiality of Religion in Early Modern English Drama* (Farnham: Ashgate Press, 2009), Coda.

[21] Jerry Brotton, *The Renaissance Bazaar*, ch. 5, and his *Trading Territories*.

Maps, too, were becoming increasingly familiar to early modern audiences due to the advent of print, though they still remained relatively rare and precious objects. Early modern maps reflected new levels of geographical accuracy, but they were also influenced by subjective geopolitical interests. If medieval 'T and O' maps privileged a Christian worldview by placing Jerusalem in the centre, early modern maps privileged other kinds of authority, such as royal dominion. For example, in the opening scene of *King Lear*, the King uses a map to illustrate the division of his kingdom into three parts, which he intends to parcel out to his daughters based on his perception of their deserts. In this way, the play models the use of a map to lay claim visually to territorial possession, power, and empire. Similarly in *1 Henry IV*, rebels plotting to overthrow the King bring a map onto the stage in order to divide the kingdom visually among each rebel leader. As John Gillies has discussed, isolated moments such as these demonstrate Shakespeare's conversance with geographic discourses and cartographic technologies, though they also distinguish his approach from playwrights such as Christopher Marlowe, whose *Tamburlaine* exhibits a cartographic knowledge that 'seems to be translated into the symbolic structures of the play as a whole'.[22]

Another localized example of Shakespeare's deployment of cartographic knowledge occurs in *The Comedy of Errors*, where the globe is metaphorically invoked to chart the foreign space of a woman's body. In this case, Dromio of Syracuse describes Nell's body as 'spherical, like a globe' (3.2.116–17) and proceeds to locate specific countries on different parts of her body. In addition to identifying a number of European countries, including Ireland, Scotland, France, England, Spain, Belgium, and the Netherlands, he also locates America and the Indies 'upon her nose', which is 'all o'er embellished with rubies, carbuncles, sapphires' (3.2.137–8). His comical charting of Nell's body inadvertently reflects a knowledge of foreign trade and colonial hierarchies. In addition to comparing the embellishments on Nell's nose to the riches of America and the Indies, Dromio of Syracuse describes how they give way to Nell's breath, thereby 'declining their rich aspect to the hot breath of Spain, who sent whole armadas of carracks to be ballast at her nose' (3.2.39–41). Spain's location underneath America and the Indies, where it provides a 'ballast' or support for receiving their riches, reflects a commercial and colonial relationship rather than a geographical one. The only play in Shakespeare's canon to invoke 'America' explicitly, *The Comedy of Errors*' mapping of America in relation to Spain, also underscores Spain's rather than England's claims to America's riches.

This is not to say that Shakespeare's plays did not freely embrace fantasies of colonial subjection and express them in both local and more general ways. At the most local level, a character such as Falstaff in *The Merry Wives of Windsor* asserts a claim of sexual mastery through a language of imperial geography. He boasts of his intention to maintain two lovers at once: 'They shall be my East and West Indies, and I will trade to them both (1.3.64–5). By contrast, a play such as *Othello* revises Venice's imperial past

---

[22] John Gillies, *Shakespeare and the Geography of Difference* (Cambridge: Cambridge University Press, 1994), 52.

by reimaging the Christian loss of Cyprus to the invading Ottomans as a Christian victory in which the Turks conveniently drown on their way to Cyprus. This bald fantasy expresses the desirability of Christian imperial conquest over the Ottoman Turks while also acknowledging its unreality. In a different way, *The Tempest* models European subjugation of a foreign colonial space as a means of resolving problems of governance at home. The questions of whether the play is set in the Mediterranean or in the New World, and whether its chief concern is colonialism or political usurpation, have prompted heated critical debates. While these debates may obscure the ways that the play disrupts these binaries, linking Old World to New and colonialism to the restoration of political power, the distinction between a Mediterranean and New World setting has crucial implications, particularly in terms of topical resonance. While European colonialism in the New World was at least tentatively under way, Europeans harboured little to no hope of colonizing Mediterranean territories controlled by the much more powerful Ottoman Empire. On the one hand, the contemporary distinctions between eastern and western geographies seem not to matter in *The Tempest*—a play whose title refers to the displacement of its characters rather than the place where they land. In addition, the island seems to be as indebted to the magical realms of romance as it does to any 'real' place. But on the other hand, even a reading of the play's setting as otherworldly must take into account the topical significance of a journey from Tunis to Naples, or of the published reports of a Bermuda shipwreck that Shakespeare drew upon, in order to understand why Shakespeare adapts these contemporary associations in the ways that he does. In addition, the resonances of individual discourses of place—ancient or contemporary, empirical or fictional, eastern or western—are not necessarily mutually exclusive. The idea of a shipwreck on the way from the North African coast to Italy could not have been received in neutral ways by early modern audiences, who were undoubtedly familiar with news of shipwrecks and other calamities experienced in the notoriously unpoliced waters of the Mediterranean. As Anthony Parr puts it, 'The crusade against Islam, the shipwreck on a desert isle, and the trope of the world turned upside-down are long-established motifs made subject to modification by the pressures of contemporary events and discoveries.'[23]

POTENTIAL CONTEMPORARY RESONANCE: *TWELFTH NIGHT*'S ILLYRIA

How can an appreciation of England's expanding worldview around 1600 help us read Shakespeare's plays better or differently? I would like to address this question by considering how the contemporary geopolitical resonances of the setting of *Twelfth*

---

[23] Anthony Parr, Introduction, *Three Renaissance Travel Plays* (Manchester: Manchester University Press, 1995), 4.

Night might open up a broader interpretation of the events and relationships depicted in the play. Like *The Tempest*, the action of *Twelfth Night* is set in motion by a shipwreck that displaces characters onto an unknown foreign coast. The specific implications of their location affect both how the characters perceive their predicament as strangers in a strange land and how the audience understands their predicament. In her first line of the play, at the opening of the second scene, Viola minces no words in posing the pointed question, 'What country, friends, is this?' (2.1.1). The 'friends' Viola addresses are her fellow shipmates, and as we later learn from the one named Antonio, the distinction between friend and foe in orienting oneself to this foreign country may indeed have dire significance. The Captain's reply, 'This is Illyria, lady', does little to quell Viola's anxieties (1.2.1). Suspecting that her brother has drowned and that she is without male protection in this strange land, Viola poses a second crucial question: 'And what shall I do in Illyria?' (1.2.3).

Questions about where exactly Viola has landed, what kind of place it is, and what kind of world it belongs to bear crucially upon what Viola 'shall do in Illyria'. Modern critics have tended to downplay Illyria's precise geographical significance by reading the play's setting as a timeless, placeless hinterland of Shakespeare's imagination.[24] Consistent with this reading, they tend to approach the play as one of Shakespeare's cross-dressing comedies, presuming that its playful negotiations of gender have nothing to do with the specificity of its setting. By contrast, I want to consider how Illyria's specific contemporary resonances might make possible a deeper understanding of the play's treatment of Viola's sexual vulnerability, her strategy of cross-dressing, and the tensions that animate the relationships between strangers and natives in this vexed setting.

For early modern audiences, Illyria's significance was informed by both classical and contemporary sources. According to classical authors such as Pliny, Ptolemy, and Thucydides, 'Illyria' referred to a vast stretch of coastline extending from modern-day Croatia to Greece. Though Greek settlements were established in the southern part of Illyria, according to Thucydides, the Greeks considered it a foreign and barbarous territory because of the different language spoken there. The characters' names in *Twelfth Night* reinforce the play's ties to a classical setting. The names Cesario, Sebastian, and Olivia all figured importantly in the life of Caesar Augustus, who lived in Illyria, had the Greek name Sebastos, and married a woman called Livia. At the same time, a number of early modern publications linked Illyria with a different kind of 'barbary', that of the contemporary Ottoman Empire and the menacing figure of the Turk. It is invoked in this context by travel writers such as George Sandys and William Lithgow.[25] Sandys explicitly notes that the Christians of Illyia must pay tribute to the

---

[24] An exception to this is Goran Stanivukovic, 'Illyria Revisited: Shakespeare and the Eastern Adriatic', in Tom Clayton, Susan Brock, and Vicentre Forés (eds.), *Shakespeare and the Mediterranean* (Newark: University of Delaware Press, 2004), who emphasizes Illyria's multivalent associations and its ties to romance.

[25] George Sandys, *A Relation of a Journey Begun Anno Domini 1610* (London: 1615), 2–3, and William Lithgow, An Admired and painful peregrination (London: 1616), 21.

Turks, in addition to gifts and entertainment provided to the 'Grandsignior', in order to 'purchase their peace and a discharge of duties throughout the Ottoman empire'.[26]

Though Illyria eludes a precise location, its positioning along the stretch of the eastern Adriatic coastline sets it on the unstable border of what would have been the Ottoman Empire at the time of Shakespeare's play. During the mid to late fifteenth-century reign of Mehmed II, the Ottomans conquered most of the territory along the Adriatic coastline of Croatia, Bosnia, Yugoslavia, Albania, and Greece. Throughout the sixteenth and early seventeenth centuries, this vast territory remained an actively contested battleground between the Venetian and Ottoman empires, marking a border zone between Christendom and Islam. As we learn in the beginning of the second act from Viola's twin brother Sebastian, he and Viola have come from Messina, Sicily, suggesting that perhaps their ship was headed east (toward the rich trading ports of the eastern Mediterranean) when it failed to clear the southern coast of Greece and instead became redirected north into the Adriatic Sea. Given the geopolitical division of territory at the time of the play's performance, Viola and Sebastian's shipwreck effectively relocates them from the then Spanish-owned territory of Sicily to the western border of the Islamic Ottoman Empire, or the dominion of the Turk.

My objective here is not to close down the ambiguities of *Twelfth Night*'s setting by aligning it with this single context, but rather to consider how its association with a border zone between East and West, Christianity and Islam, might inform the sexual implications of Viola's disguise. Toward this end, perhaps the label of 'cross-dressing' does more to obscure the precise nature of Viola's disguise in *Twelfth Night* than to clarify it. Why, we might ask instead, is *Twelfth Night* the only one of Shakespeare's cross-dressing plays to imagine the cross-dressed figure as a eunuch? The reference to Viola's eunuch disguise comes early on in the play, but it has generally been disregarded by critics. When Viola learns of the noble Duke Orsino and his hopeless suit for a noble lady named Olivia, she resolves to secure a position at Orsino's court and petitions the Captain to aid her:

> Conceal me what I am, and be my aid
> For such disguise as haply shall become
> The form of my intent. I'll serve this duke.
> Thou shalt present me as an eunuch to him.   (1.2.49–52)

To be sure, most editors have dismissed the significance of Viola's desire to pose as a eunuch, which the play refers to only once more in the same scene. But there is also reason to consider the opposite: the implicit pun of Viola's cross-dressed name, Cesario, as well as Malvolio's later reference to the 'c's, u's, and t's' that prove his lady's identity through her handwriting, may suggest that the play remembers its earlier reference to Viola's eunuch disguise. Responding to this possibility, Stephen Orgel has argued that Viola's implied surgical neutering renders her 'double-gendered'

---

[26] Sandys, *A Relation of a Journey*, 3.

and simultaneously heterosexual and homosexual.[27] But critics have not yet considered how such double-gendering might be inflected, and refigured, in a contemporary eastern context. From the perspective of early modern audiences, the Ottoman Empire was notorious for importing foreign slaves and forcibly castrating them to serve in the emperor's palace. White eunuchs served as officers of the seraglio, and black eunuchs guarded the harem; like Viola, they played a vital role in guarding the thresholds of the sultan's inner court and were used to convey messages back and forth between male and female domains. The fact of their castration enabled them to be trusted as guards of the harem; in this sense, their anatomical difference de-sexualized them rather than making them doubly-sexed.

Given this context for the play, Viola's planned disguise may be seen as providing a kind of sexual prophylactic against her vulnerability as a single maid in Orsino's court. If we think back to Orsino's opening speech of the play, we might detect hints of the stereotypical oriental despot in his sensuality, decadence, and lethargy: 'If music be the food of love, play on, | Give me excess of it, that, surfeiting, | The appetite may sicken and so die' (1.1.1–3). In other English plays of the late sixteenth and early seventeenth centuries, the stereotypical oriental despot took the specific form of a raging Turk. Plays such as Thomas Kyd's *Soliman and Perseda*, Thomas Heywood's *The Fair Maid of the West*, and Robert Daborne's *A Christian Turned Turk* featured male Turks lusting after young Christian maidens. It is perhaps no coincidence that in each of these three plays, the vulnerable female who finds herself the object of the sultan's merciless sexual persecution cross-dresses in order to protect her maidenhood. Viola's plan to disguise herself as a eunuch in order to enter into service in Orsino's court plays upon the early modern stage's frequent representation of vulnerable female sexuality in the courts of eastern tyrants. This context may also enable us to appreciate in broader terms the stakes of Viola's exogamous marriage to Orsino, the count of Illyria. Even this largely playful comedy cannot quite envision such a marriage coming to fruition: as many critics have observed, Viola never does shed her disguise and re-inhabit her maiden weeds.

If the disguise of the castrated eunuch offered a form of protection for female sexual vulnerability, it also conveyed anxieties about masculine vulnerability. In contemporary plays, male Christian characters who were tempted or forced to convert to Islam by means of enslavement, torture, sexual seduction, or the promise of wealth and social advancement sealed their conversions by undergoing circumcision. The slippery slope between circumcision and castration constituted a running joke on the stage. In Thomas Heywood's *Fair Maid of the West*, the clownish servant Clem is duped into undergoing castration by the promise of social mobility. More tragically, in John Mason's *Eunuchus*, a character described as 'a free borne Christian's sonne in Cyprus' made captive 'when Famagusta by the Turke was sackt' laments his fate at the hands of his Turkish captors: 'They wrongd nature in me, mad[e] me an Eunuch | Disabled of

[27] Stephen Orgel, *Impersonations: The Performance of Gender in Shakespeare's England* (Cambridge: Cambridge University Press, 1996), 56.

those masculine functions | Due from our sex' (1.2.89–91). In addition to completely emasculating a subject, the condition of being circumcised or castrated was frequently associated with a pronounced vulnerability to anal penetration, which Turkish males were also perceived to be notorious for desiring. Ironically, of course, while Viola's eunuch disguise protects her at least temporarily from Orsino's sexual desire, it opens her up to Olivia's desire. On the one hand, this possibility is comically defused by the fact that it does not threaten penetration; but on the other hand, the underlying fact of the actors' male bodies raises the more perverse spectre of anal penetration. The Turkish threats of castration and buggery might also vaguely inform the danger that Antonio senses in Illyria. While we never fully learn what Sebastian and Viola are doing on the ship, we learn in Act 3 that Antonio has served before as a professional seaman and that he was previously involved in a 'sea-fight' against Orsino's galleys. He warns Sebastian that the streets of Illyria could 'prove rough and unhospitable' to one who is a stranger, 'unguided and unfriended' (3.2.10–11), adding:

> I do not without danger walk these streets.
> Once in a sea-fight 'gainst the Count his galleys
> I did some service of such note indeed
> That were I ta'en here it would scarce be answered.   (3.3.25–8)

Antonio's somewhat cryptic allusion to his past offence and endangerment to captivity in Illyria suggests that he has plundered a ship of Orsino's during a sea-fight. Playgoers would have easily associated the dangers facing Antonio with the contemporary dangers of captivity, conversion, circumcision, and castration experienced by English privateers and pirates operating in the waters of the Ottoman Empire.

I have explored this potential contemporary resonance of Illyria not to suggest that it constitutes the correct or most important context for understanding *Twelfth Night*, but that it offers *one possible* context for interpreting the play's multivalent setting. As with *The Tempest*, Shakespeare seems in *Twelfth Night* to refuse the specificity of setting, instead exploiting a multiplicity of potential resonances and the extent to which geographical locations are layered by multiple temporal histories. Illyria's significance as a place of constant and violent struggle is informed by its multiple histories of Roman, Venetian, and Ottoman conquest, as well as by its location on the border between East and West. The hybrid identity of Shakespeare's Illyria sustains traces of all three conquests. Thus, in a sense, Illyria is less a timeless and placeless setting devoid of meaning (as some critics have suggested) than a place packed with too many meanings, inflected by a layered history of struggles between East and West.

SHAKESPEARE'S SETTINGS AS BORDER ZONES

The foregoing consideration of *Twelfth Night*'s temporally layered setting offers a model for approaching the multivalent settings in many of Shakespeare's plays. The

Ottoman Empire resonates in a number of these plays, including *The Comedy of Errors*, *Pericles*, *Antony and Cleopatra*, and *Othello*, all of which are set in geographical territories ultimately conquered by the Ottomans. Due to its commercial importance as well as its association with interreligious and imperial strife, the Mediterranean was considered by Shakespeare and his audiences to be one of the most highly charged regions of the world. For example, *The Comedy of Errors* engages contemporary commerce in the Mediterranean and its attendant dangers by projecting the fungibility of commodities onto human bodies. In adapting the setting of Plautus' *Menaechmi*, which is set not in Ephesus but in Epidamnum, Shakespeare presents an Ephesus defined by mercantilism that also signifies in multiple and inconsistent ways: it is both pre-Christian and post-Christian, classical and contemporary, familiar and foreign.[28] Riddled with Pauline references, the play registers Ephesus' biblical connection to St Paul, who spent two years in Ephesus converting the Gentiles to Christianity. In addition, it engages Ephesus' significance as a Mediterranean port of the Ottoman Empire, a place that Christian merchants valued for its rich trade but also entered with serious concerns about the safety of their bodies and souls. As Arthur F. Kinney has pointed out, 'the business of *The Comedy of Errors* is business'; every character in the play has some good or service to sell or trade, and the word 'gold' occurs thirty times—far more than in any other Shakespeare play.[29] The contemporary location of Ephesus meant that it was a place where English merchants and adventurers were putting their own baptisms to the test by trading and consorting with Muslims, Jews, and Catholics. In analogizing the conversions associated with Christian universalism and global commerce, the play exposes the dangers that emerge when human bodies are subsumed into cross-cultural systems of exchange.

In addition to creating settings distinguished by multiple temporal resonances, Shakespeare frequently set his plays in unstable border zones between adjacent geographical regions and imperial epochs. In this way, his settings capture cultures in contention or on the brink of transformation. For example, plays such as *Cymbeline*, *The Winter's Tale*, and *Pericles* take place on the threshold of Christianity. Ostensibly presided over by Jupiter, Apollo, and Diana, the foreign worlds of these plays exemplify crises of religious authority by fusing together pagan and Christian religious elements. Similarly, *Antony and Cleopatra* explicitly refers to the necessary conditions for Christ's birth through Octavius Caesar's prophecy of the *pax romana*, establishing

---

[28] On the complex cultural and religious resonances attached to Shakespeare's Ephesus, see Linda McJannet, 'Genre and Geography: The Eastern Mediterranean in *Pericles*; John Gillies and Virginia Mason Vaughan (eds.), *The Comedy of Errors'*, *Playing the Globe: Genre and Geography in English Renaissance Drama* (London: Associated University Presses, 1998), 86–106; and Randall Martin, 'Rediscovering Artemis in *The Comedy of Errors*', in Tom Clayton, Susan Brock, and Vicente Forés, (eds.), *Shakespeare and the Mediterranean: Selected Proceedings of the International Shakespeare Association World Congress, Valencia, 2001* (Newark: University of Delaware Press), 363–79.

[29] Arthur F. Kinney, '*The Comedy of Errors*: A Modern Perspective', *The Folger Edition The Comedy of Errors* (New York: Washington Square Press, 2004), 179–96. See also Kinney, 'Shakespeare's *Comedy of Errors* and the Nature of Kinds', *Studies in Philology* 85.1 (1998), 29–52.

the departure of Hercules as part of the providential design that overlays this Roman tragedy. At the same time, Shakespeare's portrayal of the decadent seductions of Cleopatra's Egypt registers the degeneration associated with ancient Egypt as well as with Egypt's conquest by the Ottoman Empire. John Archer has called attention to how this 'shifting discursive setting' reflects Egypt's instability as a site of both grandeur and degeneration.[30] Other plays, such as *Titus Andronicus, Troilus and Cressida, Julius Caesar*, and *Coriolanus*, represent ancient imperial clashes in ways that recreate old worlds while also evoking contemporary geopolitical concerns and interests in nation- and empire-building.

Shakespeare's *Hamlet* has been read as a timeless tragedy, but it too occupies a setting on a crucial border zone between imperial epochs. If Holinshed's *Chronicles* organized British history before 1066 into four imperial conquests or periods of foreign rule (by the Romans, the Saxons, the Danes, and the Normans), *Hamlet* begins during the Third Rule, when England is 'Denmark's faithful tributary' (5.2.39), and ends with the Norman conquest of Denmark. As Margreta de Grazia has argued, the play inhabits a particular place in world history that has been occluded by the First Folio's equation of 'history' plays with post-1066 English regnal history.[31] In addition to capturing a crucial transition in Britain's history of foreign rule, *Hamlet* engages more general concerns related to the fall of world empires and the birth of new ones. In characterizing the fall of the Danish empire, the play alludes to a number of ancient rises and falls, including those of Troy, Carthage, and Rome. In addition, it invites consideration of a future or fifth rule by a foreign power, such as the Ottoman Empire. To understand Hamlet as a play that occupies an imperial border zone in world history may also help us situate plays such as *Cymbeline, King Lear, Macbeth*, and *King John* in relation to England's historical sense of itself as a nation subjugated under foreign rule.

As I have briefly mentioned above, *Othello* revisits a much more recent imperial clash—that between the Venetian and Ottoman empires over the contested territory of Cyprus. Most recently conquered by the Ottoman Turks in 1571, the island had been hotly contested during the previous century: in 1473 the Venetians won it from the Turks, and in 1570 the Turks attempted unsuccessfully to take it back. In setting four acts of *Othello* in this contested frontier, Shakespeare crucially revises history. Though Cyprus was under Ottoman control at the time of *Othello*'s first performances in 1604, it is represented in the play as a Venetian territory, and the attacking Turks are providentially destroyed in a storm on their way to laying siege to the island. In place of an imperial battle, Shakespeare gives us a domestic tragedy. In some sense, his revision of history represents the stage's role in projecting a bald fantasy, but in another sense, it offers a story that could be more believably enacted on the stage. Othello's strangulation of Desdemona in their marriage bed lent itself to the constraints of the early modern theatre in ways that a full-scale military attack of an island did not.

---

[30] John Michael Archer, *Old Worlds: Egypt, Southwest Asia, India, and Russia in Early Modern English Writing* (Stanford, CA: Stanford University Press, 2002), ch. 1.

[31] Margreta de Grazia, *Hamlet Without Hamlet* (Cambridge: Cambridge University Press, 2007), ch. 3.

Notably, Shakespeare's Cyprus evokes very little local texture. It pales in comparison to the exotic places verbally conjured through Othello's traveller's history. Part of the sparseness of Cyprus's setting may have to do with the limited scenery, stage props, and special effects the early modern theatre had at its disposal, but leaving these conditions aside, Shakespeare's script does not endow Cyprus with exotic natives or detailed descriptions expressed through dialogue. The island's otherness is conveyed primarily through its implicit effects on the Christian characters of the play, suggested by Othello's questioning of whether his brawling men have 'turned Turks' and his own descent into tragic violence (2.3.163). This may tell us something about the early modern theatre's particular investments in realism: rather than conjure foreign places through material or descriptive details, it did so through character and action. In addition, Shakespeare seems not to have been interested in offering an accurate depiction of foreign places. Defending poets against the charge that they are 'principle liars', Philip Sidney reasoned that playwrights cannot lie because they never claim to tell the truth in the first place. He further explains that no one goes to the theatre expecting to see reality: 'What child is there, that, coming to a play, and seeing Thebes written in great letters upon an old door, doth believe that it is Thebes?'[32] Shakespeare's plays seem to be consistent with Sidney's view of the theatre. In representing foreign settings, Shakespeare may have been interested in entertainment and moral edification, but not necessarily in realistic portrayals.

THEATRICAL CONTRIVANCES OF TRAVEL

The physical movement of travel was particularly difficult to enact in the theatre. How could plays even begin to represent the traversal of wide expanses of land or sea within the finite space of the stage? Moreover, how could they capture the length of time that it took to travel to foreign places, the unpredictable nature of travel, and the often directionless wandering that travel entailed in the early modern period? *Pericles* represents Shakespeare's most ambitious attempt to represent travel across multiple geographical settings. Co-authored by George Wilkins, the play follows the journeys of Pericles and his family members to six different Mediterranean settings: Tyre, Antioch, Tarsus, Pentapolis, Mytilene, and Ephesus. In total, it charts ten different trips between these various places. *Pericles* was first printed without any act or scene divisions, and its episodic plot structure approximates the wandering quality of early modern travel. In doing so, it appropriates a structural convention of romance, which was also oriented around movements from place to place. As Cyrus Mulready has argued, travel plays tapped into audiences' thirst for foreign worlds, and often defied the Aristotelian

---

[32] Philip Sidney, 'The Defense of Poesy', in Katherine Duncan-Jones (ed.), *Sir Philip Sidney: The Major Works* (Oxford: Oxford University Press, 2002), 235.

unities of time, place, and action.[33] An exception to this is *The Tempest*, which forcefully sustains the unities, seeming to respond to (or even parody) neo-classical critiques of the travel play's episodic structure. But if *Pericles* appropriates romance's digressive nature and eschews unity, it also employs theatrical contrivances such as Gower's role as the Chorus and the use of dumbshow to compensate for the difficulty of enacting sea travel and other movement across wide geographical expanses. In the fifth scene of the play, Gower describes Pericles' departure from Tarsus by explaining 'Now the wind begins to blow', causing his ship to be 'wrecked and split' and Pericles to be 'tossed' 'from coast to coast' (Sc. 5.29, 32, 34). In effect, Gower's speech inserts chunks of romance narrative into the play to reveal what the stage cannot show. After Gower explains that 'fortune' decided to spare Pericles' life and 'threw him ashore', Pericles enters, according to the stage direction, 'wet and half naked' (1.5.38, sd.38). Gower's narrative not only stands in for action that is difficult to stage, it also lends a sense of purpose to the otherwise aimless relocations of the characters. In addition, the play's punctuation of the underlying force of providence, as well as its moments of familial recognition and reconciliation, impart a certain kind of unity on its otherwise meandering structure.

Although *Pericles* has largely been derided by modern critics for its loose, baggy structure and its one-dimensional characters, it was widely popular with early modern audiences. This clearly suggests the appeal of plays featuring travel, episodic plots, and old-fashioned discursive models drawn from romance. Shakespeare's co-author Wilkins also had a hand in writing *The Travailes of the Three English Brothers*, another popular travel play performed within the same year as *Pericles*. Though *The Travailes* is set in contemporary times and fictionalizes the adventures of the real-life Shirley brothers, it mirrors *Pericles'* episodic structure and its depiction of travel in the Mediterranean world. The success of these plays may well indicate the pleasures of seeing travel imperfectly transposed onto the stage. The task of reconciling the traveller's physical movements across vast stretches of space within the limited space of theatre was fairly impossible to accomplish in believable ways, and travel laid bare the limitations of the stage and its most unrealistic contrivances. Could it be that audiences loved *Pericles* not because it transported them to the eastern Mediterranean, but because it made them aware of the disjuncture between verisimilitude and theatricality? If so, the popularity of plays about travel and foreign worlds may take on a new significance in terms of revealing the proclivities of early modern English theatregoers. Rather than transport theatregoers into foreign worlds, plays depicting vast geographical expanses made audiences most conscious of the world of the theatre. We might thus interpret the Chorus's opening apology in *Henry V* not in terms of regret for what the stage cannot adequately represent but as a moment in which theatrical enactment is demystified for purposes of pleasure in itself. When the Chorus asks the audience to allow the events

---

[33] Cyrus Mulready, '"Asia of the One Side, Affric of the Other": Sidney's Unities and the Staging of Romance', in Valerie Wayne and Mary Ellen Lamb (eds.), *Staging Early Modern Romance: Prose Fiction, Dramatic Romance, and Shakespeare* (London: Routledge, 2008), 47–71.

depicted 'within this wooden O' to work on their 'imaginary forces' and thus 'piece out [the stage's] imperfections with [their] thoughts', he invokes the audience's active role in not only making meaning of the play but in observing with pleasure the fabrications of the stage and its inherent disjuncture from reality (Prologue, 13, 18, 23). In some sense, then, plays such as *Henry V* and *Pericles* were as much about the Globe Theatre as they were about the terrestrial globe.

Another pleasure the stage offered audiences in depicting travel to foreign worlds was observing a play's citation of other discursive treatments of place. As many examples throughout this chapter demonstrate, Shakespeare's theatrical contrivance of foreign places necessarily involved transposing information from one source or medium to another. Moreover, his settings reflect layers of multiple meanings that were temporarily and generically diverse. And, of course, Shakespeare's negotiation and synthesis of multiple sources helped make discursive treatments of place into new places. The setting of *The Tempest* fuses the geography of the Old World with topical interests in a recent shipwreck off the coast of Bermuda in 1609; it also integrates elements from romance and from Shakespeare's own imagination to create a place unlike anything that existed in the real world.[34] Quite possibly, this is how Shakespeare's settings were also received by early modern audiences—as amalgamations of multiple discourses filtered through the playwright's imagination. Othello's traveller's history, which invokes multiple geographies and discursive genres, seems to illustrate Shakespeare's process for conjuring place. Referred to by Peter Womack as a 'cocktail of discursive conventions', Othello's history integrates discourses ranging from *Mandeville's travels*, to biblical Exodus, to *Leo Africanus* (p. 148). The pleasures of listening to this speech may have come not only from its exotic foreignness but also from an audience's familiarity with its diverse conventions.

Shakespeare's foreign places may have also generated new discursive associations on the part of early modern audiences. Scattered seventeenth-century marginalia in a First Folio of Shakespeare's works housed at the Philadelphia Free Library tell us about the reading practices of one early modern reader.[35] Several of the handwritten notes cross-reference moments in Shakespeare's plays with other early modern texts: a note in *The Tempest* refers to *Purchas his Pilgrimes*; a note in *Hamlet* refers to *Tottel's Miscellany*; and a note in *Measure for Measure* references a song printed in *John Fletcher's Rollo, or The Bloody Brother*. Particularly interesting for our purposes, the marginal note in *The Tempest* links Caliban's entrance at the beginning of 2.1 to 'Setebos god of ye Canibals purch. pil. vol. 1. p. 35'. (Earlier, in 1.2, Caliban identifies Setebos as the god of his mother, Sycorax.) This reader's reference indicates a travel narrative in Samuel Purchas's

---

[34] Pamphlets reporting on the Bermuda shipwreck include Sylvester Jourdain, *Discovery of the Bermudas* (1609); Council of Virginia, *True Declaration of the State of the Colony in Virginia* (1610); and William Strachey, *True Repertory of the Wrack* (1625), which Shakespeare may have read in manuscript form.

[35] My research on this First Folio was conducted in collaboration with Cyrus Mulready. We presented our findings in a talk for the History of Material Texts Seminar at the University of Pennsylvania in 2005.

compendium that comes from the journal of Antonio Pigafetta, a member of Ferdinand Magellan's crew during his 1522 circumnavigation of the globe. On page 35 of *Purchas*, Pigafetta recounts the first contact between Magellan's men and the *Patagoni* of southern South America. He describes how they were able to capture some of the Patagonian 'giants' for slavery by using 'trifles' to lure the men into bondage. Once captured, the Patagonians are said to have 'cried upon their great devil Setebos to help them'. Interestingly Sycorax's god is connected to the geography of South America rather than to Africa, indicating an adaptation on Shakespeare's part. Before appearing in *Purchas*, Pigafetta's report was published in Richard Eden's 1577 *History of Travayle in the West and East Indies*, which was probably Shakespeare's source for Setebos. While the marginal note in the First Folio is clearly not intended to identify Shakespeare's source (since *Purchas his Pilgrimes* postdated the play's performance), it reveals how an early modern reader linked a detail in Shakespeare's play to information drawn from a more recent compendium of travel narratives. Thus it is possible that for early modern audiences and readers, Shakespeare's representations of the foreign may not only have signalled citations from older discourses, but also inspired new discursive connections.

Shakespeare's plays brought foreign worlds home to English audiences, but never in a straightforward way. To create his foreign settings, Shakespeare drew upon and synthesized a range of other discourses, conjuring settings that were at once removed from specific geographical meaning and yet too full of meaning. This chapter has implicitly argued for a reconsideration of the relationship between travel knowledge and the stage. Like all cultural content, travel knowledge underwent a transfer when it was shifted into the space of the theatre. It was necessarily reshaped by dramatic conventions, the particular social and material conditions of the early modern theatre, the strengths and limitations of performance, and the transformations carried out by theatrical enactment. Shakespeare's foreign settings were also crucially shaped by artistic licence and his imagination. What did it mean that he assigned a coastline to Bohemia in *The Winter's Tale*, when early modern maps and travel narratives reflected Bohemia's location inland? Ben Jonson taunted Shakespeare for his ignorance, when another possibility was that Shakespeare wilfully disregarded geographical accuracy.[36] His foreign settings both were and were not real places. Some critics argue that Bohemia is a screen for England; others that it merely signifies a pastoral (as opposed to courtly) setting; and still others that it signals a completely fictitious and otherworldly place. The best kinds of readings allow for a play of meanings, acknowledging the imaginative, ludic element in Shakespeare's settings. But if Shakespeare's settings are impossible to pin down, they nonetheless wield power. When Brabantio accuses Othello of practising 'witchcraft' on Desdemona, Othello counters that the only 'witchcraft' he has used are the stories he told about his travels (1.3.64, 168). But travellers' tales were like a form of witchcraft: they were powerful, seductive, ensnaring, and potentially dangerous. By 1604, when *Othello* was first performed, the

---

[36] Jonson, 'Conversations with Drummond', in Ian Donaldson (ed.), *Ben Jonson* (Oxford: Oxford University Press, 1985), 599.

'Anthropophagi' referred to in Othello's traveller's history had become code for the implausibility and wilful deception of travellers' tales. Yet it was not difficult to understand how Othello's tale of exotic worlds could serve as the basis for Desdemona's seduction, even by one 'she feared to look on' (1.3.98). The Duke proclaims, 'I think [Othello's] tale would win my daughter, too' (1.3.170). On one level he is talking about the power of travellers' tales, but on another level he speaks of the power of theatre itself. In Shakespeare's plays, the two merged. By creating settings that could be so many different things at once, the theatre conjures its own unique and distinctive 'foreign worlds'.

CHAPTER 25

....

AUDIENCE RECEPTION

....

TANYA POLLARD

How did audiences in Shakespeare's time respond to the plays they saw, and how can we know? And, for that matter, why might these questions be worth considering in the first place? Early modern ideas about audiences' reactions to plays can illuminate both the plays themselves and playwrights' goals in composing them. More broadly, they reflect on the development of the theatre as a commercial institution, and its strategies for identifying, cultivating, and pleasing the paying customers who were necessary to its success.

ALL THE WORLD'S AN AUDIENCE

....

Audiences for plays in early modern England were as diverse as the settings in which plays could be performed. In the academic realm, universities and grammar schools staged student-acted plays for audiences of students, teachers, local townspeople, and visiting dignitaries, while law students at the Inns of Court sponsored theatrical performances for themselves and their friends.[1] Among the nobility, aristocratic patrons sponsored theatrical performances in their homes for their households and guests, and the royal courts of Elizabeth I and James I hosted plays, pageants, and masques for members of the court.[2] Among a wider public, churches housed both local religious plays and plays by professional actors for their parishes until at least the

---

[1] On schools, see especially Frederick S. Boas, *University Drama in the Tudor Age* (Oxford: Clarendon Press, 1914), and T. H. Vail Motter, *The School Drama in England* (London: Longmans, 1929); on Inns of Court, see A. Wigfall Green, *The Inns of Court and Early English Drama* (New Haven, CT: Yale University Press, 1931).

[2] See Suzanne Westfall, *Patrons and Performance: Early Tudor Household Revels* (Oxford: Clarendon Press, 1990), and John Astington, *English Court Theatre 1558–1642* (Cambridge: Cambridge University Press, 1999).

middle of the seventeenth century, and the medieval tradition of street theatre continued to have an important place in many cities and towns.[3]

Both before and during the rise of the commercial playhouses, then, there were many communities watching plays in many different places. With the establishment of the commercial playhouses, these wide-ranging audiences increasingly jostled together in close quarters. Although the more expensive indoor, or roofed, theatres necessarily housed wealthier audiences than did the outdoor amphitheatres, both were open to the public, and attracted many of the same theatregoers.[4] Scholars have debated the nature of these audiences, with Alfred Harbage identifying the lower social classes as the mainstay of the amphitheatres, Ann Jennalie Cook arguing for the predominance of the educated elite at both kinds of theatres, and Andrew Gurr emphasizing the wide range of types at each.[5] Whatever the precise make-up of the commercial audiences, however, the evidence shows that they were a strikingly heterogeneous group, composed of men and women, aristocrats and commoners, locals and foreigners, scholars, poets, apprentices, servants, butchers, sailors, prostitutes, and more. And judging from the vehemence of the period's debates about plays, and from even conservative estimates of attendance, audiences seem to have responded powerfully to what they saw, and to have frequently come back for more.

Why does it matter who attended the theatre and what they made of it? The striking success of the commercial theatre in early modern England was rooted in playwrights' abilities to appeal to wide-ranging audiences. Plays had long appeared to large crowds in churches, streets, and town squares, among other places, but these performances were sponsored by institutions, guilds, or wealthy patrons. Opening up ticket sales to the general public did not mean that playwrights could afford to overlook their traditional patrons—the wealthy and elite continued to be important sponsors of household and court theatre, as well as paying customers at both the amphitheatres and the roofed theatres. But writing only for these groups would sharply limit profits at

---

[3] See John M. Wasson, 'The English Church as Theatrical Space', in John D. Cox and David Scott Kastan (eds.), *A New History of Early English Drama* (New York: Columbia University Press, 1997) 25–37; Anne Higgins, 'Streets and Markets', in *A New History of Early English Drama*, 77–92; and Anne Lancashire, 'London Street Theatre', in Richard Dutton (ed.), *The Oxford Handbook to Early Modern Theatre* (Oxford: Oxford University Press, 2009), 323–39. For more information on the range of theatrical performances and playing spaces outside the standard London sites, see the *Records of Early English Drama* publications series.

[4] Prices ranged from only one penny to stand in the yard in the amphitheatres, to more than two shillings for the most expensive seats in the indoor theatres; see Ann Jennalie Cook, *The Privileged Playgoers of Shakespeare's London: 1576–1642* (Princeton, NJ: Princeton University Press 1981), 179–85, and Andrew Gurr, *The Shakespearean Stage 1574–1642*, 3rd edn. (Cambridge: Cambridge University Press, 1992), 146–7, 197–8.

[5] See Alfred Harbage, *Shakespeare's Audiences* (New York: Macmillan, 1952); Andrew Gurr, *Playgoing in Shakespeare's London*, 3rd edn. (Cambridge: Cambridge University Press, 2004); Cook, *Privileged Playgoers*; Cook, 'Audiences', in *A New History of Early English Drama*, 305–20; also Bernard Capp, 'Playgoers, Players and Cross-Dressing in Early Modern London: The Bridewell Evidence', *The Seventeenth Century* 18 (2003), 159–71, and Duncan Salkeld, 'New Allusions to London "Shewes" and Playhouses, 1575–1604', *Early Theatre* 8 (2005), 101–8.

the playhouses, where a large number of seats were sold very cheaply. Writing for a fixed playhouse, rather than touring, also meant having to cultivate and engage a relatively fixed audience by offering a changing repertory of plays, rather than performing the same few plays to different audiences in different places. Playing companies depended heavily on their audiences, and even with strong aristocratic patronage they had a clear financial incentive to make their plays appeal to a wide general audience as well as an elite one.

The premise of the commercial theatre, then, presupposed confidence that significant numbers of the general public would be attracted to plays forcefully enough to pay their own money to see them. But how did theatre entrepreneurs and playwrights acquire this confidence, and how did they set about capturing these diverse paying customers? As many scholars have noted, England's rich pre-existing theatrical culture laid a crucial foundation for the new enterprise. Less explored, however, is the sudden surge in the period of literary conversations about the relationship between plays and their audiences. These conversations, which began in Italy but spread to England, are crucial to understanding the apparent explosion of paying audiences in the period, as well as the striking fascination with audiences' responses displayed by the stage's attackers, defenders, witnesses, and producers.

Although it may at first glance seem a distant remove from English audiences, the publication of plays by Aeschylus, Sophocles, Euripides, and Aristophanes in sixteenth-century continental Europe had a crucial role in spurring and rewriting contemporary debates about the theatre.[6] These newly discovered plays inspired translations, then imitations, and finally modern plays, which led to live performances and the construction of amphitheatres to house them. They also inspired a surge of interest in Aristotle's *Poetics*, which was first printed in Greek in 1508.[7] In contrast to Horace's *Ars Poetica*, which emphasized the importance of poetry's moral and didactic functions, the *Poetics* featured both practical advice on how to write plays and the conviction that arousing pleasure and intense emotions should be the theatre's primary goal. It offered writers, then, a recipe for drama with wide audience appeal.[8] In 1571, Castelvetro refuted arguments that poetry should be primarily didactic by finding proof in Aristotle that 'poetry was invented for the sole purpose of providing pleasure and recreation . . . to the

---

[6] On the emergence of Greek plays, see Rudolf Hirsch, 'The Printing Tradition of Aeschylus, Euripides, Sophocles and Aristophanes', *Gutenberg Jahrbuch* (1964), 138–46.

[7] On the impact of Aristotle's *Poetics*, see Joel Spingarn, *Literary Criticism in the Renaissance* (New York: Columbia University Press, 1908); Bernard Weinberg, *A History of Literary Criticism in the Italian Renaissance*, vols. 1 and 2 (Chicago, IL: University of Chicago Press, 1961), esp. 1: 349–634; and Daniel Javitch, 'The emergence of poetic genre theory in the sixteenth century', *Modern Language Quarterly* 59.2 (1998), 139–69.

[8] On the new Renaissance emphasis on audience following the printing of *The Poetics*, see Nicholas Cronk, 'Aristotle, Horace, and Longinus: the conception of reader response', *The Cambridge History of Literary Criticism*, vol. 3: *The Renaissance* Glyn Norton, (ed.) (Cambridge: Cambridge University Press, 1999), 199–204; also Timothy J. Reiss, 'Renaissance theatre and the theory of tragedy', in the same volume, esp. 242.

souls of the common people and the rude multitude'.[9] Prioritizing pleasure as the theatre's most important and desirable consequence suggested that serious plays did not require intellectually sophisticated audiences. In fact, Castelvetro claimed that the ignorant are, or ought to be, 'the very public for whom poems are primarily composed' (p. 281). Although interpretations of Aristotle were variable and contentious, Castelvetro spoke for many in taking Aristotle's account of Greek drama as a model for a widely accessible public theatre rooted in a direct appeal to audiences' pleasures.

The pleasures of theatregoing, to many of the writers who engaged with the *Poetics*, were rooted especially in the experience of intense emotions. Accordingly, both critics and playwrights began arguing that it was acceptable to break Aristotle's rules if doing so allowed one to intensify audience's emotional responses. Giraldi Cinthio, whose plays were the first to achieve popular success on the Renaissance stage, claimed that 'Aristotle himself has conceded [these revisions] to me'.[10] 'Not merely new spectators', he wrote of his play *Orbecche*, 'but those who had seen it every time it was acted were unable to restrain their sighs and sobs'.[11] As Cinthio implies, Italian responses to *The Poetics* focused especially on the idea that through arousing powerful emotions, tragedy could bring about their *catharsis*, variously understood as purgation, purification, and/or transformation.[12] In keeping with Aristotle's choice of a medical term, early modern ideas about the embodied nature of the passions held that plays' effects on audiences were not only emotional and intellectual, but physiological as well.[13] Italian accounts of the theatre, accordingly, emphasized what they saw as tragedy's therapeutic effects on audiences' bodies and souls, and extrapolated from Aristotle to construct similar arguments about comedy, and eventually tragicomedy, as well.

Although responses to *The Poetics* were most explicit in continental Europe, English critics and playwrights became familiar with these debates through a number of channels. These included the universities, where many playwrights were educated; writers such as George Puttenham, Philip Sidney, and Ben Jonson, who studied

---

[9] Lodovico Castelvetro, *Castelvetro on the Art of Poetry*, Andrew Bongiorno (ed. and trans.) (Binghamton, NY: Medieval and Renaissance Texts and Studies, 1984), 19; further citations in the text. In 1587 Jacopo Mazzoni similarly cited Aristotle for evidence that 'as a recreation [poetry] should have for its end pleasure alone' (*On the Defense of the Comedy*, in Allan H. Gilbert [ed.], *Literary Criticism: Plato to Dryden* [New York: American Book Company, 1940], 378).

[10] Giraldi Cinthio, 'The Apology for *Dido*' (1543), in *Literary Criticism*, 252.

[11] Giraldi Cinthio, 'On the Composition of Comedies and Tragedies' (1543), in *Literary Criticism*, 253.

[12] On catharsis, see Aristotle, *Poetics*, 49b20; on the particular emphasis on tragedy's therapeutic effects as a Renaissance innovation rather than an Aristotelian tradition, see Stephen Orgel, 'Shakespeare and the Kinds of Drama', *Critical Inquiry* 6.1 (1979), 107–23.

[13] On affective and physiological responses to poetry in this period, see especially Katharine Craik, *Reading Sensations in Early Modern England* (Basingstoke: Palgrave Macmillan, 2007). On theatre's effects on bodies, see Cynthia Marshall, 'Bodies in the Audience', *Shakespeare Studies* 29 (2001), 51–6, and Tanya Pollard, *Drugs and Theatre in Early Modern England* (Oxford: Oxford University Press, 2005). For more on early modern passions, see Gail Kern Paster, *Humoring the Body: Emotions and the Shakespearean Stage* (Chicago, IL: University of Chicago Press, 2004), and Paster, Katherine Rowe, and Mary Floyd-Wilson (eds.), *Reading the Early Modern Passions: Essays in the Cultural History of Emotion* (Philadelphia: University of Pennsylvania Press, 2004).

classical and Italian literary theory; and the Italian *novelle* and plays forged alongside their authors' literary theories. Works by Cinthio, for instance, ultimately became models for George Whetstone's *Promos and Cassandra*, Shakespeare's *Measure for Measure*, and *Othello*. Guarini, another Italian writer whose literary criticism responded to the *Poetics*, became a crucial inspiration for the plays of Francis Beaumont and John Fletcher. For English playwrights working to entice their newly diverse paying customers, the surge of contemporary interest in the emotional effects of classical dramatic genres offered rich possibilities. Accounts of the theatre by attackers, defenders, and playwrights themselves came to share a pervasive assumption that plays could successfully attract large paying audiences by imitating generic forms designed to manipulate emotions, appeal to the senses, and provide pleasure. These different groups, however, had very different motives for promoting this idea, and their accounts of playgoers' reactions show competing notions of what plays did to their audiences.

ANTI-THEATRICALISTS ON AUDIENCE RESPONSES

To the theatre's critics, plays were all too successful in their strategies for inflaming intense emotions. By assaulting the senses and appealing to the desire for pleasure, these writers argued, plays not only attracted the lowest sort of audiences, but encouraged those audiences to surrender to their lowest instincts. In 1579 the anti-theatricalist Stephen Gosson worried particularly that plays' powerful effects on the senses gave them a dangerous power to invade audiences' hearts, minds, and souls. With their 'strange consorts of melody, to tickle the ear; costly apparel, to flatter the sight; effeminate gesture, to ravish the sense; and wanton speech, to whet desire to inordinate lust', plays enter the body and mind by every available port: most disturbingly, they 'by the privy entries of the ear slip down into the heart, and with gunshot of affection gall the mind, where reason and virtue should rule the roost'.[14] Gosson's attention to the ear as a privileged point of entry to the heart and mind highlights contemporary ideas about the physically penetrating power of sound and the bodily vulnerability of listening.[15] Combined with his own self-consciously lavish rhetoric, it also reminds us that Gosson, a failed playwright and eventual preacher, had a significant personal investment in the ability of words to captivate and enthrall audiences. Part of the

---

[14] Stephen Gosson, *The School of Abuse* (London: 1579), printed in Tanya Pollard (ed.), *Shakespeare's Theater: A Sourcebook* (Oxford: Blackwell, 2004), 25; further citations will be to this edition unless noted.

[15] On sound and hearing, see especially Bruce Smith, *The Acoustic World of Early Modern England: Attending to the O-Factor* (Chicago, IL: University of Chicago Press, 1999), and Gina Bloom, *Voice in Motion: Staging Gender, Shaping Sound in Early Modern England* (Philadelphia: University of Pennsylvania Press, 2007).

scandal of plays' affective power, to moralizing critics, was their success at competing with the clergy's chosen media of sermons and tracts.[16]

Although anti-theatricalists worried about a wide range of plays' physical and emotional effects, their most recurring fears centred on their capacity to arouse lust. In 1583 the moralist Philip Stubbes ranted furiously on the topic:

> Do they not maintain bawdry, insinuate foolery, and renew the remembrance of heathen idolatry? Do they not induce whoredom and uncleanness? Nay, are they not rather plain devourers of maidenly virginity and chastity? For proof whereof, but mark the flocking and running to theaters and curtains, daily and hourly, night and day, time and tide, to see plays and interludes, where such wanton gestures, such bawdy speeches, such laughing and fleering, such kissing and bussing, such clipping and culling, such winking and glancing of wanton eyes, and the like is used, as is wonderful to behold.[17]

While Gosson imagines audiences as vulnerable vessels invaded and usurped through their ears, Stubbes casts them as food for plays' ravenous appetites, gobbled up by these 'plain devourers of maidenly virginity and chastity'. Yet these audiences are hardly passive—as we can see in their avid 'flocking and running to theaters', lust is not only an inevitable consequence of playgoing, but its primary attraction. People attend plays precisely because they want to watch kissing and flirting; they want to imaginatively enter these activities, and enjoy them vicariously. Stubbes and other moralizing critics drew on a literary tradition rooted in Plato and the Latin church fathers to argue that the theatrical medium itself drew audiences to identify with and imitate what they saw onstage. This identification was especially scandalous given the nature of erotic desire in plays. Not only were lovers inevitably unmarried but, with female parts played by men, they were always of the same sex. Accordingly, anti-theatricalists routinely complained that plays used their considerable affective power to encourage not only lust but effeminacy and homoerotic desire.[18]

Beyond their predominant concerns with sexual mores, attackers of the stage worried about the particular emotional consequences of dramatic genres. In 1582, Gosson wrote,

> The beholding of troubles and miserable slaughters that are in tragedies drive us to immoderate sorrow, heaviness, womanish weeping and mourning, whereby we become lovers of dumps and lamentation, both enemies to fortitude. Comedies so tickle our senses with a pleasanter vein that they make us lovers of laughter and pleasure without any mean, both foes to temperance; what schooling is this?[19]

---

[16] On competition between sermons and plays, and the recurring complaint that churches lay empty because of attendance at theatres, see Peter Lake, *The Antichrist's Lewd Hat: Protestants, Papists and Players in Post-Reformation England* (New Haven, CT: Yale University Press, 2002).

[17] Philip Stubbes, *The Anatomie of Abuses* (London: 1583), in *Shakespeare's Theater*, 121.

[18] On anti-theatricality and homoeroticism, see Jonathan Goldberg, *Sodometries* (Stanford, CA: Stanford University Press, 1992); Laura Levine, *Men in Women's Clothing: Anti-theatricality and Effeminization 1579–1642* (Cambridge: Cambridge University Press, 1994); and Stephen Orgel, *Impersonations* (Cambridge: Cambridge University Press, 1997).

[19] Gosson, *Plays Confuted*, in *Shakespeare's Theater*, 95. On this topic, see especially Matthew Steggle, *Laughing and Weeping in Early Modern Theatres* (Aldershot: Ashgate, 2007).

For Gosson, the classical genres of tragedy and comedy assault audiences with emotions beyond control or limit. Tragedies drive us to tears while comedies tickle us to laughter, in both cases weakening us and stripping us of moral agency. Both responses were widely understood as explicitly physiological processes: humoral imbalances, triggered by sensory stimulus, led inevitably to uncontrollable bodily spasms in both cases.[20] Despite, or because of, the pleasurable release they offered, tears and laughter were highly ambivalent phenomena: they brought out animal instincts, which we experience regardless of our wishes, and often against our wills. As the public setting most prominently identified with triggering both laughter and tears, the theatre was a magnet for both the pleasures and the disapproval that these symptoms generated. For moralizing critics striving to limit attendance at playhouses, the theatre's popular associations with evoking intense emotion offered a firm platform for attacking its effects as irrational and immoral.

STAGE DEFENDERS ON AUDIENCE RESPONSES

The theatre's defenders followed anti-theatricalists in assuming that plays exerted a powerful impact on audiences' senses and emotions, but differed in describing these effects as pleasurable forces that could be both innocently enjoyed and usefully harnessed. For this group—primarily composed of writers who wanted to justify their craft to its increasingly fierce critics—the new Aristotle-inspired emphasis on the pleasures of watching plays offered a crucial foundation for their arguments. In *The Arte of English Poesie* (printed 1589, though written earlier), explicitly indebted to both *The Poetics* and Italian responses to it, George Puttenham described comedies as 'the solace and recreation of the common people', and in 1570, Thomas Lodge defended plays and poetry by noting, 'I must confess, with Aristotle, that men are greatly delighted with imitation'.[21] Far from vilifying pleasure, both writers identify it with the theatre's appeal to broad general audiences. In his 1616 *Apology for Actors*, the playwright Thomas Heywood pursued an explicit defence of pleasure to rebut anti-theatrical criticisms:

> I hold them more scrupulous than well advised that go about to take from us the use of all moderate recreations. Why hath God ordained for man variety of meats, dainties and delicates, if not to taste thereof? . . . Since God hath provided us of these pastimes, why may we not use them to his glory?[22]

---

[20] See Steggle, *Laughing and Weeping*, 11–23.

[21] George Puttenham, in *Shakespeare's Theater*, 140, and Lodge, in *Shakespeare's Theater*, 54; further citations in the text.

[22] Heywood, *An Apology for Actors*, in *Shakespeare's Theater*, 224; further citations in the text.

Whereas Stubbes imagines audiences as passively devoured by plays, Heywood identifies audiences as the consumers, and suggests that as eating is a necessary act, it might
as well be an enjoyable one.[23]

Loosely echoing the Aristotelian notion of catharsis, the theatre's defenders insisted
that the pleasures and emotions it roused were not only acceptable, but crucial to its
capacity to heal and improve audiences. The Oxford professor Alberico Gentili wrote in
1593 that 'Poets are doctors. They certainly cure through the emotions in a powerful way.
And so Aristotle makes a note of that in defining tragedy.'[24] Heywood similarly found
that theatrical pleasures offered medicine to both mind and body: plays could 'recreate
such as of themselves are wholly devoted to melancholy, which corrupts the blood: or to
refresh such weary spirits as are tired with labor, or study, to moderate the cares and
heaviness of the mind, that they may return to their trades and faculties with more zeal
and earnestness, after some small soft and pleasant retirement' (p. 242). Heywood's
notion of plays as physical and spiritual medicine for melancholy was widely echoed in
the period. In fact Robert Burton, in his 1621 *Anatomy of Melancholy*, similarly urged
sufferers to 'Use . . . scenical shews, plays, [and] games' to drive away ill humuors.[25]

To many defenders, moreover, especially those versed in the traditional Horatian
defence of poetry as pleasing and instructing, the emotional intensity evoked by the
theatre could be justified as not only therapeutic, but intellectually and ethically
improving. Because plays enlivened what they presented, defenders argued, they
were an efficient vehicle for instructing audiences in history, character, and language
skills, among other things. Ideally, plays used emotion to teach moral lessons: Sidney
claimed that tragedy, 'with stirring the effects of admiration and commiseration
teacheth the uncertainty of this world, and upon how weak foundations guilded
roofs are built'.[26] Intriguingly, defenders shared anti-theatricalists' assumption that
plays would shape audiences in their own images, but emphasized the positive potential
of this imitation. Heywood argued, for instance, that powerful emotional responses
toward heroes could make audiences emulate their glory:

> what English blood, seeing the person of any bold English man presented and doth
> not hug his fame, and hunny at his valor, pursuing him in his enterprise with his
> best wishes, and as being rapt in contemplation, offers to him in his heart all
> prosperous performance, as if the personater were the man personated: so bewitch-
> ing a thing is lively and well spirited action, that it hath power to new mold the
> hearts of the spectators and fashion them to the shape of any noble and notable
> attempt.   (p. 221)

---

[23] On early modern identification of reading with eating, see especially Craik, *Reading Sensations*, 45–7
and 93–114. Jeremy Lopez discusses the recurring anti-theatrical trope of plays as food, but claims that
defenders did not use the image; see *Theatrical Convention*, 27–31.

[24] Gentili, 'Commentatio ad Legem III Codicis de professoribus et medicis', in *Latin Treatises on
Poetry from Renaissance England*, J. W. Binns, (ed. and trans.) (Signet Mountain, TN: Summertown
Texts, 1999), 91.

[25] Robert Burton, *Anatomy of Melancholy*, A. R. Shilleto (ed.) (London: George Bell, 1893), vol. 2, 142.

[26] Sidney, in *Shakespeare's Theater*, 151; further citations in the text.

Heywood's claims, notably, rest not only on the representation of the character, but especially on his conception of the contagious nature of performance. According to him, it is the 'lively and well spirited action', not simply the poetic depiction of character, that has the power to recreate itself in the hearts of spectators. And, as his blatantly nationalist example suggests, this emotional power could have political consequences as well, in its ability to direct our affections and loyalties as well as our actions.

Just as positive images might inspire audiences to emulation, moreover, Heywood and others claimed that depictions of immoral behaviour could inspire revulsion. This argument, like its corollary, had both ethical and political implications: the emotional engagement inspired by plays could inhibit unwanted behaviours. Citing Horace, Lodge defended the satire of Old Comedy as a means to strike audiences' consciences: 'there was no abuse but these men reprehended it. A thief was loath to be seen on their spectacle; a coward was never present at their assemblies; a backbiter abhorred that company' (p. 52). In a more personal vein, Heywood famously described an audience member's response to watching a play in which a woman conspired to kill her husband in order to enjoy her lover. According to him,

> As this was acted, a townswoman (till then of good estimation and report) finding her conscience (at this presentment) extremely troubled, suddenly screeched and cried out Oh my husband, my husband! I see the ghost of my husband fiercely threatening and menacing me. At which shrill and unexpected outcry, the people about her, moved to a strange amazement, inquired the reason of her clamor, when presently, unurged, she told them that seven years ago she, to be possessed of such a gentleman (meaning him) had poisoned her husband, whose fearful image perso- nated it self in the shape of that ghost: whereupon the murderess was apprehended, before the Justices further examined, and by her voluntary confession after con- demned.   (p. 245)

According to Heywood, her response was not an isolated event. In the same book, he described a similar incident in which a performance of a murder led a woman to shriek with recognition and confess that twelve years earlier she had murdered her husband in the same fashion, leading to her trial and condemnation. Again, for Heywood it is specifically the physical enactment, or personation, that evokes the intensity of the emotional response. The physical immediacy of live theatre, he suggests, exerts a more forceful impact on its audiences' senses and passions than the printed page could offer.

RECORDS OF AUDIENCE RESPONSES

Of course, neither anti-theatricalists nor defenders of the theatre are necessarily reliable witnesses of how audiences responded to plays: both groups were made up of polemi- cists with particular agendas, and the pictures they paint of audiences are inevitably exaggerated to prove their points. Playgoers attended the theatre for many reasons, some of which had little or nothing to do with its emotional impact, or even with the plays themselves. They went to see and be seen, and to identify themselves as part of particular communities; they went for wit, for entertainment, for costumes, and for recognition.[27] Yet records of playgoers' reactions to plays, though they are few and often prosaic, suggest that playwrights succeeded in evoking intense emotions in their audiences, at least much of the time.[28]

Legal records from the period suggest that anti-theatricalists were not always wrong about some of the theatre's effects. Watching plays might not have been always and inevitably a stepping stone to lust, but apparently at least some of the time it was. To mention only a few colourful examples, in 1576 the prostitute Godlyfe White described accompanying a Wallys's wife and a tailor to a play at the Bell, after which they went to a house where the tailor had sex with Wallys's wife in the kitchen; Elizabeth Everys similarly confessed that she had become Benjamin Gunston's mistress, and was later driven into prostitution, after meeting him at a play at the Bull in 1578.[29] And these consequences were not restricted to the lower classes: in 1600, Alice Pindar, a gentlewoman, admitted that Robert Welch, gentleman, who 'taking acquaintance of her coming from a playe did send for her . . . to come to him in Smythfeild where he had a cooche redy and tooke her into the cooche with him and carried her to Stratford the Bowe where he had . . . carnall knowledge of her bodye'.[30] Even in records that stop short of rape or prostitution, theatre routinely emerges as a site for amorous or lascivious behaviour. Sir Ambrose Vaux was accused in 1612 of trying to abduct Elizabeth Wybarn from her party at the Globe, and Simon Forman wooed Sarah Archdall at the Curtain playhouse in 1599.[31] There is no evidence that plays themselves prompted any of this behaviour, and there are any number of explanations—most notably the sheer fact of the large crowds at playhouses—but the incidents nonetheless confirmed critics' fears that theatre both attracted and encouraged amorous instincts, and that watching erotic liaisons onstage spurred others to do the same.

[27] On the attractions of other audience members, see Tiffany Stern, 'Actors and Audience on the stage at Blackfriars', in Paul Menzer (ed.), *Inside Shakespeare: Essays on the Blackfriars Stage* (Selinsgrove, PA: Susuehanna University Press, 2006), 35–53. Mary Bly has suggested that the sophisticated bawdy and homoerotic puns in plays staged at the Whitefriars theatre not only carried cultural caché, but created a sense of knowing community among members of a homoerotic subculture; see Bly, *Queer Virgins and Virgin Queans on the Early Modern Stage* (Oxford: Oxford University Press, 2000).

[28] On this topic, see especially Andrew Gurr, *Playgoing*; Matthew Steggle, *Laughing and Weeping*; Richard Levin, 'The Relation of External Evidence to the Allegorical and Thematic Interpretation of Shakespeare', *Shakespeare Studies* 13 (1980), 1–30; and Charles Whitney, *Early Responses to Renaissance Drama* (Cambridge: Cambridge University Press, 2006).

[29] See Capp, 'Playgoers, Players and Cross-Dressing', 160–1.

[30] Capp, 'Playgoers, Players and Cross-Dressing', 160.

[31] Gurr, *Playgoing*, 243; Mary A. Blackstone and Cameron Lewis, 'Towards "A Full and Understanding Auditory": New Evidence of Playgoers at the first Globe Theatre', *Modern Language Review* 90 (1995): 556–71; on Forman, see Barbara Traister, *The Notorious Astrological Physician of London*, 153, 169, and Gurr, *Playgoing*, 224.

Beyond documenting the lasciviousness for which plays were criticized, records of actual performances often commented on audiences' laughter, implicitly confirming anti-theatricalists' accounts, though not their displeasure. A description of the reception of Beaumont's *Masque of the Inner Temple and Grayes Inn* noted that 'the Musicke was extremely well fitted . . . but the perpetual laughter and applause was aboue the Musicke'.[32] Most accounts of audience laughter focused on clowns, and especially Richard Tarlton. One theatregoer noted that Tarlton 'brought the whole company into such a vehement laughter, that not able agayne to make them keepe silence, for that present tyme they were faine to break vppe'.[33] Audiences were apparently seized helplessly, and quickly. As Henry Peacham similarly remembered,

> Tarlton when his head was onely seene,
> The Tire-house doore and Tapistrie betweene
> Set all the multitude in such a laughter,
> They could not hold for scarse an houre after . . .[34]

Peacham's account echoes the sense of urgency, and further suggests that it was Tarlton's person, more than his words or even his actions, that triggered such powerful responses. The effects of performances, then, seem to have depended as much on audiences' fascination with charismatic stage presences as on the plays themselves.

The intensity and helplessness implicit in these descriptions of audience laughter surface as well in personal accounts of playgoers being moved to other emotions. Richard Norwood, a scholar and soldier, wrote in his diary in 1612 that he 'went often to stage plays wherewith I was as it were bewitched'.[35] William Gager, a Latin playwright at Christ Church, Oxford, acknowledged 'I haue bene often mooved by our playes to laughter, and sometimes to teares', and the essayist Thomas Browne wrote that 'I could lose an arme without a teare, and with few groanes, me thinkes, be quartered into pieces; yet can I weep most seriously at a Play, and receive with a true passion, the counterfeit griefs of those knowne and professed impostures.'[36] These men note their own susceptibility ruefully, but other records of performances suggest that their responses might be inevitable, at least if a performance succeeded. The academic Henry Jackson wrote an account of a performance of *Othello* by the King's Men in 1610, in which he noted that 'not just in their speaking, but also in their action, they moved tears', and an account of entertainments for Sir Henry Sidney (Philip Sidney's father) in

---

[32] Beaumont, *The masque of the Inner Temple and Grayes Inne* (London: 1613), sig. C3v; cited in Steggle, *Laughing and Weeping*, 79.

[33] See B. R., *Greene's Newes both from Heaven and Hell* (London: 1593), McKerrow (ed.), 58; cited in Wiles, *Shakespeare's Clown*, 22; and Steggle, *Laughing and Weeping*, 67.

[34] Henry Peacham, *Thalia's Bouquet* (London: 1620), cited in Steggle, *Laughing and Weeping*, 68.

[35] Gurr, *Playgoing*, 239; Wesley Frank Craven (ed.), *The Journal of Richard Norwood* (1945), 42; see also Charles Whitney, *Early Responses to Renaissance Drama* (Cambridge: Cambridge University Press, 2006).

[36] William Gager, quoted in John Rainoldes, *Th'overthrow of stage-playes* (London: 1599), 22; Steggle, *Laughing and Weeping*, 84; Sir Thomas Browne, *Religio Medici* (London: 1642), 127–8; Steggle, *Laughing and Weeping*, 89.

1581 noted that it 'was doon so pytyfully and of sutche Excellency that truly itt made many bothe in the bardge vppon the water as also people vpon Land to weepe and *my* Lord hym selffe to chandge countenance'.[37] Both commentaries suggest that powerful emotional responses such as tears were proof of a good play, rather than of a weak playgoer.

Contemporary witnesses, then, paint as vivid a picture of playgoers' responses as those conjured by the theatre's attackers and defenders. Their descriptions also suggest that audiences actively sought out the experience of being powerfully moved, and enjoyed it. In fact, for many the intensity of audiences' emotional responses became the primary criterion of a well-written and well-acted play. Just as disapproving anti-theatricalists feared, considerable numbers of audience members seem to have attended plays precisely in the hope of experiencing powerful emotions, whether pleasurable or uncomfortable.

PLAYWRIGHTS ON AUDIENCE RESPONSES

While many sectors of the population weighed in on how plays affected audiences, no one had as much at stake in the question as playwrights themselves. It is not surprising, then, that plays from the period reflect extensively on the experience of playgoing. Metatheatrical devices such as prologues, epilogues, and the play-within-the-play offered mechanisms for commenting on and depicting the reactions expected, hoped for, or feared from audiences. Yet although we might expect playwrights to seize these potential marketing opportunities by unequivocally advocating the plea-sures of theatregoing, this was not always the case. Playwrights routinely noted their ability to rouse emotions, but not always pleasurable ones. More perversely, play-wrights also presented audiences as making themselves vulnerable to both emotional and physical violence, as well as other unsettling transformations. If anti-theatricalists played up the theatre's power over emotions in order to discredit its moral status, and defenders emphasized its emotional effects in order to credit plays' powers for thera-peutic, ethical, and educational improvement, playwrights perhaps exaggerated the medium's effects on playgoers to sometimes outrageous degrees, precisely to ward off the possibility that spectators might leave the playhouses unmoved. Selling might not mean selling the theatre's pleasures as much as selling the certainty of some sort of tangible experience of emotional, sensory, and intellectual transformation.

Playwrights, of course, had a compelling financial interest in satisfying their wide-ranging general audiences, and they were clearly mindful of the challenges this entailed.

---

[37] See Gurr, *Shakespearean Stage*, 226, and Steggle, *Laughing and Weeping*, 88, 85; trans. Steggle from Latin, quoting from Gamini Salgado (ed.), *Eyewitnesses of Shakespeare* (London: Sussex University Press, 1975), 30; on Sidney, see 'Dr Taylor's history', quoted in J. Alan B. Somerset, *Records of Early English Drama: Shropshire*, 2 vols. (Toronto: University of Toronto Press, 1994), 1: 228–9.

The Prologue in Middleton's *No Wit, No Help Like a Woman's* (1611) catalogues some of the motives and desires:

> How is't possible to suffice
> So many Ears, so many Eyes?
> Some in wit, some in shows
> Take delight, and some in Clothes;
> Some for mirth they chiefly come,
> Some for passion, for both some;
> Some for lascivious meetings, that's their arrant;
> Some to detract and ignorance their warrant.
> How is't possible to please
> Opinion tos'd in such wilde Seas?[38]

Despite acknowledging the problem, however, as Jeremy Lopez has noted, the Prologue ultimately expresses confidence in the play's ability to capture all parts of the audience:

> Yet I doubt not, if attention
> Seize you above, and apprehension
> You below, to take things quickly,
> We shall both make you sad and tickle ye.[39]

The Prologue's solution echoes the suggestion, from both critics and witnesses, that plays successfully captured their audiences' attention and interest by moving their emotions. In promising to 'both make you sad and tickle ye', or to inspire both tears and laughter, the play gestures toward the rising appeal of tragicomedy, and suggests that if rousing one strong emotion is good, rousing two is better. More typically, however, plays offered genre-specific emotions: comedies promised audiences the pleasures of laughter, and tragedies held out the pleasurable release of tears.

Promising to make audiences laugh was a reliable line of advertisement for comedies, often explicitly announced through metatheatrical devices such as prologues and personifications of Comedy. The figure of Comedy at the start of the popular *Mucedorus* (1598), for instance, announces

> *Comedie* play thy part, and please,
> Mak merry them that coms to ioy with thee:
> Ioy then good gentilles, I hope to make you laugh.[40]

If comedies promoted laughter as the desired response to a play, tragic and mixed-genre plays similarly emphasized the appeal of tears. The figure of Tragedy in *A Warning for Faire Women* (1599) announces that she 'must moue the soule, | Make the heart heauie, and throb within the bosome, | Extorting teares out of the strictest

---

[38] Middleton, *No Wit Like a Woman's*, Prologue, 1–10.

[39] Prologue, 11–14; see Jeremy Lopez, *Theatrical Convention and Audience Response in Early Modern Drama* (Cambridge: Cambridge University Press, 2003), 19.

[40] *Mucedorus* (1598), A2 sig.r; see Steggle, *Laughing and Weeping*, 60.

eyes'.[41] As in appeals to laughter, this description points to the power of emotion to move not only the soul, but the body as well. Far from denying anti-theatrical complaints about plays' assaults on the emotions, then, playwrights actively relish and advertise this power, which seems to have lain at the heart of the theatre's commercial success.

Of course, as noted, it is not surprising to see plays advertising their ability to move audiences to tears or laughter, as these responses seem to have been widely linked with the pleasures of playgoing. Yet these were not the only, or even necessarily the most common, reactions that plays attributed to their onstage audiences. Echoing both Italian and English defences of theatre, playwrights routinely suggested that watching plays could have medicinal effects, for better and for worse. In the Induction to *The Taming of the Shrew* (1593–4), a messenger tells Sly that he is to watch a comedy,

> For so your doctors hold it very meet,
> Seeing too much sadness hath congealed your blood,
> And melancholy is the nurse of frenzy.
> Therefore they thought it good you hear a play
> And frame your mind to mirth and merriment,
> Which bars a thousand harms, and lengthens life.[42]

In practice, the actors' intentions are less generous than they suggest: they come to mock, not to cure. Sly's primary response to their performance, moreover, is desire for the young page pretending to be his wife: 'Servants, leave me and her alone. | Madam, undress you and come now to bed' (Induction, 2.115–16). The medicine the play actually offers, then, might be less gentle than abrasive, and less purgative than aphrodisiac in its effects. Yet either way, the commonsensical explanation of Sly's messenger suggests that there was nothing surprising in doctors prescribing a play as a medicine toward therapeutic ends. And Shakespeare was not the only playwright to describe plays as medicinal. In John Webster's *The Duchess of Malfi* (1612), Ferdinand arranges to have his sister regaled with a theatre of madmen as a purported medical treatment. In the realm of literary criticism, Ben Jonson regularly used a medical vocabulary to describe a playwright's moral obligation to improve his audiences, even if it meant making them uncomfortable. 'If men may by no meanes write freely, or speake truth, but when it offends not', he asked, 'why doe *Physicians* cure with sharpe medicines, or corrosives? Is not the same equally lawfull in the cure of the minde, that is in the cure of the body?'[43] Where the messenger's speech seems designed to appeal to audiences, though, Jonson's harsher notion of treatment seems designed to challenge playgoers more than

---

[41] *A Warning for Faire Women* (1599), A3 sig.r; Steggle, *Laughing and Weeping*, 94.

[42] William Shakespeare, *The Taming of the Shrew*, Induction, 2.128–33. This, along with all subsequent Shakespeare quotations, refers to *The Oxford Shakespeare: Collected Works*, Gary Taylor and Stanley Wells (eds.), 2nd edn. (Oxford: Oxford University Press, 2005).

[43] Ben Jonson, 'Explorata: or, Discoveries', in *Workes* (London, 1641), 125; see Pollard, *Drugs and Theater*, 32–3.

lure them, suggesting that not all playwrights aspired to woo their paying customers with promises of pleasure and ease.

Jonson's rigorous interest in curing the mind echoes the notion, seen in Sidney and Heywood, that the emotional intensity evoked by plays could strike the conscience, leading to confession and possibly reformation. Hamlet, famously, hits upon the idea of his trap for Claudius after being struck by the players' ability to harness emotions:

> I have heard,
> That guilty creatures sitting at a play
> Have, by the very cunning of the scene,
> Been struck so to the soul that presently
> They have proclaim'd their malefactions . . .
>   I'll have these players
> Play something like the murder of my father.   (2.2.584–91)

Although Hamlet's strategy does not go quite as planned, he succeeds in his attempt to prove Claudius's guilt through staging a play. Not only does Claudius visibly respond, but he promptly goes on to confess his crime, albeit only to himself and the audience. Similarly, Prospero in *The Tempest* successfully contrives to punish and reform his wicked brother Sebastian and his co-conspirer Alonso through producing a series of masques and illusions, beginning with their ship's apparent wreck and the presumed death of Alonso's son Ferdinand at the start of the play.

If the promise of being tested and punished does not necessarily sound like a way to lure spectators to the theatre, these were hardly the worst outcomes depicted. A number of plays suggest that watching performances makes audiences vulnerable both to disturbing emotions and to actual physical harm. In Thomas Kyd's *The Spanish Tragedy* (c.1587), the King of Spain, Viceroy of Portugal, and Duke of Castile watch the performance of a tragedy, only to learn afterward that they have witnessed the actual murders and suicide of their children. In Middleton's *The Revenger's Tragedy* (1607), Vindice seizes the opportunity of a court masque to murder all the members of the audience. Less violently, Shakespeare's recurring trope of the play as a dream staged while the audience sleeps suggests that audiences may not be fully aware of what they see, nor of its effects on them. 'If we shadows have offended', Puck tells the audience at the end of *A Midsummer Night's Dream*,

> Think but this, and all is mended:
> That you have but slumbered here,
> While these visions did appear;
> And this weak and idle theme,
> No more yielding but a dream.   (Epilogue, 1–6)

By depicting the play's external spectators as sleepers waking from a dream, Puck identifies them with Titania and the Athenian lovers, all of whom were onstage spectators at the mechanicals' play-within-the-play, and all of whom have awakened from their drugged sleeps to imagine that the strange events they have undergone must have been dreams. Is this identification a good thing, or a bad? These characters seem to be happy at the end of the play, but along the way they have passively undergone drugs, disorientation, and suffering. Sleeping figures in Shakespeare's plays, moreover, are always disturbingly vulnerable, susceptible not only to manipulation and deceit but to violence, even murder. The experience of theatregoing, Puck's address implies, is a receptive state subject to fantastical experiences and unpredictable, ambivalent, and often dangerous transformations.

While anti-theatricalists saw plays' emotional impact as corroding moral agency, then, and defenders saw it as both pleasurable and intellectually productive, playwrights borrowed from both of these groups to depict audiences as being transformed by what they saw both for better and for worse. Playwrights emphasized the theatre's power over emotions as a marketing tool to advertise their pleasures to spectators, but their messages were cautionary as well as promotional. They seem to have exaggerated the consequences of watching a performance, even when this meant attributing a negative impact. The alternative, they implicitly suggest, might be worse: plays might have no impact at all, and audiences might be bored, simply wasting their money. As noted earlier, many audience members came to the theatre for reasons that had nothing to do with the play. And audiences were not necessarily always happy with the plays being performed: Francis Beaumont's *Knight of the Burning Pestle* (1607) opens with a grocer and his wife complaining about the play being staged and demanding to replace it with a genre, and material, of their own choosing. Playwrights' insistence that plays exerted a powerful, even dangerous, impact on their audiences suggests a wishful attempt to ward off the more threatening possibility that they might fail in their efforts to engage and captivate those many patrons on whom they depended for the theatre's commercial survival.

Whether intent on attacking, defending, marketing, or entertaining, writers in early modern England were fascinated by theatre audiences and their responses to what they saw. In the wake of a new surge of European literary conversations responding to Greek plays and poetics, English writers developed new models for the relationship between plays and their audiences, models that were crucial to the rise of the commercial playhouse and its appeal to large mixed audiences. Both critics and supporters of plays insisted on the medium's ability to alter audiences' emotions in a wide range of ways, and many audience members concurred. Writings from the period suggest that audiences responded to plays with pleasure, amorous desire, laughter, tears, and more ambivalent transformations, and that the promise of these sorts of responses constituted an essential part of the theatre's attraction. Clearly aware of this appeal, playwrights deliberately aimed to achieve powerful emotional responses in their audiences. In fact, depictions of audiences and their reactions in plays suggest that playwrights would rather imagine violent and unhappy responses than no responses at all. Shakespeare's audiences may seem distant, unknowable, and irrelevant to our own experiences of the plays, but their centrality in both plays and writings about the theatre from the early modern period show how crucial they and their responses were to those who wrote for and about them.

CHAPTER 26

··

SHAKESPEARE ON FILM
AND TELEVISION

··

LAURY MAGNUS

JUST as Shakespeare's dramatic words, written for stage performance in early modern England, have had a formative relation to the English language, so in our times, Shakespeare on screen has both reflected and formed the contemporary consciousness of audiences around the globe. Dating back to 1899 when Sir Herbert Beerbohm Tree first filmed an imaginary scene from a stage production of *King John*,[1] international productions of Shakespeare on film or television have both moulded and been moulded by contemporary understandings of race, gender, politics, cultural history, human psychology, and social justice. Our internet age, privileging images and interconnecting virtual audiences, guarantees the Bard a global ubiquity, whether or not such images are accompanied by his words.

More than stage performance does, film adaptation imposes a director's point of view on audiences by showing figure against ground; film audiences are compelled both by the camera's framing focus and by music. Film can render much of what cannot be shown on stage by way of camera angle, montage and editing, compressing time, radiating motivation or exposition through actors' faces or the sudden close-up on a symbolic object, making visible worlds of fantasy or apocalypse, drawing parallels among intercut scenes, and calling attention to its own artifice—or not.

Shakespeare's plays owe much of their drive and theatricality to the split between action as representation and as performance, between locus and platea. Critical discussions of Shakespeare on screen have noted mirroring divisions in approaches to film adaptation: Jack Jorgens draws distinctions among 'realistic', 'theatrical', or 'filmic' modes;[2] Kenneth Rothwell contrasts bardolators with cineastes;[3] Jackson contrasts

---

[1] See Kenneth S. Rothwell, *A History of Shakespeare on Screen: A Century of Film and Television* (Cambridge: Cambridge University Press, 2004), 1–2; see also Judith Buchanan, *Shakespeare on Silent Film: An Excellent Dumb Discourse* (Cambridge: Cambridge University Press, 2009), 57–75.

[2] Jack Jorgens, *Shakespeare on Film* (Bloomington: Indiana University Press, 1977), 7–16.

[3] Rothwell, *A History of Shakespeare on Screen*, 3.

'continuity editing that preserves language and story', with montage, which 'fore-grounds the means by which language and story are created';[4] and Burnett contrasts 'an inherited ideal of the Shakespearean corpus as something permanent and commu-nal' with a forward-looking model that is ephemeral, deriving its authority from an 'intertextual investment in sequelization'.[5] All such ongoing taxonomic divisions are there in potential in the first stirrings of Shakespearean film-making.

The budding film industry had to reinvent Shakespeare virtually without words (except for short inter-titles and speech motion). But the silver screen was still tied to an ideal of fidelity to a storyline and to characters. It demanded a wholly new art of acting, limited at first to the ten-minute reel and to famous scenes, then gradually attempting a complete representation of plays' actions. The uncertain economics of film production and distribution, further complicated by a burgeoning film star system, forced directors 'into an inevitable synergy with popular culture',[6] which arguably remains the predominant factor in Shakespeare film aesthetics to this day.

Silent-screen film-making also had an ambivalent relationship to the stage. Its internationalism could more clearly cross cultural linguistic boundaries to cast famous stage stars like the French Sarah Bernhardt or the Danish Asta Nielsen as Hamlet. But in Europe, film's agenda was at first tied to enshrinement. France's Film d'art company was formed with the idea of immortalizing the day's great theatre artists in classic works of high culture—'serious' plays (or play fragments) like *Macbeth* and *Hamlet*, both released in 1910; *Film D'art Italiana* productions started from a stage tradition of opera, with spectacular costumes and grand tableaux.

Before the 1920s, makeshift crews staffed American film studios, usually setting up on rooftops or in glass-roofed photographic studios for lighting. Shakespearean one-reelers (with their comedy and melodrama) played in the nickelodeons alongside circus clowning, freak shows, and vaudevillian slapstick,[7] just as Shakespeare's plays originally shared stages used for bear-baiting. This irreverent, free-wheeling approach was a great advantage for the new artistic medium. Early Shakespearean film, paradoxically unable to be carried by Shakespeare's words, had to shake loose of the stage and reinvent itself in its own terms, and film's transatlantic ventures of self-discovery would, with expanding technical capabilities, become part of the creative multimedia explosion of artistic modernism. The priority of image in film, its grandeur and daring, reflected a crucial but often underappreciated aspect of Shakespeare's stagecraft, wherein word and image work in creative but not necessarily synchronized complement. Despite the silent screen and fixed cameras of early film, by the 1910s New York's Vitagraph studios began making one-reelers with some regularity, some moving out into city locations

    [4] Russell Jackson (ed.), *The Cambridge Companion to Shakespeare on Film* (Cambridge: Cambridge University Press, 2007), 15–16.
    [5] Mark Thornton Burnett, *Filming Shakespeare in the Global Marketplace* (New York: Palgrave, 2007), 29.
    [6] Rothwell, *A History of Shakespeare on Screen*, 5.
    [7] Rothwell, *A History of Shakespeare on Screen*, 5–8.

and featuring new stars in versions of *As You Like it, The Merchant of Venice, Othello, Richard III, Romeo and Juliet,* and *Twelfth Night.*[8]

Svend Gade's iconoclastic *Hamlet* of 1920 represented a great leap forward, based on a screenplay that re-gendered and rewrote Shakespeare's entire plot, foreshadowing the myriad free-handed Shakespearean adaptations/derivatives of the twentieth and twenty-first centuries. Asta Nielsen played a Hamlet who was secretly a woman, cross-dressed to disguise this great state secret while she ferreted out and revenged the royal evil, all the while hopelessly in love with Horatio and in jealous rivalry with Ophelia. If film, like almost all post-Restoration Shakespearean stagings, re-gendered Shakespeare's women's roles, Gade's film rewrote the play in such a way as to revive, reverse, and subvert original casting practices. A masterpiece of expressionist art, it combined inventive framing, symbolic shots stressing evil and subterfuge, and a star whose luminous, expressive face carried her virtuoso performance.

With the coming of synchronized sound, mainstream Shakespeare 'movies' would remain ambivalent about such avant-garde liberties, preferring straightforward story-telling—albeit with only some of the text—as more commercially viable. As Douglas Brode argues, Shakespearean drama is in any case inherently filmic, composed of short scenes analogous to film sequences (an original compositional rhythm belied by the act/scene divisions of later editorial tradition).[9] What Rothwell describes as an 'art house' tradition[10] would also permanently emerge with more modest commercial ambitions, but Hollywood and America, steadily promoting their film star system, began remaking Shakespeare in their own image. In 1929, Sam Taylor produced the first feature-length Shakespeare 'talkie': *The Taming of the Shrew*. Superimposing their contemporary Hollywood star profiles onto familiar Shakespearean combatants, Mary Pickford opened her mouth and took up her whip as Kate, and her husband, Douglas Fairbanks, king of the swashbucklers, became the swaggering Petruchio. Taylor's *Taming* boasts audacious juxtapositions of words and images, as when Fairbanks delivers his 'falcon' speech to his hound Troilus. The film's interpolated scenes and ruthless cuts (of the whole Induction and almost all of Acts 4 and 5) became something of a norm, the film retaining only about a third of Shakespeare's words and ending with an abrupt cut to Kate's speech on obedience—delivered with her famous wink to her sister. Pickford's sarcastic wink became a global icon, clearly indicating who wore the pants and empowering the apparently submissive 'little woman'.

European and American traditions soon began to converge with the rise of Facism, as creative artists fled Europe. With America in the throes of the Great Depression, Hollywood imported expressionist masters Max Reinhardt and William Dieterle to direct an enthralling *Midsummer Night's Dream* (1935). The film's brilliant filmic inventiveness captured the play's hybrid character. In the fantasy realm of the forest's gossamer, balletic fairies streamed to life to Mendelssohn's strains, with elvish mischief

---

[8] See Robert Hamilton Ball, *Shakespeare on Silent Film* (London: George Allen, 1968).

[9] Douglas Brode, *Shakespeare in the Movies* (Oxford: Oxford University Press, 2000), 6–7.

[10] Rothwell, *A History of Shakespeare on Screen*, 69–89.

FIGURE 26.1. In Sam Taylor's 1929 *The Taming of the Shrew*, Mary Pickford's Kate rolls her eyes during her 'obedience' speech, preparing for her famous sardonic wink to her sister, which became a global icon for the emancipated woman. Film's close-ups can make such iconic moments possible.

and a darker, satyr-like Oberon and his train also lurking there; the apprentice-shop world of dim-witted mechanicals reincarnated in such brash American screen idols as Jimmy Cagney and Joe E. Brown. The framing Athenian realm of courtly patriarchy and crooning lovers made it possible to recast these stars in familiar romantic/musical-comedy terms. Shakespeare was thus escapist enchantment—albeit with a surreal, 'darker gothic subtext'[11]—and as plain folks' normal screen entertainment, updating Shakespeare's joining of high and low culture with appeal to kings and commoners alike.

Still, filmed Shakespeare seemed doomed to box office failure, even with a classic, realistic style of Shakespearean adaptation that emerged from other thirties' films, notably George Cukor's 1936 production of *Romeo and Juliet*. Despite a multi-million-dollar investment to produce a lavish Renaissance mise-en-scène and closer attention to Shakespeare's words, the love of two young teenagers played by thirty-five-year-old Norma Shearer and forty-three-year-old Leslie Howard could not survive the camera's close-ups. Hollywood producers backed away from Shakespeare films until 1953's *Julius Caesar* somewhat resuscitated their box office draw. Joseph Mankiewicz's film, a grand-style Hollywood epic, was the first to achieve both artistic and reasonable commercial success, casting internationally famous British actors such as John Gielgud (Cassius)

---

[11] Rothwell, *A History of Shakespeare on Screen*, 34.

FIGURE 26.2. Laurence Olivier's *Henry V* (1944) creates a metadramatic frame in an Elizabethan playhouse that will dissolve into action sequences: the filmic prologue moves from actors dressing (and cross-dressing) backstage, to the stage with Olivier-as-Henry invoking a 'Muse of fire', and outward to include shots of the reacting audience, limning film's potential for self-reflexiveness.

and James Mason (Brutus), alongside the riveting American Marlon Brando as a Machiavellian Antony.

Change came again with the Second World War. Laurence Olivier in Britain and Orson Welles in America spearheaded a film Shakespeare movement, which, as part of the great post-war festival of the allied victory, also became an important vehicle for political statement. Even before and during the war, on-screen, modernized, politically charged Shakespeare—long a phenomenon of stage productions—could reach world audiences. Olivier, Shakespeare's first *auteur*, directed, rescripted, and starred in three Shakespeare films. From 1943 to 1944, he cut and redesigned his *Henry V* to hearten the war-weary home front and Allied troops readying themselves to invade France. His 1948 *Hamlet* superimposed an opening script with lines drawing an implied parallel between Hamlet's vacillation and the Allies' early appeasement of Nazi Germany. Olivier's *Richard III* of 1955 bore a less obvious relation to the war, but it too is a study of the vicious moral evils that characterized it.

Inventively translated to the screen, Olivier's films had a definitive impact on subsequent directors of Shakespearean films, such as Welles, who also used his camera to move deep into the psyches of his characters. Olivier's Technicolor *Henry V* invents a tripartite mise-en-scène that opens from one level of reality onto the next, approximating Shakespeare's metatheatrical strategies: an Elizabethan theatre with

FIGURE 26.3. 'The lunatic, the lover and the poet are of imagination all compact', and film-makers can be poets. Bottom and Titania in Reinhardt/Dieterle's *A Midsummer Night's Dream* (1935) typify the film's haunting concoction of moonbeams, cobwebs, and courtly lovers' intrigues.

cross-dressing players and a heckling audience at the play/film's beginning; a second, deliberately artificial storybook-type setting derived from a medieval illuminated manuscript, for a distancing effect in the wooing scenes; and a third level for the battle scenes shot in a comparatively realistic mode.

Even more impressively, Olivier's *Hamlet* featured heightened, poetic transpositions of Shakespearean text to set a high mark for film's developing self-referentiality. Olivier relied not only on stage traditions but on popular genres such as the horror film and *film noir*, with dissolves and voice-overs transporting us into Hamlet's head. An introductory bird's-eye-view shot through parting storm clouds shows us the ramparts of Elsinore (starting the film at its end-point), but then the focus narrows to tell the story of a poisonous earthly realm, with its chiaroscuro of cavernous, dark interiors in deep focus shots seen largely from Hamlet's point of view. Steeped in Freudian psychology, Olivier framed Hamlet's apparent paralysis from Ernest Jones's reading of the play as embodying strong Oedipal conflicts. Nevertheless, Olivier's often-brooding Hamlet can also be agile and heroic, as in the duel scene, with the famous shot in which he takes a dangerous leap from a high platform to kill the treacherous Claudius. The film ends as it had begun with a striking homage to the fallen prince: the figures wind their way upward in purgatorial ascent, bearing Hamlet's body 'high to the view' atop Elsinore's battlements under a dawning sky and, as in the opening sequences, amplify the film's narrowed domestic focus with a more cosmic dimension.

FIGURE 26.4. Laurence Olivier's 1948 *Hamlet* invokes a cosmic view, ending as it had begun, with a striking homage to the fallen prince. Dantesque figures wind their way upward in purgatorial ascent, bearing Hamlet's body 'high to the view' atop Elsinore's battlements under a dawning sky.

Olivier's brilliant *Hamlet*, like his *Richard III*, stood in dialogic relation both to stage traditions and to the canon of Welles's filmed Shakespeare. If Olivier was the Michelangelesque sculptor of film, honing and refining the contours of his materials and of film itself, Welles was film's Leonardo, relentlessly pushing *techné* to its limits and usually overreaching himself—and thus losing public approval and funding. But Welles's startling camerawork was his genius, infusing his three finished Shakespeare films with a raw power that few Shakespeare films have ever matched.

Welles made *Macbeth* (1948) on a shoestring budget and an impossible three-week shooting schedule, retooling ideas taken from his famous 1936 stage production, *Voodoo Macbeth*.[12] The studio's penury seems to have powerfully radicalized Welles's artistic choices. *Macbeth*'s demonic setting. With its elemental crags of rough-hewn rock wall, stone arches, and underground caverns, frames Welles's believable, weak-willed Macbeth, who succumbs to the temptations for power steeped in blood, an ostentatiously public anti-hero, whether eager for approval, sweating in terror, or murdering with joyless zest. Like Olivier, Welles cuts and transposes Shakespeare's text; he also reappropriates others' lines for himself, adding a shaman-like ancient priest to heighten the film's anti-Fascist allegory of good v. evil.

---

[12] A scene of this stage production is available at www.google.com/search?hl=en&q=welles+voodoo+macbeth&aq=f&oq=&aqi=.

FIGURE 26.5. *Macbeth*'s three witches in Orson Welles's 1948 film bear staves that are just one embodiment of his symbolic use of 'woods'. Representing runic 'charms wound up', the wooden staves morph into gibbets for traitors, Birnam Woods's marching boughs, avenging armies' cross-topped staffs, and a battering ram for Macbeth's castle door.

The critics excoriated Welles's low-budget film, a box office fiasco, released barely a month after Olivier's world-acclaimed *Hamlet*. Both films did, however, show the world what Shakespeare on film was capable of, with camerawork that took an active part in the action and created a visual language to rival Shakespeare's words. André Bazin writes that Welles relied increasingly on montage rather than long takes more out of necessity than preference[13] as he went on to make two other great Shakespeare masterworks: his 1952 *Othello* and his 1965 *Chimes at Midnight*. Welles's *Othello* is a valiant warrior whose soul and mind are unhinged completely by his

---

[13] André Bazin, *Orson Welles, A Critical View* (New York: Harper & Row, 1978), 110.

jealousy. As in *Macbeth*, a wrenching, unforgettably weird prologue prefigures the film's closure and introduces major visual symbols and motifs. Through imprisoning metal bars winched high above the rocky walls of his prison, Iago observes—wordlessly—the magnificent state funeral cortège he has engendered. These initial on-location shots anticipate the baroque Venetian decoration of gratings, slats, and grillework that gradually imprison Othello's noble figure in the bricolage of low, high-angle, canted, and deep-focus shots, embodying his psychic entrapment and disintegration. Welles's last project, *Chimes at Midnight*, takes transposition and découpage to their limits, compressing the action of the entire *Henriad* into a bi-fold story: Hal's assumption of the responsibilities/hypocrisies of kingship, and Hal's sacrifice, on kingship's altar, of his friend Falstaff, who with his mythic, Rabelaisian life-energies stripped away, is cast off as a charlatan, a dissolute, dishonourable 'old man'.

The Shakespeare films of Olivier and Welles paved the way for such international Shakespeare film-makers as, most notably, Akira Kurosowa and Grigori Kozintsev. The adaptations of these two film-makers also responded to the cataclysmic dis-locations of the Second World War and its aftermath, taking Shakespeare's words across linguistic, cultural, and political boundaries and producing apocalyptic masterpieces.

Kurosawa's Shakespeare films transfixed western audiences. His films synthesized his vast knowledge both of Asian and Western literature, art, and culture, fusing the main action of Shakespeare's plays with the vocabularies of Noh drama, Japanese scroll painting, Buddhist philosophy, Japanese history, and Samurai action films. Kurosawa's three Shakespeare films create stories that—without his words—deeply parallel Shake-speare's plays: *Throne of Blood* (*Macbeth*, 1957), *The Bad Sleep Well* (*Hamlet*, 1960), and *Ran* (*King Lear*, 1985). As Bernice W. Kliman stresses, Kurosawa 'recreates and adapts rather than interprets' Shakespeare,[14] alluding to rather than using his words, and sometimes combining multiple plots into one strand, as in *Ran*. For example, the Lear figure Hidatora encourages civil war among three sons, with a daughter-in-law, Lady Kaede, supplying the Gloucester sub-plot and all the cold-blooded malevolence of Edmund, Goneril, and Regan combined, greatly recalibrating the play's sexual politics. Sublime, austerely grand visual poetry, music, and the intense rhythms of repeated symbolic motifs recall Shakespeare's compelling lines and recreate them with thrilling visual intensity. During massive battle scenes, for example, time stops as all sound ceases. On a colour-saturated wide-screen, hordes of clashing warriors stream on horseback, bearing wind-whipped primary-coloured banners through palatial gates, but the human and natural din of war is soundless—we hear only the tragic musical score, repeated when Hidetora sits in his burning castle in trance-like fixity under his sons' thousand flaming arrows.

Whereas Kurosawa's epic cinepoems 'translated' Shakespeare without his words, Grigori Kozintsev's *Hamlet* needed the words' allegorical/topical power; the film was

---

[14] Bernice W. Kliman, *Shakespeare in Performance: Macbeth* (Manchester: Manchester University Press, 2004), 183.

FIGURE 26.6. In Akira Kurosawa's *Ran* (1985), an adaptation of *King Lear*, Hidetora (Lear) emerges in a catatonic state from his burning castle, with its thousands of flaming arrows, Kurosawa's shot renders the exact geometry of cataclysmic destruction.

made in 1963–4, at the end of the period of de-Stalinization known as the 'Thaw', a period of intellectual and artistic ferment not seen since the 1920s in Russia. Yet social and artistic repression was returning. As with his *King Lear* (1970), Kozintsev used Boris Pasternak's poetic Russian verse translation and worked with composer Dmitri Shostakovich and cinematographer Jonas Gritsius. Innokenti Smoktunovky's Hamlet is a hero of individual conscience and sensibility. Like the multitudes who hear Claudius's proclamations in a huge public square outside the castle, Hamlet is trapped in an annihilating public realm of puppet-like courtiers under Claudius's gracious-seeming, vicious rule, but he never fails to confront and reflect on the hypocrisy. Swept by expanses of sea, surrounded by massive plains and enormous skyscapes, Claudius's Elsinore is a fortress of stone whose huge iron maw immediately swallows Hamlet, a galloping rider from the sea who has returned at news of his father's death. This initial image of Hamlet establishes a hero in intense pursuit of truth and human dignity, continually affronted by his and his people's spiritual imprisonment and stultification,

FIGURE 26.7. In Grigori Kozintsev's 1971 *King Lear* (*Korol' Lir*), the mad king joins the hordes of war-driven dispossessed who nomadically stream the plains or mountains with Edgar-as-mad-Tom and Gloucester.

as voice-overs contrapuntally dramatize. Though Hamlet is also much more gifted with the common touch than Kozintsev's initially aloof and self-centred King Lear, the mad Lear later joins the hordes of war-driven dispossessed who nomadically stream across the plains or mountains, as do Edgar-as-mad-Tom, and, ultimately, Gloucester.

Despite the magnificent scale and artistic achievements of Olivier, Welles, Kurosawa, and Kozintsev among others in this first golden age, it was Franco Zeffirelli whose commercially successful *The Taming of the Shrew* (1967) and hugely profitable *Romeo and Juliet* (1968) pave the way for the twentieth century's second great era, the 1960s. The star-power of Elizabeth Taylor and Richard Burton was set off by Zeffirelli's operatically grand-scale setting, his canny interpolations and his point-of-view shots; Nino Rota's ebullient musical motifs captured the anarchic, buffo energy of the skirmishing lovers, bringing to the big screen a lively sexual dynamics. He cut the Christopher Sly induction and much else to emphasize Kate and Petruchio, turning Shakespeare's play into a popular film, though feminist critics assailed what they saw as the film's reductive reinforcement of gender stereotypes, its voyeuristic fixation on Taylor's cleavage and fetishizing of the female body. Nevertheless, point-of-view shots and slyly transgressive sequences tell the story largely from Katherina's point of view, creating a Kate who could hold her own and suggesting a mutual love that is clearly signalled in the full text.

Five years later, Zeffirelli's *Romeo and Juliet* blazed into the Vietnam War era with earthshaking relevance at a time when American youths were defying the military draft. Everything 'establishment' was suspect, and Zeffirelli cast two beautiful, talented

FIGURE 26.8. Franco Zeffirelli's duel scenes in *Romeo and Juliet* (1968) give gang warfare a twist of innocent, youthful stupidity, alternating horseplay and swordplay, which here turns deadly.

teenaged newcomers, Olivia Hussey and Leonard Whiting, in the starring roles. Notions of patriarchal, parental, or governmental authority gave way in this film to youthful freedom and spontaneity. Masterful cinematography and editing were combined with superlative performances by supporting actors by Leonard Boinstein. Zeffirelli's duel scenes gave gang warfare a twist of innocent, youthful stupidity by alternating sword-play and horseplay, aligning *Romeo and Juliet* with its prior *West Side Story* musical incarnation by Leonard Bernstein.

Zeffirelli's genius for supplying characters' back-story and instantaneous exposition in these films was carried forward decades later into his *Hamlet* (1990). Here, for example, Mel Gibson's action-hero Hamlet looks down from a window to take in Gertrude's (Glen Close's) flirtatious exuberance with Claudius, while the disgust he registers in the first soliloquy is conveyed by a voice-over reaction shot.

These great auteurs' large-screen Shakespeare adaptations, with their international audiences, played interpretive havoc with texts but thrilled movie-goers and cognos-centi alike through the late 1960s and early 1970s. Other directors of originality and daring, particularly Pier Paolo Pasolini and Peter Brooks, used the big screen to pursue nihilistic, radically destructive, or violent agendas that were box office failures, and their works have remained fairly obscure. It was the small-scale television screen, however, that could—at least in the West—enter people's lives on a regular basis and, within a few decades, give millions of viewers first-time access to great productions of both familiar and lesser-known plays and genres. Television's roots lie in radio and in the live spoken word rather than the edited photographic image, and TV productions have generally been more faithful to Shakespeare's words and textual sequencing than film, though encountering tougher commercial pressures such as stringent production budgets, advertising, time slots, and rating restrictions. Samuel Crowl distinguishes three basic types of televised Shakespeare productions: those shot in a TV studio; those moving successful stage productions into a TV studio and modifying them for broadcast reproduction; and those recording or simulcasting a successful stage production before a live audience in its original theatre.[15]

Recent advances in technological capabilities have been bringing a great number of stage productions in the second or third category to the small screen by way of videocassette or DVD, placing the media for producing Shakespearean materials into metadialogic relationships with both playtexts and with one another. Some are released on DVD along with special TV broadcasts, allowing viewers access even to sold-out world tour performances.

Produced-for-television Shakespeare did not get seriously under way until 1960, when the BBC aired *An Age of Kings*, an impressively cast 15-week series that included *Richard II*; *1* and *2 Henry IV*; *Henry V*; *1, 2,* and *3 Henry VI; and Richard III*. In 1965, *The War of the Roses*, based on a John Barton–Peter Hall teleplay, a condensed Old Vic production of the first tetralogy, set the stage for other successful famed TV productions such as *The Merchant of Venice* and *King Lear*, starring Olivier. Later, educational video series (now on DVD) such as Barton's pioneering *Playing Shakespeare* (1979) also took audiences behind the scenes, showing great RSC actors preparing soliloquies or 'Speaking the Verse'.

In America, from 1953 to 1970, Hallmark (among other commercial sponsors of TV Shakespeare) began its eight Hall of Fame Shakespeare productions, most of them directed by George Schaefer with Maurice Evans in many title roles, including *Hamlet* and *Macbeth* (co-starring Judith Anderson). *Richard II*, *The Taming of the Shrew*, *Twelfth Night*, and a memorable version of *The Tempest*, with Richard Burton as Caliban. It also produced Peter Woods's *Hamlet*, starring Richard Chamberlain as Hamlet (a production which would influence Kenneth Branagh's *Hamlet*). Another important American contribution was Joseph Papp's New York Shakespeare Festival, with its 1970s recordings of live stage productions, such as *Much Ado* and *King Lear*, featuring Sam Waterston and James Earl Jones, respectively. TV was beginning to connect live and broadcast stagings for world viewers. In our century, Hallmark has produced an inventive *Hamlet* with Campbell Scott in the lead role (2000).

The BBC between 1978 and 1985 undertook the enormous project of televising the entire 37-play canon, with three successive producers, Cedric Messina, Jonathan Miller, and Shaun Sutton. Messina's original idea (which unfortunately became a rigidly constricting directorial formula) was to present the plays uncut with authentic period costumes and minimal sets to privilege spoken language and bring 'timeless' texts to public and school audiences. For the first time, such rarely performed works as *Coriolanus, Titus Andronicus,* and *Henry VIII* became accessible.[16]

[15] Samuel Crowl, *Shakespeare and Film* (New York: W. W. Norton, 2008), 61.
[16] See Bernice W. Kliman, 'Television', in Michael Dobson and Stanley Wells (eds.), *The Oxford Companion to Shakespeare* (Oxford: Oxford University Press 2001), 464–6.

TV's then small-screen and limited camerawork options presented challenges for Shakespeare's intensely theatrical plays. The rhetorically heightened, highly-stylized identity/gender confusions of *As You Like It*, *The Comedy of Errors*, or *Twelfth Night*, for example, are nearly impossible to execute in a photorealistic medium that lends itself primarily to alternating close-ups. Grand processionals or battle scenes, too, are more easily accommodated by film's deep focus and montage capabilities. Even in productions featuring such great actors as Derek Jacobi playing *Hamlet*, 'the characters acted but did not interact'[17] as earlier TV cameras focused on faces and individual speakers. As a medium, TV's realism is better suited for problem plays with intense personal conflicts like *The Merchant of Venice*, and only a few directors developed a vocabulary for overcoming such constraints in productions like Desmond Davis's *Measure for Measure* (1979) or Jane Howell's ambitious *Henry VI* trilogy (1983). Yet television had a permanent and definitive role in enlarging the public understanding of the scope and generic complexity of Shakespeare's canon. In the 1990s, long after the BBC series, marketed internationally on videocassette, and after television recording had greatly advanced in sophistication, 'television rather than film became the preferred medium for capturing brilliant stage productions'[18] such as Trevor Nunn's *Othello* (1976) or Janet Suzman's racially charged, riveting South African *Othello* (1989), made during the last days of apartheid.

Film, though, was to regain dominance in the 1990s. Kenneth Branagh's *Henry V* (1989) inaugurated a second golden age of Shakespeare on film, a period of relative stability and economic growth coinciding with the collapse of Communism and moving through the tumultuous events of 9/11, during which film-makers have continued to reinvent themselves and their ongoing commitment to Shakespeare on screen. Financing and distribution had become especially critical as it had become tougher to find the backing to make and market Shakespeare films in an age of the Cineplex. However, more than twenty feature films of the plays and almost as many spin-offs, parodies, and other kinds of derivatives based on Shakespearean materials would be made between 1989 and 2001. Crowl, in characterizing this second wave, adds another category, that of the 'hybrid,' to Jorgens's resilient theatrical, filmic, and realistic modes of Shakespearean film. Hybrids derive inspiration 'as much from other, conventional Hollywood films and film genres as they do from their Shakespearean source material'.[19] Directors in this vein, though varied in their approaches to adaptation, include Branagh, Zeffirelli (*Hamlet*, 1990), Christine Edzard (*As You Like It*, 1992, and *The Children's Midsummer Night's Dream*, 2001), Peter Greenaway (*Prospero's Books*, 1991), Richard Loncraine (*Richard III*, 1995), Oliver Parker (*Othello* 1995), Baz Luhrman (*Romeo + Juliet*, 1996), Adrian Nobel (*A Midsummer Night's Dream*, 1996), Trevor Nunn (*Twelfth Night*, 1996), Michael Hoffman (*A Midsummer Night's Dream*, 1999), Julie Taymor (*Titus*,

---

[17] Rothwell, *A History of Shakespeare on Screen*, 109.
[18] Samuel Crowl, *Shakespeare at the Cineplex: The Kenneth Branagh Era* (Athens: Ohio University Press, 2003), 6.
[19] Crowl, *Cineplex*, 6.

FIGURE 26.9. Janet Suzman's racially charged, riveting South African *Othello* (1989) was made for television broadcast during the last days of South African apartheid. A black Othello (John Kani) embracing a white Desdemona (Joanna Weinberg) was politically explosive in 1987, and with the 2005 DVD, these images can now reach millions of viewers.

1999) Michael Almereyda (*Hamlet*, 2000), and on into the twenty-first century, Michael Radford (*The Merchant of Venice*, 2004); while John Madden and the screenwriting team of Marc Norman/Tom Stoppard would enchant movie-goers and bardolators with their indelible bio-pastiche, the Oscar-winning *Shakespeare in Love* (1998).

Branagh—'upstart crow' of auteurs—spearheaded this creative explosion, merging mass-audience and screen-Shakespeare traditions. His *Henry V* cast boasted stars such as Derek Jacobi, Judi Dench, Paul Scofield, Brian Blessed, and Ian Holm, who joined Branagh's distinguished Henry and Emma Thompson's Queen-to-Be Katherine. Branagh's cinematography used and quoted from great-screen traditions of American war and anti-war films like *The Great Escape* and *Platoon*. As auteur, Branagh learned much from Olivier's theatricality and Welles's cinematic genius, but Zeffirelli's picturesque realism most influenced his own epic ambitions.

Yet, as a movie buff and equal-opportunity-resource scavenger, Branagh was also aware of the emerging independent film tradition. He had set out to make a totally accessible, low-budget *Henry V* in the realistic mode, featuring anti-heroic battle scenes with mud, blood, and rain, showing limbs hacked and gored and corpses robbed. Patrick Doyle's Hollywood-style orchestral score helped define Branagh's directorial style, sometimes counterpointing screen images against speech and enhancing the play's foregrounded self-contradictions. Branagh included much that problematizes Henry's heroism, such as the threats of rape and pillage to Harfleur's citizenry. Unlike

Olivier's, his Henry is introspective and self-doubting, with war's personal, physical, and psychological costs emphasized, but he also finds redemption in the battlefield's brotherhood of suffering and bravery, more greatly valorized, ironically, against a background of unmitigated gore.

Branagh turned to comedy in *Much Ado About Nothing* (1993), whose commercial triumphs cinched film Shakespeare's 1990s box office draw. Branagh and Emma Thompson—a spectacularly cast 'Mistress Tongue'—headed an Anglo-American cast of stars, including Denzel Washington, Keanu Reeves, and Michael Keaton, familiar to young audiences and affiliated with diverse film genres. The famous opening sequence with triumphant horseback riders cresting a hill evoked *The Magnificent Seven*'s riders and instituted a trend of film quotation. The film's mixed casting was also colour-blind, and helped normalize future crossings of race lines in Shakespearean performance. *Much Ado* put mainstream Shakespeare film on the map, relocating its implied setting to Tuscany, recasting the play's combative repartee as 'screwball', its genre as thoroughly 'romantic' comedy, and de-emphasizing the play's satirical elements. Other comedies of the 1990s would have darker tonalities.

Branagh's marriage of updated Shakespeare and Hollywood influenced all the film-makers of the 1990s in their quoting from diverse genres—spaghetti westerns, war films, historical epics, *film noir*, musical comedy, action flicks, gangster films, and erotic thrillers—as well as from previous Shakespeare films. More conservative in his linguistic choices than his predecessors or successors, Branagh supplied the modus operandi for such paradoxically 'mainstream' post-modernist tragedies as Baz Luhrmann's, and created a contrastive model for more transgressive films by Julie Taymor, Richard Loncrain, Peter Greenaway, and Christine Edzard. The latter were buoyed by the commercial success of Shakespeare films generally, unlike transgressive films of the sixties and seventies, such as Peter Brook's bleak *King Lear* and Roman Polanski's bloody *Macbeth*, works of dark vision which were excoriated in print and shunned in theatres.

Branagh's revolution also produced the financing that allowed him to undertake the most ambitious project in the 100-year history of Shakespeare's films, his uncut, four-hour, epic *Hamlet*. Shot in 70 mm film, *Hamlet* captured wide expanses of Blenheim Palace, its grand hall-of-mirrors court and its grounds, creating the elaborate Victorian/Edwardian mise-en-scène that Branagh chose as providing a more accessible alternative than sense of the sixteenth-century mise-en-scène could provide.[20] This *Hamlet*'s wide-screen solidity stands in stark contrast with Olivier's poetic verticality, Zeffirelli's restively-moving, rapid juxtapositions, and Almereyda's jumpy agitation wrought by frequent hand-held camera sequences. Imperially enormous in its story-telling and linguistic project, it combines Folio and 1605 Quarto passages, showing that film image or interpolation need not supplant the word, though Branagh relies greatly on his actors' talents as much as on filmic resources to avoid 'iambic doze'.[21]

---

[20] Kenneth Branagh, *Hamlet, Screenplay and Introduction* (New York: Norton, 1996), p. xv.

[21] Geoffrey O'Brien, 'The Ghost at the Feast', www.geocities.com/athens/parthenon/6261/Articles/newyorkreview.htm.

Branagh as Hamlet balances the heroic man of action with the man of complex thoughts and responses. Derek Jacobi's gracious-seeming Claudius is canny, unflappable, and powerful; Julie Christie is an ageing but appealing Gertrude who becomes Hamlet's ally (downplaying Oedipal emphases of prior *Hamlet*s); Kate Winslet is an obedient but troubled, conscience-stricken, and ultimately friendless Ophelia locked away in an asylum. Branagh's reliance on world-class actors allows him to shoot soliloquies and long speeches in one take, as in Gertrude's description of Ophelia's death and Hamlet's soliloquies. Branagh's and his cast's crisp but nuanced delivery of lines keeps the language moving along. Flash-cuts create a back-story of Fortinbras's machinations, King Hamlet's murder, and, more problematically, of a sexual liaison between Hamlet and Ophelia. Montage moves the action out into the larger political sphere when Fortinbras's forces surround the fatal fencers within Denmark's throne room. Still, the film's length ran into problems of pacing for which Branagh attempted to compensate with a brilliant gravedigger scene, though his 'mass market' aesthetic of film quotation led to ridiculous swashbuckling shots of Hamlet's swooping to his revenge on a chandelier, which greatly marred the film's closure. Ultimately, *Hamlet* simultaneously evinces a certain greatness, stodginess, and bravery in its willingness to take risks. It received mixed critical responses, grudging admiration, and disappointing box office earnings. Branagh's two later films show ingenuity in matching a modernized setting suited to each play's style, *Love's Labour's Lost* (2000) cast in a retro, Astaire-Rogers-grand-musical style to fit the play's linguistic artifice, and the filmed-for-TV *As You Like It* (2006), set in nineteenth-century Japan, but both have had a narrow appeal in leaner economic times.

Comedies after Branagh's *All's Well* have received more straightforward treatments, though all have been laced with a certain *fin-de-siècle* melancholy (one which afflicts Radford's 2004 *Merchant of Venice* as well). Additionally, since Luhrmann's *Romeo + Juliet*, and through the first decade of the twenty-first century, the Shakespeare spin-off or 'derivative' has begun to dominate film adaptation. More recent derivatives completely abandon Shakespeare's language and scenic architecture, investing their energies in contemporary situational parallels and self-ironizing comedy. In 2001, *Ten Things I Hate about You*, based on *The Taming of the Shrew*, catapulted into the teen market the venerable, inventive tradition of Shakespeare derivatives of classic vintage such as *To Be or Not to Be* (1942), *Kiss Me Kate* (1953), and *Rosencrantz and Guildenstern are Dead* (1990). Such derivatives also include more serious films such as *My Own Private Idaho* (1991), based on *The Henriad*, *Scotland PA* (2001), based on *Macbeth*, and their lesser cousins, including *O* (*Othello*, 2001) and *She's the Man* (*Twelfth Night*, 2006). These, in turn, have generated popular TV spin-offs, including the ShakespeaRe-Told series (2005) and the Animated Shakespeare series (mostly in 1992 and 1994).

Tragedy, though, took accustomed first place in the outpouring of mid-nineties productions, domesticating the genre in familiar, contemporary film language, while claiming greater authority from Shakespeare's words. Oliver Parker's *Othello* (1995) is a good example. Marketed as an erotic thriller, it starred Laurence Fishburne as a sexy, dignified, yet dynamic Othello and Irène Jacob as a strong, self-possessed Desdemona. Camerawork shows us the leads' lovemaking in the lush Venetian setting, though overly literalizing sex scenes between Desdemona and Cassio are interpolated, allowing us to 'grossly gape on' in complicity with Othello's jealous imaginings. While Parker's *Othello* skillfully deploys montage to establish and develop character, situation, and psychological subtext, it does so without subterranean depth. The film's murderous denouement is daylight horror, far from the phantasmagoric psychic entrapment featured in Welles's film. While its psychological dynamics are credible, its literalizing realism eases the play's racial tensions and political implications.

A major turn from relatively strict adaptation to post-modernist découpage was taken by Baz Luhrmann, who seized the momentum of the 1990s to remake *Romeo and Juliet* as a contemporary social tragedy spoken in Shakespearean language. His instant teen smash hit, the 1996 *Romeo + Juliet*, starring Leonardo DiCaprio and Clare Danes, used crazy shots like 'slam zooms' and 'whip pans', creating a hip, MTV-type look, sound, and music. A TV anchorwoman delivers the Prologue as a breaking news story set in an alienated California-like urban wasteland ringed by beaches, mansions, and trailer parks where pop celebrities, cops, kids, punks, and Latino gangsters rub elbows. Luhrmann used Shakespearean lines but sought to convey Shakespeare's theatricality by his corresponding self-referential film-television style, his screenplay declaring his intent to 'make this movie rambunctious, sexy, violent and entertaining, the way Shakespeare himself might have if he had been a film-maker'.[22] Inventive parallels with Shakespearean tactics come through Luhrmann's iconoclasm. Like the invasive bawdy of Acts 1–3, for example, Luhrmann's punk, over-the-top opening gas station shoot-out replicates some of Shakespeare's shock value by opening what is now a 'classic' tragedy with an unexpectedly ludicrous action sequence. The leads' throw-away diction retains Shakespeare's language but naturalizes it, bringing it into line with powerful contemporary images, for example, Mercutio's masquerading as a transvestite show-girl, the Capulets' moonlit swimming pool as 'balcony', and a candlelit new-wave cathedral as the site of the dual suicide. If, as many think, the poetic sublimity of the lovers' erotic quest fails to come through, their poignancy as victims in a loveless contemporary urban wasteland does.

Julie Taymor's brilliant *Titus* of 1999, updated with similar audacity, adapted Shakespeare's most unsettling, racially-charged revenge tragedy of rape, dismemberment, and cannibalism to explore western culture's increasingly 'blood-dimmed tide' of mechanized violence and brutality from an end-of-twentieth-century perspective. Taymor's stylized treatment of violence is mixed with moments of visceral realism to arouse horror, pity, and revulsion combined with the perverse, surreal humour inherent in Shakespeare's own over-the-top stew. The film's power also lies in great performances, especially those of Anthony Hopkins's Titus and Jessica Lange's Tamora. Unlike her sole female directorial counterpart, Christine Edzard, who made low-budget, experimental versions of two comedies (*As You Like It*, 1992, and *The Children's A Midsummer Night's Dream*, 2001), Taymor had a comparatively high budget ($20 million) for her simultaneously anachronistic, futuristic, and fantastic setting. The

²² Baz Luhrmann, 'The Production: Production Notes', www.romeoandjuliet.com/players/p'n1.

film's opening framework anticipates other interpolated dream sequences, and sweeps us into a contemporary kitchen in which young Lucius sits playing with action-figure he-men. They materialize and drag him back in time to an ancient (later a Fascist) Roman coliseum, wherein Titus' mud-caked warriors march in iron-age lockstep, saluting his military victory and preparing for the ritual slaughter of Tamora's son that sets in motion the hideous dynamic of blood-for-blood revenge. Carefully balancing Aaron's vicious evil-doing against both Tamora's and Titus' revenges, *Titus* achieves questionable closure by putting to rest the savagery with the image of young Lucius picking up Aaron's baby in his arms and carrying him back (presumably) to his own twentieth century—a re-gendering, nurturing image reminiscent of the ending of Kurosawa's *Rashomon*.

Almereyda's *Hamlet 2000* spanned the turn of the century, predating 9/11. The film makes inventive use of iconic New York locales, such as the spiralling interior of the Guggenheim Museum for Ophelia's mad scene. Almereyda's Hamlet (Ethan Hawke) equipped with a video-camera and editing machinery, mumbles lines of Shakespearean verse to create his own existentialist diary as a film student hemmed in by his step-father's surveillance cameras and bodyguards. The film succeeds in dramatizing Hamlet's existential malaise within the slick facelessness and materialism of late-twentieth-century Manhattan, but its seams begin to show by the time we reach the film-within-the-film, and a rushed dénouement with its ceaseless mappings of Elsinore onto New York becomes both laboured and reductive.

The nouveau-apocalyptic tragic mode was the most conspicuous part of the 1990s story. But after Branagh's success with *Much Ado*, the 1990s revisited Shakespearean comedy with Trevor Nunn's splendid 1996 *Twelfth Night* (sequences of which fuelled *Shakespeare in Love*) and with two versions of *A Midsummer Night's Dream*, Adrian Noble's unsuccessful made-for-TV production of 1996, and Michael Hoffman's in 1999, featuring Kevin Kline as Bottom. The festive effervescence of the Hoffman film stemmed from his use of popular film and TV stars, as well as from the visual beauty of his north Italian turn-of-the-century setting, opening on Theseus' grand palazzo garden, with resplendent nuptial tables in preparation. More so than the sodden, mucky forest where the lovers wander in forlorn confusion, the sunny town market-place into which the gramophone pours glorious operatic arias becomes a kind of classless gateway to the 'rare visions' which the play-within engenders. However, Donaldson justly critiques the nobles' condescending appreciation of the play-within, arguing that the film's closure reneges on the democratizing promises inherent in the technology of the mise-en-scène's then new 'age of mechanical reproduction'.[23]

Trevor Nunn's distinguished history as artistic director of the Royal Shakespeare Theatre might have placed his *Twelfth Night* in the 'theatrical' film-making tradition. Instead it proved his gifts as film director as well, through shots on the Cornish sea coast location, inspired casting, and deftly intercut love scenes radiant with unfulfilled

---

[23] Peter Donaldson, 'Bottom and the Gramophone: Media, Class and Comedy in Michael Hoffman's *A Midsummer Night's Dream*', *Shakespeare Survey* 61 (2009), 23–35.

longings and proud disguises. Nunn's subtle juxtapositions in such scenes heighten the play's interrogation of gendered behaviour and its relation to ego and desire—without evading the play's homoerotic strain in the Antonio–Sebastian story or in its gender-bending love triangles. Metafilmic costuming shots and an eye for comic detail allow us to share Imogen Stubb's–Viola's learning curve as Renaissance 'man' who can walk, fence, smoke, ride, play, and 'sing both high and low'. We watch Viola's symbolic rebirth as a man: her floating hair is cropped after the initial shipwreck, and she binds her breasts with a kind of swaddling cloth; we see her stuff a rolled-up handkerchief into her crotch, all of which will complicate her erotic relationship both to Orsino and to Olivia. Though Nunn needlessly accentuates the *Schadenfreude* of the Malvolio plot, *Twelfth Night* conveys the text's musical love essences, love's confusions, whimsy, delight, and rediscoveries, merging our closing perspective with that of Ben Kingsley's 'wise fool' whose warbling song about the rain reverberates along the coastline and reunites the lovers in a dancing quartet aboard ship.

Far and away the 1990s' most entertaining success was *Shakespeare in Love* (1998), with its perfect collage of Shakespearean themes that combine legend, biography, and pseudo-biography, Elizabethan history and theatre history (re-imaged in light of 1990s Bankside archaeology) with interwoven scenes from *Romeo and Juliet* into its post-modernist dream of origins. Joseph Fiennes stars as a young Will with writer's block whose rapturous love affair ultimately inspires his first great tragedy. Will's artistic growth (and that of Viola and Will's company) hinges on metatheatrical–filmic conceits of playing and identity exchange, including gender exchange, that enfold the film's star 'billing': Ben Affleck plays Ned Alleyn–Mercutio; Joseph Fiennes, Will Shakespeare, then 'Wilhelmina', then Romeo; Gwyneth Paltrow plays Viola de Lessops playing Thomas Kent, then Romeo, then Juliet; and Judi Dench appears both as Her Glorious Majesty and incognito. (Colin Firth's brilliantly humourless Wessex plays only himself.) Scenes intercut between bedroom and rehearsals at the Rose theatre which limn the fertile crossovers between erotic and dramatic invention, with Will speaking Juliet's and Viola Romeo's lines. Shakespearean quotation, film quotation, and metafilmic casting create broad parodies, especially of ball and balcony scenes from Zeffirelli's *Romeo and Juliet* and of breast-binding and shipwreck scenes from Nunn's *Twelfth Night*. The creative midwifery of Imelda Staunton as Viola/Juliet's 'nurse' (Staunton also played Nunn's Maria) anticipates the film's closing shot: Viola defying a 'watery death' and walking ashore in the new world, while Will's pen inscribes *Twelfth Night*'s opening, 'What country, friends, is this?' Lovers may be sundered or suffer a transatlantic sea-change, it is implied, but they have engendered Shakespeare's immortal creative progeny and contributed to the ongoing excitement of the expanding world-Shakespearean project.

The grand film in the twenty-first century's first decade was Julie Taymor's *The Tempest*; it was released in the summer of 2010 and became the centrepiece of the Venice and New York Film Festivals. Exotic Hawaiian settings give the film the requisite strangeness and rough beauty of Prospero's magic isle, and Taymor's supreme visual wizardry goes far to create a grand mythic setting which integrates facial

FIGURE 26.10. Viola's flirtation with Will Shakespeare in the ballroom scene of *Shakespeare in Love* (1998) invokes the vertigo of Zeffirelli's ballroom scene from *Romeo and Juliet*. Such quotations are characteristic of a 'hybrid' genre of Shakespeare films of the 1990s.

'landscapes' with the specific locales the characters inhabit. Ariel's shape-changing is especially mirrored in watery images that rise up to ride the air, and in wondrously choreographed Ovidian shots, he bounds over the earth as well. Caliban (played by the African actor Djimon Hounsou) inhabits elemental volcanic formations and caves, his body bearing clay-like, scarified inscriptions of curses.

Surprisingly, Taymor's casting of Helen Mirren as Prospera, comes off quite naturally and credibly with a few interpolations in the back-story: Prospera's exile with her daughter was forced upon her with accusations of witchcraft that arose from her intense study of alchemy, which translated into her 'rough magic' on the isle. Her anger at her enemies is maternal, stemming as much from a desire to protect Miranda as from her need for revenge, and Mirren's performance is as masterful as the role demands. The comic sub-polts do not come off as well, however, and the film received mixed reviews and disappointing box office returns. Taken together with the post-2008 global economic crises and the production complications they have caused, *The Tempest* seems unlikely to inspire a new wave of ambitious Shakespeare film productions.

Nevertheless, looking back, one finds that twentieth/twenty-first-century film/TV–digital Shakespeare converges in uncanny ways with Shakespeare's own multifaceted dramatic canon: both endeavours started with and continued to gather a 'renaissance' energy born of relentlessly changing artistic, national, and international boundaries—and relations to growing English-language cultural ascendancy. Thus, Shakespeare on film and television creates analogues with original practices that have opened rather than closed questions in virtually every facet of contemporary critical enquiry. Most obvious are questions regarding 'originary art': film adaptations and even derivatives ask what exactly is the 'underlying' Shakespearean dramatic text; which of multiple texts have authority, or primacy; and what was and is the relation of these texts to original performances and to the interpretive 're-enactments' of reading? Conflicting film models—the auteur-v.-film-ensemble, with the latter's collaborative creativity of producer, director, actor, and cinematographer—reflect questions about the extent of Shakespeare as collaboration. The BBC's project of performing 'the complete' Shakespeare canon raised the obvious question of the limits and extent of his canon, still the subject of scholarly debate. Questions of canon are replayed in film's own financially constrained performance history, most dramatically exemplified, perhaps, by Welles's self-revising canon, technologically expanded in 'restored' and 'digitally remastered' films like *Othello*, whose sound tracks have, as Michael Anderegg discusses, been often questionably 'improved'.[24] Shakespeare as borrower of ancient and contemporary sources, converges, especially in the 1990s, with film's and television's elaborate filmic and metafilmic quotation, and an increasingly cross-fertilizing stage and film tradition of borrowed gesture and symbol. The metamedia performance of the Wooster Group's 2007 *Hamlet*, which reversed the process of Richard Burton's early 'electronovision' stage broadcast in a live *Hamlet* reconstructed by actors responding to film clips derived from the original 1964 performance is just one recent example. Then there is the acclaimed 2009 stage production in which David Esbornjon used a film quotation with Christian Carmargo's Hamlet appearing in a crypt-like opening sequence and scattering a handful of dust over his father's bones, quoting Gibson's gesture in the interpolated opening crypt sequence of Zeffirelli's *Hamlet*.

More difficult to compass, the new medias' divergences from Shakespeare's plays in their linguistic, cultural, and imagistic appropriations, are in some ways daunting and discouraging, in others exciting and stimulating. The standard text-cutting of half to two-thirds of Shakespeare's words has paved the way for the image but also for wordless and even 'sceneless' derivations that have run the gamut from great art to pornographic bowdlerism. Like those of modern-dress stage productions, screen's mapping of a given spatio-temporal locality onto a bare stage aesthetic has led to some of the greatest moments of artistic expression in the past century, with no reason (beyond the economic) to conjure creative diminution: one thinks of Lear's companions in the storm-scene's hovel of Kozintsev's 3.4, cast as godforsaken Gulag creatures. As reproducible on film, such creatures will always be different from human auditors whom a Lear can speak to directly across the footlights or on evenly illuminated stages like those of the New Globe or the Blackfriars of the American Shakespeare Center. Film directors will always be challenged to find strategies that can convey Shakespeare's inherent metatheatricality and the richness of his language and characters. But unless

---

[24] Michael Anderegg, *Orson Welles, Shakespeare and Popular Culture* (New York: Columbia University Press, 1988), 111–22.

contemporary Edgars and Poor Toms achieve such mythic power as Kozintsev's—
whether on stage or in film—other updated mappings continually risk failing Shakespeare's words, becoming laboured, false to a cultural moment, or passé. For example,
Crowl, in 2007, faulted the orgiastic, sexually decadent world of Taymor's Saturninus as
a mismapping, since the prudish 'West, with its "global consumerism",' is 'on a
shopping spree, not a sex spree' (though Crowl's 'correction' itself is now outdated).[25]
On the other hand, Christine Edzard's low-budget, radical, inventive 'translation' of *As
You like It*, made in 1992, seems especially prescient in having relocated our increasingly
vanishing 'green world' to a domain of playful imaginative pleasure still possible in a
decidedly burnt-out urban wilderness, where, ironically, increasing numbers of globally
dispossessed will likely be deprived of access to her imaginative films. Yet if canonical
texts and interpretations have faded or vanished, the possibilities for collaborative
invention are endless.

Auden's elegy for Yeats proclaimed, 'He has become his admirers.' For Shakespeare
in an electronic age, one could say that he has become the billions of micro- and macro-
events, visual and auditory, collaborative and reconstructive, of his global admirers.
Given the transportability of small and larger screens, the interchangeable platforms of
computer, television, and enhanced cell phone, and given the expanding capacity of

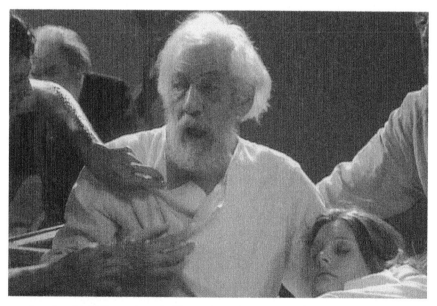

FIGURE 26.11. Ian McKellen as Lear in Trevor Nunn's *King Lear* keens over Cordelia in a 2008
made-for-television version of the RSC's world-touring stage production. He is framed as if
audiences can see him from a third-row orchestra seat: close enough to see 'this button' the king
asks to 'undo'.

---

[25] Crowl, *Cineplex*, 152.

the current video-clip (analogous, perhaps, to the one-reeler), the digital film–television performance archive has become an entertainment, news, and research vehicle, university course module, and part of a growing body of cultural history whose products can trace their ancestry back to folio and quarto.

Perhaps the most telling conclusions we can come to about the future of Shakespeare on screen were revealed in Nunn's DVD interview with Ian McKellen, who described the performance trajectory of a renowned RSC *King Lear*, from its intimate Courtyard Theatre staging through performances in grand theatres round the world, to its final incarnation as television-broadcast/DVD in 2008. 'Shakespeare's plays', McKellen avers, 'are all about the characters, and getting closer to them'. He declares that on the grand stages, he felt he was getting farther and farther away from the Courtyard's sense of intimacy until Nunn's made-for-television production restored that sense. Television viewers could once again get near enough to see what Lear feels when, with his last breath, he utters 'pray you undo this button'.

What *is* lacking about televised Shakespeare McKellen feels is the specifically gathered community whose ticket purchase and attendance creats an 'occasion' that only audiences can bestow in their collective attention to an uninterrupted performance. In theatre, this attention forges a collaborative electricity among actor and audience members. A sense of community in an uninterrupted aesthetic experience can, of course, be felt with film, or even in a classroom viewing, as many contemporary film-goers have experienced when film audiences break into applause. But to put aside the time to make an occasion of communal viewing is an increasingly rare commitment. McKellen closed by voicing the hope that the same impulse that draws folks to the increasingly isolated TV, film, or computer-screen experience might also awaken their taste and curiosity as to what their own local theatre community is doing, flowering in an age in which more modestly budgeted but abundant stage and screen productions would go hand in hand. The internet's dissemination of instant information about festival Shakespeares and myriad stage productions suggest that such a hope is currently being realized and creating an increasingly more educated, international audience, both of amateurs and connoisseurs, many of them educated for the stage by the Shakespeare films they have seen.

CHAPTER 27

MARKETING

DOUGLAS M. LANIER

AMONG the many fascinating details in Baz Luhrmann's *Romeo + Juliet* are the advertisements that litter its mise-en-scène. These advertisements have received little critical attention. Certainly they illustrate how bits of Shakespearean language or imagery can be pulled free of the plays in which they appear and attached to products to enhance their appeal. This process, as we shall see, has a long history stretching back to advertising in the nineteenth century. But Luhrmann's fictional ads also implicitly comment on that process, suggesting how thoroughly Shakespearean language has been corrupted to serve the corporate rivalry of Montague and Capulet. Some of the slogans reflect the father's patriarchalism—behind Capulet in his earliest appearance is a poster with the slogan 'experience is by industry achieved' (*Two Gentlemen of Verona* 1.3.22), and in Sycamore Grove we see a billboard for a recliner, with a smiling father-figure seated in it, which reads 'such stuff as dreams are made on' (*Tempest* 4.1.156–7). Elsewhere the violence that ultimately springs from Montague's and Capulet's commercial feud emerges in slogans like 'shoot forth thunder' (2 *Henry VI* 4.1.104, an ad for bullets) and Shakespearean brand names for guns like 'sword' and 'strongbow'. The place of advertising in Verona Beach's culture of violence becomes clear in the film's opening gunfight, where the sign at the Phoenix gas station, with its catchphrase 'add more fuel to your fire' (3 *Henry VI* 5.4.70) spins furiously as gunplay escalates, as if fanning the flames of conflict. Luhrmann suggests that Shakespearean language, once it is appropriated by advertising, becomes part of a culture of mindless violence. The alternative is provided by Romeo. We first see him far from the downtown riot, at dawn on Sycamore Beach, writing down lines of Shakespearean love verse in his journal. Thus is established a contest between two uses of Shakespeare—the love verse of the lone poet is set against the wrap-around, violence-obsessed media and commercial culture that dominates Verona Beach. And in Luhrmann's adaptation, the tragedy is that Romeo's counter-voice is eventually silenced.

Luhrmann's conviction that advertising's appropriation of Shakespeare corrupts Shakespeare's art is a cultural belief widely shared, borne of a post-Romantic faith that poetry is or should be free of the marketplace. Paradoxically, that belief has become part of why advertisers cite Shakespeare, for he has become a handy symbol for values counterposed to those of commercial culture–handcrafted quality, sophistica- tion, traditionalism, trustworthiness, gravity, rustic authenticity, and the literary. Invoking Shakespeare allows advertisers to suggest how their products transcend the mass-cultural norm. Of course, the values above can easily be reversed—traditionalism might be recast as old-fashionedness, sophistication as snobbiness, gravity as ponder- ous moralism, rustic authenticity as disconnection from modern urban life. And here too Shakespeare has proved useful, for he can also serve as a foil to brand a product as new, popular, modern, and fun. Recently a third alternative has emerged, the ironic invocation of Shakespeare which rewards the viewer's recognition of the allusion while wryly distancing the viewer from high culture, an apt mode for products directed at educated hipsters. These three modes of commercial allusion to Shakespeare have a distinct history, related to the history of advertising and Shakespeare's ideological fortunes in the last century and a half.

Before I sketch that history, two preliminary points are apropos. First, rigid distinc- tion between Shakespeare's art and the commercial realm simply will not hold, for the vitality of Shakespeare on stage, screen, and store bookshelf has long depended, at least in part, on how Shakespeare has been marketed to the public as a cultural icon. Even the success of Luhrmann's film rested in part on a marketing campaign, which appropriated Leonardo DiCaprios and Claire Danes's status as teen stars, turned a Shakespearean line turned into a slogan ('my only love sprung from my only hate'), and tied the film to a hip soundtrack. Even the 'and' in the play's title became a distinctive Goth '+' logo. This is not to single out Luhrmann as hypocritical, only to recognize that marketing helps shape the received meaning of any Shakespeare production. And despite the fact that Shakespeare is a commercial property within, not above, the marketplace, study of how Shakespeare books, plays, and films have been marketed through history is only in its infancy.[1] Second, advertising typically is not a source of new ideas about Shakespeare. Advertising deals in already familiar cultural myths, and so it tends to be a carrier and intensifier of received ideas, although it may certainly create compelling new styles for presenting them. Shakespeare ads typically dwell on a few commonplaces: the Droeshout portrait, the Globe Theatre, distinctive titles like *Much Ado About Nothing* and *The Comedy of Errors*, famous speeches such as 'to be or not to be' or Jaques's 'seven ages', major characters like Hamlet, Ophelia, Macbeth, Falstaff, and Richard III, and key images from performance like Hamlet holding Yorick's skull, Romeo courting Juliet in the balcony scene, and Titania wooing Bottom in his ass's ears. Though these offer a very incomplete view of Shakespeare, nonetheless

[1] Crucial background works are Michael Bristol, *Big-Time Shakespeare* (New York: Routledge, 2006), esp. part I, 'The Supply Side of Culture', 3–117; Barbara Hodgdon, *The Shakespeare Trade: Performances and Appropriations* (Philadelphia: University of Pennsylvania Press, 1998), esp. ch. 6, 'Stratford's Empire of Shakespeare', 191–240; Emma French, *Selling Shakespeare to Hollywood: The Marketing of Filmed Shakespeare Adaptations from 1989 into the New Millennium* (Hertfordshire: University of Hertfordshire Press, 2006); and Don-John Dugas, *Marketing the Bard: Shakespeare in Performance and Print, 1660–1740* (Columbia: University of Missouri Press, 2006).

advertising is an important discursive conduit through which the modern public learns what it knows (or thinks it knows) about Shakespeare. Despite the fact that Shakespeare-themed ads comprise quite a small segment of advertising as a whole, because advertising messages are compelling and oft-repeated they have a cultural power that exceeds their small numbers and limited range within the Shakespeare canon.

Shakespeare's use in advertising can be divided into three phases: the late Victorian period, a heyday for Shakespeare-oriented marketing; the modern period, from the First World War through the 1950s and early 1960s, in which Shakespeare played a relatively minor role in marketing; and the contemporary period, from the 1960s to the present day, in which Shakespeare-themed advertising has enjoyed a modest resurgence. Each of these periods' advertisements deploy Shakespeare in distinctive ways, for reasons arising not only from changes in media, advertising strategies, and the nature of mass production, but also from Shakespeare's changing ideological valence and relationship to the public.

The Golden Age of Shakespeare Advertising, 1875–1900

Shakespeare played little role in late eighteenth- and early nineteenth-century advertising. Though the first saturation marketing campaign in history, for Warren's Shoe Blacking in London, did include a Romeo-and-Juliet-themed advertisement,[2] there is, to my knowledge, only one Shakespearean example in the considerable canon of Warren's ads. One reason for this was that widespread regard for Shakespeare's writing fitted poorly with advertisement's reputation as mere puffery. An added practical reason was that until space restrictions and taxes on print advertising were lifted in the 1860s, there was simply no room to refer to Shakespeare—or any other artist—in a typical ad. Several changes in the last quarter of the nineteenth century led to a boom in Shakespeare-themed advertisements. First, this period witnessed the rise of mass-produced and mass-distributed commodities on a heretofore unheard-of scale. Because these industrially-produced goods sought to displace items that households would previously have made themselves (soap, biscuits, and clothing, for example), those new products needed symbolic associations and reassurances about quality that would encourage consumers to integrate them into their lives; Shakespeare—familiar, wholesome, superlative, trustworthy—supplied the need. Second, developments in image technology enabled new modes of advertising. Lithographic advances prompted the rise of the display adverts in journals; refinements in chromolithography led to development of the trade card, a card given away by manufacturers or store owners, which featured on

---

[2] John Strachan, *Advertising and Satirical Culture in the Romantic Period* (Cambridge: Cambridge University Press, 2007), 129.

one side an eye-catching illustration, on the other information about the product; improvements in offset lithography spurred new forms of advertising on packaging, particularly decorated tins, all of which offered new opportunities for yoking Shakespearean imagery with products. Third, as Lawrence Levine has noted,[3] for late-nineteenth-century America and Britain Shakespeare was an established cultural touch-stone, both popular and eminently respected, a status bolstered by Shakespeare's prominence in the theatre. Unlike that other widely-shared touchstone, the Bible, citing Shakespeare in a commercial context was neither heretical nor for most even contro-versial. Indeed, as such institutions as *Punch* and stage burlesques show, the nineteenth century already had a robust tradition of referring to Shakespeare irreverently, so that advertising merely tapped into and extended established practice.

In addition to drawing attention to their products, late nineteenth-century advertisers needed to address two questions: how to encourage customers to integrate mass-produced commodities into their lives, and how to convince a sceptical public of those goods' quality? In both cases Shakespeare proved useful. There were Cordelia sofas, Romeo and Juliet tobacco, Antony and Cleopatra cigars, Othello dresses, Hamlet stoves, Macbeth bicycles, Falstaff beer—Shakespearean names gave goods an air of quality and familiarity, even if the relationship between name and product was arbitrary. This form of loose association is central to the trade card, a ubiquitous item in Victorian popular culture.[4] Processed food manufacturers like Libby's meat in America and Liebig's meat extract in Germany, for example, issued trade card series in which images of their products were pictured alongside noteworthy Shakespeare scenes. Many of the Shakespearean images on trade cards were filtered through late nineteenth-century sentimentality or parody. Cards for Dr. King's cough syrup, for example, depicted cherub-faced children in Shakespearean roles; another series, of 'stock cards' (cards featuring generic images, on which any purveyor could stamp information), offered working-class caricatures of Shakespearean characters: Othello as a jealous farmworker in overalls, Romeo and Juliet as homespun teens kissing at a barn window. Indeed, some images were used interchangeably for different products. A version of the balcony scene in which a childish Romeo kisses Juliet as she leans over a garden wall was reused by different advertisers—in one, Romeo is perched on top of a Singer sewing machine, in another on an Osborne plough, in yet another on a giant spool of Kerr's thread.

Two things are immediately apparent to modern observers. First, the range of reference in these cards—and in late nineteenth-century Shakespeare-themed adver-tising generally—is remarkable. There are allusions not only to the major tragedies and

---

[3] See Lawrence Levine, 'William Shakespeare in America', in his *Highbrow/Lowbrow: The Emergence of Cultural Hierarchy in America* (Cambridge, MA: Harvard University Press, 1990), 3–81. Whether Levine's argument about the emergence of cultural divisions in the latter half of the century holds for England and other English-speaking countries is a matter for debate.

[4] See Robert Jay, *The Trade-Card in Nineteenth-Century America* (Columbia: University of Missouri Press, 1987), and Dave Kathman, 'Bard Cards: Shakespeare's Role in Victorian Advertising', *The Advertising Trade Card Quarterly* 8 (2001), 16–23.

comedies but also to *Love's Labour's Lost*, *King John*, *Titus Andronicus*, *Timon of Athens*, *Cymbeline*, and *The Winter's Tale*, confirmation of Lawrence Levine's claim that late nineteenth-century familiarity with Shakespeare was broad. Second, though Shakespeare and product are brought together on the same card, sometimes on different sides, there is minimal (and often no) effort to harmonize them connotatively. These juxtapositions could lead to surreal or unintentionally comic results. Liebig cards, for example, pictured jars of its meat extract at the feet of King Lear, Othello, and Richard III. To be sure, some advertisers made an effort to rationalize the link between Shakespeare and their goods. Libby's cards tells us, for instance, that Oberon bewitched Titania with tinned meat and that Lady Macbeth encouraged Macbeth to offer Banquo's ghost a can of ox tongues. Trade cards for Dobbins' Electric Soap based on the 'seven ages' speech comically linked its detergent to each age of man; for the final age, 'sans teeth, sans eyes, sans taste, sans everything', we see a boy in a bathtub, entirely obscured by suds.[5] More often, however, even this strategy made only minimal connections between Shakespeare and products. A 'seven ages' series of trade cards for Emerson ploughs was far more typical—on the recto side was an idyllic illustration of one of the seven ages, on the other detailed information about farm equipment which made no reference to Shakespeare at all.

This disjunction also operated in another popular advertising form of the day, the Shakespeare pamphlet. Such pamphlets would print extracts from Shakespeare along with product information, making their advertising less disposable and by association more respectable. O. Phelps Brown, a purveyor of herbal extracts, pioneered this strategy, issuing a series of 'Shakespearian Annual Almanacs' throughout the 1870s and 1880s to bolster his credibility as a 'doctor'. In the 1880s, the New Home Sewing Company published its notorious *Shakespeare Boiled Down*, a set of play summaries followed by adverts, all of which was intended to ease New Home's sewing machines into the cultural life of consumers. Its bizarre cover illustration, of Shakespeare literally boiling in a cauldron, made a tongue-in-cheek point about the value of subjecting a laborious task— sewing, reading Shakespeare—to mechanical processing.[6] Even so, this was perhaps too tongue-in-cheek for the age, for later editions reduce the illustration and move it to the upper margin, replacing it with more conventional engravings of Shakespearean scenes, such as Macbeth and Lady Macbeth after Duncan's murder. Ironically, Shakespeare in the

[5] The 'seven ages' speech was a favourite for late nineteenth-century advertisers, for it allowed marketers to suggest how the product might suit a variety of consumers and uses, extending its market beyond its 'natural' scope. In the first decade of the 1900s, Horlick's malted milk, originally marketed as food for infants and invalids, launched a 'seven ages' campaign touting the product's benefits for every age group. In an early version of the 'before–after' ad, a pamphlet for Hoff's malt extract contrasted passages from the 'seven ages' speech (accompanied by drawings of tired figures) with rewrites of the same passages (accompanied by robust figures) stressing that Hoff's made the difference. The 'seven ages' ad was to have a long life in advertising. There are versions for Postum coffee substitute (1943) and Bell Telephone (1957), to name two latter-day examples.

[6] Richard Halpern, *Shakespeare Among the Moderns* (Cambridge, MA: Harvard University Press, 1997), 57–8.

cauldron would itself become an object for consumption in the late twentieth century; the image was duplicated on refrigerator magnets and postcards and sold at the Folger Library giftshop, snarky post-modern kitsch for intellectuals.

A favourite gambit of nineteenth-century advertising is the testimonial, where some ordinary consumer verifies the advertiser's truthfulness and the product's efficacy. Quotations from Shakespeare, a feature of many display advertisements of the period, often have the quality of testimonials. Advertisers carefully choose their Shakespeare lines so that the text—and thus Shakespeare himself—seems to endorse the product, sometimes lightly reworking the lines so that his endorsement is even more direct. Shakespeare thereby functions as a generic voice of popular authority, akin to the male voice-over in classic television ads. An 1892 advert for Macbeth bicycles twice cites Shakespeare (appropriately from *Macbeth*)—'Horsed upon the sightless couriers of the air' (1.7.22–3) and 'Thou art so far before—the swiftest wing is slow to overtake thee' (1.4.16–18, slightly revised). Both lines testify to the bicycle's speed and, with the glance at 'horses', to a competing, inferior means of transport. The citations are prefaced with this telling phrase, 'What Shakespeare says of the "Macbeth"'. An 1885 display advert for Ridge's baby food from *The Illustrated Sporting and Dramatic News* features mutually reinforcing endorsements, one from a Dr Samuel Barker, three from Shakespeare: 'What say these young ones' (*King John* 2.1.522), 'It be wholesome food' (*The Taming of the Shrew* 4.3.16), and 'The food that to him is luscious' (*Othello* 1.3.349, slightly modified). Strung together, the Shakespeare lines provide popular testimony to Ridge's quality and appeal, while Barker provides scientific corroboration of Shakespeare's 'claims'. An 1895 advert for the cure-all Homocea takes Shakespeare proof-texting a step further, combining several man-on-the-street testimonials with nine Shakespearean quotations which list 'what Shakespeare says of Homocea' (e.g. 'A sovereign cure' [Sonnet 153, l. 8], 'It is a thing most precious' [*Cymbeline* 3.5.59], 'Made me happy, or else I often had been miserable' [*Two Gentlemen of Verona* 4.1.33–4], and the like).[7]

Like other advertising strategies, the Shakespeare testimonial invited variations and hybrids. Mellin's Food, manufacturer of a heavily advertised infant milk supplement, combined the Shakespearean testimonial and the Shakespearean pamphlet in its *Shakesperian Wisdom on the Feeding and Rearing of Infants*. Offered free at the bottom of its many print adverts, to all who wrote in, this booklet brought two forms of authority to bear on the question of what to feed infants, combining carefully chosen Shakespeare passages related to child-rearing and pictures of cute, healthy infants accompanied by parents' testimonials. Since wilful misquotation can easily shade into parody anyway, it is inevitable that some advertisers would treat the Shakespearean testimonial as an opportunity for burlesque. Such is the case with an advertising booklet issued by

[7] An escalation in the deployment of Shakespearean citations can be seen in an 1893 display ad for Darlington Dress and Fabrics in the journal *Moonshine*. This ad uses no fewer than twenty-three Shakespearean citations related to dress, stylishness, or extravagance in a single page, arranged so that the first letters of the quotations 'magically' spell out the company's name.

Cleveland Bicycles in 1892, *Shakespeare Would Ride the Bicycle If Alive Today: The Reasons Why*. The booklet features comical bicycling situations illustrated by noted comic-strip artist Frederick Opper, each captioned with an appropriate Shakespeare line. One example: a picture shows Hamlet (in dark doublet) being tossed off his bike into a ditch, with the caption, 'what a falling off was there' (*Hamlet* 1.5.47). Interestingly, even as the booklet seems to lampoon Shakespearean endorsement as a practice, it nevertheless uses the tactic, albeit with a self-reflexive irony. This anticipates how popular invocation of Shakespeare's cultural authority would become increasingly equivocal and wry in the new century.

The transfer of prestige from Shakespeare to actors, elsewhere so abundantly evident in Victorian culture, did not prompt their appearance in advertisement, as it would with Laurence Olivier, Maurice Evans, and Orson Welles in the twentieth century. Despite their considerable fame, Shakespearean actors rarely appear in advertisements, perhaps because the vulgarity of trade was felt still to be beneath their dignity, perhaps because the celebrity testimonial did not hit full stride until the rise of the cinema. There is one notable exception—Sir Henry Irving, the most eminent Shakespearean of the late Victorian period, the first actor to be knighted, arguably a model for bourgeois upward mobility. Irving and Ellen Terry were, for example, the first and only actors to appear on a decorated biscuit tin (for Macfarlane & Lang in 1890); he was the only actor to appear among the famous figures used to market Sweet Home Family Soap; and at least six adverts featured Irving testimonials, for Beecham's Pills (1889), Kropp Razors (1889), Hyomei inhalers (1896), Mariani Wine (1897), Abbey's Effervescent Salts (1898), and Proctor's Pine-lyptus Pastilles (1898–1900). The Beecham's and Abbey's advertisements are of special note. In the Beecham's advert Irving appears as Hamlet, dressed in dark doublet and cape, staring the viewer intently in the eye and playing on Hamlet's and Beecham's famous taglines: 'To Beecham or not to Beecham? That is the question, methinks I've heard they are worth a guinea a box'. It's striking how the advert complicates the issue of who offers the testimonial and in what tone—is a dyspeptic Hamlet speaking, or Irving, or Shakespeare himself? The caption at the bottom, 'with apologies to our greatest Poet, and our most renowned Actor', also reveals some reticence about deploying Shakespearean prestige in the service of a nostrum, while of course highlighting that prestige. The Abbey's Salt ad seems even more equivocal about Shakespearean endorsement. On the bottle of Abbey's, we see Shakespeare proclaiming 'Had I ever tasted Abbey's Salt, I would never had said, "Throw physic to the dogs"'.[8] As if sensing that this extravagant endorsement may admit more than it intends (Shakespeare never tasted Abbey's), it adds a backhanded testimonial from Irving, 'It has certainly not been overrated'. Both adverts reveal a growing ambivalence to using Shakespeare and Shakespeareans in testimonials, even as they do so.

By and large, late nineteenth-century advertisers did not see Shakespeare as a source of connotations for shaping a specific brand image. However, an innovation in

---

[8] Taken from *Macbeth* 5.3.49.

packaging, the decorated tin, pointed toward the future of Shakespeare in advertising. Tins became middle-class collector items, their imagery elevating their value by evoking luxury, travel, patriotism, nostalgia, or good taste. Shakespeare-themed designs were perennial favourites, and as with trade cards, Shakespeare made mass-produced foodstuffs seem familiar and wholesome. Shakespeare designs, however, had additional connotational resonances. Some tins portrayed scenes from Shakespeare plays, typically pastoral or romantic scenes (the latter evocative of Shakespeare as poet of love, appropriate for the tins' function as gifts), or scenes featuring Falstaff (evocative of conviviality and plenty). Others pictured idyllic village scenes of Stratford-upon-Avon or its Warwickshire environs. Here Shakespeare offered a bridge back to a pre-industrial, 'authentic' Britain of the village, evoking rural artisanship and pastoralism, in effect giving back to the consumer in symbolic form what mass-produced commodity culture had taken away. Pastoral scenes from *A Midsummer Night's Dream* and *As You Like It*, much favoured designs, also evoked this pastoral nostalgia. The association between Shakespeare and a native rural ideal predates this period, but its use as a marketing tool for non-souvenir commodities suggests how Shakespeare himself is becoming a distinctive brand.

The most durable Shakespeare-themed marketing campaign of this period also partakes of this association. In 1864, Charles Edward Flower, head of the local Stratford brewery, the town's biggest employer and five times its mayor, laid the groundwork for the building of a tercentenary theatre in Stratford in honour of Shakespeare's 300th birthday; Flower's donation of a substantial tract of riverside property enabled the erection of the first Shakespeare Memorial Theatre fifteen years later. His sponsorship inaugurated a long association between Flowers Brewing and Shakespeare. Shakespeare's image (taken from the funerary bust in Holy Trinity Church) became the Flowers logo, reproduced on its bottle labels and beermats above the phrase 'brewed in Stratford-upon-Avon' until Whitbread took over the brand in the 1960s. Shakespeare's considerable prestige influenced Flowers' sponsorship, but Flowers' brand identification with the Bard seems far more concerned with touting Shakespeare as a symbol of local, village craft and 'merrie ole England' than with any upmarket ambitions. Shakespeare-themed tins and Flowers' ale reveal how Shakespeare was becoming a source not of authority but of associative resonances, resonances which twentieth-century advertisers would harness to shape their brands.

SHAKESPEARE AND MODERN ADVERTISING, 1900–1960

After the turn of the century, Shakespeare-themed marketing noticeably declined, so much so that by the 1920s Shakespeare references in ads were few and far between. Some practices from the Victorian era did hang on—a few Shakespeare titles or characters were adopted as brand names, Shakespeare's face was occasionally used as a logo, and a few citations from Shakespeare appeared in ad copy (though in a much narrower range of reference). As if preserving Victorian tradition, an advertisement campaign from 1928, for example, provided 'what Shakespeare says about Coca-Cola', offering in each instalment a quotation and a cartoon of characters enjoying a Coke (including, strangely enough, Julius Caesar and King Lear). But this type of marketing was becoming scarce. The reasons for this somewhat sudden shift are many. The emergence of a pronounced cultural divide between highbrow and lowbrow, with Shakespeare increasingly coded as high culture, meant that Shakespeare could no longer be deployed as a voice of *popular* authority in advertising. This cultural divide between Shakespeare and popular culture was widened by film's (and later radio's and television's) displacement of the theatre as the dominant medium for performance, and by the academic institutionalization of Shakespeare. Cast as the very epitome of traditionalism, elitism, and specialist knowledge, Shakespeare had lost the common touch. But equally crucial was that advertising itself was shifting formats, from a product-information approach stressing the product's uses and merits, to a product-image approach stressing the product's (and brand's) symbolic significance for the consumer. Advertisers thus treated Shakespeare less as a source of legitimation and more as a bundle of connotations with which to identify or contrast their products. Unfortunately Shakespeare was increasingly out of sync with those values now favoured by advertisers—modernity, urban life, convenience, speed, accessibility, fun, democratization.

Two adverts suggest Shakespeare's changed cultural status. Although a 1920 advert for Paramount Pictures in *The American Magazine* pictures Shakespeare and quotes from his work, its headline reads 'times have changed since Shakespeare'. 'Shakespeare thought of all the world as a stage', it claims, but 'motion pictures have made that thought a fact'. The graphics underline the point, with a small picture of Shakespeare and a cramped Globe theatre performance contrasting with a spacious, luxurious film theatre.[9] A 1936 advertisement for Budweiser beer titled 'he'll have to eat his words' defends the very concept of branding, using Shakespeare as exemplar and foil. His famous phrase 'what's in a name?' is given the lie, so the copy argues, by the 'sublime quality' we associate with Shakespeare's name, an association between name and quality which Budweiser shares. The authority of Shakespeare's words is trumped by his own accordance with the inexorable power of branding. Though Shakespeare dominates the illustration, far more authoritative is the bellhop pictured in the lower

---

[9] A 1944 ad for Dumont television sets reiterated this strategy, declaring 'verily, Mr. Shakespeare, "all the world's a stage" . . . with television'. Indeed, Shakespeare is regularly used early in the marketing of new technologies to suggest both continuities with the past as well as their surpassing of earlier products. A 1947 British Overseas Airways Corporation (B.O.A.C) ad, for example, pictures Shakespeare holding a globe and crowing 'why, then the world's mine oyster' (*The Merry Wives of Windsor* 2.2.4) in praise of international air travel. The ad combines a nostalgic appeal to 'merrie ole England' with its picture of the Shakespeare birthplace (a potential destination) and evocation of Shakespeare's authority to address safety concerns (a B.O.A.C pilot is described in these terms from *Two Gentlemen of Verona* 2.4.67–8: 'his years but young, but his experience old; his head unmellow'd, but his judgement ripe').

right corner, whose recommendation for the best beer is what modern consumers seek. In the illustration of Shakespeare, the book behind him is open to the first page of *As You Like It*; below this illustration, that title is repurposed to describe how Budweiser is available in both bottles and cans 'as you like it'. Both of Budweiser's Shakespearean citations distance themselves from Shakespeare's authority even as they draw upon the reader's passing familiarity with phrases from his work.

For some luxury products, such as jewellery, cigars, liquor or chocolates, Shakespeare's association with elitism and exclusivity was useful, a means for brands to gain an upmarket sheen. A 1930 advert for DeBeers diamonds, about Christmas engagement rings, bolsters its tone of quiet luxury—it pictures a well-dressed young couple with theatre box seats—with a Shakespeare quotation ('if all year were playing holiday', incongruously from Hal's 'I know you all' speech in *1 Henry IV* 1.2.201) as well as ersatz Shakespearean diction ('Thrice fortunate, proclaim the smiling sages, the young people who announce their engagement during this blessed season'). In 1933, Whitman portrayed Romeo and Juliet embracing on the balcony as a way of lending its chocolates a touch of class. The balcony scene had long been a means for associating products with love, but striking here is that in all versions of this advert the 'modern' nature of the romance is stressed, as if the advertiser feared that by using Shakespeare the product might unwittingly be branded as old-fashioned. An ad for Old Taylor whiskey in 1936 takes up another connotation from Shakespeare—artisanship. Picturing Shakespeare admiring his freshly-completed handwritten manuscript, the advert touts that Old Taylor is 'proudly signed by the master like other noble works'; in the foreground we see a hand signing a bottle with a quill pen, conflating Taylor the brewer with Shakespeare the author.[10] Even so, it is noteworthy that the advertisement copy never refers to Shakespeare's text directly; the illustration's caption (in tiny print) identifies Shakespeare's status as a 'master in spite of dispute and criticism which began before his death and continue even to this day'.

Perhaps the clearest indication that Shakespeare had come to connote luxury and excellence can be found in a 1934 sales brochure for Cadillac. With Shakespeare's image gracing the cover, the brochure makes the case that in art, literature, and music, one artist alone is the acknowledged master, as, so the argument goes, Cadillac is in automobiles. This brochure treats Shakespeare as the exemplary exemplar, the preferred popular emblem for the idea of the 'supreme'. Though not a word of Shakespeare appears, the description of his writing emphasizes tactile craft, uniqueness, and artistic 'aura'—'just once in all the history of literature Shakespeare pressed his pen against the parchments'—qualities which when transferred to Cadillac cars lift them from the

---

[10] Shakespeare's signature also figures in a 1924 Esterbrook pen ad, which features a facsimile of the signature along with a frowning Shakespeare, quill in hand. The copy argues that because Shakespeare used a quill, he cannot be blamed for his appalling penmanship, but with an Esterbrook there is no excuse for bad writing. This and the Old Taylor ad nicely illustrate how a single Shakespearean attribute—the signature—can be coded positively (as a sign of quality hand-craftedness) or negatively (as a sign of old-fashioned practice), depending on the marketers' needs.

realm of mundane mass-manufactured products. Yet this suggestion of artistic time-lessness sits uneasily with Cadillac's equally important quality of technological innovation, and so the pamphlet is forced to qualify its analogy: 'We do not wish to infer that a motor car can be compared to a great and ageless work of art. We merely wish to have you recall that in *every* field there is always *one* that stands supreme . . . Cadillac has *always* believed that *progress* means *change*—and we have brought to America, year after year, the greatest advancement in motor cars that science could achieve' (3–4, italics in original). The ad quite overtly shows marketers negotiating between the competing qualities of exclusivity and availability, agelessness and innovation, artisanal and technological production. It clarifies why, as Shakespeare's brand image came into focus, he might be invoked less often.

To address these tensions, advertisers adopt several strategies. One is to make Shakespeare a connotative foil. A 1944 Pacquin handcream ad cites *Romeo and Juliet* 3.3.36 ('The white wonder of dear Juliet's hand') and portrays a woman with perfect hands fondling a string of pearls, but it adds the riposte 'a lovely quotation, but did "dear Juliet" ever wrestle a black pot?', underlining the point with a picture of a woman washing up. By revealing the implicitly aristocratic circumstances that underlie Juliet's beauty, the advert positions its product as popular and middle class, while still maintaining Juliet as a romantic ideal for the housewife, its target consumer. Another approach is to treat Shakespeare with humour or irreverence. In 'Why Willie Screamed', a 1949 ad for 'Sanforized' fabrics (a shrinkage control process), we see a man dressed in shrunk pajamas standing atop a tiny theatre, bellowing while a bust of Shakespeare behind him looks on with raised eyebrows; the theatre displays the label 'Midsummer Night's Scream'. Here the Shakespearean reference serves merely as a comic intensifier. Plays upon familiar Shakespeare phrases—'to be or not to be', 'much ado about nothing', 'wherefore art thou', 'such stuff as dreams are made on'—often function in the same way. By contrast, a 1949 advert for Ford pictures a sedan leaving a summer-stock theatre, driven by the cast dressed in Elizabethan costuming. Combined are playful suggestions of luxury and romance—perennial Shakespearean qualities—with comically recast quotations such as 'thou shalt like an airy spirit go . . . on "hydra-coil springs" in front, "para-flex" in back' and 'pick of new V8 or six engine . . . both warbling of one song, both in one key'. Interestingly the advert updates the play's patriarchalism. We see Egeus at the top, angry that his daughter's heart has been 'filched', yet at the bottom is his modern fatherly counterpart, pleased that his child is so well protected by Ford's superior body and brakes.

Most notably, many Shakespearean references in advertisements simply become more oblique. In some cases, Shakespeare is never explicitly identified as a reference point. A 1949 advert for Schlitz beer, for example, pictures what is clearly a rehearsal of *Romeo and Juliet* (the costuming and balcony are unmistakable), yet Shakespeare is never mentioned or quoted; pictures of Falstaff disappear entirely from adverts for Falstaff beer, with the exception of a 1953 advert in which he appears (considerably trimmed down) as an antique pencil sketch in the background, labelled 'the choicest product of the brewer's art'. Intermediaries, often actors, now imparted the aura of

Shakespearean 'class'. Orson Welles's adverts for Paul Masson wine—'we will sell no wine before its time'—are perhaps the most famous example. Maurice Evans, a British actor who enjoyed celebrity as a Shakespearean in post-Second World War America, lent his aura to various brands of liquor and other consumer items throughout the fifties, though only in a 1950 ad for Lucky Strike cigarettes is he identified as a Shakespearean (in the background he is pictured as Hamlet). Actors, however, are not the only intermediaries. In the early 1930s, Halsey drinking fountains and Georgia marble both used their association with the building of the Folger Shakespeare Library to add prestige to their brands; the Shakespeare Inn and Shakespeare Memorial Theatre in Stratford-upon-Avon have been featured in Shakespeare-themed adverts for liquor, insurance, and cars, among other products.

One last development merits special mention—Shakespeare as a vehicle for corporate image-laundering. One of the earliest examples is a 1945 advertisement for Olin Industries, a major supplier of munitions to the Allies during the Second World War. The advert pictures London in ruins, with a flower in the foreground and behind it a toppled bust of Shakespeare, a bullet hole in its temple. The copy begins with Hotspur's line from *1 Henry IV*, 'out of this nettle, danger, we pluck this flower, safety' (2.3.11), and goes on to claim that a flower sprang up in the London rubble, fertilized by the nitrates in bombs which fell on the city, an obvious metaphor for how because of the wartime activities of Olin (reframed as 'us') 'the lovely flower of peace' can now thrive. But the deployment of Shakespeare—not really needed by this advertisement—does more than just provide Shakespearean seconding of its point. It positions Olin as a defender of Shakespeare and of culture itself, by *translatio imperii* the successor to the British Empire, while it diverts attention from Olin's profits from the war. A 1947 advert for Shell Oil makes an elaborate case for the benefits of glycerine by connecting the petroleum distillate to such products as cigarettes (signifying popular sophistication) and Shakespeare (signifying high culture). A volume of Shakespeare is open to Hamlet's 'to be or not to be' speech (with an accompanying illustration), apparently printed with glycerine-based inks. The association hints that just as Hamlet's speech is suffused throughout the culture to all our benefit, so too is glycerine—Shell and Shakespeare are thereby allied. Certainly Shell is not selling glycerine per se to readers of *Life Magazine*, where this advert appeared. Rather, its purpose is to establish Shell as a good corporate citizen, producing beneficial products at a moment of post-war expansion, and also perhaps to recast the image of a compound which, the advert acknowledges, is also found in 'dynamite and nitro-glycerine'.[11] Likewise, corporate sponsorship of Shakespeare performance functioned to create a corporate image of benevolent, generous patronage. In 1964 advertisements, for example, British Petroleum publicized its support for Canada's Stratford Festival (and adverts trumpeting corporate sponsorship still pepper the festival's programmes). Fifteen years later, ExxonMobil, Metlife Insurance,

[11] For another example, see Alan Sinfield's incisive discussion of a 1989 Royal Ordnance ad in *Faultlines: Cultural Materialism and the Politics of Dissident Reading* (Berkeley: University of California Press, 1992), 1–7.

and Morgan Guaranty Trust launched a substantial campaign to highlight their sponsorship of the broadcast of the BBC–Time Life Shakespeare series on American public television. Interestingly, in those ads television was as important as was Shakespeare, suggesting that these corporations sought not just to burnish their stature by associating themselves with a high cultural icon but also to promote the conversion of traditional cultural capital into a medium conducive to their needs. Their sponsorship of Shakespeare's definitive transposition into video format suggests a convergence of interests among transnational corporations, screen media, and Shakespearean cultural capital.

SHAKESPEARE AND CONTEMPORARY ADVERTISING, 1960 TO THE PRESENT

Contemporary Shakespeare-themed marketing certainly exhibits many continuities with earlier history. Advertisers still run variations on key phrases like 'we happy few' and 'to be or not to be'—indeed, by the nineties the latter had become the favourite Shakespearean reference in advertising. As was the case with earlier innovations, when new writing technologies were introduced in the 1970s and 1980s—the electric typewriter, the copier, the word processor—Shakespeare served as one means for advertisers to highlight advances over earlier writing media and also to integrate a new, potentially intimidating device into the workplace by linking it to the handwritten word. Irreverent treatment of Shakespeare and use of Shakespeare as a high-cultural foil also remained dominant modes. A 1969 Coke advert, for example, offers a revisionary version of *Julius Caesar* with the product at its centre, suggesting that had Brutus properly understood Caesar's 'et tu, Brute' as an offer of a drink, 'things would have gone better with Coke'. Coke thereby becomes a magical means for breaking the fixities of history and high art. In a 1998 advert for a car repair scheme, a cartoon of the balcony scene features Juliet offering this line, 'Lifetime guarantee? What do you think this is, GM Goodwrench Service Plus?' Notably, nowhere is the scene identified in the ad as Shakespearean. The playful iconoclasm of these advertisements reveals that despite post-modernism's supposed levelling of high/low distinctions, Shakespeare remains a residual significer of highbrow tradition, often evoked ironically.

What is more, print advertisers, particularly those of the 1980s and after, tend to magnify the obliqueness of their Shakespearean allusions. Allusions were increasingly visual rather than textual and often referred to only a few immediately recognizable commonplaces—the balcony scene, Hamlet with Yorick's skull, variations of the Droeshout portrait. A 1987 advert for B&B Italia (a furniture store) pictures Hamlet in black doublet sprawled on a modern white sofa in the style of Ingres' *Odalisque*, with Yorick's skull on an end-table; the advert offers no explanation of the strikingly incongruous juxtaposition other than the slogan 'être ou ne pas être installeé confortablement'. Even more oblique allusions to *Hamlet* surface in two advertisements from the last decade. In one, from 2003, for Sky TV's broadcast of episodes of *Biography*, we see a frowning infant contemplating his cupped hand which will one day hold Yorick's skull, with only the caption 'William Shakespeare from the beginning'; in another, from 2007, for the Eurostar, a kneeling skeleton holds the head of a man (a reversal of Hamlet and Yorick), with the slogan 'London is changing'. The initially cryptic and visually arresting nature of these adverts is calculated to capture the viewer's attention but, more importantly, to reward his or her capacity to recognize the allusion. If earlier advertisements sought to associate some characteristically Shakespearean quality with the product, here Shakespearean citation works to place the target consumer among a knowing elite, though the bar for 'knowing' is set low.

Unlike the case of print advertisement, Shakespeare has made few substantial in-roads into radio and television advertising, perhaps because both are directed at the widest possible audience and thus antithetical to the kinds of specialist knowledge supposed necessary for understanding Shakespeare. Radio advertising has been particularly resistant to Shakespeare-themed advertising—I have found no substantial examples from American radio's 'golden age' in the 1930s and 1940s other than spots publicizing Shakespeare performances or films or using well-known Shakespearean actors. Television advertising too has been rather unamenable to Shakespearean allusion beyond the occasional 'to be or not to be' or balcony scene parody or lampoons of stuffy Shakespeare himself. A 1973 BIC pen advertisement reveals why. Here we see Shakespeare struggling to communicate with the Elizabethan court; the voice-over (supplied by comedian Mel Brooks) tells us, 'there are still people tryin' to figure out what he was talkin' about'. His modern reincarnation, using a BIC pen, immediately impresses his bohemian audience with his updated version of 'to be or not to be', 'I am, take it or leave it'. The announcer allies other ballpoint pens with Shakespeare's outdated language, whereas the BIC pen is modern and hip. A similarly stark contrast between period Shakespeare and demotic modernity suffuses a Carling Black Label lager ad of the mid-1980s. The setting is a stage performance of *Hamlet*. As Hamlet launches into his 'poor Yorick' speech, he drops the skull, only miraculously to save it with his foot before it hits the floor. The audience's cheers encourage him to show off his spectacular soccer moves using the skull as a ball, until he and Horatio send it flying into the lap of a beer-drinking spectator. The triumph of working-class sport over stolid, overly-intellectual Shakespeare brands Carling as 'popular', aligned with those who puncture the upper-class decorum associated with 'culture'. This Hamlet-as-lad displays physical skills which, so the advert suggests, surpass Shakespeare's linguistic virtuosity; his vitality breathes new life—literally—into Yorick's skull, which delivers the punchline—'I bet he drinks Carling Black Label'.[12]

This aggressive positioning of Shakespeare as a symbol of oppressive high culture, in tension with the freedom and anarchic vitality of products coded as 'popular', is

---

[12] Derek Longhurst labels this mode the 'popular grotesque'. He discusses the Carling advert in '"You base football-player!": Shakespeare in Contemporary Popular Culture', in Graham Holderness (ed.), *The Shakespeare Myth* (Manchester: Manchester University Press, 1988), 66–8.

how Shakespeare most often appears in television advertising, even in the wake of Shakespeare's cinematic repopularization in the nineties. Recent advertisements involving student performances of *Romeo and Juliet* illustrate the point. In one for Slim Jim snacks from the late 1990s, very much in the vein of the Carling Black Label advert, a Shakespearean rehearsal lorded over by an imperious director is disrupted by the explosive arrival of Randy 'Macho Man' Savage, the outrageous American wrestling star. Asking 'art thou bored?' he invites the male actors to 'snap into a Slim Jim', and with each bite of the snack, the set is blown apart, the finale occurring when a flat falls on the director. Less spectacular but more witty is a 2003 Nextel advert in which students in period costume carrying cell phones act out the plot of *Romeo and Juliet* with texted dialogue. Here is the entire script: 'Romeo', 'Juliet', 'I love you', 'Ditto', 'Die!', 'Marry him', 'Never!', 'No!', 'Better now', 'No!', 'Kids'. In both cases, the adverts lampoon *Romeo and Juliet* for being an overly-familiar, revered school text, despite the fact that the Nextel commercial depends upon (and thus rewards) the viewer's familiarity with the play for the advert's compressed action to make sense.

Even though many adverts single out Shakespeare's language for scorn, a new style of Shakespeare-themed advertising has recently emerged, one which takes the re-romanticized, re-heroicized Shakespeare of recent film adaptation as its foundation. A Levi's jeans advert from 2005 offers a particularly interesting example. In it, a young man in jeans, after passing through a gauntlet of gang members on a dangerous corner, catches the eye of a beautiful young woman who instantly declares her love for him. The dialogue is taken from Bottom's first encounter with Titania in *A Midsummer Night's Dream* (3.1), but the scene is handled as heroic and romantic rather than preposterous, its dreaminess highlighted by Mendelssohn's *Midsummer Night's Dream Suite* playing in the background. The key reference point, cued by the red curtain which opens the piece, is Luhrmann's *Romeo + Juliet* (with a distant nod to *West Side Story*), with its blend of youth culture, urban modernization, and lush passion. The spot is especially deft in using Shakespearean language to fine-tune the jeans' image. When the gang leader observes 'Bottom, thou art changed' (*Dream*, 3.1.110), he refers to Bottom's rejection of now unfashionable gang clothing, so that Bottom's bravery on the mean city streets becomes primarily sartorial; Titania's line 'So is mine eye enthralled to thy shape' (*Dream*, 3.1.132) is also redirected toward Bottom's cut of jeans, apparently magically irresistible to women. Here Shakespeare is not being used as a high-cultural foil. Instead, the hip, romantic Shakespeare of Luhrmann's film becomes a direct means for revivifying Levi's somewhat tired 'classic' brand, and without a knowing wink. A second example, for the Sony Playstation 3 in 2008, is more equivocal. The concept is simple: against a sequence of clips from Playstation 3 racing and fighting games plays a rousing rendition of Henry V's 'band of brothers' speech (4.3.20–67), accompanied by stirring music. Here the principal reference point is Branagh's *Henry V*, but the advert's tone is difficult to locate—is it intended as mock-heroic, as clips from the cartoon game 'Little Big Planet' might seem to suggest? Or is this praise of heroic camaraderie genuine, given that all the featured games are multi-player and interactive? The ambiguity seems strategic—this deployment of Shakespeare seeks to elevate the Playstation brand among young male consumers, beset by charges of nerdiness, while maintaining just enough ironic distance not to seem overly earnest. That Shakespeare has become once again useful to some advertisers as a positive connotative resource, reveals the power of recent Shakespeare films to reinvigorate Shakespearean cultural capital for a new generation.

That power has contributed to a second effect—the globalization of Shakespeare-themed advertising. In earlier phases of advertising's development, Shakespeare's strong association with British culture made him an unattractive point of reference in many non-Anglo markets.[13] One effect of the international cinematizing of Shakespeare in the past two decades has been to loosen his close identification with Anglo culture and strengthen his link to urban youth culture worldwide. The Levi's jeans advert referred to above, for example, is notable for its multi-racial casting; it was released not only in America and Britain, but also in a number of European countries in dubbed or subtitled form, suggesting that advertisers now assume youth Shakespeare has a cross-cultural appeal. Almost all global Shakespearean advertising dwells on one of three *topoi*—Shakespeare himself, *Hamlet*, and *Romeo and Juliet*—the last of which offers by far the most fruitful territory for marketers. Riffs on the balcony scene figure in, to take a few examples, adverts for Volkswagen (1999, Brazil), ice cream (2000, Portugal), heritage sites (2001, Italy), bras (2003, South Africa), chewing gum (2003, Germany), a dating service (2003, India), tea (2004, Japan), mobile service (2005, Portugal), diet drink (2006, India), condoms (2008, Poland), chewing gum (2008, Russia), televisions (2008, Turkey), insecticide (2008, Indonesia), and ceiling board (2008, Thailand). One reason *Romeo and Juliet* has been so popular with advertisers is that the tale has already been transposed into so many modern ethnic and cultural contexts by adaptors; another is that the balcony scene's earnestness is ripe for playful puncturing (few adverts treat the scene seriously). Certainly Shakespeare's increasing popularity in worldwide advertising testifies to how recent screen adaptations have increased Shakespeare's mobility across cultural borders by shifting his work from primarily textual to visual terms. Indeed, references in many of these advertisements to visual and musical details in Zeffirelli's and Luhrmann's films underline this close relationship. Which raises a provocative question: what then was (and is) the larger cultural project of recent Shakespeare on screen? Whose interests are being served by the mediatization of Shakespearean cultural capital and its recent global mobilization? Herein lies the paradox of Luhrmann's citation of Shakespearean advertising with which we began: his film laments commercialized Shakespeare in order to

---

[13] In Britain, the association between Shakespeare and national pride has been renewed in advertising of the past ten years. A recent television spot for Fuller's London Pride beer, for example, uses John of Gaunt's 'this sceptr'd isle' speech (*Richard II* 2.1.40–50) as a voice-over for shots of a filled football stadium, linking populist fandom, Shakespearean patriotism, and brand of ale in one fell swoop. Another advert, for Renault, features a friendly cultural rivalry between a fetching French woman and British man. To counter her references to French writers, the man holds up a copy of *Henry V* and whispers 'Shhhhhh-akespeare', at which the woman grimaces, apparently defeated. Ironically, the advert touts Renault's combination of French style and British engineering.

produce a newly romanticized Shakespeare which, because of the cinematic power of his adaptation, has enabled Shakespearean marketing to be extended as never before.

Why does Shakespeare in advertising matter? It is true that the history of Shakespearean advertising is largely a history of wilful mis-citation. As such, it might seem useless to those interested in uncovering what the plays 'really' mean, offering at best a detour into the entertaining realm of Shakespeare kitsch, at worst as an example of the kind of cultural rubbish that scholars struggle to clear away. Whether we can or should divide the 'real' Shakespeare from the many uses to which his work has been put, however, remains a matter of intense debate. At the least, if we take it seriously, the history of Shakespeare in advertising can illuminate how Shakespeare's cultural power has been reconceptualized over time. By its nature advertising must tap into cultural associations and hierarchies already familiar to the public, and so it can reveal popular interpretive proclivities and ideological investments linked to Shakespeare otherwise hard to unearth. But advertising is also an important force for reproducing perceptions of Shakespeare from generation to generation and for disseminating them throughout a society, in forms at least as powerful as the tomes and performances of the 'official' guardians of 'proper' Shakespeare. Even as it seeks short-term profits from its appropriations, advertising contributes, often unwittingly but quite significantly, to Shakespeare's long-term (re)capitalization in the ever-changing cultural marketplace. If we are to understand precisely how and why Shakespeare has remained so valuable a symbolic commodity for the past 400 years, we would do well to attend to how he has been 'retail'd to posterity'.

PART V

SPECULATIONS

CHAPTER 28

....

CLASSICS

....

JESSICA WOLFE

IN some commendatory verses prefixed to a 1640 edition of Shakespeare's poems, the poet and translator Leonard Digges (1588–1635) writes that 'Nature onely helpt him, for looke thorow | This whole Booke, thou shalt find he doth not borrow, | One phrase from *Greekes*, nor *Latines* imitate'.[1] Despite the oddly erroneous nature of the claim— two of the poems in the volume, *Venus and Adonis* and the *Rape of Lucrece*, derive from Latin sources—Digges represents Shakespeare as a poet inspired by nature rather than art, a writer who does not 'Plagiari-like from others gleane'.[2] Much of Digges' commendatory poem is directed against the plodding erudition of Ben Jonson (1572– 1637), whose 'tedious (though well labored)' *Catiline* and 'irksome' *Sejanus* fall short of Shakespeare's *Othello* and *Julius Caesar*. Digges' assertion that 'all that he doth write, | Is pure his owne' echoes John Milton's assessment of Shakespeare as 'fancies childe' in *L'Allegro* (*c*.1632) and simultaneously challenges some of the assumptions motivating Jonson's epitaph on Shakespeare, which celebrates labour and art over values such as nature, inspiration and fancy.[3] Whereas Jonson concedes that 'though the *Poets* matter, Nature be, | His Art doth give the fashion' such that 'a good *Poet's* made, as well as borne', Digges insists that 'Poets are borne not made'.[4] Such conflicting accounts of Shakespeare's reliance upon—or his independence from—classical models have shaped critical assessments of him for almost four centuries.

The nature and extent of Shakespeare's indebtedness to ancient models has likewise proven a persistent source of critical disagreement since the playwright's own time. Raphael Lyne has observed that Shakespearean drama is 'so complex and capacious that

[1] Leonard Digges, 'Upon Master William Shakespeare, the Deceased Authour, and his Poems', in *Poems written by Wil. Shake-speare. Gent.* (London: 1640), sig. 3.

[2] Digges, 'Upon Master William Shakespeare', sig. 3.

[3] Digges, 'Upon Master William Shakespeare', sig. 3v; John Milton, *L'Allegro*, l. 133, in Frank Allen Patterson (ed.), *The Works of John Milton*, 21 vols. (New York: Columbia University Press, 1931), 1: 1, 39.

[4] Ben Jonson, 'To the Memory of my beloved, The Author Mr. William Shakespeare: And what he hath left us', ll. 57–8, l. 64, in C. H. Hertford and Percy and Evelyn Simpson, *The Works of Ben Jonson*, 11 vols. (Oxford: Clarendon Press, 1947), 3: 392; Digges, 'Upon Master William Shakespeare', sig. 3.

it seems to incorporate whatever is culturally available with remarkable discernment, but without evidence of study', thus making it difficult to pinpoint literary influences which are often subtle and indirect rather than explicit and obvious.[5] Even so, Shakespeare's contemporaries often compared him to his Greek and Roman forerunners. In his 1598 *Palladis Tamia*, Francis Meres observes that '[a]s the soul of Euphorbus was thought to live in *Pythagoras*, so the sweet, witty soul of *Ovid* lives in mellifluous and hony-tongued Shakespeare'; around sixty years later, Thomas Fuller observes that 'three eminent Poets,' Ovid, Martial, and Plautus, 'may seem in some sort to be compounded in him', quipping that like Plautus, Shakespeare was 'an exact Comaedian, yet never any Scholar'.[6] The relative imperceptibility of Shakespeare's debts to the classical world arouses admiration among some readers and scorn among others. Whereas John Keats praises the 'innate universality' of Shakespeare's mind, a mind extraordinarily able to assimilate and digest classical sources, others have called him 'wayward' and 'hasty' in his imitation of Greek and Roman models.[7] In *Love's Labour's Lost*, Shakespeare appears to endorse the view of Digges and Keats when Holofernes observes that '*Imitari* is nothing. So doth the hound his master, the ape | his keeper, the tired horse his rider'.[8] But the bumbling schoolmaster, the limitations of whose Latinity are revealed by his frequent grammatical errors, his excessive adoration for Ovid, and his inordinate passion for etymology, is hardly an expert on matters poetical. Moreover, the imitative practices dismissed by Holofernes were a cornerstone of Shakespeare's grammar-school education. At Stratford, students would have honed their skills of imitation and adaptation by compressing, attenuating, rearranging, and transforming verses from Ovid and Virgil, their study supplemented by texts such as Richard Rainolde's *A Booke called the Foundacion of Rhetorike* (1563), an English adaptation of Aphthonius' *Progymnasmata* that helped to nurture the 'extraordinary inventiveness' of Elizabethan literary imitations.[9]

To the vexation of generations of readers and critics, little is known for certain about Shakespeare's education, which most scholars agree was undertaken at the King's New

---

[5] Raphael Lyne, 'The Authority of Prospero's Slave,' *Times Literary Supplement* 12 (13 February 1998), 12.

[6] Meres, *Palladis Tamia* (1598), in G. Gregory Smith (ed.), *Elizabethan Critical Essays* (Oxford: Clarendon Press, 1904), 2: 317–18; Thomas Fuller, *A History of the Worthies in England*, 126.

[7] For Keats' comments on the 'innate universality' of Shakespeare, see Richard Monckton Milnes (ed.), *Life, Letters, and Literary Remains* (New York: Putnam, 1848), 107; on Shakespeare as a 'wayward' and 'hasty' imitator, see Charles Martindale, 'Shakespeare's Ovid, Ovid's Shakespeare: a Methodological Postscript', ch. 13 of A. B. Taylor (ed.), *Shakespeare's Ovid: The Metamorphoses in the Plays and Poems* (New York: Cambridge University Press, 2000), 212.

[8] William Shakespeare, *Love's Labour's Lost* 4.2.126–7. All subsequent references to Shakespeare's works are cited parenthetically in the text of this essay from *The Oxford Shakespeare: Complete Works*, Stanley Wells and Gary Taylor (eds.), 2nd edn. (New York: Oxford University Press, 2005).

[9] On Shakespeare's 'extraordinary inventiveness' with his sources, see R. W. Maslen, 'Myths exploited: the metamorphoses of Ovid in early Elizabethan England', ch. 1 of Taylor (ed.), *Shakespeare's Ovid*, 17.

School at Stratford, a free school chartered in 1553. By contrast to contemporaries such as Edmund Spenser (*c*.1552–1599) and Ben Jonson, who studied respectively at the Merchant Taylors' School and Westminster School, there is little documentation concerning Shakespeare's course of instruction or the pedagogical methods of his schoolmasters. But thanks largely to T. W. Baldwin's groundbreaking 1944 study, *William Shakespere's small Latine and lesse Greek*, most contemporary scholars agree that Shakespeare's grammar-school education suffices to account for his evident familiarity with the language and literature of ancient Rome, his grasp of the rudiments of classical rhetoric, and his satirical handling of Elizabethan schoolmasters and their methods. Judging from other Elizabethan grammar school curricula as well as from the evidence contained in his plays and poems, Shakespeare probably would have studied selections from the major Latin poets, historians, and rhetoricians, including Virgil, Ovid, Livy, Cicero, and Quintilian. His education in these and other writers would almost certainly have been supplemented by grammars and textbooks such as William Lily's *Grammar*, William Baldwin's *Treatise of Moral Philosophy* (1547), and various other collections of maxims, fables, dialogues, and epithets, many of them modelled on the *Adages* and *Colloquies* of the early sixteenth-century humanist and educational reformer Desiderius Erasmus.

Several of Shakespeare's plays demonstrate a particular familiarity with Lily's *Brevissima Institutio*, an immensely popular Latin grammar first published in 1534. Many of the hackneyed Latin tags bandied about by Holofernes, including 'Novi hominem tanquam te' [I know the man as well as I know you], and 'vir sapit qui pauca loquitur' [it is a wise man who speaks little], derive from Lily, as may the schoolmaster's distinctive habits of speech, which like Lily's textbook often give multiple English synonyms for a single English word (*LLL* 5.1.9; 4.2.79). Both *Love's Labour's Lost* and *Merry Wives of Windsor* travesty humanist educational methods and mock the small Latin and less Greek possessed by schoolmasters who, as Moth puts it in *Love's Labour's Lost*, 'have been at a great feast of languages and stolen the scraps' (*LLL* 5.1.36–7).[10] At *Merry Wives* 4.1, when Sir Hugh Evans tests young William on his Latin grammar, the scene dramatizes the ease with which a lesson in accidence, drawn from Lily's textbook and delivered with Evans' strong Welsh accent, provides fodder for the kind of sexual innuendo beloved by schoolboys: *Pulcher* becomes *Polecats*; *hic, haec, hoc* becomes *hung, hang, hog*; and *vocativo* becomes *focative* (*MWW* 4.1 24–5, 37–42, 46–8). Throughout Shakespeare's plays, characters such as Holofernes (*LLL*) and Pistol (*Henry V*) misquote classical phrases to hilarious effect, simultaneously performing and parodying the art of allusion (from the Latin *ludere*, to play with) that Shakespeare would have learned from, and practiced with, Latin poets such as Ovid, Horace, and Virgil.

Many of Shakespeare's most celebrated adaptations of classical texts derive from contemporary English translations of Greek and Latin works such as Arthur Golding's

---

[10] Another allusion to Lily's *Grammar* has been detected at *Much Ado About Nothing* 4.1.121 by Colin Burrow; see his 'Shakespeare and Humanistic Culture', ch. 1 of Charles Martindale and A. B. Taylor (eds.), *Shakespeare and the Classics* (Cambridge: Cambridge University Press, 2004), 14.

translation of Ovid's *Metamorphoses* (1567) and Thomas North's translation of Plutarch's *Lives* (1579). But several of his works also suggest direct engagement with Latin (but never Greek) originals: *The Comedy of Errors* reveals familiarity with the plot, if not also the actual text, of Plautus' *Menaechmi*, a play not yet translated into English, while for *The Rape of Lucrece*, Shakespeare appears to have consulted both the text and the notes of Ovid's *Fasti* in the standard Latin edition.[11] Yet critics disagree over the extent to which these and other echoes reveal anywhere near the kind of erudition displayed by other Elizabethan and Jacobean playwrights such as Jonson and George Chapman. J. A. K. Thomson has argued that the 'superstructure' of *Comedy of Errors* is 'the work of a man who appears never to have looked at the *Latin* of Plautus at all', while the Latin motto on the title-page of *Venus and Adonis*, taken from *Amores* 1.15.35–6, may have been added by the publisher rather than the author; the lines were so well known, moreover, that Shakespeare need not have known Ovid intimately in order to cite them.[12] Furthermore, the task of identifying a single classical source for a given Shakespearean scene, or even a single line, can prove difficult, since as Robert Miola has argued, Elizabethan readers tend to value 'multiplicity over coherence', often drawing upon multiple versions of the same myth or historical event.[13] Menenius' fable of the belly (*Coriolanus* 1.1.94–153) appears in no fewer than five authors available to Shakespeare, including Plutarch, Livy, and Philip Sidney, while the plot of *Venus and Adonis* derives from Ovid's *Metamorphoses*, from Book 3, canto 6 of Spenser's *Faerie Queene* (1590), and quite possibly from other renditions of the myth found in sixteenth-century poems, mythographies, and even the visual arts, where it was a popular subject.[14] In assembling the sources for many of his plays, Shakespeare displays a gleeful disregard for chronological and cultural distinctions as he mixes together ancient and modern sources: in *Cymbeline*, for instance, Holinshed's *Chronicles* provides the setting of the play and the name of its main character, but Shakespeare also incorporates elements from Giovanni Boccaccio's *Decameron*, from a 1589 play entitled *The Rare Triumphs of Love and Fortune*, and (as most critics agree) from Heliodorus' *Aithiopika*, a third-century CE Greek romance that Shakespeare may have read in the Elizabethan translation by Thomas Underdowne or in Abraham Fraunce's The *Countesse of Pembrokes Yvychurch* (1591), the latter of which contains a short translation of the opening pages of Heliodorus' romance alongside other 'conceited tales'.[15]

---

[11] Martindale and Taylor (eds.), *Shakespeare and the Classics*, 1.

[12] J. A. K. Thomson, *Shakespeare and the Classics* (London: Allen and Unwin, 1952), 49, 39–40.

[13] Robert Miola, *Shakespeare's Reading* (Oxford: Oxford University Press, 2000), 4.

[14] Miola, *Shakespeare's Reading*, 4.

[15] Fraunce, *The Countesse of Pembrokes Yvychurch* (London: 1662), 'The Beginning of Heliodorus his Athiopical History', which runs from sigs. M1 to M3v at the end of the volume. On the sources of *Cymbeline*, see Geoffrey Bullough (ed.), *Narrative and Dramatic Sources of Shakespeare* (New York: Columbia University Press, 1957–75), vol. 8; on Shakespeare's use of Heliodorus, see also Thomson, *Shakespeare and the Classics*, 36–7, and Stuart Gillespie, 'Shakespeare and Greek Romance: "Like an Old Tale Still"', ch. 13 of Martindale and Taylor (eds.), *Shakespeare and the Classics*.

Shakespeare's tendency to rely upon multiple sources for a single play—sources that often echo or imitate each other—makes it difficult to distinguish a true source from an analogue or to discern where the playwright's chief debts reside.[16] The character of Theseus in *A Midsummer Night's Dream*, for example, is assembled out of elements from Chaucer's *Knight's Tale*, Plutarch's *Life of Theseus* (in North's translation), and Ovid's *Metamorphoses*, among other works. Although principally based on Plautus' *Menaechmi*, *The Comedy of Errors* borrows the motif of the dual identity of the servants from another Plautine play, *Amphitruo*, while the story of Egeus' separation from his wife and their ultimate reunion, which ultimately derives from the ancient novella *Apollonius of Tyre*, is probably adapted by way of John Gower's *Confessio Amantis* (1390) or by way of Laurence Twine's *Pattern of Painful Adventures* (1576; rpt. 1607), a loose adaptation of a French translation of Gower's poem in turn based on a popular story from the *Gesta Romanorum*. Such recycling of what Ben Jonson mockingly dismisses as 'mouldy tale[s]' drawn from ancient romances is hardly unique to Shakespeare during the period.[17] Many of the classical stories at the root of his dramatic plots were translated into Italian by writers such as Boccaccio, Matteo Bandello (*Novelle*, 1554), and Giraldi Cinthio (*Hecatommithi*, 1565) and then subsequently rendered into English for collections such as George Pettie's *Petite Palace of Pettie his Pleasure* (1576) and William Painter's *Palace of Pleasure* (1566; 2nd edn. 1575), three tales of which supply the plots of *All's Well That Ends Well*, *Romeo and Juliet*, and *Timon of Athens*.

Adept at stitching together elements from diverse sources, Shakespeare also returns to the same classical models again and again, reading 'retentively and reminiscently' such that '[p]ast sources . . . productively furnish present imaginings'.[18] When Shakespeare reuses classical material, he often transforms comic motifs into tragic ones or vice versa: in *Merry Wives*, for instance, Shakespeare reshapes Ovid's myth of Diana and Actaeon into the stuff of burlesque, resituating the myth in an insistently English Windsor Forest and integrating it with the cuckolding and dis-horning of Falstaff as well as with local folklore surrounding Herne the Hunter.[19] This process of reanimating classical myths by placing them in modern contexts and settings is also the trademark of Elizabethan allegorists such as Spenser, whose *Faerie Queene* puts myths and episodes from Ovid and Virgil to work in the service of Protestant theology and the defence of the Elizabethan state. But Shakespeare's use of such methods differs from that of his contemporaries in its tendency to generate irreverent humour or irony. As Jonathan Bate has pointed out, many of Shakespeare's comedies provide happy endings to tragic episodes from Ovid's *Metamorphoses*.[20] In *As You Like It*, Orlando escapes Adonis' fate when he is nipped (rather than killed) by a lion; in *Merry Wives*,

---

[16] Miola, *Shakespeare's Reading*, 13–14.
[17] Jonson, 'Ode to himselfe', l. 21, in *Works*, 6: 492.
[18] Miola, *Shakespeare's Reading*, 161.
[19] Miola, *Shakespeare's Reading*, 4, 161.
[20] Jonathan Bate, *Shakespeare and Ovid* (Oxford: Clarendon Press, 1993), 120.

Falstaff is only pricked by his horns, not mortally wounded by them, like Actaeon; and in *Two Gentlemen of Verona*, a play deeply informed by the cultural and sexual logic of Ovidian metamorphosis, Julia escapes Thetis' destiny when she is saved from Proteus' attempt to rape her. Conversely, Shakespeare also transforms some of the comic motifs found in his classical sources into disquieting, even tragic, themes. The Plautine device of the 'separated twins', first used to broadly comic effect in *Comedy of Errors*, takes on a more disturbing set of implications in *Twelfth Night*: in a plot derived from Plautus, and repackaged as the tale of Apollonius and Silla in Barnabe Riche's 1581 *Farewell his Militarie Profession*, the experiences of Viola and Sebastian unearth unsettling questions about autonomy, sexual identity, and the deceptive powers of the human imagination. In *Hamlet*, Shakespeare again employs a motif from Plautus' *Menaechmi*—the feigned madness of Plautus' traveller that threatens to become real—and transforms it into a vehicle for dramatizing the self-doubt and suspicion lurking underneath the 'antic disposition' of that play's hero. Another important example of Shakespeare's creative reuse of classical material can be found in his various permutations of Senecan tragedy: while early plays such as *Titus Andronicus* and *Richard III* adhere rather faithfully to the dramatic and moral pattern of the Roman model, later plays such as *Hamlet* and *The Tempest* experiment with the genre, their aborted revenge plots interrogating Seneca's typical narrative and ethical structure.

In each of the above examples, Shakespeare makes flexible use of classical sources in a manner similar to the habits of Elizabethan translators, who refashion both the morals and the styles of Greek and Roman texts to suit the values and tastes of contemporary readers. During the early modern period, translations and imitations of classical texts are 'always purposeful', as Jonathan Bate has observed: 'texts from the past were valued for their applicability to present endeavour'.[21] Elizabethan grammar-schools stressed various methods of accommodating ancient myth and history to modern problems: Rainolde's English version of Aphthonius, for instance, subjects a single fable to 'an astonishing range of transformations' in order to demonstrate its relevance to a wide range of political and moral questions.[22] By providing poets with a large arsenal of classical quotations, allusions, and epithets at the ready, and by encouraging them to 'interweave [intertexantur]' such material 'deftly and appropriately' in their writings, sixteenth-century lexicons, dictionaries, and other popular compilations such as Erasmus' *Adages*, Thomas Cooper's *Thesaurus*, and Natale Comes' *Mythographiae* increase the intellectual currency available to a writer such as Shakespeare while also promoting the creative reuse of such resources.[23]

---

[21] Bate, *Shakespeare and Ovid*, 9.

[22] R. W. Maslen, 'Myths exploited: the metamorphoses of Ovid in early Elizabethan England', in Taylor (ed.), *Shakespeare's Ovid*, 17.

[23] Desiderius Erasmus, *Adages*, in *Collected Works of Erasmus*, vol. 31, Margaret Mann Phillips (trans.), and R. A. B. Mynors (ed.) (Toronto: Toronto University Press, 1982). In his preface, Erasmus also invites his readers to circulate his adages, citing Varro's etymology of *adagio* as derived from 'ambagio' or 'circumagium', since they are 'something passed around' (*CWE* 31: 5, citing Varro, *De Lingua Latina* 7.31).

If Shakespeare 'remembered, misremembered and hybridised the works which we call the classics', as Colin Burrow has argued, he did so in ways which were 'distinctive to him, but which also reflect recognizably Tudor humanist methods of reading'.[24] In his classic study of Renaissance literary imitation, *The Light in Troy*, Thomas Greene outlines four basic methods of imitation that shed light on Shakespeare's transformation of Greek and Roman models. According to Greene, the four principal models of imitation practised by Renaissance poets and playwrights are (1) *reproductive or sacramental imitation*, in which a later writer essentially copies a classical model, (2) *eclectic or exploitative imitation*, in which 'heterogeneous allusions are mingled' out of a variety of different sources, (3) *dialectical imitation*, in which a later text 'actively conflicts with and dissociates itself from its classical pre-text', and (4) *heuristic imitation*, which 'in its own processes dramatises the historical difference between the poet and his precursor'.[25] Shakespeare often employs several different modes of imitation in the same play and even in the same scene; he competes with his source texts by altering and interrogating them, and, as we have already seen, he reads 'eclectically' by conjoining texts 'freely and unpredictably'.[26] In this respect, Shakespeare hardly ever treats his classical sources like 'classics' in the modern sense of the term, as works to be preserved or commemorated. Even a source such as Plutarch's *Lives*, which Shakespeare follows slavishly in certain places, is not immune to aggressive revision, often in the service of heightening dramatic tension. *Julius Caesar* passes over the first three-quarters of Plutarch's account, skipping over Julius' rise to power and his defeat of Pompey: in a 'bold strategy of omission', Shakespeare allots Caesar a mere 150 lines in only three scenes of the play, a technique which 'magnifies rather than diminishes [him]'.[27] Moreover, Shakespeare's debts to the classical world often run deepest where they are least apparent: although set in medieval Scotland, *Macbeth* has been deemed the most 'classical' of Shakespeare's tragedies: murders are performed off-stage, in the Roman style; speeches reverberate with echoes of Seneca's *Hippolytus* and *Hercules Furens*; and typically Senecan techniques of foreshadowing amplify the sense of tragic irony throughout this most Roman of Scottish plays.[28]

---

[24] Burrow, 'Shakespeare and Humanistic Culture', in Martindale and Taylor (eds.), *Shakespeare and the Classics*, 9.

[25] Thomas Greene, *The Light in Troy: Imitation and Discovery in Renaissance Poetry* (New Haven, CT: Yale University Press, 1993), 39–41. For a discussion of the relevance of Greene's arguments to Shakespeare's use of classical sources, see Bate, *Shakespeare and Ovid*, 42, 46.

[26] Miola, *Shakespeare's Reading*, 154.

[27] Miola, *Shakespeare's Reading*, 102–3.

[28] Thompson, *Shakespeare and the Classics*, 119. Thomson (120–1) detects Senecan parallels at *Macbeth* 1.7.8–11 (influenced by *Hercules Furens*, 2. 735–6) and at 2.2.39–44, a possible echo of *Hercules Furens*, ll. 1065–8 as well as of Ovid, *Metamorphoses* XI.623–7, which is the source of the Senecan passage, and quite possibly of the Shakespearean one. He detects additional parallels between Lady Macbeth's speech at 2.2.68–72 and Seneca, *Hippolytus* 715–19 and between IV.3.210–11 and *Hippolytus*, l. 607.

'SHAPES TRANSFORMDE': SHAKESPEARE'S OVIDIANISM

Ovid's influence on Shakespeare is as varied as it is complex: his poems shape Shakespeare's comprehension of dramatic genre, his treatment of gender and erotic desire, and his understanding of cosmic change and recurrence. In the comedies, many readers detect the particular influence of Books 3 and 4 of the *Metamorphoses*, where the unlucky fortunes of lovers such as Pyramus and Thisbe, Salmacis and Hermaphroditus, Narcissus and Echo, and Diana and Actaeon give shape to the romantic perplexities and the sexual confusion of plays such as *A Midsummer Night's Dream, As You Like It,* and *Twelfth Night.* *Twelfth Night* transforms the myth of Narcissus and Echo by playing up its 'resonant connotations of uncomfortable, sexual confusion' and its lessons about the elusiveness of self-knowledge; early in the play, Viola is cast as Echo, 'babbling gossip of the air', while Olivia and Malvolio each acquire characteristics of Narcissus, the former in her erotic attraction to another woman and the latter in his dangerous self-absorption (*TN* 1.5.262).[29] Recently, critics have also taken interest in the influence of Ovid's *Heroides* on comic heroines such as Katherina (*The Taming of the Shrew*) and Beatrice (*Much Ado About Nothing*), who claim for themselves many of the same 'expressive liberties Ovid takes with erotic, rhetorical, and social conventions'.[30] The epistolary exchanges in the *Heroides* inspire the rhetorical virtuosity displayed by these and other comic heroines, who 'put verbal wit in the service of love', but they also give shape to the 'rhetoric of a divided mind' in tragedies and problem plays such as *Measure for Measure, Hamlet,* and *Troilus and Cressida*.[31]

Ovid also shapes Shakespeare's representation of change on both human and cosmic levels. The sense of 'universal mutability' in English and Roman history plays such as *Antony and Cleopatra* derives from Ovidian cosmology as much as from Seneca and the ancient Stoics.[32] Shakespeare's 'skeptical, dynamic temperament' may account for his particular attraction to the *Metamorphoses*, a poem preoccupied with the vicissitudes of human passions and cosmic motions.[33] The 'monstrous changes' suffered by tragic heroes such as Othello and Lear owe their origin to Ovid's tales of grotesque transformation: Lady Macbeth is shaped by Ovid's accounts of Medea, Byblis, and Myrrha, while Richard II compares his tragic fall to that of Ovid's Phaethon.[34] The

---

[29] On the Ovidian allusions in *Twelfth Night*, see A. B. Taylor, introduction to *Shakespeare's Ovid*, 8–9, and Bate, *Shakespeare and Ovid*, 146–50.

[30] Heather James, 'Shakespeare's learned heroines in Ovid's schoolroom', in Martindale and Taylor (eds.), *Shakespeare and the Classics*, 68.

[31] Bate, *Shakespeare and Ovid*, 33.

[32] Geoffrey Miles, *Shakespeare and the Constant Romans* (Oxford: Clarendon Press, 1996), 172.

[33] Bate, *Shakespeare and Ovid*, 6.

[34] On these allusions and analogues, see Taylor, introduction to *Shakespeare's Ovid*, 4–5; Richard compares himself to Phaethon at *Richard II* 3.3.178.

variability of human affection in Shakespeare's comedies and romances is likewise inspired by Ovidian metamorphosis: as Falstaff jokes in *Merry Wives*, just as Ovid's Jove turns himself into 'a swan for the love of Leda', the power of love 'in some respects makes a beast a man; in some other, a man a beast', a transformation that Falstaff punningly refers to as a 'fowl' or 'foul fault' (5.5.4–6, 11).

The romances and non-dramatic poems reveal debts to Ovid at once more direct and more complex. *The Rape of Lucrece* and *Venus and Adonis* are based, respectively, on passages from the *Fasti* and from *Metamorphoses* X.524–738; Gordon Braden has also detected several allusions to the *Metamorphoses* in the *Sonnets*, which, like Petrarch's *Canzoniere* before them, 'rewrit[e] Ovid's long poem as erotic and professional autobiography' in which change and decay are counter-balanced by the promise of literary fame.[35] In his non-dramatic poems, Shakespeare is clearly influenced by the prevailing fashion for mannered, densely allusive erotic poems: contemporary verse epyllia such as Thomas Lodge's *Scillaes Metamorphosis* (1589) and Marlowe's *Hero and Leander* (*c*.1591) augment the rhetorical artifice and the coy self-referentiality of their Ovidian models, embellishing familiar tales with ekphrases, *blasons*, and similarly artful digressions.[36] Whereas Ovid's account of Venus and Adonis unfolds in a 100 or so lines, Shakespeare attenuates his version to over 1,000, adding elaborate conceits and protracted, highly stylized dialogue.[37] The romances, by contrast, look to Ovid in order to explore both the tragic and the comic dimensions of mutability: the *Metamorphoses* inspires the 'sea-change' of Ariel's 'Full fathom five', a dirge for bones turned to coral and eyes to pearls (*Tempest* 1.2.400–4) and it also informs the equally 'rich and strange' transformations and conversions in the final acts of *Cymbeline* and *The Winter's Tale*.

Yet as much as the romances are influenced by Ovid in both style and outlook, they also insist upon their difference from Ovid. Prospero's renunciation of magic at *The Tempest* 5.1.33–57 closely imitates Medea's catalogue of her magical powers at *Metamorphoses* VII.196–209 but critiques as well as honours its source.[38] Whereas Ovid's Medea celebrates her ability to reverse the course of streams and to 'call up dead men from their graves' with her 'Charmes and Witchcrafts', Prospero abjures his 'rough magic' in favour of 'Mercy' and 'peniten[ce]', gentler and more Christian means of reversing the natural order of things

---

[35] Gordon Braden, 'Ovid, Petrarch, and Shakespeare's *Sonnets*,' ch. 6 of Taylor (ed.), *Shakespeare's Ovid*, 101, 106.

[36] On the popularity of verse epyllia in the early 1590s, on their influence on Shakespeare's non-dramatic poems, and on their typically mannered or allusive style, see Bate, *Shakespeare and Ovid*, 48, and John Roe, 'Ovid 'renascent' in *Venus and Adonis* and *Hero and Leander*', ch. 2 of Taylor (ed.), *Shakespeare's Ovid*, 35.

[37] On the length of Shakespeare's *Venus and Adonis* compared to its Ovidian source, see Bate, *Shakespeare and Ovid*, 50.

[38] On Prospero's speech as a heuristic imitation of Ovid's Medea at *Metamorphoses* VII.196–209, see Miola, *Shakespeare's Reading*, 149, and Raphael Lyne, 'Ovid, Golding, and the "Rough Magic" of *The Tempest*', ch. 10 of Taylor (ed.), *Shakespeare's Ovid*, 150.

(*Tempest* 5.1.50; Epilogue, l. 18; 5.1.28).[39] While it has become fashionable over the course of the last several decades to interpret *The Tempest* as a play about colonial politics, a reading which displaces the influence of Ovid in favour of Virgil's *Aeneid*, *The Tempest* is indebted to both poets, placing them in opposition to one another and thus generating a tension at once ideological and generic between Vergil's imperial epic on the one hand and Ovid's counter-epic poem of 'bodies changed' on the other.[40]

Shakespeare's romances are especially saturated with allusions to classical myths that serve as vehicles for exploring the aesthetic and moral legitimacy of art and illusion. The wedding masque in Act 4 Scene 1 of *The Tempest*, in which Juno and Ceres, ancient goddesses of maternal and agricultural fecundity, bless the approaching marriage between Miranda and Ferdinand, provides a meditation on the transitoriness of art, an 'insubstantial pageant' (4.1.155) made of 'spirits' who 'mel[t] into air, into thin air' (4.1.149–50). In the final two acts of *The Winter's Tale*, Shakespeare interweaves a series of allusions to Proserpina's abduction and return, to Orpheus and Eurydice, and to Pygmalion's statue into an extended metacritical reflection on the nature of romance— on art's capacity to effect miraculous transformations and reversals of fortune, or to bring to life those who may appear to be lost or dead. Much earlier, in *The Merchant of Venice*, Shakespeare employs Orpheus as a symbol of art's power to change nature: Lorenzo invokes the poet's ability to animate 'trees [and] stones' as proof that 'music' may soften the most 'hard' and 'stockish' creature, enlivening the 'motions of his spirit' so as to 'change his nature' (*Merchant*, 5.1.80–7). Embedding allusions to Orpheus throughout its last two acts, *The Winter's Tale* goes a step further, using the Orphic powers of the poet to rewrite Orpheus' own tragedy: in the *Metamorphoses*, Eurydice's loss is irreparable, but in *The Winter's Tale*, Hermione's is not.[41]

In the preface to his translation of the *Metamorphoses*, the Elizabethan translator Arthur Golding explains that the myths may prove variously useful to different readers in different circumstances, depending upon how they 'take [them] in sundry wise, | As matter rysing giveth cause constructions to devyse'.[42] The flexible applications of Ovidian myth are especially evident in Shakespeare's recurrent use of the myth of Diana and Actaeon, the very myth which Golding encourages his readers to interpret 'in sundry wise' and which George Sandys, who translated the *Metamorphoses* into English in 1632, also subjects to a 'double construction', arguing that Ovid's best fables

[39] *The xv. bookes of P. Ouidius Naso, entytuled Metamorphosis*, Arthur Golding (trans.), fol. 83v (London: 1567) (VII.275, 263).

[40] On the relationship between Vergilian and Ovidian sources in *The Tempest*, see Martindale, 'Shakespeare and Virgil', ch. 5 of Martindale and Taylor (eds.), *Shakespeare and the Classics*, 100.

[41] On Shakespeare's use of the myths of Orpheus and Proserpina in *The Winter's Tale*, see A. D. Nuttall, '*The Winter's Tale*: Ovid Transformed', ch. 9 of Taylor (ed.), *Shakespeare's Ovid*, 135–9, which argues that, unlike Orpheus, who is instructed not to look back at Eurydice as they ascend from the depths of Hades, Leontes is explicitly told by Paulina *not* to turn away from Hermione's statue. Nuttall finds an allusion to Ovid, *Metamorphoses* X.64 at *Winter's Tale* 5.3.105–7 ('Do not shun her | Until you see her die again, for then | You kill her double').

[42] Ovid, *Metamorphoses*, Golding (trans.) 'Too the Reader', sig. A2.

are those which 'admit of most senses'.[43] In *Merry Wives* 3.5 and 5.5, an extended conceit turns Actaeon's violent death at the hands (or rather the antlers) of Diana's stags into the 'peaking cornuto' of a comically 'horn-mad' Falstaff (3.5.66; 139), whereas *Twelfth Night* and *Titus Andronicus* employ the same myth to radically different ends, the former to tease out the instability of sexual identity and the perils of unsatisfied sexual desire, and the latter to foreshadow the sexual violence and bodily dismemberment enacted upon Lavinia. In the opening lines of *Twelfth Night*, Duke Orsino compares himself to Actaeon, 'turned into a hart' at the sight of Olivia such that 'my desires, like fell and cruel hounds, | E'er since pursue me' (1.1.20–2). Yet the hounds in pursuit of Orsino are dispatched not by Olivia but rather by his own sickly appetites. Shakespeare thus turns a myth which, in Ovid's handling, dramatizes the dangers of female sexual power, into a cautionary emblem about the perversions to which the masculine 'spirit of love' (1.1.9) is subject: Orsino's '[l]ove-thoughts' are both predator and prey, 'kill[ing] the flock of all affections else' (1.1.40; 35). In a later scene, the sexual implications of Ovid's tale are further complicated when Orsino compares Viola, dressed as Cesario, to Diana, her lip as 'smooth and rubious' as the goddess of chastity, and her 'small pipe' as 'shrill and sound' (1.4.32–3). In this rendition of the myth, it is the sexually ambiguated Cesario/Diana, and not Orsino/Actaeon, who is transformed, a metamorphosis which proves not a punishment but rather a liberation inasmuch as it frees Viola from the strictures of her gender.

Titus Andronicus 2.3.61–5 proposes a much more pessimistic reading of the Diana and Actaeon myth in an allusion which reveals the bestial foundations of human nature and the transformative effects of sexual violence. When Bassanius, at the opening of the hunt scene that will take his life, sardonically compares Tamora to Diana, she replies that she wishes for the power to plant horns on Bassanius' head, as Diana did to Actaeon, 'and the hounds | Should drive upon thy new-transformèd limbs' (2.3.63–4). The allusion foreshadows Bassanius' doom—the '[s]weet huntsman' (2.3.269) is shortly stabbed by Demetrius and Chiron—and also presages the violence done to Lavinia, another Actaeon figure whose limbs are 'lopped and hewed' (2.4.17) after she is raped during the hunt. Like Cadmus' nephew in Ovid's version of the myth, who is only able to protest the attack of his own hounds with 'piteous looke in stead of hands' or speech, Lavinia is rendered mute, her tongueless mouth turned into a 'crimson river of warm blood' in an image that dramatizes with vivid horror the taint of violent sexual desire which stains the 'lively spring with Christall streame' in which Ovid's Actaeon spies the bathing Diana.[44]

These various applications of the fable of Diana and Actaeon demonstrate Shakespeare's skill at manipulating a single classical allusion across a generic spectrum

[43] *Ouids Metamorphosis Englished*, Sandys (trans.), 'Upon the Third Booke of Ovids Metamorphosis', 100. On the flexibility of Ovidian myths, see François Laroque, 'Ovidian v(o)ices in Marlowe and Shakespeare: the Actaeon variations', and Charles Martindale, 'Shakespeare's Ovid, Ovid's Shakespeare', chs. 11 and 13 of Taylor (ed.), *Shakespeare's Ovid*, 165–79, 203.

[44] Ovid, *Metamorphoses*, Golding (trans.), sigs. 33v, 32v (III.291; III.188).

in the service of different moral dilemmas. Actaeon's fate dramatizes different sexual tensions and problems from one play to another, from the playful venality of *Merry Wives*, to the tragicomic potentialities of sexual confusion and unsatisfied desire in *Twelfth Night*, to the rapacious brutality of *Titus*. Unlike Christopher Marlowe, whose dramatic heroes replicate the tragic downfalls of doomed Ovidian figures such as Icarus and Phaethon, Shakespeare unleashes both the tragic and the comic potential inherent in Ovidian metamorphosis, which may be punitive or redemptive, inhibiting or liberating. In *A Midsummer Night's Dream*, arguably Shakespeare's most Ovidian play in mood despite the absence of any direct influence on its plot, the rude mechanicals stage a farcical version of the fable of Pyramus and Thisbe, a story of 'very tragical mirth' that contains within it the potential for its own generic reversal in the tragedy of *Romeo and Juliet*, whose star-crossed lovers provide a tragic counterpoint to the antics of Bottom and Flute (*Dream*, 5.1.57). Yet despite its comedic crudeness, the staging of Pyramus and Thisbe in the final act of *A Midsummer Night's Dream* nonetheless preserves some of the pathos of Ovid's version, for it reminds us of the potentially tragic consequences of romantic love, especially love that meets parental resistance. In the constantly shifting world of *Midsummer*, a play dominated by the inconstant moon and its concomitant lunacies, Shakespeare repeatedly turns to Ovid's poem of 'shapes transformde to bodies straunge' to explore the vicissitudes of human emotion.[45] Love is the principal agent of metamorphosis in the play: as Helena argues in the opening scene, 'Things base and vile, holding no quantity, | Love can transpose to form and dignity', a paradox that presides over the play's subsequent reversals of affection (1.1.232–3).[46] Yet despite its debts to the Ovidian motif of sublunary vicissitude, *A Midsummer Night's Dream* self-consciously challenges the divine machinery of the *Metamorphoses* on a number of different levels. Helena's pursuit of Lysander turns topsy-turvy the normal gender dynamics of the Ovidian amatory hunt: 'The story shall be changed: | Apollo flies, and Daphne holds the chase' (2.1.230–1). Theseus challenges the 'shaping fantasies' of the play's lovers as 'antique fables' and 'fairy toys', fantastical stuff no more congenial to 'cool reason' than the far-fetched Centaurs and Bacchanals featured in the antique plays he then dismisses (5.1.5; 3). Yet while Bottom's transformation into an ass, inspired in part by William Adlington's 1566 translation of Apuleius' *Metamorphoses*, pulls the play toward the comic possibilities of Ovidian metamorphosis, some of *Midsummer*'s other transformations bring the play's characters to the brink of calamity, tragic possibilities also latent in the play's borrowings from Seneca's *Hippolytus*, in which Phaedra enlists her nurse to create a love-potion in order to ensnare her stepson Hippolytus, an act which mirrors Puck's pharmaceutical intervention in uniting Helena and Demetrius.

[45] Ovid, *Metamorphoses*, Golding (trans.) sig. 1(l.1).
[46] On love as the principal agent of metamorphosis in *A Midsummer Night's Dream*, see Bate, *Shakespeare and Ovid*, 133–4.

OLD BOOKS ON NEW STAGES: READING SHAKESPEARE'S READERS

Many of Shakespeare's methods of interpreting and adapting classical texts also inform the reading practices of characters who are frequently represented in the act of construing figures or episodes from classical myth or history in order better to comprehend their own dilemmas or fears. Copies of Ovid's *Metamorphoses* appear on stage at *Cymbeline* 2.2 and at *Titus Andronicus* 4.1: in both plays, these books 'speak for present occasions', reflecting, albeit imperfectly, the situations and feelings of characters on stage.[47] In *Titus*, when Lavinia is '[r]avished and wronged as Philomela was', she 'turns the leaves' of her Ovid in order to spell out both the parallels and the differences between her own narrative and one of its principal sources (4.1.52, 45). Even as her own experiences mirror those of Ovid's Philomela, Lavinia's reading of Ovid dramatizes the complex dynamic between art and life—between the knowledge contained in classical texts and the knowledge gained through experience—that informs the play as a whole. Terrified by the sight of Lavinia 'busily' turning the leaves of her book to the 'tragic tale of Philomel', Lucius' son remarks that

> ... I have heard my grandsire say full oft
> Extremity of griefs would make men mad,
> And I have read that Hecuba of Troy
> Ran mad for sorrow.
> (*Titus* 4.1.18–21)

Even as life imitates art in *Titus*, and even as the extremity of passion attained by the tragic figures of antiquity provides guidance for those weathering modern tragedies, Lucius' son is compelled 'down to throw my books and fly' (4.1.25) at the sight of the mutilated Lavinia, rejecting the very models that shape the play's tragic vision. And, while various characters in *Titus* mediate their grief and anger through classical models, they ultimately fall short of those models: Titus is no 'King Priam', the Trojan hero and father of heroes to whom he compares himself in the opening scene (1.1.80), and when he 'plays the cook' by serving up Demetrius and Chiron to their mother in a pasty, his ambiguous resolution that 'worse than Pro[c]ne I will be revenged' (5.2.194) leaves open the question of whether Titus' plan for vengeance is less effective than that of Tereus' wife in the *Metamorphoses*, more barbaric, or both. In the latter acts of the play, Titus tries on, and subsequently discards, multiple classical prototypes of the revenger: at one moment he is Procne, and at the next, he is 'as woeful as Virginius was' when, in a story derived from Livy's *Ab Urbe condita* (and later recounted in

---

[47] Colin Burrow, 'Shakespeare and Humanistic Culture', in Martindale and Taylor (ed.), *Classics*, ch. 19, argues that 'classical books speak for present occasions' and that '[the] presence of the classical book onstage menacingly registers the difference of perspective between [Immogen and Iachimo]'.

Gower's *Confessio Amantis*, the *Romance of the Rose*, and Painter's *Palace of Pleasure*), the Roman army commander murders his daughter in order to save her honour (5.3.49). Even so, Titus' protest upon killing his daughter that he has 'a thousand times more cause than he [Virginius] | To do this outrage' (5.3.50–1) only underscores the strange and haphazard brutality of the scene that unfolds, in which Titus kills Tamora, Saturnius kills Titus, and Lucius kills Saturnius.

The frenzied massacre at its conclusion is one of several ways in which *Titus* flaunts its remoteness from the Senecan tragedies that serve as its principal model. Indeed, the tragedy of *Titus* arises out of the failure of its characters to live up to the ethical ideals embodied by their classical counterparts—or, their failure to acknowledge the inadequacy of those ideals—an outlook which has prompted at least one critic to argue that *Titus* is a close forerunner to *Troilus and Cressida*, 'Shakespeare's most thoroughgoing critique of the ancient world'.[48] As in *Troilus and Cressida* and *Hamlet*, plays whose vexed relationships to classical antiquity are discussed at further length below, *Titus* conveys its ethical and affective distance from the Graeco-Roman world through the inaptness and the irony of its classical allusions. After Lavinia is raped and mutilated, Marcus compares her to Orpheus, the 'Thracian poet' able to tame wild animals with the 'heavenly harmony' of his 'sweet tongue' (2.4.51, 48–9). The unsuitability of the comparison verges on the grotesque: Lavinia cannot even speak, let alone sing, and the only version of Orpheus she resembles is the one torn to pieces by enraged Maenads during a Bacchic frenzy. Yet Lavinia does not even experience the salvific transformation that concludes Ovid's account, as Orpheus' lyre and his decapitated head flow down the Hebrus, still singing after death. The characters of *Titus* are, moreover, surrounded by ancient texts which they cannot interpret correctly, or from which no clear moral lessons may be extracted. When Titus sends Chiron and Demetrius a bundle of weapons inscribed with some verses from Horace, 'Integer vitae, scelerisque purus, | Non eget Mauri iaculis, nec arcu' [He who is spotless in life and free of crime does not need the javelin or the bow of the Moor], Chiron recognizes the well-known lines ('I read it in the grammar long ago') but fails to grasp their application to his own situation (4.2.20–1, 23).[49] If Elizabethan scholars and translators tend to regard classical texts as 'a myrrour for thy self thyne owne estate to see', as Golding puts it in his translation of Ovid, then *Titus* dramatizes the limitations of such humanist reading practices and illustrates the distortions to which ancient texts are subjected by 'modern' readers.[50]

In Shakespeare's plays, such interpretive distortions are the result of a profound sense of self-consciousness on the part of characters eerily aware of their own ancient forerunners but unable or unwilling, for better or for worse, to emulate the ancient examples after which they are modelled. In *Cymbeline*, when Iachimo enters the bedchamber of the sleeping Immogen in order to steal her bracelet and study her

---

[48] Bate, *Shakespeare and Ovid*, 109.

[49] The quotation derives from Horace, *Odes* XXII, ll. 1–2; on the significance of this scene, see Bate, *Shakespeare and Ovid*, 107.

[50] Ovid, *Metamorphoses*, Golding (trans.), 'Too the Reader', sig. A2.

birthmark, he spies a copy of Ovid's *Metamorphoses* by her bed: '[s]he has been reading late, | The tale of Tereus. Here the leaf's turned down | Where Philomel gave up' (2.2.44–6). The book accrues conflicting meanings from different perspectives: unlike Ovid's Philomela, Immogen does not 'give up' but instead survives, preserving her chastity by disguising herself as a boy in a play whose happy ending rejects the conclusion of its Ovidian model. Whereas the story of Tereus, Procne, and Philomela holds one meaning for Immogen—the feminine ability to triumph, through transformation, over male desire and deception—the same book provides Iachimo with a 'literal template' for the 'metaphorical violation of Immogen which he intends', as does his allusion to Tarquin upon emerging from Immogen's bedroom trunk: 'Our Tarquin thus | Did softly press the rushes ere he wakened | The chastity he wounded' (2.2.12–14). But Iachimo is no Tarquin: far from ravishing Immogen, he only records the contents of her room, and his actions have very different consequences for the political and social order of the play from those of his Roman alter ego. In *Cymbeline*, Shakespeare returns to characters and motifs treated in his much earlier *Rape of Lucrece*, and in so doing revises an ancient legend according to different generic specifications: in romance, the Tarquins fail and the Lucreces live. But even in *Lucrece*, set in the dawn of the Roman Republic, characters experience their destinies both through and in contradistinction to other classical texts. After her rape, Lucrece begins her long complaint by establishing her sympathies with 'lamenting Philomel' (l. 1079), but once she begins to examine a 'piece | Of skillful painting, made for Priam's Troy' (ll. 1366–7), a more complex relationship develops between the ancient text and its modern 'reader'. Seeking a 'face where all distress is stelled', Lucrece searches in the painting for a Trojan counterpart and finds it in 'despairing Hecuba' (ll. 1444, 1447). But the correspondence between the two women is hardly simple, for Lucrece 'shapes her sorrow to the beldam's woes'—she *becomes* Hecuba, using her voice to express the silent grief of Priam's widow and to 'tune [her] woes with my lamenting tongue' (ll. 1458, 1465). In *Lucrece*, ancient texts and lived experiences do not simply reflect but rather mutually shape each other: when Lucrece ventriloquizes Hecuba's grief, '[s]he lends them words, and she their looks doth borrow' (l. 1498). This process of double imitation transforms both Lucrece and her fictional counterparts: as she '[l]os[es] her woes in shows of discontent' (l. 1580), she also reinterprets the fall of Troy, 'blot[ting] old books and alter[ing] their contents' (l. 948) by interpolating herself into the narrative.

Lucrece's extended commiseration with Hecuba in *The Rape of Lucrece* provides a dress rehearsal for *Hamlet*, where an actor's extraordinary ability to perform 'in a fiction' what Hamlet cannot execute in actuality calls into doubt the empathetic 'reading' of antique characters exhibited by Lucrece. When Hamlet asks, 'What's Hecuba to him, or he to Hecuba, | That he should weep for her?'(2.2.561–2), he voices his sense of distance from the heroic world of classical antiquity, a sentiment that pervades *Hamlet* as a whole. The player's speech drives home the disparity between Hamlet and 'rugged Pyrrhus', the avenging son of Achilles from Virgil's *Aeneid* who takes bold action whereas Shakespeare's avenger, despite his 'motive and [his] cue for passion', remains 'unpregnant of my cause, | And can say nothing' (2.2.455, 563, 570–1).

Horatio is the one character in *Hamlet* who clings nostalgically to Roman values: he interprets the appearance of the ghost as a portent similar to the one which appeared 'a little ere the mightiest Julius fell' (Q2 1.1.716) and his suicidal impulse—'I am more an antique Roman than a Dane'—is stifled by the dying Hamlet (5.2.294), suggesting that the honour which accrues to such a 'Roman thought' in a play such as *Antony and Cleopatra* is stripped of its value in *Hamlet* (*Antony* 1.2.77). *Hamlet's* frequent allusions to classical myth and legend prompt readers to recall earlier texts only to be jolted by their dissimilarities to Shakespeare's Elsinore.[51] Gertrude's hasty remarriage hardly merits comparison to the perpetually grieving Niobe (*Hamlet* 1.2.149), and even in a moment of intense anger as he approaches his mother's bedchamber, Hamlet urges himself to '[l]et not ever | The soul of Nero enter this firm bosom', a resolution that hints at the incestuous desire of the son but also distances Shakespeare's hero from the Roman emperor notorious for the cruel murder of his mother Agrippina as well as (in Suetonius' account) his subsequent, highly theatrical suicide (3.2.382–3). Moreover, Hamlet dissociates himself from the heroic exploits of antiquity by describing Claudius as 'no more like my father | Than I to Hercules' and by calling himself '[a]s hardy as the Nemean lion's nerve', ironic similes which undermine the virtues of courage and strength associated with Hercules, who defeats the lion as one of his twelve labours (1.2.152–3; 1.4.60).[52]

Hercules is a frequent target of mockery in Shakespeare's plays, an embodiment of qualities such as strength, martial valour, or masculine *virtù* which are exposed as shallow, inadequate, or easily falsified. The pageant of the Nine Worthies in *Love's Labor's Lost*, in which Hercules is played by an 'imp' named Mote (or Moth), is typical of the ironic debasement to which Hercules is subject throughout Shakespeare's works (*LLL* 5.2.582). While Berowne complains that the 'scene of foolery' among his courtiers is like watching 'great Hercules whipping a jig' (*LLL* 4.3.165), the playwright himself appears to delight in discrediting the heroic excellence of figures such as Hercules, Pompey, Alexander, and Caesar. In a speech proclaiming himself 'a coward on instinct', Falstaff wryly claims that 'I am as valiant as Hercules' (*1 Henry IV* 2.5.273–6), but Shakespeare delights in exposing such sham bravery. In *The Merchant of Venice*, Bassanio attacks cowards with 'livers white as milk' who wear 'upon their chins | The beards of Hercules' as men who assume 'but valour's excrement' (3.2.83–7); in *Much Ado*, Beatrice complains that 'manhood | is melted into courtesies, valour into

---

[51] For a discussion of this style of intertextual allusion in Shakespeare, see Lyne, 'Ovid, Golding, and the "Rough Magic" of *The Tempest*', in Taylor (ed.), *Shakespeare's Ovid*, 151, which relies on Stephen Hinds' discussion of the concept of *traccie* (traces) to analyse allusions that prompt readers to recall an earlier text while at the same time prompting them to recognize the ways in which the two passages or scenes are incongruous.

[52] Yves Peyré, 'Niobe and the Nemean Lion: reading *Hamlet* in the light of Ovid's *Metamorphoses*', ch. 8 of Taylor (ed.), *Shakespeare's Ovid*, 128, discuss the Ovidian sources (*Metamorphoses* IX.197; *Amores* IX.61–2) of these and other lines; at 132–3, Peyré argues that 'Hamlet highlights the chasm between his world and the world of myth' since the play 'dissociates itself constantly from the founding text of the *Metamorphoses*'.

compliment, and . . . | He is now as valiant as Hercules | that only tells a lie and swears it' (4.1.319–23). If the virtues associated with ancient heroes are devalued and degraded by these and other characters, it is partly because courage and physical strength are not guaranteed to triumph in a world governed by fortune and cunning. When a messenger reports the death of Richard, Duke of York, to his sons in *3 Henry VI*, he moralizes that 'Hercules himself must yield to odds' just as the 'hardest-timbered oak' may be felled by 'many strokes, though with a little ax' (*3 Henry VI* 2.1.53–4). In *The Merchant of Venice*, the Prince of Morocco levels Hercules even further when he reasons that '[i]f Hercules and Lichas play at dice', Alcides may be 'beaten by his rage' (in some texts, 'page'), vanquished by his heroic passion or by an unlucky throw in a Machiavellian contest between *virtù* and *fortuna* (*Merchant* 2.1 32–5).

Shakespeare occasionally resorts to broad parody in order to deflate the martial prowess of antique worthies such as Julius Caesar, whose 'thrasonical brag' of 'I came, saw, and overcame' is travestied by Rosalind and again by the queen in *Cymbeline* (*ALYI* 5.2.30–1; *Cymbeline* 3.1.23–4). Another parodic strain seeks to deflate the amorous prowess of famous lovers. In *Merchant* 5.1, Lorenzo and Jessica undercut the sincerity of their 'vows of faith' by comparing their moment of moonlit intimacy to the night sky as seen by Troilus and Cressida, Pyramus and Thisbe, Dido and Aeneas— victims of classical love affairs gone horribly wrong.[53] In *Romeo and Juliet*, Mercutio tempers the play's dominant sentimentality with a cynical disquisition on love, asserting that Laura was 'but a kitchen-wench' to Petrarch, 'Dido a dowdy; Cleopatra a gypsy; | Helen and Hero hildings and harlots' (2.3.37–40). The lovers and heroes of antiquity are equally subject to the vicissitudes of time, providing opportunities for meditation on the transitoriness of mortal life and the ephemeral nature of fame: even Alexander the Great, muses Hamlet in the graveyard, is rendered into dust that might someday 'stop a beer barrel', while 'Imperial Caesar, dead and turned to clay, | Might stop a hole to keep the wind away' (5.1.208–9).

LIVING HISTORIES: SHAKESPEARE, ANCIENT AND MODERN

Hamlet's observations in the graveyard reveal a simultaneous sense of continuity with and alienation from the antique world. This tension also informs Shakespeare's history plays, in which Shakespeare's English kings model themselves on their Roman forerunners even as they remain painfully aware of the chronological, moral, and political divide which separates them from the Caesars. *Richard II* and *Richard III* both present

---

[53] Bate, *Shakespeare and Ovid*, reads *MV* 5.1.13–14 ironically; Martindale, 'Shakespeare's Ovid', 203, agrees that the Ovidian love affairs in Lorenzo and Jessica's catalogue 'turn out badly' but he resists the ironic reading proposed by Bate.

an ironic reminder of England's Roman heritage through allusions to the Tower of London: Richard II is imprisoned and murdered in 'Julius Caesar's ill-erected Tower', as are the two princes who fall victim to Richard III's treachery (*Richard II* 5.1.2; *Richard III* 3.1.68–78). Yet even as the imprisoned Prince Edward ominously observes that 'the truth should live from age to age', history never repeats itself perfectly in Shakespeare's English histories, and the lessons contained in ancient conflicts do not invariably apply to modern ones (*Richard III* 3.176). Mourning her murdered son Prince Edward in *3 Henry VI*, Queen Margaret declares that '[t]hey that stabbed Caesar shed no blood at all, | Did not offend, nor were not worthy blame, | If this foul deed were by to equal it' (5.5.52–4), while *Henry V* mocks the impulse to weigh ancient figures and events against modern ones through Fluellen, whose obsessive wish to adhere to the 'auncient prerogatifs and laws of the wars' (4.1.68) prompts an extended comparison between Henry and Alexander the Great that argues for the resemblance between Monmouth and Macedon and concludes that 'there is figures in all things' (4.7.32). Fluellen's desire to establish correspondences between the ancient and modern world proves both absurd and discomfiting: there may well be 'salmons in both' of the rivers near each hero's birthplace, but when Fluellen declares that Alexander the Great 'did in his ales and his angers . . . kill his best friend, Cleitus', an event he proceeds to liken to Henry's rejection of Falstaff, Gower protests that 'Our King is not like him in that. He never killed any of his friends' (4.7.30, 36–7). Whereas Gower overlooks the obvious parallels between Henry and his Greek forerunner—the King has just ordered the execution of his former friend Scrope and allowed Bardolph to be hanged for theft—Fluellen exaggerates those parallels to a ridiculous degree; for Shakespeare, the truth is somewhere in the middle.

Even in works set in Julius Caesar's Rome or Homer's Troy, Shakespeare's classical heroes are acutely aware of their status as historical legends—legends told, and perhaps misinterpreted, countless times. Sensitive to the familiarity of her own story, Lucrece fears that those who 'know not how | To cipher what is writ in learnèd books, | Will quote my loathsome trespass in my looks' (*Rape of Lucrece*, ll. 810–12). Troilus and Cressida promise, albeit rather unsuccessfully, to be '[a]s true as Troilus' and '[a]s false as Cressida', and their actions in the play are defined and limited according to prior versions of their own narrative (3.2.177, 192). Shakespeare's critics have long bemoaned the clocks in *Julius Caesar*, the eyeglasses in *Coriolanus*, and other anachronisms that belie the ancient settings of many of his plays. In an 1807 work, Francis Douce complains of *Troilus and Cressida* that 'Hector quotes *Aristotle*; Ulysses speaks of the bull-bearing *Milo*, and Pandarus of a man born in *April. Friday* and *Sunday* and even *minced-pies* with dates in them are introduced', characteristics which exemplify the 'wrenching of text out of context' typical of Shakespeare's representation of the ancient world.[54]

Shakespeare often jumbles together stories from Seneca and Plutarch with highly topical issues—*Coriolanus* is commonly interpreted as an extended commentary on the

---

[54] Francis Douce, *Illustrations of Shakespeare*, 2 vols. (London: 1807), 2: 291.

famine and riots taking place across England in 1606–7, while *Julius Caesar* has been read in light of contemporary pressures such as Elizabethan republicanism, the threat of Puritan dissent, and the rise and fall of the Earl of Essex. Yet the contemporary relevance of these and other plays does not detract from the fact that Shakespeare's Rome also presents a radically different historical and cultural situation—an 'alien polity', as A. D. Nuttall has called it, that embraces different values and adheres to a different political and cultural logic from that of Elizabethan England.[55] While Shakespeare's ancient heroes strive to 'come off | Like Romans' (*Coriolanus* 1.7.1–2) or to achieve the 'formal constancy' of 'Roman actors' (*Julius Caesar* 2.1.225–26), his English heroes assert their ethical and cultural distance from Rome by repudiating the Roman ideal of *virtus* or by refusing (as does Macbeth) to 'play the Roman fool, and die | On mine own sword' (5.10.1–2). As he transforms his antique sources for audiences at a cultural and ideological remove, Shakespeare invents for the stage a distinctly modern sensibility that grasps both its continuity to and its distance from the past. The methods used to effect these transformations continue to provide guidance for readers, teachers, directors, and film-makers as they adapt and accommodate the works of Shakespeare for future generations.

[55] A. D. Nuttall, 'Shakespeare and the Greeks', in Martindale and Taylor (eds.), *Shakespeare and the Classics*, 211.

CHAPTER 29

CHARACTER

CHRISTY DESMET

In 1827, the Romantic poet Samuel Taylor Coleridge confessed to having a 'smack of Hamlet' in him. In 1853, Mary Cowden Clarke published her three-volume work, *The Girlhood of Shakespeare's Heroines*. And in 1997, literary pundit Harold Bloom spent over 700 pages demonstrating that Shakespeare 'invented' the 'human', as we know it.[1] Each of these instances exemplifies an enduring tendency among readers and playgoers to identify Shakespeare's dramatic characters as 'real people' and, in some cases, to identify themselves *with* Shakespeare's literary persons. The intellectual figure most strongly associated with the treatment of Shakespearean plays as a 'little world of persons'[2] was Oxford Professor of Poetry A. C. Bradley, whose influential *Shakespearean Tragedy* (1904) represented the culmination of two centuries of Shakespearean character study. Bradley's pronouncements on the heroes of Shakespeare's principal tragedies were popularized widely and for a long time through literary criticism, student editions of the play, and pedagogical guides, so that Bradleyian character criticism became the default method for teaching Shakespeare's plays. In the second half of the twentieth century, however, literary critics began to scorn what Terence Hawkes has called the 'Hamlet 'n Falstaff "R" Us' school of literary appreciation and its educational ritual, the annual 'character development jamboree' in A-level examinations and their counterparts in other nations.[3]

While L. C. Knights' acerbic question, 'How Many Children Had Lady Macbeth?' (1933)[4] was a direct attack on Bradley, it also became a rallying point for later efforts among academic critics to view Shakespeare's plays through interpretive lenses that did

---

[1] Samuel Taylor Coleridge, *Lectures and Notes on Shakspere and other English Poets* (ed.) T. Ashe (London: George Bell and Sons, 1897), 531; Mary Cowden Clarke, *The Girlhood of Shakespeare's Heroines*, 3 vols. (London: Bickers and Son, 1880); Harold Bloom, *Shakespeare: The Invention of the Human* (New York: Riverhead, 1997).

[2] A. C. Bradley, *Shakespearean Tragedy* (Greenwich, CT: Fawcett, n.d.), 42.

[3] Terence Hawkes, 'Bloom with a View', *New Statesman*, 1999, reprinted in Christy Desmet and Robert Sawyer (eds.), *Harold Bloom's Shakespeare* (New York: Palgrave, 2001), 29, 27.

[4] L. C. Knights, *How Many Children Had Lady Macbeth?* (Cambridge: Minority Press, 1933).

not privilege character over other aspects of dramatic production and reception. The attack on character criticism continued unabated through the 1980s, largely through the efforts of New Historicist critics (in the US) and culturalist materialists (in the UK) who claimed Knights, Michel Foucault, and Raymond Williams as forefathers. These anti-character critics generally subscribed to Jonathan Dollimore's credo: 'Materialist theory rejects those ideologies which sustain the belief in an ultimate separation between the political, historical, and social on the one hand, and the subjective and spiritual on the other. In particular it rejects...the humanist belief in a unified, autonomous self.'[5] Construing the self as being shaped and 'contained' by social forces and institutions brought with it a sense that agency, for both literary and historical persons, was constricted. Foucault's dynamic of subversion and containment ultimately means, in Stephen Greenblatt's phrase, that there can be 'subversion, no end of subversion, only not for us'.[6]

Greenblatt used the case of Martin Guerre to argue that in the sixteenth century, personal identity was defined by social roles, not individual personality. People did not grow or develop; rather, they were shaped in response to their place in a complex network of social relations.[7] In the famous case of identity theft evoked by Greenblatt, Martin Guerre went to war and returned a changed man: a better husband, a more tractable partner in the family business, an all-round nicer man. Martin Guerre thus seems to fulfil our expectations for liberal humanist subjects. Eventually, however, the true Martin Guerre, no more pleasant than when he left but now missing a leg, returned home; the usurper of his bed and board, identified as Arnaud du Tilh, was hanged for his offence in front of Martin Guerre's home. The case of Martin Guerre thus becomes a cautionary tale of human limitation on the model of Foucault: there was subversion, no end of subversion of law and social norms, but, in the end, not for Arnaud du Tilh. While Greenblatt's account of the case of Martin Guerre makes a historicist argument, his and other materialists' conception of early modern identity extends as well to the contemporary politics of selfhood. 'We', too, can manoeuvre within social formations and find fissures within dominant ideologies, but never break free from them altogether to exercise free choice and indulge unbridled will. That illusion is what underwrites what Catherine Belsey has disparagingly called the 'liberal humanist subject'.[8]

[5] Jonathan Dollimore, *Radical Tragedy: Religion, Ideology, and Power in the Drama of Shakespeare and his Contemporaries*, 2nd edn. (Durham, NC: Duke University Press, 1993), pp. xxvii–xxviii.

[6] Stephen Greenblatt, 'Invisible Bullets: Renaissance Authority and Its Subversion, *Henry IV* and *Henry V*', in Jonathan Dollimore and Alan Sinfield (eds.), *Political Shakespeare: New Essays in Cultural Materialism* (Ithaca, NY: Cornell University Press, 1985), 45.

[7] Stephen Greenblatt, 'Psychoanalysis and Renaissance Culture', in Patricia Parker and David Quint, (eds.), *Literary Theory / Renaissance Texts* (Baltimore, MD: The Johns Hopkins University Press, 1986), 210–24.

[8] Catherine Belsey, *The Subject of Tragedy: Identity and Difference in Renaissance Drama* (London and New York: Methuen, 1985), 8 and *passim*. Belsey articulates the position that agency can be redeemed by negotiating interstices in dominant ideologies in 'Constructing the Subject: Deconstructing the Text', in Robyn R. Warhol and Diane Price Herndl (eds.), *Feminisms: An Anthology of Literary Theory and Criticism* (New Brunswick, NJ: Rutgers University Press, 1997), 657–73.

More recent attempts to recuperate literary character as a legitimate category for critical and theoretical discussion generally take as their point of departure the materialist critique of subjectivity and individualism and move the discussion in one of three directions. The first attempts to define the concept of 'character' historically, to imagine early modern dramatic persons in relation to 'real' early modern persons as products of intersecting networks of discourse. The second, a form of neo-humanism, argues that there are 'essential' continuities in human experience that permit a direct moral identification between Shakespeare's audiences and his characters. The third can be described as a 'rhetorical' approach to literary character that seeks to define the social operations of language that informed early modern and now contemporary receptions of Shakespearean character. There is a certain degree of overlap among the three approaches, but this chapter will argue that the rhetorical approach is best suited to new experiences of Shakespearean character made possible in the age of computers.

RECENT APPROACHES TO SHAKESPEAREAN CHARACTER

Historicist approaches to character accept as axiomatic the limits on individuality, self-determination, and personal freedom that are the hallmarks of an identity constructed from social roles and institutions. Elizabeth Fowler, for instance, defines characters as 'social persons', literary representations of human beings 'comparable to the representations in other spheres of cultural practice', such as economics, theology, and law.[9] Such persons are not flesh-and-blood people, but 'abstract models' that 'act as a cognitive framework' against which actual people may be measured and judged.[10] Jean-Christophe Agnew, in a compatible argument, looks at the way the concept of personhood develops in accordance with market economies. The English stage, he argues, 'developed narrative and thematic conventions that effectively reproduced the representational strategies and difficulties of the marketplace' and thus gave playgoers a toolkit for coping with social disruptions attendant on the market as an emerging institution.[11] Like Fowler, Agnew sees in this process a tension between the rhetorical simplification of social types in literature and the social complexity, even chaos, engendered by the upheavals in class structure that accompanied the development of market economies.

Neo-humanists, by contrast, push back directly against the materialists' deconstruction of notions of identity and selfhood. Some of these efforts, most notably Harold

---

[9] Elizabeth Fowler, *Literary Character: The Human Figure in Early English Writing* (Ithaca, NY: Cornell University Press, 2003), 28.

[10] Elizabeth Fowler, 'Shylock's Virtual Injuries', *Shakespeare Studies* 34 (2006), 59.

[11] Jean-Christophe Agnew, *Worlds Apart: The Market and the Theater in Anglo-American Thought, 1550–1750* (Cambridge: Cambridge University Press, 1986), 12.

Bloom's monumental *Shakespeare: The Invention of the Human*,[12] have been aggressively nostalgic for both the liberal humanist subject and the rituals of character criticism. Following in the footsteps of Bradley and Coleridge before him, Bloom celebrates Shakespeare's grasp of 'human nature' by praising the ability of his characters not only to 'develop' but also self-consciously to 'reconceive' themselves (Bloom, p.xvii). They often attain a level of philosophical wisdom unavailable to most of us (Hamlet being the paradigm here) and are, *pace* Sinfield and his fellow materialists, emphatically 'agents' rather than merely 'effects' of the clashing intellectual 'realizations' that shape their personalities: 'We are convinced of Hamlet's superior reality because Shakespeare has made Hamlet free by making him know the truth, truth too intolerable for us to bear' (p. 7). The possibility of agency, both for literary characters and for 'us', was already implicit in the concept of social persons,[13] but Bloom's humanism requires a religious vocabulary to explain how and why a character such as Falstaff is the 'mortal god' of the critic's 'imaginings' (Bloom, p.xix). Admitting Shakespeare, on the strength of his characterization, to the same intellectual pantheon that Bloom's version of Hamlet inhabits, allows the critic, by rhetorical sleight of hand, to claim for Shakespeare a 'universalism' that is 'global and multicultural' and that relieves Bloom from the necessity of attending not only to historical difference, but also to the differences of race, class, and nationality that have preoccupied post colonial critics.[14]

Another strain of neo-humanism, by contrast, concerns itself directly with literature's ethical function. The work of Canadian philosopher Charles Taylor underwrites one effort to analyse the 'orientation' of different Shakespearean characters toward the 'greatest good' as an ethical ideal.[15] Neo-humanism can address the reception as well as the production of literary character. Michael Bristol, for instance, argues that because some 'essential' features of human experience transcend historical difference, Shakespeare's characters are indeed 'like us' and 'live in a world we can understand. We don't need any specialised historical knowledge to understand Constance or Shylock or Lady Macbeth if we are really alive to our own feelings and capable of empathy with other people.' He concludes: 'Engagement with a character has a moral dimension; it corresponds to the imperative of respect for our human vulnerability to loss and grief. We learn about our own complex character by thinking about and coming to respect Shakespeare's characters.'[16]

The third approach to Shakespearean character, rhetorical criticism, emerged in the 1990s as a response to structuralist explorations of character as narrative function and

[12] (New York: Riverhead, 1998). Further citations given parenthetically in the text.

[13] For a theoretical account of agency, see Belsey, 'Constructing the Subject'. A historical study of Renaissance 'agency' can be found in Katherine Rowe, *Dead Hands: Fictions of Agency, Renaissance to Modern* (Stanford, CA: Stanford University Press, 1999).

[14] See, for instance, Alan Sinfield, 'How to Read *The Merchant of Venice* without Being Heterosexist', in Kate Chedgzoy (ed.), *Shakespeare, Feminism, and Gender* (Basingstoke: Palgrave Macmillan, 2001), 115–34; and Fowler, 'Shylock's Virtual Injuries'.

[15] Mustapha Fahmi, 'Man's Chief Good: The Shakespearean Character as Evaluator', *The Shakespearean International Yearbook* 8 (2008), 119–35.

[16] Michael Bristol, 'Confusing Shakespeare's Characters with Real People: Reflections on Reading in Four Questions', in Paul Yachnin and Jessica Slights (eds.), *Shakespeare and Character: Theory, History, Performance, and Theatrical Persons* (New York: Palgrave Macmillan, 2009), 38.

the post-structuralist dismantling of character along with other narrative elements. Rhetorical approaches to Shakespearean character might be defined as explorations of how characters as rhetorical structures are 'read' on stage and in books through processes of identification,[17] or how 'character effects' are received through structured encounters with cultural discourses.[18] In both cases, rhetorical frameworks, or tropes of character, mediate between producers and audiences, foreclosing the kind of direct emotional identification championed by neo-humanists.

The minor rhetorical form of the Theophrastan Character, which flourished in the Renaissance alongside the medically-driven model of humours characterization, offers a paradigm for how Renaissance characters are mediated through rhetorical screens. Theophrastan Characters generally work by meiosis, a systematic placing of persons into ethical or social groups based on a relentlessly satiric survey of physical characteristics and behaviours. The Character is wedded to an ideology of moral transparency. The types put on display in the genre are grotesque, diseased, smelly, and generally repellent. No one, the narrator's confident tone assures us, would be fooled by such a figure. But the narrative frame in which the portraits are cast suggests a different story. While in collections of such portraits, such as those by Thomas Overbury, Characters can sometimes be flattened into a recitation of traits, in Theophrastus characters generally are portrayed in a social situation. The Flatterer, for instance, pulls loose threads from his patron's coat and praises him loudly in front of others.[19] The narrator of this vignette therefore becomes an observer watching the parasite through the reactions of a chorus rather than participating directly in the social scene. This secondary audience becomes the medium through which these hyperbolically repulsive individuals must be approached. Only through embodied others can character be interpreted, understood, and dealt with. This emphasis on rhetorical structures as embodied mediators between literary characters and audiences will prove central to Shakespearean character in the computer age.

SHAKESPEAREAN CHARACTER AFTER COMPUTERS

Shakespearean character after the advent of computers looks less familiar and feels less comfortable than it has at any time between the invention of the stylus and film. The digital age offers something very different from what narratologist Mieke Bal tellingly

[17] See Christy Desmet, *Reading Shakespeare's Characters* (Amherst: University of Massachusetts Press, 1992).

[18] See Alan Sinfield, 'From Bradley to Cultural Materialism', *Shakespeare Studies* 34 (2006), 25–34.

[19] *Theophrastus: The Character Sketches*, Warren Anderson (trans.) (Kent, OH: Kent State University Press, 1970), 71. I discuss the Theophrastan Character as a theoretical model in 'The Persistence of Character', *Shakespeare Studies* 34 (2006): 46–55.

called 'paper persons'.[20] In her discussion of the concept of the post-human, which she sees as the ethos of the computer and information age, N. Katherine Hayles critiques the model of a binary opposition between signifier and signified that has governed our understanding of linguistic signification under the influence of deconstruction, Lacanian psychoanalysis, and other brands of post-structuralism. She imagines instead a 'flickering signification' of meaning that occurs when persons are dissolved into data, then reshaped according to an ongoing dialectic between pattern and randomness through feedback loops that alter both self and environment.[21]

The terms in which Shakespearean character had been discussed in the eighteenth and nineteenth centuries were largely Aristotelian, with 'verisimilitude' and 'consistency' being the hallmark of a credible character. With the novel providing the dominant paradigm, a believable character became one who is, in E. M. Forster's vocabulary, 'round'; a 'flat', two-dimensional figure lacks the qualities necessary to rise to the status of a character, who is an 'individual' and possesses an autonomous self.[22] By contrast, Shakespearean characters in the digital or post-human age are dispersed as packets of data that circulate through the porous membrane between self and environment.

Post-human Shakespearean character might be visualized as a computer-generated word cloud. In the word cloud produced from the complete text of *Twelfth Night*, for instance, various character names are scattered throughout the graphic, illustrating the narratological understanding of character as a 'piling up of data'.[23] Not only are characters reduced to their names,[24] but first names are severed from surnames and proper names placed on equal footing with other words—nouns, adjectives, personal pronouns, and even titles of address (e.g. 'Sir')—while the size of a word depends on its frequency of occurrence. To an uncanny degree, the narratology of this Shakespearean word cloud exhibits the rhetorical operations that Mieke Bal sees as shaping character in narrative: repetition (illustrated by word sizes), accumulation, and relations to other characters (illustrated by the spatial organization of words).[25] In the word cloud, character acquires significance based on this dialectic between pattern and randomness. Is it ironic, for instance, that Olivia and Orsino should find themselves so close to one another? Is it not allegorically appropriate for Sir Toby's last name to take up so much graphic real estate?

---

[20] Mieke Bal, *Introduction to the Theory of Narrative*, 2nd edn. (Toronto: University of Toronto Press, 1997), 116.

[21] N. Katherine Hayles, *How We Became Posthuman: Virtual Bodies in Cybernetics, Literature, and Informatics* (Chicago, IL: University of Chicago Press, 1999), 25 and *passim*.

[22] I discuss the shape of Shakespearean character criticism during those two centuries in *Reading Shakespeare's Characters: Rhetoric, Ethics, and Identity* (Amherst: University of Massachusetts Press, 1992), chs. 1 and 2. E. M. Forster outlines his well-known taxonomy of character in *Aspects of the Novel* (New York: Harcourt, Brace, and Company, 1927).

[23] Bal, *Introduction to the Theory of Narrative*, 125.

[24] On character as proper name, see Roland Barthes, *S/Z*, Richard Miller (trans.) (New York: Hill and Wang), 131.

[25] See Bal, *Introduction to the Theory of Narrative*, 126.

'tis act aguecheek aios andrew answer antonio art
away ay belch boy brother captain cesario count dark dear desire devill dost doth drink
dulo enter excellent exeunt exit eyes fabin fair faith favour fellow
feste fool gentlemen god host hath heart hold house indeed keep
knight lady leave letter life lord love mad madam
malvolio man maria marry master matter mine nature nay niece
night nono nothing officer olivia irsino peace play please pray previous
prithee re-enter reads reason scene sebastein servent sir smile soul
speak sweet thee thorofozo think thouthy tin toby topal
viola wit woman youth

While a post-human perspective on Shakespearean character as word cloud foregrounds the multiplicity, instability, and widely distributed nature of character, consideration of the computer as a practical tool puts constraints on the free flow of information. Willard McCarty explains the computer as a modelling machine. By the term 'modelling' he means 'the heuristic process of constructing and manipulating models', a model being either a 'representation of something for purposes of study' (what Clifford Geertz called a defining 'model *of*') or 'a design for realizing something new' (Geertz's 'model *for*' accomplishing some plan).[26] Models, unlike concepts, therefore have contradictory natures. On the one hand, they must be explicit and consistent; on the other, they are capable of manipulation—rigid and flexible at the same time. Because of the requirements for explicitness and consistency, models sometimes do not work, so that the gap between model and data collapses into aporia, an intellectual dead end. On the other hand, a model always mediates between observer and observed and will function as an embodied actor in that relationship.[27] Thus, the information extracted by any model is in some sense a moving target, and the post-human subject involved with a computer as modelling machine is engaged in a threesome, its relations social but always unsteady and shifting.

The mediated nature of electronic interactions requires an important shift in theories of 'reading' character. Kenneth Burke's explanation of rhetorical identification as a dialectic between identification *of* and identification *with* works well for textual relations with Shakespeare's characters,[28] but imaginatively grounded as it is in Aristotelian rhetoric and public, face-to-face oratory, Burke's paradigm still shares with neo-humanism a confidence that unmediated access to others is possible. A Shakespearean imagining of how identification might work occurs in *Cymbeline*, where the King's rusticated sons, raised in the rough Welsh mountains far from their courtly origins,

[26] Willard McCarty, *Humanities Computing* (Basingstoke: Palgrave Macmillan, 2005), 24.
[27] See McCarty, *Humanities Computing*, 38.
[28] For a discussion of Burkean identification as a model for Shakespearean identification, see Desmet, *Reading Shakespeare's Characters*, 29–33 Identification is discussed in Kenneth Burke, *A Rhetoric of Motives* (1950; rpt. Berkeley: University of California Press, 1969), 19 ff.

respond with a direct intensity to the stories their adoptive father tells them about heroic battles of his past:

> When on my three-foot stool I sit and tell
> The warlike feats I have done, his spirits fly out
> Into my story: say 'Thus mine enemy fell,
> And thus I set my foot on 's neck', even then
> The princely blood flows in his cheek, he sweats,
> Strains his young nerves, and puts himself in posture
> That acts my words.
>
> (*Cymbeline* 3.2.89–95)

The vigorous and strongly mimetic quality of the young prince's dramatic re-enactment suggest that he has what Eric Havelock, speaking of ancient epic, called a nearly pathological identification with the storyteller's subject.[29]

With a computer, by contrast, the model can get in the way of mimesis. Or to put it another way, the computer as actor can act up. The embodied nature of electronic relations is important to their success, as has been recognized recently. As Mark B. N. Hansen discusses, the body is crucial, for instance, to human interactions with virtual reality.[30] Theorists of drama, too, are acknowledging that the actor's body mediates between characters and audiences, limiting the actor's agency but opening up a space for audience participation in the assessment of character.[31] In a comparable manner, the rigidity of computer modelling limits agency for a number of participants while enabling others. Take, for instance, the example of a database extracted from texts through mark-up languages in online journals and texts such as those produced by the Internet Shakespeare Editions. The model is flexible; in mark-up languages, the salient items to be marked are determined by the software designer. But the model is also rigid; once the defining set of terms for mark-up is in place, these become the only categories that can be applied to a text. In the case of a tag set for 'genre of Shakespeare play', only those genres identified in advance can be applied to play titles. What happens if the designer forgot a genre? Or if a set of genre tags includes comedy, tragedy, history, romance, Roman play, and problem play, how might a coder identify *Troilus and Cressida*? Ambiguity and multiplicity are not allowed here: only one identification is possible, so that the database's search function for a particular genre will be limited by whichever relevant tag was chosen for *Troilus and Cressida* in any given text. The designer, the coder, the researcher: when using this database, all are limited by the computer's function as a modelling machine. When data is 'unstructured'—raw text, in a manner of speaking—the sheer power of the computer in searching for specific words can also be a hindrance to focused interpretation. In the case of the *Twelfth Night* tag

---

[29] Eric A. Havelock, *Preface to Plato* (Cambridge, MA: Harvard University Press, 1963), 20–35.

[30] Mark B. N. Hansen, *Bodies in Code: Interfaces with Digital Media* (New York: Routledge, 2006), 2.

[31] See Andrew James Hartley, 'Character, Agency, and the Familiar Actor', in Paul Yachnin and Jessica Slights (eds.), *Shakespeare and Character: Theory, History, Performance, and Theatrical Persons* (New York: Palgrave Macmillan, 2009), 174.

cloud, for instance, proper names are tied not to actions but to a host of small function words, the search engine's hunt for frequency of appearance frustrating rather than satisfying the urge to know what's in a name.

FOUR AXIOMS FOR A NEW RHETORIC OF SHAKESPEAREAN CHARACTER

The remainder of this chapter will reconsider Shakespearean character in the information age in terms of post-human engagements with computers. It begins with the assumption that literary character is always mediated rather than directly accessible and therefore focuses on its reception as well as its production. The chapter considers the 'flickering signification' generated through a dialectic between pattern and randomness. Since the medium is to some extent the message in the latest versions of Shakespearean character, the chapter focuses specifically on two exemplary digital venues: professional applications for exploring Shakespearean texts and YouTube appropriations of Shakespeare. With apologies to Kenneth Burke, the chapter concludes by offering four axioms for a rhetoric of Shakespearean character in the digital age. Often, these axioms engage with one another in a paradoxical relation.

1. Character is copious; its master trope is congeries, and its mood is hyperbolic

To some extent, this statement simply gives a new emphasis to realizations about the persistence of the 'Shakespeare effect' by materialist critics. In his retrospective look at character after the theory revolution, Alan Sinfield acknowledges that Shakespearean *character effects* prove sufficient to prompt character oriented questions', but insists that 'the plays are not organised around character in the modern sense... They effect a sequence of loosely linked glimpses of interiority, not a coherent identity.'[32] While Sinfield finds the 'looseness' of the data for interiority a problem for character criticism, recent critiques of Shakespearean character have tended to embrace that looseness, to dissolve the solid image of a social 'person' that has stood as the imagined object for character analysis into more abstract schemata that are compatible with Hayles's concept of the post-human. Fowler, for instance, speaks of cognitive 'frameworks',[33] Agnew of markets as spatial conglomerations. Both metaphors gesture toward Hayles's notion of a 'distributed cognition' embracing both

---

[32] Alan Sinfield, 'From Bradley to Cultural Materialism', *Shakespeare Studies*, 34 (2006), 29 (italics in original).

[33] Fowler, 'Shylock's Virtual Injuries', 59.

subjects and their environments in a recursive manner. But under the aegis of the computer, even 'models', 'networks', or 'frameworks' can prove to be metaphorically too iron-clad, too purposive in their import. Digital character is less organised, less intentional, than such metaphors might imply. It is governed instead by a logic of copiousness and is prone to excess.

Superfluity is generally a hallmark of digital text. As Richard Lanham has argued, in an information economy there is no shortage of information; in fact, we are drowning in data. What is in short supply is the human attention needed to sort through and make sense of that data.[34] This is true also of digital character, whose affect I suggest might be conveyed by the classical trope 'congeries'. The term refers to a technique of accumulation, sometimes of ideas but more frequently of words; it carries as well the implication of a copiousness that is chaos barely contained, a piling up of words, images, and clauses that defies logic. Renaissance rhetorician George Puttenham defines such 'heaps' of words in the following way, as 'when we lay on such [a] load and so go to it by heaps; as if we would win the game by multitude of words and speeches, not all of one, but of divers matter and sense.' The example that Puttenham gives is a character portrait that works by accumulation:

> To muse in mind how faire, how wise, how good,
> How brave, how free, how courteous, and how true,
> My Lady is doth but inflame my blood.[35]

In Puttenham's example, adjectives of praise for My Lady follow thickly upon one another, contributing to the kind of hyperbole that characterizes the epideictic tradition of praise and blame in classical rhetoric. This 'piling on' of epithets is congeries.

My first example of how the computer manages copiousness in character analysis is Hugh Craig's study of common words as an index to characterization in Shakespeare's plays. While human critics often fasten on salient, often uncommon words as an index to the subtlety and richness of Shakespeare's language,[36] the computer's capacity for large-scale analysis works best with more humble, unambiguous, 'common' words. Thus, statistical analysis of first-person singular and plural pronouns shows that at one extreme, Warwick (*3 Henry VI*) uses predominantly 'our' and 'we', while at the other Pandarus (*Troilus and Cressida*) uses 'I' in combination with 'not'. While my summary simplifies the wide range of common words 'crunched' by the computer, a generic distinction emerges not only between histories and comedies, but also between characters: Warwick fulfils a 'choric' function, Pandarus an 'interlocutory' one, which

---

[34] Richard A. Lanham, *The Economics of Attention: Style and Substance in the Age of Information* (Chicago, IL: University of Chicago Press, 2006).

[35] George Puttenham, *The Arte of English Poesie* (London: 1589) (Menston: Scolar Press, 1969), 236; Richard A. Lanham, *A Handlist of Rhetorical Terms*, 2nd edn. (Berkeley: University of California Press, 1991), 74.

[36] Jonathan Hope and Michael Witmore, 'The Very Large Textual Object: A Prosthetic Reading of Shakespeare', *Early Modern Literary Studies* 9.3, Special Issue 12 (2004), paras. 1–36, http://purl.oclc.org/emls/09-3/hopewhit.htm.

Craig sees as in keeping with the generic demands of history and comedy and also with the character typologies belonging to these genres.[37] The visual result of this kind of analysis is a series of graphs placing characters on a grid according to their use of different categories of words. Craig's essay records, for instance, the placement of characters based on the frequency of their use of the fifty most common words, the words based on their use by the fifty largest Shakespeare characters, and characters as identified by gender. There could be no more graphic representation of distributed cognition than this, where characters are divided and replicated according to the computer's 'superhuman capacity to remember and to process systematically' until they become no more than points on a graph.[38] Instead of Bradley's little world of persons, we have an abstract representation of many persons, figured as data clusters distributed over a geometrically defined space.

But despite the computer's capacity for precision, there is a cornucopia of information here, perhaps for some readers even too much information; this tension between the computer's capacity and the receiver's limitations—Lanham's economics of attention—is experienced as well in online Shakespeare editions, where the editor must adjudicate between the urge to provide readers with full information from a variety of critics in the style of a Variorum edition and any given reader's memory and attention span.[39] With a computer's capacities, data is always threatening to get out of control.

My second example of a character congeries comes from the popular YouTube genre of the video mash-up. Usually presented as a movie trailer, the mash-up combines footage from one or more films with a discordant soundtrack from another. One classic example is 'Scary Mary', in which outtakes from *Mary Poppins*, Disney's cheery film about a nanny's magical effect on the family she works for, are paired with the sound-track from the horror film *An American Haunting*. Nothing from the film is altered; the general effect depends on a precise juxtaposition of selected image and sound that makes Mary Poppins's 'spoonful of sugar' very scary, indeed.[40] In my chosen Shakespearean example, the selection and combination of both visual and aural excerpts becomes much denser. 'Hamlet is Back', a particularly viral form of Shakespearean mash-up, seamlessly combines excerpts from numerous sources to remake introspective Hamlet as Arnold Schwarzenegger.[41] *The Last Action Hero*, in which

[37] Hugh Craig, '"Speak, That I May See Thee": Shakespeare Characters and Common Words', *Shakespeare Survey* 61 (2008), 285. For discussion of human versus computer analysis, see also chs. 1 and 2 of Hugh Craig and Arthur F. Kinney (eds.), *Shakespeare, Computers, and the Mystery of Authorship* (Cambridge: Cambridge University Press, 2009), 1–39.

[38] See Craig, '"Speak, That I May See Thee"', 282.

[39] The Internet Shakespeare Editions, whose general editor is Michael Best, offer editors the possibility of *copia* in the online edition that is not afforded by the print edition of their texts (see http://internetshakespeare.uvic.ca/index.html). The problematic of editorial *copia* in the Internet Shakespeare Editions is addressed by Jennifer Forsyth in 'Playing with Wench-like Words: Copia and Surplus in the Internet Shakespeare Edition of *Cymbeline*', *Early Modern Literary Studies* 9.3, Special Issue 12 (2004), paras. 1–27, http://purl.oclc.org/emls/09-3/forsplay.html.

[40] 'Scary Mary', YouTube, http://www.youtube.com/watch?v=2T5_0AGdFic.

[41] 'Hamlet is Back', YouTube, www.youtube.com/watch?v=m1j-wvCtzuI.

Schwarzenegger plays Hamlet in a child's fantasy remake of his boring English class, predominates in the video, but the infiltration of other sources, homogenized through a consistently sepia tint and judicious editing, harmonizes the disjunctive clips to make a James Cameron epic out of Schwarzenegger's *Hamlet*.

This highly sophisticated video trailer not only depends on rhetorical excess for its witty impact, but actually thematizes the conflict between Schwarzenegger's laconic verbal style and the video's visual lavishness, including the excess of its violence. Crumbling towers, looming dragons, and horses gracefully pounding the turf are juxtaposed to 'Hamlet's (or Schwarzenegger's) terse declaration—'Claudius, you killed my fadder.... Big mistake'— as our hero hurls his nemesis through a stained-glass window and then strolls through the castle shooting medieval knights off parapets with an automatic weapon. While in the nineteenth century Charles Lamb complained about the absurdity underlying contemporary *Hamlet* productions—that this most introspective of heroes would confess his inmost thoughts to 400 spectators in the Lyceum Theatre[42]—'Hamlet is Back' is baroque, growing ever more elaborate as the video heaps up different hyperbolic snapshots of its hero.

Amateur Shakespeare videos found on YouTube often offer even clearer examples of literary congeries by virtue of the fact that they tend toward wild, improvisatory plots. 'Zombie Hamlet', for instance, starts out squarely in the 'Zombie' genre but then veers off into an entertaining mystery in which Gertrude kills Ophelia with a blow dart. The Zombies make a belated reappearance only at the end as they march in with Fortinbras, presumably to enjoy the Danish spoils in their own ghoulish way.[43] The generic pile-up, robust and exuberant, is hyperbolic and chaotic, exemplifying perfectly the trope of congeries.

2. Character is simplified; its master trope is syncope, and its mood is parodic

Although in light of the first axiom, this statement may seem counterintuitive, the drive toward *copia* of Shakespearean character in the digital age is matched by an equally strong move toward simplification. The coexistence of simple moral types in the psychomachia tradition with Bradleyian heroes and Machiavellian villains is endemic to the early modern stage, with the formal Theophrastan Character representing the dynamics by which one can metamorphose into the other. This typology of dramatic character, however, is still couched in the terms of generality and particularity that govern the novelistic distinction between flat and round characters. There is a counter-argument, however, that credible character is achieved by simplification—subtracting details—rather than by accumulation. A suitable analogy might be between literary

---

[42] Charles Lamb, 'On the Tragedies of Shakespeare', in Jonathan Bates (ed.), *The Romantics on Shakespeare* (London: Penguin, 1992), 115.

[43] 'Zombie *Hamlet*', YouTube, www.youtube.com/watch?v=deXZl8QBBh8.

character and sculpture, where form is created by carving away matter to release the inner form, rather than painting. A rhetoric of character by simplification might be said to work by syncope, a rhetorical term for the removal of letters or syllables from the middle of a word.[44] Lanham offers as examples the substitution of 'heartly' for 'heartily' and 'ignomy' for 'ignominy'. The term can also refer to the reduction of syllables, for instance in the service of regularizing metre, as when Hamlet, speaking to Horatio about his desire to know what the ghost imparted to him, recommends that Horatio 'O'ermaster't as you may' (*Hamlet* 1.5.144).[45] A related trope is metonymy, which Kenneth Burke defines as transformation by 'reduction'.[46] Another is ellipsis, the elimination of chronological information in a narrative, but syncope expresses best not merely the simplification, but also the material depletion of data in digital character construction.

Creation of meaning by subtraction is typical of computer applications, although not obviously, because such applications are rigid models. Thus, in a simple word search in an online text, one can seek out instances of 'black' and 'white', but not (without other reading methods) 'ivory' and 'coal'. Craig notes as well that statistical study 'begins with a drastic subtraction of all but a very few of the created and perceived materials that make for meaning in drama'. It defines 'a small set of features to count and chooses one limited context [e.g., gender or genre] in which to make comparisons among the results'.[47] The yield of data is rich, but limited by the terms of the original search.

The operations of subtraction or syncope are more obvious in the world of YouTube. This particular social medium works largely by miniaturization, and the constraints placed on users are reinforced by a constant oscillation between immediacy (where the illusion of reality is complete) and hypermediacy (where one is aware of the intervening medium), as defined by Jay David Bolter and Richard Grusin in *Remediation*.[48] A YouTube page is far from a transparent window on the world. Rather, it is a layered composite of different frames. The actual video is a small screen embedded in a Web page that includes other kinds of information, from the submitter's description and metadata to viewer comments and suggested videos for further viewing. Sometimes even advertising intervenes between the viewer and the video's virtual reality, so that the viewer of a YouTube page moves constantly between looking at and looking through the screen. These visual disruptions, making viewers at times hyper-aware of the medium in which the videos are received, contribute to a generic tendency toward parody, and at the other end of the spectrum, exoticism.

A good example of syncope and the rhetoric of simplification can be found in the emerging genre of Lego Shakespeares, *Hamlet* and *Macbeth* being the two most

---

[44] Lanham, *Handlist*, 147.

[45] This example comes from the online dictionary of rhetorical tropes, *Silva Rhetoricae*, http://humanities.byu.edu/rhetoric/Silva.htm.

[46] Kenneth Burke, 'Four Master Tropes', in *A Grammar of Motives* (New York: G. Braziller, 1955), 305–17.

[47] Craig, '"Speak, That I may See Thee"', 288.

[48] Jay David Bolter and Richard Grusin, *Remediation* (Cambridge, MA: MIT Press, 1991).

popular subjects. The genre is governed generally by a rhetoric of simplification. On the level of plot, the plays are reduced to one scene, or at most a selection of scenes. A common narrative method is to intersperse animated vignettes featuring Lego figures and stage sets with snippets of text in the style of silent movies, creating in effect a new media version of the collection of Shakespearean 'beauties' popular in the eighteenth century. On the level of technology, these videos work also by stringing together small segments of film in stop-action sequence. As is typical of electronic Shakespeares, aesthetics and technology work hand in glove and are difficult to differentiate from one another; both contribute to syncope, the slicing of existing narrative segments to fit the constraints of technology, online medium, and local genre.

One exemplary Lego *Hamlet*, a nicely produced version of the closet scene, has a stylized setting (castle) and props (blockish wine cups over which Hamlet and Gertrude argue). The principals' physical appearance, of course, is necessarily simplified by the toy's structure: Gertrude, for instance, is identified by her skirt and page-boy hairdo; Hamlet's black clothing and blond bob, reminiscent of both Laurence Olivier's and Kenneth Branagh's appearance in well-known film versions of the play, identify the prince. The focus on particular details in these videos also remediates film. For instance, although Polonius's choice of an arras behind which to hide is textually determined, the expansive pool of blood round his prostrate figure derives from the film tradition. The amount of blood increases from the Olivier to the Franco Zeffirelli films, reaching a level of hyperbolic excess in Branagh's version, so that by the time Branagh's Hamlet is ready to 'lug the guts into the neighbour room' (*Hamlet* 3.4.186), the pool of blood emanating from Polonius's wound has spread almost completely throughout Gertrude's closet, transforming the domestic interior into a gothic charnel house. In 'Lego Hamlet', Hamlet's sword draws out blobs of ketchup, playfully scaling down Branagh's epic mise en scène to suit the affordances of amateur film-making and YouTube as a social medium.

3. Character works by repetitive form; its dominant trope is exergasia, and its mood is rhapsodic

YouTube Shakespeare puts little stock in originality. Its producers, by contrast, often note proudly how quickly their videos were put together. The result is a rapid development of genres and sub genres within YouTube Shakespeare. There are not only the ever-growing number of Lego *Hamlet*s and *Macbeth*s, but also a substantial body of Barbie *Hamlet*s and mash-ups consisting of a montage of scenes, taken from Branagh's film, in which Hamlet physically abuses Ophelia, that are set to romantic music celebrating young love from contemporary pop groups. Narratives play off one another, so that Lego creators select scenes used by previous Lego film-makers and riff on their staging; favourite tropes, such as the suburban swimming pool as a site for Ophelia's drowning, emerge.

The classical trope for the repetition of a single idea in many figures is exergasia.[49] Writ large, exergasia produces repetitive form. Kenneth Burke, in his rhetorical lexicon of 'psychology and form', identifies 'repetitive form' as 'the restatement of a theme by new details'.[50] In the case of YouTube, repetitive form is fostered by the application's status as a database, a 'structured collection of data' shaped by mathematical algorithms.[51] YouTube's threading of videos according to metadata recorded by those who upload them, for instance, provides both viewers and potential producers with a handy taxonomy of previous examples that YouTube film-makers clearly rely on when consulting their own personal muses; in many ways, YouTube's function as a database of videos works like handbooks giving formulas for writing romance novels. Paradoxically, this structural approach to Shakespeare can produce new and idiosyncratic character effects, as one video suggesting that Gertrude may have murdered Ophelia, for instance, gives rise to others, the principal variation being in the Queen's chosen instrument for murder. In the database, pieces of characterological 'data' relate to one another paradigmatically, in terms of hierarchical semantic relations; thus, Gertrude is an Ophelia-murderer, a narrative function that does not necessarily tie in neatly with the other roles given to her by Shakespeare. Connections between the video's linear narrative and its dramatic actors on the syntagmatic level are therefore at best episodic, at worst illogical, producing wildly aberrant characterizations. The overall literary effect of repetitive form, as produced through a database, is rhapsodic, each video functioning as a quasi-musical string of events and people that play out in changing combinations.

4. Character is appropriation: its master trope is metalepsis, and its mood moves between irony and exoticism

The dominant ethos of Web 2.0, which includes such social networking sites as YouTube, is appropriation. This aspect of the new media has been met with ambivalence. While Lawrence Lessig celebrates the ability of amateur Web 2.0 authors to appropriate and recombine materials freely in their own art, others have seen this appropriation as nothing more than the theft of others' intellectual property.[52] In either case, appropriation is very much part of the YouTube ethos. Amateur film-makers take not only ideas, but also pieces of visual and verbal data from one another, which often are applied to new narrative situations that seem to have no logical connection to their source; ease of access seems to be the primary criterion for selection. This is most

---

[49] Lanham, *Handlist*, 74.

[50] Kenneth Burke, *Counter-statement* (Berkeley: University of California Press, 1931), 125–7.

[51] Lev Manovich, *The Language of New Media* (Cambridge, MA: MIT Press, 2001), 218.

[52] The first argument is made by Lawrence Lessig, *Code, and other Laws of Cyberspace, Version 2.0* (New York: Basic Books, 2006); the second by Andrew Keen, *The Cult of the Amateur: How Today's Internet is Killing Our Culture* (New York: Bantam Bell Publishing Group, 2007).

obvious in mash-ups that take wholesale footage from other videos and either add to or subtract from it, but there are also more isolated examples in which the relation between source and appropriation is notably strained. For example, another Lego *Hamlet* enacts 1.5, Hamlet's confrontation with the Ghost, using music appropriated from the mash-up 'Hamlet is Back'. A soundtrack that in its original context evoked the epic scope of a James Cameron film has now been applied to a miniaturization of Hamlet's encounter with the Ghost, whose low-tech effects put its visuals into an ironic relation with the soundtrack.[53]

In this way, appropriation on YouTube works as metalepsis, the trope by which a present effect is traced to a distant cause, the interim logical connections between them generally having been erased. The relation is not strictly one of substitution, which might more properly be labelled metaphor, for the simple reason that the YouTube database intrudes on any single interaction between video and receivers, who always are being invited to look at related videos. While YouTube videos that respond intentionally to one another create a relatively (or perhaps deceptively) clear relation between source and appropriation, the greater the response to any given video, the more diffuse the artistic genealogy becomes, thus producing metalepsis as a master trope.

Metalepsis characterizes Web-based databases generally, which operate by a logic of what John Unsworth has called 'sampling':

> Sampling is the result of selection according to a criterion, really: the criterion could be a search term (in which case the sample that results from selection would be a sample of the frequency with which the thing searched for occurs in the body of material searched). In another case, the criterion might itself be a rate of frequency, for example 'five frames per second', in which case the sample that results would be a series of images sampling the world inside the camera's frame every five seconds.[54]

Within not only YouTube, but also scholarly databases, the selection and isolation of pieces of video, audio, visual, or textual data can strain the already tenuous relations between Shakespearean appropriation or performance and its original context. To give a straightforward example, the Shakespeare in Performance database at the Internet Shakespeare Editions groups its artefacts in terms of subject: one can search for audio, costume design, graphic, flier, etc., although subsidiary links make other searches possible.[55] As is typical of library databases, paradigmatic relations (e.g. moving from one audio clip to another) offer themselves on an equal footing with syntagmatic relations (e.g. viewing all artefacts from one performance). The collected artefacts, furthermore, relate to the performances with which they are associated by the relatively weak trope of metonymy; they are associated with one another, but the online artefact offers only a miniature

---

[53] 'Lego *Hamlet*', YouTube, http://web.mit.edu/shakespeare/asia/collections/catalogue.html.

[54] John Unsworth, 'Scholarly Primitives: what methods do humanities researchers have in common, and how might our tools reflect this?', www3.isrl.illinois.edu/~unsworth//Kings.5-oo/primitives.html.

[55] Shakespeare in Performance, Internet Shakespeare Editions, http://internetshakespeare.uvic.ca/Theater/sip/browse.html.

excerpt from the whole performance and represents, rather than simply reproduces that performance, placing the copy at a double remove from its original.

Within museum environments such as the Internet Shakespeare Editions, the scholarly apparatus provided by editors underwrites, guides, and perhaps even disciplines the possibilities for interpretation of any given artefact. The more separated the user of such a database is from the context from which the artefacts were extracted, however, the greater the possibility for an audience response that is grounded in exoticism. I use this term in preference to orientalism (which suggests a more coherent ideological position vis-à-vis the other) because the database's ability to deliver data as cultural 'snapshots' is disorienting in an ideological sense, in part because websites lack, to a greater or lesser extent, the surrounding material or paratext that shapes a scholarly response to unfamiliar art. On the scholarly end of the spectrum is MIT's Shakespeare Performance in Asia collection, which houses records of more than 240 performances and adaptations and twenty-two video clips. The second clip, 'I have killed my wife', in which Othello soliloquizes after having killed his Desdemona, comes with the following bibliographical information:

> *Clip Title:* I have killed my wife
> *Production Title:* Desdemona (Tokyo)
> *Description:* Othello confesses to killing Desdemona.
> *Shakespeare Reference:* Othello
> *Language:* English, Japanese, Burmese, Sanskrit, and Korean
> *Tags:* patriarchy and video[56]

All of this metadata helps viewers unfamiliar with the dramatic tradition being recorded in the 2:51 minute clip understand its relation to Shakespeare, despite obvious barriers such as language and performance conventions. Subtitles also prove helpful, indicating that Othello's tragedy is linked to his desire for a son that this marriage presumably has not given him.

Contrast the scholarly apparatus that guides neophyte scholars of Asian Shakespeare on this website to the relative lack of contextual information provided by YouTube. In one clearly parodic, yet uncontextualized clip, a Japanese Hamlet (identified as Tatsuja Fujiwara) is confronted by a ghost that, by Shakespearean standards, seems excessively abject, at the exact moment when, as the video's description tells us, Hamlet in his underwear is 'just about to get it on with a Valkyri'.[57] From the YouTube posting, we can glean that this is a musical, from the video itself can we sense that a comic mood predominates, and from other threaded videos we can see more selections from the musical. But that is all. YouTube uncouples multimedia clips on the Web from their

---

[56] Shakespeare Performance in Asia, http://web.mit.edu/shakespeare/asia/collections/catalogue. html.

[57] 'Hamlet (Tatsuya Fujiwara) meets his "Ghost Dad"', YouTube, http://www.youtube.com/watch? v=l_xRLAd5CQI.

cultural contexts according to the logic of metalepsis, encouraging an attitude of exotic wonder and perhaps intellectual confusion.

Perhaps what distinguishes most clearly the production and reception of Shakespearean characters in new media, Web 2.0, and other electronic environments from other current approaches to character is the way in which the mediation of code between receiver and character brackets together the issue of morality in identification. One can respond with a nearly voyeuristic curiosity or with a burst of simple appreciation, the ubiquitous 'lol' of YouTube commentary. Because the medium intervenes always between us and the characters, however, the possibility of moral improvement and a sharing of essential human experiences are precluded.

Coda

This chapter has sought to explain what happens when Shakespearean plays and their characters are catapulted onto the World Wide Web by a variety of computer applications. It does not argue, however, that either the operations of identification or defamiliarization are restricted to particular media or historical moments. Robert Greene, in disparaging Shakespeare as an 'upstart Crowe', equated him with his historical invention, the character of Margaret of Anjou as witch and national pariah. Charles Whitney has shown as well that early modern audiences identified with dramatic characters, in particular Falstaff and Tamburlaine, in often idiosyncratic ways.[58] In many ways, despite vast differences in technology and medium, Shakespeare's audiences in the age of computers struggle, as his contemporaries did, against the mediated quality of 'Shakespeare' to make their own, equally idiosyncratic identifications with the playwright.

[58] Charles Whitney, *Early Responses to Renaissance Drama* (Cambridge: Cambridge University Press, 2006).

CHAPTER 30

....

LAW

....

REBECCA LEMON

It is equitable to pardon human weaknesses, and to look, not to the law but to the legislator; not to the letter of the law but to the intention of the legislator; not to the action itself, but to the moral purpose; not to the part, but to the whole; not to what a man is now, but to what he has been, always or generally.

—Aristotle, *The 'Art' of Rhetoric*[1]

SHAKESPEARE's plays could be called courts of equity. Like equity courts, which provide a corrective to harsh legal justice by offering pardon to condemned criminals, Shakespeare's plays weigh up, and often pardon, various human failings. Literature more broadly offers judgements and pardons, of course. Shakespeare is particularly attuned to legal dilemmas, however. Through a combination of his education, observation of life in London and Stratford, and personal experience, he gathered enough fluency with the law to fill his poems and plays with legal insights.[2] From contract in *The Comedy of Errors* and *The Merchant of Venice* to treason in *Richard II* and *Macbeth* to adultery in *Measure for Measure* to property in *King Lear*, he explores some of the central legal questions of his day. In doing so, his plays, like Aristotle's equity, move beyond the precise letter of the law to interpret its spirit. He surveys traitors and petty criminals, adulterers, heretics, tyrants, thieves, and murderers, giving his audience a world of human failings and the power to pardon them.

---

[1] Aristotle, *The 'Art' of Rhetoric*, John Henry Freese (ed. and trans.), Loeb Classical Library (Cambridge, MA: Harvard University Press, 1926), I: xiii.1374*b*, 146–7.

[2] Shakespeare and his family were repeatedly engaged in lawsuits. His father John, as well as violating usury laws and failing to appear in court at Westminster, also defaulted on a contract; as a result he lost the family property in Wiltshire, which would have come to his son William. The lawsuit surrounding this property dragged on for decades. Shakespeare brought several legal suits to court, including a suit against a neighbour in 1604, another suit for money owed him in 1608, and a suit in Chancery (the court of equity) in 1609 over tithes in Stratford in which he had invested. See Daniel Kornstein, *Kill All the Lawyers?: Shakespeare's Legal Appeal* (Lincoln: University of Nebraska Press, 2005).

But before examining Shakespeare's spirit of the law, let us first turn to the letter of it. Aristotle's formulation (law v. legislator, letter v. spirit) might suggest that the 'law' is coherent and material, a 'letter' to be followed. Against the letter of the law stands equity, the power to pardon. But such an opposition is misleading. The law is not singular. Indeed, attempting to write a chapter about the law in Shakespeare forces us to pause and ask, what is the law? This chapter strives to answer that question. It does so by addressing, in its first two sections, the variety of law in Shakespeare's England. This variety challenges any misconception that law might be stable and entirely specialized. Instead, law in the early modern period proves capacious and multi-jurisdictional. It also appears heavily implicated in social relations: the politics of gender, class, race, religion, and nation, among other social formations, press upon legal form and interpretation. The chapter's third section turns to Shakespeare's *The Merchant of Venice* to explore this notion of law's sociability. This section demonstrates how even at a moment of firm articulation of 'stony' law (4.1.3) the process of invested interpretation remains paramount.[3] Shakespeare repeatedly illuminates law not as a force of transhistorical custom, shoring up order amid chaos, but instead as one among many tools available to secure and occasionally challenge existing social relations. Thus, for an imaginative, humanistic writer like Shakespeare, the *copia* of the law—its various histories, courts, and social dimensions—provided ingredients for legally-themed plays that move far beyond technicalities and proceduralism. Finally, in its closing section, the chapter explores this notion of law's social relations in order to suggest potentially new directions for the study of Shakespeare and the law.[4]

LAW IN EARLY MODERN ENGLAND

In answering the question 'what is the law?' we might begin by noting the variety of laws in early modern England. This section will briefly survey these various legal forms and practices. Such a survey is a necessary starting point because it can be easy to approach the study of Shakespeare and the law from the vantage point that 'law' can be neatly reflected, represented, and thematized in literature. Instead, even the shortest survey of England's legal variety helps reveal the continual process of interpretation and jurisdictional boundary-hunting that goes into not only the practice of the law, but also its literary representation. To put this another way, such a survey helps reinforce one of the most basic premises of the law and literature movement: that both fields are

---

[3] *The Comical History of the Merchant of Venice, or Otherwise Called the Jew of Venice (1596–7)*, in *The Oxford Shakespeare*, 2nd edn., Gary Taylor and Stanley Wells (eds.), with John Jowett and William Montgomery (Oxford: Oxford University Press, 2005). All citations are to this edition.

[4] I am grateful to Penelope Geng, Constance Jordan, Arthur F. Kinney, and Genevieve Love for commenting on drafts of this chapter.

equally marked by an investment in language, interpretation, and social forms, making their encounter at once structurally rich and textually dense.

Early modern England drew from at least three legal traditions, which at times competed with one another. First, and most influential, is English common law. Common law continues to be the law of the land in England, drawn from customs from time immemorial (in practice, from the reign of William I). It is established through a set of judicial rulings; it was traditionally unwritten, and emerged from an ancient constitution—the existence of which has provoked significant historical debate.[5]

In the early modern period, common law courts were arguably the most powerful in the land. The courts were arranged hierarchically, from local to state level. The local magistrates' courts addressed legal issues brought by justices of the peace in quarter sessions. The most serious of these cases then went to the assize courts, comprised of justices from the court of the King's or Queen's Bench who travelled on commissions around the country. The central, state courts included the court of common pleas, which heard the majority of common law cases, as well as the exchequer, which dealt with financial cases such as debts owed to the Crown.

In addition to these common law courts, the equity courts, most notably the court of Chancery, allowed judges to deliver pardons when legal rulings failed to produce justice.[6] Specifically, as William Lambarde and Christopher St German both explore, the court of Chancery allowed a judge, according to his conscience, to free a petitioner trapped by the letter of the law: Chancery, Lambard writes, 'doth so cancell and shut up the rigour of the generall *Law*, that it shall not breake forth to the hurt of some one singular Case and person'.[7] Lambarde's claim, that equity can 'cancel' and 'shut up' the general law might sound like reckless suspension of legal precedent. But J. H. Baker explains the process this way: 'The chancellor [in the equity court] came not to destroy law, but to fulfil it by ordering what conscience demanded. In doing so, he did not thwart the common law, because the law did not forbid the conscientious

---

[5] Glen Burgess, *The Politics of the Ancient Constitution* (University Park, PA: Pennsylvania State University Press, 1992); J. G. A. Pocock, *The Ancient Constitution and the Feudal Law: A Study of English Historical Thought in the Seventeenth Century* (Cambridge: Cambridge University Press, 1957). On legal precedent, see Christopher Brooks, *Law, Politics and Society in Early Modern England* (Cambridge: Cambridge University Press, 2008).

[6] The country's most notorious court, the Star Chamber, had originally served like Chancery as an equity court. By the early modern period, however, Star Chamber became associated instead with the exercise of sovereign prerogative over and above the law to the point that Star Chamber is a term synonymous with tyrannical rule and judgements delivered through sovereign caprice.

[7] William Lambarde, *Archeion or, A Discourse upon the High Courts of Justice in England* (London: 1591), Charles H. McIlwain and Paul L. Ward (eds.) (Cambridge, MA: Harvard University Press, 1957), 31–2. I am grateful to Constance Jordan for drawing this quote to my attention and for sharing her work on equity before its publication. See Constance Jordan, 'Law', in Patricia Parker (ed.), *Shakespeare Encyclopedia*, forthcoming. On equity, see also Arthur F. Kinney, 'Sir Philip Sidney and the Uses of History', in Heather Dubrow and Richard Strier (eds.), *The Historical Renaissance*, (Chicago, IL: University of Chicago Press, 1988), 293–314, and Louis A. Knafla, *Law and Politics in Jacobean England* (Cambridge: Cambridge University Press, 1977), 155–82, who explores the relationship between equity and common law.

result.'[8] Thus judges were not to deviate significantly from positive law but instead temper it in extraordinary cases.

While the common law and its related courts were dominant, there were other practices of law in early modern England. Civil law training and practise flourished after Henry VIII's split with Rome, as ecclesiastical courts turned from canon law (the ecclesiastical law of the Catholic Church) to civil law instead. Practised throughout continental Europe, civil law emerged out of written Roman traditions, and was codified by the emperor Justinian in the monumental *Corpus Juris Civilis*. Unlike the common law, then, civil law was written and international. It relied not on judicial precedent but on code for its legal authority. Probate, marriage, and sexual behaviour all fell under the civil law of the ecclesiastical courts. These courts included the court of high commission, which was the highest ecclesiastical court in England, as well as the consistory court and the archdeaconry courts presided over by bishops and arch-bishops; and finally the various courts of appeal before ecclesiasts, including the court of audience, the court of delegates, and the court of arches. Further, dealing in maritime issues, the admiralty courts were also governed by civil law.

Finally, in addition to these common and civil law traditions, there were sovereign proclamations and statutes. Increasingly in the early modern period monarchs turned to statutes to effect legal changes, most obviously with Henry VIII, who used statutes passed in Parliament to effect the Reformation. The resulting tension between legislative and judicial powers in the early modern period continued until after the English Civil War.[9]

With multiple legal systems and multiple courts came multiple sites of legal training. Common law lawyers were trained at the Inns of Court (in London: Lincoln's Inn, Grey's Inn, Middle Temple, and Inner Temple), while civil lawyers went to Oxford and Cambridge. All of these future lawyers needed to command a range of languages: English, Latin, and law French. In a final emphasis on the multiplicity of the law, these future lawyers and barristers learned, in their schools, various methods of interpretations.[10]

This survey of the range of laws, courts, schools, languages, and methods of interpretation helps to demonstrate the impossibility of invoking 'law' as a stable category. To speak of 'law' as a singular force is to collapse a set of diverse and often competing practices. Written law is not singular: civil v. statute law reveals this. Law is

---

[8] J. H. Baker, *The Oxford History of the Laws of England*, vol. 6 (Oxford: Oxford University Press, 2003), 42; see especially 'Equity and Conscience', 39–48. On conscience and law, see Christopher St German, *Doctor and Student* T. F. T. Plucknett and J. L. Barton (eds.) (London: Selden Society, 1974), 94–7, 101–7. As Baker explores, St German's view of conscience as an objective ideal to which judges refer in their equity rulings was controversial since other early modern legal theorists saw equity as a potentially arbitrary ruling by a single judge.

[9] On the role of statute, see J. H. Baker, *An Introduction to English Legal History*, 3rd edn. (London: Butterworths, 1990), and G. R. Elton, *Policy and Police: The Enforcement of the Reformation in the Age of Thomas Cromwell* (Cambridge: Cambridge University Press, 1972).

[10] On methods of judicial interpretation, see Peter Goodrich, *Reading the Law: A Critical Introduction to Legal Methods and Techniques* (Oxford: Blackwell, 1986), 57.

not evenly applied: the role of chancery (i.e. equity) proves this. And law is not consolidated in the monarch alone: the status of custom and judicial precedent shows this. Law is thus diverse on multiple fronts: because the original written law might be interpreted in a restrictive or expansive sense; because laws can be altogether supplemented or changed, depending upon political need; and because the application of this law in the hands of the judges, juries, and sovereigns might differ. Further, law is in transition in this period. Not only did the Henrican Reformation generate enormous legal changes, but also the influence of continental humanism, urbanization, and other social and intellectual changes of the period further advanced the practice of law. Finally, this period saw the emergence of law as a profession, with specialized training and methods.[11]

I labour this point about the diversity of the law because it only compounds the challenge of studying the law in Shakespeare. After all, 'Shakespeare' is equally diverse. Of course, this is also one of the pleasures of pursuing the study of literature and law. As Frances E. Dolan writes of studying law in the early modern period,

> One appeal is that there was not anything as homogeneous, coherent, or originary as 'the law' in this period. Instead, there were various and competing bodies of law, operating through numerous tribunals.[12]

Recognizing this appeal—the appeal of heterogeneity—we can now turn to scholarship on Shakespeare and the law itself.

LAW IN SHAKESPEARE STUDIES

As the above survey of early modern laws and courts might suggest, the difficulty and indeed opportunity facing scholars who work in the field of law and Shakespeare is the sheer range of approaches to the topic. If 'law' is multi-vocal, so too is Shakespeare. In writing about the law and Shakespeare, the challenge lies, as with other interdisciplinary relations, with 'and'. We might study the law 'in' Shakespeare or the law 'through' Shakespeare; or we might study the fields side by side. This section offers a brief illustration of approaches to the law and Shakespeare, suggesting the extensive and varied nature of this interdisciplinary topic.

Plays such as *Measure for Measure* and *The Merchant of Venice* have attracted particular attention for their extended engagements with the law. In *Measure for Measure*, Shakespeare depicts a Duke seeking to reinforce lapsed laws. But the tyranny

---

[11] David Dean, *Law Making and Society in Late Elizabethan England* (Cambridge: Cambridge University Press, 2002); Edward Gieskes, *Representing the Professions: Administration, Law, and Theatre in Early Modern England* (Newark: University of Delaware Press, 2006).

[12] Frances E. Dolan, 'Early Modern Literature and the Law', *Huntington Library Quarterly* 71.2 (June 2008), 352.

of his deputy, Angelo, leads to a host of new legal problems, among them slander, sexual betrayal, and injustice. The problem with this 'problem play' lies in the instability of the law, a force offered as at once the source of and solution to Vienna's problems. *The Merchant of Venice*, a play discussed below, reveals an equal density of legal issues. Among the questions of contract, criminality, and citizenship posed by both plays, Shakespeare draws particular attention to the legal ins and outs of marriage. At what point is a union legally binding? What obligation do spouses have to one another? How do past attachments—to friends and/or lovers—impact marital relations? Both *Merchant* and *Measure* explore such questions through complex triangles of affection and aversion: Antonio, Bassanio, and Portia go to court with Shylock, just as Isabella, Mariana, and the Duke legally contend with Angelo.

Marriage is a topic Shakespeare repeatedly engages, not only in these two famously legal plays but also in a range of texts, spanning *The Taming of the Shrew* through the Sonnets and *The Rape of Lucrece* to *Cymbeline*.[13] In a period of shifting conceptions of marriage and changing legal opportunities for women, Shakespeare depicts the challenges of union for both men and women. And marriage law is only one of many forms of law in Shakespeare. His legal range includes nearly all aspects of law. A host of critics probe the relationship between particular forms of the law and specific plays, from Roman law to constitutional law, from *Coriolanus* to *The Tempest*.[14] Shakespeare represents specific legal codes (on contract, property, and equity), as well as general legal philosophy: what, his plays ask, is the nature of citizenship and subjectivity? How does the law understand human action and intention?[15]

Shakespeare's plays repeatedly explore the interplay between forms of law and literature, as characters debate, uphold, and undermine legal principles familiar (or perhaps foreign) to their audiences. Rather than survey all of the legal practices and philosophies engaged by Shakespeare, a gargantuan task, instead one example, that of

---

[13] On marriage see Frances E. Dolan, *Marriage and Violence: The Early Modern Legacy* (Philadelphia: University of Pennsylvania Press, 2008); Subha Mukherji, *Law and Representation in Early Modern Drama* (Cambridge: Cambridge University Press, 2006); B. J. Sokol and Mary Sokol, *Shakespeare, Law, and Marriage* (Cambridge: Cambridge University Press, 2003).

[14] On Roman law, see Lorna Hutson, *The Invention of Suspicion: Law and Mimesis in Shakespeare and Renaissance Drama* (Oxford: Oxford University Press, 2007); Rebecca Lemon, 'Arms and Laws in Shakespeare's *Coriolanus*', in Karen Cunningham and Constance Jordan (eds.), *The Law in Shakespeare* (New York: Palgrave Macmillan, 2007), 233–48; Charles Ross, *Elizabethan Literature and the Law of Fraudulent Conveyance: Sidney, Spenser, and Shakespeare* (Aldershot: Ashgate, 2003). On constitutional law, see Peter C. Herman, '*Macbeth*: Absolutism, the Ancient Constitution, and the Aporia of Politics', in Cunningham and Jordan (eds.), *The Law in Shakespeare*, 208–32; Ian Ward, *Shakespeare and the Legal Imagination* (London: Butterworths, 1999).

[15] On property, see Jill Phillips Ingram, *Idioms of Self-interest: Credit, Identity, and Property in English Renaissance Literature* (New York: Routledge, 2006), and Joseph Loewenstein, *The Author's Due: Printing and the Prehistory of Copyright* (Chicago, IL: University of Chicago Press, 2002). On equity, see Mark Fortier, *The Culture of Equity in Early Modern England* (Aldershot: Ashgate, 2005); Andrew J. Majeske, *Equity in English Renaissance Literature: Thomas More and Edmund Spenser* (New York: Routledge, 2006); and Elliott Visconsi, *Lines of Equity: Literature and the Origins of Law in Later Stuart England* (Ithaca, NY: Cornell University Press, 2008).

succession, might be used to indicate the range and impact of his legal interests. When the Archbishop of Canterbury offers a long genealogical exposition on the legality of Henry V's claim to France (1.2.33–95), he summarizes the Salic law argument, namely the French tradition that kingship may never be claimed through descent from a woman. Audience members may or may not have known about Salic law. But, as so often happens in Shakespeare's plays, this speech in *Henry V* educates its audience on legal principles and practises. While this speech can be read as a flimsy legalistic excuse allowing Henry to invade France, critics have also explored how, as Katherine Eggert writes, the play is 'deeply concerned with Salic law', particularly with the law's implication that 'an English king might legitimately claim political power without having derived any of that power from a woman'.[16]

Arcane or foreign legal principles provide, in Shakespeare's drama, matter for political debates with immediate contemporary relevance. Through Canterbury's discourse on Salic law, Shakespeare raises the issue of succession, a crucial and forbidden topic in 1599. *Henry V* is, of course, not the only one of his plays to address the succession issue. Shakespeare refers, for example, to Scottish and English practises of succession in *Macbeth*: he invokes the ancient Gaelic model of tanistry, even as he also depicts, in Duncan, a king who follows primogeniture by nominating his son as his successor.[17] In *Coriolanus* and *Julius Caesar*, Shakespeare shows, in the form of senatorial tensions, the opposition between monarchical and republican forms of government. Such struggles resonate with, and arguably weigh into, Elizabethan and Jacobean debates about the relation of king and parliament: is England a country ruled by a king, by a king-in-parliament, or by king and parliament together?[18]

Shakespeare poses questions of succession in comedies and romances as well, from *As You Like It* to *The Tempest*. But it is, most obviously, in his history plays from the late 1580s and 1590s that Shakespeare addresses issues resonant with the Elizabethan succession crisis, when the Queen forbade publications on, or discussions of, the issue. In his preoccupation with dynastic politics onstage, evident in the first and second tetralogies, Shakespeare participated in this barred but nonetheless omnipresent

---

[16] Katherine Eggert, 'Nostalgia and the Not Yet Late Queen: Refusing Female Rule in *Henry V*', *ELH* 61.3 (1994), at 523, 524. On Salic law and *Henry V* see also Andrew Gurr, (ed.), *King Henry V* (Cambridge: Cambridge University Press, 1992); Clayton G. MacKenzie, 'Henry V and the Invasion of France: Rethinking the Moral Justification', *Upstart Crow* 25 (2005), 65–70; Michio Tokumi, 'The *Salic Law* in *Henry V*', *Shakespeare Studies* 37 (1999), 45–61.

[17] David Norbrook, '*Macbeth* and the Politics of Historiography', in Kevin Sharpe and Steven N. Zwicker (eds.), *Politics of Discourse: The Literature and History of Seventeenth-Century England* (Berkeley: University of California Press, 1987), 78–116.

[18] Both of these Roman plays have been read in light of significant constitutional debates about the relationship of king to parliament, as well as the viability of an English republic or the British Union. See Alex Garganigo, '"Coriolanus", the Union Controversy, and Access to the Royal Person', *Studies in English Literature, 1500–1900* 42.2 (2002), 335–59; Shannon Miller, 'Topicality and Subversion in William Shakespeare's *Coriolanus*', *SEL* 32.2 (Spring 1992), 287–310; Neil Rhodes, 'Wrapped in the Strong Arms of the Union: Shakespeare and King James', in Willy Maley and Andrew Murphy (eds.), *Shakespeare and Scotland* (Manchester: Manchester University Press, 2004), 37–52.

conversation about succession. He may have contributed to the conversation in very specific ways, as recent studies of the relationship between *Richard II* and Robert Persons' controversial polemic, *A Conference about the Next Succession*, suggest.[19] More generally, as Peter Lake puts it, history plays from the 1580s on are 'obsessed with dynastic civil wars, rebellion, usurpation and the nature of legitimacy, with narratives often organized around competing claims to both the English and the French thrones, noble faction and feud, and campaigns in and against France.'[20]

The legal ins and outs of succession—be it in France, Scotland, classical Rome, or medieval England—thus provide an occasion for Shakespeare to explore the broader and more immediate questions of Elizabethan and Jacobean governance. Recognizing the tangle of legal issues surrounding succession in his plays, we might go a step further and acknowledge how Shakespeare poses questions about the fundamental conditions necessary for rule of law and stable governance. On the one hand, in the first tetralogy Shakespeare examines the rule of law: he depicts a social and legal world so corroded as to rely on brute force rather than legal procedure.[21] On the other hand, in the second tetralogy Shakespeare depicts competing models of governance, exploring the interplay of law and sovereignty. The rhetoric of absolutism, divine right, and tyranny fills *Richard II*, as the king suspends law and seizes property. Bolingbroke responds by asserting his quasi-legal rights against the reigning King, usurping the throne, and consolidating his own shaky claims to sovereignty through wars against foreign rebels. On his deathbed, he famously advises his son to 'busy giddy minds | With foreign quarrels' (2 *Henry IV* 4.3.342–3). In contrast to the absolute sovereignty of *Richard II*, the two *Henry IV* plays thus explore notions of popular and national sovereignty.

Questions of succession lead to questions of sovereignty, as Shakespeare repeatedly stages the challenges of rulership. From *Richard III* through *Hamlet* to *King Lear*, the plays ask, what legal actions might be taken when a ruler makes bad decisions, or gains the throne under suspicious circumstances? Can a ruler be held accountable?[22] And, when a ruler or subject has strayed, what constitutes appropriate punishment? Shakespeare carefully accounts for every stage of the legal process—from the creation or suspension of law to the process of enforcement through arrest, imprisonment, and punishment.[23]

[19] Cyndia Susan Clegg, 'Censorship and the Problems with History in Shakespeare's England', in Richard Dutton and Jean Elizabeth Howard (eds.), *A Companion to Shakespeare's Works: The Histories* (Oxford: Blackwell, 2003), 48–69; Rebecca Lemon, *Treason by Words: Literature, Law, and Rebellion in Shakespeare's England* (Ithaca, NY: Cornell University Press, 2006), esp. ch. 2 on *Richard II*.

[20] Peter Lake, 'The King (The Queen) and the Jesuit: James Stuart's "True Law of Free Monarchies" in Context/s', *Transactions of the Royal Historical Society*, 6th series, xiv (2004), 243–60, at. 244.

[21] Eric Heinze, 'Power Politics and the Rule of Law: Shakespeare's First Historical Tetralogy and Law's "Foundations"', *Oxford Journal of Legal Studies* 29.1 (2009), 139–68.

[22] Theodor Meron, 'Crimes and Accountability in Shakespeare,' *The American Journal of International Law* 92.1 (1998), 1–40.

[23] Harry Keyishian, 'Henry de Bracton, Renaissance Punishment Theory, and Shakespearean Closure', *Law and Literature* 20.3 (2008), 444–58, 487–8.

In depicting law ranging from contract to property to constitution, from marriage to succession, Shakespeare's plays engage the central legal questions of the day. In a period of tremendous legal change, the plays help audiences, both early modern and modern, grapple with legal issues. This emphasis on legal change, and Shakespeare's role in navigating through this change, cannot be over emphasized. The early modern period arguably witnessed transformation of English law: this period saw the rise of the jury and concepts of probability, the rise of the common law, a shift in attitudes toward human volition and action, and the emergence of a culture of fact.[24] Amid such shifts and changes, Shakespeare's plays educate modern readers, as well as early modern audiences, on diverse principles and practises of the law in literature.

'I CRAVE THE LAW': INTERPRETING LAW IN *THE MERCHANT OF VENICE*

The Merchant of Venice is an instructive place to examine the diversity of law in Shakespeare. Its Venice is not only a multi-ethnic and multi-religious city but also a multi-legal one. The play engages multiple legal issues: property, paternity, marriage, contract, crime, and citizenship. Multiple laws are invoked in the course of the play: Venetian law, natural law, biblical law, and the laws of the market. And finally, much legal scholarship concentrates on this particular play.[25]

The most obvious legal issue is Shylock's contract. Shylock mocks the 'soft and dull-eyed fool' who might 'relent, and sigh, and yield | To Christian intercessors' (3.3.14–16). He, by contrast, is 'a stony adversary' (4.1.3) who pursues 'a rigorous course' (4.1.7). His rigid legal contract stands temporarily against human or even divine law. If God commands 'thou shalt not murder', Shylock's contract defies even this divine will. In transgressing divine dictates, characters repeatedly deem Shylock a devil and a beast. Bassanio calls him a 'cruel devil' (4.1.214); Lancelot deems him 'a kind of devil' (2.2.21) and 'the very devil incarnation' (2.2.25); while Jessica, too, claims, 'our house is hell' (2.3.2). Gratiano indicts Shylock as a 'damned, inexorable dog' (4.1.127), with a 'currish spirit | Governed by a wolf' (4.1.132–3), while to Solanio he is 'the dog Jew' (2.8.14).

---

[24] On juries and probability, see Hutson, *The Invention of Suspicion*; on the common law, see Bradin Cormack, *A Power to Do Justice: Jurisdiction, English Literature, and the Rise of the Common Law, 1509–1625* (Chicago, IL: University of Chicago Press, 2007). On action and intention, see Luke Wilson, *Theaters of Intention: Drama and the Law in Early Modern England* (Stanford, CA: Stanford University Press, 2000); on facts and evidence, see Barbara Shapiro, *A Culture of Fact; England, 1550–1730* (Ithaca, NY: Cornell University Press, 2000).

[25] See, for example, *Cardozo Studies in Law and Literature* 5.1, A Symposium Issue on 'The Merchant of Venice' (Spring 1993), and the collection *Shakespeare and the Law*, Paul Raffield and Gary Watt (eds.) (Oxford: Hart Publishing, 2008), which features a special section on *Merchant*. In that volume see especially Charles Spinosa, 'Shylock and Debt and Contract in *The Merchant of Venice*', 65–85, which examines the play in relationship to the landmark Slade's Case.

Since Venetian citizens accuse Shylock of transgressing human and biblical law, it would seem natural to overturn his contract as illegitimate. This is the position that Bassanio takes when he pleads with Balthasar:

> I beseech you
> Wrest once the law to your authority.
> To do a great right, do a little wrong,
> And curb this cruel devil of his will.   (4.1.211–14)

The authority of Balthasar, he argues, should supersede the law, transcending problematic positive law (i.e. written, earthly law) in the name of the superior moral authority, the 'great right' of Venetian Christians. Nevertheless Shylock, the Duke, and Portia uphold the contract—it may be murderous but in terms of Venetian law it is legitimate. As Portia, in the guise of Balthasar, claims,

> There is no power in Venice
> Can alter a decree establishèd.
> 'Twill be recorded for a precedent,
> And many an error by the same example
> Will rush into the state.   (4.1.215–19)

Portia articulates how common law is established through judicial rulings: were s/he to alter a decree, a new precedent would be established.[26] Even Antonio admits, as he realizes Shylock's murderous designs on him, that 'The duke cannot deny the course of law' (3.3.26). And Shylock, of course, reminds the counsellors that the law is on his side: 'If you deny me, fie upon your law: | There is no force in the decrees of Venice. | I stand for judgement' (4.1.100–2); 'I stand here for law' (141); 'I crave the law, | The penalty and forfeit of my bond' (203–4).

Both the Duke and Portia recognize legal necessity and uphold the bond. Only mercy, they argue, can temper its terms. As the Duke puts it,

> The world thinks—and I think so too—
> That thou but lead'st this fashion of thy malice
> To the last hour of act, and then 'tis thought
> Thou'lt show thy mercy.   (4.1.16–19)

Portia, too, invokes the notion of pity and mercy against the contract, exploring how 'the quality of mercy is not strained' (4.1.181).

The resulting opposition, between Shylock's legalism and Portia's pleas, has been characterized as one between Old Testament justice and New Testament mercy, between law and equity. The Christian Venetians counsel the Jewish Shylock to forgo his temporary legal power over one of them in the name of humanity. In refusing to

---

[26] Her eventual ruling, however, sets judicial precedent in a potentially much more damaging manner, as Thomas C. Bilello argues in 'Accomplished with What She Lacks: Law, Equity, and Portia's Con', *Law and Literature* 16.1 (2004), 28–9. Bilello explores how Portia introduces a method of strict interpretation of contract that could shake commercial confidence in Venice.

suspend the contract, Shylock is deemed a beast, a wolf. In showing mercy, he would instead prove himself human and noble. Portia's famous speech calls mercy the purview of kings and gods: "tis mightiest in the mightiest' (4.1.185).[27]

Pushing this point about the role of mercy in the trial scene further, Stephen A. Cohen has identified Portia's ruling as an Aristotelian notion of equity (invoked at the opening of this chapter). Specifically, Cohen argues, Portia practises equity in rising above the law to suspend the injustice that would result from enforcing the bond itself.[28] Along similar lines the legal theorist and judge Richard Posner argues that 'Portia personifies the spirit of equity—the prudent recognition that strict rules of law, however necessary to a well-ordered society, must be applied with sensitivity and tact so that the spirit of the law is not sacrificed unnecessarily to the letter'.[29] We might hear, in Posner's argument, echoes of Aristotle's language of spirit and letter. We might also note, in his framing of Portia, how the equitable judge not only *follows* the spirit of the law but also *personifies* it, standing as body and spirit simultaneously. The judge occupies a position of sovereign heroism against the ferocity of the law itself.

As this section will go on to argue, however, the play's legal conflict only *appears* to hang on the opposition of the stony law of Shylock's contract to the mercy of Venetian equity.[30] Instead, the play repeatedly stages scenes of legal investment. It demonstrates, again and again, the law's implication in political, religious, and national ideologies— and in so doing, it highlights for readers the ways in which law is never neutral; it is never above human prejudices or failings.[31] Of course, judicial rulings might invoke law, written with apparent objectivity or practised through long custom, as a superior force of truth, transcendence, justice, or equality. But, as the following discussion will emphasize, the law is equally historical, particular, invested, and prejudicial.

The play demonstrates the law's ideological biases at all levels, from the creation of law, to its application, its interpretation, and its suspension. At the level of creation, we see the prejudices of the written law in the play's two contracts: Shylock's bond and Portia's father's will. Shylock's contract is meant as a form of revenge—its 'law' masks personal biases, and it does so quite poorly. Spectators fairly wonder how Antonio could be so blind, as he naively deems Shylock 'kind' in crafting the patently murderous contract. Portia's father, while his motives might be more sympathetic than Shylock's,

---

[27] Mercy and equity are not the same thing, as George Williams Keeton notes in *Shakespeare and His Legal Problems* (London: A&C Black, 1930), 19 n. 6.

[28] Stephen A. Cohen, '"The quality of mercy": Law, Equity, and Ideology in *The Merchant of Venice*', *Mosaic* 27.4 (1994), 35–54.

[29] Richard A. Posner, *Law and Literature* (Cambridge, MA: Harvard University Press, 1998), 109.

[30] Significant scholarly attention has been paid to the role of equity in the play, although recent critics have been much more sceptical about its relevance. See Bilello, 'Accomplished with What She Lacks', and B. J. Sokol and Mary Sokol, 'Shakespeare and the English Equity Jurisdiction: *The Merchant of Venice* and the Two Texts of *King Lear*', *Review of English Studies*, NS. 50.200 (1999), 417–39, which surveys the scholarship on this topic in order to challenge the assumption that the play engages concepts of equity.

[31] Indeed, the law can be all too prejudicial. See István Pogány, 'Shylock in Transylvania: Anti-Semitism and the Law in East Central Europe', *Shakespeare and the Law*, Raffield and Watt (eds.), 253–70.

also creates a prejudicial law. He wants to protect his estate and his daughter from fortune hunters, but in devising the casket contest as a feature of his will he also controls her choice of mate. As she says: 'I may neither choose who I would nor refuse who I dislike; so is the will of a living daughter curb'd by the will of a dead father. Is it not hard, Nerissa, that I cannot choose one, nor refuse none?' (1.2.22–6). Her language of hardness echoes the descriptions of Shylock's stony bond. Both Shylock and Portia's fathers, then, deploy law to enforce their own beliefs and protect their own interests. This may seem unproblematic until we consider that contracts should be entered into by equals, as a consensual exchange. But we might question Antonio's legal capacity: is he in a position to give meaningful consent when he seems all too eager to prove his love by risking death? And as for the request to Portia, she too lacks capacity and the law manipulates her through a phony choice.[32]

Not only are laws prejudicially constructed, but they are capriciously enforced as well. At times, custom reigns, but at other moments it is suspended to suit a character's best interests. The play begins with Antonio saying, 'to supply the ripe wants of my friend, | I'll break a custom' (1.3.61–2). He ordinarily shuns usurious lending but, setting aside precedent, he will borrow money from Shylock. To legally-minded readers, this is an anxious moment—deviation from custom has significant consequences. It upsets the legal order, as Portia states in the lines cited above. If such a move is sympathetic, it is also foolhardy and prejudicial, as Antonio suspends his habitual law for a favourite.

Bassanio, too, sidesteps law and custom. Of course he relies on the law of contract to advance himself: he is the beneficiary of Antonio's contract with Shylock, and of Portia's father's will. But in the climactic trial scene, Bassanio is the one who asks Balthasar to sidestep the law: 'wrest once the law to your authority' (4.1.212). Here, Bassanio asks to suspend law in order to achieve his own ends. He commits a further, more egregious transgression of the law when he offers his wife to the devil in order to save Antonio from the contract. Speaking of his life, his wife, and 'all the world', he tells Antonio, 'I would lose all, ay, sacrifice them all | Here to the devil, to deliver you' (4.1.279–83). Shylock recognizes the infidelity of such a pledge, saying simply, 'These be the Christian husbands!' (292) as he mourns the marriage of his own daughter to one such man.

If Antonio and Bassanio suspend the law in the name of friendship, then their pleas to Shylock to suspend the contract might seem consistent: they want him to do what they routinely do themselves. But there is a problem with this logic. The Christian Venetians, including Antonio and Bassanio, are in a position of social and cultural dominance; they suspend law to uphold friendship and their own interests. By contrast, Shylock is expected to suspend the law for the opposite reason: he should curtail his own desires. In a position of political vulnerability, he finds in the law a source of

---

[32] On homoeroticism in the play, see Steve Patterson, 'The Bankruptcy of Homoerotic Amity in Shakespeare's *Merchant of Venice*', *Shakespeare Quarterly* 50.1 (1999), 9–32, and Alan Sinfield, 'How to Read *The Merchant of Venice* without Being Heterosexist', in Terence Hawkes (ed.), *Alternative Shakespeares*, vol. 2 (London: Routledge, 1996), 122–39.

temporary power. Indeed, his sole source of power lies in this contract.[33] It is note-worthy that Venetians refuse to recognize Shylock's sovereignty at any other point in the play. His attempts to rule his own household are ridiculed; as Solanio puts it, in describing Shylock's loss of his household, including his daughter, his money, and his servant, 'I never heard a passion so confused, | So strange, outrageous, and so variable | As the dog Jew did utter in the streets' (2.8.12–14). It isn't simply Solanio's lack of sympathy that we might note here. The Venetian dismisses Shylock's response as foreign, 'strange,' and as illegitimate, 'outrageous'. The terms of his condemnation suggest that Shylock had no right to rule his own home. One might call Portia's father's will, or Bassanio's borrowing, or Lorenzo's courting strange and outrageous, for each deviates from social norms. But it is only Shylock's self-sovereignty, his rule of his own house, which draws condemnation. Not surprisingly, then, Shylock exercises sovereign-ty in the form of his contract when the Venetians expect him to suspend his legal claim. They counsel him to forgo his power; indeed, they demand it as a condition of humanity.

When Shylock refuses to yield, then a faulty court, a kangaroo court if you will, appears with a cross-dressed justice and clerk impersonating legal authority; the judgement against Shylock, clever as it is, is a sham. Legal scholar Thomas C. Bilello puts it this way: 'by inserting herself by artifice into the legal proceedings to enforce the bond, Portia converts the law to an instrumentality of her will. Interestingly, the criticisms of the court scene largely ignore the significance of Portia's fraud'.[34] The literalist arguments of Portia are a set-up for Shylock—she initially hooks him into a method of judicial interpretation that apparently favours him; but her method merely presages the radical literalism (flesh but no blood) that she will use against him in establishing the contract as unenforceable and forfeit.

As the scene proceeds to reveal, even the stoniest of stony laws comes down to a matter of interpretation. If prejudice appears in written law and its application, then the trial scene reveals the potential partiality of judicial judgement. The written law is unfavourable; it cannot be suspended, so in a final stand for Christian Venice judicial interpretation must save the day. It is as if Shakespeare has offered a catalogue of the law's prejudices, from construction to application to interpretation of the law. And, in the end, even mercy is questionably invested: Shylock is dispossessed of his fortune, his faith, and his family. This 'mercy' of the Venetians tips their hand, showing their partiality and prejudice even in their application of equity. James Shapiro describes the end of the trial scene this way: 'Venetian society is able to have it both ways: while the city's charter guarantees equity before the law, a feature that has attracted foreigners to Venice, it retains legislation that renders this equality provisional, if not fictional.'[35] Invoking the ancient law that protects Venetians against foreigners, the Christians shift the legal playing field at the eleventh hour, from the law of contract to the laws of nations.

---

[33] Anton Schütz explores Shylock's ferocity in sticking to his contract in precisely these terms: through upholding his contractual rights Shylock strategizes for Venetian citizenship; see 'Shylock as a Politician', *Shakespeare and the Law*, Raffield and Watt (eds.), 271–88.

[34] Bilello, 'Accomplished with What She Lacks', 12.

[35] James Shapiro, *Shakespeare and the Jews* (New York: Columbia University Press, 1996), 188.

What is at stake in this issue of legal malleability, at the levels of creation, enforcement, interpretation, and application of law? We might say that equity and mercy are at stake. Flexible law allows for diverse applications, and allows judges to temper their justice with mercy. But the play suggests otherwise. Flexible law favours those in power. Discretion, innovation, and pragmatism are all the tools of those who govern. The Christian male characters repeatedly encourage one another to break the law as a sign of sovereignty, independence, mercy, generosity, and liberality. Through the figures of Bassanio and Antonio, the play invokes law only to challenge it. The law is prejudicially constructed, whimsically applied, conveniently suspended, and will-fully interpreted. Neither law, nor judicial judgement, is ever impartial. Instead, in order to uphold bonds between Christian men, characters lobby for breaking oaths taken between these Venetian citizens and the Jews (and women) to whom they have contracted themselves.

Thus, *The Merchant of Venice* repeatedly represents the waywardness of Venetian citizens as regards the law, whether human law of contract or divine law of salvation (offering one's wife to the devil clearly messes with divine providence). But the play suppresses its own troubling insights about legal manipulation and prejudice. It does so in two ways. First, the characters—from the Duke to Antonio and Bassanio to Balthazar—repeatedly insist that the problem with contract is Shylock, not the law; Shylock is not, the Venetians claim, willing to offer mercy. As a result, the legal problems of the play—problems with unenforceable contracts, with judicial interpretation, with political and religious bias—are displaced as singular problems rather than systemic ones. The problem, the Venetians suggest, is with the Jew; if it weren't for Shylock's temporary power, the system of law and equity would run smoothly, and precedent and contract could be upheld.

Second, the play ends by turning the chaos of broken contracts into a joke. It does so by comically invoking a second broken contract, beyond Shylock's: the marriage contract. Portia gives her husband a ring in order to establish their marital bond. The ring is, she tells him, 'a thing stuck on with oaths upon your finger' (5.1.168). According to the terms of this oath, Bassanio is to have Portia so long as he does not take the ring off his finger. But this marriage contract is quickly abandoned. Antonio convinces Bassanio to give up the ring to Balthasar: 'Let his deservings and my love withal | Be valued 'gainst your wife's command-ment' (4.1.446–7). To Antonio, who had earlier set aside custom to help his friend, contracts are not necessarily binding. Bassanio, too, holds a malleable view of law and, despite his initial hesitation, breaks his recently-taken oath.

This broken oath could upset the play's comic ending. Early modern marriage, as Andrew Zurcher has most recently explored, is 'a species of what we would today call "contract", exhibiting close parallels with other social and legal bonds'.[36] This marriage

---

[36] Andrew Zurcher, *Spenser's Legal Language: Law and Poetry in Early Modern England* (Woodbridge: D. S. Brewer, 2007), 90. See also Gary Watt, 'The Law of Dramatic Properties in *The Merchant of Venice*', *Shakespeare and the Law*, 237–52, which examines the relationships between the marriage contract and its various 'props' (oaths, rings), and Richard H. Weisberg's chapter on *Merchant* in *Poethics: and other Strategies of Law and Literature* (New York: Columbia University Press, 1992).

contract, like Shylock's, should not be suspended or ignored. Indeed, all the elements of the earlier legal struggle with Shylock appear here. Two contracts are broken, Shylock's and Portia's. Antonio appears as surety in both cases. In the first case he offers his flesh, and in the second his soul: 'I dare be bound again,' he claims, 'My soul upon the forfeit, that your lord | Will never more break faith advisedly' (5.1.251–3). Having spent the greater part of the play bound by an unorthodox contract, Antonio's willingness to increase the contractual stakes, from body to soul, from pound of flesh to eternity, should be alarming.

But, of course, Antonio's gesture is not alarming, at least not from a legal perspective. Instead, in the final exchange of soul as surety we find *contract* invoked as a metaphor, as a rhetorical flourish. Contract is not, here, a legal matter, but instead a form of hyperbolic reassurance. We might argue that such a flourish is necessary since it restores the primacy of the marital bond over Antonio's potentially threatening friendship with Bassanio. But regardless of the gesture's emotional power, the point is that it holds no *legal* power: law has been displaced in the name of love and friendship. In emptying out contract of its legal power in the final exchange, Shakespeare's play ends by restoring community at the expense of law. Good citizens, the happy ending implies, have no need of the law; they can work out disputes through sociable exchanges, witty promises, and confident gestures.

Thus, this legal play ends with a curiously anti-legal resolution. Despite the preponderance of oaths and contracts, the play nevertheless stages an ever-receding positive law, written in a contract or oath but ultimately laughed out of court. By the end of the play, the language of 'bond' and 'oath' has been so tainted by Shylock's overuse that the terms are corrupted—to call on the power of a bond is to be hardened and obdurate. Instead, characters simply reaffirm good intentions. Legal questioning and judicial habits serve as sexual foreplay: 'Let us go in, | And charge us there upon inter'gatories' (5.1.297–8), Portia says to Bassanio, while Gratiano claims, 'I should wish it dark | Till I were couching with the doctor's clerk' (5.1.304–5). The contractual ring becomes a bawdy pun in the play's last line, delivered by Gratiano: 'Well, while I live I'll fear no other thing | So sore, as keeping safe Nerissa's ring' (5.1.306–7). Bonds are less entrapping than titillating; they are velvet ropes to secure love and desire. This comic resolution represses all trace of the law's prejudices evident throughout the first four acts of the play. But the marriage contract, like any other, can lead to significant legal disputes. If the play's newlyweds have forgotten this fact, perhaps the audience's more seasoned members have not.

Legal Investments

When Portia dresses as a lawyer and debates with Antonio and Shylock about the interpretation of contract, she demonstrates, perhaps unwittingly, the way in which the law is forged in practise and interpretation rather than as written impartial code.[37] And this process of interpretation, as argued above, is open to manipulation. Portia's strict literalism in the interpretation of Shylock's contract contrasts deeply with her leniency when it comes to her own contract with Bassanio. She employs radically different interpretive techniques, suggesting a problematically variant method as regards legal ruling.

These Shakespearean insights about law and its prejudices anticipate the analysis of legal theorist Peter Goodrich. Goodrich highlights the ways in which the law is enacted through interpretation, despite the disproportionate affirmation accorded legal rules and procedures:

> What is peculiar to the legal institution is not that it has rules of office, of ritual procedures, of doctrine and heresy, as well as specific methods of interpretation and application of its rules but rather that such a tremendous degree of social affirmation is lavished upon those rules and procedures.... [L]egal administrative power—in both its formal and substantive aspects—is much less regulated and far more open to manipulation, negotiation and technique generally, interpretation and abuse, than is admitted by legal doctrine.[38]

Portia's manipulation of law in *The Merchant of Venice* exhibits precisely Goodrich's point. She is a doctor of law speaking in the language of rules, procedures, and compulsion: 'It must not be' (4.1.215), 'it cannot be' (4.1.219), 'you must prepare' (4.2.242), 'you must cut' (4.1.299). Further, her language insists upon the law as impersonal: 'The law allows it, and the court awards it' (4.1.300); 'the court awards it, and the law doth give it' (4.1.297). The impersonality, the formality of these statements obscures what Goodrich deems the 'manipulation', the 'negotiation', the 'interpretation', and the 'abuse' that can mark the exercise of legal power if it is left unexamined or unregulated. The ability of lawyers, judges, and sovereigns to manipulate law becomes all the stronger when the law is perceived to be an arena of such specialist expertise that it appears beyond investigation. When viewed as a specialist pursuit, which is incomprehensible to the lay person, the law is no longer positioned as one among many social forces acting upon citizens but instead as an arena of unassailable authority. Indeed, legal doctrine often obscures this connection of law to other social discourses. As Goodrich writes, however, the law is in fact one among many discursive tools: 'legal discourse is...simply one of many competing normative disciplinary discourses, discourses of morality, religion and social custom to which it is closely related and from which it draws many if not all of its justificatory arguments'.[39]

---

[37] Debora Shuger, writing about censorship, makes a point equally apt for contract: 'Laws, decrees, verdicts, and ordinances are not well-wrought urns; they are intended to do certain things in the world, and those contexts are part of their meaning', in *Censorship and Cultural Sensibility: The Regulation of Language in Tudor-Stuart England* (Philadelphia: University of Pennsylvania Press, 2006), 8.

[38] Peter Goodrich, *Reading the Law: A Critical Introduction to Legal Methods and Techniques* (Oxford: Blackwell, 1986), 17.

[39] Goodrich, *Reading the Law*, 20.

In thinking with Goodrich about the law as a social form, this chapter has suggested some of the ways in which Shakespeare's work proves ideal for legal analysis. In *Merchant*, and in many of his other works, Shakespeare meditates precisely on the cultural and political questions raised by the law's practise. He does so in the many ways outlined throughout this chapter. It is worth considering, in thinking about future paths for the study of Shakespeare and the law, Shakespeare's singular contribution to what we might call legal geography. Shakespeare experienced legal suits in cosmopolitan and town settings, in London and Stratford. His plays also saw legal performances in a variety of London settings, with the appearance of *Comedy of Errors, Twelfth Night, Troilus and Cressida*, and *Midsummer Night's Dream* at the Inns of Court.[40] But he depicts a much greater geographical range than London or even England: from the succession disputes of England, Scotland, Rome, and Denmark, to criminal claims in Venice and Vienna, Shakespeare's plays ask the audience to examine the relation between law and space, both theatrical and imaginary: how is law different in Egypt, Illyria, Sicilia, or Wales? In such varied spaces, who has access to formal law? Who must turn instead to vigilantism or impromptu rulings? Shakespeare's depiction of foreign and ancient spaces gives us the continual interplay between formal law and its more renegade expansions. In these spaces, evidence ranges from circumspect to substantial, from dreams to handkerchiefs to bloody daggers. This imaginative range challenges law even as it invokes it, asking the audience repeatedly to ponder the nature of evidence, judgement, and interpretation. And we ponder these legal questions through the compelling testimonies of Shakespeare's imaginative characters, who face the forms and investments of law onstage, in performance, every night, before an audience of paying judges.

---

[40] On plays at the Inns of Courts, see Dennis Kezar (ed.), *Solon and Thespis: Law and Theater in the English Renaissance* (Notre Dame, IN: University of Notre Dame Press, 2007); Michelle O'Callaghan, *The English Wits: Literature and Sociability in Early Modern England* (Cambridge: Cambridge University Press, 2007).

CHAPTER 31

....

FORMATION OF NATIONHOOD

....

CATHY SHRANK

As the soule of *Euphorbus* was thought to live in *Pythagorus*: so the sweete wittie soule of *Ovid* lives in mellifluous & hony-tongued *Shakespeare* [...] As *Plautus* and *Seneca* are accounted the best for Comedy and Tragedy among the Latines: so *Shakespeare* among the English is the most excellent in both kinds for the stage [...] As *Epius Stolo* said, that the Muses would speake with *Plautus* tongue, if they would speake Latine: so I say that the Muses would speake with *Shakespeares* fine filed phrase, if they would speake English.[1]

IN 1598, in the earliest printed work to praise Shakespeare by name, Francis Meres celebrates the poet-dramatist in a list of English authors who are placed in direct comparison—and competition—with the great 'Greeke, Latine and Italian Poets' (fol. 279r). The moment is illustrative of a mode of national consciousness that was articulated toward the end of the Elizabethan era through a new-found confidence in English as a literary language. True, Chaucer had gestured toward an emulative relationship with classical authors in the *envoi* to *Troilus and Criseyde* (c.1381–88): 'Kis the steppes, where as thow seest space | Virgile, Ovide, Omer, Lucan, and Stace', he instructs his 'litel book'.[2] Chaucer himself was posthumously declared, in the 1540s, an English 'Petrarch' and 'Dante'.[3] Yet neither of these instances bespeak the confidence of

Unless otherwise stated, all Shakespeare quotations are from *The Oxford Shakespeare: The Complete Works*, (ed. Stanley Wells et al.), 2nd edn. (Oxford: Oxford University Press, 2005). Except for Shakespeare's plays, early modern works are quoted in old spelling; in these cases i/j and u/v have been regularized and thorns transcribed as 'th'.

[1] Francis Meres, *Palladis Tamia* (London, 1598), fols. 281v–282.

[2] Geoffrey Chaucer, *Troilus and Criseyde*, *The Riverside Chaucer*, Larry D. Benson (ed.), 3rd edn. (Oxford: Oxford University Press, 1988), ll. 1791–2, 1789.

[3] John Leland, *Commentarii de Scriptoribus Britannicis*, Anthony Hall (ed.), 2 vols. (Oxford, 1709), 2: 422.

Meres's list: Chaucer's self-comparison has a (mock) humility; and the comparisons with Dante and Petrarch are to vernacular, not classical, authors. Moreover, Meres's eulogy to Shakespeare is just part of a roll-call of around eighty English writers lauded in similarly superlative terms.

Shakespeare lived toward the end of a century that had seen a deliberate investment on the part of its writers in developing and promoting their native tongue and in building a national literary canon.[4] Meres's encomia are the direct result of this process, as well as a contribution to it. Literature and language were not the only aspects of national identity that found new forms of expression during the Tudor period, however. Henry VIII's split from the Church of Rome in the 1530s, and the subsequent phases of religious Reformation under his children Edward VI and Elizabeth I, also impacted on the English sense of themselves. By the 1570s—exacerbated by the Northern Rising (1569) and the papal bull *Regans in Excelsis* (1570), which excommunicated Elizabeth and absolved her subjects of allegiance to her—national identity increasingly crystallized along religious lines. Writing in response to the Northern Rising, the author and Parliament-man Thomas Norton represented the opinion of many when he equated 'true Englishe subiectes' with 'true Christians', denouncing 'every such English papist' as 'a traytor to the Queene of England' and 'a speciall traytor to the realme of England'.[5]

England's rejection of the Roman Church also heightened a sense of belligerent, if vulnerable, isolation, faced as it was across the sea by the strong Catholic powers of France and (stronger still) Spain. English writers, not least among them Shakespeare, had frequent recourse to the image of England as an island fortress, a misrepresentation of geographic reality, which effectively appropriated—and rhetorically annulled the threat from—its old enemy and neighbour, Scotland. The Duke of Austria in Shakespeare's *King John* exemplifies this motif, as he reiterates England's status as an island using the rhetorical figures of *exergasia* (repeating the same idea in different ways) and *anaphora* (repeating a word at the start of successive clauses). 'That pale, that white-faced shore, | Whose foot spurns back the ocean's roaring tides | And coops from other lands her islanders,' he muses: 'that England, hedged in with the main, | That water-wallèd bulwark, still secure | And confident from foreign purposes' (2.1.23–8). This seemingly comforting image of England's natural defences is, however, undercut by the fact that it comes in a speech in which Austria pledges to take up arms against it and force it to recognize a monarch of his and the French king's choosing. All too often, then, the bolstering of England as an island stronghold, safely sealed from enemy approaches, is tempered by an awareness that its boundaries are permeable (as the Jesuit mission to reconvert England in the 1580s highlighted for anxious English Protestants), or that it is threatened by treachery. 'I had no peere, yf to my self I were

---

[4] Richard Foster Jones, *The Triumph of English* (Stanford, CA: Stanford University Press, 1953); Cathy Shrank, *Writing the Nation in Reformation England, 1530–1580* (Oxford: Oxford University Press, 2004).

[5] Thomas Norton, *A warning agaynst the dangerous Translations practises of papists* (London: 1569), sigs. B1–B1v.

trewe,' confesses a stereotypical Englishman in 1547,[6] a motif which echoes on into the closing words of Shakespeare's *King John*: 'Naught shall make us rue | If England to itself do rest but true' (5.7.117–118). The conditional *if* suggests alternative possibilities. In the words of Touchstone, there is 'much virtue [power] in "if"'.[7]

Englishness in the period was not only thought to be threatened by external invasion or internal perfidy. According to humoural theory, on which early modern medical practice relied, temperament and physical make-up were not fixed, but were in constant flux, subject to the influence of factors such as diet and climate.[8] Hence the English abroad would be conscious of their body changing. Travelling in Italy, for instance, the writer William Thomas 'that before time could in maner brooke no fruite' 'after [he] had been a while in Italie [. . .] fell so in love withal, that as long as [he] was there, [he] desired no meate more'.[9] Whereas Thomas's comment remains an interested observation, this sense of metamorphosis assumes a hysterically polemic note in the works of Cambridge-educated humanists like Thomas Wilson or Roger Ascham. 'I know [. . .] many,' laments Ascham, 'who, partyng out of England fervent in the love of Christes doctrine, and well furnished with the feare of God, returned out of *Italie* worse transformed, than ever was any in *Circes* Court.' He proceeds to describe how such men, tainted with 'Italian' vices (such as Machiavellianism), 'returned verie Swyne and Asses home agayne: [. . .] verie Foxes with sutlie and busie heades: and where they may, verie wolves, with cruell malicious hartes'.[10]

This chapter explores the ways in which Shakespeare probes the nature of national identity in *King John* (c.1596) and *The Merry Wives of Windsor* (c.1597–8), two plays that display revealingly different approaches to 'England': where the former—a history play—examines the idea of England as a realm (a kingdom), the latter—a comedy—considers it as a community of people who, for better or worse, are bound by co-residence and language. These two plays not only allow us to explore how genre might affect the representation of nationhood; the Englishness of both has also been singled out by critics and practitioners, often at moments of national stress (*King John*) or celebration (*Merry Wives*). The eighteenth century saw revivals of *King John* in 1745 (the year of the Second Jacobite Rising), when Colly Cibber staged his adaptation, *Papal Tyranny in the Reign of King John*, 'to capitalize on anti-Jacobite sentiments', and in 1800, when Richard Valpy had it performed by the boys of Reading School to raise money 'for the subscription of the naval pillar, to be erected in honour of the naval

---

[6] Andrew Borde, *The Fyrst Boke of the Introduction to Knowledge* (London: 1547?), sig. A4.

[7] Shakespeare, *As You Like It*, 5.4.100–1.

[8] Cathy Shrank, 'Foreign Bodies: Politics, Polemic and the Continental Landscape', in Mike Pincombe (ed.), *Travels and Translations in the Sixteenth Century* (Aldershot: Ashgate, 2004), 31–44.

[9] William Thomas, *The Historie of Italie* (London: 1549), sig. 2v.

[10] Compare Thomas Wilson, *The Arte of Rhetorique* (London: 1553): 'Some farre jorneid jentlemen at their returne home, like as thei love to go in forrein apparell, so thei wil pouder their talke w[i]t[h] ouersea language'; 'He that cometh lately out of France, wil talke Frenche English, & never blushe at the matter. Another choppes in with Angleso Italiano' (fol. 86).

victories of the present war [against Napoleon]'.[11] When explaining his decision to stage *Merry Wives* at the Festival of Britain in 1951, the director Hugh Hunt declared that 'he would like to justify showing it by showing the English humour of the play— the merry England which has played so large a part in the building of our institutions and national character'.[12] These sentiments are echoed by Fredson Bowers almost a decade later: '*The Merry Wives of Windsor* may even be called a patriotic play. Despite its contrivances, it is a very English one. We should be thankful for it.'[13] In contrast to these earlier voices, this chapter suggests that Shakespeare's attitude to England and Englishness is less straightforwardly eulogistic; he does not so much praise it as investigate the assumptions on which national identity rests. The chapter ends with an afterword on *Cymbeline* (*c*.1610–11) and the way in which this Jacobean play engages with notions of Britain when the Union of the crowns under James I and VI in 1603 had brought into focus a new form of national identity.

KING JOHN AND THE QUESTION OF ENGLAND

Shakespeare's *King John* could have been what Bowers calls 'a patriotic play'. The reworking of English history that occurred after and in response to Henry VIII's rejection of the authority of the Pope on English soil rehabilitated King John as a proto-Protestant hero, remembered not for the loss of his French territories and his rapaciousness in accruing funds for campaigns to recover them, but for his ultimately doomed resistance to papal authority.[14] Shakespeare thus inherited a tradition in which John had become 'the standard symbol for English Protestant writers of the patriot-martyr', poisoned by a monk, an agent of the Catholic Church, for his attempts to throw off the papal yoke.[15] There are moments in Shakespeare's *King John* which certainly seem to echo this jingoistic agenda. 'What earthy name to interrogatories | Can task the free breath of a sacred king?' John demands (3.1.73–4). As he derides the name of 'pope' as 'slight, unworthy, and ridiculous' (3.1.76) and denounces the 'usurped authority' of the

---

[11] Eugene Waith, '*King John* and the Drama of History', *Shakespeare Quarterly*, 29 (1978), 193; Richard Valpy, *King John, an historical tragedy, altered from Shakespeare* (Reading: 1800). John Middleton Murray also describes the Bastard as 'manifestly Shakespeare's ideal of an Englishman', *Selected Criticism* (Oxford: Oxford University Press, 1960), 154; cited by Virginia Mason Vaughan, 'Between Tetralogies: *King John* as Transition', *Shakespeare Quarterly*, 35 (1984), 414.

[12] Cited in Leah Marcus, *Unediting the Renaissance* (London: Routledge, 1996), 76.

[13] Cited in Marcus, *Unediting the Renaissance*, 83.

[14] See, for example, Leland, *Commentarii*, 1: 248; John Bale, *King Johan*, Peter Happé (ed.) *Four Morality Plays* (Harmondsworth: Penguin, 1979).

[15] John R. Elliott, 'Shakespeare and the Double Image of King John', *Shakespeare Studies* 1 (1965), 68; cited by Virginia Mason Vaughan, '*King John*: A Study in Subversion and Containment', in Deborah T. Curren-Aquino (ed.), *King John: New Perspectives* (Newark: University of Delaware Press, 1989), 63.

papacy (3.1.86), his words would have struck a familiar—and no doubt stirring—chord among his original audiences. John speaks the language of Reformist propaganda and of the English statutes which effected the break with Rome.[16] 'Tell him this tale,' he insists:

> and from the mouth of England
> Add thus much more: that no Italian priest
> Shall tithe or toll in our dominions.   (3.1.78–80)

The play also refracts the idiom of Reformation and Counter-Reformation polemic, setting up a conflict between rival mothers: the mother church (the 'whorish mother church' for Reformers) and mother England.[17] 'Let the Church, our mother, breathe her curse, | A mother's curse, on her revolting son', declares the papal legate Pandolf (3.1.182–3). Two acts later, the mother is England, and the unnatural rebellion against its sovereign, not the Pope: 'you degenerate, you ingrate revolts, | You bloody Neros, ripping up the womb | Of your dear mother England,' spits the Bastard (5.2.151–3), stripping the rebels of their nationality through the term 'degenerate' (from the Latin *degenerare*, to 'become unlike from one's race').[18]

It is the presence of a hostile Other that helps forge identity. John becomes 'English John' in the mouth of his then enemy Philip, the French king (2.1.10). It is also noticeable that in Act 5, when the full machinery of the Roman Church and the invading foreign forces that it commands are weighed against John, the Bastard calls him 'our English king' (5.2.128), a noun phrase which knits him—through the possessive pronoun and premodifying adjective—more tightly to a sense of national identity than the alternative noun phrase 'the king of England', with its postmodifying prepositional phrase ('of England').

Yet, despite the fact that *King John* offers rich potential for rallying national sentiment round the anti-papal flag, these moments are strikingly sparse in Shakespeare's play. Gone are scenes designed to play up to stereotypical images of the hypocrisy, greed, and lechery of the Catholic clergy as found in the probable source play, *The Troublesome Reign of King John* (printed in 1591), with its comically venal friars and saucy nun secreted in the abbot's treasure chest. So too, as Jean Howard and Phyllis Rackin write, 'Shakespeare's amoral portrait of John resists the patriotic appropriations of humanist historiography'.[19] It was exactly this lost opportunity that Cibber lamented in 1745. 'In all the historical Plays of *Shakespeare* there is scarce any Fact that might better have employed his Genius than the flaming Contest between his insolent *Holiness* and *King John*,' he states: 'It seems surprising that our *Shakespeare* should have taken no more Fire at it'. 'This Coldness' consequently 'incited' Cibber to adapt

---

[16] For these statutes, see G. R. Elton (ed.), *The Tudor Constitution: Documents and Commentary* (Cambridge: Cambridge University Press, 1982), 338–68, 372–7.

[17] William Thomas, *Pelegrine* (1547), British Library Additional MS 33383, fol. 56v.

[18] 'Dē-generō, āre', in William Smith (ed.), *Latin–English Dictionary*, rev. edn. (London: John Murray, 1933).

[19] Jean E. Howard and Phyllis Rackin, *Engendering a Nation* (London: Routledge, 1997), 125. Cf. Vaughan, '*King John*: A Study in Subversion and Containment'.

Shakespeare's play, and 'to inspirit King *John* with a Resentment that justly might become an *English* Monarch, and to paint the intoxicated Tyranny of *Rome* in its proper Colours'.[20]

The fact that Cibber needed to rewrite *King John* (or '*tortur[e] Shakespeare*', as one anonymous reviewer put it) highlights the way in which Shakespeare desists from religious and indeed nationalistic propaganda.[21] The play invokes England not to rouse Shakespeare's compatriots to patriotic indignation against the Roman Church, but to interrogate what is meant by England. 'My kyng, my Contry, alone for whome I lyve', wrote the poet-diplomat Thomas Wyatt in the late 1530s.[22] His asyndetic conflation of king and country highlights the same conundrum that Shakespeare's *King John* explores. What constitutes 'England': the land, the monarch, or (absent from both Wyatt's poem and—as we shall see—Shakespeare's play) the people? When John talks of his rebuttal of the Pope coming 'from the mouth of England' in the above-cited passage, 'England' stands for the king of England, and for the first half of the play it is the use of 'England' (or 'France') to mean 'monarch' that dominates.[23] Yet this association of king and country is far from triumphal. The word *right* punctuates the play, mentioned more times (30) in *King John* than in any other Shakespeare play; even bearing in mind other usages (e.g. 'catch you right'), this indicates the significance of legitimacy within the drama.[24] However, the frequency with which 'rights' are over-ridden, or what previously deemed 'right' is suddenly revoked, serves to undercut the pomp of kingship;[25] by Act 4, the Bastard (who recurrently acts as sardonic chorus on events) is describing 'majesty' as a 'bare-picked bone' (4.3.149). There is also something grimly comical in the way the Bastard literalizes the metaphor of the head-of-state, the ruler as head of the body politic, reducing the Duke of Austria's severed head to a stage property: 'Austria's head lie there,' he crows (3.2.3). As Peter Womack points out, 'the action [of *King John*], which largely consists of highly public interstate diplomacy, is informed by the assumption that the monarch is the effective embodiment of the realm [. . .]. However, this assumption is not substantiated by the play.' Instead, 'the

[20] Colley Cibber, dedication to *Papal Tyranny in the Reign of King John*, in Brian Vickers (ed.), *Shakespeare: The Critical Heritage*, vol. 3 (London: Routledge & Kegan Paul, 1975), 135–6.

[21] *A Letter to Colley Cibber, Esq: on his Transformation of 'King John'* (1745), in Vickers (ed.), *Shakespeare: The Critical Heritage*, 3: 156.

[22] Thomas Wyatt, 'Tagus Farewell', in Kenneth Muir and Patricia Thomson (eds.), *Collected Poems of Sir Thomas Wyatt* (Liverpool: Liverpool University Press, 1969), 7.

[23] Of the 47 instances of 'England' or 'England's' in Shakespeare's *King John*, 21 refer to England as monarch; a further 4 uses are ambiguous. *2 Henry VI* is the only other play to use 'England' or 'England's' more than *King John* (56 combined instances); *Henry V* has 44 combined instances. Figures collated using www.opensourceshakespeare.com.

[24] For the centrality of legitimacy to *King John*, see Howard and Rackin (ed.), *Engendering a Nation*, 127; Tom McAlindon, 'Swearing and Forswearing in Shakespeare's Histories: The Playwright as Contra-Machiavel', *Review of English Studies* 51 (2000), 208–29.

[25] Edward S. Brubaker gives a director's perspective on the way in which *King John* eschews ceremony, 'Staging *King John*: A Director's Observations', in Curren-Aquino (ed.), *King John*, 165–72.

comically arbitrary events, the magniloquent postures and grubby deals, have the effect of hollowing out the royal claims to representative status'.[26]

If sovereign right looms large, then, it is neither revered nor unproblematic. Both John and the child Arthur have claims to be 'England', as even the Bastard (otherwise loyal to John) recognizes as he addresses Hubert, Arthur's erstwhile jailer, who holds the boy's corpse in his arms: 'How easy dost thou take all England [i.e. Arthur] up!' (4.3.143). Monarchs in *King John* also show a cruel disregard for the subjects they govern: their concern for sovereign right takes precedence over their attention to sovereign duty. 'We'll [. . .] | Wade to the market-place in Frenchmen's blood, | But we will make it subject to this boy', vaunts Philip, the French king, for example (2.1.41–3), a wanton destructiveness later highlighted by the Bastard, talking of both John and Philip:

> Ha, majesty! How high thy glory towers
> When the rich blood of kings is set on fire!
> O, now doth Death line his dead chaps with steel;
> The swords of soldiers are his teeth, his fangs;
> And now he feasts, mousing the flesh of men
> In undetermined differences of kings.   (2.1.350–5)

When monarch is equitable with and emblematic of country, obvious tensions arise if the interests of the monarch conflict with those of the country, as the latter half of *King John* dramatizes. What should be unified splits into two distinct entities, as Philip's words on John's departure highlight, by bringing two different senses of the term 'England' into play within the same line: 'And bloody England into England gone' (3.4.8).

King John has often been decried by critics for its lack of coherence. However, viewing it as a play that tests the question 'what is England?' reveals its finely balanced construction and the way that Shakespeare paces his deployment of alternative senses of the term, so that various meanings come to the fore in different phases of the drama. With John's return to England, the second half of the play, as Womack notes, 'bring[s] home [. . .] the action of the play'.[27] In the process, the use of 'England' to refer predominantly to its monarch falls away, to be replaced by its growing tendency to define a territory, a land that consumes the bodies of those who fight over it. 'Heaven take my soul, and England keep my bones!' cries the dying Arthur (4.3.10). Increasingly, too, characters start to link their identity and loyalty to their native soil. The rebel Salisbury mulls on the injury that he and his compatriots feel bound to inflict upon their homeland in the name of (what he sees as) 'right' (5.2.21):

[26] Peter Womack, 'Imagining Communities: Theatres and the English Nation in the Sixteenth Century', in David Aers (ed.), *Culture and History, 1350–1600: Essays on English Communities, Identities and Writing* (Detroit, MI: Wayne State University Press, 1992), 119–20.

[27] Womack, 'Imagining Communities', 126.

> And is't not pity, O my grievèd friends,
> That we the sons and children of this isle
> Was [sic] born to see so sad an hour as this,
> Wherein we step after a stranger, march
> Upon her gentle bosom [. . .]   (5.2.24–8)

In this latter part of the play, as England is imagined corporally—a living being that can be wounded—John's rhetoric of kingship also changes. He still sees himself as synonymous with his country, but he no longer relies on the apparent power resident in the title 'England' (as he had in his earlier rejection of papal authority). Rather, he becomes the land itself, imagining himself anaphorically as 'this fleshly land, | This kingdom, this confine of blood and breath' (4.2.246–7). As civil war erupts within his realm, John finds himself subject to similar internal conflict: within his 'fleshly land' 'Hostility and civil tumult reigns | Between [his] conscience and [his] cousin's [Arthur's] death' (4.2.248–9). His deathbed words take a similarly topographical thrust, as he longs for his 'kingdom's rivers [to] take their course | Through [his] burned bosom', as if he were the land itself (5.7.38–9).[28]

In contrast, a third meaning of 'England' (besides territory or monarch) is notably absent from much of *King John*, namely its use as a collective term for the inhabitants of England (as in *Henry V*, when the Archbishop of Canterbury advises Henry to 'Divide your happy England into four' and 'take [. . .] one quarter into France', 1.2.214–15). In *King John* this sense of England as its people is downplayed. The commons remain a shadowy presence off stage, in thrall to gossip and superstition. Act 4, for example, finds them 'strangely fantasied, | Possessed with rumours, full of idle dreams, | Not knowing what they fear, but full of fear' (4.2.144–6). Or they feature merely in an allusion to the prophecies of 'old men and beldams in the street' (4.2.186); age here lends these representatives of the popular voice not authority, but an impression of them being impotent and marginal.[29] W. H. Auden attributes the 'loss of the sense of the whole of society' in *King John* and *Richard II* to the lack of a sub-plot.[30] However, in *King John*, this denuding effect is also emphasized by the way in which Shakespeare manipulates the different meanings of the term 'England'. If 'England' in the first phase of the play denotes the monarch, to be replaced in the second by the land, then toward the very end of the play, we start to see 'England' standing for its people. After Arthur's death (an indirect result of John's attempt to assassinate him, but the catalyst in provoking open revolt), 'England' emerges, on the Bastard's lip, as a synonym for its people, as he moves from imagining England as the body of the dead Arthur

---

[28] Howard and Rackin also draw attention to John's image of himself as a piece of burning parchment in this scene, which they link to the idea of a national, written history that proves all too fragile; *Engendering a Nation*, 125.

[29] 'Beldam', for instance, has a frequently perjorative sense (*Oxford English Dictionary*, http://dictionary.oed.com, 'beldam', 3).

[30] W. H. Auden, '*The Taming of the Shrew, King John*, and *Richard II*', *Lectures on Shakespeare* (Princeton, NJ: Princeton University Press, 2001), 65.

('How easy dost thou take all England up!', 4.3.143) to the way in which 'England now is left | To tug and scramble, and to part by th' teeth | The unowed interest of proud swelling state' (4.3.146–8). By the time 'England' appears in the final couplet of the play, there is no doubt that it means its people: 'Naught shall make us rue | If England to itself do rest but true' (5.7.117–18).

Although not defined formally as such, the Bastard's closing words act to some extent like an epilogue, addressing the members of the audience as much, if not more, than the characters on stage. They issue a challenge, prescribing future behaviour. As such, they are also a reminder that, if the people have been noticeably absent from the action onstage, then they are far from disengaged from it offstage. Virginia Mason Vaughan has drawn attention to how *King John* involves its audience, highlighting the way 'the scenes are arranged so as to give the audience divided loyalties': 'through a series of debate-like scenes, the play probes rather than pronounces. [. . .] In *King John* the issues of sovereignty and legitimacy cloud any facile moralizing on the evils of civil war and hence represent a deeper exploration of political realities.'[31] The audience, in other words, cannot merely watch that complacently, but are required to form judgements on the action before them. This is nowhere more pertinent than at the end of the play, when the audience is induced to consider how they might manage to be 'true' and, indeed, what is 'true' after watching a play that has constantly placed notions of truth and right under pressure. Yet even as spectators in contemplating these questions are forced to recognize their embodiment as 'England', they are also reminded of the inherent lack of cohesion provided by that label: England is not one thing ('itself'), but comprises many, and—as noted earlier—the possibility of all remaining 'true' is contingent on that destabilizing word 'if'.

Nor has the play made it clear who or what is 'England' or 'English'. *King John* is set at a time when English kings had territories both sides of the Channel; losing these, John became the first king for generations to be based solely in England.[32] Being the 'King of England's subjects' (as are the citizens of Angers, 2.1.267) is not synonymous with being English. The play shows the intertwined heritages of France and England. 'My grandsire was an Englishman,' declares Count Melun, explaining why he betrays his compatriots (warning the English rebels that the Dauphin intends to kill them) before dying on English soil (5.4.42). Two scenes later, the Bastard's request that Hubert tell him the news 'sans compliment' (without formality, 5.6.17) is a further, linguistic reminder of the culture that the two nations share. It is to ideas of linguistic nationhood that the next section of this chapter turns.

[31] Vaughan, 'Between Tetralogies', 412; Vaughan's argument regarding the way in which the play's use of debate draws the audience into an active role resonates with Lorna Hutson's thesis of the engaged, forensic role of playhouse audiences in *The Invention of Suspicion: Law and Mimesis in Shakespeare and Renaissance Drama* (Oxford: Oxford University Press, 2007).

[32] The loss of English territories in France would also be within living memory in the 1590s, since the last English outpost (Calais) had been lost, humiliatingly, in 1558.

MERRY WIVES AND 'FRITTERS OF ENGLISH'

In *King John*, representatives of 'the people' are, as we have seen, decidedly thin on the ground. The Windsor of *Merry Wives*, in contrast, is shown as much more socially diverse. As Anne Barton notes, the 'comic community' of the play comprises 'children, adolescents, mature married couples, bachelor members of the professional classes, servants, and postmaster's boys: only the very old are excluded from the panorama of life at Windsor'.[33] The focus is on the urban, the domestic, the 'middling sort'; the court is kept very much to the fringes, a presence alluded to (Caius leaves for court in 1.4, where Mistress Page believes he has 'potent' friends, 4.4.87; Falstaff worries about news of his humiliation reaching 'the ear of the court' at 4.5.89) or evoked in refracted form (for example, through the name of the inn—the Garter—which gestures somewhat irreverently toward the royal Order of the Garter).[34] Those courtiers who are present onstage, Falstaff and Fenton, seem alienated from their earlier, favoured *milieu*: Falstaff is clearly down on his luck ('almost out at heels', 1.3.27) and is forced to cast off some of his retinue, persuading Bardolph to become a tapster in our first meeting with him (1.3); Fenton once 'kept company with the wild prince and Poins' (3.2.66–7), but there is no sign of these unruly friends now, and Fenton is very much a lone operator, devoid of companionship.

In light of the removal of the play's setting from the centre of national politics (the court at Westminster and other royal palaces, such as the castle at Windsor), it is entirely fitting that the focus shift from king and realm to the people. 'England' as a word does not feature at all in the Quarto version of this 'most English of Shakespeare's plays',[35] and only once in the Folio (1.1.271); the word 'English'—denoting the language which its inhabitants speak and which, to some extent, defines them—does figure: eight times in the Folio, a sum only equalled by *Henry V*.[36] It is also striking, considering the play's concern with language, that *Merry Wives* is the only time that Shakespeare uses the verb 'Englished' (i.e. translated into the vernacular, 1.3.43). Language is one of the ways in which community is forged. As Thomas Smith wrote in 1565, 'our tongue, our

---

[33] Anne Barton, 'Falstaff and the Comic Community', *Essays Mainly Shakespearean* (Cambridge: Cambridge University Press, 1994), 84.

[34] For an account of connections between *Merry Wives* and the Feast of the Garter in 1597, see Leslie S. Katz, '*The Merry Wives of Windsor*: Sharing the Queen's Holiday', *Representations* 51 (1995): 77–93.

[35] The phrase is from H. M. Burton's illustrated introduction to Shakespeare for children, *Shakespeare and his Plays* (London: Metheun, 1958), 24; it is, however, a commonplace description of *Merry Wives*, as any Google search on 'Merry Wives'+'most English of' will reveal. Marcus (*Unediting the Renaissance*) gives an account of the difference between the Quarto and Folio versions, which highlights the more urban dynamic of the former, but does not bring out the greater attention to linguistic play in the latter.

[36] There are 38 references to 'English' in *Henry V*, but only 8 of those refer to the language.

laws and our religion [. . .] be the true bands of commonwealth'.[37] Communities, though, depend on excluding as well as including members.[38] In *Merry Wives*, these outsiders are ostensibly provided by the French doctor, Caius, and the Welsh parson and schoolmaster, Sir Hugh Evans. Certainly Windsor is a community with a propensity for stereotypically xenophobic insults, such as 'Flemish drunkard' (2.1.23) or 'base Hungrian wight' (1.3.19): 'I will rather trust a Fleming with my butter, Parson Hugh the Welshman with my cheese, an Irishman with my aqua-vitae bottle, or a thief to walk my ambling gelding, than my wife with herself,' expostulates Ford (2.2.291–4).[39] Evans and Caius thus attract scornful comments from their native neighbours, derision that focuses above all on their language. Evans makes 'fritters of English' (5.5.142); he and Caius 'hack our language' (3.1.72). The audience too is encouraged to mock their stage-accents. Evans cannot voice plosive and fricative consonants, substituting 'p' for 'b' (pottle), 't' for 'd' (goot), 'f' for 'v' (fery), or drops consonants at the start of words ('oman, 'ork, 'udge); he also muddles parts of speech (using 'absence' for 'absent'). Caius struggles with 'wh' and 'th', so that 'third' becomes, with predictable puerility, 'turd' ('I shall make-a the turd', 3.3.225). The Folio version of *Merry Wives* recurrently increases the opportunities for highlighting Evans's and Caius's linguistic strangeness (as here; the turd quotation does not appear in the Quarto), inserting scenes, for example, such as the Latin lesson conducted by Evans (4.1), or increasing the amount of lines given to the doctor (in Folio 1.4, for example, he speaks 34 lines; in the Quarto equivalent, 16).

However, it is not just Caius and Evans who are guilty of 'abusing [. . .] the King's English' (1.4.5). The Folio's alterations and additions also heighten the linguistic bumblings and quirks of its native English speakers. The revised first scene, for instance, plunges the audience into a veritable Babel, akin to the situation lamented by Thomas Wilson in his *Arte of Rhetorique* half a century earlier:

> He that cometh lately out of France, wil talke Frenche English, & never blushe at the matter. Another choppes in with Angleso Italiano: the lawyer wil store his stomack with the pratyng of Pedlers. The Auditour in makyng his accompt and rekenyng, cometh in with sise sould, and cater denere, for vi. s iiii.d. The fine Courtier wil talke nothyng but Chaucer. The misticall wise menne, and Poeticall Clerkes, will speake nothyng but quaint proverbs, and blynd allegories, delityng muche in their awne darkenesse, especially, when none can tell what thei dooe saie. The unlearned or foolishe phantasticall, that smelles but of learnyng (suche felowes as have seen learned men in their daies) will so latine their tongues, that the simple cannot but wonder at their talke, and thynke surely thei speake by some Revelacion.   (87–87v)

---

[37] Cited in Mary Dewar, *Thomas Smith: A Tudor Intellectual in Office* (London: Athlone Press, 1964), 157.

[38] Phil Withington and Alexandra Shepard, Introduction, in Withington and Shepard (eds.), *Communities in Early Modern England* (Manchester: Manchester University Press, 2000), 6–7.

[39] Flemings (the Dutch) were notorious for their love of butter and alcohol; the Welsh, cheese; the Irish, aqua-vitae (distilled spirit). Hugarians are 'base' (i.e. wretched) thanks to a pun on 'hungry'. For early modern national European stereotypes, see Borde, *Fyrst Boke of the Introduction of Knowledge*.

So in that opening scene, besides Evans's 'petter' (better), 'prains' (brains) and 'prings' (brings, 1.1.38–40), we have Shallow's and Slender's mangled law Latin ('Coram', 'Custalorum', 'Ratolorum', 1.1.5–7). This is quickly followed by the 'cony-catching' (1.1.117) slang of Bardolph, Nim, and Pistol. As Slender says of Bardolph's speech ('being fap, sir, was, as they say, cashiered', 1.1.162–3), 'you spake in Latin, then' (that is, incomprehensibly, 1.1.164). In the following act, Page comments that Nim likewise 'frights English out of his [its] wits' (2.1.131).

Where the jargon of Pistol and Nim with their references to 'labras' (Spanish for lips, 1.1.149) and 'nuthook' (constable, 1.1.153) seems designed to impress or bewilder, Bardolph's use of language borders on the incompetent, as he confuses 'sentences' with 'senses' ('I say the gentleman had drunk himself out of his five sentences', 1.1.159–60), a mistake which even the non-native speaker Evans notices. Nor is Bardolph the only inept English-speaker: Slender and Mistress Quickly similarly massacre their mother tongue. Slender, like Wilson's 'foolishe phantasticall, that smelles but of learnyng', attempts to reach for higher register words, but ends up saying the opposite of what he wishes by choosing the wrong word. For example, within five lines, he mistakes 'decrease' for 'increase', 'contempt' for 'content', 'dissolved' and 'dissolutely' for 're-solved' and 'resolutely' (1.1.229–33). Again, it is the non-native speaker Evans who comments on this malapropism, but who also deciphers it and understands that 'his meaning is good' (1.1.236). The fact that Slender misuses words of long-standing (however Latinate they sound) demonstrates his imbecility. Likewise, when endeavour-ing to woo Anne Page, he manages to mistake her question 'What is your will?' (your wish, 3.4.54) for an enquiry as to whether or not he has made his last will and testament.

Quickly, too, misconstrues Latinate, but time-honoured words, usually with scato-logical or ribald effect: on her lips, 'virtuous' becomes 'fartuous' (2.2.96), affection 'infection' (raising the possibility of sexually transmitted disease, 2.2.112), and 'direc-tion' 'erection' (3.5.38). In this way, her English raises as much of a bawdy laugh as does the 'turd' of her master, the French doctor. The addition of the Latin-lesson scene in the Folio, therefore, does not simply provide another opportunity to showcase Evans's stage-Welsh: if we snigger at Evans's 'focative' ('vocative', 4.1.45), then we must also laugh at Quickly, as she recurrently misinterprets William's Latin (hearing the genitive case *horum* as 'whorum', i.e. whore, 4.1.61) and understands '*caret*' (lacking)—with a strong suggestion of double-entendre, thanks to its phallic shape—as carrot, 'a good root' (4.1.49).

Caius and Evans are no more linguistically incompetent, and therefore to be excluded from a community of English-speakers, than many of their neighbours. Both are valued members of Windsor society, as the Host, a man of some authority within the play, observes, as he stops the duel between the two men. 'Shall I lose my doctor?' he asks: 'No, he gives me the potions and the motions [i.e. through laxatives]. Shall I lose my parson, my priest, my Sir Hugh? No, he gives me the Proverbs [biblical] and the No-verbs [Evans' linguistic errors]' (3.1.93–6). There is even a hint of affection here, in the possessive pronoun '*my* Sir Hugh', and certainly a wry acceptance of his linguistic alterity, which becomes part of his identity and a way of placing him within,

rather than extraneous to, the community. That Evans takes a key role in the humiliation of Falstaff further signals his absorption into the Windsor community as he trains
the children for their part in the masquerade ('I will teach the children their behaviours', 4.4.66). It is also Evans who speaks on behalf of that community, articulating its
norms as he lectures both the discomfited knight and the unreasonably jealous
husband Ford in the final scene, although both Falstaff and Ford try to save some
face here, by jeering at Evans's accent. 'I will never mistrust my wife again,' begins Ford
with seeming humility, before finishing 'till thou art able to woo her in good English'
(5.5.132–3), while Falstaff maintains a steady barrage of mocking banter, including the
insult 'fritters of English' (5.5.142).

Like *King John*, then, *Merry Wives* recognizes and legitimates a degree of cultural
hybridity. As Barton writes, 'it is one of Windsor's strengths as a society that it is
remarkably inclusive and willing to absorb foreign elements'.[40] Falstaff and Ford
might mock Evans to the end, but neither man is exactly the hero or moral centre of
the piece. Whereas many sixteenth-century writers anxiously policed the boundaries of
Englishness, reflecting woefully on the Italianate Englishman as the devil incarnate[41] or
trying—as Sir John Cheke did—to purge English of foreign loanwords, so that it might
be 'cleane and pure, unmixt and unmangeled with borowing of other tunges'[42]—these
plays of Shakespeare appear to acknowledge and even celebrate the way England's
heritage was intermingled with those of its continental neighbours, be it in terms of
blood (as with *King John*'s Count Melun) or language. The Folio version of *Merry Wives*
not only amplifies the linguistic errors of native and non-native speakers alike, it also
highlights the polyglot nature of Tudor English, its ability—like Windsor—to draw in
and make use of foreign terms. Pistol plays on the semantic variety and nuances of
standard Tudor English, counterpoising Anglo-Saxon and long-accepted Latinate
derivatives, whilst throwing in a smattering of foreign (Spanish) slang: '"Convey"' the
wise call it. "Steal"? Foh, a fico [fig] for the phrase' (1.3.26–7). The Host, a slightly more
respectable figure (if still a schemer), shows a similar fondness for multilingual terms.
'Cavaliero Justice', he calls Shallow (2.1.184); 'Will you go, mijn'heers?' he bids Shallow
and Page (2.1.205–6).[43] Indeed, elements of the play's humour even rely on intralingual
puns, such as that between Anne (Page) and *an* (French for 'arse').[44]

A full understanding of the exchange round the verb 'Englished' (Shakespeare's sole
usage of the word) also relies on audience members being able to comprehend a
complex semantic and etymological interplay. 'The hardest voice of her [Mistress
Ford's] behaviour, to be Englished [translated, understood] rightly, is "I am Sir John

---

[40] Barton, 'Falstaff and the Comic Community', 85.

[41] Roger Ascham, *The Scholemaster* (London: 1570), fol. 26; cf. Wilson, *Arte of Rhetorique*, fol. 86;
Thomas Smith, *Communicacion of the Queenes Highnes Mariage* (c.1561), British Library Additional MS
48047, fol. 97v.

[42] John Cheke to Thomas Hoby, appended to Hoby, *The Courtyer* (London: 1561), sig. 2Z5.

[43] Cavaliero (for 'Cabaliero'), Spanish (sir, knight); mijn heers, Dutch (gentlemen).

[44] Will Stockton, '"I am made an ass": Falstaff and the scatology of Windsor's polity', *Texas Studies in
Literature and Language* 49 (2007), 340–60.

Falstaff's," the fat knight declares' (1.3.41–3). 'He hath studied her well,' responds Pistol, 'and translated her will: out of honesty, into English' (1.1.44–5). Pistol's 'translated' can also mean 'changed' (that is, Pistol is aware that Falstaff has *mis*construed Mistress Ford); 'English' here represents the *vulgar* language, that of the people (*vulgus*), but also—by extension—common. To grasp what Pistol means (Falstaff has misread Mistress Ford and changed her behaviour from that of an honest wife to a common slut), spectators need to be able to bring the layered and varied roots of English into dialogue with each other. The hybrid nature of English, its very lack of impurity, is what gives it creative energy. It is instructive to read *Merry Wives* (and Shakespeare's meditations on his native tongue) against its sibling play, *Henry V*—an intertext, as David Landreth states, 'that *Merry Wives* can't deny'.[45] *Henry V* is notable for its portrayal of an English army which includes representatives from all four kingdoms comprising the 'Atlantic Archipelago' (England, Wales, Ireland, Scotland), which co-exist in slightly testy fellowship. What interests us here, though, is the way in which the linguistic hybridity of the final wooing scene between Henry and Katherine proves generative. Henry and Katherine both mingle French and English; between them they will 'compound a boy, half-French, half-English' (5.2.205). Henry expresses hope in the productive union of difference, albeit a wish that is ultimately doomed: the reign of the bilingual, bi-national son (Henry VI) will bring humiliation abroad and civil war at home, as the final chorus tells us.

CONCLUSION: *CYMBELINE*'S BRITAIN

When Shakespeare was celebrated, posthumously, through the 1623 Folio of his works, he was constructed as a national poet, belonging to many, the 'great Variety of Readers'.[46] Whereas Meres had fashioned Shakespeare as one of a series of English authors of credit to their nation, the Folio presents him in a class of his own ('outshin[ing]' Lyly, 'sporting Kyd' and 'Marlowe's mighty line', sig. A4) and as British: 'Triumph, my Britain, thou has one to show | To whom all scenes of Europe homage owe,' declares Ben Jonson (sig. A4v); 'Britons brave' are asked by Hugh Holland to mourn his passing (sig. A5). The English tendency to appropriate 'Britain' as a synonym for 'England' is centuries old, as Bale's elision of 'our Englyshe or Bryttysh nacyon' shows, and earlier poets, such as Wyatt and Henry Howard, Earl of Surrey, had been celebrated for their work 'for Brytayns gaine'.[47] After 1603, however, and the Union of the crowns under

---

[45] David Landreth, 'Once More into the Preech: *The Merry Wives'* English Pedagogy', *Shakespeare Quarterly* 55 (2004), 443.

[46] William Shakespeare, *Comedies, Histories, & Tragedies* (London, 1623), sig. A4.

[47] John Bale and John Leland, *The laboryouse Journey & serche of Johan Leylande* (London: 1549), sig. B8; Henry Howard, 'Wyat resteth here', *An excellent epitaffe of syr Thomas Wyat* (London: 1545?), sig. A1; George Turberville, 'Verse in prayse of Henry Howarde, Earle of Surrey', *Epitaphes, epigrams, songs and sonnets* (London, 1567): sig. C1.

James I and VI, Britishness took on a new dimension: to be British was not simply to annex England's neighbours but to contemplate union with them. When Shakespeare had recourse to national history as a Jacobean writer, he generally turned not to an English, medieval past (as he had in the first and second tetralogies in the 1590s) but to an older, less Anglocentric tradition.[48] An interest in Englishness recedes, to be replaced by a surge in the use of terms such as 'Britain' and 'Briton'.[49] Of all Shakespeare's Jacobean plays it is *Cymbeline* that shows the most sustained interest in Britishness.[50]

Set in pre-Roman Britain, *Cymbeline* displays many of the motifs of the rhetoric of nationhood that we have seen in Shakespeare's Elizabethan works. Britain is celebrated (more accurately than England) as an island fortress: it 'stands | as Neptune's park, ribbed and paled in | With banks unscalable and roaring waters' (3.1.18–20). As elsewhere, national identities are again constructed in opposition to something else, or come into focus when someone is removed from their native environment. Hence, Posthumus becomes 'the Briton' when exiled in Rome (1.4.26); Lucius is 'the Roman' when on embassy to Britain (3.5.31). Characters also resort to national stereotypes. Pisanio wonders 'what false Italian, | As poisonous tongued as handed, hath prevailed | On [Posthumus'] too ready hearing' (3.2.4–6); Innogen similarly deduces 'that drug-damned Italy hath out-craftied him' (3.4.15)—assumptions that both transpire to have a grain of truth.

However, just as with Englishness in *King John* and *Merry Wives*, so Britishness in *Cymbeline* proves to be more hybrid than it at first appears, and the play ultimately more open to inculturation than to belligerent isolation. The celebration of Britain's insular status is, for instance, put in the mouth of the wicked Queen, as she urges her husband, Cymbeline, to break faith with the Romans. The play itself ends celebrating union and thus laying the groundwork for the part that the Romans played in the heritage and history of Britain: 'Let | A Roman and a British ensign wave, | Friendly together,' affirms Cymbeline (5.6.480–2). Yet even before this formal peace, British culture seems Romanized. Innogen falls asleep reading Ovid's *Metamorphoses*, 'the lea[f] turned down | Where Philomel gave up' (2.2.45–6). Posthumus Leonatus ('the Briton') has a distinctly Latinate nomen and cognomen, and both Britons and Romans worship Jupiter, frequently invoking him by name, while the peace is to be ratified in his temple (5.6.483).[51]

Shakespeare's plays grow out of a tradition that tends to celebrate and cherish what set his nation apart from its neighbours, not least its insularity and (increasingly, if initially wishfully) a sense of emergent literary superiority. Hybridity for many Tudor and Stuart writers was something to be reviled; Shakespeare, in contrast, evinces no

---

[48] The co-authored play *Henry VIII* is an exception.

[49] 'Britain' appears three times in Shakespeare's Elizabethan plays (twice in *2 Henry VI*, once in *Love's Labour's Lost*); the terms Briton(s) and British do not appear.

[50] 'Briton/Britons' appears 17 times in *Cymbeline*; 'British', 5 times; 'Britain', 24 times.

[51] Among those Britons who invoke Jupiter are Cloten (3.5.84), Belarius (3.6.42), and the first captain (5.5.84). Jupiter, who is named more times in *Cymbeline* (12 references) than in any other Shakespeare play, also appears onstage in 5.5.

such discomfort with embracing difference or recognizing a mongrel past (be it of blood or language). At the same time, he shows himself resistant to the type of polemical history found in Reformation hagiographies of King John, which rely on a simplistic division between right/wrong, them/us. MacMorris in *Henry V* famously asks 'What ish my nation?' (3.2.66). It is not a question he actually answers, and not one which seems to offer easy definitions. MacMorris had every reason to be confused. As Richard Dutton points out, as a 'gentleman' (3.3.12), he is almost certainly one of the 'Old English', long-denizened in Ireland and regarded by many as 'degenerated and growne almost mere Irish'.[52] When Shakespeare's plays beg the same question of his compatriots (what is—what comprises—my nation?), they too provide no neat and ready categories, but remind us of the hotchpotch nature of the English, or British, national heritage.

---

[52] Richard Dutton, '"Methinks the truth should live from age to age": The Dating and Contexts of *Henry V*', *Huntington Library Quarterly* 68 (2005), 199; Edmund Spenser, *A View of the Present State of Ireland*, Andrew Hadfield and Willy Maley (eds.), (Oxford: Blackwell, 1997), 54.

CHAPTER 32

....

REPUBLICANISM

....

ANDREW HADFIELD

THE questions of Shakespeare's politics and the history of republicanism in early modern England are likely to remain controversial issues, especially when the two are considered together.[1] The problems are all too obvious. Shakespeare is elusive even by the standards of early modern English dramatists and it is hard to pin down his political—and religious—affiliations: that is, assuming he had any.[2] For many historians there can be no meaningful sense of republicanism before the establishment of a republic during the interregnum. Moreover, attempting to isolate a strain of republicanism in early modern England, even using a model based on Patrick Collinson's influential notion of the 'monarchical republic', risks distorting our understanding of early modern political culture and, crucially, downplaying the importance of religion. Therefore, the attempt to align Shakespeare with any republican sympathies is doomed to failure.[3]

Nevertheless, stubborn facts remain behind, which might suggest that the subject has some substance and reports of its death are premature. It is clear that many writers were especially keen to make comparisons between the bloody transition from the Roman Republic to the Roman Empire and the potential fate of England after the death of Elizabeth with the attendant uncertainty regarding the succession. One of the key authors for Elizabethans was, after all, Marcus Tullius Cicero (106–43 BCE), and it is hard to believe that no one made the connection between the circumstances of his

---

[1] For recent overviews, see Martin van Gelderen and Quentin Skinner (eds.), *Republicanism: A Shared European Heritage*, 2 vols. (Cambridge: Cambridge University Press, 2002); Andrew Hadfield, *Shakespeare and Renaissance Politics* (London: Thomson, 2003).

[2] Blair Worden, 'Shakespeare and Politics', *Shakespeare Survey* 44 (1991), 1–15. See also the discussions in David Armitage, Conal Condren, and Andrew Fitzmaurice (eds.), *Shakespeare and Early Modern Political Thought* (Cambridge: Cambridge University Press, 2009).

[3] For a sceptical approach, see Peter Lake, '"The Monarchical Republic of Queen Elizabeth I" (and the Fall of Archbishop Grindal) Revisited', in John McDiarmid (ed.), *The Monarchical Republic of Early Modern England: Essays in Response to Patrick Collinson* (Aldershot: Ashgate, 2007), 132–6; Patrick Collinson, 'The Monarchical Republic of Queen Elizabeth I', in *Elizabethans* (London: Hambledon, 2003), 31–57.

writings and their application to contemporary events. Cicero defended the institutions of the republic until he felt that they had become so corrupted that they could no longer function as they were designed to do. Instead, he concentrated on the virtue of friendship, the private relationship between individuals that cut across hierarchical boundaries, and promised to deliver a more egalitarian conversation between equals. Again, the parallel to Shakespeare's England is obvious enough, given the weight that was frequently placed on the value of friendship as a means of escaping from the tyranny of ordinary life. Ben Jonson's epigram 'Inviting a Friend to Supper' makes precisely this connection between the value of privacy in the contemporary world and the tyranny of public existence. While the friends are eating Jonson declares that his man 'Shall read a piece of Virgil, Tacitus, | Livy, or of some better book to us, | Of which we'll speak our minds, amidst our meat[.]' The poem concludes:

> And we will have no Poley or Parrot by,
> Nor shall our cups make any guilty men,
> But at our parting we will be as when
> We innocently met. No simple word
> That shall be uttered at our mirthful board
> Shall make us sad next morning, or afright
> The liberty that we'll enjoy tonight.[4]

Poley and Parrot were two notorious spies, Poley having been involved in the Babington Plot, which led to the execution of Mary Stuart (1587), as well as the strange death of Christopher Marlowe (1593).[5] They were probably the two spies who tried to force a confession out of Jonson when he was imprisoned for writing the notorious play *The Isle of Dogs*, with Thomas Nashe (1597). As David Riggs has noted, 'the very mention of their names reminds the reader that Jonson's "libertie" is imperilled by state-supported surveillance and repression.'[6] Jonson's point is that at supper the two men can talk and debate as equals, enjoying proper liberty, the freedom to say what they think without fear of reprisal so that they can both wake up happily refreshed the next morning, safe in the knowledge that they will not be sent off to prison for speaking out of turn. It is important that they will reflect on the complexities of life after having heard some history and poetry written just before and just after the transformation of the republic into the empire, further suggesting that many who lived through the final years of Elizabeth's reign thought about their times in terms of the end of the Roman Republic. Livy, Tacitus, and Virgil might be said to form a nicely balanced trinity of positions regarding the republic: Livy in favour of it; Tacitus could be read as a supporter or a hard-headed realist; and Virgil as a supporter of the imperial regime of Augustus, albeit by no stretch of the imagination an uncritical one. If the poem cannot be defined as

---

⁴ Ben Jonson, 'Inviting a Friend to Supper', ll. 21–3, 36–42, in Ian Donaldson (ed.), *Poems* (London: Oxford University Press, 1975), 31–4, *passim*.

⁵ Charles Nicholl, *The Reckoning: The Murder of Christopher Marlowe* (London: Picador, 1993), *passim*.

⁶ David Riggs, *Ben Jonson: A Life* (Cambridge, MA: Harvard University Press, 1989), 231.

'republican' it is certainly very close to the mark, juxtaposing equality and free discussion between friends with the harsh repression of society outside.[7] Furthermore, the expression of this republican impulse takes place in a literary text, providing evidence—if any were needed—that literature often served writers and readers as a means of solving insoluble problems, and of opening up a space for free thinking.

Jonson, like Shakespeare, has often been read as a conservative figure, principally because he produced masques for the Stuart court, a judgement that undoubtedly obscures more than it reveals.[8] Jonson's theatrical rivalry with Shakespeare is well-attested, but the relationship between their Roman plays has not received much serious comment. *Julius Caesar* was either the first—or one of the first—plays at the newly founded Globe Theatre in 1599, indicating that it fed a clear topical interest in political assassination and its consequences in the last years of Elizabeth's reign. It is likely that *Antony and Cleopatra*, the next instalment of the story, was meant to follow soon afterward. However, for some reason, perhaps because putting two plays on which narrated the story of the end of the Roman Republic was simply too controversial, especially in the wake of the Essex rising, the play was not performed until *c.*1607.[9] Jonson wrote two plays about Roman coups d'état, *Sejanus His Fall* (1603), which attracted the hostile attention of the authorities perhaps because it was assumed that it was a reflection on the Essex rebellion and in what circumstances rebellion could be countenanced, and *Catiline His Conspiracy* (1611), which led to further trouble when it was assumed that the play was a reflection on the Gunpowder Plot.[10] In between these two Shakespeare produced *Coriolanus* (*c.*1608), which attracted no hostile attention that has been recorded. The evidence suggests that Roman plays were in demand, but often the reason why they were popular also explains why there were not that many of them: they ran the risk of proving too topical and controversial.

Shakespeare wrote about Rome and Roman subjects throughout his two-and-a-half decade writing career. In the early 1590s he co-wrote *Titus Andronicus* with George Peele, a play set in the last days of imperial Roman, that begins with a long discussion of different constitutional positions before an election. It is likely that Shakespeare was employed because of his facility with Ovidian verse, and that Peele, a more learned classicist, produced the opening scene.[11] Nevertheless, even if Shakespeare did not actually write this scene, he was clearly involved in a project that posed political questions about how government should function. It is possible that Shakespeare was

---

[7] For a spirited case about Jonson's drama, see Julie Sanders, *Ben Jonson's Theatrical Republics* (Basingstoke: Macmillan, 1998).

[8] An assumption that is implicit even in Peter Womack's otherwise perceptive study, *Ben Jonson* (Oxford: Blackwell, 1986).

[9] Geoffrey Bullough, *Narrative and Dramatic Sources of Shakespeare*, 8 vols. (London: Routledge, 1957–75), 5: 216.

[10] For comment, see Janet Clare, '*Art made tongue-tied by authority*': *Elizabethan and Jacobean Dramatic Censorship*, 2nd edn. (Manchester: Manchester University Press, 1990), 132–5; Riggs, *Jonson*, 176–7.

[11] On the authorship of the play and the probable scene divisions, see Brian Vickers, *Shakespeare, Co-Author* (Oxford: Oxford University Press, 2002), ch. 3.

asked to co-write the play because he had already produced work on Roman subjects, perhaps an early version of *Venus and Adonis* (published 1593): we cannot be confident of the chronology of these early works. What we do know is that when the theatres were closed because of plague he published the *Rape of Lucrece* (1594), which might have been written earlier, a serious narrative poem that tells the story of the act that led to the banishment of the last Roman kings, the Tarquins, and the establishment of the republic.

Of course, writing plays or poems about Rome is not in itself proof of a serious interest in republicanism, and it is possible that they were written as discrete and isolated works. Moreover, it is often easy enough to show that when read on their own plays do not necessarily express a commitment to an ideal or lead the audience in any particular direction. This is especially true of Shakespeare, who has usually been seen to be 'myriad-minded', multiple, and above the vulgar fray of the political commitment.[12] But such objections are in danger of missing the point. Interest in republicanism becomes more obvious when the plays are read as a group, demonstrating a series of concerns. And they are plays, designed to be challenging and dramatic, arguing a case *pro* and *contra* in line with the rhetorical and educational principle of *in utramque partem*, weighing up the evidence by representing each side of the argument.[13] It would be unthinkable that anyone might find an undiscovered play written in the later 1590s entitled *Brutus the Heroic Tyrant-Slayer*. We do, however, find a pamphlet on this subject, and plays that tell what look like related stories.[14] It is possible that the stage was used as a tool of government propaganda to persuade the citizens of London to obey their lords and masters and not to challenge the status quo.[15] But if that were the case we would expect the authorities to have been rather less nervous about what appeared on the stage than they clearly were.[16] Read together, Shakespeare's three Roman plays tell the story of the fall of the Roman Republic and the establishment of the empire, as well as a notorious episode when the republic was nearly destroyed by a fatal combination of external and internal forces. The plays perhaps follow on from Thomas Lodge's *The Wounds of Civil War*, performed either just before or just after Marlowe's *Tamburlaine* in the late 1580s but first published in 1594. That important play told the story of the vicious civil war between Marius and the dictator

[12] 'Myriad-minded' is Coleridge's phrase, adopted by Ernst Honigmann for his collection *Myriad-Minded Shakespeare: Essays on the Tragedies, Problem Comedies and Shakespeare the Man* (Basingstoke: Macmillan, 1989). See also Brian Gibbons, *Shakespeare and Multiplicity* (Cambridge: Cambridge University Press, 1993).

[13] Quentin Skinner, 'Afterword: Shakespeare and humanist culture', in Armitage et al. (eds.), *Shakespeare and Early Modern Political Thought*.

[14] Brutus, Stephanus Junius, the Celt, *Vindiciae, Contra Tyrannos, or, concerning the legitimate power of a prince over the people, and of the people over a prince* (1579), George Garnett (ed.) (Cambridge: Cambridge University Press, 1994).

[15] See the lively debate in Anthony B. Dawson and Paul Yachnin, *The Culture of Playgoing in Shakespeare's England: a Collaborative Debate* (Cambridge: Cambridge University Press, 2001).

[16] There is now a large literature on censorship on the stage: in addition to Clare, 'Art made tongue-tied by authority', see Cyndia Clegg, *Press Censorship in Elizabethan England* (Cambridge: Cambridge University Press, 1997); Richard Dutton, *Licensing, Censorship and Authorship in Early Modern England: Buggeswords* (Basingstoke: Palgrave Macmillan, 2000).

Sulla, the conflict that was commonly seen to have initiated the destruction of republican government.[17] *Julius Caesar* shows us a system of government in terminal decline. None of the great institutions of republican government work: we see no debates in the senate, only the murder of the man whose dictatorship signals its final end. Cicero is shown to be ineffective and weak, neither joining the conspirators nor helping to moderate Caesar's rule and preserve some form of reasonable, workable government. Brutus, in many ways an honourable man, is vain and easily manipulated by those less principled than he. He cannot see through the ruse of the fraudulent letters that are delivered to him by Cassius, pretending that their conspiracy enjoys widespread support. Most striking of all, given the carefully constructed arguments within the play, Brutus' rhetorical gifts are limited. Perhaps this is not really his fault as he has no opportunity to speak in public until he has to persuade the crowd that the killing of Caesar was a justifiable action.

Significantly enough, his first major speech is a soliloquy in his own orchard, not an address to the senate, a sign of how far republican Rome has decayed from its heyday of public participation. Brutus meditates on the need for Caesar's assassination as a means of curing Rome's ills:

> It must be by his death; and, for my part,
> I know no personal cause to spurn at him,
> But for the general; he would be crowned.
> How that might change his nature, there's the question.
> It is the bright day that brings forth the adder,
> And that craves wary walking. Crown him that,
> And then, I grant, we put a sting in him
> That at his will he may do danger with.
> Th'abuse of greatness is when it disjoins
> Remorse from power, and, to speak truth of Caesar,
> I have known when his affections swayed
> More than his reason. But 'tis a common proof
> That lowliness is a young ambition's ladder,
> Whereto the climber-upward turns his face;
> But when he once attains the upmost round
> He then unto the ladder turns his back,
> Looks in the clouds, scorning the base degrees
> By which he did ascend. So Caesar may.[18]

The speech reverses and overturns the normal process of logical reasoning based on the building-block of the syllogism ('Socrates is a man. All men are mortal. Therefore Socrates is mortal'). Here Brutus starts with the conclusion, using the imperative 'must', and ends the sequence of thought with the evidence, which is based on a series of conjectures, using the conditional, 'may'. He begins asking himself a question, how

[17] Andrew Hadfield, 'Thomas Lodge and Elizabethan Republicanism', in Anna Fåhraeus and Per Sivefors (ed.), *Nordic Journal of English Studies* 4.2, Special Issue on Early Modern Drama (2005), 91–105.

[18] William Shakespeare, *Julius Caesar*, Arthur Humphreys (ed.) (Oxford: Oxford University Press, 1984), 2.1.10–27. All subsequent references to this edition in parentheses in the text.

might Caesar change if he is crowned, and proceeds to an analogy, suggesting that, if crowned, Caesar's bad inner nature might come to the fore and everyone might suffer as a result. Brutus then asserts that great people can become dangerous when their human emotions (here, remorse) are separated from the harsh reality of the need to govern. Brutus cites as evidence the fact that he has observed Caesar's affections dominate his reason, which is not quite the same process, nor can it be taken as useful supporting evidence. He then resorts to a cliché, that the ambitious forget who their real friends are when they rise to power, a general observation that he does not bother to support with any reference to how Caesar has behaved or may behave in the near future.

This is a speech that we know would have been ripped to shreds had it been aired in public. In the last days of the republic, the great arts that it inspired—most importantly, oratory and debate—have been reduced to ill-thought-out parodies of their former glory. The audience can see the play and see what is wrong with the arguments represented within it, which might be seen as a republican argument for the need for political participation. The characters cannot. In itself this important point shows that *Julius Caesar* asks the audience one of the fundamental republican questions: do institutions cause men to degenerate when they go wrong? Or do bad men undermine institutions? Perhaps this question is even more fundamental than the more familiar one of whether Brutus was actually right to assassinate Caesar.[19] The play also works as an example of the principle of *in utramque partem*, asking the audience to choose and decide what is the meaning of what they have seen and what they think should have happened. But that is exactly what is denied to Brutus and Cassius, who have to try to reinvent the republic. They manage to produce only a parody of its violent founding action when Brutus' namesake and ancestor banished the Tarquins after the rape and suicide of Lucrece, a story Shakespeare had already told.[20]

Julius Caesar shows us the republic deprived of its public purpose, its private world similarly corrupted. The play also represents Brutus and Cassius' disastrous but affectionate friendship. We see this begin with Cassius' successful attempt to delude Brutus into joining the conspiracy and end with their deaths at the Battle of Philippi. Act 4 witnesses the disintegration of their friendship after they have fled Rome and raised an army to fight a civil war with the forces of the Triumvirate. Brutus accuses Cassius of corruption and makes an unwise speech which concludes with the accusation that he would rather 'be a dog and bay at the moon | Than such a Roman as Cassius' (4.2.78–9), which leads, unsurprisingly, to a heated argument that reveals Brutus as aloof and devoid of proper affection toward his fellows, and Cassius as impulsive and morally weak, as he confesses in stating his love for his friend with the rhetorical question: 'Have you not love enough to bear with me, | When that rash humour which my mother gave me | Makes me forgetful?' (4.2.170–2). Anyone who loves Cassius has to accept his impulsiveness and his inability to control himself at crucial moments; anyone who loves Brutus has to accept his self-

[19] Robert Miola, '*Julius Caesar* and the Tyrannicide Debate', *Renaissance Quarterly* 36 (1985), 271–90.
[20] For comment, see Andrew Hadfield, *Shakespeare and Republicanism* (Cambridge: Cambridge University Press, 2005), 136–53.

righteousness and inability to act appropriately at equally vital times. The effect of their dispute is to undermine the morale of their army and extinguishes any last chance they had of achieving victory against determined and angry opponents.

Shakespeare has expanded what he discovered in his source, Plutarch's *Lives*, in line with Renaissance ideals of friendship. Plutarch describes a meeting of the two halves of the republican army at the city of Sardis, where each division addresses the leader as 'emperor', a sign in itself that the republic is doomed. Plutarch, in North's translation, one of the books that Shakespeare would have had in his small library, comments:

> Now, as it commonly happeneth in great affairs between two persons, both of them having many friends, and so many captains under them, there ran tales and complaints betwixt them. Therefore, before they fell in hand with any other matter, they went into a little chamber together, and bade every man avoid, and did shut the doors to them. Then they began to pour out their complaints one to the other, and grew hot and loud, earnestly accusing one another, and at length fell both a-weeping.[21]

Shakespeare has transformed Plutarch's narrative, extending Brutus and Cassius' quarrel to show how isolated they are from the rest of the army and how passionate they are in their professions of friendship. Most of all, the episode shows how much they have corrupted, and been corrupted by, the decayed and now pernicious values they are trying to defend. Just as assassination has taken the place of public debate, so have the selfish passions and needs of friendship replaced its enabling virtues. What should bind men together is actually undermining their efforts to preserve the political system they support. We find similar instances of this malign transformation throughout the play. Portia, the daughter of the great Stoic, Cato, demonstrates her great love for her husband by enduring a self-inflicted wound in her thigh, which she shows to him in order to gain his approval and access to his thoughts, a corruption of Stoic values of the indifference to the passions. In the same way, republican ideals of friendship work to undermine the social fabric rather than bind the body politic together, especially if we consider the effect of Antony's fierce loyalty and devotion to his dead friend.

Act 4 of *Julius Caesar* was, I suspect, written with Cicero's dialogue *De Amicitia* (*On Friendship*) in mind.[22] Cicero, following Aristotle, argues that friendship is a virtue that can only exist between good men who are already virtuous, 'who so act and so live as to give proof of loyalty and uprightness, or fairness and generosity; who are free from al passion, caprice, and insolence, and have great strength of character.'[23] Friendship is

---

[21] Plutarch, *Selected Lives*, Judith Mossman (ed.) (Ware: Wordsworth, 1998), 843. On Shakespeare's library, see Stuart Gillespie (ed.), *Shakespeare's Books: A Dictionary of Shakespeare Sources* (London: Athlone, 2001), 425–36.

[22] There was a convenient English translation available had Shakespeare needed to cross-reference the Latin text: *Fowre Severall Treatises of M. Tullius Cicero: Conteyninge his most learned and eloquent discourses of Frendshippe, Oldage, Paradoxes: and Scipio his Dreame*, Thomas Newton (trans.) (London: 1577).

[23] Cicero, *De Senectute, De Amicitia, De Divinatione*, William Armistead Falconer (trans.) (Cambridge, MA: Harvard University Press, 1959), 129. All subsequent references to this edition in parentheses in the text.

defined as a 'nothing else than an accord in all things, human and divine, conjoined with mutual goodwill and affection', so that 'no better thing has been given to man by the immortal gods' (131). Cassius has undermined the ideal of friendship through his deviousness: 'in friendship there is nothing false, nothing pretended; whatever there is is genuine and comes of its own accord . . . friendship springs rather from nature than from need, and from an inclination of the soul joined with a feeling of love rather than calculation of how much profit the friendship is likely to afford' (139). Certainly, Cassius becomes more noble as the play continues, and his natural affection for his friend either develops or comes to the fore, as his self-interest recedes. Equally important for Cicero's disputants is the need for warmth and affection in friendship, qualities that are conspicuously lacking in Brutus. They also argue that self-reliance is a virtue in itself, which makes a man reach out to others in friendship: 'For to the extent that a man relies upon himself and is so fortified by virtue and wisdom that he is dependent on no one and considers al his possessions to be within himself, in that degree is he most conspicuous for seeking out and cherishing friendships' (143). Brutus might well be read as a parody of this ideal, so self-reliant that he has excessive confidence in his judgements—most notably his speech over the dead body of Caesar being a key example, along with his poor military decisions—that he drives his wife to suicide and fails to notice how dependent on him Cassius has become. Dying by his own hand only emphasizes his—and our—sense of him as a proud man apart, the noblest Roman who has become an outdated remnant of the republic. Rome needs to move forward to a more practical, Tacitean phase of its history based on various forms of self-interest, which, in such times, is safer and makes more sense for everyone.

My point is not that *Julius Caesar* is republican propaganda, endorsing Roman ideals without qualification and attempting to persuade the Elizabethan audience to adopt them. It is far too nuanced, balanced, and complicated to betray any such message. Rather, the play demonstrates just how interested Shakespeare was in the history, culture, and importance of the Roman Republic, adding to his principal source to make his play more concerned with republican values than Plutarch was. What *Julius Caesar* does show us is the decay and impending death of an ideal, a society in which every action designed to save and preserve its values serves only to undermine them and hasten its doom. The play is indeed as elusive as admirers of Shakespeare have invariably claimed. But this does not mean that it endorses the status quo and has an uncritical perception of monarchy. Instead, it forces the audience to think and choose. What is the most appropriate form of government? What is the most appropriate form of behaviour under any regime? How should a nation facing a change which might be every bit as cataclysmic as the transformation of Rome from republic to monarchy act? Can values be transferred across such regime changes, or is a new way of behaving appropriate? In actually asking the audience to think, even if we assume that his motives were cynical, self-interested, and designed to make a profit, Shakespeare's play had already taken a step toward republican values. If it is true that *Antony and Cleopatra* was postponed because it was likely to lead to trouble, then the reasons are easy to understand, especially after the historical links that had been made before and after the Essex uprising, which, of course, involved a work probably written by Shakespeare.[24]

Antony and Cleopatra does read best as a companion piece to *Julius Caesar*. While the ancient world is shown balanced between public and private ideals in the earlier play, the later one shows us the exhaustion and desperation of the principal protagonists of the republican age and their need to retreat into a private world to escape the forces of modernity. The fate of Cleopatra in particular should be read against that of Dido, Queen of Carthage, abandoned by her lover, Aeneas, whose destiny is to found the new Rome and leave behind the old world, whatever its attractions. Shakespeare's play can be seen as a belated response to that of his precursor and sometime rival, Christopher Marlowe.[25] Whereas Aeneas could never be defined by the role of lover, Antony is prepared to cast in his lot with the ineffective queen whose country will become the first victim of the new Roman war-machine led by Octavius/Augustus.

Even Enorbarbus' famous description of Cleopatra in her barge demonstrates the transitory and limited nature of her power:

> The barge she sat in, like a burnished throne
> Burned on the water; the poop was beaten gold,
> Purple the sails, and so perfumèd that
> The winds were love-sick with them; the oars were silver,
> Which to the tune of flutes kept stroke, and made
> The water which they beat to follow faster,
> As amorous of their strokes. For her own person,
> It beggared all description: she did lie
> In her pavilion—cloth-of-gold of tissue—
> O'er-picturing that Venus where we see
> The fancy out-work nature. On each side her
> Stood pretty dimpled boys, like smiling Cupids,
> With divers-coloured fans, whose wind did seem
> To glow the delicate cheeks which they did cool,
> And what they undid did.[26]

Cleopatra's regal appearance would undoubtedly have reminded many theatregoers of their late queen's imperious style and love of opulent public display (something that James usually avoided).[27] The description also appears as notably 'Spenserian' in character, reinforcing our understanding that, although Cleopatra's public staging of

---

[24] Paul E. J. Hammer, 'Shakespeare's *Richard II*, the Play of 7 February 1601, and the Essex Rising', *Shakespeare Quarterly* 59 (2008), 1–35.

[25] See James Shapiro, *Rival Playwrights: Marlowe, Jonson, Shakespeare* (New York: Columbia University Press, 1991).

[26] William Shakespeare, *Antony and Cleopatra*, Michael Neill (ed.) (Oxford: Clarendon Press, 1994), 2.2.198–212. All subsequent references to this edition in parentheses in the text.

[27] Helen Hackett, *Virgin Mother, Maiden Queen: Elizabeth I and the Cult of the Virgin Mary* (Basingstoke: Palgrave Macmillan, 1995), 41–9, *passim*; Curtis Perry, *The Making of Jacobean Culture* (Cambridge: Cambridge University Press, 1997), pt. 3.

her beauty is impressive, it is an end in itself: vain, self-regarding, and ineffective as a means of serious government.[28] Certainly, such magnificent displays have an impact on observers, as Enobarbus' lyrical description indicates. But, in the hard world of realpolitik, Cleopatra is simply demonstrating what the audience already knows, that she is no match for the brutal new world run by Octavius, a man ruthless enough to discard and destroy his rival triumvirs, as well as the old republican opposition. While Antony and Cleopatra retreat into private spaces to die, Octavius takes centre stage. In the final scene, the triumphant new Caesar orders the burial of his dead foes, Cleopatra's body remaining on stage still in the bed where she had lived with Antony and died. Augustus and his army will 'In solemn show attend the funeral—| And then to Rome' (5.2.362–3), having the task of founding the imperial dynasty.

Even the most perfunctory knowledge of Roman history, one outlined in any number of translations and histories published in late Elizabethan England, would have told the reader that Augustus' dynasty, the Julio-Claudians, soon degenerated into tyranny in the reigns of Tiberius, Caligula, and Nero.[29] *Antony and Cleopatra*, especially when read as a sequel to *Julius Caesar*, shows us the republican government of Rome transformed into distorted and equally unpalatable male and female halves. On the one hand we have the appealing but dangerously ineffective 'petticoat' government of Cleopatra. Under her influence the once powerful Antony becomes indifferent to the political world, valuing personal relationships above all else, as he proudly proclaims to his lover:

> Let Rome in Tiber melt, and the wide arch
> Of the ranged empire fall! Here is my space.
> Kingdoms are clay. Our dungy earth alike
> Feeds beast as man. The nobleness of life
> Is to do thus, when such a mutual pair
> And such a twain can do't—in which I bind,
> On pain of punishment, the world to weet
> We stand up peerless.   (1.1.35–42)

Antony establishes his union with Cleopatra as a means of standing apart and retreating into a private space at odds with the world outside. Playgoers who had seen *Julius Caesar* would not have been witnessing a surprising transformation. Antony, despite his fearsome reputation as a valiant soldier in the past, is shown to value the personal over the political from his first appearance and was prepared to 'let slip the dogs of war' (2.1.273) in order to avenge his friend. Ranged against them we witness the brutal masculine might of Rome and the inexorable rise of Octavius, who has no time for frivolous displays, or friendship and loyalty, as we witness him grow in frightening

---

[28] For other connections between the play and Spenser, see Judith H. Anderson, 'Beyond Binarism: Eros/Death and Venus/Mars in Shakespeare's *Antony and Cleopatra* and Spenser's *Faerie Queene*', in J. B. Lethbridge (ed.), *Shakespeare and Spenser: Attractive Opposites* (Manchester: Manchester University Press, 2008), 54–78.

[29] Hadfield, *Shakespeare and Republicanism*, pt. 1.

stature until he assumes command of the Roman Empire in the final act of *Antony and Cleopatra*. Octavius understands people but makes use of his insights to manipulate, undermine, and, usually, destroy them. He passes on advice to his trusted servants, telling Thidias to 'Observe how Antony becomes his flaw' (3.12.35). When he confronts Antony and Cleopatra's forces, Octavius has prepared for battle thoroughly and developed just the right tactics to defeat his former ally. His speech is not notable for its eloquence but it reveals a mind focused entirely on what needs to be done to achieve victory:

> Let our best heads
> Know that tomorrow the last of many battles
> We mean to fight. Within our files there are,
> Of those that served Mark Antony but late,
> Enough to fetch him in. See it done,
> And feast the army—we have store to do't,
> And they have earned the waste. Poor Antony!   (4.1.10–16)

The last lines are especially revealing and show that Caesar has truly assumed command and knows that he has the means to crush his enemy, so much so that he can afford to pity the once-powerful general in advance. Octavius knows that this will be the decisive battle of the campaign. He has assembled an army that contains men carefully selected for the tasks ahead, those who know and recognize Antony. And, even though we know that he does not enjoy or approve of excessive consumption, Octavius knows that it is worth his while to feast his soldiers on the eve of the battle to ensure their loyalty. The speech is that of a successful general: it is focused, prosaic, and devoid of both persuasive strategies and rhetorical flourishes. Caesar is truly Caesar. He does not have to try to convince his audience that what he is doing is right. He knows that he is and he expects them to obey or to suffer the consequences.

The rise of Octavius is at the expense of the political and intellectual culture of the Republic. We no longer witness a society of equals—or friends—who respect each other's opinions and judgements and are prepared to listen and debate. Instead, we have a military dictatorship ruled by an astute man who knows how to make his society successful and defeat rivals and opponents, internal and external. In contrast to the other characters in both plays, Octavius appears relatively untroubled by the ties of human relationships and does not allow them to complicate the goals of his life. Even when he consoles his sister, Octavia, Antony's wife, for Antony's desertion to Cleopatra, he places the emphasis on the political effects of her errant husband's actions. Octavius states that Antony 'hath given his empire | Up to a whore' (3.6.66–7), and then lists the kings with whom Antony has allied (3.6.69–76), which suggests that even when he may have some personal feelings, political considerations provide the major influence on his words and actions. With the transformation of Octavius into Augustus, we have moved a long way from the world of Cicero.

Julius Caesar and *Antony and Cleopatra* can be read as plays that show us negative examples of government: or, rather, government moving in the wrong direction. Like all other early modern English playwrights, Shakespeare frequently represents the worst form of government, tyranny, on the stage, inviting the audience to make what comparisons they will, from the first tetralogy through *Hamlet* and *Macbeth* to *The Winter's Tale* and, arguably, *The Tempest*.[30] In itself this does not necessarily make Shakespeare especially remarkable, and, inevitably, drama will supply us with negative rather than positive images of government because of the need to tell a good story. But we do have at least one important representation of good government in the plays, which stands as a pointed contrast to the often horrifying examples of evil and tyrannous rule in the histories, tragedies, and many comedies: the opening act of *Othello*. Venice was one of the rare examples of republican government known to English readers in the sixteenth century (the other principal example was the Dutch Republic besieged by the Spanish for most of Elizabeth's reign).[31] The city-state was especially attractive for English visitors and readers, partly owing to the famed beauty of its courtesans, its spectacular wealth, and its cosmopolitan culture as the gateway to the East. But it is too easy to be cynical about its appeal. Venice was also valued because of its stability and the political liberty it afforded its diverse range of citizens, many of whom were foreigners and who had adopted Venetian values, exactly like Othello. In his influential *History of Italy* (1549), which, as the standard English work on Italy Shakespeare was likely to have known, William Thomas argues that 'their [the Venetians'] principal profession is liberty, and he that should usurp upon another should incontinently be reputed a tyrant, which name of all things they cannot abide. For when a subject of theirs says, "Sir, you are my lord, you are my master," he takes it for the greatest villainy of the world.'[32] If we bear in mind the political charge that the word 'tyrant' possessed in this period, a description that no political leader could ever accept, then we should realize the radical statement that Thomas is making here.[33] For Venetians, tyranny is a present danger, and they have to be constantly on guard against threats to their liberty, in itself a true sign of virtue, and something that promotes virtue, suggesting that Thomas was aware of the nature of political debate in sixteenth-century Italy.[34]

---

[30] Rebecca Bushnell, *Tragedies of Tyrants: Political Thought and Theater in the English Renaissance* (Ithaca, NY: Cornell University Press, 1990).

[31] For comment and analysis see Martin Van Gelderen, *The Political Thought of the Dutch Revolt, 1555–1590* (Cambridge: Cambridge University Press, 1992); Martin Van Gelderen (ed.), *The Dutch Revolt* (Cambridge: Cambridge University Press, 1993).

[32] Angelo Deidda, Maria Grazia Dongu, and Laura Sanna (eds.), *Lezioni ai Potenti: William Thomas e l'Italia, con una selezione da The Historie of Italie* (Cagliari: CUEC, 2002), 244. All subsequent references to Thomas's *History* in parentheses in the text.

[33] On 'tyranny' in the early modern period, see Robert M. Kingdon, 'Calvinism and Resistance Theory, 1550–1580', in J. H. Burns and Mark Goldie (eds.), *The Cambridge History of Political Thought, 1450–1700* (Cambridge: Cambridge University Press, 1991), 193–218; Bushnell, *Tragedies of Tyrants*.

[34] On the concept of liberty, see Quentin Skinner, *Liberty Before Liberalism* (Cambridge: Cambridge University Press, 1998). On Italian political debate, see James Hankins (ed.), *Renaissance Civic Humanism* (Cambridge: Cambridge University Press, 2000); Peter Stacey, *Roman Monarchy and the Renaissance Prince* (Cambridge: Cambridge University Press, 2007).

Othello was written with a clear knowledge of republican Venice. In the opening act we witness one of the most satisfactory and straightforward resolutions of a legal case in Shakespeare's works—perhaps designed as a pointed contrast to Portia's subtle legal trickery in the earlier *Merchant of Venice*, probably the first representation of the city-state on the English stage.[35] Indeed, by the end of the opening act Othello would appear to be in the most fortunate position of any of Shakespeare's tragic figures: his marriage has been upheld as legal and proper against the designs of his enemies, he is very much in love with his wife, and he has been supported by the state he serves and given an important command. Of course, this only serves to make his tragic fall all the more terrible. But the point that needs to be made is that Othello's success is bound up with the political achievement of the Republic; his downfall, his distance from it.

We are aware that there is another side to Venice. In the opening scene we witness Iago and Roderigo referring to Othello in overtly racist terms as the 'thick-lips', and conjuring up a grotesque pornographic scenario to force Brabantio to take action against his daughter:

> 'Swounds, sir, you're robbed; for shame, put on your gown!
> Your heart is burst, you have lost half your soul:
> Even now, now, very now, an old black ram
> Is tupping your white ewe. Arise, arise!
> Awake the snorting citizens with the bell,
> Or else the devil will make a grandsire of you.
> Arise, I say![36]

Iago skilfully packs a great deal into a short space. Brabantio is robbed; his daughter has been transformed into an animal by her new husband; and Othello is a devil. While the city sleeps soundly its most sacred values are undermined by the forces of darkness. This is popular racism at its most potent. Probably the most haunting image is that of Desdemona as a ewe, sired by Othello the black ram. Brabantio has to respond that his 'house is not a grange [a country estate]' (1.1.106), but that is precisely what Iago is warning him that it has become. While Brabantio imagines that he lives in the centre of the most civilized city on earth, Iago warns him that the barbarians are already through the gates, let in by the overly tolerant city governors, and are swamping the true, civilized culture of Europe. Shakespeare makes it clear that Iago has struck a chord with the fears of the old man. When Brabantio realizes that Desdemona and Othello really are married he finally rouses himself and comments, 'This accident is not unlike my dream; | Belief of it oppresses me already' (1.1.141–2). He has already seen the image in his nightmares. Venetians are obsessed with the visual signs of racial difference, which haunt them and determine how they think and act. A more benign—but perhaps equally worrying—corollary to the graphic imagery of Brabantio, Roderigo, and Iago is

---

[35] For discussion, see Andrew Hadfield, 'Shakespeare and Republican Venice', in Shaul Bassi and Lauri Tosi (eds.), *Shakespeare and Venice* (Aldershot: Ashgate, forthcoming, 2011).

[36] William Shakespeare, *Othello*, Michael Neill (ed.) (Oxford: Oxford University Press, 2006), 1.1.66, 86–92. All subsequent references to *Othello* in parentheses in the text.

Desdemona's innocent defence of her husband in the trial scene: 'I saw Othello's visage in his mind' (1.3.250), to which the Duke eventually responds by telling Brabantio, 'If virtue no delighted beauty lack, | Your son-in-law is far more fair than black' (1.3.287–8). Even the nicest people in cosmopolitan Venice see the world in terms of black and white. The Duke, in upholding Venice's republican values cannot hide the fact that he still thinks in terms of black republicans and white republicans.

But if these are the popular forces within Venice that are ranged against the newly-weds, they also have powerful allies among the city's governing elite and state institutions, support from its republican heart. We witness the efficiency and humanity of the city's legal processes in the scenes immediately following Iago's and Roderigo's attempts to undermine the newlyweds. Othello is summoned to the Duke's palace where the senate is in emergency session to counter the Turkish threat to the Venetian outpost, Cyprus. Brabantio, after confronting Othello and demanding that he be sent to prison to await trial for his actions, insists on attending the meeting and having his demands met, as he is certain that his judgement will be upheld. In 1.3 we see the Duke and senators plan their military actions with great speed, appointing Othello as the best available military commander to deal with the situation. They then turn to the matter of the marriage and hear the evidence on each side. According to Brabantio, Desdemona must be abused because the only reason she could have married Othello was through witchcraft and the 'spells and medicines of mountebanks', the only reason for 'nature so preposterously to err' (1.3.62–3). Othello's defence is that he won the heart of Desdemona through the art of rhetoric, the chief republican virtue. After his defence of his actions the Duke admits that Othello's tales of his escapades among the cannibals and monsters who inhabit the most remote corners of the globe, 'would win my daughter too' (1.3.171). Accordingly, the Duke judges that the marriage can stand, despite the bitter protestations of Brabantio.

The scene shows Shakespeare's imagination to be absorbed in the world of the late sixteenth-century Venetian Republic and he had undoubtedly read the recently published works that described the city's people, institutions, and culture, most notably Lewis Lewkenor's translation of Gaspar Contarini's *Commonwealth and Government of Venice* (1599).[37] In departing so radically from his source, Giraldi Cinthio's sensationalist novella about the Moor of Venice, Shakespeare shows that he has much sympathy for the ways in which the Venetian senate deals with the evidence in a trial.[38] The Duke will not take Brabantio's assertions that Othello has drugged Desdemona as evidence and reprimands him for seeming to claim that his rank and status will carry the day:

> To vouch this is no proof
> Without more wider and more overt test

---

[37] Gaspar Contarini, *The Commonwealth and Government of Venice*, Lewis Lewkenor (trans.), (London: 1599). For comment see David McPherson, *Shakespeare, Jonson, and the Myth of Venice* (Newark: University of Delaware Press, 1990).

[38] Bullough, *Narrative and Dramatic*, 7: 193–252.

> Than these thin habits and poor likelihoods
> Of modern seeming do prefer against him.   (1.3.97–100)

What the Duke accepts as proof is persuasive argument and we have a striking contrast established in the first act between the value placed on rhetorical skill by the republican authorities and the impact of the visual imagination on the wider Venetian public (which, of course, also includes many of the same people). There is a utopian aspect to republicanism, a potential fault line between its hopes and expectations and the stubborn reality of the confusions and prejudices of ordinary people and daily life. *Othello* forces the audience to think about republican values and the means of fostering and enforcing them, perhaps the key issue in republican thinking. Can Venice impose the liberty it desires to preserve the city as its rulers think it should be? Or should its citizens have the liberty to think as they please and, if they so wish, choose freely to undermine that liberty? In essence, this is yet another version of the republican conundrum: do republican institutions make people virtuous or do republican institutions only work when people are already virtuous? According to Polybius, the Roman Republic undermined itself when it expanded too far and included too many people, very few of whom were actually committed to the Republic's original ideals.[39] Perhaps we are witnessing the same process happening to Shakespeare's Venice.[40]

In *Othello*, the Venetian state is strong enough to control its citizens. But when the action is translated to Cyprus, popular prejudices, sexual as well as racial, are overwhelmingly powerful. The city's institutions, under strain but functioning at home, are not there to prevent the tragedy unfolding.[41] It is worth noting further that only the women, Desdemona and Emilia, are actually Venetian. Othello, Iago, Roderigo, and Cassio are all foreigners in the service of Venice, a further indication that Venice is populated by people who do not understand its values yet who absorb its myths, including the belief that Venetian women were of great beauty and easy virtue.[42] At the end of *Othello* Venice looks vulnerable and isolated, safe only because the Turks were unfortunately destroyed in a storm, not because the city-state is robust enough to protect itself. Iago is led off to be tortured to reveal a truth that no one in the audience can believe will ever be revealed. Suddenly Venice looks rather like besieged England in the 1590s, not the perfect constitution that had endured for a millennium.

Shakespeare never abandoned his interest in republican topics or his interest in the crucial stages of Roman republican history. *Coriolanus* appears after the major

---

[39] Polybius, *The Rise of the Roman Empire*, Frank W. Walbank (trans.) (Harmondsworth: Penguin, 1979), pt. 6.

[40] It is an interesting, but probably unanswerable, question, how much Shakespeare actually knew about recent Venetian history. Venice, despite its spectacular victory over the Turks in the Battle of Lepanto (1571), was in terminal decline and the Turks already had effective domination of the Mediterranean.

[41] On sexual prejudice in *Othello* see Lisa Jardine, *Reading Shakespeare Historically* (London: Routledge, 1996), ch. 1.

[42] Virginia Mason Vaughan, *Othello: A Contextual History* (Cambridge: Cambridge University Press, 1994), ch. 4.

tragedies and just before the advent of the late plays, a sign that Shakespeare felt that republican subjects still had life left in them and an audience who wanted to witness them. *Coriolanus* cannot easily be reduced to any one particular message, or easily appropriated for a political cause, as its complicated critical history indicates.[43] But it is interesting to note that its opening scene involves a crisis in Rome and the citizens convinced that they have the right to revolt against the senators who they believe are hoarding food (a question that the play never actually answers). The situation recalls the opening of *Titus Andronicus*, Shakespeare's first Roman play. In *Coriolanus* Menenius appears to confront the arguments of the First Citizen with his fable of the belly. Menenius employs the ubiquitous image of the body politic, the most frequently used metaphor for the state in early modern political discourse.[44] For Menenius the rebellious members are mistaken in regarding the belly as 'idle and unactive' (1.1.98); they should accept the argument that

> The senators of Rome are this good belly,
> And you the mutinous members: for examine
> Their counsels and their cares, digest things rightly
> Touching the weal o'th'common, you shall find
> No public benefit which you receive
> But it proceeds or comes from them to you,
> And no way from yourselves.   (1.1.147–53)

Menenius' argument—admittedly, produced in difficult circumstances—presents an authoritarian model of society. Menenius sarcastically dismisses the First Citizen as 'the great toe of this assembly' because he is 'one o'th'lowest, basest, poorest | Of this most wise rebellion' (1.1.156–7). However, immediately before Menenius' explanation, it is not at all obvious that the First Citizen's ability to manipulate the political metaphor is any less convincing or plausible than that of Menenius, or that Menenius has the best of the argument. The citizen parrots the explanation he expects Menenius to give after his patrician adversary has introduced the image of the body politic:

> FIRST CIT: Your belly's answer—what?
> The kingly crown'd head, the vigilant eye,
> The counsellor heart, the arm our soldier,
> Our steed the leg, the tongue our trumpeter,
> With other muniments and petty helps
> In this our fabric, if that they—
> MEN: What then?
> 'Fore me, this fellow speaks! What then? What then?

---

[43] See David George (ed.), *Coriolanus: Shakespeare: The Critical Tradition* (London: Continuum, 2004).

[44] See D. G. Hale, *The Body Politic: A Political Metaphor in Renaissance English Literature* (The Hague: Mouton, 1971); Peter Burke, 'Tacitism, scepticism, and reason of state', in J. H. Burns and Mark Goldie (eds.), 479–98.

FIRST CIT: Should by the cormorant belly be restrain'd,
            Who is the sink o'th'body—
MEN: Well, what then?
First CIT: The former agents, if they did complain,
            What could the belly answer?

(1.1.113–24)

The First Citizen's notion of an integrated body politic, with different parts of the body dependent on others, all working together to produce a healthy whole, stands against the more authoritarian model adopted by Menenius.[45] The play does not force us to decide who is right, but leaves these images with us as a mirror through which to consider the action of the play. In the second act Coriolanus shows utter contempt for the citizens when he is obliged to display his wounds in order to be elected as consul, eschewing any notion of democracy or the need to answer to the necessities and desires of ordinary people. This failing leads to his banishment and persuades him, against his better judgement, to help the Volscians in their campaign against Rome. The scene (2.2) is, as Mark Kishlansky has pointed out, based on Shakespeare's observation of either 'wardmote selections of the London Common Council or of parliamentary selections'.[46] Clearly the electoral and political machinery of ancient Rome is being seen in terms of that of contemporary London. Shakespeare might not have been arguing a fiercely partisan republican or democratic case in 1608, but he was certainly showing that thinking of Jacobean London in terms of Rome's republican political structure was a valid enterprise. Furthermore, it is hard to make a case for Coriolanus' behaviour, which suggests a sympathy for the rights of the citizens, and perhaps indicates that Shakespeare felt that his best interests lay with the cause of urban freemen.[47]

Shakespeare probably thought that republican values and virtues were unlikely to be adopted in England in his lifetime.[48] Often, republican ideals of liberty, justice, and stability were simply not practical solutions to problems in a world that had never been able to rise above its dangerous divisions and prejudices, and had a complicated history which could not easily be unwritten. Nevertheless, his plays usually represent republican ideals positively, even when they do not succeed, as is the case in the first two Roman plays and *Othello*. Certainly no one seeing the plays on stage would prefer to live in fifteenth-century England instead of Venice, or imperial rather than republican Rome. Perhaps republican society, like Montaigne's cannibals, opened up a critical utopian space which could be used to think constructively about contemporary issues and problems.

---

[45] Andrew Gurr, '*Coriolanus* and the Body Politic', *Shakespeare Survey* 28 (1975), 63–9; D. G. Hale, '*Coriolanus*: The Death of a Political Metaphor', *Shakespeare Survey* 22 (1971), 197–202.

[46] Mark A. Kishlansky, *Parliamentary Selection: Social and Political Choice in Early Modern England* (Cambridge: Cambridge University Press, 1986), 5.

[47] See Phil Withington, *The Politics of Commonwealth: Citizens and Freemen in Early Modern England* (Cambridge: Cambridge University Press, 2005).

[48] Compare Sir Philip Sidney's reaction to Venice: Alan Stewart, *Philip Sidney: A Double Life* (London: Pimlico, 2001), 116.

CHAPTER 33

··

EMPIRE

··

BRIAN C. LOCKEY

'O Wisdom Imperiall: most diligently, to be Imitated.'[1]

THE ancient Roman Empire loomed large in the early modern imagination. William Shakespeare wrote and co-wrote a number of plays and poems about ancient Rome, the most important of which, *Julius Caesar* and *Antony and Cleopatra*, recount the last days of the Roman Republic and the empire's foundation. It is often assumed that, in contrast to Shakespeare's source, Plutarch, whose sympathies were with the Roman Republic, early modern English playwrights and spectators were predisposed to see imperial rule in positive terms. After all, the emperor of Rome was essentially a monarch, who ruled in a manner that was familiar to European subject and sovereign alike.[2] But the political views of Shakespeare were in all probability more complex. Andrew Hadfield has recently argued that, based on some of his earliest printed works, *Titus Andronicus*, the *Rape of Lucrece*, and *Venus and Adonis*, the young Shakespeare was at least initially seeking to fashion himself as a republican author.[3] And despite whatever might be assumed about the early modern audiences' sympathies for the wielders of Roman imperial might, it is clear that the plays themselves are complex, displaying dramatic tensions between the sympathy that is exhibited for the opponents and defenders of centralized imperial rule.

During the early modern period, most European sovereigns sought to identify themselves with ancient Roman imperial power, but England carved out an imperial identity both in imitation of ancient Rome and in competition with contemporary Rome. The English Crown had a history of tension with the Roman curia that went

---

[1] John Dee, *General And Rare Memorials pertayning to the Perfect Arte of Navigation* (London, 1577), sig. G4.

[2] See for example, the introduction to *Julius Caesar* in G. Blakemore Evans et al. (eds.), *The Riverside Shakespeare*, 2nd edn. (New York: Houghton Mifflin, 1997), 1147.

[3] Andrew Hadfield, *Shakespeare and Republicanism* (Cambridge: Cambridge University Press, 2005), 100.

back to the medieval period. The first statute of *praemunire*, passed during the reign of Edward III, constituted an attempt to block the ability of the Church's canon law courts from drawing 'all persons of the king's ligeance' to venues that owed their allegiance to the Church. Subsequent statutes of *praemunire* restricted the right of the Church and its courts to transfer tribute or other forms of imposition outside of the realm.[4] During the late medieval period, the writ of *praemunire* declined in importance, but during the years leading up to the Reformation, it once again became an important royal tool used to restrain the power of the clergy.[5]

The Statute in Restraint of Appeals of 1533, which famously refers to the kingdom of England as an empire, is an important part of this history. The act forbade appeals to the Pope in religious matters and made King Henry VIII Head of the Church, declaring that 'this realm of *England* is an Empire, and so hath been accepted in the World, governed by one Supreme Head and King, having the Dignity and Royal Estate of the Imperial Crown of the same'.[6] Effectively granting the king power over the spiritual and temporal realms, the statute went on to make direct reference to the statutes of *praemunire* that were passed during the fourteenth century, which restricted the ability of English subjects to appeal to the Roman curia. The most significant formal declaration of empire during the period was therefore based on a defensive conception of sovereignty, according to which the English Crown should have complete control over its own internal affairs, whether they be temporal or spiritual. The connotation of overseas expansion and colonization is a later development that literary historians normally associate with the late sixteenth- and early seventeenth-century settlements in Ireland and Virginia.[7]

William Shakespeare's late play, *Cymbeline*, reflects the early modern tensions within English and British imperial ideology concerning identification with and rejection of Roman imperialism. Based on Raphael Holinshed's *Chronicles of England, Scotland, and Ireland* (1577, 1587), *Cymbeline* dramatizes the story of the legendary king of Britain, who led the Britons in a successful rebellion against the Roman Empire. At the centre of the tensions between Britain and Rome is a dispute over tribute, which the British Crown owes to imperial Rome. In the middle of the play, Cymbeline addresses the Roman ambassador, Caius Lucius, declaring, 'You must know, | Till the injurious Romans did extort | This tribute from us we were free' (3.1.46–8).[8] As a result, he explains that the Britons intend 'to shake off' the Roman 'yoke' (3.1.51). Cymbeline's declaration of

---

[4] See 27 Edw. III stat. I, c. I (1353) in *The Statutes at large, from Magna Charta to the Thirtieth Year of King George II, inclusive*, in 6 vols. (London: 1758), 1, sigs. 2N2–2N2v. See also 35 Edw. I stat. I, c. 2 [1, sig. x4v], 25 Edw III stat. 6 (1350) [1, sig. 2M4], and 16 Ric. II c. 5 (1392) [1, sigs. 3G1v–3G2v].

[5] J. A. Guy, 'Henry VIII and the Praemunire Maneuvers of 1530–31', *The English Historical Review* 97.384 (1982), 481–503.

[6] See 24 Henry VIII. c. 12 (1533), in *The Statutes*, 2, sig. A1v.

[7] Tristan Marshall, *Theatre and Empire: Great Britain on the London Stages under James VI and James I* (Manchester: Manchester University Press, 2000), 11–28; Walter S. H. Lim, *The Arts of Empire: The Poetics of Colonialism from Ralegh to Milton* (Newark: University of Delaware Press, 1998).

[8] All citations from Shakespeare are from *The Complete Works*, Stanley Wells and Gary Taylor (eds.), 2nd edn. (Oxford: Oxford University Press, 2005).

independence from Roman rule sets in motion a military conflict in which the Britons successfully repel the invading Roman army.

Paradoxically, after having successfully gained the British Crown's independence from the Roman Empire, Cymbeline decides in the last scene to re-submit himself to Roman rule. Having at first condemned to death a diverse collection of Italian and British prisoners-of-war, including Caius Lucius, Cymbeline suddenly reverses his decision, applying the legal principle of equity to the judgements, and sparing the prisoners' lives.[9] Having successfully taken up arms in order to gain back self-determination for Britain, Cymbeline decides after all that Britain will submit itself to Roman imperial rule, even agreeing to pay the disputed tribute. The imperial logic at work in the play is an example of what medieval and Renaissance writers called *translatio imperii*, the transfer of empire from East to West, Troy to Greece to Rome to Britain.[10] Britain becomes the inheritor of Roman imperial might, a new power in the West that could literally take the place of Rome in terms of spreading civilization to the 'barbarians'. Thus, in the final verses of the play, the Soothsayer declares the fulfilment of his own earlier prediction, namely that 'the Roman eagle | From south to west of wing soaring aloft' would vanish into the 'sun', the radiant Cymbeline, 'which shines here in the west' (5.6.471–7). Finally, Cymbeline himself announces that 'A Roman and a British ensign [will] wave | Friendly together' (5.6.481–2). Not surprisingly, the notion of *translatio imperii* permeated James I's court as well. Throughout his reign (1603–25), James I presented himself as a modern instantiation of Augustus Caesar, and the composite monarchy of Britain was central to this self-presentation. In contrast to Elizabeth who, like her father, presented her imperial rule as encompassing England only, James presented himself as the emperor of Britain, the new or, should we say, ancient British polity comprising England, Scotland, Wales, and sometimes Ireland. The king's court, the architecture of his palaces, the frontispieces on the title-pages of books associated with the king and his court all bore signs of imperial Roman influence.[11]

Much of the dramatic tension in *Cymbeline* centres around a struggle between the forces of retrogression that threaten to return Britain to its own 'barbaric' past and the hope that the Britons have attained civility through their contact with Rome. Throughout Cymbeline's Britain, rumours abound of the reputed barbarity of outlying Britons. Innogen describes Belarius and the prince's cave-dwelling as 'some savage hold' and Cloten's speaks of 'some villain mountaineers', invoking rumours that savage elements still exist on the margins of Britain (3.6.18; 4.2.73). Shakespeare owed this less mythologized, less romanticized notion of ancient Britain to antiquarians such as William Camden and John Speed, who portrayed the ancient Britons as savage barbarians, to whom the

---

[9] Brian Lockey, *Law and Empire in English Renaissance Literature* (Cambridge: Cambridge University Press, 2006), 183–4.

[10] Anthony Pagden, *Lords of All the World, Ideologies of Empire in Spain, Britain, and France c.1500–c.1800* (New Haven, CT: Yale University Press, 1995), 11–28.

[11] Jonathan Goldberg, *James I and the Politics of Literature: Jonson, Shakespeare, Donne, and Their Contemporaries* (Baltimore, MD: The Johns Hopkins University Press, 1983), 33.

Roman conquest had introduced civility.[12] Perhaps the most notable and graphic representation of the idea that imperial Rome had introduced civility into Britain can be found in the frontispiece to Speed's *The Theatre of the British Empire*, a detailed atlas and historical and geographical description of the kingdoms comprising the British archipelago. The frontispiece of the 1616 Latin edition is a Romanesque series of five arches and columns, containing pictorial representatives of the five nations that had inhabited the islands. And in contrast to earlier romanticized accounts of the ancient Britons, Speed's Britannia is represented by a painted savage, wearing only a loin cloth and a robe (see Figure 33.1).[13] Contemporary readers of Edmund Spenser's *A View of the Present State of Ireland* would have been reminded of the English poet's descriptions of the wild Irish, who supposedly scorned English clothing for a simple mantle or cloak.[14]

On the other hand, Shakespeare includes indications that the Roman conquest has recently introduced civility into barbaric Britain. Thus Posthumus tells his Italian friend, Philario, that the Britons are now 'more ordered than when Julius Caesar | Smiled at their lack of skill' (2.4.21–2). He goes on to remark that the Britons are 'people such | That mend upon the world', effectively describing a progression through which the Britons have developed greater 'discipline' and order (2.4.25–6; 23). The *translatio imperii* at work in such passages ultimately suggests an important parallel: just as Rome introduced civility to a rapidly mending Britain, so James's newly united Britain could introduce civility through its conquest of Ireland and other 'savage' territories such as Virginia.[15]

But while certain passages of the play present Cymbeline's Britain as inheriting the glory of Rome, other passages gesture in the opposite direction, presenting Britain as a kind of imperial 'Anti-Rome'. In contrast to the new antiquarians, medieval chroniclers such as Geoffrey of Monmouth had presented the ancient history of Britain not as one mired in savagery and barbarism, but one that was based on a Britain that wielded imperial might that made it Rome's rival of the ancient world.[16] A second inheritance, akin to the traditional form of *translatio imperii*, was therefore not one in which Britain would inherit empire from Rome but rather a British Empire that would emerge from

[12] William Camden, 'Of the Diversity of Names of this Island' (1604), in *A Collection of Curious Discourses Written by Eminent Antiquaries*, T. Hearne (ed.) (Oxford, 1720), sigs. T3, T4; Camden, *Britannia*, trans. and enlarged by Richard Gough (London, 1789), sig. S2; Mark Netzloff, *England's Internal Colonies: Class, Capital, and the Literature of Early Modern English Colonialism* (Basingstoke: Palgrave Macmillan, 2003), 177; Debora Shuger, 'Irishmen, Aristocrats, and other White Barbarians', *Renaissance Quarterly* 50 (1997): 494–525.

[13] John Speed, *Theatrum imperii Magnae Britanniae* (London, 1616), sig. A1.

[14] Edmund Spenser, *A View of the Present State of Ireland*, Rudolf Gottfried (ed.), in *The Works of Edmund Spenser: A Variorum Edition* (Baltimore, MD: The Johns Hopkins University Press, 1949), 9, ll. 1514–1663.

[15] Nicholas Canny, *The Elizabethan Conquest of Ireland: A Pattern Established 1565–76* (New York: Barnes and Noble, 1976), 128–9, Andrew Hadfield, *Shakespeare, Spenser, and the Matter of Britain* (Basingstoke: Palgrave Macmillan, 2004), 17–19, 90–104.

[16] Geoffrey of Monmouth, *The History of the Kings of Britain*, Sebastian Evans (trans.) (New York: E. P. Dutton, 1958), 9.16.206. See also Christopher Hodgkins, *Reforming Empire: Protestant Colonialism and Conscience in British Literature* (Columbia: University of Missouri Press, 2002), 12–17.

FIGURE 33.1. John Speed, *Theatrum imperii Magnae Britanniae* (London, 1616), title-page. By permission of the Folger Shakespeare Library.

ancient Britain itself. In addition to the inheritance from Rome, *Cymbeline* bears signs of this native imperial inheritance. In declaring Britain's independence from Rome, Cymbeline alludes to a self-determining organic British identity that had its own integrity independent of Roman influences. Thus, in a speech that is, in equal parts, rambling and eloquent, the king declares to Caius Lucius,

> We do say then to Caesar,
> Our ancestor was that Mulmutius which
> Ordained our laws, whose use the sword of Caesar
> Hath too much mangled, whose repair and franchise
> Shall by the power we hold be our good deed,

Though Rome be therefore angry. Mulmutius made our laws,
Who was the first of Britain which did put
His brows within a golden crown and called
Himself a king.   (3.1.53–61)

In contrast with the work of Camden and other antiquarians, this speech presents the ancient Britons not as savage and lawless barbarians who were civilized by the invading Romans, but rather as a people blessed with their own independent political and legal traditions that have legitimacy apart from any contact with the Roman Empire. Cymbeline seeks to throw off Roman rule not in imitation of Roman self-determination and imperial might but rather in order to restore a native British model of self-determination. In this respect, Cymbeline's speech alludes to contemporary common lawyers such as Sir Edward Coke, who had followed Geoffrey's medieval account of Britain's ancient history, according to which the island had been settled and founded by ancient Trojan refugees led by Brutus. According to this account of the common law, Brutus had not founded a new political and legal regime of Britain, but rather he had exported an existing political structure from ancient Trojan law. According to Coke, Mulmutius was the first of the ancient kings of Britain to record the law that Brutus exported to Britain and established there.[17]

In declaring independence from Rome, then, Cymbeline would be restoring the kingdom to its ancient pre-Roman grandeur and to its Trojan roots. To contemporaries, aware that James I himself favoured greater political and legal union with Scotland as well as the revival of the ancient identity of Britain based on such a union, Cymbeline must have been perceived as reflecting back to James his own plans to restore a reinvigorated Britain to its ancient greatness.[18] Shakespeare and James were not the only ones of the period to see the mythical polity of Britain as a model on which to base a contemporary conception of imperial rule. John Dee was perhaps the first English writer to apply the phrase 'British Empire' to an imperial polity with overseas territories.[19] And for Dee, the model for such an entity was not the Roman Empire—it was rather a united Britain governed by the 'Peaceable, and Prouident Saxon, King Edgar', who established a 'Grand Nauy of 4000 Sayle' in order to guard and protect the island and project its power. He goes on to admonish Queen Elizabeth with the example of King Edgar, the imperial monarch: 'shall we . . . not Iudge it, some part of Wisdome, to Imitate carefully, in some little Proportion, (though not with so many Thousands,) the prosperous Pastimes of Peaceable King Edgar, that Saxonicall Alexander?'[20] Later in the century, Dee's portrayal of King Edgar as a model for imperial glory was incorporated by Richard

[17] Sir Edward Coke, *The Selected Writings of Sir Edward Coke*, Steve Sheppard (ed.), vol. 1 (Indianapolis, IN: Liberty Fund, 2003), 66–7.

[18] For a discussion of diverse views on the union, see Galloway, *The Union of England and Scotland* (Edinburgh: John Donald Ltd, 1986), 30–55.

[19] Netzloff, *England's Internal Colonies*, 9.

[20] John Dee, *General and Rare Monuments pertaining to the Perfect Arte of Navigation*, sigs. G4v; G4v–H1.

Hakluyt into his collection of English and European accounts of exploration. The first volume of the 1599 edition of the *Principal Navigations* begins with a transcription of Dee's account of King Edgar, the first 'imperial' monarch of the British Isles.[21] In promoting such an imperial identity for Britain, both Dee and Hakluyt were simply following the precedent established by Geoffrey himself, whose *Historia regum Britanniae* presented the mythical King Arthur as a conqueror, whose imperial rule supposedly stretched from Greenland to the edge of Rome itself.[22]

***

This famous Iland in the Virginian Sea.

—Fynes Moryson[23]

Many early modern historians and literary scholars view the English conquest of Ireland as an important step on the way to the eventual emergence of the British Empire. According to this historical account, the strategies and patterns of English settlement within the New World were modelled after those that occurred first in Ireland.[24] The historical account by which Ireland became a stepping stone on the way to English expansionism into the Atlantic has become an important paradigm within historiographical and literary studies. Within Shakespeare studies, this 'Atlanticist paradigm' has been successfully applied to *The Tempest*, such that Caliban is viewed as an early modern allegory for either the native Irishman or the Amerindian or alternatively as an amalgamation of a number of different portrayals of the exotic or colonized other.[25] And just as the English invasion of Ireland was justified partly on the basis of reforming 'barbaric' Irish customs, Prospero's conquest of the island is meant to instruct the islander, Caliban, in the ways of civility.

In addition to the Atlanticist paradigm, there exists a competing approach to the relationship between England and Ireland. Andrew Murphy has called this second

[21] Richard Hakluyt, *The Principal Navigations, Voyages, Traffiques, & Discoveries of the English Nation*, vol. 1 (New York: Macmillan, 1903), 16–24.

[22] Hodgkins, *Reforming Empire*, 14–17.

[23] Fynes Moryson, *The Itinerary of Fynes Moryson*, Moryson describing Ireland during his travels, vol. 4 (Glasgow: James MacLehose and Sons, 1908), 185.

[24] Canny, *The Elizabethan Conquest of Ireland*, and Hans Pawlisch, *Sir John Davies and the Conquest of Ireland: A Study in Legal Imperialism* (Cambridge: Cambridge University Press, 1985). More recently, see Christopher Highley, *Shakespeare, Spenser, and the Crisis in Ireland* (Cambridge: Cambridge University Press, 1997), and Canny, *Making Ireland British 1580-1650* (Oxford: Oxford University Press, 2003). For some context on what has been called the Atlanticist paradigm in literary studies, see Andrew Murphy, 'Revising Criticism: Ireland and the British Model', in David J. Baker and Willy Maley (eds.), *British Identities and English Renaissance Literature* (Cambridge: Cambridge University Press, 2002), 24–36; and Patricia Palmer, *Language and Conquest in Early Modern Ireland: English Renaissance Literature and Elizabethan Imperial Expansion* (Cambridge: Cambridge University Press, 2001), 15–39.

[25] Paul Brown, '"This Thing of Darkness I Acknowledge Mine": *The Tempest* and the Discourse of Colonialism', in *Political Shakespeare: New Essays in Cultural Materialism* (Manchester: Manchester University Press, 1985), 48–71; Barbara Fuchs, 'Conquering Islands: Contextualizing *The Tempest*', *Shakespeare Quarterly* 48.1 (1997), 45–62.

historical approach the 'archipelagic paradigm', while others have referred to it more generally as the 'British paradigm'. According to this approach, the English Crown's *dominium* over Ireland had little in common with other sixteenth-century colonialist ventures. Rather, because parts of Ireland had been subject to English governance, at least since the early Anglo-Norman settlers established settlements there during the twelfth century, the history of English governance in Ireland should be viewed according to the similarities between the routines of governance in Ireland and in England. Accordingly, English officials in Ireland intended to assimilate Ireland into English rule in the same way as the English countryside was being assimilated into more centralized government.[26] Irish revolt and rebellion are explained 'in terms of malfunction in administration' rather than as part of a larger historical process of Irish rebels unshackling the Irish from England's colonial rule.[27]

In turn, Ireland becomes less a model for invasion and conquest from which to base the future expansion of the British Empire than it is an integral, albeit outlying and rebellious, kingdom within an emerging British polity, governed by what David Armitage calls a composite monarchy (whereby a monarch ruled over separate and distinct kingdoms that were to be unified by their combined Britishness).[28] And if we take the building of British identity as integral to the eventual construction of a British imperial identity, then the integration and assimilation of Ireland into a framework of English governance would still be an important step for imagining and understanding the empire. At first glance, such an approach might seem to be reductively Anglocentric, but if one takes as one's starting point the history of interactions, conflicts, and encounters between the nations of the British archipelago, then a 'British' approach might be the opposite, effectively interrogating the Anglocentric nature of traditional history and literary criticism.[29]

David J. Baker has approached *Henry V* from the 'British' perspective, beginning with the premiss that the play presents an ideal whereby the various nationalities that comprise the Atlantic archipelago are meant to unite in Henry V's conquest of France. *Henry V* (1599) predates the attempts to unite politically the kingdoms of Scotland and England under James I. Even so, the play celebrates the union of disparate ethnic identities—comprising what Jonathan Dollimore and Alan Sinfield call the 'hoped-for unity of Britain'—as a way of promoting Anglo patriotism.[30] The play begins with the

---

[26] Murphy, 'Revising criticism', 29–30. See Brendan Bradshaw, *The Irish Constitutional Revolution in the Sixteenth Century* (Cambridge: Cambridge University Press, 1979).

[27] Canny, *Kingdom and Colony: Ireland in the Atlantic World, 1560–1800* (Baltimore, MD: The Johns Hopkins University Press, 1988), 11.

[28] Armitage, *The Ideological Origins of the British Empire* (Cambridge: Cambridge University Press, 2000), 22–3.

[29] J. G. A. Pocock, 'British History: A Plea for a New Subject', *Journal of Modern History* 47 (1975), 601–28; David J. Baker, *Between Nations: Shakespeare, Spenser, Marvell, and the Question of Britain* (Stanford, CA: Stanford University Press, 1997), 1–16; Willy Maley, *Nation, State and Empire in English Renaissance Literature* (Basingstoke: Palgrave Macmillan, 2003), 7–29.

[30] Jonathan Dollimore and Alan Sinfield, 'History and Ideology: the Instance of *Henry V*', in John Drakakis (ed.), *Alternative Shakespeares* (London: Methuen, 1985), 21. See also Claire McEachern, '*Henry V* and the Paradox of the Body Politic', *Shakespeare Quarterly* 45 (1994), 44.

threat that regional feuding may be on the verge of breaking out. Henry V acknowledges early in the first act that invading France carries certain risks with it, chief among them that Scotland 'hath been still a giddy neighbour to us' (1.2.145). After invoking this threat from the north, the play seems to point in the opposite direction, illustrating a version of history in which the representatives of the 'other' island nationalities of Britain swear allegiance to and facilitate the dominance of England's political hegemony. Indeed, the play assimilates and makes British the nationalities that comprise the archipelago by showing how willingly and loyally the Welsh, Scottish, and Irish soldiers serve Henry and his cause, and how they submit their own national identity to the English identity, speaking the English language, however imperfectly, rather than their own.

Note then that this imperial paradigm stands in stark contrast to the Atlanticist paradigm, by which the conquest of Ireland serves as the model on which other expansionist ventures in the Americas and elsewhere could be patterned. Within the archipelagic or British paradigm, the other nationalities that comprise the British Isles assimilate themselves into English or British expansionism in such a way that they become stakeholders in the imperial venture. Most importantly, while English commoners from Cheapside such as Pistol and Bardolph treat the invasion of France as an opportunity for self-enrichment, the Irishman MacMorris, the Welshman Fluellen, and the Scotsman Jamy selflessly throw themselves into the fight. And to the extent that Henry identifies himself as Fluellen's countryman, telling him after the Battle of Agincourt, 'I am Welsh, you know, good countryman', the play simultaneously re-centres and decentres the locus of power from England to Wales and back again (4.7.103).[31] In effect, the marginal kingdom of Wales becomes a centre from which to marshal a multivalent English or British nationalism that encompasses the surrounding kingdoms as well.

But, as Baker has shown, there are problems with this thesis as well, especially having to do with anxiety over the question of Ireland. In 1599, Robert Devereux, Earl of Essex and the Queen's favourite, led a failed campaign of 16,000 troops to vanquish the Irish rebel Hugh O'Neill, Earl of Tyrone.[32] After he had made a humiliating truce with O'Neill, he directly disobeyed Queen Elizabeth, returning to court and intruding upon the Queen in her bedchamber when she was not properly dressed, an offence for which he was eventually arrested and tried for treason. The first version of *Henry V* to be staged in London seems to have been written during the period between March 27 1599 when Essex departed for Ireland and September 28 1599 when he returned to London. During the last appearance of the Chorus, Shakespeare celebrates Henry's return to London after the Battle of Agincourt by comparing it to Essex's eventual triumphant return to London from Ireland:

> But now behold,
> In the quick forge and working-house of thought,

[31] Baker, *Between Nations*, 50–62.
[32] Baker, *Between Nations*, 25.

> How London doth pour out her citizens.
> The Mayor and all his brethren, in best sort,
> Like to the senators of th'antique Rome,
> With the plebeians swarming at their heels,
> Go forth and fetch their conqu'ring Caesar in—
> As by a lower but high-loving likelihood,
> Were now the general of our gracious Empress—
> As in good time he may—from Ireland coming,
> Bringing rebellion broachèd on his sword,
> How many would the peaceful city quit
> To welcome him! Much more, and much more cause,
> Did they this Harry.   (5.0.22–35)

Note that this passage begins with a standard expression of *translatio imperii*, in which Henry V's triumphant return to London after having defeated the French is compared to Julius Caesar's triumphant return to Rome. Toward the end of the passage, the comparison extends to Essex's future return to London from Ireland, and once again, the Chorus invokes the crowds of tumultuous Londoners that will presumably welcome him.

Given what we have already said about the way in which this play seems to assimilate the national and ethnic differences within the British Isles into an English or proto-British nationalism, this passage describing Essex's conquest of Ireland seems oddly out of place. The series of analogies drawn here, between Caesar's conquests during the Roman Empire and Henry V's conquest of France and then between the latter and Essex's invasion of Ireland, better fits the Atlanticist paradigm that views Ireland as a separate and independent polity that was invaded and conquered by the Elizabethan English in order to submit that polity to the English Crown and the empire that it was establishing. The notion that Ireland's inhabitants were not committed and loyal subjects of the English Crown in 1599 would therefore belie the notion, seemingly put forward throughout so much of the play, that an Irishman such as MacMorris could be a loyal soldier in Henry's invading army. Of course, as David J. Baker and others have noted, after Essex's disastrous return to London, the comparisons that were made in the original version of the play had suddenly become politically dangerous. And this is, in effect, the reason why two versions of the play exist: the version printed in the 1623 First Folio, which makes naive reference to Essex's Irish campaign and a second version that edits out the references to Essex as well as some of the scenes that are most damning of the King's cause in France, including the early scene in which the Church officials scheme to manipulate Henry into invading France.[33]

This second version of the play, printed in the 1600 Quarto edition, omits two of the characters, the Irishman, MacMorris, and the Scotsman, Jamy, that are so crucial to the assimilationist thesis that I have put forward above. Perhaps, in light of Essex's disastrous campaign in Ireland, any reference to the other British nationalities that England sought either to eliminate or assimilate into itself was seen as dangerous. If this

---

[33] Baker, *Between Nations*, 25–9.

is the case, then it is worth reconsidering whether such characters are really assimilated into a coherent Anglo patriotism or proto-British nationalism during the course of the play. Indeed, it is even possible that Shakespeare is advancing a critique of imperial ideology from the perspective of the British nationalities that existed on the margins of the English centre.

One such critique involves the Welshman, Fluellen, who appears in both the Quarto and the Folio versions of the play. At issue is Fluellen's signature mispronunciations of the English language and his incendiary habit of comparing the present to the classical Roman and Greek past. At one point, Fluellen compares King Henry to Alexander the Great, or as he terms him, 'Alexander the Pig' (Fluellen frequently pronounces the English 'b' as a 'p') (4.7.12–13). Fluellen goes into great detail about the parallels between Henry and Alexander, the most important being that both killed their best friends:

> As Alexander killed his friend Clietus, being in his ales and his cups, so also Harry Monmouth, being in his right wits and his good judgements, turned away the fat knight with the great-belly doublet—he was full of jests and gipes and knaveries and mocks—I have forgot his name.   (4.7.43–8)

As Stephen Greenblatt has noted, the comparison is 'potentially devastating', because it records and remembers uncomfortable historical facts about Henry's past friendship with Falstaff that would better be forgotten.[34] Of course, there is an obvious irony here as well—Fluellen is either too naive or too circumspect to extend the comparison of Alexander enjoying 'his ales and his cups' to Henry, but spectators would have immediately remembered that young Harry also had a fondness for drunken revelry. Most importantly, as Leeds Barroll has noted, the comparison reminds the reader that, more than anything else, Alexander was remembered during the Renaissance through the lens of the pirate who, when accused by Alexander of the crime of robbery, compared his own minor thievery to Alexander's greater robbery through conquest.[35] Indeed, Shakespeare's play implies precisely the same comparison when one considers the proximity of Henry's speech threatening rape and pillage before the gates of Harfleur to the subsequent execution of Bardolph for the minor crime of stealing a pax (3.3.84–126, 3.6.38). Ultimately, it seems that Fluellen's comparison functions to disrupt the coherent British imperial identity that Henry's invasion of France seeks to establish. Hence, disruptive aspects inhering in the plurality of British identities serve to counter the notion of a coherent British Empire. In other words, Shakespeare could critique empire as well as promote it.

---

[34] Stephen Greenblatt, *Shakespearean Negotiations: The Circulation of Social Energy in Renaissance England* (Berkeley: University of California Press, 1989), 57.

[35] Leeds Barroll, *Shakespearean Tragedy: Genre, Tradition, and Change in Antony and Cleopatra* (London: Associated University Presses, 1984), 250–1. See also Patricia Parker, 'Uncertain Unions: Welsh Leeks in *Henry V*', in David J. Baker and Willy Maley (eds.), *British Identities and English Renaissance Literature* (Cambridge: Cambridge University Press, 2002), 85.

***

> The Gaules used to drinke their enemyes blodd and to painte themselves therewith So allsoe they write that the owlde Irishe weare wonte And so have I sene some of the Irishe doe.[36]

More than any other Shakespeare play, *The Tempest* lends itself to the topic of empire. The truth, however, is that other than the *translatio imperii* implicit in Gonzalo's comparison in Act 2 of Princess Claribel's marriage to the King of Tunis with Aeneas' love affair with Queen Dido of Carthage, *The Tempest* has little to do with the traditional questions of identity that accompany empire building (2.1.7–102). Rather, *The Tempest* more directly addresses the related subject of how to justify conquest of overseas populations and colonization of unfamiliar lands, enterprises that came to be seen as concomitant to the establishment of an overseas empire.[37] At least three significant justifications for establishing colonies and conquering foreign populations existed during this period: the argument that the native population had failed to cultivate the land properly; the argument that the native population could be conquered because they were unbelievers; and finally the argument that the barbarous or unnatural behaviour of the native populations justified conquest.

The first of the three, called the *res nullius* argument, held that populations that did not cultivate their land could be justly conquered. Interestingly, this argument emerges in the first important fictional account of the New World published in England, Sir Thomas More's *Utopia*. Toward the beginning of his account of Utopian customs, Raphael Hythloday discusses the island nation's policy on establishing colonies on the mainland. He explains that if the population of the entire island exceeds a certain quota, 'then they enrol citizens out of every city and plant a colony under their own laws on the mainland near them, wherever the natives have plenty of unoccupied and uncultivated land'. Hythloday explains that normally the natives want to live with the Utopians, especially since the Utopians 'make the land yield an abundance for all'; however, if the natives do not submit to the Utopian laws, then the Utopian settlers 'drive them out of the land they claim for themselves'. Furthermore the Utopians feel perfectly justified in doing so since they say it is 'justifiable to make war on people who leave their land idle and waste, yet forbid the use of it to others who, by the law of nature ought to be supported from it'.[38] It is worth noting that John Locke popularized precisely the same justification for colonization toward the end of the seventeenth century, and well into the eighteenth century, the *res nullius* argument was seen as the most persuasive justification of British and French conquest and colonization of the New World.[39]

---

[36] Spenser, *A View of the Present State of Ireland*, ll. 1933–6.
[37] Dee, *General and Rare Monuments*, sigs. G4v–H1.
[38] Sir Thomas More, *Utopia*, Robert M. Adams (trans. and ed.) (New York: Norton 1992), 41.
[39] Pagden, *Lords of All the World*, 77–86.

During the century that preceded Shakespeare's career, however, there existed other impetuses for overseas settlement that had little to do with the *res nullius* argument. Indeed, more important than any other factor in the construction of the British Empire was the prior existence of the Spanish Empire and especially the English perception of the hegemony of the Spanish imperial crown.[40] One of the earliest English responses to the Spanish Empire during this period was Richard Eden's translation of portions of Peter Martyr's *De orbe novo decades*, a work of early modern humanism that recounted the history of Spanish overseas expansion (1555). Translated during the reign of Catholic Queen Mary Tudor, *The Decades of the new worlde*, as the work was called in the English translation, was prefaced by expressions of effusive praise for the Spanish conquest of the Americas. Eden saw the Spanish conquests as fulfilling a religious mission that had been assigned to the Spanish Crown by God, and he urged the English Crown to emulate them.[41]

During the reign of the Protestant Queen of England, Elizabeth I, English perceptions of Spain changed dramatically. Partly due to the threat that Spain presented to England itself and partly as a result of written accounts of Spanish atrocities in the New World by Bartolomé de las Casas and others, the English began to see the Spanish conquistadores as cruel and merciless. In contrast, England's own expansion into the Americas was viewed as liberating enslaved and persecuted subjects from Spanish oppression. In the *Discovery of Guiana* (1596), Sir Walter Ralegh recounts his encounter with the inhabitants of Trinidad:

> I called all the captains [of the native inhabitants] of the island together that were enemies to the Spaniards.... And by my Indian interpreter, which I carried out of England, I made them understand that I was the servant of a queen who was the great cacique of the north, and a virgin, and had more caciqui under her than there were trees in that island; that she was an enemy to the Castellani in respect of their tyranny and oppression, and that she delivered all such nations about her, as were by them oppressed; and having freed all the coast of the northern world from their servitude, had sent me to free them also, and withal to defend the country of Guiana from their invasion and conquest.[42]

In response to Las Casas, the idea that Englishmen should 'deliver' or liberate those peoples oppressed by the bloodthirsty Spanish took on a life of its own. Late sixteenth- and early seventeenth-century Englishmen repeatedly saw their nation in competition with Spain, and much of this competition involved the idea that England had a more ethical strategy of foreign engagement than Spain had.[43] Ironically, their own legal and moral justifications for claiming dominion over Ireland and the New World largely

---

[40] For the literary history of English perceptions of Spain, see Eric Griffin, *English Renaissance Drama and the Specter of Spain: Ethnopoetics and Empire* (Philadelphia: University of Pennsylvania Press, 2009), and Barbara Fuchs, *Mimesis and Empire: The New World, Islam and European Identities* (Cambridge: Cambridge University Press, 2001), 118–38.

[41] Pietro Martire, *The Decades of the newe worlde or west India*, in *The first Three English books on America, Being chiefly Translations, Compilations, Etc by Richard Eden*, Edward Arber (ed.) (Birmingham: 1885), 49–60.

[42] Sir Walter Ralegh, *The Discovery of Guiana* (Hoboken, NJ: BiblioBytes, 1998).

[43] See William S. Maltby, *The Black Legend in England: the Development of Anti-Spanish Sentiment, 1558–1660* (Durham, NC: Duke University Press, 1971), 1–60; Richard McCabe, *Spenser's Monstrous Regiment: Elizabethan Ireland and the Poetics of Difference* (Oxford: Oxford University Press, 2002), 226–7; and Lockey, *Law and Empire*, 65–9.

replicated the logic that the Spanish had used, even if the English never presented the issues as lucidly as Spanish theologians previously had.[44]

The first justification for Spanish imperial expansion came in the form of the papal bulls of 1493 and the Treaty of Tordesillas of 1494, the purpose of which was to limit future rivalry between Castile and Portugal. The papal bulls conceded to Ferdinand and Isabella the right to rule over and occupy 'such islands and lands as you have discovered or are about to discover'.[45] According to the Pope, the justification for Spanish dominion over the Americas was religious: the bulls effectively deprived the inhabitants of the New World of their land and liberty by virtue of their unbelief. Accordingly, Spanish dominion over the Americas derived from God's grace such that no non-Christian could lawfully claim the right to own property or to sovereignty.[46]

English writers emulated the Spanish with regard to religion as a justification for expansionism and conquest. While Protestant England owed no allegiance to the Pope or any other religious authority beyond the Crown itself, Richard Hakluyt nevertheless claimed that the kings and queens of England 'have the name of Defendors of the Faithe' and that they had an obligation 'to mayneteyne and patronize the faith of Christe, but also to inlarge and advaunce the same',[47] In addition, the Jamestown charter of 1609 proclaimed that the purpose of the settlement was to serve 'in propagating of Christian religion to such people'.[48] In spite of such early declarations of faith as a rationale for imperial expansionism, there is considerable debate among historians and literary critics on the extent to which the religious mission was central to English imperial ventures. While emulation of the Spanish religious mission was an important justification for expansion into the Americas, it is also clear that the English colonists lacked the same code of religious uniformity enjoyed by their Spanish counterparts. To the extent that there was some loose form of uniformity in the English colonies, one might argue that the religious belief of all the English colonists could be broadly described as Calvinist. However, as Anthony Pagden has noted, 'such men had little real interest in converting the Native Americans'.[49] Indeed, as David Armitage has shown in great detail, the establishment and expansion of the British Empire was not primarily driven by religious concerns, but rather commercial, ideological, and political concerns, and this was mainly due to the fact that there simply was no uniform religious doctrine to which all English colonists could subscribe.[50]

---

[44] Lockey, *Law and Empire*, 113–41; Lockey, 'Conquest and English Legal Identity in Renaissance Ireland', *Journal of the History of Ideas* 65.4 (2004), 543–58.

[45] Cited in Pagden, *Lords of All the World*, 32.

[46] See Pagden, *Lords of All the Worlds*, 32.

[47] Richard Hakluyt, *The Original Writings & Correspondence of the Two Richard Hakluyts*, E. G. R. Taylor (ed.) (Cambridge: Cambridge University Press, 1935), 215.

[48] *The Three Charters of the Virginia Company of London with Seven Related Documents*, Intro. Samuel M. Bemiss (Williamsburg: Virginia 350th Anniversary Celebration Corporation, 1957), 2.

[49] Pagden, *Lords of All the World*, 36.

[50] Armitage, *The Ideological Origins*, 61–99.

In any case, the notion that legitimate dominion was granted only by God's grace was not without controversy. In Spain, the neo-scholastics, led by Francisco de Vitoria and Domingo de Soto, recognized the Pope as the spiritual head of all Christians but rejected the notion that he had any authority over non-Christians such as the inhabitants of the New World. As a result, they rejected the notion that the Pope had the authority to grant *dominium* over the Amerindians to Christian princes.[51] A more formidable argument in favour of conquest and colonization, put forward by John Major and Spanish humanist Juan Ginés de Sepúlveda, held that the Amerindians were the natural slaves, whom Aristotle had described in the first and third books of his *Politics*.[52] According to Major and Sepúlveda, the Amerindians practised unnatural customs such as cannibalism and human sacrifice, which justified their enslavement, according to Aristotle's claim that some humans are inherently slave-like (see Figure 33.2).[53] According to jurists such as Italian Protestant émigré Alberico Gentili, 'The cause of the Spaniards is just when they make war upon the Indians, who practiced abominable lewdness even with beasts, and who ate human flesh, slaying men for that purpose.'[54]

In response, Vitoria and other Dominicans such as Las Casas argued that, in fact, the Amerindians did live according to a recognizable order and that, although the Amerindians did sometimes indulge in so-called 'unnatural' vices, Christians had also been known to commit such vices. Vitoria concluded that the Amerindians could be conquered to advance the cause of reforming them or in order to rescue innocent people persecuted by such unnatural practises, but that such a war must not continue after the 'barbarians' had ceased them. Most importantly, Vitoria argued that a Christian prince could not legally dispossess or enslave conquered 'barbarians' in perpetuity. In effect, once the Amerindians had been reformed, the prince had a duty to restore their liberty and property to them.[55]

It is clear that Shakespeare's *The Tempest* participates in such debates about the justification for conquest and dominion over the so-called barbarian. Aristotle's natural slave was a being who to all outward appearances seemed human but who lacked the crucial faculties of reason and judgement that Aristotle postulated as crucial to human

---

[51] See Francisco de Vitoria, *On Dietary Laws, or Self Restraint* in *Political Writings*, Anthony Pagden et al. (eds.) (Cambridge: Cambridge University Press, 1991), 205–30, esp. 223–4.

[52] Pagden, *The Fall of Natural Man: The American Indian and the Origins of Comparative Ethnography* (Cambridge: Cambridge University Press, 1986), 38–41.

[53] John Major, *In secundum librum sentiarum* (Paris, 1519); Juan Ginés de Sepúlveda, *Democrates Segundo, o de las Justas causas de la Guerra contra los indios*, Angel Losada (ed.) (Madrid: Consejo Superior de Investigaciones Científicas, Institute Francisco de Vitoria, 1984).

[54] Alberico Gentili, *De Jure Belli Libri Tres*, James Scott Brown, (ed.), John C. Rolfe (trans.), Coleman Philipson (intro.), vol. 1: photographic reproduction of 1612 edn., vol. 2: English translation (Oxford: Clarendon Press, 1933) 1: 198; 2: 122. For consideration of the British context with regard to this topic, see Philip D. Morgan, 'Encounters between British and "indigenous" peoples, c. 1500–1800', in *Empire and Others: British Encounters with Indigenous Peoples, 1600–1850*, Martin Daunton et al. (ed.) (Philadelphia: University of Pennsylvania Press, 1999), 52–3.

[55] Vitoria, *On the American Indians*, in *Political Writings*, 250; Vitoria, *On Dietary Laws, or Self-Restraint*, in *Political Writings*, 207–30; Pagden, *The Fall*, 57–108.

FIGURE 33.2. Theodor de Bry, *America* [i.e. *Grands Voyages*] (Frankfurt, 1590–1620), III, 127. By permission of the Folger Shakespeare Library.

faculties. According to Aristotle, such creatures were in their proper state when they were subjected to the superior reason and judgement of natural masters.[56] The idea that Caliban is the embodiment of Aristotle's natural slave is not a new idea. As long ago as the early 1950s, in an introduction to *The Tempest*, Frank Kermode wrote that Caliban embodied the characteristics of Aristotle's notion of the natural slave.[57] At the beginning of the play, of course, we immediately understand that Caliban is Prospero's slave, but what is less clear is Prospero's justification for having enslaved the islander. Early in the first act, Prospero suggests that Caliban's enslavement was the result of base behaviour—in particular, his attempt to rape Prospero's daughter, Miranda. When Caliban complains about the terms of his servitude, Prospero claims to have

> used thee [i.e. Caliban],
> Filth as thou art, with human care, and lodged thee
> In mine own cell, till thou didst seek to violate
> The honour of my child.   (1.2.347–50)

But Caliban's response to Prospero, 'O ho, O ho! Would't had been done! | Thou didst prevent me; I had peopled else | This isle with Calibans', suggests that Prospero may already have enslaved Caliban before he assaulted Miranda and that the attempted rape was in response to Prospero's unjust subjection of Caliban (1.2.351–2).

---

[56] Aristotle, *The Politics of Aristotle*, Peter L. Phillips Simpson (ed. and trans.) (Chapel Hill: University of North Carolina Press, 1997), 1253*a*2 ff; 1338*b*19 ff.

[57] William Shakespeare, *The Tempest*, Frank Kermode (ed.) (Cambridge, MA: Harvard University Press, 1954), xlii. For a more recent take on such matters, see Julia Reinhard Lupton, 'Creature Caliban', *Shakespeare Quarterly* 51.1 (2000), 1–23.

From the very beginning of the sub-plot concerning Caliban, Shakespeare creates considerable ambiguity about Caliban's nature: it is unclear whether he is human, whether he is animal, or whether he is something between human and animal. In his opening conversation with Ariel, Prospero describes Caliban's nature, using what seems to be an intentionally confusing locution:

> Then was this island—
> Save for the son that she [Sycorax] did litter here,
> A freckled whelp, hag-born—not honoured with
> A human shape.   (1.2.282–3)

When analysing such a sentence, one should first note the difference between the experience of hearing and reading the words. It is almost impossible to hear this sentence spoken and not understand that the phrase, 'not honoured with | A human shape', is adjectival and refers to Caliban. In effect, when experienced aurally, the sentence seems to imply after all that Caliban is not human or at least that he is 'not honoured with | A human shape'. When one reads the sentence, however, it is clear that Prospero intends precisely the opposite. Paraphrased, the sentence indicates that, before Prospero's arrival, the island had no human shape, except for Caliban. In effect, Caliban was the only inhabitant on the island that had anything resembling a human shape, which would suggest that Caliban is in fact human. Unfortunately, the way that Prospero describes Caliban indicates even more ambiguity. Prospero claims that Sycorax 'littered' Caliban, the 'whelp'—both words that indicate animal offspring. The fact that Caliban is 'hag-born' moreover suggests that he may be the offspring of a demon. Later in Act 2, the matter of Caliban's nature is once again left ambiguous. When a drunken servant named Trinculo encounters Caliban hiding under his gabardine on the shore, he wonders whether Caliban is a 'man or a fish' (2.2.25). He calls him a 'monster', remarking that he has 'fins like arms' (2.2.30, 34). Finally, he concludes that 'this is no fish, but an islander, that hath lately suffered by a thunderbolt' (2.2.35–6). Of course, Trinculo's final conclusion is no more accurate than any other description of Caliban. In the end, the cumulative effect of these descriptions indicates both the difficulty of determining Caliban's nature as well as the necessity for the spectator or reader to enquire into and speculate about his nature.

Ultimately, the play sets aside the ambiguity of visual evidence and justifies Prospero's conquest and enslavement of Caliban based on Caliban's behaviour, which is precisely what both Vitoria and Sepúlveda, from two conflicting positions, used to make their arguments about whether or not the Amerindians could be justly conquered and enslaved by Spanish conquistadores.[58] At the end of Act 1, Prospero orders Caliban to fetch wood for the fire. When we see him in Act 2, Caliban is fulfilling Prospero's order, albeit with a great deal of protest and complaint. By the end of Act 2, however, Caliban has rebelled against Prospero's order, having been persuaded by Stephano's bottle that Stephano is a god who can challenge Prospero's rule over the island.

---

[58] Pagden, *The Fall*, 27–56.

Meanwhile, Prospero has encountered Ferdinand, the royal heir to the throne of Naples, and promptly enslaves him and tasks him with fetching wood for the fire. Ferdinand carries out this task without complaint, while Caliban foolishly submits himself to the authority of Stephano, in the hope that Stephano can supplant his current master. By the end of the play, Ferdinand's willing submission has been rewarded with freedom and with Miranda's hand in marriage, while Caliban continues in the state of natural servitude, with which the drama began.

Although the contest may seem 'rigged' from our own twenty-first-century perspective, the play is structured around a competition between Ferdinand and Caliban. According to the logic of this competition, Ferdinand and Caliban are placed into comparable states of servitude to Prospero. And whereas Caliban is unable to control his baser instincts, attempting to rape Miranda, Ferdinand controls his sexual desire when he is alone with Miranda. As a result, Ferdinand is ultimately rewarded with liberty and the ability to enter into human fellowship with Prospero. At the end of his subjugation of Ferdinand, Prospero confides in Ferdinand that 'All thy vexations | Were but my trials of thy love, and thou | Hast strangely stood the test' (4.1.5–7). Ferdinand has effectively passed the exam, by maintaining his civility and controlling his sexual desire. When given the same test, Caliban failed. More telling, when Caliban attempts to gain his freedom from Prospero, he ends up submitting himself to another servant, Stephano.

Ultimately, *The Tempest* is constructed like a rigged 'television reality show', in which the producers have determined in advance which contestant shall take home the grand prize. The test is whether each of the contestants can submit himself to what the play portrays as legitimate rule while controlling his sexual appetite, at the same time that he is isolated from civilization on a deserted island in the face of great temptation. Ferdinand's success at this endeavour proves that he is worthy of being a master, while Caliban's failure justifies his perpetual servitude at the hands of Prospero and others. Like Aristotle's description of the natural slave, who is 'as widely separated from others as are soul and body or human and beast', Caliban must perpetually be under the government of a master.[59] Most important of course is the allegorical significance of all of this. According to numerous critics, Caliban represents the colonized subjects of Ireland or the New World. And just as Sepúlveda and others justified conquest and enslavement of the Amerindians based on reports of their unnatural vices, Caliban's failure to control his appetites serves as justification of his enslavement. Thus, by means of a narrative logic which compares Ferdinand's 'civility' favourably with Caliban's 'degeneracy', the play justifies imperial dominion over people in other countries that exhibit behaviour deemed 'unnatural' or 'uncivilized'.

Not surprisingly, a consideration of colonial contexts throughout history illustrates that imperial masters tend to fixate on the colonial subjects' acts of 'degeneracy' and 'barbarism', while remaining oblivious to the justice or injustice of their own acts of

---

[59] Aristotle, *Politics*, 1254b15–16.

violence against the colonial subject. In the case of *The Tempest*, of course, the question of which act of violence comes first, Prospero's enslavement of Caliban or Caliban's attempted violation of Miranda, is not clear. But according to the imperial logic at work in the contest between Caliban and Ferdinand, it may not matter. What is crucial is that Caliban's lack of self-restraint stands in contrast to Ferdinand, who is able to restrain his sexual appetite in a comparable state of enslavement. The play justifies Prospero's favourable treatment of Ferdinand, even if it is obvious from the beginning that the nature of the competition seems to favour the charming Italian prince. In the process, any desire on Prospero's part for advantage or power or dominion is occluded from view. In the end, the perception of the colonial subjects' barbarism and degeneracy occludes any suggestion of cruelty or self-interest on the part of the conqueror. The conqueror's violent actions are presented as having been taken in the colonial subject's interests. Colonial violence is legitimized, rendered invisible, by seemingly serving as a means to reform or to control the colonial subject's barbaric behaviour.

CHAPTER 34

....

PHILOSOPHY

....

TZACHI ZAMIR

I.

....

SHAKESPEARE's poems and plays frequently offer sententious speculations about life, its meaning (or lack of it); about love, friendship, trust, pain; language (or speechlessness); action (or the inability to act); about the meaning of being a parent, or a friend; or the loss of self-respect; about honour and reputation; about the theatricality that imbues action. Philosophy is the reflective activity whereby such existential spheres and processes are rigorously examined. Pithy articulations of such experiential kernels would, accordingly, appear to be natural candidates for Shakespeare's 'relevance' to philosophers.

While such lofty speculations immediately come to mind when thinking of Shakespeare and philosophy, when one actually attempts to think through such a linkage in a specific textual moment, one comes up with very little. Consider, for example, Macbeth's equating life with a poor player who 'struts and frets his hour upon the stage and then is heard no more', or Hamlet's 'to be or not to be' soliloquy, debating the pros and cons of existence, or Ulysses and his reflections on value in the eyes of others, or Falstaff's philosophizing about honour emptying into a mere word, or Timon's insights regarding the corrupting power of money. All of these are surely deep moments in the plays. Such moving speeches suggest the philosopher's capacity to rise above the quotidian hustle and bustle, coolly and dispassionately apprehending a facet of life and issuing its succinct articulation.

But suppose now that such claims are removed from their context and introduced as proposed truths in a gathering of philosophers. 'I can perhaps see why Hamlet might believe that he should either live and suffer life's humiliations or die and risk afterlife punishment, but why should one hold that this disjunction is applicable to the lives of other individuals?' would ask one puzzled philosopher. 'May we know what necessary and sufficient conditions are being presupposed with regard to "life" and "acting" when

Macbeth identifies "life" with a poor player?' demands another philosopher. 'Why should one hold that 'honor travels in a strait so narrow where one but goes abreast'?' wonders a third, upon pondering Ulysses' remark, 'Does Ulysses ground this claim regarding honour's limited distribution on empirical fact or on conceptual necessity?' The problem is obvious: such claims about life or honour, moving and effective as they are in their dramatic contexts, are partial, vague, and unsupported when examined as proposed truths. Furthermore, since such generalizations are (thankfully) not being argued for in their fictional context, they are not even candidates for philosophical scrutiny. Such statements can, at best, embellish an independent philosophical argument. They add spice that might appeal to the bookish. No more.

II.

A second unpromising route through which Shakespeare's philosophical import may be established is to place his work in dialogue with themes developed more systematically by his contemporaries. Thinkers such as Montaigne, Bodin, Hooker, More, or Calvin have formulated elaborate ideas regarding the limits of knowledge, the illusiveness of free will, or the nature of salvation. Why not examine the explicit and implicit interplay between Shakespeare's work and such an established philosophical corpus? There are three reasons that advise against this. Firstly, we are either faced with the daunting—and probably ultimately futile—task of attempting to distill Shakespeare's own thoughts from his plays, or the equally unappealing project of hounding implied philosophical positions in the plays. The problem with implied positions is that the plays offer too many varied and conflicting ideas and attitudes. One would have to flatten the numerous incoherent and ad hoc reflections found in them into some coherent 'idea'. 'Reason and love keep little company together' says Bottom, and it will not be hard to find a critic capable of interweaving this observation into debates regarding the place of the passions in the good life in early modern England. But how to square this remark with the opposite process at work in some of the plays or particularly in the sonnets, whereby love occasions a privileged access to reality, a sharper penetration into it rather than mere insulation?

Secondly, even when philosophical positions can actually be discerned, they are formulated by characters with whom we sympathize to a limited degree or not at all. What, for example, is the significance of Shakespeare's allocating the remark above to Bottom? Does Bottom's low status undermine the statement? Or perhaps, on the contrary, it being uttered by a fool strengthens it? Both options are interpretively viable. Moreover, how should one approach the complex, sometimes contradictory relations between asserted content and overall effect? Hamlet's dismissals of life are rendered through powerful images that energize both language and actor to an extraordinary degree. Such lines constitute a celebration of life even when life is being disparaged. Which idea is unfolded at such moments? Are we witnessing an articulation of nihilism or its opposite? Jaques finds nothing but theatricality in the lives he dispassionately views around him. In old age—the last of the seven ages of man—he sees no more than disability and dependency. But it is often unnoted that just after the famous speech, Shakespeare has Orlando entering carrying an old loyal servant, frantically looking for scraps of food through which Orlando can nourish him. Is Jaques a mouthpiece for Shakespeare's own view of life as nothing more than a stage? Is Shakespeare alternatively, subtly criticizing Jaques's lugubrious and reductive stance by showing how old age can become an opportunity to give (and receive)?

Finally, to historicize Shakespeare's philosophical relevance means to relegate his philosophical significance to the history of philosophy (and not to one of its grander moments at that) rather than making him a partner to contemporary thought. Granted, for some philosophers philosophy *is just* its history. But even for such philosophers, one would have to demonstrate that Shakespeare is an important player in the evolution and refinement of some concepts or themes. But it seems strained to claim that Rosalind's jolly disregard of Jaques's cynicism plays a similar role to, say, Locke's criticism of the theory of innate ideas. After Locke's critique, it was no longer possible merely to iterate the idea that universally accepted propositions imply innateness. In what sense is Rosalind's sprightly dismissal of Jaques's morbid stance a critique? In what way is our sympathy for her an argument that should counteract nihilism? Does the exchange truly advance our sense of the shortcomings of nihilism? Can it be reapplied? Does it expose nihilism's limitations in the same way in which, say, Kant exposes a possible error in Anselm's ontological argument by undermining the presupposition that existence is a predicate?

If not the memorable contemplative statements or the interplay between such statements and ideas, what can philosophers qua philosophers achieve by immersing themselves in Shakespeare's works? And what can literary critics gain if they eavesdrop on (or risk undertaking) such philosophically-oriented readings of Shakespeare?

III.

No longer mourn for me when I am dead
Than you shall hear the surly sullen bell
Give warning to the world that I am fled
From this vile world with vilest worms to dwell.
Nay, if you read this line, remember not
The hand that writ it; for I love you so
That I in your sweet thoughts would be forgot
If thinking on me then should make you woe.
O, if, I say, you look upon this verse
When I perhaps compounded am with clay,
Do not so much as my poor name rehearse,
But let your love even with my life decay,

> Lest the wise world should look into your moan
> And mock you with me after I am gone.

The 'world' opens and closes Sonnet 71.[1] It is introduced as the unimpressed abstract recipient of the news concerning the speaker's death. Then it becomes a detested, 'vile' context, acoustically and graphically resonating in the world–worm reverse rhyme. Finally, the 'wise world' poses the threat of external ridicule. Shakespeare's sonnet thus construes the poem's intimacy—the poem as an enactment of intimacy with a projected recipient and an eavesdropping reader—as a private space, predicated on the positing (or invention) of an opposing and externalised 'world'.

But what does the speaker infuse into this loving space upon insulating it from the world? Surprisingly, what we hear are thoughts of death. The sonnet catalogues prescriptions to the beloved, forbidding the latter to mourn over the speaker once he is gone. The speaker offers to spare the beloved the pain and scorn such grief would inevitably evoke. A profoundly selfless loving gesture seems to be extended. And yet, the mere verbalization of the possibility (not to say the wish) to be forgotten by the beloved amounts to conjuring up a nightmare. The injunction to forget becomes particularly poignant if the sonnet is read (as Joseph Pequigney reads the entire sequence) as a homoerotic disclosure. Following such reading, the world will 'mock you with me after I am gone' reveals the maddening loneliness of same-sex grief in Shakespeare's cultural context.[2] The plea to be forgotten comes to entail an earnest wish that the beloved will move on and thereby spare himself additional suffering.

But we are also aware of an unmistakable counter-movement: the self-reinstatement paradoxically constituted by this repetitive command to be erased from consciousness. We might also glimpse the attempt to control the beloved's thoughts after the poet is gone. Should he read this line, the beloved is asked to perform the impossible—to disremember the very hand that wrote it. The ostensibly selfless, other-oriented surface of the argument thus gives way to an opposing self-centred refusal to be erased from thought. The beloved is not really allowed to move on. He is, rather, being cleverly manipulated into grief when the speaker can no longer wring a binding attachment in person.

The combination of selflessness and aggression is not being merely described, disclosed, or expressed. The relations between emotion and language are more complex than implied by these categories. A sonnet is not merely a linguistic formulation of

---

[1] I reproduce the sonnet's text and punctuation as given by Stanley Wells and Gary Taylor (eds.), *William Shakespeare: The Complete Works*, The Oxford Shakespeare (Oxford: Clarendon Press, 1989), 759. Other editions give a slightly different punctuation that will not modify my claims.

[2] 'The character of the relationship between the speaker and his beloved [in Sonnet 71] is not greatly changed whether the beloved was a man or a woman', Jack M. Davis and J. E. Grant assert in 'A Critical Dialogue on Shakespeare's Sonnet 71', *Texas Studies in Language and Literature* 1 (1959), at 215. Yet the nature of the 'mock' alluded to does depend heavily on the kind of eroticism one imagines to be articulated and, in this particular sonnet, renders the homoerotic reading far more moving. For Pequigney's argument, see *Such is My Love: A Study of Shakespeare's Sonnets* (Chicago, IL: University of Chicago Press, 1985).

a pre-existing sentiment. A Shakespearean sonnet (to follow Helen Vendler) is an action performed in language whereby a distinct thread of love is being created. The speaker evolves through this action, allowing the reader not merely to comprehend a state or grasp a truth, but to follow sympathetically the temporal steps through which a distinct and personal sentiment is being crystallized. The sonnet allows its reader to eavesdrop into this private process. It also invites the reader to partake in the temporality entailed in following a creative act. The sonnet thereby forms an unstable mixture of descriptive, expressive, and generative elements. Each of these elements can turn out to be a mere façade, momentarily assumed by the speaker only to conceal the fact that another aspect is being mobilized.

Once a sonnet ceases to be regarded as a linguistic construction which simply mediates between an independently existing emotion and the real/imagined beloved or the real/imagined reader, once a sonnet is regarded as, in part, a performative creation of a distinct strand of love, its reader accesses an experiential configuration that, if aesthetically persuasive, does not constitute a stylized mimetic copy of reality or some elaborate formal description of it, but is a feature of emotional reality directly encountered. The reality unveiled is not the material one of sticks and stones. It encompasses, rather, intricately subtle states made up of a dynamic interplay between feeling, image, and words. These states are fictional; they are proposed as experiences of the fictional speaker who may or may not mirror the thoughts and feelings of the living poet. But if the sonnet is aesthetically successful, it convinces its reader of its plausibility as the articulation of a mindscape in love.

IV.

With this view of poetic language, let us return to Sonnet 71, this time with an eye for detail. I claimed that we are not relating to the sonnet as an expression or a description. Instead, we regard it as the means whereby an evolving sentiment is being progressively created before us, different from the experiences that precede and follow it in the sonnet sequence as a whole.

The first four lines could be read in one breath[3]: "No longer mourn for me when I am dead | Than you shall hear the surly sullen bell | Give warning to the world that I am fled | From this vile world, with vilest worms to dwell.' The scene of the speaker's imagined funeral, which is evoked as the very last event in which he asks to be moaned for by the beloved then gives way to an articulation of the moment of reading: 'Nay, if you read this line, remember not | The hand that writ it'. Collin Burrow notes the complex 'you' of the love sonnets aligns the sonnet's reader with the real/imagined beloved, and that also

---

[3] In 'Breath, Today: Celan's Translation of Sonnet 71' (*Comparative Literature* 57.4 [2005], 328–51) Sara Guyer interestingly suggests that the reading of the first sentence effects a thematically-relevant effect of *breathlessness*.

occasions a metafictional unification of the speaker/poet.[4] The beloved reads the speaker's line; the reader reads the poet's line. The sonnet is thus able to question its status as mere fictional or stylized disclosure, exhorting the reader to ponder on the identity of the addressee. The poet is not here speaking to the reader over the beloved's head (as he does in Sonnet 18, for example), but draws on the first-person pronoun and on the invocation of the non-fictional moment of reading 'this line' to fuse rhetorically the beloved and the reader in the same posthumous action and moment.

The rhetorical objective of this ploy is, I think, to originate the broaching of a critical distance between reader and beloved. The self-humbling, self-abnegating prescriptions generated by the speaker to the beloved might suit the latter. But once the reader is subtly united with the beloved, the nature of such a plea potentially encourages readers to refrain from following such implausible demands. Why this request to be forgotten so quickly? Why this plea to go on after you die as if nothing had happened? The more the beloved is construed as someone who might actually abide by a prescription of this kind, the more the reader is likely to withdraw from sharing such a cold stance. Rhetorically positioned as implied addressees, readers can thus perceive and resent more acutely the beloved's flippant and carefree mindset, one that can occasion such words of parting in the first place.

The sonnet's counter-theme is now introduced through a reversed chronology: the speaker invites the beloved to place himself in the position of loss and to then relate to him afresh. Under the guise of a poem about death and the relations between the living and the deceased, there hides a poem about life and the present bond between the living lovers. The sonnet thus mobilizes a familiar manoeuvre in erotic psychology (which will be rendered explicit in Sonnet 73): an intensification of feelings by way of imagining the death of the beloved. This thematic counterpoint—the introduction of life while referring to death—is reflected in word choice. The repetitive injunctions not to imagine the hand that is writing, or to forget the speaker's name, are being beautifully undercut by an obsessive iteration of the first person 'I,' 'me' and 'my' that permeate the sonnet's remaining lines.

Line six provides the transitional point between the imagined future moment of grief and the present: 'for I love you so | That I in your sweet thoughts would be forgot, | If thinking on me then should make you woe'. The simple, unadorned 'for I love you so', its shift from future to present tense, reinforce the naked, non-stylized sentiment that presses itself into the sonnet's figuratively dense surface. The disturbing request to forget the departed loved one betrays love's contradictions. Disappearance from memory through the imagined burial in the beloved's 'sweet thoughts' acts as a mental analogue for the material decomposition evoked at the sonnet's opening (one hears echoes of *hearse* in 'do not so much as my poor name rehearse', affiliating the beloved's verbalization of the poet's name with a burial). The 'make you woe' which closes line eight gives way to the expressive 'O' that opens line nine, thus uniting through acoustics and performed action ('woe'/'o') the speaker and the beloved. The speaker's

---

[4] Introduction to the Oxford edition of Shakespeare's *The Complete Poems and Plays* (New York: Oxford University Press, 2002), 122.

exclamation not only audibly and semantically duplicates the beloved's 'woe' but also rhymes with 'love you so', echoing, as it were, the loving sentiment conveyed by that suspended sentence in the following lines, carrying on the contradictory sentiment that prescribes forgetting while powerfully soliciting remembrance.

Detectable too, is the hurtful imbalance—reiterated time and again in the sonnet sequence as a whole—between the loving speaker and the betraying and evasive youth. Your 'woe' is conditional and uncertain ('*If* thinking on me then should make you woe'). The speaker's 'O', on the other hand, is unconditional. As commentators have repeatedly noted, behind this disturbing expression of utmost self-negation there lies the gnawing suspicion that the speaker will hardly be mourned at all.[5] One facet constituting the richness of the evolving sentiment is thus the speaker's attempt to reinterpret the beloved's potentially wounding future disregard of his death. By *not* moaning for him, the beloved would be dutifully *complying* with the speaker's death wish. The process, which the speaker undergoes in the sonnet, thus also includes an attempt to make peace with a loved one moving on.

The speaker is thereby able to combine, on the one hand, loving sacrifice which is conditioned by the limitations of same-sex grief and the—to my mind authentic— benevolent willingness to release the youth from the obligation to grieve. On the other hand, one may sense a tacit yet marked complaint that the speaker will not be sufficiently mourned and that he is already disappearing from the beloved's carefree heart. The request not to be mourned would render bearable the inevitable prediction that the speaker will soon be forgotten by this lover anyway. The speaker is, accordingly, compelled to recreate his fading presence in a mind already forgoing and forgetting. This contradictory (but emotionally consistent) combination of egocentric and selfless attitudes tinged with the pain that issues from thoughts of loss, of a mocked beloved, of envy and rage upon being already forgotten concludes the sonnet.

V.

How does Sonnet 71 inform philosophy? The sonnet does not offer arguments or striking generalizations or memorable sententious statements about life or love. Moreover, unlike some other forms of literature, the Shakespearean sonnet (like the Shakespearean play) is not designed to instruct, demonstrate a point, or improve us. At the same time, it informs. How?

[5] Helen Vendler, *The Art of Shakespeare's Sonnets* (Cambridge, MA: Harvard University Press, 1999), 329. For similar impressions, see Burrow, *The Complete Sonnets and Poems* (New York: Oxford University Press), 122; and J. Pequigney's 'Sonnets 71–74: Texts and Contexts', in James Schiffer (ed.), *Shakespeare's Sonnets: Critical Essays* (New York: Garland 1999), 287.

The sonnet extends an invitation to share a highly particular moment in the poet/ speaker's experience. The wish to establish connection with another may account for our need to read poetry in the first place. When the poetry is of superior quality, the connection also yields valuable insights, leading to a refined understanding of (in the case of the Shakespearean sonnets) love and its surprising modalities. Though non-general, highly contextual and private, the descriptions of such modalities remain potentially applicable to other contexts. Such renderings thereby become *truth claims*, potential truths. The fictional and artificial nature of the sonnet form does not undermine its claim to capture and convey a truth adequately. On the contrary, stylization enables a slowing down of perception, hampering, and de-automatizing smooth processing. Stylization elicits a pause, an uncertainty in the reader, and thus enables the unfolding of an intimate experience.

The core of the response regarding a literary work's contribution to philosophy lies in this combination of an articulated potential truth with the configuration of a not-to-be-taken-for-granted attuned state of mind created in the reader by a well-written text. Literature at its best captures evasive and nuanced truth-claims. It does so in a way that makes these claims resonate meaningfully within the reader. This reply is loosely satisfactory. To appease a philosopher it would need to establish further both the epistemic and the rhetorical components. Philosophers would wish to understand how poetic claims become upgraded into *truth*-claims. They would also like to know more about the responsive state created in the reader and how such engaged suasion contributes to (rather than undermines) knowledge.

VI.

How do we know that a particular poetic articulation is a truth-*claim* (which is not to be confused with a true *proposition*) rather than an idiosyncratic assertion? Defenders of literature's philosophical import would often respond by arguing that literary insights can be poetically compelling because they cohere with the reader's sense of the depicted experience. Not that readers already know what Shakespeare is about to unravel. But they do relate to the articulated sentiment as a *successful* rendering of what they have already vaguely experienced. Yet the question remains: How do we know that a proposed poetic articulation of what we already independently fuzzily sense constitutes an enhanced rendering in the progressive mapping of our internal lives? How can we distinguish between successful articulations that we ought to embrace and unsuccessful ones that we are unable to reject precisely because of our own unclarity regarding inner states?

While we are not utterly helpless regarding such matters (I have elsewhere investigated this problem in greater detail),[6] the answer is that we do not have at our disposal

---

[6] Tzachi Zamir, *Double Vision: Moral Philosophy and Shakespearean Drama* (Princeton, NJ: Princeton University Press, 2007), 35–8.

conceptual tools that can fully satisfy us on this score. This inability accounts for the sceptical, hesitant, uncategorical, and suggestive nature which characterize the discourse of literary interpretation as in the cautious nature of the claims above regarding Sonnet 71. Successful poetic articulations are *potentially* true (hence: truth-*claims*). Surprisingly, we are willing to allow them to *remain* in this state. We ascribe explanatory power to such claims, without turning them into demonstrable truths (whatever 'demonstrable' can mean in the context of contingent truths). This is to take a step beyond a highly fruitful insight offered by Peter Lamarque and Stein Olsen whereby they claim that 'thematic statements' can be understood without being construed as assertions.[7] One can agree with Lamarque's and Olsen's view that literary or literary-interpretive statements should not be regarded as *assertions*. At the same time, such statements are also not merely comprehended. They are articulated as potential truths, as truth-claims.

Since anything can be 'potentially' true, philosophers might wonder how meaningful such an ascription ultimately is. Even when recognizing the contingent nature of claims regarding, for instance, the uneasy connections between generosity and control in a love relation, as formulated in Sonnet 71, and the implication which such contingent status entails vis-à-vis the unavailability of proof, the philosopher would strive to know what makes the successfully poetic articulation a *potential* truth. If the sonnet does not constitute an argument, if it does not merely fancifully recreate an experience akin to that which the reader has independently already sensed, in what other way can it support its particular observations? I, for one, have neither experienced myself nor detected in others the precise unstable combination of self-marginalization and self-reinstatement that I have just postulated as the leading sentiment developed in Sonnet 71. On what basis, then, am I willing to accept the sonnet as deeply informing my sense of what love might involve?

VII.

The response to the above question begins by denying that the 'plausibility' in question relates merely or primarily to *descriptive* adequacy. The disanalogy between material reality and mindscapes dissuades a brash acceptance of the 'inner' as some pre-existing immaterial correlate to material objects. We thus arrive at a more nuanced and interesting position: the poetic articulation is only *partly* a description that conforms to what one imprecisely senses to be the case in another's love. The apprehension of such conformity is not based on some arbitrary intuition. It rests, rather, upon familiarity with other lives, sensitivities, difficulties, and forms of attraction and erotic dependency. Thus, even if I do not possess first-hand familiarity with the experience

7 *Truth, Fiction, and Literature: A Philosophical Perspective* (Oxford: Clarendon Press, 1994), 328.

portrayed, the patterns I have been discussing harmonize with my previous sense of the plausible scope of erotic dependency and manipulation.

At the same time, and beyond its status as a description of experience, the poetic articulation is also partly a proposed *intensification* of that experience. Richard Shusterman aptly formulates such a thought in his attempt to articulate art as dramatization in the following way: 'Art distinguishes itself from ordinary reality not by its fictional frame of action but by its greater vividness of experience and action, through which art is opposed not to the concept of *life* but rather to that which is lifeless and humdrum'.[8] The precision we attribute to successful art and literature involves both ingredients: the descriptive *and* the intensifying. The poet—at least this kind of poet—convinces us with his eye for lived detail even when we have not undergone such experience ourselves, as well as with his capacity to offer a distilled expression of a vivid experience which readers are invited to sense.

What characterizes this 'intensity'? Take, for example, the discussion of the speaker's transition in Sonnet 71 from (your conditional) 'woe' to (the speaker's unconditional) 'O'. This linkage between unification in voice/action and complaint does not merely entail a description regarding how some pre-existing love happens to operate; nor is it some stylistically pleasing way of dressing up an independently existing sentiment. It constitutes 'intensification' in the sense of capturing in miniature, in the movement between two words, an emotional world encompassing several (three) distinct strands: utmost, genuine sympathy extended to the beloved's future pain (captured by the acoustic unification); the opposite, i.e. selfish concern that the beloved's future pain over the speaker's death would be insufficient (captured by the contrast between the beloved's conditional woe and the speaker's unconditional 'O'); and (thirdly) the dreadful thought that one will truly disappear from the beloved's world.

'Intensification' can take the form of this capacity to encapsulate into a detail numerous distinct *descriptively plausible* strands. It is opposed to what Shusterman calls 'humdrum' reality because the humdrum entails precisely the deflation of content, the act of seeing and experiencing very little. By contrast, the best works of art and literature often attain their status by inviting absorption in a detail. The detail becomes 'intense' because so many distinct threads are woven into it.

Such quantitative concentration of independently valued, descriptively plausible components that are distilled into a condensed stylized form is what provides some art at some moments with the energized quality of a presentation of *heightened* experience. Rather than a set of descriptively correct observations on actual loves, poetic articulations operate modally: they suggest that life *could* attain the precise blend of precision and richness that we perceive in the work. When 'accepting' such articulations as plausible and rewarding, we do not merely regard them as adequately capturing a complex state of affairs, but as a plausible intensification of experience as opposed to the 'humdrum'.

---

[8] *Surface and Depth: Dialectics of Criticism and Culture* (Ithaca, NY: Cornell University Press, 2002), 234.

Apart from the dense richness, in which independently valued insights are crowded into the space of a detail, intensity also often denotes a quality marking the details themselves. Note, for instance, the bitter-sweet mood through which the speaker imagines his dissipation in the beloved's thoughts in 'for I love you so | that I in your sweet thoughts would be forgot'. Surrounded as this image is by two discomforting glimpses into material decomposition—the subterranean aggression in this seemingly soft-spoken line, turns the beloved's mind (should he comply and forget the speaker as the latter supposedly asks) into a grave. The images thus militate against the mellifluous surface meaning in which the speaker is pleading to spare the beloved pain. This is not 'irony' in the sense of asserting X and meaning Y. *Both* meanings, the selfless and the hostile, are being genuinely endorsed, and this contrapuntal movement of meaning lends a qualitative intensity to the line.

Such use of language is, again, opposed to the 'humdrum' and is, in this sense, 'intense'. This time, though, the contrast is not between quantitative richness of detail encountered in poetry and some watered-down version of reality which we ordinarily experience. Intensity, here, denotes a quality of the language: the planned organization of sense in such a way that it is able to capture and voice the shades of emotion that are at work in a lived context. The 'voicing' is sometimes an amplifying. To tacitly present the beloved's mind as a grave transmits rage. The speaker does not curse or blame the future forgetful beloved. He is, rather, subliminally turning him into a sarcophagus, a locus of decomposition in which death takes place. The beloved becomes 'death' not in its abstract, conceptual sense but in its material and terrifying one. The *quality* of the line lies in this mixture: the powerful contrast between the genuine caring consideration extended to the beloved, and the underlying rage that cannot be fully repressed. Perhaps this is a sharper form of resentment than what people actually feel when imagining themselves being forgotten by their lovers. But the equation carries expressive precision, since it brings out and conveys an aspect of this state. The 'humdrum' is the opposite of this: it lies rather in the obtuseness involved in the inability to register or express adequately such subtle ripples. Intensity thus entails both the weaving of many observations in a detail and a dimension pertaining to the formulation of the details themselves, an amplification of that which quietly throbs beside the louder, more noticeable movements of the inner life.

Return now to the question of what accepting a poetic articulation means. Literary works offer various forms of experiential extension. These are accepted not only because they are descriptively accurate. Such articulations become opportunities for imaginative participation. Readers participate with a planned organization of experience in which far more takes place (in contrast to non-fictional life) and in which minor inner movements are played up. Accordingly, when accepting a poetic articulation as a potential truth, we grant it both descriptive force *and* the capacity to enable imaginative identification with an intense experience. Intensity itself relates both to descriptive richness and amplification. It is, accordingly, on the one hand an experience of an imagined state, and, on the other, an experience that is not divorced from, and is in fact intimately tied up with, truth. Such is the route whereby poetry is able to generate not truth, but a *potential* truth.

VIII.

While the discussion above is pertinent to art and literature in general in their relationship with philosophy, it is particularly apt to the particular merits characterizing Shakespeare's works; specifically, the fascinating quality of his language. I have suggested that the intensity of a work is predicated on its descriptive density and on its power to metamorphose weak and marginal movements of thought and feeling into moments of heightened awareness. We admire works that repay scrutiny of details and reveal more upon further perusal. But we are also moved by them because they enable imaginatively accessing an intensified state. This linkage is not universally applicable to all major works of poetry. Spenser's allegorical poetry, for example, is morally illuminating and intellectually profound at its best, yet its emotional appeal revolves around charged mental images and the transition between them, and is less attuned to the kind of intensity described above. But this linkage does hold true for Shakespeare's poetry, whether dramatized or not, possessing, as his work does, an experiential precision in its descriptive and expressive modes, coupled with a capacity to move its reader/audience powerfully and even sometimes to effect a transformation in inner experience when verbalized and acted.

Such an effect on the reader/audience constitutes a second, additional source for Shakespeare's particular relevance to philosophy. Apart from the intensity of his language—and perhaps because of it—the reader/audience often undergoes unique experiences when engaging with Shakespeare's works. When Helena reminds Hermia about the meaning of friendship, when Coriolanus banishes Rome, when Lorenzo woos Jessica through a disquisition over music, when Lear denounces filial betrayal, Hamlet philosophizes about replacing one's lover, Shylock about Judaism, Lady Macbeth contemplates murder, Claudius probes the meaning of prayer, or Isabella explicates justice—we are moved. What renders such experiences unique is not the strength of the effect. A well-made horror movie can shock us to a greater extent. What Shakespeare offers is, rather, the combination of the depth in which a state is explored by the character (to employ the terms above, the 'intensity' of the character's language) and the experience this creates within the reader/audience.

IX.

What are these experiences? How do they differ from ordinary, non-literary experiences? How do they lead to knowledge? Let us respond to these in turn. The first question as to the nature of these experiences cannot be answered by appealing to some incontestable established experience that a literary work universally generates in every reader/audience. If the experience of a work was of such nature, we would have no need of literary critics. However, a thoughtful criticism of a work is not a report, but is, in part, a proposal opening up fruitful and rewarding ways of experiencing the text. We need critics precisely because we sense that the more rewarding experiences are often not immediately accessible. In Sonnet 71, for example, I *suggested* that the reader's experience includes a sense of amused sympathy for the speaker's capacity to transform a painful forgetting into the loving compliance with a death wish. I have also *proposed* that the speaker succeeds in involving us in his state, suspended as he is between painful alternatives, which unfold in their indismissable force as the sonnet progresses. These feelings intertwine with the more immediate experience of attending another (the lover) who is disclosing a painfully torn inner state.

How do such literary experiences differ from non-literary ones? They do not. True, some experiences are distinctly literary; pitying a fictional character, while it certainly takes place as part of experienced reading, is never simply the same as feeling sorry for a non-fictional person. But this does not necessitate upholding a belief in some unique 'aesthetic experience' that characterizes all valued engagements with art. All of the elements that I have catalogued can be encountered in a living exchange, unmediated by art or literature. The problem with lived experience is that life too rarely offers the kind of experiences that are the focus of literary works. When it does, we are usually belaboured by pragmatic concerns. Some action usually needs to be undertaken in response to what is being disclosed. We are also typically overwhelmed by the strength of such experiences (whereas experiences in art or literature are heightened and vivid, not strong).

Finally, how are such experiences connected with knowledge? Gary Iseminger has usefully distinguished between two different ways in which experiences as part of art have been traditionally associated with knowledge. The first—which Iseminger calls 'phenomenological'—refers to experiencing what something is like. The second—labelled by him as 'epistemic'—relates to non-inferential knowledge, 'a non-inferential way of coming to know something—comparable, say, to seeing that something is a chair'.[9] Iseminger's terms are, I think, confusing (since the 'phenomenological'—the knowing what some state is like—is itself a mode of non-inferential knowledge). Yet we can still relate to the distinction as offering two distinct routes through which experiences act as non-inferential knowledge. The first of these relies on empathy, whereas the second relates to a state akin to witnessing or perceiving. Both modes of associating the experiences created by art and literature (with or without invoking the problematic construction of 'aesthetic experience') can illuminate the unique ways through which literature informs philosophy in a manner that philosophy on its own cannot access. Literature enables us to relate to its insights while undergoing an experience created by the work. According to the reading above, for example, Sonnet 71 offers a plausible articulation of what it might be like to come to terms with the additional pain of secrecy in grief as part of homoerotic love in a hostile cultural context. This would be the *phenomenological* linkage between experience and knowledge.

[9] 'Aesthetic Experience', in Jerrold Levinson (ed.), *The Oxford Handbook of Aesthetics* (Oxford: Oxford University Press, 2005), ch. 3.

The epistemic formulation of the claim for the knowledge-yielding capacities of literature asserts that the experience of a powerful literary work is never an argument that supports the insights the poem presents, but rather functions as what I have elsewhere called a 'ground'.[10] The 'ground' is an element relating to justification in the sense of correcting beliefs (or modifying conduct or decision-making) because one is exposed to some new experience. Such experiences (literary or non-literary) have the power to turn some claims from formulations that are cerebrally acknowledged as potentially plausible, into vividly accepted truth-claims. In Sonnet 71 we move from knowing that lovers are possessive to a specific and direct presentation of such possessiveness. The sonnet turns the dread of being forgotten by a beloved into an elaborate and anxious manipulation in which one seemingly releases the beloved only to keep asserting control over his future once the speaker is dead. The sonnet allows us to *experience* erotic possessiveness by witnessing its unfolding, by following its temporal evolving from generosity to anger. Our familiarity with erotic possessiveness has not changed in terms of new propositions that we are accepting now and which we rejected before (even if such changes occur, new beliefs of this kind could easily be paraphrased and removed from the context of the literary work). Rather, literary experiences modify the *relation* between agents and beliefs, qualitatively enhancing the beliefs and thereby changing their place and import for the reader.

X.

....

Martha Nussbaum opens her *Love's Knowledge* with the following question: 'How should one write, what words should one select, what forms and structures and organization, if one is pursuing understanding? (Which is to say, if one is, in that sense, a philosopher?).'[11] The bracketed sentence, identifying philosophers with those who seek understanding, is difficult to reject: no philosopher would endorse a self-characterization that does not involve the pursuit of understanding. The controversy would relate to what philosophers mean by the term 'understanding'.

I have been advocating the following: Shakespeare advances our understanding in several distinct ways. Firstly, his poetic insights constitute descriptively accurate statements of inner reality. Secondly, these insights are often condensed into a narrow textual space, creating 'intensity', a term denoting both a denser and richer experience of reality than what one ordinarily undergoes, and a qualitative amplification of understudied, weak inner structures. Such intensity offers itself to the philosopher both as an opportunity for studying reality and also as an experiential invitation. When probed, such moments enable a slowing down of perception and a taking into account of the complexities within

---

[10] Zamir, *Double Vision*, 11–14.
[11] *Love's Knowledge: Essays on Philosophy and Literature* (Oxford: Oxford University Press, 1990), 3.

seemingly simple, one-dimensional processes. When embraced as an invitation to be moved, such moments enable the philosopher to undergo an interpenetration of descriptive insight and experience (to invoke the terms of Aristotelian rhetoric: to merge *logos* and *pathos*). 'Understanding' is both the broadening of accessible potential truths and the modification in one's experience of particular truth-claims.

Such a position holds for art and literature in general, not just for Shakespeare's work. But it is exceptionally suited to the merits characterizing his dramatized and non-dramatized poetic language. Other virtues of his work—such as characterisation, an eye for dialogue and emotional development, a sensitivity to images (spoken or staged), multifaceted humour, a gendered-specific attunement to affective shades, and political sophistication in which the conservative is played against the subversive—might relate to philosophy in other ways. Here I have confined myself to the distinctiveness of the most salient feature of his art—his language and how it can contribute to understanding. A deep response to Shakespeare's works promotes understanding in both senses spelled out above. After writing this essay and spending time with Sonnet 71, I know more about seemingly generous erotic gestures. This understanding is couched both in what the sonnet conveys, at least what I take it to mean, and how it makes me relate to such content.

If the above is correct, philosophers access important insights by engaging in dialogue with Shakespeare's works. Should literary critics be concerned with philosophical criticism of this kind? I suggest the following five reasons why they should. Firstly, the idea that a literary work may offer knowledge and anchor it in unique ways creates a powerful bridge between literary studies and philosophy. We read Shakespeare's works not only because they provide pleasure, or enable us to access the implicit ideological formations in early modern England, or because of their canonical status and poetic merits. Such works can become pivotal in promoting understanding, and examining them can become a facet of the examined life.

Secondly, as shown in the above analysis, a philosophical reading is always attentive to the specific contribution that the literary work makes *as* literature. The philosopher will always be concerned with justifying the detour to knowledge by way of literature. What accordingly ensues is an examination of the features that make up literariness (in the analysis above, 'intensity'). Far from being an instrumentalization of literature as some might fear, philosophical criticism reopens the question of the literary, and provides a range of answers that relate to the specific contributions of literature to knowledge or to moral attunement.

Thirdly, by specifying such contributions, philosophical criticism is able to advance the political objectives of much contemporary work undertaken in literary studies. The focus in the last decades on forms of marginalization and ideology formation as these operate in literary works, is complemented and sharpened once one is also equipped with a reasoned position regarding the specific ways by which literature can articulate suffering, or the specific ways by which it recreates a power nexus. A sophisticated and nuanced version of the 'cultural turn' cannot mean flattening all practices to some all-enveloping discursive network, in which the distinct rhetoric of literature is ignored.

One must attend the actual contours of specific formations—specifically, literary formations—and the particular ways in which they can promote or undermine power. Philosophical readings of literary works pinpoint the uniqueness of specifically literary depictions in their relation to knowledge, thereby contributing to the understanding of such representations as constituents of power.

Fourthly, philosophical criticism's focus on understanding enables justifying the non-arbitrary attribution of aesthetic value to a literary work. A 'great' or 'canonical' literary work is one that, among other virtues, provides and promotes understanding. Since such understanding is not merely reducible to paraphrasable content, but is rooted in forging an experiential connection with that content, a work attains high merit if it invites visitation and revisitation. Philosophical readings elucidate this content and the contact with it, thereby justifying the return to the specific work and its high valuation. While such merit can be ideologically exploited in various ways and harnessed to various non-aesthetic goals, the attributing of aesthetic merit, if based on the rich understanding provided by the work, also implies recognizing an intrinsically valuable aspect inherent in the work as such.

Fifthly, critical schemes in literary studies are never evaluated merely relative to whether or not they are internally consistent or defensible. What ultimately matters is whether they can mobilize interesting and rewarding readings. Philosophical criticism facilitates such readings. It justifies approaching a work not by evaluating it on its own terms (whatever that may mean), or as a prism through which one studies its formative culture, but by attending to how the work and its close-reading informs our own autonomous engagement and interest in a particular dimension of life (love in Sonnet 71). The close-reading becomes concept-oriented, in the sense of asking what the work might tell us about an important concept, one that underlies many of our concerns. The reading also becomes rhetorically oriented, in the sense of examining the nature of the experience created by the work. The dialogue with the work—a reading—thereby becomes an interplay between what a text might be saying about life and literature's particular way of making such claims. Philosophical readings thereby turn literature into a contemporary guide and partner in an examined life.

XI.

Where would philosophical studies of Shakespeare go in the future? Books on Shakespeare and philosophy are published all the time (I count six of them in the last three years). This growing interest need not imply a distinct orientation within Shakespeare studies. Much of this work searches for abstract thoughts in Shakespeare's plays or suggests tacit links between Shakespeare and the philosophical concerns explicitly voiced in the theology, philosophy, law, or political thought of his time. Such scholarship can obviously be profound and rewarding to read, but it does not differ significantly from other forms of contextualization routinely performed by literary critics.

The challenge facing work on Shakespeare and philosophy is whether it can amount to a fruitful, theoretically distinct approach to Shakespeare. From the standpoint of philosophers, the test for such fruitfulness is whether scrutinizing Shakespeare's works promotes understanding and the pressurizing of one's vocabulary, which is what philosophy is. For literary critics, fruitfulness would consist in the interpretive pay-offs that a concept-oriented reading yields. The disciplines need not be united in their verdict: philosophers might benefit from engagement with Shakespeare while literary critics gain little. Alternatively, literary critics might welcome readings by philosophers in a way that strikes other philosophers as intellectually shallow. Literary critics frequently cite and rely upon philosophers in their readings, often without the familiarity with the underlying philosophical motivations that philosophers bring to their enquiries. Philosophers might hesitate advocating practising philosophy when it is unhappily liberated from the restrictions posed by a rigorous conceptual analysis once it is exported into the context of a literary interpretation. Such philosophizing can deteriorate into the production of seemingly profound yet ultimately vague statements being applauded by practitioners of another discipline who lack the training enabling them to sift the wheat from the chaff.

Disciplinary labels aside, if the argument above regarding the different epistemologies underlying philosophy and literature is correct, literary interpretations (good ones) will often be philosophical—without mentioning it—by virtue of the unique interpenetration of insight and reader positioning that they explain and promote. An explicitly philosophical criticism would complement such interpretation with an examination of the epistemological state itself, what it includes or omits, and why it cannot be established by argumentation alone. The problem facing philosophical criticism here is the current disinterest in interpretation and close-reading within Shakespeare studies, and the preference for literary-oriented anthropology of various kinds. Shakespeareans, it seems, now restrict close-reading to their classrooms, allowing very little of it to trickle into their talks and publications. Given this context, any reading-oriented, text-oriented (rather than culture-oriented) approach will be suspected of a regressive agenda, a return to 'new criticism' and its latent conservative politics. Would developments within literary studies such as 'new aestheticism' or philosophical criticism recentralize the literary work? It is too early to tell.

By contrast to Shakespeare studies, the shifts within moral philosophy suggest a more optimistic future for philosophical criticism. The epistemic limitations of proposition-based, argument-based accounts regarding what it means to know are increasingly recognized. Alternatives to argument-based accounts are being sought. Literary works are being read with an eye to one compensatory thesis or another, in which literature is seen as able to bypass limitations built into standard philosophical argumentation or into its default modes of moral reflection. There is a perceptible stream of work by philosophers who have not been daunted by Shakespeare or by the fear of being off-courted by Shakespeareans. Most of this work is anecdotal, in the sense of producing an insightful reading of one play or another. Rich and engaging as such interpretations often are, the greater philosophical challenge is to come up with a theoretically comprehensive project, in the sense of interpretations that are not haphazardly collected, but are rooted in an overarching position regarding the relations between philosophy and literature.

Since experience-based epistemological frameworks are proposed with growing refinement and sophistication within aesthetics, one can expect these to inform future philosophically-oriented readings of Shakespeare. I will risk a more specific guess (or hope) as to the contours of the next significant contribution to work done on the philosophy/Shakespeare trajectory. Philosophers in the Anglo-American tradition (such as Shaun Gallagher, Mark Johnson, and Richard Shusterman) are very recently rethinking the body and the role of embodiment in world-processing (Continentalists have been doing this longer). This development could prove important to Shakespeare's philosophical critics. It could mean that Shakespeare's appeal as an author of *dramatic* poetry might begin to be focalized by aestheticians who are willing to experiment with the *enactment* of a poetically intense text and how theatricalizing words modifies understanding.[12] If the grasp of meaning is more than comprehension of a statement, if it can be significant to process propositional meaning when one's state is modified as well, if imaginative response to fictional characters qualitatively shapes and thus deepens what one understands, how would the dramatic acting of a text—its fuller embodiment— augment and consolidate what one knows? For example, what would a Stanley Cavell know, say, about the meaning of shame, if after completing his *Lear* interpretation, he acts (however amateurishly, but in earnest) in a performance of the play? I have recently watched a brilliant ageing actor remain naked before a large audience in the 'off, off you lendings' scene. How does an experience of this kind affect one's sense and grasp of shame? The Shakespearean text is obviously pushing the actor deeper into exposure by enforcing partial or complete nakedness before others. What can such fuller imaginative embodiment teach?

Shakespeare is obviously not the only playwright whose work facilitates such enquiry in the context of dramatized poetry (not to mention non-poetic drama). But which other author furnishes a more fertile ground through which such a study can be undertaken?

---

[12] Philosophical criticism would thereby reach out to include recent developments within performance studies regarding the unique status of the dramatic text. On this issue see W. B. Worther, *Drama: Between Poetry and Performance* (Chichester: Wiley-Blackwell, 2010).

....

CHAPTER 35

PRAGMATISM

....

LARS ENGLE

THIS chapter addresses three questions: What is pragmatism? How is it related to theatre? How might it be helpful to think of Shakespeare as a pragmatist? While it returns to some arguments made in my book *Shakespearean Pragmatism* (1993), I focus on work on pragmatism, theatre, and Shakespeare that has been done since then. Having offered the caveat that pragmatism does not provide a distinctive method for literary critics or a reliable weapon in their disputes with one another, I close with a reading of *Macbeth* that aligns what might seem Shakespeare's least pragmatic play with pragmatist thought.

WHAT IS PRAGMATISM?

....

Philosophy has always had therapeutic as well as constructive aims. It has aspired to provide discursive cures to deep sources of human unhappiness: the disaster-prone changefulness of social arrangements, the ways fairness is undermined by the self-serving opinions of other people, the instability of evaluation, the elusiveness of truth, even mortality itself and the progressive extinction of selfhood that appears to accompany decay and death. Pragmatism, a distinctively American contribution to the history of philosophy, is as therapeutic as other kinds of philosophy, but its aim is to cure us of some of these traditional philosophic aspirations, or at least to get us to accept that the cure is never going to be entirely different in kind from the ailment. Pragmatism teaches that we are stuck with social mutability, with ungrounded commitments to what is right and wrong, with evaluative instability, with truth that is an honorific term applied by communities to useful reliable beliefs, and with our own status as sentient but evanescent nodes in an ongoing exchange of words, things, genes, and commitments. As a critique of modern philosophy, it attacks the idea that the goal of philosophy and science is to provide true representations of nature, where 'true' means 'independent of the position of the judger', 'getting at the real relations of things to each other'. Since, according to pragmatists, we cannot get outside human communities of discourse, truth cannot involve independence of them. Pragmatists propose instead the idea that the true is what has the best consequences in action, and they suggest that this has always already been the case.

From the viewpoint of contemporary theoretically-oriented students of Shakespeare, pragmatism cuts two ways. It points on the one hand toward an anti-foundational critique that pragmatism shares with a variety of loosely-grouped post-structuralist positions, and thus cuts against dominant realist positions among scientists and some philosophers. Literary critics are on the whole very comfortable with anti-foundationalism. But pragmatism also points toward the view that there has always been a working system for the emergence of truths. Assertions of philosophical crisis in, for instance, the way reference to objects does not fix the meanings of words, or of ethical crisis in the way the vocabulary of a given community can support and naturalize its wicked patterns of behaviour, are from a pragmatist viewpoint exaggerations of the way things have always been into a shocking discovery. If language is always already in some sense broken, it is also always already in some sense fixed, in that everyone is making it work for a variety of ends. Pragmatism offers a view of how we arrive at truths that resists the reification of language, or of ideology, as a constructor of consciousness, a view that sets itself, in Donald Davidson's famous phrase, against 'the very idea of a conceptual scheme'.[1] Historically, it is optimistic about democracy and reluctant to embrace ideas that reduce the agency of ordinary people by suggesting that expert insight is needed to see through the mystifications that govern society. With this aspect of pragmatism—as an anti-realist position that questions the more exciting, and self-privileging, anti-realist claim that social power conditions subjectivity in such a way as to determine truth—contemporary literary critics are on the whole less comfortable.[2]

Pragmatism proposed itself as a third way at the beginning of the twentieth century when the philosophical alternatives were realism and idealism. William James gives a much-quoted description of pragmatism that illustrates its substitution of quasi-Darwinian historical processes for Platonic or empiricist ones in accounting for truth:

> That new idea is truest which performs most felicitously its function of satisfying our double urgency [for accommodation of new observations and consistency with accumulated beliefs]. It makes itself true, gets itself classed as true, by the way it works; grafting itself then upon the ancient body of truth, which thus grows much as a tree grows by the activity of a new layer of cambium....
>
> Purely objective truth ... is nowhere to be found.
> The trail of the human serpent is thus over everything.[3]

[1] Donald Davidson, 'On the Very Idea of a Conceptual Scheme', in Davidson, *Inquiries into Truth and Interpretation* (Oxford: Clarendon Press, 1984), 183–98.

[2] For a remarkable account of realism, pragmatism, and constructivism as the three options for justifying any assertion, and for readings of Shakespeare related to this idea, see Rob Carson, 'Digesting the Third: Reconfiguring Binaries in Shakespeare and Early Modern Thought' (Dissertation, University of Toronto, 2008).

[3] William James, *Pragmatism: A New Name for Some Old Ways of Thinking* (1907), in Bruce Kuklick (ed.), *William James: Writings 1902–1910* (New York: Library of America, 1987), 514–15, cited

James moves on to claim that '*The true is the name of whatever proves itself to be good in the way of belief, and good, too, for definite, assignable reasons*'.[4] The 'definite, assignable reasons' here hark back to Charles Peirce, who, in an 1878 paper in *Popular Science Monthly* entitled 'How to Make Our Ideas Clear', defined a relation between conceptual clarity and action that James regards as crucial: 'Consider what effects, which might conceivably have practical bearings, we conceive the object of our conception to have. Then, our conception of those effects is the whole of our conception of the object.'[5] Peirce's maxim points toward the insistence on the inseparability of mind and experience, fact and value, which is the heart of pragmatism. Such an insistence does no harm to truth or to the quest to seek truths that are as solid as evidence and argument can make them. It does, however, undermine the idea that such a quest has as its aim incorrigible and thus extra-human truth, truth that has somehow escaped the history of human thought. Pragmatism does not propose new truth-seeking practices; it interrogates reigning theories about what truth-seeking is.

Pragmatism invites awareness (of what we would now call a 'presentist' kind) of the way claims of philosophic truth-seeking function in scholarship. As literary scholar-critics who teach would-be scholar-critics, our writings perforce model and participate in a ceaseless struggle for rhetorical advantage in an ongoing conversation. The conversation itself needs to be mobile, because its mobility is the main sign of life for the discursive institution of literary or cultural studies, which cannot replicate itself without also changing itself. To launch a book or article with a gesture toward methodological superiority—by way of historical accuracy, or of philosophic rigour, or of a proper understanding of the special nature of art, to cite three ways of claiming rhetorical high ground that have been prominent in the past few generations of literary criticism—gives one's piece a handle so that others can pick it up to use in their own rhetorical struggles. In preparing graduate students for future professional life, we need to be giving them such tools, and they may need to be, in effect, edged tools: sword/ploughshares that will both break new ground and take or defend contested territory. One of the virtues of presentist positions in the current presentist/historicist debate is that presentists acknowledge their participation in a struggle for rhetorical advantage in the here and now, and thus can seem less mystified about what they are doing than historicists. But historicist claims offer a huge research programme, backed by the ethical energy that comes with respect for the genuine difference of past from present.

---

parenthetically henceforth. It is amusing to notice that 'the trail of the serpent', here a vivid condensation of the way pragmatists deny that we can get outside the 'fallen' world of human values, appears with an entirely different valence in *The Varieties of Religious Experience* (1902): 'But surely the systematic theologians are the closet-naturalists of the deity . . . What is their deduction of these metaphysical attributes [of God] but a shuffling and matching of pedantic dictionary adjectives, aloof from morals, aloof from human needs . . . They have the trail of the serpent over them' (*Writings*, 400–1).

  [4] William James, *Writings*, 520.

  [5] Charles S. Peirce, 'How to Make Our Ideas Clear', in Peirce Edition Project (eds.), *Writings of Charles S. Peirce: A Chronological Edition*, vol. 3 (Bloomington, IN: Indiana University Press, 1982), 266. For James on this passage, see e.g., *Writings*, 506–7.

The pragmatist attack on both realist descriptions of objectivity and idealist descriptions of transcendence may seem a deflating or negative one. At the same time, however, pragmatist philosophers consistently present the abandonment of a quest for certainty as part of a broad acceptance of the openness of human futures. John Dewey and Richard Rorty both suggest, for instance, that the increase in the technical powers of science, and the partly consequent rise of a greatly enlarged group of educated people with reflective leisure who at least potentially participate in political life, may result in productive experiments in new and better forms of living that may lead eventually to better, more democratic, more thoughtful, more innovative lives for the people of the future. 'What is needed', as Dewey says, 'is intelligent examination of the consequences that are actually effected by inherited institutions and customs, in order that there may be intelligent consideration of the ways in which they are to be intentionally modified in behalf of generation of different consequences.'[6] This is a very American way of looking at things. At the same time, both Dewey and Rorty caution that there is no extra human–factor—no abstract immutable distinction between good and evil—that can protect us from the development of bad social forms, no truth that will set us free.

There have been sporadic attempts to make use of pragmatism in literary criticism and theory. The main such attempt focuses on an aspect of pragmatism that Louis Menand articulates when discussing the legal theorizing of Oliver Wendell Holmes Jr: the idea that practice or experience precedes logic or theory, and that it is thus always a mistake to put theory before practice.[7] According to Holmes, the decisions of a judge are not determined by the theory of the law the judge holds. 'Holmes said that common law judges decided the result first and figured out a plausible account of how they got there afterward' (p. 340). Holmes sums up this view in one sentence from *The Common Law*: 'The life of the law has not been logic; it has been experience' (p. 341). 'Even people who think their thinking is guided by general principles, in other words, even people who think thought is deductive, actually think the way everyone else does—by the seat of their pants' (p. 342). Menand goes on to argue attractively that this is the core of pragmatism. 'Pragmatism is an account of the way people think—the way they come up with ideas, form beliefs, and reach decisions' (p. 351). Pragmatists are Darwinists about truth, and Menand quotes James on how 'all our thoughts are *instrumental*, and mental modes of *adaptations* to reality, rather than revelations' (p. 358).

Pragmatism exalts what in contemporary administrative jargon are called 'best practices': if you want to do something right, do it according to what are the best-known practices for doing it. That means acquiring habits and entering into conversation with your betters, and mastering various vocabularies in which to describe your decisions; it does not (according to pragmatists) involve getting the nature of reality or language right so that the opinions of others will give way to a non-human truth. In

---

6 John Dewey, *The Quest for Certainty* (New York: Capricorn, 1960), 273.

7 Louis Menand, *The Metaphysical Club: A Story of Ideas in America* (New York: Farrar, Straus, and Giroux, 2001), 339. Further page references are given parenthetically in the text.

recent culture wars this aspect of pragmatism has aroused the criticism that pragmatists do not believe in firm standards by which one activity can be judged to be better than another. Rorty replies to this criticism in a response to the realist philosopher John Searle. Since the issue is important, I quote at some length.

> Here is an example of the kind of rhetoric which Searle quotes with relish as an illustration of the evil influence of views like mine: 'As the most powerful modern philosophies and theories have been demonstrating, claims of disinterest, objectivity, and universality are not to be trusted, and themselves tend to reflect local historical conditions.' I have to admit to Searle that the committee which produced that dreadful sentence included people who really do believe that the philosophical views I share with Kuhn and Derrida entail that the universities have no further use for notions like 'disinterest' and 'objectivity.'
>
> But these people are wrong. What we deny is that these notions can be explained or defended by reference to the notion of 'correspondence to mind-independent reality'. Philosophers on my side of the argument think that we can only explain what we mean when we say that academic research should be disinterested and objective by pointing to the ways in which free universities actually function.[8]

Rorty makes clear that he believes that the best practices of the academy—practices involving fairness in evaluation, the need to back claims with evidence, and the right to make unpopular arguments—need to be defended, and that the view that the university is just a political power-centre like any other should be deplored. But he believes we should defend these practices, and a view of a university as a special kind of place where special kinds of conversation occur, out of intelligent loyalty to our own institutions, not because we think we know how to arrive at a special inhuman form of truth-seeking.

In the same way, on a pragmatist account, resistance to evil has to be undertaken in the name of desirable and undesirable practices, not the idea that one is on the side of truth against error or of God against the devil. Joseph Schumpeter comments on defending democracy in this frame of mind: 'to realize the relative validity of one's convictions and yet stand for them unflinchingly is what distinguishes a civilized man from a barbarian'.[9]

If action, including heroic self-sacrificial right action, precedes theory in this way, literature can be seen as a repository of human experience, less organized than the law, but arguably broader or deeper, that impinges on practical judgement and itself is an object of such judgement. Literature can both redescribe human relations to make us aware of cruelty that needs attention, and make us aware of new possibilities of social and mental life.[10] *Pace* the claim occasionally made in the name of pragmatism by

---

[8] Richard Rorty, 'Does Academic Freedom Have Philosophical Presuppositions?', in Louis Menand (ed.), *The Future of Academic Freedom* (Chicago, IL: University of Chicago Press, 1996), 26–7.

[9] Schumpeter, *Capitalism, Socialism, and Democracy*, rpt. (London: George Allen and Unwin, 1976), 243.

[10] See Rorty, *Contingency, Irony, and Solidarity* (Cambridge: Cambridge University Press, 1989), *passim*, esp. 189–98.

followers of Stanley Fish that theory should end,[11] this is not a principled objection to the use of philosophic vocabularies by literary interpreters, but it is an objection to what they may think they are doing with philosophy: that is, *applying* a set of truths about the nature of language, or the relation of the subject to reality, to the experience of reading. Rorty caustically dismisses the possibility that pragmatism could serve as a 'literary theory'.

> When people got bored with New Criticism, they turned to other things. But the idea was always to, first, master a set of principles and then to apply them. This is a terrible way to be a critic, as people are now, perhaps, beginning to realize. This idea of 'applying a theory' would never have arisen if it weren't for the need to give credentials to thousands of members of departments of English literature. But I think that now everybody is so sick of formulaic criticism that we don't need to worry about literary theories anymore. In particular we don't need to worry about whether pragmatism counts as one of them.[12]

Pragmatism can, however, be more than simply a twentieth-century therapy against essentialism: it can on the one hand be a mode or tendency of thought in an author—a tendency to see the realm of value and interest as extending beyond the marketplace and pervading the realms where transcendence claims are routinely made—and on the other it can point us toward kinds of crisis that emerge around issues of causation and predictive truth, tensions around the relations between system and experience that emerge when choices must be made. I myself believe, and will argue in the rest of this chapter, that drama's general way of presenting experience is, in fact, illuminated by comparison to pragmatism's account of theory–practice relations, and that Shakespeare is an author with pragmatic intellectual habits. I illustrate the first point by reference to a powerful recent redescription of drama, and the second by reference to *Macbeth*.

PRAGMATISM AND SHAKESPEARE'S THEATRE

Let me begin with yet another evocation of pragmatism in relation to philosophy, this one from Richard Rorty's *Consequences of Pragmatism*. It is one of his many provocative thumbnail sketches of intellectual history:

> [My preferred] . . . way of characterizing pragmatism . . . focus[es] on a funda-mental choice which confronts the reflective mind: that between accepting the

---

[11] Steven Knapp and Walter Benn Michaels, 'Against Theory', in W. J. T. Mitchell (ed.), *Against Theory: Literary Studies and the New Pragmatism* (Chicago, IL: University of Chicago Press, 1985), 11–30.
[12] Richard Rorty, *Take Care of Freedom and Truth Will Take Care of Itself: Interviews with Richard Rorty*, Eduardo Mendieta (ed.) (Stanford, CA: Stanford University Press, 2006), 127.

contingent character of starting-points, and attempting to evade this contingency. To accept the contingency of starting-points is to accept our inheritance from, and our conversation with, our fellow-humans as our only source of guidance. To attempt to evade this contingency is to hope to become a properly-programmed machine. This was the hope which Plato thought might be fulfilled at the top of the divided line, when we passed beyond hypotheses. Christians have hoped it might be attained by becoming attuned to the voice of God in the heart, and Cartesians that it might be fulfilled by emptying the mind and seeking the indubitable. Since Kant, philosophers have hoped that it might be fulfilled by finding the a priori structure of any possible inquiry, or language, or form of social life. If we give up this hope, we shall lose what Nietzsche called 'metaphysical comfort,' but we may gain a renewed sense of community. Our identification with our community—our society, our political tradition, our intellectual heritage—is heightened when we see this community as *ours* rather than *nature's, shaped* rather than *found*, one among many which men have made. In the end, the pragmatists tell us, what matters is our loyalty to other human beings clinging together against the dark, not our hope of getting things right. James, in arguing against realists and idealists that 'the trail of the human serpent is over all,' was reminding us that our glory is in our participation in fallible and transitory human projects, not in our obedience to permanent non-human constraints.[13]

In one way, an emphasis on the contingency of starting points, alongside a goal of clinging together against (and maybe in) the dark, seems a good opening to a description of drama in general and of the way Shakespeare's plays operate, from which it may be an easy step to a description of the way Shakespeare thinks in his plays. Contingent starting points, after all, are what the first acts of plays lay out, and plays are also relentlessly concerned with the consequences of choice and with the communality of experience. Rorty's metaphor of 'clinging together against the dark' may well be connected with audience experiences at plays like *King Lear* or *Macbeth*, though he is equally likely to be thinking of Matthew Arnold's 'Dover Beach' or Samuel Beckett's *Waiting for Godot*.

In another way, however, the invocation of distinguished theorists beginning with Plato and running implicitly through Augustine and Aquinas and then explicitly through Descartes, Kant, and modern analytic philosophy seems unpromising in relation to Shakespeare. Philosophic tradition does not seem to have interested Shakespeare much. The name 'Plato', for instance, never appears in the works of Shakespeare, nor do the words 'republic' and 'symposium' that might bespeak Shakespearean awareness of Platonic themes. Shakespeare shows relatively little interest in, or respect for, contemplative self-isolation as a means to wisdom or truth.[14] And most of the figures Rorty cites as

[13] Richard Rorty, *Consequences of Pragmatism* (Minneapolis: University of Minnesota Press, 1980), 165–6.

[14] For argument along these lines, see Jonathan Bate, *Soul of the Age: A Biography of the Mind of Shakespeare* (New York: Random House, 2009), 360–72, and Lars Engle, 'Shame and Reflection in Montaigne and Shakespeare', *Shakespeare Survey* 63 (2010), 244–61.

guides toward evading the contingency of starting-points postdate Shakespeare. So it may seem oddly anachronistic to invoke philosophic pragmatism in an attempt to describe how Shakespeare thinks.

Nonetheless, William James's book *Pragmatism*, the first large-scale introduction of the term, is subtitled 'A New Name for Some Old Ways of Thinking'. 'Some old ways of thinking' sounds simple and turns out to be subtle. Ways of thinking are not beliefs; they can be conscious methods or unconscious habits; as 'ways' rather than 'a way' they need not be entirely coherent; 'ways' may also be found, followed, or made, may be lost and rediscovered, and may need mapping or repair. To see pragmatism as 'some old ways of thinking' involves identifying it with traditions of thought that evaluate concepts by investigating their practical consequences.

Socratic interrogations, as James points out, involve pragmatic enquiry,[15] but these evolve into Plato's vigorous indictments of sophistic rhetoric and, in related ways, of theatre and poetry, indictments that amount to the argument, basic to Platonism, that modes of discourse that merely follow the trail of the human serpent can never guide us in the direction of the truly good. Are theatre, poetry, and rhetoric, then, to be regarded as limbs of an implicit pragmatic doppelgänger shadowing philosophy from the start?

Paul Woodruff, in *The Necessity of Theater*, implicitly answers yes to this question. His book offers an impressive new theory of theatre that, without mentioning pragmatism, situates Shakespeare alongside Sophocles and Brecht and Beckett against Plato as offering a kind of wisdom or truth-seeking experience that is anti-Platonic in embracing contingent starting and ending points, but is nonetheless (as are James and Dewey and, less obviously, Rorty) reverent about the ideals of wisdom and right-living through reflective activity.[16] Woodruff claims that theatrical experience, broadly seen as watching significant human action in a measured time and space, is central to well-lived life and is absent from no life that can be considered human. Though Woodruff does not mention Dewey, his account of the necessity of measure and significance resembles arguments made in Dewey's chapter 'Having an Experience' in *Art as Experience*.[17] Thus theatre is 'necessary'. Woodruff has several examples from outside the realm of art theatre to which he returns repetitively, elaborating and deepening his account of them as he goes along: a wedding, a football game, a lynching, children demanding the attention of parents as they play, students and teachers in the theatrical activity of teaching and being taught. Woodruff sees watching and being watched as a sine qua non of human life, and he sees watching well and feeling worth watching by others as essential to good living:

---

[15] See, James, *Writings*, 508, where James conscripts Socrates, Aristotle, Locke, Berkeley, and Hume into the project 'to find out what definite difference it will make to you and me, at definite instants of our life, if this world-formula or that world-formula be the true one'.

[16] Paul Woodruff, *The Necessity of Theater: The Art of Watching and Being Watched* (Oxford and New York: Oxford University Press, 2008).

[17] John Dewey, *Art as Experience* (1934; rpt. New York: Putnam, 1980), 35–57.

Theater is the art of finding human action worth watching, and it mostly does this by finding human characters worth caring about. We need to practice that art, on both sides—to find people worth watching and, for ourselves, to make ourselves worth watching when we need to be watched (when we are getting married, for example). The grounds of this need are psychological (we dry up if we feel that no one is noticing us), social (a community comes apart if it attempts to secure justice in a forum that is not watched), and ethical (I cannot exercise human virtues unless I practice the art of watching). Willing or not, at one time or another, each of us will be among the watchers and the watched.[18]

As he develops this argument, with much circling back and gradual complication of various key examples (*Hamlet, Antigone*, weddings), it becomes clearer that Woodruff is to some degree relocating truth from its ancient association with contemplation and transcendence toward a social location in a mixed experience of critique and solidarity through theatre. This is, however, a relocation he does not want to argue for or about explicitly:

Plato . . . was right about this: theater is no place to learn the truth about justice. But then neither is the world in which we live. Justice does not live here; it does not live even in heaven, according to Plato.   (p. 214)

This is gentler and more fondly evocative than Rorty's comment on how Plato thought we could find proper programming at the top of the line, but it makes the same point. The project of finding non-contingent starting points such as the truth about justice has to take us out of this world, and, Rorty adds (while Woodruff holds his tongue) no one has succeeded yet in doing that. Woodruff continues, rather, by conceding philosophy its aspirations to transcendence but insisting that his expanded view of theatre is a necessary path to what is useful to us in the lives we actually live:

This earth is no place for the wisdom that would know the true nature of justice; I will not challenge Plato on that point. But this earth is the place for another kind of wisdom, and so is theater.   (p. 214)

Thus Woodruff's exaltation of theatre asserts that theatre offers necessary wisdom in the realm in which the trail of the human serpent is over all. Moreover, as Woodruff points out, much of the initial power of philosophy comes from theatre: what Socrates provided for the bright young men of Athens was what he calls 'direct theater' or 'extreme theater', theatre in which we cross the line between watching and participating (p. 214). Woodruff makes theatre into a school of participation in community life that is philosophical in a very Deweyan way, not 'in any sense whatever a form of knowledge' but rather 'a form of desire, of effort at action—a love, namely, of wisdom'.[19] As Dewey comments toward the end of *Art as Experience*, 'works of art are the most intimate and energetic means of aiding individuals to share in the arts of

---

[18] Woodruff, *Necessity*, 18. Further page references are given parenthetically in the text.

[19] John Dewey, 'Philosophy and Democracy', quoted in Robert Westbrook, *John Dewey and American Democracy* (Ithaca, NY: Cornell University Press, 1991), 145.

living'.[20] Woodruff shows how this rather banal-sounding observation of Dewey's has special application to theatre.

Woodruff's book on this description sounds very normative, as though comedy that affirms social cohesion were more basic than tragedy that exposes social faultlines. But the power of his claims can be seen when we look at the processes by which watching and being watched are just as central to the discursive establishment and propagation of new norm-altering practices, through, as he suggests, making us care for characters and simultaneously making us see that the realm of choices they inhabit is wrongly limited. The life lesson here involves stepping between being good at listening and watching and being good at talking and being watched:

> Learning when to speak and when to listen is the hardest lesson for a language learner. Many of us never get it right, and none of us gets it right all the time.
>
> So it is with theater, but it is even harder there, and less obvious that we must. . . . The performer must learn to watch, and the watcher must learn to perform. . . . How may this man become an agent of change, when he has so long been only a disaffected spectator? Or how may this colleague step back from the turbulence . . . and watch?
>
> . . . [T]heater is most theater when it is not theater at all, when the arts of watching and being watched merge and give way to shared action, shared experience.[21]

That is, the meaning of theatre lies in its capacity for consequences, some subtle and reflective, others overt and public.

Shakespearean Pragmatism in *Macbeth*

What does it mean to suggest that Shakespeare was a pragmatist, as I did in a book published in the early 1990s?[22] I focused on Shakespeare's frequent invocation of contingent evaluation systems like markets, and on his interest in the mutability of social forms over time. Shakespeare and other early modern thinkers were in no position to anticipate Darwin, but they were to varying degrees aware of economic processes that framed social forms and undergirded or undermined hierarchies; they also experienced the mutability of belief systems vividly because of the Reformation.

My suggestion was that in Shakespeare's dramas and poems, we find a pragmatic way of thinking about the way characters work toward understanding of the world, what I called a persistent tendency to redescribe fixed structures as mutable economies of value, and that the large-scale understanding of a social order in Shakespeare turned

---

[20] Dewey, *Art as Experience*, 336.
[21] Woodruff, *Necessity*, 229.
[22] Lars Engle, *Shakespearean Pragmatism: Market of His Time* (Chicago, IL: University of Chicago Press, 1993).

out to be, in a way that was distinctive to Shakespeare, a recognition of complex interdependence of one value on another, and a persistent exposure of absolutist language to evidence of its functions in an economy of values that to some extent undermines any claim it has to give access to certainty. I should add here that if *Shakespearean Pragmatism* had any impact, it was in providing generalizations (including some tentative historical generalizations) useful to critics involved in a small movement to see Shakespeare as an economic thinker, not in establishing a practice of pragmatist reading among Shakespeareans.

Macbeth was a worry, not a topic, in that project. The Shakespearean play that seems least anticipatory of modern enlightened attitudes, it barely features the overt dialogue between scepticism and credulousness, or realism and idealism, so prominent in other plays of the second part of Shakespeare's career. In *Macbeth*, Shakespeare does not seem very concerned with markets, or with market-like processes of evaluation. Shakespeare seems aware that *Macbeth* looks back to medieval society, and accordingly emphasizes gift-exchange, yet *Macbeth*'s treatment of Scottish feudalism does not think through the consequences of different political economies in the manner of *Timon*, *Troilus*, and the Roman plays. Nonetheless, I hope to show that *Macbeth* can be rewardingly redescribed in pragmatist terms, and specifically in terms suggested by Peirce, James, and Rorty.

Macbeth's supernaturalism and absolutism are aspects of what makes it the most clearly topical (and thus locally contingent) of Shakespeare's tragedies. Almost everything that happens in it can be brought into relation to the new reign of James I: into general relation to James's published opinions about sacred monarchy and about witchcraft and demonic agency and into more specific relation to James's survival of the Gunpowder Plot of 1605 and to the sermons and trials that were under way in late 1605 and 1606 as Shakespeare (we think) composed the play.[23]

While *Macbeth* may in some sense lie at the end of a causal chain that includes King James's writings, his coronation, and the plots against his rule, its relation to such a chain of causes remains a puzzle.[24] In fact, the play is preoccupied with just such puzzles, which engage Macbeth himself as well as readers of the play, and some of them can be elucidated by reference to Peirce's maxim: 'Consider what effects, which might

---

[23] For an imaginative historian's view of the play's topicality, see Garry Wills, *Witches and Jesuits: Shakespeare's 'Macbeth'* (New York: Oxford University Press, 1995); for an illustration of how a wealth of topicality can flow from the contextualization of a single line of *Macbeth*, see Arthur F. Kinney, 'Macbeth's Knowledge', *Shakespeare Survey* 57 (2004), 11–26. For an intelligent summary account illustrating that in *Macbeth* 'Shakespeare was by now well and truly the King's Man', see Jonathan Bate, *Soul of the Age*, 326.

[24] See, e.g., Alan Sinfield, 'History, Ideology, and Intellectuals', in Sinfield (ed.), *New Casebooks: Macbeth* (New York: St Martin's, 1992), 121–35; David Scott Kastan, 'Macbeth and the "Name of King"', *Shakespeare After Theory* (New York: Routledge, 1999), 165–92; Arthur F. Kinney, *Lies Like Truth: Shakespeare, 'Macbeth', and the Cultural Moment* (Detroit, MI: Wayne State University Press, 2001), 259–68 and *passim*; Jonathan Gil Harris, *Untimely Matter in the Time of Shakespeare* (Philadelphia: University of Pennsylvania Press, 2009), 119–40.

conceivably have practical bearings, we conceive the object of our conception to have. Then, our conception of those effects is the whole of our conception of the object.'

Macbeth offers a dramatic meditation on the relation among broader ideas of causal influence and on the future-oriented idea of meaning as practical consequence that is at the heart of pragmatism. The word 'consequence' is relatively rare in Shakespeare—*Hamlet* is the only play where it occurs more often than in *Macbeth*, and then only because Polonius's near-senility causes a triple repetition of his phrase 'closes in the consequence' in his conversation with Reynaldo (*Hamlet* 2.1.45–54).[25] In *Macbeth* the word occurs thrice, and each instance is crucial. Banquo cautions Macbeth that

> oftentimes to win us to our harm
> The instruments of darkness tell us truths,
> Win us with honest trifles to betray's
> In deepest consequence.   (1.3.121–4)

Macbeth, in a soliloquy, postulates a conditional, 'If th'assassination | Could trammel up the consequence, . . . | We'd jump the life to come' (1.7.2–7). And as Macbeth prepares to meet the English invasion, he asserts that the witches have given him a way to trammel up consequences:

> What's the boy Malcolm?
> Was he not born of woman? The spirits that know
> All mortal consequences have pronounced me thus:
> 'Fear not, Macbeth. No man that's born of woman
> Shall e'er have power upon thee.'   (5.3.3–7)

Thus *Macbeth* raises, quite overtly, a question that pragmatists often face: if you confine truth and morality to this-worldly consequences of actions, how do you distinguish successful action in a bad social order from good action, or successful intellectual conformity in a lying social order from truth?[26] Can you guarantee that it is possible in a range of social situations to be, by your own lights, good? Is it possible, for instance, to be good in the play's Scotland? For 'deepest consequence' here—by which Banquo means 'salvation' and 'damnation'—here has everything to do with works, not faith, with what characters do, not what they believe. This brings us to the question of what the play's contingent starting point actually is.

Few of Macbeth's actions in the play escape critical censure, but he is not often condemned for saving Duncan. By personally killing the rebel Macdonald on one battlefield and defeating the Norwegian king on another, Macbeth (with Banquo as a second) rescues Duncan's kingship. In Shakespeare's sources Duncan has been a poor king, incapable of maintaining order because of his meek gentleness. In this play, no reason whatsoever is given for the rebellion except Macdonald's 'villainies of nature'

---

[25] See Marvin Spevack, *The Harvard Concordance to Shakespeare* (Cambridge, MA: Harvard University Press, 1973), 232.

[26] On this see James Ryerson, 'The Quest for Uncertainty: Richard Rorty's Pilgrimage', in Mendieta (ed.), *Take Care of Freedom*, 13–15.

(1.2.11) and, arguably, the 'Norwegian lord ... surveying vantage' (1.2.31). Something about Scotland causes villainy to 'swarm' (1.2.12) and enemies to seek to take advantage of its weakness.

Thus Macbeth's first line, 'So foul and fair a day I have not seen' (1.3.36), registers an ambivalence that may extend beyond the weather and his possible ambivalence about killing people, to attach also to what he, or he and Banquo, have just done in political terms: sustained with enormous risk and effort a king whom many want to overthrow, and thus committed Scotland to the likelihood of continued political disruption. Harry Berger has an influential and insightful account of the early scenes of the play that suggests some of this. He surveys the disorder Duncan presides over, and discerns also 'that those who speak with Duncan respond to him with varying degrees of barely concealed constraint, irritability, perhaps condescension'.[27]

But even Berger, who sees Duncan's speeches to Macbeth registering Duncan's embarrassment in being the loser in a gift-exchange, does not quite capture the sheer administrative incompetence of Duncan's well-intentioned behaviour toward Macbeth and Banquo. Having sent Ross and Angus to tell Macbeth that he is now Thane of Cawdor 'for an earnest of a greater honour' (1.3.102), Duncan greets Macbeth as 'worthiest cousin' (1.4.14), then reproaches Macbeth for doing so much ('Would thou hadst less deserved' [1.4.18]) and goes on to say that '"More is thy due than more than all can pay"' (1.4.21). This forces Macbeth into an embarrassed civics lesson directed at someone who either proposes to abdicate in his favour (a plausible construal of the 'all' in Duncan's 'more than all') or has temporarily lost sight of the central monarchical idea that kings are founts of honour:

> Your highness' part
> Is to receive our duties, and our duties
> Are to your throne and state children and servants
> Which do but what they should by doing everything
> Safe toward your love and honour.   (1.4.23–7)

Duncan goes on immediately to tell Banquo that, despite the (accurate) description of Macbeth as 'worthiest', Banquo has 'no less deserved, nor must be known | No less to have done so' (1.4.30–1)—thus sowing doubt between Banquo and Macbeth about which of them deserves 'more than all', and rhetorically undercutting his recent evaluation of Macbeth. Finally, bursting into tears, and having failed, as Berger points out, to deliver Macbeth anything new and Banquo anything more than a hug, Duncan begins the big announcement he and his messenger led Macbeth and the audience to expect: 'Sons, kinsmen, thanes, | And you whose places are the nearest' (1.4.35–6)—the 'you ... nearest' being Macbeth and Banquo—

---

[27] 'The Early Scenes of *Macbeth*', in Harry Berger, Jr, *Making Trifles of Terrors: Redistributing Complicities in Shakespeare* (Stanford, CA: Stanford University Press, 1997), 95.

> know
> We will establish our estate upon . . .   (1.4.37–8)

Upon whom? It is important to recognize that, to someone seeing or reading *Macbeth* for the first time without knowing what is going to happen, the next line comes as a surprise: 'Our eldest, Malcolm, whom we name hereafter | The Prince of Cumberland' (1.4.38–9).

What a disappointment, after this build-up! And what a humiliation for Macbeth! Of course one can understand that Duncan feels the need to defend himself against his obligation to Macbeth and against Macbeth's superiority in battle to Malcolm, but surely he should not take this moment to assert a succession that cannot be automatic, since it has hitherto been unestablished. Moreover, having promised Macbeth something special beyond Cawdor's thaneship, Duncan should also not follow the gift of 'all' to Malcolm with vague never-realized offers of promotion to practically everyone without any specific individual reward for Macbeth:

> . . . The Prince of Cumberland; which honour must
> Not unaccompanied invest him only,
> But signs of nobleness, like stars, shall shine
> On all deservers.   (1.4.39–42)

No wonder Macbeth mutters 'stars, hide your fires' (1.4.50) a few lines later. Duncan has made it a humiliation rather than a pleasure to have this sort of star shine on him.

Perhaps Duncan's well-intentioned awkwardness (which has an endearing quality: he makes everyone feel awful about their relations with him while wishing all of them the very best) arises partly from his grief over the first Thane of Cawdor's betrayal. This Cawdor is one of a series of alter egos to Macbeth himself (a man whose title and 'robes' Macbeth assumes before he does Duncan's). We know that Duncan regarded Cawdor highly: Duncan orders his abrupt, trial-free execution with the comment 'No more that Thane of Cawdor shall deceive | Our bosom interest. Go pronounce his present death, | And with his former title greet Macbeth' (1.2.63–5). Duncan greets Macbeth under the influence of regret and confusion, the immediate aftermath of betrayal by a 'bosom' friend, 'a gentleman on whom I built | An absolute trust' (1.4.14–16). The play sounds a note of disappointment in absolute commitments that reverberates later. It seems possible, moreover, that the Scottish succession, oddly suspended until its untimely announcement in Malcolm's favour, may have somehow been linked to Cawdor. Macbeth replies to the witches' hailing him as 'Thane of Cawdor' with the comment 'The Thane of Cawdor lives | A prosperous gentleman, and to be king | Stands not within the prospect of belief, | No more than to be Cawdor' (1.3.70–2). That Macbeth should link the incredibility of the two titles in this way suggests that Duncan's 'prosperous' intimate stands between Macbeth and the throne, a 'step | On which I must fall down or else o'erleap' (1.4.48–9), as Malcolm becomes after Duncan announces the succession.

Cawdor, it turns out, has sided with Norway against a king who favoured him more highly than any other thane. When that attempt fails, Cawdor makes the best he can of the consequences of his actions, and does so with considerable grace, as Malcolm reports:

> Nothing in his life
> Became him like the leaving it. He died
> As one that had been studied in his death
> To throw away the dearest thing he owed
> As 'twere a careless trifle.   (1.4.7–11)

This decorous action elevates Cawdor in our mind and deepens the pathos of his betrayal, but also makes betrayal by such a smooth performer more significant.[28] Either Cawdor felt that Duncan was fated to fall, or he felt that Duncan ought to fall. Certainly the set of political conditions surrounding Duncan at the outset makes his fall seem likely, and we have seen in Duncan's reception of Macbeth's victories how self-undermining a king Duncan is when he is trying to confer favour on someone.

Given this, Macbeth must begin the play in doubt that he has done the right thing by saving Duncan (a similar doubt may contribute to the 'cursèd thoughts | Nature gives way to in repose' [2.1.8–9] mentioned by Banquo). Such doubt may contribute to the complexity of Macbeth's thinking about murdering him—Macbeth both needs to reassure himself that Duncan is worth having saved—that he is 'meek' and 'clear' of abuse of power (1.7.17–18), *and* that it may be the effective, self-enhancing thing to murder him.

If, as pragmatists assert, moral truths are condensations of principles by which communities thrive, and communities are constantly evolving and developing new norms, then a moral choice will often be a choice between longer-term, more stable, less immediate community-oriented values and shorter-term, less stable, more immediate self-oriented values. Apparent absolutes, like 'thou shalt not kill', turn out to mean in most instances something like 'thou shalt not kill unless your community requires you to do so for its collective good (as, say, a soldier) or unless your community regards you as having an imperative justification of a kind it collectively accepts (defending your family or yourself against an assault with intent to kill)'. That is, it means something like 'thou shalt not kill well-behaved members of your community, and thou shalt check carefully before killing outsiders'.[29]

'Thou shalt not commit regicide' in 1605–6 might seem to permit fewer qualifications, since God sends the monarch in theory to centre the community as a parent does a family, but a community-injuring monarch does much to thin the hedge of divinity that protects him, as sixteenth-century resistance theorists argued. The historical Macbeth was linked to justified resistance.[30] Some surprisingly Machiavellian

---

[28] See Rebecca Lemon, 'Scaffolds of Treason in *Macbeth*', *Theatre Journal* 54.1 (2002), 25–43, for an argument that Cawdor's scaffold confession should be seen as conventional and perhaps unreliably reported.

[29] See Rorty, *Contingency*, 194–5.

[30] See, for a particularly strong claim along these lines from a Catholic, Juan de Mariaga, *De Rege et Regis Institutione* (Toledo, 1599), Robert S. Miola (trans. and ed.), *Macbeth: A Norton Critical Edition* (New York: Norton, 2004), 154–9. For discussion of George Buchanan and other Protestant resistance theorists see David Norbrook, '*Macbeth* and the Politics of Historiography', in Kevin Sharpe and Steven Zwicker (eds.), *Politics of Discourse: The Literature and History of Seventeenth-Century England* (Berkeley: University of California Press, 1987), 78–116; Kinney, *Lies Like Truth*, 103–24; and William

comments made by Macduff to Malcolm in Act 4 suggest his awareness of both practice and theory of resistance. After Malcolm describes himself as a voluptuary, Macduff says 'Boundless intemperance | In nature is a tyranny. It hath been | Th'untimely emptying of the happy throne, | And fall of many kings' (4.3.67–70). But Macduff thinks Scotland has 'willing dames enough' to endure or exhaust such a king (4.3.74), and Macduff's regime-change commentary might just be general analysis of the falls of princes. When Malcolm goes on to describe himself as full of avarice, Macduff brings his reflections on regicide home: 'This avarice... hath been | The sword of our slain kings' (4.3.88). In other words, Scotland routinely empties its thrones of misbehaving kings, often by murder.[31] The ways Malcolm employs arts of deception similar to Macbeth's and Cawdor's has often been remarked, but Macduff's frank confirmation of deposition and regicide as habitual consequences of royal error is more startling than Malcolm's double-talk in a play sometimes thought to be absolutist.[32]

Macbeth takes up short-term versus long-term consequences, and I-intentions versus we-intentions, more systematically and philosophically than any other Shakespeare play. A. C. Bradley writes that Lady Macbeth and Macbeth are linked in having a limited social conception of themselves:

> We observe in them no love of country, and no interest in the welfare of anyone outside their family. Their habitual thoughts and aims are, and, we imagine, long have been, all of station and power.... Not that they are egoists, like Iago; or if they are egoists, theirs is an *egoïsme à deux*.[33]

As Bradley's phrase suggests, it is hard in their case to separate dual intentions from individual ones, at least early in the play, but when it is possible to make this separation, the differences are fascinating. The 'we' of Macbeth and Lady Macbeth *à deux* in early scenes is far less prone to long-term thinking, and to recognition of patterns of communal health, than the 'I' or the free-floating 'we' of Macbeth's soliloquies in 1.3 and 1.7. Indeed, what triggers Lady Macbeth's extraordinary assault on her husband's masculinity is a signal from Macbeth that he is thinking of a 'we' that is larger than the two of them:

MACBETH: Hath he asked for me?
LADY MACBETH: Know you not he has?

C. Carroll, '"Two Truths are Told": Afterlives and Histories of Macbeths', *Shakespeare Survey* 57 (2004), 69–80.

[31] Machiavelli in ch. XVII of *The Prince* cautions that clemency is more dangerous in a prince than cruelty, because it is better to be feared than loved. But one must avoid being hated, which the prince can do as long as he abstains from the property of his citizens and subjects and from their women. 'If [the Prince] must take someone's life, he should do so when there is proper justification and manifest cause; but, above all, he should avoid the property of others; for men forget more quickly the death of their father than the loss of their patrimony.' Peter Bondanella and Mark Musa (eds. and trans.), *The Portable Machiavelli* (New York: Penguin, 1979), 132.

[32] For Malcolm's resemblance to Macbeth and to Cawdor, see Lemon, 'Scaffolds of Treason'.

[33] A. C. Bradley, *Shakespearean Tragedy* (1904; London: Macmillan, 1965), 293.

MACBETH: We will proceed no further in this business.
         He hath honoured me of late, and I have bought
         Golden opinions from all sorts of people,
         Which would be worn now in their newest gloss,
         Not cast aside so soon.
LADY MACBETH: Was the hope drunk
         Wherein you dressed yourself? Hath it slept since?
         And wakes it now to look so green and pale
         At what it did so freely? From this time
         Such I account thy love.

                                (1.7.30–9)

And she proceeds to her fantasia on the nursing child that does so much, as Janet Adelman and others have shown, to set masculinity in this play in opposition to any sort of fruitful social interdependence.[34] Lady Macbeth's cue is, however, Macbeth's quite ordinary response to suddenly being well-thought-of by those who watch him: it endears his local community to him (doubtless a largely male community), and she violently brings him back to the limited and focused nuptial 'we' of claims like 'But screw your courage to the sticking-place | And we'll not fail' (1.7.60–1).

As we have already seen, non-supernatural lines of causation of a Machiavellian kind meet in the death of Duncan. What lines of causation spread from it? How does Macbeth's own sense of causality and existence in time focus on the killing? Insofar as *Macbeth* treats Macbeth's consciousness as a central realm of investigation, what the play does is to unpack the practical consequences of an initial conception:

         My thought, whose murder yet is but fantastical,
         Shakes so my single state of man that function
         Is smothered in surmise, and nothing is
         But what is not.   (1.3.138–41)

The first consequence is radical self-division, the shaking of Macbeth's 'single state of man'. A second imagined consequence is that Macbeth might recover a 'single state of man' by doing the deed, or by achieving the bright circular singular crown, 'the golden round' (1.5.27), 'that | Which thou esteem'st the ornament of life' (1.7.41–2).

This view is strongly urged by Lady Macbeth. Macbeth's submission to her is also a resolution to unify himself: 'I am settled, and bend up | Each corporal agent to this terrible feat' (1.7.79–80). In other words, Macbeth seeks to end self-division by rallying all his internal forces to this one goal and achieving peace through what Lady Macbeth calls 'our great quell' (1.7.72). This 'quell' is referred to in causal and euphemistic terms as a quintessential transformative and unifying action by both of them: 'the nearest way' (1.5.17), 'Th'effect' (1.5.46), 'This night's great business... | Which shall to all our nights and days to come | Give solely sovereign sway and masterdom' (1.5.67–9), 'this

---

[34] See Janet Adelman, *Suffocating Mothers: Fantasies of Maternal Origin in Shakespeare's Plays, 'Hamlet' to 'The Tempest'* (London: Routledge, 1992), 130–47.

business' (1.7.31), 'the hope . . . | Wherein you dressed yourself' (1.7.35-6), 'To be the same in thine own act and valour | As thou art in desire' (1.7.40-1), 'this enterprise' (1.7.48), 'to be more than what you were' (1.7.50), 'this' (1.7.59), 'What . . . you and I [can] perform' (1.7.69), ' 't' (1.7.77), 'it' (1.7.77), 'the way that I was going' (2.1.42), 'the bloody business' (2.1.48), 'it' (2.1.62), 'He is about it' (2.2.4), ''t' (2.2.10), 'the deed' (2.2.10), ''t' (2.2.13), 'I have done the deed' (2.2.14). The maximal contraction to a repeated ''t' ('Will it not be received | . . . | That they have done't?'[1.7.74-7], 'I am afraid . . . | . . . , 'tis not done' [2.2.9-10], 'Had he not resembled | My father as he slept, I had done't' [2.2.12-13]) offers a typographical registration of the way the Macbeths have reduced this action to a decisive transformative moment in which cause and effect join to satisfy desire and end frustration, encoding the unity of personal being, mutual happiness, and future security.

Or rather, this is what Macbeth does under the insistent pressure of Lady Macbeth's power to shame him. When he is alone, as we have already seen in his comment on how the thought of murder 'shakes . . . my single state of man', Macbeth has a considerably wider sense of the web of consequences that denies control of the meaning of an action to its actor. After all, Macbeth articulates both the hope and the near-impossibility that 'th'assassination | Could trammel up the consequence, and catch | With his surcease, success' (1.7.2-4). In this, Macbeth applies Peirce's maxim to his own aspirations: 'consider what effects, which might conceivably have practical bearings, we conceive [the murder of Duncan | becoming King of Scotland] to have. Then, our conception of those effects is the whole of our conception of the object'. This sets the meaning of an act in the future, but offers a way of limiting the consequences to 'practical' ones. Macbeth first uses this maxim to cut off otherworldly judgement from consideration, at least as most interpreters understand his lines:

> If it were done when 'tis done, then 'twere well
> It were done quickly. If th'assassination
> Could trammel up the consequence, and catch
> With his surcease success: that but this blow
> Might be the be-all and the end-all, here,
> But here upon this bank and shoal of time,
> We'd jump the life to come.   (1.7.1-7)

The indefinition of both 'it' and 'we' creates an oscillation between the general situation of human action undertaken in the desire to cut off forking paths of consequence and the particular murder in question. We find the same sort of oscillation in Hamlet's 'To be, or not to be' (*Hamlet* 3.1.58-90) , or Macbeth's later 'Tomorrow, and tomorrow, and tomorrow' (5.5.18-27). Shakespearean philosophizing has this quality of circling mysteriously around the particular in generally suggestive ways. The 'we' might plausibly be Macbeth and Lady Macbeth, but if so it is a far less contracted and purposeful 'we' than the one Lady Macbeth enforces. The 'we' of 'we'd jump' reaches out to include the audience or reader in a general reflection on action amid uncertainty about consequences. If 'jump' means 'hazard', as editors suggest, Macbeth anticipates the terms of Pascal's wager but refuses to accept its argument for longest-term thinking.

Returning to this-worldly considerations, Macbeth then reasons morally by exploring middle-term consequences of the murder of Duncan:

> But in these cases
> We still have judgement here, that we but teach
> Bloody instructions which, being taught, return
> To plague th'inventor. This even-handed justice
> Commends th'ingredience of our poisoned chalice
> To our own lips.   (1.7.7–12)

Sounding like someone who has the final scene of *Hamlet* in mind ('purposes mistook | Fall'n on th'inventors' heads' [*Hamlet* 5.2.338–9], 'Drink off this potion' ([*Hamlet* 5.2.278] '[The King] is justly served. It is a poison tempered by himself' [*Hamlet* 5.2.279–80]) Macbeth recognizes that the middle-term social consequences of violent usurpation may threaten the usurper. He then begins to think in less exclusively political (but still, from a pragmatic viewpoint, practical) terms about the communal norms he will violate by killing Duncan:

> He's here in double trust:
> First, as I am his kinsman and his subject,
> Strong both against the deed; then, as his host,
> Who should against his murderer shut the door,
> Not bear the knife myself. Besides, this Duncan
> Hath borne his faculties so meek, hath been
> So clear in his great office, that his virtues
> Will plead like angels, trumpet-tongued against
> The deep damnation of his taking-off,
> And pity, like a naked new-born babe,
> Striding the blast, or heaven's cherubin, horsed
> Upon the sightless couriers of the air,
> Shall blow the horrid deed in every eye
> That tears shall drown the wind.   (1.7.12–25)

All these disincentives are cast in terms of a metaphoric storm of social grief and reproach. Macbeth imagines himself assailed at both ear and eye by a set of regrets occasioned by the very characteristics in Duncan that seem to have made him ripe for usurpation: his meekness and his innocence. The 'angels' and 'cherubin' here are present in simile as hypostatized guardians of apolitical virtues, the areas of inhibition that protect the 'naked new-born babe' from harm. Lady Macbeth shows how well she knows her husband's imagination when she chastises him by slaughtering another hypothetical infant.

Two directions of consequentiality govern Macbeth's evolution in the play, and both are forecast in the early soliloquies and exchanges with his wife. The first is the diminution of meaningful action by the elimination of a meaningful community of fellow-humans, the 'watchers' whose moral centrality Paul Woodruff asserts. Lady

Macbeth sees such watchers as subject to the will of the strong, saying of her very sketchy plan to pin guilt for Duncan's murder on the guards: 'Who dares receive it other?' (1.7.77). Macbeth retains some sense of this community of watchers when he tells the murderers that he could 'With barefaced power sweep [Banquo] from my sight | And bid my will avouch it, yet I must not, | For certain friends that are both his and mine, | Whose loves I may not drop' (3.2.120–3). But by the time Macbeth revisits the witches and receives a second set of prophecies, he has rhetorically at least divested himself of communal concerns: 'For mine own good | All causes shall give way. I am in blood | Stepped in so far that, should I wade no more, | Returning were as tedious as go o'er' (3.4.134–7). Macbeth fords this wide river of blood by himself because he has redescribed Lady Macbeth not as co-actor but as audience for the murder of Banquo: 'Be innocent of the knowledge, dearest chuck, | Till thou applaud the deed' (3.3.46–7). Tedium emerges as a problem because the vital contribution to meaning made by the watchers of one's actions is denied. The full-blown expression of this nihilistic view emerges when Lady Macbeth, the residual audience, dies, and Macbeth sees life as an entirely meaningless succession because a performance unworthy of being seriously watched:

> Tomorrow, and tomorrow, and tomorrow
> Creeps in this petty pace from day to day
> To the last syllable of recorded time,
> And all our yesterdays have lighted fools
> The way to dusty death. Out, out, brief candle.
> Life's but a walking shadow, a poor player
> That struts and frets his hour upon the stage,
> And then is heard no more. It is a tale
> Told by an idiot, full of sound and fury,
> Signifying nothing.   (5.5.18–27)

One can agree with Tzachi Zamir that 'through Macbeth, Shakespeare captures an intellectual nihilism that emerges from a psychological and existential context'.[35] But it is important to see also that another direction of consequentiality runs through Macbeth's own perspective on the action that enmeshes him. Macbeth himself has diagnosed the conditions for meaningful action in the play. When the witches assure Macbeth that he will reign until Birnam Wood comes to Dunsinane, Macbeth responds:

> Sweet bodements, good!
> Rebellious dead, rise never till the wood
> Of Birnam rise, and on's high place Macbeth
> Shall live the lease of nature, pay his breath
> To time and mortal custom.   (4.1.112–16)

---

[35] Tzachi Zamir, *Double Vision: Moral Philosophy and Shakespearean Drama* (Princeton, NJ: Princeton University Press, 2007), 107.

Thus time and mortal custom—the conditions of endurance through change by way of ingrained community habit—will carry Macbeth through. Even up to the end Macbeth keeps evoking harmonious communality wistfully as something he has forgone:

> My way of life
> Is fall'n into the sere, the yellow leaf,
> And that which should accompany old age,
> As honour, love, obedience, troops of friends,
> I must not look to have, but in their stead
> Curses, not loud but deep, mouth-honour, breath
> Which the poor heart would fain deny and dare not.
>   (5.3.24–30)

Macbeth invokes the community of watchers as here offering a meaningful response to his choices: they curse him subvocally while fearing him.

   What could lead Macbeth to this point? He is repeatedly seduced, as a pragmatist would see it, by a quest for certainty. He imagines what he does to those he kills as supplying them a certainty he himself desires: the bell that sends him to Duncan's chamber is 'a knell | That summons thee to heaven or to hell' (2.1.63–4), and after sending out the murderers, he says 'Banquo, thy soul's flight, | If it find heaven, must find it out tonight' (3.1.142–3). (There is no purgatory in Macbeth's imagination of death: it is an immediate up or down. Though Catholic in its orientation toward works rather than faith, *Macbeth* shows no nostalgia for Catholic afterlives.) Macbeth cannot rest in a kingship that does not somehow conquer the future: 'To be thus is nothing | But to be safely thus' (3.1.49–50). Having conferred certainty of status on others, he envies them his gift:

> Better be with the dead,
> Whom we to gain our peace have sent to peace,
> Than on the torture of the mind to lie
> In restless ecstasy. Duncan is in his grave.
> After life's fitful fever he sleeps well.
> Treason has done his worst. Nor steel nor poison,
> Malice domestic, foreign levy, nothing
> Can touch him further.   (3.3.21–8)

Duncan's life was 'fitful' because of the uncertain and conflict-laden relation he had with his primary watchers, the thanes who revolted against him, allied themselves with foreign levies, and finally took steel to his body. The same uncertainty seizes Macbeth when he learns that the murderers have not killed Fleance:

> Then comes my fit again; I had else been perfect,
> Whole as the marble, founded as the rock,
> As broad and general as the casing air,
> But now I am cabined, cribbed, confined, bound in
> To saucy doubts and fears.   (3.4.20–4)

By the play's end, Macbeth has in effect emptied out the world to a point where his own action has no significance because a meaningful audience has been entirely alienated. Each recollection of meaningful living turns out to be a remembrance of a community of watchers; each complaint turns out to be a recognition of being bound in to a chain of consequences that is not worth watching.

I have argued in this chapter that pragmatism can offer plausible paradigms for how theatre engages philosophic issues, and that it is helpful and plausible to think of pragmatism as a description of how Shakespeare's thought achieves such power while evading the fixed starting points available to thinkers of his era. The effort to delineate the local historical processes in which a work of art from the past participated is thus a kind of pragmatism: many aspects of *Macbeth* can plausibly be seen as practical consequences of the accession of King James. Moreover, *Macbeth* can also be seen as a meditation on the ways that trying to exhibit 'pragmatism' in the ordinary-language sense of focusing on practical consequences and setting aside emotions or ideals to do so can be destructive for persons and for states.

More importantly, *Macbeth* also anticipates philosophic pragmatism's critique of certainty claims and of aspirations to certainty. The play focuses insistently on how attempts to close off the openness of the future lead to cruelty and to self-reduction. Indeed, the play offers something surprisingly close to a pragmatist moral: if you attempt to guarantee your own future security by foreclosing the future possibilities of others like you, the watchers who give your actions meaning, you may destroy yourself as well as them. You are social, not individual; mutable and fallible, not fixed and unerring; and your relation to your own future must acknowledge this and thus admit insecurity and rivalry. As a moral, this may seem banal. It is certainly an easy point for readers and playgoers to get, given that Middleton, the play's first interpreter, makes Hecate state something very like it: 'You all know security | Is mortal's greatest enemy' (3.5.32–3). But it is not banal. Attempts to negotiate between greater certainty and individual control, on one hand, and on the other, less certainty, more social participation, and the possibility of more harmony, constitute from a pragmatist viewpoint the centre of moral reasoning. *Macbeth* shows the tragic social and personal consequences of a quest for certainty.

CHAPTER 36

....

RELIGION

....

BRIAN CUMMINGS

WHAT did Shakespeare believe? Religion appears to be the last great mystery in Shakespeare studies. For much of the twentieth century the topic appeared marginal, in the same way that the Reformation seemed marginal to the English Renaissance, or perhaps in the way that belief and devotion appeared marginal to the study of English literature more widely. In contrast to this, more has been written on the question in the last decade than perhaps at any point in 300 years of Shakespearean scholarship. This has accompanied, and is obviously related to, a transformation in the field by means of which post-Reformation religion, of late, has become the most widely discussed question in early modern literature. Yet Shakespeare's religion remains an enquiry that evokes a special form of quizzicality. David Bevington, in a magisterial, articulate and wisely judicious essay on *Shakespeare's Ideas*, for a series of books on great human thinkers, takes on the topic of religion almost last of all, just before that of scepticism. Moreover, like others, he is more certain of establishing grounds for Shakespeare's scepticism than for his belief. Bevington opens his chapter on faith with a paragraph that contains six questions and only one statement, and that statement sums up the opinion of someone else, not his own.[1]

Opinion about Shakespeare's religion, while more vocal than ever, is still openly divided. In a recent interview, Stephen Greenblatt confirmed his view that Shakespeare lived a life:

> in the shadow of Catholic belief. Shakespeare loved damaged institutional goods, and he drew upon them for aesthetic purposes all his life. My opinion is that he did this because he had a close personal relationship with them, but whether or not that's true, their presence can be felt in all his work.[2]

---

[1] *Shakespeare's Ideas: More Things in Heaven and Earth*, Blackwell Great Thinkers (Oxford: Wiley-Blackwell, 2008), 106.

[2] Massachussetts Institute of Technology, forum on 'literature/ history/ biography', October 14, 2008, http://web.mit.edu/comm-forum/forums/greenblatt.html.

In complete contrast, a year before, at the end of another long career in Shakespearean commentary, A. D. Nuttall came to the opposite conclusion: Shakespeare, Nuttall says, 'writes as if the Reformation hasn't even happened'.[3]

The Reformation in Shakespeare's England

Each of these statements, disarmingly made, is more complex than it looks. Greenblatt carefully distances himself from a biographical assumption while also drawing on its power as an imaginative matrix. He is careful not to say that Shakespeare had Catholic beliefs, only that he lived 'in the shadow' of such belief. Nuttall does not say that Shakespeare did not notice the Reformation, but that somehow he effaces it, writing 'as if' it had not taken place. In other words, for Greenblatt, the Reformation deeply matters to Shakespeare whether or not he acknowledged it, whereas for Nuttall the Reformation is irrelevant to Shakespeare, in whatever way he personally responded to it. Yet despite the gulf between these scholars, what is striking, from the point of view of the history of Shakespearean interpretation, is that religion plays such a prominent role in defining the terms of discussion.

Even as an absence, the Reformation now holds a powerful meaning in Shakespearean studies. This would have seemed strange a generation ago, when religion was held to be irrelevant to a writer pre-eminently secular in tone. As a sign of this prejudice, a predecessor to the current volume, *The Cambridge Companion to Shakespeare*, in both its first and its second editions, felt no need to include religion as a topic.[4] Yet we might ask in response how could the most divisive and dramatic events of his century pass Shakespeare by? Religion is the dominant landscape behind the cultural structures of the sixteenth century. No musical or visual history of the period would make sense without religion, and the same is beginning to be held true in literary history. Religion transformed the material, ideological, and imaginative contexts of books and writing.[5] Yet in understanding this, we have also come to see how a cultural history, perhaps especially a literary history bound up with the study of words and their meanings, also makes the idea of the Reformation itself much more complex.

The Reformation was perhaps at one time seen primarily in terms of linear events of change: a transformation in doctrine and in institutions, and in English terms, in one revolutionary direction from 'Catholic' to 'Protestant'. The picture as now seen in historical studies is much more varied. The break with Rome initiated by Henry VIII's

---

[3] *Shakespeare the Thinker* (New Haven, CT: Yale University Press, 2007), 20.

[4] *The Cambridge Companion to Shakespeare Studies*, Stanley Wells (ed.) (Cambridge: Cambridge University Press, 1986); *The Cambridge Companion to Shakespeare*, Margreta de Grazia and Stanley Wells (ed.) (Cambridge: Cambridge University Press, 2001). A projected third edition will finally make up the gap.

[5] Brian Cummings, 'Reformed Literature and Literature Reformed', in, David Wallace (ed.), *The Cambridge History of Medieval English Literature* (Cambridge: Cambridge University Press, 1999), 821–51.

divorce and subsequently enacted by the Act of Supremacy in 1534 accompanied wide-spread conflict over belief and ritual, much of it prompted by revolutions in Martin Luther's Germany and Huldrych Zwingli's Switzerland. Henry's religious policy of the 1530s was at first radical and then increasingly conservative, attempting to shore up traditional practices around the Mass and prayers for the dead, while destroying the monasteries in which so much of medieval English cultural life was embodied, and attacking the cult of the saints. Under Henry's son, Edward VI, a second Protestant Reformation was much more decisively revolutionary, with iconoclasm a visible sign of an onslaught on traditional religion which brought with it a vernacular Book of Common Prayer containing a different concept of religious ritual. The bodily performance of the Mass, the elaborate material culture of gesture, offering, censing, and blessing, and its attendant culture of procession and communal celebration, was swept away in favour of a system of mental observation and assent, a hegemony of internalized faith. Yet this revolution lasted only five years; under Mary I, a counter-Reformation took place, reversing the previous legislation and combining the reinstitution of traditional practice with persecution of Protestants. By the time of Shakespeare's childhood, England was under the sway of a further religious regime, the fifth in thirty years.

Elizabeth's religious 'settlement', which appeared to make permanent the Protestant face of England, did nothing of the kind in practice. Outward religious conformity, built round a new edition of the Book of Common Prayer, concealed a panoply of religious positions. Division took place on family, social, and regional lines and frequently interrelated with political factions, but it also reflected a widespread anxiety and uncertainty. What were people supposed to believe in times of such volatility? A footnote in the 1552 Book of Common Prayer took the trouble to explain that in requiring that the congregation kneel at certain points in the service, 'it is not ment thereby, that any adoracion is doone, or oughte to bee doone, eyther unto the Sacramentall bread or wyne there bodily receyved, or unto anye reall and essencial presence there beeyng of Christ's naturall fleshe and bloude'.[6] Yet even in making this injunction, the rubric acknowledges differences of belief and practice. Many people still meant exactly that when they knelt; and many others no doubt were not sure what they believed. The Reformation involved profound arguments about fundamental concepts in identity. It is therefore a cultural as much as a theological phenomenon, as many recent studies have emphasized.[7] Rather than looking for religion in terms of historical

---

[6] From 'The order for the administracion of the Lordes supper, or holye Communion' (the so-called 'Black Rubric'), *The Boke of Common Prayer* (London: 1552).

[7] For example, the pioneering essay by Patrick Collinson, 'Protestant Culture and the Cultural Revolution', in *The Birthpangs of Protestant England: Religious and Cultural Change in the Sixteenth and Seventeenth Centuries* (London: Macmillan, 1988), 94–116, and his earlier *The Religion of Protestants* (Oxford: Clarendon Press, 1982); and with a literary emphasis, Alison Shell, *Catholicism, Controversy and the English Literary Imagination, 1558–1660* (Cambridge: Cambridge University Press, 1999); Brian Cummings, *The Literary Culture of the Reformation: Grammar and Grace* (Oxford: Oxford University Press, 2002); and Peter Lake with Michael Questier, *The Anti-Christ's Lewd Hat: Protestants, Papists and Players in Post-Reformation England* (New Haven, CT: Yale University Press, 2002).

events and then applying them to Shakespeare, it may be just as instructive to look for religion in Shakespeare and apply the vicissitudes of dramatic and poetic interpretation back to the historical events.

How for instance, does the word 'religion' appear in Shakespeare's works? We are used to seeing religion in the twenty-first century in individual and in internalized terms. This is why we ask the question, 'what did Shakespeare believe?' Yet in the plays, 'religion' is almost always a matter of public display and performance. In the first scene of *1 Henry VI*, Gloucester warns Winchester:

> Name not religion, for thou lov'st the flesh,
> And ne'er throughout the year to church thou goest—
> Except it be to pray against thy foes   (1.1.41–3)

Religion is a thing one does rather than something one thinks. It is also a mark of politics and the state: it delineates affiliation and loyalty and defines social identity. This distinction in the resonance of the word is something we should keep constantly in mind in approaching the issue.

THE RELIGION OF SHAKESPEARE'S FAMILY

What has happened to bring about Shakespeare's latter-day turn to religion? Nothing in this debate is quite as it seems, and there is no one simple explanation. The proximate cause, however, can be said to be a revival of interest in a set of leads and assumptions in Shakespeare's biography. One of the earliest memorials of Shakespeare's personal life consists in a series of jottings by a chaplain of Corpus Christi College, Oxford, Richard Davies. In a footnote concerning Shakespeare's burial stone, on which Davies does not elaborate, he adds the words 'he dyed a papist'.[8] This obscure speculation has had a curious half-life in Shakespearean studies. Forty years ago, it was commonplace to dismiss it. Now it is quoted as without authority yet in sympathy. Stephen Greenblatt calls it 'intriguing' but no more than a curious echo of the turmoils of religion associated with Shakespeare's Catholic youth.[9] Greenblatt is circumspect in his use of evidence here: in *Will in the World*, as elsewhere, he is highly cautious of documentary proof.

The materials for a spiritual autobiography of William Shakespeare are manifestly missing. He wrote no doctrinal pamphlets or devotional verse. He hardly wrote even in the first person, except for the *Sonnets*: and on religion, as well as sex, the *Sonnets* are notoriously hard to read. Indeed, the first observable fact about narratives of Shakespearean belief is that they all concern someone other than Shakespeare himself.

---

[8] Oxford, Corpus Christi College MS 309; text reproduced in full in E. K. Chambers, *William Shakespeare: A Study of Facts and Problems*, 2 vols. (Oxford: Clarendon Press, 1930), 2: 257.

[9] *Will in the World: How Shakespeare became Shakespeare* (London: Jonathan Cape, 2004), 387.

Primary among these stories are ones concerned with Shakespeare's father, John. John Shakespeare was cited for 'not comminge monethlie to the churche' in Stratford-upon-Avon in 1592.[10] Failing to attend church in the Elizabethan period came to be known as 'recusancy'. This was politically sensitive because one of the primary reasons for such behaviour was affiliation to the Catholic rite. The exiled head of the English Catholics, Cardinal William Allen, warned his flock from corrupting their souls by submitting to a heretical form of ritual, although he also urged compassion toward backsliders.[11] For some years, non-attendance was tolerated by the Elizabethan government. Whether they liked it or not, attachment to the old ways of religion was so widespread that enforcement was futile. After 1570, however, when Queen Elizabeth was excommunicated and her replacement with a Catholic monarch was made an article of faith, the Privy Council reversed its attitude. In a circuitous but vicious way, non-conformity became a test of treason. One reason for this was precisely because it was so trivial and easy to prove. Religious *belief*, as more recent political legislations have discovered, is hard to establish by legal process. Failure to attend church is a lazier but more stringent means of enforcement.

John Shakespeare's recusancy has been known since the mid-nineteenth century. The fortunes of the archival record of the Stratford Corporation, and of the interpretation given to it, often tell us as much about the scholar involved as they do about Shakespeare's father. On one side it will be said, correctly, that the legal deposition stipulates the reason for his recusancy as debt, not religion. On the other hand, it is equally true that debt was often used as a cover for religion, so that faith could be kept without incurring political penalty. At times in the past, it has also been pointed out, correctly, that some recusants were Puritans, equally opposed for their own reasons to the established liturgy of the Book of Common Prayer. The idea of a Puritan Shakespeare is now outlandish, but in support it used to be said, in the nineteenth century, by those wishing to establish William Shakespeare's perfect credentials as a national poet, that John Shakespeare as Chamberlain of Stratford had paid for the reparations by which the wall paintings in the Guild Chapel of the Holy Cross were whitewashed in accordance with Puritan iconoclasm. Both of these actions in the name of political religion, we notice—enforcement of church attendance, and destruction of church ornament—involve a similar mix of ideology and bad faith. These actions are also, we begin to notice, notoriously difficult to interpret according to a simple index of individual belief. One person may continue to attend church while despising the beliefs he appears to profess, out of a desire to save his political skin. Another person may agree to whitewash a devotional painting, as many church wardens did, while intending to restore the icon at the first opportunity. Still a third person might be in two minds on both opposing occasions.

---

[10] Chambers, *William Shakespeare*, 1: 15.

[11] Alexandra Walsham, *Church Papists: Catholicism, Conformity and Confessional Polemic in Early Modern England* (Woodbridge: Boydell, 1999), 68–9.

The other line of enquiry associated with John Shakespeare is the document which has come to be known as his 'Spiritual Testament'. This was discovered by chance, according to the story, in 1757, by a bricklayer working in the house at Henley Street, 'between the rafters and the tiling'. It was passed on some years later to Edmond Malone, at first accepted by him as genuine, and later dismissed as a probable forgery. Malone failed to explain his reasoning fully in either direction. The original in any case did not survive, but only a transcription. The idea remained dormant for over a century and a half, until it was discovered that Shakespeare's Testament closely corresponded to an authentic original, the *Testament of the Soul* by Cardinal Carlo Borromeo, in an English translation unknown in the eighteenth century when the Henley Street document was first examined by Malone. The suggestion has been made that it was promulgated as part of the mission of Edmund Campion which led to his execution as traitor or martyr in 1581.

The Testament is still disputed. Robert Bearman has pointed out that the existence of the Borromeo text may show only that the forgery is a sophisticated one.[12] Yet his argument that the 1757 version is a doctored transcription, a true document altered by the addition of Shakespeare's signature, is itself a conjecture. Others have questioned the exact status of Borromeo's testament for devotional purposes and its use as a missionary artefact.[13] Satisfying these questions lies beyond the scope of the present enquiry, although eminent historians both of Elizabethan Catholicism (Eamon Duffy) and Puritanism (Patrick Collinson) have endorsed the likelihood that John Shakespeare was a Stratford Catholic recusant.

CATHOLIC SHAKESPEARE?

The more significant point—as Collinson argues—is whether this does anything to alter the issue of whether William was also a Catholic.[14] We recall here that Henry VIII's father was a Catholic, as was also Martin Luther's. Young William is harder to track down than either of these apostates. His name does not appear among lists of Elizabethan recusants. Yet it may be just as significant that his name does not either appear in any roll of those attending church. Against this evidence of silence comes a possible counter-argument. More significant than the religion of one's parents in designating personal affiliation may be the religion of one's children. William's three children were all baptized in Holy Trinity Church in Stratford. Baptism according to the rites of the Book of Common Prayer was heretical to true Catholics. However, church

---

[12] Roger Bearman, 'John Shakespeare's "Spiritual Testament": A Reappraisal', *Shakespeare Survey* 56 (2003): 184–202.

[13] Peter Davidson and Thomas McCoog, 'Unreconciled: what evidence links Shakespeare and the Jesuits?' *Times Literary Supplement*, March 16, 2007.

[14] Patrick Collinson, 'William Shakespeare's Religious Inheritance and Environment', in *Elizabethan Essays* (London: Hambledon Press, 1994), 252.

papists often made such deals with their consciences to allow belief some room for manoeuvre under strenuous laws of religious enforcement. Perhaps it is worth considering the known habits of his children in later life. Susanna, his elder daughter, was cited in 1606 for failure to attend church. Was she a recusant? On the other hand, a year later she married John Hall, a staunch Protestant. Yet again the bare documents can lead to different conclusions.

Sadly, even the tiny traces of Shakespeare's life that he left behind give no definitive answers. So the fitful trail of his religious life has led instead to other proxy forms of religious identity. Most persistent has been another tale of recusant association. In 1923 the eminent Shakespearean E. K. Chambers included in his monumental documentary encyclopaedia of *The Elizabethan Stage* a transcript of the will of Alexander Hoghton of Hoghton Tower in Lancashire. The will was made out in August 1581 in the wake of the scandal surrounding the arrest (and subsequent trial and execution) of the Jesuit Campion. It makes provision for the livelihood of the players in his household, passing them on, with his stock of play clothes and musical instruments, to his brother Thomas, or if his brother chose not to keep players, to Sir Thomas Hesketh. Hoghton then adds to his will a specific codicil 'And I most heartily require the said Sir Thomas to be friendly unto Fulk Gillom & William Shakeshafte now dwelling with me & either to take them unto his service or else to help them to some good master'.[15]

Supposition can be added to supposition here. Chambers did not immediately suggest a connection between Shakeshafte and Shakespeare, which was first made instead by Oliver Baker in 1937.[16] But Chambers already thought Shakeshafte was probably a player, and in 1944 he speculated further, recalling that the poet's grandfather, Richard, sometimes used a variant spelling for his name.[17] Although it has often been repeated recently in the Catholic Shakespeare debate that this family variant was 'Shakeshafte', in fact the nearest equivalent Richard Shakespeare used was 'Shakestaff'.[18] Chambers was himself habitually cautious about conclusions on this question, as on others, but felt that the case merited more investigation. In 1970 Douglas Hamer refuted the connection; in 1985 E. A. J. Honigmann revived it at great length in a kind of archival detective mystery about Shakespeare's 'Lost Years'—a fanciful if agreeably romantic epithet long given to what is in fact a perfectly normal archival gap in the biographical record whereby we know nothing of the playwright's life between the birth of his twins in 1585 and his presence in the London literary world in 1592.[19] Honigmann admitted that there were many surviving problems with the evidence—not least of which is that the Shakeshafte story does not fall into the 'Lost Years' period at all, but

[15] E. A. J. Honigmann, *Shakespeare: the 'Lost Years'* (Manchester: Manchester University Press, 1985), 136 ('Appendix A: Extracts from Wills').

[16] Oliver Baker, *In Shakespeare's Warwickshire and the Unknown Years* (London: Simpkin Marshall, 1937), 297–319.

[17] E. K. Chambers, 'William Shakeshafte', in *Shakespearean Gleanings* (Oxford: Oxford University Press, 1944), 52–6.

[18] Honigmann, *Shakespeare: the 'Lost Years'*, 18.

[19] Douglas Hamer, 'Was William Shakespeare William Shakeshafte?', *Review of English Studies* 21 (1970), 41–8.

creates a new conundrum, that of Shakespeare commuting between Lancashire in 1581 and Warwickshire, where in 1582 he got married. But Honigmann also felt there was a series of apparent coincidences between the Shakespeare story and Lancashire. The most exciting of these was one which linked the Hesketh household with the entourage of the Stanley family, the Earls of Derby. This was the source of Chambers's fascination. Henry, the fourth Earl, kept an extravagant estate of entertainments in his family seat in Lancashire, and for a while supported a troupe of players known as Lord Derby's Men. His son, Ferdinando, Lord Strange, was also a patron of theatre; and Chambers demonstrated at length that several of the players in what later became the Lord Chamberlain's Men had previously been among Strange's Men. The Shakeshafte story thus joined the links in a narrative, which not only took Shakespeare out of Stratford, but also eventually to London and directly into the theatre.

This is the great 'missing link' in Shakespearean biography. Almost in an undertow, however, another link came with it. The common factor among all these patrons is not only Lancashire but Catholic recusancy. Hoghton gave Campion room in his house and got into trouble for it. Hesketh was mentioned in official documents as being under similar suspicion. The Stanleys were grander and closer to the heart of Protestant establishment, but like other grand families, their private ties to Catholicism were well known and tolerated. Henry, the fourth Earl, prosecuted recusants in the Lancashire region in the 1570s but also assisted Catholics with allegiances to his family. He was accused of being lax toward Catholics in 1587.[20] Ferdinando, on succeeding Henry as the fifth Earl, was the figurehead for a Catholic plot in 1593; Richard Hesketh, third son of Sir Thomas, was executed for his part in the affair.[21] Thomas, Richard's elder brother, was also known as a recusant.[22]

Honigmann's fastidious and sympathetic work in the archive connected many trails. He intertwined the story of Shakeshafte the itinerant player with the older rumours of young Shakespeare the schoolmaster. To tie the strands together he followed the fortunes of John Cottam, the master of the Stratford grammar school between 1579 and 1581 or 1582. Honigmann found Cottam was originally a native of a Lancashire town just a few miles from the Hoghtons, and his brother Thomas was a Catholic priest executed in 1582. An earlier master at the school, Simon Hunt, had left Stratford for Douai, where he became a Jesuit.[23]

Shakespeare's religious life has a symptomatic relationship with the documentary conundrum that surrounds his life in general. Honigmann admitted the tenuous link between many parts of the evidence, but he also argued that since we have nothing

---

[20] Louis A. Knafla, 'Stanley, Henry, fourth earl of Derby (1531–1593)', *Oxford Dictionary of National Biography* (Oxford: Oxford University Press, 2004), http://www.oxforddnb.com/view/article/26272.

[21] David Kathman, 'Stanley, Ferdinando, fifth earl of Derby (1559?–1594)', *Oxford Dictionary of National Biography* (Oxford: Oxford University Press, 2004), http://www.oxforddnb.com/view/article/26269.

[22] Honigmann, *Shakespeare: the 'Lost Years'*, 37.

[23] Honigmann, *Shakespeare: the 'Lost Years'*, 5.

better to go on, spectacular coincidences may have more meaning than had been allowed in more conservative scholarship, and imagination could be employed in creating a plausible new picture. It was worth entertaining the possibility, he said, that Shakespeare was brought up a Catholic, had close ties to a network of Catholic families throughout the realm, and worked in such circles once he moved to London. It was also worth considering the effect this might have on interpretations of the plays, especially if this meant working against the grain of the traditions of Shakespearean scholarship, founded as it was, in large part, in the myth of English Protestant national triumph and the cult of Queen Elizabeth. That this popular myth of Englishness is still allied to an anti-Catholic bias can be seen in the celluloid imagery of both John Madden's *Shakespeare in Love* (1998) and Shekhar Kapur's *Elizabeth* (1998) and its 2007 sequel.

RELIGION IN SHAKESPEARE'S PLAYS

Several plays offered themselves immediately as capable of new interpretation in this light. The sympathetic portraits of Friar Lawrence in *Romeo and Juliet* and Friar Francis in *Much Ado About Nothing* could be seen not only as implying affection for older religious practices but as invoking a theology in which the mediation of the church redeems human love from evil will. Isabella in *Measure for Measure*, in more complex fashion, defends the female Catholic religious life against the predatory advances of a Puritan-seeming magistrate, Angelo, who applies with evident corruption a rigid and new-fangled form of tyrannical religious and ethical doctrine. The tragedies from late in the reign of Elizabeth and early in the reign of James I also seemed to Honigmann and others as offering a Catholic trajectory. Hamlet's father's lines, uttered from beyond the grave, had long-since occasioned questions as to the theological origins of the play:

> I am thy father's spirit,
> Doom'd for a certain term to walk the night,
> And for the day confin'd to fast in fires,
> Till the foul crimes done in my days of nature
> Are burnt and purg'd away.
> (*Hamlet*, 1.5.9–13)

Old Hamlet apparently hailed from the realm of purgatory, outlawed under the Forty-Two Articles of Religion in 1553. The world of *Macbeth*, with its specific reference to the practice of equivocation, the Jesuit form of casuistry developed in response to the methods of torture used by the Elizabethan regime against recusants, suggested a direct reference to the events of the Gunpowder Plot, which (according to one theory in dating the play) were contemporary with *Macbeth*'s first staging. *King Lear* contains similarly buried references to the sensational uncovering of Catholic practices of exorcism revealed in Samuel Harsnett's *Declaration of the Egregious Impostures* (1603), the source for many of Edgar's apparently rambling speeches on the heath.

These references were not new, and had been examined in relation to Catholic theology before. Greenblatt's well-known essay 'Shakespeare and the Exorcists', originally published in 1984, alluded to the performance of *King Lear*, along with *Pericles*, in front of recusants in Yorkshire in 1610.[24] On the other hand, Honigmann pointed to passages which posed an obvious difficulty to a Catholic Shakespeare as author. Primary among them was the prophecy made by Archbishop Cranmer at the end of Shakespeare's last play, *Henry VIII*, the history of the monarch who brought about the English Reformation:

> This royal infant—heaven still move about her—
> Though in her cradle, yet now promises
> Upon this land a thousand thousand blessings,
> Which time shall bring to ripeness. She shall be—
> But few now living can behold that goodness—
> A pattern to all princes living with her,
> And all that shall succeed.
>
> (*Henry VIII* 5.4.17–23)

Could a Catholic have endorsed this singing exultation of the future Queen Elizabeth, here presented in terms which anticipate Cate Blanchett's thrilling portrait in all its propagandist flair?

Perhaps these lines could be put down to a later conversion from childhood Catholicism to conformist royalist middle age. Yet there are stirrings of anti-Catholic fervour in *1* and *2 Henry VI*, often dated the earliest of Shakespeare's plays. Most striking of all is the representation of arguments about the prerogatives of papal and royal power in *King John*.

> Thou canst not, cardinal, devise a name
> So slight, unworthy and ridiculous,
> To charge me to an answer, as the pope.
> Tell him this tale; and from the mouth of England
> Add thus much more, that no Italian priest
> Shall tithe or toll in our dominions;
> But as we, under God, are supreme head,
> So under Him that great supremacy,
> Where we do reign, we will alone uphold
> Without th' assistance of a mortal hand:
> So tell the pope, all reverence set apart
> To him and his usurp'd authority.
>
> (*King John* 3.1.149–60)

If the anti-papal remarks in *1 Henry VI* can be put down to historical accuracy or even to character sketching, no spectator or reader of *King John* could fail to note its trenchant applicability to the Tudor polity.

---

[24] *Shakespearean Negotiations: The Circulation of Social Energy in Renaissance England* (Oxford: Oxford University Press, 1988), 122. At this point, however, Greenblatt fell specifically short of giving the play a Catholic agenda; see 190–1.

One response to these anti-Catholic references might be to dispute the accuracy of authorial attribution. *1* and *2 Henry VI, King John*, and *Henry VIII* are all plays of multiple or disputed authorship. Yet Honigmann, with characteristic frankness, suggested a much more fruitful and ambiguous explanation, to which we will return, that the plays give evidence not only of good faith but of bad faith. Shakespeare might be a Catholic boy, he thought, but he was not necessarily a good Catholic boy. This only makes the politics of affiliation the more problematic for dramatic and literary interpretation.

RELIGIOUS IDENTITY IN SHAKESPEARE

Much of the best scholarship attached to the new argument about Shakespeare's religion came about as a result of engrafting a revisionist historiography of the English Reformation into the life of the national poet. Works such as J. J. Scarisbrick's *The Reformation and the English People* (1984) and Eamon Duffy's *The Stripping of the Altars* (1992), along with a series of polemical articles by Christopher Haigh, have created a major reappraisal of the religious upheavals of the sixteenth century. Haigh in particular argued that the longstanding narrative of the groundswell of English Protestantism overturning medieval superstition, summed up in A. G. Dickens's classic *The English Reformation* (1964), was an ideological fiction little different in outline from the providential iconoclasm of John Foxe's *Actes and Monuments* (1563–96), which had seen the reign of Elizabeth as the result of divine necessity and election.

In another sense, however, the Catholic Shakespeare is still disputed from a different point of view. In a sceptical spirit, Samuel Schoenbaum once listed a series of claims about Shakespeare's religion and characterized them all as *parti pris*. With Olympian detachment, Schoenbaum described how Richard Simpson (an Anglican priest who converted to Catholicism) proved Shakespeare a Catholic, while Thomas Carter (a Presbyterian minister) proved him a Puritan; whereas William John Birch, a rationalist humanist, demonstrated irrefutably that he was an atheist; and the *Franciscan Annals* of 1898 suggested that he became a Franciscan, and was even buried in Franciscan garb—the origin of the gravestone malediction to leave his bones undisturbed. 'Thus does each man convert Shakespeare to his own belief or infidelity'.[25]

This was part of Schoenbaum's more general thesis that Shakespeare's biography had become mirrored in the image of the biographer. The thesis contains a deal of truth. We could conclude, and probably should, that Shakespearean biography is an interminable mystery of dead ends and impossible suppositions. Yet it is also too easy to dismiss all argument on this front as vested interests. More generally, after all, we could observe that the historiography of the English Reformations is enmeshed in

---

[25] *Shakespeare's Lives*, new ed. (Oxford: Oxford University Press, 1991), 331.

sectarian conflicts that are still unresolved. Rather than assume this is the end of the matter, it may be time to turn the argument on its head and see how far the history of religion is intertwined at every level with subsequent experience and interpretation, and also that this vexed relationship also applies to arguments about secularization, too. Schoenbaum's irony in turn pulls us toward identifying Shakespeare with a modern, liberal scepticism. But this may be just as much a feature of *parti pris* as any other position. There has been an equally biased motivation in the traditional disinclination to see religion in Shakespeare. Secular Shakespeare—as in Harold Bloom's famous dictum that Shakespeare provides a 'secular scripture'—is a historical fabrication with its roots in a modernist ideology.[26]

If only, we think, we had the right evidence, we could solve the mystery and discover Shakespeare's faith. It is as if we could discover Shakespeare's personal creed: 'I, William Shakespeare, believe in . . .' Yet this could be said to be the first fallacy of the religion of Shakespeare, a mirror image of the second, that if we cannot identify such a creed, we must conclude that he had no beliefs, that he is a modern agnostic. Shakespeare, we are told in this latter version, is sceptical, secular, and humanist to the core, an atheist before his time. In that way, he succeeds in being a person unlike anybody else in his century. This is a much more unlikely eventuality than the concoction that he is a Presbyterian or a Franciscan.

Is this, though, a matter of missing evidence? The difficulty that bedevils Shakespeare's religion is not just an absence of facts, it is the kind of label we wish to appropriate. 'Was Shakespeare a Catholic?' may not only be a question we cannot precisely answer, it may be the wrong question in the first place. In the sixteenth century, 'Catholic' often means something other, and indeed has a variety of meanings according to who is speaking. 'Catholic' and 'Protestant', terms used readily in twenty-first-century attempts to make hard and fast distinctions between religious groups, when used in a sixteenth-century context (especially together) almost always connote a polemical argument rather than a demographic observation. Religious identities after the Reformation in England were plural, mobile, and even volatile. As one author put it in 1581, within a single man's memory (we might say, for example, within the lifetime of Richard Shakespeare, the poet's grandfather) one king had abolished the Pope's authority while in other points keeping the faith of his fathers; in the name of his son, a child, was then abolished the whole ancient religion; he was followed as prince by his sister who restored the same again and sharply punished heretics; then she was followed lastly by her younger sister, her majesty that now is, who has used the same laws to bring everything down again. All these strange differences, the author states, have taken place within thirty years.[27] Another writer could say, a year before, that

---

[26] *Shakespeare and the Invention of the Human* (London: Longman, 1998), 3, borrowing a phrase from Northrop Frye.

[27] Cited in Peter Lake, 'Religious Identities in Shakespeare's England', in David Scott Kastan (ed.), *A Companion to Shakespeare* (Oxford: Blackwell, 1999), 57, who also quotes the following citation.

there was one inevitable result of this confusion: no single faith now prevailed but 'fower knowen religions, and the professors thereof, distinct both in name, spirite, and doctrine'.[28] He divided the religious nation into four—Catholics, Protestants, Puritans, and the Family of Love. Beyond these groups there were multiples of petty sects, new born every day, grovelling on the ground.

It is hardly surprising, given these testimonies of contemporaries, if we find it hard to categorize religion at a distance of 400 years. Yet these witnesses themselves are not impartial. One author is Cardinal William Allen, founder of the seminary mission in Douai and leader of the English Catholics; the second is Robert Persons, Jesuit priest and the companion of Campion on his last journey to England. The representation of the nation as fragmented and ruptured, while no doubt accurate, is also part of a theological argument in which 'Catholic' is a word signifying unity while Protestant is a mark of schism and disorder. The Elizabethan government, meanwhile, with a sense of menace, configured religion by the 'Act of Uniformity' of 1559 as a form of social order, which depended on conformity to a *reformed* religious practice. Although some Protestants certainly desired that uniformity should be along the lines of belief and doctrine, statutes, royal proclamations, and church visitations construed religious conformity as a visible practice rather than as a window into the soul. John Whitgift, Archbishop of Canterbury, and William Cecil, Lord Burghley, who took responsibility for the temporal control of religion, seem to have preferred to leave belief out of statute. Yet, of course, there was no rigid way of distinguishing belief from practice, either.

Lord Burghley had a map drawn up around 1590 of which the section for Lancashire survives in the British Library. Crosses have been placed next to some houses.[29] They indicate the houses of Catholic gentry whom Burghley felt he might not be able to trust. It is a political map, showing safe areas where loyalists might be relied on to quash a rebellion, and beacons from which servants of the Crown could send messages quickly back to London. It is no doubt rough and ready, and even here we do not know on what basis Burghley established loyalty or religious identity. Was Ferdinando Strange a Catholic or a loyalist? Evidence can be read both ways, as it can for Henry Wriothesley, Earl of Southampton, Shakespeare's only known literary patron. What are we looking for when we ask such questions? What do we expect to learn, especially in the act of reading poetry or watching drama?

Henry Howard, Earl of Northampton (1540–1614), was the son of a poet (another Henry Howard, Earl of Surrey) executed for treason in 1547. The tutor of the younger Howard for the next six years was John Foxe, later the Protestant martyrologist; but Howard then served as a page to a staunch Catholic bishop under Mary. Under Elizabeth he was frequently suspected of involvement in plots to replace the Queen with Mary, Queen of Scots. Yet he also wrote to Burghley professing his fidelity to the

[28] Robert Persons, *A brief discours contayning certayne reasons why Catholiques refuse to goe to church* (Douai: 1580), sig. 3.

[29] London, British Library, Royal MS 18.D.III, fo.81.

Crown and offering his services in the Navy during the Armada. Under James I, he was a conspicuous client of Burghley's son, Sir Robert Cecil.[30] Howard was something of a philosopher and intellectual, and a writer of a number of treatises. His writing shows Catholic sympathies and yet also includes a conformist defence of the Bishops against the Puritans. He seems to have tried to observe the Catholic ritual at some points of his life but at others became attached to a devotional use of the Book of Common Prayer, especially surrounding its order for Communion.

RELIGION AND IDENTITY IN SHAKESPEARE'S PLAYS

How do we learn to read the runes of Shakespeare's writing in the light of this complexity? One way of interpreting Shakespeare which has emerged strongly through the Catholic Shakespeare debate has been to see a series of plays as participating in a kind of coterie language with other recusants. In Sonnet 29, the speaker declares:

> When in disgrace with Fortune and men's eyes
> I all alone beweep my outcast state

Is this a Catholic bemoaning persecution and suppression? Is the reference in *Hamlet* to 'Denmark's a prison' a way of imagining the play as an allegory of the tyrannical treatment of the old religion in Elizabethan England? More complex coded references to the fortunes of individual Catholic magnates have been explored in plays such as *Love's Labour's Lost* and *The Winter's Tale*. This raises several kinds of scepticism. One arises from the fact that there is only one surviving record of an identifiable English Catholic reading from a copy of Shakespeare, which is a Second Folio of 1632, once the possession of the English Seminary College in Valladolid, and now in the Folger Library. This copy was systematically inspected by Father William Sankey, under his Spanish *nom de plume* of Guillermo Sanchez, on behalf of the Inquisition as part of the routine censorship of books. If Shakespeare was writing for recusants, this reader failed to notice. On the contrary, he crossed out a large number of lines felt to be injurious to the Catholic faith—including the passages from *King John* and *Henry VIII* quoted above—along with the entire text of *Measure for Measure*, a play that has received some of the most imaginative and subtle religious rereadings in the last few years of post-Reformation scrutiny.

It would be equally mistaken, though, to interpret Sankey's reading as the only one available to a recusant mind. What it does show is that a play is an ambiguous genre in which to encode a message to co-religionists. Allegorical plays, of course, do exist. But

---

[30] Pauline Croft, 'Howard, Henry, earl of Northampton (1540–1614)', *Oxford Dictionary of National Biography* (Oxford: Oxford University Press, 2004), http://www.oxforddnb.com/view/article/13906.

drama as a medium plays out to multiple voices and multiple ways of thinking. It is possible, in fact, that this is the best way forward for a reinterpretation of Shakespeare in the light of the Reformation. The initial energies of the argument were in the direction of finding a single authorial perspective from which to view religious controversy. The more productive route might be to recognize not only that Shakespeare's plays and poems give voice to hybrid and plural imaginings of the Reformation, but also that in this way they are a powerful index of the traumatic anxieties that the Reformation produced.

Measure for Measure, whatever the reason for Sankey's misgiving, is a play which readily demonstrates the richness of the post-Reformation legacy. Let us take a seemingly throw-away line by Lucio, near the beginning of the play, to a nearby gentleman:

> Lucio: Ay, why not? Grace is grace, despite of all controversy; as for example, thou thyself art a wicked villain, despite of all grace.
>
> (1.2.25–6)

The line is offered in casual jest, typical of Lucio's louche linguistic style. He drops slanders gratuitously throughout the play, as if with no sense of the value or significance of words. Yet here he simultaneously indulges himself in a piece of acutely specific controversy. 'Grace' was one of the key words of the Reformation. It was the scene of Luther's first crisis, with his assertion that salvation must be given freely by God, with no conditions, or else, in the words of St Paul, *gratia iam non est gratia*, 'grace is no more grace' (Romans 11.6). Grace is given *gratis*, for free. Man's own works can have no merit in this transaction. Luther's analysis in turn was exposed to line by line refutation at the Council of Trent at its sixth session, meeting just months after Luther's death in 1546. Trent confirmed the gratuitousness of grace but nonetheless allowed some part to man's cooperation with grace by freely assenting to it; and some merit to the works that a man does, with grace's prompting, after baptism.

Lucio alludes to this 'controversy' with a theologian's subtlety. The gentleman he talks to, he jokes, has no merit, he is an utter 'villain', deprived of all grace. At the same time he conceals his own theological position—he takes an each way bet. In any case, his scoffing manner shows what he thinks of public religion. Yet this play also bristles with political theology, just as the nation did, while watching the play being performed, probably within the first two years of the accession of James I in 1603. This is a play in which religious performance is a matter of life and death.

The word 'grace' recurs through the early scenes of *Measure for Measure* with a tour-de-force mixture of exactitude and ambiguity. The sense of the word metamorphoses in front of us. In the same scene, the gentlemen argue over the import of 'grace' in 'the thanksgiving before meat' (1.2.13). In the one scene, therefore, the power of religious language is revealed across a tortuous range of registers. Grace at a meal was a daily observance, but it was also fraught with confessional power. The use of words to empower acts of ritual performance, as we saw earlier with the example of kneeling at prayer, made Puritans full of suspicion. Such practices easily merged into what they saw as the superstitious magic of Catholicism, in which the priest performs a range of sacred actions through sacred words. Puritans said grace at mealtimes as a thanksgiving, but worried that the blessing might carry more weight.

Angelo the Governor is presented through the play as a Puritan magistrate in action. In the next scene but one, Lucio again alludes to the strain on the vocabulary of grace, as he asks whether Isabella the novitiate nun has

> the grace by your fair prayer
> To soften Angelo   (1.4.69)

What does he mean by this? Is he thinking of her soft feminine grace, which shortly turns out to have all too easy entrance to Angelo's passions? Or is he referring to the power of prayer? In which case, he could be equivocating in another sense, either in the sense of the intercession of the Catholic Church, or in the idea of a direct appeal to a Calvinist interpretation of divine authority.

A theological argument about grace can be traced through the whole play: indeed, it gives rise to the play's title. God's justice works through the strict application of a law, the title implies: it gives measure for measure, an eye for an eye. Yet here again there is the presence of a pun, as the title means both the rod of the law and yet also suggests the tempering 'measure' of mercy. Grace, whether in a Catholic or a Lutheran interpretation, involves an interruption of rigid enforcement of human rules. Grace has its own rule, a rule of forgiveness.

Yet within this framework the play tests the audience's viewpoint over and over again. We could therefore justifiably ask from what position it approaches the issue, or where it ends up. Yet in asking this question, just as in asking the question about Shakespeare's own religion, we may be applying pressure in the wrong place. One of the hindrances in the historiography of religion is that it often establishes the groundwork of its terminology and methodology by the examination of an exaggerated form of religious literacy. To find out what Calvinists think, we turn naturally to the works of Calvin. In fact, Calvin is a much more complex writer than he is often taken to be, who writes in a huge variety of genres and rhetorical registers. We do not discover directly from him what English Puritans such as the Calvinist writer William Perkins thought, in the next generation. Perkins in some sense is more properly called a Calvinist than Calvin. Yet even so, reading Perkins may not tell us how to understand a lay Puritan such as Shakespeare's son-in-law, Dr Hall.

Before we try to identify Shakespeare's religious affiliation, it is worth thinking first what we mean by religious identity. It was a completely different concept in the society Shakespeare lived in than it is today. We imagine religion, in the modern West, primarily in terms of private beliefs. We expect these to correspond to a kind of personal philosophy. While the sixteenth and seventeenth centuries produced reams of sophisticated religious literature and philosophy, religion was not a private but a *public* domain. It was also, as I have been stressing, as much about practice as about belief, even though the issue of belief was also discussed openly and with public complexity. This insight has already produced some notable new readings of Shakespeare's plays. We are beginning to rethink the place of ritual in Shakespeare, and of the human body and its social meanings and performances. Yet we need to read those practices also in the light of the profound changes they were then undergoing. A taxonomy of practice according to 'Catholic' and 'Protestant' affinities is no easier than one of doctrine.

Greenblatt's analysis of *Hamlet in Purgatory*, which accompanied the first fanfare of the renewed interest in Shakespeare's religion, articulated the play's religious ambiguity by saying that it shows a Catholic father in posthumous debate with a Protestant-leaning son from Luther's university of Wittenberg. The sixteenth century is full of such conflicts—whether personal—in the conversion of Ben Jonson to Catholicism and John Donne away from it—or political, in the endless confessional wars and purges. Whatever we think of Shakespeare, father and son, we are never going to know for sure where their affiliation lay. But perhaps we should stop seeing this as a problem and instead see it as an opportunity. In this very impenetrability of evidence, in this hard core of resistance in the trace of religious language and its operation, Shakespeare's work allows us to see the extraordinary historical, intellectual, and emotional fall-out of the Reformation in its largest sense. Indeed, one symptom of this profound change is the richness of Shakespeare's own language. The whole kaleidoscope of Shakespeare's dramatic and poetic register is now offering itself for re-examination in this light. In that sense religion is indeed the undiscovered country of his writing. What is clear is that it will be much more difficult in the future to go back to a time when religion in Shakespeare could be resolutely ignored.

CHAPTER 37

···

ARCHITECTURE

···

FREDERICK KIEFER

Hardwick Hall in Derbyshire claims several distinctions: it was built by a woman, Bess of Hardwick, who married four times, accumulating the vast fortune that financed her home; it was designed by the most accomplished architect in Elizabethan England, Robert Smythson; and it is among the most perfectly preserved of Elizabethan homes. Thanks to the National Trust, the house today looks very much the way it did when Bess took up residence in 1597.[1]

No evidence exists that Shakespeare ever visited Hardwick Hall, situated in the north of England, far from London. Nor can we say that Shakespeare's company of players ever found a venue for acting there, though troupes of actors often toured the countryside, and the Queen's Men played at Hardwick in 1600.[2] My purpose here is neither to hypothesize a visit to the house by Shakespeare nor to suggest that Hardwick provided a performance space for any particular play. Instead, I seek to look closely at the building, outside and in, and thereby to explore what is admittedly a speculation: that aesthetic principles guiding Elizabethan architecture and interior design have implications for drama. In particular, I am interested in the relationship between the plastic arts and the elaborate plots that characterize plays by Shakespeare and his contemporaries.

I.

···

A visitor to Hardwick Hall finds a towered three-storey structure with a façade that seems largely made of glass.[3] That glass may have been the most conspicuous feature of

---

[1] Most scholars suggest the date of completion as 1600. For a documentary account of the construction, see Basil Stallybrass, 'Bess of Hardwick's Buildings and Building Accounts', *Archaeologia* 64 (1913), 347–98. The first inventory of Hardwick's contents was made in 1601.

[2] David N. Durant, *Bess of Hardwick: Portrait of an Elizabethan Dynast*, rev. edn. (London: Peter Owen, 1999), 185.

[3] Photos by Nick Meers in Mark Girouard, *Hardwick Hall* (1989; rpt. London: The National Trust, 1994) and 12; by Mike Williams in Malcolm Airs, *The Tudor and Jacobean Country House: A Building History* (1995; rpt. Phoenix Mill: Sutton in association with The National Trust, 1998).

the building in its own time: according to the local jingle, 'Hardwick Hall, more glass than wall'. In an era when most homes were rather dark, Hardwick floods its interior with sunlight, not unlike a late Gothic church in which the walls become curtains of glass. The windows at Hardwick become higher with each storey, reflecting the importance of the rooms within, and they evoke another feature of Gothic style. Because the windows are taller than they are wide—they look like elongated rectangles standing on end—they lead the eye upward, our view culminating in six vertical projections that defy the roof line, creating the impression of towers reaching skyward like those in medieval cathedrals. Finally, a series of chimneys pushes through the roof, echoing in miniature the form of the towers (see Figure 37.1).

In one major respect, however, Hardwick Hall would defy the expectations of most sixteenth-century visitors. Instead of an irregular agglomeration of architectural elements—like that at Compton Wynyates in Warwickshire or Little Moreton Hall in Cheshire—Hardwick is perfectly symmetrical.[4] That is, the east and west sides are identical in size and shape as are the north and south. So concerned with overall symmetry is the architect that he creates false windows, concealing chimneypieces within. Such emphasis on regularity of form does not belong to the Gothic past. Instead, it finds inspiration in the newer style of architecture that originated in

FIGURE 37.1. Hardwick Hall, Derbyshire. Photo courtesy of Wikimedia Commons.

---

[4] In this respect Hardwick marks a departure from the nearby Hardwick Old Hall, which grew piecemeal. For a reconstruction and photos of the ruins, see Lucy Worsley, *Hardwick Old Hall* (London: English Heritage, 1998).

quattrocento Italy, as Filippo Brunelleschi and Leon Battista Alberti rediscovered and redeployed structural features of ancient building. Gradually these features gained popularity, making their way northward through France and the Low Countries, finally reaching England. Fittingly, the ground floor of the east and west façades, between the towers at Hardwick, consists of a loggia featuring Doric columns, evocative of Greek and Roman precedent. By those columns Robert Smythson signals his knowledge of ancient architectural forms.

A double agenda, then, dictates the architecture of Hardwick Hall. With the towers and upended rectangles of glass, Smythson means to recollect the Gothic past still visible nearly everywhere in the form of cathedrals like those at Lincoln and York, Salisbury and Ely. At the same time, he means to evoke classical antiquity by the structure's regularity and symmetry. Another way of understanding this dual impulse is to think of the façade as a balance of vertical and horizontal elements. The towers, chimneys, and fenestration combine to lead the eye skyward, while the loggia, the entablatures of each storey, the balustrade on the roof, and general dimensions of a house wider than it is tall on east and west, emphasize a broad horizontal line. Robert Smythson's genius lies in achieving a balance of elements that, despite disparate inspiration, creates a cohesive ensemble.

Although Hardwick Hall marks the culmination of Smythson's work, earlier projects made his reputation and undoubtedly led Bess to select him as her architect. The features that characterize his earlier houses are much the same features that find expression at Hardwick. Consider, for example, Wollaton Hall in Nottingham, built between 1580 and 1588 for Sir Francis Willoughby. Bess knew Willoughby, and in 1591 John Rodes, 'a master mason from Wollaton, signed a contract with Bess for all the remaining stonework for the new house [Hardwick Hall]'.[5] Earlier, Bess had lent her marble carver, Thomas Accres, to Willoughby, and in the summer of 1592, on her way home from London, she visited Wollaton herself.[6]

Perched atop a hill, Wollaton is essentially a two-storey house with three-storey towers at its four corners; these, in turn, are surmounted by obelisks, statuary, and chimneys that draw the eye skyward.[7] The most conspicuous feature of this home is the rectangular central block that rises even higher than the four towers and contains both the Great Hall and, above it, a Prospect Room from which to survey the surrounding countryside. The clerestory windows of this central section are, like those of Hardwick Hall, rectangles of glass set on end so that they are much taller than they are wide. And if the second-storey windows of the surrounding house are higher than those on the first, the windows in the central block, which retain their original tracery, are still taller.

---

[5] Durant, *Bess of Hardwick*, 163.

[6] Durant, *Bess of Hardwick*, 176–7. E. Carleton Williams, in *Bess of Hardwick* (1959; rpt. London: Longmans, 1960), writes of Bess: 'As she gazed at the vast pile of Wollaton Hall with its bold outlines, symmetry and exotic towers, she must have wondered if it would serve as a model for a house of hers which as yet lay in the future' (p. 206).

[7] Photo in Pamela Marshall, *Wollaton Hall and the Willoughby Family* (Nottingham: Nottingham Civic Society, 1999), illus. 1.

In the profusion of glass, 'Wollaton is one of the most sensational of Elizabethan lantern-houses'.[8] That is, lit from within at night, the expanse of lighted glass would have seemed a giant lantern. Clinging to each corner of the central block and projecting above its roof are cylindrical turrets (bartizans) that reach even higher. Finally, chimneystacks surmount the Great Hall and Prospect Room (or High Hall), echoing the vertical emphasis of those turrets. Seen from afar, Wollaton Hall, with its flamboyance and exuberance, evokes the silhouette of a medieval castle (see Figure 37.2).

Yet as we look more closely, we realize that this structure belongs to a movement that originated in the pioneering work of Brunelleschi, Alberti, and such followers as Andrea Palladio and Sebastiano Serlio, who specialized in rehabilitating classical forms. For one thing, the house, which follows an overall square plan, is symmetrical: the east and west façades are identical in shape and dimension, as are the north and south. For another, the upper two storeys of the towers have niches with round Roman arches that seem intended to accommodate statuary. Beside the niches on each storey are pilasters culminating in Doric, Ionic, and Corinthian capitals. Atop the towers are gables featuring obelisks, and above the gables are triangular shapes that look like the pediments of classical temples; each triangle supports a statue.[9] Those cylindrical turrets on the central block, moreover, culminate in domes, which had become popular as ancient architectural features were revived, rather than the pinnacles or spires of a

FIGURE 37.2. Wollaton Hall, Nottingham. Photo by author.

[8] Mark Girouard, *Robert Smythson and the Elizabethan Country House* (New Haven, CT: Yale University Press, 1983), 101.

[9] Photo by Edward Piper in Girouard, *Elizabethan Country House*, colour pl. VI.

Gothic building. Inset in the surfaces of the façade are another recollection of the ancient world: medallion busts of Greek and Roman philosophers and writers. Collectively, all of these features announce Smythson's allegiance to classicism.

Smythson's capacity for synthesizing and thereby creating 'the most innovative house in English architectural history'[10] appears in his perspective drawing for one of the four towers of Wollaton Hall. '[T]hought to be the earliest English example of its kind,'[11] the drawing shows three floors, the tallest at the bottom, the shortest at the top. On the façade of each storey are banded pilasters, narrower as they rise floor by floor, and culminating in capitals. The pilasters and the progression of the capitals upward from Doric to Corinthian bespeak a classical ancestry. When we reach the roofline, however, we find an assemblage of features that emulate no ancient structure.[12] Most prominent among these is strapwork in stone: that is, '[o]rnament consisting of interlaced bands, reminiscent of leather thongs or carved fretwork'.[13] No Greek or Roman eyes ever beheld such a feature. Above the strapwork at Wollaton is a pediment, modelled on that of an ancient temple. But it is very small and unconnected with the columned temple front that, in ancient times, would support such an element. In short, although the pediment itself originates in antiquity, here it lacks a classical context of supporting columns. Finally, on either side of the strapwork, at each corner of the tower, stands a small obelisk. This feature was hardly unknown to the ancient world—it has its origins in pharaonic Egypt—but it did not adorn the tops of Greek and Roman buildings. In sum, Smythson has adopted some classical features, combined them with a modern form (strapwork), and organized them in a way that has no precedent in the ancient world or the medieval. In assembling this particular collection of elements, Smythson seems chiefly guided by precedent in the Low Countries, as architects there adapted classical forms to local tastes.[14]

The house that launched Robert Smythson's career and led to the commission at Wollaton Hall is Longleat in Wiltshire, called by John Summerson 'the first great monument of Elizabethan architecture'.[15] Admittedly, Smythson was not completely

---

[10] Timothy Mowl, *Elizabethan and Jacobean Style* (London: Phaidon, 1993), 100.

[11] Marshall, *Wollaton Hall*, 34. Marshall reproduces the drawing, illus. 10.

[12] Photos by Martin Charles in Mowl, *Elizabethan and Jacobean Style*, 97; and by Mark Fiennes in Susan Watkins, *In Public and in Private: Elizabeth I and Her World* (London: Thames & Hudson, 1998), 140 and 143.

[13] John Fleming, Hugh Honour, and Nikolaus Pevsner, *The Penguin Dictionary of Architecture*, 4th edn. (London and New York: Penguin, 1991), 424. According to Alan and Ann Gore, 'Strapwork first appeared in England when Henry VIII brought over artists from the Continent to decorate Nonsuch Palace at Ewell in Surrey, where building began in 1538. Strapwork . . . was either carved or, more usually, moulded in plaster' (*The History of English Interiors* [Oxford: Phaidon, 1991], 23).

[14] Wollaton displays the self-conscious style known as Mannerism, especially as it was practised in the Low Countries and transmitted to England by pattern books. Margaret Jourdain, in *English Interior Decoration, 1500–1830: A Study in the Development of Design* (London: Batsford, 1950), notes that books of design by Jan Vredeman de Vries, published between 1563 and 1585, were 'accessible to English craftsmen during the great building period of the late sixteenth and early seventeenth century' (p. 7).

[15] John Summerson, *Architecture in Britain, 1530 to 1830*, 9th edn. Pelican History of Art (New Haven, CT: Yale University Press, 1993), 60.

responsible for the house. Built for Sir John Thynne, Longleat saw four identifiable periods of construction, beginning in 1547 and culminating *c*.1580. From the adaptation of a Carthusian priory, the house evolved in size and ambition to match the aspirations of its wealthy owner. Before Smythson arrived in March 1568, Longleat was 'a kind of degenerate Gothic cake, enriched with occasional classical cherries'.[16] For a dozen years (until 1580 when he began working at Wollaton Hall), Smythson contributed his talents as a stonemason. Over time his responsibilities grew, and he had a hand in the fourth phase of construction, which essentially wrapped a new façade around the existing building.

In its final incarnation Longleat departs markedly from the typical houses of its day.[17] Much the same regularity and symmetry that would later characterize both Wollaton and Hardwick mark Longleat (see Figure 37.3). The emulation of classical practice extends to the pilasters on all four sides. Those pilasters culminate in a sequence of capitals dictated by classical precedent: Doric, Ionic, then Corinthian. Visitors must have been awed by the height and mass of Longleat, which dwarfed conventional homes of the nobility, and by the sheer expanse of glass. Whereas most earlier houses combined the functions of home and fortress and thereby reserved glass and graceful design for interior courtyards, Longleat represents a 'turning inside out of the courtyard house' and invites the observer to admire 'symmetry and decoration' on

FIGURE 37.3. Longleat, Wiltshire. Photo courtesy of Wikimedia Commons.

[16] Mark Girouard, *Robert Smythson and the Architecture of the Elizabethan Era* (South Brunswick: Barnes, n.d. [1967]), 55.
[17] Photo by Clay Perry in Lionel Esher, *The Glory of the English House* (Boston: Bulfinch, 1991), 6–7.

the exterior.[18] Because we cannot see with sixteenth-century eyes, we cannot fully appreciate the novelty of the house for an onlooker accustomed to rambling structures that grew by accretion. John Summerson points to its uniqueness when he writes of Longleat: 'It stands alone in the European architecture of its time.'[19]

What marks Smythson's originality is his capacity for synthesizing, nowhere more evident than in the Longleat façades; their most conspicuous feature consists of thirteen enormous bay windows (25 feet wide, 10 feet deep, and 65 feet high), a distinctively English contribution to house construction, encouraged by the cold, damp climate and by the paucity of sunlight for much of the year.[20] The infatuation with glass and light has its origins in late Gothic ecclesiastical style. But if one stands immediately in front of the house, the observer sees no towers of the kind that characterize Smythson's later homes; instead, the horizontal emphasis of cornice and balustrade seems paramount here. As one moves farther away from the house, however, something interesting happens: the roofline assumes more prominence not only in the decoration at the parapet (statuary and ornamental stonework) but also in the assemblage of rooftop structures, the most prominent of which are banqueting houses, used when diners, after their meal in the hall, retired to the roof for wine, fruit, and views of the surrounding countryside. If one enters the house and climbs the stairs to the top, one finds a conglomeration of chimneys, staircase turrets, and heraldic beasts, along with the surviving pointed gables (on an interior court) that characterized the house before its final modification.[21] All of these bespeak the vitality of the Gothic past and anticipate the later vertical emphases of Wollaton and Hardwick. To move from Longleat to Wollaton to Hardwick is to appreciate the continuity of Robert Smythson's architectural design, even though he stamps each house with a distinctive look.

As Smythson's houses demonstrate, Elizabethan architects and builders were mindful of classical precedent, even as they created structures that were daringly new. Ironically, that newness was inextricably connected to the past, as William Harrison indicates in his *Description of England*: 'Those [houses] of the nobility are . . . wrought with bricke and hard stone, as provision may best be made: but so magnificent and statelie as the basest house of a baron dooth often match in our daies with some honours of princes in old time. So that if ever curious [ingenious, skilful] building did florish in England, it is in these our yeares, wherin our workemen excell, and are in maner comparable in skill with old *Vitruvius, Leo[n] Baptista [Alberti]*, and *[Sebastiano] Serl[i]o.'*[22] The three men Harrison names share a commitment to antique design. Thus John Shute, in *The First and Chief Groundes of Architecture* (1563), invokes the name of Vitruvius, the first-century Roman whose treatise on architecture

[18] Eric Mercer, 'The Houses of the Gentry', *Past and Present* 5 (1954), 13.

[19] Summerson, *Architecture in Britain*, 61.

[20] Photos in Girouard, *Elizabethan Country House*, figs. 31 and 32.

[21] Photos in Girouard, *Elizabethan Country House*, figs. 20 and 21, and colour pl. II; Airs, *The Tudor and Jacobean Country House*, 134.

[22] William Harrison, *An Historicall description of the Iland of Britaine*, in Raphael Holinshed, *The First and second volumes of Chronicles* (London, 1587), 188.

became a handbook in the fifteenth and sixteenth centuries.[23] (Sir Francis Willoughby owned a copy.) Alberti, who 'made sense of Vitruvius for a modern audience',[24] designed San Lorenzo in Florence, the first church 'to use generally Classical forms'.[25] And Serlio, who also saw himself as applying Vitruvian principles in the modern world, became the single most influential Italian architect in England.[26] According to Shute, Serlio is 'a mervelous conning artificer in our time'.[27] (Willoughby also owned Serlio's *Architecture*.) What the Italian architects share is a conviction that nothing is more conducive to designing contemporary structures than studying ancient architecture, and Shute himself emulates their method. At the beginning of his treatise, 'the only theoretical work on any of the visual arts published in England before the very end of the sixteenth century',[28] Shute recalls that the Duke of Northumberland had sent him to Italy 'ther to confer with the doinges of y skilful maisters in architectur, & also to view such auncient Monumentes hereof as are yet extant'.[29] To adopt modern Italian principles, then, is to embrace the latest and most fashionable guidelines that should guide new construction. For Alberti, Serlio, and their contemporaries, the route to architectural excellence may be described as 'Back to the Future'!

The corollary of viewing the Romans with admiration is turning against longstanding Gothic features, including pointed arches, bell towers, battlements, and buttresses. Thus Giorgio Vasari, in his *Lives of the Artists*, couples Brunelleschi's enthusiasm for the ancients with his contempt for the Gothic. Vasari tells us that during Brunelleschi's sojourn in Rome, where he recorded the ruins, 'he was able to give himself completely to his studies, not caring whether he went without food and sleep and concentrating utterly on the architecture of the past [i.e. antiquity], by which I mean the good ancient orders and not the barbarous German style [i.e. Gothic] which was then fashionable'.[30] By 'ancient orders' Vasari means the recovery of classical columns and their capitals: 'he rediscovered the use of the antique cornices and restored the Tuscan, Corinthian,

---

[23] John Shute, in *The First and Chief Groundes of Architecture used in all the auncient and famous monymentes* (London: 1563), writes: 'Architectur (by the common consent of many notable men) . . . ys of all artes, the most noble and excellent, Contayning in it sundrie sciences and knowlaiges wherwyth it is furnished and adourned, as full well Vitruvius doth affyrme and declare by his writinge' (sig. B2v). According to Frederick Hard, Shute coined the word 'symmetry' (Hard [ed.], *The Elements of Architecture* [Charlottesville: University Press of Virginia, 1968], p. lxv).

[24] Robert Tavernor, *On Alberti and the Art of Building* (New Haven, CT: Yale University Press, 1998), 15.

[25] John Onians, *Bearers of Meaning: The Classical Orders in Antiquity, the Middle Ages, and the Renaissance* (Princeton, NJ: Princeton University Press, 1988), 127.

[26] Nikolaus Pevsner, in 'Old Somerset House', *Architectural Review* 116 (1954), 163–7, writes that 'Serlio's *Architecture*—this can now be taken as universally accepted—was of the greatest importance for the development of classical forms in England', p. 164.

[27] Shute, *The First and Chief Groundes*, sig. A3.

[28] David Evett, *Literature and the Visual Arts in Tudor England* (Athens: University of Georgia Press, 1990), 55.

[29] Shute, *The First and Chief Grounds*, sig. A2.

[30] Giorgio Vasari, *Lives of the Artists*, George Bull (trans.), 2 vols. (1965; rpt. with rev., London: Penguin, 1987), 1: 139.

Doric, and Ionic orders to their original forms'.[31] So painstaking and thorough was Brunelleschi that 'in his mind's eye he could see Rome as it had stood before it fell into ruins'.[32] Arriving at this reconstruction, Brunelleschi found the starting point for his own designs. The previous centuries of Gothic style, now regarded as a degeneration, ceased to have any appeal.

In much the same way, Leon Battista Alberti, a generation later, also turned his back on the Gothic. His church of San Lorenzo in Florence not only embraced classical forms but also had the distinction of being 'the first in Italy to reject Gothic'.[33] Alberti's most characteristic design was his transformation of the church of San Francesco in Rimini, which has become known as the Tempio Malatestiano in honour of the patron (Sigismondo Malatesta), who financed the rebuilding.[34] Alberti encased the Gothic building in a marble and porphyry shell and based the façade on the Arch of Augustus in Rimini, thereby concealing the pointed arches of the original church; he also probably supervised the decoration of the interior with bas reliefs of putti and personifications that have no specifically Christian significance.[35] So successful was Alberti's effort to suppress Gothic features and evoke ancient Rome that the Pope felt obliged to decry the result. Pius II described the transformed church as 'so full of pagan images that it seems like a temple for the worshippers of demons, and not for Christians'.[36]

In view of the commanding status that Roman architecture achieved among the cognoscenti, it is hardly surprising that English writers should prize the ancients and look disapprovingly upon their own traditions. For example, Henry Wotton, who, as a former ambassador to Venice, had first-hand knowledge of new building in Italy (including Palladio's Venetian churches of San Giorgio Maggiore and Il Redentore), disdains the Gothic arch: 'such as these, both for the naturall imbecility of the sharpe *Angle* it selfe, and likewise for their very *Uncomelinesse*, ought to bee exiled from judicious eyes, and left to their first inventors, the *Gothes* or *Lumbards*, amongst other *Reliques* of that barbarous *Age*'.[37] And yet it would be a mistake to think that Wotton speaks for all or even most of his countrymen; Gothic buildings continued to enjoy favour. William Camden in *Britannia* singles out the Gothic chapel of King's College, Cambridge, as 'one of the fairest buildings in the whole world'.[38] He also praises Lincoln Cathedral as 'all throughout not onely most sumptuously, but also passing beautifull, and that with rare and singular workmanship: but especially that forefront at

[31] Vasari, *Lives*, 172.

[32] Vasari, *Lives*, 141.

[33] Onians, *Bearers of Meaning*, 127.

[34] Photo of the (unfinished) façade in Franco Borsi, *Leon Battista Alberti*, Rudolf G. Carpanini (trans.) (New York: Harper & Row, 1977), fig. 149.

[35] For the bas reliefs by Agostino di Duccio and Matteo de' Pasti, see the photos in Borsi, *Leon Battista Alberti*, figs. 184–201.

[36] Quoted by Ludwig H. Heydenreich and Wolfgang Lotz, *Architecture in Italy, 1400–1600*, Mary Hottinger (trans.), Pelican History of Art (Harmondsworth: Penguin, 1974), 31.

[37] Henry Wotton, *The Elements of Architecture* (London: 1624), 51.

[38] William Camden, *Britain, or a Chorographicall Description of the Most flourishing Kingdomes, England, Scotland, and Ireland*, Philemon Holland (trans.), rev. edn. (London: 1610), 487.

the West end, which in a sort ravisheth and allureth the eies of all that judiciously view it'.[39] Clearly, Camden and his countrymen had not entirely lost their appreciation for the Gothic style.

Although Robert Smythson left no written record to indicate whether he was closer to Wotton's judgement or Camden's, we may deduce his attitudes from the houses he built. Those structures reveal that he did not feel a need to embrace one ideal or the other exclusively; his houses accommodate both. Indeed, the hallmark of their design is the simultaneous coupling of ancient forms and indigenous Gothic features. Why is it that Smythson departs from the principles recommended by Brunelleschi, Alberti, and Serlio? Because the Gothic style in England had a hold on the imagination that it never achieved in Italy, where architects had been surrounded for a millennium by ruins of the ancient Romans.[40] Significantly, Gothic style had its genesis not in Italy but just outside Paris, a long way from the centre of Roman civilization in the Mediterranean. The farther one moves into the cooler and darker climes of Europe—into Germany, the Low Countries, northern France, and England—the more deeply grow Gothic roots and the less likely are architects, artists, and artisans to repudiate their medieval past. Both of these movements—classical and Gothic—which seem to point in opposite directions, appealed to English eyes, and the most innovative English builders combined them to create uniquely powerful and pleasing buildings.

The Gothic style in England not only continued to exert an appeal but also enjoyed new favour toward the end of the sixteenth century and the beginning of the seventeenth, as national pride burgeoned following the defeat of the Spanish Armada. Eric Mercer writes of the Gothic style's renewed popularity: 'This is sometimes called a "survival" and sometimes a "revival". It was in fact both, and it could only be revived by some men because it had survived amongst others.'[41] And so just as classical forms in art, architecture, and sculpture began to appear nearly everywhere in England, there was, paradoxically, a simultaneous enthusiasm for the Gothic, which manifests itself throughout the arts, from architecture to courtly tournaments, from painting to poetry. Nowhere is it more apparent than in buildings like Wollaton Hall. As John Summerson writes, 'The Serlian plan rises into a sort of fantastic castle, something Arthurian or like the symbolic castles of Spenser or the pasteboard castles which were besieged and captured, with their fair garrisons, at Court junketings.'[42] And as the Elizabethan era gave way to the Jacobean, the Gothic would enjoy even more favour. A case in point is Bolsover Castle, located not far from Hardwick Hall and designed by John Smythson,

[39] Camden, *Britain*, 539.

[40] It is precisely the strength of this Gothic inspiration that Mark Girouard finds behind the appeal of architecture in the second half of the sixteenth century: 'it seems to me that it was responsible for nearly everything that is most interesting and alive about Elizabethan architecture'. See Girouard, 'Elizabethan Architecture and the Gothic Tradition', *Architectural History* 6 (1963), 30.

[41] Eric Mercer, *English Art, 1553–1625*, Oxford History of English Art 7 (Oxford: Clarendon Press, 1962), 85.

[42] Summerson, *Architecture in Britain*, 64.

the son of Robert.[43] Built for Sir Charles Cavendish in 1612–21, Bolsover 'is the most exhilarating and perfect of all the Jacobean fantasy castles'.[44] The exterior resembles a battlemented medieval fortress, self-contained and forbidding, largely devoid of the classical values that characterize Hardwick Hall and the other buildings of Robert Smythson.[45] It is as though the Gothic style insisted on one last burst of popularity before it would surrender to the chilly aesthetic of neo-classicism.

II.

If the exterior of Hardwick Hall impresses the eye by its soaring towers of glass and disciplined symmetry, the interior works its magic by different means. Surviving in numerous rooms are the accoutrements of daily life: fireplaces, overmantels, portraits, tapestries, embroideries, cushion covers, and even a few pieces of furniture, all of which belonged to the house c.1600. It is exceedingly rare to find such an assemblage of furnishings dating to the 1590s; in most other houses of the era, successive remodellings have completely destroyed the original interiors and scattered their contents. Of course, many of the furnishings have been lost at Hardwick, too, as the inventory of 1601 reveals. Nevertheless, among houses contemporaneous with Shakespeare, Hardwick is the great exception, a house that still retains much of its Elizabethan decoration.[46]

The single most important room of Hardwick Hall is the High Great Chamber, a state room on the uppermost floor used for entertaining visitors, for performances by musicians and actors, for dining and dancing.[47] Such chambers had taken over the function of the great hall in medieval houses. (Hardwick's vestigial entry hall, located on the ground floor, is too small for most entertaining.) If the Great Chamber has a centre of visual interest, it is the chimneypiece, the work of Thomas Accres, a marble mason who had previously worked at Wollaton. Instead of the figures and complicated decoration sculpted in so many sixteenth-century fireplaces, this one is simplicity itself: a plain pair of banded Doric columns symmetrically placed on either side of the

---

[43] According to P. A. Faulkner, *Bolsover Castle*, An English Heritage Handbook (1972; rpt. London: Historic Buildings and Monuments Commission for England, 1985), 'There has been a castle at Bolsover since the twelfth century' (p. 5). John Smythson's structure, known as the Little Castle, was built on the site of its medieval predecessor.

[44] Malcolm Airs, *The Buildings of Britain: Tudor and Jacobean* (London: Barrie and Jenkins, 1982), 141.

[45] Only the substantial windows defy medieval precedent. Photo by Martin Charles in Mowl, *Elizabethan and Jacobean Style*, 118.

[46] For a specific analysis of the contents, see 'The Hardwick Hall Inventory of 1601', Lindsay Boynton (ed.), with an introduction by Boynton and a commentary by Peter Thornton, *Furniture History* 7 (1971), 1–14.

[47] The High Great Chamber is essentially 'a rectangular box extended on one side by a window embrasure, itself as big as a normal parlour, which occupies the whole space within one of the turrets' (Nigel Nicolson, *The National Trust Book of Great Houses of Britain* [London: The National Trust and Weidenfeld & Nicolson, 1978], 93).

fireplace and, above, panels of geometric forms carved in alabaster and blackstone and arranged within a subdued strapwork design.[48] The huge royal coat of arms, representing Bess of Hardwick's loyalty to the queen, surmounts the chimneypiece and fills the wall right up to the ceiling.

As one begins to explore the room, the plaster frieze that runs around the perimeter commands attention. Executed by Abraham Smith and his team of twenty-one artisans, the frieze constitutes a band occupying roughly the top half of the walls.[49] A woodland scene, the plants and animals are in high relief and painted so that they stand out against the white background.[50] The plasterers have obviously been inspired by their knowledge of the Derbyshire countryside. Indeed, 'the plasterer used real branches and leaves for forms'[51] that copied the look of local vegetation. So, for example, we may identify not only various trees but also foxgloves, lilies, and gilly-flowers. Wildlife also populates the frieze in the form of stags, bears, horses, birds, and other beasts. There are classical deities too (more of them in a moment), but these have been domesticated, set within the context of the woodlands just beyond the house and its garden. That dense plasterwork forest in the High Great Chamber is much more than a background for the human and animal figures; 'it is as important as the figures and determines the mood of the room'.[52]

Who precisely are the classical figures in the frieze and what are they doing in the High Great Chamber? One, a nude woman with flowers in her hair and right hand, may be identified as a personification of Spring.[53] But because her left hand grasps the arm of Cupid, as though in reproof, scholars sometimes identify her as Venus. The conflation of Spring and Venus has a certain logic. After all, romantic passion is frequently identified with this season, as sixteenth-century engravings demonstrate. For example, a print by Jan Sadeler after Dirk Barentsz (Theodor Bernards) depicts Spring with a flowerpot balanced on one leg, another flowerpot beside her; in the background we see an amorous couple in a bower.[54] At Hardwick the plasterers base their Spring/Venus on a

[48] Photos by James Pipkin in Gervase Jackson-Stops and James Pipkin, *The English Country House: A Grand Tour* (Boston: Little, Brown; Washington, DC: National Gallery of Art, 1985), 83; and by Graham Challifour in Girouard, *Hardwick Hall*, 33.

[49] Geoffrey Beard, *Stucco and Decorative Plasterwork in Europe* (London: Thames & Hudson, 1983. Although most scholars credit Smith with responsibility for the plasterwork, David Bostick, in 'Plaster Puzzle Decoded', *Country Life* 184.30 (July 26 1990), 76–9, credits Richard Orton and John Marker.

[50] Geoffrey Beard, in *The National Trust Book of the English House Interior* (London: Viking in association with The National Trust, 1990), writes: 'Had the Hardwick frieze been left white, washed with a solution of Crich lime as all else in the house was, its spirited reliefwork would still amaze us. But the effect is made more dramatic . . . by the use of colour' (p. 56).

[51] Watkins, *In Public and in Private*, 147.

[52] Olive Cook, *The English Country House: An Art and a Way of Life* (1974; rpt. London: Thames & Hudson, 1984), 90.

[53] Photo by Pipkin in Jackson-Stops and Pipkin, *The English Country House*, 82; and by Mike Williams in Girouard, *Hardwick Hall*, 21.

[54] Reproduced by Frederick Kiefer, *Shakespeare's Visual Theatre: Staging the Personified Characters* (Cambridge: Cambridge University Press, 2003), fig. 5.

print by Crispin van der Passe after a design by Maarten de Vos.[55] Another plasterwork figure is a seated woman, her right arm resting upon a sheaf of grain while her right leg is propped upon another sheaf; and her left hand grasps still another; grain adorns even her hair.[56] This figure has been identified as Summer, and a print by Maarten de Vos, probably used as a model by the plasterers, is labelled 'Aestas'.[57] But the woman may just as easily be identified as the classical Ceres, who is similarly represented in the arts.[58] What Spring/Venus and Summer/Ceres express symbolically is the fertility of the earth, the seasons particularly identified with growth and maturation, and the bounty of the land that supports both wildlife and humankind.

Although the plasterwork represents the most unusual treasure of Hardwick's High Great Chamber and has even been called 'the supreme achievement of Elizabethan plasterers',[59] the room boasts another work of art, too, a series of eight tapestries that fill the lower half of the walls around the perimeter.[60] Made in Belgium and based on designs by Michiel Coxie, they tell the story of Ulysses. Interestingly, Bess bought the tapestries in 1587, before construction of her house began. This suggests that they were from the beginning intended for display in the High Great Chamber: 'The room in which they still hang was clearly planned to contain them, for they fill exactly in width and height the available space.'[61] The implication for the design of this most important of Elizabethan rooms[62] seems inevitable: the plaster frieze above and the tapestries, situated below and separated by a white cornice, were conceived of as an ensemble; the room was proportioned to accommodate both.

What links the Flemish tapestries and English plaster? On the most obvious level we find similarities in setting. Most of the tapestries depict, at least in the background, mature trees of the kind that appear in the plasterwork. So, for example, the panel depicting Ulysses battling the boar that gores him in the leg takes place in woodland. Another panel, in which Ulysses feigns insanity, is placed outdoors. Even the panel of Ulysses taking leave of his wife seems set in a landscape: although two classical columns are visible immediately behind Ulysses and must support some kind of structure above

[55] Girouard, *Hardwick Hall*, 20. The same print was also used for the design of a tapestry of the Four Seasons (1611) at Hatfield House, near London. Reproduced by Mowl, *Elizabethan and Jacobean Style*, [158].

[56] Photo in Margaret Jourdain, *English Decorative Plasterwork of the Renaissance* (London: Batsford, 1926), fig. 20.

[57] Reproduced by Jourdain, *English Decorative Plasterwork*, fig. 19.

[58] See Kiefer, *Shakespeare's Visual Theatre*, 169–74.

[59] Beard, *The National Trust Book of the English House Interior*, 56.

[60] The tapestries occupy 'just over half the height of the room' (Alan and Ann Gore, *The History of English Interiors*, 27). For the plasterwork and tapestries together, see the photo by Robert Thrift in Anthony Wells-Cole, *Art and Decoration in Elizabethan and Jacobean England: The Influence of Continental Prints, 1558–1625* (New Haven, CT and London: Yale University Press, 1997), fig. 460; by Pipkin in Jackson-Stops and Pipkin, *The English Country House*, 83.

[61] Marcel Roethlisberger, 'The Ulysses Tapestries at Hardwick Hall', *Gazette des Beaux-Arts* 79 (February 1972), 111. Roethlisberger reproduces the tapestries.

[62] Sacheverell Sitwell, in *British Architects and Craftsmen*, 4th edn. (London: Batsford, 1948), wrote that the Chamber is 'the most beautiful room, not in England alone, but in the whole of Europe' (p. 27).

that is unseen by the viewer, the setting is clearly outside; Ulysses and his wife stand on the ground, not on a paved floor; in the background the Greek hero leads a group of soldiers in a field bordered by forest.[63] A panel depicting the discovery of Achilles among the daughters of Lycomedes has for its setting a combination of the natural and the man-made: in the background stands some sort of classical pavilion that features Corinthian columns supporting a roof. Because the structure lacks walls, the surrounding forest, seen through the columns, becomes the backdrop. Meanwhile the contest over the arms of Achilles takes place before Agamemnon, seated in his tent, while in front of him stands Ulysses, a massive tree at his back, a vine growing up the trunk. Even the homecoming of Ulysses, depicted within a classical structure, reveals trees in the distance, seen through the home's arches. All of these panels, which have broad borders filled with foliage and fruit, anchor the human drama in the world of nature.

In addition to the greenery of both tapestries and plasterwork, there is something else that connects them: their classicism. The story of Ulysses is, of course, the subject of Homer's *Odyssey*, itself an inspiration for Virgil's *Aeneid*. And, like the Greek poet, the plasterers of Hardwick Hall represent certain ancient deities, hardly surprising at a time when classical culture represented in so many ways the aesthetic ideal for Elizabethans. The most prominent of these is Diana the huntress, seen from across the room as one enters the High Great Chamber.[64] The plaster Diana sits in the forest holding a large arrow and bow, attended by seven (smaller) standing nymphs, who wield their own bows and arrows. Beside Diana grows a giant oak tree of the kind that provided the structural support for Elizabethan half-timbered buildings (and for the framework and columns at the Globe Theatre). The ensemble is framed by stags and rampant horses on the one side, elephants and camels on the other.

In the representation of Diana, we may detect a pragmatic compliment to Queen Elizabeth, often identified in the arts with the virgin goddess.[65] And, of course, the royal coat of arms dominates the room. Bess must have hoped that the Queen would visit Hardwick one day, though by the time the house was completed, the Queen's advanced age made a lengthy trek to the north of England unlikely. Is it possible, however, that something other than a simple compliment may be implied by that plasterwork? Might the representation of Diana convey a subtle jibe at the powerful Queen? Diana, after all, could be capricious: she turns Actaeon into a stag hunted and killed by his own hounds when he happens upon the goddess bathing in a sylvan pool. Here a hunting scene in plaster reveals yet another expression of Diana's cruelty: 'a nymph, who has been

---

[63] Reproduced by Santina M. Levey, *Elizabethan Treasures: The Hardwick Hall Textiles* (London: The National Trust, 1998), fig. 17.

[64] Photo by Mark Fiennes in Watkins, *In Public and in Private*, 148–9.

[65] In *The Arraignment of Paris*, a comedy performed *c*.1581–4, George Peele recasts the Judgement of Paris so that it no longer celebrates the victory of Venus. Instead, Diana puts the golden apple into the hands of Queen Elizabeth. Diana makes explicit the parallel between her realm and Elizabeth's: 'The place Elizium hight, and of the place, | Her name that governes there Eliza is, | A kingdome that may well compare with mine' (5.1.1150–2). See Charles Tyler Prouty (gen. ed.), *The Life and Works of George Peele*, 3 vols. (New Haven, CT: Yale University Press, 1952–70), vol. 3.

turned into a bear by Diana as a punishment for losing her chastity, is being killed by a pack of brutal hunters'.[66] Timothy Mowl observes that had the Queen visited Hardwick, she would have been seated directly in front of Diana and her attendants: 'It is a place in which to savour the ambivalent relationship between two strong-minded old women',[67] one of them celebrated for her virginity, the other married four times and the mother of eight children. Mowl goes no further in speculating about Bess of Hardwick's motives for the symbolism in plaster, but he proffers the plausible suggestion that the representation of Diana may be something less than a straightforward compliment to the Queen. 'A state of something like armed neutrality existed between Bess of Hardwick and Elizabeth I who was rightly suspicious of the former's ambitions for her granddaughter and ward, Arabella Stuart, a possible claimant to the throne.'[68] For her part, Bess resented the task of keeping Mary Queen of Scots under what amounted to house arrest; in 1568, Queen Elizabeth gave this assignment to George Talbot, Earl of Shrewsbury, who had married Bess a year earlier.[69] For sixteen years Bess would endure the psychological and financial strain of looking after a woman who would be charged with conspiring against the Queen.

Whatever the representation of the virgin goddess may hint to the knowledgeable viewer, the casual observer of the High Great Chamber would find in the plasterwork Diana an embodiment of sexual discipline and steadfastness of purpose. The tapestry, for its part, celebrates not only the story of Ulysses but also that of his wife Penelope. One panel, depicting Ulysses' leave-taking, illustrates the husband's entrusting of his wife to the care of his father 'as though to reinforce Penelope's importance in the narrative'.[70] Penelope, who patiently waits for her husband's return, became synonymous with feminine rectitude. The particular virtue celebrated in Penelope is echoed in wall hangings elsewhere in the house, which celebrate women of the ancient world. An appliqué hanging of Penelope, for instance, depicts her pointing to heaven with her right hand, while her left hand rests upon a cylindrical object, which evokes a broken column, the familiar symbol of Fortitude.[71] On one side of Penelope stands personified Patience while Perseverance stands on the other.[72] Another appliqué artwork represents Lucrece, who killed herself after her rape by Tarquin and who was henceforth regarded as a model of probity; on either side of Lucrece stands a personified virtue:

---

[66] Mowl, *Elizabethan and Jacobean Style*, 116. Photo in Jourdain, *English Decorative Plasterwork*, fig. 35.

[67] Mowl, *Elizabethan and Jacobean Style*, 116.

[68] Jackson-Stops and Pipkin, *The English Country House*, 84.

[69] With this marriage Bess became known formally as Elizabeth, Countess of Shrewsbury.

[70] Don E. Wayne, ' "A More Safe Survey": Social-Property Relations, Hegemony, and the Rhetoric of Country Life', in Peter E. Medine and Joseph Wittreich (eds.), *Soundings of Things Done: Essays in Early Modern Literature in Honor of S. K. Heninger Jr.* (Newark: University of Delaware Press; London: Associated University Presses, 1997), 280. Wayne reproduces the tapestry panel, 282.

[71] Santina M. Levey, in *The Embroideries at Hardwick Hall: A Catalogue* (London: The National Trust, 2008), describes the object as 'an upright roll of fabric'. But the 'apparently ribbed surface of the fabric is also reminiscent of a fluted column and, as such, could symbolise Constancy or Fortitude, both virtues appropriate to' Penelope (80). Levey reproduces the artwork, fig. 1D, 80.

[72] Reproduced by Girouard, *Hardwick Hall*, 23.

Chastity and Liberality.[73] Bess must have felt a particular connection with this figure from Roman history, for she had 'her last child christened Lucretia in 1557'.[74] It is hardly surprising that the woman responsible for building and furnishing Hardwick Hall should celebrate feminine puissance. After all, she had spent her entire life in a world largely dominated by men. Only her iron will, ambition, and shrewdness allowed her to become the richest woman in England after the Queen. In her private life, moreover, she did not hesitate to defy and mock her fourth husband, the Earl of Shrewsbury. Edmund Lodge's description captures her feisty spirit: 'she was a woman of a masculine understanding and conduct; proud, furious, selfish, and unfeeling'.[75] Why should such a formidable woman not celebrate female virtue and achievement?

To summarize, the High Great Chamber contains two principal artistic works; they were created in different countries and executed in different forms at different times, and yet they complement one another when seen together. If the exterior of Hardwick Hall represents a conjunction of the Gothic and the classical, of the vertical and the horizontal, the High Great Chamber also represents a combination. The plasterwork and tapestries, outwardly so different, share something in common: an appreciation for the fecundity of nature and a celebration of female power. The more one's eyes move from plaster to textile, the more apparent this parallel becomes.

III.

What Hardwick Hall provides is an aesthetic paradigm expressive of Elizabethan and Jacobean culture. Energizing that paradigm are disparate inspirations, foreign and domestic, ancient and modern. Far from clashing, these meld, for the paradigm prizes assimilation. Indeed, the essence of the paradigm resides in the ways that it achieves a synthesis of diverse forms, materials, and impulses. Because it embraces heterogeneity, the paradigm provides for unusually powerful and complex effects. That is, one component capitalizes upon and/or balances another. Together, they generate an emotional force greater than any constituent part would possess.

In the civic pageantry that greeted King James's coronation passage through London, we find that paradigm at work. The seven triumphal arches marking the route represent an amalgam of the arts: architecture, sculptural decoration, painting, street theatre, music, and poetry (in the form of speeches recited by actors). The first of these arches, at Fenchurch, is exemplary, and we possess not only a splendid print

---

[73] Reproduced by Levey, *Elizabethan Treasures*, fig. 68.

[74] Levey, *Elizabethan Treasures*, 69.

[75] Edmund Lodge, *Illustrations of British History, Biography, and Manners, in the Reigns of Henry VIII, Edward VI, Mary, Elizabeth, and James I, Exhibited in a Series of Original Papers*, 3 vols. (London: G. Nicol, 1791), 1: xvii.

showing how it looked (in Stephen Harrison's *Arches of Triumph*) but also Ben Jonson's detailed commentary about what the crowds saw and heard.

The most visually striking section of the Fenchurch structure is a detailed panorama of London, which stretches across the fifty-foot width of the arch and occupies its upper portion. The artisans render individual features of the city in such a way that they are immediately recognizable. According to Gilbert Dugdale's first-hand account, 'In *Fanchurch street* was erected a stately Trophie or Pageant, at the Citties Charge, on which stood such a show of workmanship and glorie as I never saw the like .... The Cittie of London [was] very rarely and artificially made, where no church, house nor place of note, but your eye might easilye find out, as the *Exchange, Coleharber, Powles, Bowe Church, &c.*'[76] The panorama, 'adorn'd with houses, towres, and steeples, set off in prospective' (ll. 3–5),[77] depicts an essentially medieval city, one that would not survive the great fire of 1666 and the subsequent ascendancy of neo-classicism. Medieval London had abandoned the gridwork established by the Romans when they settled Londinium. As a consequence the buildings were arranged higgledy-piggledy along crooked streets. In the panorama, houses and larger structures are crowded cheek by jowl, a jumble shaped by the Gothic past: St Paul's Cathedral is the largest structure visible, and other medieval churches are identifiable by their spires (see Figure 37.4).

If the city atop the arch belongs to the Gothic heritage, the section beneath has a very different origin. Here we find two parallel archways arranged as they might appear in an ancient triumphal monument. The symmetry extends to the decorative programme.[78] Carefully balanced on right and left are square compartments within each of which stand three musicians. In the middle sit seven figures arranged on the form of a stepped gable; at the top is Monarchia Britannica; to one side are Gladness, Loving Affection, and Unanimity, and to the other, Veneration, Promptitude, and Vigilance. Below (and between the arches) stands Genius Urbis flanked by a figure on either side and beneath this trio lies a personification of the River Thames, as though carved by an ancient sculptor. Creating a sense of stylistic cohesion is the strapwork situated above both of the square compartments, on either side of the central stepped section, and at the base of the arch in the centre. Such strapwork represents the same kind of decoration visible atop the towers of Wollaton Hall and in the cresting of Hardwick Hall where it flanks Bess's initials (ES for Elizabeth of Shrewsbury).

Scholars assign Ben Jonson a share of the credit for designing the edifying entertainment at Fenchurch Street,[79] and the fact that a dramatist should contribute to the arch

---

[76] Gilbert Dugdale, *The Time Triumphant* (London, 1604), sig. B2v.

[77] Ben Jonson, *Part of the King's Entertainment in Passing to His Coronation*, in C. H. Herford and Percy and Evelyn Simpson (eds.), *Ben Jonson*, 11 vols. (Oxford: Clarendon Press, 1925–52), 7: 83.

[78] For a good account of this and the other arches, see David M. Bergeron, *English Civic Pageantry, 1558–1642* (Columbia: University of South Carolina Press, 1971), 75–91. Bergeron reproduces the arch, pl. 2.

[79] Sara van den Berg, in 'The Passing of the Elizabethan Court', *Ben Jonson Journal* 1 (1994), 31–61, writes: 'When King James entered London as its new king, the entertainment welcoming him was funded and controlled not by the Court but by the City of London'; Ben Jonson and Thomas Dekker 'were commissioned to design this event'; and Stephen Harrison 'designed triumphal arches' (p. 44).

FIGURE 37.4. The Fenchurch arch in the coronation procession of James I. Printed in *The Arches of Triumph* by Stephen Harrison (1604). By permission of the British Library Board (G.10866).

suggests the degree to which the various arts converge in this era. Later Jonson would become the chief writer of masques for the king's court and in this capacity became the collaborator of Inigo Jones, who designed costumes and scenery and who became the most important architect of early seventeenth-century London. As masque-maker, Jones, who had studied in Italy, would design scenery that evokes the buildings of antiquity.[80] Although Jonson himself never travelled to Italy, he was probably the foremost classicist of his age, and he must therefore have recognized and approved the adoption of ancient precedent in the triumphal arch. But he must also have recognized the indigenous Gothic features of the panorama above. How did he conceive of the relationship between sections of the arch? Jonson himself provides an insight into the aesthetic principle informing the Fenchurch structure:

> Thus farre the complementall part of the first; wherein was not onely labored the expression of state and magnificence (as proper to a triumphall Arch) but the very site, fabricke, strength, policie, dignitie, and affections of the Citie were all laid downe to life: The nature and propertie of these Devices being, to present alwaies

[80] See, for example, John Harris and Gordon Higgott, *Inigo Jones: Complete Architectural Drawings* (New York: The Drawing Center, 1989), fig. 95: design for the masque *Albion's Triumph*.

some one entire bodie, or figure, consisting of distinct members, and each of those expressing it selfe, in the owne active sphaere, yet all, with that generall harmonie so connexed, and disposed, as no one little part can be missing to the illustration of the whole (ll. 243–53)[81]

Writing these words, Jonson 'stands at the crossroads of architecture and drama'.[82] Significantly, Jonson's words have been interpreted both as an allusion to Aristotle's *Poetics* and as an allusion to Vitruvius, 'perhaps being echoed by way of Alberti or Palladio, or both'.[83] Whether the words' intended import is literary or architectural, the organizing principle is the same.

When Jonson turns to the theatre, he follows much the same principle of construction apparent in the Fenchurch arch: that is, he creates 'one entire bodie or figure, consisting of distinct members'. What this means in structural terms is that he organizes his materials by a double (or multiple) plot, which accommodates the constituent parts. This dramaturgical feature characterizes not only Jonson's plays but also those of contemporaries. For much of the twentieth century, sub-plots were regarded as blemishes in otherwise splendid drama. By the time Richard Levin wrote *The Multiple Plot in English Renaissance Drama* (1971),[84] however, the critical consensus had shifted: multiple-plot plays were seen as enjoying a unity that had eluded earlier generations of readers and playgoers. Today few critics complain that sub-plots are superfluous, tedious, or grotesque.

Shakespeare resembles Jonson and their contemporaries in creating double, triple, or even quadruple plots; he revels in copiousness and complexity. By orchestrating the plots,[85] Shakespeare incorporates an aesthetic principle manifest in the other arts, and this is nowhere plainer than in *King Lear*. The story he dramatizes reaches deep into medieval history: Geoffrey of Monmouth provides an account in his *Historia Regum Britanniae* (c.1135). Subsequent writers who treat the story include Robert Fabyan, Raphael Holinshed, John Higgins in *A Mirror for Magistrates*, William Camden, Edmund Spenser, and William Warner. However much Shakespeare owes to these authors, he finds his immediate source in *King Leir and His Three Daughters*, a play almost certainly performed in 1594 and probably earlier. *Leir*, moreover, may have been revived shortly before Shakespeare's version reached the London stage, though the

---

[81] Ben Jonson, *Part of the King's Entertainment in passing to his Coronation*, in *Ben Jonson*, 7: 90–1.

[82] Alan T. Bradford, 'Use and Uniformity in Elizabethan Architecture and Drama', *John Donne Journal* 5 (1986), 43.

[83] Bradford, 'Use and Uniformity', 43. For a subtle treatment of Jonson's debt to Vitruvius, see A. W. Johnson, *Ben Jonson: Poetry and Architecture* (Oxford: Clarendon Press, 1994), esp. ch. 1, 'Jonson and the Vitruvian Aesthetic', 9–35.

[84] Richard Levin, *The Multiple Plot in English Renaissance Drama* (Chicago, IL: University of Chicago Press, 1971).

[85] Jean E. Howard, in *Shakespeare's Art of Orchestration: Stage Technique and Audience Response* (Urbana: University of Illinois Press, 1984), uses the term 'orchestration' as I do here—metaphorically: 'By it I wish to suggest that drama, like dance and music, is a serial art in which the audience sees and hears things in a predetermined order' (2).

evidence is equivocal. In any event, there is no question that Shakespeare knew the earlier play well. Richard Knowles observes, 'Shakespeare's *Lear* shows in nearly a hundred significant details a close familiarity with the old play as it exists in the 1605 edition'.[86]

Like so many earlier plays of the sixteenth century, *Leir* is a generic mongrel. Grace Ioppolo describes it as 'comedy, tragedy, history, and romance'.[87] In the entry for May 8, 1605 the Stationers' Register gives the title as 'the Tragecall [changed from *Tragedie*] historie of kinge Leir and his Three Daughters'. The title-page of the 1605 Quarto, however, calls the play *The True Chronicle History of King Leir and His Three Daughters, Gonorill, Ragan, and Cordella*. The play may perhaps best be termed tragicomic, for *Leir* dramatizes a series of tragic (or potentially tragic) events before concluding happily. In this it resembles much of the drama in preceding decades. Like those earlier plays, *King Leir* demonstrates its heritage by dramatizing temptation, moral error, redemption, and forgiveness. The mercenary Messenger, tempted with riches by Gonorill and Ragan, agrees to murder Leir and Perillus, a good counsellor. But at the last moment remorse deflects him from the evil deed: 'Oh, but my conscience for this act doth tell, | I get heavens hate, earths scorne, and paynes of hell' (ll. 1646–7).[88] As for Leir, guilt-ridden on account of his harsh treatment of Cordella, Perillus assures him that his daughter, moved by divine grace, will reconcile with him: 'No worldly gifts, but grace from God on hye, | Doth nourish vertue and true charity' (ll. 1772–3). And so a penitent Leir appeals to his virtuous daughter: 'it is my part to kneele, | And aske forgivenesse for my former faults' (ll. 2299–2300). As these incidents suggest, *King Leir* is fundamentally Gothic in its preoccupations.[89] That is, like the sixteenth-century moral drama, the play is replete with the concepts and language of Christian belief: church, repentance, prayers and beads, nun, cloisters, palmer, soul, heaven, hell, devil, pity, blessing, conscience, charity, forgiveness, grace, Saviour, and God. In the view of Geoffrey Bullough, *King Leir* 'justifies the ways of God to men'.[90]

To the story he found in *King Leir*, Shakespeare adds that of the Paphlagonian king and his sons. Unlike the account of Leir, this obscure tale has no precedent in earlier

---

[86] Richard Knowles, 'How Shakespeare Knew *King Leir*', *Shakespeare Survey* 55 (2002), 35. Knowles provides an extraordinarily thorough account of Shakespeare's knowledge of the earlier play. Similarly, R. A. Foakes, in his edition of *King Lear*, Arden Shakespeare 3 (Walton-on-Thames: Nelson, 1997), writes of *Leir*, 'This play had a powerful impact on Shakespeare, whose close reading of it suggests that he studied the printed book' (90).

[87] Grace Ioppolo, ' "A Jointure more or less": Re-measuring *The True Chronicle History of King Lear and his three daughters*', *Medieval and Renaissance Drama in England* 17 (2005), 171.

[88] *'The History of King Leir', 1605*, W. W. Greg (ed.), Malone Society Reprints (Oxford: Oxford University Press, 1907/[1908]).

[89] Some of these are apparent in *King Lear*. According to Emrys Jones, in *The Origins of Shakespeare* (Oxford: Clarendon Press, 1977), Shakespeare's play 'makes extensive use of morality play features', 59. For his indebtedness to the morality plays, see also John Reibetanz, *The 'Lear' World: A Study of 'King Lear' in its Dramatic Context* (Toronto: University of Toronto Press, 1977), 33–55.

[90] Geoffrey Bullough (ed.), *Narrative and Dramatic Sources of Shakespeare*, 8 vols. (London: Routledge & Kegan Paul; New York: Columbia University Press, 1957–75), 7: 282.

drama. In fact, Shakespeare found it in the pages of an immensely long narrative, Sir Philip Sidney's *Arcadia* (published in 1590). It is highly ironic that Shakespeare should have resorted to this work since Sidney so thoroughly disdained the popular drama of Elizabethan England. In any event, Sidney's *Arcadia* draws upon ancient Greek prose fiction and, in adapting it, Shakespeare enters a realm far distant from that of indigenous English drama. Greek romance has little to do with free will and moral choice, with human accountability, with salvation or damnation, with a rational and just God presiding over the world. As S. L. Wolff writes, 'The paradoxical, the bizarre, the inconsistent, the self-contradictory—these were the stock in trade with the writers of Greek romance.'[91]

Grafting the ancient tale of the Paphlagonian king onto that of King Leir allows Shakespeare to create an elaborate symmetry that is classical in its precision. Both stories dramatize a father's relationship with his progeny, and the characters of those fathers are uncannily similar. Lear and Gloucester share a common failing: they grievously err in judging the natures of their children, and through that misjudgement both fathers suffer a cruel calamity. In adversity Lear and Gloucester come to understand their culpability in giving life to children deficient in basic decency, children who lack any feeling for the claims of natural bonds. Such acknowledgement, in turn, entails a threat to the fathers' reason and a sharp challenge to comforting assumptions about the world's nature. The symmetry of the two plots extends even further. The youngest daughter of Lear is the very antithesis of her sisters; similarly, Edgar is the opposite of Edmund. And in each family the vicious victimize the virtuous in a way that underscores the powerlessness of the innocent. Ultimately, the wronged children forgive their credulous fathers, but that charity is unable to arrest the momentum of events, leading ineluctably to tragedy. John Reibetanz best summarizes the play's tendency to align every character and action with a moral template: 'Actions and characters in the *Lear* world define themselves at irreversible extremes. When they are good, they are very good, and when they are bad they are unspeakable.'[92] Nowhere else in Shakespeare's plays is this divide so stark and so consistently maintained. No wonder Maynard Mack applies the word 'diagrammatic' to *King Lear*.[93]

It is difficult to imagine two works more dissimilar than *King Leir* and the story of the Paphlagonian king. One belongs to the tradition of a Christianized medieval England, the other to the vanished world of pagan antiquity.[94] And yet, as Kenneth Muir observes, *King Lear*, 'far from exhibiting any signs of loose, episodic structure, is

---

[91] Samuel Lee Wolff, *The Greek Romances in Elizabethan Prose Fiction* (1912; rpt. New York: Burt Franklin, 1961), 5. According to Wolff, Sidney found the story of the Paphlagonian King in Heliodorus (pp. 312–13).

[92] Reibetanz, *The 'Lear' World*, 16.

[93] Maynard Mack, *'King Lear' in Our Time* (1965; rpt. Berkeley: University of California Press, 1972), 95.

[94] As scholars have exhaustively demonstrated, *King Lear* is indebted to various works, including Samuel Harsnett's *A Declaration of Egregious Impostures* (1603) and John Florio's translation of Montaigne (1603). Here I am dealing only with the basic elements of the two plots.

more closely knit than any of the tragedies, except *Othello*'.[95] In *The Sources of Shakespeare's Plays*, Muir adds, 'The two plots are ingeniously linked together'[96]—so much so that a playgoer new to *King Lear* would almost certainly fail to guess that the plots have utterly different origins. The jointure is purposeful, of course: Jay Halio remarks that by conflating the stories of the Paphlagonian king and King Leir, Shakespeare 'universalised his theme and raised it to "cosmic" proportions'.[97] That Shakespeare should have synthesized such disparate stories (while simultaneously changing both) is a tribute not only to his own creative imagination but also to the aesthetic paradigm that shaped the design of Longleat, Wollaton, Hardwick Hall, and numerous other creations of Elizabethan–Jacobean England.

[95] Kenneth Muir (ed.), *King Lear*, Arden Shakespeare (1952; rpt. with corrections, Cambridge, MA: Harvard University Press, 1959), xliii.
[96] Kenneth Muir, *The Sources of Shakespeare's Plays* (New Haven, CT: Yale University Press, 1978), 207.
[97] Jay L. Halio, (ed.), *The Tragedy of King Lear: Updated Edition*, New Cambridge Shakespeare (Cambridge: Cambridge University Press, 2005), 4.

CHAPTER 38

SCIENCE AND TECHNOLOGY

ADAM MAX COHEN

A careful historical and artefactual study of the Elizabethan–Jacobean period yields evidence that the period experienced a multifaceted technology boom. Elizabethan and Jacobean Englishmen did not routinely use the word *technology* to mean the study of an industrial field, though the *Oxford English Dictionary* notes one use of *technology* in something approximating its modern sense in 1615, one year prior to Shakespeare's death. To describe individuals working in what we today would consider technological fields Englishmen preferred terms such as mechanical, mechanician—which could be narrowed down further to speculative mechanician or mathematical mechanician— Latinate terms such as *artifex mathematicus*, less exalted terms like common artificer, and more laudatory terms like ingenious practisers. Latin terms for the new tools crafted by these practitioners included *instrumenta nova*, *nova reperta*, and *novitates*, and the new arts and practices were called *artes novae* and the *artes mechanicae*.

I.

The technological revolutions in the realms of information technology, navigation, optics, surveying, and other fields in the fifteenth, sixteenth, and early seventeenth centuries may have helped lay the ground for the rise of science in Europe in the second half of the seventeenth century. Because the history of science is sometimes considered a branch of philosophy, and thus fair game for scholars trained in the humanities, most early modern literary scholars who are willing to cross disciplinary lines usually focus on the history of science instead of the history of technology. The protoscientific theory and practice that was often referred to in the period as *natural philosophy* was closely intertwined with humanistic study. While a significant gap may exist today between the humanities and the sciences, no such disciplinary gap existed during the early modern period. Indeed *science* as it is now conceived did not exist either as a disciplinary category or as a habit of thought. What did exist was an array of practices and artefacts associated with newly invented or recently updated instruments, tools, and machines. Some innovations quickly translated into widely available products such as printed books, glass mirrors, lantern clocks, or globes, and some were so impractical that they served only to satisfy the public's mounting fascination with marvellous and impossible machines. While 'technology' in the modern sense of the word had not yet emerged as a discrete disciplinary category, a wide variety of mechanical practices and artefacts did exist, and artisans, craftsmen, students, and scholars employed these practices and artefacts in ways that helped to redefine early modern English culture.

These studies of early modern mechanical artefacts are complicated by the fact that only a fraction of the technologies designed and built during the Elizabethan–Jacobean period survive. Among those that do survive there are more expensive tools and instruments than their cheaper, more mass-produced counterparts. Despite the challenges of artefactual research, ample evidence of a technological boom in England exists in the form of treatises on the mechanical and mathematical arts, almanacs, records of public lectures delivered in Latin and in English, and the extant physical artefacts themselves.

Some literary scholars are reluctant to consider the representations of tools, instruments, and machines. A few are unconvinced that the study of technological artefacts and practices is necessary for the study of literary history. In R. G. W. Anderson's foreword to Gerard L'E. Turner's book *Elizabethan Instrument Makers*, Anderson encourages these scholars to reconsider their position by asserting that

> instruments are not an alternative source of knowledge to manuscripts and printed books; they are complementary, and without them our understanding of important areas of cultural history could not be illuminated.'[1]

II.

How might Shakespeare have come to know so much about many different types of mechanical innovations both ancient and modern? This question is difficult to answer in part because we know so little about Shakespeare's life, but the few details we do know offer possible explanations. As a boy in Stratford, Shakespeare probably would have learned how to use a few tools and implements while observing and perhaps working in his father's glove-making shop. At the King's New School he would have read about marvellous and powerful ancient machines. At school he also would have been introduced to the wealth of mechanical metaphors that were invoked by classical, medieval, and early modern rhetoricians to describe the human body, human ingenuity, the state, and the cosmos.

---

[1] In Gerard L'E. Turner, *Elizabethan Instrument Makers: The Origins of the London Trade in Precision Instrument Making* (Oxford: Oxford University Press, 2000), v.

Upon moving to London and entering the professional theatre Shakespeare would have been introduced to the tools of that trade. As a playwright, an actor, and ultimately a sharer in the Lord Chamberlain's Men/King's Men he needed to be at least somewhat familiar with the mechanical contrivances used in stage effects he integrated into his plays, including flying entrances enabled by cranks and pulleys in the 'Heavens', gunpowder pyrotechnics, sound effects ranging from thunder to the tolling of bells, and even the magical disappearance of a banquet in *The Tempest*. As a resident in the Blackfriars parish in the latter part of his theatrical career, he would very likely have met technicians and instrument-makers, since residents of that parish were well known for designing, manufacturing, and marketing new instruments, tools, and machines.

III.

Hundreds of new tools, inventions, and machines were developed during Shakespeare's lifetime. In the field of navigation the innovations included new types of compasses, quadrants, astrolabes, armillary spheres, globes, staffs, and sea-rings. In the field of gunnery, sectors, quadrants and gunner's levels helped aim various large ordnance including iron and brass cannon as well as hand-held gunpowder weapons such as the arquebus, the caliver, and the musket. In timekeeping, sundials equipped with compasses, spring-driven clocks, and weight-driven cathedral and chamber clocks were all in use. In surveying instrument-makers perfected theodolites, carpenters' rules, various sorts of squares, and backstaffs. Some of these tools were designed and built by professional instrument-makers, some were made by mechanics or mathematicians hired by noble households, and some were built by amateurs who had seen or read of a new technology in an almanac or a *Description and Use* treatise. The playwright was thus well aware of the overlapping and interlocking technological revolutions that took place in England during his career.[2]

Moreover, if it is true that the purpose of 'playing' was to hold a mirror up to nature, and if it is also true that a technology boom took place during Shakespeare's career, then it seems reasonable to look to Shakespeare's plays for evidence of technological shifts. Theatrical culture was a dominant element of popular culture that portrayed and appealed to the learned and the illiterate alike.[3] Both groups designed and built

[2] This same human–machine fusion is also evident in the technical literature of the period. For example, in Robert Recorde's *Grounde of Artes* the reader's hands become calculating tools. The left hand is used to count from 1 to 99, and the right is used to count larger numbers. See Robert Recorde, *The Grounde of Artes* (London: 1542), sigs. P1–P2. Recorde was not the first to describe human digits as counting instruments. In 1533, Peter Apian's *Instrument Buch* included a chapter on the 'naturlich instrument die Finger der Hande' after a series of chapters on the construction of quadrants and sectors.

[3] Even though members of different classes viewed the same technologies differently, technological shifts were of interest to all classes of English subjects. Deborah Harkness notes, 'Unlike other forms of natural science practice, instrumentation and engineering caught the attention of both common citizens and high-placed officials in Elizabeth's government' (Deborah Harkness, ' "Strange" Ideas and "English" Knowledge: Natural Science Exchange in Elizabethan London,' in Pamela H. Smith and Paula Findlen

mechanical marvels, and both groups purchased and used them. By studying the appearance of technological metaphors in the plays we can learn a great deal about how technologies pervaded the different strata of English society.

The theatre seems a natural place to seek out representations of technologies because of the cross-fertilization between technological and theatrical imagery in the technological treatises published during the period. Between 1400 and 1620 a new genre of technical literature appeared called the *theatrum mechanorum*, the machine theatre.[4] These machine theatres often included elaborate engravings of semi-mythical inventions, and they presented technology as a spectacle for the enjoyment of readers and viewers. While instrument-makers, printers, engravers, and cartographers presented their works as theatres or spectacles, Elizabethan and Jacobean playwrights employed a variety of technological tropes in their plays.

Shakespeare's imagery engages with his dramaturgy from many different perspectives. It considers individual words, enigmatic passages, characterization, plot development, genre, theatre history, notions of theatrical space, and paradigms depicting the purpose of playing.

IV.

What happened in London between 1550 and 1616 to transform the city and the country from a technological backwater rife with anti-mathematical prejudice into one of Europe's leading producers of new technologies? England was indeed lacking technological advancement until the mid-sixteenth century. Up to this time, England had remained primarily a wool producer and exporter. Much of the manipulation of the wool was left to England's more technologically sophisticated continental neighbours.

But, by the sixteenth century, there were several factors that encouraged the Elizabethan–Jacobean technology boom:

1. a general mathematical renaissance engineered by John Cheke, John Dee, Robert Recorde, and others;
2. the publication of almanacs that disseminated information about the latest advances in technical fields;
3. the rise in English literacy during the sixteenth century;
4. the establishment of multiple public lecture series in applied mathematics;
5. the influx of foreign craftsmen from the Continent;
6. the work of English instrument-makers;

[eds.], *Merchants and Marvels: Commerce, Science, and Art in Early Modern Europe*, [New York: Routledge, 2002], 150).

[4] Otto Mayr, *Authority, Liberty and Automatic Machinery in Early Modern Europe* (Baltimore, MD: The Johns Hopkins University Press, 1986), 213–14. For more on uses of the word 'mechanical' see Christopher Hill, *Change and Continuity in Seventeenth-Century England* (London: Weidenfeld & Nicolson, 1974), 255–60.

7. the threat of Spanish invasion;
8. the increase in overseas exploration and trade;
9. the relatively fluid land market that followed the dissolution of the monasteries in the 1530s;
10. the impact of previous technological breakthroughs;
11. the increase in domestic production of the raw materials needed for instrument manufacture;
12. limited guild acceptance.

New technologies usually develop from pre-existing technologies, and this was certainly true in England. After examining the history of technology during the early modern period as a whole, Carlo Cipolla concluded that technological innovations of the fifteenth century encouraged and facilitated the technological innovations of the sixteenth century. For instance, the proliferation of firearms, improvements in ship-building, and the refinement of navigational tools in the fifteenth century enabled the Age of Discovery, and journeys of discovery encouraged demand for cannon, cannon balls, anchors, and sophisticated new machines to pump water out of mines and haul minerals. The invention of printing with movable type in the fifteenth century enabled the proliferation of technical literature in the sixteenth century, which led to innovation in many fields.[5]

The availability of raw materials is also a critical prerequisite for technological development. In the fifteenth and early sixteenth centuries, brass had to be imported into England, and brass was very expensive. In May 1568, Queen Elizabeth granted royal charters to the Company of Mineral and Battery Works and the Company of Mines Royal, which encouraged them to produce brass and brass plate. The subsequent increase in domestic brass production provided the raw materials needed for the manufacture of a wide variety of precision instruments. Initially England's mining industry relied on assistance from German technicians, but over time the Germans trained Englishmen to do their own prospecting, mining, and metalworking.

No English craft or trade could survive without at least tacit acceptance by one of the twelve great livery companies. While most instrument-makers attempted to circumvent guild restrictions by settling in the suburbs or the liberties, some received guild protection. Joyce Brown has recently shown that many instrument-makers were eventually absorbed into the Grocers' Company, in part because many early instrument-makers were the sons of Grocers, and a young man was usually permitted the chance to join his father's company.[6]

---

[5] See Carlo Cipolla, *Clocks and Culture, 1300–1700* (New York: Norton, 1977), 23.

[6] For more on the unique place of instrument-makers within the guild structure see Joyce Brown, *Mathematical Instrument-Makers in the Grocers' Company, 1688–1800* (London: Science Museum, 1979). Despite the dates noted in her title, Brown's work begins with a discussion of instrument-makers in the sixteenth century. See also Joyce Brown, 'Guild Organisation and the Instrument-Making Trade, 1500–1830: The Grocers' and Clockmakers' Companies', *Annals of Science* 36 (1979), 1–34.

The mathematical renaissance that occurred in England beginning in the middle of the sixteenth century both encouraged and benefited from the Elizabethan technology boom. John Dee was a key figure in England's mathematical renaissance. After completing his university training, Dee visited Paris, Brussels, and Louvain from 1547 to 1550. In each city he studied the design and manufacture of instruments for surveying, navigation, cartography, gunnery, and dialling. He also met some of the leading instrument-makers of the day, including Gemma Frisius (1508–1555) and Gerard Mercator (1512–1594).

Dee's *Mathematicall Preface* to Billingsley's translation of Euclid's *Geometry* (1570) was a mathematical manifesto intended 'to stirre the imagination mathematicall' and 'to inform the practiser mechanicall'.[7] The work presented a taxonomy of the mathematical arts and emphasized that each branch produced practical improvements in English culture. Some of Dee's terms have fallen out of use, and a few of his branches of applied mathematics have fallen out of practise, but most persist in some form. The branches include 'Geographie'; 'Chorographie' (mapmaking); 'Hydrographie' (the charting of coastal waters); 'Stratarithmetrie' (the numbering of soldiers in military formations); 'Perspective,' 'Acoptrike' (the study of mirrors and reflections); 'Astronomie,' 'Cosmographie' (the 'whole and perfect description of the heauenly, and also elementall parte of the world'); 'Astrologie' ('the operations and effectes, of the naturall beames, of light, and secrete influence of the Sterres and Planets: in euery element and elementall body at all times'); 'Statike' ('the causes of heauynes, and lightnes of all thynges: and of motions and properties'); 'Anthropographie' ('the Number, Measure, Waight, figure, Situation, and colour of euery diuerse thing, conteyned in the perfect body of MAN; with certain knowledge of the Symmetrie, figure, waight, Characterization, and due locall motion, of any parcell of the sayd body'); 'Trochilike' ('the properties of all Circular motions, Simple and Compounde,' such as clockworks and millworks); 'Helicosophie' ('the scrue, used in diverse instrumentes and engines'); 'Pneumatithmie' ('the straunge properties . . . of the Water, Ayre, Smoke, and Fire, in theyr continuitie, and as they are ioyned to the Elementes next them'); 'Menadrie' (the art by which 'Cranes, Gybbettes, & Engines do lift up'); 'Hypogeiodie' (the determination of underground property rights for mining purposes); 'Hydragogie' (irrigation); 'Horometrie' ('the precise usuall denomination of time'); 'Zographie' (the art of perspective applied exclusively to painting); and 'Architecture', 'Nauigation', and 'Thaumaturgike' (displays which evoked awe or wonder).

Dee claimed that different types of mathematical practitioners were needed to master different types of tools, inventions, and machines. The ship's pilot, for instance, needed to be able to make and use 'Quadrantes, The Astronomers Ryng, The Astronomers staffe, The Astrolabe uniuersall. An Hydrographicall Globe. Charts Hydrographicall . . . The common Sea Compas: The Compas of variacion: The Proportionall, and Paradoxall Compasses . . . clockes with spryng: houre, halfe houre, and three houre

---

[7] In E. G. R. Taylor, *The Mathematical Practitioners of Tudor and Stuart England* (Cambridge: Cambridge University Press, 1954), 320.

Sandglasses; & Sundry other instrumentes.'[8] Dee was widely criticized for his fascination with prophecy and mirror scrying, but this work and others helped to nurture a whole host of mathematical practices.

A different type of public education also played a role in fostering the technology boom. As the preparations for war with Spain reached a fever pitch in 1588, Sir Thomas Smythe and John, Lord Lumley established a public lecture on mathematics to train captains in the military arts. Another series of mathematical lectures was founded in 1597 at Gresham House, and these lectures attracted an even wider audience. To ensure that the lectures were accessible to all, they were first delivered in Latin and then repeated the same day in English.

V.

To this point we have focused on English contributions to the Elizabethan–Jacobean technology boom, but it is important to note that many of the key figures in the movement came from the continent. The boom was caused in large part by an influx of highly skilled Continental artisans and craftsmen who fled their homelands to escape war and/or religious persecution. The Franco-Spanish Wars of 1494–1559 caused a steady migration of skilled craftsmen out of Italy; France was torn apart by feuding religious and political groups after 1560; and during the sixteenth century war and religious persecution caused a flight of Protestant craftsmen and technicians from the Low Countries.

Pressing foreign policy concerns also fuelled English technical innovation during the Elizabethan period. After 1580, England faced the imminent threat of Spanish invasion, and this threat encouraged innovation in firearms manufacture as well as ship design, ballistics, and fortification. Partly as a response to the escalating hostilities between England and Spain, English overseas exploration and trade also increased dramatically during the period. The Merchant Adventurers Company, the Muscovy Company, the Levant Company, and the East India Company all worked to establish commerce abroad to rival Spain's growing empire. While plying coastal waters English pilots could rely on visual landmarks and the lead and line technique, but in open ocean navigation more sophisticated tools were needed to determine orientation and to compute position.

Domestic political upheavals also encouraged the spike in English technological development. In the field of surveying, the dissolution of the monasteries and the redistribution of church lands in the 1530s created a fluid land market that led to

---

[8] John Dee, sig. D3v. Many influential Elizabethans shared Dee's faith in the redeeming power of mathematical practice. In B. W. Beckingsale's biography of William Cecil, Beckingsale asserts that John Dee was but 'preaching what Burghley encouraged in practice' (B. W. Beckingsale, *Burghley, Tudor Statesman 1520–1598* [London: St Martin's Press, 1967], esp. ch. 17).

what several historians of early modern English cartography have described as a 'surveying revolution'.

Gunpowder, the printing press, and the compass had all been in use in Europe for quite some time prior to the mid-sixteenth century. The fact that these three technologies were often grouped together in a culture familiar with the belief in a Father, a Son, and a Holy Spirit may simply be a coincidence, but it is a rather suggestive one. Lynn White Jr has gone so far as to call the grouping a 'secular trinity'.[9] Perhaps it was only in the mid-sixteenth century, as the multiple effects of technological change were manifesting themselves in overlapping and interlocking ways, that faith in the secular trinity became conventional. Francis Bacon mentions the secular trinity on more than one occasion. In a fragment of an unpublished court masque of 1592 that Bacon presented to Essex, Bacon praises gunpowder, the printing press, and the compass.[10] In 1620, four years after Shakespeare's death, Bacon reiterated the importance of these three inventions in his *Novum Organon*:

> Again, it helps to notice the force, power, and consequences of discoveries, which appear at their clearest in three things that were unknown to antiquity, and whose origins, though recent, are obscure and unsung: namely the art of printing, gunpowder, and the nautical compass. In fact these three things have changed the face and condition of things all over the globe; the first in literature; the second in the art of war; the third in navigation; and innumerable changes have followed; so that no empire or sect or star seems to have exercised greater power and influence on human affairs than those mechanical things.[11]

During the late sixteenth and early seventeenth centuries, certain London parishes became hotbeds of technological innovation. In his *New Atlantis* (1627) Bacon depicted a scientific and technological utopia called Solomon's House where inventors and their inventions were immortalized in 'two very long and fair galleries'.[12] One gallery contained 'patterns and samples' of key inventions, and the other contained statues of 'all principal inventors', both those known to Europeans and those known only to the islanders. The statues, which indicated a heroic inventor theory of innovation, were

---

[9] Lynn White Jr, *Medieval Religion and Technology: Collected Essays* (Berkeley: University of California Press, 1978), xiii.

[10] In *Authorizing Words: Speech, Writing, and Print in the English Renaissance* (Ithaca, NY: Cornell University Press, 1989), Martin Elsky notes that the court masque contained the 'kernel for many ideas that Bacon was to develop later in his philosophical works' (p. 195). For the masque excerpt see Francis Bacon, *The Works of Francis Bacon*, James Spedding, Robert Leslie Ellis, and Douglas Denon Heath (eds.), 14 vols. (London: Longman, 1857–74; rpt. New York: Garrett Press, 1968), 8: 123–6.

[11] For a new English translation of *Novum Organon*, see *Francis Bacon: The New Organon*, Lisa Jardine and Michael Silverthorne (eds.) (Cambridge: Cambridge University Press, 2000). The passage cited here comes from Book I, aphorism 129. According to Jardine, 'To understand the *New Organon* in the spirit in which it was written, we need to be clear that it is driven by a strong commitment to new technical scientific instruments and the increasing variety of experiments on nature they made possible' (p. ii).

[12] References to Francis Bacon's work come from *The New Atlantis* (London: 1627), Jerry Weinberger (ed.) (Arlington Heights, IL: Harlan Davidson, 1989), 79–90.

made of brass, marble, touchstone, 'other special woods gilt and adorned', iron, silver, and gold. Deborah Harkness has noted that Solomon's House, which was ostensibly located in the Pacific Islands discovered by Europeans in 1568, closely resembled Bacon's own St Clement–St Dunstan neighbourhood. Bacon's neighbourhood was well known for its instrument-makers working on what Bacon's narrator describes as 'engines and instruments for all sorts of motions', 'diverse curious clocks', and 'all instruments, as well of geometry as astronomy, exquisitely made'. Bacon's Solomon's House served as the model for the Philosophical College that met in 1646 in the Bullhead Tavern in Cheapside. In 1662 the college was incorporated as The Royal Society of London for Improving Natural Knowledge. While the Royal Society is usually described as a scientific organization, technological innovation was also a top priority. In fact the first of the original eight standing committees set up in 1662 were created to 'consider and improve all mechanical inventions'.

VI.

Shakespeare began his playwriting career at the height of the 'ancients versus moderns' debate, which focused on the relative merits of older versus newer military technologies. The 'ancients' argued for the continued use of the longbow, while the 'moderns' argued that firearms should replace longbows in English military formations. Shakespeare's career also spanned the foreign policy shift from militarism to pacifism that took place after James's accession. What impact might this shift to pacifism have had on Shakespeare's representations of gunpowder weaponry? Shakespeare's culture was deeply ambivalent about gunpowder weapons, and this ambivalence led Shakespeare's characters to portray gunpowder weapons both positively and negatively. When one traces the development of Shakespeare's representations of gunpowder weapons over the course of his entire career, one finds that on balance Shakespeare's characters find gunpowder weapons repulsive for a wide variety of reasons. While warfare or the threat of warfare was constant during Shakespeare's lifetime, the nature of armed conflict seems to have undergone significant changes. Michael Roberts was the first to claim that a 'military revolution' took place in Europe between 1560 and 1660.[13] Roberts asserted that the key facets of this revolution were the introduction of the musket and the longbow to replace the lance and the pike, the overall increase in the size of armies, the use of smaller divisions within those armies, and war's increased impact on the populace.

We can analyse the relationship between Shakespeare's plays and their immediate military historical context because many English military treatises survive

---

[13] See Michael Roberts, *The Military Revolution 1560–1660* (Belfast: Marjory Boyd, 1956). See also Sir George Clark, *War and Society in the Seventeenth Century* (Cambridge: Cambridge University Press, 1958), esp. 73–5.

from the sixteenth and seventeenth centuries. Some of these treatises were printed and others were disseminated in manuscript form; some were written by Englishmen and others were written by foreigners; and some were newly composed while others recycled material from previously published texts.

As with initial advances in printing, engraving, and instrument-making in the mid-sixteenth century, English innovation in the field of artillery production was spurred by the recruitment of continental know-how. In part because of English success with the longbow during the Hundred Years War against France, England fell behind the Continent in the manufacture of gunpowder weapons during the fourteenth and fifteenth centuries. That trend began to change in the last decades of the fifteenth century when Henry VII encouraged French gunners to set up a weapons foundry in Ashdown Forest, Sussex. English munitions manufacture increased after Henry VIII appointed William Levett subtenant of the royal iron works at Newbridge in 1541.

By the turn of the seventeenth century English gun foundries were producing 800 to 1,000 tons of artillery each year. English cast iron guns were heavier than bronze cannon, but they captured a larger market because they were significantly cheaper than their bronze counterparts and they were of relatively high quality. England was the world's leading producer of heavy iron cannon.

English cannon remained superior to cannon produced in other European countries until at least the 1620s when Swedish gunmaking techniques began to rival English manufacture. At a time when many Elizabethans were complaining about the number and variety of foreign imports, iron cannon created lucrative export opportunities. English arms production impacted England, Europe, and lands all over the globe. At home the fuelling of the massive wood-burning furnaces exacerbated deforestation and contributed to a fuel crisis. In Europe, cannon manufacture helped England challenge Spain, and beyond Europe coordinated advances in ship design and the manufacture and use of sea-borne cannon and culverin enabled European powers to colonize much of the earth's land mass. Because English armament production had so many local, regional, and global effects during Shakespeare's career, it is hardly surprising that Shakespeare employs so many gunpowder metaphors in his plays.

Gunpowder imagery served Shakespeare well in different types of plays. In the histories, gunpowder served primarily as a foil for chivalry and honour, as in the disfigurement of Salisbury (*Henry V* 4.7.177) or the popinjay's complaint to Hotspur (*1 Henry IV* 1.3). In the tragedies, gunpowder blasts symbolized a human mind or soul out of balance, a self incapable of achieving the *festina lente* ideal of proper self-regulation. The comedies and the comic portions of the histories employed gunpowder imagery in witty jokes and puns.

Except for the occasional praise of the swiftness or power of a bullet or cannonball, most gunpowder references have negative connotations in Shakespeare's plays. Shakespeare's working-class characters were painfully aware that, despite their popularity among some of the rank and file, gunpowder weapons often transformed poor ragamuffins into cannon fodder.

Studies of Shakespeare's relationship to the print revolution usually fall into one of two categories: source scholarship interested in Shakespeare's reading, and bibliographical study of multiple editions of Shakespeare's plays. Source scholars consider which texts Shakespeare may have owned, borrowed, adapted, or recalled from his school days. Robert S. Miola has referred to scholarly interest in Shakespeare's reading as 'The Dream of Shakespeare's Library'.[14] Bibliographers and textual editors prefer to trace the various forms in which Shakespeare's works migrated 'from the playhouse to the printing house'.[15] These scholars consider why some plays appeared in print soon after their stage performances while others did not, why different versions of a play were published and by whom, which edition provides the best glimpse into what the playwright may have intended, and which edition offers the clearest picture of a play's original stage performance. One may take a slightly different approach to the investigation of Shakespeare's relationship to the print revolution by contextualizing what Shakespeare's characters have to say about print technology itself. While many of the books, volumes, and pages that Shakespeare mentions in his plays refer to holographic manuscripts, Shakespeare's decision to textualize so many of his characters is probably a response to the proliferation of printed materials during his lifetime. In many plays we see the metaphorical union between the human body and print technology. Shakespeare routinely describes human beings as presses, printed books, and manuscript texts (*Troilus and Cressida* 3.2.205; Sonnet 59, 7; *Love's Labour's Lost* 5.2.3).

One does recognize some early modern English scepticism regarding print technology. This is certainly not meant to suggest that Shakespeare or his contemporaries had nothing but scorn for it. Attitudes toward the technology of movable type seem to have varied widely even among members of a single socioeconomic class. Some illiterate individuals may have resented the role of print in the stratification of English society, but university wits from working-class families who managed to find jobs in England's growing bureaucracy viewed print technology more favourably since their book learning facilitated meritocratic preferment. Among nobles, print may initially have seemed a debased, anonymous form of mass reproduction, but nobles eventually accepted print as a valid information technology through which even the most intimate love lyrics could be disseminated.

Because Protestants valued the private reading and interpretation of the Bible, print technology was closely associated with the Reformation. During this period attitudes toward print technology were likely influenced to some extent by religious beliefs because print technology and printed texts played such critical roles in the religious upheavals at this time.

---

[14] Robert S. Miola, *Shakespeare's Reading* (New York: Oxford University Press, 2000), 164.

[15] See Douglas Brooks, *From Playhouse to Printing House: Drama and Authorship in Early Modern England* (Cambridge: Cambridge University Press, 2000); and David Scott Kastan's chapter 'From Playhouse to Printing House; or Making a Good Impression', in *Shakespeare and the Book* (Cambridge: Cambridge University Press, 2001), 14–49.

Since English mathematical practitioners of the 1580s and 1590s lavished so much attention on the compass, it is not surprising that Shakespeare's plays contain some very intriguing compass references. For Shakespeare and his contemporaries the compass represented a series of interconnected synecdoches. The compass eventually came to symbolize a host of navigational technologies including the sternpost rudder, the astrolabe, the cross-staff, and the quadrant. In certain situations the compass was even used to symbolize other improvements that aided navigation such as improvements in cartography and even advances in ship design.

If one were to contemplate the history of early modern navigation from the broadest possible perspective, and look to Shakespeare's plays for a complete catalogue of these advances, one would soon notice what might seem at first to be an inexplicable omission. Shakespeare's plays do not mention celestial navigational tools like the quadrant, the cross-staff, and the astrolabe even though these tools were present on English vessels. Why is there no mention of them in the plays? It is entirely possible that Shakespeare was not interested in celestial navigation or that he found these technologies less compelling from a literary standpoint. Perhaps this lacuna may also have had something to do with England's geographical location. In the Middle Ages celestial navigation using astrolabes and quadrants first became popular in and around the Mediterranean Sea because the water was so deep near the shoreline that it was impossible to take soundings from the seafloor. Sounding is one of Shakespeare's favourite metaphors for the investigation of an individual's interior. Allusions to sounding often reflect a character's psychological or personal depth (cf. *Romeo and Juliet* 1.1.147).

VII.

In addition to the secular trinity of gunpowder, the printing press, and the compass, mechanical clocks and mirrors provided a wide and deep reservoir of secular and religious metaphors from which Shakespeare drew. In early modern England clocks and watches symbolized the inventiveness of humankind, the divine design of the universe, and modernity's superiority over classical and medieval civilization.[16] When Shakespeare described stage characters as clockwork components (*1 Henry IV* 1.2.8), he was not only continuing a long literary tradition, he was also acknowledging a growing trend in clock manufacture. Klaus Maurice and Otto Mayr have shown that while poets often depicted their characters or parts of their characters as clockwork technologies, clockmakers enjoyed making clocks and automata in the shape of human beings.[17]

---

[16] For more on the clock's symbolic resonances see Gerhard Dohrn-van Rossum, *History of the Hour: Clocks and Modern Temporal Orders*, Thomas Dunlap (trans.), (Chicago, IL: University of Chicago Press, 1996), 8.

[17] Klaus Maurice and Otto Mayr (eds.), *The Clockwork Universe: German Clocks and Automata 1550–1650* (Washington, DC: Smithsonian, 1980).

Some of the most popular automata were Christ figures on the cross, clockwork Madonnas, trumpeters, men on horses, and even men sailing ships. Nobility spent huge sums on gilded and jewel-encrusted clocks depicting Bacchus drinking on the hour, Diana on a stag, St George the Dragonslayer, Minerva, a Cupid figure who shot an arrow, and countless golden animals. Popular automated animals included actual beasts such as parrots, bears, lions, camels, elephants, dogs, and turtles, and more fanciful creatures such as griffins and unicorns. Many of these clockwork beasts had eyes that shifted back and forth with the tick-tock of their verge-and-foliot escapements, and some moved or performed on the hour. At her palace at Whitehall, Queen Elizabeth had 'a piece of clockwork consisting of an Aethiop riding upon a rhinoceros, with four attendants, who all make their obeisance when it strikes the hour'.[18] With early clockmakers crafting increasingly elaborate and increasingly lifelike automata it was only a matter of time before a few attempted to build life-sized human and animal automata.

According to Otto Mayr, early modern Europeans generally embraced mechanical clocks, but there was a vocal minority that resisted the clock's authority. Mayr states that many Englishmen believed that the mechanical clock represented a form of regimentation that conflicted with burgeoning notions of individual liberty. Perhaps Shakespeare did not emphasize the authoritarianism of mechanical timepieces because timepieces were not very reliable timekeepers during his career. While there was often considerable enthusiasm for the idea of the reliable clock, there was almost universal disdain for the unreliability of actual pre-eighteenth-century timepieces (*As You Like It* 3.2.294–5).

Shakespeare did not simply acknowledge the unreliability of mechanical timepieces, he capitalized upon it by developing a theory of temporal relativity that roughly resembles one consequence of Albert Einstein's theory on special relativity. Einstein speculated that if a light-clock that ticked once with each rebound of a beam of light was placed on a spaceship and accelerated to a speed approaching the speed of light, observers on the spaceship and observers on earth would measure the behaviour of the light-clock differently. While observers on the spaceship would see the light-clock progressing normally, observers on earth would see the light-clock's ticking beam slow down, producing an effect which physicists call *time dilation*. I will not argue here that Shakespeare discovered relativity theory before Einstein did. Such a claim would not only be preposterous, it would also efface important differences between Shakespeare's understanding of temporal relativity and Einstein's. However, it does seem to be the case that Shakespeare provided a humanistic parallel to Einstein's theory in several plays in which time appears to pass at different rates for characters in different frames of mind (as in *Romeo and Juliet* and *Othello*).

Shakespeare and his contemporaries registered their fascination by integrating a wide variety of clockwork metaphors into their writing. Some of the more sophisticated

---

[18] This is reported by Paul Hentzner, one of Elizabeth's contemporaries, and quoted in James Kendal, *A History of Watches and other Timekeepers* (London: Crosby Lockwood, 1892), 64.

mechanical clocks and watches produced in Elizabethan England included minute hands, and soon *minutes* became a standard chronological concept. Shakespeare uses the word *minute* to denote one-sixtieth of an hour more than sixty times in his poems and his plays. While minutes are often mentioned to denote fine temporal distinctions, there are no references to *seconds* in Shakespeare because seconds were just beyond the cutting edge of horological technology during his career.

Shakespeare was an astute observer of the horological technology around him. He was well aware that changes in the design, manufacture, and proliferation of timepieces were transforming his society's ideas about the well-ordered universe, the ideal commonwealth, and the anatomy, physiology, and psychology of the individual human being. If Shakespeare's horological metaphors seem to anticipate futuristic phenomena like automata, cyborgs, and theories of relativity, it is only because the horological revolution going on all around him helped lay the groundwork for the scientific revolution.

If it is true, as former Royal Shakespeare Company director John Barton has claimed, that *time* is the most important word in Shakespeare's plays, then it may also be true that the mirror is one of Shakespeare's most important metaphors. Because mirror imagery is so prevalent in the plays it has received a great deal of critical attention.[19] In his comprehensive study of mirror imagery in medieval and early modern English literature, Herbert Grabes dedicates a chapter to the study of Shakespeare's seventy mirror passages; the most famous is that in *Richard II* (4.1.255). Grabes claims that even though Shakespeare's mirror imagery covers conventional territory, he often 'exploits conventions of metaphor, extending, varying and combining them contextually and enriching them functionally.'[20]

Shakespeare used mirror metaphors to represent individual virtues, individual body parts, and the entire human body. Shakespeare also employed a conventional mirror metaphor to describe the 'end' or purpose of the entire dramatic enterprise (*Hamlet* 3.2.22). Because a variety of mirror types were available to members of Shakespeare's heterogeneous Globe audience, different subgroups might have envisioned different types of mirrors. Nobles might have envisioned the small glass convex mirrors that they carried on their belts or kept on their dressing tables. If they were nobles of considerable means they might have imagined a flat glass dressing mirror. The small convex mirror would have suggested a distorted or stylized representation of nature while the flat glass dressing mirror would have suggested more accurate, realistic, or naturalistic mimesis. Divines in the audience who had recently been reading the religious tracts

---

[19] For studies of mirror scenes and mirror passages see H. T. Price, 'Mirror Scenes in Shakespeare', in J. G. McManaway, et al. (eds.), *Joseph Quincy Adams Memorial Studies*, (Washington, DC: Folger Shakespeare Library, 1948), 103–13; and Rudolf Stamm, 'The Glass of Pandar's Praise: The Word-Scenery, Mirror Passages, and Reported Scenes in *Troilus and Cressida*', in *The Shaping Powers at Work: Fifteen Essays on Poetic Transmutation* (Heidelberg: Carl Winter, 1967), 32–51; Arthur F. Kinney, *Shakespeare's Webs* (London: Routledge, 2004), ch. 1.

[20] Herbert Grabes, *The Mutable Glass: Mirror Imagery in Titles and Texts of the Middle Ages and the English Renaissance* (Cambridge: Cambridge University Press, 1982), 204.

that described how concave mirrors symbolized the way a good Christian could focus God's diffuse divinity into a powerful spiritual light may have imagined a concave mirror when they heard Prince Hamlet's instructions to the Players. Captains, soldiers, and military engineers in the audience may also have pictured concave mirrors because Elizabethan military treatises often noted that Archimedes used concave mirrors at Syracuse to set fire to the invading Roman fleet. The more prurient, lascivious, politically subversive, or heretical members of the audience might have thought of cylindrical mirrors as they contemplated the bawdy puns, the veiled political portrayals, and the religious heterodoxy of some Elizabethan–Jacobean plays. Artisans, craftsmen, apprentices in the trades, and Englishmen visiting London from the countryside might have envisioned a cheap mirror made of polished steel or tin.

Shakespeare's characters often describe exemplary individuals as mirrors. Shakespeare does not discuss the technical details of mirror foiling, but he does refer several times to the related use of metallic foils in jewellery settings. At key moments in his tragedies and one of his history plays (*Antony and Cleopatra* 1.4.24; *Coriolanus* 1.9.48; *Hamlet* 5.2.201; *Richard III* 5.5.204; *Richard II* 1.3.255), four characters use metallic foiling metaphors to highlight or intensify comparisons or contrasts. The foiling metaphors fall into three categories: beautiful foils framing base gemstones, dull foils framing beautiful gemstones, and beautiful foils framing beautiful gemstones.

By the end of Elizabeth's reign, courtiers relied heavily upon maps for the planning and implementation of domestic and foreign policy; nobles perused maps to facilitate the management of their estates; and pilots used charts, maps, and globes to plan and execute expeditions. The print revolution also fuelled the cartographic revolution because it enabled the proliferation, comparison, and revision of ancient, medieval, and early modern maps during the fifteenth and sixteenth centuries. Improvements in cartography merit inclusion in a study of early modern technological revolutions because maps, charts, and globes were graphic tools that revolutionized navigation, education, and surveying. In Shakespeare's plays we see several references to maps, charts, and globes.

In Shakespeare's plays the growing importance of estate maps is evident. Peter Eden claims that a 'golden age of estate cartography' occurred in England from 1585 to 1615, a period that happens to coincide almost precisely with Shakespeare's theatrical career.[21] By the time Shakespeare began his career as a playwright, estate maps and other types of maps were as ubiquitous as books, sundials, clocks, and mirrors. During Shakespeare's career surveying matured into an independent technical field that relied increasingly upon its own specialized technologies. Two surveying tools that were commonly used to draw estate maps in the late sixteenth century were the plane table upon which directions or features were drawn by collecting field measurements, and the theodolite. In Elizabethan–Jacobean England some degree of technological confluence is evident

---

[21] Peter Eden, 'Three Elizabethan Estate Surveyors: Peter Kempe, Thomas Clerke, and Thomas Langdon', in Sarah Tyacke (ed.), *English Map-Making 1500–1650* (London: British Library, 1983), 76.

in almost every technical field, but confluence seems particularly apparent in the field of surveying.

Globe references appear in Shakespeare's earliest plays. Since Shakespeare's early work is so classically allusive it is not surprising that the first reference to a *globe* in a tragedy comes in a gnarled recapitulation of the myth of Phaeton pulling Hyperion's chariot through the sky (e.g. *Richard II* 1.3.177). Witnessing the rising and setting of the heavenly bodies often encouraged Shakespeare's characters to contemplate life from a global perspective. Metaphorical equations between a rotund human frame and a terrestrial globe are twice employed for humorous effect in Shakespeare's plays (*Comedy of Errors* 3.2.116; *2 Henry IV* 2.4.288). England's enthusiasm for globes intensified after the production of Molyneux's globes in 1592, and this enthusiasm affected Shakespeare and his company in multiple ways. Not only did it influence the naming of the newly-constructed theatre space, it also seems to have encouraged Shakespeare's use of technical vocabulary associated with the construction and use of celestial and terrestrial globes.

In Elizabethan–Jacobean England, globalism manifested itself in an increase in open ocean sea voyages, the authorship and sale of travel narratives, the importation of exotic items, the desire for new markets for English exports, geopolitical competition with Spain, and the design and manufacture of a diverse array of new navigational technologies produced by foreigners and Englishmen alike. For evidence of this new globalism, where better to look than to the work of a theatre company that renamed the planks of its generic theatre the Globe in 1599–1600, saw that structure burn to the ground in 1613, and then named its new theatre the Globe once more?

When the Lord Chamberlain's Men ultimately lost the lease on the land upon which their theatre stood, they decided to recycle the theatre's timbers, hauling them from Shoreditch to Bankside to build their new playing space, but they did not recycle the theatre's name. Many factors may have led them to choose the Globe for the name of the rebuilt structure, ranging from England's growing colonial ambitions to the proliferation of travel narratives, charts, and maps.[22]

When Shakespeare's company renamed their rebuilt theatre the Globe, they capitalized on the prevailing metaphorical potential of terrestrial and celestial globes. They also created a space that could represent metaphysical and socioeconomic aspects of their culture. The platform upon which the players moved functioned like a terrestrial globe in that it could transport the audience members from one location to the next instantaneously; the underside of the Heavens was decorated with some of the same

---

[22] John Gillies locates the Globe within the rich cartographic tradition of the early modern period, asserting that the theatre was a 'quasi-cartographic product of the same type of cosmographic imagination which produced the world maps of Ortelius and Mercator' (p. 70). Many early modern atlases referred to themselves as a *Theatrum*, including Ortelius's groundbreaking *Theatrum Orbis Terrarum*, or *The Theatre of the Terrestrial World*. Emphasizing the symbiotic relationship between cartography and theatre, Gillies has claimed that the 'difference between the poetic map-maker and the cartographic poet is less important than their similarity' (p. 182). See John Gillies, *Shakespeare and the Geography of Difference* (Cambridge: Cambridge University Press, 1994).

stars, planets, and signs of the zodiac that could be found on a celestial globe; the trap beneath the stage provided a portal through which the players could access metaphysical space; and the various seating options for audience members—all these served as a subtle reminder that despite increasing opportunities for social advancement England remained socioeconomically stratified.

While early modern terrestrial and celestial globes were valued first and foremost as navigators' tools, some were certainly fetishized as art objects. By the end of Elizabeth's reign the globe had become an overdetermined symbol. It was routinely invoked to represent travel, exploration, discovery, the classical past, the potential for empire, learning, the individual, the stage, the nation, the earth, and the cosmos. Shakespeare's contemporaries were well aware of the symbolic potential of the globe. Even the technical manuals describing the globe's usefulness mentioned its analogical power. Today most globes are decorative objects or aids to students learning geography, but late sixteenth-century globes were essential navigational tools, and sixteenth-century globe-makers consistently emphasized the globe's utility.

Elizabethans and Jacobeans may have embraced certain tools with a quasi-religious fervour, but early modern English faith in revolutionary technologies, while ultimately quite durable, was certainly not an unexamined faith. Shakespeare's plays reflect the fact that Englishmen held a wide variety of views regarding revolutionary technologies, ranging from enthusiastic embrace to grudging acceptance to occasional suspicion to the firm conviction that certain tools, inventions, and machines were instruments of the devil. In an attempt to make sense of these strange new artefacts and practices, authors like Shakespeare often depicted them in human terms, and they also described human beings themselves as technologies. Ambivalence regarding technology's impact on the self and society seems only to have intensified during the Tudor industrial revolution.

CHAPTER 39

....

SHAKESPEARE AND AMERICA

....

FRAN TEAGUE

IN 1939, Esther Cloudman Dunn produced the first scholarly examination of Shakespeare in America, averring that 'Some magic in his pages, either truly felt or taken for granted, has made Shakespeare, along with the Bible, a constant companion of American development.'[1] Other important studies followed, by Westfall, Wright, Shattuck, Levine, Bristol, Sturgess, and the Vaughans, all documenting the role Shakespeare has played in American life.[2] In short, scholars agree that Shakespeare matters in America, although they assess that importance differently.[3] This account, necessarily a condensed one (one recalls that American institution, *Reader's Digest*), begins with a brief overview of how Shakespeare entered American life in the eighteenth century as colonists began to imagine a national identity separate from

---

[1] Esther Cloudman Dunn, *Shakespeare in America* (New York: Macmillan, 1939), 3. I understand the title 'Shakespeare and America' to be synonymous with 'Shakespeare and the United States', although a much longer and more nuanced chapter on 'Shakespeare and the Americas' would include a distinguished national tradition in Canada, as well as a lively theatrical and intellectual history in Central and South America.

[2] Alfred Van Rensselaer Westfall, *American Shakespearean Criticism, 1607–1865* (New York: H. W. Wilson, 1939); Lois B. Wright, *The Cultural Life of the American Colonies: 1607–1763* (New York: Harper, 1957; rpt. 1962); Charles Shattuck, *Shakespeare on the American Stage*, 2 vols. (Washington, DC: Folger Shakespeare Library, 1976–1987); Lawrence Levine, 'William Shakespeare and the American People: A Study in Cultural Transformation', in *The Unpredictable Past: Explorations in American Cultural History* (New York: Oxford University Press, 1993), 139–71; Michael Bristol, *Shakespeare's America, America's Shakespeare* (London: Routledge, 1990); Kim C. Sturgess, *Shakespeare and the American Nation* (Cambridge: Cambridge University Press, 2004); Virginia Mason and T. Alden Vaughan (eds.), *Shakespeare in American Life* (Washington, DC: Folger Shakespeare Library, 2007).

[3] It is also worth considering alternate histories. As Kim Sturgess remarks: 'there is much to suggest that if citizens of the United States in the nineteenth century had followed rhetoric of the original leaders of the Revolution, Americans might have been expected to reject Shakespeare as an unwanted English anachronism' (*Shakespeare and the American Nation* [Cambridge: Cambridge University Press, 2004], 3).

England's. The bulk of the chapter explains how he provided Americans with a means of thinking about personal identity (particularly class identity) in the nineteenth century. In the twentieth century, Shakespeare's importance for America changes. An increased international engagement means that Shakespeare references also increased since his figure has global currency: one finds this phenomenon in film production, for example, since that industry has worked on an international scale from its inception. Yet while Shakespeare references within American culture increase, those specific to America are more difficult to identify. Nevertheless, Shakespeare's place in American mass culture is important, particularly given America's pre-eminence in that area during the twentieth century.

BEGINNINGS

The first sign that America was at all aware of William Shakespeare seems to have come around 1750. A copy of *Macbeth* is inventoried in the estate of a Virginian, Captain Arthur Spicer, and that record is the first proof of a Shakespeare play in America, although copies of the plays might well have gone unrecorded. Virtually no allusions to Shakespeare nor quotations from his plays exist in American writing before 1750. Yet suddenly he made an appearance. After ignoring Shakespeare throughout the sixteenth and seventeenth centuries, American colonists suddenly began citing Shakespeare in newspapers and private papers, using Shakespearean images in home furnishings, and, most importantly, watching his plays. Shakespeare became a way of showing a serious turn of mind; Shakespearean images marked one's gentility, and his plays were a pleasure to attend. One can trace this abrupt interest both to Shakespeare's rising stock in eighteenth-century London, which strongly influenced America's colonial taste, and to the increased awareness of America's relationship to England in the years leading up to the American Revolution. Finally, the anti-theatrical prejudice commonly found in the settlements of New England began to diminish just as Shakespeare's reputation in London was rising, a coincidence that led to a renewed interest in him both as dramatist and as cultural icon in the years before the outbreak of the American Revolution.

In the database, 'Early American Newspapers, series 1, 1690–1876', a quick search for 'Shakespeare' between 1690 and 1776 shows eighty-four references, only two of which date before 1750.[4] Yet when one searches during 1750–5, the twenty-five years before the American Revolution, Shakespeare is repeatedly mentioned in political discussions of America's relationship to England, both to persuade and to dissuade. Moreover, parodies of Shakespeare passages can be found, and such parodies would simply make no sense unless the readers knew something of the original. In particular, Hamlet's 'To be or not to be' soliloquy was used by one writer opposed to British taxes:

[4] http://www.galileo.uga.edu.

> Be taxt or not be taxt—that is the question.
> Whether 'tis nobler in our minds to suffer
> The sleights and cunning of deceitful statesmen
> Or to petition 'gainst illegal taxes
> And by opposing, end them?

while another parodied the same speech to protest the pressure by American rebels to sign an article of association to fight the British:

> To sign, or not to sign? that is the question.
> Whether 'tis better for an honest man
> To sign—and so be safe; or to resolve,
> Betide what will, against 'associations,'
> And, by retreating, shun them.

The first uses Shakespeare to oppose the British, while the second resists the emerging spirit of American nationalism by citing Shakespeare. In short, Shakespeare is abruptly introduced into American life as a representative of Britain, who can be co-opted for rebellious ends or recruited for loyalist ends. He is a useful figure as tension increased during the years prior to the American Revolution. Furthermore, the references in political letters and editorials complement journalism about the plays in performance. Starting from no productions of Shakespearean plays, American theatres put on around 500 productions in these years. There are several candidates for the honour of being the first American Shakespeare production, but a 1730 *Romeo and Juliet* production remains the likeliest contender, while a 1750 *Richard III* was the first professional production. Those plays became particular favourites, along with *Taming of the Shrew*, *1 Henry IV*, and *Macbeth*, in early America. During the war itself, both British and American soldiers took part in or watched productions of Shakespeare's plays, even though the new American Continental Congress had prohibited performances. George Washington saw occasional performances, however, and a memorable production of *Coriolanus* was staged by American soldiers in New Hampshire during 1778. After the war, the number of Shakespeare productions initially diminished, but by the nineteenth century, Shakespeare was the playwright most often performed in American playhouses.

Perhaps more telling, Shakespeare and his characters suddenly appeared on china, in paintings, and on handsome domestic furnishings like busts, mantelpieces, and even a chess set. In 1754, an advertisement appeared for 'A beautiful Statuary Marble-carved Chimney-Piece and Picture; two fine China Chandeliers, fitted with Flowers and Branches; with three Plaister Figures of Shakespear, Milton, and Pope', and a magnificent Wedgwood chess set with chess pieces modelled on the performers in the Charles Kemble and Sarah Siddons *Macbeth* was sold to an American colonist. Such luxury items were expensive ways for American colonists to mark their social status, and occasionally to indicate their political loyalty to England. (The former motive seems to have been the more important.) Even after the Revolution, this interest in Shakespeare remained. Both Kim Sturgess and I have written elsewhere of the political potency that Shakespeare had from 1750 until the end of the Jacksonian period.[5] Employing Shakespeare, whether in an office, a drawing room, or a theatre, allowed Americans to indicate their most serious thoughts, their claims to social position, and their taste in amusements. Yet it would be a mistake to assume that Americans were universally interested by, or even aware of, Shakespeare.

Among the founding fathers, however, two were deeply engaged by Shakespeare: John Adams and Thomas Jefferson. Other leading figures of the American Revolution seem to have enjoyed attending an occasional performance, but were otherwise largely indifferent. For Jefferson and Adams, Shakespeare was something more, a writer whose political instincts engaged them and whose social views, as Adams and Jefferson understood them, pleased them. After America had won its independence, the new government sent Adams as its representative to London, and Jefferson to Paris; they joined forces on one memorable occasion to make a pilgrimage to Stratford-upon-Avon to visit Shakespeare's birthplace. The 1786 trip offered them the opportunity to reflect on what they regarded as a major English shortcoming, the neglect of the past. Not only were the Americans saddened to find little regard for the battlefields of the English Civil War, which they regarded as a war in which English commoners fought for liberty as Americans had so recently done, but they were also troubled by the neglect of the birthplace. Their reverence may be seen by Jefferson's kneeling to kiss the ground at Stratford-upon-Avon, and by Adams's lecturing locals at Edgehill and Worcester, asking them,

> And do Englishmen so soon forget the Ground where Liberty was fought for? Tell your Neighbors and Your Children that this is holy Ground, much holier than that on which your Churches stand. All England should come in Pilgrimage to this Hill, once a year.[6]

The lack of memorials at the birthplace and general air of disrepair elicited scorn, for it was, as Adams reported, 'as small and mean, as you can conceive'.[7] Clearly these two Americans felt that Shakespeare was less valued in his homeland than in America, and they were not alone, as Washington Irving's essay on Stratford-upon-Avon shows. Irving reported that the birthplace 'is a small mean-looking edifice of wood and plaster', unconsciously echoing what Adams had said about two decades before.

Despite such enthusiasts, the post-war years saw some diminution of Americans making Shakespearean references, but as Sturgess has shown, Shakespeare quickly rebounded by claiming a place in American civic culture, especially in the oratory associated with the Fourth of July. Nevertheless, from 1776 to 1825, American attitudes toward Shakespeare were inevitably affected by their attitudes toward England, and

---

[5] See Sturgess, *Shakespeare and the American Nation*, and Frances Teague, *Shakespeare and the American Popular Stage* (Cambridge: Cambridge University Press, 2004).

[6] John Adams, *Diary and Autobiography of John Adams*, ed. L. H. Butterfield (Cambridge, MA: Belknap Press of Harvard University Press, 1961) ser. 1, vol. 3, 185.

[7] Adams, *Diary and Autobiography of John Adams*, 185

while some resisted his charms because of Anglophobia, others seemed intent on reclaiming Britain's national poet as an American. By 1831, Alexis de Tocqueville remarked that 'There is hardly a pioneer's hut which does not contain a few odd volumes of Shakespeare. I remember that I read the feudal drama of Henry V. for the first time in a log house.'[8]

SHAKESPEARE MAKES GENTLEMEN

After 1825 or so, America certainly felt the pull of Shakespeare's glamour. As Gary Taylor points out, 'Shakespeare's [nineteenth-century] American admirers . . . began to discover that his culture was perhaps not so different from their own. . . . You could say—and Americans wanted to be able to say—that Whitman had more in common with Shakespeare than Tennyson did' (204). This perceived affinity resulted in splendid accomplishments: H. H. Furness revolutionized the editing of Shakespearean texts; others began the great collections that form the basis of the Folger and Huntington Libraries; while American actors like Ira Aldridge, Edmund Booth, Charlotte Cushman, Edwin Forrest, and James Henry Hackett electrified audiences. In the late nineteenth century, America contributed enormously to the study of Shakespeare. But what has Shakespeare provided America? More specifically, setting aside all artistic or scholarly considerations, what did nineteenth-century Americans find so attractive about Shakespeare?[9]

Of particular interest is the American desire to use Shakespeare as a model for conduct and social decorum. This development is perhaps not surprising. In America's post-bellum years, 'Reading and discussion of Shakespeare's plays was a social activity rather than a specialized academic *métier*', and it had an 'avocational and leisure class orientation'.[10] Thus collecting Shakespeareana and studying the plays 'are the expression of a particular structure of feeling in which class interests and political power are powerfully mediated'.[11] Because this attitude originates in a complex of social forces, one looks in vain for a single source to establish Shakespeare as a guide for America's social conduct. As Marovitz remarks, one must not reduce the issue of class and Shakespeare in America 'to a two-sided struggle . . . , whether between proponents of British culture as opposed to American, upper class as opposed to working class, or aristocrats as opposed to democrats',[12] for all of these groups attempted to claim

---

[8] Alexis de Tocqueville, *Democracy in America*, introduction by Arthur Goldhammer (New York: Library of America, 2004), 538.

[9] Michael Bristol points out, 'A detailed critical history of Shakespeare's position within American culture has not yet been written' (*Shakespeare's America, America's Shakespeare* [London: Routledge, 1990], 52). In particular, we need a serious reception study of Shakespeare's social function in America.

[10] Bristol, *Shakespeare's America*, 64, 65.

[11] Bristol, *Shakespeare's America*, 66.

[12] Sanford E. Marovitz, 'America vs. Shakespeare: From the Monroe Doctrine to the Civil War', *Zeitschrift für Anglistik und Amerikanistik* 34 (1986): 33–46, at 34.

Shakespeare as their own. What Marovitz says may suggest a link between Shakespeare and violence, and several incidents in the nineteenth century would support such an association. Certainly both Jefferson and Adams particularly admired those scenes in Shakespeare's plays that showed the violent overthrow of tyrants. During the Civil War, Abraham Lincoln also found such moments fascinating, and he had a particular interest in the speeches of Claudius and Macbeth. Lincoln's assassin, John Wilkes Booth, cited Shakespeare's work in his justification for Lincoln's murder.

Perhaps the 1849 Astor Place Riot gives the clearest indication of how sharply attitudes in the New World changed from indifference to passion. The English actor William Charles Macready performed *Macbeth* at the Astor Place Opera House while American actor Edwin Forrest deliberately mounted a rival production across town at the Bowery Theatre. Stirred up by Forrest's nativist followers and incendiary newspaper coverage, Macready's production was greeted with disruptions when it opened on May 7, and on May 10 the disruptions became a riot. When a mob gathered outside the theatre, soldiers were summoned and fired on the crowd with disastrous results. About one century after the very first Shakespeare production in America, a fiction about a Scots king became so powerful an embodiment of America's national pride that men were willing to kill to defend that fiction as more suitable for an American performer than an English actor. The Astor Place Riot illustrates the tension between the pro-American working class and the privileged upper class, but 'both sides could employ the work of Shakespeare in helping to support their view' (Marovitz, 36).[13]

Moving from violence to issues of decorum, one can trace three nineteenth-century American responses to Shakespeare. The first of these responses is to insist on Shakespeare as an arbiter of good conduct. Writing in 1849, the same year as the Astor Place Riots, Emerson insists that

> He wrote the airs for all our modern music; he wrote the text of modern life; *the text of manners*: he drew the man of England and Europe; the father of the man in America ... (emphasis added)

Thus, the essay continues, 'What point of morals, of manners, of economy, of philosophy, or religion, of taste, of the conduct of life, has he not settled?' (p. 721). Shakespeare determines morals and manners, philosophy and the conduct of life; thus, superior conduct arises from understanding the moral philosophy of his plays. A Renaissance Englishman becomes a model to guide a properly 'Shakspearized' nineteenth-century American's thought and behaviour. Another Emerson essay, on 'Manners', uses Shakespeare, 'the best-bred man in England, and Christendom', as an exemplar of the manners best suited to American life (p. 528). Americans who praise Shakespeare as a man representing the best qualities in humanity remark on his power to raise the level of social conduct.[14]

---

[13] Marovitz, 'America vs. Shakespeare', 36.

[14] Emerson's essays, 'Shakespeare' and 'Manners', are in (New York: Library of America, 1983), 710–26, 511–32. The bits I quote serve simply to illustrate an American attitude; Emerson's regard for Shakespeare was never solely or even principally based on an admiration for the playwright's contributions to American

In the nineteenth century, when Americans sought to promote the study of Shakespeare, they often offered his beneficent effect on public morality and manners as justification. Shakespeare and his works became a sort of moral nostrum for the populace. Less widely acknowledged is the nineteenth-century belief that to study Shakespeare is to become more genteel, to raise one's class. Turning to England at this same period, one could undoubtedly find writers who thought of Shakespeare in the same way. What one could not find so easily there, however, is sharp resistance to the gentlemanly Shakespeare and furious counter-resistance. In America, one finds both.

That resistance takes two different forms, both accepting the idea of Shakespeare as an index to Americans' social value, but denying the specifically social formulation of value. One form of resistance is to deny the gentlemanly model of Shakespeare and regard Shakespeare as quintessentially American (i.e. commercial) instead. The counter-resistance, however, accepts the gentlemanly model and then denies its worth. Shakespeare, in this approach, is to be admired in America for his power and genius, and yet he offends an American sensibility that values democracy, regarded as antithetical to everything in Shakespeare's plays. While one group of Americans wants to claim Shakespeare in an effort to raise the level of American manners, another group resists this attempt, either by insisting that Shakespeare's manners were like those of the common American or, in contradistinction, by denying the value of what the plays embody as a social agenda. In all cases, however, the definition and delineation of who Shakespeare was and what he stands for is crucial to the effort of defining and delineating what it is to be American.

If Emerson is the central figure for Americans who regard Shakespeare as the catalyst in creating gentlemen, Herman Melville might be considered the locus for the idea of Shakespeare as American. His response readily appropriates Shakespeare and others to American culture: '[American] ancestry is lost in the universal paternity; and Caesar, and Alfred, St Paul and Luther, and Homer and Shakespeare are as much ours as Washington.'[15] Melville's bold claim appropriates Shakespeare, along with other exemplary men, to American culture, which is in this formulation a synthesis of all that is excellent in the past. The essayist clearly does not ground his claim to Shakespeare in the playwright's being well-bred or upper-class (as Emerson seems to do). In another essay, Melville identifies the playwright as 'only Master William Shakespeare of the shrewd, thriving business firm of Condell, Shakespeare and Co.', a description that makes Shakespeare appear to be a clever Yankee businessman. This

---

etiquette. For more, see Esther Cloudman Dunn, Westfall, and Bristol (*American Shakespearean Criticism, 1607–1865* [New York: The W. H. Wilson Company, 1939]), all of whom point to Emerson's essay in *Representative Men* as enormously influential in America. Joseph Crosby, whom I discuss below, knew the essay and admired it (cf. his letter, 151).

[15] Herman Melville, *Redburn* (New York: Library of America, 1983), 185; elsewhere in *Redburn*, however, he suggests that an old family book is more valuable than Shakespeare. Other passages that I quote are from 'Hawthorne and His Mosses'. As with Emerson, my use of Melville is admittedly arbitrary, a thorough study is Julian Markels, *Melville and the Politics of Identity: From 'King Lear' to 'Moby Dick'* (Urbana: University of Illinois, 1993), esp. ch. 3, 'Melville's Route to *King Lear*', 35–54.

identification is not unconsidered. The essay insists that those who would regard Shakespeare as unapproachable are unAmerican and unprogressive:

> ... I am not willingly one of those who, as touching Shakespeare at least, exemplify the maxim of Rochefoucauld, that 'we exalt the reputation of some, in order to depress that of others'—who, to teach all noble-spirited aspirants that there is no hope for them, pronounce Shakespeare absolutely unapproachable ... this absolute and unconditional adoration of Shakespeare has grown to be part of our Anglo-Saxon superstitions. The Thirty-Nine Articles are now forty. Intolerance has come to exist in this matter. You must believe in Shakespeare's unapproachability, or quit the country. But what sort of belief is this for an American, a man who is bound to carry republican progressiveness into Literature as well as into Life?[16]

This discussion of Shakespeare and his excellence takes a nationalistic turn: to misread or misvalue Shakespeare is to be a bad American, one opposed to 'republican progressiveness' who seeks to add a point to the Britisher's Thirty-Nine Articles of faith. Shakespeare's excellence consists not of 'unapproachable' superiority, but rather abides in his ability to give the people what they want in his role as shrewd Yankee trader. (Since Melville himself is playing a role in this essay, pretending to be a Virginian instead of a New Yorker, this recasting of Shakespeare is not particularly surprising. For the purpose of praising Hawthorne, Melville was willing to remake the English national poet into a Yankee.) If one American response is to consider Shakespeare as the epitome of gentlemanly conduct, the resistance to that response is to consider the playwright as the epitome of American progressiveness.

A different counter-response is to admire Shakespeare, yet to regard his power as fundamentally alien to the American spirit. Here, the central figure is probably Walt Whitman. In an essay, he remarks, 'The great poems, Shakespeare included, are poisonous to the idea of the pride and dignity of the common people, the life-blood of democracy,' and what he identifies in Shakespeare's work as contrary to American ideals is precisely what others would value: a sense that Shakespeare is not appropriate to the *common people*, but rather to the upper-class reader. Shakespeare is sometimes linked to 'feudalism'.[17] One such passage will illustrate the general tone of the rest:

> He seems to me of astral genius, first class, entirely fit for feudalism. His contributions, especially to the literature of the passions, are immense, forever dear to humanity—and his name is always to be reverenced in America. But there is much in him ever offensive to democracy. He is not only the ally of feudalism, but I should say Shakspere is incarnated, uncompromising feudalism, in literature. Then one seems to detect something in him—I hardly know how to describe it— even amid the dazzle of his genius; and, in inferior manifestations, it is found in

---

[16] Herman Melville, 'Hawthorne and His Mosses', in George Wilkes, *Shakespeare, from an American Point of View* (New York: Appleton, 1877).

[17] Whitman, *Works* (New York: Library of America, 1982), 1058. A textual analysis shows that Whitman links variants of 'Shakspere' and 'feudalism' fifteen times in his work: twice in *Leaves of Grass* (1891) and thirteen times in *The Complete Prose*, particularly in 'Democratic Vistas'.

nearly all leading British authors. (Perhaps we will have to import the words Snob, Snobbish, &c., after all.)[18]

In this counter-response to the 'gentlemanly' view, the power ascribed to Shakespeare threatens America's democratic achievement.

THE COST OF GENTILITY

I have sketched three disparate appropriations of Shakespeare: as a model of social conduct, as a model of commerce and progress, and as a model of feudalism to be rejected. The letters of one nineteenth-century Shakespeare scholar, Joseph Crosby, illustrate that these attitudes are not limited to the popular writing of nineteenth-century America, but extend to those men learned in matters Shakespearean and to ordinary citizens.[19] When one examines what Crosby has to say, one finds a blend of Emerson's and Melville's Shakespeare, as well as a furious rejection of Whitman's. Shakespeare's works become a way of justifying American values. Shakespearean study provides a model for American moral and educational uplift, and Shakespearean social activities separate worthy citizens from those of less worth because of social status or conduct. In appropriating Shakespeare as an American institution, nineteenth-century Americans show both anxiety about their culture and aggression in recreating Shakespeare as one of their own.

Joseph Crosby was a leading citizen of Zanesville, Ohio, and a naturalized American citizen (born in Northumbria). A businessman who sold groceries and insurance, he was also an avid amateur Shakespearean, who owned one of the finest Shakespeare collections in the country and corresponded with virtually all the important Shakespearean scholars of his day. Among these were H. H. Furness and Richard Grant White, who are better known today, but who might be regarded as his contemporary peers, and Joseph Parker Norris, a prominent Philadelphia lawyer; extant letters from Crosby to Norris span the years 1875 to 1878. A leading light of Zanesville culture, Crosby enjoyed participating in the Zanesville Shakespeare Reading Club; he rarely missed lectures about or performances of the plays, and the city authorities asked his help in examining those preparing to be teachers. His letters consistently return to the social importance Shakespeare's works have for his fellow citizens.

To study Shakespeare is to be a gentleman, and Shakespeare lectures and performances drew attendance from the socially distinguished. When actor and elocutionist James Murdoch gave a public Shakespeare reading, 'He had a very fine audience

---

[18] Whitman, *Works*, 1058.

[19] Crosby's letters to the Philadelphia lawyer and Shakespearean, Joseph Parker Norris, are found in Folger Library Manuscript Y. c.1372. Since I am quoting from the manuscript rather than the Velz and Teague edition, *One Touch of Shakespeare*, I give the number of the letter, followed by the sheet letter and side number. Thus 104b3 means the third side of the second sheet in letter 104.

(probably 500) of our most cultivated people, & was well received' (235e1). At the first meeting of the Zanesville Shakespeare Reading Club, which Crosby helped organize, 'There were present about <u>twenty</u> ladies & gentlemen—all the <u>nicest</u>, and most intelligent, people of our city' (183a1). Repeatedly, Shakespeare serves Crosby as a way of identifying the nice, the cultivated, the gentle classes in his community. Indeed the enjoyment of Shakespeare, in addition to being a 'polite accomplishment', was a means of excluding the socially undesirable. When forming the Reading Club, Crosby deliberately evaded a potentially awkward social problem: 'As only a certain number could be included, I foresaw that there would be an inevitable clamour among those omitted, & I got out of <u>that</u> scrape, by leaving it with a committee of 3 ladies' (184a3). Crosby's premonition was correct. Charles Goddard, a 'gentleman' by birth and education, had behaved in a socially unacceptable manner and was excluded. Goddard sneered at the club to Norris, who gleefully passed his complaints on. Crosby replied:

> I could not help laughing at Charlie's malignity in the description he gave you. There is considerable <u>malice</u> mixed up with it. <u>He</u> was left out in the organization & membership; and that accounts for the milk in the cocoa-nut all turning so suddenly <u>sour</u>.... Some months ago, perhaps a year, a 'Murdoch Club' was formed in Z., for the purpose of <u>performing plays</u> on the regular stage. It was composed of many of our nicest young folks, and Goddard was one. It went on for some time, but much complaint began to spring up against Charlie for being tipsy at rehearsals, & sometimes at the performance. Finally one night he was absolutely so <u>drunk</u> that he could not perform his part—hardly could stand up—and when, in the play, he had to pretend to kiss a young lady, he insulted her by catching hold of her, & kissing her in reality.... And, <u>entre nous</u>, I have no doubt <u>that</u> was the reason he was not invited to belong to the 'Zanes. Sh. Reading Club'; and <u>hinc illae lachrymae</u>! (189a1–a3)

As a gentleman who did not behave like one, Goddard was punished socially by exclusion from Shakespearean activity. Inevitably Crosby and his contemporaries felt troubled when those who clearly knew the works of Shakespeare violated social norms.

Crosby may be unusual in the extent to which he valorizes Shakespeare study as a concomitant of American social gentility, but he is not unique. Nor did he always overlook bad behaviour. Crosby comments, extensively and furiously, on George Wilkes, a proponent of the sort of countering tactic found in Whitman's work, denying the value of the 'gentlemanly' Shakespeare and 'feudal values' for Americans. *The Spirit of the Times* was a sporting paper that published a series of Wilkes's essays, later collected as *Shakespeare from an American Point of View*. Wilkes associates Shakespeare with the aristocracy of England, of whom he has a low opinion; he becomes sidetracked by the Baconian theory. Wilkes prefers Shakespeare as author to Bacon, but regards both men as sorry specimens of humanity:[20]

---

[20] The Baconian heresy flourished in nineteenth-century America. It is clearly linked, with its claims and counter-claims about aristocratic authoring v. poetry produced by a commoner, to a number of the issues I am raising in this chapter. Although Wilkes summons a variety of reasons for thinking Shakespeare rather than Bacon wrote the plays, the one he found most powerful goes unspoken: Bacon was an aristocrat, and hence to be despised by Wilkes, while Shakespeare, for all his shortcomings in Wilkes's eyes, was a commoner.

Shakespeare commenced life as a deer-stealer and a drunkard, had a child born to him less than six months after marriage, and lived in London during all his theatrical career without his wife. He was so mean as to sue one man for a debt of £6, and another for £1 19s. 10d., when he had an income of 1000l. a year, and died, at the age of fifty-two, from the effect of too much drink at dinner. Sir Francis Bacon, on the other hand, was all his life a clamorous office-seeker, a time-server, and a corrupt judge.[21]

Like Crosby and Norris, Wilkes argued against the Baconian theory of authorship, but what more orthodox Shakespeareans found unforgiveable was that Wilkes, while agreeing with their assignment of authorship, then attacked Shakespeare as a toady to aristocrats and an adherent of Roman Catholicism. Furthermore, Wilkes sets his arguments firmly within a nationalistic context, insisting that he writes as an American for Americans, and vigorously spurns the idea that Shakespeare embodies moral uplift or social grace:

> ...Shakespeare is a character of much more consequence to Englishmen, and especially to the ruling classes of Great Britain, than he can ever be to the republican citizens of the United States. With us, he is but the poet, mighty beyond all comparison; but to the ruling classes of Great Britain he is not only the Poet, but the Patron of their order, and also the tireless inculcator of those forms of popular obsequiousness, which long have been the marvel of the civilized world, under the almost purely personal form of English patriotism.[22]

Given an argument like this one, those who argued against the Baconians, maintaining Shakespeare's position as author and authority, found Wilkes a decidedly uncomfortable ally.

Save for his rejection of British importance, what Wilkes does is very much as Crosby does. Confronted with a distortion of his own attitudes toward Shakespeare, Crosby is appalled—and quick to condemn Wilkes on the grounds that he is a blackguard, not a gentleman. Two years later when Crosby bought his book and re-read Wilkes, he had even stronger things to say. Wilkes is a 'd—d, ignorant fool, and conceited puppy,' who

> doubtless thinks he is <u>Smart</u> in his silly attempts to drag Sh. down from his throne in the hearts of the American people, by abusing, & trying to ridicule (bless the mark!) him, both in his character as a <u>man</u> and as a <u>poet</u>. It is truly the most sickening, ignorant <u>trash</u> that was ever printed.   (176c2)

Crosby advocates violence: 'Nothing could give me greater happiness than to <u>cowhide</u> him. . . . a good <u>physical</u> punishment would only meet his case.' He continues in the same vein, sneering at Wilkes as low, an ass, a pig, who uses 'whangdoodle sapience, and owlish pedantry' to gain notoriety for himself (176c2–c3). Crosby vows to leave

[21] Wilkes, *Shakespeare from an American Point of View* (New York: D. Appleton, 1877), 8–10.
[22] Wilkes, *Shakespeare from an American Point of View*.

Wilkes and his book 'severely alone', although he returns to these subjects again in this and three later letters. The point of all this anger, surely, is that Wilkes threatens something that Crosby holds dear, the valorized association between Shakespeare and class, not by denying such an association, but rather by denying its worth for Americans.

Crosby passionately believed that reading, studying, and owning Shakespeare would make one a better man, and, as important, a better gentleman. The final irony, then, is that Crosby's study of Shakespeare destroyed him, morally and socially. In the financial panics of the 1880s, the huge sums he had invested in his collection of Shakespeareana resulted in a debt of $20,000. In 1884, he forged his father-in-law's name to a promissory note, and the fraud was found out. After Crosby was arrested, he abandoned family, friends, and books, fleeing to Montreal, where he died in 1891. One can tell the story of Crosby's fall with smug irony: so much for the synonymous nature of Shakespearean and gentleman. But to do so is to fail to understand a central feature of nineteenth-century America. More important than the irony is recognizing how desperately Crosby and many of his contemporaries wanted to create an American social system based on Shakespeare rather than trade, yearning for a means of raising American character and conduct through the model of art. Shakespeare's function as social perquisite may now seem naive or hypocritical, but the need for such perquisites was real. Reading Crosby's story, the issues that it raises are not really about the definition of American culture in the shadow of Britain, but rather about the need to control that culture and themselves. Someone like Crosby wanted to believe that the absence of a controlling power to ensure gentlemanly conduct could be filled by Shakespeare, that appropriating Shakespeare would raise one to virtue and goodness. Crosby felt the need for Shakespeare's power, but inevitably that power failed him. That failure should not obscure recognition that the need was urgent and terrible.

SHAKESPEARE FOR THE MASSES

The publisher Henry Luce famously termed the twentieth century 'the American century' to describe American hegemony in political and economic arenas. Yet one could make the case that the century was notably American because of the way that the United States dominated mass culture and saturated the world with its amusements. As Shakespeare and his works entered American mass culture, the relationship between Shakespeare and America changed. Rather than employing Shakespeare to define themselves, America began using Shakespeare as a convenient brand name. Shakespeare became an efficient way of suggesting a complex of intellectual and cultural values. Because his plays were already familiar through the many nineteenth-century productions, a creator could cite Shakespeare easily to add value to a work, and because the works were already many centuries old, they were freely available without concerns about copyright.

In the late nineteenth and early twentieth centuries, the audience for Shakespeare increased dramatically. Instead of an audience that would fill a theatre for a specific staged production, the audience for the new form of the film was limitless because the same film could be run over and over; the coming of sound in 1927 and later technological developments kept the audiences coming back throughout the century. Meanwhile newspapers began to publish comics for a national audience in the 1890s, at roughly the same time that pulp fiction sprang up. Print technology made possible the printing of inexpensive paperbacks, beginning in the 1930s with Penguins in the United Kingdom and Pocketbooks in the United States. This development in turn led to a corresponding rise in the potential audience for genre novels. It suddenly became possible to buy mysteries or romances at a fraction of the price that one paid for mainstream novels. In 1920, radio became a national medium, as KDKA began transmitting under the first federal licence. Westinghouse soon opened its own station, and others joined to draw huge audiences who were content to be amused in their homes, without making a trip to a vaudeville or movie house. In a few decades the start of television displaced radio as a socially central entertainment form. Each of these forms needed fresh material: voracious audiences demanded new products.

The burgeoning of mass culture forms like film and television introduced a complex, even contradictory value system. In describing a radio series, Douglas Lanier has a good description. The series shows

> ... the conviction that mass culture, as the creature of corporate capitalism, is merely a series of degraded commodities fashioned for consumption by a gullible public. Despite the show's skewering of Shakespearean theater as outmoded and pompous, Shakespeare nevertheless emerges as the unequivocal standard of quality against which commercial media always come up short. Even so, the show also purveys a parallel ideology, what one might call 'the ideology of high culture,' the conviction that high culture is little more than a means through which a certain social class lays claim to privilege.[23]

The complexity of this response means that Shakespeare simultaneously is and is not available to all Americans because he operates as a marker of high-class status, as a marker of deadly culture, and as a democratically available cultural icon. While radio has been less powerful in the United States than elsewhere, as Lanier points out, television's penetration of American culture is inarguable.

In television one can see that complex relationship, both in arts programming that tries to provide Shakespeare for all and in the more casual references of situation comedies, cartoons, science fiction series, and so on. By and large, American television has linked Shakespeare's plays to education, and today the Public Broadcasting Service (PBS) takes a lead role in presenting Shakespeare productions, with many British

[23] Lanier, 'WSHX: Shakespeare and American Radio', in Richard Burt (ed.), *Shakespeare after Mass Media* (New York: Palgrave, 2002), 195–219, at 121. In this section, I have also found the Internet Movie Database invaluable.

imports and mixed results. Thus television has continued to follow the earliest American encounters with Shakespeare by using him as a token of Anglophilia. One of the most interesting television experiments with an American inflection has its origins in the United Kingdom. When Laurence Olivier made *Richard III* (1955), he released it to movie theatres in the United States after the day that NBC broadcast it on television. The plan was daring: to appeal to the vast audience of American television viewers that was, even in 1955, already much larger than Britain's, or indeed any other nation's. Presumably seeing the film in miniature black and white images could make viewers want to see it a second time on a big screen in Technicolor. But the film's producers judged wrong; the film did not make a profit in America. Thus in the middle of the twentieth century, the mass medium that would displace film as the most popular form of American entertainment was already affecting other mass Shakespeare productions.

The form that Shakespeare takes in American television varies. The uses of Shakespeare move from straightforward productions, to slightly less straightforward raids on his plots and characters, to playful twisting of Shakespearean elements. Although a full-scale television production of one of his plays is fairly common, as are anthology programmes and the occasional documentary, the more difficult shows to categorize are those that employ Shakespeare and his plays to make a thematic point, as well as those that allude to Shakespeareana, often in the form of a burlesque. The productions that employ Shakespeare to their own ends are, however, by far the most interesting ways that television uses Shakespeare and his works.

To begin with the straight productions, the principal networks have offered a variety of plays, weighted toward the tragedies, as 'quality' shows that have helped to justify their social and cultural worth since the 1950s. Particularly through such important series as *Studio One* and *Hallmark Hall of Fame*, Shakespeare productions have served to establish a network's bona fides, an important mission in the years when the Federal Communication Commission checked such things while renewing licences and policing the airwaves. The great bulk of these productions are uninspiring, although the plays that George Schaefer directed for the *Hallmark Hall of Fame* between 1954 and 1960—*Richard II, Macbeth* twice, *The Taming of the Shrew* and *Kiss Me, Kate*, and *The Tempest*—are good. Since PBS began broadcasting in 1970, it has offered a number of Shakespeare productions and documentaries, many rich in Anglophilia. Occasionally, an educational production breaks loose from preconceptions about class or culture and is distinctively American: the New York Shakespeare Festival's 1973 *Much Ado About Nothing* (CBS) that reset the action to the Spanish-American war, the flying Karamazov Brothers' New Vaudeville adaptation of *The Comedy of Errors* (PBS, 1987), and *Play On!* (PBS, 1998), an adaptation that incorporated Duke Ellington's music with the plot line of *Twelfth Night* and reset the action to the Harlem Renaissance. Each of these was emphatically entertaining, moving, and all-American. In addition, each was a television adaptation of a successful stage production. Television productions of Shakespeare have largely depended on the originality of the theatre, transmitting that energy and freshness to a huge audience that would otherwise be unable to gain access to such elite productions.

References in popular television series generally burlesque plays like *Hamlet* and *Romeo and Juliet*, which are often taught in schools and thus widely familiar. The castaways on *Gilligan's Island* presented a musical version of *Hamlet* in a 1964 episode, 'The Producer'. Family situation comedies concentrated their Shakespeare citations on teenagers in school plays: *The Brady Bunch* cast Marcia as Juliet ('Juliet is the Sun' 1971), *Happy Days* cast the Fonz as Hamlet ('A Star is Bored' 1974), and *Family Matters* cast Urkel as Romeo ('The Show Must Go On' 1991). Perhaps the cleverest use of Shakespeare by a sitcom was *Just Shoot Me*'s episode 'King Lear Jet' (1997), which used *Lear* to reflect the tensions among the characters and included a retelling of the play in a Manhattan bar to a moved audience of media and publishing workers. Even most dramatic series tend to use Shakespeare playfully, as the famous 'Atomic Shakespeare' (1986) episode of *Moonlighting* showed when the characters re-enacted *Taming of the Shrew* with a feminist twist.

The most playful of all are the Shakespeare references found in cartoon series. While some are banal, such as the episode of *Archie's Fun House* (1970) in which Shakespeare becomes a source for lines to pick up girls, others take sophisticated aim at both an adult and a children's audience. *Garfield and Friends* had a reflexive 1994 episode where a pig from the network wanted to recast Shakespeare tales in nursery rhyme form because it was an educational project, only to learn they were completely unsuitable for children. *The Simpsons* often burlesques Shakespearean plays. Perhaps the most famous is the rewriting of *Hamlet* in which the over-achieving Lisa took the role of Ophelia and declared, 'Nobody out-crazies Ophelia', a nice comment on both her own character and Shakespeare's. Finally the infamous 'Scott Tenorman Must Die' episode of *South Park* (2001) retells *Titus Andronicus*. Seeking revenge on Tenorman, Eric Cartman persuades him to eat chili that has been made from Scott's parents. By moving the plot to an elementary school, one might think the plot would lighten Shakespeare's horror, but the script retains moments of sexual violation, which are made simultaneously more disturbing and more ridiculous because they involve an obnoxious brat in elementary school. Eric Cartman, who combines elements of both Titus and Lavinia, is clearly a megalomaniac, while the abrupt ending cites the Looney Tunes closing with Cartman as Porky Pig declaring 'That's all, Folks!' Because cartoons are inherently unserious, they seem able to take more risks than regular situation comedies. Their lack of reverence can offer a refreshing, if sometimes alarming, view of Shakespeare.

In most mass culture forms, Shakespeare may serve as a way to suggest affiliation with Anglophilia or whatever the culture deems to be traditional values; a further purpose for citing Shakespeare is to suggest that a particular genre is more complex than most of its kind, and to amuse audiences who understand the references. One form of genre fiction that does occasionally interrogate what Shakespeare means is science fiction. American science fiction series often handle Shakespeare substantively, much as the UK's *Doctor Who* does.

Many people know about the Shakespeare references found throughout the *Star Trek* television series, as well as the paperbacks and films; some of those references are quite sophisticated, and they have been well examined by critics. In the original series, for example, the episode 'Elaan of Troyius' (1968) refers to both Homer and *Taming of the Shrew*, while the later series, *Star Trek: The Next Generation*, featured Patrick Stewart, who had great success with the Royal Shakespeare Company. *The Next Generation* often interpolated references: among the more memorable were 'The Defector' (1989) in which Picard (played by Stewart) helped the android Data with the proper interpretation of *Henry V*'s 'Upon the King' scene, or 'Time's Arrow, Part II' (1992), which recreated *A Midsummer Night's Dream*. One of the series' final episodes was 'Emergence' (1994), which borrowed from *The Tempest* in a reflexive script about endings. In all, the uses of Shakespeare are respectful, without being reverential. In *Star Trek*, the series uses the plays to comic effect and to reflect the events in the production, and other science fiction television programmes have also employed that double purpose.

In *The Twilight Zone*, the final episode of the fourth season, 'The Bard' (1963), was clearly a comment on the fickle nature of popular television, A hack writer summons William Shakespeare to provide him with material he can steal. Dealing with both the hack and with the idiots who run television infuriates Shakespeare, whose contempt for the whole process seems a clear comment on both the mediocrity of what television offers, as well as frustration about the magic it could provide. Another 1960s sci-fi series uses Shakespeare more reverently: Bruce Wayne enters the Batcave using a trick bust of Shakespeare, while one of his most dangerous enemies is the Puzzler, who adores Shakespeare. In this instance Shakespeare is a clear index of social and professional power. The use of Shakespeare's bust unintentionally harks back to the colonial Americans who acquired such busts to indicate their social importance. (Nor is Batman the only programme to involve a bust of Shakespeare. In *Murder She Wrote*'s 1994 episode 'School for Murder', a Shakespeare bust is replaced by an Elvis bust at a preparatory school shortly before the school faces disorder and murder of a faculty member. Clearly the Great Chain of Being continues to operate in popular television.)

The comic tenor continues in *Third Rock from the Sun*, when the alien leader Dick directs a production of *Romeo and Juliet* ('Romeo & Juliet & Dick' 1997) to rescue it from a teacher who fails to understand the play. The human thinks the play is about adolescent sex, while the alien thinks it is about passion and art; the production is, of course, a disaster, suggesting that however inadequate humans are, aliens are even less effectual. The inverse of that episode might be found in the *Mystery Science 3000* episode in 1999 when the space travellers watch and comment on a film of *Hamlet*. In their flip commentary, one sees that mediocrity cannot be saved from mockery by even the most potent of names and (the central point of this sci-fi series) that television can easily make film look idiotic.

It seems altogether appropriate that science fiction, a form that depends on ideas about technology and interrogations of institutions, should simultaneously refer to Shakespeare and be so strongly associated with America, a nation that has also depended on technology and interrogated institutions from its inception. The continuing interest that Americans have with Shakespeare, whether as a marker of attitudes toward England, an indication of social status, an institution to be mocked or revered, remains constant from the colonial to the post-colonial nation.

CHAPTER 40

....

SHAKESPEARE AND THE WORLD

....

TON HOENSELAARS

THE work of Shakespeare may be read as a Renaissance attempt to absorb and represent the known physical world, the assumed laws governing that world, and the potentialities of the non-material, spiritual world. The world we inhabit has, in turn, absorbed and represented 'Shakespeare'—the man, his work, and his reputation. In the course of the centuries, and by many indirections, the early modern playwright and poet from Stratford has acquired a unique world status, with multiple local Shakespeares discernible around the globe. This expansive movement has not been due merely to what were traditionally defined as humanist values inherent in the plays and poems, to the distinguished arts of Shakespeare's language, or to any form of beauty associated with him. There are other factors that determine and steer what has symbolically come to be known as the Shakespeare Industry. Shakespeare's work captures the concerns and anxieties of a writer at the dawn of world capitalism, but the playwright has also posthumously fallen victim to that ideology himself. His name and his work have also become a commodity, a brand in the anonymous global market networks that have emerged since the seventeenth century.[1] We must be aware of the forces that determine the current status of Shakespeare worldwide, but, amidst the profiteering and trading that characterize the Shakespearean afterlives, we should also continually ask ourselves if and how traditional humanist values survive or cede to new modes of engaging with Shakespeare.

Describing the spread of Shakespeare's name and fame across the globe, we must of necessity be modest and selective. Studying the multiple afterlives of Shakespeare beyond the English Channel, this chapter first devotes attention to the theatrical history of the playwright abroad. It then follows his poetry and plays in translation, across the

---

[1] See Michael D. Bristol, *Big-Time Shakespeare* (London: Routledge, 1996), and Jyotsna Singh (ed.), *A Companion to the Global Renaissance: English Literature and Culture in the Age of Expansion* (Oxford: Wiley-Blackwell, 2009).

language barriers that continue to fracture the world, despite the fact that English as the *lingua franca* might suggest otherwise. This chapter continues to devote attention to the ways in which nations and cultures, inspired by his work, have appropriated it to produce new plays, new poems, and original genres that Shakespeare himself did not practise, like the novel or film. Part of this process involves the phenomenon whereby new artists appropriate the dramatic work or the poems to write back to Shakespeare after years of political and cultural suppression in colonial situations serving mainly British interests.

In the course of the centuries, Shakespeare has not only crossed geographical, linguistic, and generic borders. He has also entered into new media, undergoing a veritable metamorphosis, also to convey his message in opera, ballet, and dance, on the radio as on the cinematic and television screens, which unlock the global space (and global always means commercial), where 'Shakespeare' has become a supranational brand; a household word worldwide with significance also to those who may have never seen or read a play or a sonnet, but who choose Ophelia fish soup on the tourist menu at Elsinore, like to smoke Hamlet cigars produced by Japan Tobacco, innocently sharpen their black German-made Othello pencils from Stabilo, or dream of ever owning one of Alfa Romeo's vintage two-seater Giulietta models produced in Milan between 1954 and 1965.

If the various globalizing tendencies have significantly affected the traditional, consciously or unconsciously local identifications with Shakespeare, it is worth realizing that they may have affected no nation more than Shakespeare's own. Also, witnessing how the commodification of Shakespeare has been accompanied by a gradual erosion of the humanist values traditionally associated with him, thus confirming the playwright's own worst anxieties, it is worth recognizing that, even if rare, certain values continue to be associated with Shakespeare and continue to shape communities of readers, writers, players, audiences, as well as critics.

TOURING

The plays of Shakespeare began their conquest of the globe by way of strolling players. Already during Shakespeare's lifetime, in the 1580s, travelling players crossed the Channel from England to the rest of Europe where they performed in marketplaces and at courts across the Continent. They were sighted in the Low Countries, at Hamlet's Elsinore, at Gdansk, Wolfenbüttel, Heidelberg, Nürnberg, Graz, Prague, and in a host of other European venues. The earliest recorded continental production of the strolling players dates from April 23, 1586. In the train of the Earl of Leicester— Elizabeth I's viceroy in the Low Countries during the war against Spain—a company of actors visited the garrison town of Utrecht, and treated the authorities to 'The Forces of Hercules', a more or less acrobatic show of strength involving the construction of a human pyramid. Leicester must have realized that on the day, which until the sixteenth century and the Reformation had been known as St George's Day, it was more appropriate to celebrate national military strength by way of the achievements of a safely classical hero like Hercules than a challenged Catholic saint.

Initially, the stage plays by Shakespeare's contemporaries were more popular abroad than his own. The earliest Elizabethan and Jacobean play to appear in the Low Countries was a version of Thomas Middleton's *The Revenger's Tragedy* (1618) translated by Theodore Rodenburgh, the Flemish trade representative in London during the 1600s. There were also scrambled versions of Thomas Kyd's *The Spanish Tragedy*, including Adriaen van den Bergh's *Ieronimo* (Utrecht, 1621), and the anonymous *Don Jeronimo* (Amsterdam, 1638).

Although in 1605 the French king Henry IV is reported to have seen a play that featured the character of Falstaff brought on stage by some English travelling players at the court of France, we have, strictly speaking, no reliable traces of Shakespeare's work on the European continent until 1620. That year saw the edition in German of *Englische Comedien und Tragedien* [English comedies and tragedies] that marks for the first time how many Shakespeare plays were really involved in an intertextual engagement on the European continent. They included *Titus Andronicus*, the perennially popular 'Pyramus and Thisbe' sequence from *A Midsummer Night's Dream*, *The Merchant of Venice*, and *Twelfth Night*, as well as the play entitled *Der bestrafte Brudermord* (Fratricide Punished), containing many intriguing similarities with the First Quarto edition of *Hamlet*.[2]

The itinerant companies performed the plays in their own early modern English, and it is remarkable, as the players' popularity suggests, and as is confirmed by specific instances of audience response, that they communicated so well on the non-Anglophone Continent. In *An Apology for Actors*, Thomas Heywood writes of a woman in Amsterdam who was reminded by the murder in the play that she saw staged by the English comedians of the way in which she had murdered her own husband twelve years before. Many of the plays were 'spectacular' in the literal sense of the word, designed to be seen rather than heard. Gesture, costume, music, song, dance, and acrobatics all seem to have contributed to communicate what the English language under those trying circumstances could not. The impact of the itinerant companies cannot be underestimated. A number of the plays put on were soon made available in translation and absorbed by the vernacular drama. Also, as in Amsterdam, the rivalry that the strolling players presented to the local amateur chambers of rhetoric, spurred the latter's incentive to go professional too.

The dissemination of Shakespeare by native Englishmen on the nearby continent of Europe did not end with the strolling players of the early seventeenth century. Touring Shakespeare's works never ceased to play a vital role in the economy of the theatre and its culture of performance, and the practise continues unabated to the present day. Inevitably, political differences between nations have tended to affect the theatrical

---

[2] Ernest Brennecke and Henry Brennecke, *Shakespeare in Germany, 1590–1700. With Translations of Five Early Plays* (Chicago, IL: University of Chicago Press, 1964).

fortunes of touring companies. The early nineteenth-century visits to Paris by prominent English actors provide a case in point. In 1822, one company of players nearly caused a riot performing *Othello* in Paris. One of the reasons for this reception was that the French were still accustomed to the domesticated, neo-classical adaptation of the play by Jean-François Ducis and could not stomach the 'real' Shakespeare. Another, related reason for the players' failure in Paris was that the performance of *Othello* took place barely seven years after the defeat of Napoleon at Waterloo. This certainly explains the cries from the audience of 'Down with Shakespeare! He's Wellington's lieutenant.' Toward the end of the 1820s, however, the memories of Waterloo seem to have faded, and a Romantic urge to embrace the English bard—furthered by Stendhal's *Racine et Shakespeare* (1823)—explains the triumphant success on September 11, 1827 of Charles Kemble's *Hamlet* at the Paris Odéon. Suddenly, Shakespeare turned out to be a catalyst for the initially still sceptical but ultimately convinced French Romantics in the audience, including the young French composer Hector Berlioz. Watching Kemble's Ophelia, the Irish Harriet Smithson, Berlioz developed a desperate love for the actress, but he also contracted Shakespearomania, a creative disease from which French opera was to derive immense profit.[3]

By the nineteenth century, touring Shakespeare had long ceased to be the privilege of the English. Traffic was dense across Europe, but also across the Atlantic. Stars like Adelaide Ristori (1822–1906), Tommaso Salvini (1829–1915), and Ernesto Rossi (1827–1896), who performed across the European continent from Amsterdam to Moscow and from Odessa to Madrid, seem to have found a more cordial reception in Britain and the United States than they did in Italy, where neo-classical notions of dramatic style persisted well into the nineteenth century.[4] Between 1873 and 1889, Salvini made no fewer than five visits to America, where he played King Lear in 1882–3—an interpretation admired by Henry James, who reviewed the Boston production for the *Atlantic Monthly*—as well as the title role of *Othello* with the celebrated American actor Edwin Booth as Iago.[5]

By the nineteenth century, of course, the native American theatre tradition had also started to send its players to Europe. One of the more notorious American touring stars in Europe was the African-American actor Ira Aldridge (1807–1867). He became a celebrity in Britain, but also travelled and performed often and with great success on the Continent. There he would—as was customary also with other star colleagues performing in foreign lands—play his part, like his favourite Othello, in English,

[3] For an account of these events see Peter Raby, *'Fair Ophelia': A Life of Harriet Smithson Berlioz* (Cambridge: Cambridge University Press, 1982), 46; and Peter Holland, 'Touring Shakespeare', in Stanley Wells and Sarah Stanton (eds.), *Cambridge Companion to Shakespeare on Stage* (Cambridge: Cambridge University Press, 2002), 203–5.

[4] Marvin Carlson, *The Italian Shakespearians: Performances by Ristori, Salvini, and Rossi in England and America* (Washington, DC: Folger Shakespeare Library, 1985).

[5] 'Foreign Visitors and the New Realism', in Charles Harlen Shattuck, *Shakespeare on the American Stage: From Booth and Barrett to Sothern and Marlowe* (Washington, DC: Folger Shakespeare Library, 1976), 142–209.

surrounded by a supporting cast performing the rest of the play in the local vernacular. Symbolically, Ira Aldridge died prematurely, while on tour in the Polish town of Łodz, during what was already his eighth visit there in fourteen years.

The conspicuous tours of the British Council, the Royal Shakespeare Company, the Shenandoah Shakespeare Express, Yukio Ninagawa's strolling players from Japan, Ariane Mnouchkine's Théâtre du Soleil, and countless other companies during the late twentieth and early twenty-first centuries, continue a long tradition. It is almost surprising that such intensive touring to theatres and festivals persists into our own time. It occurs in spite of the fact that audiences, too, have started to tour to see their own Shakespeare, but also in spite of the fact that Shakespeare today may also be enjoyed in the various new media.[6] Surprise fades into appreciation when we study the personal records of the performance tours, which have become fashionable. They make fascinating reading, as descriptions of the productions, naturally, but also in capturing the unexpected ways in which a live show may impact on a foreign audience, or how the audience may communicate its feelings to affect the players in turn. Records kept by actors, directors, and roadies confirm that the type of theatre performance to which Shakespeare dedicated most of his career is a mode of artistic exchange, releasing reciprocal energies in ways that are unmatched by any other. Moreover, crossing geographical borders and seeking new cultural contexts for performance creates new plays out of old texts. Touring creates multiple Shakespeares, and enables performances to become a revelation for both the audience and the actors. This was Ian McKellen's experience when playing Richard II in Czechoslovakia during the Russian occupation in 1969, and Alan Howard's when acting the lead in *Coriolanus* with the Royal Shakespeare Company across the still politically disturbed European continent during the late 1970s.[7] Michael Bogdanov, Michael Pennington, and their English Shakespeare Company, touring the world with *The Wars of the Roses* in the 1980s, ironically found that they were better understood abroad than in Thatcherite Britain whose society they originally sought to challenge, shock, and change. It made Bogdanov wonder: 'Why is it that one had to go to Australia, Canada, provincial America, to get some coherent views (good or bad) of what we were attempting? . . . It merely confirms one's impression that London is the real provincial, bourgeois capital of the world. . . . In a way, it is lucky for London that America exists.'[8]

Shakespeare's journey to Asia and Africa seems to have begun at a surprisingly early date, before America came into the picture. The first plays travelled to Asia with the East India Company. We know that there were performances of *Hamlet* and *Richard II* aboard the *Red Dragon*, off the west coast of Africa in 1607. But the real absorption of Shakespeare by Indian culture, of course, took place on stage and in the classroom as

---

[6] Dennis Kennedy, 'Shakespeare and the Global Spectator', *Shakespeare-Jahrbuch* 131 (1995), 50–64.

[7] David Daniell, *Coriolanus in Europe* (London: Athlone Press, 1980); Ronald Harwood (ed.), *A Night at the Theatre* (London: Methuen, 1982), 108.

[8] Michael Bogdanov and Michael Pennington, *The English Shakespeare Company: The Story of 'The Wars of the Roses', 1986–1989* (London: Nick Hern Books, 1992), 181.

the British settlers boosted a sense of English superiority over the native inhabitants, in terms of both language and culture. The Englishman may have introduced Shakespeare in India, but he could not control his subsequent reception there. Somehow, the colonizer never managed to prevent Indians from interpreting *Othello* as the tragedy of 'caste'. During the early twentieth century India's film industry—mostly after the First World War—arose to rival the local stage, and challenge the original reverence for Shakespeare.

By the early 1800s, Shakespeare had also reached Australia, but he really settled there only after overcoming prolonged reservations about the merits of introducing his drama in a colony of convicts. For a number of reasons, Australian Shakespeare remains a terra incognita on the world map. Systematic approaches to Shakespeare on the Australian stage are rare, but a closer look at the theatrical tradition as well as the emerging scholarly tradition there suggests that the story of this continent would make at least as unique a chapter in the history of the British Empire and post-colonialism as India has yielded.[9]

TRANSLATION

Shakespeare has reached the outermost parts of the globe not only by way of the ancient and still active touring networks, but also through the printed text of his work in translation. The translation of Shakespeare's early modern English into other world languages since the early seventeenth century represents a fascinating process of cultural mobility, expansion, and exchange, with Shakespeare's major medium of language at the centre of attention. Significantly, translation was not a new invention when Shakespeare's work travelled abroad, and it has, in fact, been rightly defined as the core business of the Renaissance itself. Translation and interpretation perform a central role in *Henry V*, during the Princess of France's language lesson and King Henry's subsequent courtship of her, but also on the battlefield of Agincourt where the Boy acts as interpreter between Pistol and Monsieur le Fer, language is an issue. Anglo-Welsh relations in the first part of *Henry IV* require a similar kind of mediation, when it turns out that the daughter of Owen Glendower speaks Welsh and her husband Mortimer only English.

Looking at translations of Shakespeare's plays and poems themselves, we witness the multiple ways and byways by which their message has travelled around the globe, across linguistic and cultural barriers. It helps us to appreciate why the earliest practitioners of the art used Shakespeare's work as the raw material for a stage product that would satisfy the taste of the new audience in locations ever further removed from the omphalos that was London. One might deplore the fact that the earliest translations

[9] *O Brave New World: Two Centuries of Shakespeare on the Australian Stage*, John Golder and Richard Madelaine (eds.) (Sydney: Currency Press, 2002).

were often free, target audience-oriented rewrites. But from our present-day perspective we can no longer argue that this process only involved loss. In fact, it is precisely because of its departure from the Shakespeare text that Abraham Sybant's Dutch *Taming of the Shrew* of 1654 is now an ideal textual site to compare contemporary views of women and marital partnership on either side of the English Channel.

Generations of critics have tended to interpret these seventeenth- and eighteenth-century audience-oriented adaptations of Shakespeare as a mark of disrespect. However, this was far from the translators' objectives. Rather, within the context of the then prevailing poetics, translation was seen as the first step in a more elaborate process that further included the imitation and preferably also the emulation of the source text. It is such neo-classical poetics—which cannot be dissociated either from the way in which Shakespeare himself ransacked his sources to work a sea-change—which explain the veritable metamorphosis that Shakespeare's texts underwent after crossing the Channel. This was emphatically not a matter of iconoclasm—like some manifestations of Shakespeare in our time—but of interactive creativity within the established rules.

Toward the end of the eighteenth century, as Shakespeare came to be appreciated more as a genius in his own right, as a unique poet whose work commanded respect, new demands were made on translators. They no longer sought to please their own audiences but tried to do justice to the demands of the dead poet and his increasingly sacrosanct text. By the turn of the century, the creative and often misunderstood type of free translation was a thing of the past.

Some of the translations that were produced during the Romantic period have almost reached the status of national literature in their own right. The German translation of Shakespeare's plays by August Wilhelm Schlegel and Ludwig Tieck, produced during the early nineteenth century, is still a standard text in the German-speaking world. Just as the English language in Shakespeare's time achieved the triumph of the language partly through successful attempts to prove that the native tongue could render the nuance of the classics, so the German language—to a certain extent, anyway—created and empowered itself through the work of Shakespeare. The Germans called the man from Stratford 'unser Shakespeare' (our Shakespeare), someone born in Britain, but alive across Germany. The issue also entered the political discourse of the First World War when writers such as Ludwig Fulda in his *Deutsche Kultur und Engländerei* (1916) argued that the issue of Shakespeare's nationality should be settled once and for all during the forthcoming peace negotiations between Germany and Britain.

Romantic and post-Romantic translations have been produced by people with literary reputations in their own right, such as Johann Wolfgang Goethe and Friedrich Schiller, Chr. M. Wieland, Stefan George, Karl Kraus, Paul Celan, Marcel Schwob, Marcel Pagnol, André Gide, Jean Anouilh, Boris Pasternak, G. Ungaretti, Eduardo de Filippo, Ramón de la Cruz, Leandro Fernándes de Moratín, José Maria Valverde, Per Hallström, Adriaan Roland Holst, Martinus Nijhoff, and Hugo Claus. The list of major poets—which continues to grow—forces us to readjust our perception of Shakespeare in translation. We are still more inclined to assume that translation involves loss rather than gain. Significantly, though, close attention to the interlingual creativity that Shakespeare generates enables one to appreciate even better the energies that make up the original texts.

The study of translation teaches us much, not only about the ways in which languages interact, but also about the cultures within which those languages function. For example, the translation and reception history of Shakespeare's Sonnet 66 ('Tired with all these, for restful death I cry') shows that this particular sonnet has been more popular in translation than it has ever been in English. Particularly in the course of the twentieth century, Sonnet 66, with its Hamlet-like reflection on the multiple ills of society and on suicide as an option to escape from these, has been taken most seriously on the continent of Europe, while in Britain it seems to have been marginalized. During the Nazi era in Germany, it was the signature tune for intellectuals disgusted with war. In 1940, Dimitri Shostakovich composed music to Boris Pasternak's translation of Sonnet 66, and in total produced three versions of the sonnet as part of his *Six Romances after Raleigh, Burns, and Shakespeare*. Indeed, the many translations made in communist Europe after the Second World War help trace the developing frustration with a system whose collapse would only be definitive with the razing of the Berlin Wall in 1989.[10]

Even though English has in the course of the twentieth century become the lingua franca, the original practice of translating Shakespeare's work has not come to a stop, and is not likely to, because theatre productions worldwide will continue to be presented in the native vernaculars. This situation brings into focus the curious paradox that the playwright and poet who is currently taught, read, played, and revered worldwide because of his unique verbal artistry, is, more often than not, read and performed in a language other than his own early modern English. This situation raises a number of questions to which there are no easy answers. Does Shakespeare's work have a special quality that explains how it may communicate its message also 'without his language'? Is it anything universal, as, for example, the global film industry would have us believe? Or, do we argue, as some do, that Shakespeare 'in other words' is not Shakespeare? One thing is certain: 'Shakespeare' simply would not enjoy his current worldwide status if he had not been available in so many translations.

This current debate over the translation of Shakespeare still has its roots very much in the Romantic period when the author came to be revered as a unique medium, and the text came to be edited and read as the most personal expression of this unique personality, to be respected in its purest form. This sacrosanct status of the text and its bardic author explains the persistent anxiety over Shakespeare's assumed loss of authenticity and authority, especially when it concerns the intralingual translation of Shakespeare into modern English. It also explains that the translator (*traduttore*) who replaces Shakespeare's early modern English words with his own foreign vocabulary is

---

[10] Manfred Pfister, 'Route 66: The Political Performance of Shakespeare's Sonnet 66 in Germany and Elsewhere', in Angel Luis Pujante and Ton Hoenselaars (eds.), *Four Hundred Years of Shakespeare in Europe*, (Newark: University of Delaware Press, 2003), 70–88.

also sometimes seen as a traitor (*tradittore*). And if the translator is not a traitor, he or she is certainly deemed incapable of rendering Shakespeare as in the original, which, in turn, explains why instead of saying that this mediator on Shakespeare's behalf produces a translation, the translator is said to be producing an adaptation.

ADAPTATION

Surveying the international afterlives of Shakespeare and seeing how his name and fame have spread across the globe, one must draw a distinction between an adaptation as a pejorative term for an imperfect translation, and an adaptation defined as a creative product involving a metamorphosis, a reappraisal, or rewriting of the work and ideas of Shakespeare. Adaptation—although it acquired an unfavourable ring in the context of Shakespearean translation—was not a negative term in the seventeenth or eighteenth century when Dryden, Davenant, Garrick, Voltaire, Ducis, and a host of others revised the Shakespearean playtexts to meet the then prevailing taste and poetic justice.[11] Shakespeare came to inspire a vast canon of creative adaptations, personal appropriations (not necessarily hostile) of the plays and poems, and of characters, themes, and lines, as well as his biography. Johann Wolfgang Goethe's novel *Wilhelm Meister's Apprentice Years* features an eponymous character who is an aspiring actor with a number of remarkable ideas about *Hamlet* that were soon to acquire household status in academic Shakespeare criticism worldwide. Welcome Msomi's stage play *uMabatha* (1970) is a Zulu adaptation of *Macbeth* that performed a vital role in South Africa, both during apartheid and the turbulent years that followed, just as Heiner Müller's *Hamletmaschine* showed how Shakespeare's tragedy could be rewritten for a stark and trenchant analysis of the twentieth-century predicament in Europe: 'I was Hamlet. I stood on the shore and talked with the surf BLABLA, the ruins of Europe in back of me.'

With the post-Second World War upsurge of the nationalist and independence movements in what had long been European colonies, a new type of Shakespearean adaptation emerged when Shakespeare and his work were used to write back to the omphalos of the European empire. Characteristic of such post-colonial adaptation is *A Tempest* (1969) by the Martinique-born playwright Aimé Césaire, presenting a company of black actors who stage their own version of Shakespeare's last comedy. The new play reveals a very special interest in the fate of Caliban, and draws on contemporary Caribbean society and the African-American experience in an attempt to reflect on colonialism and racism, and to suggest alternative perceptions. There is a veritable abundance of post-colonial rewritings of Shakespeare, generally but not

---

[11] A useful introduction to the phenomenon is in Daniel Fischlin and Mark Fortier (eds.), *Adaptations of Shakespeare: A Critical Anthology of Plays from the Seventeenth Century to the Present* (New York: Routledge, 2000).

exclusively produced by representatives from those areas of the globe where the European colonizer with the Shakespearean canon imposed his rule for centuries. Rather than reject Shakespeare altogether, post-colonial writing engages in an act of mimicry, suggesting either that the playwright is merely useful as a shared frame of reference, or that he has welded so closely with the original cultures as to be inseparable from them, or that he presents the richness and complexity required for this intercultural debate.[12]

The post-colonial discussion has tended to focus not only on Shakespeare's plot and characters, but also on his language, as the suppressed or ignored minorities have sought to assert a new and independent vernacular with Shakespeare as the vital touchstone. A case in point was the Latin American 'Shakespeare for Writers' project of the 1990s, seeking to provide an outlet for Shakespeare not in Iberian Spanish (which still dominates the publishing world in Latin America) but in independent regional Spanish idioms. Arguably the most effective response to this challenge was the Cuban Omar Pérez's translation of *As You Like It* (entitled *Como les guste*).

Comparable post-colonial rewriting may also be found in Canada, where aspirations for an independent Quebec province between the late 1960s and roughly 1980 produced a brand of Shakespeare in the local so-called *joual* dialect (after its pronunciation of the French word *cheval*), drastically rewritten to meet the theatre's political objectives. This unique form of Shakespearean appropriation, depending on a deft combination of linguistic factors and immediate political interests of an emancipatory kind, was labelled with a new term, tradaptation. It has produced plays of lasting value such as Jean-Pierre Ronfard's raucous *Lear* (1977) whose Quebec dialect iconoclastically combines with stage images that challenge traditional French and English views of the old king, whose crown is now a baseball cap, whose throne is a wooden Coca Cola crate, and whose 'kingdom' to be divided among his daughters is a pizza.

Post-colonial tendencies may also be discerned in Britain, where Ireland, Scotland, and Wales have for decades been seeking to realize the devolution of power based in London. During the 1990s, several Scottish attempts were undertaken to reclaim the nation's political and cultural identity by translating *Macbeth* into Scots. At the time when the Scottish nation pursued home rule, both David Purves and R. L. C. Lorimer sought to return to Macbeth and Lady Macbeth their own voice:

> The corbie himsell is hairse
> that craiks the fatal entrie o Duncan
> ablo ma battilments. Cum ben ye spreits
> that tends on deidlie thochts; tak awa ma sex
> an fill me pang fou frae croun ti tae
> wi utmaist crueltie! Mak ma bluid thick!
> Clag aw springheids o peitie or compassion
> in ma saul, latna ma naitur hinner me
> in ma fell purpose, an lat me hae nae peace

---

[12] Ania Loomba and Martin Orkin (eds.), *Post-Colonial Shakespeare* (London: Routledge, 1998). See also Martin Orkin, *Local Shakespeares: Proximations and Power* (London: Routledge, 2005).

or it's fulfilled! Cum til ma wumman's breists
an chynge ma milk for gaw, ye murderin agents,
whare'er ye byde ti steir up naitur's mischief![13]

NEW MEDIA

In the case of a wordsmith like Shakespeare, it is natural and appropriate to focus on matters of language. However, the works have also been metamorphosed into stage images, paintings, cartoons, and graphic novels, as well as musical compositions, including songs, choral works, symphonies, and operas. Trying to appreciate the ways in which Shakespeare's name and fame have spread across the globe, it is difficult to underestimate the role played by the intersemiotic transfer of Shakespeare's words into new sign systems (images, gestures, sound), and the often accompanying inter-medial shifts (stage, musical score, television and cinematic screens). For reasons of space, this section focuses on several musical traditions, including opera, the musical, as well as classical and popular songs.[14]

Between 300 and 400 operas have been written around Shakespearean materials, and composers continue to take up the challenge.[15] Appropriately, the career of Shakespearean opera started in England, with Henry Purcell's *The Fairy Queen* (1692). The opera does not really set *A Midsummer Night's Dream* itself to music, but the authenticity of the music explains how its four acts may have been performed between the five acts of Shakespeare's comedy. Purcell started a long tradition leading by way of Benjamin Britten—whose play-within-the-play in *The Midsummer Night's Dream* parodies native and foreign operatic styles that range from Gilbert and Sullivan to Donizetti and Verdi—to Thomas Adès (b. 1971), whose opera based on Shakespeare's most operatic play, *The Tempest*, premiered in 2004.

Shakespearean opera began in England, but in the course of the years, the continental European tradition of opera—effectively begun by Shakespeare's Italian contemporary Claudio Monteverdi—was to dwarf it by comparison. Since opera's interest in history tended toward romance, Shakespeare's history plays have so far proved to be of little or no interest to librettists. Memorable, no doubt, is Camille Saint-Saëns's *Henry VIII*, with a libretto that rewrites Shakespeare's final history, and Calderón's *Schism in England* (1627), as well as Giorgio Battistelli's *Richard III* (2005). The comedies and tragedies, however, have been put to music over and over again, though relatively few have stood the test of time. The nineteenth century was the golden age of opera,

---

[13] J. Derrick McClure, 'Scots for Shakespeare', in Ton Hoenselaars (ed.), *Shakespeare and the Language of Translation* (London: Thomson Learning, 2004), 237. The quotation is from R. L. C. Lorimer's translation.

[14] For a detailed discussion of the cinematic afterlives of Shakespeare, see the chapter by Laury Magnus, pp. 475–98.

[15] See Gary Schmidgall, *Shakespeare and Opera* (New York: Oxford University Press, 1990), and Julie Sanders, *Shakespeare and Music: Afterlives and Borrowings* (Oxford: Polity Press, 2007).

producing such Shakespearean masterpieces as Gioachino Rossini's *Otello* (1816), Richard Wagner's radical reading of *Measure for Measure* as *Das Liebesverbot* [*The Ban on Love*] (1836), Otto Nicolai's *Die lustigen Weiber von Windsor* [*The Merry Wives of Windsor*] (1849), Hector Berlioz's *Béatrice et Bénédict* (1862), Charles Gounod's *Roméo et Juliette* (1867), and Ambroise Thomas's *Hamlet* (1866–8). It may seem difficult to imagine and also listen to a mid-nineteenth-century Hamlet singing 'Être ou ne pas être' as part of a tragedy that also has a happy ending! However, such prejudice would deprive one of an acquaintance not only with a carefully crafted opera, but also with a most intriguing reflection on the monarchic system during the French Restoration, on the eve of the Third Republic, when the happy ending to *Hamlet* served to convey that despite the political friction that may exist in royal families, they can take good care of themselves if necessary. It is with such a vision of the monarchy that Napoleon III appears to have welcomed Thomas's *Hamlet*, unlike the English at Covent Garden in 1869, when they were adamant that after killing Claudius, Hamlet should also kill himself, and had their way.

Of all nineteenth-century opera, Giuseppe Verdi's *Otello* (1887) with its Darwinian Iago, and his *Merry Wives* opera entitled *Falstaff* (1893), both emulating the original plays in a highly original and inspired manner, deserve recognition as the most complex Shakespearean contributions to the operatic genre. The many ensemble pieces that make up much of Verdi's *Falstaff* represent a subtle translation of the civic spirit of Shakespeare's Windsor into music, with its unique potential of simultaneous expression, where the spoken word, if it wishes to preserve intelligibility, can only be linear. The ensemble pieces, however, also set off the character of Falstaff, who acquires near-tragic grandeur as he begins to acknowledge his age and its limitations: 'Va, vecchio John, va per la tua via; camminsa finchè tu muoia'—'Go, old Jack, go thy ways; travel until thou'rt dead.'

The success of Falstaff abroad was not lost on composers in England, and this also explains repeated attempts to reclaim Sir John for the English, like Gustav Holst's sombre *At the Boar's Head* (1924) or Ralph Vaughan Williams's exquisite *Sir John in Love* (1924–8). Yet, Verdi's *Falstaff* still reigns supreme, as a comic ensemble opera about bourgeois virtues and vices, but also (as demonstrated by the Jamaica-born baritone Willard White in the leading role at Aix-en-Provence festival of 2001) as a subtle means of studying society and its scapegoating of the other.

If Europe first developed the operatic tradition, it was the United States that developed the Shakespearean musical that would reach worldwide fame. Easily the most famous American musical version of Shakespeare is Leonard Bernstein's *West Side Story* (1949)—which transfers the scene of *Romeo and Juliet* from Renaissance Verona to post-Second World War New York, with the Jets and the Sharks as the rival street gangs who cause the death of Italian-American Tony (Romeo) but leave Maria (who is of Cuban extraction) alive to rue his death. But Cole Porter's *Kiss Me, Kate* (1948), based on *the Taming of the Shrew*, has also been performed frequently, making 'Brush Up Your Shakespeare' and 'I've Come to Wive it Wealthily in Padua' household songs the world over.

Shakespeare and musical drama have also entered non-western culture, as with the Chinese Kunju opera adaptation of *Macbeth* entitled *Story of Bloody Hands* (dir. Huang Zuolin, 1987). However, this never rivalled the popularity of that other *Macbeth*, the Peking opera *The Kingdom of Desire* (1986), conceived, directed, and performed by Wu Hsing-kuo of Taiwan's Contemporary Legend Theatre. Shakespeare the man has entered the Asian operatic scene in the *Ghost Opera* (1994) by the Chinese composer Tan Dun, whose opening scene presents how 'Bach, Monks, and Shakespeare Meet in Water'. As the opera bridges eastern and western musical systems, Shakespeare emerges as a world classic.

Shakespeare on the operatic stage represents only a fraction of the musical afterlives to which the Stratford playwright and his work have given rise. Indeed, we ourselves would need multiple afterlives to hear and appreciate all the classical songs (such as Franz Schubert's version of 'Who is Sylvia?' from *The Two Gentlemen of Verona*, Mario Castelnuovo-Tedesco's multiple Shakespeare songs, or Erich Korngold's exquisite *Songs of the Clown* based on *Twelfth Night* lyrics), symphonic spin-offs (like Tchaikovsky's *Romeo and Juliet* overture), the Shakespearean jazz heritage (with Duke Ellington and Billy Strayhorn's Shakespeare suite entitled *Such Sweet Thunder* of 1957, but also with Cleo Laine and her concert of Shakespeare songs set to music by her husband John Dankworth), the ballet music of Sergei Prokofiev (*Romeo and Juliet*, completed in 1935), and all the film scores (from Max Reinhardt and William Dieterle's 1935 Hollywood film version of *A Midsummer Night's Dream* to Baz Luhrmann's lush and excentric *Romeo + Juliet*). Finally, there have been the popular songs quoting Shakespeare, including work of Barclay James Harvest ('Welcome to the Show', 1992), the Bee Gees ('To be or not to be', 1965), The Band ('Ophelia'), The Beatles ('I am the Walrus', 1967), David Bowie ('Cracked Actor', 1973), John Cale ('Macbeth', 1973), Clinic (who recorded 'Falstaff' on their *Winchester Cathedral* CD), Elvis Costello ('Miss Macbeth', 1989), The Eagles ('Get Over It', 1994), Dire Straits ('Romeo and Juliet', 1980), The Grateful Dead ('Althea', 1980), Jack Panzer ('Thane to the Throne', 2000), Peggy Lee ('Fever', 1958), Fleetwood Mac ('Then Play On', 1969), Madonna ('Cherish', 1989), Elvis Presley ('I'll Take Love', 1967), Sting ('Nothing Like the Sun', 1987), as well as Mark Wahlberg and Marvyn Warren (whose 'Hamlet Rap' featured prominently in the *Renaissance Man* film, 1994).[16]

ENGLAND AND/IN THE WORLD

In the course of the past few decades, we have gradually turned our main gaze away from Stratford as the centre of the Shakespeare industry, and have started to appreciate how people around the globe have developed ever new sites for appropriating the work of

---

[16] The richest resource on Shakespearean references and allusions in the modern media is Richard Burt (ed.), *Shakespeares after Shakespeare: An Encyclopedia of the Bard in Mass Media and Popular Culture*, 2 vols. (Westport, CT: Greenwood Press, 2007).

the alien Englishman, both on the stage and in ever more advanced media, both in early modern English and in ever new vernaculars, both in high and in popular culture. As a consequence, we see how the traditional category of Shakespeare by country has been complemented with terms marking Shakespearean practice by continent (European and Asian Shakespeares), as well as region (Arab world, the Caribbean, the former USSR). Despite this decentring focus and our increasing interest in transnational and intercultural processes facilitated by the global world, England, and its specific engagement with world Shakespeare remains unique.

In recent years, many attempts have been undertaken in England to open the nation's doors to other Shakespeares, but the reception has not been unproblematic. In 1994, Michael Kustow devised a season optimistically entitled 'Everybody's Shakespeare' at the Barbican Theatre in London, with productions from America, Japan, Germany, Israel, and Georgia. The response from the press was unusually prejudiced and xenophobic, and displayed a distinctly dated attitude of cultural superiority. How, the press wondered, could one expect foreign companies to convey the message of the Bard correctly?[17] Although the climate has changed since the early 1990s, English audiences still have a hard time evaluating the world's Shakespeare that descends on its local stages. A case in point was the RSC's Complete Works Festival, with the ambition to stage every play in the canon in Stratford between April 2006 and April 2007, and to allow for a broad range of non-native productions, from Germany, Poland, South Africa, Japan, and other countries. English responses on this occasion were not xenophobic, perhaps, but the reviews do capture how hard it has been for a cosmopolitan English observer to accept the foreign production's right to speak its Shakespeare, and at the same time to be duly critical on those occasions where gratuitous irreverence or iconoclasm seems to have been a conscious part of the director's strategy.[18]

The unprecedented expansion and repositioning of Shakespeare worldwide has challenged not only England's perception of other nations and regions, but also its perception of Shakespeare and of itself as a nation. It has really become one nation among so many global players, and it has been challenged more than ever before to define its notion of Englishness.[19] This is perhaps best illustrated with reference to BBC 1's screen adaptation of *Much Ado About Nothing*, *Macbeth*, *The Taming of the Shrew*, and *A Midsummer Night's Dream*, first presented together as *ShakespeaRe-Told* in November 2005.[20] All four of these adaptations are, as the BBC puts it, 'updatings'.

---

[17] Peter Holland, 'Festivals and Foreigners', in his *English Shakespeares: Shakespeare on the English Stage in the 1990s* (Cambridge: Cambridge University Press, 1997), 253–70.

[18] Michael Dobson, 'Shakespeare Performances in England, 2006', *Shakespeare Survey* 60 (2007), 284–91, and Michael Dobson, 'Shakespeare Performances in England, 2007', *Shakespeare Survey* 61 (2008), 318–50.

[19] For a more detailed treatment of this issue, which is closely related to the devolution of power in Britain over the past two decades, see Willey Maley and Margaret Clayton-Tudeau (eds.), *This England, That Shakespeare: New Angles on Englishness and the Bard* (London: Ashgate, 2010).

[20] *Much Ado About Nothing* (dir. David Nicholls), November 7, 2005; *Macbeth* (dir. Peter Moffat), November 14, 2005; *The Taming of the Shrew* (dir. Sally Wainwright), November 21, 2005; and

Significantly, they are also (with the exception of *Macbeth*) instances of relocation. *The Taming of the Shrew* is relocated in present-day London, and, seeking to show how Katherina will become the next prime minister of Britain, is set in and around the Houses of Parliament. The original Padua setting that cosmopolitan Shakespeare used for his main plot has become a vaguely defined Italian location, best described as Chiantishire (the Englishman's image of Tuscany), and it is here that Petruchio and Katherina spend their honeymoon. Like *The Taming of the Shrew*, the BBC's *Much Ado About Nothing* has been transposed from Sicily to the south of England, where both Beatrice and Benedick are presenters for a television channel in a news bulletin which is in Hardyesque terms called 'Wessex Tonight'. Hero is cast as the pretty weather girl who is going to marry dashing sports reporter Claude, until her ex-lover Don Reid (as the reincarnation of Don John) interferes. *A Midsummer Night's Dream* takes place no longer in Athens or even the forest of Athens, but in a holiday park in the British Midlands during an engagement party for Hermia and Demetrius.

The BBC series has deservedly received much credit for this highly imaginative and playful retelling of Shakespeare's plays. However, the updating tendency presents fewer questions than the relocation of the plays. Significantly, the *ShakespeRe-Told* project deprives Shakespeare's plays of a broader world vision, and creates a Shakespeare who is narrowly British. At a juncture in world history where the Kuwaiti writer and director Sulayman Al-Bassam—notably upon the invitation of the RSC—shows the world how a play like *Richard III* may tell an Arab story, the BBC broadcasts a Shakespeare to tell a native British story all its own. Operating in the multicultural anonymity of the 'global' world, all nations are more or less equal in their need to appropriate Shakespeare for themselves, and this does not exclude Britain vis-à-vis its own, native Shakespeare. This change, more complex than space allows here, explains the foundation of the British Shakespeare Association in the 1990s—nearly 130 years after the foundation of the Deutsche Shakespeare-Gesellschaft in 1864, and dozens of other Shakespearean associations in the years that followed—which serves, among other things, to cater to local British interests and needs. Its 2009 conference at the University of London was appropriately devoted to the topic of 'Local and Global Shakespeares'.

Replicas

The spread of Shakespeare's name worldwide and his commodified absorption into anonymous global networks is marked by a massive outpouring of stage productions and translations, as well as many other forms of local adaptation and updating.

A Midsummer Night's Dream (dir. Peter Bowker), November 28, 2005. For a detailed discussion of the series, see Clara Calvo and Ton Hoenselaars, 'Shakespeare Uprooted: The BBC and ShakespeaRe-Told (2005)', in Graham Bradshaw and Tom Bishop (eds.), *The Shakespearean International Yearbook* vol. 8 (London: The Athlone Press, 2008), 82–96.

However, there has also been a search for authenticity. This process may be witnessed in multiple attempts to reconstruct the Globe, the theatre for which Shakespeare wrote most of his plays, or any theatre with which Shakespeare is closely associated.

In the early twentieth century, William Poel—inspired by the discovery in 1888 of the De Witt drawing of the bare interior of the Swan, made during the 1590s—believed that our appreciation of Shakespeare would benefit from staging his plays under the original conditions, on the empty stage, and not from perpetuating the then current Victorian attempts at spectacular realism. Unfortunately, Poel's early attempts to rebuild a playhouse for his Elizabethan Stage Society failed, but Sam Wanamaker was more successful. In 1970 he conceived of the idea to rebuild Shakespeare's Globe as close as possible to the site where the first had been constructed on London's South Bank in December 1599, and although Wanamaker did not live to see the theatre's official opening on June 12, 1997 with Richard Olivier's *Henry V*, the venture has gone from strength to strength, both as a unique form of theatrical entertainment, and as a laboratory for actors and audiences who try to gain a better understanding of the plays of Shakespeare and his fellow playwrights by experiencing them under more or less similar, simulated conditions.

There have been many attempts worldwide to reconstruct not only the Globe, but also the Fortune, and the Blackfriars playhouse. As early as 1934, J. C. Adams produced a Globe replica for the World's Fair in Chicago (now in the Folger Library), and many ventures soon followed, including the construction of The Old Globe Theatre in San Diego (built in 1935 as part of the California Pacific International Exposition), the roofed Tokyo Globe (1988), and the Globe playhouse with its annual festival in the German town of Neuss (1991). Unfortunately, the Globe replica in Prague of 1999 was destroyed by fire in November 2005 (much like its early modern predecessor during a performance of *Henry VIII* in 1613), but since 2005 Rome has had its own Silvano Toti Globe Theatre in the park of Villa Borghese, and in 2009, the cornerstone was laid on the site of a lost Elizabethan theatre constructed in seventeenth-century Gdansk, whose architecture was based upon the London Fortune playhouse that Shakespeare knew. At the American Shakespeare Center in Staunton, Virginia, a replica of Blackfriars Playhouse opened its doors in September 2001.

Replicas of Shakespeare's theatres have been produced not only on a more or less life-size scale, but also, on occasion, as models. The most famous model of the Globe worldwide is the one that features in the opening sequence of Laurence Olivier's 1944 film version of *Henry V*. Here the camera, in an aerial movement, pans from Tower Bridge (as it might have looked in Shakespeare's time) to an obvious replica of the Globe theatre. It zooms in and enters the 'Wooden O' from above where a production of Shakespeare's *Henry V* is about to begin, and soon we enter the film world, and are allowed to forget about the artifice. Famous worldwide is also the replica of the Rose theatre, designed for the set of the film *Shakespeare in Love* (1998). It was rescued from destruction by Dame Judi Dench, with the objective to re-erect it as a performing space and training facility for young actors.

Easily the most relevant and beneficial appropriation of the Globe replica occurred in Wieland Wagner's 1963 production of *Die Meistersinger von Nürnberg*. With Hitler's Nuremberg rallies still fresh in people's memories as well as the Führer's passion for Richard Wagner's operas (including *Die Meistersinger von Nürnberg*, featuring the story of the sixteenth-century playwright Hans Sachs arguing for the narrow cultivation of one's national arts), it was nearly impossible to stage the *Meistersinger* again in post-war Bayreuth. Wieland's solution to this very real problem was to include Shakespeare's Globe in the Bayreuth stage set for the *Meistersinger*—a move that may have been suggested by the fact that the opera is also one of the subtlest rewritings of *A Midsummer Night's Dream*. It was also historically right for the opera's sixteenth-century setting about a contemporary of Shakespeare's. By incorporating Shakespeare's symbolic Globe into his production of Wagner's *Meistersinger*, Wieland Wagner managed to graft onto the tainted opera the perspective that we associate with a worldwide Shakespeare possibly endowed with supranational values, a vital alternative to the narrow national perception of art that developed in the nineteenth century. It is not at all certain that Shakespeare's work is as apolitical or wholesome as the 1963 adoption of the Globe on the Bayreuth stage suggested, but the real point from a cultural-historical perspective is that Wieland Wagner believed that he could cleanse the tainted image of his grandfather's operatic masterpiece with the assistance of Shakespeare. Two world wars have engendered serious doubts about the viability of Renaissance humanism. A tiny, supranational Shakespearean gesture like Wieland Wagner's, however, may help restore some of the confidence lost.

References and Further Reading
....

Chapter 1 Authorship

Abrams, Richard. 'Breaching the Canon: *Elegy by W. S.*: The State of the Argument', *The Shakespeare Newsletter* (1995), 51–2, 54.

Anonymous, *The Returne from Pernassus: or the Scourge of Simony* (London, 1606).

Brooks, Alden, *Will Shakspere and the Dyer's Hand* (New York: Scribner, 1943).

Burrow, Colin (ed.), *Shakespeare: The Complete Sonnets and Poems* (Oxford: Oxford University Press, 2002).

Byrne, M. St. C., 'Bibliographical Clues in Collaborate Plays', *The Library*, 4th series, 13 (1932), 21–48.

Chambers, E. K., *The Disintegration of Shakespeare*, The British Academy: The Annual Shakespeare Lecture (London: Oxford University Press, 1924).

Cheney, Patrick, *Shakespeare's Literary Authorship* (Cambridge: Cambridge University Press, 2008).

Craig, Hugh, 'The 1602 Additions to *The Spanish Tragedy*', in Craig and Kinney (eds.), *Shakespeare, Computers, and the Mystery of Authorship*, 162–80.

——, 'Common-Words Frequencies, Shakespeare's Style, and the *Elegy* by W. S', *Early Modern Literary Studies* 8.1 (2002), http://purl.oclc.org/emls/081/craistyl.htm.

——, and Arthur F. Kinney (eds.), *Shakespeare, Computers, and the Mystery of Authorship* (Cambridge: Cambridge University Press, 2009).

de Grazia, Margreta, *Shakespeare Verbatim: The Reproduction of Authenticity and the 1790 Apparatus* (Oxford: Clarendon Press, 1991).

Elliott, Ward, and Robert J. Valenza, 'Did Shakespeare Write *A Lover's Complaint*? The Jackson Ascription Revisited', *Words That Count: Essays on Early Modern Authorship in Honor of MacDonald P. Jackson*, Brian Boyd (ed.) (Newark: University of Delaware Press, 2004), 117–39.

Erne, Lukas, *Shakespeare as Literary Dramatist* (Cambridge: Cambridge University Press, 2003).

Faulkes, Fred, *Tiger's Heart in Woman's Hide*, vol. 1 (Victoria: Trafford, 2007).

Foster, Donald W., *Elegy by W.S.: A Study in Attribution* (Newark: University of Delaware Press, 1989).

——, '*A Funeral Elegy*: W[Illiam] S[Hakespeare]'s "Best-Speaking Witnesses"', *PMLA* 111 (1996), 1080–95.

Gililov, Ilya, *The Shakespeare Game: The Mystery of the Great Phoenix* (New York: Algora, 2003).

Harbage, Alfred, and S. Schoenbaum, *Annals of English Drama 975–1700* (2nd edn. Philadelphia: University of Pennsylvania Press, 1964).

Heywood, Thomas, *The English Traveller* (London, 1633).

Ioppolo, Erace, *Dramatists and their manuscripts in the Age of Shakespeare, Jonson, Middleton and Heywood: Authorship, Authority and the Playhouse* (London: Routledge, 2006).

Jackson, Macdonald P., 'The Date and Authorship of Hand D's Contribution to *Sir Thomas More*: Evidence from "Literature Online"', *Shakespeare Survey* 59 (2006), 69–78.

——, '*A Lover's Complaint* Revisited', *Shakespeare Studies* 32 (2004), 267–94.

——, 'Shakespeare and the Quarrel Scene in *Arden of Faversham*', *Shakespeare Quarterly* 57.3 (2006), 249–93.

James, Brenda, and William Rubenstein, *The Truth Will Out: Unmasking the Real Shakespeare* (Harlow: Pearson Education, 2005).

Kerrigan, John (ed.), *Motives of Woe: Shakespeare and The 'Female Complaint': A Critical Anthology* (Oxford: Clarendon Press, 1991).

Kinney, Arthur F., 'Authoring *Arden of Faversham*', in Craig and Kinney (eds.), *Shakespeare, Computers, and the Mystery of Authorship* (Cambridge, Cambridge University Press), 78–99.

Marlowe Society Hoffman Prize, www.marlowe-society.org/reading/info/hoffmanprize.html.

Meres, Francis, *Palladis Tamia: Wit's Treasury* (London, 1598).

Metz, G. Harold (ed.), *Sources of Four Plays Ascribed to Shakespeare: 'The Reign of King Edward III,' 'Sir Thomas More,' 'The History of Cardenio,' 'The Two Noble Kinsmen'* (Columbia: University of Missouri Press, 1989).

Monsarrat, G. D., '*A Funeral Elegy*: Ford, W.S., and Shakespeare', *The Review of English Studies* 53 (2002), 186–203.

Oliphant, E. H. C., 'How Not to Play the Game of Parallels', *Journal of English and German Philology* 28 (1929), 1–15.

Palmer, Philip, '*Edmond Ironside* and the Question of Shakepearean Authorship', in Craig and Kinney (eds.), *Shakespeare, Computers, and the Mystery of Authorship*, 100–115.

Pendleton, Thomas A., 'The Non-Shakespearian Language of "Shall I Die?" ', *The Review of English Studies* 40 (1989), 323–51.

Pollard, Alfred W. (ed.), *Shakespeare's Hand in the Play of 'Sir Thomas More': Papers* (Cambridge: Cambridge University Press, 1923).

Posner, Michael, 'Rethinking Shakespeare', *Queen's Quarterly* 115 (2008), 247–59.

Schoenbaum, S., *Internal Evidence and Elizabethan Dramatic Authorship: An Essay in Literary History and Method* (London: Edward Arnold, 1966).

——, *Shakespeare's Lives*, new edn. (Oxford: Clarendon Press, 1991).

Sharon-Zisser, Shirley (ed.), *Critical Essays on Shakespeare's 'A Lover's Complaint': Suffering Ecstasy* (London: Ashgate, 2006).

Stevenson, Warren, *Shakespeare's Additions to Thomas Kyd's 'The Spanish Tragedy': A Fresh Look at the Evidence Regarding the 1602 Additions* (Lewiston, NY: Edwin Mellen, 2008).

Taylor, Gary, *Reinventing Shakespeare: A Cultural History, from the Restoration to the Present* (New York: Weidenfeld & Nicolson, 1989).

Vickers, Brian, *Shakespeare, 'A Lover's Complaint', and John Davies of Hereford* (Cambridge: Cambridge University Press, 2007).

——, *Shakespeare, Co-Author: A Historical Study of Five Collaborative Plays* (Oxford: Oxford University Press, 2002).

——, 'Thomas Kyd, Secret Sharer', *Times Literary Supplement* (18 April 2008), 13–15.

Watt, Timothy Irish, 'The Authorship of the Hand-D Addition to *The Book of Sir Thomas More*', in Craig and Kinney (eds.), *Shakespeare, Computers, and the Mystery of Authorship*. 134–61.

WATT, TIMOTHY IRISH, 'The Authorship of *The Raigne of Edward the Third*', in Craig and Kinney (eds.), *Shakespeare, Computers, and the Mystery of Authorship*, 116–32.

WELLS, STANLEY, and GARY TAYLOR (eds.), *The Complete Oxford Shakespeare*, 3 vols. (Oxford: Clarendon Press, 1987).

—— ——, *William Shakespeare: A Textual Companion* (Oxford: Clarendon Press, 1987).

WILLIAMS, ROBIN P., *Sweet Swan of Avon: Did a Woman Write Shakespeare?* (Berkeley, CA: Peachpit Press, 2006).

CHAPTER 2 COLLABORATION

BENTLEY, GERALD EADES, *The Profession of Dramatist in Shakespeare's Time, 1590–1642* (Princeton, NJ: Princeton University Press, 1971).

BRAUNMULLER, A. R., and MICHAEL HATTAWAY (eds.), *The Cambridge Companion to English Renaissance Drama* (Cambridge: Cambridge University Press, 1990).

BURNS, EDWARD (ed.), *King Henry VI Part 1* (London: Arden Shakespeare, 2000).

CARROLL, JAYNE M., and MacD. P. JACKSON, 'Shakespeare, *Arden of Faversham*, and "Literature Online"', *Shakespeare Newsletter* 54 (2004), 3–4, 6.

CHAMBERS, E. K., *William Shakespeare: A Study of Facts and Problems*, 2 vols. (Oxford: Clarendon Press, 1930).

——, *The Elizabethan Stage*, 4 vols. (Oxford: Clarendon Press, 1923).

CHAMBERS, R. W., 'Shakespeare and the Play of *More*', in *Man's Unconquerable Mind* (London: Cape, 1939, rpt. 1952), 204–49.

CRAIG, HUGH, and ARTHUR F. KINNEY (eds.), *Shakespeare, Computers, and the Mystery of Authorship* (Cambridge: Cambridge University Press, 2009).

DAWSON, ANTONY B., and GRETCHEN E. MINTON (eds.), *Timon of Athens* (London: Arden Shakespeare, 2008).

EDWARDS, PHILIP, *Shakespeare and the Confines of Art* (London: Methuen, 1968).

ELLIOTT, WARD E. Y., and ROBERT J. VALENZA, 'Two tough nuts to crack: Did Shakespeare write the "Shakespeare" portions of *Sir Thomas More* and *Edward III*? Part 1 and Part II: Conclusion', *Literary and Linguistic Computing* 25 (2010), 67–83, 165–77.

HARBAGE, ALFRED, and S. SCHOENBAUM (rev. edn.), *Annals of English Drama 975–1700* (London: Methuen, 1964).

HOPE, JONATHAN, *The Authorship of Shakespeare's Plays* (Cambridge: Cambridge University Press, 1994).

JACKSON, MACDONALD P., 'Compound Adjectives in *Arden of Faversham*', *Notes and Queries* 250 (2006), 51–5.

——, *Defining Shakespeare: 'Pericles' as Test Case* (Oxford: Oxford University Press, 2003).

——, 'Determining Authorship: A New Technique', *Research Opportunities in Renaissance Drama* 41 (2002), 1–14.

——, 'Is "Hand D" of *Sir Thomas More* Shakespeare's? Thomas Bayes and the Elliott–Valenza Authorship Tests', *Early Modern Literary Studies* 12.3 (2007), 11–36, http://purl.oclc.org/emls/12-3/jackbaye.htm.

——, 'Shakespeare and the Quarrel Scene in *Arden of Faversham*', *Shakespeare Quarterly* 57 (2006), 249–93.

——, 'Shakespearean Features of the Poetic Style of *Arden of Faversham*', *Archiv für das Studium der neueren Sprachen und Literaturen* 230 (1993), 279–304.

——, 'The Date and Authorship of Hand D's Contribution to *Sir Thomas More*: Evidence from "Literature Online"', *Shakespeare Survey* 59 (2006), 69–78.

KNAPP, JEFFREY, 'What is a Co-Author?', *Representations* 89 (2005), 1–29.

——. 'Shakespeare as Coauthor', *Shakespeare Studies* 36 (2008), 49–59.

LEECH, CLIFFORD, *The John Fletcher Plays* (London: Chatto & Windus, 1962).

LOVE, HAROLD, *Attributing Authorship: An Introduction* (Cambridge: Cambridge University Press, 2002).

McGUIRE, PHILIP C., 'Collaboration', in Arthur F. Kinney (ed.), *A Companion to Renaissance Drama* (Oxford: Blackwell, 2002), 540–52.

MASTEN, JEFFREY, *Textual Intercourse: Collaboration, Authorship, and Sexualities in Renaissance Drama* (Cambridge: Cambridge University Press, 1997).

MAXWELL, J. C. (ed.), *Henry the Eighth* (Cambridge: Cambridge University Press, 1962).

MELCHIORI, GIORGIO (ed.), *King Edward III* (Cambridge: Cambridge University Press, 1998).

MERRIAM, THOMAS, 'Edward III', *Literary and Linguistic Computing* 15 (2000), 157–86.

METZ, G. HAROLD (ed.), *Sources of Four Plays Ascribed to Shakespeare* (Columbia: University of Missouri Press, 1989).

MINCOFF, MARCO, 'Henry VIII and Fletcher', *Shakespeare Quarterly* 12 (1961), 239–60.

MUIR, KENNETH, *Shakespeare as Collaborator* (London: Methuen, 1960).

POOLER, C. KNOX (ed.), *The Famous History of the Life of King Henry VIII* (London: Methuen, 1915).

SWINBURNE, ALGERNON CHARLES, *A Study of Shakespeare* (London, Chatto & Windus, 1879; Heinemann, 1918).

TARLINSKAJA, MARINA, 'Looking for Shakespeare in *Edward III*', forthcoming in *Shakespeare Yearbook* (private communication, Sept. 2009).

TAYLOR, GARY, 'Shakespeare and Others: The Authorship of *Henry the Sixth, Part One*', *Medieval and Renaissance Drama in England* 7 (1995), 145–205.

——, and JOHN LAVAGNINO (eds.), *Thomas Middleton and Early Modern Textual Culture: A Companion to the Collected Works* (Oxford: Clarendon Press, 2007).

——, and JOHN LAVAGNINO (eds.), *Thomas Middleton: The Collected Works* (Oxford: Clarendon Press 2007).

TIMBERLAKE, PHILIP W., *The Feminine Ending in English Blank Verse: A Study of its Use by Early Writers in the Measure and its Development in the Drama up to the Year 1595* (Menasha, WI: George Banta, 1931).

VICKERS, BRIAN, 'Incomplete Shakespeare: Or, Denying Coauthorship in *1 Henry IV*', *Shakespeare Quarterly* 58 (2007), 311–52.

——, *Shakespeare, Co-Author: A Historical Study of Five Collaborative Plays* (Oxford: Oxford University Press, 2002).

VINCENT, PAUL, *When 'harey' Met Shakespeare: The Genesis of the First Part of Henry the Sixth* (Saarbrücken: DVM Verlag Dr Müller, 2008).

WAITH, EUGENE (ed.), *The Two Noble Kinsmen* (Oxford: Clarendon Press, 1989).

WELLS, STANLEY, and GARY TAYLOR (eds.), *William Shakespeare: The Complete Works* (Oxford: Clarendon Press, 1986; 2nd edn. 2005).

——, with JOHN JOWETT and WILLIAM MONTGOMERY, *William Shakespeare: A Textual Companion* (Oxford: Clarendon Press, 1987).

WINE, M. L. (ed.), *The Tragedy of Arden of Faversham* (London: Methuen, 1973).

CHAPTER 3 MANUSCRIPT CIRCULATION

BAKER, JOHN, 'Found: Shakespeare's Manuscript of *Henry IV*', *Elizabethan Review* 4 (1996), 14–46.

BEAL, PETER (comp.), *Index of Early Modern English Literary Manuscripts*, vol. 1, pt. 2: 1450–1625 (London: Mansell, 1980).

BROWN, CEDRIC C., and ARTHUR F. MAROTTI (eds.), *Texts and Cultural Change in Early Modern England* (Basingstoke: Palgrave Macmillan, 1997).

BURROW, COLIN (ed.), *The Complete Sonnets and Poems*, The Oxford Shakespeare (Oxford: Oxford University Press, 2002).

CRANE, MARY THOMAS, *Framing Authority: Sayings, Self, and Society in Sixteenth-Century England* (Princeton, NJ: Princeton University Press, 1997).

DE GRAZIA, MARGRETA, and PETER STALLYBRASS, 'The Materiality of the Shakespearean Text', *Shakespeare Quarterly* 14.3 (Fall 1993), 255–83.

DUNCAN-JONES, KATHERINE (ed.), *Shakespeare's Sonnets*, The Arden Shakespeare (London: Thomson Learning, 1997).

EMSLIE, MACDONALD, 'Pepys' Shakespeare Song', *Shakespeare Quarterly* 6.2 (1955), 159–70.

ERNE, LUKAS, *Shakespeare as Literary Dramatist* (Cambridge: Cambridge University Press, 2003).

EVANS, G. BLAKEMORE, 'Shakespeare's *Julius Caesar*—A Seventeenth-Century Manuscript', *Journal of English and Germanic Philology* 41 (1942), 401–17.

——, 'The Douai Manuscript—Six Shakespearean Transcripts (1694–95)', *Philological Quarterly* 41 (1962), 158–72.

——, 'The Merry Wives of Windsor: The Folger Manuscript', in Bernhard Fabian and Kurt Tetzeli von Rosador (eds.), *Shakespeare, Text, Language, Criticism: Essays in Honor of Martin Spevack* (Zurich and New York: Olms-Weidman, 1987), 57–79.

EVANS, WILLA MCCLUNG, 'Lawes' Version of Shakespeare's Sonnet CXVI', *PMLA* 51.1 (1936), 120–22.

GABRIELI, VITTORIO, and GIORGIO MELCHIORI (eds.), *Sir Thomas More* (Manchester: Manchester University Press, 1990).

HAO, TIANHU, '*Hesperides, or the Muses' Garden*: Commonplace Reading and Writing in Early Modern England' (PhD dissertation, Columbia University, 2006).

HEDBÄCK, ANN-MARI, 'The Douai Manuscript Reexamined', *Papers of the Bibliographical Society of America* 73.1 (1979), 1–18.

HOBBS, MARY, *Early Seventeenth-Century Verse Miscellany Manuscripts* (Aldershot: Ashgate, 1992).

——, 'Shakespeare's Sonnet II: A "sugred sonnet"?', *Notes and Queries* 224 (1979), 112–13.

HUNTER, G. K., 'The Marking of *Sententiae* in Elizabethan Printed Plays, Poems, and Romances', *The Library* 6, nos. 3–4 (1951), 171–88.

JORGENS, ELISE BICKFORD, *English Song 1600–1675: Facsimiles of Twenty-six Manuscripts and an Edition of the Text* (New York: Garland, 1987).

JOWETT, JOHN, WILLIAM MONTGOMERY, GARY TAYLOR, and STANLEY WELLS (eds.), *The Oxford Shakespeare: The Complete Works* (Oxford: Clarendon Press, 2005).

KELLIHER, HILTON, 'Unrecorded Extracts from Shakespeare, Sidney, and Dyer', *English Manuscript Studies 1100–1700* 2 (1990), 163–88.

KERRIGAN, JOHN (ed.), *The Sonnets and A Lover's Complaint* (New York: Viking, 1986).

KIRSCH, ARTHUR C., 'A Caroline Commentary on the Drama', *Modern Philology* 66.3 (1969), 256–61.

LEVIN, RICHARD, 'The Longleat Manuscript and *Titus Andronicus*', *Shakespeare Quarterly* 53.3 (2002), 323–40.

LONG, JOHN H., *Shakespeare's Use of Music: The Histories and the Tragedies* (Gainesville: University of Florida Press, 1971).

MARCUS, LEAH, 'The Veil of Manuscript', *Renaissance Drama*, New Series 30 (1999–2000), 115–31.

MAROTTI, ARTHUR F., 'Shakespeare's Sonnets and the Manuscript Circulation of Texts in Early Modern England', in Michael Schoenfeldt (ed.), *A Companion to Shakespeare's Sonnets* (Oxford: Blackwell, 2007), 185–203.

——, 'The Cultural and Textual Importance of Folger MS V.a.89', *English Manuscript Studies 1100–1700* 11 (2002), 70–92.

MASTEN, JEFFREY, *Textual Intercourse: Collaboration, Authorship, and Sexualities in Renaissance Drama* (Cambridge: Cambridge University Press, 1997).

MCMANAWAY, JAMES G., 'Excerpta Quaedam per A. W. Adolescentem', in Thomas P. Harrison et al. (eds.), *Studies in Honor of DeWitt T. Starnes* (Austin: University of Texas Press, 1967), 117–29.

MERES, FRANCIS, *Palladius Tamia* (1598), in G. Gregory Smith (ed.), *Elizabethan Critical Essays*, vol. 2 (Oxford: Oxford University Press, 1904).

MOSS, ANN, *Printed Commonplace Books and the Structuring of Renaissance Thought* (Oxford: Clarendon Press, 1996).

PALFREY, SIMON, and TIFFANY STERN, *Shakespeare in Parts* (Oxford: Oxford University Press, 2007).

REDDING, DAVID COLEMAN, 'Robert Bishop's Commonplace Book: An Edition of a Seventeenth-Century Miscellany' (PhD dissertation, University of Pennsylvania, 1960).

REES, JULIET, 'Shakespeare and Edward Pudsey's Booke, 1600', *Notes & Queries* 39.3 (1992), 330–31.

——, (née GOWAN), 'An Edition of Edward Pudsey's Commonplace Book (c. 1600–1615) from the Manuscript in the Bodleian Library' (MPhil Thesis, University of London, 1967).

ROBERTS, SASHA, *Reading Shakespeare's Poems in Early Modern England* (Basingstoke: Palgrave Macmillan, 2003).

SENG, PETER J., *The Vocal Songs in the Plays of Shakespeare: A Critical History* (Cambridge, MA: Harvard University Press, 1967).

STALLYBRASS, PETER, et al., 'Hamlet's Tables and the Technologies of Writing in Renaissance England', *Shakespeare Quarterly* 55.4 (2004), 379–419.

STERN, TIFFANY, *Making Shakespeare: From Stage to Page* (New York: Routledge, 2004).

TAYLOR, GARY, 'Some Manuscripts of Shakespeare's Sonnets', *Bulletin of the John Rylands Library* 68 (1985–86), 210–46.

WILLIAMS, GEORGE WALTON, and GWYNNE BLAKEMORE EVANS (eds.), *The History of King Henry the Fourth, as revised by Sir Edward Dering, Bart.* (Charlottesville: University of Virginia Press, 1974).

WOUDHUYSEN, HENRY, 'The Foundations of Shakespeare's Text', *Proceedings of the British Academy* 125 (2004), 69–100.

YEANDLE, LAETITIA, 'The Dating of Sir Edward Dering's Copy of "The history of King Henry the Fourth"', *Shakespeare Quarterly* 37.2 (1986), 224–26.

CHAPTER 4 QUARTO AND FOLIO

BATE, JONATHAN, and ERIC RASMUSSEN (eds.), *William Shakespeare, Complete Works: The RSC Shakespeare* (London: Macmillan, 2007).

BRANAGH, KENNETH, *Hamlet: Screenplay and Introduction* (London: Chatto & Windus, 1996).

DESSEN, ALAN C., and LESLIE THOMPSON, *A Dictionary of Stage Directions in English Drama, 1580-1642* (Cambridge: Cambridge University Press, 1999).

ELAM, KEIR (ed.), *Twelfth Night* (London: Cengage Learning, 2008).

ERNE, LUKAS, *Shakespeare as Literary Dramatist* (Cambridge: Cambridge University Press, 2003).

GREENBLATT, STEPHEN, WALTER COHEN, JEAN E. HOWARD, and KATHARINE EISAMAN MAUS (eds.), *The Norton Shakespeare based on the Oxford Edition* (New York: Norton, 1997).

JENKINS, HAROLD (ed.), *Hamlet*, Arden Shakespeare, 2nd series (London: Methuen, 1982).

HOWARD, TONY, 'Tragedy Transplanted', *Around the Globe* 23 (Spring 2003), 28–29.

MAGUIRE, LAURIE E., *Shakespearean Suspect Texts: The 'Bad' Quartos and their Contexts* (Cambridge: Cambridge University Press, 1996).

MARCUS, LEAH, *Unediting the Renaissance: Shakespeare, Marlowe, Milton* (New York: Routledge, 1996).

MOWAT, BARBARA, 'The Form of *Hamlet*'s Fortunes', *Renaissance Drama* 19 (1988), 97–126.

ROSENBAUM, ROD, 'Shakespeare in Rewrite', *The New Yorker* (13 May 2002), 68–77.

TAYLOR, GARY, and MICHAEL WARREN (eds.), *The Division of the Kingdoms: Shakespeare's Two Versions of 'King Lear'* (Oxford: Clarendon Press, 1983).

TAYLOR, GARY, et al. (eds.), *Collected Works of Thomas Middleton*, 2 vols. (Oxford: Oxford University Press, 2007).

THOMPSON, ANN, and NEIL TAYLOR (eds.), *Hamlet*, The Arden Shakespeare, 3rd series (London: Thomson Learning, 2006).

—— —— (eds.), *Hamlet: The Texts of 1603 and 1623*, The Arden Shakespeare, 3rd series (London: Thomson Learning, 2006).

VAUGHAN, VIRGINIA MASON, and ALDEN T. VAUGHAN (eds.), *The Tempest* (London: Thomas Nelson, 1999).

WELLS, STANLEY, *Re-editing Shakespeare for the Modern Reader* (Oxford: Oxford University Press, 1984).

——, and GARY TAYLOR (gen. eds.), *William Shakespeare: The Complete Works* (Oxford: Clarendon Press, 1986).

—— —— ——. *William Shakespeare: A Textual Companion* (Oxford: Clarendon Press, 1987).

——, 'The Oxford Shakespeare Re-viewed by the General Editors', *Analytical and Enumerative Bibliography* 4 (1990), 6–20.

CHAPTER 5 REVISION

ADAMS, JOSEPH QUINCY (ed.), *The Dramatic Records of Sir Henry Herbert, Master of the Revels, 1623-1673* (New Haven, CT: Yale University Press, 1917).

BALE, JOHN, *John Bale's King Johan*, Barry B. Adams (ed.) (San Marino, CA: Huntington Library Press, 1969).

BAWCUTT, N. W. (ed.), *The Control and Censorship of Caroline Drama, The Records of Sir Henry Herbert, Master of the Revels: 1623-73* (Oxford: Clarendon Press, 1996).

BENTLEY, G. E., *The Profession of Dramatist 1590-1642* (Princeton, NJ: Princeton University Press, 1971).

BLAYNEY, PETER W. M., 'The *Booke of Sir Thomas Moore* Re-Examined', *Studies in Philology* 69 (1972), 167–91.

——, *The Printing of Playbooks*, in John D. Cox and David Scott Kastan (ed.), *A New History of Early English Drama* (New York: Columbia University Press, 1997), 383–422.

FOAKES, R. A., *Hamlet versus Lear: Cultural Politics and Shakespeare's Art* (Cambridge: Cambridge University Press, 1993).

GLAPTHORNE, HENRY. *The Lady Mother by Henry Glapthorne*, Arthur Brown (ed.) (Oxford: Oxford University Press), 1959.

GREENE, ROBERT. *The Historie of Orlando Furioso* (London: John Dante for Cuthbert Burbie, 1594).

GREGG, W. W. (ed.), *The Book of Sir Thomas More* (Oxford: Oxford University Press, 1911).

——, 'Massinger's Autograph Corrections in *The Duke of Milan*', and 'More Massinger Corrections', in J. C. Maxwell (ed.), *Collected Papers* (Oxford: Clarendon Press, 1966), 110–148.

——, *The Shakespeare First Folio* (Oxford: Clarendon Press, 1955).

——, *Two Elizabethan Stage Abridgements: The Battle of Alcazar & Orlando Furioso* (Oxford: Clarendon Press, 1923).

——, *Collections Vol. II. Part III* (Oxford: Oxford University Press, 1931; rpt. New York: AMS Press, 1985).

GURR, ANDREW J., *The Shakespeare Company, 1594–1642* (Cambridge: Cambridge University Press, 2004).

HAAKER, ANN, 'The Plague, the Theater and the Poet', *Renaissance Drama*, ns. 1 (1968), 283–306.

HENSLOWE-ALLEYN DIGITISATION PROJECT: www.henslowe-alleyn.org.uk.

Henslowe's Diary, R. A. Foakes (ed.), 2nd ed. (Cambridge: Cambridge University Press, 2002).

HEYWOOD, THOMAS, *The Captives by Thomas Heywood*, Arthur Brown (ed.) (Oxford: Oxford University Press, 1953).

——, *The Escapes of Jupiter*, Henry D. Janzen (ed.) (Oxford: Oxford University Press, 1978).

HONIGMANN, E. A. J., *The Stability of Shakespeare's Text* (London: E. Arnold, 1965).

HOWARD-HILL, T. H., 'Crane's 1619 "Promptbook" of *Barnavelt* and Theatrical Processes', *Modern Philology* 86 (1988), 146–70.

——, 'Ralph Crane, Shakespeare's Earliest Editor', *Shakespeare Survey* 44 (1992), 113–29.

IOPPOLO, GRACE, *Dramatists and their Manuscripts in the Age Shakespeare, Jonson, Middleton and Heywood: Authorship, Authority and the Playhouse* (London: Routledge, 2006).

——, *Revising Shakespeare* (Cambridge, MA: Harvard University Press, 1991).

JONSON, BEN, *Poetaster* (London: 1602).

——, *The Works of Beniamin Jonson* (London, 1616).

——, *Bartholomew Fair*, in *The Works of Benjamin Jonson: The Second Volume* (London: 1640).

——, *The Gypsies Metamorphosed*, George Watson Cole (ed.) (New York: MLA, 1931).

LEVER, J. W., and G. R. PROUDFOOD (eds.), *The Wasp or Subjects Precedent* (Oxford: Oxford University Press, 1976).

MASSINGER, PHILIP, *Believe as You List by Philip Massinger*, C. J. Sisson (ed.) (Oxford: Oxford University Press, 1927).

MCMILLIN, SCOTT, *The Elizabethan Theatre and The Book of Sir Thomas More* (Ithaca, NY: Cornell University Press, 1987).

MIDDLETON, THOMAS, *Hengist, King of Kent by Thomas Middleton*, Grace Ioppolo (ed.) (Oxford: Oxford University Press, 2004).

RENWICK, WILLIAM LINSDAY, and W. W. GREG (eds.), *John of Bordeaux* (Oxford: Oxford University Press, 1936).

SHAKESPEARE, WILLIAM, *A Midsommer nights dreame* (London: 1600).

SHAKESPEARE, WILLIAM, *A Midsummer Night's Dream*, Arthur Quiller-Couch and John Dover Wilson (eds.) (Cambridge: Cambridge University Press, 1924).

——, *The Second part of Henrie the fourth* (London: 1600).

——, *The Tragicall Historie of Hamlet* (London: 1603).

——, *The Tragicall Historie of Hamlet* (London: 1604).

——, *Mr William Shak-speare: His True Chronicle Historie of the life and death of King Lear and his three Daughters* (London: 1608).

——, *Mr William Shakespeares Comedies, Histories & Tragedies* (London: 1623).

TAYLOR, GARY, and MICHAEL WARREN (eds.), *The Division of the Kingdoms: Shakespeare's Two Versions of 'King Lear'* (Oxford: Oxford University Press, 1986).

URKOWTIZ, STEVEN, *Shakespeare's Revision of King Lear* (Princeton, NJ: Princeton University Press, 1980).

WELLS, STANLEY, GARY TAYLOR, JOHN JOWETT and WILLIAM MONTGOMERY, *William Shakespeare: A Textual Companion* (Oxford: Clarendon Press, 1987).

WICKHAM, GLYNNE, HERBERT BERRY and WILLIAM INGRAM, *English Professional Theatre 1530–1660* (Cambridge: Cambridge University Press, 2000).

CHAPTER 6 DRAMATIC METRE

BARISH, JONAS, 'Mixed Prose-Verse Scenes in Shakespearean Tragedy', in W. R. Elton and William B. Long (eds.), *Shakespeare and Dramatic Tradition: Essays in Honor of S. F. Johnson* (Newark: University of Delaware Press, 1989), 32–46.

BAXTER, JOHN. *Shakespeare Poetic Styles: Verse into Drama* (London: Routledge, 1980).

BROOK, G. L., *The Language of Shakespeare* (London: Deutsch, 1976).

CHENEY, PATRICK, 'Poetry in Shakespeare's Plays', in Patrick Cheney (ed.), *The Cambridge Companion to Shakespeare's Poetry* (Cambridge: Cambridge University Press, 2007), 221–40.

HALLIDAY, F. E., *The Poetry of Shakespeare's Plays* (New York: Barnes & Noble, 1964).

HARDISON, O. B., *Prosody and Purpose in the English Renaissance* (Baltimore MD: The Johns Hopkins University Press, 1989).

HUDSON, KENNETH, 'Shakespeare's Use of Colloquial Language', *Shakespeare Survey* 23 (1970), 39–48.

HYLAND, PETER, *An Introduction to Shakespeare's Poems* (New York: Palgrave Macmillan, 2003).

McDONALD, RUSS, *Shakespeare and the Arts of Language* (Oxford: Oxford University Press, 2001).

——, 'Shakespeare's Verse', in Stanley Wells and Lena Cowen Orlin (eds.), *Shakespeare: An Oxford Guide* (Oxford: Oxford University Press, 2003), 79–92.

MUIR, KENNETH, 'Shakespeare and the Metamorphosis of the Pentameter', *Shakespeare Survey* 50 (1997), 147–50.

——, 'Shakespeare the Professional', *Shakespeare Survey* 24 (1971), 37–46.

SIPE, DOROTHY L., *Shakespeare's Metrics* (New Haven, CT: Yale University Press, 1968).

SPOLSKY, ELLEN, 'The Limits of Literal Meaning', *New Literary History* 19 (1988), 419–40.

TARLINSKAJA, MARINA, *Shakespeare's Verse: Iambic Pentameter and the Poet's Idiosyncrasies* (New York: Peter Lang, 1987).

VICKERS, BRIAN, *The Artistry of Shakespeare's Prose* (London: Routledge, 1979).

WOMACK, MARK, 'Shakespearean Prosody Unbound', *Texas Studies in Literature and Language* 45.1 (Spring 2003), 1–19.

WRIGHT, GEORGE T., 'Shakespeare's Metre Scanned', in Sylvia Adamson, et al. (eds.), *Reading Shakespeare's Dramatic Language: A Guide* (London: Thomson Learning, 2001), 51–70.

——, *Shakespeare's Metrical Art* (Berkeley: University of California Press, 1988).

——, 'Troubles of a Professional Meter Reader', in Russ McDonald (ed.), *Shakespeare Reread: The Texts in New Contexts* (Ithaca, NY: Cornell University Press, 1994), 56–76.

CHAPTER 7 BOOK TRADE

BLAYNEY, PETER W. M., *The First Folio of Shakespeare* (Washington, DC: Folger Shakespeare Library, 1991).

——, 'The Publication of Playbooks', in John D. Cox and David Scott Kastan, (eds.), *A New History of Early English Drama* (New York: Columbia University Press, 1997), 383–422.

BRAYMAN HACKEL, HEIDI, *Reading Material in Early Modern England: Print, Gender, and Literacy* (Cambridge: Cambridge University Press, 2005).

BROOKS, DOUGLAS, *From Playhouse to Printing House* (Cambridge: Cambridge University Press, 2000).

CHARTIER, ROGER, and PETER STALLYBRASS, 'Reading and Authorship: The Circulation of Shakespeare 1590–1619', in Andrew Murphy (ed.), *A Concise Companion to Shakespeare and the Text* (Oxford: Blackwell, 2007), 35–56.

CHENEY, PATRICK, *Shakespeare's Literary Authorship* (Cambridge: Cambridge University Press, 2008).

——, *Shakespeare, National Poet-Playwright* (Cambridge: Cambridge University Press, 2004).

DE GRAZIA, MARGRETA, and PETER STALLYBRASS, 'The Materiality of the Shakespearean Text', *Shakespeare Quarterly* 44.3 (1993), 255–83.

ERNE, LUKAS, *Shakespeare as Literary Dramatist* (Cambridge: Cambridge University Press, 2003).

FARMER, ALAN B., and ZACHARY LESSER, 'The Popularity of Playbooks Revisited', *Shakespeare Quarterly* 56.1 (2005), 1–32.

HOOKS, ADAM G., 'Booksellers' Catalogues and the Classification of Printed Drama in Seventeenth-Century England', *Papers of the Bibliographical Society of America* 102.4 (2008), 445–64.

JOWETT, JOHN, *Shakespeare and Text* (Oxford: Oxford University Press, 2007).

KASTAN, DAVID SCOTT, *Shakespeare After Theory* (New York: Routledge, 1999).

——, *Shakespeare and the Book* (Cambridge: Cambridge University Press, 2001).

LESSER, ZACHARY, *Renaissance Drama and the Politics of Publication* (Cambridge: Cambridge University Press, 2004).

MAGUIRE, LAURIE, *Shakespearean Suspect Texts: The 'Bad' Quartos and their Contexts* (Cambridge: Cambridge University Press, 1996).

MASSAI, SONIA, *Shakespeare and the Rise of the Editor* (Cambridge: Cambridge University Press, 2007).

MASTEN, JEFFREY, *Textual Intercourse: Collaboration, Authorship, and Sexualities in Renaissance Drama* (Cambridge: Cambridge University Press, 1997).

MERES, FRANCIS, *Palladis Tamia* (London: 1598).

MURPHY, ANDREW, *Shakespeare in Print* (Cambridge: Cambridge University Press, 2003).

PRYNNE, WILLIAM, *Histrio-Mastix* (London, 1633).

ROBERTS, SASHA, *Reading Shakespeare's Poems in Early Modern England* (Basingstoke: Palgrave Macmillan, 2003).

STERN, TIFFANY, *Making Shakespeare: From Stage to Page* (New York: Routledge, 2004).

STRAZNICKY, MARTA (ed.), *The Book of the Play: Playwrights, Stationers, and Readers in Early Modern England* (Amherst: University of Massachusetts Press, 2006).

TAYLOR, GARY, and STANLEY WELLS (eds.), *William Shakespeare: A Textual Companion* (Oxford: Oxford University Press, 1987).

WEST, ANTHONY JAMES, *The Shakespeare First Folio: The History of the Book*, 2 vols. (Oxford: Oxford University Press, 2001–2003).

WRIGHT, THOMAS, *The Passions of the Minde* (London: 1601).

CHAPTER 8 EARLY READERS

BATE, JONATHAN (ed.), *Titus Andronicus*, the Arden Shakespeare, 3rd Series (London and New York: Routledge, 1995).

BLAYNEY, PETER, 'The Publication of Playbooks', in John D. Cox and David Scott Kastan (eds.), *A New History of Early English Drama* (New York: Columbia University Press, 1997).

——, 'The Alleged Popularity of Playbooks', *Shakespeare Quarterly* 56 (2005), 32–50.

BURROW, COLIN (ed.), *Complete Sonnets and Poems*, The Oxford Shakespeare (Oxford: Oxford University Press, 2002).

CORMACK, BRADIN, and CARLA MAZZIO, *Book Use, Book Theory: 1500–1700* (Chicago, IL: University of Chicago Press, 2005).

DE GRAZIA, MARGRETA, 'Shakespeare in Quotation Marks', in Jean I. Marsden (ed.), *The Appropriation of Shakespeare: Post-Renaissance Reconstructions of the Works and the Myth* (New York: St. Martin's Press, 1991).

DOBSON, MICHAEL, *The Making of the National Poet: Shakespeare, Adaptation and Authorship, 1660–1769* (Oxford, Clarendon Press, 1992).

ECKHARDT, JOSHUA, *Manuscript Verse Collectors and the Politics of Anti-Courtly Love Poetry* (Oxford: Oxford University Press, 2009).

ERNE, LUKAS, 'The "Making" of Shakespeare', in his *Shakespeare as Literary Dramatist* (Cambridge: Cambridge University Press, 2003).

FARMER, ALAN B., 'Shakespeare, Revision, and the Ephemerality of Playbooks', delivered at the International Shakespeare Conference, Shakespeare Institute, Stratford-upon-Avon, Aug. 2008.

——, and ZACHARY LESSER, 'The Popularity of Playbooks Revisited', *Shakespeare Quarterly* 56 (2005), 1–32.

—— ——, 'Structures of Popularity in the Early Modern Book Trade', *Shakespeare Quarterly* 56 (2005), 206–13.

HACKEL, HEIDI BRAYMAN, *Reading Material in Early Modern England: Print, Gender, and Literacy* (Cambridge: Cambridge University Press, 2005).

HUNTER, GEORGE K., 'The Marking of Sententiae in Elizabethan Printed Plays, Poems, and Romances', in *The Library*, 5th ser., 6 (1951–1952), 171–88.

INGLEBY, CLEMENT MANSFIELD, *The Shakespeare Allusion Book*, 2 vols. (London: 1909).

KASTAN, DAVID SCOTT (ed.), *Henry IV, Part 1*, The Arden Shakespeare, 3rd Series (London: Thomson Learning, 2002).

——, 'Plays into Print: Shakespeare to His Earliest Readers', in Jennifer Andersen and Elizabeth Sauer (ed.), *Books and Readers in Early Modern England* (Philadelphia: University of Pennsylvania Press, 2002).

KELLIHER, HILTON, 'Contemporary Manuscript Extracts from Shakespeare's *1 Henry IV*', in *English Manuscript Studies*, vol. 1 (1988).

LENHAM, T. N. S., 'Sir Edward Dering's Collection of Playbooks, 1619–1624', *Shakespeare Quarterly* 16 (1965): 145–53.

LESSER, ZACHARY, and PETER STALLYBRASS, 'The First Literary *Hamlet* and the Commonplacing of Professional Plays', *Shakespeare Quarterly* 59 (2008): 371–420.

MACK, PETER, 'Rhetoric, Ethics and Reading in the Renaissance', *Renaissance Studies* 19 (2005): 1–21.

MAGUIRE, LAURIE, *Shakespearean Suspect Texts: The 'Bad' Quartos and their Context* (Cambridge: Cambridge University Press, 1996).

MASSAI, SONIA, *Shakespeare and the Rise of the Editor* (Cambridge: Cambridge University Press, 2007).

——, 'Editorial Pledges in Early Modern Dramatic Paratexts', in Helen Smith and Louise Wilson (eds.), *Renaissance Paratexts* (Cambridge: Cambridge University Press, 2011).

MAYER, JEAN-CHRISTOPHE, 'Shakespeare's Commonplacing Readers', delivered at the 'Shakespeare Reconfigured' Conference, University of York, Oct. 2009.

MOSS, ANN, *Printed Commonplace Books and the Structuring of Renaissance Thought* (Oxford: Clarendon Press, 1996).

ROBERTS, SASHA, *Reading Shakespeare's Poems in Early Modern England* (Basingstoke: Palgrave Mcmillan, 2003).

'Shakespeare in Quarto,' database, http://www.bl.uk/treasures/treasuresinfull.html.

SHARPE, KEVIN, *Reading Revolutions: The Politics of Reading in Early Modern England* (New Haven, CT: Yale University Press, 2000).

SHERMAN, WILLIAM H., *John Dee: The Politics of Reading and Writing in the English Renaissance* (Amherst: University of Massachusetts Press, 1995).

——, *Used Books: Marking Readers in Renaissance England* (Philadelphia: University of Pennsylvania Press, 2008).

STALLYBRASS, PETER, and ROGER CHARTIER, 'Reading and Authorship: The Circulation of Shakespeare, 1590–1619', in Andrew Murphy (ed.), *A Concise Companion to Shakespeare and the Text* (Oxford: Blackwell, 2007).

TAYLOR, GARY, 'Why Publish Shakespeare's Works?', in 'The McKenzie Lectures', delivered at the University of Oxford, Feb. 2006.

VICKERS, BRIAN, *Shakespeare, Co-Author: A Historical Study of Five Collaborative Plays* (Oxford: Oxford University Press, 2002).

WALCOTT, MACKENZIE EDWARD CHARLES, *The Memorials of Westminster* (London: 1851).

WERSTINE, PAUL, 'A Century of "Bad" Quartos', *Shakespeare Quarterly* 50 (1999), 310–33.

WEST, ANTHONY JAMES, *The Shakespeare First Folio: The History of the Book*, vol. 2, *A New Worldwide Census of First Folios* (Oxford: Oxford University Press, 2003).

WILSON, JOHN DOVER (ed.), *Titus Andronicus*, The New Shakespeare (Cambridge: Cambridge University Press, 1948).

WOUDHUYSEN, HENRY, 'Early Play Texts: Forms and Formes', in *In Arden: Editing Shakespeare, Essays in Honour of Richard Proudfoot* (London: Thomson Learning, 2003).

ZWICKER, STEVEN N., 'The constitution of opinion and the pacification of reading', in Kevin Sharpe and Zwicker (eds.), *Reading Society and Politics in Early Modern England* (Cambridge: Cambridge University Press, 2003).

CHAPTER 9 ECONOMY

AGNEW, JEAN-CHRISTOPHE, *Worlds Apart: The Market and the Theater in Anglo-American Thought, 1550–1750* (Cambridge: Cambridge University Press, 1986).

ARCHER, IAN W., 'Commerce and Consumption' in Norman Jones and Susan Doran (eds.), *The Elizabethan World* (New York: Routledge, 2011).

BEARMAN, ROBERT, 'John Shakespeare: A Papist or Just Penniless?', *Shakespeare Quarterly* 56 (2005): 411–33.

BEIER, A. L., and ROGER A. P. FINLAY, *London 1500–1700: The Making of the Metropolis* (London: Longman, 1986).

BRITNELL, RICHARD, *The Commercialisation of English Society 1000–1500*, 2nd edn. (Manchester: Manchester University Press, 1997).

BROCKBANK, PHILIP, *On Shakespeare: Jesus, Shakespeare, and Karl Marx, and other Essays* (Oxford: Blackwell, 1989).

BRUSTER, DOUGLAS, *Drama and the Market in the Age of Shakespeare* (Cambridge: Cambridge University Press, 1992).

——, 'On a Certain Tendency in Economic Criticism of Shakespeare', in Linda Woodbridge (ed.), *Money and the Age of Shakespeare* (Basingstoke: Palgrave Macmillan, 2003).

CERASANO, SUSAN, 'Edward Alleyn, 1566–1626', in Aileen Reid and Robert Maniwa (eds.), *Edward Alleyn: Elizabethan Actor, Jacobean Gentleman* (London: Dulwich Picture Gallery, 1994).

——, 'Theatre Entrepreneurs and Theatrical Economics', in Richard Dutton (ed.), *The Oxford Handbook of Early Modern Theatre* (Oxford: Oxford University Press, 2009).

CHAMBERS, E.K. (ed.), *William Shakespeare: A Study of Facts and Problems*, 2 vols. (Oxford: Clarendon Press, 1930).

CLARK, PETER (ed.), *The Cambridge Urban History of Britain*, Vol. 2: *1540–1840* (Cambridge: Cambridge University Press, 2000).

CLAY, C. G. A., *Economic Expansion and Social Change. England 1500–1700*, vol. 1: *People, land and Towns*; vol. 2: *Industry, Trade and Government* (Cambridge: Cambridge University Press, 1984).

DEKKER, THOMAS, *The Gull's Horn Book* (London: 1609).

DEWAR, MARY (ed.), Sir Thomas Smith. *De Republica Anglorum*, (London: 1605) (Cambridge: Cambridge University Press, 1982).

DUTTON, RICHARD (ed.), *The Oxford Handbook of Early Modern Theatre* (Oxford: Oxford University Press, 2009).

DYER, ALAN, 'Crisis and Recovery. Government and Society in Stratford, 1540–1640', in Robert Bearman (ed.), *The History of an English Borough. Stratford-upon-Avon, 1196–1996* (Stroud: Alan Sutton for the Shakespeare Birthplace Trust, 1997).

ECCLES, M., *Shakespeare in Warwickshire* (Madison: University of Wisconsin Press, 1961).

EDELEN, GEORGES (ed.), William Harrison's *The Description of England* (Ithaca, NY: Cornell University Press, 1968).

FLEAY, F., *Chronicle History of the London Stage 1559–1642* (London: Reeves and Turner, 1890).

FOAKES, R. A., and R. T. RICKERT (eds.), *Henslowe's Diary* (Cambridge: Cambridge University Press, 1961).

FOX, LEVI, (ed.), *Minutes and Accounts of the Corporation of Stratford-upon-Avon*, vol. 5: *1593–1598* (Stratford-upon-Avon, 1990).

FRIPP, E. I., *Master Richard Quyny. Bailiff of Stratford-upon-Avon and Friend of William Shakespeare* (London and New York: Oxford University Press, 1924).

GRADY, HUGH, 'Timon of Athens. The Dialectic of Usury, Nihilism and Art', in Richard Dutton and Jean E. Howard (eds.), *A Companion to Shakespeare's Works*, vol. 1: *The Tragedies* (Oxford: Blackwell, 2003), 430–51.

GRASSBY, RICHARD, 'The Personal Wealth of the Business Community in Seventeenth Century' London', *Economic History Review*, 2nd series, 23 (1970), 220–34.

GREENBLATT, STEPHEN, *Will in the World. How Shakespeare became Shakespeare* (New York: W. W. Norton, 2004).

GURR, ANDREW, *The Shakespeare Company, 1594–1642* (Cambridge: Cambridge University Press, 2004).

HALPERN, RICHARD, *The Poetics of Primitive Accumulation: Renaissance Culture and the Genealogy of Capital* (Ithaca, NY: Cornell University Press, 1991).

HARRIS, JONATHAN GIL, *Sick Economies. Drama, Mercantilism, and Disease in Shakespeare's England* (Philadelphia: University of Pennsylvania Press, 2004).

HAWKES, DAVID, *Idols of the Marketplace. Idolatry and Commodity Fetishism in English Literature, 1580–1700*, (Basingstoke: Palgrave Macmillan, 2001).

HAZLITT, W. C. (ed.), *The English Drama and Stage under the Tudor and Stuart princes, 1543–1664* (London, 1869).

HOLBROOK, PETER, 'Class X: Shakespeare, Class and the Comedies', in R. Dutton and J. E. Howard (eds.), *A Companion to Shakespeare's Works*, vol. 3: *The Comedies* (Oxford: Blackwell, 2003), 67–89.

HONIGMANN, E. A. J., 'There is a World Elsewhere': William Shakespeare, Businessman', in Werne Habicht, D. J. Palmer, and Roger Pringle (eds.), *Images of Shakespeare: Proceedings of the Third Congress of the International Shakespeare Association* (Newark: University of Delaware Press, 1988).

INGRAM, WILLIAM, *The Business of Playing: The Beginnings of Adult Professional Theater in Elizabethan London* (Ithaca, NY: Cornell University Press, 1992).

JONES, NORMAN, *God and the Moneylenders: Usury and Law in early Modern England* (Oxford: Blackwell, 1989).

KEENE, DEREK, 'Material London in Time and Space', in Lena Orlin (ed.), *Material London, c.1600* (Pittsburg: University of Pennsylvania Press, 2000).

KLEIN, KARL, (ed.), *Timon of Athens* (Cambridge: Cambridge University Press, 2001).

KNUTSON, R. L., *Playing Companies and Commerce in Shakespeare's Time* (Cambridge: Cambridge University Press, 2005).

KORDA, NATASHA, 'Household Property, Stage Property: Henslowe as pawnbroker', *Theatre Journal* 48 (1996), 85–95.

——, *Shakespeare's Domestic Economies: Gender and Property in Early Modern England* (Philadelphia: University of Pennsylvania Press, 2002).

LEINWAND, THEODORE, *Theatre, Finance and Society in Early Modern England* (Cambridge: Cambridge University Press, 1999).

Martin, J. W., 'A Warwickshire Market Town in Adversity: Stratford-upon-Avon in the Sixteenth and Seventeenth Centuries', *Midland History* 7 (1982), 26–41.

Muldrew, Craig, *The economy of obligation: the culture of credit and social relations in early modern England* (Basingstoke: Macmillan, 1998).

Orlin, Lena, *Private Matters and Public Culture in Early Modern England* (Ithaca, NY: Cornell University Press, 1994).

——, 'Shakespearean Comedy and Material Life', in R. Dutton and J. E. Howard (eds.), *A Companion to Shakespeare's Works*, vol. 3: *The Comedies* (Oxford: Blackwell, 2003), 159–81.

Overton, Mark, et al., *Production and Consumption in English Households, 1600–1750* (London: Routledge, 2004).

Palliser, D. M., *The Age of Elizabeth: England under the later Tudors 1547–1603*, 2nd edn. (London: Longman, 1992).

Palmer, B. D., 'Early Modern Mobility: Players, Payments, and Patrons', *Shakespeare Quarterly* 56 (2005), 259–305.

Perry, Curtis, 'Commerce, Community, and Nostalgia in *The Comedy of Errors*', in Linda Woodbridge (ed.), *Money and the Age of Shakespeare* (Basingstoke: Palgrave Macmillan, 2003), 39–51.

Scott, W. R., *The Constitution and Finance of English, Scottish, and Irish Joint Stock Companies to 1720*, 3 vols. (Cambridge: Cambridge University Press, 1910–12).

Shapiro, James, *1599: A Year in the Life of William Shakespeare* (London: Faber, 2005).

Shell, Marc, *Money, Language, and Thought: Literary and Philosophic Economics from the Medieval to the Modern Era* (Berkeley: University of California Press, 1982).

Shepard, Alexandra, 'Manhood, Credit and Patriarchy in Early Modern England c.1580–1640', *Past and Present* 167 (2000), 75–106.

——, *Meanings of Manhood in Early Modern England* (Oxford: Oxford University Press, 2003).

Skipp, V. H. T., *Crisis and Development: An Ecological Case Study of the Forest of Arden, 1570–1674* (Cambridge: Cambridge University Press, 1978).

Stewart, Alan, 'Shakespeare and the Carriers' *Shakespeare Quarterly* 58 (2007), 431–64.

Streitbger, W. R., 'Adult Playing Companies to 1583', in Richard Dutton (ed.), *The Oxford Handbook of Early Modern Theatre* (Oxford: Oxford University Press, 2009), 19–35.

Thirsk, Joan (ed.), *The Agrarian History of England and Wales*, vol. 4: *1500–1640*. (Cambridge: Cambridge University Press, 1967).

——, *Economic Policy and Projects: The Development of a Consumer Society in Early Modern England* (Oxford: Clarendon Press, 1975).

Wilson, Richard, *Will Power: Essays on Shakespearean authority* (Detroit, MI: Wayne State University Press, 1993).

Woodbridge, Linda (ed.), *Money and the Age of Shakespeare* (Basingstoke: Palgrave Macmillan, 2003).

Wrightson, Keith, *English Society 1580–1680* (London: Hutchinson, 1982).

——, *Earthly Necessities: Economic Lives in Early Modern Britain* (New Haven, CT: Yale University Press, 2000).

Xenophon *Treatise of householde*, John Allde (trans.) (London: 1573).

Chapter 10 Status

BARRY, JONATHAN, and CHRISTOPHER BROOK (eds.), *The Middling Sort of People: Culture, Society, and Politics in England, 1550–1800* (New York: St Martin's Press, 1994).

BEDNARZ, JAMES, *Shakespeare and the Poets' War* (New York: Columbia University Press, 2001).

BERRY, RALPH, *Shakespeare and Social Class* (Atlantic Highlands, NJ: Humanities Press International, 1988).

BURNETT, MARK THORNTON, *Masters and Servants in English Renaissance Drama and Culture: Authority and Obedience* (New York: St Martin's Press, 1997).

CARROLL, WILLIAM, *Fat King, Lean Beggar: Representations of Poverty in the Age of Shakespeare* (Ithaca, NY: Cornell University Press, 1996).

CRESSY, DAVID, 'Describing the Social Order of Elizabethan and Stuart England', *Literature and History* 3 (1976), 29–44.

DE GRAZIA, MARGRETA, 'The Ideology of Superfluous Things: *King Lear* as Period Piece', in de Grazia, Maureen Quilligan, and Peter Stallybrass (eds.), *Subject and Object in Renaissance Culture* (Cambridge: Cambridge University Press, 1996), 17–42.

DEWAR, MARY, 'A Question of Plagiarism: The "Harrison Chapters" in Sir Thomas Smith's *De Republica Anglorum*', *The Historical Journal* 22.4 (1979), 921–9.

DUNCAN-JONES, KATHERINE, *Ungentle Shakespeare: Scenes from His Life* (London: Arden, 2001).

EVETT, DAVID, *Discourses of Service in Shakespeare's England* (New York: Palgrave Macmillan, 2005).

GREENBLATT, STEPHEN, *Will in the World: How Shakespeare became Shakespeare* (New York: W. W. Norton, 2004).

GURR, ANDREW, *Playgoing in Shakespeare's London*, 2nd edn. (Cambridge: Cambridge University Press, 1996).

HELGERSON, RICHARD, *Forms of Nationhood: The Elizabethan Writing of England* (Chicago, IL: University of Chicago Press, 1992).

HONIGMANN, E. A. J., '"There is a World Elsewhere": William Shakespeare, Businessman', Werner Habicht, D. J. Palmer, Roger Pringle (eds.), *Images of Shakespeare: Proceedings of the Third Congress of the International Shakespeare Association* (London: Associated University Presses, 1988), 40–6.

HOWARD, JEAN E., *The Stage and Social Struggle in Early Modern England* (New York: Routledge, 1994).

JONSON, BEN, *Every Man Out of his Humour*, Helen Ostovich (ed.) (Manchester: Manchester University Press, 2001).

KASTAN, DAVID SCOTT, 'Is There a Class in This (Shakespearean) Text?' *Renaissance Drama* 24 (1993), 101–21.

KEARNEY, JAMES, 'Idleness', in Brian Cummings and James Simpson (eds.) *Cultural Reformations: Medieval and Renaissance in Literary History* (Oxford: Oxford University Press, 2010), 570–88.

LASLETT, PETER, *The World We have Lost* (New York: Scribner, 1965).

LEINWAND, THEODORE, 'Shakespeare and the Middling Sort', *Shakespeare Quarterly* 44.3 (1993), 284–303.

MONTROSE, LOUIS, *The Purpose of Playing: Shakespeare and the Cultural Politics of the Elizabethan Theatre* (Chicago, IL: University of Chicago Press, 1996).

NASHE, THOMAS, *The Unfortunate Traveler and other Works*, J. B. Steane (ed.) (New York: Penguin Books, 1985; first published 1972).

NORBROOK, DAVID, '"What Cares these Roarers for the Name of King?": Language and Utopia in *The Tempest*', in *The Politics of Tragicomedy: Shakespeare and After*, Gordon McMullan and Jonathan Hope (eds.) (London: Routledge, 1992), 21–54.

PARKER, PATRICIA, 'Preposterous Events', *Shakespeare Quarterly* 43.2 (1992), 186–213.

PATTERSON, ANNABEL, *Shakespeare and the Popular Voice* (Oxford: Blackwell, 1989).

RACKIN, PHYLLIS, *Stages of History: Shakespeare's English Chronicles* (Ithaca, NY: Cornell University Press, 1990).

SCHALKWYK, DAVID, *Shakespeare, Love and Service* (Cambridge: Cambridge University Press, 2008).

SCHOENBAUM, SAMUEL, *William Shakespeare: A Documentary Life* (New York: Oxford University Press, 1975).

SHAKESPEARE, WILLIAM, *The Riverside Shakespeare*, G. Blakemore Evans et al. (eds.), 2nd edn. (Boston: Houghton Mifflin, 1997).

SHARPE, J. A., *Early Modern England: A Social History 1550–1760* (London: Edward Arnold, 1987).

SHEPHARD, ALEXANDRA, 'Poverty, Labour and the Language of Social Description in Early Modern England'. *Past and Present* 201 (2008), 51–95.

TEST, EDWARD, '*The Tempest* and the Newfoundland Cod Fishery', in Barbara Sebek and Stephen Deng (eds.), *Global Traffic: Discourses and Practices of Trade in English Literature and Culture from 1550 to 1700* (New York: Palgrave Macmillan, 2008), 201–20.

WEIL, JUDITH, *Service and Dependency in Shakespeare's Plays* (Cambridge: Cambridge University Press, 2005).

WELLS, STANLEY, and GARY TAYLOR (eds.), *William Shakespeare: The Complete Works*, 2nd edn. (Oxford: Clarendon Press, 2005).

WILSON, RICHARD, *Will Power: Essays on Shakespearean Authority* (Detroit, MI: Wayne State University Press, 1993).

WRIGHTSON, KEITH, *Earthly Necessities: Economic Lives in Early Modern Britain* (New Haven, CT: Yale University Press, 2000).

——. 'Estates, Degrees, and Sorts: Changing Perceptions of Society in Tudor and Stuart England', in Penelope Corfield (ed.), *Language, History, and Class* (Oxford: Blackwell, 1991), 30–52.

YACHNIN, PAUL, and ANTHONY DAWSON, *The Culture of Playgoing in Shakespeare's England: A Collaborative Debate* (Cambridge: Cambridge University Press, 2001).

CHAPTER 11 DOMESTIC LIFE

DE SOUSA, GERALDO V., *At Home in Shakespeare's Tragedies* (Aldershot: Ashgate, 2010).

DUBROW, HEATHER, *Shakespeare and Domestic Loss: Forms of Deprivation, Mourning and Recuperation* (Cambridge: Cambridge University Press, 2003).

HARRIS, JONATHAN GIL, *Untimely Matter in the Time of Shakespeare* (Philadelphia: University of Pennsylvania Press, 2009).

JARDINE, LISA, *Reading Shakespeare Historically* (London: Routledge, 1996).

KORDA, NATASHA, *Shakespeare's Domestic Economies, Gender and Property in Early Modern England* (Philadelphia: University of Pennsylvania Press, 2002).

ORLIN, LENA COWEN, 'The Performance of Things in *The Taming of the Shrew*', *Yearbook of English Studies*, Early Shakesepare Special Number, 23 (1993), 167–88.

——, *Private Matters and Public Culture in Post-Reformation England* (Ithaca, NY: Cornell University Press, 1994).

RICHARDSON, CATHERINE, *Domestic Life and Domestic Tragedy in Early Modern England: The Material Life of the Household* (Manchester: Manchester University Press, 2006).

CHAPTER 12 GENDER

ADELMAN, JANET, *Suffocating Mothers: Fantasies of Maternal Origin in Shakespeare's Plays, Hamlet to The Tempest* (New York: Routledge, 1992).

BULLINGER, H. EINRICH, *The golden boke of christen matrimonye* (London: 1542).

CALLAGHAN, D., *Shakespeare Without Women: Representing Gender and Race on the Renaissance Stage* (London: Routledge, 2000).

CAVENDISH, MARGARET, *CCXI sociable letters* (London: 1664).

CLELAND, JAMES, *Hero-Paideia: of the Institution of a Young Nobleman* (London: 1607).

CORYATE, THOMAS, *Coryats crudities* (London: 1611).

DONNE, J., *The Sermons of John Donne*, George R. Potter and Evelyn M. Simpson (eds.), vol. 4 (Berkeley: University of California Press, 1959).

DUSINBERRE, JULIET, *Shakespeare and the Nature of Women* (London: Macmillan, 1975).

HARTLEY, T. E., *Proceedings in the Parliaments of Elizabeth I*, vol. 1: *1558–1581* (Leicester: Leicester University Press, 1981).

HODGDON, BARBARA, 'Sexual Disguise and the Theatre of Gender', in A. Leggatt (ed.), *The Cambridge Companion to Shakespearean Comedy* (Cambridge: Cambridge University Press, 2002), 179–97.

'Homilee', see 'An Homilee of the state of Matrimonie', in *The second tome of homilees* (London: 1571; 1st pub. 1562).

JARDINE, LISA, 'Boy Actors, Female Roles, and Elizabethan Eroticism', in D. S. Kastan and P. Stallybrass (eds.), *Staging the Renaissance: Reinterpretations of Elizabethan and Jacobean Drama* (New York and London: Routledge, 1991), 57–67.

MAZZIO, CARLA, *The Inarticulate Renaissance: Language Trouble in an Age of Eloquence* (Philadelphia: University of Pennsylvania Press, 2009).

MONTAGU, ELIZABETH R., *An essay on the writings and genius of Shakespear* (London: 1769).

MULCASTER, RICHARD, *Positions wherein those primitiue circumstances be examined, which are necessarie for the training vp of children* (London: 1581).

OVERBURY, THOMAS, *A wife now the widow* (London: 1614).

PASTER, GAIL KERN, *Humoring the Body: Emotions and the Shakespearean Stage* (Chicago, IL: University of Chicago Press, 2004).

SINFIELD, ALAN, 'How to Read *The Merchant of Venice* Without Being Heterosexist', in Kate Chedgzoy (ed.), *Shakespeare, Feminism and Gender* (Basingstoke: Palgrave Macmillan, 2001), 115–34.

SMITH, THOMAS, *De republica Anglorum* (London: 1583).

SPRENGNETHER, MABELON GOHLKE, '"I wooed thee with my sword": Shakespeare's Tragic Paradigms', in R. McDonald (ed.), *Shakespeare: An Anthology of Criticism and Theory 1945-2000* (Oxford: Blackwell, 2004), 591–605.

STUBBES, PHILLIP, *The Anatomie of Abuses* (London: 1583).

WHATELY, WILLIAM, *A bride-bush, or A wedding sermon* (London: 1617).

CHAPTER 13 LANGUAGE

ADAMSON, SYLVIA, et al. (eds.), *Reading Shakespeare's Dramatic Language: A Guide* (London: Arden Shakespeare, 2001).

ALEXANDER, CATHERINE M. S. (ed.), *Shakespeare and Language* (Cambridge: Cambridge University Press, 2004).

BAKHTIN, M. M., 'Discourse in the Novel', in Micheal Holquist (ed.), *The Dialogic Imagination: Four Essays* (Austin: University of Texas Press, 1981), 259–422.

BLAKE, N. F., *A Grammar of Shakespeare's Language* (Basingstoke: Palgrave Macmillan, 2002).

BLANK, PAULA, *Broken English: Dialects and the Politics of Language in Renaissance Writings* (London: Routledge, 1996).

BOLTON, W. F., *Shakespeare's English: Language in the History Plays* (Cambridge, MA: Basil Blackwell, 1992).

CICERO, *DE INVENTIONE*, H. M. HUBBELL (trans.) (Cambridge, MA: Harvard University Press, 1949).

COOPER, ROBIN, and RUTH KEMPSON (eds.), *Language in Flux: Dialogue Coordination, Language Variation, Change and Evolution* (London: King's College, College Publications, 2008).

CRESSY, DAVID, *Literacy and the Social Order: Reading and Writing in Tudor and Stuart England* (Cambridge: Cambridge University Press, 1980).

CRYSTAL, DAVID, *The Cambridge Encyclopedia of the English Language* (Cambridge: Cambridge University Press, 1995).

——, *'Think on my Words': Exploring Shakespeare's Language* (Cambridge: Cambridge University Press, 2008).

FITZMAURICE, SUSAN M., and IRMA TAAVITSAINEN (eds.), *Methods in Historical Pragmatics: Approaches to Negotiated Meaning in Historical Contexts* (Berlin: Mouton de Gruyter, 2007).

FOX, ADAM, *Oral and Literate Culture in England, 1500–1700* (Oxford: Clarendon Press, 2000).

GARNER, BRYAN A., 'Shakespeare's Latinate Neologisms', rpt. in Salmon and Burness (eds.), *A Reader in the Language of Shakespearean Drama*, 207–28.

GÖRLACH, MANFRED, *Introduction to Early Modern English* (Cambridge: Cambridge University Press, 1991).

HOPE, JONATHAN, 'Shakespeare and Language: An Introduction', in Alexander (ed.), *Shakespeare and Language*, 1–17.

——, *Shakespeare's Grammar* (London: Arden Shakespeare, 2003).

LASS, ROGER (ed.), *The Cambridge History of the English Language*, vol. 3: *1476–1776* (Cambridge: Cambridge University Press, 1999).

McDONALD, RUSS, *Shakespeare and the Arts of Language* (Oxford: Oxford University Press, 2001).

MAGNUSSON, LYNNE, *Shakespeare and Social Dialogue: Dramatic Language and Elizabethan Letters* (Cambridge: Cambridge University Press, 1999).

NEVALAINEN, TERTTU, and HELENA RAUMOLIN-BRUNBERG, *Historical Sociolinguistics: Language Change in Tudor and Stuart England* (London: Longman, 2003).

ONG, WALTER J., *Orality and Literacy: The Technologizing of the Word* (London: Methuen, 1982).

PARKER, PATRICIA A., *Literary Fat Ladies: Rhetoric, Gender, Property* (London: Methuen, 1987).

SALMON, VIVIAN, and EDWINA BURNESS (eds.), *A Reader in the Language of Shakespearean Drama* (Amsterdam and Philadelphia: John Benjamins, 1987).

SCHÄFER, JÜRGEN, *Shakespeares Stil* (Frankfurt am Main: Athenäum Verlag, 1973).

CHAPTER 14 DRAMATURGY

ALTMAN, JOEL, *The Tudor Play of Mind* (London: University of California Press, 1978).

BECKERMAN, BERNARD, *Shakespeare at the Globe 1599–1603* (New York: Macmillan, 1962).

BRADBROOK, M. C., *Themes and Conventions of Elizabethan Tragedy* (Cambridge: Cambridge University Press, 1935).

EMPSON, WILLIAM, *Some Versions of Pastoral* (London: Chatto & Windus, 1935).

GIBBONS, BRIAN, *Shakespeare and Multiplicity* (Cambridge: Cambridge University Press, 1993; rpt. 2006).

HONIGMANN, E. A. J., 'Shakespeare's Mingled Yarn in *Measure for Measure*', in *Proceedings of the British Academy LXVII* (London, 1983).

LEVIN, RICHARD, *The Multiple Plot in English Renaissance Drama* (Chicago, IL: University of Chicago Press, 1971).

NIMS, JOHN FREDERICK (ed.), *Ovid's Metamorphoses, the Arthur Golding Translation (1567)* (New York: Macmillan, 1965), pp. xiii–xxxv.

ROSSITER, A. P., *Angel with Horns* (London: Longmans, 1961).

SPIVACK, BERNARD, *Shakespeare and the Allegory of Evil* (New York: Columbia University Press, 1958).

CHAPTER 15 CENSORSHIP

BAWCUTT, N.W. (ed.), *The Control and Censorship of Caroline Drama: the Records of Sir Henry Herbert, Master of the Revels* (Oxford: Clarendon Press, 1996).

BRIGGS, JULIA (ed.), *The Lady's Tragedy* in Gary Taylor and John Lavagnino (eds.), *Thomas Middleton: The Collected Works* (Oxford: Clarendon Press, 2007), 833–906.

BURT, RICHARD, *Licensed by Authority: Ben Jonson and the Discourses of Censorship* (Ithaca, NY: Cornell University Press, 1993).

CHAMBERS, E. K., *The Elizabethan Stage*, 4 vols. (Oxford: Oxford University Press, 1923).

CLARE, JANET, *Art Made Tongue-Tied by Authority: Elizabethan and Jacobean Dramatic Censorship*, 2nd edn. (Manchester: Manchester University Press, 1999).

——, 'Historicism and the Question of Censorship in the Renaissance', *English Literary Renaissance* 27:2 (1997): 155–76.

CLEGG, CYNDIA, *Press Censorship in Elizabethan England* (Cambridge: Cambridge University Press, 1997), 57–65.

——, *Press Censorship on Jacobean England* (Cambridge: Cambridge University Press, 2001).

DUTTON, RICHARD, *Mastering the Revels: the Regulation and Censorship of English Renaissance Drama* (London: Macmillan, 1991), 125.

——, *Licensing, Censorship and Authorship in Early Modern England: Buggeswords* (Basingstoke: Palgrave Macmillan, 2000).

HADFIELD, ANDREW (ed.), *Literature and Censorship in Renaissance England* (London: Palgrave Macmillan, 2001), 149–65.

HOWARD-HILL, T. H. (ed.), *Shakespeare and Sir Thomas More: Essays on the Play and its Shakespearian Interest* (Cambridge: Cambridge University Press, 1989).

IOPPOLO, GRACE, *Dramatists and their Manuscripts in the Age of Shakespeare, Jonson, Middleton and Heyward: Authorship, Authority and the Playhouse* (London: Routledge, 2006).

PATTERSON, ANNABEL, *Censorship and Interpretation: the Conditions of Writing and Reading in Early Modern England* (Madison: University of Wisconsin Press, 1984).

CHAPTER 16 THE EARLY SHAKESPEARE

BATE, JONATHAN (ed.), *Titus Andronicus*. The Arden Shakespeare, 3rd series (London: Routledge, 1995).

BERRY, EDWARD I., *Patterns of Decay: Shakespeare's Early Histories* (Charlottesville: University Press of Virginia, 1975).

BISHOP, T. G., *Shakespeare and the Theatre of Wonder* (Cambridge: Cambridge University Press, 1996).

BOWERS, FREDSON T., *Elizabethan Revenge Tragedy, 1587–1642* (Princeton, NJ: Princeton University Press, 1940).

BROWN, JOHN RUSSELL, and BERNARD HARRIS (eds.), *Early Shakespeare*, Stratford-upon-Avon Studies 3 (New York: Schocken, 1961).

BURKE, WILLIAM KENNETH, *A New Approach to Shakespeare's Early Comedies: Theoretical Foundations* (New York: Vantage, 1998).

CARROLL, WILLIAM C., *The Great Feast of Language in 'Love's Labour's Lost'* (Princeton, NJ: Princeton University Press, 1976).

COX, JOHN D., and ERIC RASMUSSEN (eds.), *King Henry VI Part III*, The Arden Shakespeare 3rd series (London: Thomson Learning, 2001).

DUTTON, RICHARD, and JEAN E. HOWARD (eds.), *A Companion to Shakespeare's Works*, vol. 2: *The Histories* (Oxford: Blackwell Publishing, 2003).

——— (eds.), *A Companion to Shakespeare's Works*, vol. 3: *The Comedies* (Oxford: Blackwell, 2003).

ELAM, KEIR, *Shakespeare's Universe of Discourse: Language-Games in the Comedies* (Cambridge: Cambridge University Press, 1984).

HAMILTON, A. C., *The Early Shakespeare* (San Marino, CA: Huntington Library, 1967).

KASTAN, DAVID SCOTT, *Shakespeare and the Shapes of Time* (Hanover, NH: University Press of New England, 1982).

KELLY, HENRY ANSGAR, *Divine Providence in the England of Shakespeare's Histories* (Cambridge, MA: Harvard University Press, 1970).

KINNEY, ARTHUR F., 'Shakespeare's *Comedy of Errors* and the Nature of Kinds', *Studies in Philology* 85 (1988), 25–52.

KNOWLES, RONALD (ed.), *King Henry VI Part II*. The Arden Shakespeare, 3rd series (London: Thomas Nelson, 1999).

LEVINE, NINA S., *Women's Matters: Politics, Gender, and Nation in Shakespeare's Early History Plays* (Newark: University of Delaware Press, 1998).

MASTEN, JEFFREY, 'Playwriting: Authorship and Collaboration', in John D. Cox and David Scott Kastan (eds.), *A New History of Early English Drama* (New York: Columbia University Press, 1997), 357–82.

TAYLOR, GARY, 'Shakespeare and Others: the Authorship of *Henry the Sixth, Part I*', *Medieval and Renaissance Drama in England* 7 (1995), 145–205.

TILLYARD, E. M. W., *Shakespeare's History Plays* (London: Chatto & Windus, 1944 and 1961).

TRAVERSI, DEREK, *William Shakespeare: The Early Comedies.* (London: Longmans, Green, 1960).

VICKERS, BRIAN, *Shakespeare, Co-Author: A Historical Study of Five Collaborative Plays.* (Oxford: Oxford University Press, 2002).

WILSON, F. P., *Marlowe and the Early Shakespeare* (Oxford: Clarendon Press, 1953).

CHAPTER 17 MIDDLE SHAKESPEARE

BEDNARZ, JAMES P., *Shakespeare and the Poets' War* (New York: Columbia University Press, 2001).

BEVINGTON, DAVID, et al. (eds.), *English Renaissance Drama: A Norton Anthology* (New York: Norton, 2002).

CHAMBERS, E. K., *William Shakespeare: A Study of Facts and Problems*, 2 vols. (Oxford: Clarendon Press, 1930).

DUTTON, RICHARD (ed.), *The Oxford Handbook of Early Modern Theatre* (Oxford: Oxford University Press, 2009).

KNIGHTS, L. C., "Shakespeare: King Lear and the Great Tragedies," in Boris Ford (ed.), *The New Pelican Guide to English Literature, Vol. 2: The Age of Shakespeare* (Harmondsworth: Penguin, 1982), 327–56.

MAXWELL, J. C., "Shakespeare: The Middle Plays," in Boris Ford (ed.), *The New Pelican Guide to English Literature, Vol. 2: The Age of Shakespeare* (Harmondsworth: Penguin, 1982), 300–26.

MERES, FRANCIS, *Palladis Tamia: Wit's Treasury* (London: 1598).

PREISS, RICHARD, 'Robert Armin Do the Police in Different Voices', in Peter Holland and Stephen Orgel (eds.), *Performance to Print in Shakespeare's England* (Basingstoke: Palgrave Macmillan, 2006), 208–27.

SHAPIRO, JAMES, *A Year in the Life of William Shakespeare: 1599* (New York: HarperCollins, 2005).

STERN, TIFFANY (ed.), *King Leir* (New York: Routledge, 2003).

TAYLOR, GARY, and JOHN LAVIGNANO (eds.), *Thomas Middleton and Early Modern Textual Culture: A Companion to the Collected Works* (Oxford: Clarendon Press, 2007).

VICKERS, BRIAN, *Shakespeare, Co-Author: A Historical Study of Five Collaborative Plays* (Oxford: Oxford University Press, 2002).

WOFFORD, SUSANNE L. (ed.), *Shakespeare's Late Tragedies: A Collection of Critical Essays* (Englewood Cliffs, NJ: Prentice Hall, 1996).

YOUNG, DAVID (ed.), *Shakespeare's Middle Tragedies: A Collection of Critical Essays* (Englewood Cliffs, NJ: Prentice Hall, 1992).

CHAPTER 18 POETRY

BATE, JONATHAN, *Shakespeare and Ovid* (Oxford: Oxford University Press, 1993).

BOOTH, STEPHEN, *An Essay on Shakespeare's Sonnets* (New Haven, CT: Yale University Press, 1969).

CHENEY, PATRICK (ed.), *The Cambridge Companion to Shakespeare's Poetry* (Cambridge: Cambridge University Press, 2007).

DONALDSON, IAN, *The Rapes of Lucretia: A Myth and Its Transformations* (Oxford: Oxford University Press, 1982).

DUBROW, HEATHER, *Captive Victors: Shakespeare's Narrative Poems and Sonnets* (Ithaca, NY: Cornell University Press, 1987).

——, *Echoes of Desire: English Petrarchism and its Counterdiscourses* (Ithaca, NY: Cornell University Press, 1995).

——, *Shakespeare and Domestic Loss* (Cambridge: Cambridge University Press, 1999).

ENTERLINE, LYNN, *The Rhetoric of the Body: From Ovid to Shakespeare* (Cambridge: Cambridge University Press, 2000).

FINEMAN, JOEL, *Shakespeare's Perjured Eye: The Invention of Poetic Subjectivity in the Sonnets* (Berkeley: University of California Press, 1986).

HULSE, CLARK, *Metamorphic Verse: The Elizabethan Minor Epic* (Princeton, NJ: Princeton University Press, 1981).

KAY, DENNIS, *William Shakespeare: Sonnets and Poems* (New York: Twayne, 1998).

KEACH, WILLIAM, *Elizabethan Erotic Narratives: Irony and Pathos in the Ovidian Poetry of Shakespeare, Marlowe, and their Contemporaries* (New Brunswick, NJ: Rutgers University Press, 1977).

KOLIN, PHILIP (ed.), *Venus and Adonis: Critical Essays* (New York: Routledge, 1997).

LANHAM, RICHARD, *The Motives of Eloquence: Literary Rhetoric in the Renaissance* (New Haven, CT: Yale University Press, 1976).

MORTIMER, ANTHONY, *Variable Passions: A Reading of Shakespeare's Venus and Adonis* (New York: AMS Press, 2000).

ROBERTS, SASHA, *Reading Shakespeare's Poems in Early Modern England* (Basingstoke: Palgrave Macmillan, 2003).

SCHIFFER, JAMES (ed.), *Shakespeare's Sonnets: Critical Essays* (New York: Garland, 1999).

SCHOENFELDT, MICHAEL (ed.), *A Companion to Shakespeare's Sonnets* (Oxford: Blackwell, 2007).

SHARON-ZISSER, SHIRLEY (ed.), *Critical Essays on Shakespeare's* A Lover's Complaint: *Suffering Ecstasy* (Aldershot: Ashgate, 2006).

TAYLOR, A. B. (ed.), *Shakespeare's Ovid: The* Metamorphoses *in the Plays and Poems* (Cambridge: Cambridge University Press, 2000).

VENDLER, HELEN (ed.), *The Art of Shakespeare's Sonnets* (Cambridge, MA: Harvard University Press, 1997).

Chapter 19 Late Shakespeare

Adams, Robert Martin, *Shakespeare: The Four Romances* (New York: Norton, 1989).

Foster, Verna A., *The Name and Nature of Tragicomedy* (Burlington, VT: Ashgate, 2004).

Henke, Robert, *Pastoral Transformations* (London: Associated University Presses, 1997).

Jordan, Constance, *Shakespeare's Monarchies: Ruler and Subject in the Romances* (Ithaca, NY: Cornell University Press, 1997).

McDonald, Russ, *Shakespeare's Late Style* (Cambridge: Cambridge University Press, 2006).

McMullan, Gordon, *Shakespeare and the Idea of Late Writing: Authorship in the Proximity of Death* (Cambridge: Cambridge University Press, 2007).

—— and Jonathan Hope (eds.), *The Politics of Tragicomedy: Shakespeare and After* (London: Routledge, 1992).

Palfrey, Simon, *Late Shakespeare: A New World of Words* (Oxford: Oxford University Press, 1997).

Platt, Peter, *Reason Diminished: Shakespeare and the Marvelous* (Lincoln: University of Nebraska Press, 1997).

Richards, Jennifer, and James Knowles (eds), *Shakespeare's Late Plays: New Readings* (Edinburgh: Edinburgh University Press, 1999).

Shannon, Laurie, *Sovereign Amity: Figures of Friendship in Shakespearean Contexts* (Chicago, IL: University of Chicago Press, 2002).

Traversi, Derek, *Shakespeare: The Last Phase* (New York: Harcourt, Brace, 1955).

Chapter 20 Local Records

Barish, Jonas, *The Anti-Theatrical Prejudice* (Berkeley: University of California Press, 1985).

Bearman, Robert, 'John Shakespeare's "Spiritual Testament": A Reappraisal', *Shakespeare Survey* 56 (2003), 184–202.

——, *Shakespeare in the Stratford Records* (Stroud, Glocs.: Sutton, 1994).

Bentley, G. E., *The Jacobean and Caroline Stage*, 7 vols. (Oxford: Clarendon Press, 1941–68).

——, *The Profession of Player in Shakespeare's Time, 1590–1642* (Princeton, NJ : Princeton University Press, 1984).

Brooke, C. F. Tucker (ed.), *The Shakespeare Apocrypha* (Oxford: Clarendon Press, 1908).

Chambers, E. K., *The Elizabethan Stage*, 4 vols. (Oxford: Clarendon Press, 1923).

——, *William Shakespeare: A Study of Facts and Problems*, 2 vols. (Oxford: Clarendon Press, 1930).

Coletti, Theresa, 'Reading REED: History and the Records of Early English Drama', in Lee Patterson (ed.), *Literary Practice and Social Change in Britain, 1380–1530* (Berkeley: University of California Press, 1990), 248–84.

Dawson, Giles, 'John Payne Collier's Great Forgery', *Studies in Bibliography* 24 (1971), 1–26.

—— (ed.), *Records of Plays and Players in Kent, 1450–1642*, Malone Society Collections VII (Oxford: Oxford University Press, 1965).

Freeman, Arthur, 'A New Victim for the Old Corrector', *Times Literary Supplement*, (April 22, 1983), 391.

——, and Janet Ing Freeman, *John Payne Collier: Scholarship and Forgery in the Nineteenth Century*, 2 vols. (New Haven, CT: Yale University Press, 2004).

GALLOWAY, D., and J. WASSON (eds.), *Records of Plays and Players in Norfolk and Suffolk, 1330–1642*, Malone Society Collections XI (Oxford: Oxford University Press, 1981).

GIBSON, JAMES (ed.), *Kent: Diocese of Canterbury*. Records of Early English Drama, 2 vols. (Toronto: University of Toronto Press, 2002).

GURR, ANDREW, *The Shakespeare Company 1594–1642* (Cambridge: Cambridge University Press, 2004).

HONIGMANN, E. A. J., and S. BROCK, *Playhouse Wills, 1558–1642: An Edition of Wills by Shakespeare and his Contemporaries in the London Theatre* (Manchester: Manchester University Press, 1993).

NOLEN, STEPHANIE, *Shakespeare's Face* (Toronto: Knopf, 2002).

PALMER, BARBARA D., ' "Towneley Plays" or "Wakefield Cycle" Revisited,' *Comparative Drama* 21.4 (Winter 1987–8), 318–49.

PIERCE, PATRICIA. *The Great Shakespeare Fraud: The Strange, True Story of William-Henry Ireland* (Stroud: Sutton, 2004).

ROWAN, DONALD F., ' "Inns, Inn-Yards, and Other Playing Places" ', *The Elizabethan Theatre IX* (Port Credit: P. D. Meany, 1981).

SCHOENBAUM, SAMUEL, *Shakespeare's Lives*, 2nd. edn. (New York: Oxford University Press, 1991).

——, *William Shakespeare: A Documentary Life* (New York: Oxford University Press, 1975).

SOMERSET, ALAN. 'James Orchard Halliwell-Phillipps and his Scrapbooks', *REED Newsletter* (1979), 8–17.

——, *Halliwell-Phillipps Scrapbooks: An Index* (Toronto: REED, 1979).

——, ' "Label me a Sceptic", Tentatively—I Think', International Conference, 'Picturing Shakespeare,' University of Toronto, November 2002. Canadian Shakespeares website, University of Guelph: http://www.canadianshakespeares.ca/multimedia/imagegallery/m_i_13.cfm

—— (ed.), *Shropshire*. Records of Early English Drama, 2 vols. (Toronto: University of Toronto Press, 1994).

VELZ, JOHN, 'The Collier Controversy Redivivus', *Shakespeare Quarterly* 36 (1985), 106.

WICKHAM, GLYNNE, WILLIAM INGRAM, and HERBERT BERRY (eds.), *English Professional Theatre, 1530–1660* (Cambridge: Cambridge University Press, 2000).

CHAPTER 21 PATRONAGE

BLY, MARY, 'The Boy Companies, 1599–1613', in Richard Dutton (ed.), *The Oxford Handbook of Early Modern Theatre* (New York: Oxford University Press, 2009), 136–50.

BRUSTER, DOUGLAS, *Drama and the Market in the Age of Shakespeare* (Cambridge: Cambridge University Press, 1992).

CHAMBERS, E. K., *The Elizabethan Stage*, 4 vols. (Oxford: Clarendon Press, 1923).

DUTTON, RICHARD, 'The Revels Office and the Boy Companies, 1600–1613: New Perspectives', *English Literary Renaissance* 32 (2002), 324–51.

GREENFIELD, PETER., 'Touring', in Richard Dutton (ed.), *The Oxford Handbook of Early Modern Theatre* (New York: Oxford University Press, 2009), 292–306.

GURR, ANDREW, *The Shakespearian Playing Companies* (Oxford: Clarendon Press, 1996).

——, *The Shakespearean Stage 1574–1642* (Cambridge: Cambridge University Press, 2008).

McLUSKIE, KATHLEEN E., and FELICITY DUNSWORTH, 'Patronage and the Economics of Theater', in John D. Cox and David Scott Kastan (eds.), *A New History of Early English Drama*, (New York: Columbia University Press, 1997), 423–40.

McMillin, Scott, and Sally-Beth MacLean, *The Queen's Men and their Plays* (Cambridge: Cambridge University Press, 1998).

Somerset, Alan, 'Not just Sir Oliver Owlet: From Patrons to "Patronage" of Early Modern Theatre', in Richard Dutton (ed.), *The Oxford Handbook of Early Modern Theatre* (New York: Oxford University Press, 2009), 343–61.

White, Paul Westfield, and Suzanne R. Westfall, *Shakespeare and Theatrical Patronage* (Cambridge: Cambridge University Press, 2002).

Chapter 22 Repertory System

Adams, Joseph Quincy (ed.), *The Dramatic Records of Sir Henry Herbert* (New Haven, CT: Yale University Press, 1917).

Barroll, J. Leeds, *Politics, Plague, and Shakespeare's Theater: The Stuart Years* (Ithaca, NY: Cornell University Press, 1991).

Bentley, G. E., 'Shakespeare and the Blackfriars Theatre', *Shakespeare Survey* 1 (1948), 38–50.

Chambers, E. K., *The Elizabethan Stage*, 4 vols. (Oxford: Clarendon Press, 1923).

——, *William Shakespeare: A Study of Facts and Problems*, 2 vols. (Oxford: Clarendon Press, 1930).

Cook, David, and F. P. Wilson (eds.), *Dramatic Records in the Declared Accounts of the Treasurer of the Chamber 1558–1642*, Malone Society Collections, VI, 1 (1961).

Erne, Lukas, *Beyond The Spanish Tragedy: A Study of the Works of Thomas Kyd* (Manchester: Manchester University Press, 2001).

Fleay, F. G., *A Chronicle History of the English Stage: 1559–1642* (London: Reaves and Turner, 1891).

Foakes, R. A. (ed.), *Henslowe's Diary*, 2nd edn. (Cambridge: Cambridge University Press, 2002; edition with R. T. Rickert, 1961).

Greg, W. W. (ed.), *Henslowe Papers* (London: A. H. Bullen, 1907).

Gurr, Andrew. 'London's Blackfriars Playhouse and the Chamberlain's Men', in Paul Menzer (ed.), *Inside Shakespeare: Essays on the Blackfriars Stage* (Selinsgrove, PA: Susquehanna University Press, 2006), 17–30.

——, 'Privy Councilors as Theatre Patrons', in Paul Whitfield White and Suzanne R. Westfall (eds.), *Shakespeare and Theatrical Patronage in Early Modern England* (Cambridge: Cambridge University Press, 2002), 221–45.

——, 'Shakespeare's Playhouses', in David Scott Kastan (ed.), *A Companion to Shakespeare* (Oxford: Blackwell, 1999), 362–76.

——, *The Shakespeare Company 1594–1642* (Cambridge: Cambridge University Press, 2004).

——, *The Shakespearian Playing Companies* (Oxford: Clarendon Press, 1996).

Ingram, William, *A London Life in the Brazen Age: Francis Langley 1548–1602* (Cambridge, MA: Harvard University Press, 1978).

Knutson, Roslyn L., 'Evidence for the Assignment of Plays to the Repertory of Shakespeare's Company', *Medieval and Renaissance Drama in England* 4 (1989), 63–89.

——, 'Love's Labor's Won in Repertory', *Publications of the Arkansas Philological Association* 11 (1985), 45–57.

——, *The Repertory of Shakespeare's Company, 1594–1613* (Fayetteville: University of Arkansas Press, 1991).

KNUTSON, ROSLYN L., 'The Start of Something Big', in Helen Ostovich et al. (eds.), *Locating the Queen's Men: Material Practices and Conditions of Playing, 1583-1603* (Aldershot: Ashgate, 2009), 99–108.

——, 'Two Playhouses, Both Alike in Dignity', *Shakespeare Studies* 30 (2002), 111–17.

——, 'What if there wasn't a "Blackfriars Repertory"?' in Paul Menzer (ed.), *Inside Shakespeare: Essays on the Blackfriars Stage* (Selinsgrove: Susquehanna University Press, 2006), 54–60.

——, 'What was James Burbage *Thinking*???', in Peter Kanelos and Matt Kozusko (eds.), *Thunder at a Playhouse: Essays on Shakespeare and the Early Modern Stage* (Selinsgrove, PA: Susquehanna University Press, 2010).

Lost Plays Database, http://lostplays.org.

LOGAN, ROBERT A., *Shakespeare's Marlowe: The Influence of Christopher Marlowe on Shakespeare's Artistry* (Aldershot: Ashgate, 2007).

MCMILLIN, SCOTT, and SALLY-BETH MACLEAN, *The Queen's Men and their Plays*, (Cambridge: Cambridge University Press, 1998).

MANLEY, LAWRENCE, 'Playing with Fire: Immolation and the Repertory of Strange's Men', *Early Theatre* 4 (2001), 115–29.

REED Patrons and Performances Web Site, http://link.library.utoronto.ca/reed.

SHARPE, ROBERT B., *The Real War of the Theaters.* (Boston: D. C. Heath, 1935).

SKURA, MEREDITH ANNE. *Shakespeare the Actor and the Purposes of Playing* (Chicago, IL: University of Chicago Press, 1993).

WICKHAM, GLYNNE, HERBERT BERRY, and WILLIAM INGRAM, (eds.), *English Professional Theatre, 1530 1660* (Cambridge: Cambridge University Press, 2000).

WRIGHT, JAMES. *Historia Histrionica* (London, 1699).

CHAPTER 23 THEATRE AS BUSINESS

AARON, MELISSA D., *Global Economics: A History of the Theatre Business, the Chamberlain's/ King's Men, and Their Plays, 1599-1642* (Wilmington: University of Delaware Press, 2005).

AGNEW, J. C., *Worlds Apart: The Market and the Theatre in Anglo-American Thought, 1550-1750* (Cambridge: Cambridge University Press, 1986).

BALDWIN, T. W., *The Organization and Personnel of the Shakespearean Company* (Princeton, NJ: Princeton University Press, 1927; rpt. New York: Russell and Russell, 1961).

BARROLL, J. Leeds, *Politics, Plague and Shakespeare's Theatre: The Stuart Years* (Ithaca, NY: Cornell University Press, 1991).

BLAYNEY, PETER W. M., *The First Folio of Shakespeare* (Washington, DC: Folger Shakespeare Library, 1991).

BRADLEY, DAVID, *From Text to Performance in the Elizabethan Theatre: Preparing the Play for the Stage* (Cambridge: Cambridge University Press, 1992).

BRUSTER, DOUGLAS, *Drama and the Market in the Age of Shakespeare* (Cambridge: Cambridge University Press, 1992).

CARSON, NEIL, *A Companion to Henslowe's Diary* (Cambridge: Cambridge University Press, 1988).

EGAN, GABRIEL, 'John Heminges's Tap-House at the Globe', *Theatre Notebook* 55 (2001), 72–77.

FORSE, JAMES H., *Art Imitates Business: Commercial and Political Influence in Elizabethan Theatre* (Bowling Green, OH: Bowling Green State University Popular Press, 1993).

GRAVES, R. B., *Lighting the Shakespearean Stage, 1567–1642* (Carbondale and Edwardsville: Southern Illinois University Press, 1999).

GURR, ANDREW. *Playgoing in Shakespeare's London* (Cambridge: Cambridge University Press, 1987).

——, *The Shakespeare Company, 1594–1642* (Cambridge: Cambridge University Press, 2004).

——, *The Shakespearian Playing Companies* (Oxford: Clarendon Press, 1996).

HENSLOWE, PHILIP, *Henslowe's Diary*, R. A. Foakes and R. I. Rickert (eds.) (Cambridge: Cambridge University Press, 1961).

HENTZNER, PAUL, 'A Journey into England. By Paul Hentzner, in the year 1598', Horace Walpole (trans.), *Fugitive Pieces on Various Subjects by Several Authors*. 2 vols. Vol. 2 (London, 1761).

INGRAM, WILLIAM, *The Business of Playing: The Beginnings of the Adult Professional Theater in Elizabethan London* (Ithaca, NY: Cornell University Press, 1992).

KNUTSON, ROSLYN LANDER, *Playing Companies and Commerce in Shakespeare's Time* (Cambridge: Cambridge University Press, 2001).

——, *The Repertory of Shakespeare's Company, 1594–1613* (Fayetteville: University of Arkansas Press, 1991).

LEINWAND, THEODORE, *Theatre, Finance and Society in Early Modern England* (Cambridge: Cambridge University Press, 1999).

MacINTYRE, JEAN, *Costumes and Scripts in the Elizabethan Theatres* (Edmonton: University of Alberta Press, 1992).

PLATTER, THOMAS, *Thomas Platter's Travels in England 1599*, Clare Williams (trans.) (London Jonathan Cape: 1937).

RUTTER, CAROL CHILLINGTON (ed.), *Documents of the Rose Playhouse*, The Revels Play Companion Library (Manchester: Manchester University Press, 1984).

SOMERSET, J. A. B., ' "How Chances It They Travel?": Provincial Touring, Playing Places, and the King's Men', *Shakespeare Survey* 47 (1994), 45–60.

WALLACE, CHARLES WILLIAM, *The First London Theatre: Materials for a History* (London: Benjamin Bloom, 1969).

——, 'Shakespeare and his London Associates as Revealed in Recently Discovered Documents', *University of Nebraska Studies* 10.4 (1910), 261–360.

CHAPTER 24 FOREIGN WORLDS

ANDREWS, KENNETH R., *Trade, Plunder and Settlement: Maritime Enterprise and the Genesis of the British Empire 1480–1630* (Cambridge: Cambridge University Press, 1984).

ARCHER, JOHN MICHAEL, *Old Worlds: Egypt, Southwest Asia, India, and Russia in Early Modern English Writing* (Stanford: Stanford University Press, 2001).

BARTELS, EMILY C., *Speaking of the Moor: From Alcazar to Othello* (Philadelphia: University of Pennsylvania Press, 2008).

BRAUDEL, FERNAND, *The Mediterranean and the Mediterranean World in the Age of Philip II*, Sian Reynolds (trans.), 2 vols. (New York: Harper & Row, 1972).

BRENNER, ROBERT, *Merchants and Revolution: Commercial Change, Political Conflict, and London's Overseas Traders, 1550–1653* (London: Verso, 2003).

BROTTON, JERRY, *The Renaissance Bazaar: From the Silk Road to Michelangelo* (Oxford: Oxford University Press, 2002).

CLAYTON, TOM, SUSAN BROCK, and VICENTE FORÉS (eds.), *Shakespeare and the Mediterranean: Selected Proceedings of the International Shakespeare Association World Congress, Valencia, 2001* (Newark: University of Delaware Press, 2004).

CORYAT, THOMAS, *Coryat's Crudities* (London: 1611).

EDEN, RICHARD (trans.), *Decades of the Newe Worlde* (London: 1555).

FULLER, MARY C., *Voyages in Print: English Travel to America, 1576–1624* (Cambridge: Cambridge University Press, 1995).

GILLIES, JOHN, *Shakespeare and the Geography of Difference* (Cambridge: Cambridge University Press, 1994).

——, and VIRGINIA MASON VAUGHAN (eds.), *Playing the Globe: Genre and Geography in English Renaissance Drama* (Cranbury, NJ: Associated University Presses, 1998).

HADFIELD, ANDREW, *Literature, Travel, and Colonial Writing in the English Renaissance, 1545–1625* (Oxford: Oxford University Press, 2007).

HAKLUYT, RICHARD, *The Principall Navigations, Voyages, and Discoveries of the English Nation* (London: 1589, 1598–1600).

HARRIOT, THOMAS, *A Brief and True Report of the Newfoundland of Virginia* (London, 1588, 1590).

LOOMBA, ANIA, 'Outsiders in Shakespeare's England', in Margreta de Grazia and Stanley Wells (eds.), *The Cambridge Companion to Shakespeare* (Cambridge: Cambridge University Press, 2001).

MAQUERLOT, JEAN-PIERRE, and MICHELE WILLEMS (eds.), *Travel and Drama in Shakespeare's Time* (Cambridge: Cambridge University Press, 1996).

MARKLEY, ROBERT, *The Far East and the English Imagination, 1600–1730* (Cambridge: Cambridge University Press, 2006).

RALEIGH, WALTER, *Discoverie of Guiana* (London: 1596).

SINGH, JYOTSNA G., *A Companion to the Global Renaissance: English Literature and Culture in the Era of Expansion* (Chichester: Wiley-Blackwell, 2009).

SMITH, D. K., *The Cartographic Imagination in Early Modern England* (Aldershot: Ashgate, 2008).

CHAPTER 25 AUDIENCE RECEPTION

BARISH, JONAS, *The Antitheatrical Prejudice* (Berkeley: University of California Press, 1981).

BLACKSTONE, MARY A., and CAMERON, LEWIS, 'Towards "A Full and Understanding Auditory": New Evidence of Playgoers at the first Globe Theatre', *MLR* 90 (1995), 556–71.

CAPP, BERNARD. 'Playgoers, Players and Cross-Dressing in Early Modern London: The Bridewell Evidence', *The Seventeenth Century* 18 (2003), 159–71.

COOK, ANN JENNALIE. *The Privileged Playgoers of Shakespeare's London: 1576–1642* (Princeton, NJ: Princeton University Press 1981).

GURR, ANDREW, *Playgoing in Shakespeare's London*, 3rd edn. (Cambridge: Cambridge University Press, 2004).

HARBAGE, ALFRED, *Shakespeare's Audiences* (New York: Columbia, 1941).

LEVIN, RICHARD, 'The Relation of External Evidence to the Allegorical and Thematic Interpretation of Shakespeare', *Shakespeare Studies* 13 (1980), 1–30.

LEVINE, LAURA, *Men in Women's Clothing: Anti-theatricality and Effeminization 1579–1642* (Cambridge: Cambridge University Press, 1994).

LOPEZ, JEREMY, *Theatrical Convention and Audience Response in Early Modern Drama* (Cambridge: Cambridge University Press, 2003).

MARSHALL, CYNTHIA, 'Bodies in the Audience', *Shakespeare Studies* 29 (2001), 51–6.

POLLARD, TANYA, *Drugs and Theater in Early Modern England* (Oxford: Oxford University Press, 2005).

—— (ed.), *Shakespeare's Theater: A Sourcebook* (Oxford: Blackwell, 2004).

SMITH, BRUCE, *The Acoustic World of Early Modern England: Attending to the O-Factor* (Chicago, IL: University of Chicago Press, 1999).

SOMERSET, J. ALAN B. (ed.), *Records of Early English Drama: Shropshire*, 2 vols. (Toronto: University of Toronto Press, 1994).

STEGGLE, MATTHEW, *Laughing and Weeping in Early Modern Theatres* (Aldershot: Ashgate, 2007).

WHITNEY, CHARLES, *Early Responses to Renaissance Drama* (Cambridge: Cambridge University Press, 2006).

CHAPTER 26 SHAKESPEARE ON FILM AND TELEVISION

ANDEREGG, MICHAEL, *Orson Welles, Shakespeare and Popular Culture* (New York: Columbia University Press, 1988).

BALL, ROBERT HAMILTON, *Shakespeare on Silent Film* (London: George Allen and Unwin, 1968).

BAZIN, ANDRÉ, *Orson Welles, A Critical View* (New York: Harper & Row, 1978).

BRANAGH, KENNETH, *Hamlet, Screenplay and Introduction* (New York: Norton, 1996).

BRODE, DOUGLAS, *Shakespeare in the Movies* (Oxford: Oxford University Press, 2000).

BUCHANAN, JUDITH, *Shakespeare on Silent Film: An Excellent Dumb Discourse* (Cambridge: Cambridge University Press, 2009).

BURNETT, MARK THORNTON, *Filming Shakespeare in the Global Marketplace* (New York: Palgrave, 2007).

CROWL, SAMUEL, *Shakespeare at the Cineplex: The Kenneth Branagh Era* (Athens, OH: Ohio University Press, 2003).

——, *Shakespeare and Film* (New York: Norton, 2008).

DONALDSON, PETER, 'Bottom and the gramophone: Media, Class and Comedy in Michael Hoffman's A Midsummer Night's Dream', *Shakespeare Survey* 61 (2009), 23–35.

JACKSON, RUSSELL (ed.), *The Cambridge Companion to Shakespeare on Film* (Cambridge: Cambridge University Press, 2007).

JORGENS, JACK, *Shakespeare on Film* (Bloomington: Indiana University Press, 1977).

KLIMAN, BERNICE W., 'Television', in Michael Dobson and Stanley Wells (eds.), *The Oxford Companion to Shakespeare* (Oxford: Oxford University Press, 2001).

KLIMAN, BERNICE W., *Shakespeare in Performance: Macbeth* (Manchester: Manchester University Press, 2004).

LUHRMANN, BAZ, 'The Production: Production Notes', http://www.romeoandjuliet.com/players/pn.1.html.

O'BRIEN, GEOFFREY, 'The Ghost at the Feast', www.geocities.com/athens/parthenon/6261/Articles/newyorkreview.htm.

ROTHWELL, KENNETH, *A History of Shakespeare on Screen: A Century of Film and Television* (Cambridge: Cambridge University Press, 2004).

Voodoo, Macbeth, www.google.com/search?hl=en&q=welles+voodoo+macbeth&aq=f&oq=&aqi=.

CHAPTER 27 MARKETING

BRISTOL, MICHAEL, *Big-Time Shakespeare* (New York: Routledge, 2006).

DANESI, MARCEL, *Brands* (London: Routledge, 2006).

DUGAS, DON-JOHN, *Marketing the Bard: Shakespeare in Performance and Print, 1660–1740* (Columbia: University of Missouri Press, 2006).

FRENCH, EMMA, *Selling Shakespeare to Hollywood: The Marketing of Filmed Shakespeare Adaptations from 1989 into the New Millennium* (Hertfordshire: University of Hertfordshire Press, 2006).

GARBER, MARJORIE, *Shakespeare and Modern Culture* (Cambridge, MA: Harvard University Press, 2008).

HALPERN, RICHARD, *Shakespeare Among the Moderns* (Cambridge, MA: Harvard University Press, 1997).

HARDISON, FELICIA, and ROBERT J. WATERMEIER, 'Shakespeare Selling Shakespeare: Festival Commodities as Bait and as Pre-Conditioning', *Litteraria Pragensia* 6.12 (1996), 51–6.

HODGDON, BARBARA, *The Shakespeare Trade: Performances and Appropriations* (Philadelphia: University of Pennsylvania Press, 1998).

HOLDERNESS, GRAHAM, and BRYAN LOUGHREY, 'Shakespeare's Features', in Graham Holderness (ed.), *Cultural Shakespeare: Essays in the Shakespeare Myth* (Hertfordshire: University of Hertfordshire Press, 2001), 141–59.

HOLT, LIZ, 'Mass Storytelling and the Power of Advertising', in Jim Davies, John Simmons, and Rob Williams (eds.), *The Bard & Co: Shakespeare's Role in Modern Advertising* (London: Cyan Books, 2007), 86–93.

JAY, ROBERT, *The Trade-Card in Nineteenth-Century America* (Columbia: University of Missouri Press, 1987).

JHALLY, SUT, *The Codes of Advertising: Fetishism and the Political Economy of Meaning in the Consumer Society* (New York: Routledge, 1990).

KATHMAN, DAVE, 'Bard Cards: Shakespeare's Role in Victorian Advertising', *The Advertising Trade Card Quarterly* 8 (Spring 2001), 16–23.

LANDAUER, BELLA C., 'Literary Allusions in American Advertising as Sources of Social History', *New York Historical Society Quarterly* 31.3 (1947), 148–59.

——, 'When Advertisers Discovered Shakespeare', (1937). Unpublished ms.

LEISS, WILLIAM, STEPHEN KLINE, SUT JHALLY, and JACQUELINE BOTTERILL, *Social Communication in Advertising: Consumption in the Mediated Marketplace*, 3rd edn. (New York: Routledge, 2005).

LEVINE, LAWRENCE, *Highbrow/Lowbrow: The Emergence of Cultural Hierarchy in America* (Cambridge, MA: Harvard University Press, 1990).

LONGHURST, DEREK, '"You base football-player!": Shakespeare in Contemporary Popular Culture', in Graham Holderness (ed.), *The Shakespeare Myth* (Manchester: Manchester University Press, 1988), 59–73.

MCLUSKIE, KATHLEEN E., 'Shakespeare and the Millennial Market: The Commercial Bard', *Renaissance Drama* 30 (1999–2001), 161–81.

MUKERJI, CHANDRA, 'Shakespeare in L. A.: A Commentary on "Shakespeare and Modern Commercial Culture"', *Litteraria Pragensia* 6.12 (1996), 13–25.

PRESBEY, FRANK, *The History and Development of Advertising* (New York: Doubleday, 1929).

RIDDEN, GEOFF, 'Trade Marks of Shakespeare', *Shakespeare Yearbook* 11 (2000), 36–49.

SINFIELD, ALAN, *Faultlines: Cultural Materialism and the Politics of Dissident Reading* (Berkeley: University of California Press, 1992).

STRACHAN, JOHN, *Advertising and Satirical Culture in the Romantic Period* (Cambridge: Cambridge University Press, 2007).

TERRIS, OLWEN, 'Shakespeare and Television Advertising', in Olwen Terris, Eve-Marie Oesterlen, and Luke McKernan (eds.), *Shakespeare on Film, Television and Radio: The Researcher's Guide* (London: British Universities Film & Video Council, 2009), 40–50.

TRANTER, SUSAN, 'Selling Shakespeare', *Around the Globe* (1999), 22–3.

TWITCHELL, JAMES B., *Twenty Ads that Shook the World* (New York: Crown Publishers, 2000).

CHAPTER 28 CLASSICS

BALDWIN, T. W., *William Shakespeare's small Latine & lesse Greeke* (Urbana: University of Illinois Press, 1944).

BARKAN, LEONARD, 'What did Shakespeare Read?' in Margreta de Grazia and Stanley Wells (eds.), *The Cambridge Companion to Shakespeare* (Cambridge: Cambridge University Press, 2001), 31–47.

BATE, JONATHAN, *Shakespeare and Ovid* (Oxford: Clarendon Press, 1993).

BRADEN, GORDON, *Renaissance Tragedy and the Senecan Tradition: Anger's Privilege* (New Haven, CT: Yale University Press, 1985).

BULLOUGH, GEOFFREY (ed.), *Narrative and Dramatic Sources of Shakespeare*, 8 vols. (New York: Columbia University Press, 1957–75).

DIGGES, LEONARD, 'Upon Master William Shakespeare, the Deceased Authour, and his Poems', in *Poems written by Wil. Shake-speare. Gent.* (London: 1640).

DOUCE, FRANCIS, *Illustrations of Shakespeare* 2 vols. (London, 1807).

ERASMUS, DESIDERIUS, *Collected Works*, vol. 31: *Adages I.i.1 to I.v.100*, Margaret Mann Phillips (trans.) and R. A. B. Mynors (ed.) (Toronto: University of Toronto Press, 1982).

FRAUNCE, ABRAHAM, *The Countesse of Pembrokes Yvychurch* (London: 1591).

FULLER, THOMAS, *A History of the Worthies in England* (London: 1662).

GILLESPIE, STUART, *Shakespeare's Books: A Dictionary of Shakespeare Sources* (London: Athlone, 2001).

GREENE, THOMAS, *The Light in Troy: Imitation and Discovery in Renaissance Poetry* (New Haven, CT: Yale University Press, 1993).

HADFIELD, ANDREW, *Shakespeare and Republicanism* (Cambridge: Cambridge University Press, 2005).

HAMILTON, DONNA, *Virgil and the Tempest: The Politics of Imitation* (Columbus: Ohio State University Press, 1990).

HINDS, STEPHEN, *Allusion and Intertext: Dynamics of Appropriation in Roman Poetry* (Cambridge and New York: Cambridge University Press, 1998).

JAMES, HEATHER, *Shakespeare's Troy: Drama, Politics, and the Translation of Empire* (Cambridge: Cambridge University Press, 1997).

JONSON, BEN, *The Works of Ben Jonson*, C. H. Herford and Percy and Evelyn Simpson (eds.), 11 vols. (Oxford: Clarendon Press, 1947).

KEATS, JOHN, *Life, Letters, and Literary Remains of John Keats*, Richard Monckton Milnes (ed.) (New York: Putnam, 1848).

LYNE, RAPHAEL, 'The Authority of Prospero's Slave', *Times Literary Supplement* 12 (February 13, 1998).

MARTINDALE, CHARLES (ed.), *Ovid Renewed: Ovidian Influences on Literature and Art from the Middle Ages to the Twentieth Century* (Cambridge: Cambridge University Press, 1988).

——, *Shakespeare and the Uses of Antiquity, An Introductory Essay* (London: Routledge, 1990).

——, and A. B. TAYLOR (eds.), *Shakespeare and the Classics* (Cambridge: Cambridge University Press, 2004).

MERES, FRANCIS, *Palladis Tamia* (1598), rpt. in *Elizabethan Critical Essays*, G. Gregory Smith (ed.), 2 vols. (Oxford: Clarendon Press, 1904).

MILES, GEOFFREY, *Shakespeare and the Constant Romans* (Oxford: Clarendon Press, 1996).

MILTON, JOHN, *The Works of John Milton*, ed. Frank Allen Patterson 18 vols (ed.) in 21 (New York: Columbia University Press, 1931).

MIOLA, ROBERT, *Shakespeare and Classical Comedy: The Influence of Plautus and Terence* (Oxford: Oxford University Press, 1994).

——, *Shakespeare's Reading* (Oxford: Oxford University Press, 2000).

——, *Shakespeare's Rome* (Cambridge: Cambridge University Press, 1983).

Ovid, *The. xv. bookes of P. Ouidius Naso, entytuled Metamorphosis* Arthur Golding (trans.) (London: 1567).

——, *Ouids Metamorphosis Englished, Mythologiz'd, and Represented in Figures*, G[eorge] S[andys] (trans.) (Oxford: 1632).

TAYLOR, A. B. (ed.), *Shakespeare's Ovid: the Metamorphoses in the Plays and Poems* (New York: Cambridge University Press, 2000).

THOMSON, J. A. K., *Shakespeare and the Classics* (London: Allen and Unwin, 1952).

CHAPTER 29 CHARACTER

BELSEY, CATHERINE, *The Subject of Tragedy: Identity and Difference in Renaissance Drama* (London and New York: Methuen, 1985).

BLOOM, HAROLD, *Shakespeare: The Invention of the Human* (New York: Riverhead, 1998).

BOLTER, JAY DAVID, and RICHARD GRUSIN, *Remediation* (Cambridge, MA: MIT Press, 1991).

BRADLEY, A. C., *Shakespearean Tragedy* (Greenwich, CT: Fawcett, n.d.).

CRAIG, HUGH, '"Speak, That I May See Thee": Shakespeare Characters and Common Words', *Shakespeare Survey* 61 (2008), 281–8.

DESMET, CHRISTY, *Reading Shakespeare's Characters: Rhetoric, Ethics, and Identity* (Amherst: University of Massachusetts Press, 1992).

——, 'Paying Attention in Shakespeare Parody: From Tom Stoppard to YouTube', *Shakespeare Survey* 61 (2008), 227–38.

GREENBLATT, STEPHEN, 'Psychoanalysis and Renaissance Culture', in Patricia Parker and David Quint (eds.), *Literary Theory / Renaissance Texts* (Baltimore, MD: The Johns Hopkins University Press, 1986), 210–24.

HAYLES, N. KATHERINE, *How We Became Posthuman: Virtual Bodies in Cybernetics, Literature, and Informatics* (Chicago, IL: University of Chicago Press, 1999).

HOPE, JONATHAN, and MICHAEL WITMORE, 'The Very Large Textual Object: A Prosthetic Reading of Shakespeare', *Early Modern Literary Studies* 9.3, Special Issue 12 (January 2004), paras. 1–36, http://purl.oclc.org/emls/09-3/hopewhit.htm.

LANHAM, RICHARD, *The Economics of Attention: Style and Substance in the Age of Information* (Chicago, IL: University of Chicago Press, 2006).

MCCARTY, WILLARD, *Humanities Computing* (Basingstoke: Palgrave Macmillan, 2005).

MANOVICH, LEV, *The Language of New Media* (Cambridge, MA: MIT Press, 2001).

SINFIELD, ALAN, 'From Bradley to Cultural Materialism', *Shakespeare Studies* 34 (2006), 25–34.

CHAPTER 30 LAW

BROOKS, PETER, and PAUL GEWIRTZ (eds.), *Law's Stories: Narrative and Rhetoric in the Law* (New Haven, CT: Yale University Press, 1996).

COLCLOUGH, DAVID, *Freedom of Speech in Early Stuart England* (Cambridge: Cambridge University Press, 2005).

CORMACK, BRADIN, *A Power to Do Justice: Jurisdiction, English Literature, and the Rise of the Common Law, 1509–1625* (Chicago, IL: University of Chicago Press, 2007).

CUNNINGHAM, KAREN, *Imaginary Betrayals: Subjectivity and the Discourses of Treason in Early Modern Literature* (Philadelphia: University of Pennsylvania Press, 2002).

——, and CONSTANCE JORDAN (eds.), *The Law in Shakespeare* (Basingstoke: Palgrave Macmillan, 2007).

EDEN, KATHY, *Friends Hold All Things in Common: Tradition, Intellectual Property, and the Adages of Erasmus* (New Haven, CT: Yale University Press, 2001).

GOODRICH, PETER, *Reading the Law: A Critical Introduction to Legal Methods and Techniques* (Oxford: Blackwell, 1986).

HUTSON, LORNA, *The Invention of Suspicion: Law and Mimesis in Shakespeare and Renaissance Drama* (Oxford: Oxford University Press, 2007).

JORDAN, CONSTANCE, *Ruler and Subject in the Romances* (Ithaca, NY: Cornell University Press, 1997).

KAHN, VICTORIA, and LORNA HUTSON (eds.), *Rhetoric and Law in Early Modern Europe* (New Haven, CT: Yale University Press, 2001).

KEZAR, DENNIS D. (ed.), *Solon and Thespis: Law and Theater in the English Renaissance* (Notre Dame, IN: University of Notre Dame Press, 2007).

LEMON, REBECCA, *Treason by Words: Literature, Law and Rebellion in Shakespeare's England* (Ithaca, NY: Cornell University Press, 2006).

LOCKEY, BRIAN, *Law and Empire in English Renaissance Literature* (Cambridge: Cambridge University Press, 2006).

MUKHERJI, SUBHA, *Law and Representation in Early Modern Drama* (Cambridge: Cambridge University Press, 2006).

O'CALLAGHAN, MICHELLE, *English Wits: Literature and Sociability in Early Modern England* (Cambridge: Cambridge University Press, 2007).

POSNER, RICHARD, *Law and Literature: A Misunderstood Relation* (Cambridge, MA: Harvard University Press, 1988).

RAFFIELD, PAUL, *Images and Cultures of Law in Early Modern England* (Cambridge: Cambridge University Press, 2004).

—— and GARY WATT (eds.), *Shakespeare and the Law* (Oxford and Portland, OR: Hart Publishing, 2008).

ROSS, CHARLES, *Elizabethan Literature and the Law of Fraudulent Conveyance: Sidney, Spenser and Shakespeare* (Aldershot: Ashgate, 2003).

SHAPIRO, BARBARA, *A Culture of Fact: England, 1550–1730* (Ithaca, NY: Cornell University Press, 2000).

SHEEN, ERICA, and LORNA HUTSON (eds.), *Literature, Politics and Law in Renaissance England* (Basingstoke: Palgrave Macmillan, 2005).

SHUGER, DEBORA, *Censorship and Cultural Sensibility: The Regulation of Language in Tudor-Stuart England* (Philadelphia: University of Pennsylvania Press, 2006).

SOKOL, B. J., and MARY SOKOL, *Shakespeare, Law, and Marriage* (Cambridge: Cambridge University Press, 2003).

WILSON, LUKE, *Theaters of Intention: Drama and the Law in Early Modern England* (Stanford, CA: Stanford University Press, 2000).

CHAPTER 31 FORMATION OF NATIONHOOD

AUDEN, W. H., '*The Taming of the Shrew, King John*, and *Richard II*', *Lectures on Shakespeare* (Princeton, NJ: Princeton University Press, 2001), 63–74.

BALE, JOHN, *King Johan*, Peter Happé (ed.), *Four Morality Plays* (Harmondsworth: Penguin, 1979).

BARTON, ANNE, 'Falstaff and the Comic Community', *Essays Mainly Shakespearean* (Cambridge: Cambridge University Press, 1994), 70–90.

BRUBAKER, EDWARD S., 'Staging *King John*: A Director's Observations', in Deborah T. Curren-Aquino (ed.), *King John: New Perspectives* (Newark: University of Delaware Press, 1989), 165–72.

DEWAR, MARY, *Thomas Smith: A Tudor Intellectual in Office* (London: Athlone Press, 1964).

DUTTON, RICHARD, '"Methinks the truth should live from age to age": The Dating and Contexts of *Henry V*', *Huntington Library Quarterly* 68 (2005), 173–204.

ELTON, G. R. (ed.), *The Tudor Constitution: Documents and Commentary* (Cambridge: Cambridge University Press, 1982).

HOWARD, JEAN E., and PHYLLIS RACKIN, *Engendering a Nation* (London: Routledge, 1997).

HUTSON, LORNA, *The Invention of Suspicion: Law and Mimesis in Shakespeare and Renaissance Drama* (Oxford: Oxford University Press, 2007).

JONES, RICHARD FOSTER, *The Triumph of English* (Stanford, CA: Stanford University Press, 1953).

KATZ, LESLIE S., 'The Merry Wives of Windsor: Sharing the Queen's Holiday', *Representations* 51 (1995), 77–93.

LANDRETH, DAVID, 'Once More into the Preech: *The Merry Wives'* English Pedagogy', *Shakespeare Quarterly* 55 (2004), 420–49.

McALINDON, TOM, 'Swearing and Forswearing in Shakespeare's Histories: The Playwright as Contra-Machiavel', *Review of English Studies* 51 (2000), 208–29.

MARCUS, LEAH, *Unediting the Renaissance* (London: Routledge, 1996).

SHRANK, CATHY, 'Foreign Bodies: Politics, Polemic and the Continental Landscape', in Mike Pincombe (ed.), *Travels and Translations in the Sixteenth Century* (Aldershot: Ashgate, 2004), 31–44.

——, *Writing the Nation in Reformation England, 1530–1580* (Oxford: Oxford University Press, 2004).

STOCKTON, WILL, ' "I am made an ass": Falstaff and the scatology of Windsor's polity', *Texas Studies in Literature and Language* 49 (2007), 340–60.

VALPY, RICHARD, *King John, an historical tragedy, altered from Shakespeare* (Reading: 1800).

VAUGHAN, VIRGINIA MASON, 'Between Tetralogies: *King John* as Transition', *Shakespeare Quarterly* 35 (1984), 407–20.

——, '*King John*: A Study in Subversion and Containment', in Deborah T. Curren-Aquino, (ed.), *King John: New Perspectives* (Newark: University of Delaware Press, 1989), 62–75.

VICKERS, BRIAN (ed.), *Shakespeare: The Critical Heritage*, 6 vols. (London: Routledge and Kegan Paul, 1975).

WAITH, EUGENE, '*King John* and the Drama of History', *Shakespeare Quarterly* 29 (1978), 192–211.

WITHINGTON, PHIL, and ALEXANDRA SHEPARD, 'Introduction', in Withington and Shepard (eds.), *Communities in Early Modern England* (Manchester: Manchester University Press, 2000), 1–15.

WOMACK, PETER, 'Imagining Communities: Theatres and the English Nation in the Sixteenth Century', in David Aers (ed.), *Culture and History, 1350–1600: Essays on English Communities, Identities and Writing* (Detroit, MI: Wayne State University Press, 1992), 91–143.

CHAPTER 32 REPUBLICANISM

ARMITAGE, DAVID, CONAL CONDREN, and ANDREW FITZMAURICE (eds.), *Shakespeare and Early Modern Political Thought* (Cambridge: Cambridge University Press, 2009).

BUSHNELL, REBECCA, *Tragedies of Tyrants: Political Thought and Theater in the English Renaissance* (Ithaca, NY: Cornell University Press, 1990).

COLLINSON, PATRICK, 'The Monarchical Republic of Queen Elizabeth I', in Patrick Collinson (ed.), *Elizabethans* (London: Hambledon, 2003), 31–57.

HADFIELD, ANDREW, *Shakespeare and Renaissance Politics* (London: Arden Critical Companions, 2003).

——, *Shakespeare and Republicanism* (Cambridge: Cambridge University Press, 2005).

McDiarmid, John (ed.), *The Monarchical Republic of Early Modern England: Essays in Response to Patrick Collinson* (Aldershot: Ashgate, 2007).

McPherson, David, *Shakespeare, Jonson, and the Myth of Venice* (Newark: University of Delaware Press, 1990).

Miola, Robert, '*Julius Caesar* and the Tyrannicide Debate', *Renaissance Quarterly* 36 (1985), 271–90.

Van Gelderen, Martin, *The Political Thought of the Dutch Revolt, 1555–1590* (Cambridge: Cambridge University Press, 1992).

——, and Quentin Skinner (eds.), *Republicanism: A Shared European Heritage*, 2 vols. (Cambridge: Cambridge University Press, 2002).

Vaughan, Virginia Mason, *Othello: A Contextual History* (Cambridge: Cambridge University Press, 1994).

Chapter 33 Empire

Armitage, David, *The Ideological Origins of the British Empire* (New York: Cambridge University Press, 2000).

Baker, David J., *Between Nations: Shakespeare, Spenser, Marvell, and the Question of Britain* (Stanford, CA: Stanford University Press, 1997).

Canny, Nicholas, *The Elizabethan Conquest of Ireland: A Pattern Established 1565–76* (New York: Barnes and Noble, 1976).

——, *Making Ireland British, 1580–1650* (New York: Oxford University Press, 2001).

Dauntan, M., and R. Halpern (eds.), *Empire and Others: British Encounters with Indigenous Peoples, 1600–1850* (Philadelphia: University of Pennsylvania Press, 1999).

Fuchs, Barbara, *Mimesis and Empire: The New World, Islam and European Identities* (New York: Cambridge University Press, 2001).

Greenblatt, Stephen (ed.), *New World Encounters* (Berkeley: University of California Press, 1993).

Griffin, Eric, *English Renaissance Drama and the Specter of Spain: Ethnopoetics and Empire* (Philadelphia: University of Pennsylvania Press, 2009).

Hadfield, Andrew, *Shakespeare, Spenser, and the Matter of Britain* (Basingstoke: Palgrave Macmillan, 2004).

Highley, Christopher, *Shakespeare, Spenser, and the Crisis in Ireland* (New York: Cambridge University Press, 1997).

Lockey, Brian, *Law and Empire in English Renaissance Literature* (New York: Cambridge University Press, 2006).

Maley, Willy, *Nation, State and Empire in English Renaissance Literature* (Basingstoke: Palgrave Macmillan, 2003).

Marshall, Tristan, *Theatre and Empire: Great Britain on the London Stages under James VI and James I* (Manchester: Manchester University Press, 2000).

Netzloff, Mark, *England's Internal Colonies: Class, Capital, and the Literature of Early Modern English Colonialism* (Basingstoke: Palgrave Macmillan, 2003).

Pagden, Anthony, *Lords of All the World, Ideologies of Empire in Spain, Britain, and France c.1500–c.1800* (New Haven, CT: Yale University Press, 1995).

——, *The Fall of Natural Man: The American Indian and the Origins of Comparative Ethnography* (Cambridge: Cambridge University Press, 1986).

CHAPTER 34 PHILOSOPHY

BURROW, COLLIN, *The Complete Sonnets and Poems* (New York: Oxford University Press 2002).

DAVIS, JACK M., and J. E. GRANT, 'A Critical Dialogue on Shakespeare's Sonnet 71', *Texas Studies in Language and Literature* 1 (1959): 214–32.

GUYER, SARA, 'Breath, Today: Celan's Translation of Sonnet 71', *Comparative Literature* 57.4 (2005): 328–51.

ISEMINGER, GARY, 'Aesthetic Experience', in Jerrold Levinson (ed.), *The Oxford Handbook of Aesthetics*, (Oxford: Oxford University Press, 2005), 99–116.

LAMARQUE, PETER, and STEIN OLSEN, *Truth, Fiction, and Literature: A Philosophical Perspective* (Oxford: Clarendon Press, 1994).

NUSSBAUM, MARTHA, *Love's Knowledge: Essays on Philosophy and Literature* (Oxford: Oxford University Press, 1990).

PEQUIGNEY, JOSEPH, *Such is My Love: A Study of Shakespeare's Sonnets* (Chicago, IL: University of Chicago Press, 1985).

——, 'Sonnets 71–74: Texts and Contexts', in J. Schiffer (ed.), *Shakespeare's Sonnets: Critical Essays*, (New York: Garland, 1999), 285–304.

SHUSTERMAN, RICHARD, *Surface and Depth: Dialectics of Criticism and Culture* (Ithaca, NY: Cornell University Press, 2002).

VENDLER, HELEN, *The Art of Shakespeare's Sonnets* (Cambridge, MA: Harvard University Press, 1999).

WORTHEN, W. B., *Drama: Between Poetry and Performance* (Chichester: Wiley-Blackwell, 2010).

ZAMIR, TZACHI, *Double Vision: Moral Philosophy and Shakespearean Drama* (Princeton, NJ: Princeton University Press, 2007).

CHAPTER 35 PRAGMATISM

ADELMAN, JANET, *Suffocating Mothers: Fantasies of Maternal Origin in Shakespeare's Plays, 'Hamlet' to 'The Tempest'* (London: Routledge, 1992).

BATE, JONATHAN, *Soul of the Age: A Biography of the Mind of Shakespeare* (New York: Random House, 2009).

BERGER JR, HARRY, *Making Trifles of Terrors: Redistributing Complicities in Shakespeare* (Stanford, CA: Stanford University Press, 1997).

BRADLEY, A. C., *Shakespearean Tragedy* (London: Macmillan, 1965).

CARSON, ROB, 'Digesting the Third: Reconfiguring Binaries in Shakespeare and Early Modern Thought' (Dissertation, University of Toronto 2008).

DAVIDSON, DONALD. 'On the Very Idea of a Conceptual Scheme', in Donald Davidson, *Inquiries into Truth and Interpretation* (Oxford, Clarendon Press, 1984), 183–98.

DEWEY, JOHN, *Art as Experience* (New York, Putnam, 1980).

DEWEY, JOHN, *The Quest for Certainty* (New York: Capricorn, 1960).

ENGLE, LARS, *Shakespearean Pragmatism: Market of His Time* (Chicago, IL: University of Chicago Press, 1993).

HARRIS, JONATHAN GIL, *Untimely Matter in the Time of Shakespeare* (Philadelphia: University of Pennsylvania Press, 2009).

HOLLAND, PETER (ed.), *Shakespeare Survey 57: Macbeth and its Afterlife* (Cambridge: Cambridge University Press, 2004).

JAMES, WILLIAM, *William James: Writing 1902–1910*, Bruce Kuklick (ed.) (New York: Library of America, 1987).

KASTAN, DAVID SCOTT, *Shakespeare After Theory* (New York: Routledge, 1999).

KINNEY, ARTHUR F., *Lies Like Truth: Shakespeare, Macbeth, and the Cultural Moment* (Detroit, MI: Wayne State University Press, 2001).

——, 'Macbeth's Knowledge', *Shakespeare Survey* 57 (2004): 11–26.

LEMON, REBECCA, 'Scaffolds of Treason in Macbeth', *Theatre Journal* 54.1 (2002): 25–43.

MENAND, LOUIS, *The Metaphysical Club: A Story of Ideas in America* (New York: Farrar, Straus, and Giroux, 2001).

PEIRCE, CHARLES S., 'How to Make Our Ideas Clear', in The Peirce Edition Project *Writings of Charles S. Peirce: A Chronological Edition*, vol. 3 (Bloomington: Indiana University Press, 1982–).

RORTY, RICHARD, *Consequences of Pragmatism: Essays, 1972–1980* (Minneapolis: University of Minnesota Press, 1980).

——, *Contingency, Irony, and Solidarity* (Cambridge: Cambridge University Press, 1989).

——, 'Does Academic Freedom Have Philosophical Presuppositions?', in Louis Menand (ed.), *The future of Academic Freedom* (Chicago, IL: University of Chicago Press, 1996), 21–42.

——, *Take Care of Freedom and Truth Will Take Care of Itself: Interviews with Richard Rorty*, Eduardo Mendieta (ed.) (Stanford, CA, Stanford University Press, 2006).

WILLS, GARRY, *Witches and Jesuits: Shakespeare's 'Macbeth'* (New York: Oxford University Press, 1995).

WOODRUFF, PAUL, *The Necessity of Theater: The Art of Watching and Being Watched* (Oxford and New York: Oxford University Press, 2008).

ZAMIR, TZACHI, *Double Vision: Moral Philosophy and Shakespearean Drama* (Princeton, NJ: Princeton University Press, 2007).

CHAPTER 36 RELIGION

COLLINSON, PATRICK, *The Birthpangs of Protestant England: Religious and Cultural Change in the Sixteenth and Seventeenth Centuries* (London: Macmillan, 1988).

——, 'William Shakespeare's Religious Inheritance and Environment', in *Elizabethan Essays* (London: Hambledon Press, 1994), 219–52.

CUMMINGS, BRIAN, *The Literary Culture of the Reformation: Grammar and Grace* (Oxford: Oxford University Press, 2002).

DIEHL, HUSTON, *Staging Reform, Reforming the Stage: Protestantism and Popular Theater in Early Modern England* (Ithaca, NY: Cornell University Press, 1997).

DÖRING, TOBIAS, *Performances of Mourning in Shakespearean Theatre and Early Modern Culture* (London: Palgrave Macmillan, 2006).

DUFFY, EAMON, *The Stripping of the Altars: Traditional Religion in England, 1400–1580* (New Haven, CT: Yale University Press, 1992).

DUTTON, RICHARD, ALISON FINDLAY, and RICHARD WILSON (eds.), *Region, Religion and Patronage: Lancastrian Shakespeare* (Manchester: Manchester University Press, 2004).

——, ——, —— (eds.), *Theatre and Religion: Lancastrian Shakespeare* (Manchester: Manchester University Press, 2004).

GREENBLATT, STEPHEN, *Hamlet in Purgatory* (Princeton, NJ: Princeton University Press, 2001).

——, *Will in the World: How Shakespeare became Shakespeare* (London: Jonathan Cape, 2004).

HOLLAND, PETER (ed.), *Shakespeare Survey 54: Shakespeare and Religions* (2005).

HONIGMANN, E. A. J., *Shakespeare: The 'Lost Years'* (Manchester: Manchester University Press, 1985).

JENSEN, PHEBE, *Religion and Revelry in Shakespeare's Festive World* (Cambridge: Cambridge University Press, 2008).

KNAPP, JEFFREY, *Shakespeare's Tribe: Church, Nation, and Theater in Renaissance* (Chicago, IL: Chicago University Press, 2002).

LAKE, PETER, 'Religious Identities in Shakespeare's England', in David Scott Kastan (ed.), *A Companion to Shakespeare* (Oxford: Blackwell, 1999), 57–84.

——, and MICHAEL QUESTIER, *The Anti-Christ's Lewd Hat: Protestants, Papists and Players in Post-Reformation England* (New Haven, CT: Yale University Press, 2002).

MCEACHERN, CLAIRE, and DEBORA SHUGER, (eds.), *Religion and Culture in Renaissance England* (Cambridge: Cambridge University Press, 1985).

MAROTTI, ARTHUR, *Religious Ideology and Cultural Fantasy: Catholic and Anti-Catholic Discourses in Early Modern England* (Notre Dame, IN: University of Notre Dame Press, 2005).

NUTTALL, A. D., *Shakespeare the Thinker* (New Haven, CT: Yale University Press, 2007).

POOLE, KRISTEN, *Radical Religion: Figures of Nonconformity from Shakespeare to Milton* (Cambridge: Cambridge University Press, 2000).

SCHOENBAUM, SAMUEL, *Shakespeare's Lives*, new edn. (Oxford: Oxford University Press, 1991).

SHAHEEN, NASEEB, *Biblical References in Shakespeare's Plays* (Newark: University of Delaware Press, 1999).

SHELL, ALISON, *Catholicism, Controversy and the English Literary Imagination, 1558–1660* (Cambridge: Cambridge University Press, 1999).

SIMPSON, JAMES, *Burning to Read: English Fundamentalism and Its Reformation Opponents* (Cambridge, MA: Harvard University Press, 2007).

WILSON, RICHARD, *Secret Shakespeare: Studies in Theatre, Religion and Resistance* (Manchester: Manchester University Press, 2004).

CHAPTER 37 ARCHITECTURE

AIRS, MALCOLM, *The Buildings of Britain: Tudor and Jacobean* (London: Barrie & Jenkins, 1982).

——, *The Tudor and Jacobean Country House* (1995; reprint Stroud: Sutton 1998).

BEARD, GEOFFREY, *The National Trust Book of the English House Interior* (London: Viking in association with The National Trust, 1990).

BEARD, GEOFFREY, *Stucco and Decorative Plasterwork in Europe* (London: Thames & Hudson, 1983).

GIROUARD, MARK, *Hardwick Hall* (rpt. London: The National Trust, 1994).

——, *Robert Smythson and the Elizabethan Country House* (New Haven, CT: Yale University Press, 1983).

JOHNSON, A. W., *Ben Jonson: Poetry and Architecture* (Oxford: Clarendon Press, 1994).

JOURDAIN, MARGARET, *English Decorative Plasterwork of the Renaissance* (London: Batsford, 1926).

MOWL, TIMOTHY, *Elizabethan and Jacobean Style* (London: Phaidon, 1993).

WELLS-COLE, ANTHONY, *Art and Decoration in Elizabethan and Jacobean England: The Influence of Continental Prints, 1558–1625* (New Haven, CT: Yale University Press, 1997).

CHAPTER 38 SCIENCE AND TECHNOLOGY

BACON, FRANCIS, *Francis Bacon: The New Organon*, Lisa Jardine and Michael Silverthorne (eds.) (Cambridge: Cambridge University Press, 2000).

CIPOLLA, CARLO, *Clocks and Culture, 1300–1700* (New York: Norton, 1977).

——, *Guns and Sails in the Early Phase of the European Expansion 1400–1700* (London: Collins, 1965).

COHEN, ADAM MAX, *Shakespeare and Technology: Dramatizing Early Modern Technological Revolutions* (New York: Palgrave, 2006).

DE GRAZIA, MARGRETA, 'Imprints, Descartes, Shakespeare, and Gutenberg', in Terence Hawkes (ed.), *Alternative Shakespeares*, vol. 2 (New York: Routledge, 1996).

GILLIES, JOHN, *Shakespeare and the Geography of Difference* (Cambridge: Cambridge University Press, 1994).

GRABES, HERBERT, *The Mutable Glass: Mirror Imagery in Titles and Texts of the Middle Ages and the English Renaissance* (Cambridge: Cambridge University Press, 1982).

GRAFTON, ANTHONY, *New Worlds, Ancient Texts: The Power of Tradition and the Shock of Discovery* (Cambridge, MA: Harvard University Press, 1992).

HARKNESS, DEBORAH, '"Strange" Ideas and "English" Knowledge: Natural Science Exchange in Elizabethan London', in Pamela H. Smith and Paula Findlen (eds.), *Merchants and Marvels: Commerce, Science, and Art in Early Modern Europe* (New York: Routledge, 2002).

MASTEN, JEFFREY, PETER STALLYBRASS, and NANCY J. VICKERS (eds.), *Language Machines: Technologies of Literary and Cultural Production* (New York: Routledge, 1997).

MAYR, OTTO, *Authority, Liberty, and Automatic Machinery in Early Modern Europe* (Baltimore, MD: The Johns Hopkins University Press, 1986).

MIOLA, ROBERT S., *Shakespeare's Reading* (New York: Oxford University Press, 2000).

RHODES, NEIL, and JONATHAN SAWDAY (eds.), *The Renaissance Computer: Knowledge Technology in the First Age of Print* (London: Routledge, 2000).

TAYLOR, E. G. R., *The Mathematical Practitioners of Tudor and Stuart England* (Cambridge: Cambridge University Press, 1954).

TURNER, GERARD L'E., *Elizabethan Instrument Makers: The Origins of the London Trade in Precision Instrument Making* (Oxford: Oxford University Press, 2000).

WHITE JR, LYNN, *Medieval Religion and Technology: Collected Essays* (Berkeley: University of California Press, 1978).

Chapter 39 Shakespeare and America

Bristol, Michael, *Shakespeare's America, America's Shakespeare* (London: Routledge, 1990).

Burt, Richard (ed.), *Shakespeare after Mass Media* (New York: Palgrave, 2002).

——, *Shakespeares after Shakespeare: An Encyclopedia of the Bard in Mass Media and Popular Culture* (Westport, CT: Greenwood Press, 2007).

Dunn, Esther Cloudman, *Shakespeare in America* (New York: Macmillan, 1939).

Levine, Lawrence, 'William Shakespeare and the American People: A Study in Cultural Transformation', in *The Unpredictable Past: Explorations in American Cultural History* (New York: Oxford University Press, 1993), 139–71.

Marovitz, Sanford E., 'America vs. Shakespeare: From the Monroe Doctrine to the Civil War', *Zeitschrift für Anglistik und Amerikanistik* 34 (1986), 33–46.

Shattuck, Charles H. *Shakespeare on the American Stage*, 2 vols. (Washington, DC: Folger Shakespeare Library, 1976, 1987).

Sturgess, Kim C., *Shakespeare and the American Nation* (Cambridge: Cambridge University Press, 2004).

Teague, Frances, *Shakespeare and the American Popular Stage* (Cambridge: Cambridge University Press, 2006).

Vaughan, Virginia Mason, and T. Alden (eds.), *Shakespeare in American Life* (Washington, DC: Folger Shakespeare Library, 2007).

Westfall, Alfred Van Rensselaer, *American Shakespearean Criticism, 1607–1865* (New York: H. W. Wilson, 1939).

Wilkes, George, *Shakespeare from an American Point of View* (New York: D. Appleton, 1877).

Wright, Louis B., *The Cultural Life of the American Colonies: 1607–1763* (New York: Harper, 1957, rpt. 1962).

Chapter 40 Shakespeare and the World

Bristol, Michael D., *Big-Time Shakespeare* (London: Routledge, 1996).

Burt, Richard (ed.), *Shakespeares after Shakespeare: An Encyclopedia of the Bard in Mass Media and Popular Culture*, 2 vols. (Westport, CT: Greenwood Press, 2007).

Fischlin, Daniel, and Mark Fortier (eds.), *Adaptations of Shakespeare: A Critical Anthology of Plays from the Seventeenth Century to the Present* (New York: Routledge, 2000).

Golder, John, and Madelaine Richard (eds.), *O Brave New World: Two Centuries of Shakespeare on the Australian Stage* (Sydney: Currency Press, 2002).

Hoenselaars, Ton (ed.), *Shakespeare and the Language of Translation* (London: Thomson Learning, 2004).

—— (ed.), *Shakespeare's History Plays: Performance, Translation and Adaptation in Britain and Abroad* (Cambridge: Cambridge University Press, 2004).

Hortmann, Wilhelm, *Shakespeare on the German Stage: The Twentieth Century* (Cambridge: Cambridge University Press, 1998).

Huang, Alexander C. Y., *Chinese Shakespeares: Two Centuries of Cultural Exchange* (New York: Columbia University Press, 2009).

JOHNSON, DAVID, *Shakespeare and South Africa* (Oxford: Clarendon Press, 1996).

KENNEDY, DENNIS (ed.), *Foreign Shakespeare: Contemporary Performance* (Cambridge: Cambridge University Press, 1993).

——, 'Shakespeare and the Global Spectator', *Shakespeare-Jahrbuch* 131 (1995), 50–64.

KNOWLES, RIC, *Shakespeare and Canada: Essays on Production, Translation, and Adaptation* (Brussels: Peter Lang, 2004).

LEITER, SAMUEL L. (ed.), *Shakespeare Around the Globe: A Guide to Notable Postwar Revivals* (New York: Greenwood Press, 1986).

LOOMBA, ANIA, and MARTIN ORKIN (eds.), *Post-Colonial Shakespeare* (London: Routledge, 1998).

MASSAI, SONIA (ed.), *Worldwide Shakespeares: Local Appropriations in Film and Performance* (New York: Routledge, 2005).

ORKIN, MARTIN, *Drama and the South African State* (Manchester: Manchester University Press, 1991).

——, *Local Shakespeares: Proximations and Power* (London: Routledge, 2005).

PUJANTE, ANGEL LUIS, and TON, HOENSELAARS (eds.), *Four Hundred Years of Shakespeare in Europe* (Newark: Delaware University Press, 2003).

SANDERS, JULIE, *Shakespeare and Music: Afterlives and Borrowings* (Oxford: Polity Press, 2007).

SASAYAMA, TAKASHI, J. R. MULRYNE, and MARGARET SHEWRING (eds.), *Shakespeare and the Japanese Stage* (Cambridge: Cambridge University Press, 1999).

SCHMIDGALL, GARY, *Shakespeare and Opera* (New York: Oxford University Press, 1990).

SHANKAR, D. A. (ed.), *Shakespeare in Indian Languages* (Shimla: Indian Institute of Advanced Study, 1999).

TATLOW, ANTONY, *Shakespeare, Brecht, and the Intercultural Sign* (Durham, NC: Duke University Press, 2001).

TAYLOR, GARY, *Reinventing Shakespeare: A Cultural History from the Reformation to the Present* (London: Hogarth Press, 1990).

INDEX
....

Note: page numbers in *italic* refer to illustrations and tables.

Lightning Source UK Ltd.
Milton Keynes UK
UKOW05f0741301015

261728UK00002B/2/P